Mike Holt's Illustrated Guide to

UNDERSTANDING NEC® REQUIREMENTS FOR
SOLAR PHOTOVOLTAIC
AND ENERGY STORAGE SYSTEMS

BASED ON THE
2020 NEC®

NOTICE TO THE READER

The text and commentary in this book is the author's interpretation of the 2020 Edition of NFPA 70®, the *National Electrical Code*®. It shall not be considered an endorsement of or the official position of the NFPA® or any of its committees, nor relied upon as a formal interpretation of the meaning or intent of any specific provision or provisions of the 2020 edition of NFPA 70, *National Electrical Code*.

The publisher does not warrant or guarantee any of the products described herein or perform any independent analysis in connection with any of the product information contained herein. The publisher does not assume, and expressly disclaims, any obligation to obtain and include information other than that provided to it by the manufacturer.

The reader is expressly warned to consider and adopt all safety precautions and applicable federal, state, and local laws and regulations. By following the instructions contained herein, the reader willingly assumes all risks in connection with such instructions.

Mike Holt Enterprises disclaims liability for any personal injury, property or other damages of any nature whatsoever, whether special, indirect, consequential or compensatory, directly or indirectly resulting from the use of this material. The reader is responsible for understanding what a Qualified Person is and determining safety and appropriate actions in all circumstances based on the applicable safety standards such as NFPA70E and OSHA.

The publisher makes no representation or warranties of any kind, including but not limited to, the warranties of fitness for particular purpose or merchantability, nor are any such representations implied with respect to the material set forth herein, and the publisher takes no responsibility with respect to such material. The publisher shall not be liable for any special, consequential, or exemplary damages resulting, in whole or part, from the reader's use of, or reliance upon, this material.

Mike Holt's Illustrated Guide to Understanding NEC® Requirements for Solar Photovoltaic and Energy Storage Systems, based on the 2020 NEC®

Second Printing: February 2023

Author: Mike Holt
Technical Illustrator: Mike Culbreath
Cover Design: Bryan Burch
Layout Design and Typesetting: Cathleen Kwas

COPYRIGHT © 2020 Charles Michael Holt
ISBN 978-1-950431-05-2

Produced and Printed in the USA

All rights reserved. No part of this work covered by the copyright hereon may be reproduced or used in any form or by any means graphic, electronic, or mechanical, including photocopying, recording, taping, or information storage and retrieval systems without the written permission of the publisher. You can request permission to use material from this text by e-mailing Info@MikeHolt.com.

For more information, call 888.632.2633, or e-mail Info@MikeHolt.com.

NEC®, NFPA 70®, NFPA 70E® and *National Electrical Code*® are registered trademarks of the National Fire Protection Association.

 This logo is a registered trademark of Mike Holt Enterprises, Inc.

If you are an instructor and would like to request an examination copy of this or other Mike Holt Publications:

Call: 888.632.2633 • Fax: 352.360.0983

E-mail: Info@MikeHolt.com • Visit: MikeHolt.com/Instructors

You can download a sample PDF of all our publications by visiting MikeHolt.com/Products.

I dedicate this book to the
Lord Jesus Christ, *my mentor and teacher.*
Proverbs 16:3

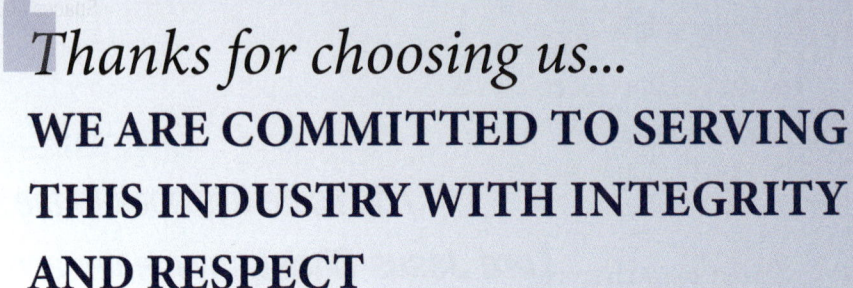

> *Thanks for choosing us...*
> **WE ARE COMMITTED TO SERVING THIS INDUSTRY WITH INTEGRITY AND RESPECT**

Since 1975, we have worked hard to develop products that get results, and to help individuals in their pursuit of success in this exciting industry.

From the very beginning we have been committed to the idea that customers come first. Everyone on my team will do everything they possibly can to help you succeed. I want you to know that we value you and are honored that you have chosen us to be your partner in training.

You are the future of this industry and we know that it is you who will make the difference in the years to come. My goal is to share with you everything that I know and to encourage you to pursue your education on a continuous basis. I hope that not only will you learn theory, *Code*, calculations, or how to pass an exam, but that in the process, you will become the expert in the field and the person others know to trust.

To put it simply, we genuinely care about your success and will do everything that we can to help you take your skills to the next level!

We are happy to partner with you on your educational journey.

God bless and much success,

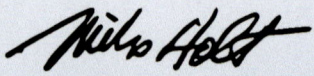

TABLE OF CONTENTS

About This Textbook xv

Additional Products to Help You Learn xviii

How to Use the *National Electrical Code* 1

Article 90—Introduction to the *National Electrical Code* 7
- 90.1 Purpose of the *NEC* 7
- 90.2 Scope of the *NEC* 8
- 90.3 *Code* Arrangement 10
- 90.4 Enforcement 11
- 90.5 Mandatory Requirements and Explanatory Material 13
- 90.7 Examination of Equipment for Product Safety 14

CHAPTER 1—GENERAL RULES 15

Article 100—Definitions 17
- 100 Definitions 17

Article 110—Requirements for Electrical Installations 45
Part I. General Requirements 45
- 110.1 Scope 45
- 110.2 Approval of Conductors and Equipment 45
- 110.3 Use and Product Listing (Certification) of Equipment 46
- 110.4 Voltage Rating of Electrical Equipment 46
- 110.5 Conductor Material 46
- 110.6 Conductor Sizes 46
- 110.7 Wiring Integrity 47
- 110.8 Suitable Wiring Methods 47
- 110.9 Interrupting Rating (Overcurrent Protective Devices) 47
- 110.10 Equipment Short Circuit Current Rating 48
- 110.11 Deteriorating Agents 49
- 110.12 Mechanical Execution of Work 50
- 110.13 Mounting and Cooling of Equipment 52
- 110.14 Conductor Termination and Splicing 52
- 110.15 High-Leg Conductor Identification 59
- 110.16 Arc Flash Hazard Warning 59
- 110.21 Markings 61
- 110.22 Identification of Disconnecting Means 62
- 110.24 Available Fault Current 63
- 110.25 Lockable Disconnecting Means 63

Part II. 1,000V, Nominal, or Less 63
- 110.26 Spaces About Electrical Equipment 63
- 110.28 Enclosure Types 72

CHAPTER 2—WIRING AND PROTECTION 73

Article 200—Use and Identification of Grounded Conductors 75
- 200.1 Scope 76
- 200.2 General 76
- 200.4 Neutral Conductor 76
- 200.6 Identification of Grounded Conductors 77
- 200.7 Use of White or Gray Color 79

Article 210—Branch Circuits 81
Part I. General Provisions 81
- 210.1 Scope 81
- 210.4 Multiwire Branch Circuits 82
- 210.5 Identification for Branch Circuits 84
- 210.7 Multiple Branch Circuits 85

Part II. Branch-Circuit Ratings 86
- 210.18 Branch-Circuit Rating 86
- 210.19 Conductor Sizing 86
- 210.20 Overcurrent Protection 88
- 210.21 Receptacle Rating 89
- 210.23 Permissible Loads, Multiple-Outlet Branch Circuits 90

Article 215—Feeders 91
- 215.1 Scope 91
- 215.2 Conductor Sizing 92
- 215.3 Overcurrent Protection Sizing 96
- 215.10 Ground-Fault Protection of Equipment 97
- 215.12 Conductor Identification 97

Article 225—Outside Branch Circuits and Feeders 99
Part I. General 99
- 225.1 Scope 99
- 225.6 Minimum Conductor Size and Support 99
- 225.16 Attachment of Overhead Conductors 100
- 225.17 Masts as Supports 100

225.18	Clearance for Overhead Conductors	101	Part VI. Service Disconnect—Disconnecting Means		124
225.19	Clearances from Buildings	102	230.70	Service Disconnect Requirements	124
225.22	Raceways on Exterior Surfaces of Buildings or Other Structures	103	230.71	Number of Service Disconnects	125
			230.72	Grouping of Disconnects	125
225.26	Trees for Conductor Support	103	230.76	Manually or Power Operated	126
225.27	Raceway Seals	104	230.79	Rating of Disconnect	126
Part II. Buildings or Other Structures Supplied by a Feeder		104	230.82	Connected on Supply Side of the Service Disconnect	126
225.30	Number of Supplies	104	230.85	Emergency Disconnects	128
225.31	Disconnecting Means	105	Part VII. Service Disconnect Overcurrent Protection		128
225.32	Disconnecting Means Location	105	230.90	Overload Protection—Where Required	128
225.33	Maximum Number of Disconnects	105	230.91	Location	129
225.34	Grouping of Disconnects	106	230.95	Ground-Fault Protection of Equipment	129
225.37	Identification of Multiple Supplies	106			
225.39	Rating of Disconnecting Means	106	**Article 240—Overcurrent Protection**		**131**
			Part I. General		132
Article 230—Services		**107**	240.1	Scope	132
Part I. General		107	240.2	Definitions	132
230.1	Scope	107	240.3	Other Articles (Overcurrent Protection of Equipment)	133
230.2	Number of Services	107	240.4	Overcurrent Protection of Conductors	133
230.3	Not to Pass Through a Building	109	240.5	Protection of Flexible Cords, Flexible Cables, and Fixture Wires	137
230.6	Conductors Considered Outside a Building	109			
230.7	Service Conductors Separate from Other Conductors	109	240.6	Standard Ampere Ratings	137
230.8	Raceway Seals	110	240.10	Supplementary Overcurrent Protection	138
230.9	Clearances on Buildings	110	240.13	Ground-Fault Protection of Equipment	138
230.10	Vegetation as Support	110	240.15	Phase Conductor Overcurrent Device	139
Part II. Overhead Service Conductors		111	Part II. Location		140
230.23	Overhead Service Conductor Size and Rating	111	240.21	Location in Circuit	140
230.24	Vertical Clearance for Overhead Service Conductors	112	240.24	Location of Overcurrent Protective Devices at Premises	145
230.26	Point of Attachment	112	Part III. Enclosures		147
230.27	Means of Attachment	113	240.33	Vertical Position	147
230.28	Service Masts as Support	113	Part IV. Disconnecting and Guarding		147
Part III. Underground Service Conductors		114	240.40	Disconnecting Means for Fuses	147
230.30	Installation	114	Part V. Plug Fuses, Fuseholders, and Adapters		147
230.31	Underground Service Conductor Size and Rating	114	240.51	Edison-Base Fuses	147
230.32	Protection Against Damage	114	Part VI. Cartridge Fuses and Fuseholders		148
Part IV. Service-Entrance Conductors		115	240.60	General	148
230.40	Number of Service-Entrance Conductor Sets	115	240.67	Arc Energy Reduction—Fuses	149
230.42	Conductor Sizing	115	Part VII. Circuit Breakers		149
230.43	Wiring Methods	119	240.81	Indicating	149
230.46	Spliced Conductors	119	240.83	Markings	149
230.50	Protection Against Physical Damage	120	240.85	Applications	150
230.51	Cable Supports	120	240.86	Series Ratings	151
230.53	Raceways to Drain	121	240.87	Arc Energy Reduction—Circuit Breakers	152
230.54	Overhead Service Locations	121	240.88	Reconditioned Equipment	153
230.56	High-Leg Conductor Identification	122			
Part V. Service Disconnect—General		122	**Article 250—Grounding and Bonding**		**155**
230.62	Service Equipment—Enclosed or Guarded	122	Part I. General		155
230.66	Marking for Service Disconnect	123	250.1	Scope	155
230.67	Surge Protection	123	250.4	Performance Requirements for Grounding and Bonding	156

250.6	Objectionable Current	162
250.8	Connection of Grounding and Bonding Connectors	166
250.10	Protection of Ground Clamps and Fittings	166
250.12	Clean Surfaces	166

Part II. System Grounding and Bonding 167

250.20	Systems Required to be Grounded	167
250.21	Ungrounded Systems	168
250.24	Grounding	168
250.25	Grounding for Supply Side of the Service Disconnect	172
250.28	Main Bonding Jumper and System Bonding Jumper	173
250.30	Separately Derived Systems	174
250.32	Buildings Supplied by a Feeder	183
250.34	Generators—Portable and Vehicle- or Trailer-Mounted	185
250.36	High-Impedance Grounded Systems	186

Part III. Grounding Electrode System and Grounding Electrode Conductor 186

250.50	Grounding Electrode System	186
250.52	Grounding Electrode Types	187
250.53	Grounding Electrode Installation Requirements	190
250.54	Auxiliary Grounding Electrodes	195
250.58	Common Grounding Electrode	196
250.62	Grounding Electrode Conductor	196
250.64	Grounding Electrode Conductor Installation	196
250.66	Sizing Grounding Electrode Conductor	200
250.68	Grounding Electrode Conductor and Bonding Jumper Connection to Grounding Electrodes	201
250.70	Grounding Electrode Conductor Termination Fittings	203

Part IV. Enclosure, Raceway, and Service Cable Connections 204

250.80	Service Raceways and Enclosures	204
250.86	Other Enclosures	204

Part V. Bonding for Fault Current 204

250.90	General	204
250.92	Bonding Equipment Containing Service Conductors	204
250.94	Bonding Communications Systems	207
250.96	Bonding Other Enclosures	208
250.97	Bonding Metal Parts Containing 277V and 480V Circuits	209
250.98	Bonding Loosely Jointed Metal Raceways	209
250.102	Neutral Conductor, Bonding Conductors, and Bonding Jumpers	210
250.104	Bonding of Piping Systems and Exposed Structural Metal	212
250.106	Lightning Protection Systems	216

Part VI. Equipment Grounding and Equipment Grounding Conductors 216

250.109	Metal Enclosures	216
250.114	Equipment Connected by Cord and Plug	216
250.118	Types of Equipment Grounding Conductors	218
250.119	Identification of Equipment Grounding Conductors	221
250.120	Equipment Grounding Conductor Installation	222
250.121	Restricted Use of Equipment Grounding Conductors	223
250.122	Sizing Equipment Grounding Conductors	223

Part VII. Methods of Equipment Grounding Conductor Connections 226

250.134	Equipment Connected by Permanent Wiring Methods	226
250.136	Equipment Secured to Grounded Metal Supports	227
250.138	Cord-and-Plug-Connected	227
250.140	Frames of Ranges, Ovens, and Clothes Dryers	227
250.142	Neutral Conductor for Effective Ground-Fault Current Path	228
250.146	Connecting Receptacle Grounding Terminal to an Equipment Grounding Conductor	229
250.148	Continuity and Attachment of Equipment Grounding Conductors in Boxes	232

CHAPTER 3—WIRING METHODS AND MATERIALS 235

Article 300—General Requirements for Wiring Methods and Materials 239

Part I. General Requirements 239

300.1	Scope	239
300.3	Conductors	240
300.4	Protection Against Physical Damage	243
300.5	Underground Installations	246
300.6	Protection Against Corrosion and Deterioration	250
300.7	Raceways Exposed to Different Temperatures	251
300.9	Raceways in Wet Locations Above Grade	251
300.10	Electrical Continuity	252
300.11	Securing and Supporting	252
300.12	Mechanical Continuity	254
300.13	Mechanical and Electrical Continuity of Conductors-Splices and Pigtails	255
300.14	Length of Free Conductors	256
300.15	Boxes or Fittings	257
300.17	Number and Size of Conductors in a Raceway	259
300.18	Inserting Conductors in Raceways	261
300.19	Supporting Conductors in Vertical Raceways	261
300.20	Induced Alternating Currents in Ferrous Metal Parts	262
300.21	Spread of Fire or Products of Combustion	264
300.22	Wiring in Ducts and Plenum Spaces	265
300.23	Panels Designed to Allow Access	267
300.25	Exit Enclosures (Stair Towers)	267

Article 310—Conductors for General Wiring 269

Part I. General 269

310.1	Scope	269
310.3	Conductors	269

Part II. Construction Specifications 270

310.4	Conductor Construction and Application	270
310.6	Conductor Identification	273

Article 312 | Table of Contents

Part III. Installation		273
310.10	Uses Permitted	273
310.12	Single-Phase Dwelling Services and Feeders	276
310.14	Ampacities for Conductors Rated 0V to 2,000V	279
310.15	Ampacity Tables	280
310.16	Ampacities of Insulated Conductors in Raceways, Cables, or Buried	287

Article 312—Cabinets 289

Part I. Scope and Installation		289
312.1	Scope	289
312.2	Damp or Wet Locations	289
312.3	Position in Walls	290
312.4	Repairing Gaps in Noncombustible Surfaces	290
312.5	Enclosures	290
312.6	Deflection of Conductors	292
312.8	Overcurrent Device Enclosures	292
Part II. Construction Specifications		294
312.10	Material	294

Article 314—Outlet, Pull, and Junction Boxes; Conduit Bodies; and Handhole Enclosures 295

Part I. Scope and General		295
314.1	Scope	295
314.3	Nonmetallic Boxes	295
314.4	Metal Boxes	296
Part II. Installation		296
314.15	Damp or Wet Locations	296
314.16	Sizing Outlet Boxes	296
314.17	Conductors That Enter Boxes or Conduit Bodies	304
314.20	Flush-Mounted Box Installations	304
314.21	Repairing Noncombustible Surfaces	305
314.22	Surface Extensions	306
314.23	Support of Boxes	306
314.25	Covers and Canopies	308
314.27	Outlet Box Requirements	309
314.28	Sizing Pull and Junction Boxes	311
314.29	Wiring to be Accessible	314
314.30	Handhole Enclosures	315

Article 320—Armored Cable (Type AC) 317

Part I. General		317
320.1	Scope	317
320.2	Definition	317
320.6	Listing Requirements	317
Part II. Installation		318
320.10	Uses Permitted	318
320.12	Uses Not Permitted	318
320.15	Exposed Work	318
320.17	Through or Parallel to Framing Members	318
320.23	In Accessible Attics or Roof Spaces	319
320.24	Bending Radius	319
320.30	Securing and Supporting	319
320.40	Boxes and Fittings	321
320.80	Conductor Ampacity	321
Part III. Construction Specifications		322
320.100	Construction	322
320.108	Equipment Grounding Conductor	322

Article 330—Metal-Clad Cable (Type MC) 323

Part I. General		323
330.1	Scope	323
330.2	Definition	323
330.6	Listing Requirements	324
Part II. Installation		324
330.10	Uses Permitted	324
330.12	Uses Not Permitted	325
330.15	Exposed Work	325
330.17	Through or Parallel to Framing Members	325
330.23	In Accessible Attics or Roof Spaces	326
330.24	Bending Radius	326
330.30	Securing and Supporting	326
330.80	Conductor Ampacities	328
Part III. Construction Specifications		329
330.108	Equipment Grounding Conductor	329

Article 334—Nonmetallic-Sheathed Cable (Type NM) 331

Part I. General		331
334.1	Scope	331
334.2	Definition	331
334.6	Listing Requirements	331
Part II. Installation		332
334.10	Uses Permitted	332
334.12	Uses Not Permitted	333
334.15	Exposed Work	333
334.17	Through or Parallel to Framing Members	334
334.23	Accessible Attics and Roof Spaces	335
334.24	Bending Radius	335
334.30	Securing and Supporting	336
334.40	Boxes and Fittings	337
334.80	Conductor Ampacity	337
Part III. Construction Specifications		338
334.108	Equipment Grounding Conductor	338

Article 336—Power and Control Tray Cable (Type TC) 339
Part I. General 339
336.1 Scope 339
336.2 Definition 339
336.6 Listing Requirements 339
Part II. Installation 339
336.10 Uses Permitted 339
336.12 Uses Not Permitted 340
336.24 Bending Radius 340

Article 338—Service-Entrance Cable (Types SE and USE) 341
Part I. General 341
338.1 Scope 341
338.2 Definitions 341
338.6 Listing Requirements 342
Part II. Installation 342
338.10 Uses Permitted 342
338.12 Uses Not Permitted 343
338.24 Bending Radius 343

Article 340—Underground Feeder and Branch-Circuit Cable (Type UF) 345
Part I. General 345
340.1 Scope 345
340.2 Definition 345
340.6 Listing Requirements 345
Part II. Installation 345
340.10 Uses Permitted 345
340.12 Uses Not Permitted 346
340.24 Bends 346
340.80 Ampacity 346
Part III. Construction Specifications 346
340.108 Equipment Grounding Conductor 346
340.112 Insulation 346

Article 342—Intermediate Metal Conduit (Type IMC) 347
Part I. General 347
342.1 Scope 347
342.2 Definition 347
342.6 Listing Requirements 347
Part II. Installation 348
342.10 Uses Permitted 348
342.14 Dissimilar Metals 348
342.20 Trade Size 348
342.22 Number of Conductors 348
342.24 Bends 348
342.26 Number of Bends (360°) 348
342.28 Reaming 348
342.30 Securing and Supporting 349
342.42 Couplings and Connectors 350
342.46 Bushings 350
342.60 Equipment Grounding Conductor 351

Article 344—Rigid Metal Conduit (Type RMC) 353
Part I. General 353
344.1 Scope 353
344.2 Definition 353
344.6 Listing Requirements 354
Part II. Installation 354
344.10 Uses Permitted 354
344.14 Dissimilar Metals 354
344.20 Trade Size 354
344.22 Number of Conductors 354
344.24 Bends 355
344.26 Number of Bends (360°) 355
344.28 Reaming 355
344.30 Securing and Supporting 355
344.42 Couplings and Connectors 357
344.46 Bushings 358
344.60 Equipment Grounding Conductor 358

Article 348—Flexible Metal Conduit (Type FMC) 359
Part I. General 359
348.1 Scope 359
348.2 Definition 359
348.6 Listing Requirements 359
Part II. Installation 359
348.10 Uses Permitted 359
348.12 Uses Not Permitted 359
348.20 Trade Size 360
348.22 Number of Conductors 360
348.24 Bends 361
348.26 Number of Bends (360°) 361
348.28 Trimming 361
348.30 Securing and Supporting 361
348.60 Equipment Grounding and Bonding Conductors 362

Article 350—Liquidtight Flexible Metal Conduit (Type LFMC) 363
Part I. General 363
350.1 Scope 363
350.2 Definition 363
350.6 Listing Requirements 363

Article 352 | Table of Contents

Part II. Installation	363
350.10	Uses Permitted	363
350.12	Uses Not Permitted	364
350.20	Trade Size	364
350.22	Number of Conductors	364
350.24	Bends	365
350.26	Number of Bends (360°)	365
350.28	Trimming	365
350.30	Securing and Supporting	365
350.60	Equipment Grounding and Bonding Conductors	366

Article 352—Rigid Polyvinyl Chloride Conduit (Type PVC) 369

Part I. General 369
- 352.1 Scope 369
- 352.2 Definition 369

Part II. Installation 369
- 352.10 Uses Permitted 369
- 352.12 Uses Not Permitted 370
- 352.20 Trade Size 371
- 352.22 Number of Conductors 371
- 352.24 Bends 372
- 352.26 Number of Bends (360°) 372
- 352.28 Trimming 372
- 352.30 Securing and Supporting 372
- 352.44 Expansion Fittings 373
- 352.46 Bushings 373
- 352.48 Joints 374
- 352.60 Equipment Grounding Conductor 374

Article 356—Liquidtight Flexible Nonmetallic Conduit (Type LFNC) 377

Part I. General 377
- 356.1 Scope 377
- 356.2 Definition 377
- 356.6 Listing Requirements 377

Part II. Installation 377
- 356.10 Uses Permitted 377
- 356.12 Uses Not Permitted 378
- 356.20 Trade Size 378
- 356.22 Number of Conductors 378
- 356.24 Bends 379
- 356.26 Number of Bends (360°) 379
- 356.30 Securing and Supporting 379
- 356.42 Fittings 379
- 356.60 Equipment Grounding Conductor 379

Article 358—Electrical Metallic Tubing (Type EMT) 381

Part I. General 381
- 358.1 Scope 381
- 358.2 Definition 381
- 358.6 Listing Requirements 381

Part II. Installation 382
- 358.10 Uses Permitted 382
- 358.12 Uses Not Permitted 382
- 358.20 Trade Size 382
- 358.22 Number of Conductors 383
- 358.24 Bends 383
- 358.26 Number of Bends (360°) 383
- 358.28 Reaming 383
- 358.30 Securing and Supporting 384
- 358.42 Couplings and Connectors 385
- 358.60 Equipment Grounding Conductor 385

Article 362—Electrical Nonmetallic Tubing (Type ENT) 387

Part I. General 387
- 362.1 Scope 387
- 362.2 Definition 387
- 362.6 Listing 387

Part II. Installation 387
- 362.10 Uses Permitted 387
- 362.12 Uses Not Permitted 389
- 362.20 Trade Sizes 389
- 362.22 Number of Conductors 389
- 362.24 Bends 390
- 362.26 Number of Bends (360°) 390
- 362.28 Trimming 390
- 362.30 Securing and Supporting 390
- 362.46 Bushings 391
- 362.48 Joints 391
- 362.60 Equipment Grounding Conductor 391

Article 376—Metal Wireways 393

Part I. General 393
- 376.1 Scope 393
- 376.2 Definition 393

Part II. Installation 393
- 376.10 Uses Permitted 393
- 376.12 Uses Not Permitted 394
- 376.20 Conductors Connected in Parallel 394
- 376.22 Number of Conductors and Ampacity 394
- 376.23 Wireway Sizing 395
- 376.30 Supports 396
- 376.56 Splices, Taps, and Power Distribution Blocks 397

Part III. Construction Specifications 398
376.100   Construction 398

Article 380—Multioutlet Assemblies 399
Part I. General 399
380.1   Scope 399
Part II. Installation 399
380.10   Uses Permitted 399
380.12   Uses Not Permitted 399
380.76   Through Partitions 399

Article 386—Surface Metal Raceways 401
Part I. General 401
386.1   Scope 401
386.2   Definition 401
386.6   Listing Requirements 402
Part II. Installation 402
386.10   Uses Permitted 402
386.12   Uses Not Permitted 402
386.21   Size of Conductors 402
386.22   Number of Conductors 402
386.30   Securing and Supporting 403
386.56   Splices and Taps 403
386.60   Equipment Grounding Conductor 403
386.70   Separate Compartments 403

Article 392—Cable Trays 405
Part I. General 405
392.1   Scope 405
392.2   Definition 405
Part II. Installation 405
392.10   Uses Permitted 405
392.12   Uses Not Permitted 407
392.18   Cable Tray Installations 407
392.20   Cable and Conductor Installation 408
392.30   Securing and Supporting 408
392.44   Expansion Splice Plates 408
392.46   Bushed Conduit and Tubing 408
392.56   Cable Splices 408
392.60   Equipment Grounding Conductor 409

CHAPTER 4—EQUIPMENT FOR GENERAL USE 411

Article 400—Flexible Cords and Flexible Cables 413
400.1   Scope 413
400.3   Suitability 413
400.4   Types of Flexible Cords and Flexible Cables 414
400.5   Ampacity of Flexible Cords and Flexible Cables 414
400.10   Uses Permitted 414
400.12   Uses Not Permitted 415
400.14   Pull at Joints and Terminals 416
400.17   Protection from Damage 417

Article 404—Switches 419
Part I. Installation 419
404.1   Scope 419
404.2   Switch Connections 419
404.3   Switch Enclosures 421
404.4   Damp or Wet Locations 422
404.7   Indicating 422
404.8   Accessibility and Grouping 423
404.9   General-Use Snap Switches, Dimmers, and Control Switches 425
404.10   Mounting of Snap Switches, Dimmers, and Control Switches 426
404.12   Grounding of Enclosures 427
404.14   Rating and Use of Snap Switches 427
Part II. Construction Specifications 427
404.20   Switch Marking 427
404.22   Electronic Control Switches 428

Article 408—Switchboards and Panelboards 429
Part I. General 429
408.1   Scope 429
408.3   Arrangement of Busbars and Conductors 429
408.4   Field Identification 430
408.5   Clearance for Conductors Entering Bus Enclosures 431
408.6   Short-Circuit Current Rating 432
408.7   Unused Openings 432
408.8   Reconditioning of Equipment 432
Part II. Switchboards and Switchgear 432
408.18   Clearances 432
Part III. Panelboards 432
408.36   Overcurrent Protection 432
408.37   Panelboards in Damp or Wet Locations 433
408.40   Equipment Grounding Conductor 433
408.41   Neutral Conductor Terminations 434
408.43   Panelboard Orientation 434

Article 445—Generators 435
445.1   Scope 435
445.6   Listing 435
445.11   Marking 435
445.13   Ampacity of Conductors 436
445.18   Disconnecting Means and Emergency Shutdown 436

Article 450 | Table of Contents

Article 450—Transformers 439
450.1	Scope	439
450.3	Overcurrent Protection	439
450.9	Ventilation	440
450.10	Grounding and Bonding	440
450.13	Transformer Accessibility	440
450.14	Disconnecting Means	441

Article 480—Storage Batteries 443
480.1	Scope	443
480.2	Definitions	443
480.4	Battery and Cell Terminations	444
480.5	Wiring and Equipment Supplied from Batteries	445
480.7	Direct-Current Disconnect Methods	445
480.8	Insulation of Batteries	445
480.9	Battery Support Systems	445
480.10	Battery Locations	446
480.12	Battery Interconnections	446
480.13	Ground-Fault Detection	446

CHAPTER 6—SPECIAL EQUIPMENT 447

Article 690—Solar Photovoltaic (PV) Systems 449

Part I. General 449
690.1	Scope	449
690.2	Definitions	451
690.4	General Requirements	454
690.6	Alternating-Current Modules and Systems	455

Part II. Circuit Requirements 456
690.7	Maximum PV System Direct-Current Circuit Voltage	456
690.8	Circuit Current and Conductor Sizing	460
690.9	Overcurrent Protection	465
690.10	Stand-Alone Systems	467
690.11	Arc-Fault Circuit Protection	467
690.12	Rapid Shutdown	467

Part III. Disconnect 469
690.13	PV System Disconnect	469
690.15	PV Equipment Disconnecting Means to Isolate PV Equipment	470

Part IV. Wiring Methods 472
690.31	Wiring Methods	472
690.32	Component Interconnections	477
690.33	Connectors (Mating)	477
690.34	Access to Boxes	478

Part V. Grounding and Bonding 478
690.43	Equipment Grounding and Bonding	478
690.45	Size of Equipment Grounding Conductors	479
690.47	Grounding Electrode System	480

Part VI. Markings and Labels 481
690.53	Direct-Current PV Circuit Label	481
690.54	Interactive System Point of Interconnection	482
690.55	Energy Storage	482
690.56	Identification of Power Sources	482

Part VII. Connections to Other Sources 483
690.59	Connection to Other Power Sources	483

Part VIII. Energy Storage Systems 483
690.71	Energy Storage Systems	483
690.72	Self-Regulated PV Charge Control	484

Article 691—Large-Scale Photovoltaic (PV) Electric Supply Stations 485
691.1	Scope	485
691.2	Definitions	485
691.4	Special Requirements for Large-Scale PV Electric Supply Stations	485
691.5	Equipment	486
691.6	Engineered Design	486
691.7	Conformance of Construction to Engineered Design	486
691.8	Direct-Current Operating Voltage	486
691.9	Disconnect for Isolating Photovoltaic Equipment	486
691.10	Arc-Fault Mitigation	486
691.11	Fence Bonding and Grounding	486

CHAPTER 7—SPECIAL CONDITIONS 487

Article 705—Interconnected Electric Power Production Sources 489

Part I. General 489
705.1	Scope	489
705.2	Definitions	489
705.6	Equipment Approval	490
705.8	System Installation	490
705.10	Identification of Power Sources	490
705.11	Supply-Side Source Connections	491
705.12	Load-Side Source Connections	493
705.13	Power Control Systems	499
705.16	Interrupting and Short-Circuit Current Rating	500
705.20	Disconnect	500
705.25	Wiring Methods	500
705.28	Circuit Sizing and Current	500
705.30	Overcurrent Protection	501
705.32	Ground-Fault Protection	502
705.40	Loss of Utility Power	502
705.45	Unbalanced Interconnections	502

Part II. Microgrid Systems 504
705.50	System Operation	504
705.60	Primary Power Source Connection	504

Article 706—Energy Storage Systems 505
Part I. General 505
- 706.1 Scope 505
- 706.2 Definitions 506
- 706.3 Qualified Personnel 506
- 706.4 System Requirements 506
- 706.5 Listing 507
- 706.6 Multiple Systems 507
- 706.8 Storage Batteries 507
- 706.9 Maximum Voltage 507

Part II. Disconnect 507
- 706.15 Disconnect 507

Part III. Installation Requirements 508
- 706.20 General 508
- 706.21 Directory (Identification of Power Sources) 509

Part IV. Circuit Requirements 509
- 706.30 Circuit Sizing and Current 509
- 706.31 Overcurrent Protection 510
- 706.33 Charge Control 510

Part V. Flow Battery Energy Storage Systems 511

Article 710—Stand-Alone Systems 513
- 710.1 Scope 513
- 710.6 Equipment Approval 513
- 710.10 Identification of Power Sources 514
- 710.12 Stand-Alone Inverter Input Circuit Current 514
- 710.15 General 514

Practice Questions 517

Final Exam A—Straight Order 551

Final Exam B—Random Order 563

INDEX 573

About the Author 583

About the Illustrator 584

About the Mike Holt Team 585

Notes

ABOUT THIS TEXTBOOK

Mike Holt's Illustrated Guide to Understanding NEC® Requirements for Solar Photovoltaic and Energy Storage Systems, based on the 2020 NEC®

This textbook covers the *National Electrical Code®* requirements as they relate to Solar Photovoltaic (PV) systems. While some may think that only Articles 690 and 691 relate to Solar PV installations, the reality is that almost every chapter in the *NEC* pertains to some part of a PV installation or to a location where PV may be installed. This text covers not only the conductors and equipment that are directly responsible for the production of power, but it also covers the rules that apply to conversion and delivery of this power to the end user and the utility. The *NEC®* rules that govern PV systems are very complex and as a result, could easily be misinterpreted. The intent of this textbook is to help you narrow down which rules relate to a PV installation and to better understand how and when they should be applied. Changes to these *NEC* rules for 2020 are indicated by underlining in the chapter color.

Mike's writing style is informative, practical, easy to understand, and applicable for today's electrical professional. As with all of Mike Holt's textbooks, this one is built around hundreds of full-color illustrations and photographs that show the requirements of the *National Electrical Code* in a practical setting. The images provide a visual representation of the information being discussed, helping you to better understand how the *Code* rules are applied.

This material also explains possible conflicts or frequently misinterpreted *NEC* requirements, tips on proper electrical installations, and the hazards related to improper installations. Sometimes a rule seems confusing or it may be difficult to understand its actual application. Where this is the case, you will find additional content and videos that further explain how to apply the *NEC*. Our intention is to help the industry better understand the *NEC* and encourage all *Code* users to be a part of the change process that helps create a better *NEC* for the future.

As with all of Mike Holt's textbooks, this one is supported by in-depth videos that will take your understanding of PV systems to another level. The panel that was assembled for the making of this video was selected from the top experts in the PV industry and they bring a unique perspective to this discussion of *NEC* requirements for solar installations. As the installations of PV systems become more prevalent, the chances that you'll need to work on them will greatly increase. If you haven't participated in any additional training for PV systems, you could create a hazard for both yourself and the end user by working on the system.

Keeping up with the current requirements of the *NEC* should be the goal of everyone involved in the electrical industry, whether you are an installer, contractor, inspector, engineer or instructor, and this textbook is designed to help you do so.

The Scope of This Textbook

This textbook, Mike Holt's *Illustrated Guide to Understanding NEC Requirements for Solar Photovoltaic and Energy Storage Systems, based on the 2020 NEC*, focuses on the *NEC* rules that apply to Solar PV systems. The scope of the textbook covers the general requirements contained in Articles 90 through 480, that every solar installer should know, as well as the rules specific to these systems found in Articles 690, 691, 705, 706, and 710.

This program is based on solidly grounded alternating-current systems, 1,000V or less, using 90°C insulated copper conductors sized to 60°C rated terminals for 100A and less rated circuits, and 75°C rated terminals for over 100A rated circuits, unless indicated otherwise.

How to Use This Textbook

This textbook is intended to help you interpret the *NEC* and is not a replacement for it, so be sure to have a copy of the 2020 *National Electrical Code* handy. You will notice that we have paraphrased a great deal of the wording, and some of the article and section titles appear different than those in the actual *Code* book. We believe doing so makes it easier to understand the content of the rule, so keep that in mind when comparing this textbook to the *NEC*.

Technical Questions | About This Textbook

Always compare what is being explained in this textbook to what the *Code* book says and underline or highlight pertinent rules. Get with others who are knowledgeable about the *NEC* to discuss any topics you find difficult to understand or join our free *Code* Forum at MikeHolt.com/Forum to post your question.

NEC Content. This textbook follows the *Code* format, but it does not cover every requirement. For example, it does not include every article, section, subsection, exception, or Informational Note. So, do not be concerned if you see that the textbook contains Exception 1 and Exception 3, but not Exception 2.

Cross-References. Many *NEC* rules refer to requirements located in other sections of the *Code*. This textbook does the same with the intention of helping you develop a better understanding of how the *NEC* rules relate to one another. These cross-references are indicated by *Code* section numbers in brackets, an example of which is "[90.4]."

Informational Notes. Informational Notes contained in the *NEC* will be identified in this textbook as "Note."

Exceptions. Where shown in this textbook, Exceptions to *NEC* rules will be identified as simply "Ex" and not spelled out.

As you read through this textbook, allow yourself enough time to review the text using the outstanding graphics and follow the step-by-step examples meant to assist you in a more in-depth understanding of the *Code*.

Technical Questions

As you progress through this textbook, you might find that you don't understand every explanation, example, calculation, or comment. Don't become frustrated, and don't get down on yourself. Remember, this is the *National Electrical Code*, and sometimes the best attempt to explain a concept isn't enough to make it perfectly clear. If you're still confused, visit MikeHolt.com/Forum, and post your question on our free Code Forum. The forum is a moderated community of electrical professionals.

Textbook Corrections

We're committed to providing you the finest product with the fewest errors and take great care to ensure our textbooks are correct. But we're realistic and know that errors might be found after printing. If you believe that there's an error of any kind (typographical, grammatical, technical, etc.) in this textbook or in the Answer Key, please visit MikeHolt.com/Corrections and complete the online Correction Form.

Key Features

The layout and design of this textbook incorporate special features and symbols designed to help you navigate easily through the material, and to enhance your understanding.

 A **QR Code** under the section number can be scanned with a smartphone app to take you to a sample video clip to see Mike and the video panel discuss this rule. For a complete list of all the videos that accompany this product call 888.632.2633.

Caution, Warning, and Danger Icons

These icons highlight areas of concern.

Caution
Caution: An explanation of possible damage to property or equipment.

Warning
Warning: An explanation of possible severe property damage or personal injury.

Danger
Danger: An explanation of possible severe injury or death.

Formulas

$$P = I \times E$$

Formulas are easily identifiable in green text on a gray bar.

Modular Color-Coded Page Layout

Chapters are color-coded and modular to make it easy to navigate through each section of the textbook.

About This Textbook | **Key Features**

Code Rule Headers. The *Code* rule being taught is identified with a chapter color bar and white text.

Author's Comments. These comments provide additional information to help you understand the context.

Code Change text. Underlined text denotes changes to the *Code* for the 2020 *NEC*.

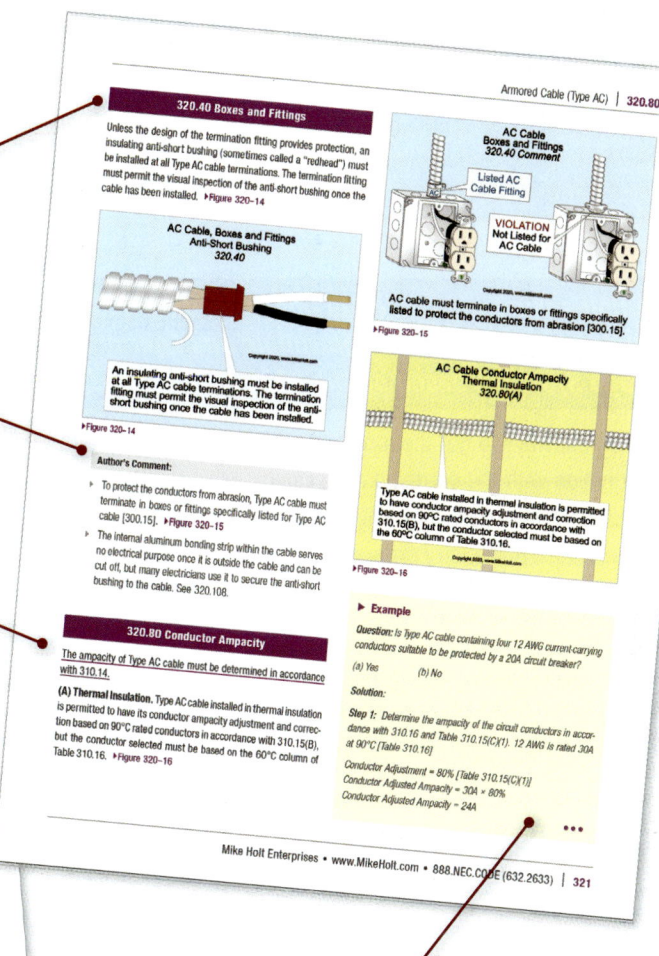

Examples. These practical application questions and answers are contained in yellow boxes.

If you see an ellipsis (• • •) at the bottom corner of a text box or example, it is completed on the following page.

Additional Background Information Boxes. Where information unrelated to the specific rule will help you understand the concept being taught, we include these topics, easily identified in boxes that are shaded gray.

ADDITIONAL PRODUCTS TO HELP YOU LEARN

Mike Holt's Illustrated Guide to Understanding NEC® Requirements for Solar Photovoltaic and Energy Storage Systems, based on the 2020 NEC® Videos

One of the best ways to get the most out of this textbook is to use it in conjunction with the corresponding videos. Mike Holt's videos provide a 360° view of each topic with specialized commentary from Mike and his panel of industry experts. Whether you're a visual or an auditory learner, watching the videos will enhance your knowledge and understanding.

 To add the videos that accompany this textbook, scan the QR code, call our office at 888.632.2633 and ask for product code 20SOLUPGRADEVI, or visit MikeHolt.com/upgrade20SOL.

Mike Holt's Business Success Program

It's time to take your business skills to the next level. Whether you have recently passed an exam, recently opened a business or are just looking to understand the electrical business from a different vantage point, Mike's Business Success Program can help you in the following areas:

Estimating. You will understand estimating and make sure that all your jobs are profitable, with this step-by-step Estimating training program.

Business Management. Part Motivation, part Business Wisdom, this module will help you get where you want to go faster.

Leadership. This program distills Mike's knowledge on running a successful business for over 40 years into the primary building blocks of being a leader.

Understanding the NEC Complete Training Library

When you really need to understand the *NEC*, there's no better way to learn it than with Mike's *NEC* Complete Training Library. It takes you step-by-step through the *NEC*, in *Code* order with detailed illustrations, great practice questions, and in-depth analysis on the videos. This library is perfect for engineers, electricians, contractors, and electrical inspectors.

Understanding the NEC—Volume 1 Textbook
▶ *Understanding the NEC Volume 1 videos*

Understanding the NEC Workbook, Articles 90-480

Understanding the NEC—Volume 2 Textbook
▶ *Understanding the NEC Volume 2 videos*

Bonding and Grounding Textbook
▶ *Bonding and Grounding videos*

NEC Online Quiz

Digital answer keys

Plus! A digital version of each book

Product Code: [20UNDLIBMM]

Mike Holt's Life Skills Program

This program explores the core skills of success. It is a life skills primer that gives you the roadmap to build the life you want and reach all your goals. Learn with Mike as he shares his ups and downs and the skills and wisdom that have made him successful in business for over 40 years. This program is a step-by-step training to help you improve your ability to reach your goals in your professional and personal life.

To order visit MikeHolt.com/Products or call 888.632.2633.

HOW TO USE THE *NATIONAL ELECTRICAL CODE*

The original *NEC* document was developed in 1897 as a result of the united efforts of various insurance, electrical, architectural, and other cooperative interests. The National Fire Protection Association (NFPA) has sponsored the *National Electrical Code* since 1911.

The purpose of the *Code* is the practical safeguarding of persons and property from hazards arising from the use of electricity. It isn't intended as a design specification or an instruction manual for untrained persons. It is, in fact, a standard that contains the minimum requirements for an electrical installation that's essentially free from hazard. Learning to understand and use the *Code* is critical to you working safely; whether you're training to become an electrician, or are already an electrician, electrical contractor, inspector, engineer, designer, or instructor.

The *NEC* was written for qualified persons; those who understand electrical terms, theory, safety procedures, and electrical trade practices. Learning to use the *Code* is a lengthy process and can be frustrating if you don't approach it the right way. First, you'll need to understand electrical theory and if you don't have theory as a background when you get into the *NEC*, you're going to struggle. Take one step back if necessary and learn electrical theory. You must also understand the concepts and terms in the *Code* and know grammar and punctuation in order to understand the complex structure of the rules and their intended purpose(s). The *NEC* is written in a formal outline which many of us haven't seen or used since high school or college so it's important for you to pay particular attention to this format. Our goal for the next few pages is to give you some guidelines and suggestions on using your *Code* book to help you understand that standard, and assist you in what you're trying to accomplish and, ultimately, your personal success as an electrical professional!

Language Considerations for the *NEC*

Terms and Concepts

The *NEC* contains many technical terms, and it's crucial for *Code* users to understand their meanings and applications. If you don't understand a term used in a rule, it will be impossible to properly apply the *NEC* requirement. Article 100 defines those that are used generally in two or more articles throughout the *Code*; for example, the term "Dwelling Unit" is found in many articles. If you don't know the *NEC* definition for a "dwelling unit" you can't properly identify its *Code* requirements. Another example worth mentioning is the term "Outlet." For many people it has always meant a receptacle—not so in the *NEC*!

Many *Code* articles use terms unique to that specific article, and the definitions of those terms only apply to that given article. Definitions for them are usually found in the beginning of the article. For example, Section 250.2 contains the definitions of terms that only apply to Article 250—Grounding and Bonding. Whether definitions are unique to a specific article, or apply throughout the *NEC*, is indicated at the beginning of the definitions (xxx.2) section of the article. For example, Article 690 contains definitions (in 690.2) that apply ONLY to that article while Article 705 introduces definitions (in 705.2) that apply throughout the entire *Code*.

Small Words, Grammar, and Punctuation

Technical words aren't the only ones that require close attention. Even simple words can make a big difference to the application of a rule. Is there a comma? Does it use "or," "and," "other than," "greater than," or "smaller than"? The word "or" can imply alternate choices for wiring methods. A word like "or" gives us choices while the word "and" can mean an additional requirement must be met.

An example of the important role small words play in the *NEC* is found in 110.26(C)(2), where it says equipment containing overcurrent, switching, "or" control devices that are 1,200A or more "and" over 6 ft wide require a means of egress at each end of the working space. In this section, the word "or" clarifies that equipment containing any of the three types of devices listed must follow this rule. The word "and" clarifies that 110.26(C)(2) only applies if the equipment is both 1,200A or more and over 6 ft wide.

NEC Style and Layout | How to Use the *National Electrical Code*

Grammar and punctuation play an important role in establishing the meaning of a rule. The location of a comma can dramatically change the requirement of a rule such as in 250.28(A), where it says a main bonding jumper shall be a wire, bus, screw, or similar suitable conductor. If the comma between "bus" and "screw" was removed, only a "bus screw" could be used. That comma makes a big change in the requirements of the rule.

Slang Terms or Technical Jargon

Trade-related professionals in different areas of the country often use local "slang" terms that aren't shared by all. This can make it difficult to communicate if it isn't clear what the meaning of those slang terms are. Use the proper terms by finding out what their definitions and applications are before you use them. For example, the term "pigtail" is often used to describe the short piece of conductor used to connect a device to a splice, but a "pigtail" is also used for a rubberized light socket with pre-terminated conductors. Although the term is the same, the meaning is very different and could cause confusion. The words "splice" and "tap" are examples of terms often interchanged in the field but are two entirely different things! The uniformity and consistency of the terminology used in the *Code*, makes it so everyone says and means the same thing regardless of geographical location.

NEC Style and Layout

It's important to understand the structure and writing style of the *Code* if you want to use it effectively. The *National Electrical Code* is organized using twelve major components.

1. Table of Contents
2. Chapters—Chapters 1 through 9 (major categories)
3. Articles—Chapter subdivisions that cover specific subjects
4. Parts—Divisions used to organize article subject matter
5. Sections—Divisions used to further organize article subject matter
6. Tables and Figures—Represent the mandatory requirements of a rule
7. Exceptions—Alternatives to the main *Code* rule
8. Informational Notes—Explanatory material for a specific rule (not a requirement)
9. Tables—Applicable as referenced in the *NEC*
10. Annexes—Additional explanatory information such as tables and references (not a requirement)
11. Index
12. Changes to the *Code* from the previous edition

1. Table of Contents. The Table of Contents displays the layout of the chapters, articles, and parts as well as the page numbers. It's an excellent resource and should be referred to periodically to observe the interrelationship of the various *NEC* components. When attempting to locate the rules for a specific situation, knowledgeable *Code* users often go first to the Table of Contents to quickly find the specific *NEC* rule that applies.

2. Chapters. There are nine chapters, each of which is divided into articles. The articles fall into one of four groupings: General Requirements (Chapters 1 through 4), Specific Requirements (Chapters 5 through 7), Communications Systems (Chapter 8), and Tables (Chapter 9).

Chapter 1—General
Chapter 2—Wiring and Protection
Chapter 3—Wiring Methods and Materials
Chapter 4—Equipment for General Use
Chapter 5—Special Occupancies
Chapter 6—Special Equipment
Chapter 7—Special Conditions
Chapter 8—Communications Systems (Telephone, Data, Satellite, Cable TV, and Broadband)
Chapter 9—Tables–Conductor and Raceway Specifications

3. Articles. The *NEC* contains approximately 140 articles, each of which covers a specific subject. It begins with Article 90, the introduction to the *Code* which contains the purpose of the *NEC*, what is covered and isn't covered, along with how the *Code* is arranged. It also gives information on enforcement, how mandatory and permissive rules are written, and how explanatory material is included. Article 90 also includes information on formal interpretations, examination of equipment for safety, wiring planning, and information about formatting units of measurement. Here are some other examples of articles you'll find in the *NEC*:

Article 110—Requirements for Electrical Installations
Article 250—Grounding and Bonding
Article 300—General Requirements for Wiring Methods and Materials
Article 430—Motors, Motor Circuits, and Motor Controllers
Article 500—Hazardous (Classified) Locations
Article 680—Swimming Pools, Fountains, and Similar Installations
Article 725—Remote-Control, Signaling, and Power-Limited Circuits
Article 800—General Requirements for Communications Systems

4. Parts. Larger articles are subdivided into parts. Because the parts of a *Code* article aren't included in the section numbers, we tend to forget to what "part" an *NEC* rule is relating. For example, Table 110.34(A) contains working space clearances for electrical equipment. If we aren't careful, we might think this table applies to all electrical installations, but Table 110.34(A) is in Part III, which only contains requirements for "Over 1,000 Volts, Nominal" installations. The rules for working clearances for electrical equipment for systems 1,000V, nominal, or less are contained in Table 110.26(A)(1), which is in Part II—1,000 Volts, Nominal, or Less.

5. Sections. Each *NEC* rule is called a "*Code* Section." A *Code* section may be broken down into subdivisions; first level subdivision will be in parentheses like (A), (B),..., the next will be second level subdivisions in parentheses like (1), (2),..., and third level subdivisions in lowercase letters such as (a), (b), and so on.

For example, the rule requiring all receptacles in a dwelling unit bathroom to be GFCI protected is contained in Section 210.8(A)(1) which is in Chapter 2, Article 210, Section 8, first level subdivision (A), and second level subdivision (1).

Note: According to the *NEC Style Manual*, first and second level subdivisions are required to have titles. A title for a third level subdivision is permitted but not required.

Many in the industry incorrectly use the term "Article" when referring to a *Code* section. For example, they say "Article 210.8," when they should say "Section 210.8." Section numbers in this textbook are shown without the word "Section," unless they're at the beginning of a sentence. For example, Section 210.8(A) is shown as simply 210.8(A).

6. Tables and Figures. Many *NEC* requirements are contained within tables, which are lists of *Code* rules placed in a systematic arrangement. The titles of the tables are extremely important; you must read them carefully in order to understand the contents, applications, and limitations of each one. Notes are often provided in or below a table; be sure to read them as well since they're also part of the requirement. For example, Note 1 for Table 300.5 explains how to measure the cover when burying cables and raceways and Note 5 explains what to do if solid rock is encountered.

7. Exceptions. Exceptions are *NEC* requirements or permissions that provide an alternative method to a specific rule. There are two types of exceptions—mandatory and permissive. When a rule has several exceptions, those exceptions with mandatory requirements are listed before the permissive exceptions.

Mandatory Exceptions. A mandatory exception uses the words "shall" or "shall not." The word "shall" in an exception means that if you're using the exception, you're required to do it in a specific way. The phrase "shall not" means it isn't permitted.

Permissive Exceptions. A permissive exception uses words such as "shall be permitted," which means it's acceptable (but not mandatory) to do it in this way.

8. Informational Notes. An Informational Note contains explanatory material intended to clarify a rule or give assistance, but it isn't a *Code* requirement.

9. Tables. Chapter 9 consists of tables applicable as referenced in the *NEC*. They're used to calculate raceway sizing, conductor fill, the radius of raceway bends, and conductor voltage drop.

10. Informative Annexes. Annexes aren't a part of the *Code* requirements and are included for informational purposes only.

Annex A. Product Safety Standards
Annex B. Application Information for Ampacity Calculation
Annex C. Raceway Fill Tables for Conductors and Fixture Wires of the Same Size
Annex D. Examples
Annex E. Types of Construction
Annex F. Critical Operations Power Systems (COPS)
Annex G. Supervisory Control and Data Acquisition (SCADA)
Annex H. Administration and Enforcement
Annex I. Recommended Tightening Torques
Annex J. ADA Standards for Accessible Design

11. Index. The Index at the back of the *NEC* is helpful in locating a specific rule using pertinent keywords to assist in your search.

12. Changes to the *Code*. Changes in the *NEC* are indicated as follows:

▸ Rules that were changed since the previous edition are identified by shading the revised text.

▸ New rules aren't shaded like a change, instead they have a shaded "N" in the margin to the left of the section number.

▸ Relocated rules are treated like new rules with a shaded "N" in the left margin by the section number.

▸ Deleted rules are indicated by a bullet symbol " • " located in the left margin where the rule was in the previous edition. Unlike older editions the bullet symbol is only used where one or more complete paragraphs have been deleted. There's no indication used where a word, group of words, or a sentence was deleted.

▸ A "Δ" represents text deletions and figure/table revisions.

How to Locate a Specific Requirement

How to go about finding what you're looking for in the *Code* book depends, to some degree, on your experience with the *NEC*. Experts typically know the requirements so well that they just go to the correct rule. Very experienced people might only need the Table of Contents to locate the requirement for which they're looking. On the other hand, average users should use all the tools at their disposal, including the Table of Contents, the Index, and the search feature on electronic versions of the *Code* book.

Let's work through a simple example: What *NEC* rule specifies the maximum number of disconnects permitted for a service?

Using the Table of Contents. If you're an experienced *Code* user, you might use the Table of Contents. You'll know Article 230 applies to "Services," and because this article is so large, it's divided up into multiple parts (eight parts to be exact). With this knowledge, you can quickly go to the Table of Contents and see it lists the Service Equipment Disconnecting Means requirements in Part VI.

Author's Comment:

▶ The number "70" precedes all page numbers in this standard because the *NEC* is NFPA Standard Number 70.

Using the Index. If you use the Index (which lists subjects in alphabetical order) to look up the term "service disconnect," you'll see there's no listing. If you try "disconnecting means," then "services," you'll find that the Index indicates the rule is in Article 230, Part VI. Because the *NEC* doesn't give a page number in the Index, you'll need to use the Table of Contents to find it, or flip through the *Code* book to Article 230, then continue to flip through pages until you find Part VI.

Many people complain that the *NEC* only confuses them by taking them in circles. Once you gain experience in using the *Code* and deepen your understanding of words, terms, principles, and practices, you'll find it much easier to understand and use than you originally thought.

With enough exposure in the use of the *NEC*, you'll discover that some words and terms are often specific to certain articles. The word "solar" for example will immediately send experienced *Code* book users to Article 690—Solar Photovoltaic (PV) Systems. The word "marina" suggests what you seek might be in Article 555. There are times when a main article will send you to a specific requirement in another one in which compliance is required in which case it will say (for example), "in accordance with 230.xx." Don't think of these situations as a "circle," but rather a map directing you to exactly where you need to be.

Customizing Your *Code* Book

One way to increase your comfort level with your *Code* book is to customize it to meet your needs. You can do this by highlighting and underlining important *NEC* requirements. Preprinted adhesive tabs are also an excellent aid to quickly find important articles and sections that are regularly referenced. However, understand that if you're using your *Code* book to prepare to take an exam, some exam centers don't allow markings of any type. For more information about tabs for your *Code* book, visit MikeHolt.com/Tabs.

Highlighting. As you read through or find answers to your questions, be sure you highlight those requirements in the *NEC* that are the most important or relevant to you. Use one color, like yellow, for general interest and a different one for important requirements you want to find quickly. Be sure to highlight terms in the Index and the Table of Contents as you use them.

Underlining. Underline or circle key words and phrases in the *Code* with a red or blue pen (not a lead pencil) using a short ruler or other straightedge to keep lines straight and neat. This is a very handy way to make important requirements stand out. A short ruler or other straightedge also comes in handy for locating the correct information in a table.

Interpretations

Industry professionals often enjoy the challenge of discussing, and at times debating, the *Code* requirements. These types of discussions are important to the process of better understanding the *NEC* requirements and applications. However, if you decide you're going to participate in one of these discussions, don't spout out what you think without having the actual *Code* book in your hand. The professional way of discussing a requirement is by referring to a specific section rather than talking in vague generalities. This will help everyone involved clearly understand the point and become better educated. In fact, you may become so well educated about the *NEC* that you might even decide to participate in the change process and help to make it even better!

Become Involved in the *NEC* Process

The actual process of changing the *Code* takes about two years and involves hundreds of individuals trying to make the *NEC* as current and accurate as possible. As you advance in your studies and understanding of the *Code*, you might begin to find it very interesting, enjoy it more, and realize that you can also be a part of the process. Rather than sitting back and allowing others to take the lead, you can participate by making proposals and being a part of its development. For the 2020 cycle, there were 3,730 Public Inputs and 1,930 comments. Hundreds of updates and five new articles were added to keep the *NEC* up to date with new technologies and pave the way to a safer and more efficient electrical future.

Here's how the process works:

STEP 1—Public Input Stage

Public Input. The revision cycle begins with the acceptance of Public Input (PI) which is the public notice asking for anyone interested to submit input on an existing standard or a committee-approved new draft standard. Following the closing date, the committee conducts a First Draft Meeting to respond to all Public Inputs.

First Draft Meeting. At the First Draft (FD) Meeting, the Technical Committee considers and provides a response to all Public Input. The Technical Committee may use the input to develop First Revisions to the standard. The First Draft documents consist of the initial meeting consensus of the committee by simple majority. However, the final position of the Technical Committee must be established by a ballot which follows.

Committee Ballot on First Draft. The First Draft developed at the First Draft Meeting is balloted. In order to appear in the First Draft, a revision must be approved by at least two-thirds of the Technical Committee.

First Draft Report Posted. First revisions which pass ballot are ultimately compiled and published as the First Draft Report on the document's NFPA web page. This report serves as documentation for the Input Stage and is published for review and comment. The public may review the First Draft Report to determine whether to submit Public Comments on the First Draft.

STEP 2—Public Comment Stage

Public Comment. Once the First Draft Report becomes available, there's a Public Comment period during which anyone can submit a Public Comment on the First Draft. After the Public Comment closing date, the Technical Committee conducts/holds their Second Draft Meeting.

Second Draft Meeting. After the Public Comment closing date, if Public Comments are received or the committee has additional proposed revisions, a Second Draft Meeting is held. At the Second Draft Meeting, the Technical Committee reviews the First Draft and may make additional revisions to the draft Standard. All Public Comments are considered, and the Technical Committee provides an action and response to each Public Comment. These actions result in the Second Draft.

Committee Ballot on Second Draft. The Second Revisions developed at the Second Draft Meeting are balloted. To appear in the Second Draft, a revision must be approved by at least two-thirds of the Technical Committee.

Second Draft Report Posted. Second Revisions which pass ballot are ultimately compiled and published as the Second Draft Report on the document's NFPA website. This report serves as documentation of the Comment Stage and is published for public review.

Once published, the public can review the Second Draft Report to decide whether to submit a Notice of Intent to Make a Motion (NITMAM) for further consideration.

STEP 3—NFPA Technical Meeting (Tech Session)

Following completion of the Public Input and Public Comment stages, there's further opportunity for debate and discussion of issues through the NFPA Technical Meeting that takes place at the NFPA Conference & Expo®. These motions are attempts to change the resulting final Standard from the committee's recommendations published as the Second Draft.

STEP 4—Council Appeals and Issuance of Standard

Issuance of Standards. When the Standards Council convenes to issue an NFPA standard, it also hears any related appeals. Appeals are an important part of assuring that all NFPA rules have been followed and that due process and fairness have continued throughout the standards development process. The Standards Council considers appeals based on the written record and by conducting live hearings during which all interested parties can participate. Appeals are decided on the entire record of the process, as well as all submissions and statements presented.

After deciding all appeals related to a standard, the Standards Council, if appropriate, proceeds to issue the Standard as an official NFPA Standard. The decision of the Standards Council is final subject only to limited review by the NFPA Board of Directors. The new NFPA standard becomes effective twenty days following the Standards Council's action of issuance.

Temporary Interim Amendment—(TIA)

Sometimes, a change to the *NEC* is of an emergency nature. Perhaps an editing mistake was made that can affect an electrical installation to the extent it may create a hazard. Maybe an occurrence in the field created a condition that needs to be addressed immediately and can't wait for the normal *Code* cycle and next edition of the standard. When these circumstances warrant it, a TIA or "Temporary Interim Amendment" can be submitted for consideration.

The NFPA defines a TIA as, "tentative because it has not been processed through the entire standards-making procedures. It is interim because it is effective only between editions of the standard. A TIA automatically becomes a Public Input of the proponent for the next edition of the standard; as such, it then is subject to all of the procedures of the standards-making process."

Author's Comment:

▸ Proposals, comments, and TIAs can be submitted for consideration online at the NFPA website, nfpa.org. From the homepage, look for "Codes & Standards," then find "Standards Development," and click on "How the Process Works." If you'd like to see something changed in the *Code*, you're encouraged to participate in the process.

2020 *Code* Book and Tabs

The ideal way to use your *Code* book is to tab it for quick reference—Mike's best-selling tabs make organizing the *NEC* easy.

If you're using your *Code* book for an exam, you'll need to confirm with your testing authority that a tabbed *Code* book is allowed into the exam room.

Order your tabs today, at MikeHolt.com/Tabs.

ARTICLE 90

INTRODUCTION TO THE *NATIONAL ELECTRICAL CODE*

Introduction to Article 90—Introduction to the *National Electrical Code*

Article 90 opens by saying the *National Electrical Code* (*NEC/Code*) is not intended as a design specification or instruction manual. It has one purpose only, and that is the "practical safeguarding of persons and property from hazards arising from the use of electricity." That does not necessarily mean the installation will be efficient, convenient, or able to accommodate future expansion; just safe. The necessity of carefully studying the *Code* rules cannot be overemphasized, and the step-by-step explanatory design of a textbook such as this is to help in that undertaking. Understanding where to find the requirements in the *NEC* that apply to the installation is invaluable. Rules in several different articles often apply to even a simple installation. You are not going to remember every section of every article of the *Code* but, hopefully, you will come away with knowing where to look after studying this textbook.

Article 90 then goes on to describe the scope and arrangement of the *NEC*. The balance of it provides the reader with information essential to understanding the *Code* rules.

Most electrical installations require you to understand the first four chapters of the *NEC* (which apply generally) and have a working knowledge of the Chapter 9 tables. That understanding begins with this article. Chapters 5, 6, and 7 make up a large portion of the *Code* book, but they apply to special occupancies, special equipment, or special conditions. They build on, modify, or amend the rules in the first four chapters. Chapter 8 contains the requirements for communications systems, such as radio and television equipment, satellite receivers, antenna systems, twisted pair conductors, and coaxial cable wiring. Communications systems are not subject to the general requirements of Chapters 1 through 4, or the special requirements of Chapters 5 through 7, unless there is a specific reference to a rule in the previous chapters.

90.1 Purpose of the *NEC*

(A) Practical Safeguarding. The purpose of the *National Electrical Code* is to ensure electrical systems are installed in a manner that protects people and property by minimizing the risks associated with the use of electricity. The *NEC* is not a design specification standard nor is it an instruction manual for the untrained and unqualified. ▶Figure 90–1

Author's Comment:

▶ The *Code* is intended to be used by those who are skilled and knowledgeable in electrical theory, electrical systems, building and electrical construction, and the installation and operation of electrical equipment.

▶Figure 90–1

90.2 | Introduction to the National Electrical Code

(B) Adequacy. The *NEC* contains the requirements considered necessary for a safe electrical installation. If one is installed in compliance with the *Code*, it is considered essentially free from electrical hazards.

The requirements contained in the *NEC* are not intended to ensure an electrical installation will be efficient, convenient, adequate for good service, or suitable for future expansion. ▶Figure 90-2

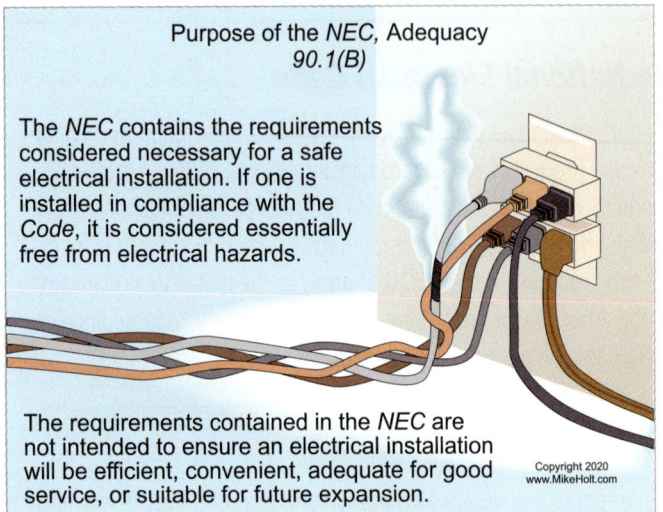
▶Figure 90-2

Author's Comment:

▸ Electrical energy management, equipment maintenance, power quality, or suitability for future loads are not issues within the scope of the *Code*.

Note: Hazards often occur because the initial wiring did not provide for increases in the use of electricity and therefore wiring systems become overloaded. ▶Figure 90-3

Author's Comment:

▸ The *NEC* does not require electrical systems to be designed or installed to accommodate future loads. However, the electrical designer (typically an electrical engineer) is concerned with not only ensuring electrical safety (*Code* compliance), but also that the electrical system meets the customers' needs, both for today and in the coming years. To satisfy their needs, electrical systems are often designed and installed above the minimum requirements contained in the *NEC*.

(C) Relation to International Standards. The requirements of the *Code* address the fundamental safety principles contained in the International Electrotechnical Commission (IEC) Standard.

▶Figure 90-3

Note: IEC 60364-1, Section 131, contains fundamental principles of protection for safety that encompass protection against electric shock, protection against thermal effects, protection against overcurrent, protection against fault currents, and protection against overvoltage. All of these potential hazards are addressed by the requirements in this *Code*. ▶Figure 90-4

▶Figure 90-4

90.2 Scope of the NEC

(A) What is Covered by the NEC. The *NEC* covers the installation and removal of electrical conductors, equipment, and raceways; signaling and communications conductors, equipment, and raceways; and optical fiber cables and raceways for the following: ▶Figure 90-5

Introduction to the *National Electrical Code* | 90.2

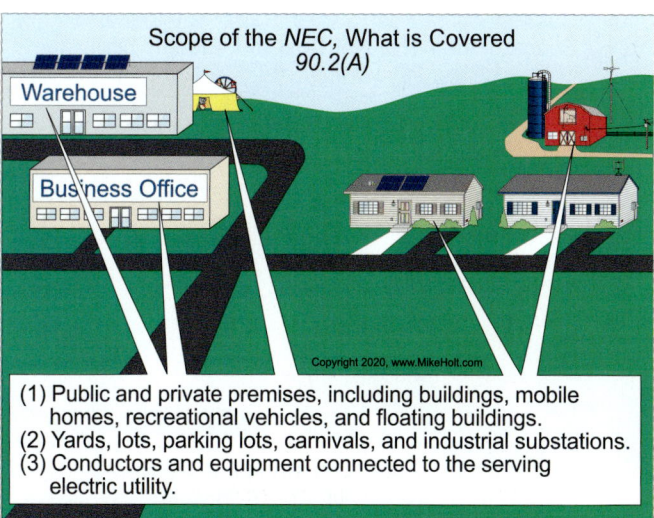
▶Figure 90-5

▶Figure 90-7

(1) Public and private premises including buildings, mobile homes, recreational vehicles, and floating buildings.

(2) Yards, lots, parking lots, carnivals, and industrial substations.

(3) Conductors and equipment connected to the serving electric utility.

(4) Installations used by a serving electric utility such as office buildings, warehouses, garages, machine shops, recreational buildings, and other electric utility buildings that are not an integral part of a utility's generating plant, substation, or control center. ▶Figure 90-6

Author's Comment:

▸ The new item in Article 90's scope, 90.2(A)(5), appears to include the power cable between the pedestal and the boat in the scope of the *NEC*, but there are no specific rules in Article 555 covering that power-supply cord.

▸ The text in 555.35(B) requires leakage detection equipment to detect leakage current from boats and applies to the load side of the supplying receptacle.

(6) Installations used to export electric power from vehicles to premises wiring or for bidirectional current flow ▶Figure 90-8

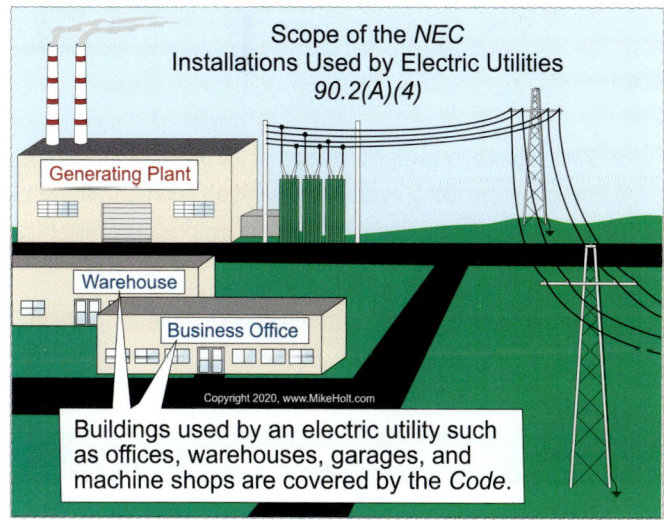
▶Figure 90-6

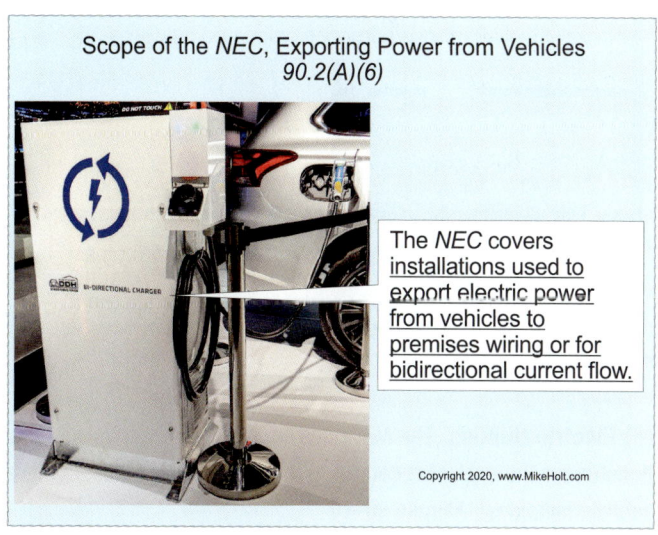
▶Figure 90-8

(5) Installations supplying shore power to watercraft in marinas and boatyards, including monitoring of leakage current. ▶Figure 90-7

90.3 | Introduction to the *National Electrical Code*

Author's Comment:

▸ The battery power supply of an electrical vehicle can be used "bidirectionally" which means it can be used as a backup or alternate power source to supply premises wiring circuits in the event of a power failure. The rules for this application can be found in Article 625.

(B) What is not Covered by the *NEC*. The *Code* does not apply to the installation of electrical or communications systems for:

(1) Transportation Vehicles. The *NEC* does not apply to installations in ships and watercraft other than floating buildings, and automotive vehicles other than mobile homes and recreational vehicles.

(2) Mining Equipment. The *Code* does not apply to installations underground in mines, and in self-propelled mobile surface mining machinery and its attendant electrical trailing cables.

(3) Railways. The *NEC* does not apply to railway power, signaling, energy storage, and communications wiring.

(4) Communications Utilities. The *Code* does not apply to installations under the exclusive control of the communications utility located in building spaces used exclusively for these purposes or located outdoors. ▸Figure 90–9

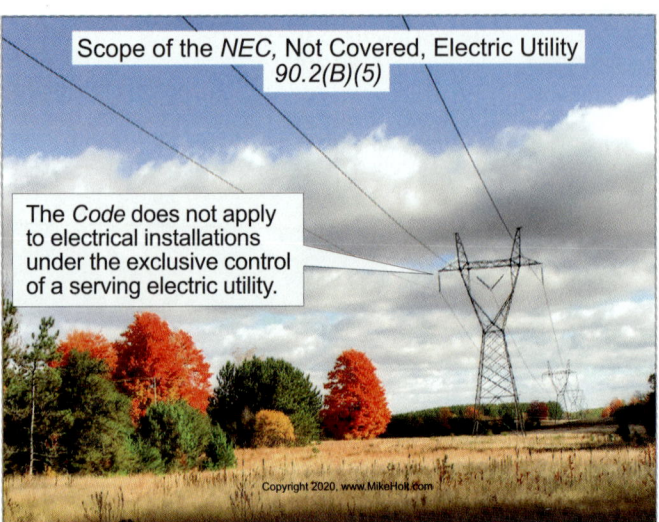

▸Figure 90–10

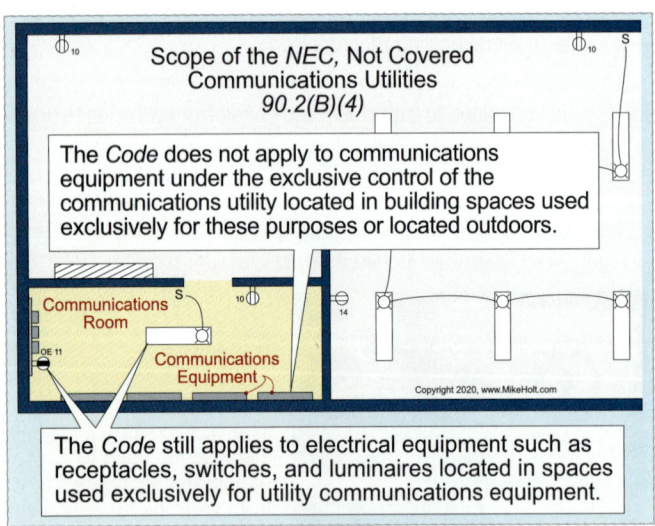

▸Figure 90–9

(5) Electric Utilities. The *NEC* does not apply to electrical installations under the exclusive control of a serving electric utility where such installations: ▸Figure 90–10

 a. Consist of service drops or service laterals and associated metering, or ▸Figure 90–11

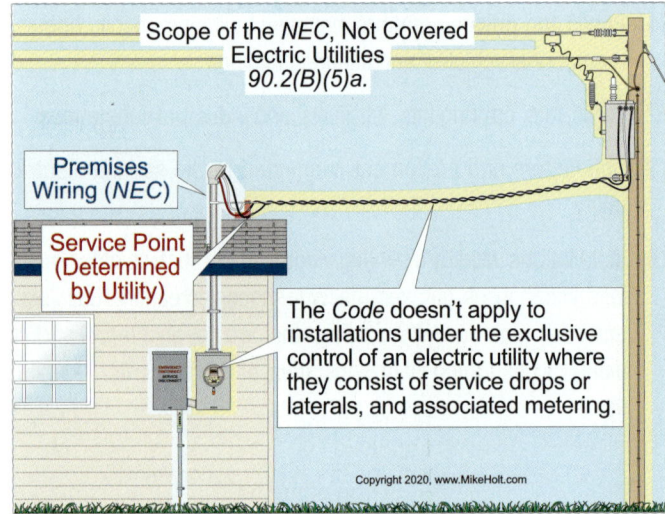

▸Figure 90–11

 b. Are on property owned or leased by the utility for the purpose of communications, metering, generation, control, transformation, transmission, energy storage, or distribution of electrical energy, or ▸Figure 90–12

 c. Are located in legally established easements or rights-of-way ▸Figure 90–13

90.3 *Code* Arrangement

General Requirements. The *Code* is divided into an introduction and nine chapters followed by informative annexes. Chapters 1, 2, 3, and 4 are general conditions. ▸Figure 90–14

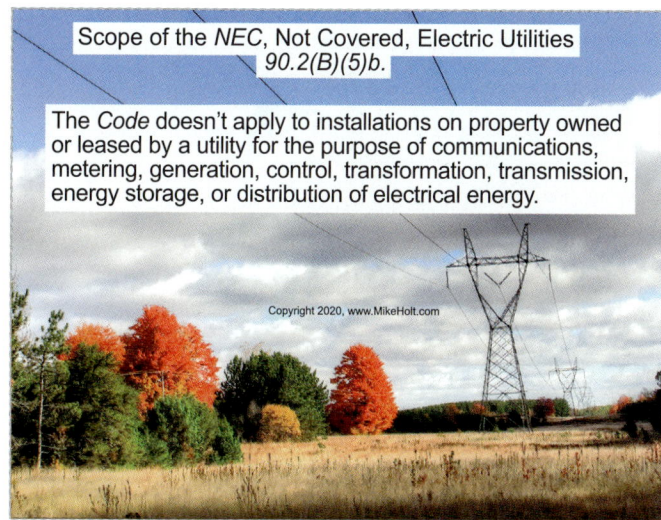
▶Figure 90–12

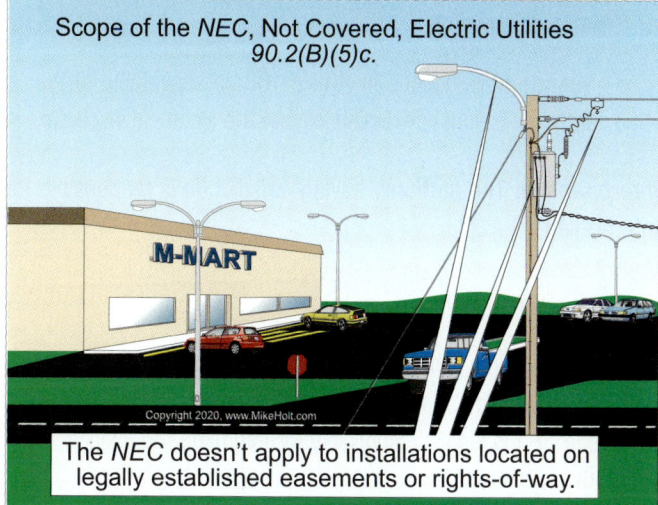
▶Figure 90–13

The requirements contained in Chapters 5, 6, and 7 apply to special occupancies, special equipment, or other special conditions, which may supplement or modify the requirements contained in Chapters 1 through 7; but not Chapter 8.

Chapter 8 contains the requirements for communications systems (twisted wire, antennas, and coaxial cable) which are not subject to the general requirements of Chapters 1 through 4, or the special requirements of Chapters 5 through 7, unless a specific reference in Chapter 8 is made to a rule in Chapters 1 through 7.

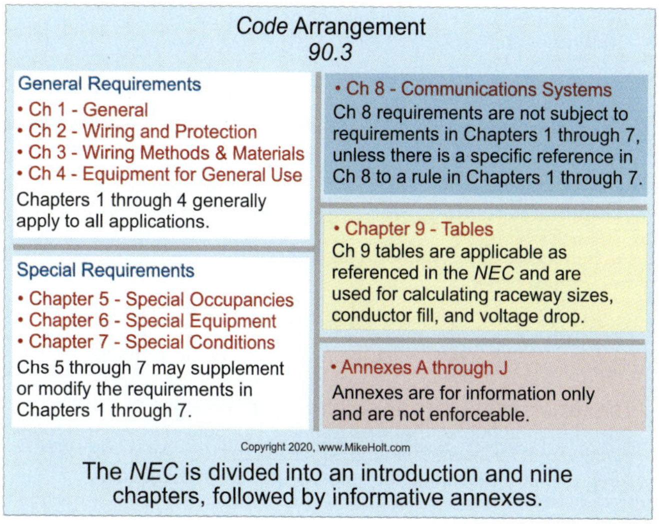

▶Figure 90–14

Chapter 9 consists of tables applicable as referenced in the *NEC*. The tables are used to calculate raceway sizing, conductor fill, the radius of raceway bends, and conductor voltage drop.

Annexes are not part of the requirements of the *Code* but are included for informational purposes. There are ten annexes:

▸ Annex A. Product Safety Standards
▸ Annex B. Application Information for Ampacity Calculation
▸ Annex C. Raceway Fill Tables for Conductors and Fixture Wires of the Same Size
▸ Annex D. Examples
▸ Annex E. Types of Construction
▸ Annex F. Critical Operations Power Systems (COPS)
▸ Annex G. Supervisory Control and Data Acquisition (SCADA)
▸ Annex H. Administration and Enforcement
▸ Annex I. Recommended Tightening Torques
▸ Annex J. ADA Standards for Accessible Design

90.4 Enforcement

The *NEC* is intended to be suitable for enforcement by governmental bodies that exercise legal jurisdiction over electrical installations for power, lighting, signaling circuits, and communications systems such as: ▶Figure 90–15

90.4 | Introduction to the *National Electrical Code*

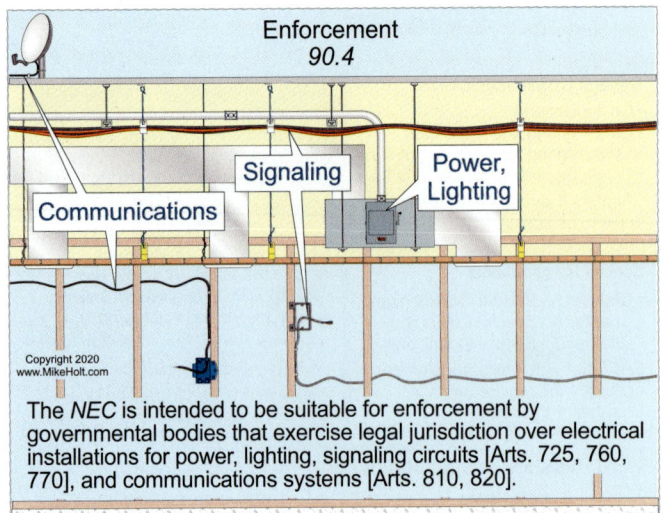

▶Figure 90–15

The *NEC* is intended to be suitable for enforcement by governmental bodies that exercise legal jurisdiction over electrical installations for power, lighting, signaling circuits [Arts. 725, 760, 770], and communications systems [Arts. 810, 820].

Signaling circuits include:

- Article 725. Remote-Control, Signaling, and Power-Limited Circuits
- Article 760. Fire Alarm Systems
- Article 770. Optical Fiber Cables

Communications systems which include:

- Article 810. Radio and Television Equipment (Satellite Antenna)
- Article 820. Community Antenna Television and Radio Distribution Systems (Coaxial Cable)

Author's Comment:

- Once adopted (in part, wholly, or amended), the *National Electrical Code* becomes statutory law for the adopting jurisdiction and is thereby considered a legal document.

Enforcement. The enforcement of the *NEC* is the responsibility of the authority having jurisdiction, who is responsible for interpreting requirements, approving equipment and materials, waiving *Code* requirements, and ensuring equipment is installed in accordance with listing instructions. ▶Figure 90–16

Author's Comment:

- "Authority Having Jurisdiction" is defined in Article 100 as the organization, office, or individual responsible for approving equipment, materials, an installation, or a procedure. See 90.4 and 90.7 for more information.

▶Figure 90–16

The enforcement of the *NEC* is the responsibility of the authority having jurisdiction, who is responsible for interpreting requirements, approving equipment and materials, waiving *Code* requirements, and ensuring equipment is installed in accordance with listing instructions.

Author's Comment:

- "Approved" is defined in Article 100 as acceptable to the authority having jurisdiction, usually the electrical inspector.

Interpretation. The authority having jurisdiction is responsible for interpreting the *NEC*.

Author's Comment:

- The authority having jurisdiction's decisions must be based on a specific *Code* requirement. If an installation is rejected, the AHJ is legally responsible for informing the installer of the specific *NEC* rule that was violated.

- The art of getting along with the AHJ consists of doing good work and knowing what the *Code* says (as opposed to what you think it says). It is also useful to know how to choose your battles when the inevitable disagreement does occur.

Approval of Equipment and Materials. Only the authority having jurisdiction has the authority to approve the installation of equipment and materials. ▶Figure 90–17

▶Figure 90–17

Author's Comment:

▸ Typically, the AHJ will approve equipment listed by a product testing organization such as Underwriters Laboratories, Inc. (UL). The *NEC* does not require all equipment to be listed, but many state and local authorities having jurisdictions do. See 90.7, 110.2, and 110.3 and the definitions for "Approved," "Identified," "Labeled," and "Listed" in Article 100.

▸ According to the *Code*, the authority having jurisdiction determines the approval of equipment. This means he or she can reject an installation of listed equipment and can approve the use of unlisted equipment. Given our highly litigious society, approval of unlisted equipment is becoming increasingly difficult to obtain.

Approval of Alternate Means. By special permission, the authority having jurisdiction may approve alternate methods where it is assured equivalent safety can be achieved and maintained.

Author's Comment:

▸ "Special Permission" is defined in Article 100 as the written consent of the AHJ.

Waiver of Product Requirements. If the *Code* requires products, constructions, or materials that are not yet available at the time the *NEC* is adopted, the authority having jurisdiction can allow products that were acceptable in the previous *Code* to continue to be used.

Author's Comment:

▸ Sometimes it takes years for testing laboratories to establish product standards for new *NEC* product requirements; then it takes time before manufacturers can design, manufacture, and distribute those products to the marketplace.

90.5 Mandatory Requirements and Explanatory Material

(A) Mandatory Requirements. The words "shall" or "shall not" indicate a mandatory requirement.

Author's Comment:

▸ For greater ease in reading this textbook, we will use the word "must" instead of "shall," and "must not" will be used instead of "shall not."

(B) Permissive Requirements. When the *Code* uses "shall be permitted" it means the action is permitted, but not required. Permissive rules are often contained in exceptions to the general requirement.

Author's Comment:

▸ For greater ease in reading, the phrase "shall be permitted" (as used in the *NEC*) has been replaced in this textbook with "is permitted" or "are permitted."

(C) Explanatory Material. References to other standards or information related to a *Code* rule are included in the form of "Informational Notes." Such notes are for informational purposes only and are not enforceable as an *NEC* requirement.

For example, Informational Note No. 3 in 210.19(A)(1) recommends that the voltage drop of a circuit not exceed 3 percent; this is a recommendation—not a *Code* requirement.

Author's Comment:

▸ For convenience and ease in reading this textbook, "Informational Notes" will simply be identified as "Note."

> **Caution**
> ⚡ Informational notes are not enforceable but notes to tables are. Within this textbook, we will call notes contained in a table a "Table Note."

(D) Informative Annexes. Informative annexes contained in the back of the *Code* book are for information only and are not enforceable as requirements of the *NEC*.

90.7 Examination of Equipment for Product Safety

Product evaluation for *Code* compliance, approval, and safety is typically performed by a nationally recognized testing laboratory in accordance with the listing standards.

Except to detect alterations or damage, listed factory-installed internal wiring of equipment that has been processed by a qualified testing laboratory does not need to be inspected for *NEC* compliance at the time of installation. ▶Figure 90–18

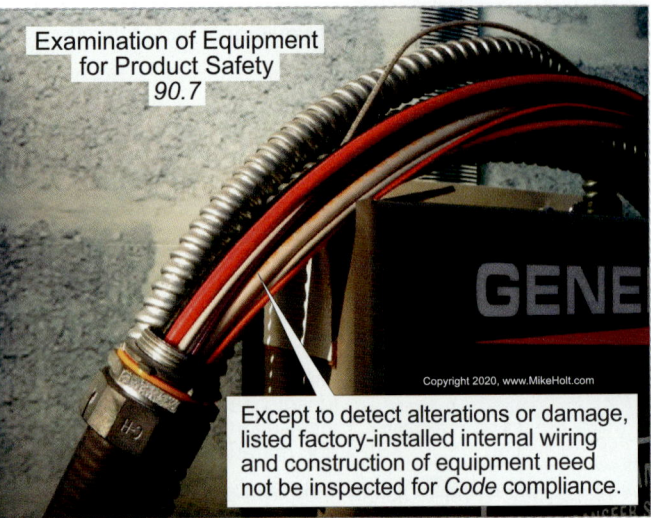

▶Figure 90–18

Note 1: The requirements contained in Article 300 do not apply to the integral parts of electrical equipment. See 110.3(B).

Note 2: "Listed" is defined in Article 100 as equipment or materials included in a list published by a testing laboratory acceptable to the authority having jurisdiction. The listing organization must periodically inspect the production of listed equipment or material to ensure it meets appropriate designated standards and is suitable for a specified purpose.

CHAPTER 1

GENERAL RULES

Introduction to Chapter 1—General Rules

Before you can make sense of the *NEC*, you must become familiar with its general rules, concepts, definitions, and requirements. Chapter 1 consists of two topics; Article 100 which provides definitions that help ensure consistency when *Code*-related matters are the topic of discussion, and Article 110 which supplies the general requirements needed to correctly apply the *NEC*.

After gaining an understanding of Chapter 1, some of the *Code* requirements that might be confusing to many, will become increasingly clear to you. *NEC* requirements will make more sense to you because you will have the foundation from which to build upon your understanding and application of the rules.

▶ **Article 100—Definitions.** Article 100 is organized into three parts. Part I contains the definitions of terms used throughout the *Code* for systems that operate at 1,000V, nominal, or less. The definitions of terms in Part II apply to systems that operate at over 1,000V, nominal, are not within the scope of this textbook. Part III contains definitions applicable to "Hazardous (Classified) Locations" found in Chapter 5 of the *NEC*.

This article overall, only contains terms used in more than one article. Definitions of standard terms, such as volt, voltage drop, ampere, impedance, and resistance, are not contained in Article 100. If the *NEC* does not define a term, then a dictionary or building code acceptable to the authority having jurisdiction should be consulted.

Definitions are sometimes located at the beginning of an article. When this occurs, those terms only apply to that given article. There is uniformity in the location of the definitions specific to an article in that the article number will be followed by ".2." For example, definitions specific to solar photovoltaic (PV) systems are found in 690.2.

▶ **Article 110—Requirements for Electrical Installations.** This article contains general requirements applicable to all electrical installations.

Notes

ARTICLE 100 DEFINITIONS

Introduction to Article 100—Definitions

Have you ever had a conversation with someone only to discover that what you said and what he or she heard were completely different? This often happens when people have different definitions or interpretations of the words being used, and that is why the definitions of key *NEC* terms are located at the beginning of the *Code* (Article 100), or at the beginning of each article. If we can all agree on important definitions, then we speak the same language and avoid misunderstandings. Words taken out of context have created more than their fair share of problems. Because the *NEC* exists to protect people and property, it is very important for you to be able to convey and comprehend the language used. Review and study Article 100 until you are confident you know the definitions presented.

100 Definitions

Scope. This article contains definitions essential to the application of this *Code*; it does not include general or technical terms from other *code*s and standards. In general, only those used in two or more articles are defined in Article 100.

Definitions are also found in the xxx.2 sections of other articles.

- Part I of this article contains definitions intended to apply wherever the terms are used throughout the *NEC*.
- Part III contains definitions applicable to Hazardous (Classified) Locations.

Accessible (as applied to equipment). Capable of being reached for operation, renewal, and inspection. ▶Figure 100–1

Accessible, Readily (Readily Accessible). Capable of being reached quickly for operation, renewal, or inspection without requiring those to whom ready access is necessary to use tools (other than keys), climb over or under obstructions, remove obstacles, resort to using portable ladders, and so forth. ▶Figure 100–2

Note: The use of keys for locks on electrical equipment, and locked doors to electrical equipment rooms and vaults is a common practice and permitted by the *NEC*. ▶Figure 100–3

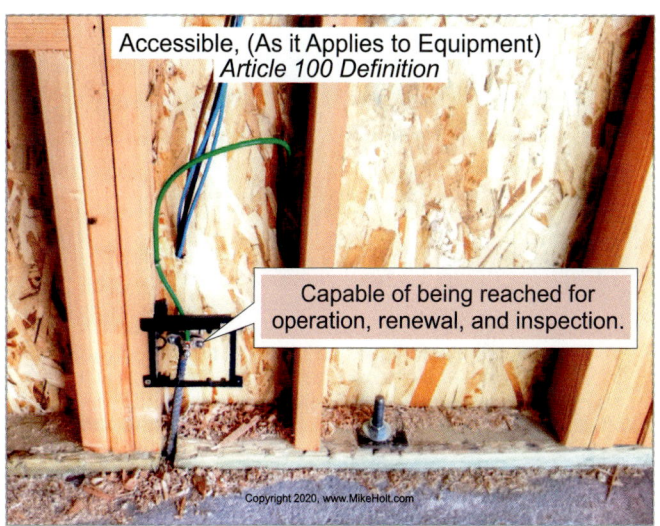

▶Figure 100–1

Ampacity. The current, in amperes, a conductor can carry continuously under its conditions of use without exceeding its temperature rating. ▶Figure 100–4

Author's Comment:

- See 310.10 and 310.15 for details and examples.

Approved. Acceptable to the authority having jurisdiction; usually the electrical inspector. ▶Figure 100–5

100 | Definitions

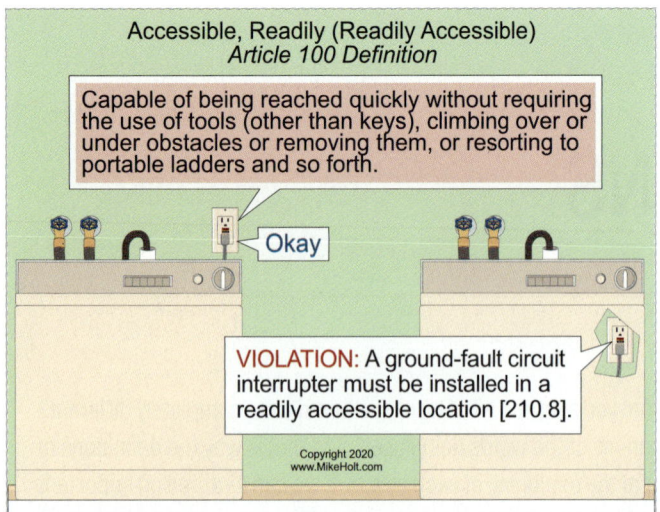
▶Figure 100–2

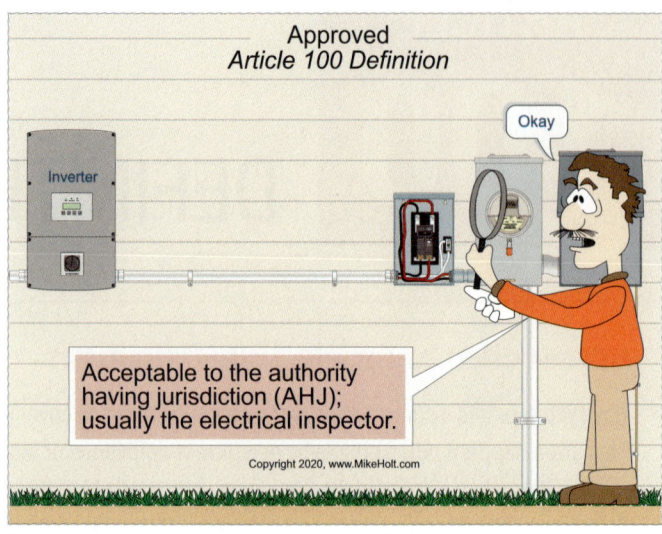
▶Figure 100–5

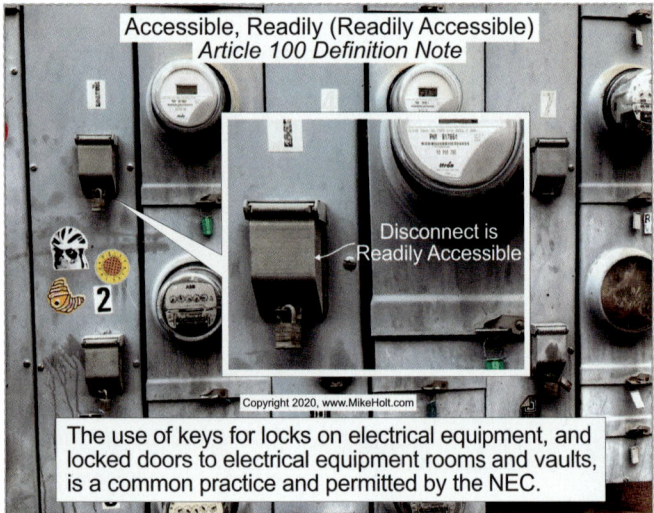
▶Figure 100–3

Author's Comment:

▸ Product listing does not mean the product is approved, but it can be a basis for approval. See 90.4, 90.7, and 110.2 and the definitions in this article for "Authority Having Jurisdiction," "Identified," "Labeled," and "Listed."

Attachment Fitting. A device that, by insertion into a locking support and mounting receptacle, establishes a connection between the conductors of the attached utilization equipment and the branch-circuit conductors connected to the locking support and mounting receptacle.

Note: An attachment fitting is different than an attachment plug, because no cord is associated with the fitting. An attachment fitting in combination with a locking support and mounting receptacle secures the associated utilization equipment in place and supports its weight.

Attachment Plug (Plug Cap), (Plug). A wiring device at the end of a flexible cord intended to be inserted into a receptacle in order to make an electrical connection. ▶Figure 100–6

Authority Having Jurisdiction (AHJ). The organization, office, or individual responsible for approving equipment, materials, an installation, or a procedure. See 90.4 and 90.7 for more information.

Note: The authority having jurisdiction may be a federal, state, or local government department or individual such as a fire chief, fire marshal, chief of a fire prevention bureau, labor or health department, a building official, electrical inspector, or others having statutory authority. In some circumstances, the property owner or his or her agent assumes the role, and at government installations, the commanding officer or departmental official may be the authority having jurisdiction.

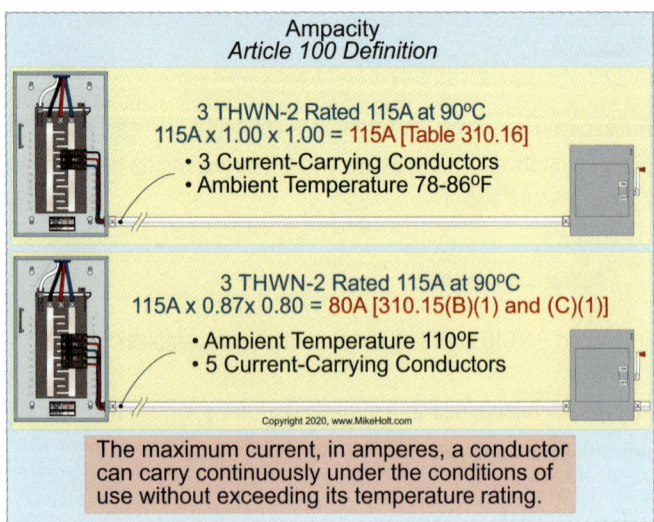
▶Figure 100–4

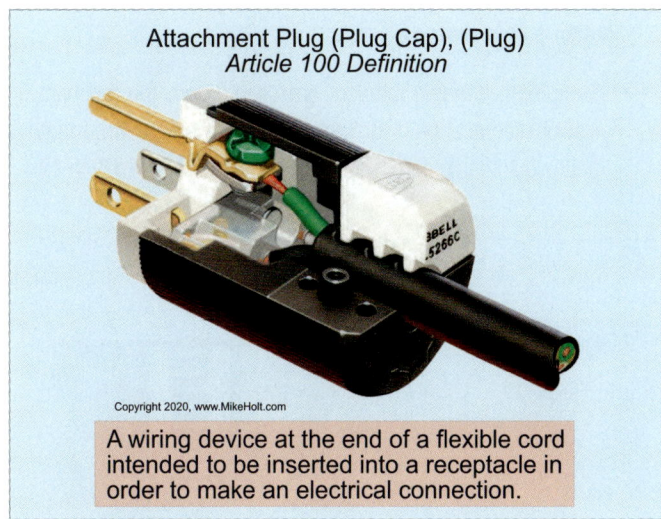
▶Figure 100–6

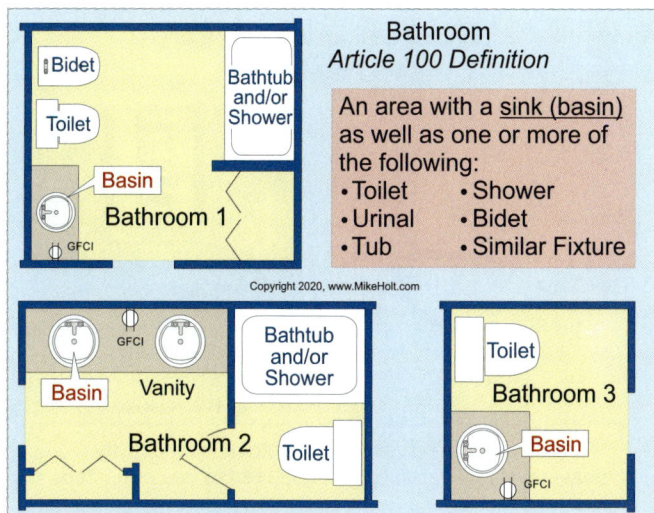
▶Figure 100–7

Author's Comment:

▸ The authority having jurisdiction is typically the electrical inspector who has legal statutory authority. In the absence of federal, state, or local regulations, the operator of the facility or his or her agent (such as an architect or engineer of the facility) can assume the role.

▸ Most expect the "authority having jurisdiction" to have at least some prior experience in the electrical field, such as having studied electrical engineering or having obtained an electrical contractor's license. In a few states this is a legal requirement. Memberships, certifications, and active participation in electrical organizations such as the International Association of Electrical Inspectors (IAEI) speak to an individual's qualifications. Visit www.IAEI.org for more information about that organization.

Automatic. Functioning without needing human intervention.

Bathroom. An area that includes a sink (basin) as well as one or more of the following: a toilet, urinal, tub, shower, bidet, or similar plumbing fixture. ▶Figure 100–7

Bonded (Bonding). Connected to establish electrical continuity and conductivity. ▶Figure 100–8 and ▶Figure 100–9

Bonding Conductor or Jumper. A conductor that ensures electrical conductivity between metal parts of the electrical installation. ▶Figure 100–10

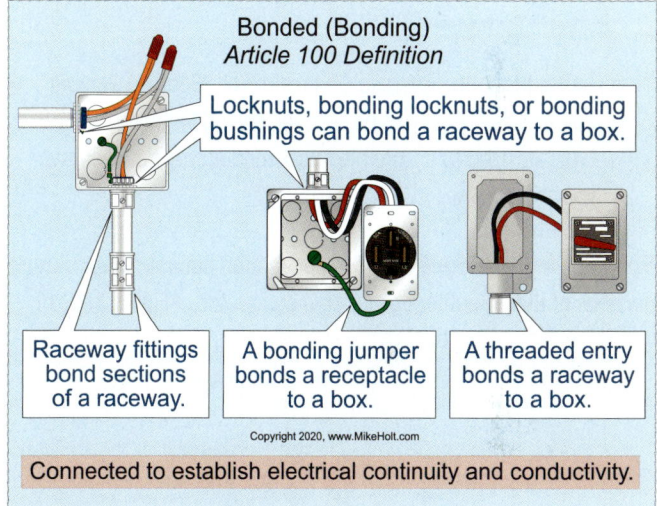
▶Figure 100–8

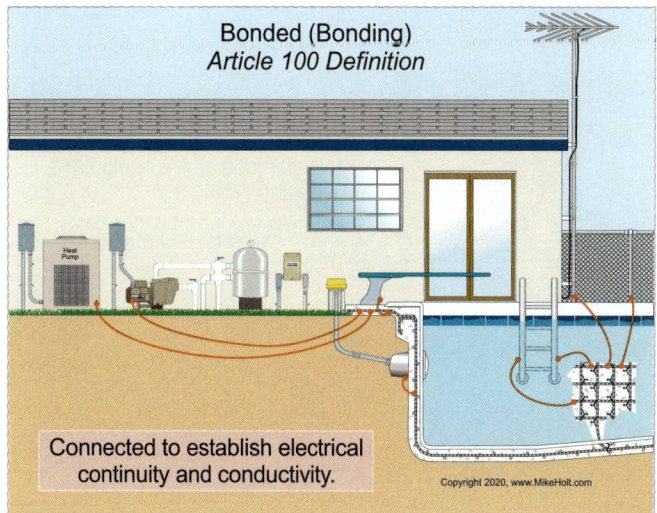
▶Figure 100–9

100 | Definitions

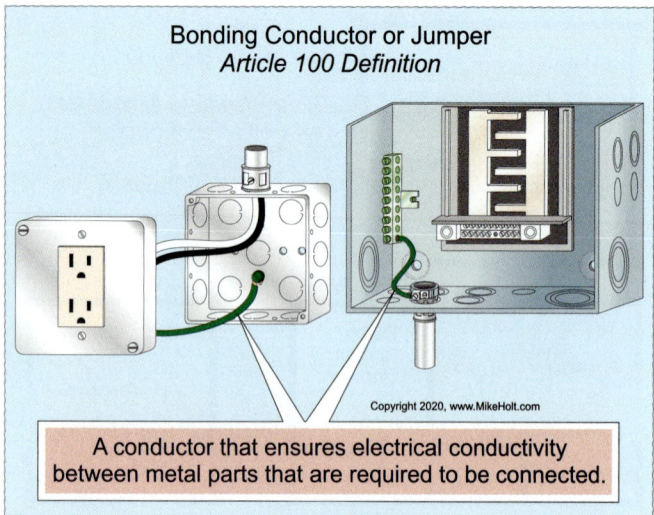

▶Figure 100–10

Author's Comment:

▸ Either the term "Bonding Conductor" or "Bonding Jumper" can be used. They can be short or several feet long and are typically used to ensure electrical conductivity between two metallic objects.

Bonding Jumper, Equipment. A connection between two or more portions of the equipment grounding conductor. ▶Figure 100–11

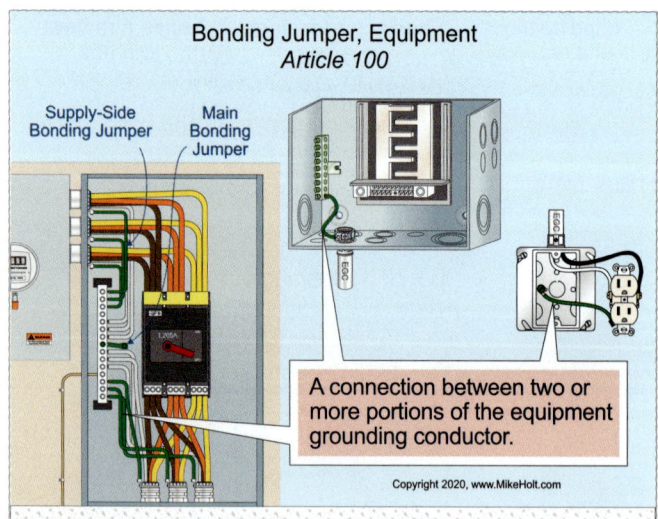

▶Figure 100–11

Author's Comment:

▸ Equipment bonding jumpers are used where the mechanical or electrical path for the effective ground-fault current path would be compromised or interrupted. ▶Figure 100–12

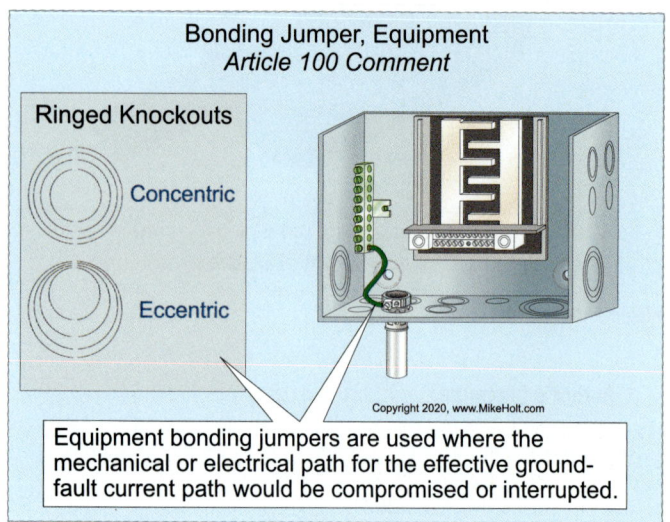

▶Figure 100–12

Bonding Jumper, Main. A conductor, screw, or strap used to connect the circuit equipment grounding conductor to the neutral conductor or to the supply-side bonding jumper at the service equipment in accordance with 250.24(B). ▶Figure 100–13 and ▶Figure 100–14

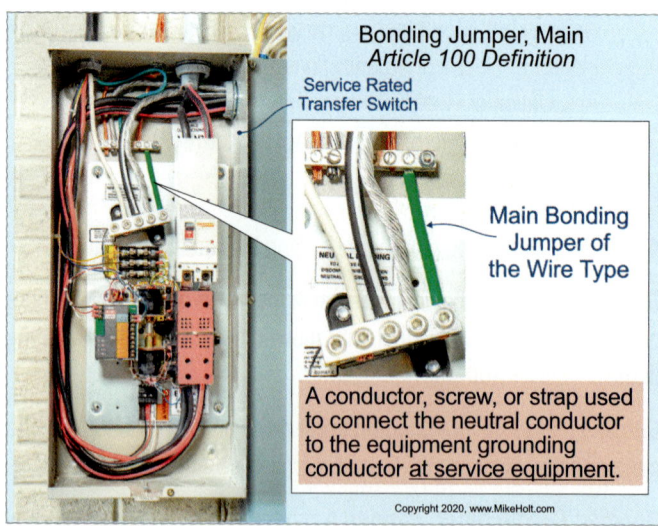

▶Figure 100–13

Definitions | **100**

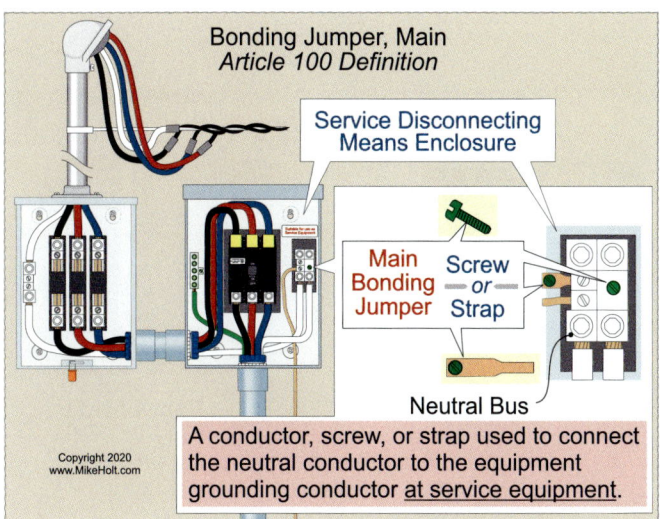
▶Figure 100-14

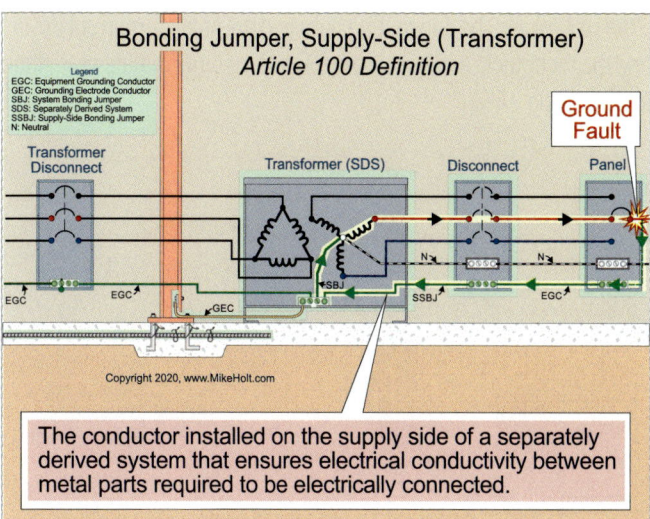
▶Figure 100-16

Bonding Jumper, Supply-Side. The conductor installed on the supply side of a service or separately derived system that ensures conductivity between metal parts required to be electrically connected. ▶Figure 100-15, ▶Figure 100-16, and ▶Figure 100-17

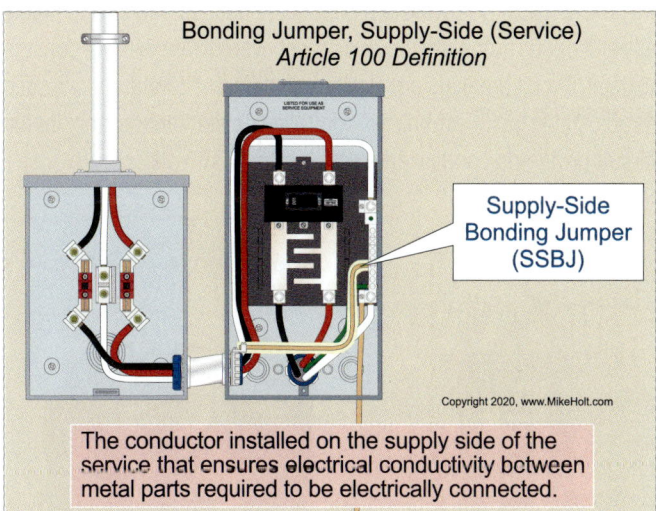
▶Figure 100-15

Bonding Jumper, System. The connection between the neutral conductor or grounded-phase conductor and the supply-side bonding jumper or equipment grounding conductor, or both, at a separately derived system transformer. ▶Figure 100-18

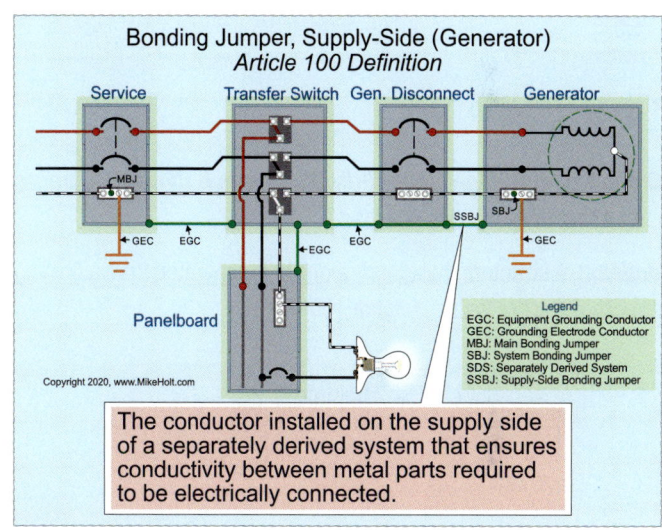
▶Figure 100-17

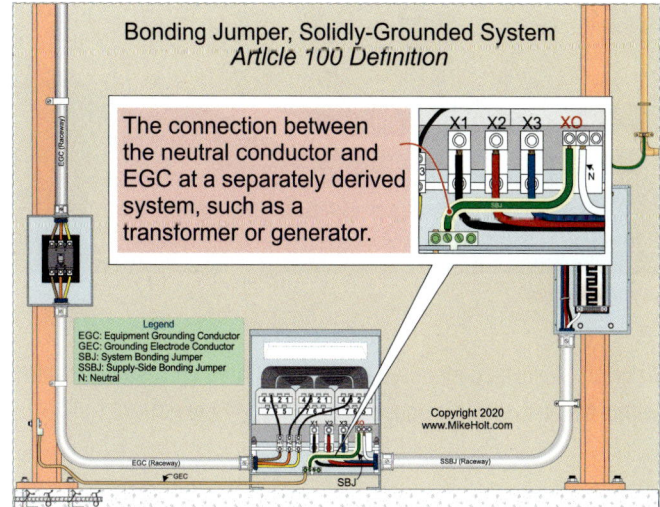
▶Figure 100-18

2nd Printing | 2020 NEC Requirements for Solar PV and Energy Storage Systems | MikeHolt.com | **21**

100 | Definitions

Branch Circuit. The conductors between the final overcurrent device and the receptacle outlets, lighting outlets, or other outlets as defined in this article. ▶Figure 100–19

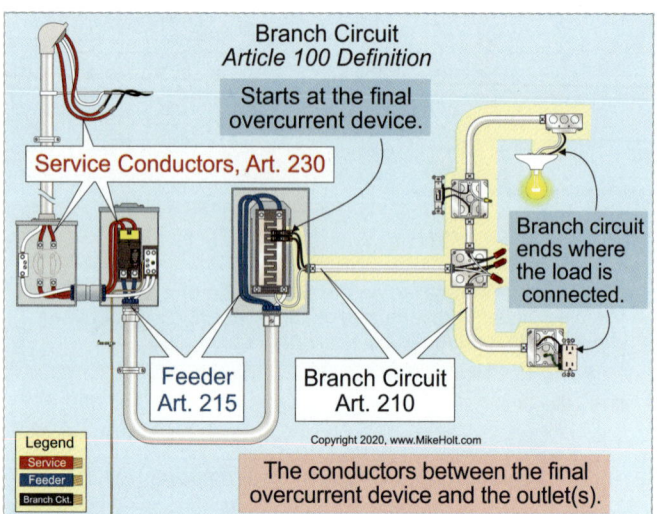

▶Figure 100–19

Branch Circuit, Individual (Individual Branch Circuit). A branch circuit that only supplies one load.

Building. A structure that stands alone or is separated from adjoining structures by fire walls. ▶Figure 100–20

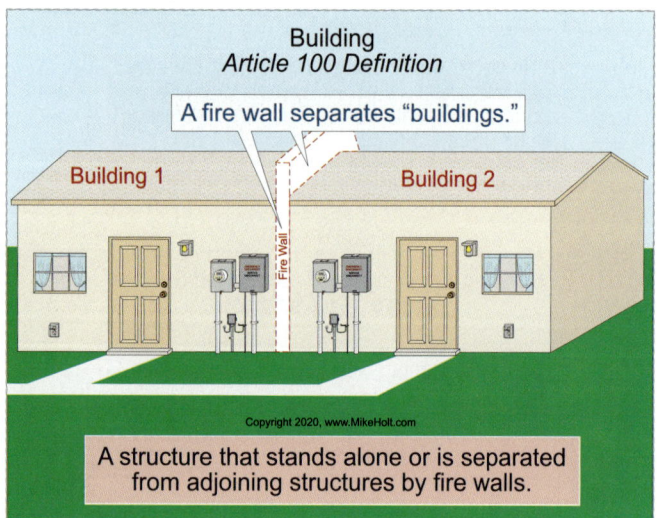

▶Figure 100–20

Cabinet. A surface-mounted or flush-mounted enclosure provided with a frame in which a door can be hung. ▶Figure 100–21

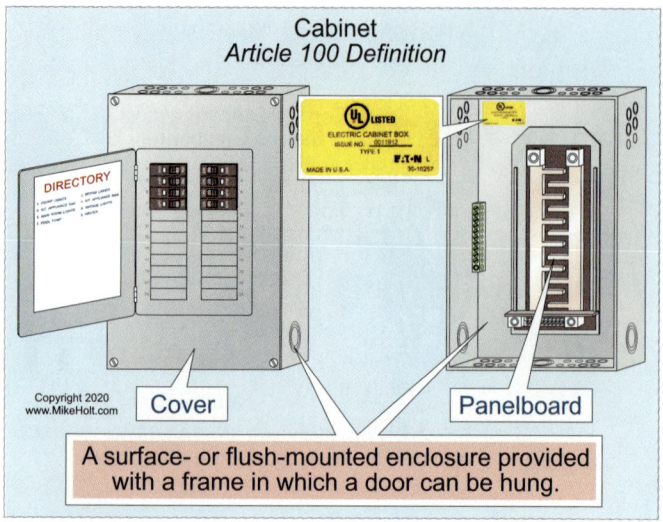

▶Figure 100–21

Author's Comment:

▸ Cabinets are used to enclose panelboards. See the definition of "Panelboard" in this article.

Circuit Breaker. A device designed to be opened and closed manually and opens automatically at a preset overcurrent without damage to itself. Circuit breakers are available in different configurations such as adjustable trip (electronically controlled), instantaneous trip/motor-circuit protectors, and inverse time. ▶Figure 100–22

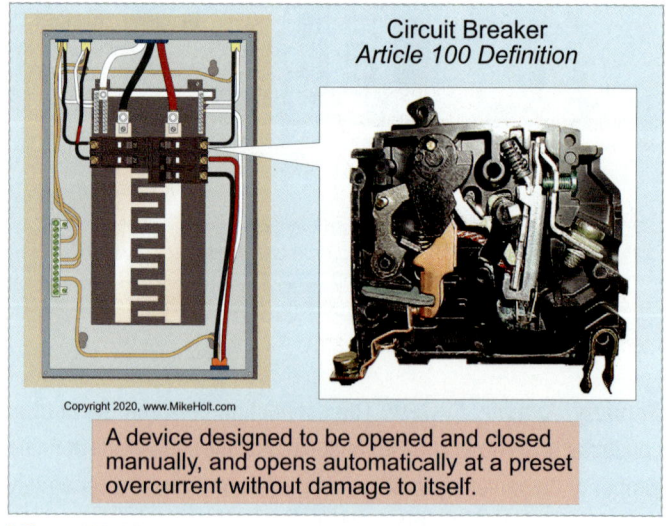

▶Figure 100–22

Circuit Breaker, Adjustable. Adjustable circuit breakers permit the circuit breaker to be set to trip at various values of current, time (or both), within a predetermined range.

Circuit Breaker, Instantaneous Trip. Instantaneous trip breakers only operate on the principle of electromagnetism and are used for motors. These devices are sometimes called "motor-circuit protectors." This type of overcurrent protective device does not provide overload protection. It only provides short-circuit and ground-fault protection; overload protection must be provided separately.

Author's Comment:

▸ Instantaneous trip circuit breakers have no intentional time delay and are sensitive to current inrush, vibration, and shock. Consequently, they should not be used where these factors are known to exist.

Circuit Breaker, Inverse Time. This type of circuit breaker is purposely designed to delay its tripping action during an overcurrent condition. The intent is to compensate for the inrush of current during the normal start-up of equipment such as vacuum cleaners or air conditioners and helps avoid "nuisance tripping."

Author's Comment:

▸ Inverse time breakers operate on the principle that as the current increases, the time it takes for the devices to open decreases. They provide ordinary overcurrent protection during overload, short-circuit, or ground-fault conditions. This is the most common type of circuit breaker purchased over the counter.

Class 1 Circuit. The wiring system between the load side of a Class 1 circuit overcurrent protective device and the connected equipment. ▸Figure 100–23

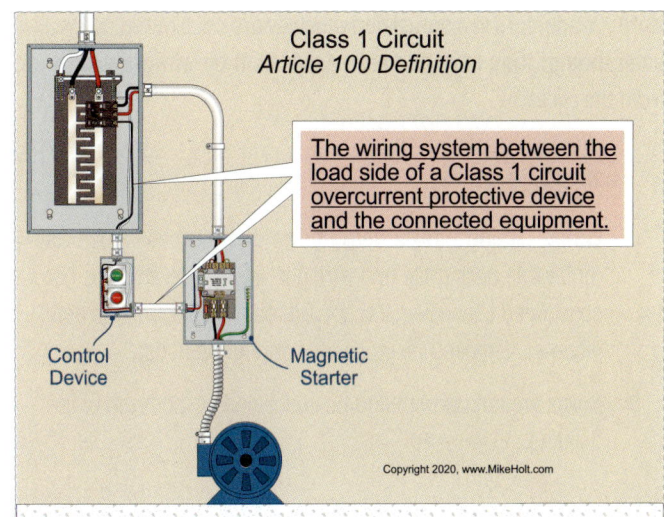
▸Figure 100–23

Note: See 725.41 for the voltage and power limitations of Class 1 circuits.

Clothes Closet. A nonhabitable room or space intended primarily for the storage of garments and apparel. ▸Figure 100–24

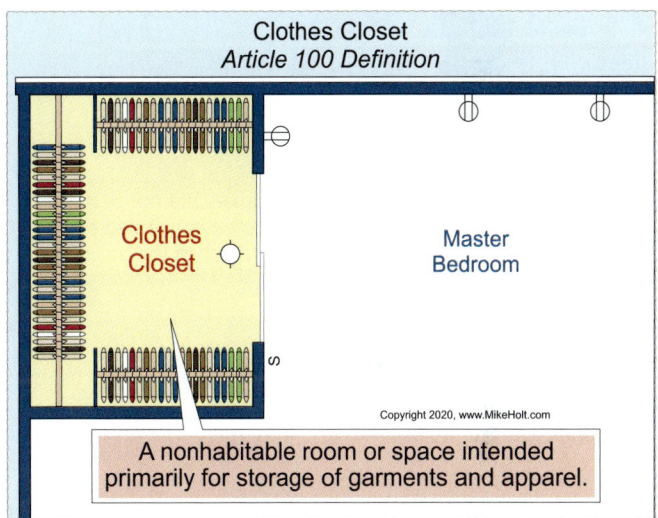
▸Figure 100–24

Author's Comment:

▸ The definition of a "Clothes Closet" provides clarification in the application of overcurrent protective devices [240.24(D)] and luminaires [410.16] in clothes closets.

Concealed. Rendered inaccessible by the structure or finish of the building. ▸Figure 100–25

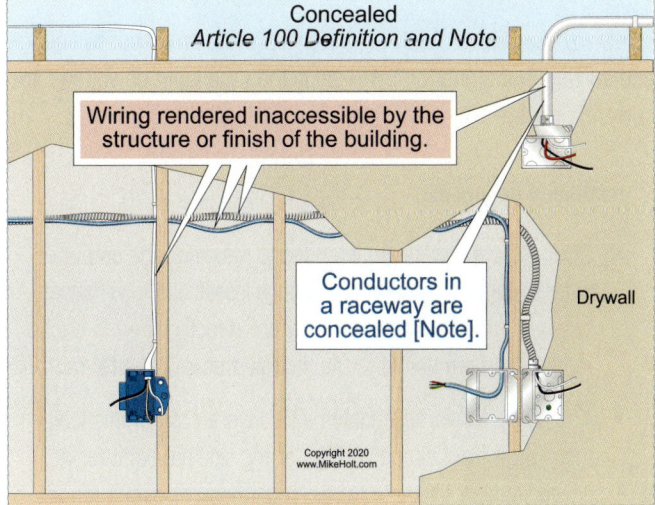
▸Figure 100–25

100 | Definitions

Note: Conductors in a concealed raceway are considered concealed even though they may be made accessible by withdrawing them from the raceway.

Author's Comment:

- Wiring behind panels designed to allow access, such as removable ceiling tile and wiring in accessible attics, is not considered concealed; it is considered exposed. See the definition of "Exposed (as applied to wiring methods)."
- Boxes are not permitted to be concealed by the finish of the building. ▶Figure 100–26

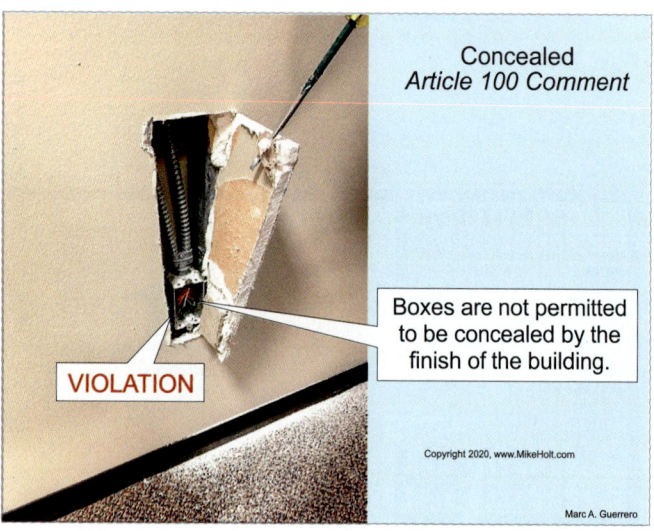

▶Figure 100–26

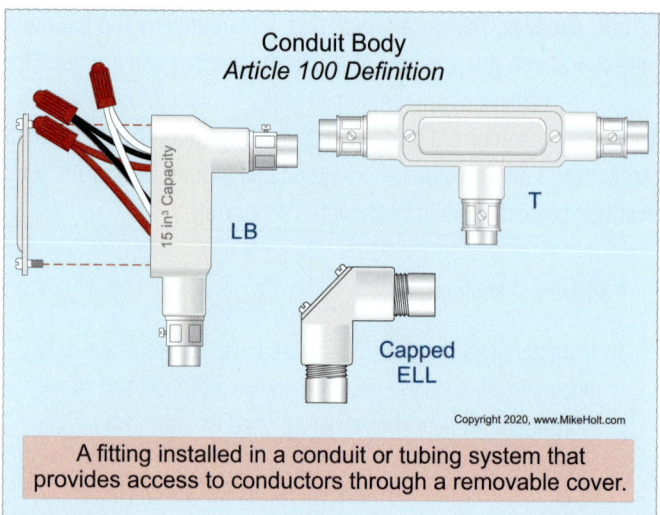

▶Figure 100–27

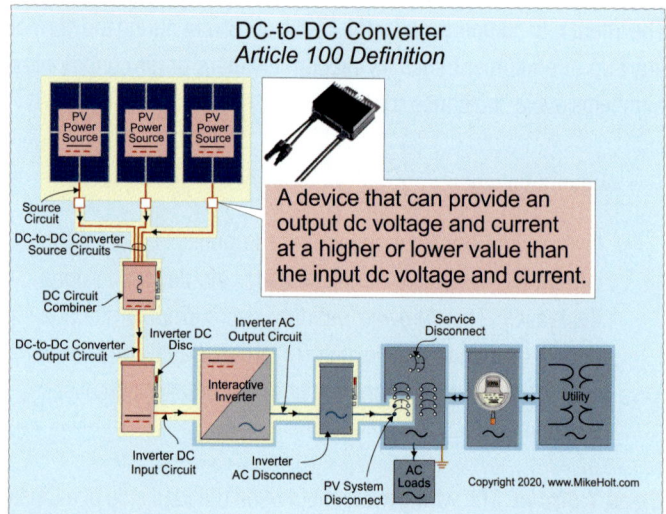

▶Figure 100–28

Conduit Body. A fitting installed in a conduit or tubing system that provides access to conductors through a removable cover. ▶Figure 100–27

DC-to-DC Converter. A device that can provide an output dc voltage and current at a higher or lower value than the input dc voltage and current. ▶Figure 100–28

Author's Comment:

- DC-to-DC converters are intended to maximize the output of independent PV modules and reduce losses due to variances between modules' outputs. They are directly wired to each module and are bolted to the module frame or the PV rack.
- A dc-to-dc converter enables a PV inverter to automatically maintain a fixed circuit voltage, at the optimal point for dc/ac conversion by the inverter, regardless of circuit length and individual module performance.

Device. A component of an electrical installation, other than a conductor, intended to carry or control electric energy as its principal function. ▶Figure 100–29

Author's Comment:

- Devices generally do not consume electric energy and include receptacles, switches, illuminated switches, circuit breakers, fuses, time clocks, controllers, attachment plugs, and so forth. Some (such as illuminated switches, contactors, or relays) consume very small amounts of energy and are still classified as a device based on their primary function.

Disconnecting Means (Disconnect). A device that disconnects the circuit conductors from their power source. Examples include switches, attachment plugs, and circuit breakers. ▶Figure 100–30

Definitions | 100

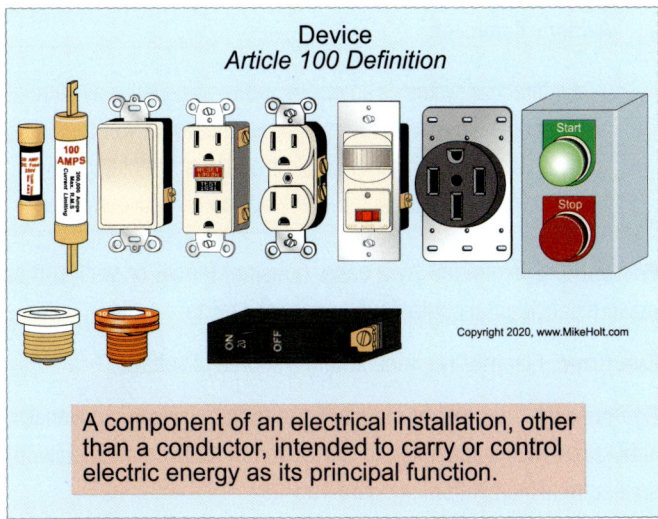
▶Figure 100–29

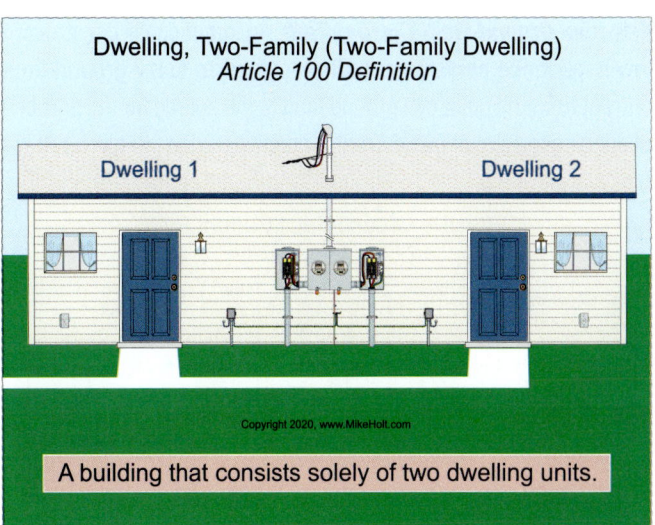
▶Figure 100–31

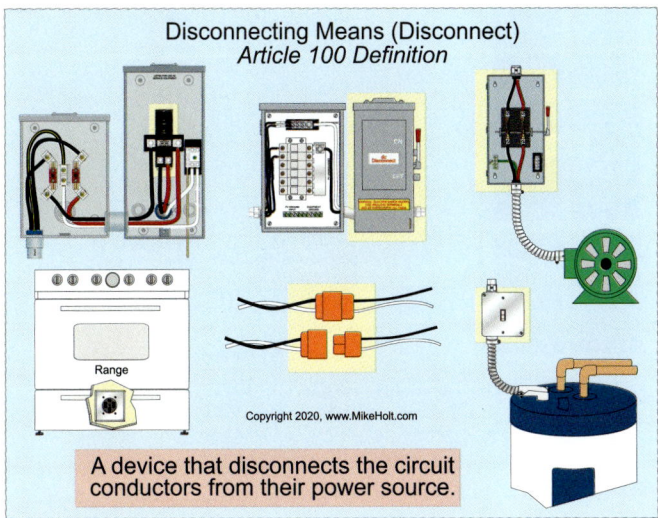
▶Figure 100–30

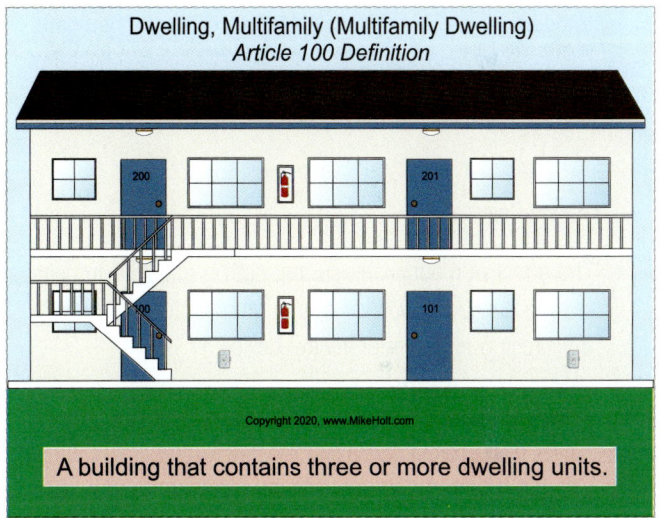
▶Figure 100–32

Dwelling, One-Family (One-Family Dwelling). A building that consists solely of one dwelling unit.

Dwelling, Two-Family (Two-Family Dwelling). A building that consists solely of two dwelling units. ▶Figure 100–31

Dwelling, Multifamily (Multifamily Dwelling). A building that contains three or more dwelling units. ▶Figure 100–32

Dwelling Unit. A space that provides independent living facilities with space for eating, living, sleeping, and permanent provisions for cooking and sanitation. ▶Figure 100–33

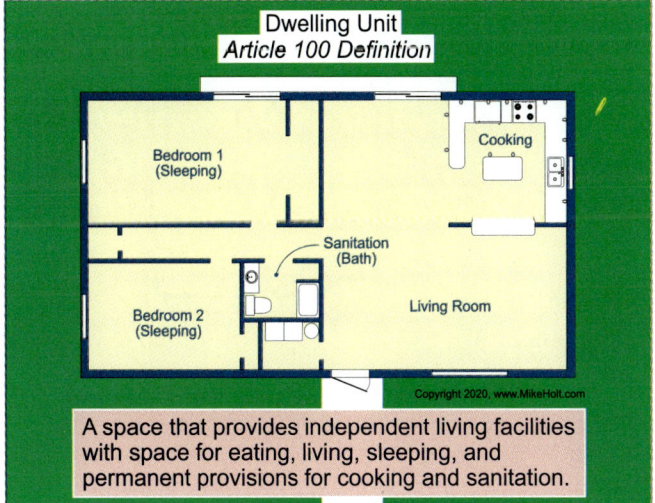
▶Figure 100–33

100 | Definitions

Effective Ground-Fault Current Path. An intentionally constructed low-impedance conductive path designed to carry ground-fault current from the point of a ground fault to the source for the purpose of opening the circuit overcurrent protective device. ▶Figure 100-34

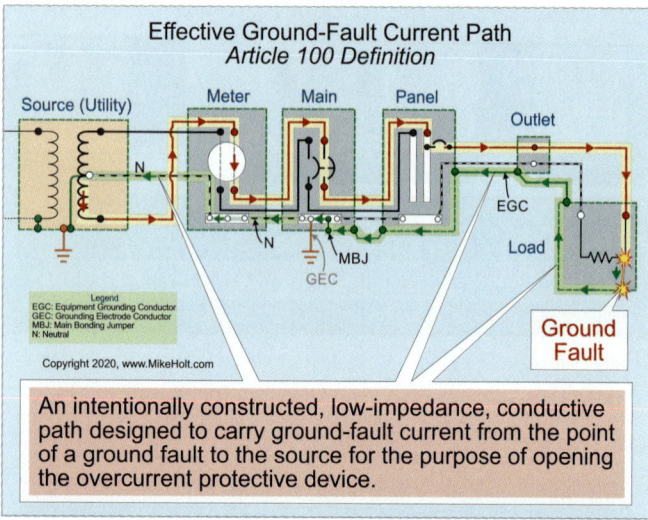
▶Figure 100-34

Author's Comment:

▸ The effective ground-fault current path is intended to help remove dangerous voltage from a ground fault by opening the circuit overcurrent protective device.

Electric Power Production and Distribution Network. A serving electric utility that is connected to premises wiring and is not controlled by an interactive system. ▶Figure 100-35

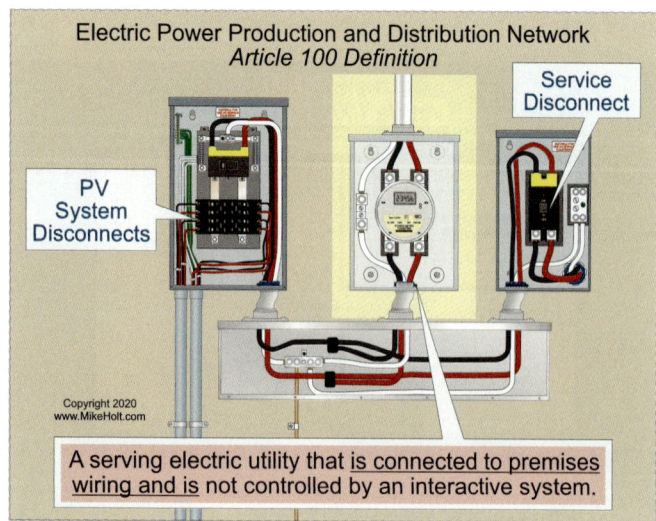
▶Figure 100-35

Author's Comment:

▸ An interactive system is an electric power production system that operates in parallel with, and may deliver power to, the serving electric utility. An example is a PV system interactively connected in parallel to the utility by an interactive inverter.

Enclosed. Surrounded by a case, housing, fence, or wall(s) that prevents accidental contact with energized parts.

Energized. Electrically connected to a source of voltage.

Equipment. A general term including fittings, devices, appliances, luminaires, machinery, and the like as part of (or in connection with) an electrical installation. ▶Figure 100-36

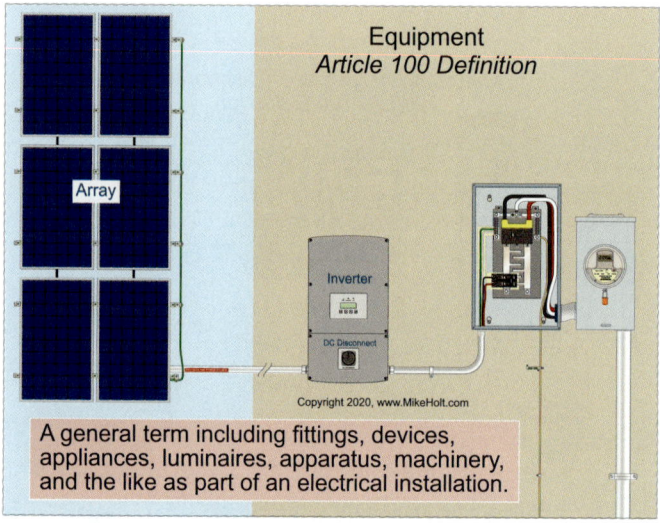
▶Figure 100-36

Exposed (as applied to live parts). Capable of being accidentally touched or approached nearer than a safe distance. ▶Figure 100-37

Note: This term applies to parts that are not suitably guarded, isolated, or insulated for the condition such as line-side lugs in a meter socket or panelboard.

Exposed (as applied to wiring methods). On or attached to the surface of a building, or behind panels designed to allow access. ▶Figure 100-38

Fault Current. The current delivered at a point on the system during a short-circuit condition. ▶Figure 100-39

Note: A short circuit can occur during abnormal conditions such as a fault between circuit conductors or a ground fault.

Definitions | 100

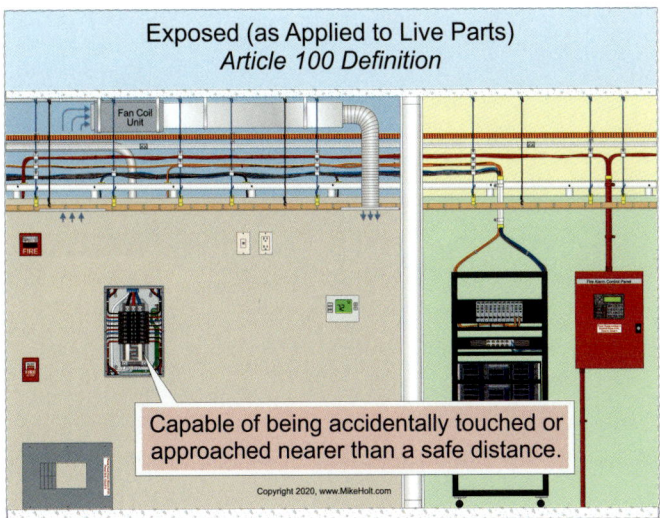
▶Figure 100-37

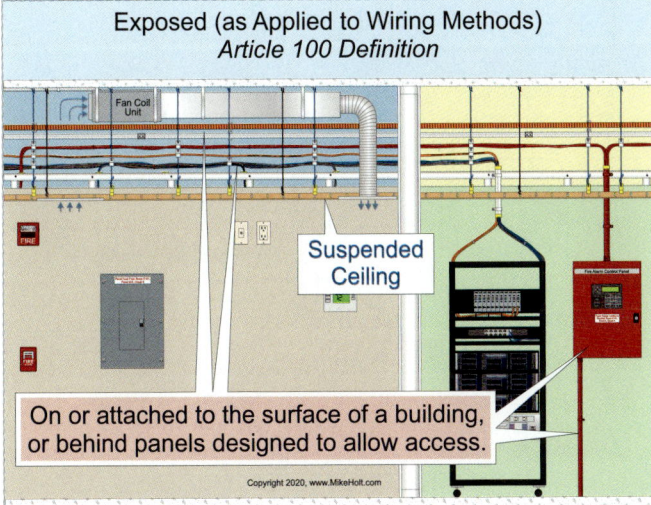
▶Figure 100-38

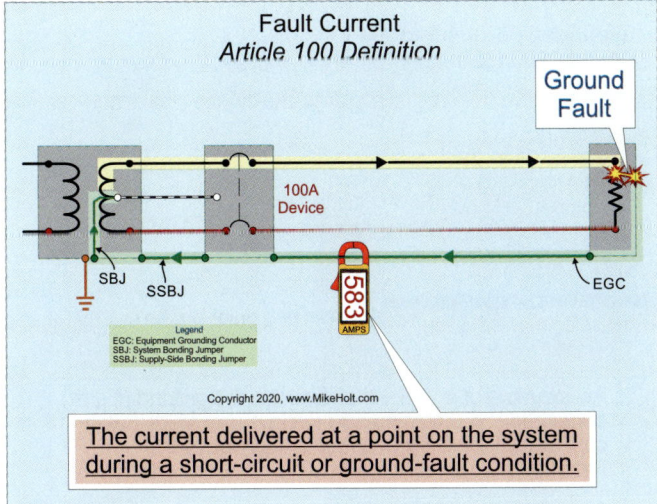
▶Figure 100-39

Feeder. The conductors between the service disconnect, a separately derived system (typically a transformer), or other power-supply source and the final branch-circuit overcurrent device. ▶Figure 100-40

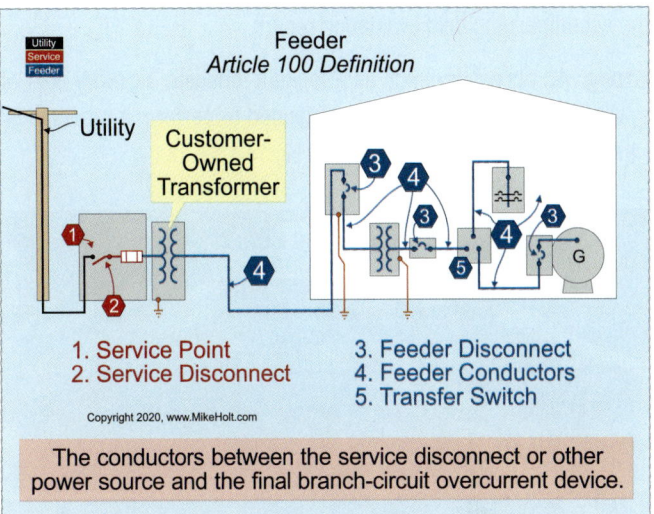
▶Figure 100-40

Author's Comment:

▸ An "other power-supply source" includes solar PV systems or conductors from generators. ▶Figure 100-41

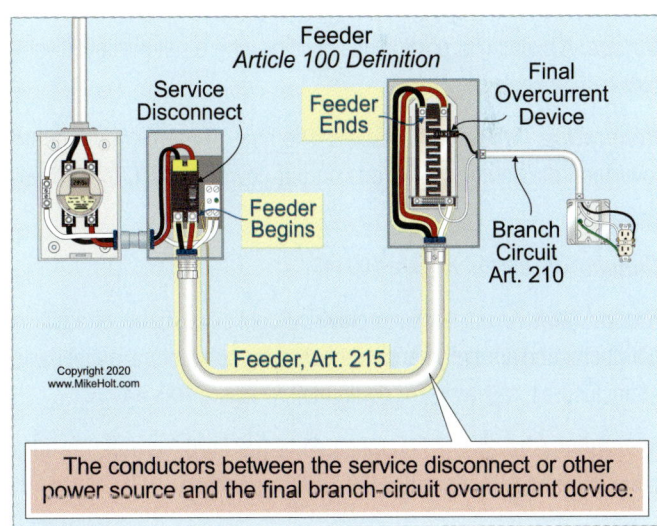
▶Figure 100-41

Field Evaluation Body (FEB). An organization or part of an organization that performs field evaluations of electrical equipment and materials.

100 | Definitions

Field Labeled (as applied to evaluated products). Equipment or materials which have a label, symbol, or other identifying mark of a field evaluation body (FEB) indicating the equipment or materials were evaluated and found to comply with the requirements described in the accompanying field evaluation report.

Fitting. An accessory such as a locknut, bushing, or other part of a wiring system that is primarily intended to perform a mechanical rather than an electrical function. ▶Figure 100–42

▶Figure 100–42

Garage. A building or portion of a building where self-propelled vehicles can be kept.

Generating Capacity, Inverter. The sum of parallel-connected inverters' maximum continuous output power at 40°C in watts or kilowatts.

Ground. The Earth. ▶Figure 100–43

Ground Fault. An unintentional electrical connection between a phase conductor and normally noncurrent-carrying conductors, metal parts of enclosures, raceways, or equipment. ▶Figure 100–44

Grounded (Grounding). Connected to the Earth (ground) or to a conductive body that extends the Earth connection. ▶Figure 100–45

> **Author's Comment:**
> ▸ An example of a "body that extends the ground (earth) connection" is a termination to structural steel that is connected to the Earth either directly or by the termination to another grounding electrode in accordance with 250.52.

▶Figure 100–43

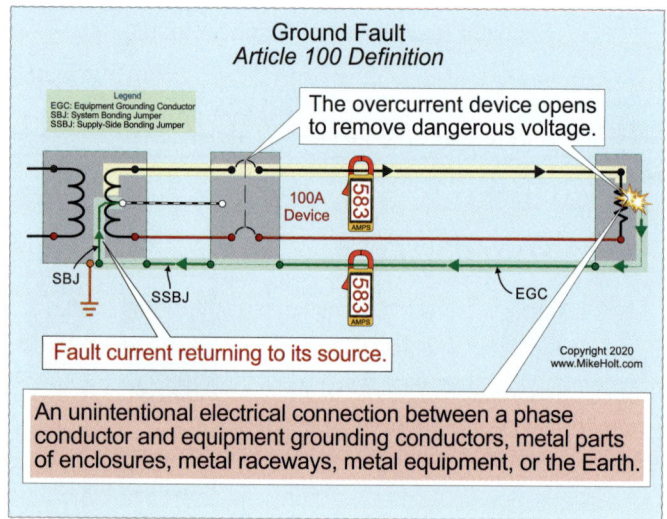

▶Figure 100–44

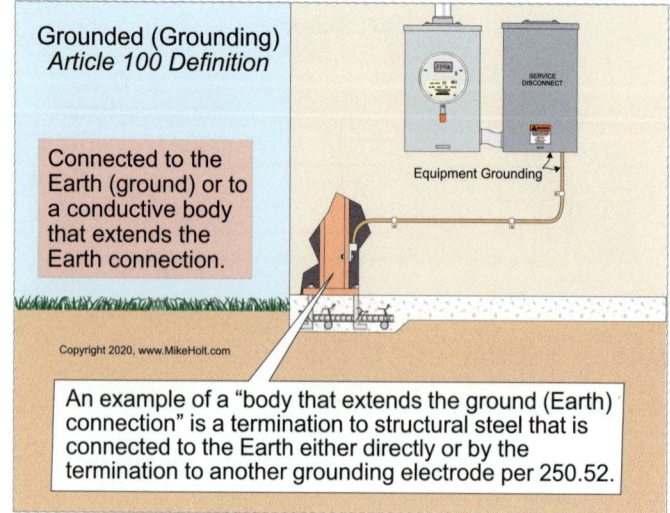

▶Figure 100–45

Grounded Conductor. The system or circuit conductor that is intentionally connected to the Earth (ground). ▶Figure 100–46

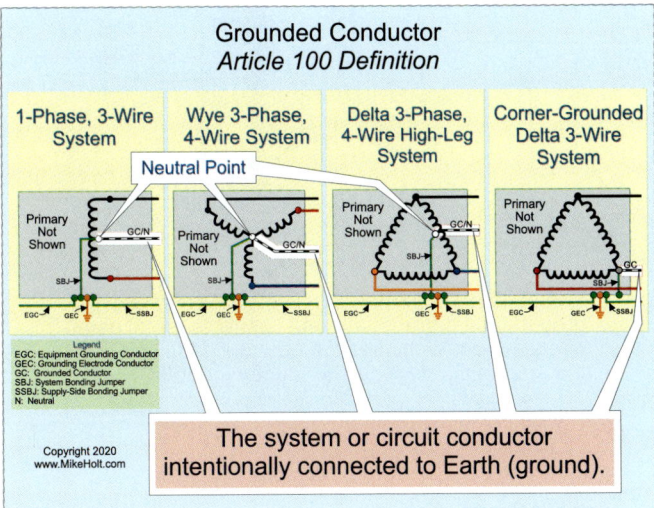

▶Figure 100–46

Note: Although an equipment grounding conductor is grounded, it is not considered a grounded conductor.

Author's Comment:

▸ There are two types of grounded conductors: neutral conductors and grounded-phase conductors. A system where the transformer secondary is wye connected with the neutral point grounded will have a neutral. ▶Figure 100–47

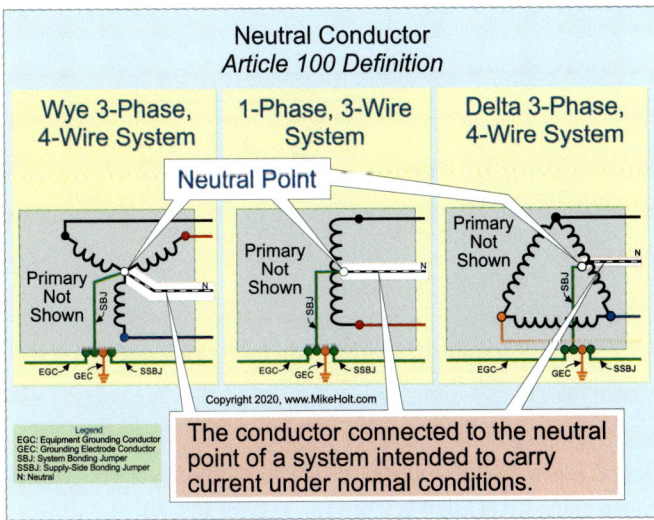

▶Figure 100–47

Author's Comment:

▸ A system where the transformer secondary is delta connected with one corner winding grounded will have a grounded-phase conductor. ▶Figure 100–48

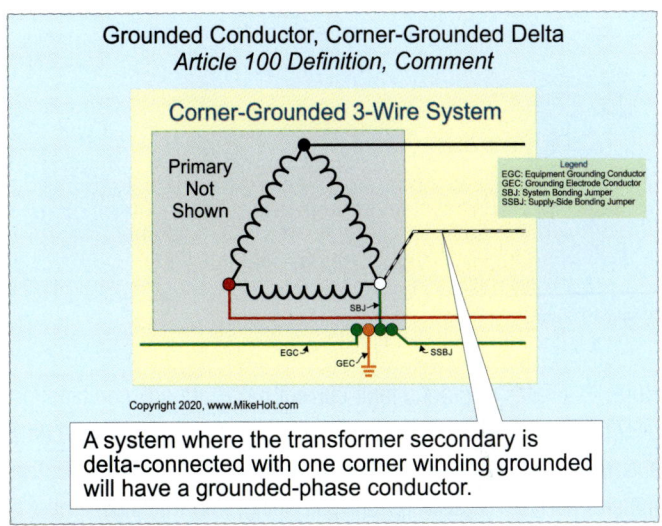

▶Figure 100–48

Grounded, Solidly (Solidly Grounded). Connected to ground (earth) without inserting any resistor or impedance device. ▶Figure 100–49

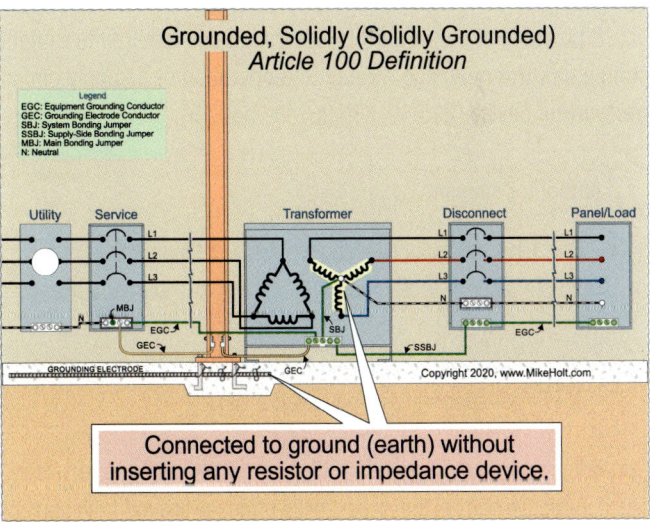

▶Figure 100–49

Ground-Fault Current Path. An electrically conductive path from the point of a ground fault on a wiring system through normally noncurrent-carrying conductors, neutral conductors, equipment, or the Earth to the electrical supply source. ▶Figure 100–50

100 | Definitions

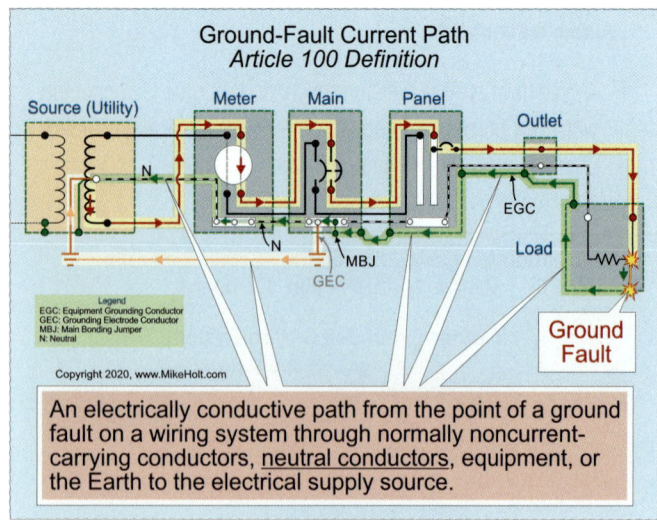

▶Figure 100-50

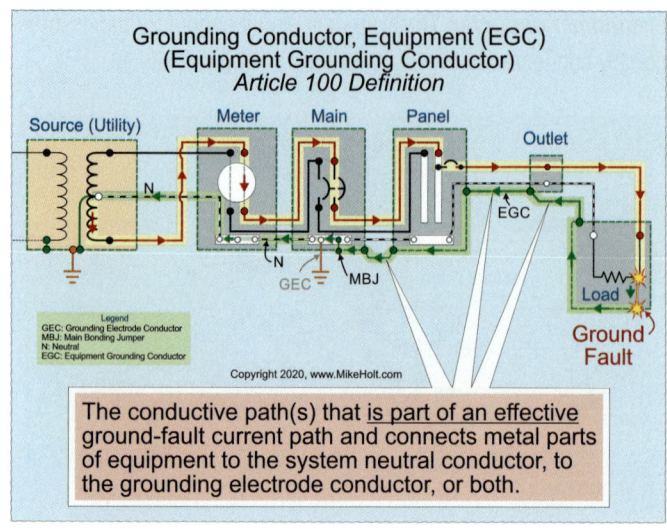

▶Figure 100-51

Note: Examples of ground-fault current paths are any combination of equipment grounding conductors, metallic raceways, metal cable sheaths, electrical equipment, and any other electrically conductive material such as metal, water, and gas piping; steel framing members; stucco mesh; metal ducting; reinforcing steel; shields of communications cables; neutral conductors; and the Earth itself.

Ground-Fault Protection of Equipment. A system intended to provide protection of equipment from damaging ground-fault currents by opening all phase conductors of the faulted circuit. This protection is provided at current levels less than those required to protect conductors from damage through the operation of a supply circuit overcurrent device [215.10, 230.95, and 240.13].

Author's Comment:

▸ This type of protective device is not intended to protect people since it trips (opens the circuit) at a higher current level than that of a "Class A" GFCI-protective device. It is typically referred to as ground-fault protection for equipment, or GFPE; but should never be called a GFCI.

Grounding Conductor, Equipment (Equipment Grounding Conductor). The conductive path(s) that is part of an effective ground-fault current path and connects metal parts of equipment to the system neutral conductor or grounded-phase conductor [250.110 through 250.126]. ▶Figure 100-51

Note 1: The circuit equipment grounding conductor also performs bonding.

Author's Comment:

▸ To quickly remove dangerous touch voltage on metal parts from a ground fault, the equipment grounding conductor (EGC) must be connected to the system neutral conductor at the source and have low enough impedance so fault current will quickly rise to a level that will open the circuit's overcurrent protective device [250.4(A)(3)]. ▶Figure 100-52

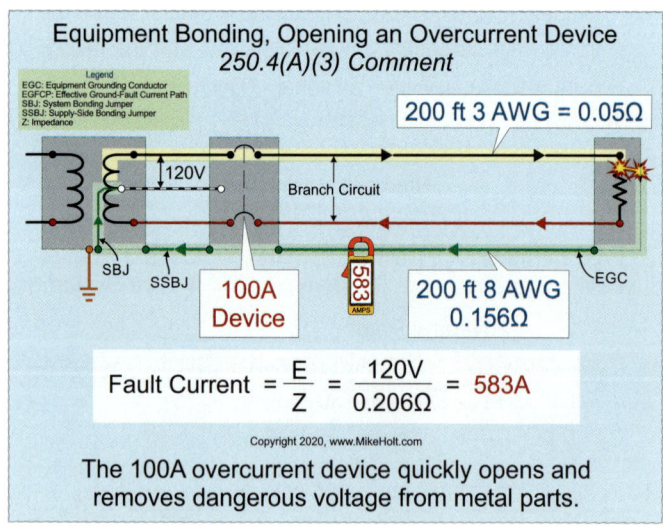

▶Figure 100-52

Note 2: An equipment grounding conductor can be any one or a combination of the types listed in 250.118. ▶Figure 100-53

Definitions | **100**

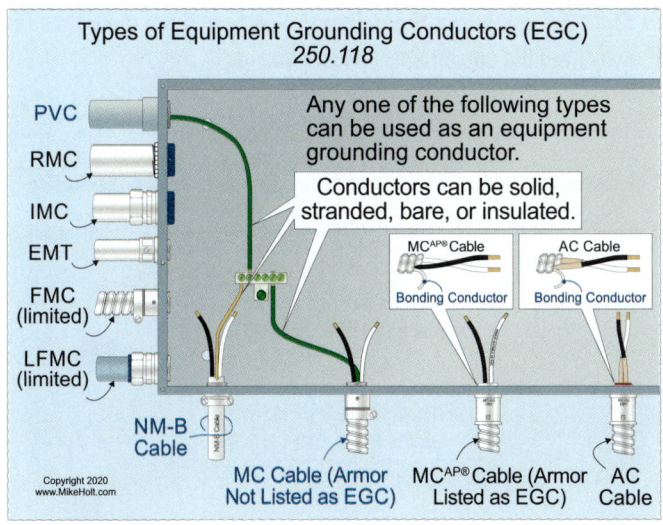
▶Figure 100–53

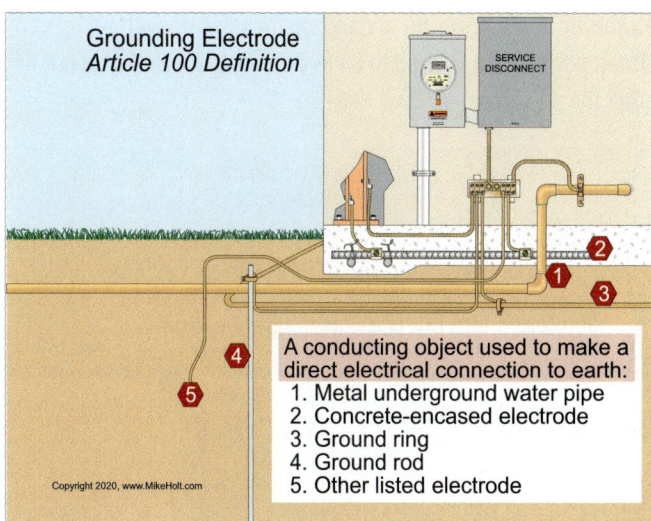
▶Figure 100–54

Author's Comment:

▸ Equipment grounding conductors include:

  ▸ A bare or insulated conductor
  ▸ Rigid metal conduit
  ▸ Intermediate metal conduit
  ▸ Electrical metallic tubing
  ▸ Listed flexible metal conduit as limited by 250.118(5)
  ▸ Listed liquidtight flexible metal conduit as limited by 250.118(6)
  ▸ Armored cable
  ▸ The copper metal sheath of mineral-insulated cable
  ▸ Metal-clad cable as limited by 250.118(10)
  ▸ Metal cable trays as limited by 250.118(11) and 392.60
  ▸ Electrically continuous metal raceways listed for grounding
  ▸ Surface metal raceways listed for grounding
  ▸ Metal enclosures

Grounding Electrode. A conducting object used to make a direct electrical connection to the Earth [250.50 through 250.70]. ▶Figure 100–54

Grounding Electrode Conductor. The conductor used to connect the system neutral conductor or grounded-phase conductor, or the equipment to the grounding electrode system. ▶Figure 100–55

Guest Room. An accommodation combining living, sleeping, sanitary, and storage facilities. ▶Figure 100–56

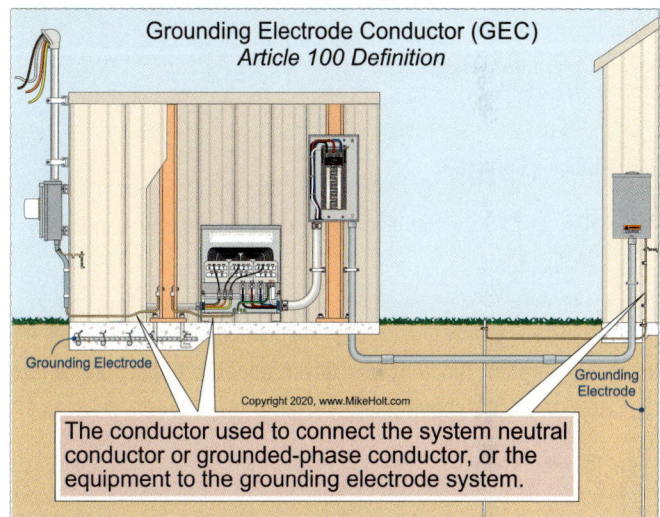
▶Figure 100–55

▶Figure 100–56

100 | Definitions

Handhole Enclosure. An underground enclosure with an open or closed bottom that is sized to allow personnel to reach into but not enter the enclosure. ▶Figure 100-57

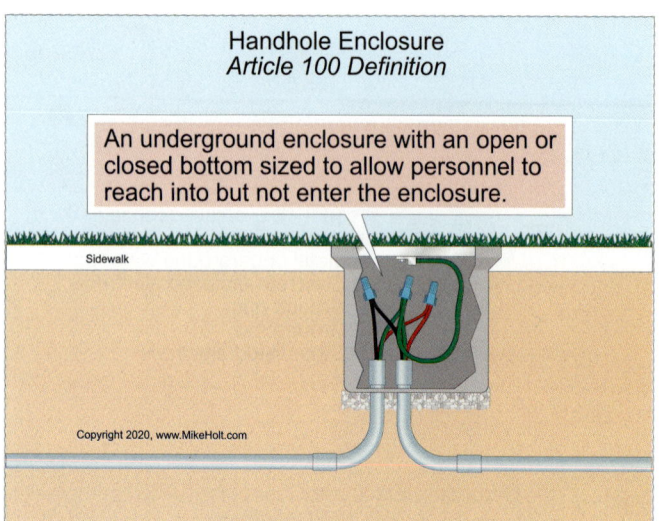
▶Figure 100-57

Author's Comment:

▸ See 314.30 for the installation requirements for handhole enclosures.

Identified (as applied to equipment). Recognized as suitable for a specific purpose, function, use, environment, or application where described in a *Code* requirement. ▶Figure 100-58

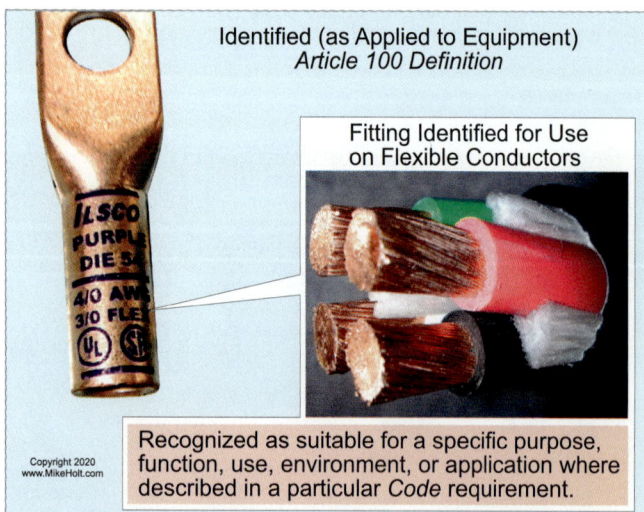
▶Figure 100-58

Author's Comment:

▸ See 90.4, 90.7, and 110.3(A)(1) and the definitions for "Approved," "Labeled," and "Listed" in this article.

In Sight From (Within Sight From). Visible and not more than 50 ft away from the equipment. ▶Figure 100-59

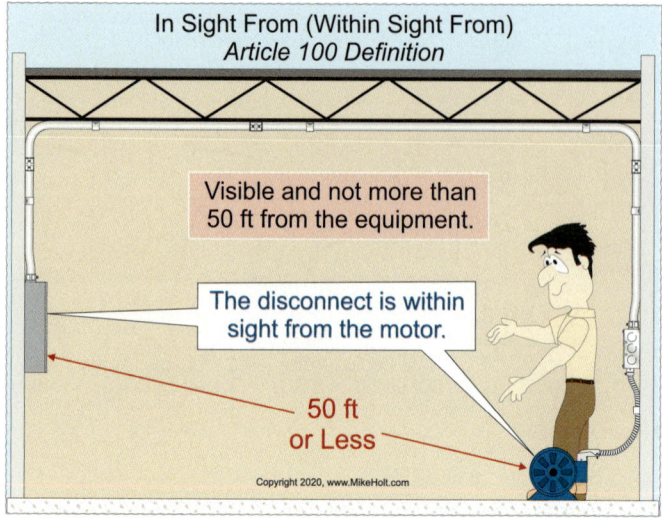
▶Figure 100-59

Interactive Inverter. An inverter intended to be used in parallel with a power source(s), such as the serving electric utility, to supply common loads and is capable of delivering power to the serving electric utility. ▶Figure 100-60

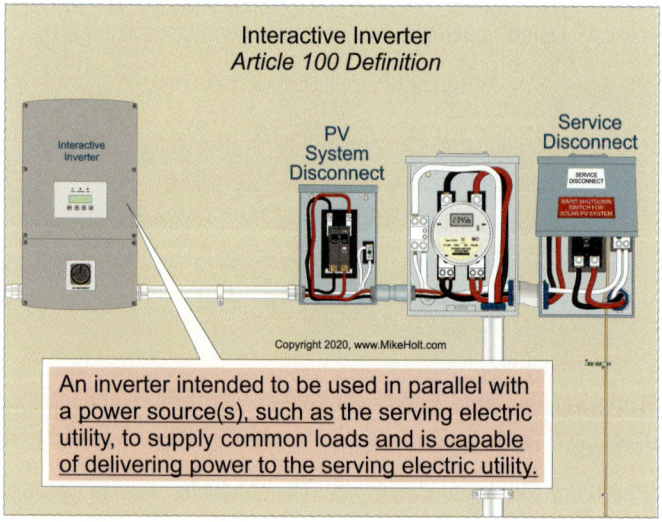
▶Figure 100-60

Author's Comment:

▸ A listed interactive inverter automatically stops exporting power upon loss of utility voltage and cannot be reconnected until the voltage has been restored. Interactive inverters can automatically or manually resume exporting power to the utility once the utility source is restored.

Interactive System. An electric power production system that operates in parallel with, and may deliver power to, the serving electric utility. ▶Figure 100-61

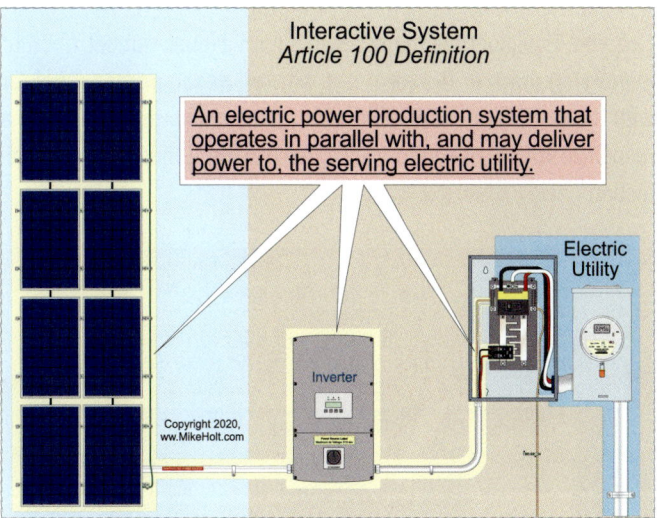

▶Figure 100-61

Interrupting Rating. The highest short-circuit current at rated voltage the device is identified to safely interrupt under standard test conditions.

Intersystem Bonding Termination. A device that provides a means to connect intersystem bonding conductors for communications systems (twisted wire, antennas, and coaxial cable) to the grounding electrode system, in accordance with 250.94. ▶Figure 100-62

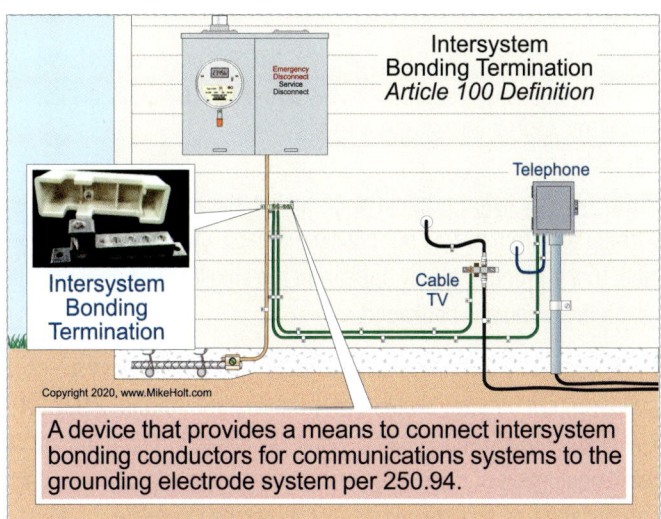

▶Figure 100-62

Author's Comment:

▸ Overcurrent protective devices have two current ratings, "rated current" and "fault current." Rated current protects circuits under normal conditions and the rating is labeled on the handle of the circuit breaker. The fault current rating or "ampere interrupting capacity" (AIC) is the amount of current the device can safely handle during a ground fault or short circuit. Fault current ratings range up to the tens, or even hundreds, of thousands of amperes!

▸ For more information, see 110.9 in this textbook.

Inverter. Equipment that changes direct current to alternating current. ▶Figure 100-63

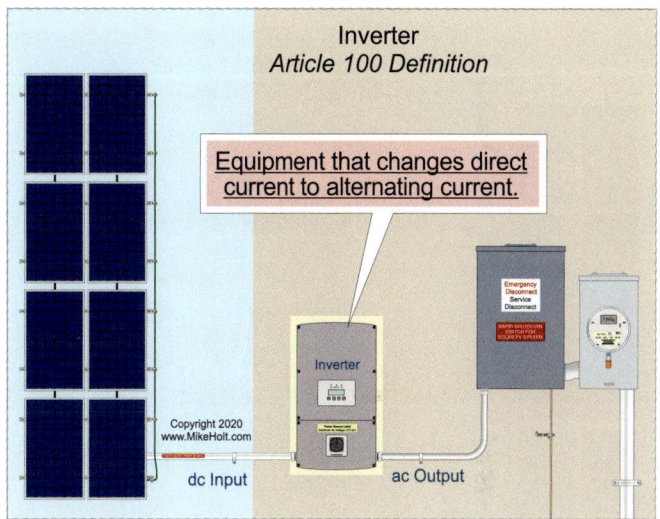

▶Figure 100-63

Inverter Input Circuit. Conductors connected to the direct-current input of an inverter. ▶Figure 100-64

Inverter Output Circuit. The circuit conductors connected to the alternating-current output of an inverter. ▶Figure 100-65

Inverter, Multimode. Equipment having the capabilities of both interactive and stand-alone inverters. ▶Figure 100-66

100 | Definitions

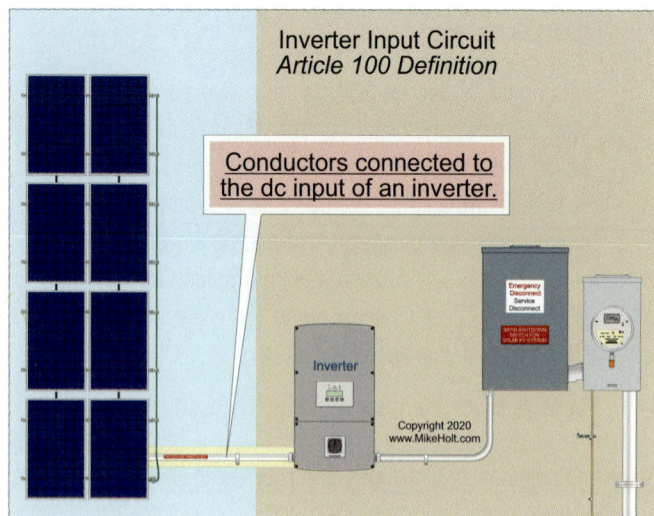
▶Figure 100-64

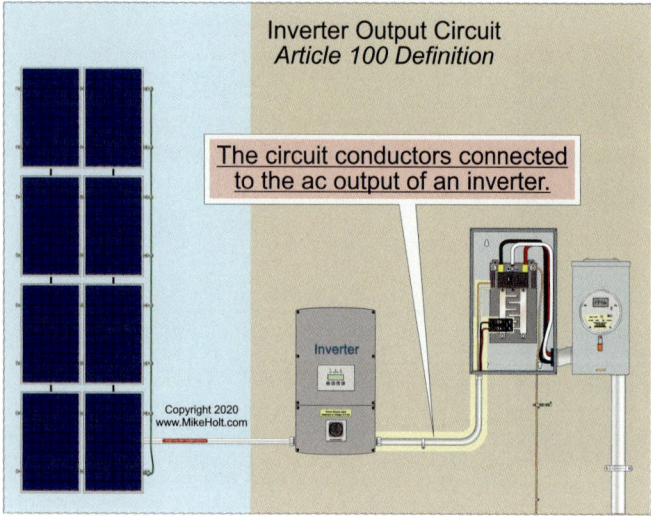
▶Figure 100-65

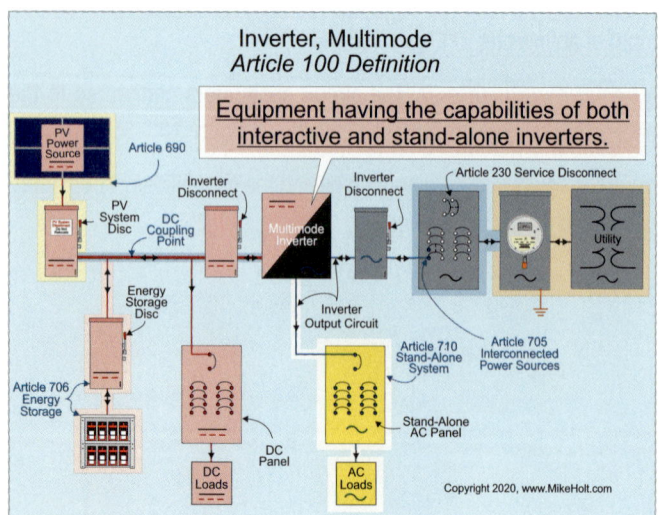
▶Figure 100-66

Island Mode. The operational mode for stand-alone power production equipment or an isolated microgrid (or for a multimode inverter or an interconnected microgrid) that is disconnected from an electric power production and distribution network or other primary power source.

Labeled. Equipment or materials that have a label, symbol, or other identifying mark in the form of a sticker, decal, printed label, or with the identifying mark molded or stamped into the product by a recognized testing laboratory acceptable to the authority having jurisdiction. ▶Figure 100-67

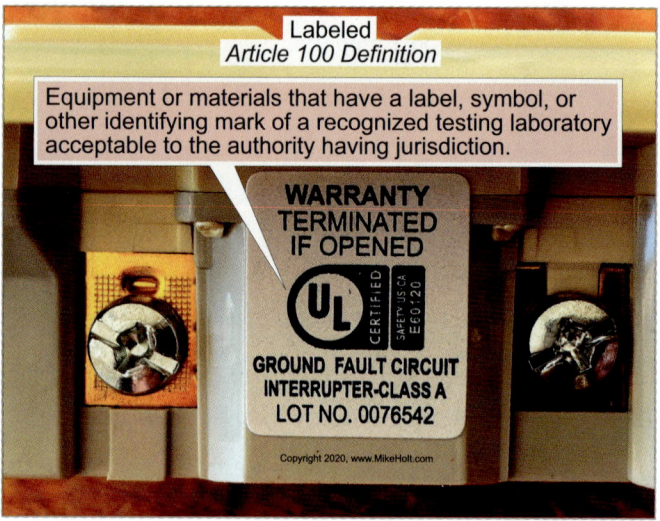
▶Figure 100-67

Author's Comment:

▸ Labeling and listing of equipment typically provides the basis for equipment approval by the authority having jurisdiction [90.4, 90.7, 110.2, and 110.3].

Note: When a listed product is of such a size, shape, material, or surface texture that it is not possible to legibly apply the complete label to the product, it may appear on the smallest unit container in which the product is packaged.

Listed. Equipment or materials included in a list published by a recognized testing laboratory acceptable to the authority having jurisdiction. The listing organization must periodically inspect the production of listed equipment or material to ensure they meet appropriate designated standards and are suitable for a specified purpose.

Note: Examples of nationally recognized testing laboratories (NRTLs) are Underwriters Laboratory (UL) and Canadian Standards Association (CSA). Both are accepted in either the United States or Canada and most electrical equipment is marked by both agencies. Always look for at least one of these seals and accept no imitations or counterfeits.

Definitions | 100

Author's Comment:

▸ The *NEC* does not require all electrical equipment to be listed, but some *Code* requirements do specifically call for product listing. Organizations such as OSHA are increasingly requiring listed equipment to be used when such equipment is available [90.7, 110.2, and 110.3].

Location, Damp (Damp Location). Locations protected from weather and not subject to saturation with water or other liquids. ▸Figure 100–68

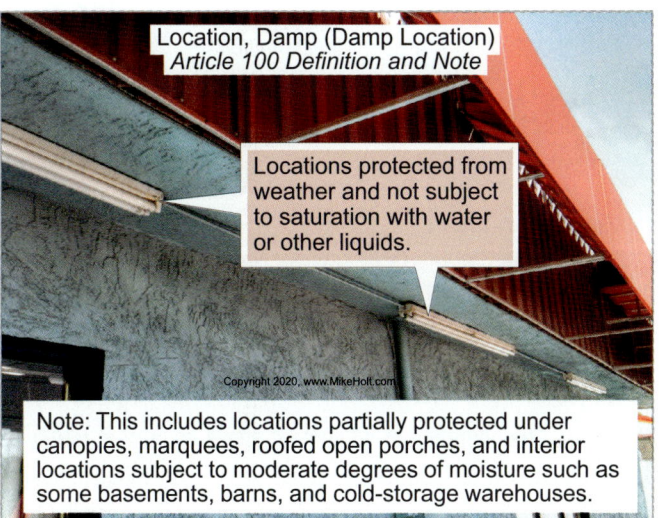
▸Figure 100–68

Note: This includes locations partially protected under canopies, marquees, roofed open porches, and interior locations subject to moderate degrees of moisture such as some basements, barns, and cold-storage warehouses.

Location, Dry (Dry Location). An area not normally subjected to dampness or wetness, but which may temporarily be subjected to dampness or wetness, such as a building under construction.

Location, Wet (Wet Location). An installation underground, in concrete slabs in direct contact with the Earth, areas subject to saturation with water, and unprotected locations exposed to weather. ▸Figure 100–69 and ▸Figure 100–70

Neutral Conductor. The conductor connected to the neutral point of a system that is intended to carry current under normal conditions. ▸Figure 100–71

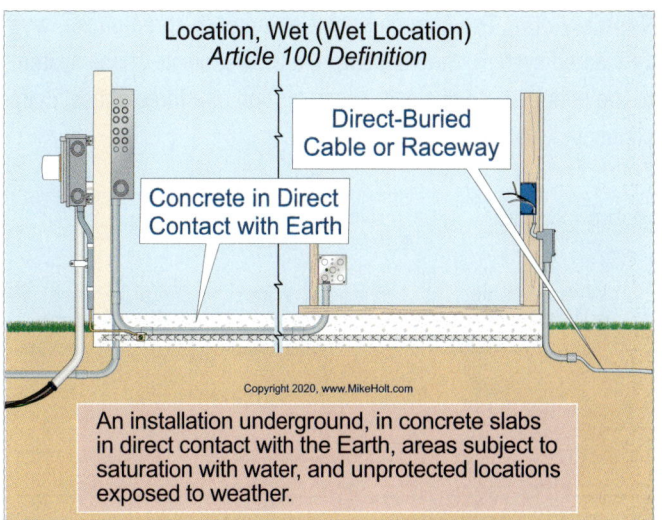
▸Figure 100–69

▸Figure 100–70

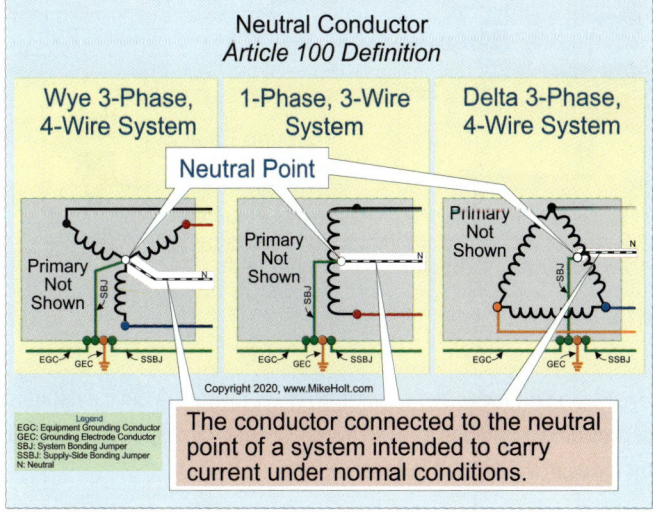
▸Figure 100–71

Neutral Point. The common point of a 4-wire, three-phase, wye-connected system; the midpoint of a 3-wire, single-phase system; or the midpoint of the single-phase portion of a three-phase, delta-connected system. ▶Figure 100-72

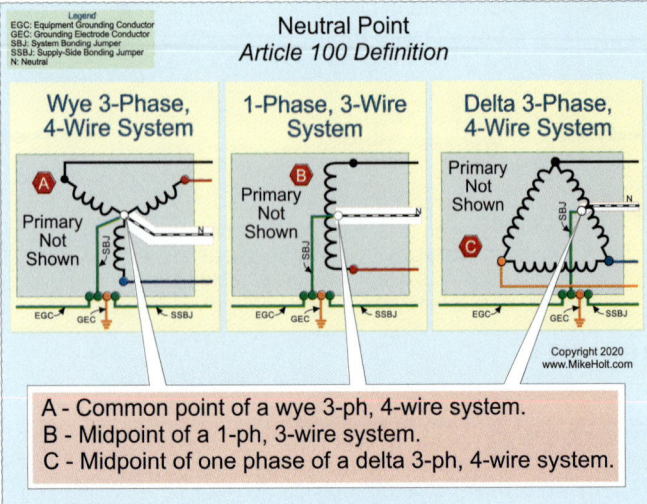

▶Figure 100-72

Nonautomatic. Requiring human intervention to perform a function.

Overcurrent. Current in excess of the equipment's current rating or a conductor's ampacity caused by an overload, short circuit, or ground fault. ▶Figure 100-73

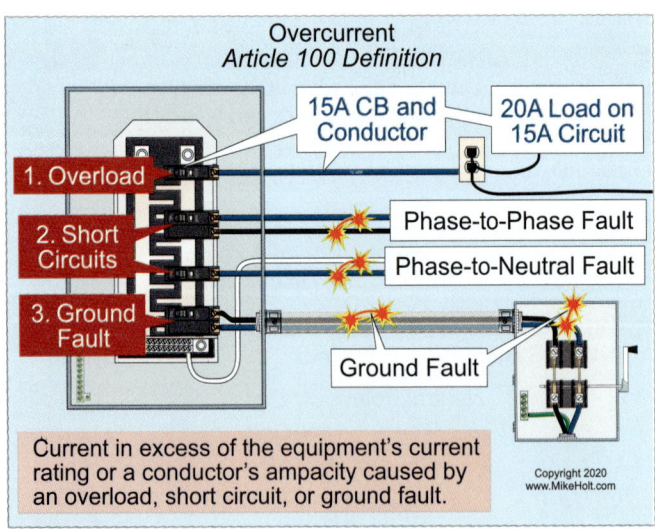

▶Figure 100-73

Overcurrent Protective Device, Branch Circuit. A device capable of providing protection from an overload, short circuit, or ground fault for service, feeder, and branch circuits.

Overcurrent Protective Device, Supplementary. A device intended to provide limited overcurrent protection for specific applications and utilization equipment, such as luminaires and appliances. This limited protection is in addition to the protection required and provided by the branch-circuit overcurrent protective device. ▶Figure 100-74

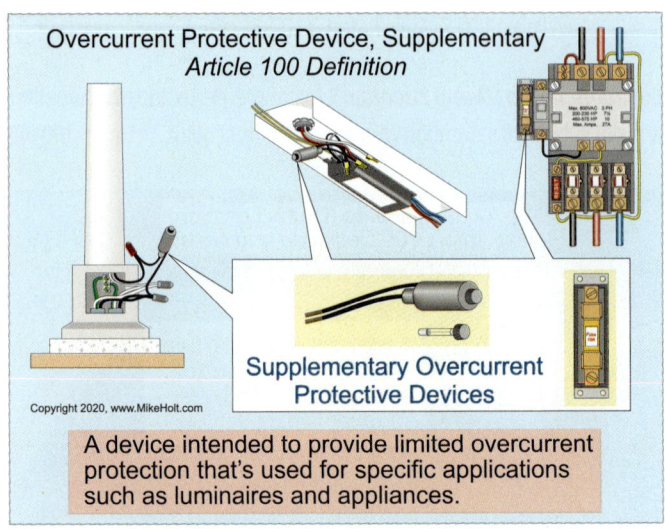

▶Figure 100-74

Overload. The operation of equipment above its current rating, or current in excess of a conductor's ampacity. If an overload condition persists long enough, the result can be equipment failure or a fire from damaging or dangerous overheating. A fault, such as a short circuit or ground fault, is not an overload. ▶Figure 100-75

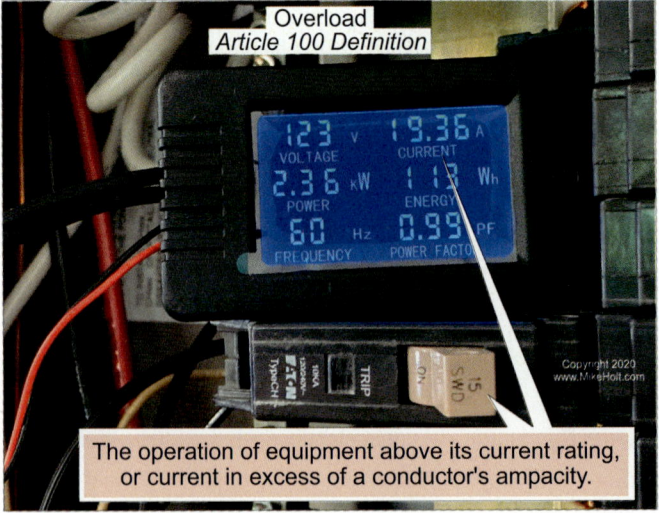

▶Figure 100-75

Panelboard. An assembly designed for the distribution of light, heat, or power circuits with overcurrent devices and typically placed in a cabinet. ▶Figure 100-76

Definitions | 100

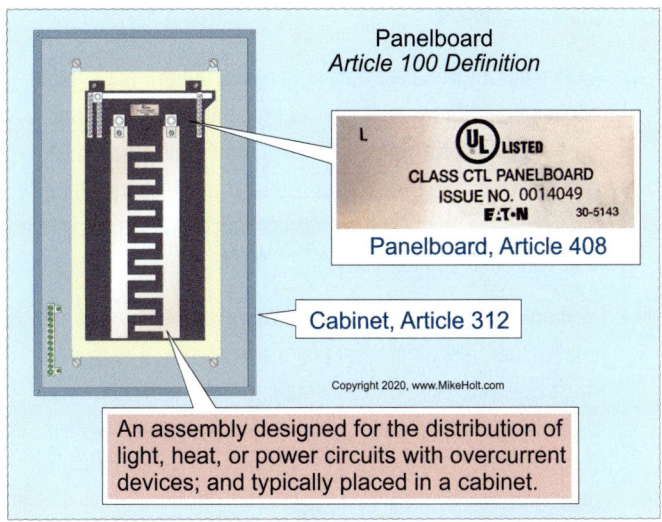
▶Figure 100-76

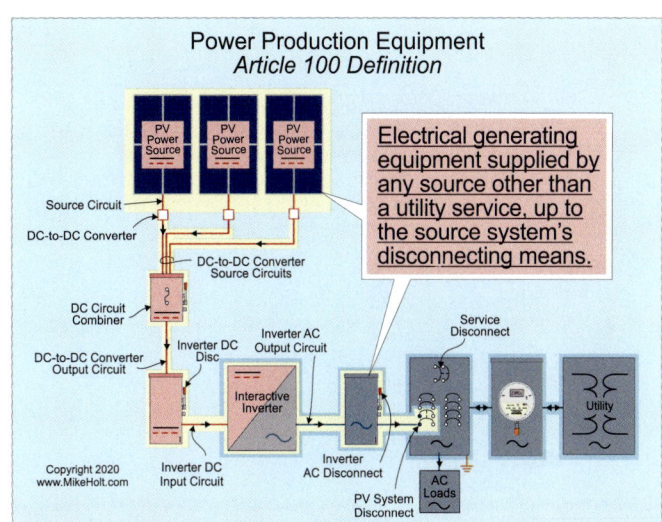
▶Figure 100-78

Author's Comment:

▸ See the definition of "Cabinet" in this article.

▸ The slang term in the electrical field for a panelboard is "the guts." This is the interior of the panelboard assembly and is covered by Article 408, while the cabinet is covered by Article 312.

Photovoltaic (PV) System. The combination of all components and subsystems, including the PV system disconnecting means, that convert solar energy into electric energy for utilization loads. ▶Figure 100-77

Note: Examples of power production equipment include such items as generators, solar photovoltaic systems, and fuel cell systems.

Premises Wiring. The interior and exterior wiring including power, lighting, control, and signaling circuits, and all associated hardware, fittings, and wiring devices. This includes permanently and temporarily installed wiring from the service point to the outlets. Where there is no service point, it is the wiring from and including the electric power source (such as a generator, transformer, or PV system) to the outlets.
▶Figure 100-79

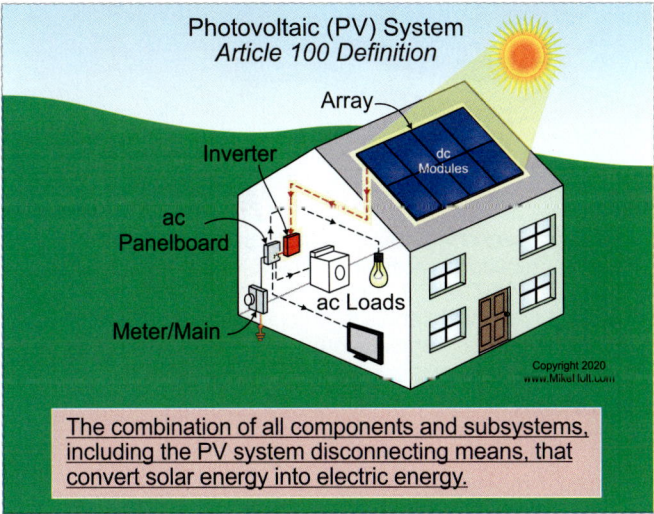
▶Figure 100-77

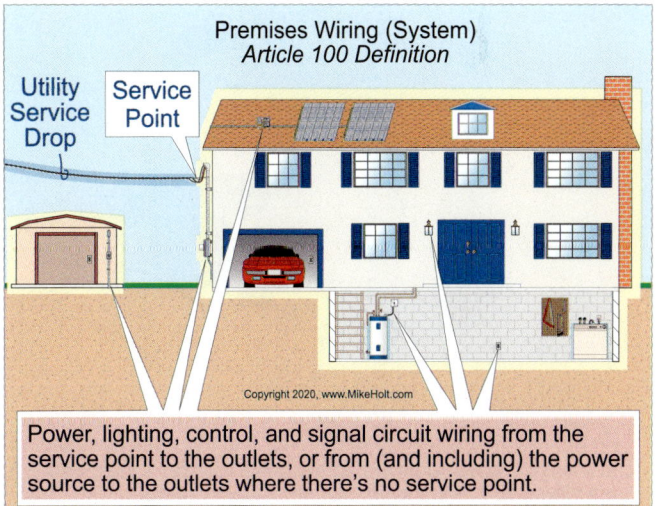
▶Figure 100-79

Power Production Equipment. Electrical generating equipment supplied by any source other than a utility service, up to the source system's disconnecting means. ▶Figure 100-78

Premises wiring does not include the internal wiring of electrical equipment and appliances such as luminaires, dishwashers, water heaters, motors, controllers, motor control centers, air-conditioning equipment, and so on [90.7 and 300.1(B)]. ▶Figure 100-80

100 | Definitions

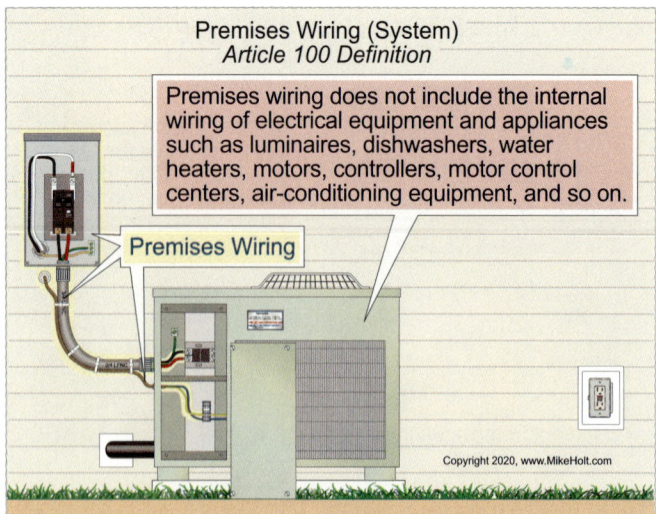
▶Figure 100–80

Note: Electric power sources include (but not limited to) interconnected or stand-alone batteries, PV systems, other distributed generation systems, and generators.

Prime Mover. The machine that supplies mechanical horsepower to a generator.

Qualified Person. A person who has the skill and knowledge related to the construction and operation of electrical equipment and its installation. This person must have received safety training to recognize and avoid the hazards involved with electrical systems. ▶Figure 100–81

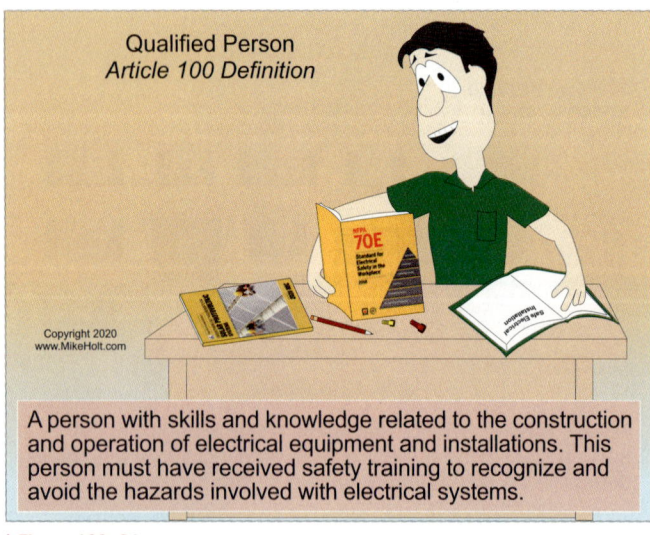
▶Figure 100–81

Note: NFPA 70E, *Standard for Electrical Safety in the Workplace*, provides information on the safety training requirements expected of a "qualified person."

Author's Comment:

▸ Examples of this safety training include, but are not limited to, training in the use of special precautionary techniques, personal protective equipment (PPE), insulating and shielding materials, and the use of insulated tools and test equipment when working on or near exposed conductors or circuit parts that can become energized.

▸ In many parts of the United States, electricians, electrical contractors, electrical inspectors, and electrical engineers must complete from 6 to 24 hours of *NEC* review each year as a requirement to maintain licensing. This, in and of itself, does not make one qualified to deal with the specific hazards involved with electrical systems.

Raceway. A channel designed for the installation of conductors, cables, or busbars.

Raceway, Communications. An enclosed nonmetallic channel designed for holding communications wires and cables; optical fiber cables; data cables associated with information technology and communications equipment; Class 2, Type PLTC, and power-limited fire alarm cables in plenum spaces, risers, and general-purpose applications. ▶Figure 100–82

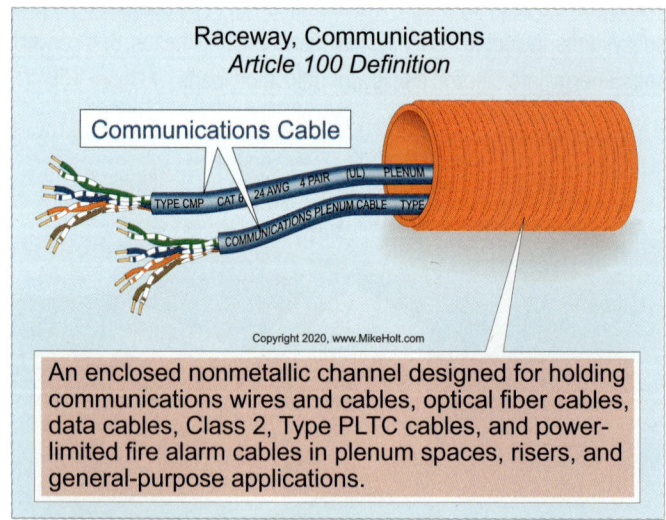
▶Figure 100–82

Author's Comment:

▸ A cable tray system is not a raceway; it is a support system for cables and raceways [392.2].

Definitions | 100

Rainproof. Constructed, protected, or treated to prevent rain from interfering with the successful operation of the apparatus under specified test conditions.

Raintight. Constructed or protected so exposure to a beating rain will not result in the entrance of water under specified test conditions.

Remote-Control Circuit. An electric circuit that controls another circuit by a relay or equivalent device installed in accordance with Article 725. ▶Figure 100-83

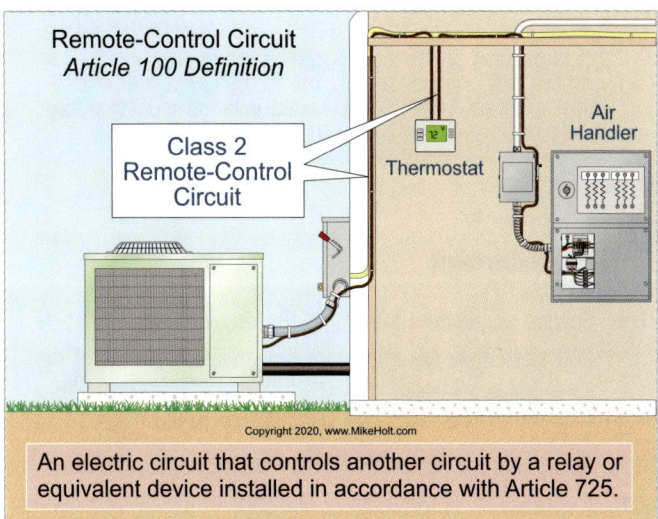

▶Figure 100-83

Service [Article 230]. The conductors and equipment connecting the serving electric utility to the wiring system of the premises served. ▶Figure 100-84

▶Figure 100-84

Author's Comment:

▸ A service can only be supplied by the serving electric utility and is not covered by the *NEC*. If power is supplied by other than the serving electric utility, the conductors and equipment are part of a feeder and covered by the *Code*.

▸ Conductors from UPS systems, solar PV systems, generators, or transformers are not service conductors. See the definitions of "Feeder" and "Service Conductors" in this article.

Service Conductors. The conductors from the serving electric utility service point to the service disconnect. ▶Figure 100-85

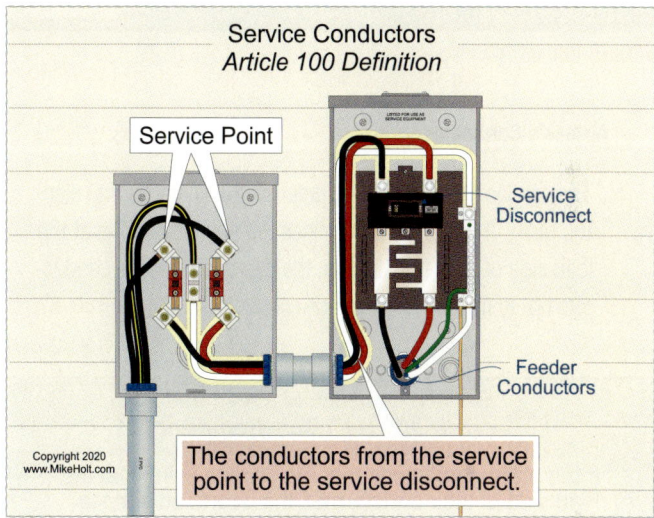

▶Figure 100-85

Author's Comment:

▸ Service conductors can include overhead service conductors, overhead service-entrance conductors, and underground service conductors. These conductors are not under the exclusive control of the serving electric utility, which means they are owned by the customer and are covered by the requirements in Article 230.

Service Conductors, Overhead (Overhead Service Conductors). Overhead conductors between the serving electric utility service point and the first point of connection to the service-entrance conductors at the building. ▶Figure 100-86

100 | Definitions

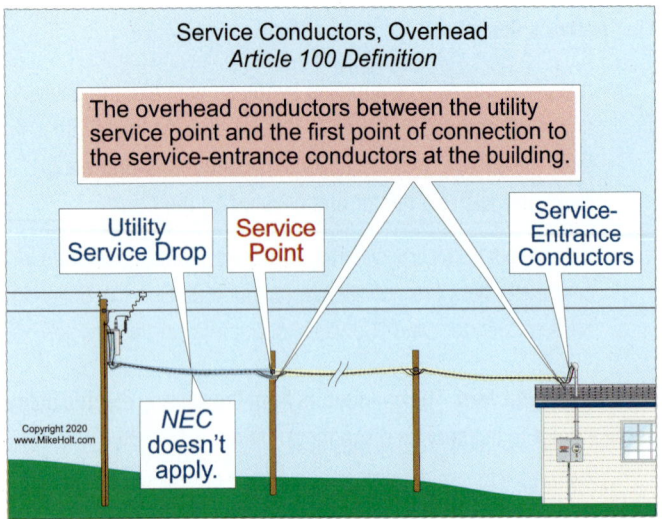
▶Figure 100–86

Author's Comment:

▶ The service point is typically determined by the serving electric utility. If the utility determines the service point is at the load side of their transformer, the overhead service conductors run to the service-entrance conductors. ▶Figure 100–87

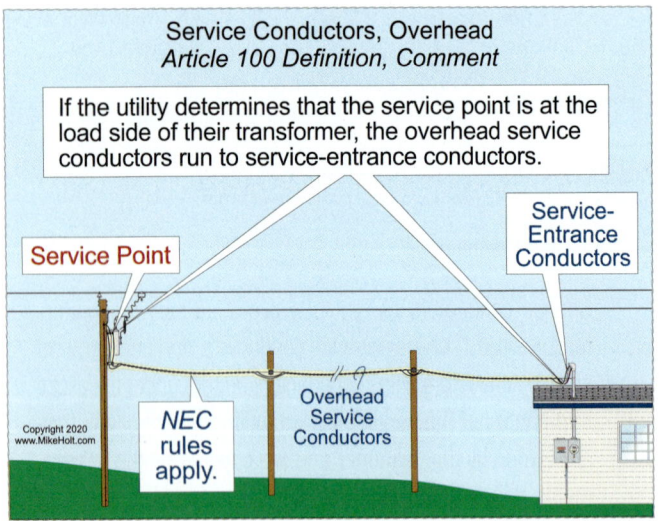
▶Figure 100–87

Service Conductors, Underground (Underground Service Conductors). Underground conductors between the service point and the first point of connection to the service-entrance conductors in a terminal box, meter, or other enclosure; inside or outside the building wall. ▶Figure 100–88

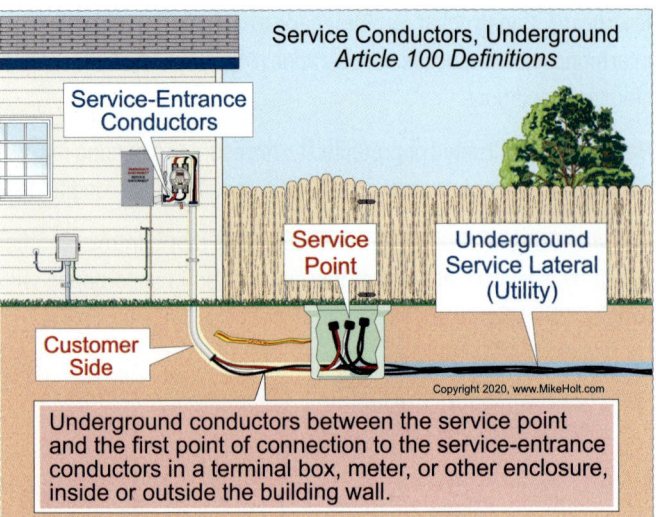
▶Figure 100–88

Author's Comment:

▶ Service conductors fall within the requirements of Article 230 since they are not under the exclusive control of the serving electric utility.

Note: Where there is no terminal box, meter, or other enclosure the point of connection is the point of entrance of the service conductors into the building.

Service Drop. Utility-owned overhead conductors between the serving electric utility and the service point. ▶Figure 100–89

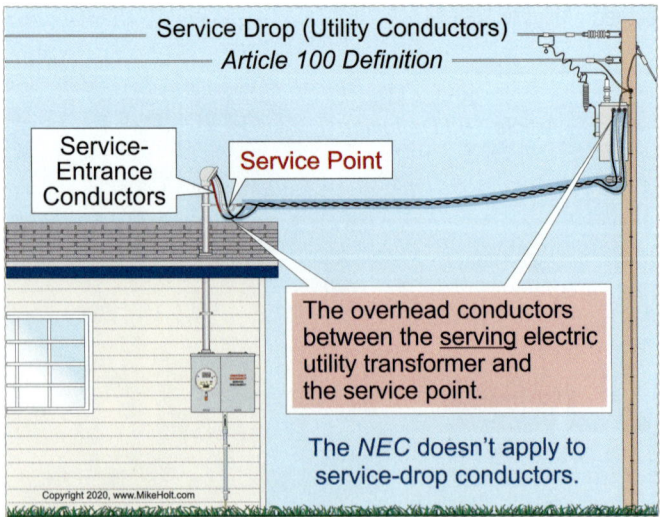
▶Figure 100–89

Author's Comment:

▸ The *NEC* does not apply to service drops.

Service-Entrance Conductors, Overhead (Overhead Service-Entrance Conductors). The conductors between the terminals of the service disconnect and service drop or overhead service conductors. ▸Figure 100-90

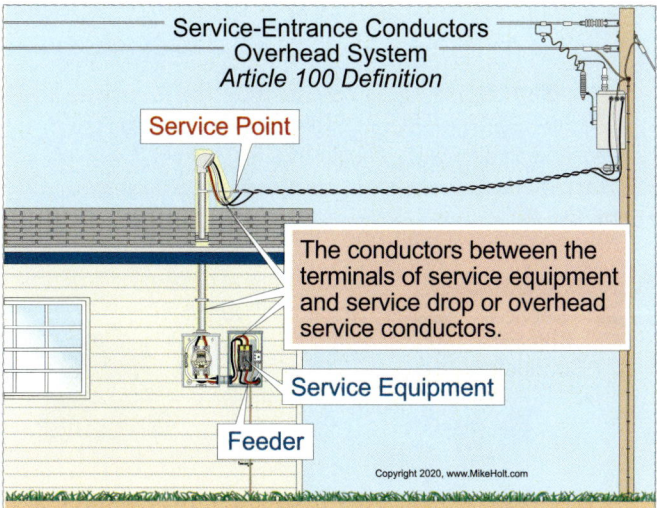

▸Figure 100-90

Author's Comment:

▸ Overhead service-entrance conductors are covered by the requirements of Article 230, since they are not under the exclusive control of the serving electric utility.

Service-Entrance Conductors, Underground (Underground Service-Entrance Conductors). The conductors between the terminals of the service disconnect and underground service point. ▸Figure 100-91

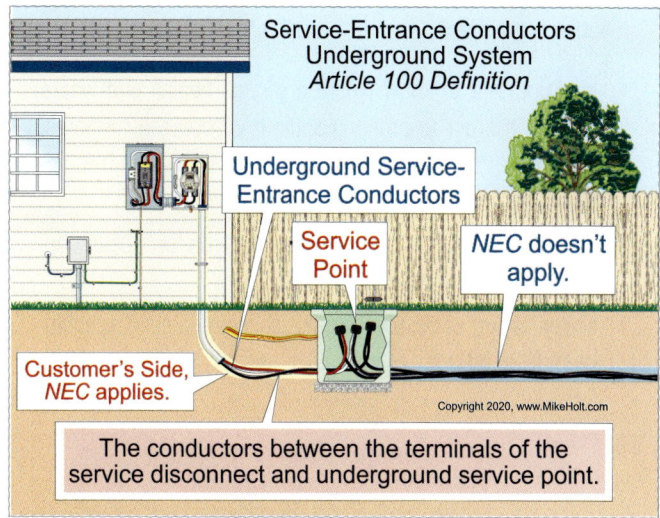

▸Figure 100-91

Author's Comment:

▸ Underground service-entrance conductors fall within the requirements of Article 230 since they are not under the exclusive control of the serving electric utility.

Service Equipment (Service Disconnect). Disconnects such as circuit breakers or switches connected to the serving electric utility, intended to control and disconnect the power from the serving electric utility. ▸Figure 100-92

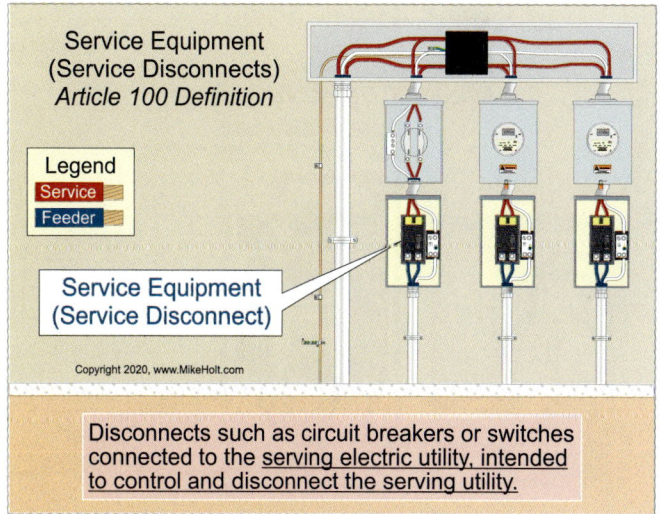

▸Figure 100-92

100 | Definitions

Author's Comment:

- It's important to know where a service begins and where it ends in order to properly apply the *Code* requirements. Sometimes the service ends before the metering equipment. ▶Figure 100-93 and ▶Figure 100-94
- Service equipment is often referred to as the "service disconnect" or "service main."
- Meter socket enclosures are not considered service equipment [230.66].

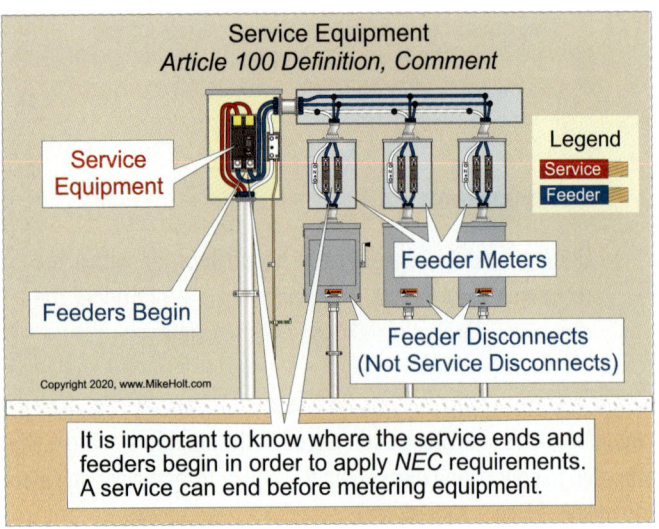

▶Figure 100-93

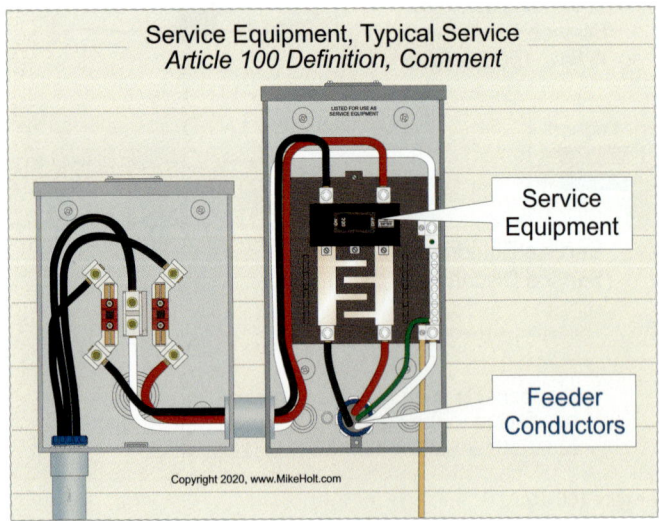

▶Figure 100-94

Service Lateral. Utility-owned underground conductors between the serving electric utility transformer and the service point. ▶Figure 100-95 and ▶Figure 100-96

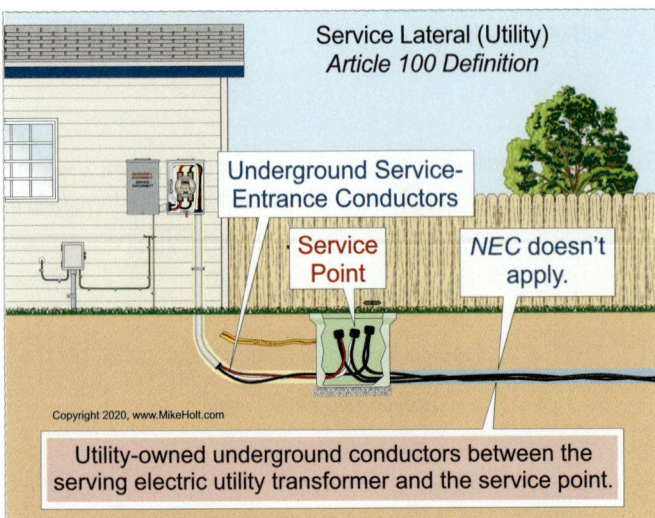

▶Figure 100-95

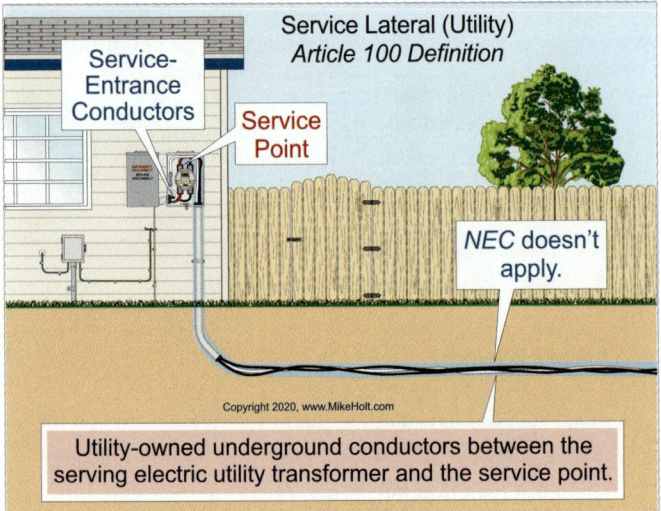

▶Figure 100-96

Service Point. The point where the serving electric utility conductors connect to customer-owned wiring. ▶Figure 100-97

Author's Comment:

- The service point is typically determined by the serving electric utility and may vary with different utilities and different types of occupancies.
- For utility-owned transformers, the service point will be at the serving electric utility's transformer secondary terminals, at the service drop, or at the meter socket enclosure depending on where their conductors terminate. ▶Figure 100-98
- For customer-owned transformers, the service point will be at the termination of the serving electric utility's conductors, often at the utility's pole. ▶Figure 100-99

Definitions | **100**

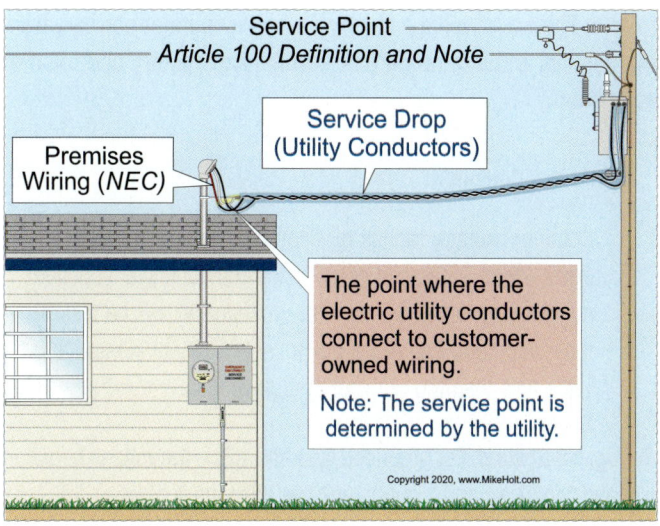
▶Figure 100-97

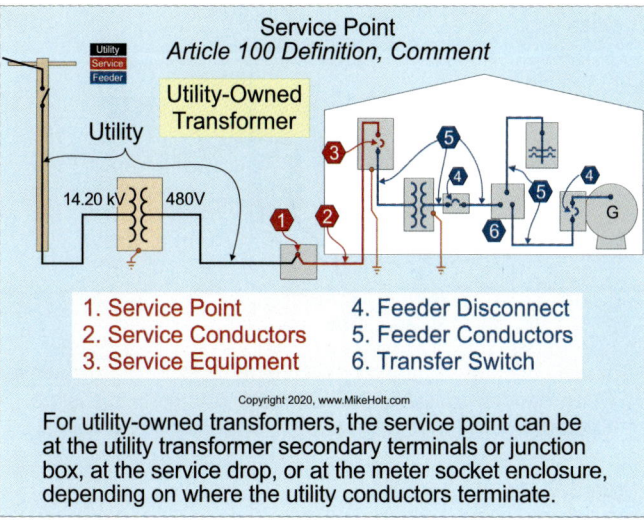
▶Figure 100-98

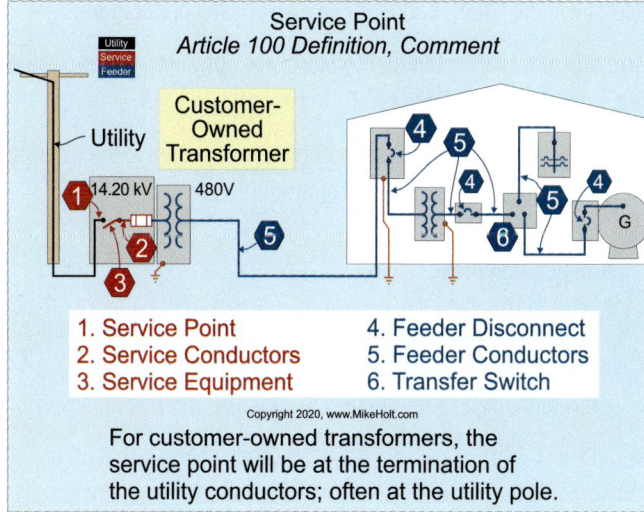
▶Figure 100-99

Short-Circuit Current Rating. The prospective symmetrical fault current at a nominal voltage to which electrical equipment can be connected without sustaining damage exceeding defined acceptance criteria.

Special Permission. Written consent from the authority having jurisdiction.

Author's Comment:

▸ See the definition of "Authority Having Jurisdiction."

Stand-Alone System. A system capable of supplying power independently of a serving electric utility. ▶Figure 100-100

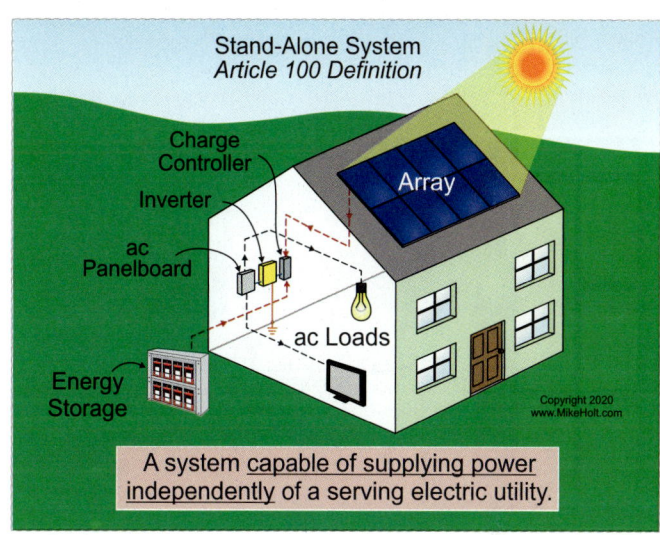
▶Figure 100-100

Author's Comment:

▸ Although stand-alone systems can operate independently of the serving electric utility, they may include a connection to the serving electric utility for use when not operating in stand-alone mode ("island mode").

Structure. That which is built or constructed, other than equipment. ▶Figure 100-101

Voltage of a Circuit. The greatest effective root-mean-square (RMS) difference of voltage between any two conductors of the circuit. ▶Figure 100-102

Voltage, Nominal (Nominal Voltage). A value assigned for conveniently designating voltage classes. Examples are 120/240V, 120/208V, or 277/480V [220.5(A)]. ▶Figure 100-103

2nd Printing | 2020 NEC Requirements for Solar PV and Energy Storage Systems | MikeHolt.com | **43**

100 | Definitions

▶Figure 100–101

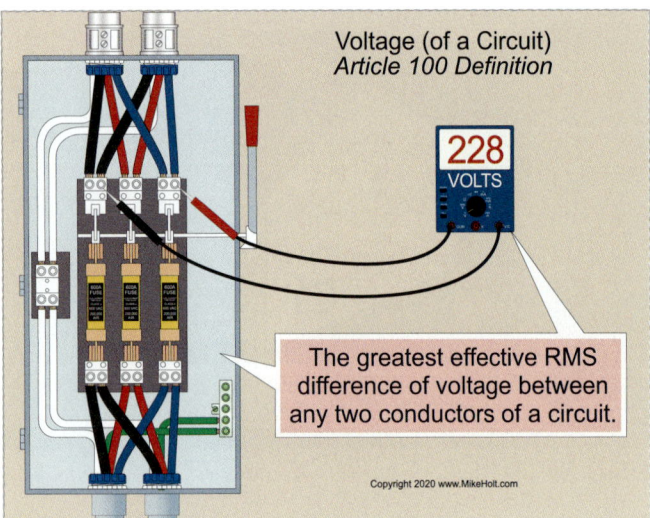
▶Figure 100–102

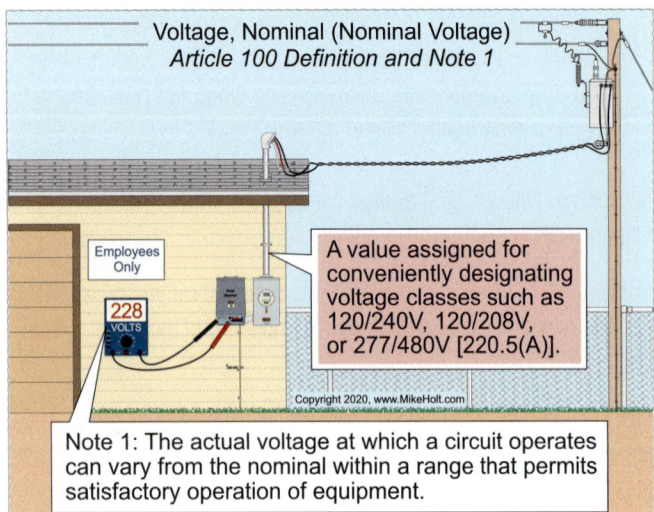
▶Figure 100–103

Note 1: The actual voltage at which a circuit operates can vary from the nominal within a range that permits satisfactory operation of equipment.

> **Author's Comment:**
>
> ▸ Common voltage ratings of electrical equipment are 115V, 200V, 208V, 230V, and 460V. The electrical power supplied might be at the 240V, nominal, voltage but will be less at the equipment. Therefore, electrical equipment is rated at a value less than the nominal system voltage.

Voltage to Ground. For grounded systems, this is the voltage between a phase conductor and ground; typically, the neutral. ▶Figure 100–104

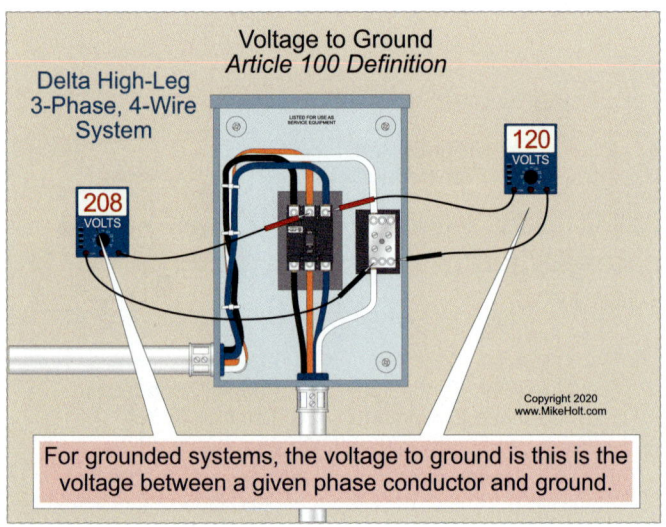
▶Figure 100–104

For ungrounded systems, the voltage to ground is the greatest difference of voltage (RMS) between any two phase conductors.

Watertight. Constructed so moisture will not enter the enclosure under specific test conditions.

Weatherproof. Constructed or protected so exposure to the weather will not interfere with successful operation.

> **Author's Comment:**
>
> ▸ Article 100 now includes a "Part III" which contains definitions specific to Hazardous (Classified) Locations. While a few of the definitions are new to the *Code*, most were moved from Chapter 5 to this new part.

ARTICLE 110 — REQUIREMENTS FOR ELECTRICAL INSTALLATIONS

Introduction to Article 110—Requirements for Electrical Installations

Article 110 sets the stage for how the rest of the *NEC* is implemented. It is critical for you to completely understand all aspects of this article since it is the foundation for much of the *Code*. As you read and master Article 110, you are building your foundation for correctly applying the *NEC*. While the purpose of the *National Electrical Code* is to provide a safe installation, this article is perhaps focused a little more on providing an installation that is safe for the installer and maintenance electrician, so time spent here is a good investment.

Part I. General Requirements

110.1 Scope

Article 110 covers the general requirements for the examination and approval, installation and use, and access to spaces about electrical equipment. ▶Figure 110–1

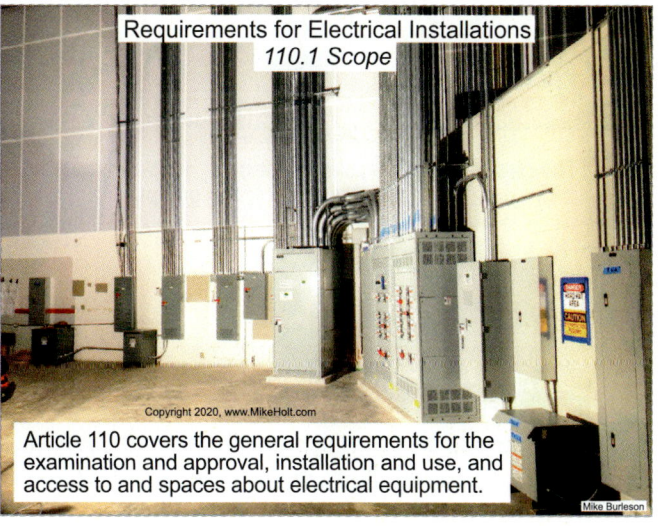

▶Figure 110–1

Note: See Annex J for information regarding ADA accessibility design.

Author's Comment:

▸ Requirements for people with disabilities include things like mounting heights for switches and receptacles, and requirements for the distance that objects (such as wall sconces) protrude from a wall.

110.2 Approval of Conductors and Equipment

The authority having jurisdiction must approve all electrical conductors and equipment. ▶Figure 110–2

▶Figure 110–2

Author's Comment:

▸ For a better understanding of product approval, review 90.4, 90.7, and 110.3 and the definitions for "Approved," "Identified," "Labeled," and "Listed" in Article 100.

110.3 Use and Product Listing (Certification) of Equipment

(A) Guidelines for Approval. The authority having jurisdiction must approve equipment. In doing so, consideration must be given to the following:

(1) Suitability for installation and use in accordance with the *NEC*

Note 1: Equipment may be new, reconditioned, refurbished, or remanufactured.

Note 2: Suitability of equipment use may be identified by a description marked on, or provided with, a product to identify the suitability of the product for a specific purpose, environment, or application. Special conditions of use or other limitations may be marked on the equipment, in the product instructions, or included in the appropriate listing and labeling information. Suitability of equipment may be evidenced by listing or labeling.

(2) Mechanical strength and durability

(3) Wire-bending and connection space

(4) Electrical insulation

(5) Heating effects under all conditions of use

(6) Arcing effects

(7) Classification by type, size, voltage, current capacity, and specific use

(8) Other factors contributing to the practical safeguarding of persons using or in contact with the equipment

(B) Installation and Use. Equipment that is listed, labeled, or both must be installed and used in accordance with any instructions included in the listing or labeling. ▶Figure 110-3

(C) Product Listing. Product testing, evaluation, and listing must be performed by a recognized qualified testing laboratory in accordance with standards that achieve effective safety to comply with the *NEC*.

Note: OSHA recognizes qualified electrical testing laboratories that provide product certification that meets their electrical standards.

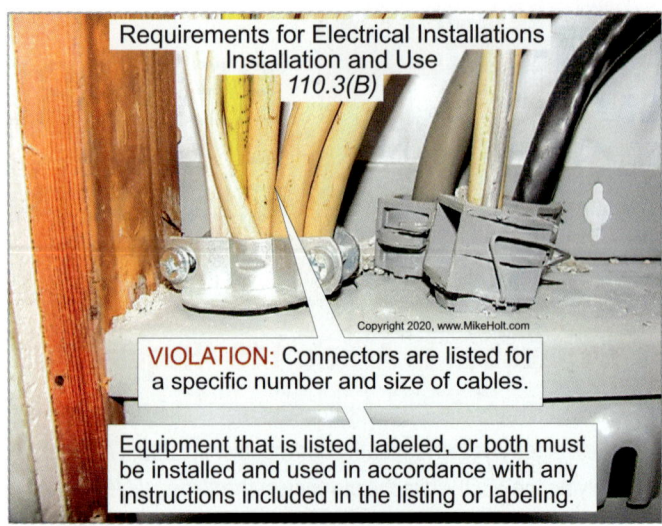

▶Figure 110-3

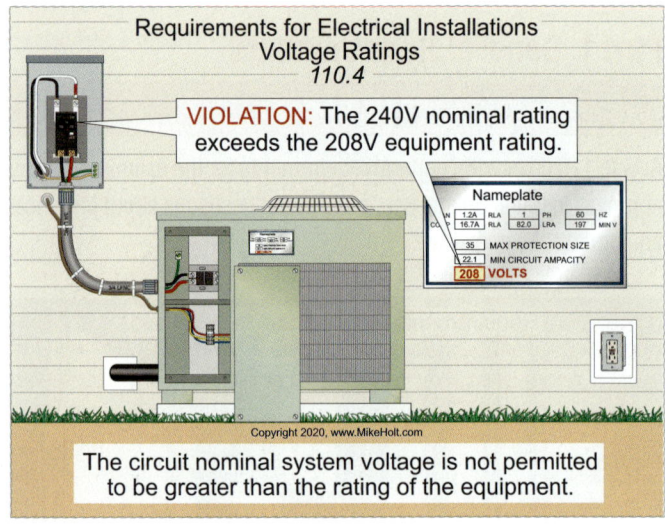

▶Figure 110-4

110.4 Voltage Rating of Electrical Equipment

The circuit nominal system voltage is not permitted to be greater than the rating of the equipment. ▶Figure 110-4

110.5 Conductor Material

Conductors must be copper, aluminum, or copper-clad aluminum unless otherwise provided in this *Code*; and when the conductor material is not specified in a rule, the sizes given in the *NEC* are based on a copper conductor. ▶Figure 110-5

110.6 Conductor Sizes

Conductor sizes are expressed in American Wire Gage (AWG) or circular mils (cmil). ▶Figure 110-6

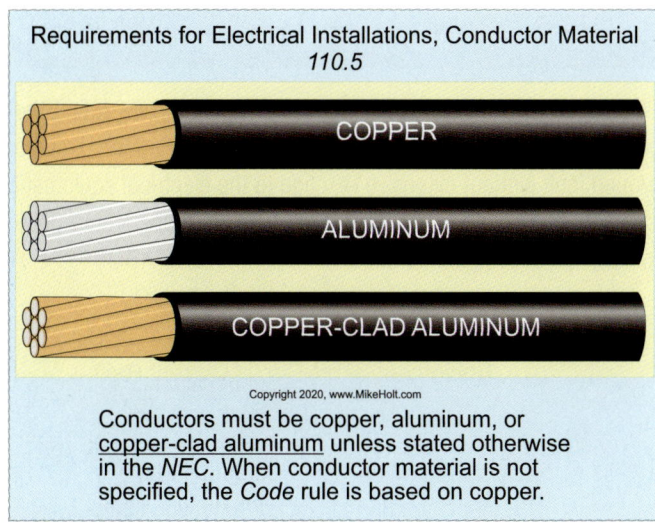
▶Figure 110–5

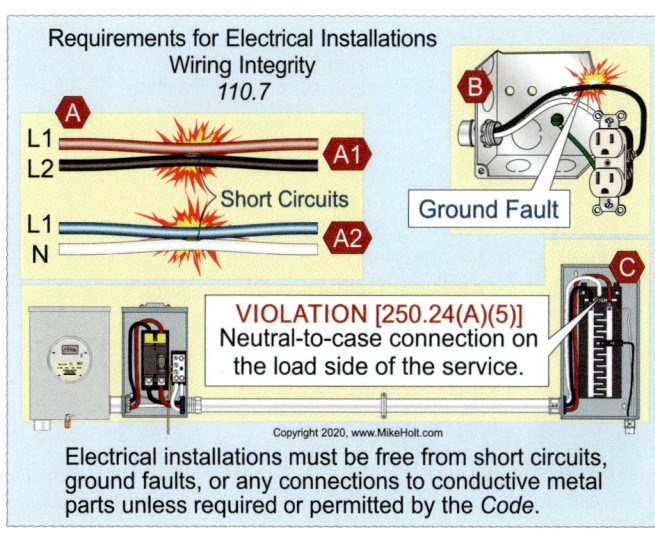
▶Figure 110–7

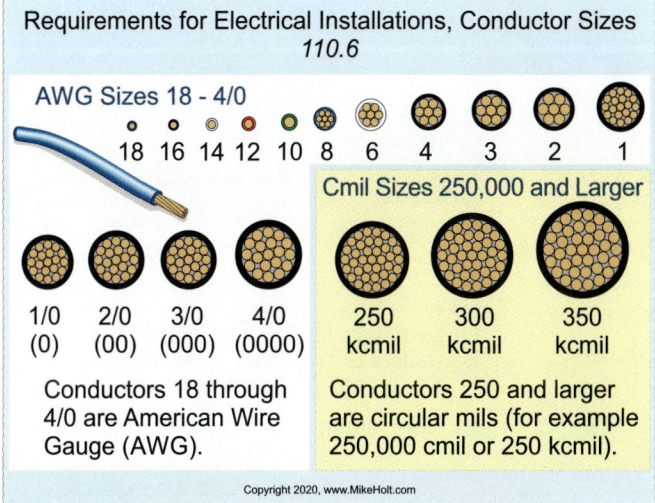
▶Figure 110–6

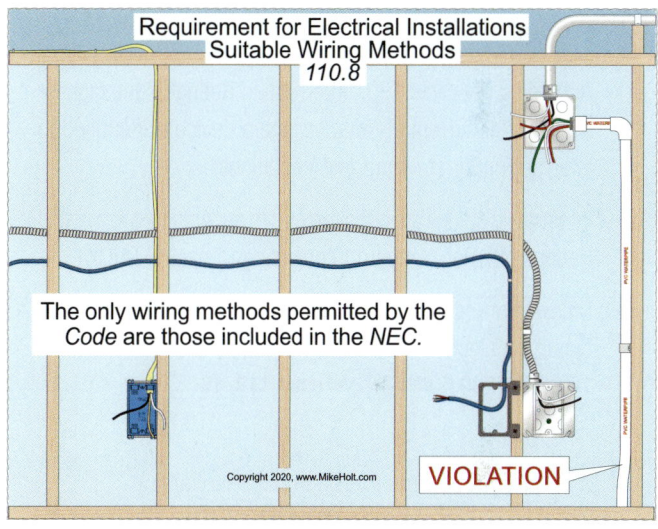
▶Figure 110–8

110.7 Wiring Integrity

Electrical installations must be free from short circuits, ground faults, or any connections to conductive metal parts unless required or permitted by the *Code*. ▶Figure 110–7

110.8 Suitable Wiring Methods

The only wiring methods permitted by the *NEC* are those included in the *Code*. ▶Figure 110–8

Author's Comment:

▸ See Chapter 3 for power and lighting wiring methods; Chapter 7 for signaling, remote-control, and power-limited circuit wiring methods; and Chapter 8 for communications circuits wiring methods.

110.9 Interrupting Rating (Overcurrent Protective Devices)

Overcurrent protective devices, such as circuit breakers and fuses, must have an interrupting rating capacity (AIC) equal to or greater than the fault current available at the line terminals of the equipment. ▶Figure 110–9

110.10 | Requirements for Electrical Installations

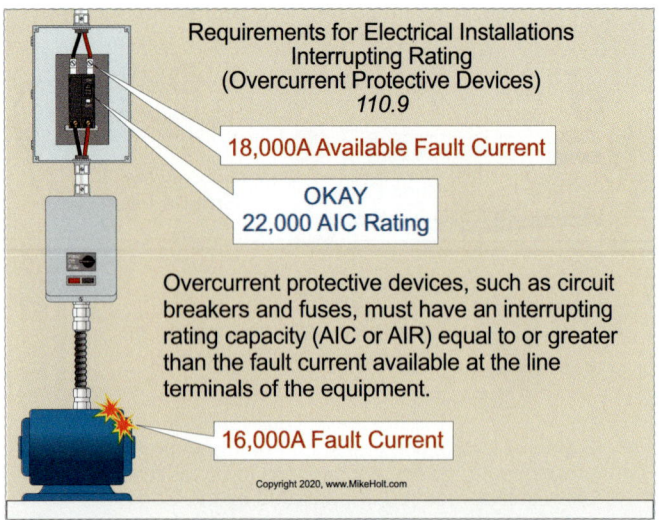
▶Figure 110–9

Author's Comment:

▶ According to Article 100, "Interrupting Rating" is the highest short-circuit current at rated voltage a device is identified to interrupt under standard test conditions.

▶ Interrupting ratings are often referred to as "Ampere Interrupting Rating" (AIR) or "Ampere Interrupting Capacity" (AIC).

▶ Unless marked otherwise, the ampere interrupting rating for circuit breakers is 5,000A [240.83(C)], and for fuses it is 10,000A [240.60(C)(3)]. ▶Figure 110–10

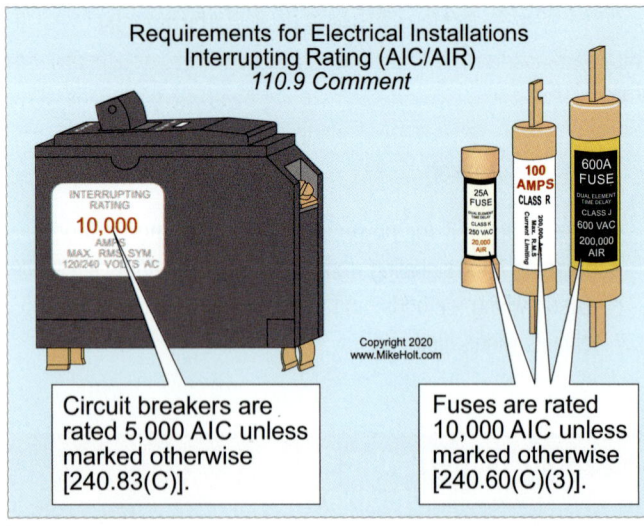
▶Figure 110–10

110.10 Equipment Short-Circuit Current Rating

Electrical equipment must have a short-circuit current rating that permits the circuit protective device to open due to a short circuit or ground fault without extensive damage to the electrical equipment. Listed equipment applied in accordance with its listing is considered to have met this requirement. ▶Figure 110–11 and ▶Figure 110–12

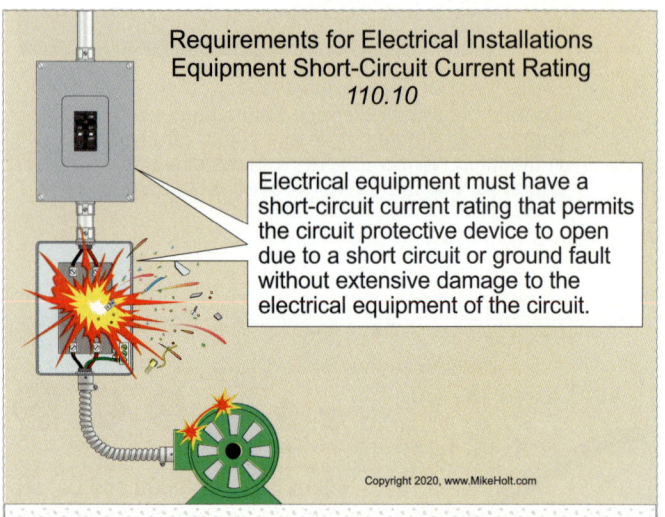
▶Figure 110–11

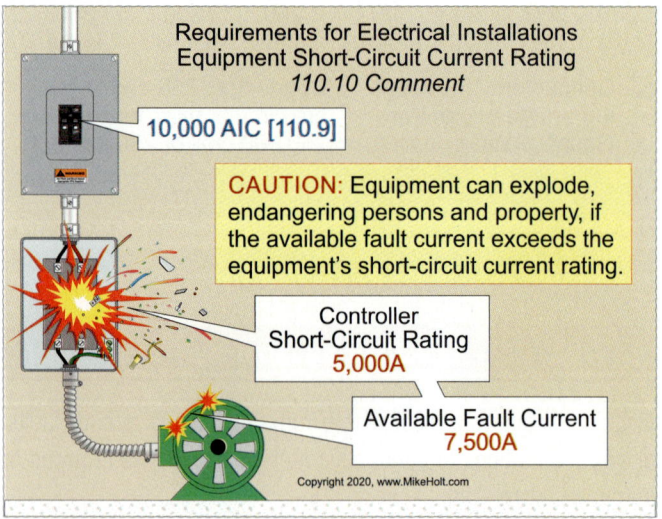
▶Figure 110–12

Available Short-Circuit Current

Sections 110.9 and 110.10 use similar sounding terms making it a bit challenging to understand the differences. Be careful not to confuse the term "interrupting rating" with "short-circuit rating."

Available short-circuit current is the current, in amperes, available at a given point in the electrical system. It is first determined at the secondary terminals of the serving electric utility transformer, as given by the serving electric utility's engineer. After that, it is calculated at the terminals of the service disconnect, then panelboards and other equipment as various connections are made downstream from the main service. Beginning at the serving electric utility transformer, the available short-circuit current decreases at each down-stream connection point of the electrical system.

The available short-circuit current at any point depends on the impedance of the circuit. As the circuit impedance increases, the available short-circuit current decreases. ▶Figure 110–13

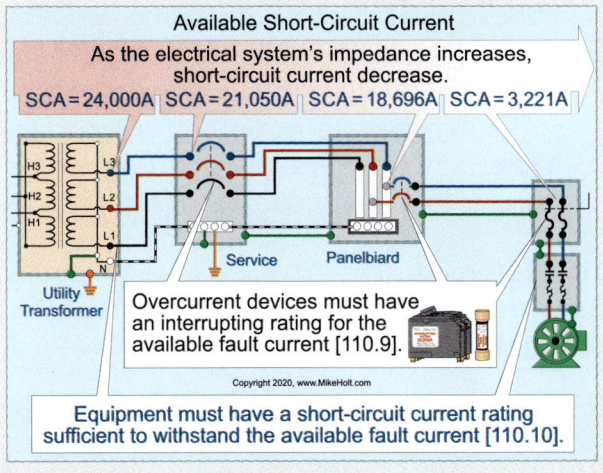

▶Figure 110–13

Factors that affect the available short-circuit current at the serving electric utility transformers are the system voltage, transformer kVA rating, and impedance. Properties that have an impact on the impedance of the circuit include the conductor material (copper versus aluminum), conductor size, conductor length, raceway type (metallic versus nonmetallic), ambient temperature, and motor loads.

Caution

⚠️ Extremely high values of current flow caused by short circuits or ground faults produce tremendously destructive thermal and magnetic forces. If an overcurrent protective device is not rated to interrupt the current at the available fault values it can explode and literally vaporize metal components which can cause serious injury or death, as well as property damage and electrical system down time. ▶Figure 110–14

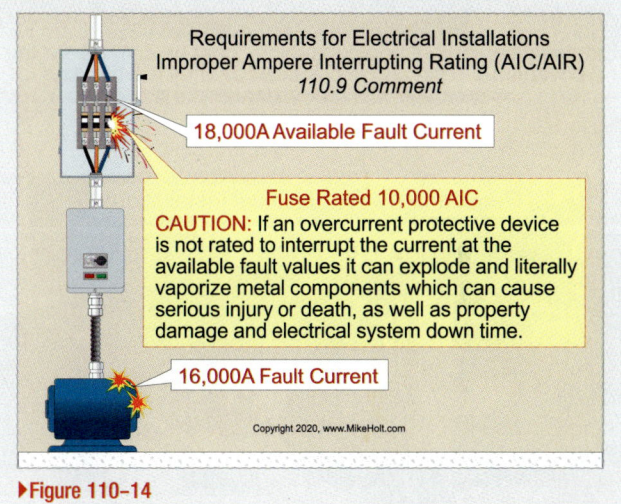

▶Figure 110–14

110.11 Deteriorating Agents

Electrical equipment and conductors must be suitable for the environment and the conditions for which they will be used. Consideration must also be given to the presence of corrosive gases, fumes, vapors, liquids, or other substances that can have a deteriorating effect on conductors and equipment. ▶Figure 110–15

Note 1: Raceways, cable trays, cablebus, cable armor, boxes, cable sheathing, cabinets, elbows, couplings, fittings, supports, and support hardware must be suitable for the environment; see 300.6. ▶Figure 110–16

Note 2: Some cleaning and lubricating compounds contain chemicals that can cause plastic to deteriorate.

Equipment identified for indoor use must be protected against damage from the weather during construction.

Note 3: See Table 110.28 for NEMA enclosure-type designations.

Note 4: For minimum flood provisions, see the *International Building Code (IBC)* and the *International Residential Code* (IRC).

110.12 | Requirements for Electrical Installations

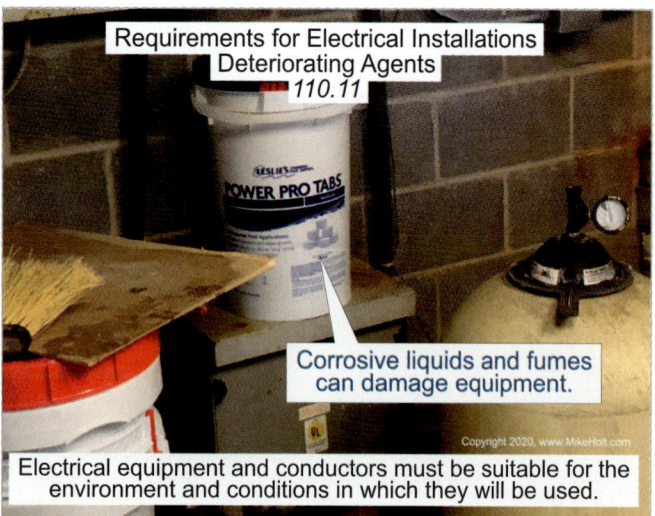
▶Figure 110–15

▶Figure 110–17

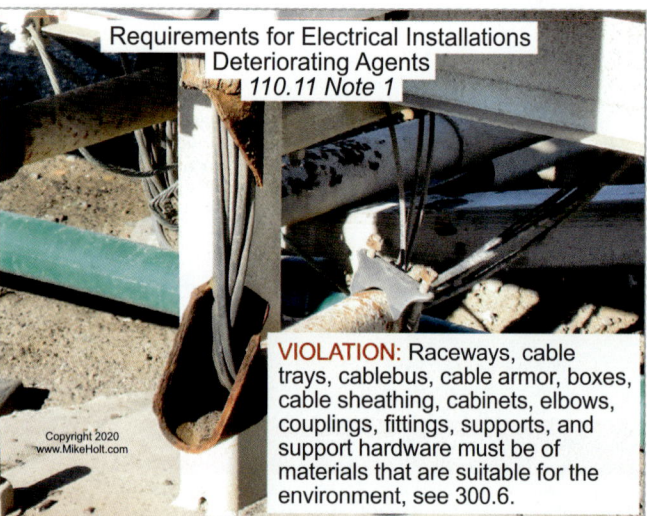
▶Figure 110–16

110.12 Mechanical Execution of Work

Electrical equipment must be installed in a neat and workmanlike manner. ▶Figure 110–17

Author's Comment:

▶ This rule is perhaps one of the most subjective of the entire *Code* and its application is still ultimately a judgment call made by the authority having jurisdiction.

Author's Comment:

▶ The National Electrical Contractors Association (*NECA*) created a series of *National Electrical Installation Standards* (NEIS)® that established the industry's first quality guidelines for electrical installations. These standards define a benchmark (baseline) of quality and workmanship for installing electrical products and systems. They explain what installing electrical products and systems in a "neat and workmanlike manner" means. For more information about these standards, visit www.NECA-NEIS.org.

(A) Unused Openings. Unused openings must be closed by fittings that provide protection substantially equivalent to the wall of the equipment. ▶Figure 110–18

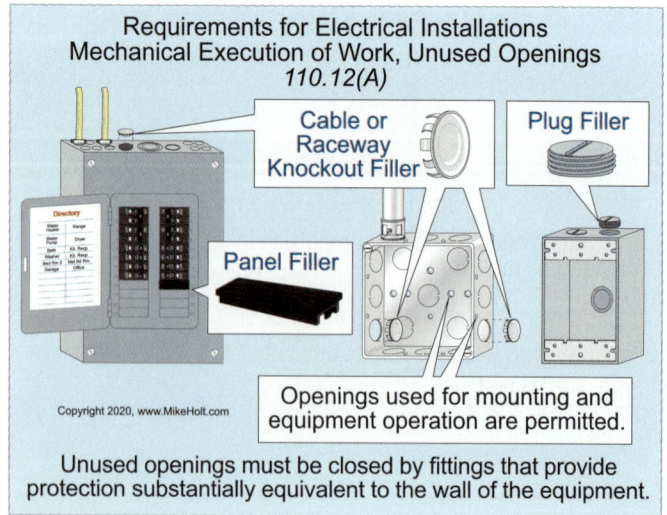
▶Figure 110–18

(B) Integrity of Electrical Equipment. Internal parts of electrical equipment must not be damaged or contaminated by foreign material, such as paint, plaster, cleaners, and so forth. ▶Figure 110–19

Electrical equipment containing damaged (such as items broken, bent, or cut) parts, or those that have been deteriorated by corrosion, chemical action, or overheating are not permitted to be installed. ▶Figure 110–21

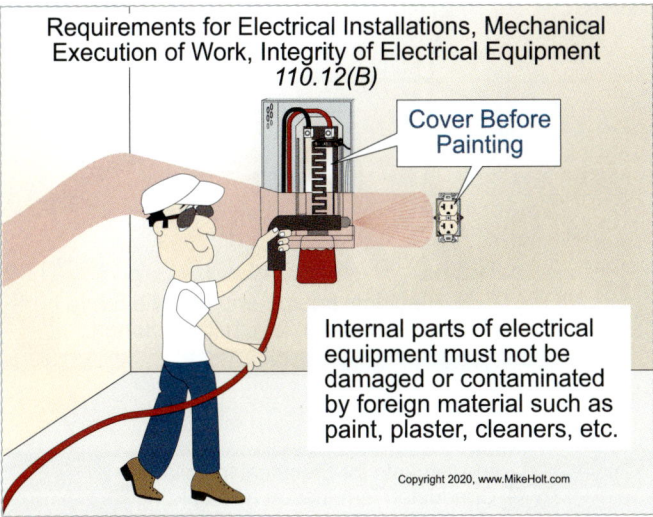

▶Figure 110–19

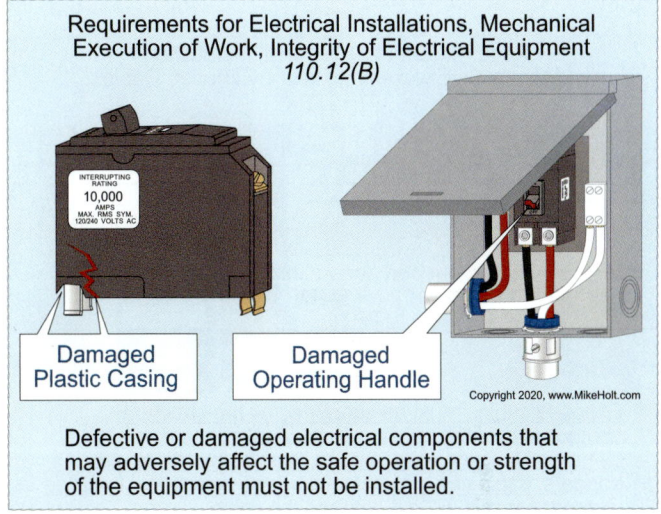

▶Figure 110–21

Author's Comment:

▶ Precautions must be taken to provide protection from contamination of the internal parts of panelboards and receptacles during building construction. Be sure the electrical equipment is properly masked and protected before sheetrock, painting, or other phases of the project that can contaminate or cause damage begins. ▶Figure 110–20

Author's Comment:

▶ Damaged parts include cracked insulators, arc shields not in place, overheated fuse clips, and damaged or missing switch handles or circuit-breaker handles.

(C) Cables and Conductors. Cables and conductors must be installed in a neat and workmanlike manner. ▶Figure 110–22

▶Figure 110–20

▶Figure 110–22

Exposed cables must be supported by the structural components of the building so they will not be damaged by normal building use. Support must be by straps, staples, hangers, cable ties, or similar fittings designed and installed in a manner that will not damage the cable. ▶Figure 110-23

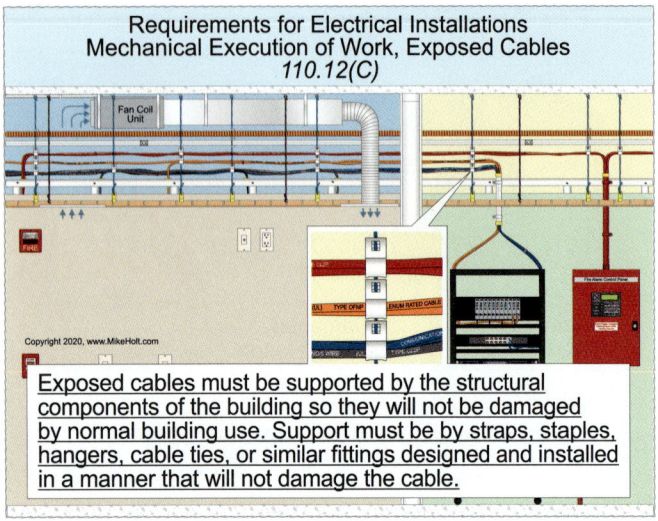

▶Figure 110-23

Note 1: Industry practices are described in ANSI/NECA/FOA 301, *Standard for Installing and Testing Fiber Optic Cables*, and other ANSI-approved installation standards.

Note 3: Paint, plaster, cleaners, abrasives, corrosive residues, or other contaminants can result in an undetermined alteration of optical fiber cable properties.

110.13 Mounting and Cooling of Equipment

(A) Mounting. Electrical equipment must be firmly secured to the surface on which it is mounted. ▶Figure 110-24

110.14 Conductor Termination and Splicing

Conductor terminal and splicing devices must be identified for the conductor material and must be properly installed and used in accordance with the manufacturer's instructions [110.3(B)]. ▶Figure 110-25

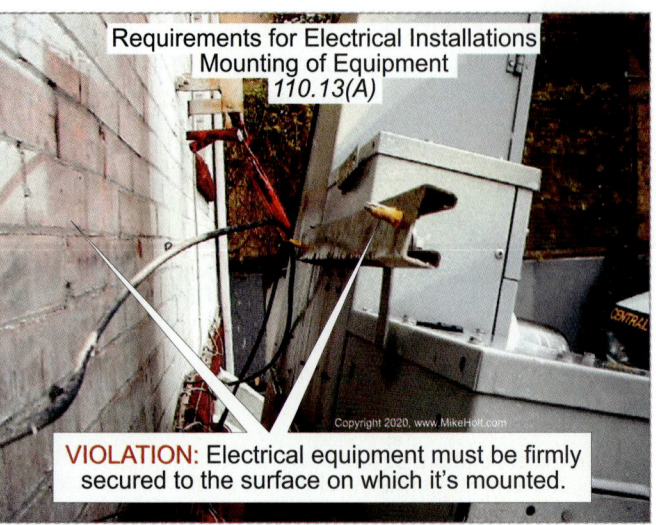

▶Figure 110-24

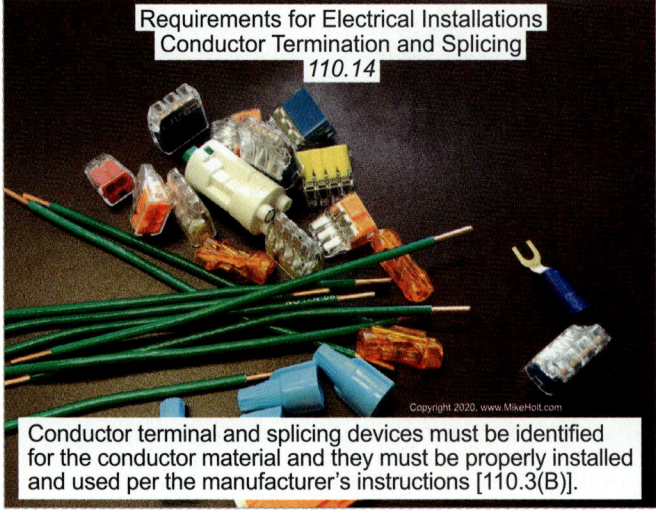

▶Figure 110-25

Author's Comment:

▸ Conductor terminals suitable for aluminum wire only will be marked "AL." Those acceptable for copper wire only will be marked "CU." Terminals suitable for both copper and aluminum will be marked "CU-AL" or "AL-CU." For 6 AWG and smaller, the markings can be printed on the container or on an information sheet inside the container. A "7" or "75" indicates a 75°C rated terminal, and a "9" or "90" indicates a 90°C rated terminal. If a terminal bears no marking, it can be used only with copper conductors. ▶Figure 110-26

Connectors and terminals for conductors more finely stranded than Class B and Class C must be identified for the use of finely stranded conductors. ▶Figure 110-27

Copper and Aluminum Mixed. Copper and aluminum conductors (dissimilar metals) are not permitted to contact each other in a device unless the device is listed and identified for this purpose.

Author's Comment:

▸ Few terminations are listed for mixing aluminum and copper conductors, but if they are, that will be marked on the product package or terminal device. The reason copper and aluminum should not be in contact with each other is because corrosion develops between the two different metals due to galvanic action, resulting in increased contact resistance at the splicing device. This increased resistance can cause the splice to overheat and result in a fire.

(A) Conductor Terminations. Conductor terminals must ensure a good connection without damaging the conductors.

Terminals are listed for one conductor unless marked otherwise. Terminals for more than one conductor must be identified for this purpose, either within the equipment instructions or on the terminal itself. ▸Figure 110-28

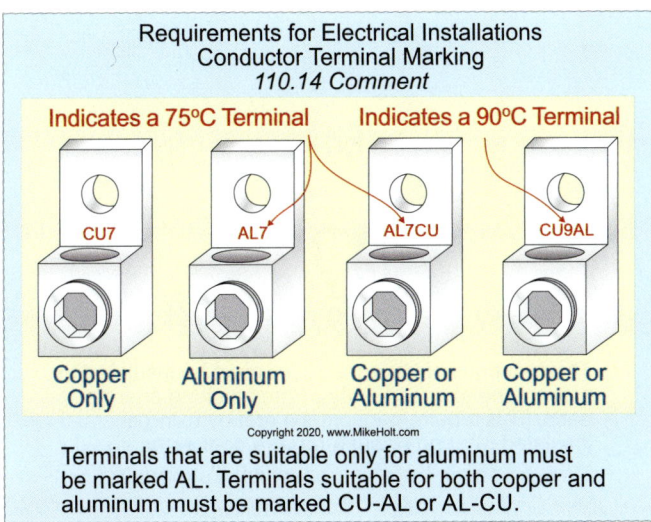
▸Figure 110-26

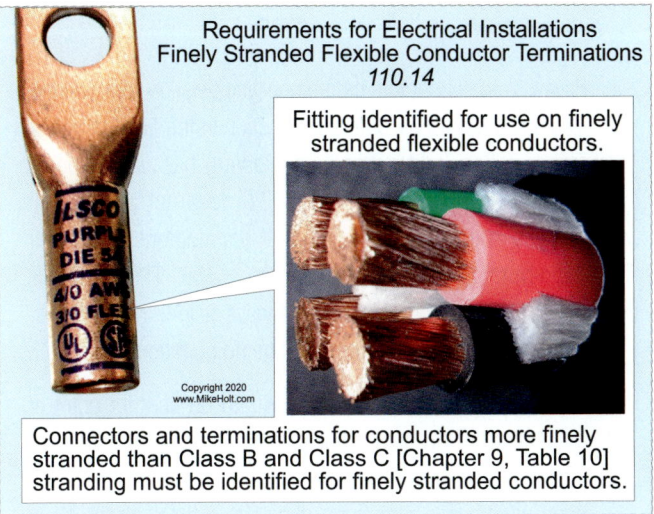
▸Figure 110-27

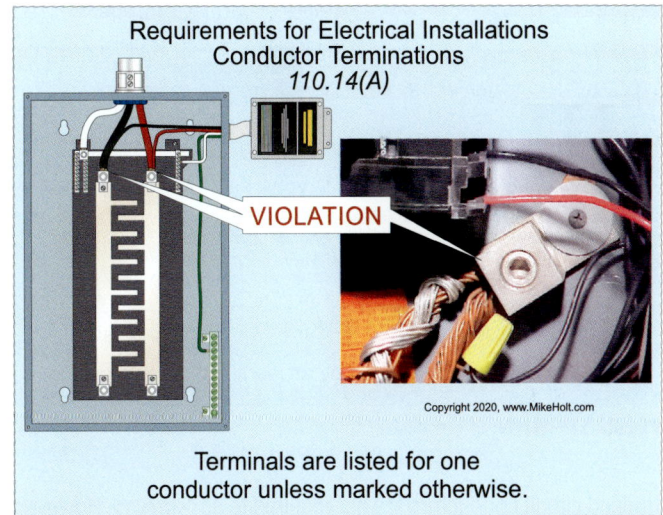
▸Figure 110-28

Author's Comment:

▸ According to Article 100, "Identified" means the item is recognized as suitable for a specific purpose, function, or environment by listing, labeling, or other means approved by the authority having jurisdiction.

▸ Conductor terminations must comply with the manufacturer's instructions as required by 110.3(B). For example, if the instructions for the device say, "Suitable for 18-12 AWG Stranded," then only stranded conductors can be used with the terminating device. If they say, "Suitable for 18-12 AWG Solid," then only solid conductors are permitted, and if the instructions say, "Suitable for 18-12 AWG," then either solid or stranded conductors can be used with the terminating device.

Author's Comment:

▸ Split-bolt connectors are commonly listed for only two conductors, although some are listed for three. However, it is a common industry practice to terminate as many conductors as possible within a split-bolt connector, even though this violates the *NEC*. ▸Figure 110-29

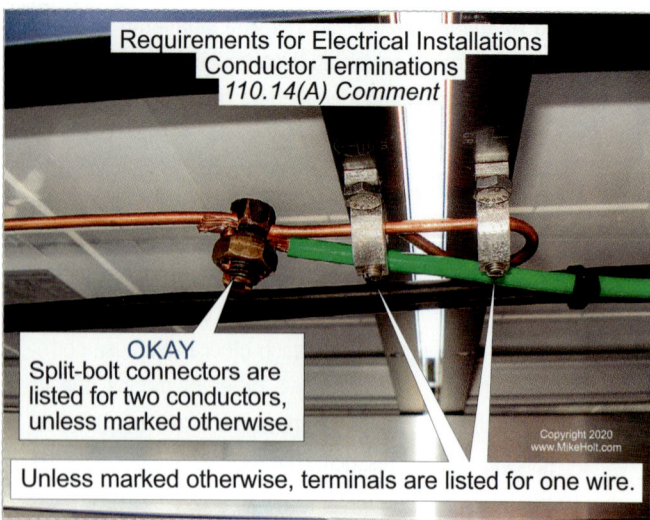

▶Figure 110–29

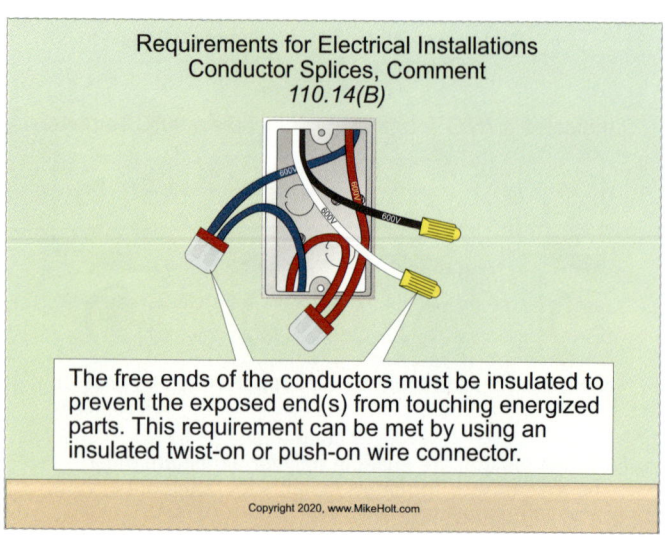

▶Figure 110–31

(B) Conductor Splices. Conductors must be spliced by a splicing device that is identified for the purpose. ▶Figure 110–30

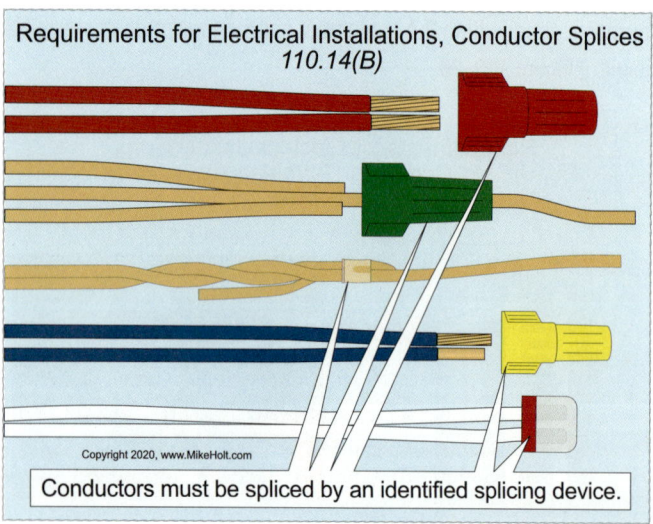

▶Figure 110–30

Unused circuit conductors are not required to be removed. However, to prevent an electrical hazard, the free ends of the conductors must be insulated to prevent the exposed end(s) from touching energized parts. This requirement can be met by using an insulated twist-on or push-on wire connector. ▶Figure 110–31

Author's Comment:

▸ According to Article 100, "Energized" means electrically connected to a source of voltage.

Author's Comment:

▸ Pre-twisting conductors before applying twist-on wire connectors has been a very common practice in the field for years. The question (and subsequent debate) has always been, "Is pre-twisting required?" The *NEC* does not require that practice and, in fact, Ideal® made a statement about their Wing-Nut® twist-on connectors which said, "Pre-twisting is acceptable, but not required." Always follow the manufacturer's instructions and there will be no question [110.3(B)].

▸ Reusing twist-on connectors seems to be another point of contention in the field. Should they be reused? Some say that they just never seem quite the same once they have been used, while others say they reuse them all the time. Defer to the manufacturer's instructions; Ideal® and 3M® both indicate in their information that it is perfectly fine to reuse their twist-on connectors. ▶Figure 110–32

Underground Splices, Single Conductors. Single direct burial types UF or USE conductors can be spliced underground with a device listed for direct burial [300.5(E) and 300.15(G)]. ▶Figure 110–33

Underground Splices, Multiconductor Cable. The individual conductors of multiconductor UF or USE cable can be spliced underground with a listed splice kit that encapsulates the conductors and cable jacket.

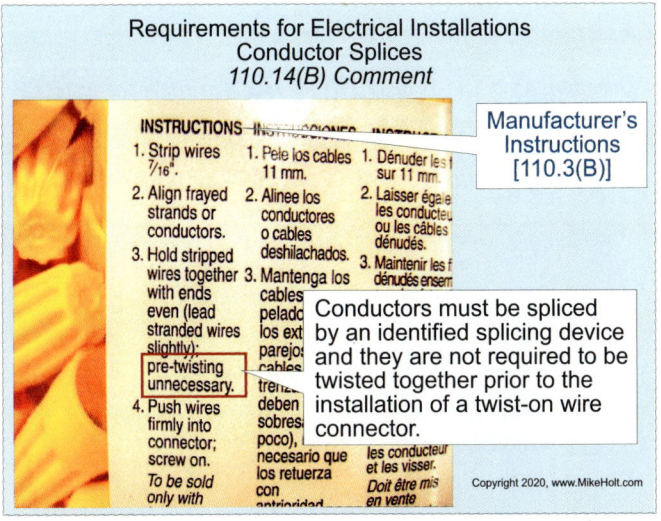

▶Figure 110-32

(2) Conductors with an insulation temperature rating greater than 60°C are permitted, but the conductor must be sized in accordance with the ampacities in the 60°C temperature column of Table 310.16.
▶Figure 110-34

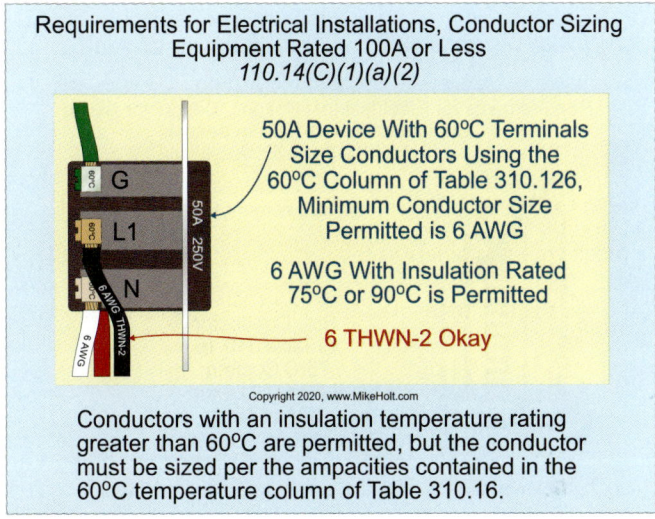

▶Figure 110-34

▶ **Example**

Question: According to Table 310.16, what size THWN-2 conductor is required for a circuit rated 50A?

(a) 10 AWG   (b) 8 AWG   (c) 6 AWG   (d) 4 AWG

Answer: (c) 6 AWG rated 55A at 60°C [110.14(C)(1)(a)(2) and Table 310.16]

(3) Conductors terminating on terminals rated 75°C can be sized in accordance with the ampacities in the 75°C temperature column of Table 310.16. ▶Figure 110-35

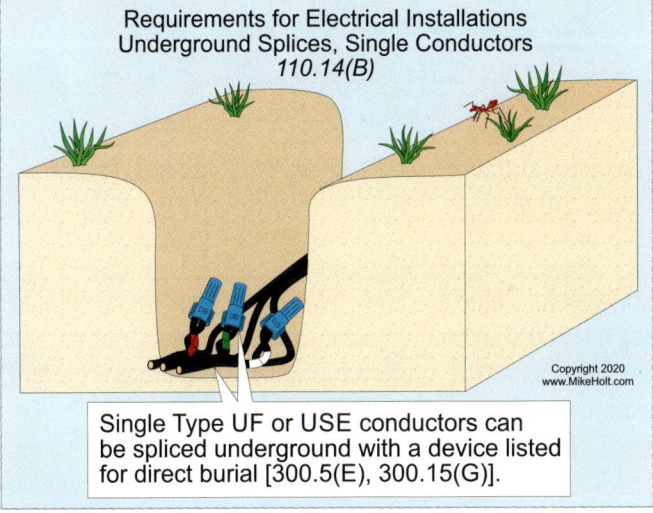

▶Figure 110-33

Author's Comment:

▸ Electrical connection failures are the cause of many equipment and building fires. Improper terminations, poor workmanship, not following the manufacturer's instructions, and improper torqueing can all cause poor electrical connections. Improper electrical terminations can damage and melt conductor insulation resulting in short circuits and ground faults.

(C) Conductor Size to Terminal Temperature Rating. Conductors are sized in accordance with 110.14(C)(1) and (2).

(1) Equipment Terminals. Unless equipment is listed and marked otherwise, conductors are sized in accordance with (a) or (b) as follows:

(a) Equipment Rated 100A or Less

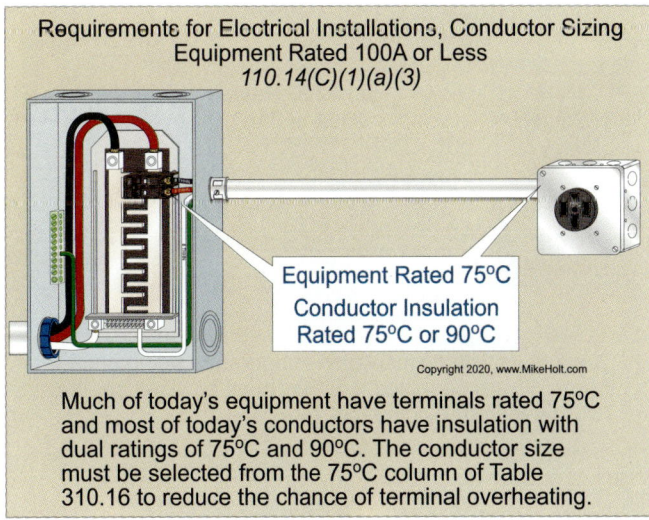

▶Figure 110-35

110.14 | Requirements for Electrical Installations

▶ **Example**

Question: *According to Table 310.16, what size THHN conductor is required for a 50A circuit where the equipment is listed for use at 75°C?* ▶Figure 110-36

(a) 10 AWG (b) 8 AWG (c) 6 AWG (d) 4 AWG

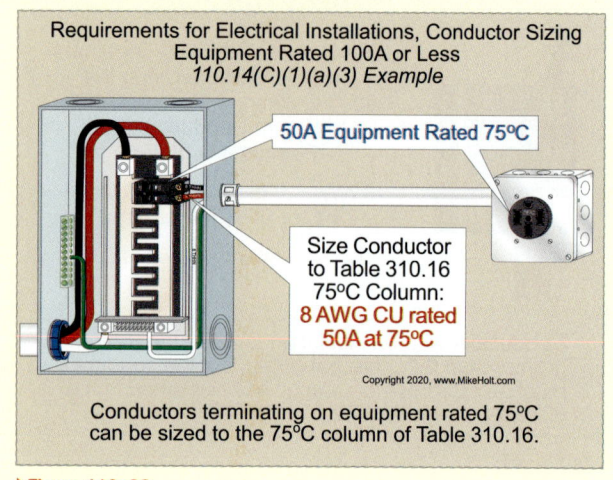

▶Figure 110-36

Answer: *(b) 8 AWG rated 50A at 75°C [110.14(C)(1)(a)(3) and Table 310.16]*

(b) Equipment Rated Over 100A.

(2) Conductors with an insulation temperature rating greater than 75°C are permitted, but the conductor must be sized in accordance with the ampacities in the 75°C temperature column of Table 310.16. ▶Figure 110-37

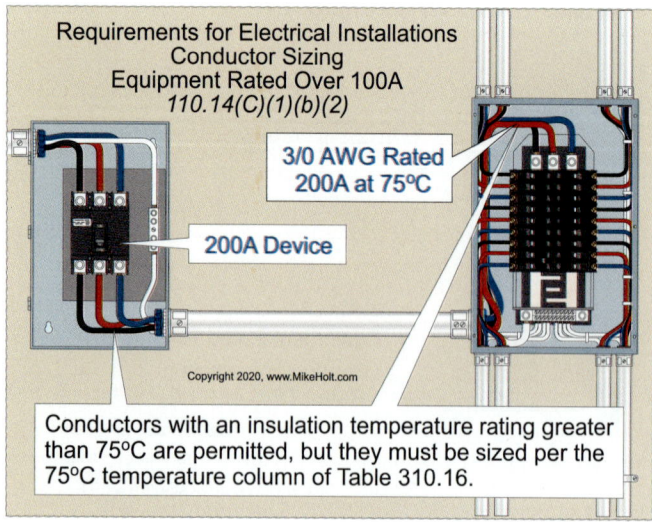

▶Figure 110-37

▶ **Example**

Question: *According to Table 310.16, what size THHN conductor is required to supply a 150A feeder?* ▶Figure 110-38

(a) 1/0 AWG (b) 2/0 AWG (c) 3/0 AWG (d) 4/0 AWG

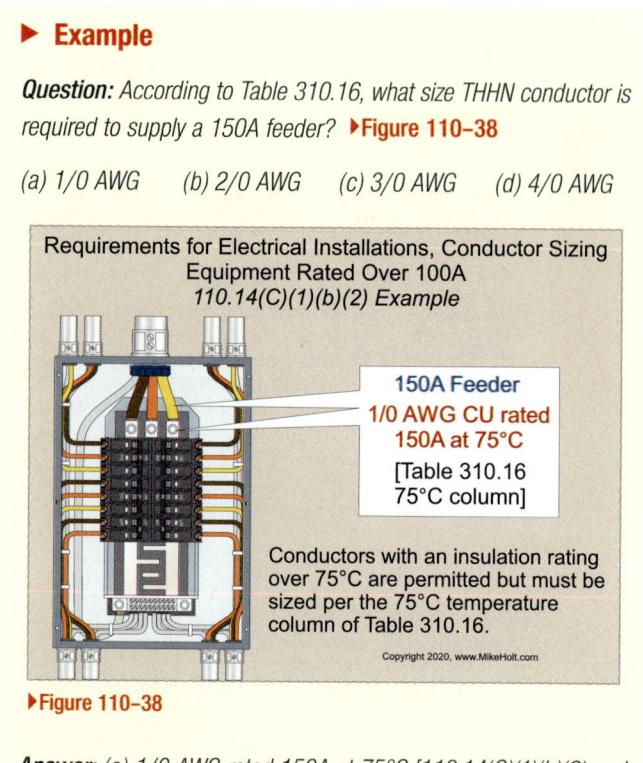

▶Figure 110-38

Answer: *(a) 1/0 AWG rated 150A at 75°C [110.14(C)(1)(b)(2) and Table 310.16]*

(2) Separate Connector. Splicing and terminating devices with terminals rated 90°C and not connected to electrical equipment can have the conductors sized in accordance with the ampacities in the 90°C temperature column of Table 310.16. ▶Figure 110-39

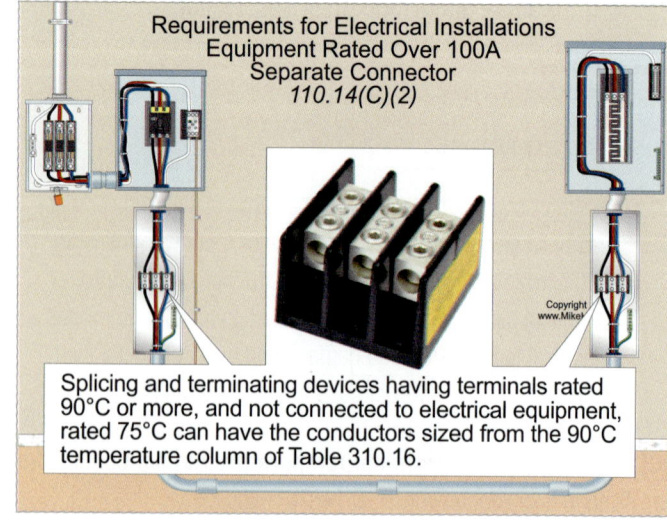

▶Figure 110-39

Table 310.16 Ampacities of Insulated Conductors
Based on Not More Than Three Current-Carrying Conductors and Ambient Temperature of 30°C (86°F)

Size AWG kcmil	60°C (140°F) TW UF	75°C (167°F) RHW THHW THW THWN XHHW USE	90°C (194°F) RHH RHW-2 THHN THHW THW-2 THWN-2 USE-2 XHHW XHHW-2	60°C (140°F) TW UF	75°C (167°F) THW THWN XHHW	90°C (194°F) THHN THW-2 THWN-2 THHW XHHW XHHW-2	Size AWG kcmil
	Copper			Aluminum/Copper-Clad Aluminum			
14	15	20	25				14
12	20	25	30	15	20	25	12
10	30	35	40	25	30	35	10
8	40	50	55	35	40	45	8
6	55	65	75	40	50	55	6
4	70	85	95	55	65	75	4
3	85	100	115	65	75	85	3
2	95	115	130	75	90	100	2
1	110	130	145	85	100	115	1
1/0	125	150	170	100	120	135	1/0
2/0	145	175	195	115	135	150	2/0
3/0	165	200	225	130	155	175	3/0
4/0	195	230	260	150	180	205	4/0
250	215	255	290	170	205	230	250
300	240	285	320	195	230	260	300
350	260	310	350	210	250	280	350
400	280	335	380	225	270	305	400
500	320	380	430	260	310	350	500

110.14 | Requirements for Electrical Installations

▶ **Example 1**

Question: According to Table 310.16, what size aluminum conductor can be used to interconnect busbars protected by a 200A overcurrent protective device if all terminals are rated 90°C?

(a) 1/0 AWG (b) 2/0 AWG (c) 3/0 AWG (d) 4/0 AWG

Answer: (d) 4/0 AWG aluminum rated 205A at 90°C [Table 310.16]

▶ **Example 2**

Question: What size XHHW-2 copper conductor can be used to interconnect 90°C rated power distribution blocks protected by a 400A overcurrent protective device serving a 320A continuous load? ▶Figure 110–40

(a) 250 kcmil (b) 300 kcmil (c) 350 kcmil (d) 400 kcmil

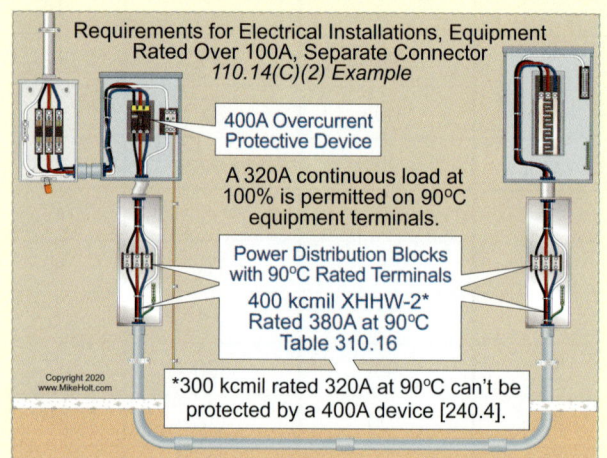

▶Figure 110–40

Note: 350 kcmil is rated 350A at 90°C; however, 350 kcmil cannot be used because it cannot be protected by a 400A overcurrent protective device [240.4].

Answer: (d) 400 kcmil rated 380A at 90°C [Table 310.16]

▶ **Example 3**

Question: What size XHHW-2 copper conductor can be used to interconnect 90°C rated power distribution blocks protected by a 400A overcurrent protective device serving a 375A continuous load? ▶Figure 110–41

(a) 250 kcmil (b) 300 kcmil (c) 350 kcmil (d) 400 kcmil

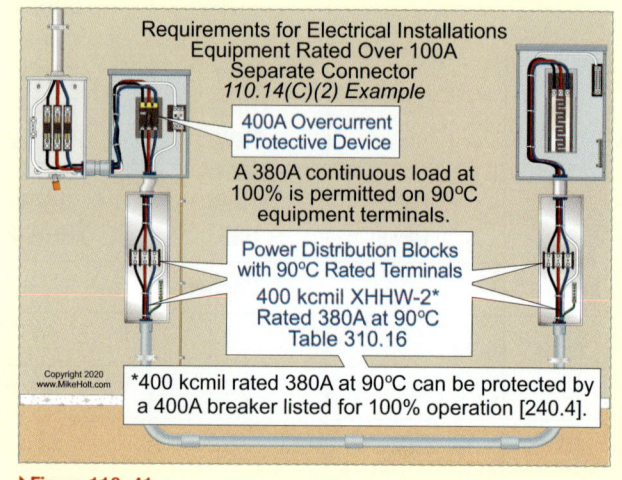

▶Figure 110–41

Answer: (d) 400 kcmil rated 380A at 90°C [Table 310.16]

(D) Terminal Connection Torque. Tightening torque values for terminal connections must be as indicated on equipment or installation instructions. An approved means (a torque tool) must be used to achieve the indicated torque value. ▶Figure 110–42

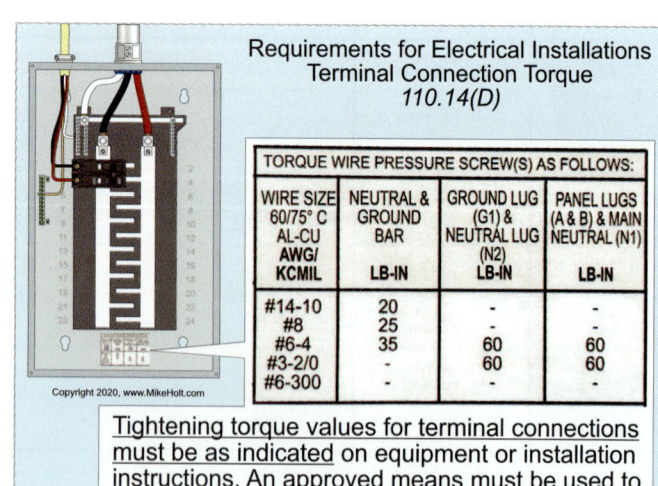

▶Figure 110–42

Author's Comment:

▶ Conductors must terminate in devices that have been properly tightened in accordance with the manufacturer's torque specifications included with equipment instructions. Failure to torque terminals properly can result in excessive heating of terminals or splicing devices due to a loose connection. A loose connection can also lead to arcing which increases the heating effect and may also lead to a short circuit or ground fault. Any of these can result in a fire or other failure, including an arc flash event. Improper torqueing is also a violation of 110.3(B), which requires all equipment to be installed in accordance with listing or labeling instructions.

Note 1: Examples of approved means of achieving the indicated torque values include the use of torque tools or devices such as shear bolts or breakaway-style devices with visual indicators that demonstrate the proper torque has been applied. ▶Figure 110–43

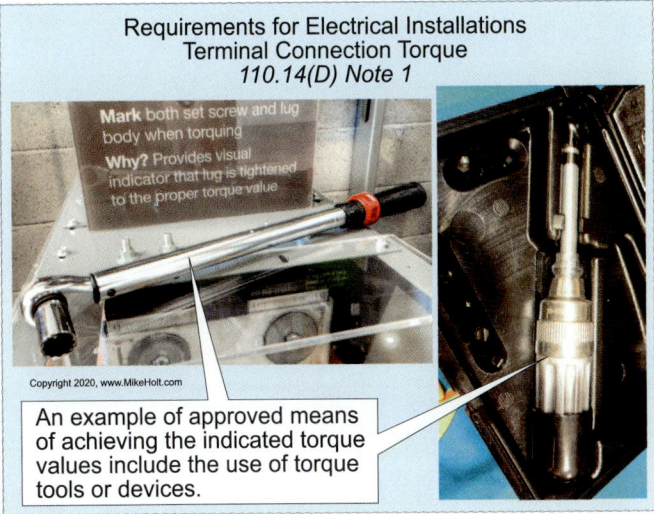

▶Figure 110–43

Note 2: The equipment manufacturer can be contacted if numeric torque values are not indicated on the equipment, or if the installation instructions are not available. Annex I of UL Standard 486A-486B, *Standard for Safety-Wire Connectors,* provides torque values in the absence of manufacturer's recommendations.

Note 3: Additional information for torqueing threaded connections and terminations can be found in Section 8.11 of NFPA 70B, *Recommended Practice for Electrical Equipment Maintenance.*

110.15 High-Leg Conductor Identification

On a 4-wire, delta-connected, three-phase system (where the midpoint of one phase winding of the secondary is grounded) the conductor with the resulting 208V to ground (high-leg) must be durably and permanently marked by an outer finish (insulation) that is orange in color or other effective means. Such identification must be placed at each point where a connection is made if the neutral conductor is present [230.56]. ▶Figure 110–44

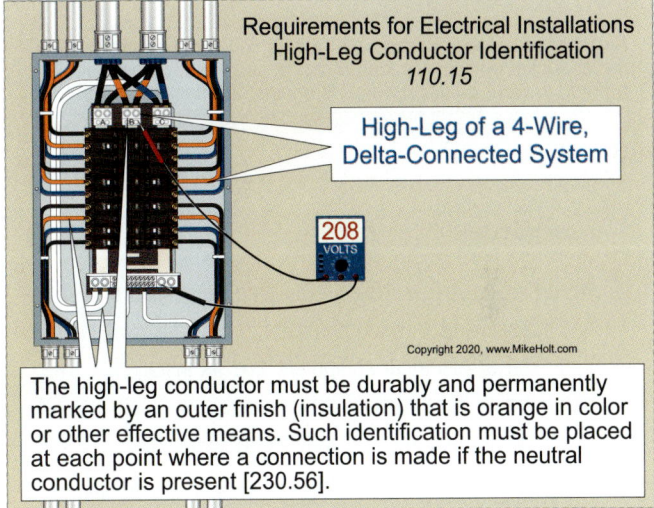

▶Figure 110–44

Author's Comment:

▶ The high-leg conductor is also called the "wild leg" or "stinger leg."

110.16 Arc Flash Hazard Warning

(A) Arc Flash Hazard Warning Label. In other than dwelling units, switchboards, switchgear, panelboards, industrial control panels, meter socket enclosures, and motor control centers must be marked to warn qualified persons of the danger associated with an arc flash resulting from a short circuit or ground fault. The arc flash hazard warning label must be permanently affixed, have sufficient durability to withstand the environment involved [110.21(B)], and be clearly visible to qualified persons before they examine, adjust, service, or perform maintenance on the equipment. ▶Figure 110–45

110.16 | Requirements for Electrical Installations

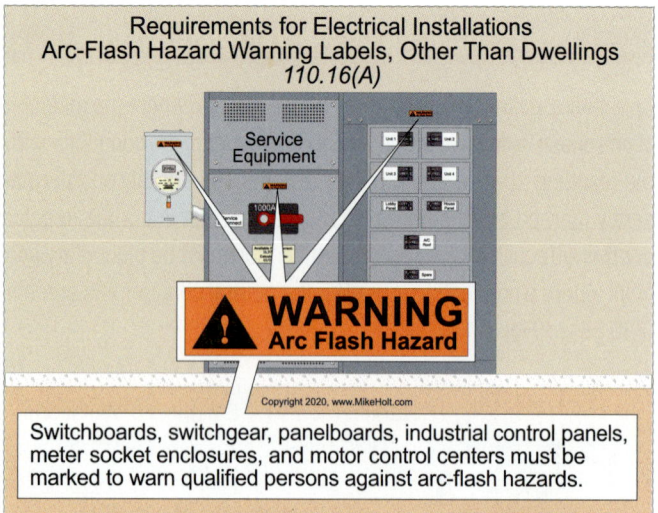

▶Figure 110–45

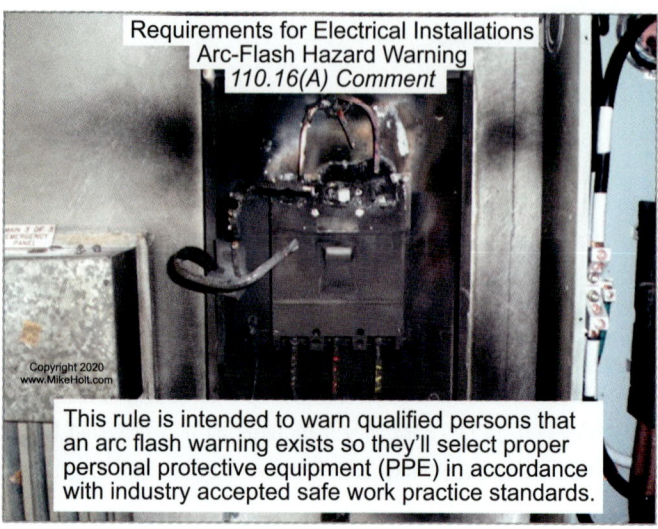

▶Figure 110–46

Author's Comment:

▸ According to Article 100, a "Qualified Person" is one who has the skill and knowledge related to the construction and operation of electrical equipment and its installation. This person must have received safety training to recognize and avoid the hazards involved with electrical systems.

▸ NFPA 70E, *Standard for Electrical Safety in the Workplace*, provides information on the safety training requirements expected of a "qualified person."

▸ Examples of this safety training include (but are not limited to) training in the use of special precautionary techniques, personal protective equipment (PPE), insulating and shielding materials, and in the use of insulated tools and test equipment when working on or near exposed conductors or circuit parts that can become energized.

▸ In many parts of the United States, electricians, electrical contractors, electrical inspectors, and electrical engineers must complete from 6 to 24 hours of *NEC* review each year as a requirement to maintain licensing. This does not necessarily make one qualified to deal with the specific hazards involved with electrical systems.

▸ This rule is intended to warn qualified persons who work on energized electrical systems that an arc flash hazard exists and to the level of danger present. They will then be able to select the necessary personal protective equipment (PPE) in accordance with industry accepted safe work practice standards. ▶Figure 110–46

(B) Service Disconnect. In addition to the requirements in 110.16(A), a service disconnect rated 1,200A or more must have a field or factory installed label containing the following details and have sufficient durability to withstand the environment: ▶Figure 110–47

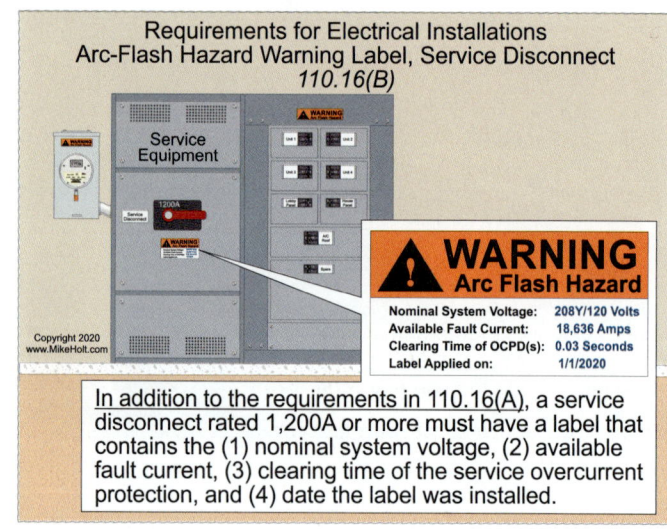

▶Figure 110–47

(1) Nominal system voltage

(2) Available fault current at the line-side of the service overcurrent protective device

(3) Clearing time of the service overcurrent protective device

(4) Date the label was installed

Author's Comment:

▸ Determining the available fault current on the line side of equipment terminals requires you to know the available fault current (provided by the electric utility), the conductor material, the length of the conductors, and the wiring method used to install the conductors. With this information, you can use an app or computer software to determine the available fault current at the line terminals.

Ex: Service disconnect fault current labeling is not required if an arc flash label in accordance with NFPA 70E, Standard for Electrical Safety in the Workplace, *is applied. See Note 3.* ▸Figure 110–48

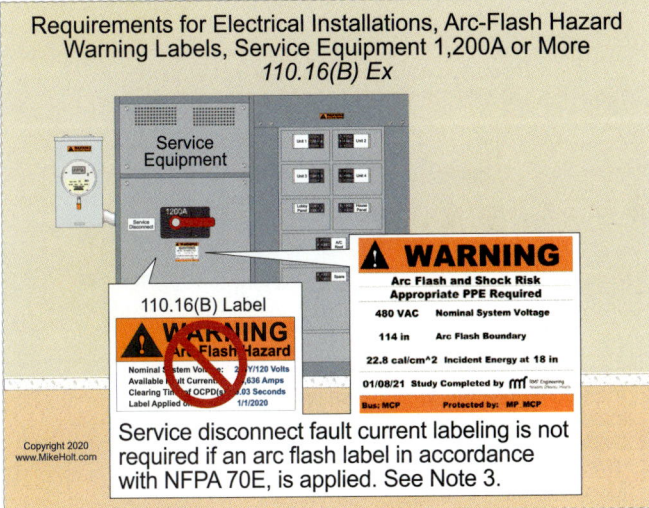

▸Figure 110–48

Note 1: NFPA 70E, *Standard for Electrical Safety in the Workplace,* provides guidance in determining the severity of potential exposure, planning safe work practices, arc flash labeling, and selecting personal protective equipment. ▸Figure 110–49

Note 3: NFPA 70E, *Standard for Electrical Safety in the Workplace* provides specific criteria for developing arc flash labels such as nominal system voltage, incident energy levels, arc flash boundaries, and selecting personal protective equipment.

Author's Comment:

▸ The information required by 110.16(B)(1), (2), and (3) is necessary in order to determine the incident energy and arc flash boundary distance by using of an app or computer software to ensure the label complies with NFPA 70E to increase safety during future work on service equipment.

▸Figure 110–49

110.21 Markings

(A) Equipment Markings

(1) General. The manufacturer's name, trademark, or other descriptive marking by which the organization responsible for the product can be identified must be placed on all electrical equipment. Other markings indicating voltage, current, wattage, or other ratings must be provided as specified elsewhere in this *Code*. The marking or label must be of sufficient durability to withstand the environment involved.

(2) Reconditioned Equipment

Reconditioned equipment must be marked with the name, trademark, or other descriptive marking by which the organization responsible for its reconditioning can be identified, along with the date of the reconditioning.

Reconditioned equipment must be identified as "reconditioned" and the original listing mark removed. Approval of the reconditioned equipment must not be based solely on the equipment's original listing.

Ex: In industrial occupancies, where conditions of maintenance and supervision ensure that only qualified persons service the equipment, the markings indicated in 110.21(A)(2) are not required for equipment that is reconditioned by the owner or operator as part of a regular equipment maintenance program.

Note 1: Industry standards are available for the application of reconditioned and refurbished equipment.

Note 2: The term "reconditioned" may be interchangeable with terms such as "rebuilt," "refurbished," or "remanufactured."

Note 3: The original listing mark may include the mark of the certifying body and not the entire equipment label.

(B) Field-Applied Hazard Markings. Where caution, warning, or danger labels are required, the labels must meet the following requirements:

(1) The markings must warn of the hazards using effective words, colors, symbols, or a combination of the three. ▶Figure 110–50

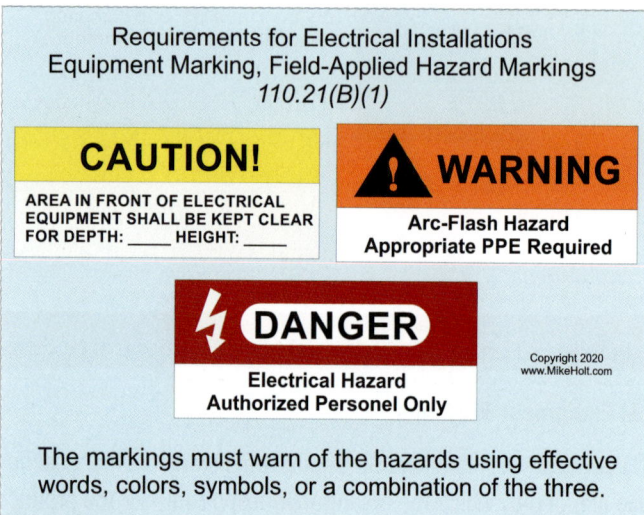

▶Figure 110–50

Note: ANSI Z535.4, *Product Safety Signs and Labels,* provides guidelines for the design and durability of signs and labels.

(2) The label cannot be handwritten and must be permanently affixed to the equipment. ▶Figure 110–51

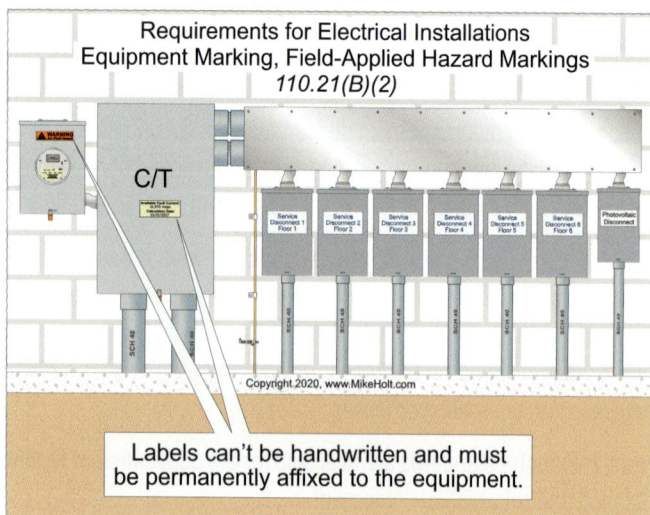

▶Figure 110–51

Ex: Labels containing information that is likely to change can be handwritten, if it is legible.

(3) The marking must be of sufficient durability to withstand the environment involved.

110.22 Identification of Disconnecting Means

(A) General. Each disconnect must be legibly marked to indicate its purpose unless located and arranged so the purpose is evident. In other than one- or two-family dwellings, the marking must include the identification of the circuit source that supplies the disconnecting means. The marking must be of sufficient durability to withstand the environment involved. ▶Figure 110–52

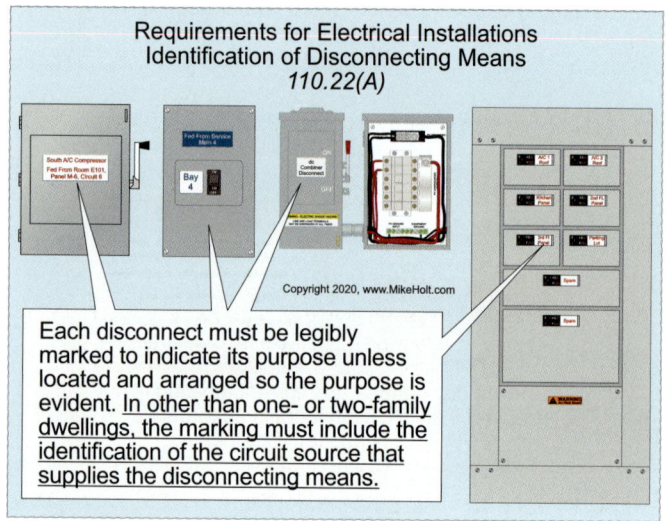

▶Figure 110–52

Author's Comment:

▸ See 408.4 for additional requirements for identification markings on circuit directories for switchboards and panelboards.

(C) Tested Series Combination Systems. Tested series-rated installations must be legibly field marked to indicate the equipment has been applied with a series combination rating in accordance with 240.86(B), be permanently affixed, and have sufficient durability to withstand the environment involved in accordance with 110.21(B) and state:

> **CAUTION—SERIES COMBINATION SYSTEM**
> **RATED _____ AMPERES. IDENTIFIED REPLACEMENT**
> **COMPONENTS REQUIRED**

110.24 Available Fault Current

(A) Field Marking. In other than dwelling units, service disconnects must be field marked with the available fault current on the line side of the service disconnect, the date the fault current calculation was performed, and the marking must be of sufficient durability to withstand the environment present.

The available fault current calculation must be documented and available to those who are authorized to design, install, inspect, maintain, or operate the system. ▶Figure 110-53

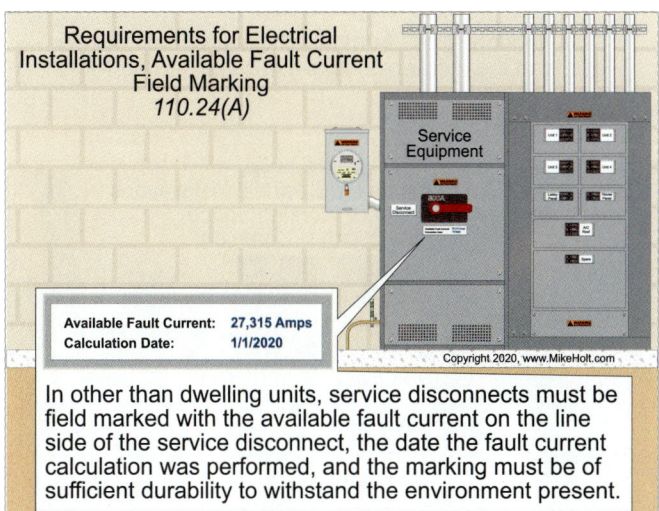

▶Figure 110-53

Note 1: The available fault current markings required by this section are related to the short-circuit current and interrupting ratings of equipment required by 110.9 and 110.10. They are not intended to be used for arc flash analysis. Arc-flash hazard information is available in NFPA 70E, *Standard for Electrical Safety in the Workplace*.

Note 2: Values of available fault current for use in determining short-circuit current and interrupting ratings of service equipment are available from electric utilities in published or other forms.

(B) Modifications. When modifications to the electrical installation affect the available fault current at the service disconnect, the available fault current must be recalculated to ensure the short-circuit current ratings at the service disconnect is sufficient for the available fault current. The required field marking(s) in 110.24(A) must be adjusted to reflect the new level of available fault current.

Author's Comment:

▶ It is common for electrical systems to be modified to accommodate growth. When the capacity of the system increases, equipment is installed to increase efficiency or alternative energy systems are added to the existing installation. These factors can all influence the available fault current if the utility transformer is changed. This increase in available fault current could end up exceeding the short-circuit current ratings of equipment in violation of 110.9 and 110.10.

Ex: Field markings required in 110.24(A) and 110.24(B) are not required for industrial installations where conditions of maintenance and supervision ensure that only qualified persons service the equipment.

110.25 Lockable Disconnecting Means

If the *Code* requires a disconnect to be lockable in the open position, the provisions for locking must remain in place whether the lock is installed or not. ▶Figure 110-54

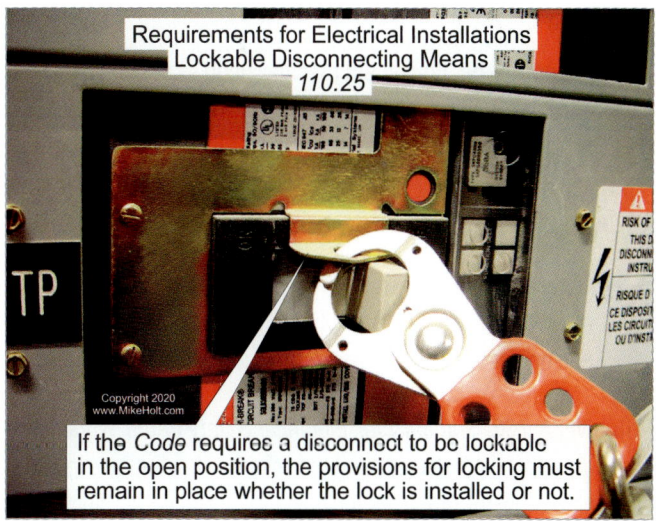

▶Figure 110-54

Part II. 1,000V, Nominal, or Less

110.26 Spaces About Electrical Equipment

For the purposes of safe operation and maintenance of equipment, access and working space must be provided around all electrical equipment. ▶Figure 110-55

110.26 | Requirements for Electrical Installations

▶Figure 110-55

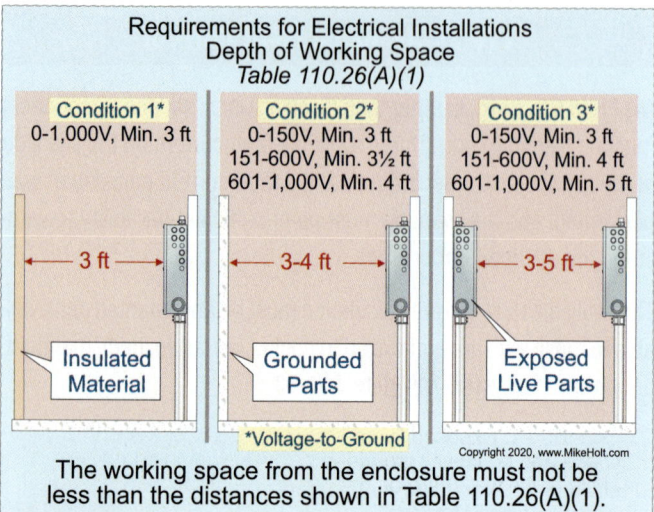
▶Figure 110-56

Author's Comment:

▸ Spaces around electrical equipment (width, depth, and height) consist of working space for worker protection [110.26(A)] and dedicated space to provide access to, and protection of, equipment [110.26(E)].

(A) Working Space. Equipment that may need examination, adjustment, servicing, or maintenance while energized must have working space provided in accordance with 110.26(A)(1), (2), (3), and (4):

Author's Comment:

▸ The phrase "while energized" is the root of many debates. As always, check with the authority having jurisdiction to see what equipment he or she believes needs a clear working space.

Note: NFPA 70E, *Standard for Electrical Safety in the Workplace*, provides guidance in determining the severity of potential exposure, planning safe work practices <u>including establishing an electrically safe work condition</u>, arc flash labeling, and selecting personal protective equipment.

(1) Depth of Working Space. The depth of working space, which is measured from the enclosure front, cannot be less than the distances contained in Table 110.26(A)(1), which are dependent on voltage and three different conditions. ▶Figure 110-56

Author's Comment:

▸ Depth of working space must be measured from the enclosure front, not the live parts. ▶Figure 110-57

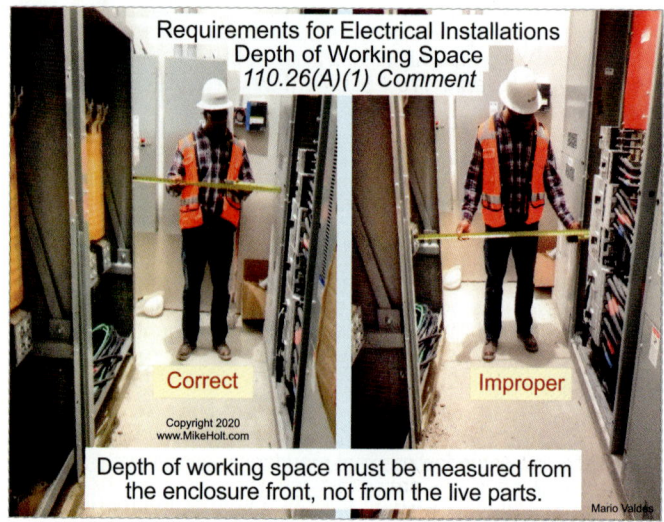
▶Figure 110-57

Table 110.26(A)(1) Working Space			
Voltage-to-Ground	Condition 1	Condition 2	Condition 3
0–150V	3 ft	3 ft	3 ft
151–600V	3 ft	3½ ft	4 ft
601–1,000V	3 ft	4 ft	5 ft

▶Figure 110-58, ▶Figure 110-59, and ▶Figure 110-60

Requirements for Electrical Installations | 110.26

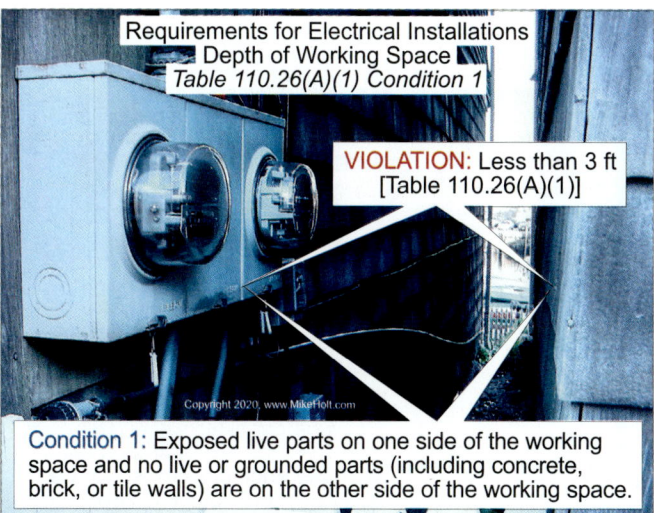
▶Figure 110–58

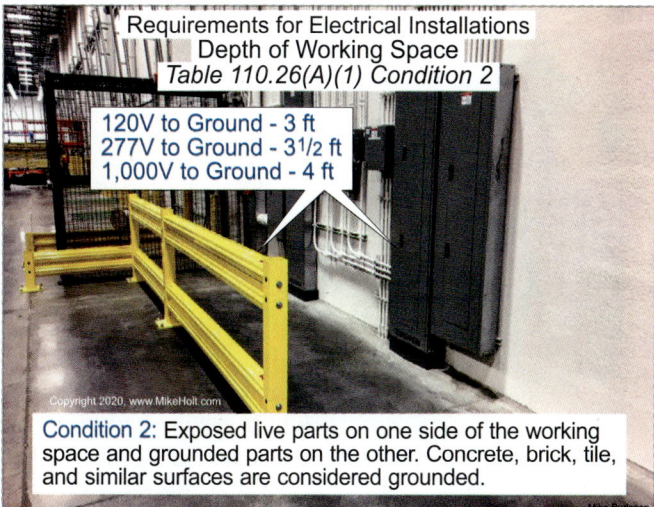
▶Figure 110–59

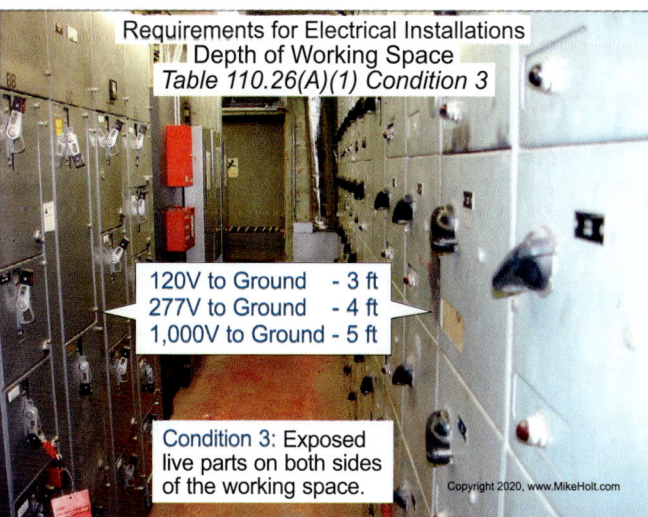
▶Figure 110–60

Author's Comment:

▶ If the working space is a platform, it must be sized to the working space requirements. ▶Figure 110–61

▶Figure 110–61

(a) Rear and Sides of Dead-Front Equipment. Working space is not required at the back or sides of equipment where all connections and all renewable, adjustable, or serviceable parts are accessible from the front. ▶Figure 110–62

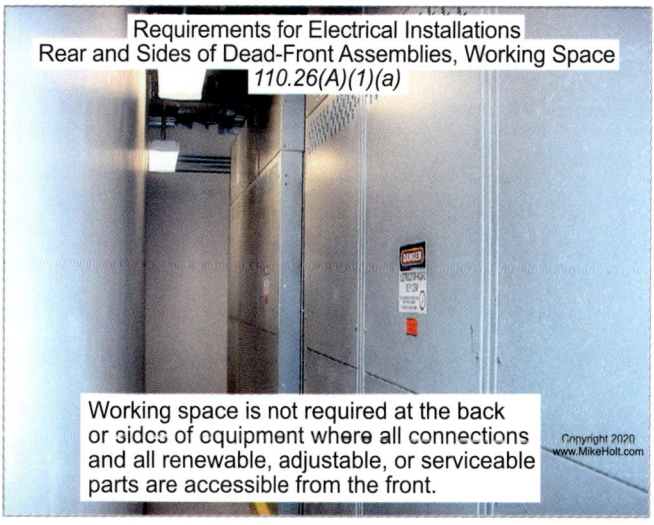
▶Figure 110–62

Author's Comment:

▶ Sections of equipment that require rear or side access to make field connections must be marked by the manufacturer on the front of the equipment. See 408.18(C).

110.26 | Requirements for Electrical Installations

(c) Existing Buildings. If electrical equipment is being replaced, Condition 2 working space is permitted between dead-front switchboards, switchgear, panelboards, or motor control centers located across the aisle from each other where conditions of maintenance and supervision ensure that written procedures have been adopted to prohibit equipment on both sides of the aisle from being open at the same time, and only authorized, qualified persons will service the installation.

(2) Width of Working Space. The width of the working space must be a minimum of 30 in., but in no case less than the width of the equipment. ▶Figure 110–63

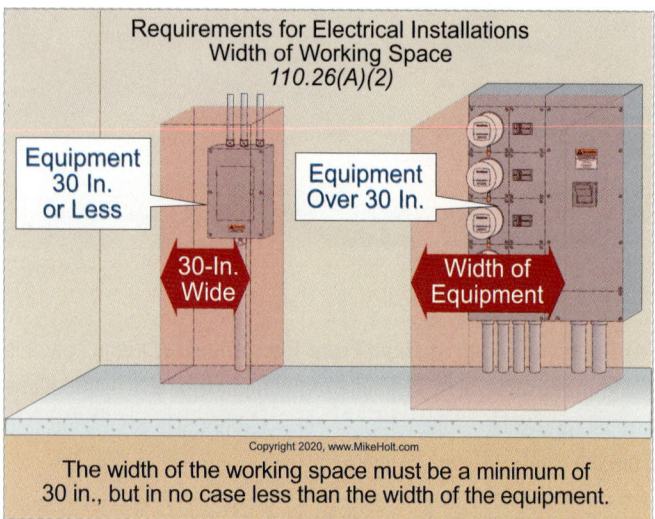

▶Figure 110–63

Author's Comment:

▶ The width of the working space can be measured from left-to-right, from right-to-left, or simply centered on the equipment and can overlap the working space for other electrical equipment. ▶Figure 110–64 and ▶Figure 110–65

The working space must be of sufficient width, depth, and height to permit equipment doors to open at least 90 degrees. ▶Figure 110–66

(3) Height of Working Space. The height of the working space must be clear and extend from the grade, floor, or platform to a height of 6½ ft or the height of the equipment. ▶Figure 110–67

Other equipment such as raceways, cables, wireways, transformers, or support structures (such as concrete pads) are permitted to extend not more than 6 in. beyond the front of the electrical equipment. ▶Figure 110–68 and ▶Figure 110–69

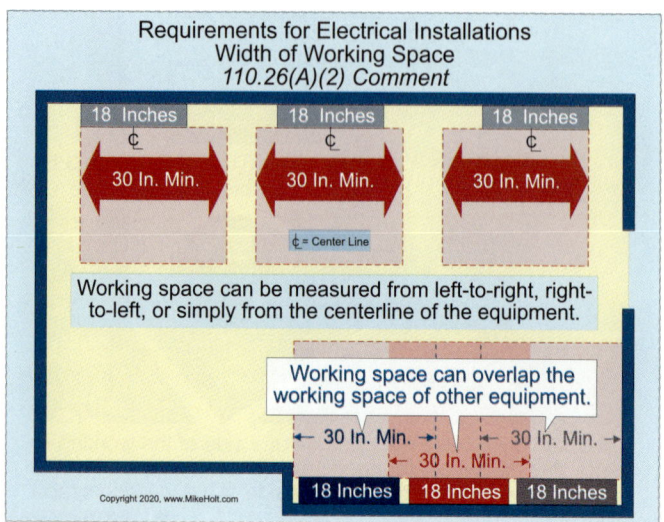

▶Figure 110–64

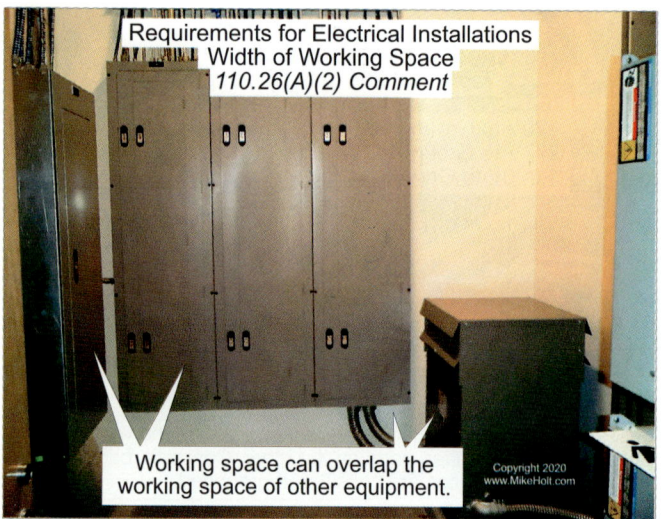

▶Figure 110–65

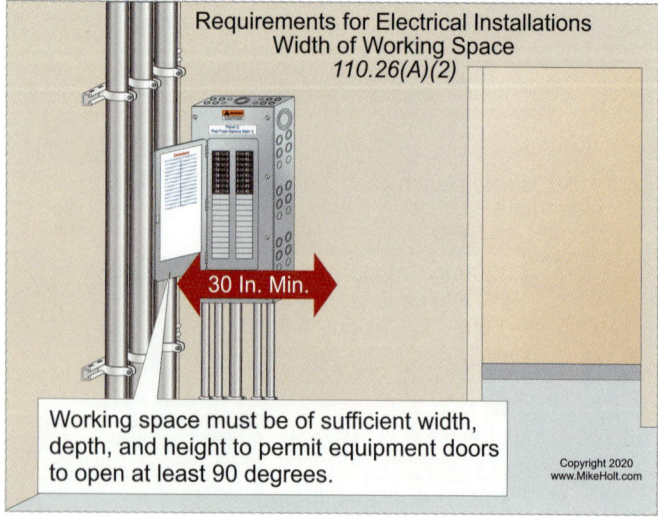

▶Figure 110–66

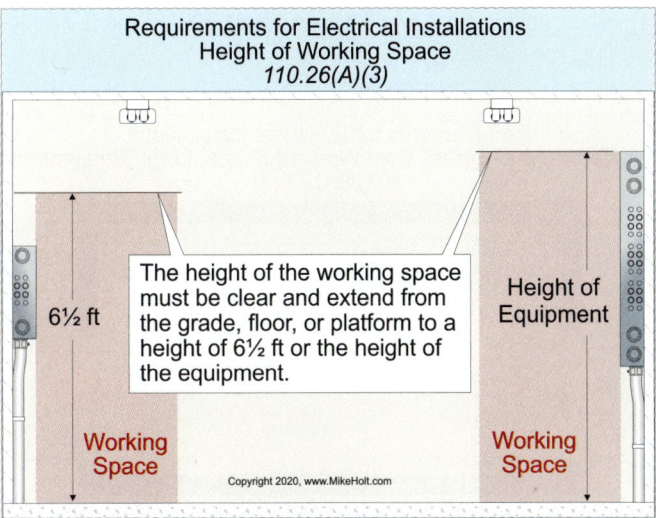
▶Figure 110-67

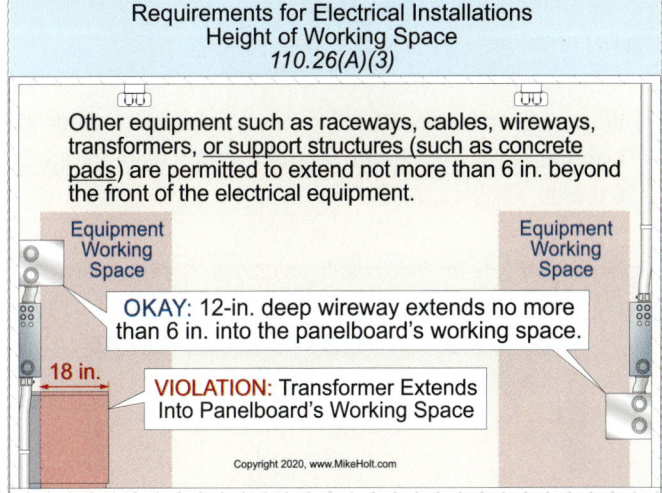
▶Figure 110-68

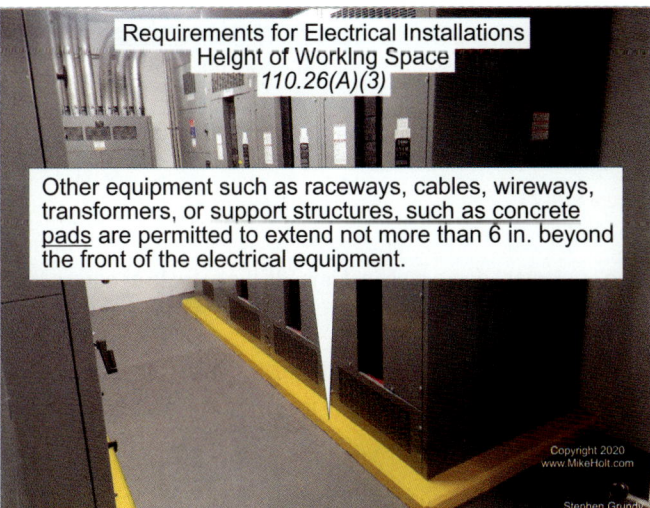
▶Figure 110-69

Ex 2: The minimum height of working space does not apply to a service disconnect or panelboards rated 200A or less located in an existing dwelling unit.

Ex 3: Meters are permitted in the working space.

(4) Limited Access. Where equipment is likely to require examination, adjustment, servicing, or maintenance while energized is located above a suspended ceiling or crawl space, all the following conditions apply:

(1) Equipment installed above a suspended ceiling must have an access opening not smaller than 22 in. × 22 in., and equipment installed in a crawl space must have an accessible opening not smaller than 22 in. × 30 in.

(2) The width of the working space must be a minimum of 30 in., but in no case less than the width of the equipment.

(3) The working space must permit equipment doors to open 90 degrees.

(4) The working space in front of equipment must comply with the depth requirements of Table 110.26(A)(1). Horizontal ceiling structural members are permitted in this space.

(B) Clear Working Space. The working space required by this section must always be clear; therefore, this space is not permitted for storage. ▶Figure 110-70

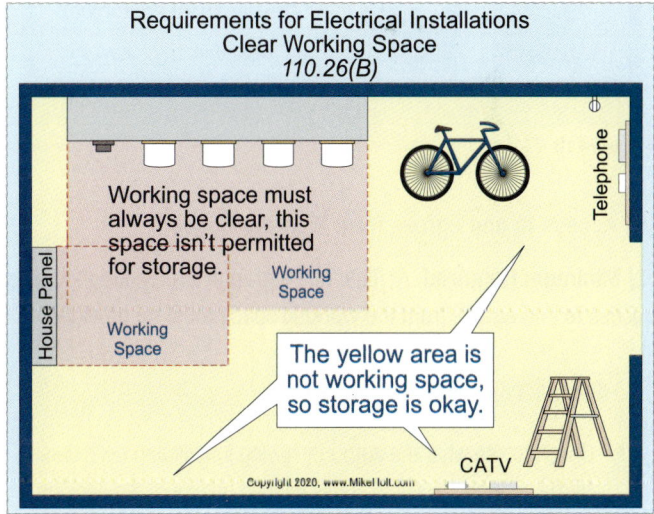
▶Figure 110-70

Caution

⚠ It is very dangerous to service energized parts in the first place, and unacceptable to be subjected to additional dangers by working around bicycles, boxes, crates, appliances, and other impediments.

110.26 | Requirements for Electrical Installations

When live parts are exposed for inspection or servicing, the working space (if in a passageway or open space) must be suitably guarded.

Author's Comment:

▸ When working in a passageway, the working space should be guarded from use by occupants. When working on electrical equipment in a passageway one must be mindful of a fire alarm. If one occurs, many people will need to be evacuated and will be congregating and moving through the area.

▸ Signaling and communications equipment are not permitted to be installed in a manner that encroaches on the working space of the electrical equipment. ▸Figure 110-71

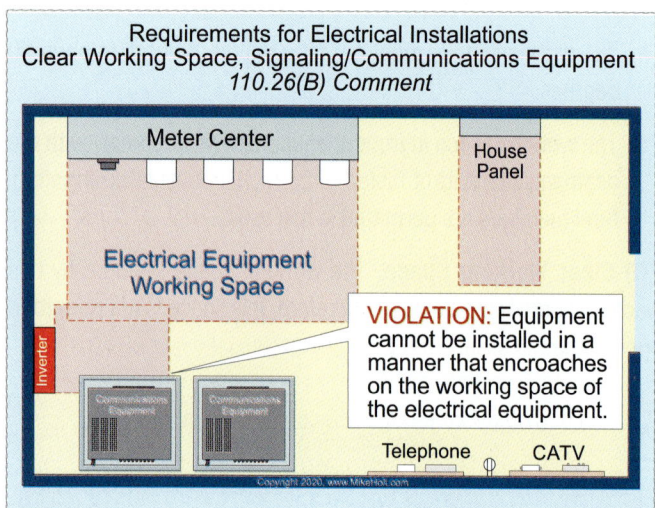

▸Figure 110-71

(C) Access to and Egress from Working Space

(1) Minimum Required. At least one entrance large enough to give access to and egress from the working space must be provided.

Author's Comment:

▸ Check to see what the authority having jurisdiction considers "large enough." Building *code*s contain minimum dimensions for doors and openings for personnel travel.

(2) Large Equipment. For large equipment containing overcurrent, switching, or control devices, an entrance to and egress from the required working space not less than 24 in. wide and 6½ ft high is required at each end of the working space. This requirement applies for either of the following conditions:

(1) Where equipment is over 6 ft wide rated 1,200A or more ▸Figure 110-72

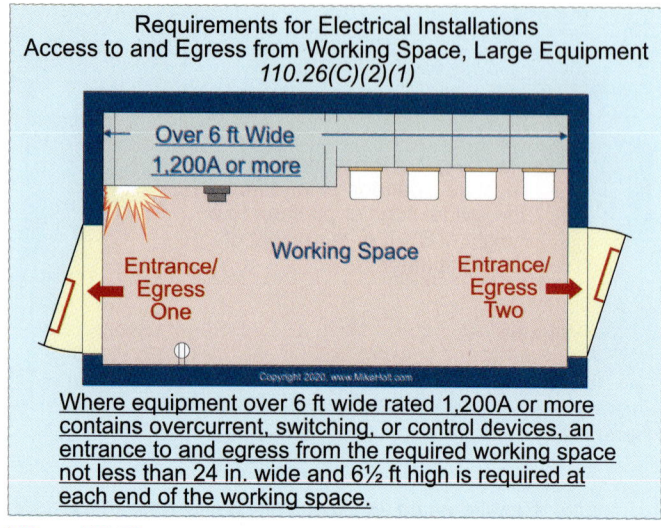

▸Figure 110-72

(2) Where the service disconnecting means installed in accordance with 230.71 has a combined rating of 1,200A or more and is over 6 ft wide ▸Figure 110-73

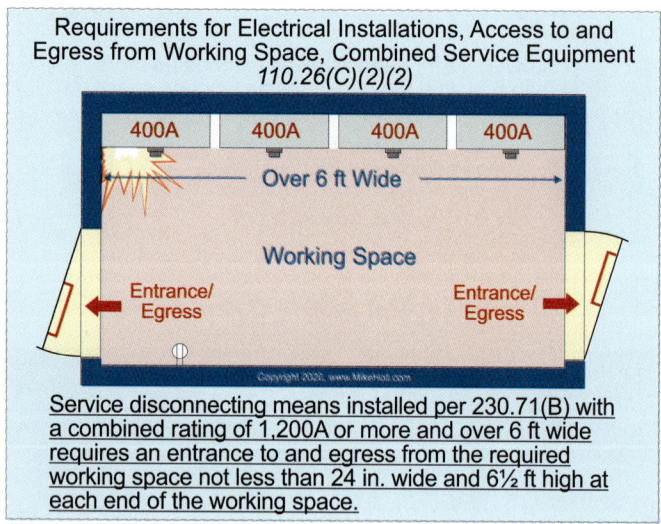

▸Figure 110-73

Open equipment doors must not impede the entry to or egress from the working space.

A single entrance for access to and egress from the required working space is permitted where either of the following conditions are met:

(a) Unobstructed Egress. Where the location permits a continuous and unobstructed way of egress travel. ▸Figure 110-74

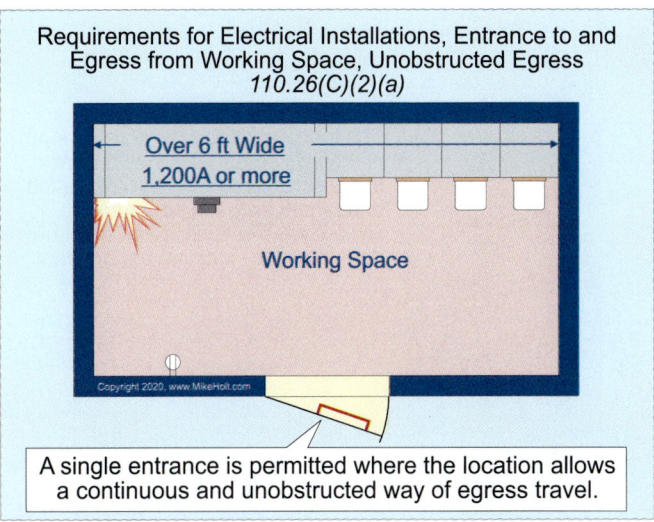

▶Figure 110–74

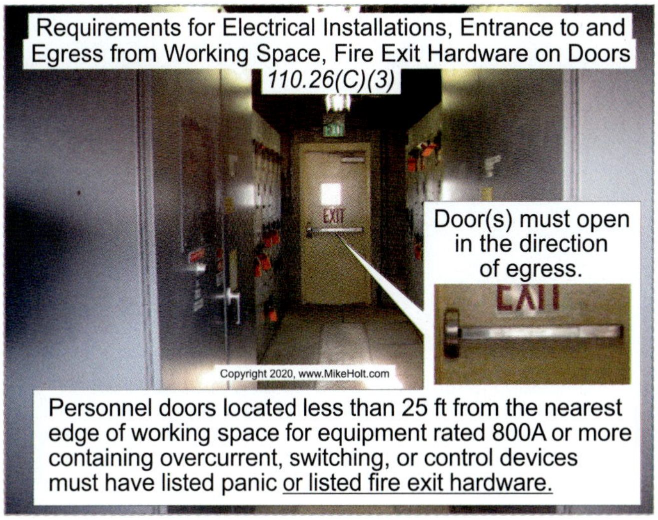

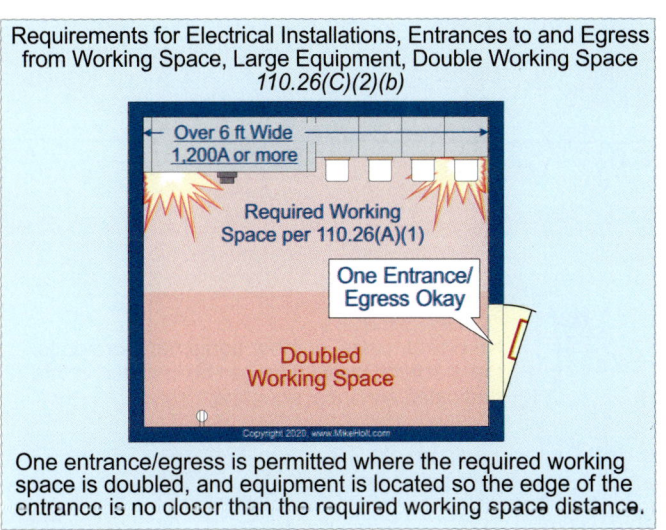

▶Figure 110–76

(b) Double Working Space. Where the required working space depth is doubled and the equipment is located so the edge of the entrance is no closer than the required working space distance. ▶Figure 110–75

▶Figure 110–75

(3) Fire Exit Hardware on Personnel Doors. Where equipment rated 800A or more contains overcurrent, switching, or control devices is installed and there is a personnel door(s) intended for entrance to and egress from the working space less than 25 ft from the nearest edge of the working space, the door(s) are required to open in the direction of egress and be equipped with listed panic or listed fire exit hardware.
▶Figure 110–76

Author's Comment:

▸ History has shown that electricians who suffer burns on their hands in electrical arc flash or arc blast events often cannot open doors equipped with knobs that must be turned or doors that must be pulled open.

▸ Since this requirement is in the *NEC*, electrical contractors are responsible for ensuring panic hardware is installed where required. Some are offended at being held liable for nonelectrical responsibilities, but this rule is designed to save the lives of electricians. For this and other reasons, many construction professionals routinely hold "pre-construction" or "pre-con" meetings to review potential opportunities for miscommunication—before the work begins.

(D) Illumination. Illumination is required for all working spaces about service equipment, switchboards, switchgear, panelboards, or motor control centers installed indoors. Control by automatic means is not permitted to control all illumination within the working space. ▶Figure 110–77 and ▶Figure 110–78

Additional lighting outlets are not required where the working space is illuminated by an adjacent light source, or as permitted by 210.70(A)(1) Ex 1 for switched receptacles.

Author's Comment:

▸ The *Code* does not identify the minimum foot-candles required to provide proper illumination even though it is essential in electrical equipment rooms for the safety of those qualified to work on such equipment.

110.26 | Requirements for Electrical Installations

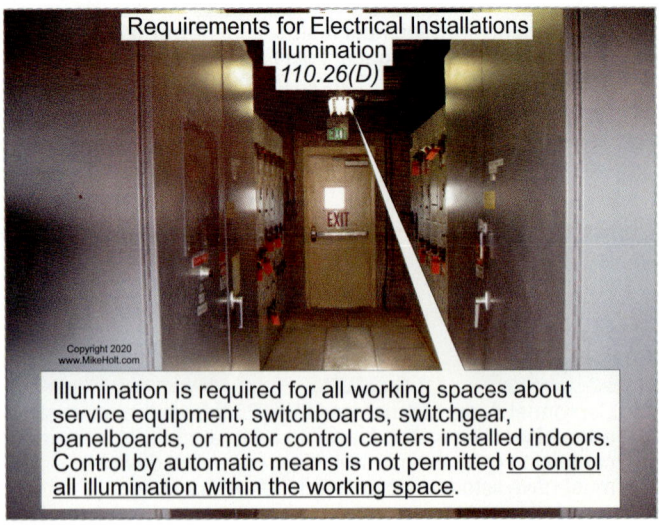
▶Figure 110–77

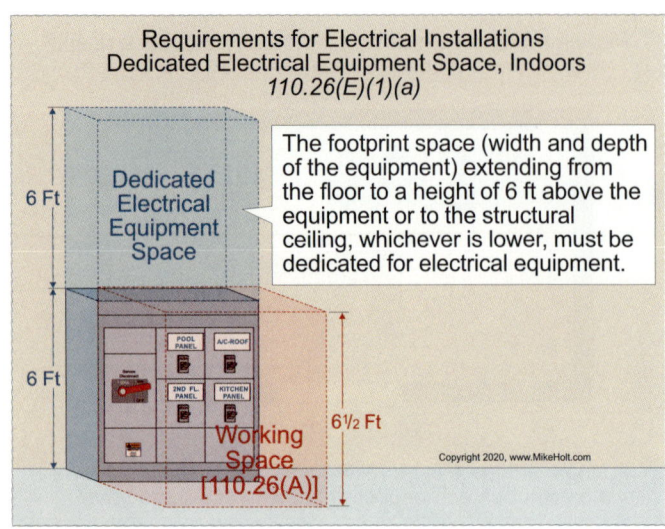
▶Figure 110–79

No piping, ducts, or other equipment foreign to the electrical system can be installed in this dedicated electrical equipment space. ▶Figure 110–80

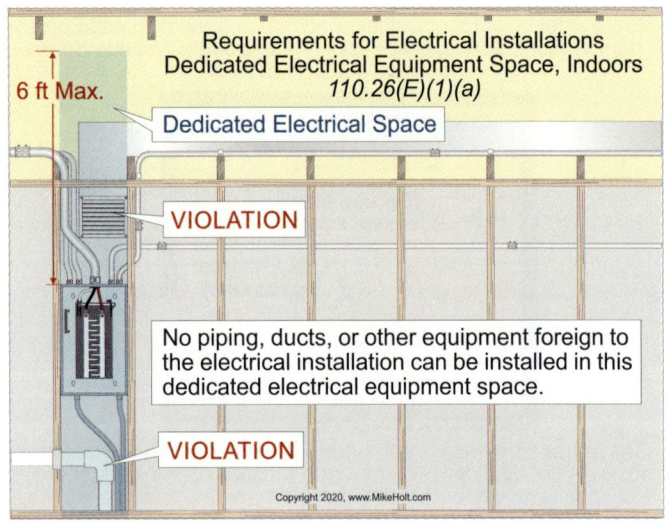
▶Figure 110–80

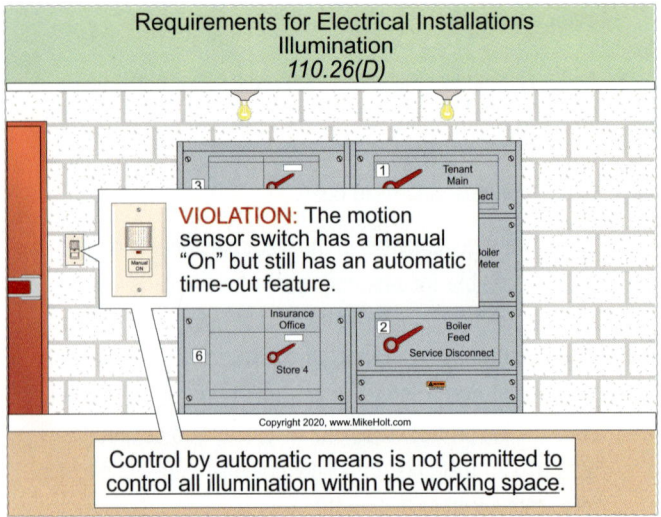
▶Figure 110–78

(E) Dedicated Electrical Equipment Space. Switchboards and panelboards must have dedicated equipment space and be protected from damage that could result from condensation, leaks, breaks in the foreign systems, and vehicular traffic as follows:

(1) Indoors. Switchboards and panelboards installed indoors must comply with the following:

(a) Equipment Space. The footprint space (width and depth of the equipment) extending from the floor to a height of 6 ft above the equipment or to the structural ceiling, whichever is lower, must be dedicated for electrical equipment. ▶Figure 110–79

Author's Comment:

▶ Electrical equipment such as raceways and cables not associated with dedicated space can be in dedicated space. ▶Figure 110–81

Ex: Suspended ceilings with removable panels can be within the dedicated space [110.26(E)(1)(d)].

Requirements for Electrical Installations | 110.26

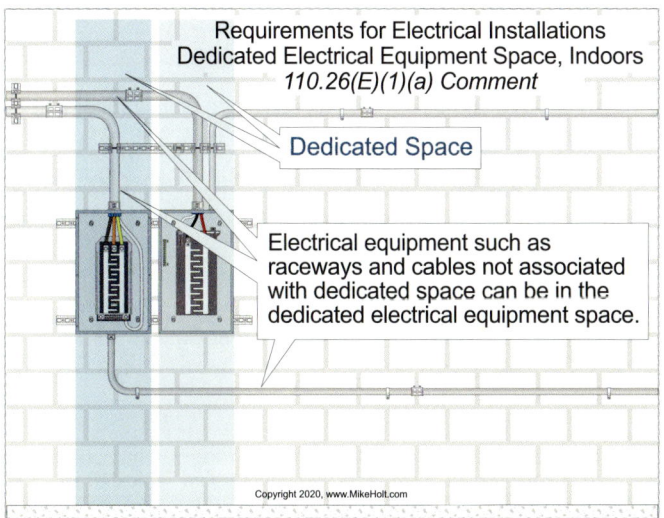
▶Figure 110–81

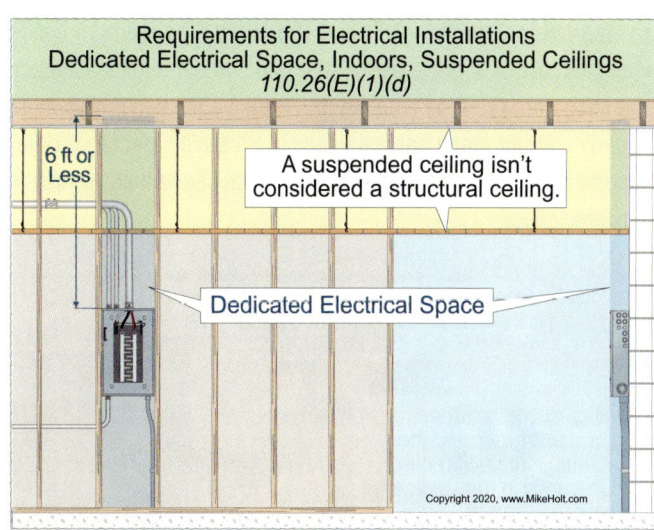
▶Figure 110–83

(b) Foreign Systems. Foreign systems can be located above the dedicated space if protection is installed to prevent damage to the electrical equipment from condensation, leaks, or breaks in the foreign systems. Such protection can be as simple as a drip-pan. ▶Figure 110–82

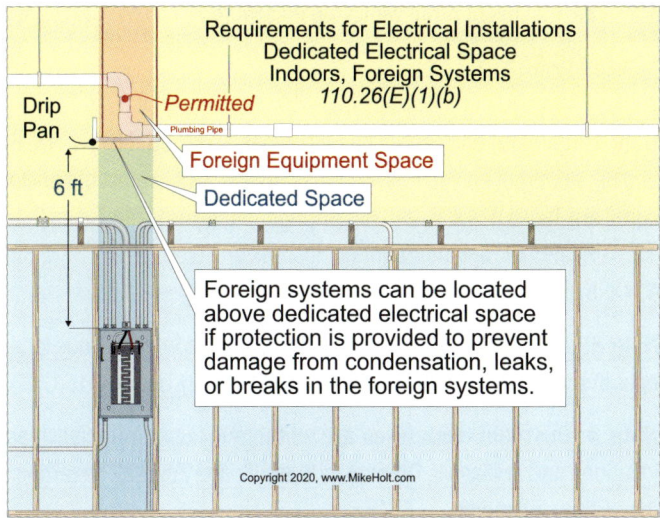
▶Figure 110–82

(c) Sprinkler Protection. Sprinkler protection piping is not permitted in the dedicated space, but the *NEC* does not prohibit sprinklers from spraying water on electrical equipment.

(d) Suspended Ceilings. A dropped, suspended, or similar ceiling is not considered a structural ceiling. ▶Figure 110–83

(2) Outdoor. Outdoor installations for switchboards and panelboard must comply with the following:

(a) Installation Requirements.

(1) Installed in identified enclosures

(2) Protected from accidental contact by unauthorized personnel or by vehicular traffic ▶Figure 110–84

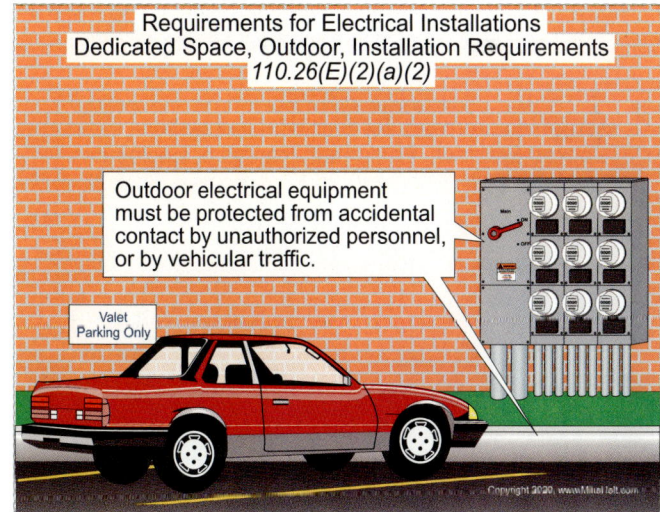
▶Figure 110–84

(3) Protected from accidental spillage or leakage from piping systems

(b) Working Space. The working clearance space includes the zone described in 110.26(A). Architectural appurtenances or other equipment are not permitted within this zone.

(c) Dedicated Equipment Space Outdoors. The footprint space (width and depth of the equipment) of the outdoor dedicated space extending from grade to a height of 6 ft above the equipment must be dedicated for electrical installations. No piping, ducts, or other equipment foreign to the electrical installation can be installed in this dedicated space. ▶Figure 110–85

▶Figure 110–85

(F) Locked Electrical Equipment Rooms or Enclosures. Rooms or enclosures containing electrical equipment controlled by a lock are considered accessible to qualified persons. ▶Figure 110–86

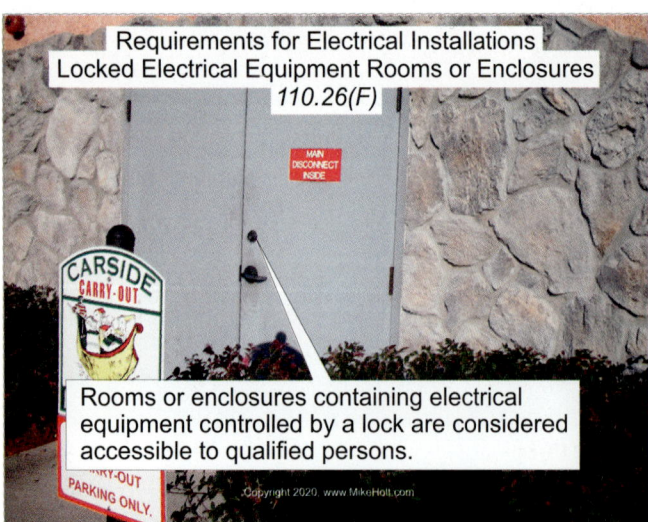

▶Figure 110–86

110.28 Enclosure Types

Enclosures must be marked with an enclosure-type number and be suitable for the location in accordance with Table 110.28. They are not intended to protect against condensation, icing, corrosion, or contamination that might occur within the enclosure or that enters via a raceway or unsealed openings. ▶Figure 110–87

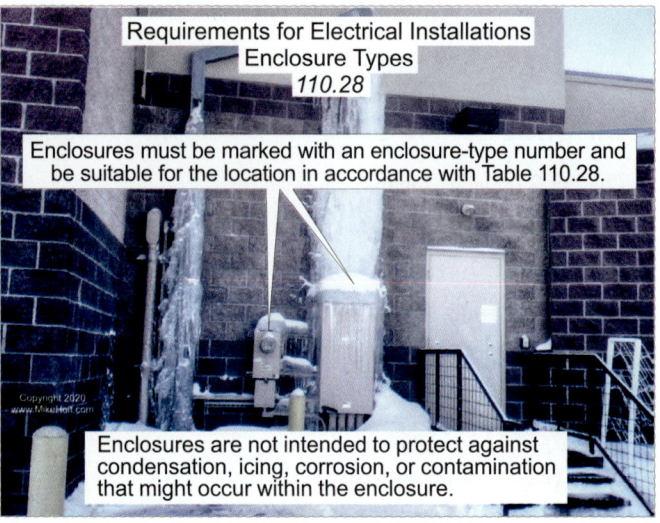

▶Figure 110–87

Note 1: Raintight enclosures include Types 3, 3S, 3SX, 3X, 4, 4X, 6, and 6P; rainproof enclosures are Types 3R and 3RX; watertight enclosures are Types 4, 4X, 6, and 6P; driptight enclosures are Types 2, 5, 12, 12K, and 13; and dusttight enclosures are Types 3, 3S, 3SX, 3X, 4, 4X, 5, 6, 6P, 12, 12K, and 13.

Note 3: Dusttight enclosures are suitable for use in hazardous locations in accordance with 502.10(B)(4), 503.10(A)(2), and 506.15(C)(9).

Note 4: Dusttight enclosures are suitable for use in unclassified locations and in Class II, Division 2; Class III; and Zone 22 hazardous (classified) locations.

CHAPTER 2

WIRING AND PROTECTION

Introduction to Chapter 2—Wiring and Protection

Chapter 2 provides the general rules for wiring and sizing services, feeders, and branch overcurrent protection of conductors, and proper grounding and bonding of electrical circuits and systems. The rules in this chapter apply to all electrical installations covered by the *NEC*—except as modified in Chapters 5, 6, and 7 [90.3].

Communications Systems [Chapter 8] (twisted-pair conductors, antennas, and coaxial cable) are not subject to the general requirements of Chapters 1 through 4, or the special requirements of Chapters 5 through 7, unless there is a specific reference in Chapter 8 to a rule in Chapters 1 through 7 [90.3].

As you go through Chapter 2, remember that it is primarily focused on correctly sizing and protecting circuits. Every article in this chapter deals with a different aspect of providing a safe installation.

- **Article 200—Use and Identification of Neutral and Grounded-Phase Conductors.** This article contains the requirements for the use and identification, of the grounded conductor, which (in most cases) is the neutral conductor.

- **Article 210—Branch Circuits.** Article 210 contains the requirements for branch circuits, such as conductor sizing, identification, AFCI and GFCI protection, as well as receptacle and lighting outlet requirements.

- **Article 215—Feeders.** This article covers the requirements for the installation and ampacity of feeders.

- **Article 225—Outside Feeders.** This article covers the requirements for wiring methods located outside (both overhead and underground). It includes feeders that run on or between buildings, poles, and other structures which may be present on the premises and used to feed equipment.

- **Article 230—Services.** Article 230 covers the installation requirements for service conductors and equipment. It is very important to know where the service begins and ends when applying Article 230.

- **Article 240—Overcurrent Protection.** This article provides the requirements for overcurrent protection and overcurrent protective devices. Overcurrent protection for conductors and equipment is provided to open the circuit if the current reaches a value that will cause an excessive or dangerous temperature on the conductors or conductor insulation.

- **Article 250—Grounding and Bonding.** Article 250 covers the grounding requirements for providing a path to the Earth to reduce overvoltage from lightning, and the bonding requirements for the low-impedance fault current path necessary to facilitate the operation of overcurrent protective devices in the event of a ground fault.

Notes

ARTICLE 200 — USE AND IDENTIFICATION OF GROUNDED CONDUCTORS

Introduction to Article 200—Use and Identification of Grounded Conductors

This article contains the requirements for the identification of grounded conductors and their terminals. There are two types of grounded conductors: neutral conductors and grounded-phase conductors. A conductor connected to the transformer secondary neutral point is both a grounded conductor and a neutral conductor. ▶Figure 200-1

A conductor connected to the secondary of one corner winding is a grounded-phase conductor. ▶Figure 200-2

A system where the transformer secondary is delta-connected with one winding or coil grounded at its midpoint will have a neutral but will also produce one phase with a higher voltage-to-ground known as a "high-leg." ▶Figure 200-3

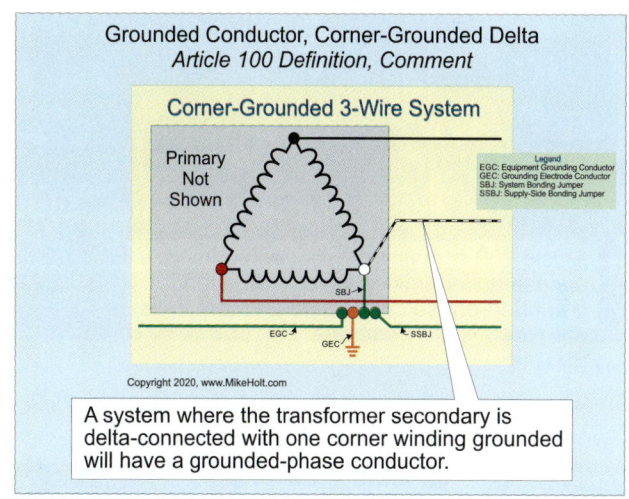
▶Figure 200-2

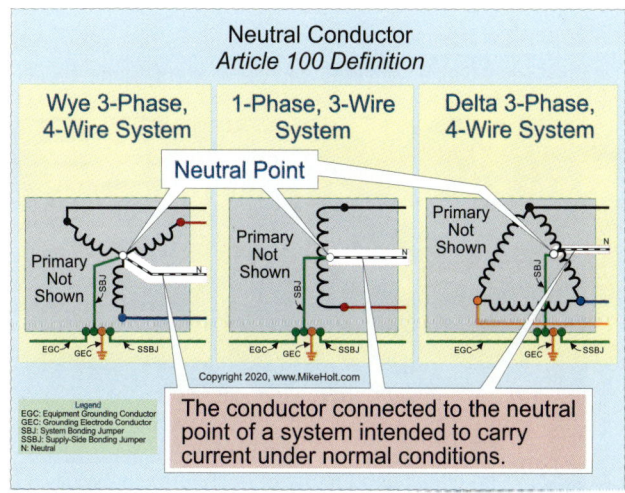
▶Figure 200-1

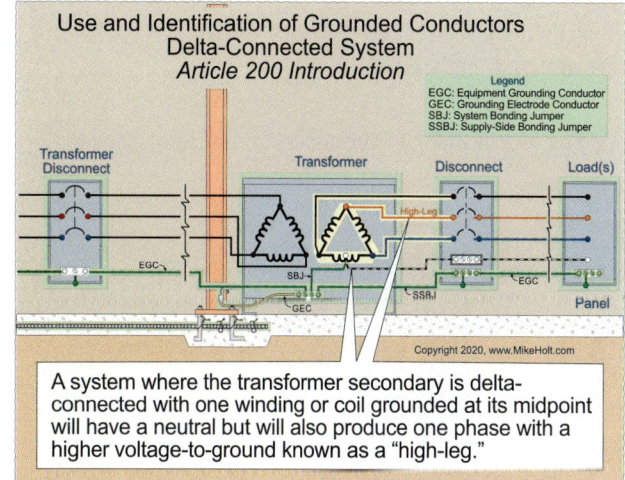
▶Figure 200-3

200.1 | Use and Identification of Grounded Conductors

200.1 Scope

Article 200 contains the requirements for the use and identification of neutral and grounded-phase conductors and terminals. ▶Figure 200–4

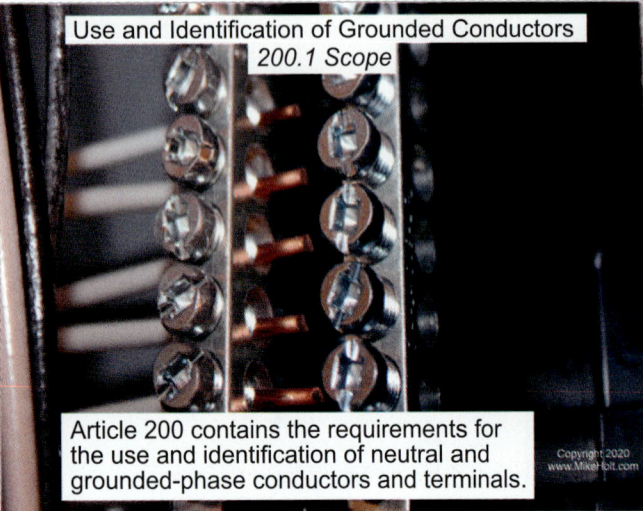

▶Figure 200–4

200.2 General

(B) Continuity. The continuity of neutral and grounded-phase conductors is not permitted to be dependent on metal enclosures, raceways, or cable armor. ▶Figure 200–5

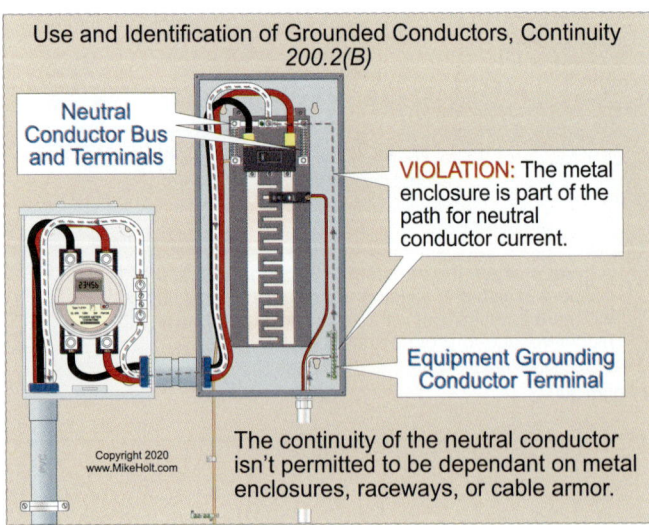

▶Figure 200–5

200.4 Neutral Conductor

Neutral conductors must comply with (A) and (B).

(A) Installation. A single neutral conductor cannot be used for more than one branch circuit or multiwire branch circuit.

(B) Multiple Circuits. The circuit conductors of each branch circuit must be identified or grouped together by cable ties or similar means in every enclosure. ▶Figure 200–6 and ▶Figure 200–7

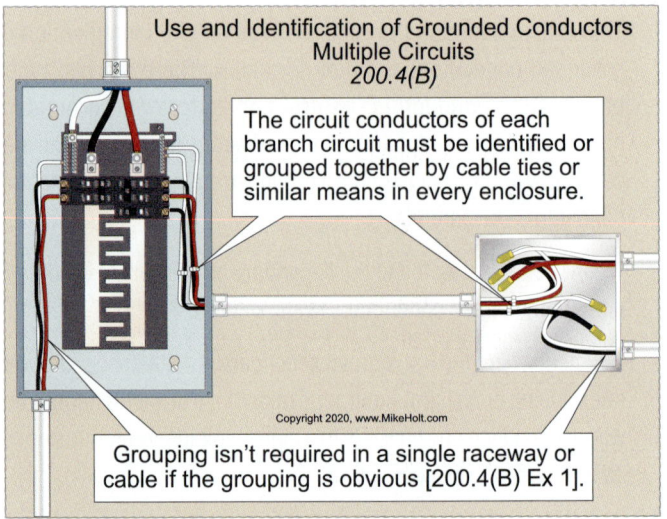

▶Figure 200–6

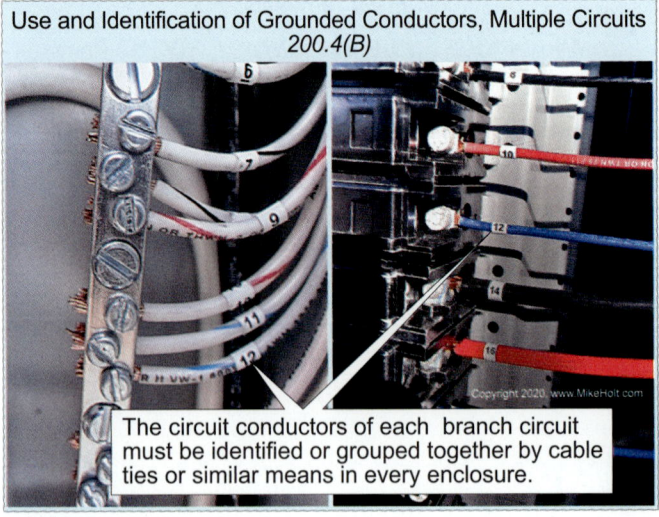

▶Figure 200–7

Ex 1: Grouping is not required where the circuit conductors are contained in a single raceway or cable unique to that circuit making the grouping obvious.

Ex 2: Grouping is not required if the conductors pass through a box or conduit body without any splices or terminations.

Author's Comment:

▸ Grouping all associated conductors by cable ties or other means within the point of origination makes it easier to visually identify conductors of individual branch circuits. Grouping assists in ensuring the correct neutral conductor is paired with the intended phase conductors at junction and splice points, particularly when connecting multiwire branch-circuit conductors to circuit breakers.

Caution

If the phase conductors of a multiwire circuit are not terminated to different phases or lines, the currents on the neutral conductor will be additive and will not balance out or reduce the neutral current. This increased current might exceed the ampere rating of the neutral conductor which in turn may damage the insulation and create a fire hazard. ▸Figure 200-8

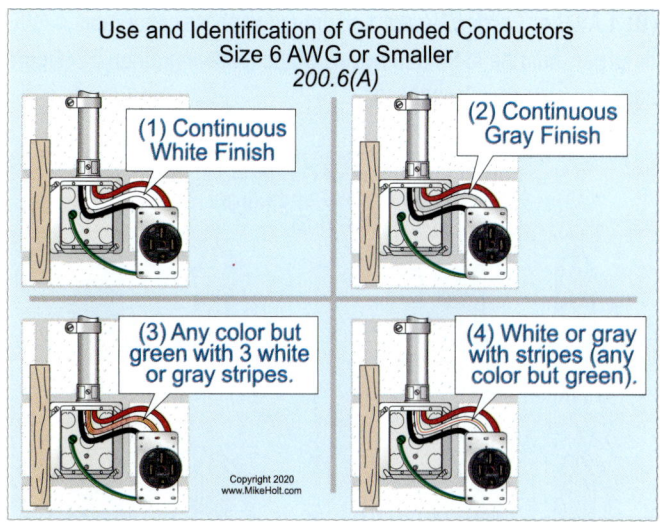

▸Figure 200-9

(1) Insulated conductors with a continuous white outer finish.

(2) Insulated conductors with a continuous gray outer finish.

(3) Insulated conductors with three continuous white or gray stripes along their entire length on other than green insulation.

(4) Insulated conductors with their outer covering finished to show a white or gray color but have colored tracer threads in the braid identifying the source of manufacture.

Author's Comment:

▸ The use of white tape, paint, or other methods of identification is not permitted for neutral and grounded-phase conductors 6 AWG and smaller. ▸Figure 200-10

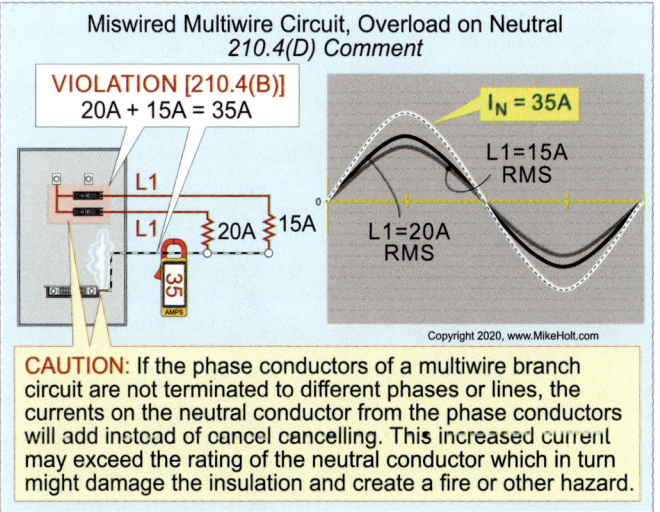

▸Figure 200-8

200.6 Identification of Grounded Conductors

(A) 6 AWG or Smaller. Neutral and grounded-phase conductors 6 AWG and smaller must be identified by any of the following means: ▸Figure 200-9

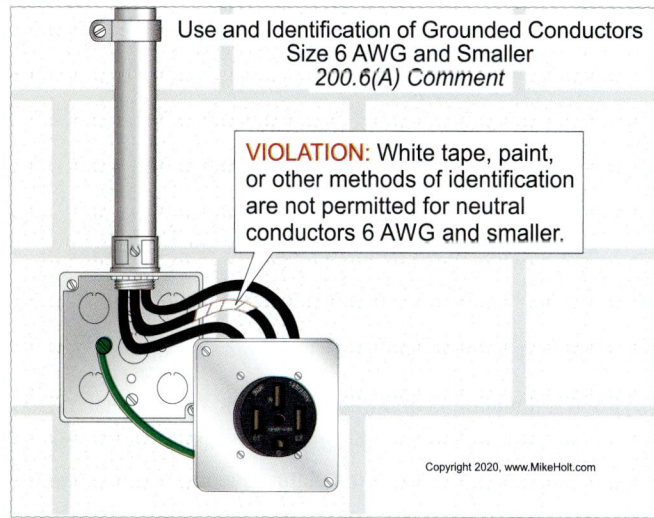

▸Figure 200-10

200.6 | Use and Identification of Grounded Conductors

(B) 4 AWG or Larger. Neutral and grounded-phase conductors 4 AWG or larger must be identified by any of the following means: ▶Figure 200-11 and ▶Figure 200-12

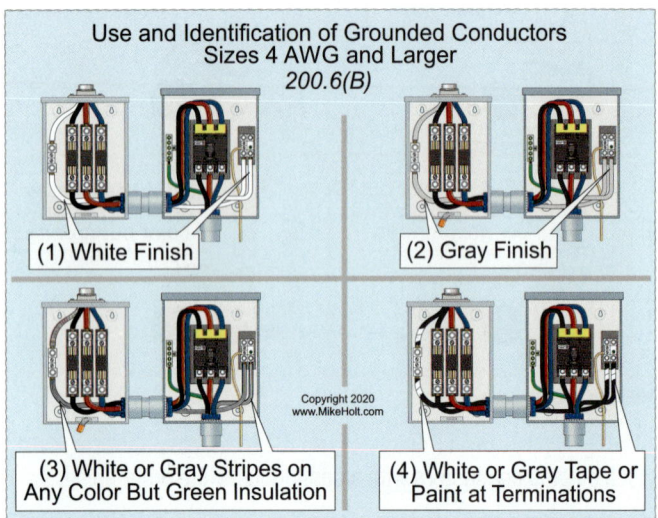

▶Figure 200-11

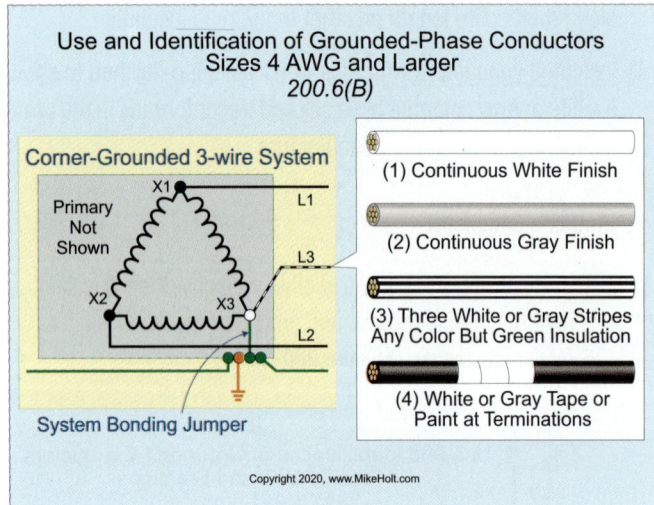

▶Figure 200-12

(1) A continuous white outer finish along their entire length.

(2) A continuous gray outer finish along their entire length.

(3) Three continuous white or gray stripes along their length.

(4) White or gray tape or markings at the terminations.

(D) Neutral Conductors of Different Systems. When neutral conductors of different voltage systems are installed in the same raceway, cable, or enclosure each system neutral conductor must be individually identified by:

(1) A continuous white or gray outer finish along its entire length. ▶Figure 200-13

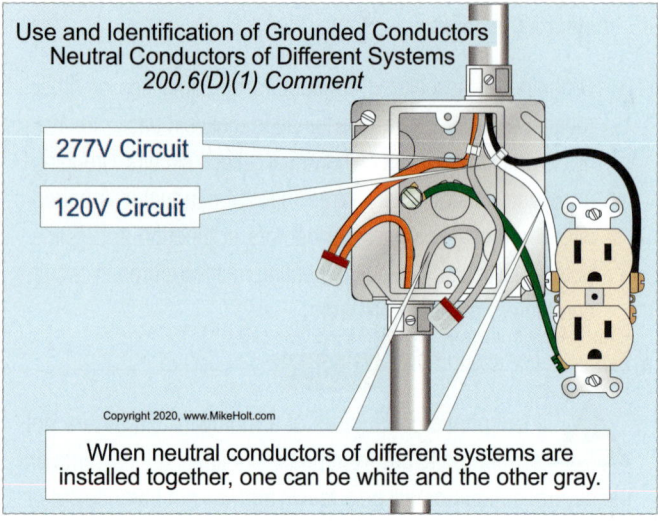

▶Figure 200-13

(2) The neutral conductor of the other system must have a different outer covering of continuous white or gray outer finish along its entire length, or an outer covering of white or gray with a readily distinguishable color stripe (other than green) along its entire length. ▶Figure 200-14

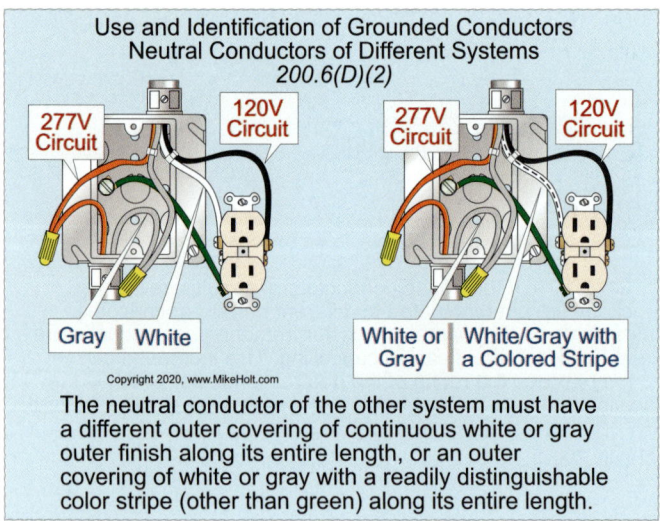

▶Figure 200-14

(3) Other identification allowed by 200.6(A) or 200.6(B) that will distinguish each system's neutral conductor. ▶Figure 200-15

Author's Comment:

▸ The method used to uniquely identify the neutral conductors of different voltage systems should remain consistent throughout the premises.

Use and Identification of Grounded Conductors | 200.7

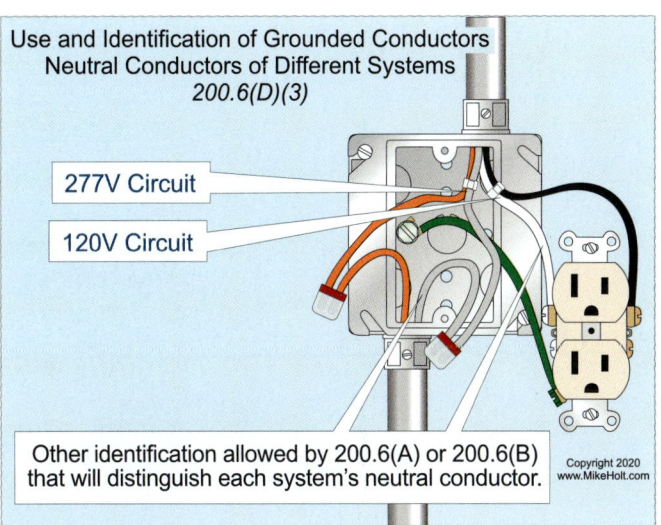
▶Figure 200–15

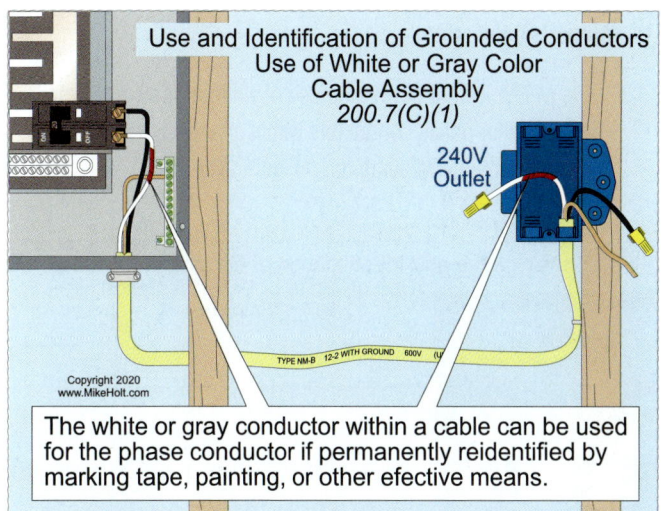
▶Figure 200–16

(E) Neutral Conductors in Multiconductor Cables. Insulated neutral conductor(s) sized 6 AWG and smaller in multiconductor cables must be identified by a continuous white or gray outer finish, or by three continuous white or gray stripes. Conductors in multiconductor cables sized 4 AWG or larger can have the neutral conductor identified in accordance with 200.6(B).

Ex 1: Neutral conductors within multiconductor cables are permitted to be reidentified at their terminations at the time of installation by a distinctive white or gray marking.

200.7 Use of White or Gray Color

(A) General. Insulated conductors identified with white or gray markings can only be used for the neutral or grounded-phase conductor except as permitted in 200.7(C).

(C) Circuits of 50V or More, Reidentification. A conductor with white or gray insulation used as a phase conductor is permitted as follows:

(1) Cable Assembly. The white or gray conductor within a cable can be used for the phase conductor if the white conductor is permanently reidentified as a phase conductor by marking tape, painting, or other effective where the conductor is visible. Identification must encircle the insulation and must be of a color other than white, gray, or green.
▶Figure 200–16

The white or gray conductor within a cable can be used to supply power to switches if the conductor is reidentified as a phase conductor by marking tape, painting, or other effective where the conductor is visible. ▶Figure 200–17 and ▶Figure 200–18

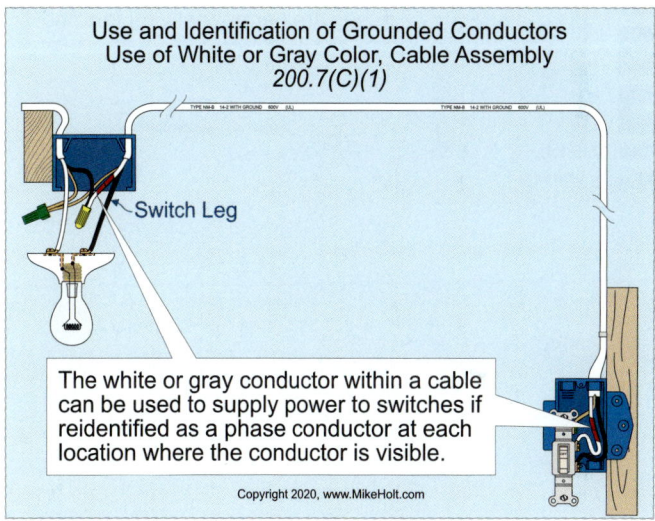
▶Figure 200–17

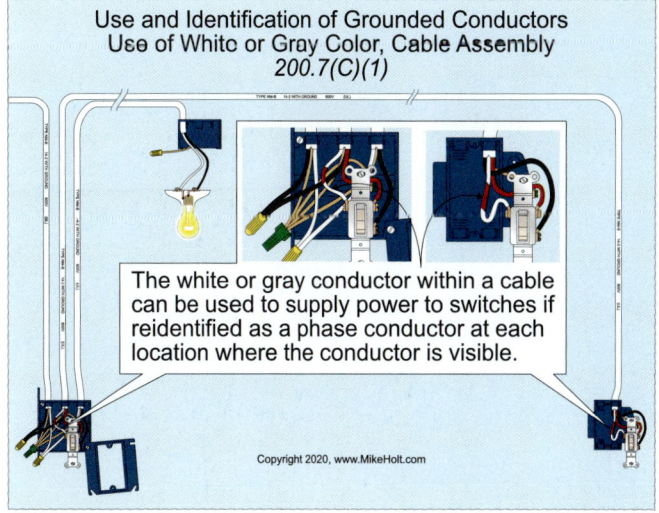
▶Figure 200–18

200.7 | Use and Identification of Grounded Conductors

Author's Comment:

▸ The *NEC* does not permit the use of white or gray conductor insulation for phase conductors within a raceway, even if they are permanently reidentified. ▸Figure 200–19

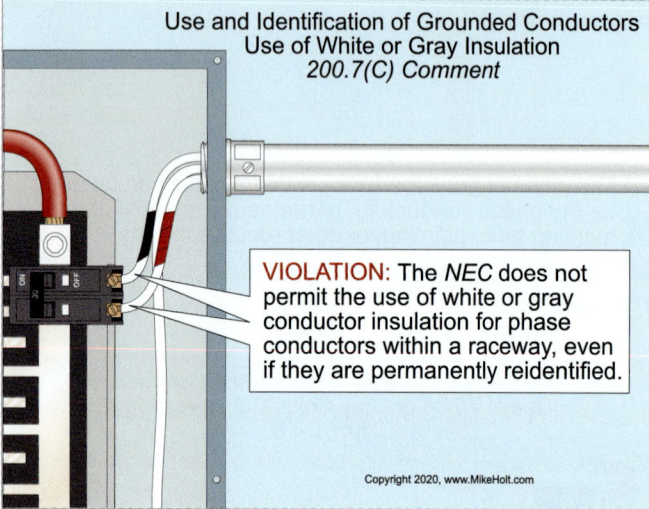

▸Figure 200–19

ARTICLE 210
BRANCH CIRCUITS

Introduction to Article 210—Branch Circuits

This article contains branch-circuit requirements such as those for conductor sizing and identification, GFCI and AFCI protection, and receptacle and lighting outlet requirements. It consists of three parts:

- Part I. General Provisions
- Part II. Branch-Circuit Ratings
- Part III. Required Outlets

Table 210.3 in this article identifies specific-purpose branch circuits. Its provisions for those that supply the equipment listed amend or supplement the requirements in Article 210 for branch circuits, so it is important to be aware of the contents of this table.

Part I. General Provisions

210.1 Scope

Article 210 provides the general requirements for branch circuits such as conductor sizing, overcurrent protection, identification, GFCI and AFCI protection, as well as receptacle outlet and lighting outlet requirements. ▶Figure 210–1

Author's Comment:

- According to Article 100 a "Branch Circuit" consists of the conductors between the final overcurrent protective device and the receptacle outlets, lighting outlets, or other outlets. ▶Figure 210–2

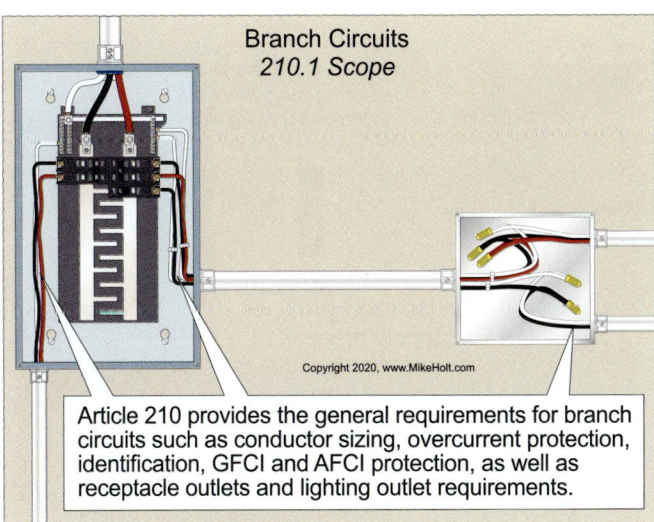

▶Figure 210–1

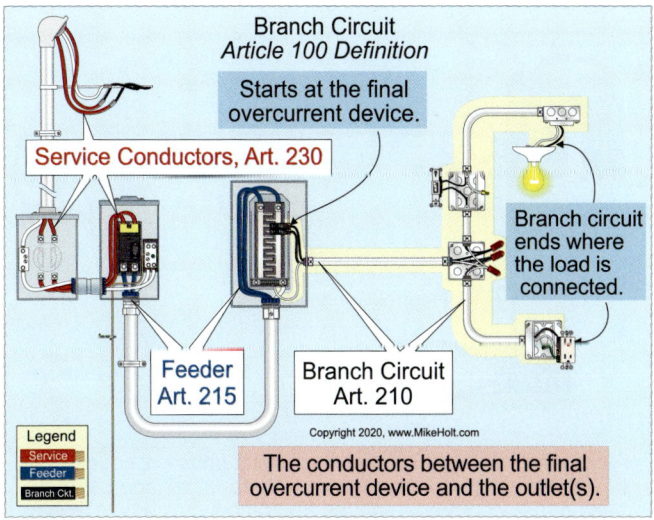

▶Figure 210–2

210.4 | Branch Circuits

210.4 Multiwire Branch Circuits

(A) General. All conductors of a multiwire branch circuit must originate from the same panelboard. ▶Figure 210-3

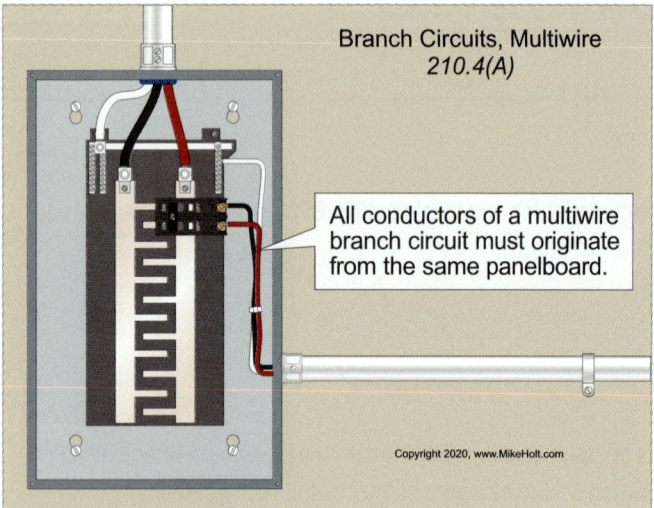

▶Figure 210-3

Author's Comment:

▸ According to Article 100, a "Multiwire Branch Circuit" consists of two or more circuit phase conductors with a common neutral conductor. This type of circuit has a voltage between the phase conductors and an equal difference of voltage from each phase conductor to the common neutral conductor. ▶Figure 210-4

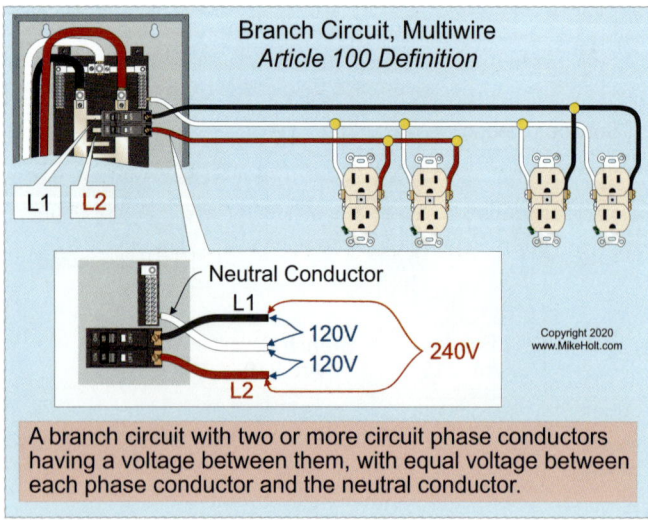

▶Figure 210-4

All conductors of a circuit (including the neutral and equipment grounding conductors) must be installed together in the same raceway, cable, trench, cord, or cable tray [300.3(B)], except as permitted by 300.3(B)(1) through (4).

Note 2: See 300.13(B) for the requirements relating to the continuity of the neutral conductor on multiwire branch circuits.

(B) Disconnecting Means. Each multiwire branch circuit must have a means to simultaneously disconnect all phase conductors at the point where the circuit originates. ▶Figure 210-5

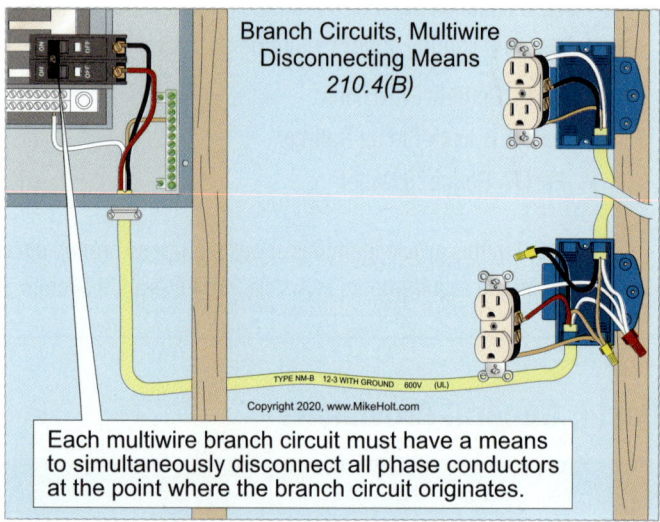

▶Figure 210-5

Note: Individual single-pole circuit breakers with handle ties identified for the purpose or a circuit breaker with a common internal trip can be used for this application [240.15(B)(1)]. ▶Figure 210-6

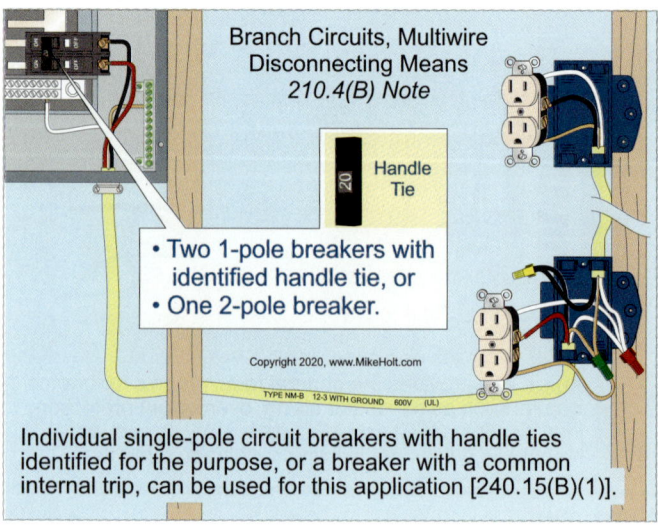

▶Figure 210-6

> **Caution**
> This rule is intended to prevent people from working on energized circuits they thought were disconnected.

(C) Line-to-Neutral Loads. Multiwire branch circuits must supply only line-to-neutral loads.

Ex 1: A multiwire branch circuit can supply an individual piece of line-to-neutral utilization equipment such as a range or dryer. ▶Figure 210–7

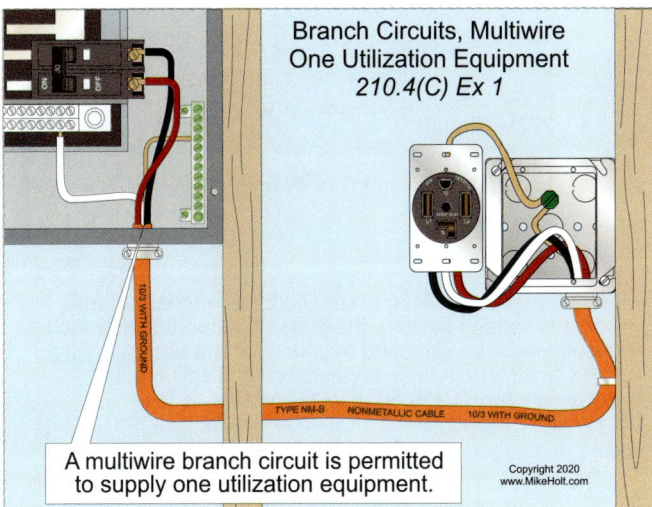

▶Figure 210–7

Ex 2: A multiwire branch circuit can supply both line-to-neutral and line-to-line loads if the circuit is protected by a device such as a multi-pole circuit breaker with a common internal trip that opens all phase conductors of the multiwire branch circuit simultaneously under a fault condition.

(D) Grouping. Phase and neutral conductors of a multiwire branch circuit must be identified or grouped together by cable ties or similar means in every enclosure in accordance with 200.4(B). ▶Figure 210–8

> **Author's Comment:**
>
> ▸ Grouping is not required where the circuit conductors are contained in a single raceway or cable unique to that circuit making the grouping obvious [200.4(B) Ex 1].
>
> ▸ If the conductors pass through a box or conduit body without any splices or terminations, then grouping is not required [200.4(B) Ex 2].

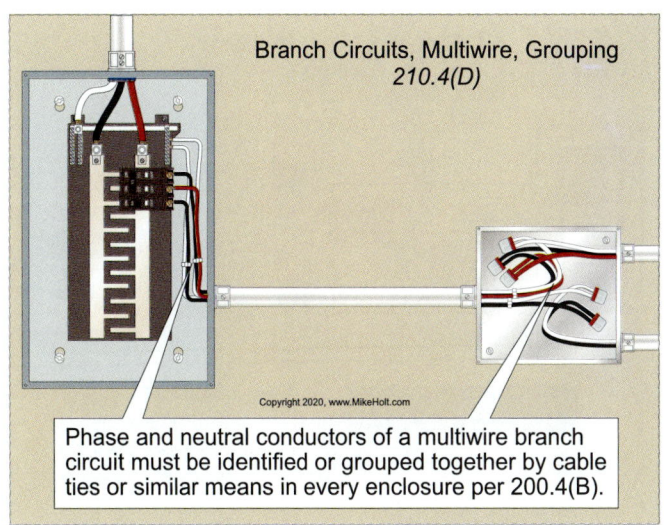

▶Figure 210–8

> **Author's Comment:**
>
> ▸ Grouping all associated conductors of a multiwire branch circuit together by cable ties or other means at the point of origin makes it easier to visually identify the conductors of each multiwire branch circuit. The grouping assists in ensuring the correct neutral is paired with the intended circuit conductors at junction points, and in correctly connecting multiwire branch-circuit conductors to circuit breakers. If proper care is not exercised when making these connections, two circuit conductors can be accidentally connected to the same phase or line.

> **Caution**
> If the phase conductors of a multiwire branch circuit are not terminated to different phases or lines, the currents on the neutral conductor from the phase conductors will be additive and will not cancel. This increased current may exceed the rating of the neutral conductor which in turn might damage the insulation and create a fire or other hazard. ▶Figure 210–9 and ▶Figure 210–10

210.5 | Branch Circuits

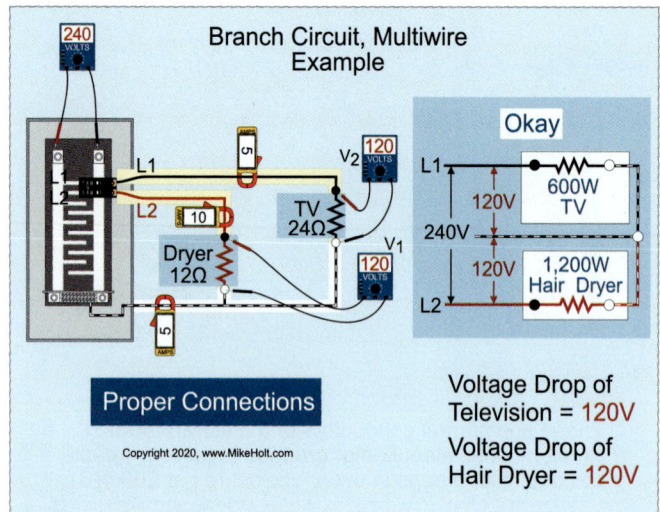

▶Figure 210–9

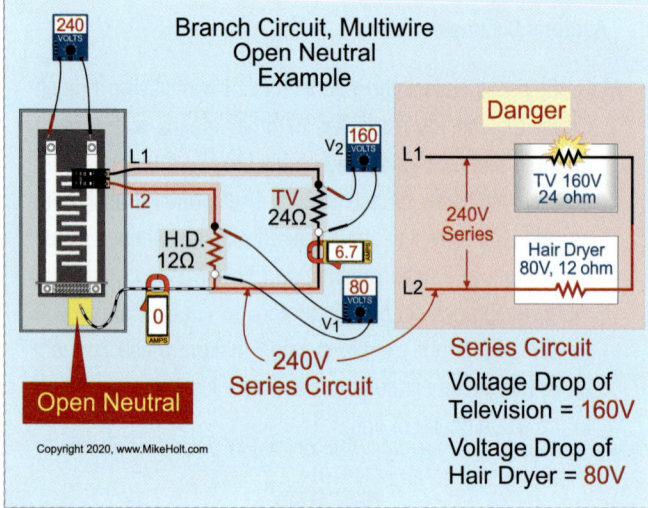

▶Figure 210–10

210.5 Identification for Branch Circuits

(A) Neutral Conductor. The branch-circuit neutral conductor must be identified in accordance with 200.6.

(B) Equipment Grounding Conductor. Equipment grounding conductors can be bare, covered, or insulated. Insulated equipment grounding conductors 6 AWG and smaller must have a continuous outer finish either green or green with one or more yellow stripes [250.119].

Insulated equipment grounding conductors 4 AWG and larger can be permanently reidentified with green marking at the time of installation where accessible [250.119(A)].

(C) Identification of Phase Conductors. Circuit phase conductors must be identified as follows:

(1) More Than One Voltage Distribution System. Where premises wiring is supplied from more than one nominal voltage system, the phase conductors of branch circuits must be identified by phase or line and by voltage class at all termination, connection, and splice points in accordance with 210.5(C)(1)(a) and (b). Different systems within the premises with the same system voltage class can use the same method of identification. ▶Figure 210–11

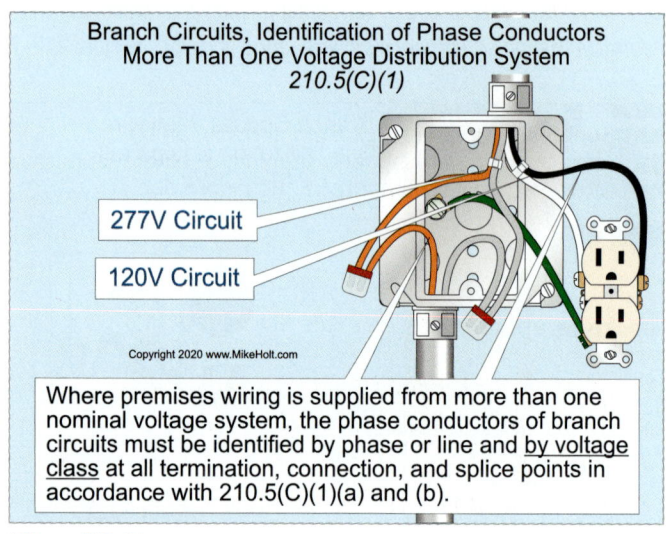

▶Figure 210–11

Author's Comment:

▶ "Voltage class" should be read as "nominal" voltage as used here. For example, a premises with two sources of 120/208V nominal such as a separately derived system, can use the same conductor identification scheme (which in this case would typically be black, red, blue, and white) because the "voltage class" (nominal voltage) is the same.

(a) Means of Identification. Identification of the phase conductors can be by color coding, marking tape, tagging, or other means approved by the authority having jurisdiction. ▶Figure 210–12

(b) Posting of Identification. The method of identification must be readily available or permanently posted at each branch-circuit panelboard, not be handwritten, and be sufficiently durable to withstand the environment involved. ▶Figure 210–13

Ex: Where a different voltage system is added to an existing installation, branch-circuit identification is only required for the new one. Each voltage system distribution equipment must have a label with the words "other unidentified systems exist on the premises." ▶Figure 210–14

Branch Circuits | 210.7

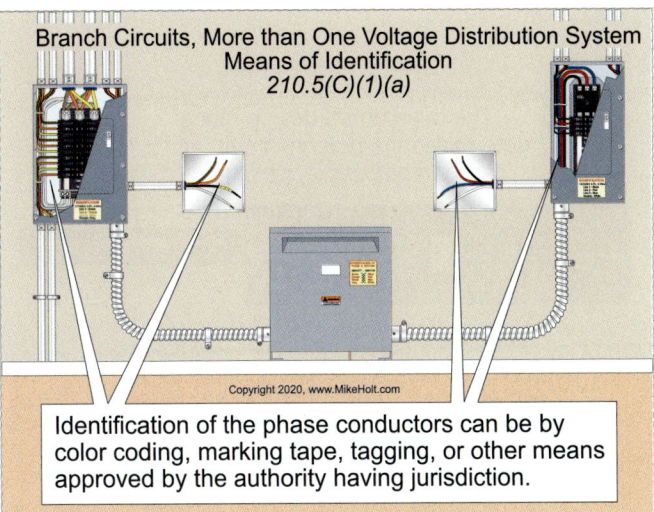

▶Figure 210–12

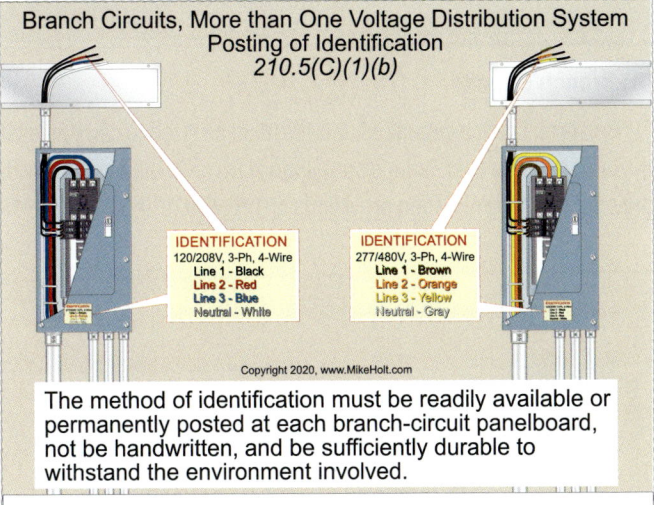

▶Figure 210–13

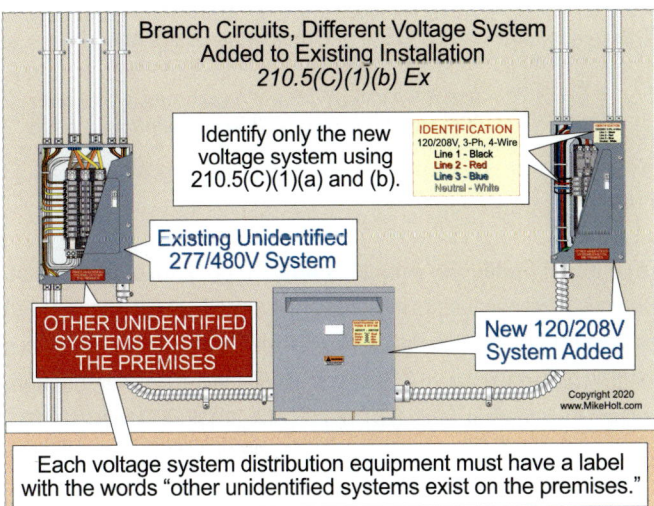

▶Figure 210–14

Author's Comment:

▶ When a premises has more than one voltage system supplying branch circuits, the phase conductors must be identified by phase and system. This can be done by permanently posting an identification legend that describes the method used, such as color-coded marking tape or color-coded insulation.

▶ Although the *NEC* does not require a specific color code for phase conductors, electricians often use the following system: ▶Figure 210–15

- 120/240V, single-phase—black, red, and white
- 120/208V, three-phase—black, red, blue, and white
- 120/240V, three-phase (high-leg)—black, orange, blue, and white
- 277/480V, three-phase—brown, orange, yellow, and gray; or, brown, purple, yellow, and gray

▶ Whichever color scheme is used, it is important for it to remain consistent wherever phase conductors are terminated or accessible throughout the entire premises. This is especially important when identifying different system voltages and neutrals.

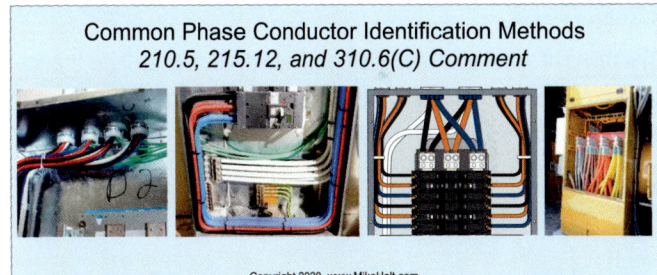

▶Figure 210–15

210.7 Multiple Branch Circuits

If two circuits supplying devices or equipment are on the same strap or yoke, all phase conductors must be disconnected at the point where the branch circuit originates. ▶Figure 210–16

210.18 | Branch Circuits

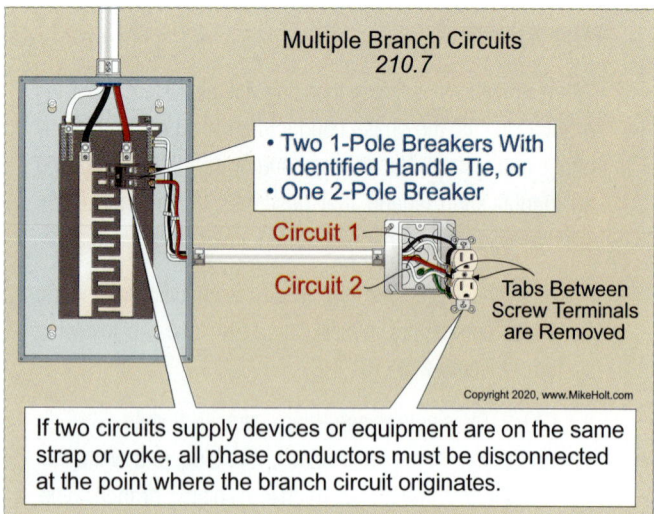
▶Figure 210–16

Author's Comment:

▸ Individual single-pole circuit breakers with handle ties identified for the purpose, or a circuit breaker with a common internal trip, can be used for this application [240.15(B)(1)].

Part II. Branch-Circuit Ratings

210.18 Branch-Circuit Rating

The rating of a branch circuit is determined by the rating of the branch-circuit overcurrent protective device, not by the ampacity rating of the conductor. ▶Figure 210–17

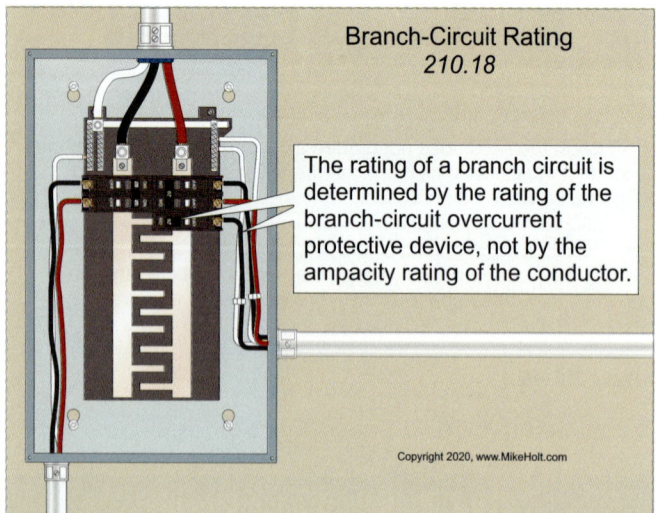
▶Figure 210–17

Author's Comment:

▸ 10 THHN rated 30A at 60°C protected by a 20A circuit breaker is a 20A rated circuit. ▶Figure 210–18

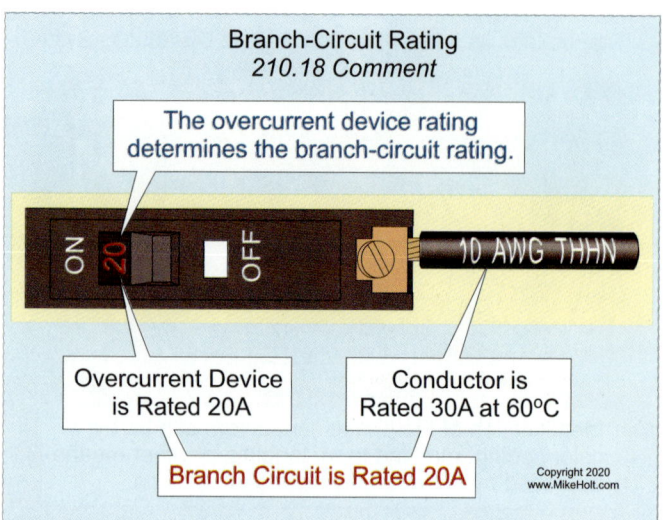
▶Figure 210–18

210.19 Conductor Sizing

(A) Branch Circuits

(1) General. Branch-circuit conductors must be sized to carry at least the largest of the calculations contained in (a) or (b) and comply with the equipment termination provisions of 110.14(C). ▶Figure 210–19

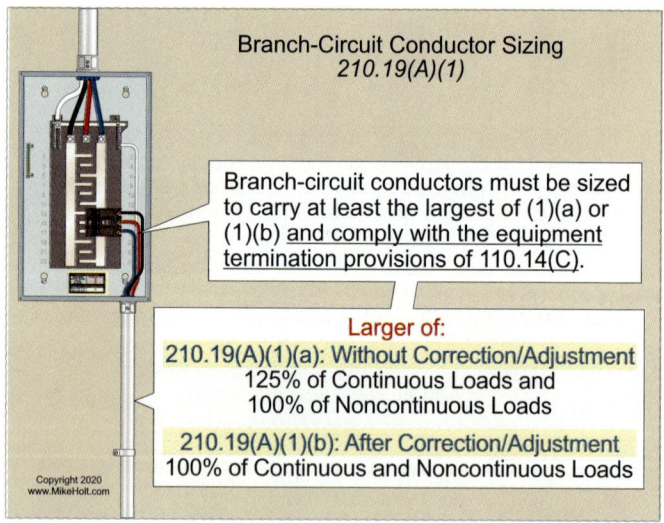
▶Figure 210–19

(a) Without Conductor Ampacity Adjustment and/or Correction. Branch-circuit conductors must have an ampacity of not less than 125 percent of the continuous loads, plus 100 percent of the noncontinuous loads in accordance with 310.14; based on the terminal temperature rating ampacities in Table 310.16 [110.14(C)(1)]. ▶Figure 210–20

Branch Circuits | 210.19

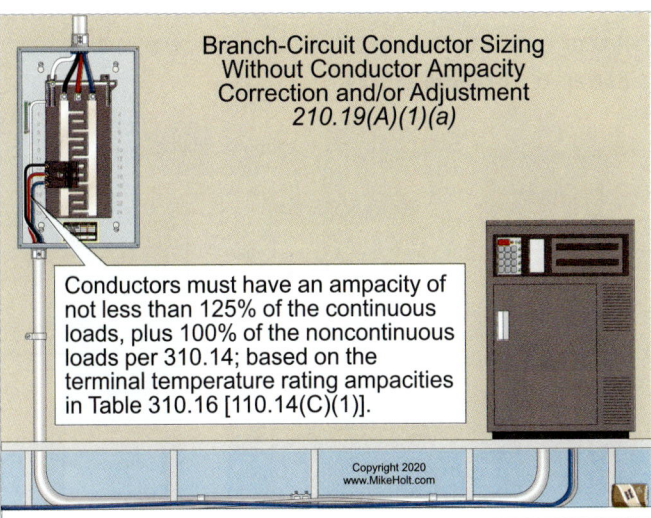

▶Figure 210–20

(b) After Conductor Ampacity Adjustment and Correction. Branch-circuit conductors must be sized to carry not less than 100 percent of the continuous load, plus 100 percent of the noncontinuous load after conductor ampacity adjustment and/or correction in accordance with Table 310.15(B)(1) and Table 310.15(C)(1). ▶Figure 210–22

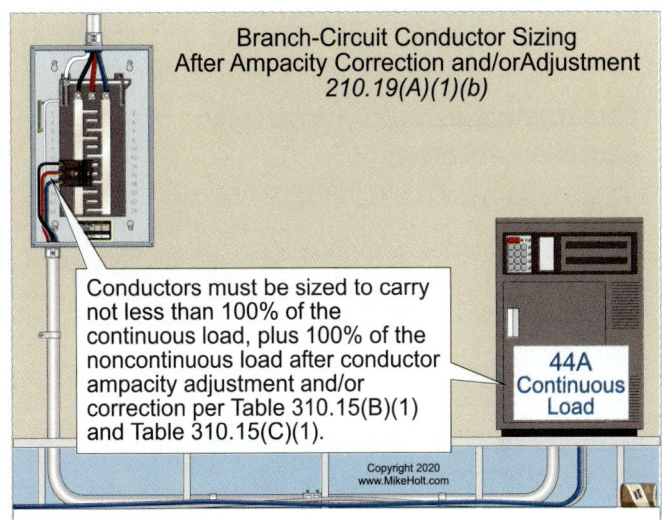

▶Figure 210–22

▶ Example 1

Question: What size conductors rated 90°C are required for a circuit supplying a 44A continuous load where the equipment terminals are rated 75°C? ▶Figure 210–21

(a) 8 AWG   (b) 6 AWG   (c) 4 AWG   (d) 3 AWG

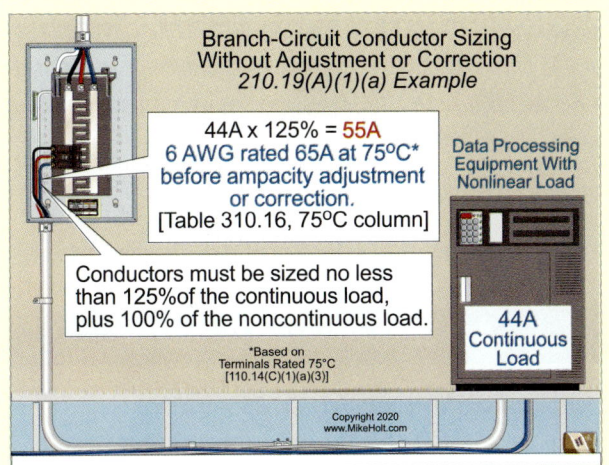

▶Figure 210–21

Solution:

Step 1: *Conductor Ampacity.* The conductor must have an ampacity of at least 55A (44A × 125%).

Step 2: Size conductors in accordance with 110.14(C)(1)(a)(3) and Table 310.16.

6 AWG is rated 65A and is suitable to be used [Table 310.16, 75°C column].

Answer: (b) 6 AWG

▶ Example

Question: What size conductors rated 90°C are required for a circuit containing four current-carrying conductors supplying a 44A continuous load in an ambient temperature of 100°F where the equipment terminals are rated 75°C? ▶Figure 210–23

(a) 10 AWG   (b) 8 AWG   (c) 6 AWG   (d) 4 AWG

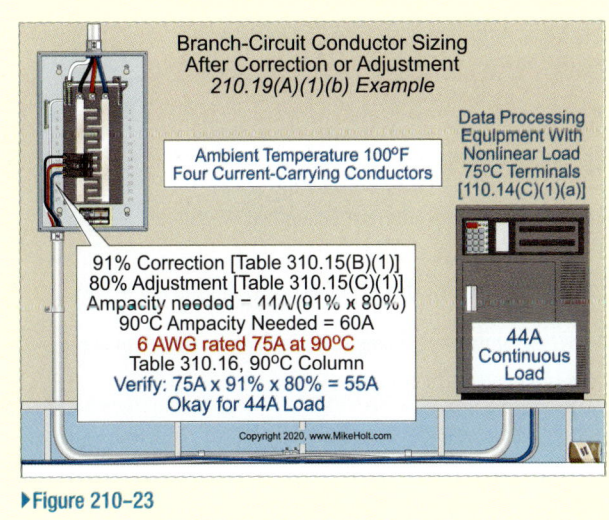

▶Figure 210–23

Solution:

Step 1: The circuit conductors must have an ampacity of not less than 44A after conductor ampacity temperature correction [Table 310.15(B)(1)] and adjustment [Table 310.15(C)(1)], based on the conductor insulation rating of 90°C [110.14(C)(1)(a)]. One way to find the conductor size is to determine the conductor ampacity required to supply a 44A load at 100% after correction and adjustment.

Conductor Ampacity at 90°C = Actual Load/ (Correction × Adjustment)

Actual Load = 44A

Correction [Table 310.15(B)(1)] = 91% (100°F with 90°C Conductor)

Adjustment [Table 310.15(C)(1)] = 80% (four current-carrying conductors)

Conductor Ampacity at 90°C Column = 44A/(91% × 80%)
Conductor Ampacity at 90°C Column = 44A/73%
Conductor Ampacity at 90°C Column = 60A

Step 2: Select the conductors from the 90°C column of Table 310.16.

6 AWG is suitable because it has an ampacity of 75A at 90°C before any correction and adjustment. In addition, 6 AWG is the minimum conductor size allowed according to 210.19(A)(1)(a).

Step 3: Verify that the ampacity of 6 AWG after correction and adjustment is capable of carrying 100 percent of the 44A continuous load at 90°C.

Conductor Ampacity after Correction and Adjustment = Conductor Ampacity × Correction × Adjustment

Conductor Ampacity at 90°C = 75A*
(*Note: 75A is from Step 2.)

Correction = 91%
Adjustment = 80%

Conductor Ampacity after Correction and Adjustment =
 75A × 91% × 80%
Conductor Ampacity after Correction and Adjustment = 55A

6 AWG has an ampere rating of 55A which is more than enough for the 44A continuous load.

Step 4: Verify that the ampacity of 6 AWG at 75°C without correction and adjustment is capable of carrying 125 percent of the 44A continuous load in accordance with 210.19(A)(1)(a).

Conductor Ampacity at 125% = 44A × 125%
Conductor Ampacity at 125% = 55A

According to Table 310.16, 6 AWG is suitable because it is rated 65A at 75°C. ▶Figure 210–24

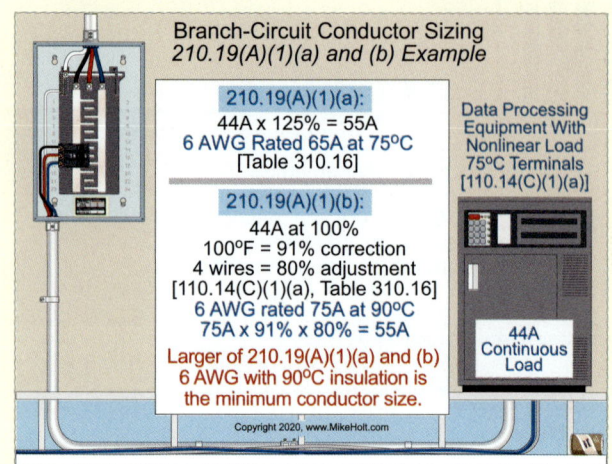

▶Figure 210–24

The branch-circuit conductors cannot be sized less than determined using 210.19(A)(1)(a). In this case, based on the conditions specified in this example, 6 AWG is the minimum permitted size.

The conductor cannot be sized less than the load at 100 percent based on the 75°C terminals specified in the question (60°C when not specified [110.14(C)]). In this case, the minimum conductor size for 44A circuit conduction using the 75°C column of Table 310.16 is 8 AWG; but, since 210.19(A)(1)(a) only permits a minimum of 6 AWG, the 8 AWG cannot be used.

Answer: (c) 6 AWG

210.20 Overcurrent Protection

Branch-circuit conductors and equipment must be protected by overcurrent protective devices with a rating or setting that complies with 210.20(A) through (D).

(A) Continuous and Noncontinuous Loads. Branch-circuit overcurrent devices must have a rating of not less than 125 percent of the continuous loads, plus 100 percent of the noncontinuous loads. ▶Figure 210–25

Branch Circuits | 210.21

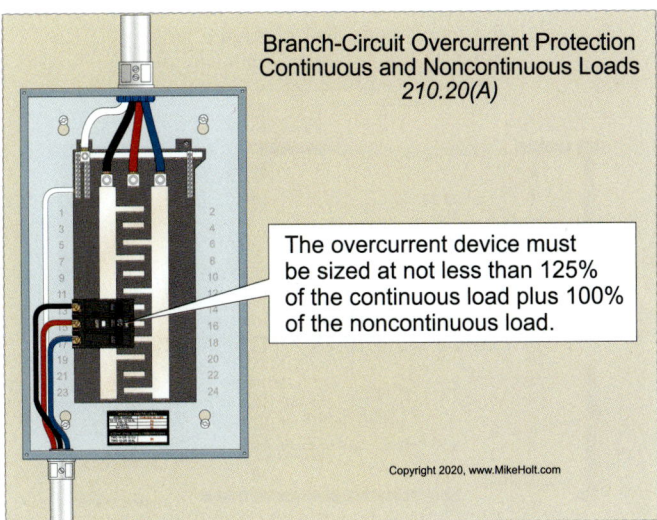
▶Figure 210-25

210.21 Receptacle Rating

(B) Receptacles—Rating and Load Capacity

(1) Single Receptacle. A single receptacle must have an ampere rating of not less than the rating of the circuit overcurrent protective device. ▶Figure 210-27

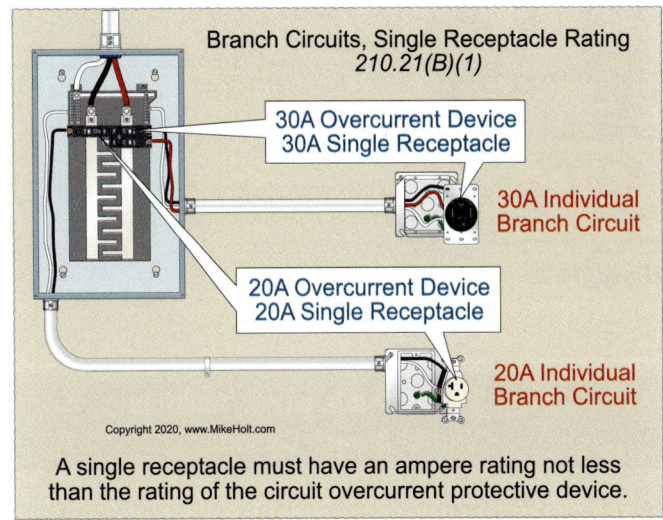
▶Figure 210-27

Note: A single receptacle has only one contact device on its yoke [Article 100]; a duplex receptacle is not a single receptacle since it has two receptacles on the yoke.

(3) Multiple Receptacles. Where multiple receptacles are connected to a branch circuit, their ampere ratings must be in accordance with Table 210.21(B)(3).

Author's Comment:

▸ Table 210.21(B)(3) permits both 15A and 20A receptacles on a 20A multioutlet circuit. ▶Figure 210-28

Table 210.21(B)(3) Receptacle Ratings	
Circuit Rating	Receptacle Rating
15A	15A
20A	15A or 20A
30A	30A
40A	40A or 50A
50A	50A

▶ **Example**

Question: What size circuit breaker is required for a branch circuit that has a 44A continuous load? ▶Figure 210-26

(a) 20A　　(b) 30A　　(c) 50A　　(d) 60A

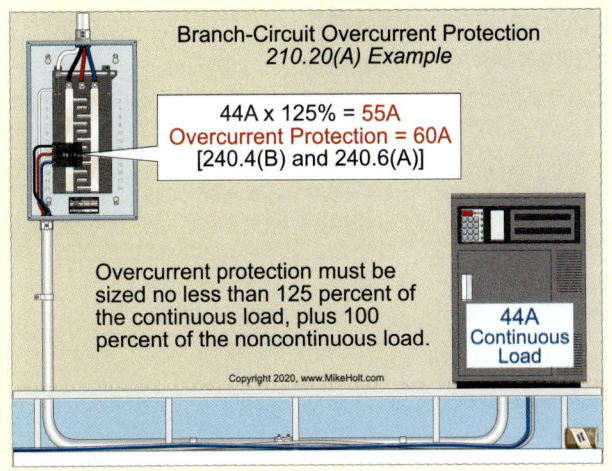
▶Figure 210-26

Solution:

Protection Rating = 44A × 125%

Protection Rating = 55A; the next size up is permitted [240.4(B)]: 60A per 240.6(A).

Answer: (d) 60A

210.23 | Branch Circuits

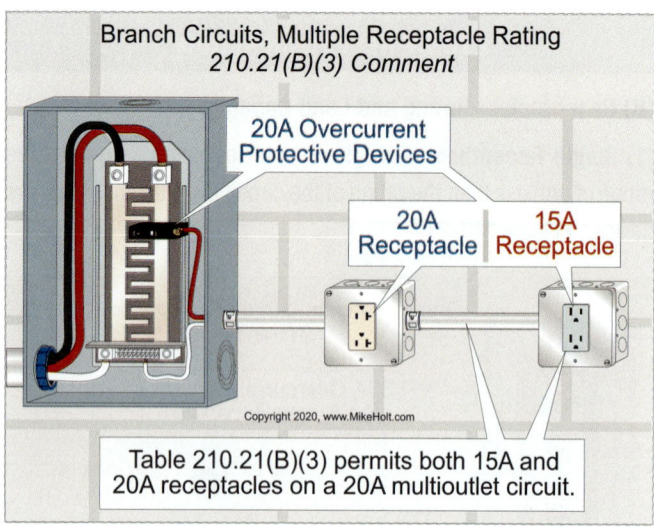
▶Figure 210–28

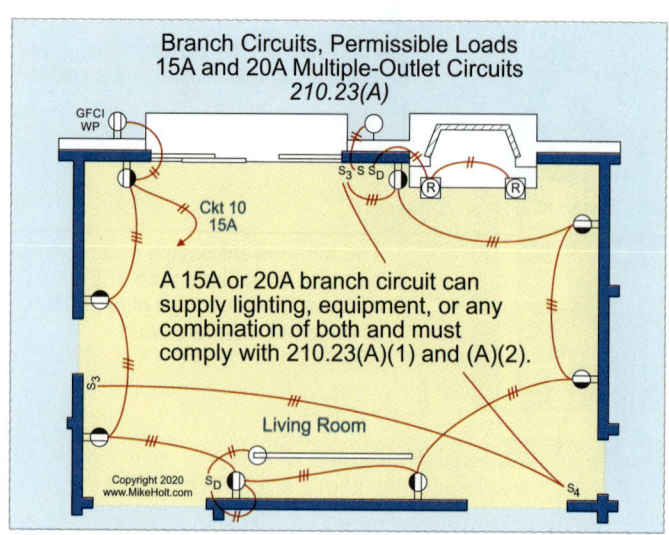
▶Figure 210–29

210.23 Permissible Loads, Multiple-Outlet Branch Circuits

(A) 15A and 20A Branch Circuits. A 15A or 20A branch circuit can supply lighting, equipment, or any combination of both. ▶Figure 210–29

(1) Cord-and-Plug Equipment. Cord-and-plug-connected equipment is not permitted to be rated more than 80 percent of the branch-circuit ampere rating.

(2) Equipment Fastened in Place. Equipment fastened in place is not permitted to be rated more than 50 percent of the branch-circuit rating that supplies more than one outlet. ▶Figure 210–30

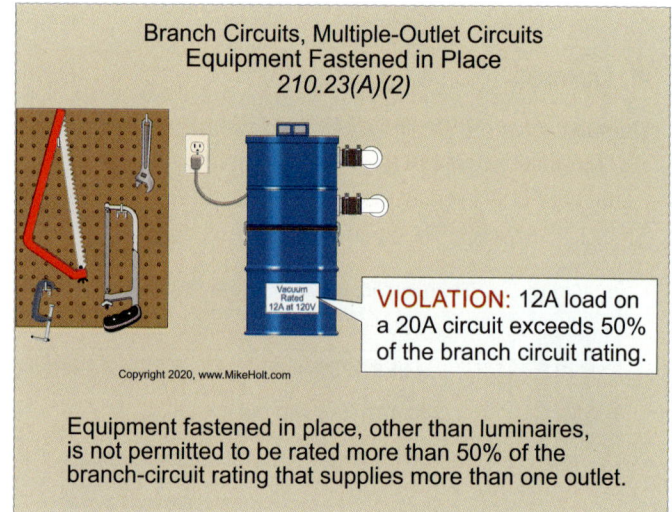
▶Figure 210–30

ARTICLE 215 FEEDERS

Introduction to Article 215—Feeders

Article 215 covers the rules for the installation and ampacity of feeders. The requirements for feeders have some similarities to those for branch circuits, and in some ways, feeders resemble service conductors. It is important to understand the distinct differences between these three types of circuits in order to correctly apply the *Code* requirements.

Feeders are the conductors between the service disconnect, the separately derived system, or other supply source, and the final branch-circuit overcurrent protective device. Conductors past the final overcurrent protective device protecting the circuit and the outlet are branch-circuit conductors and fall within the scope of Article 210 [Article 100 Definitions]. ▶Figure 215–1

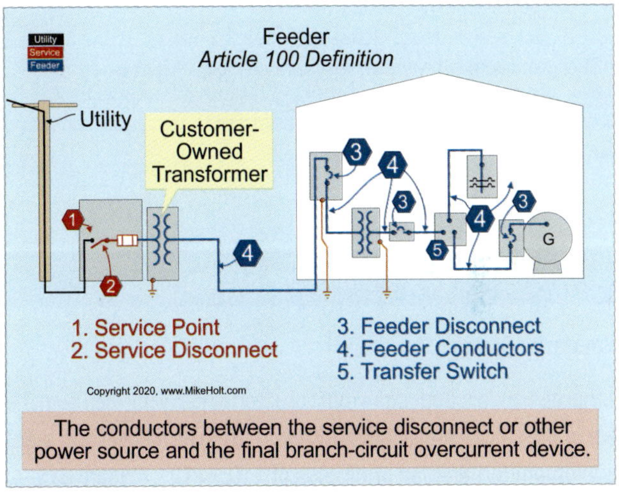

Service conductors are the conductors from the service point to the service disconnect [Article 100 Definitions]. If there is no serving utility, and the electric power is derived from a generator or other on-site electric power source, then the conductors from the supply source are defined as feeders and there are no service conductors.

It is easy to be confused between feeder, branch-circuit, and service conductors so it is important to evaluate each installation carefully using the Article 100 Definitions to be sure the correct *NEC* rules are followed.

▶Figure 215–1

215.1 Scope

Article 215 covers the installation, conductor sizing, and overcurrent protection requirements for feeder conductors. ▶Figure 215–2

Author's Comment:

▶ Article 100 defines "Feeders" as the conductors between the service disconnect, a separately derived system, or other power supply and the final branch-circuit overcurrent protective device. ▶Figure 215–3

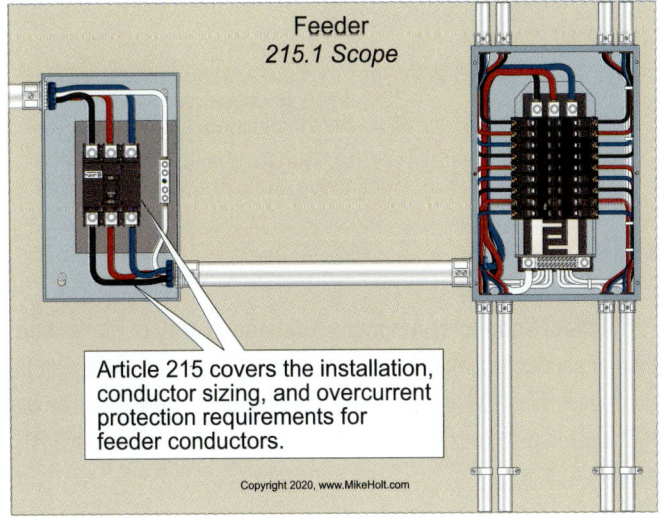

▶Figure 215–2

215.2 | Feeders

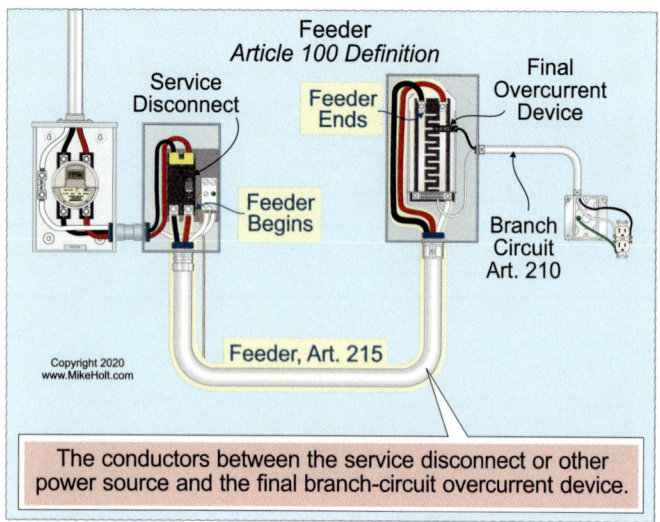
▶Figure 215-3

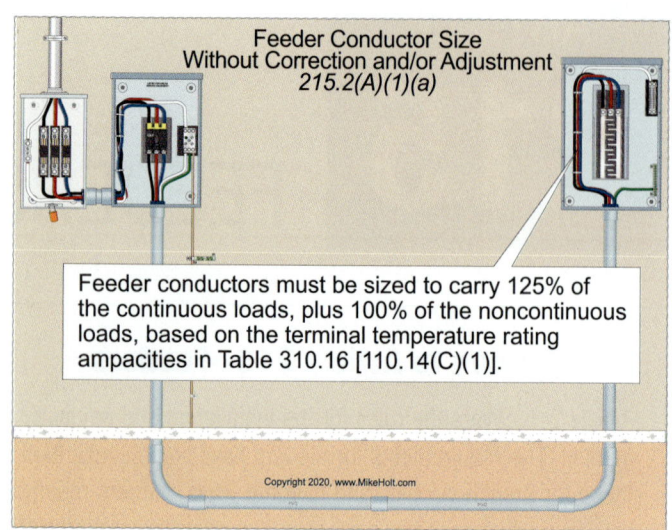
▶Figure 215-5

215.2 Conductor Sizing

(A) Feeders—Sizing

(1) General. Feeder conductors must be sized to carry not less than the largest of the calculations contained in (a) or (b) as follows and meet the equipment termination provisions of 110.14(C). ▶Figure 215-4

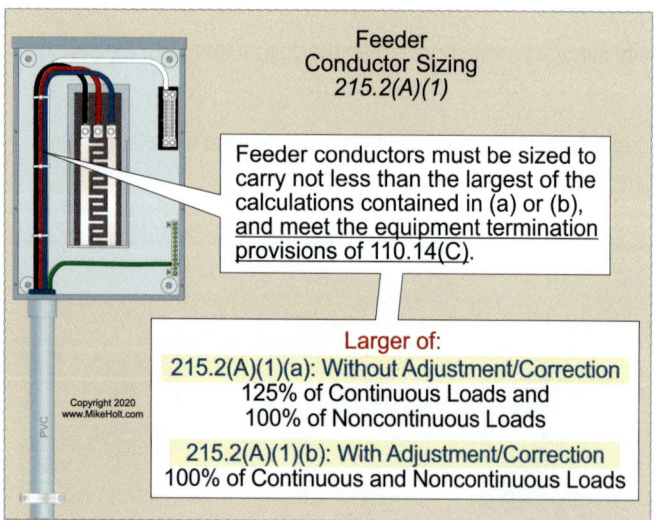
▶Figure 215-4

(a) Without Conductor Ampacity Adjustment and/or Correction. Feeder conductors must be sized to carry 125 percent of the continuous loads, plus 100 percent of the noncontinuous loads, based on the terminal temperature rating ampacities in Table 310.16 [110.14(C)(1)]. ▶Figure 215-5

▶ **Example 1**

Question: What size conductors rated 90°C are required for a feeder supplying a 180A continuous load where the equipment terminals are rated 75°C? ▶Figure 215-6

(a) 3/0 AWG (b) 4/0 AWG (c) 300 kcmil (d) 350 kcmil

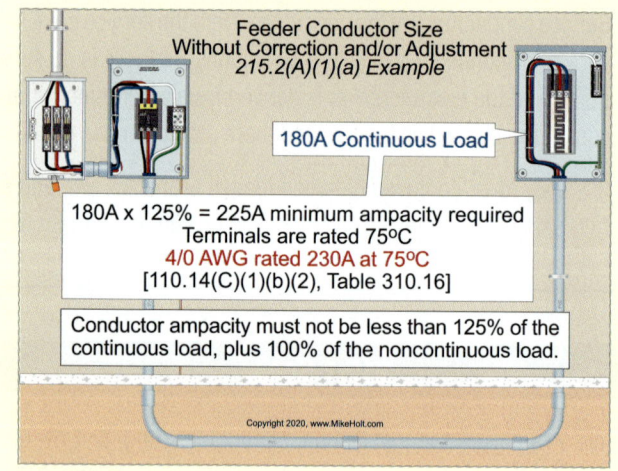
▶Figure 215-6

Solution:

Step 1: *Conductor Ampacity.* The conductor must have an ampacity of at least 225A (180A × 125%).

Step 2: Size the conductors in accordance with 110.14(C)(1)(b)(2) and Table 310.16.

4/0 AWG is rated 230A and is suitable to used [Table 310.16, 75°C column].

Answer: (b) 4/0 AWG

Example 2

Question: What size conductors rated 90°C are required for a feeder installed between the panelboard with 75°C rated terminals and distribution block with 75°C rated terminals supplying a 320A continuous load? ▶Figure 215-7

(a) 300 kcmil   (b) 400 kcmil   (c) 500 kcmil   (d) 600 kcmil

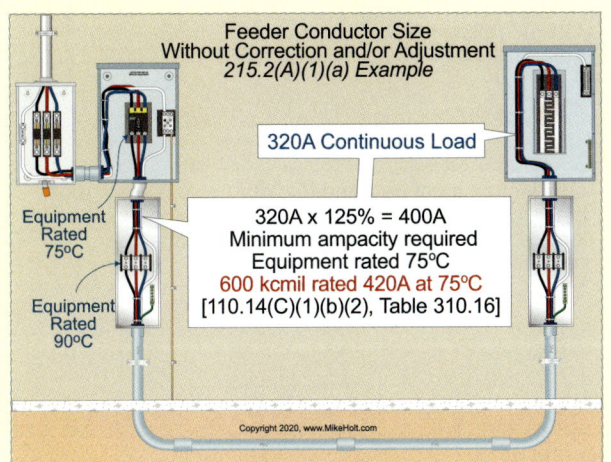
▶Figure 215-7

Solution:

Step 1: *Conductor Ampacity.* The conductor from the panelboard to the distribution block must have an ampacity of at least 400A (320A × 125%).

Step 2: Size the conductors in accordance with 110.14(C)(1)(b)(2) and Table 310.16. Where conductors terminate at terminals with different temperature ratings (such as 75°C and 90°C), the terminals with the lower temperature rating must be used when sizing conductors [110.14(C)]. The 75°C terminals are the lower rated.

600 kcmil is rated 420A and is therefore suitable to used [Table 310.16, 75°C column].

Answer: (d) 600 kcmil

Ex 2: A section of conductors that terminates in a junction box at both ends to 90°C terminals in accordance with 110.14(C)(2) are permitted to have an ampacity of not less than 100 percent of the continuous and 100 percent of the noncontinuous loads, based on the 90°C column of Table 310.16 for 90°C conductor insulation. The 100 percent at 90°C conductors are not permitted to extend into the supply or the load terminations to the circuit. ▶Figure 215-8

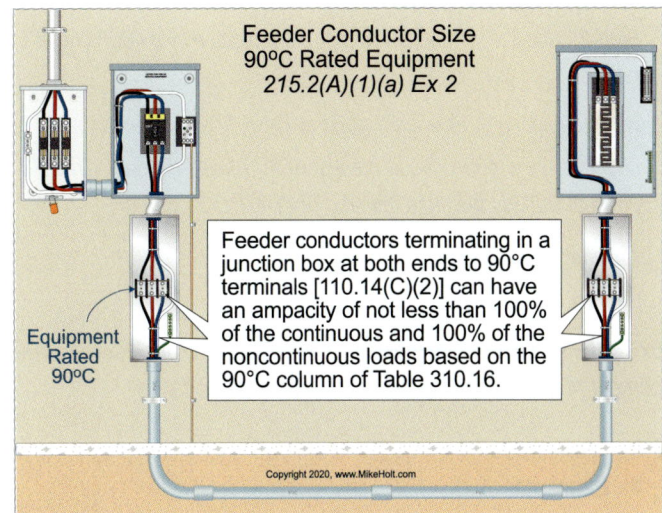
▶Figure 215-8

Example

Question: What size feeder conductors rated 90°C are required between terminals rated 90°C for a circuit supplying a 320A continuous load where the circuit overcurrent protection is 400A? ▶Figure 215-9

(a) 250 kcmil   (b) 300 kcmil   (c) 400 kcmil   (d) 500 kcmil

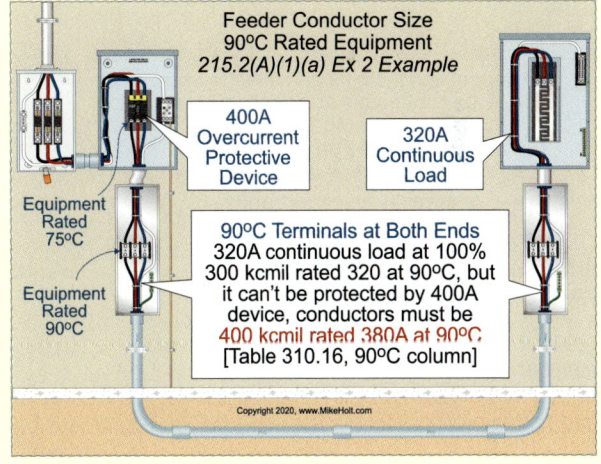
▶Figure 215-9

Solution:

Step 1: Size the conductors between the 90°C terminals to carry 100 percent of the 320A continuous load. When terminals of separately installed connectors at each end of a conductor are rated 90°C, the feeder conductor between the 90°C terminals can be sized to the 90°C column of Table 310.16 [215.2(A)(1)(a) Ex 2].

300 kcmil is rated 320A at 90°C.

215.2 | Feeders

Step 2: Size the conductors so they are protected by a 400A circuit breaker.

A 300 kcmil conductor rated 320A at 90°C is not permitted to be protected by a 400A circuit breaker. A 400 kcmil conductor rated 380A at 90°C is therefore required [240.4(B)].

Answer: (c) 400 kcmil

Ex 3: Neutral conductors must have an ampacity of not less than 100 percent of the continuous and noncontinuous loads.

▶ **Example**

Question: What size neutral conductor rated 90°C is required for a 200A continuous neutral load if the terminals are rated 75°C? ▶Figure 215-10

(a) 3/0 AWG   (b) 4/0 AWG   (c) 250 kcmil   (d) 300 kcmil

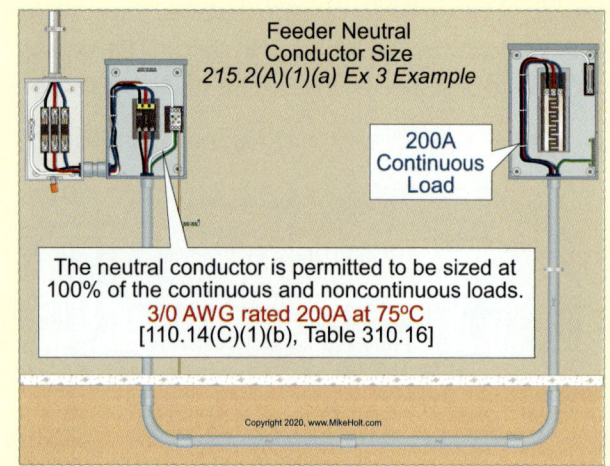

▶Figure 215-10

Solution:

Step 1: The neutral conductor is sized to the 200A continuous load at 100 percent.

Step 2: Size the conductors in accordance with 110.14(C)(1)(b)(2) and Table 310.16.

3/0 has an ampacity of 200A [Table 310.16, 75°C column].

Answer: (a) 3/0 AWG [110.14(C)(1)(b)]

(b) With Conductor Ampacity Adjustment and Correction. Conductors must be sized to carry not less than 100 percent of the continuous load, plus 100 percent of the noncontinuous load after conductor ampacity adjustment and/or correction in accordance with 310.14. ▶Figure 215-11

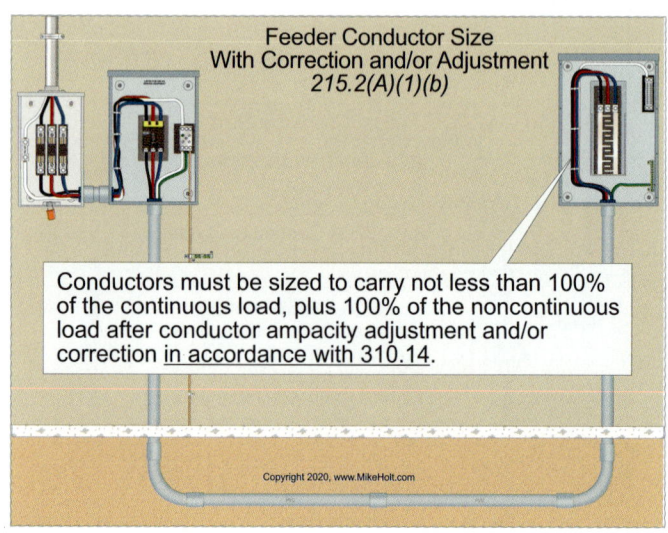

▶Figure 215-11

▶ **Example 1**

Question: What size conductors rated 90°C are required for a feeder containing four current-carrying conductors supplying a 180A continuous load in an ambient temperature of 100°F where the equipment terminals are rated 75°C? ▶Figure 215-12

(a) 4/0 AWG   (b) 300 kcmil   (c) 500 kcmil   (d) 600 kcmil

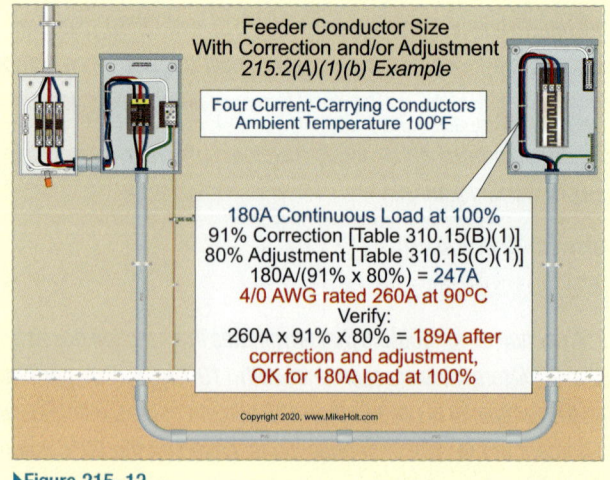

▶Figure 215-12

Author's Comment:

▶ According to 215.2(A)(1), the feeder conductor size is determined by the larger of 215.2(A)(1)(a) and (b).

Solution:

Step 1: The circuit conductors must have an ampacity of not less than 180A after conductor ampacity temperature correction [Table 310.15(B)(1)] and adjustment [Table 310.15(C)(1)], based on the conductor's insulation rating of 90°C. One way to find the conductor size is to determine the conductor ampacity required to supply a 180A continuous load at 100% after correction and adjustment.

Conductor Ampacity at 90°C = Continuous Load at 100%/ (Correction × Adjustment)

Continuous Load = 180A

Correction [Table 310.15(B)(1)] = 91% (100°F with 90°C Conductor)

Adjustment [Table 310.15(C)(1)] = 80% (four current-carrying conductors)

Conductor Ampacity at 90°C Column = 180A/(91% × 80%)
Conductor Ampacity at 90°C Column = 180A/73%
Conductor Ampacity at 90°C Column = 247A

Step 2: Select the conductors from the 90°C column of Table 310.16 [110.14(C)(1)(b)(2)].

4/0 AWG is suitable because it has an ampacity of 260A at 90°C before any correction and adjustment.

Step 3: Verify that the ampacity of 4/0 AWG after correction and adjustment is capable of carrying 100 percent of the 180A continuous load at 90°C.

Conductor Ampacity after Correction and Adjustment = Conductor Ampacity × Correction × Adjustment

Conductor Ampacity at 90°C = 260A* (*Note: 260A is from Step 2.)
Correction = 91%
Adjustment = 80%

Conductor Ampacity after Correction and Adjustment = 260A × 91% × 80%
Conductor Ampacity after Correction and Adjustment = 189A

4/0 with 90°C insulation has an ampere rating of 189A which is more than enough for the 180A continuous load.

Step 4: Verify that the ampacity of 4/0 AWG at 75°C without correction and adjustment is capable of carrying the 180A continuous load at 125 percent in accordance with 215.2(A)(1)(a).

Conductor Ampacity at 125% = 180A × 125%
Conductor Ampacity at 125% = 225A

4/0 AWG is suitable because it is rated 230A at 75°C [Table 310.16].

Answer: (a) 4/0 AWG

▶ **Example 2**

Question: What size conductors rated 90°C are required for a feeder containing four current-carrying conductors supplying a 320A continuous load in an ambient temperature of 100°F where the equipment terminals are rated 75°C? ▶Figure 215–13

(a) 300 kcmil (b) 400 kcmil (c) 500 kcmil (d) 600 kcmil

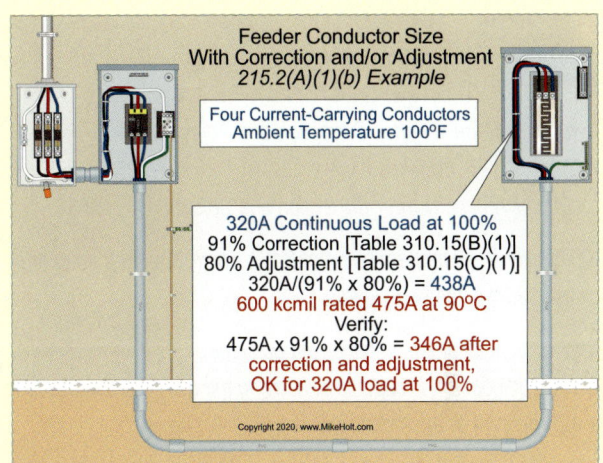

▶Figure 215–13

Solution:

Step 1: The circuit conductors must have an ampacity of not less than 320A after conductor ampacity temperature correction [Table 310.15(B)(1)] and adjustment [Table 310.15(C)(1)], based on the conductor insulation rating of 90°C. One way to find the conductor size is to determine the conductor ampacity required to supply a 320A continuous load at 100% after correction and adjustment.

Conductor Ampacity at 90°C = Continuous Load at 100%/ (Correction × Adjustment)

Continuous Load = 320A

Correction [Table 310.15(B)(1)] = 91% (100°F with 90°C Conductor)

Adjustment [Table 310.15(C)(1)] = 80% (four current-carrying conductors)

Conductor Ampacity at 90°C Column = 320A/(91% × 80%)
Conductor Ampacity at 90°C Column = 320A/73%
Conductor Ampacity at 90°C Column = 438A

Step 2: Select the conductor from the 90°C column of Table 310.16.

600 kcmil is suitable because it has an ampacity of 475A at 90°C before any correction and adjustment.

215.3 | Feeders

Step 3: Verify that the ampacity of 600 kcmil after correction and adjustment is capable of carrying 100 percent of the 320A continuous load at 90°C.

Conductor Ampacity after Correction and Adjustment =
Conductor Ampacity × Correction × Adjustment

Conductor Ampacity at 90°C = 475A*
(*Note: 475A is from Step 2.)
Correction = 91%
Adjustment = 80%

Conductor Ampacity after Correction and Adjustment =
475A × 91% × 80%
Conductor Ampacity after Correction and Adjustment = 346A

600 kcmil has an ampere rating of 346A which is more than enough for the 320A continuous load.

Step 4: Verify that the ampacity of 600 kcmil at 75°C without correction and adjustment is capable of carrying the 320A continuous load at 125 percent in accordance with 215.2(A)(1)(a).

Conductor Ampacity at 125% = 320A × 125%
Conductor Ampacity at 125% = 400A

600 kcmil is suitable because it is rated 420A at 75°C [Table 310.16].

Answer: (d) 600 kcmil

Note 2: To provide reasonable efficiency of operation of electrical equipment, feeder conductors should be sized to prevent a voltage drop from exceeding 3 percent. In addition, the total voltage drop on both feeders and branch circuits should not exceed 5 percent.

Note 3: See 210.19(A) Note 3 for voltage drop for branch circuits.

(2) Neutral Conductor Size. The neutral conductor must be sized to carry the maximum unbalanced load in accordance with 220.61 and is not permitted to be smaller than contained in 250.122, based on the rating of the feeder overcurrent protective device.

▶ **Example**

Question: What size neutral conductor is required for a feeder consisting of 250 kcmil phase conductors and one neutral conductor protected by a 250A overcurrent protective device, where the unbalanced load is 50A with 75°C terminals? ▶Figure 215-14

(a) 8 AWG   (b) 6 AWG   (c) 4 AWG   (d) 2 AWG

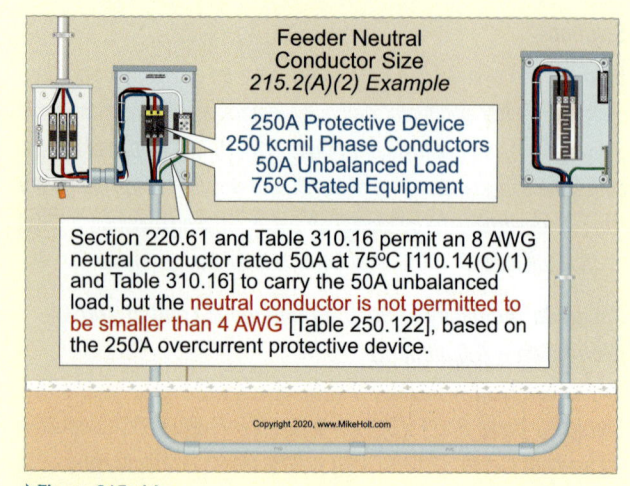

▶Figure 215-14

Solution:

Section 220.61 and Table 310.16 permit an 8 AWG neutral conductor rated 50A at 75°C [110.14(C)(1) and Table 310.16] to carry the 50A unbalanced load, but the neutral conductor is not permitted to be smaller than 4 AWG [Table 250.122], based on the 250A overcurrent protective device.

Answer: (c) 4 AWG

215.3 Overcurrent Protection Sizing

Feeder overcurrent protective devices must have a rating of not less than 125 percent of the continuous loads, plus 100 percent of the noncontinuous loads.

▶ **Example**

Question: What size feeder overcurrent protection is required for a 100A continuous load and a 100A noncontinuous load? ▶Figure 215-15

(a) 200A   (b) 225A   (c) 250A   (d) 300A

Solution:

100A Continuous Load × 125% + 100A Noncontinuous Load = 225A [240.6(A)]

Answer: (b) 225A

Feeders | 215.12

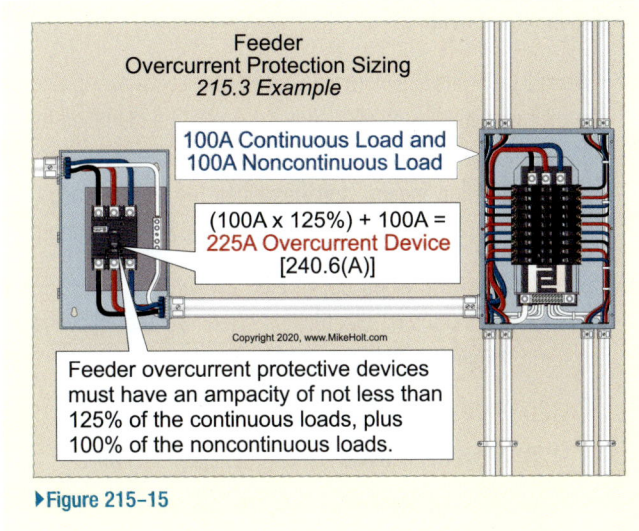
▶Figure 215-15

215.12 Conductor Identification

(A) Neutral Conductor. The feeder neutral conductor must be identified in accordance with 200.6.

(B) Equipment Grounding Conductor. Equipment grounding conductors can be bare, covered, or insulated. Insulated equipment grounding conductors 6 AWG and smaller must have a continuous outer finish either green or green with one or more yellow stripes [250.119]. ▶Figure 215-17

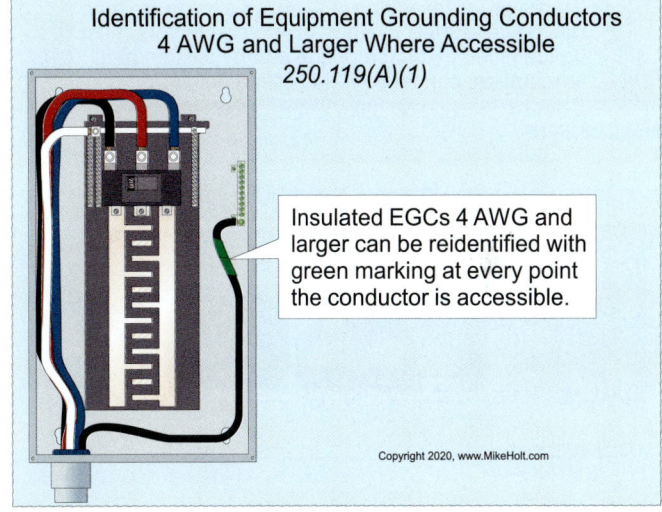
▶Figure 215-17

Ex 1: Where the assembly, including the overcurrent devices protecting the feeder(s), is listed for operation at 100 percent of its rating, the ampere rating of the overcurrent device can be sized at 100 percent of the continuous and noncontinuous loads. ▶Figure 215-16

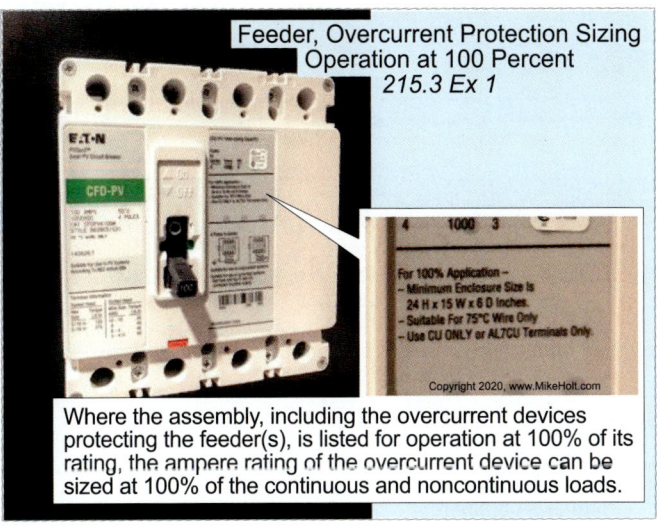
▶Figure 215-16

Insulated equipment grounding conductors 4 AWG and larger can be permanently reidentified with green marking at the time of installation where accessible [250.119(A)].

(C) Identification of Phase Conductors. Circuit phase conductors must be identified as follows:

(1) More Than One Voltage Distribution System. Where premises wiring is supplied from more than one power-supply system, phase conductors must be identified by phase or line and by system at all termination, connection, and splice points as follows: ▶Figure 215-18

(a) Means of Identification. Identification of the phase conductors can be by color coding, marking tape, tagging, or other means approved by the authority having jurisdiction. ▶Figure 215-19

(b) Posting of Identification. The method of identification must be readily available or permanently posted at each branch-circuit panelboard, not be handwritten, and be of sufficiently durable to withstand the environment involved. ▶Figure 215-20

215.10 Ground-Fault Protection of Equipment

Each feeder disconnect rated 1,000A or more supplied by a 4-wire, three-phase, 277/480V wye-connected system must be provided with ground-fault protection of equipment in accordance with 230.95 and 240.13.

215.12 | Feeders

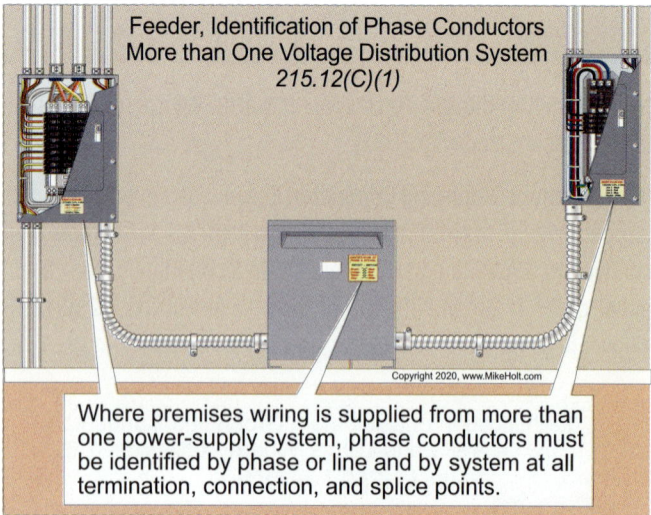

▶Figure 215–18

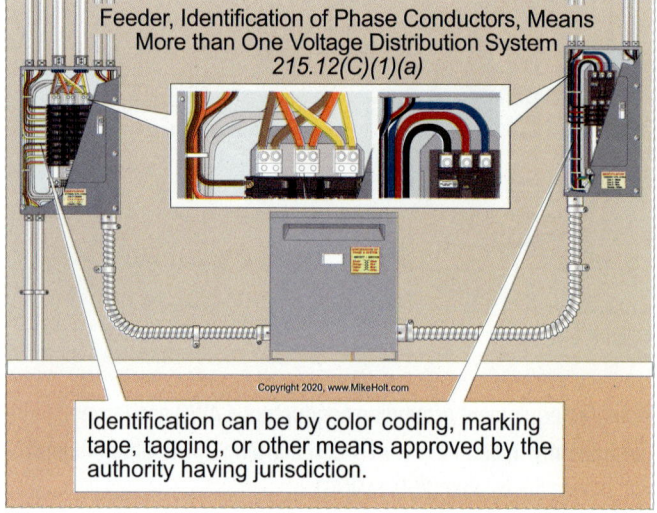

▶Figure 215–19

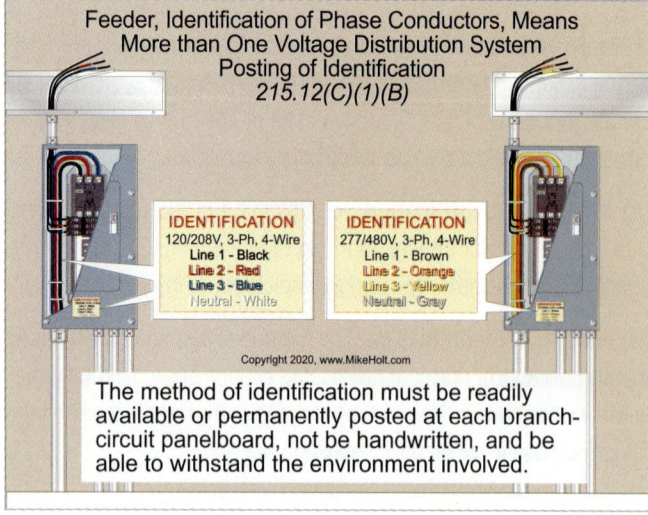

▶Figure 215–20

Author's Comment:

▸ When a premises has more than one voltage system supplying branch circuits, the phase conductors must be identified by phase and system. This can be done by permanently posting an identification legend that describes the method used, such as color-coded marking tape or color-coded insulation.

▸ Although the *NEC* does not require a specific color code for phase conductors, electricians often use the following system: ▶Figure 215–21

  ▸ 120/240V, single-phase—black, red, and white
  ▸ 120/208V, three-phase—black, red, blue, and white
  ▸ 120/240V, three-phase—black, orange, blue, and white
  ▸ 277/480V, three-phase—brown, orange, yellow, and gray; or, brown, purple, yellow, and gray

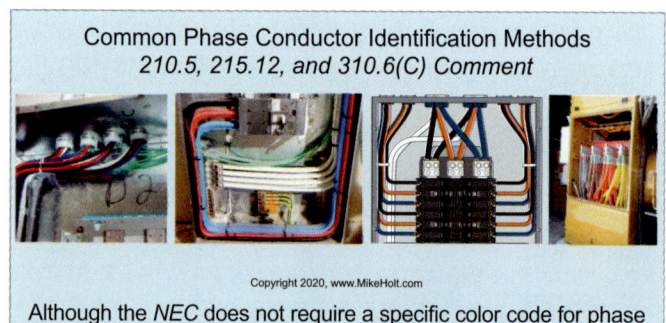

▶Figure 215–21

Author's Comment:

▸ Whichever color scheme is used, it is important for it to remain consistent wherever phase conductors are terminated or accessible throughout the entire premises. This is especially important when identifying different system voltages and neutrals.

98 | Mike Holt Enterprises | *2020 NEC Requirements for Solar PV and Energy Storage Systems*

ARTICLE 225 — OUTSIDE BRANCH CIRCUITS AND FEEDERS

Introduction to Article 225—Outside Branch Circuits and Feeders

This article covers the installation requirements for equipment, including overhead and underground branch-circuit and feeder conductors located outdoors on or between buildings, poles, and other structures on the premises. Conductors installed outdoors can serve many purposes such as area lighting, power for outdoor equipment, or for providing power to separate buildings or structures. It is important to remember that the power supply for buildings is not always a service conductor but may be feeder or branch-circuit conductors originating in another building. Never just assume that the conductors supplying power to a building are service conductors until you have identified where the service point is [Article 100] and reviewed the Article 100 definitions for feeders, branch circuits, and service conductors. If you have correctly determined the conductors are service conductors, then use Article 230.

Part II of this article limits the number of feeders plus branch circuits to a building and provides rules regarding their disconnects. These requirements include the disconnect rating, construction characteristics, labeling, where to locate the disconnect, and the grouping of multiple disconnects.

Part I. General

225.1 Scope

Article 225 contains the installation requirements for outside branch circuits and feeders installed on or between buildings, structures, or poles. ▶Figure 225–1

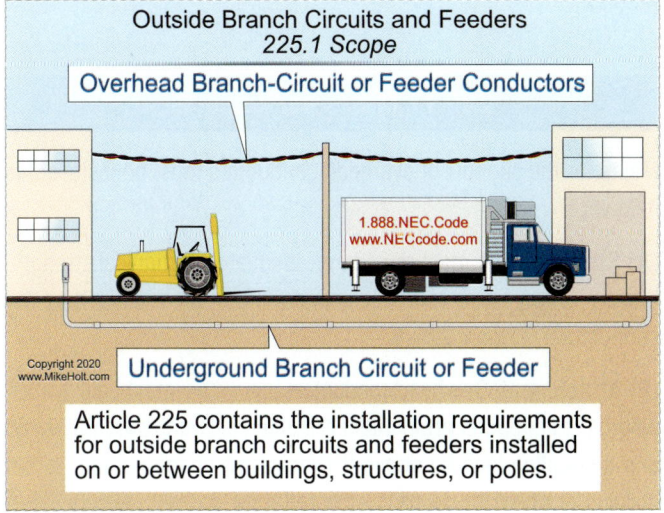

▶Figure 225–1

Author's Comment:

▸ Review the following in Article 100:
  ▸ "Branch Circuit"
  ▸ "Building"
  ▸ "Feeder"
  ▸ "Structure"

225.6 Minimum Conductor Size and Support

(A) Overhead Spans

(1) Conductor Size. Conductors 10 AWG and larger are permitted for overhead spans up to 50 ft long. For spans over 50 ft, the minimum size conductor is 8 AWG, unless supported by a messenger wire. ▶Figure 225–2

(B) Festoon Lighting. Overhead conductors for festoon lighting are not permitted to be smaller than 12 AWG and must be supported by messenger wire (with strain insulators) whenever the spans exceed 40 ft in length. ▶Figure 225–3

225.16 | Outside Branch Circuits and Feeders

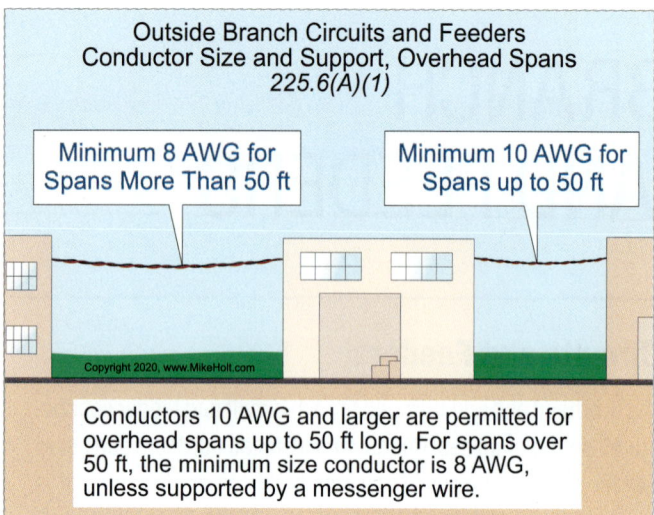

▶Figure 225-2

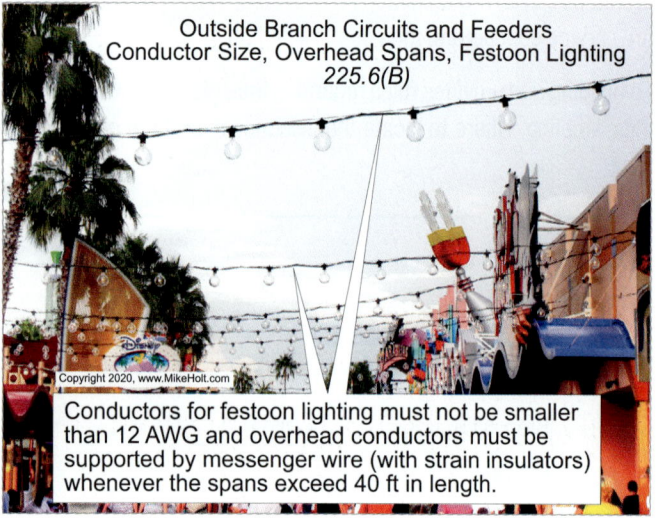

▶Figure 225-3

Author's Comment:

▸ According to Article 100 "Festoon Lighting" is a string of outdoor lights suspended between two points. Festoon lighting is commonly used at carnivals, circuses, fairs, Christmas tree lots [525.20(C)], and as temporary lighting at construction sites [590.4(F)].

225.16 Attachment of Overhead Conductors

(A) Point of Attachment. The point of attachment for overhead conductors must not be less than 10 ft above the finished grade [230.26]. ▶Figure 225-4

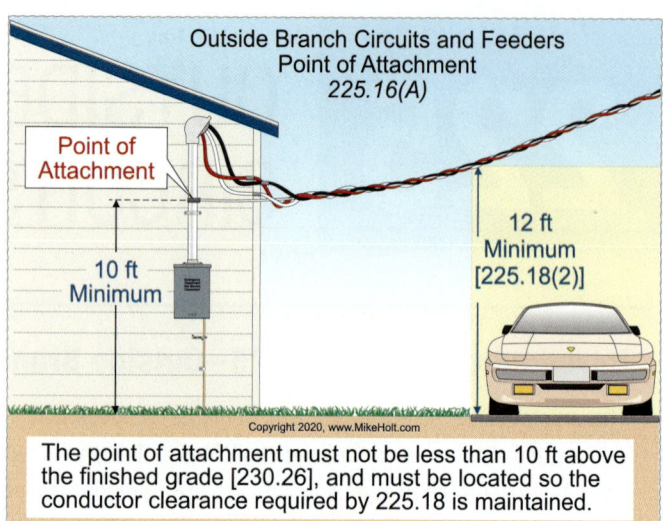

▶Figure 225-4

Author's Comment:

▸ The point of attachment must also be located so the minimum conductor clearances required by 225.18 can be maintained.

> **Caution**
> Conductors might need to have the point of attachment raised so the overhead conductors will comply with the clearances from building openings and other building areas required by 225.19.

(B) Means of Attachment to Buildings. Open conductors must be attached to fittings identified for use with conductors or to noncombustible, nonabsorbent insulators securely attached to the building [230.27].

225.17 Masts as Supports

Masts for the support of overhead conductors must be installed as follows:

(A) Strength. The mast must have adequate mechanical strength, braces, or guy wires to safely withstand the strain caused by the conductors. ▶Figure 225-5

(B) Attachment. Overhead conductors cannot be attached to a mast where the conductor attachment is located between a weatherhead and a coupling located above the last point of securement to the building, or where the coupling is located above the roof. ▶Figure 225-6

Outside Branch Circuits and Feeders | 225.18

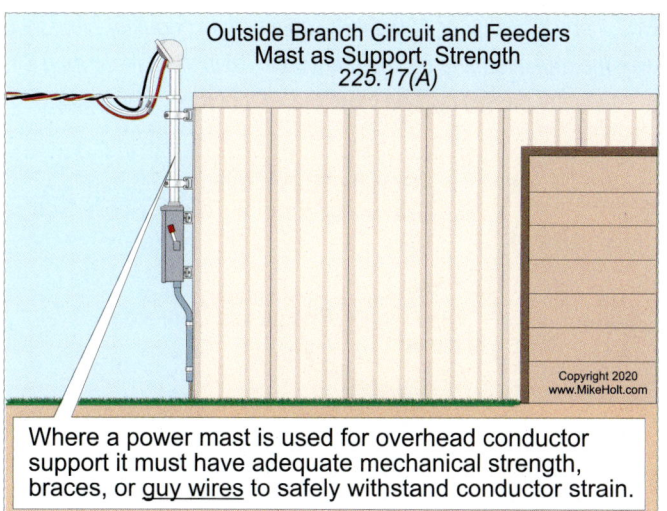
▶Figure 225-5

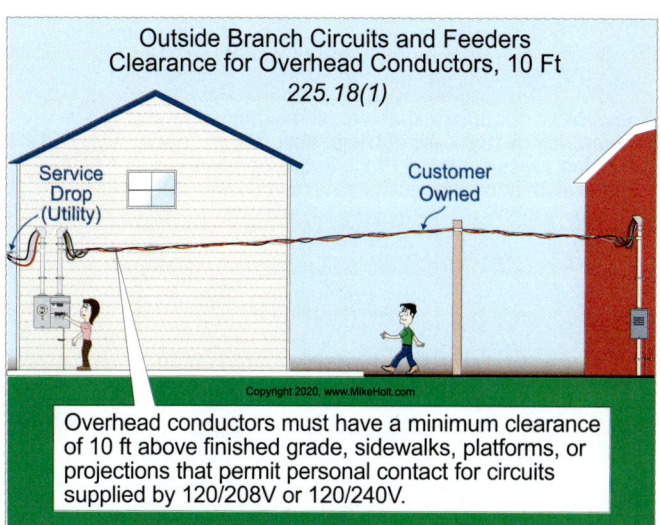
▶Figure 225-7

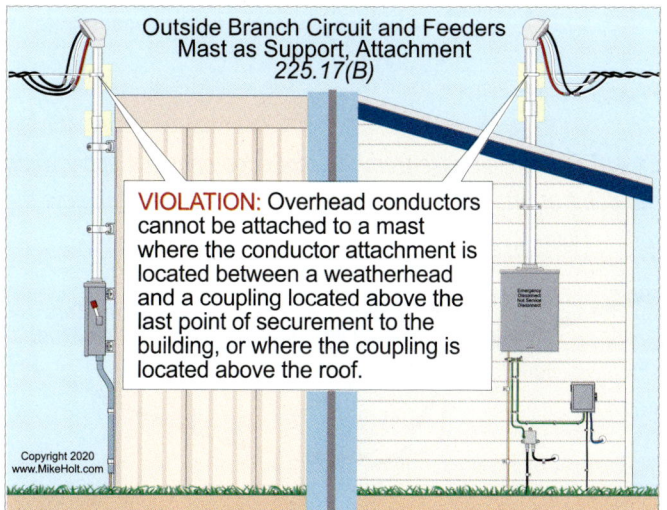
▶Figure 225-6

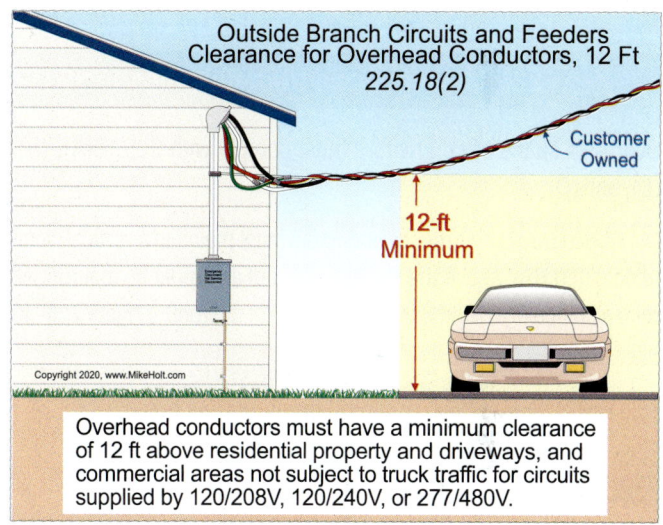
▶Figure 225-8

225.18 Clearance for Overhead Conductors

Overhead conductor spans must maintain vertical clearances of:

(1) 10 ft above finished grade, sidewalks, platforms, or projections that permit personal contact for circuits supplied by 120/208V or 120/240V. ▶Figure 225-7

(2) 12 ft above residential property and driveways, and commercial areas not subject to truck traffic for circuits supplied by 120/208V, 120/240V, or 277V/480V. ▶Figure 225-8

(3) 15 ft above residential property and driveways, and commercial areas not subject to truck traffic for circuits supplied by a system having a voltage exceeding 300V to ground.

(4) 18 ft over public streets, alleys, roads, parking areas subject to truck traffic, driveways on other than residential property, and other areas traversed by vehicles such as those used for cultivation, grazing, forestry, and orchards. ▶Figure 225-9

Author's Comment:

▶ Overhead conductors located above pools, outdoor spas, outdoor hot tubs, diving structures, observation stands, towers, or platforms must be installed in accordance with the clearance requirements in 680.9.

225.19 | Outside Branch Circuits and Feeders

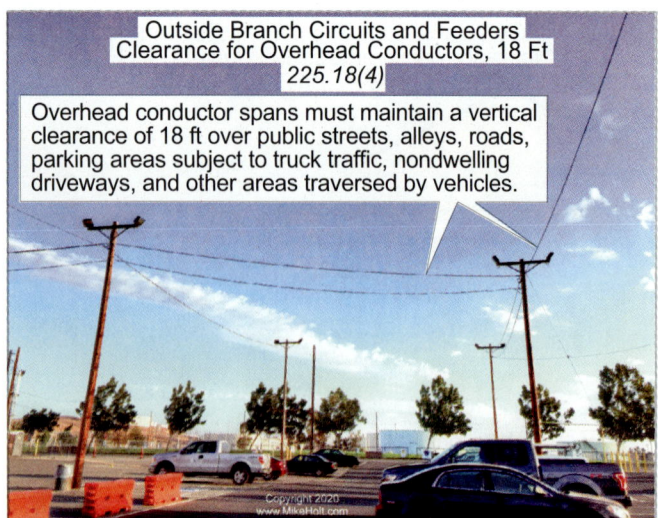

▶Figure 225–9

225.19 Clearances from Buildings

Overhead spans of conductors must comply with 225.19(A), (B), (C), and (D).

(A) Above Roofs. Overhead conductors must maintain a vertical clearance of 8 ft 6 in. above the surface of a roof and must be maintained for a distance of at least 3 ft from the edge of the roof. ▶Figure 225–10

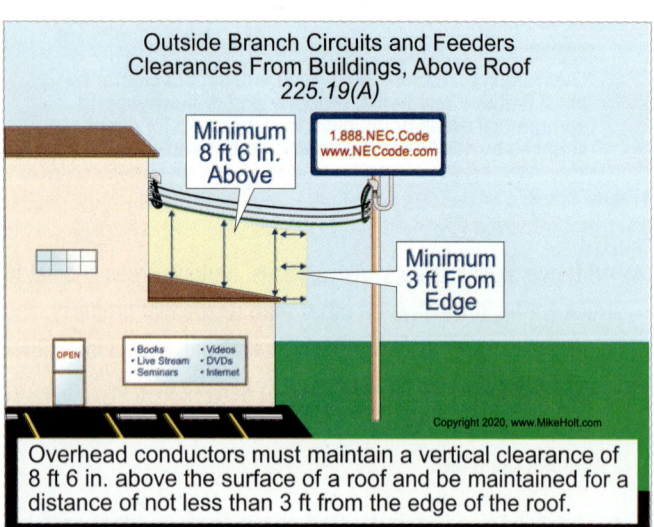

▶Figure 225–10

Ex 2: The overhead conductor clearances from the roof can be reduced to 3 ft if the slope of the roof meets or exceeds 4 in. of vertical rise for every 12 in. of horizontal run.

Ex 3: For 120/208V or 120/240V circuits, the conductor clearance over the roof overhang can be reduced to 18 in. if no more than 6 ft of conductor passes over no more than 4 ft of roof. ▶Figure 225–11

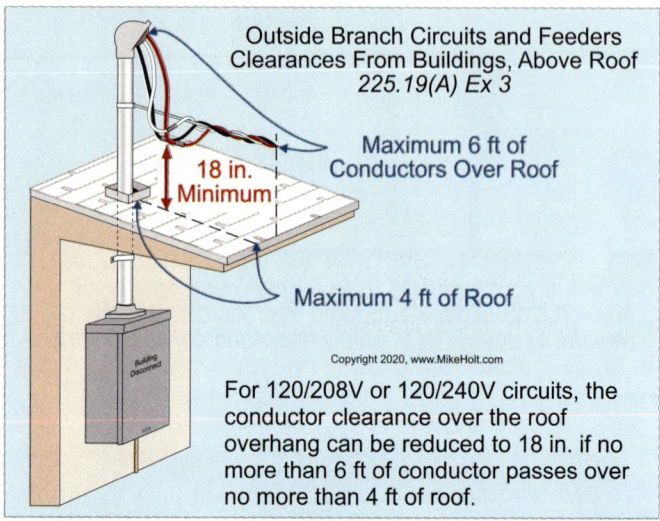

▶Figure 225–11

Ex 4: The 3-ft clearance from the roof edge does not apply when the point of attachment is on the side of the building below the roof. ▶Figure 225–12

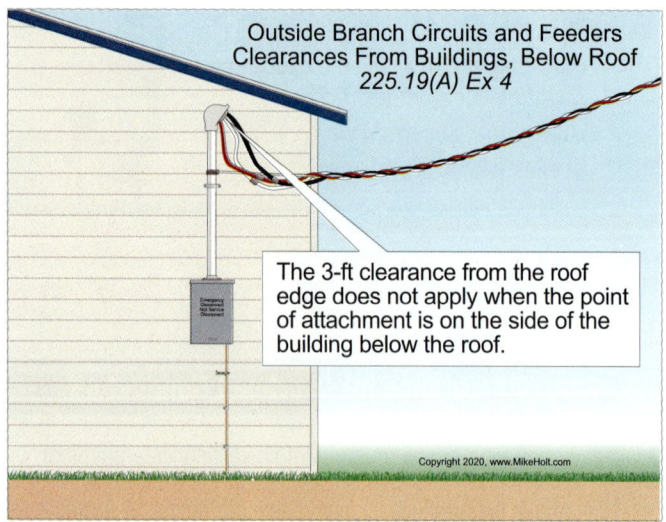

▶Figure 225–12

(B) From Other Structures. Overhead conductors must maintain a clearance of at least 3 ft from signs, chimneys, radio and television antennas, tanks, and other nonbuilding structures.

(D) Final Span Clearance

(1) Clearance from Windows. Overhead conductors must maintain a clearance of 3 ft from windows that open, doors, porches, balconies, ladders, stairs, fire escapes, or similar locations. ▶Figure 225–13

Outside Branch Circuits and Feeders | 225.26

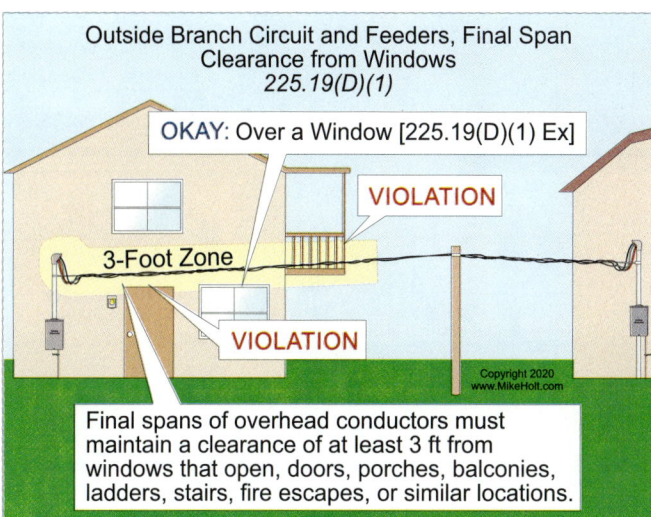
▶Figure 225-13

Ex: Overhead conductors installed above a window are not required to maintain the 3-ft distance from the window.

(2) Vertical Clearance. Overhead conductors must maintain a vertical clearance of at least 10 ft above platforms, projections, or surfaces that permit personal contact in accordance with 225.18. This vertical clearance must be maintained for 3 ft measured horizontally from the platforms, projections, or surfaces from which they might be reached.

(3) Below Openings. Overhead conductors are not permitted to be installed under an opening through which materials might pass, and they must not be installed where they will obstruct an entrance to these openings. ▶Figure 225-14

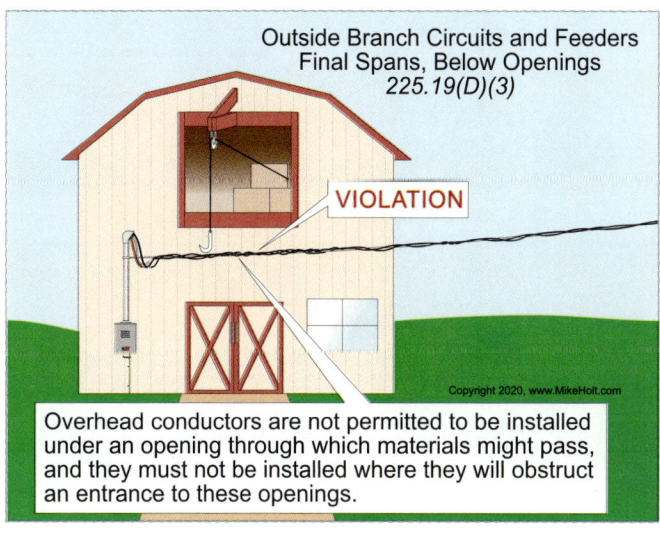
▶Figure 225-14

225.22 Raceways on Exterior Surfaces of Buildings or Other Structures

Raceways on exteriors of buildings or other structures must be arranged to drain <u>and be listed or approved for use in wet locations</u>. ▶Figure 225-15

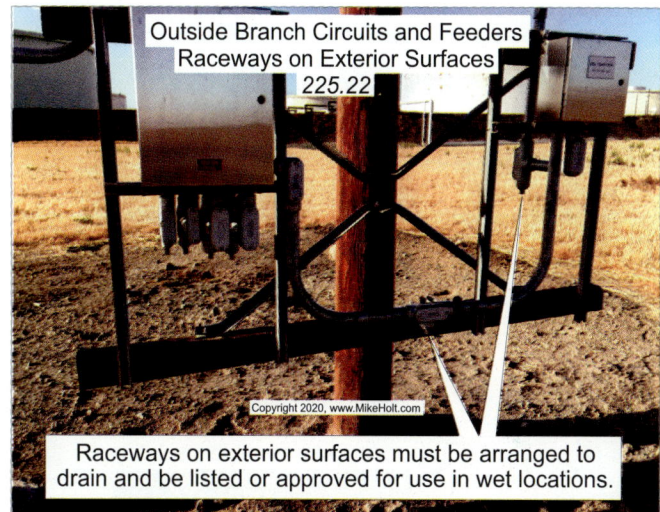
▶Figure 225-15

225.26 Trees for Conductor Support

Trees and other vegetation must not be used for the support of overhead conductor spans. ▶Figure 225-16

▶Figure 225-16

225.27 | Outside Branch Circuits and Feeders

Author's Comment:

▸ Overhead conductor spans for services [230.10] and temporary wiring [590.4(J)] are not permitted to be supported by vegetation.

225.27 Raceway Seals

Raceways (used or unused) entering buildings from outside must be sealed with a sealant identified for use with the conductor or cable insulation. ▸Figure 225-17

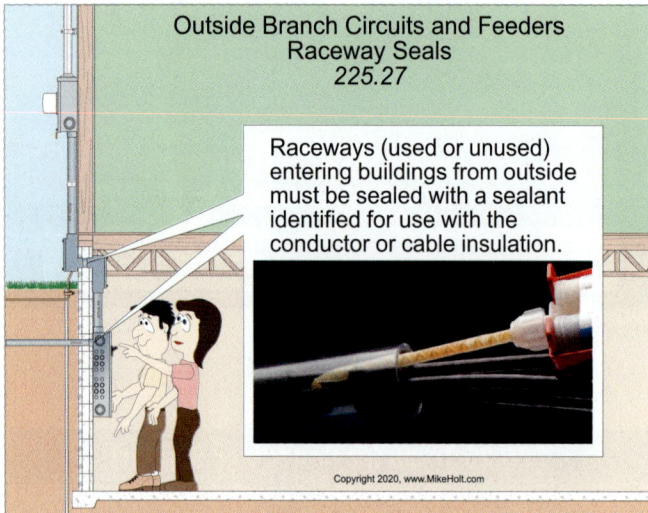

▸Figure 225-17

Part II. Buildings or Other Structures Supplied by a Feeder

225.30 Number of Supplies

A building can only be supplied by a single feeder unless otherwise permitted in 225.30(A) through (E). ▸Figure 225-18

(A) Special Conditions. Additional feeders are permitted to supply:

(1) Fire pumps.

(2) Emergency systems.

(3) Legally required standby systems.

(4) Optional standby systems.

(5) Parallel power production sources.

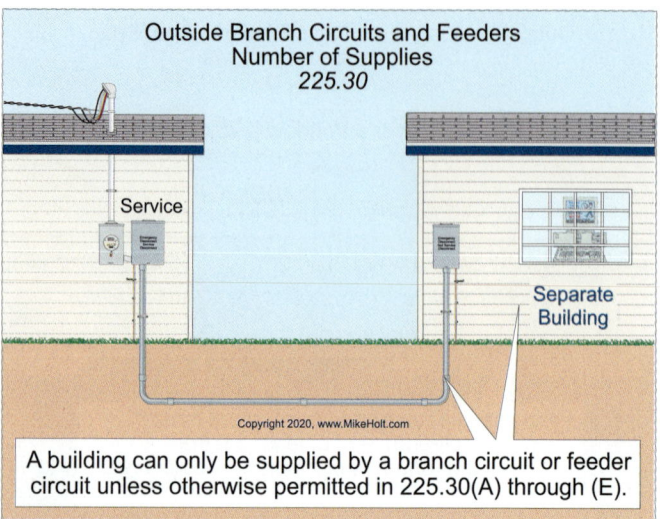

▸Figure 225-18

(6) Systems designed for connection to multiple sources of supply for the purpose of enhanced reliability.

(7) Electric vehicle charging systems listed, labeled, and identified for more than a single branch circuit or feeder.

(8) Docking facilities and piers.

(B) Common Supply Equipment. Where feeder conductors originate in the same panelboard, switchboard, or other distribution equipment, and each one terminates in a single disconnecting means, not more than six feeders are permitted. ▸Figure 225-19

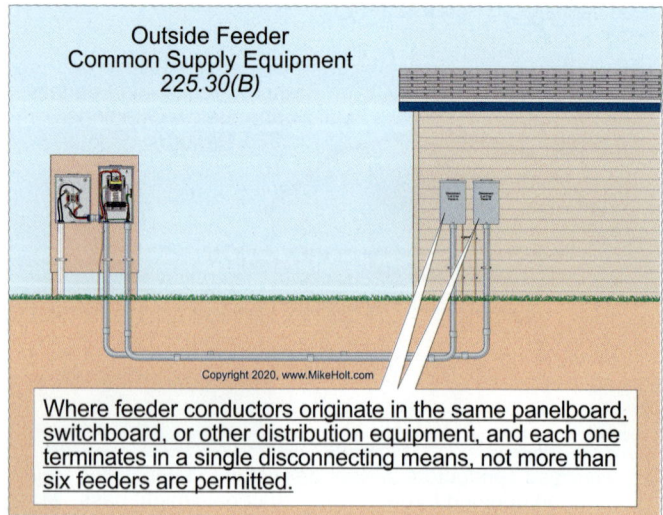

▸Figure 225-19

Where more than one feeder is installed, all feeder disconnects supplying the building must be grouped in the same location. Each disconnect must be marked to indicate the load served.

Outside Branch Circuits and Feeders | 225.33

(C) Special Occupancies. By special permission, additional feeders are permitted for:

(1) Multiple-occupancy buildings where there is no available space for supply equipment accessible to all occupants, or

(2) A building so large that two or more supplies are necessary.

(D) Capacity Requirements. Additional supplies are permitted for a building where the capacity requirements exceed 2,000A.

(E) Different Characteristics. Additional supplies are permitted for different voltages, frequencies, or uses, such as controlling outside lighting from multiple locations.

(F) Documented Switching Procedures. Additional supplies are permitted where documented safe switching procedures are established and maintained for disconnection.

225.31 Disconnecting Means

A disconnect is required for all feeder conductors that enter a building.
▶Figure 225–20

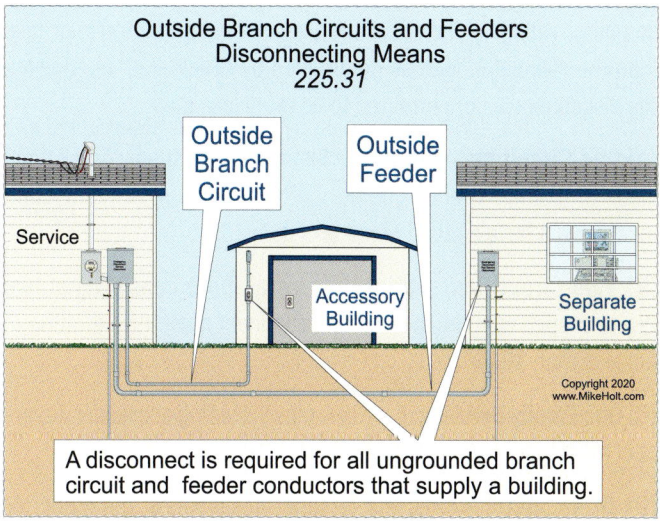
▶Figure 225–20

225.32 Disconnecting Means Location

The feeder disconnect must be installed at a readily accessible location either outside or inside nearest the point of entrance of the conductors.
▶Figure 225–21

Feeder conductors are considered outside a building where they are encased or installed under not less than 2 in. of concrete or brick [230.6].
▶Figure 225–22

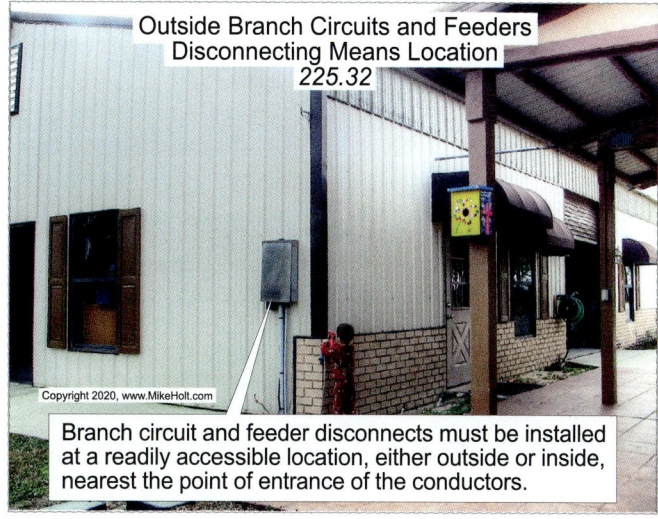
▶Figure 225–21

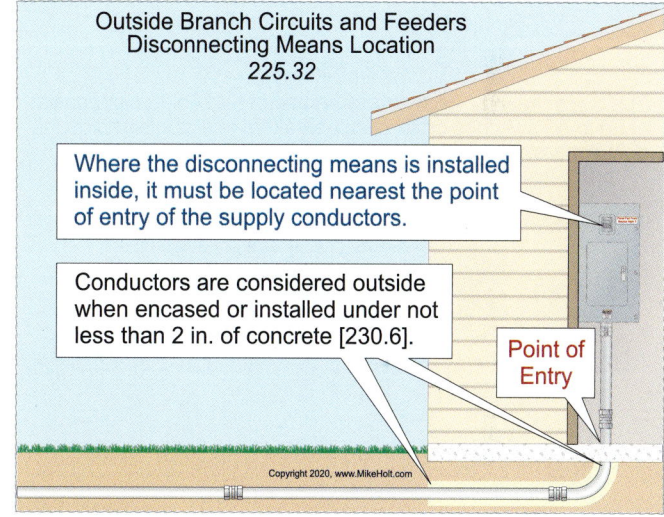
▶Figure 225–22

Ex 3: A disconnect is not required for poles that support luminaires.
▶Figure 225–23

225.33 Maximum Number of Disconnects

(A) General. The disconnecting means for each supply permitted by 225.30 can consist of no more than six switches or six circuit breakers in a single enclosure, or in separate enclosures grouped in one location [225.34]. ▶Figure 225–24

225.34 | Outside Branch Circuits and Feeders

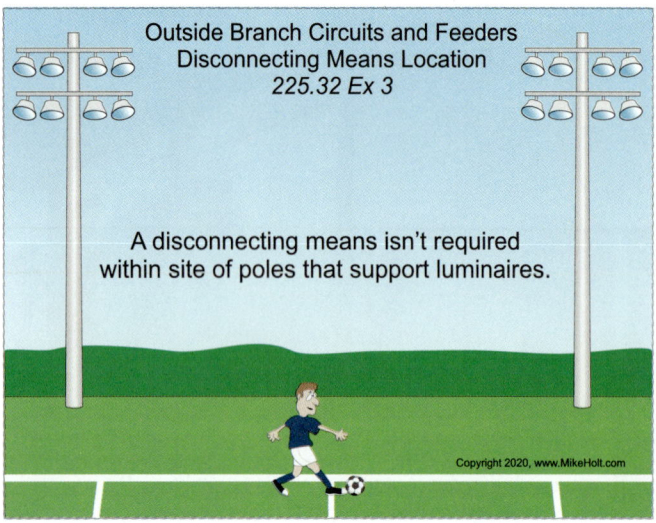

▶Figure 225–23

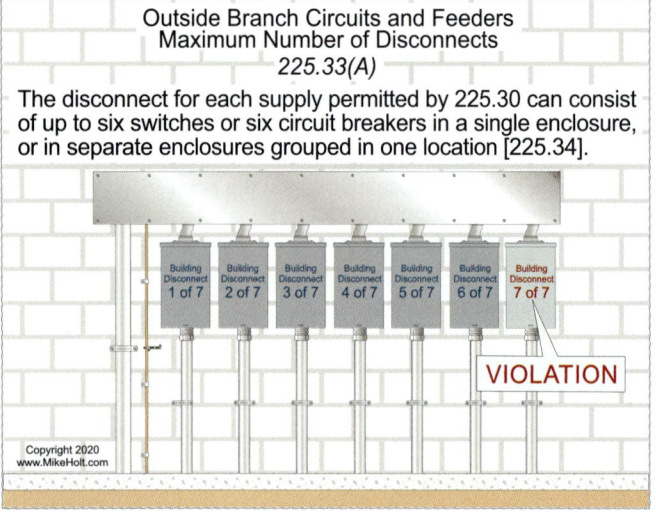

▶Figure 225–24

225.34 Grouping of Disconnects

(A) General. The building disconnects must be grouped in one location and marked to indicate the loads they serve [110.22].

(B) Additional Disconnects. To minimize the possibility of accidental interruption of critical power systems, the disconnect for a fire pump or for standby power must be located remotely from the normal power disconnect.

225.37 Identification of Multiple Supplies

If a building is fed by more than one supply, a permanent plaque or directory must be installed at each feeder disconnect location denoting all other feeders supplying that building, and the area served by each.

225.39 Rating of Disconnecting Means

A single disconnect for a building must have an ampere rating of not less than the calculated load as determined by Article 220. If the disconnect consists of more than one switch or circuit breaker, the combined ratings of the circuit breakers are not permitted to be less than the calculated load as determined by Article 220. In addition, the disconnect is not permitted to be rated less than:

(A) One-Circuit Installation. For installations to supply only limited loads of a single branch circuit, the branch-circuit disconnecting means must have a rating of not less than 15A.

(B) Two-Circuit Installation. For installations consisting of two 2-wire branch circuits, the feeder disconnect must have a rating of not less than 30A.

(C) One-Family Dwelling. For a one-family dwelling, the feeder disconnect must have a rating of not less than 100A, 3-wire.

(D) Other Installations. For all other installations, the feeder or branch-circuit disconnect must have a rating of not less than 60A.

ARTICLE 230 SERVICES

Introduction to Article 230—Services

This article covers the installation requirements for service conductors and their first means of disconnect. The requirements for service conductors differ from those for other conductors. For one thing, service conductors for one building cannot pass through the interior of another [230.3], and different rules are applied depending on whether a service conductor is inside or outside a building. When are they "outside" as opposed to "inside"? The answer may seem obvious, but 230.6 will help you determine when (and if) service conductors are considered to be outside. Article 230 consists of seven parts:

- Part I. General
- Part II. Overhead Service Conductors
- Part III. Underground Service Conductors
- Part IV. Service-Entrance Conductors
- Part V. Service Disconnect
- Part VI. Disconnecting Means
- Part VII. Overcurrent Protection

Part I. General

230.1 Scope

Article 230 covers the installation requirements for service conductors and service disconnects. ▶Figure 230-1

Author's Comment:

▶ The "Service Point" [Article 100] determines where the utility ends and the *NEC* requirements for a service begins. The electric utility typically determines the service point. Understanding the Article 100 definitions related to service disconnects and conductors are critical for understanding Article 230. ▶Figure 230-2

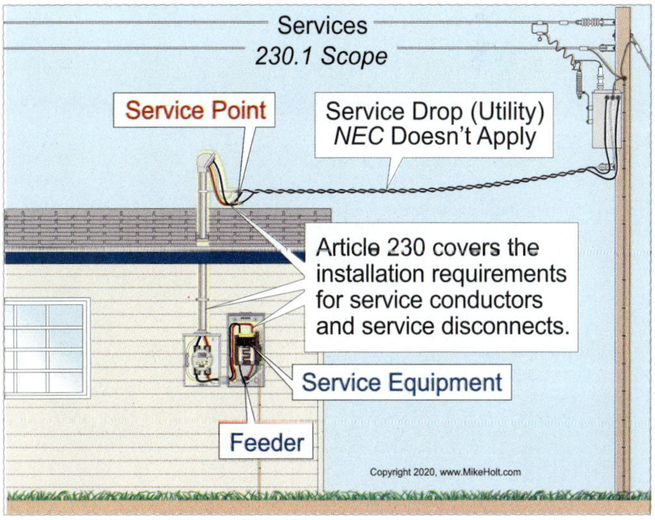

▶Figure 230-1

230.2 Number of Services

A building can only be served by one service drop or service lateral except as permitted by (A) through (D). ▶Figure 230-3 and ▶Figure 230-4

230.2 | Services

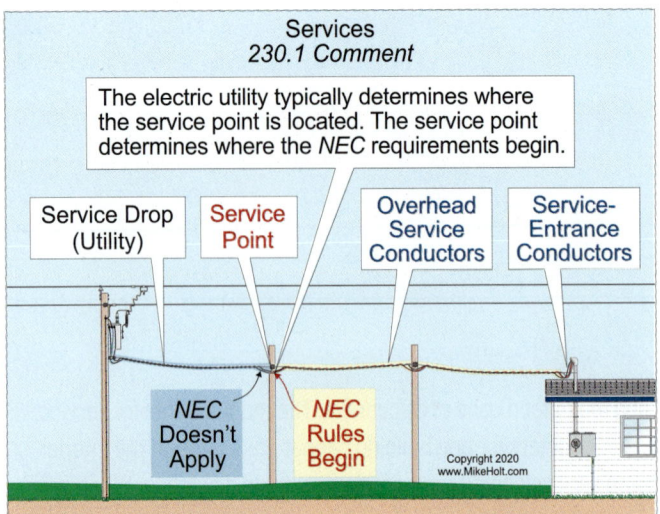
▶Figure 230-2

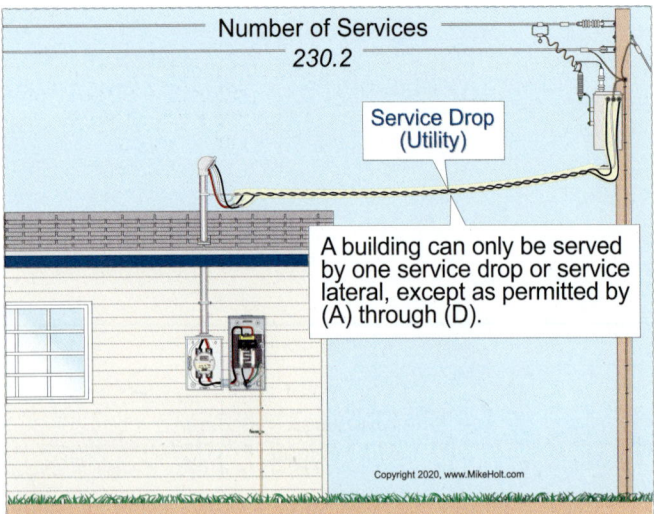
▶Figure 230-3

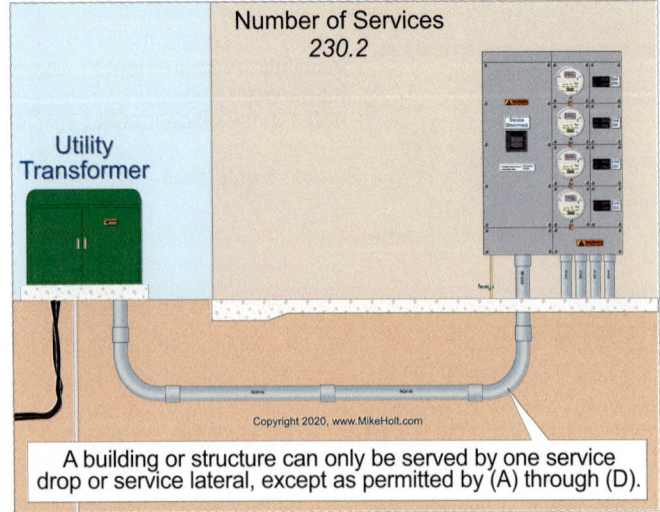
▶Figure 230-4

For the purposes of 230.40 Ex 2, underground sets of conductors 1/0 AWG and larger running to the same location and connected to each other at their supply end (but not connected together at their load end) are considered to be supplying one service.

Author's Comment:

▸ There are many possible combinations of what is considered one service drop or one service lateral. When required, one service drop (or lateral) can typically be split and connected to multiple service disconnects. When services are run in parallel, with multiple sets of conductors, they are still considered one service. See 230.40 and Ex 1 through 5. ▶Figure 230-5

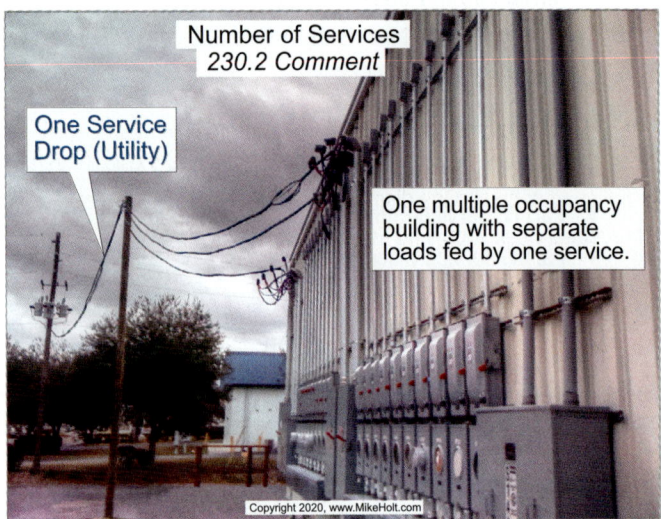
▶Figure 230-5

(A) Special Conditions. Additional services are permitted for the following:

(1) Fire pumps.

(2) Emergency systems.

(3) Legally required standby systems.

(4) Optional standby power.

(5) Parallel power production sources.

(6) Systems designed for connection to multiple sources of supply to enhance reliability.

(B) Special Occupancies. By special permission, additional services are permitted for:

(1) Multiple-occupancy buildings where there is no available space for supply equipment accessible to all occupants, or

(2) A building so large that two or more supplies are necessary.

(C) Capacity Requirements. Additional services are permitted:

(1) If the capacity requirements exceed 2,000A, or

(2) If the load requirements of a single-phase installation exceed the serving electric utility's power capacity, or

(3) By special permission.

> **Author's Comment:**
>
> ▸ According to Article 100, "Special Permission" means the written consent of the authority having jurisdiction.

(D) Different Characteristics. Additional services are permitted for different voltages, frequencies, or phases, or for different uses such as different electricity rate schedules.

(E) Identification of Multiple Services. If a building is supplied by more than one service, a permanent plaque or directory must be installed at each service disconnect location indicating the location of other services supplying that building. ▸Figure 230-6

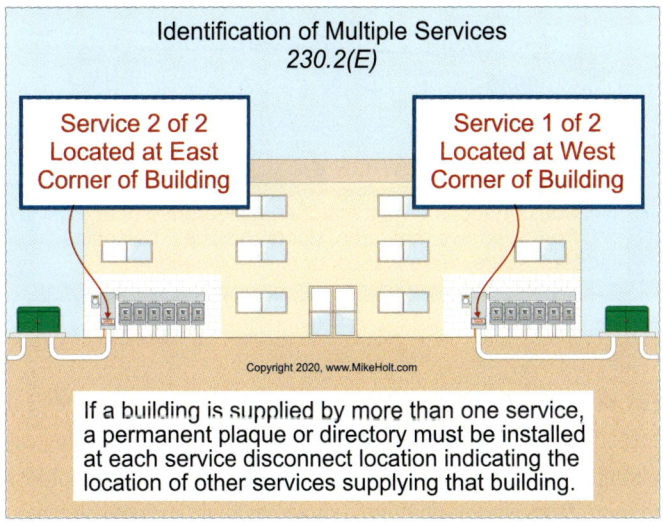
▸Figure 230-6

230.3 Not to Pass Through a Building

Service conductors must not pass through the interior of a building to supply another building.

230.6 Conductors Considered Outside a Building

Conductors are considered outside a building when they are installed:

(1) Under not less than 2 in. of concrete beneath a building. ▸Figure 230-7

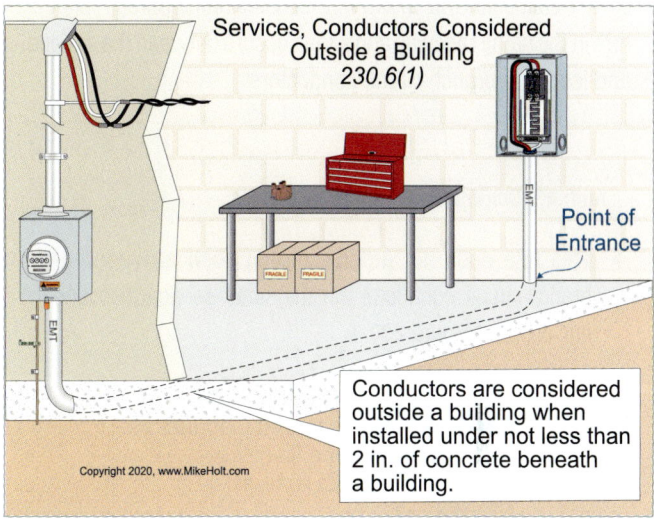
▸Figure 230-7

(2) Within a building in a raceway encased in not less than 2 in. of concrete or brick.

230.7 Service Conductors Separate from Other Conductors

Feeder and branch-circuit conductors are not permitted to be installed in a raceway containing service conductors. ▸Figure 230-8

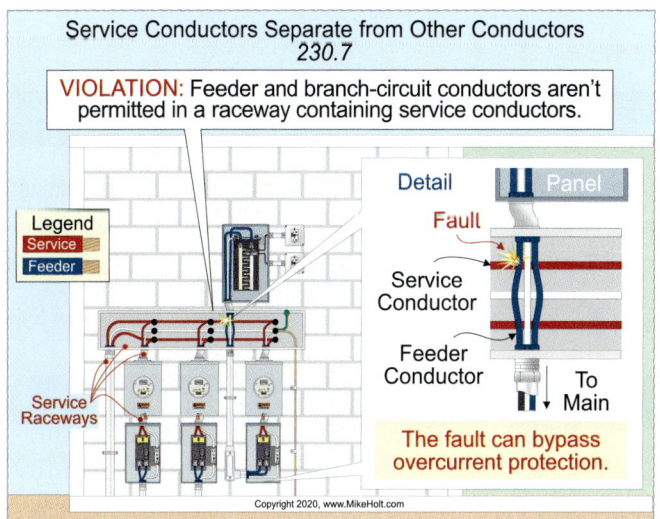
▸Figure 230-8

230.8 | Services

Ex 1: Grounding electrode conductors or supply-side bonding jumpers can be in a service raceway with service conductors.

> **Warning**
> ⚡ Overcurrent protection for feeder or branch-circuit conductors can be bypassed, or a fault can occur, if service conductors are mixed with feeder or branch-circuit conductors in the same raceway and a fault occurs between the service and feeder or branch-circuit conductors.

Author's Comment:

▸ This rule does not prohibit mixing service, feeder, and branch-circuit conductors in the same service disconnect enclosure. ▶Figure 230-9

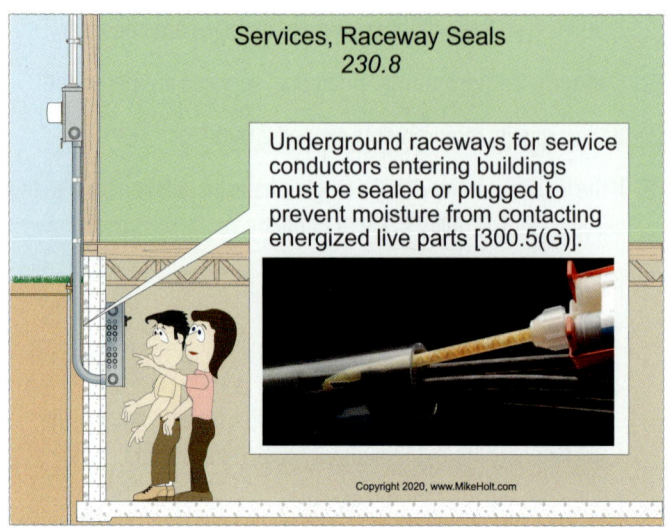
▶Figure 230-10

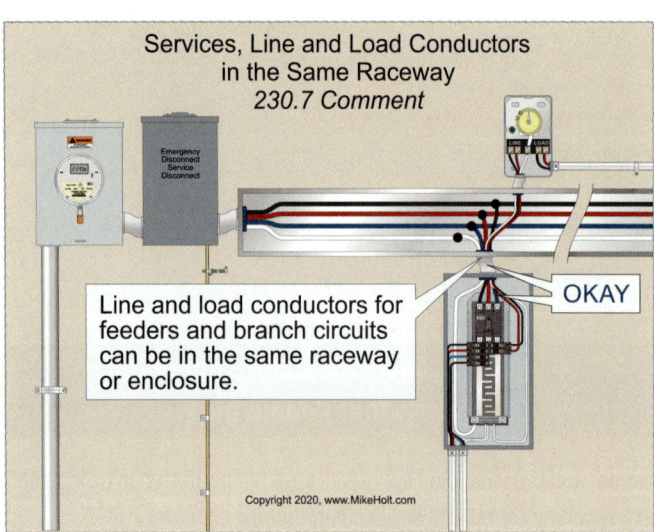
▶Figure 230-9

230.8 Raceway Seals

Underground raceways for service conductors entering buildings must be sealed or plugged to prevent moisture from contacting energized live parts [300.5(G)]. Sealants must be identified for use with the conductor or cable insulation. ▶Figure 230-10

230.9 Clearances on Buildings

(A) Clearance. Overhead service conductors must maintain a clearance of 3 ft from windows that open, doors, porches, balconies, ladders, stairs, fire escapes, or similar locations. ▶Figure 230-11

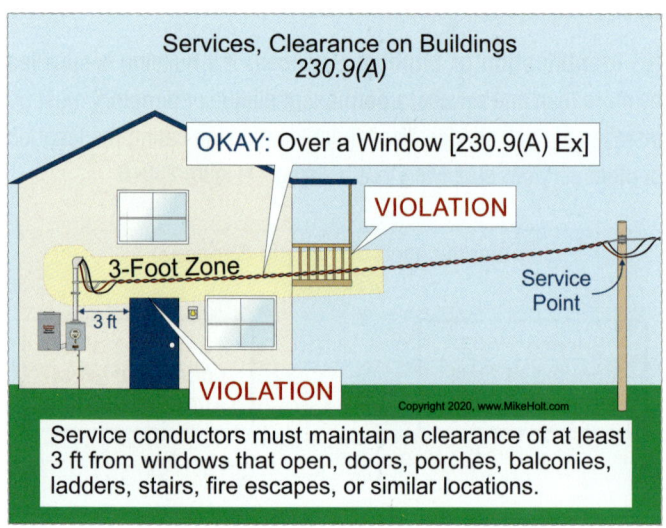
▶Figure 230-11

(B) Vertical Clearance. Overhead service conductors within 3 ft measured horizontally of platforms, projections, or surfaces that will permit personal contact must have a vertical clearance of not less than 10 ft above the platforms, projections, or surfaces in accordance with 230.24(B).

(C) Below Openings. Service conductors cannot be installed under an opening through which materials might pass, and they are not permitted to be installed where they will obstruct entrance to building openings. ▶Figure 230-12

230.10 Vegetation as Support

Trees or other vegetation must not be used for the support of overhead service conductor spans or service disconnects. ▶Figure 230-13

Services | 230.23

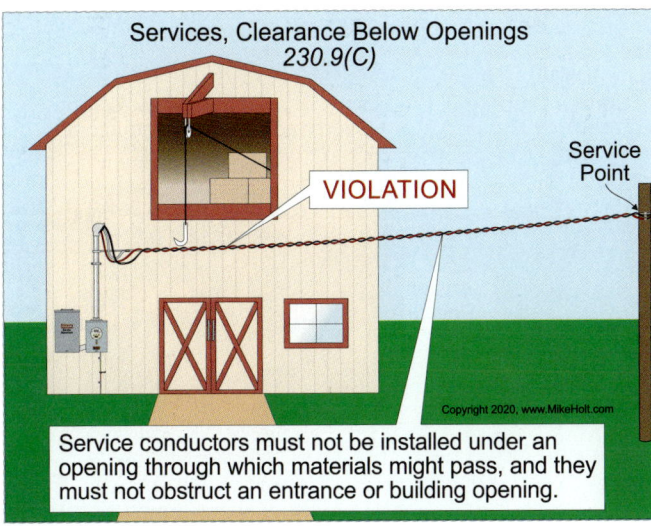

▶Figure 230–12

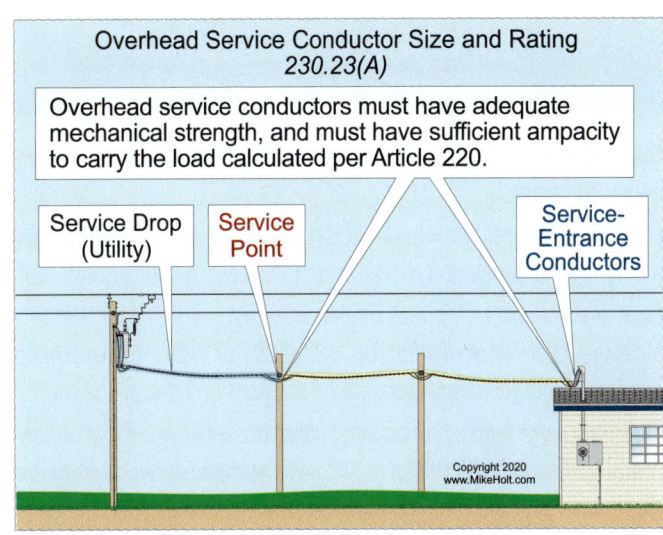

▶Figure 230–14

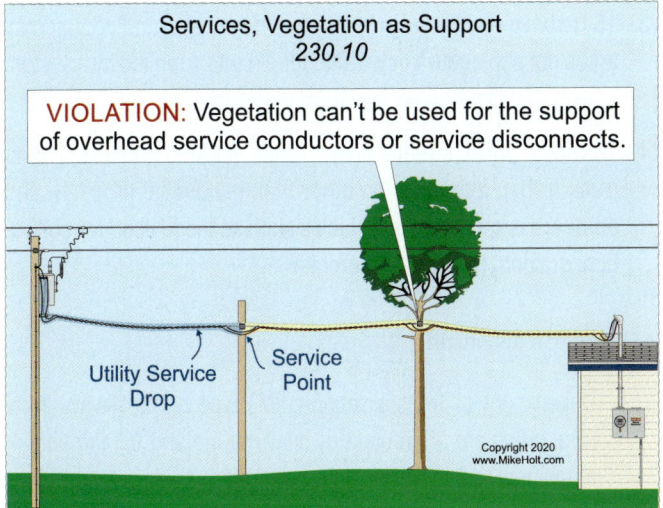

▶Figure 230–13

Part II. Overhead Service Conductors

230.23 Overhead Service Conductor Size and Rating

(A) General. Overhead service conductors must have adequate mechanical strength and enough ampacity to carry the load as calculated in accordance with Article 220. ▶Figure 230–14

(B) Phase Conductor Size. Overhead service conductors cannot be smaller than 8 AWG copper or 6 AWG aluminum.

Ex: Overhead service conductors can be as small as 12 AWG for limited-load installations.

(C) Neutral Conductor Size. The neutral conductor for overhead service conductors must be sized to carry the maximum unbalanced load in accordance with 220.61 and must be sized no smaller than required by 250.24(C).

> **Warning**
> The service neutral conductor size must not be smaller than that required by 250.24(C) to ensure it has sufficiently low impedance and current-carrying capacity to safely carry fault current in order to facilitate the operation of the overcurrent protective device [250.4(A)(5)].

▶ **Example**

Question: What size neutral conductor is required for a structure with a 400A service supplied with 500 kcmil conductors if the maximum line-to-neutral load is no more than 100A?

(a) 1/0 AWG   (b) 2/0 AWG   (c) 3/0 AWG   (d) 4/0 AWG

Solution:

According to Table 310.16, a 3 AWG conductor rated 100A at 75°C [110.14(C)(1)(b)(1)] is sufficient to carry 100A of neutral current. However, the service neutral conductor cannot be smaller than 1/0 AWG according to Table 250.102(C)(1), based on the size/area of the 500 kcmil service conductors [250.24(C)].

Answer: (a) 1/0 AWG

230.24 Vertical Clearance for Overhead Service Conductors

Overhead service conductor spans must maintain vertical clearances as follows:

(A) Above Roofs. A minimum of 8 ft above the surface of a roof for a minimum distance of 3 ft in all directions from the edge of the roof.

Ex 2: If the slope of the roof meets or exceeds 4 in. of vertical rise for every 12 in. of horizontal run, 120/208V or 120/240V overhead service conductor clearances can be reduced to 3 ft over the roof.

Ex 3: If no more than 6 ft of conductors pass over no more than 4 horizontal ft of roof, 120/208V or 120/240V overhead service conductor clearances over the roof overhang can be reduced to 18 in. ▶Figure 230-15

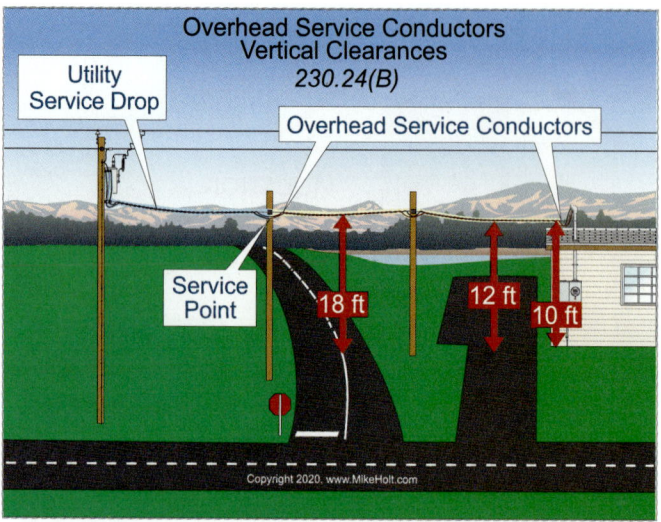
▶Figure 230-16

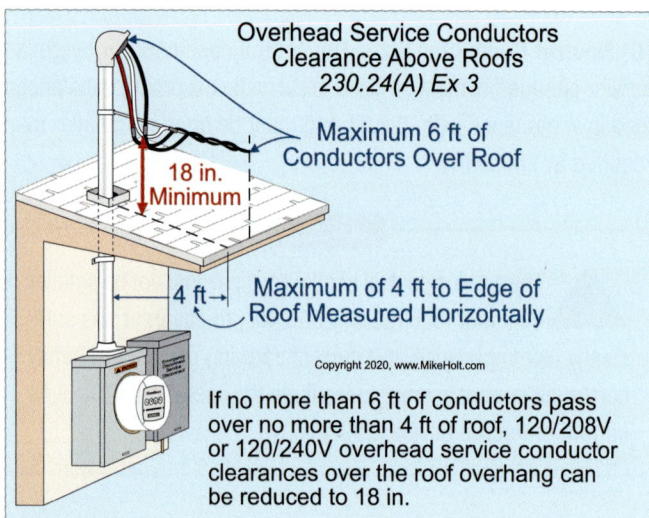
▶Figure 230-15

Ex 4: The 3-ft vertical clearance for overhead service conductors that extends from the roof does not apply when the point of attachment is on the side of the building below the roof.

Ex 5: If the voltage between conductors does not exceed 300V and the roof area is guarded or isolated, the clearance can be reduced to 3 ft.

(B) Vertical Clearance for Overhead Service Conductors. Overhead service conductor spans must maintain the following vertical clearances: ▶Figure 230-16

(1) 10 ft above finished grade, sidewalks, platforms, or projections that permit personal contact for circuits supplied by 120/208V or 120/240V.

(2) 12 ft above residential property and driveways, and commercial areas not subject to truck traffic for circuits supplied by 120/208V, 120/240V, or 277/480V.

(3) 15 ft above residential property and driveways, and commercial areas not subject to truck traffic for circuits supplied by a system having a voltage exceeding 300V to ground.

(4) 18 ft over public streets, alleys, roads, parking areas subject to truck traffic, driveways on other than residential property, and other areas traversed by vehicles such as those used for cultivation, grazing, forestry, and orchards.

Author's Comment:

▸ Department of Transportation (DOT) type rights-of-ways in rural areas are often used by slow-moving and tall farming machinery to avoid impeding road traffic.

(5) 24 ft 6 in. over tracks of railroads.

(D) Swimming Pools. Overhead service conductors not under the exclusive control of the serving electric utility located above pools, outdoor spas, outdoor hot tubs, diving structures, observation stands, towers, or platforms must be installed in accordance with the clearance requirements in 680.9.

230.26 Point of Attachment

The point of attachment for overhead service conductors is not permitted to be less than 10 ft above the finished grade and must be located so the minimum service conductor clearances required by 230.9 and 230.24 can be maintained. ▶Figure 230-17

Services | 230.28

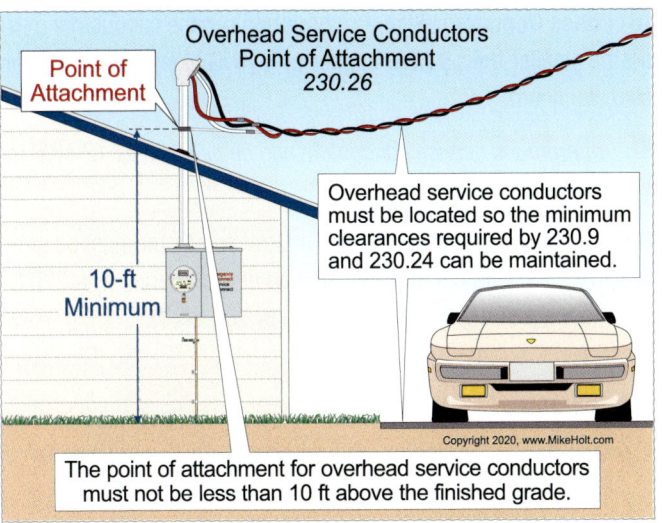
▶Figure 230-17

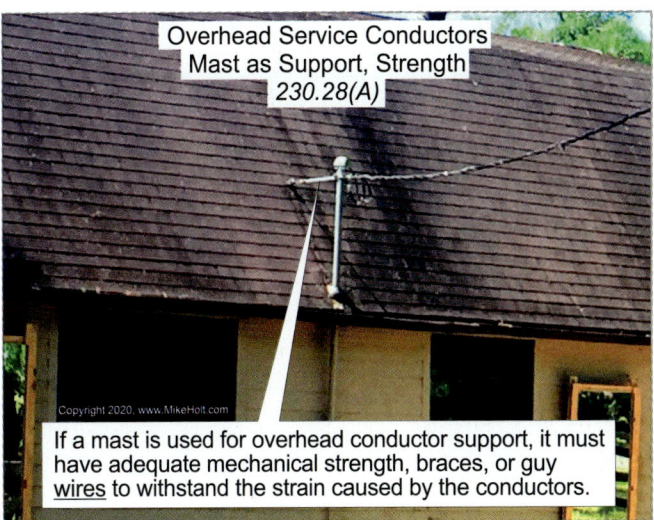
▶Figure 230-18

Caution

⚡ The point of attachment for conductors might need to be raised so the overhead service conductors will comply with the clearances from building openings required by 230.9 and from other areas as required by 230.24.

230.27 Means of Attachment

Open conductors must be attached to fittings identified for use with service conductors or to noncombustible, nonabsorbent insulators securely attached to the building.

230.28 Service Masts as Support

Masts used for the support of overhead service conductors or service drops must be installed in accordance with (A) and (B).

(A) Strength. If a mast is used for overhead conductor support, it must have adequate mechanical strength, braces, or guy wires to withstand the strain caused by the conductors. ▶Figure 230-18

(B) Attachment. Conductors cannot be attached to a mast between a weatherhead or end of the conduit and a coupling if the coupling is above the last conduit support, or if the coupling is above the building.
▶Figure 230-19

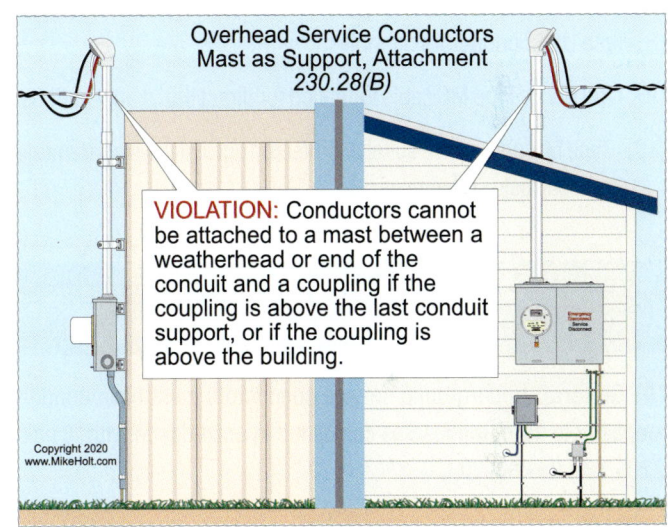
▶Figure 230-19

Author's Comment:

▸ Some local codes or utilities require a minimum trade size 2 rigid metal conduit to be used for the service mast. In addition, many electric utilities contain specific requirements for the installation of the service mast.

2020 NEC Requirements for Solar PV and Energy Storage Systems | MikeHolt.com | 113

230.30 | Services

Part III. Underground Service Conductors

230.30 Installation

(B) Wiring Methods. Only the following wiring methods are permitted to contain service conductors:

(1) Type RMC.

(2) Type IMC.

(3) Type NUCC.

(4) Type HDPE conduit.

(5) Type PVC conduit.

(6) Type RTRC.

(7) Type IGS cable.

(8) Type USE conductors or cables.

(9) Type MV or Type MC cable identified for direct burial applications.

(10) Type MI cable where suitably protected against physical damage and corrosive conditions.

230.31 Underground Service Conductor Size and Rating

(A) General. Underground service conductors must have enough ampacity to carry the load as calculated in accordance with Article 220. ▶Figure 230–20

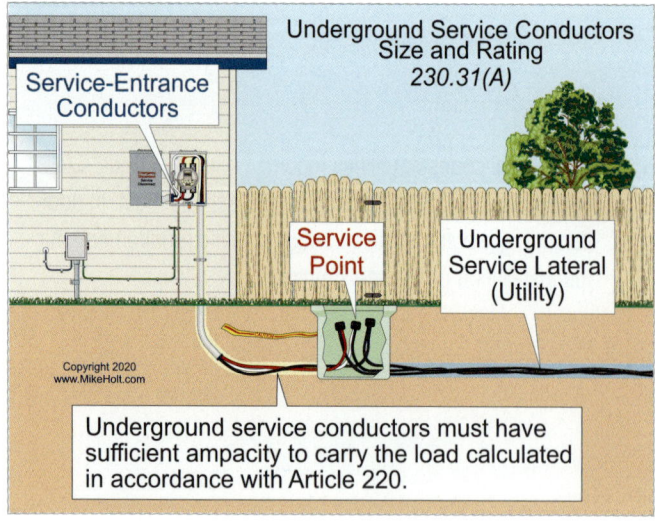

▶Figure 230–20

(B) Phase Conductor Size. Underground service conductors must not be smaller than 8 AWG copper or 6 AWG aluminum or copper-clad aluminum.

Ex: Underground service conductors can be as small as 12 AWG for limited-load installations.

(C) Neutral Conductor Size. The neutral conductor must be sized to carry the maximum unbalanced load in accordance with 220.61 and must not be smaller than required by 250.24(C).

> ▶ **Example**
>
> **Question:** What size neutral conductor is required for a structure with a 400A service supplied with 500 kcmil conductors if the maximum line-to-neutral load is no more than 100A?
>
> (a) 1/0 AWG   (b) 2/0 AWG   (c) 3/0 AWG   (d) 4/0 AWG
>
> **Solution:**
>
> According to Table 310.16, a 3 AWG conductor rated 100A at 75°C [110.14(C)(1)(b)(1)] can carry 100A of neutral current. However, the service neutral conductor must not be smaller than 1/0 AWG according to Table 250.102(C)(1), based on the size/area of the 500 kcmil service conductors [250.24(C)].
>
> **Answer:** (a) 1/0 AWG

230.32 Protection Against Damage

Underground service conductors must be installed in accordance with 300.5 and the minimum cover must be in accordance with Table 300.5. ▶Figure 230–21

▶Figure 230–21

Part IV. Service-Entrance Conductors

230.40 Number of Service-Entrance Conductor Sets

Each service drop, service lateral, or set of underground or overhead service conductors can only supply one set of service-entrance conductors.

Ex 2: Service conductors can supply two to six service disconnects as permitted in 230.71(B).

> **Author's Comment:**
>
> ▸ Underground sets of conductors 1/0 AWG and larger running to the same location and connected at their supply end, but not at their load end, are considered to supply one service [230.2].

Ex 5: One set of service-entrance conductors connected to the supply side of the normal service disconnect can supply standby power systems, fire pump equipment, fire and sprinkler alarms [230.82(5)], and solar PV systems [230.82(6)]. ▸Figure 230-22

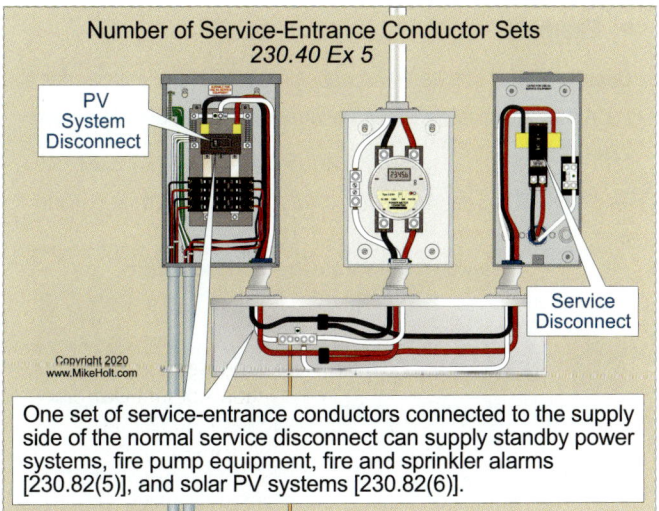

▸Figure 230-22

230.42 Conductor Sizing

(A) General. Conductors must be sized to carry not less than the largest of the calculations contained in 230.42(A)(1) or (2).

Conductor ampacity must be determined in accordance with 310.14 and the conductors must be sized to the terminal temperature rating in accordance with 110.14(C)(1). ▸Figure 230-23

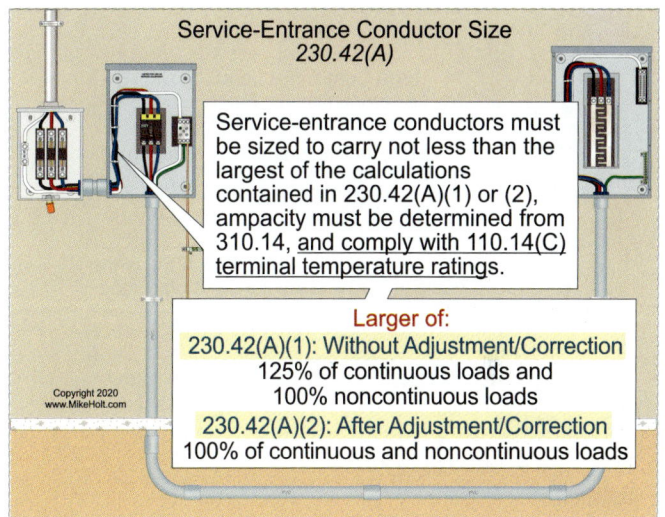

▸Figure 230-23

(1) Without Conductor Ampacity Adjustment and/or Correction. Conductors must be sized to carry 125 percent of the continuous loads, plus 100 percent of the noncontinuous loads, based on the terminal temperature rating ampacities contained in Table 310.16 [110.14(C)(1)]. ▸Figure 230-24

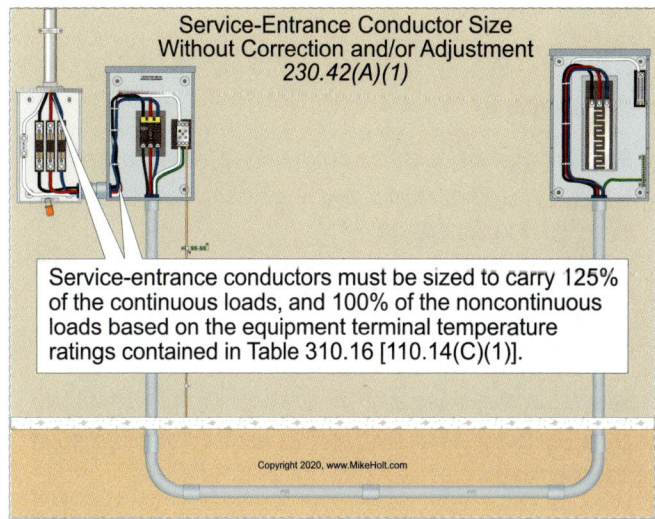

▸Figure 230-24

230.42 | Services

▶ Example 1

Question: What size conductors rated 90°C are required for a service supplying a 180A continuous load where the equipment terminals are rated 75°C? ▶Figure 230–25

(a) 3/0 AWG   (b) 4/0 AWG   (c) 300 kcmil   (d) 350 kcmil

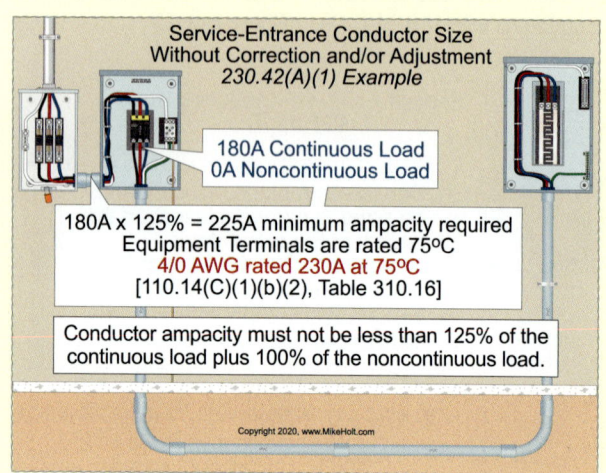

▶Figure 230–25

Solution:

Step 1: Conductor Ampacity. The conductors must have an ampacity of at least 225A (180A × 125%).

Step 2: Size the conductors in accordance with 110.14(C)(1)(b)(2) and Table 310.16.

According to the 75°C column of Table 310.16, 4/0 AWG is rated 230A and is therefore suitable to be used.

Answer: (b) 4/0 AWG

▶ Example 2

Question: What size conductors rated 90°C are required for a service supplying a 320A continuous load where the equipment terminals are rated 75°C? ▶Figure 230–26

(a) 300 kcmil   (b) 400 kcmil   (c) 500 kcmil   (d) 600 kcmil

Solution:

Step 1: Conductor Ampacity. The conductors from the panelboard to the distribution block must have an ampacity of at least 400A (320A × 125%).

Step 2: Size the conductors in accordance with 110.14(C)(1)(b)(2) and Table 310.16.

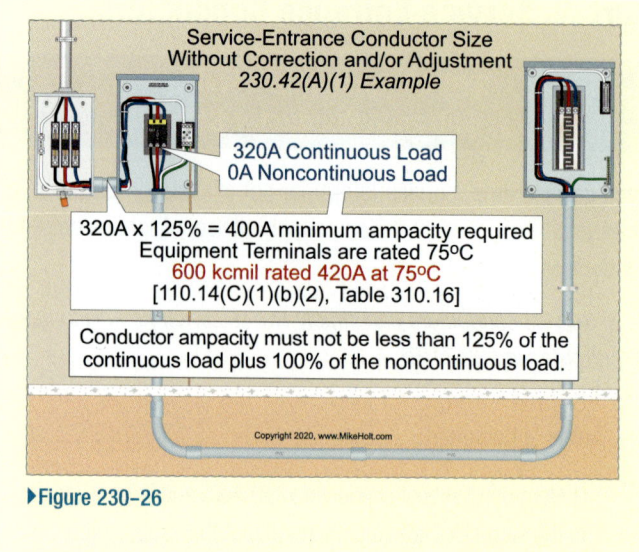

▶Figure 230–26

According to the 75°C column of Table 310.16, 600 kcmil is rated 420A and is therefore suitable to be used.

Answer: (d) 600 kcmil

Ex 1: Neutral conductors must have an ampacity of not less than 100 percent of the continuous and noncontinuous loads.

▶ Example

Question: What size neutral conductor rated 90°C is required for a 200A continuous neutral load if the terminals are rated 75°C? ▶Figure 230–27

(a) 3/0 AWG   (b) 4/0 AWG   (c) 250 kcmil   (d) 300 kcmil

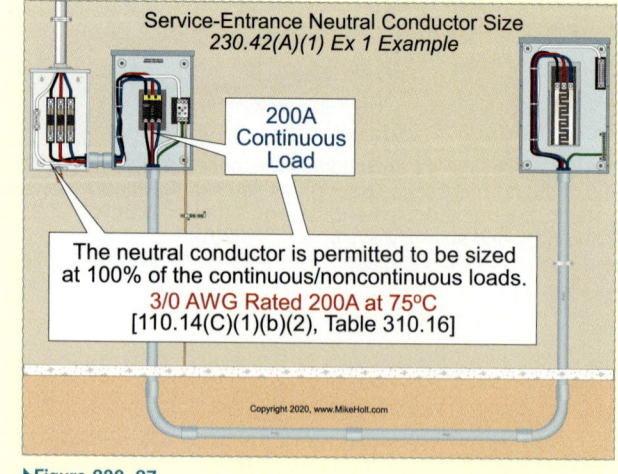

▶Figure 230–27

Solution:

Step 1: The neutral conductor is sized to the 200A continuous load (100 percent).

Step 2: Size conductors in accordance with 110.14(C)(1)(b)(2) and Table 310.16.

According to the 75°C column of Table 310.16, 3/0 AWG has an ampacity of 200A.

Answer: (a) 3/0 AWG [110.14(C)(1)(b)(2) and Table 310.16]

(2) With Conductor Ampacity Adjustment and Correction.

Conductors must be sized to carry not less than 100 percent of the continuous load, plus 100 percent of the noncontinuous load after conductor ampacity adjustment and/or correction in accordance with 310.14.
▶Figure 230–28

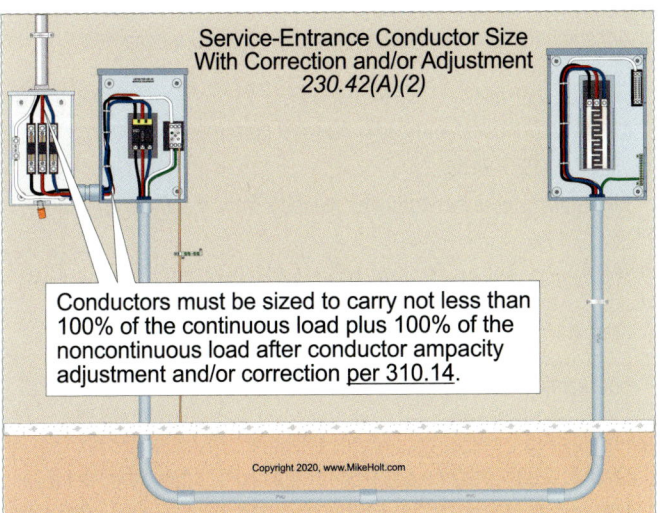
▶Figure 230–28

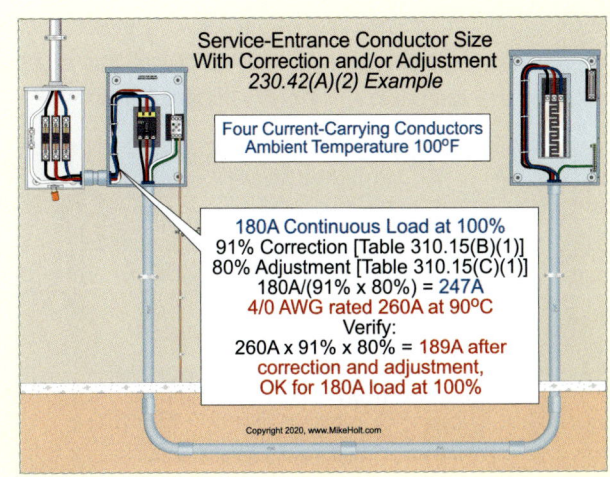
▶Figure 230–29

Continuous Load = 180A

Correction [Table 310.15(B)(1)] = 91% (100°F with 90°C Conductor)

Adjustment [Table 310.15(C)(1)] = 80% (four current-carrying conductors)

Minimum Conductor Ampacity Needed from the 90°C Column = 180A/(91% × 80%)

Minimum Conductor Ampacity Needed from the 90°C Column = 180A/73%

Minimum Conductor Ampacity Needed from the 90°C Column = 247A

Step 2: Select the conductor from the 90°C column of Table 310.16 [110.14(C)(1)(b)(2)].

4/0 AWG is suitable because it has an ampacity of 260A at 90°C before any correction and adjustment.

Step 3: Verify that the ampacity of 4/0 AWG after correction and adjustment can carry 100 percent of the 180A continuous load at 90°C.

Conductor Ampacity after Correction and Adjustment = Conductor Ampacity × Correction × Adjustment

Conductor Ampacity at 90°C = 260A

Corroction = 91%

Adjustment = 80%

Conductor Ampacity after Correction and Adjustment = 260A × 91% × 80%

Conductor Ampacity after Correction and Adjustment = 189A

4/0 AWG with 90°C insulation has an ampere rating of 189A which is more than enough for the 180A continuous load.

▶ **Example 1**

Question: *What size conductors rated 90°C are required for a service containing four current-carrying conductors supplying a 180A continuous load in an ambient temperature of 100°F where the equipment terminals are rated 75°C?* ▶Figure 230–29

(a) 4/0 AWG   (b) 300 kcmil   (c) 500 kcmil   (d) 600 kcmil

Solution:

Step 1: *The conductors must have an ampacity of not less than 180A after conductor ampacity temperature correction [Table 310.15(B)(1)] and adjustment [Table 310.15(C)(1)], based on the conductor insulation rating of 90°C. One way to find the conductor size is to determine the conductor ampacity required to supply a 180A continuous load at 100 percent after correction and adjustment.*

Conductor Ampacity at 90°C = Continuous Load at 100%/ (Correction × Adjustment)

Step 4: Verify that the ampacity of 4/0 AWG at 75°C without correction and adjustment can carry the 180A continuous load at 125 percent in accordance with 230.42(A)(1). ▶Figure 230–30

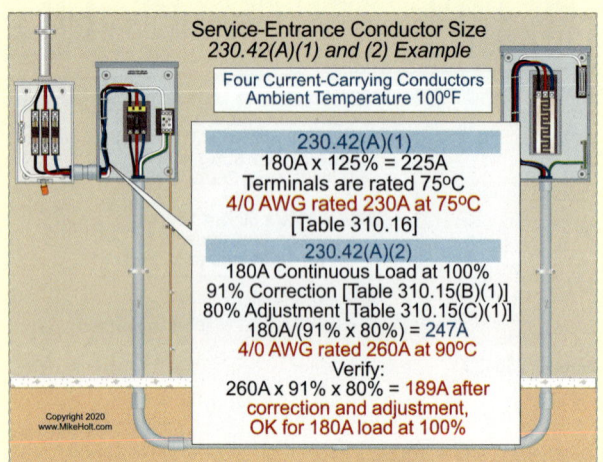

▶Figure 230–30

Conductor Ampacity Needed = Continuous load at 125%
Conductor Ampacity Needed = 180A × 125%
Conductor Ampacity needed = 225A

According to Table 310.16, 4/0 AWG is suitable because it is rated 230A at 75°C.

Answer: (a) 4/0 AWG

▶ **Example 2**

Question: What size conductors rated 90°C are required for a service containing four current-carrying conductors supplying a 320A continuous load in an ambient temperature of 100°F where the equipment terminals are rated 75°C? ▶Figure 230–31

(a) 300 kcmil   (b) 400 kcmil   (c) 500 kcmil   (d) 600 kcmil

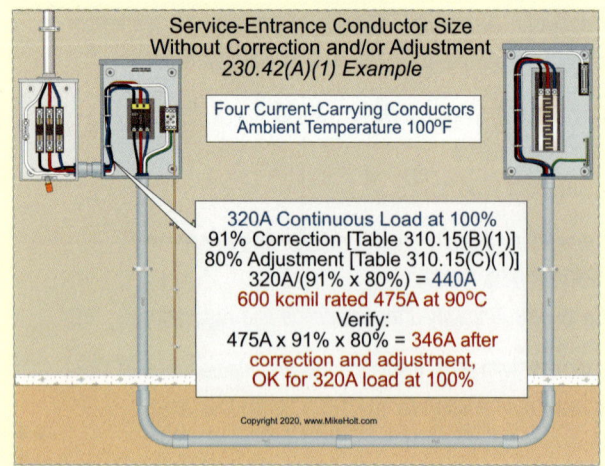

▶Figure 230–31

Solution:

Step 1: The conductors must have an ampacity of not less than 320A after conductor ampacity temperature correction [Table 310.15(B)(1)] and adjustment [Table 310.15(C)(1)], based on the conductor insulation rating of 90°C. One way to find the conductor size is to determine the conductor ampacity required to supply a 320A continuous load at 100 percent after correction and adjustment.

Conductor Ampacity at 90°C = Continuous Load at 100%/ (Correction × Adjustment)

Continuous Load = 320A

Correction [Table 310.15(B)(1)] = 91% (100°F with 90°C Conductor)

Adjustment [Table 310.15(C)(1)] = 80% (four current-carrying conductors)

Minimum Conductor Ampacity Needed from the 90°C Column = 320A/(91% × 80%)
Minimum Conductor Ampacity Needed from the 90°C Column = 320A/73%
Minimum Conductor Ampacity Needed from the 90°C Column = 438A

Step 2: Select the conductor from the 90°C column of Table 310.16.

600 kcmil is suitable because it has an ampacity of 475A at 90°C before any correction and adjustment.

Step 3: Verify that the ampacity of 600 kcmil after correction and adjustment can carry 100 percent of the 320A continuous load at 90°C.

Conductor Ampacity after Correction and Adjustment = Conductor Ampacity × Correction × Adjustment

Conductor Ampacity at 90°C = 475A
Correction = 91%
Adjustment = 80%

Conductor Ampacity after Correction and Adjustment = 475A × 91% × 80%
Conductor Ampacity after Correction and Adjustment = 346A

600 kcmil has an ampere rating of 346A which is more than enough for the 320A continuous load.

Step 4: Verify that the ampacity of 600 kcmil at 75°C without correction and adjustment can carry the 320A continuous load at 125 percent in accordance with 230.42(A)(1).

Conductor Ampacity Needed = Continuous load at 125%
Conductor Ampacity Needed = 320A × 125%
Conductor Ampacity Needed = 400A

According to Table 310.16, 600 kcmil is suitable because it is rated 420A at 75°C.

Answer: (d) 600 kcmil

(C) Neutral Conductor Size. The service neutral conductor must be sized to carry the maximum unbalanced load in accordance with 220.61 and must not be smaller than required by 250.24(C).

> **Warning**
>
> In no case can the service neutral conductor size be smaller than required by 250.24(C) to ensure it has sufficiently low impedance and current-carrying capacity to safely carry fault current in order to facilitate the operation of the overcurrent protective device.

▶Figure 230-32

230.43 Wiring Methods

Service-entrance conductors can be installed with any of the following wiring methods:

(1) Open wiring on insulators.

(3) Rigid metal conduit (RMC).

(4) Intermediate metal conduit (IMC).

(5) Electrical metallic tubing (EMT).

(6) Electrical nonmetallic tubing (ENT).

(7) Service-entrance cables.

(8) Wireways.

(11) PVC conduit.

(13) Type MC cable.

(15) Flexible metal conduit (FMC) or liquidtight flexible metal conduit (LFMC) in lengths not longer than 6 ft.

(16) Liquidtight flexible nonmetallic conduit (LFNC). ▶Figure 230-32

(17) High-density polyethylene conduit (HDPE).

(18) Nonmetallic underground conduit with conductors (NUCC).

(19) Reinforced thermosetting resin conduit (RTRC).

(20) Type TC-ER cable.

230.46 Spliced Conductors

Service-entrance conductors can be spliced or tapped in accordance with 110.14, 300.5(E), 300.13, and 300.15.

Pressure connectors and devices for splices and taps must be listed. Power distribution blocks installed on service conductors must be listed and marked "suitable for use on the line side of the service equipment" or equivalent. ▶Figure 230-33

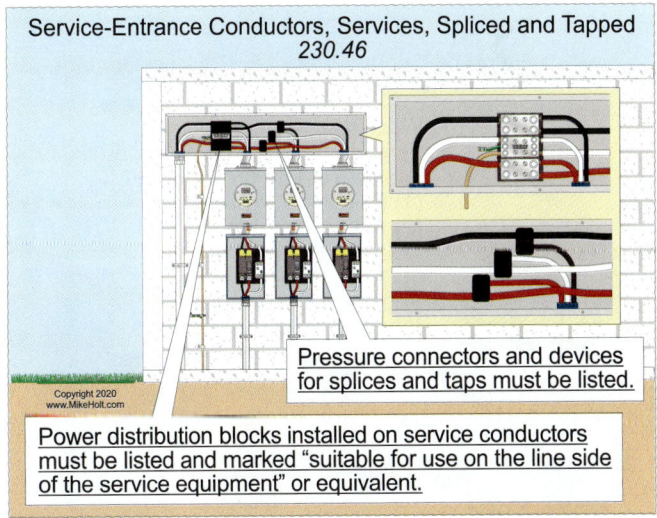

▶Figure 230-33

Note: Effective January 1, 2023, pressure connectors and devices for splices and taps installed on service conductors must be marked "suitable for use on the line side of the service equipment" or equivalent.

230.50 Protection Against Physical Damage

(A) Underground Service-Entrance Conductors. Underground service-entrance conductors must be protected against physical damage in accordance with 300.5. ▶Figure 230–34

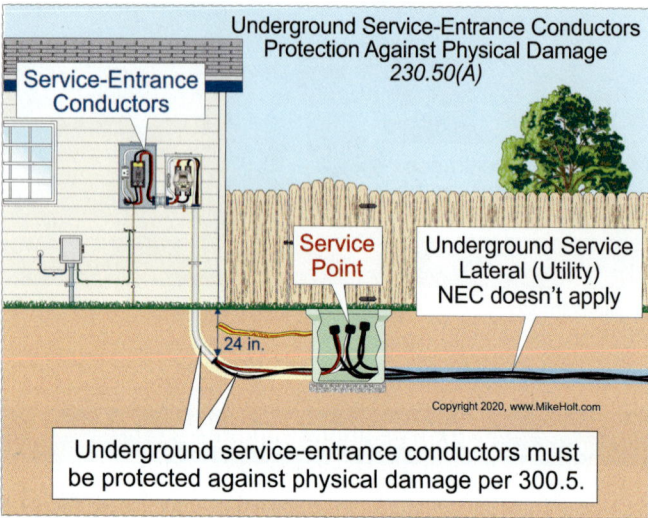

▶Figure 230–34

(B) Service-Entrance Cables Subject to Physical Damage.

(1) Service-Entrance Cables. Service-entrance cables that are subject to physical damage must be protected by any of the following: ▶Figure 230–35

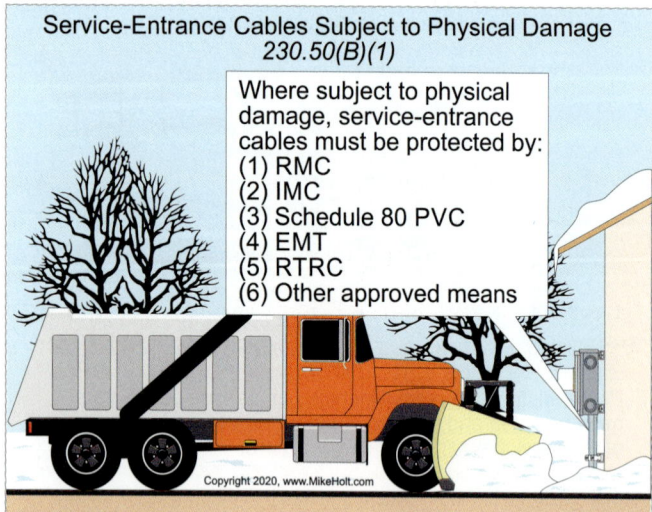

▶Figure 230–35

(1) Rigid metal conduit (RMC).

(2) Intermediate metal conduit (IMC).

(3) Schedule 80 PVC conduit.

Author's Comment:

▸ If the authority having jurisdiction determines the raceway is not subject to physical damage, Schedule 40 PVC conduit can be used. ▶Figure 230–36

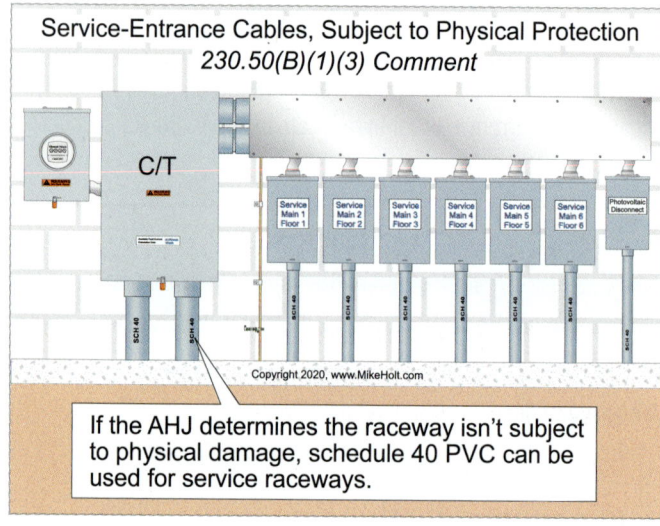

▶Figure 230–36

(4) Electrical metallic tubing (EMT).

(5) Reinforced thermosetting resin conduit (RTRC), Type XW [355.10(F) Note].

(6) Other means approved by the authority having jurisdiction.

(2) Other Than Service-Entrance Cable. Individual open conductors and cables, other than service-entrance cables, must not be installed within 10 ft of grade level or where exposed to physical damage.

230.51 Cable Supports

(A) Service-Entrance Cable Supports. Service-entrance cable must be supported within 1 ft of the weatherhead, gooseneck, raceway connections, or enclosure. Supports must be at intervals not exceeding 30 in. ▶Figure 230–37

Services | 230.54

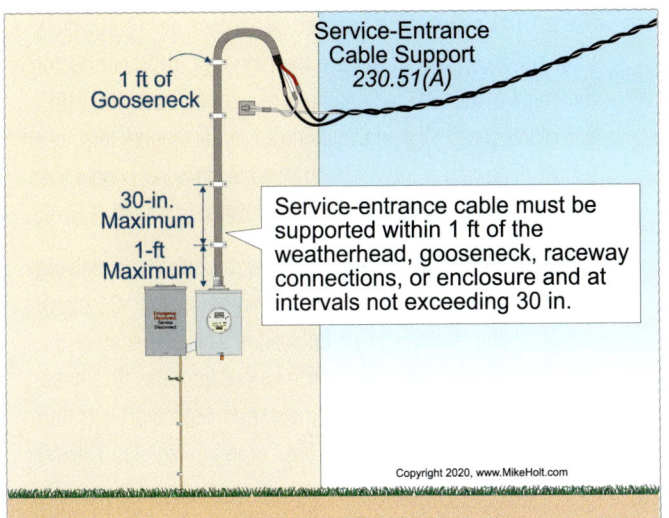

▶Figure 230-37

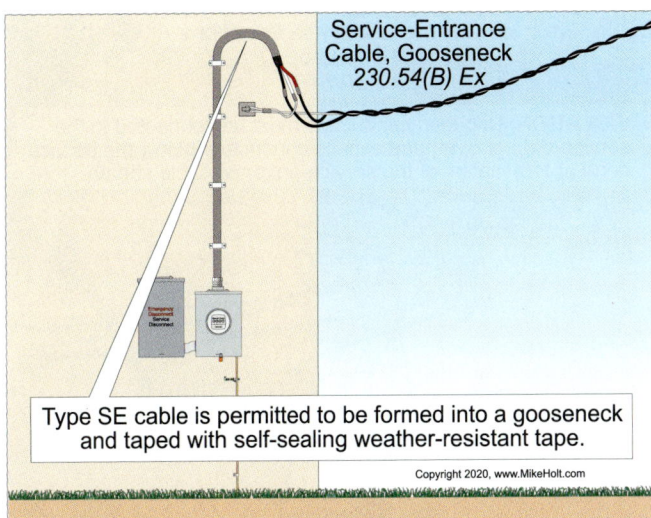

▶Figure 230-38

230.53 Raceways to Drain

Where exposed to the weather, raceways enclosing service-entrance conductors must be listed or approved for use in wet locations and arranged to drain. Where embedded in masonry, raceways shall be arranged to drain.

230.54 Overhead Service Locations

(A) Service Head. Raceways for service drops or overhead service conductors must have a weatherhead listed for wet locations.

(B) Service-Entrance Cable. Service-entrance cables must be equipped with a weatherhead listed for wet locations.

Ex: Type SE cable is permitted to be formed in a gooseneck and taped with a self-sealing weather-resistant tape. ▶Figure 230-38

(C) Above the Point of Attachment. Service heads on raceways or service-entrance cables must be located above the point of attachment [230.26] for service-drop or overhead service conductors. ▶Figure 230-39

Ex: If it is impractical to locate the service head above the point of attachment, it must be located within 2 ft of the point of attachment.

(D) Secured. Service-entrance cables must be held securely in place.

(E) Opposite Polarity Through Separately Bushed Holes. Service heads must provide a bushed opening and phase conductors must be in separate openings.

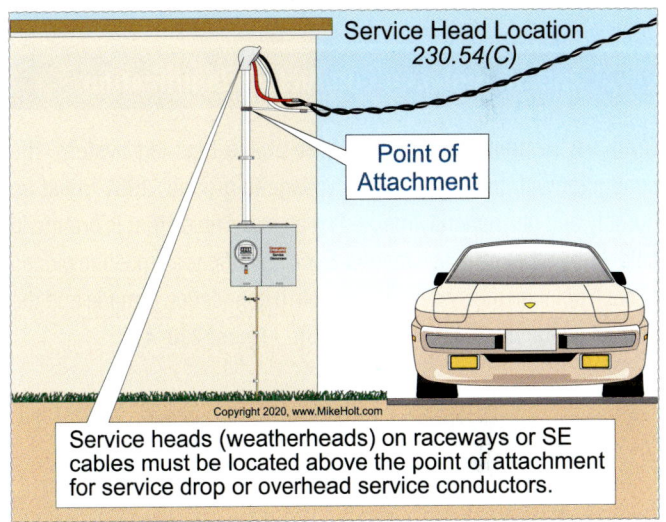

▶Figure 230-39

(F) Drip Loops. Drip loop conductors must be connected to the service-drop or overhead service conductors below the service head or termination of the service-entrance cable sheath. ▶Figure 230-40

(G) Arranged so Water Will Not Enter. Service-entrance and overhead service conductors must be arranged to prevent water from entering the service disconnect.

230.56 | Services

▶Figure 230–40

- Since 1975, panelboards supplied by a 4-wire, delta-connected, three-phase system must have the high-leg (208V) conductor terminate to the "B" (center) phase of a panelboard [408.3(E)]. For many years, high-leg marking of larger conductors was usually done with orange phasing tape but individual conductors are now manufactured with orange insulation in almost all sizes.

- The ANSI standard for meter equipment requires the high-leg conductor (208V to neutral) to terminate on the "C" (right) phase of the meter socket enclosure. This is because the demand meter needs 120V which comes from the "B" phase. Hopefully, the electric utility lineman is not colorblind and does not inadvertently cross the "orange" high-leg (208V) conductor with the red (120V) service conductor at the weatherhead. It has happened before... ▶Figure 230–42

230.56 High-Leg Conductor Identification

On a 4-wire, delta-connected, three-phase high-leg system, the conductor with the higher phase voltage-to-ground (208V) must be durably and permanently marked by an outer finish that is orange in color or by other effective means. Such identification must be placed at each point on the system where both a connection is made and the neutral conductor is present [110.15]. ▶Figure 230–41

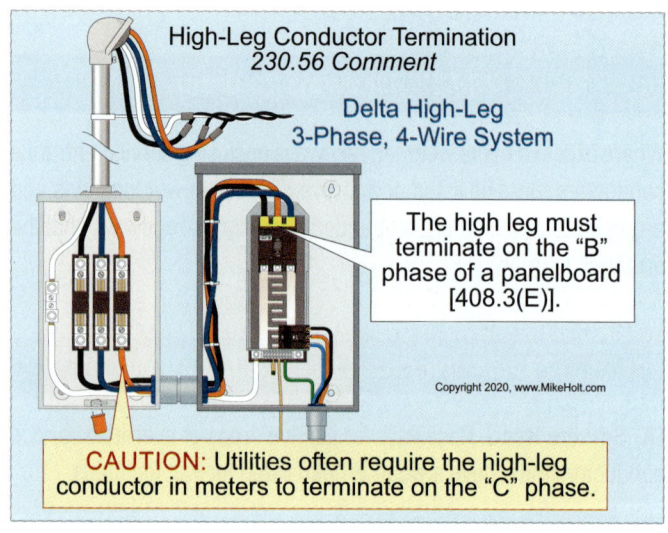
▶Figure 230–42

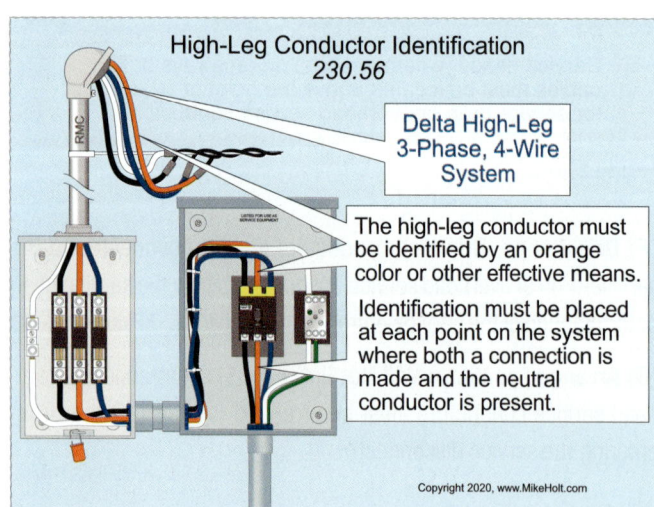
▶Figure 230–41

Author's Comment:

- The high-leg conductor is also called the "Wild Leg" or "Stinger Leg."

Part V. Service Disconnect—General

230.62 Service Equipment—Enclosed or Guarded

Energized parts of service equipment must be enclosed as specified in 230.62(A) or guarded as specified in 230.62(B).

(A) Enclosed. Energized parts must be enclosed so they will not be exposed to accidental contact or must be guarded in accordance with 230.62(B).

(B) Guarded. Energized parts that are not enclosed must be installed on a switchboard, panelboard, or control board and guarded in accordance with 110.18 and 110.27. Where energized parts are guarded as provided in 110.27(A)(1) and (A)(2), a means for locking or sealing doors providing access to energized parts must be provided.

(C) Barriers. Barriers must be placed in service equipment so no uninsulated, phase service busbar, or service terminal is exposed to inadvertent contact by persons or maintenance equipment while servicing load terminations. ▶Figure 230-43

▶Figure 230-43

230.66 Marking for Service Disconnect

(A) General. The service disconnect must be marked to identify it as being suitable as service equipment and be listed or field evaluated. ▶Figure 230-44

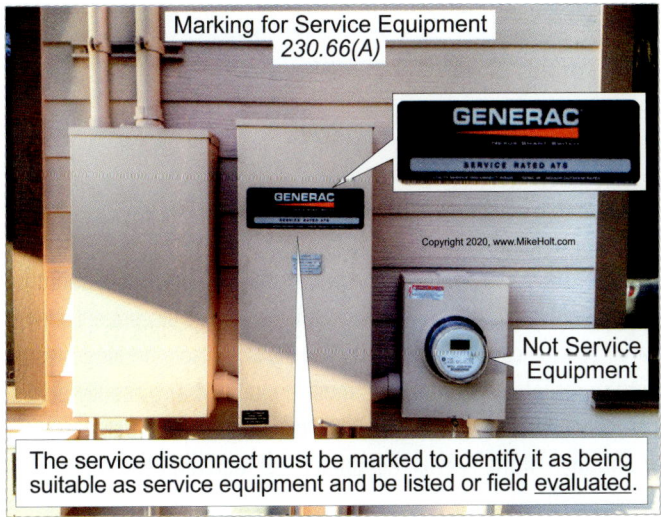
▶Figure 230-44

(B) Meter Sockets. Meter sockets must be listed and rated for the voltage and current rating of the service. ▶Figure 230-45

▶Figure 230-45

Ex: Meter socket enclosures supplied by, and under the exclusive control of, a serving electric utility are not required to be listed.

230.67 Surge Protection

(A) Surge Protective Device. All services supplying dwelling units must be provided with a surge protective device.

(B) Location. The required surge protective device for a dwelling unit must be an integral part of the service disconnect or be located immediately adjacent to the service disconnect. ▶Figure 230-46

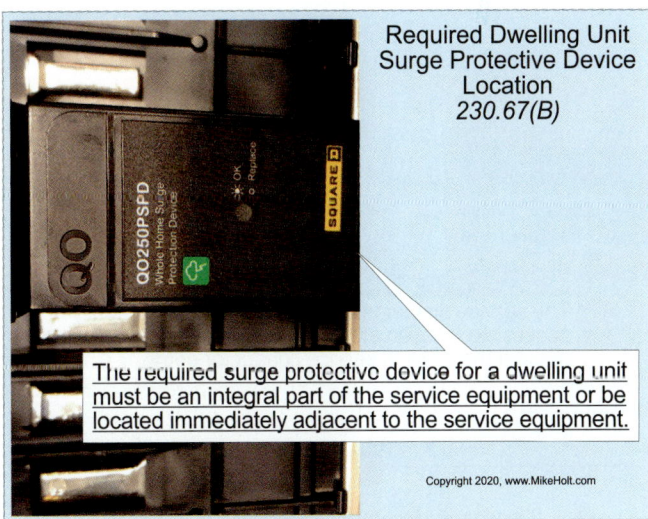
▶Figure 230-46

Ex: The surge protective device is permitted to be in the downstream panelboard.

Author's Comment:

▸ An example of the application of this exception is where there is an exterior meter main that feeds an interior panel. The SPD could be installed at the interior panel using the exception.

▸ See Parts I and II of Article 242 for the installation requirements that apply to SPDs.

(C) Type. The surge protective device must be a Type 1 or Type 2 SPD.

(D) Replacement. Where service equipment is replaced, surge protection must be installed.

Part VI. Service Disconnect—Disconnecting Means

230.70 Service Disconnect Requirements

The service disconnect must open all phase conductors.

(A) Location.

(1) Readily Accessible. The service disconnect must be placed at a readily accessible location either outside the building or inside nearest the point of conductor entry. ▸Figure 230–47

▸Figure 230–47

Warning

⚠ Because service-entrance conductors do not have short-circuit or ground-fault protection, they must be limited in length when installed inside a building. Some local jurisdictions have a specific requirement as to the maximum length permitted within a building. ▸Figure 230–48

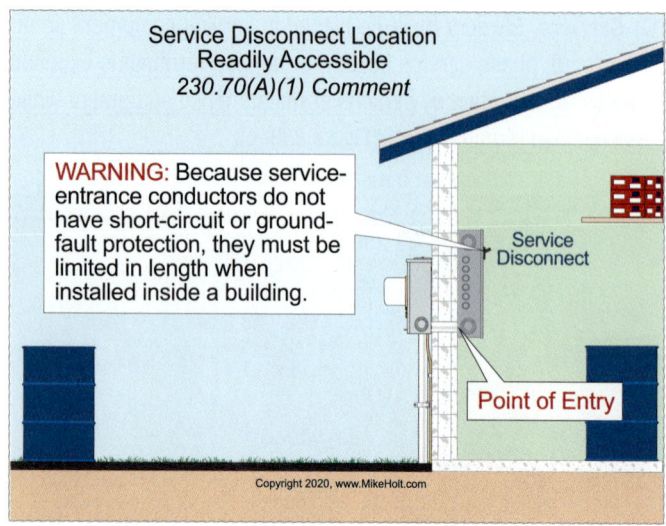
▸Figure 230–48

(2) Bathroom Areas. Service disconnects are not permitted to be installed in a bathroom area. ▸Figure 230–49

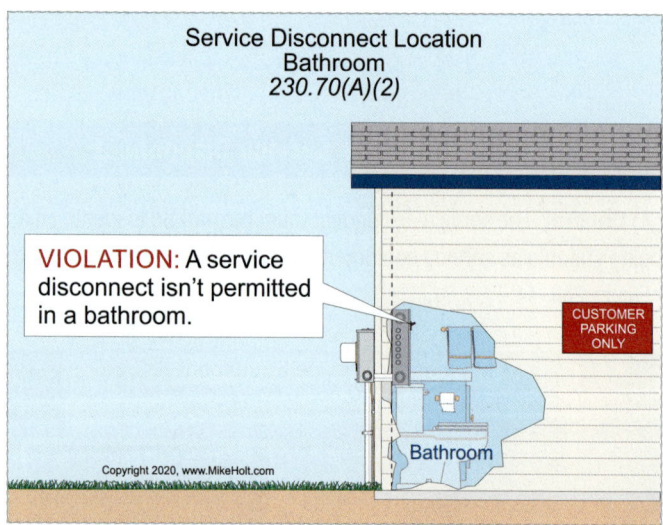
▸Figure 230–49

(3) Remote Control. A remote-control device (such as a pushbutton for a shunt-trip breaker) used to activate the service disconnect cannot serve as the service disconnect. The service disconnecting means, not the remote-control device, must be located at a readily accessible location either outside the building, or if inside, nearest the point of entrance of the service conductors as required by 230.70(A)(1).
▸Figure 230–50

Services | 230.72

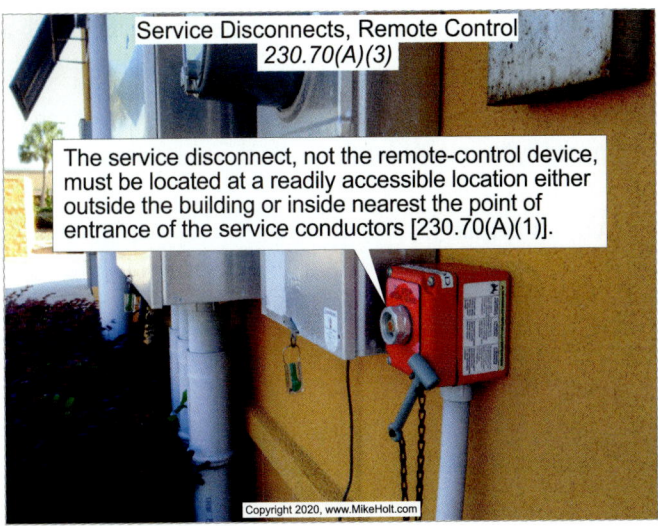

▶Figure 230–50

Author's Comment:

▸ The service disconnect must consist of a manually operated switch, or a power-operated switch or circuit breaker that is also capable of being operated manually [230.76]. The remote-control device is not permitted to serve as the service disconnect.

(B) Disconnect Identification. Each service disconnect must be permanently marked to identify it as a service disconnect. ▶Figure 230–51

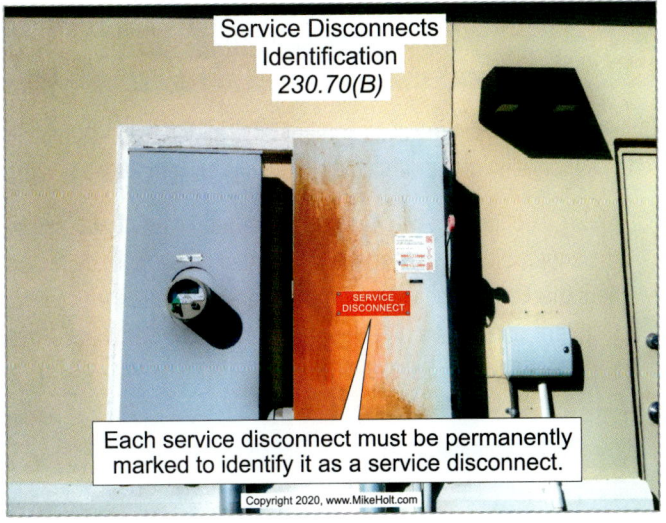

▶Figure 230–51

230.71 Number of Service Disconnects

Each service must have only one disconnecting means except as permitted in 230.71(B).

(B) Two to Six Service Disconnecting Means. Up to six service disconnects are permitted for each service allowed by 230.2, or for each set of service-entrance conductors permitted by 230.40 Ex 1, 3, 4, or 5.

The two to six service disconnecting means must consist of a combination of any of the following:

(1) Separate enclosures with a main service disconnecting means in each enclosure

(2) Panelboards with a main service disconnecting means in each panelboard

(3) Switchboard(s) where there is only one service disconnect in each separate vertical section where there are barriers separating each vertical section

(4) Service disconnects in switchgear or metering centers where each disconnect is in a separate compartment

Note 2: Examples of separate enclosures with main service disconnecting means in each enclosure include (but are not limited to) motor control centers, fused disconnects, circuit breaker enclosures, and transfer switches that are suitable for use as service equipment.

> **Caution**
> ⚠ The rule is six disconnects for each service, not for each building. If the building has two services, then there can be a total of 12 service disconnects (six disconnects per service).
> ▶Figure 230–52

230.72 Grouping of Disconnects

(A) Two to Six Disconnects. The service disconnects for each service must be grouped and marked to indicate the load served.

(B) Additional Service Disconnecting Means. To minimize the possibility of simultaneous interruption of power, the disconnect for fire pumps [Article 695], emergency systems [Article 700], legally required standby systems [Article 701], or optional standby systems [Article 702] must be located remote from the service disconnect(s) for normal service.

230.76 | Services

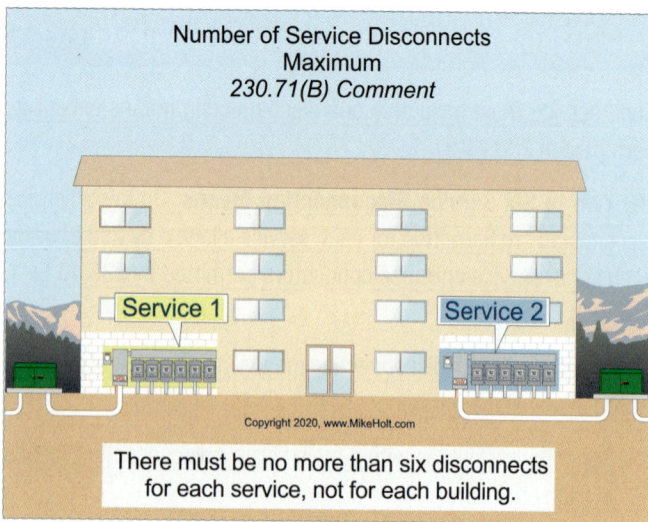
▶Figure 230-52

Author's Comment:

▸ Because emergency systems are just as important as fire pumps and standby systems, they need to have the same safety precautions to prevent unintended interruption of the supply of electricity.

▸ The authority having jurisdiction is responsible for determining what a sufficiently remote distance is for an additional service disconnect.

230.76 Manually or Power Operated

The service disconnect can consist of: ▶Figure 230-53

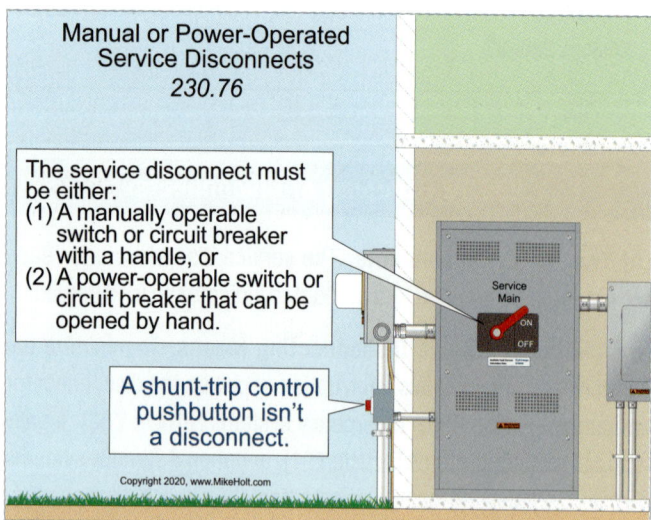
▶Figure 230-53

(1) A manually operable switch or circuit breaker equipped with a handle.

(2) A power-operated switch or circuit breaker provided it can be opened by hand in the event of a power supply failure.

Author's Comment:

▸ A shunt-trip button does not qualify as a service disconnect because it does not meet any of the above requirements.

230.79 Rating of Disconnect

The service disconnect for a building must have an ampere rating of not less than the calculated load according to Article 220 and in no case can it be less than:

(A) One-Circuit Installation. For installations consisting of a single branch circuit, the disconnect must have a rating of not less than 15A.

(B) Two-Circuit Installation. For installations consisting of two 2-wire branch circuits, the disconnect must have a rating or not less than 30A.

(C) One-Family Dwelling. For a one-family dwelling, the disconnect must have a rating of not less than 100A, 3-wire.

(D) Other Installations. For all other installations, the disconnect must have a rating of not less than 60A.

230.82 Connected on Supply Side of the Service Disconnect

Only the following electrical equipment is permitted to be connected to the supply side of the service disconnect. ▶Figure 230-54

(3) Meter disconnect switches are permitted to be connected to the supply side of the service disconnect. They must be legibly field marked on the exterior in a manner suitable for the environment as follows: **METER DISCONNECT NOT SERVICE EQUIPMENT** ▶Figure 230-55

Author's Comment:

▸ Some electric utilities require a disconnect switch ahead of the meter enclosure for 277/480V services for the purpose of enhancing safety for the serving electric utility's personnel when they install or remove a meter socket.

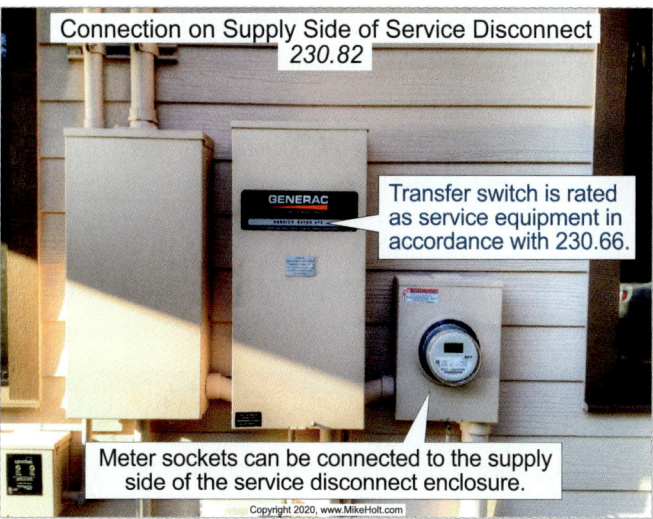
▶Figure 230-54

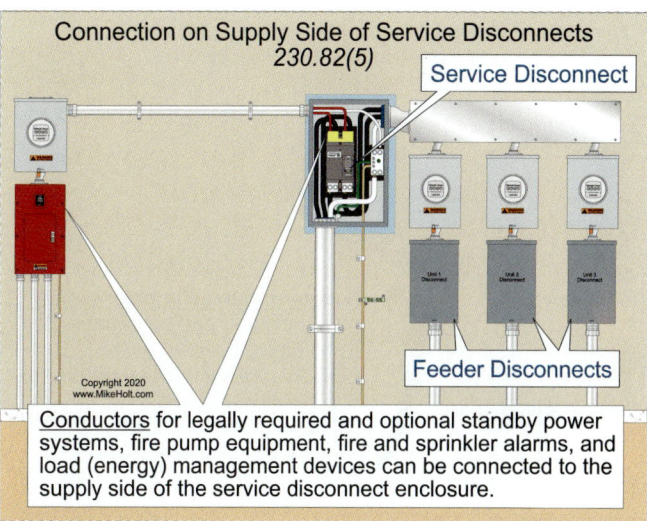
▶Figure 230-56

▶Figure 230-55

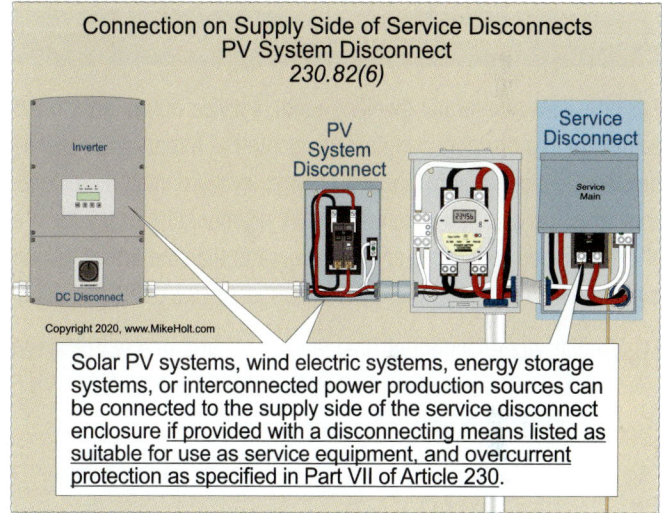
▶Figure 230-57

(5) Conductors for legally required and optional standby power systems, fire pump equipment, fire and sprinkler alarms, and load (energy) management devices can be connected to the supply side of the service disconnect enclosure. ▶Figure 230-56

(6) Solar PV systems, wind electric systems, energy storage systems, or interconnected power production sources can be connected to the supply side of the service disconnect enclosure if provided with a disconnecting means listed as suitable for use as service equipment and overcurrent protection as specified in Part VII of Article 230. ▶Figure 230-57

(10) Emergency disconnects in accordance with 230.85.

(11) Meter-mounted transfer switches that have a short-circuit current rating equal to or greater than the available fault current. A meter-mounted transfer switch must be listed and be capable of transferring the load served. A meter-mounted transfer switch must be marked on its exterior the following manner: ▶Figure 230-58

(a) Meter-mounted transfer switch

(b) Not service equipment

230.85 | Services

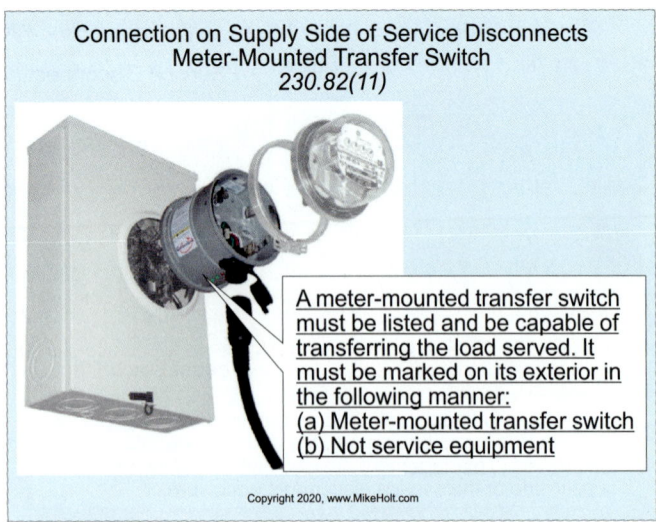
▶Figure 230-58

(3) Switch(es) or circuit breaker(s) on the supply side of the service disconnect(s) and marked: EMERGENCY DISCONNECT, NOT SERVICE EQUIPMENT

Markings must be permanently affixed and be sufficiently durable to withstand the environment involved in accordance with 110.21(B).

Part VII. Service Disconnect Overcurrent Protection

230.90 Overload Protection—Where Required

Each service phase conductor must have overload protection. ▶Figure 230-60

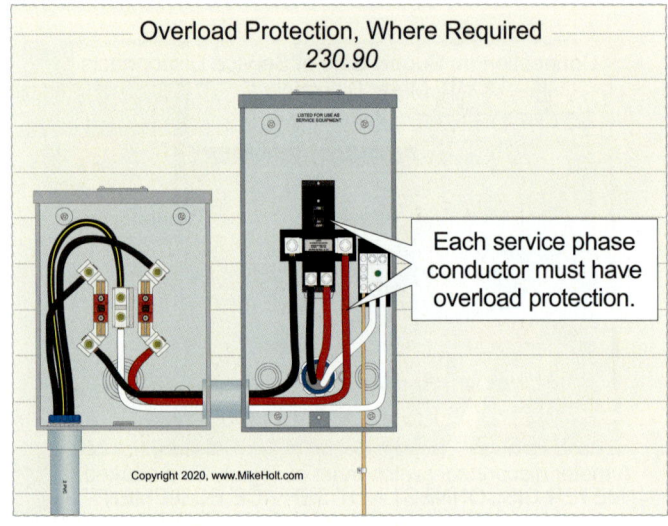
▶Figure 230-60

230.85 Emergency Disconnects

For one- and two-family dwelling units, service conductors must terminate in a disconnecting means located at a readily accessible outdoor location. If more than one emergency disconnect is provided, they must be grouped. The emergency disconnect(s) must have a short-circuit current rating equal to or greater than the available fault current. The emergency disconnect(s) must be one of the following:

(1) The service disconnect [installed in accordance with Part VI of Article 230] marked: EMERGENCY DISCONNECT, SERVICE DISCONNECT ▶Figure 230-59

▶Figure 230-59

(2) Meter disconnects [installed accordance with 230.82(3)] marked: EMERGENCY DISCONNECT, METER DISCONNECT, NOT SERVICE EQUIPMENT

(A) Overcurrent Protective Device Rating. The rating of the overcurrent protective device must not be greater than the ampacity of the service phase conductors. ▶Figure 230-61

Ex 2: If the ampacity of the phase conductors does not correspond with the standard rating of overcurrent protective devices as listed in 240.6(A), the next higher overcurrent protective device can be used if it does not exceed 800A [240.4(B)]. ▶Figure 230-62

Ex 3: The combined ratings of two to six service disconnects can exceed the ampacity of the service conductors provided the calculated load, in accordance with Article 220, does not exceed the ampacity of the service conductors. ▶Figure 230-63

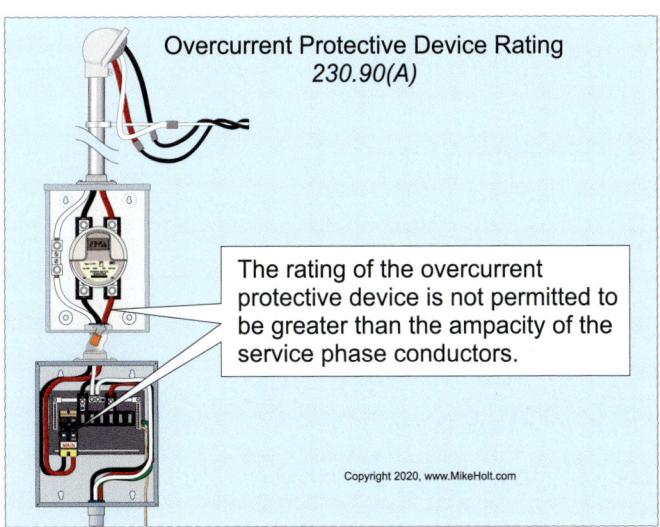

▶Figure 230-61

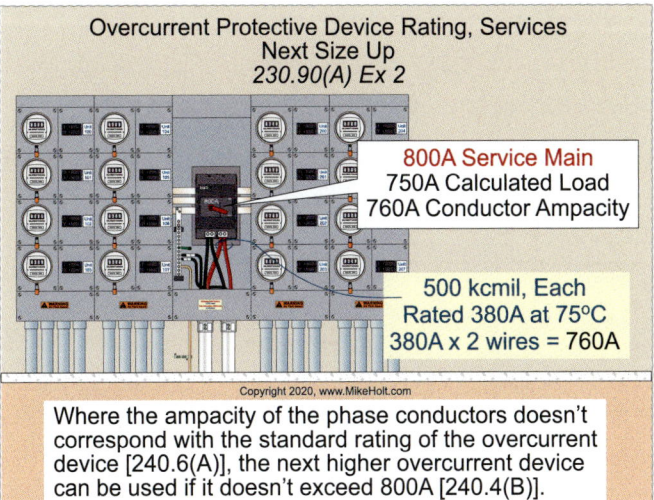

▶Figure 230-62

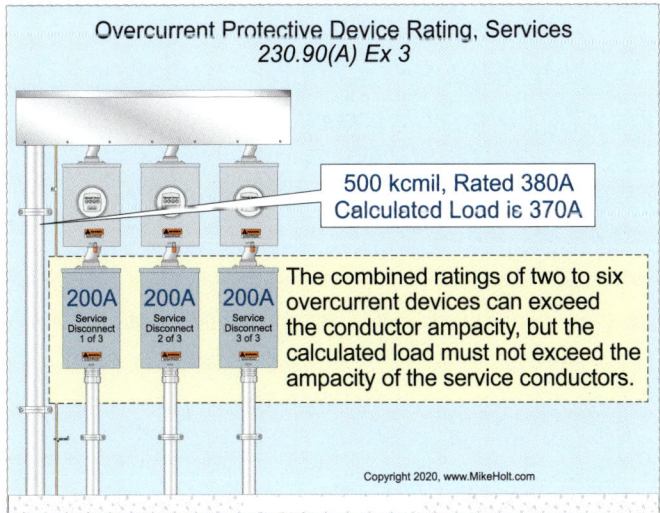

▶Figure 230-63

Ex 5: Overload protection for 120/240V, 3-wire, single-phase dwelling services is permitted in accordance with the requirements 310.12.

230.91 Location

The service overcurrent device must be an integral part of the service disconnecting means or be located immediately adjacent to the service disconnecting means. Where fuses are used as the service overcurrent device, the disconnecting means must be located ahead of the supply side of the fuses. ▶Figure 230-64

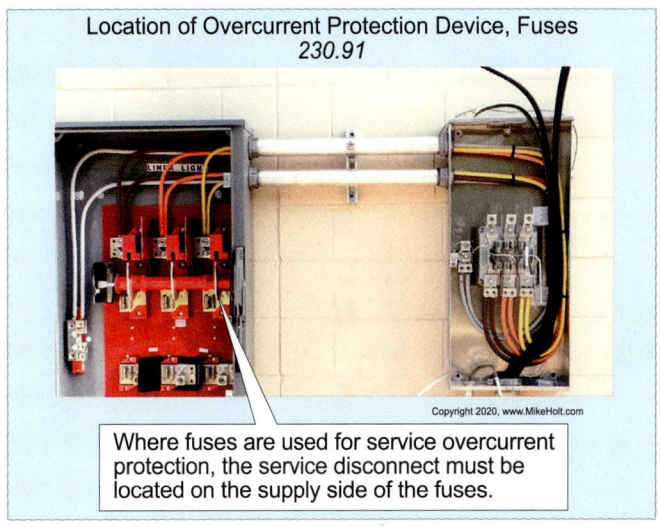

▶Figure 230-64

230.95 Ground-Fault Protection of Equipment

Ground-fault protection of equipment is required for 277/480V service disconnects rated 1,000A or more. The rating of the service disconnect is based on the rating of the largest fuse that can be installed or the circuit breaker's highest continuous current trip setting.

Notes

ARTICLE 240 — OVERCURRENT PROTECTION

Introduction to Article 240—Overcurrent Protection

This article provides the requirements for overcurrent protection and selecting and installing overcurrent protective devices—typically circuit breakers or fuses. Overcurrent exists when current exceeds the rating of equipment or the ampacity of a conductor due to an overload, short circuit, or ground fault [Article 100]. ▶Figure 240–1

- *Overload.* An overload is a condition where equipment or conductors carry current exceeding their current rating [Article 100]. A fault, such as a short circuit or ground fault, is not an overload. An example of an overload is plugging two 12.50A (1,500W) hair dryers into a 20A branch circuit.

- *Short Circuit.* A short circuit is the unintentional electrical connection between any two normally current-carrying conductors of an electric circuit, either line-to-line or line-to-neutral.

- *Ground fault.* A ground fault is an unintentional, electrically conducting connection between a phase conductor of an electric circuit and the normally noncurrent-carrying conductors, metal enclosures, metal raceways, metal equipment, or the Earth [Article 100]. When a ground fault occurs, dangerous voltages is present on metal parts until the circuit overcurrent protective device opens and clears the fault.

▶Figure 240–1

Overcurrent protective devices protect conductors and equipment. Selecting the proper overcurrent protection for a specific circuit can be more complicated than it sounds. The general rule for overcurrent protection is that conductors must be protected in accordance with their ampacities at the point where they receive their supply [240.4 and 240.21]. The asterisks next to the small conductor sizes in Table 310.16 refer to a footnote directing you to 240.4(D). That section contains the general rules for small conductors which limit the rating of the overcurrent devices protecting small conductors. There are quite a few circumstances that deviate from this and seem to "break" those rules. Table 240.4(G) lists articles in the *Code* that modify the basic rules of 240.4(D). There are also several rules allowing tap conductors (with much lower ampacities than the overcurrent device protecting them seems to allow) in specific situations [240.21(B)].

Author's Comment:

- The tripping action of an overcurrent protective device during an overload is based on a "time-curve," which essentially means that the higher the current, the faster the device will trip. Because of this "time-curve," conductors with lower ampacities than the overcurrent protective device protecting them, may seem to break the rules, but the overcurrent condition will be present only for a very short and safe amount of time.

An overcurrent protective device must be capable of opening a circuit when an overcurrent situation occurs and must also have an interrupting rating sufficient to avoid damage in fault conditions [110.9]. Carefully study this article to be sure you provide enough overcurrent protection in the correct location(s).

240.1 | Overcurrent Protection

Part I. General

240.1 Scope

Article 240 covers the general requirements for overcurrent protection and the installation requirements of overcurrent protective devices. ▶Figure 240–2

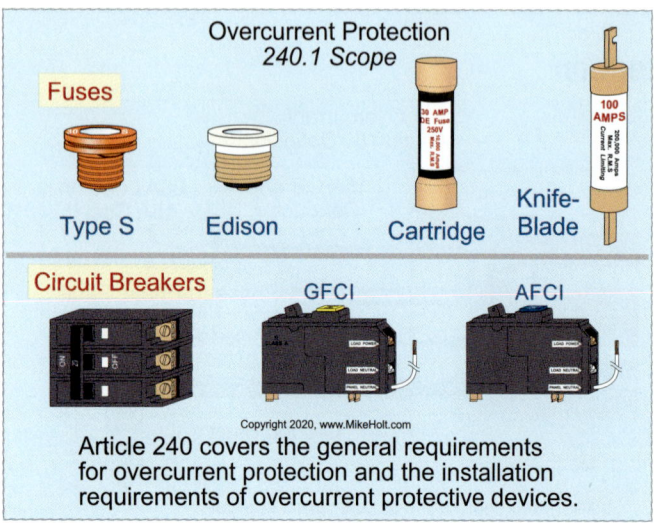

▶Figure 240–2

Author's Comment:

▸ Overcurrent is a condition where the current exceeds the rating of equipment or the ampacity of a conductor due to overload, short circuit, or ground fault [Article 100].

Note: An overcurrent protective device protects the circuit by opening the device when the current reaches a value that will cause excessive or dangerous temperature rise (overheating) in conductors. Overcurrent protective devices must have an interrupting rating sufficient for the maximum possible fault current available on the line-side terminals of the equipment [110.9]. Electrical equipment must have a short-circuit current rating that permits the circuit's overcurrent device to clear short circuits or ground faults without extensive damage to the circuit's electrical components [110.10].

Author's Comment:

▸ Perhaps one of the most critical points to understand is that a fault or other overcurrent condition will eventually occur in even the best electrical system. Our job is to ensure the overcurrent protection equipment can handle the conditions safely, and with little or no damage. Proper overcurrent protection is a critical step in this process.

240.2 Definitions

Current-Limiting Overcurrent Protective Device. An overcurrent protective device (typically a fast-acting fuse) that reduces the fault current to a magnitude substantially less than that obtainable in the same circuit if the current-limiting device was not used. See 240.40 and 240.60(B). ▶Figure 240–3

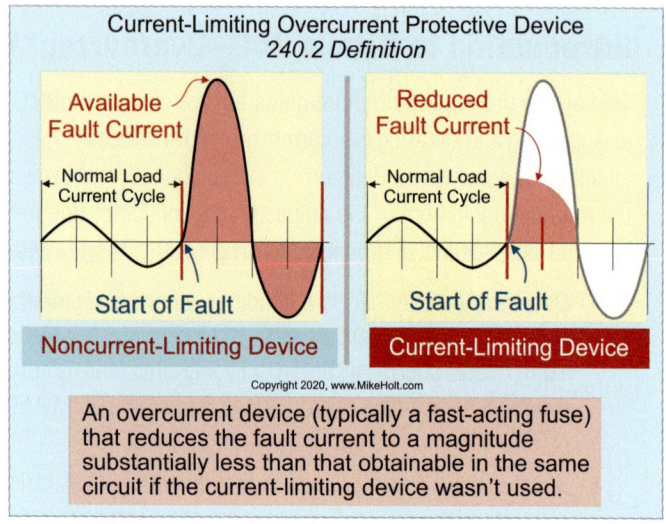

▶Figure 240–3

Author's Comment:

▸ A current-limiting fuse is designed for operations related to short circuits only. When a fuse operates in its current-limiting range, the fusible link will begin to melt in less than a quarter of a cycle, and it will open a bolted short circuit in less than half a cycle. This type of fuse limits the instantaneous peak let-through current to a value substantially less than what might occur in the same circuit if the fuse is replaced with a solid conductor of equal impedance. If the available short-circuit current exceeds the equipment's or conductor's short-circuit current rating, the thermal and magnetic forces can cause the equipment circuit conductors (as well as the circuit equipment grounding conductors) to vaporize. The only solutions to the problem of excessive available fault current are to:

▸ Install equipment with a higher ampere interrupting capacity (AIC) rating, or

▸ Protect the components of the circuit using a current-limiting overcurrent protective device such as a fast-clearing fuse, which can reduce the let-through energy.

Overcurrent Protection | 240.4

▸ While a breaker or a fuse does limit current, it may not be listed as a current-limiting device. A thermal-magnetic circuit breaker typically clears fault current in less than three to five cycles when subjected to a short circuit or ground fault of 20 times its rating. A standard fuse will clear the same fault in less than one cycle and a current-limiting fuse in less than half of a cycle.

Tap Conductors. A conductor, other than a service conductor, with overcurrent protection rated more than the ampacity of the conductor. See 240.21(A) and 240.21(B) for details. ▸Figure 240-4

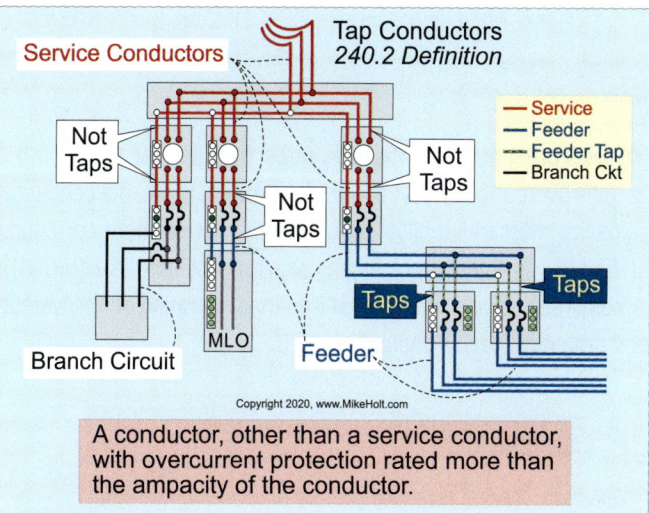
▸Figure 240-4

240.3 Other Articles (Overcurrent Protection of Equipment)

The following equipment and their conductors must be protected against overcurrent in accordance with the article for that type of equipment:

Table 240.3—Other Articles		
Equipment	Article	Section
Air-Conditioning and Refrigeration Equipment	440	440.22
Appliances	422	All
Audio Circuits	640	640.9
Branch Circuits	210	210.20

Table 240.3—Other Articles (continued)		
Equipment	Article	Section
Class 1, 2, and 3 Circuits	725	All
Feeder Conductors	215	215.3
Flexible Cords	240	240.5(B)(1)
Fire Alarms	760	All
Fire Pumps	695	All
Fixed Electric Space-Heating Equipment	424	424.22
Fixture Wire	240	240.5(B)(2)
Panelboards	408	408.36
Service Conductors	230	230.90(A)
Transformers	450	450.3

240.4 Overcurrent Protection of Conductors

Except as permitted by (A) through (G), conductors must be protected against overcurrent in accordance with their ampacity after ampacity correction and adjustment as specified in 310.14. ▸Figure 240-5

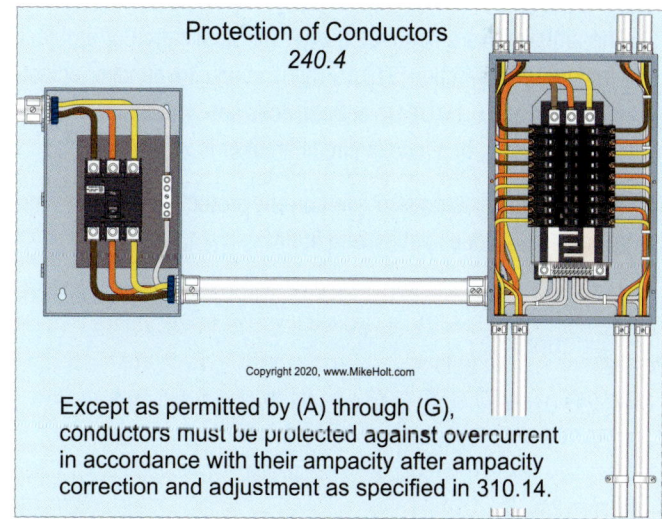
▸Figure 240-5

240.4 | Overcurrent Protection

Author's Comment:

▸ Table 310.16 contains conductor ampacities based on up to three current-carrying conductors in a raceway and in an ambient temperature of 86°F or 30°C at up to 2,000V. If any other conditions apply such as more than three current-carrying conductors, or a different ambient temperature, the ampacities found in Table 310.16 must be corrected in accordance with 310.15(B), and/or adjusted in accordance with 310.15(C).

▸ Overcurrent protection of conductors is a critical safety component to ensure an electric circuit will fail properly. Bypassing overcurrent protection is extremely dangerous to persons and property.

(A) Power Loss Hazard. Conductor overload protection is not required but short-circuit overcurrent protection is required where the interruption of the circuit will create a hazard, such as in a material-handling electromagnet circuit or fire pump circuit.

(B) Overcurrent Protective Devices Rated 800A or Less. The next higher standard rating of overcurrent protective device in 240.6 (above the ampacity of the phase conductors being protected) is permitted to be used, provided all the following conditions are met:

(1) The conductors are not part of a branch circuit supplying more than one receptacle for cord-and-plug-connected loads.

(2) The ampacity of a conductor, after the application of ambient temperature correction [310.15(B)(1)], conductor bundling adjustment [Table 310.15(C)(1)], or both, does not correspond with the standard rating of a fuse or circuit breaker in 240.6(A).

(3) The next higher standard overcurrent protective device rating from 240.6(A) does not exceed 800A.

▶ **Example**

Question: According to Table 310.16, what is the maximum size overcurrent protective device that can be used to protect 500 kcmil conductors where each conductor has an ampacity of 380A at 75°C? ▶Figure 240-6

(a) 300A   (b) 350A   (c) 400A   (d) 500A

Answer: (c) 400A [240.6(A)]

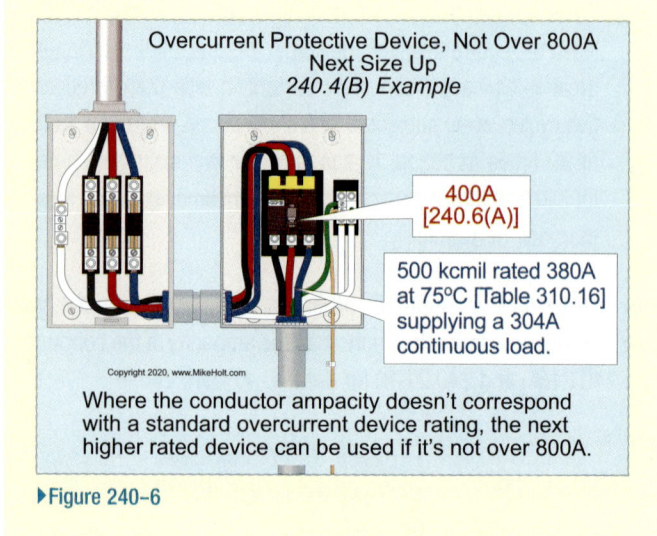
▶Figure 240-6

(C) Overcurrent Protective Devices Rated Over 800A. If the circuit's overcurrent protective device exceeds 800A, the conductor ampacity, after the application of ambient temperature correction [310.15(B)(1)], conductor bundling adjustment [Table 310.15(C)(1)], or both, must have a rating of not less than the rating of the overcurrent protective device defined in 240.6.

▶ **Example**

Question: What is the minimum size of conductor, paralled in three sets, and protected by a 1,200A overcurrent protective device? ▶Figure 240-7

(a) 400 kcmil   (b) 500 kcmil   (c) 600 kcmil   (d) 750 kcmil

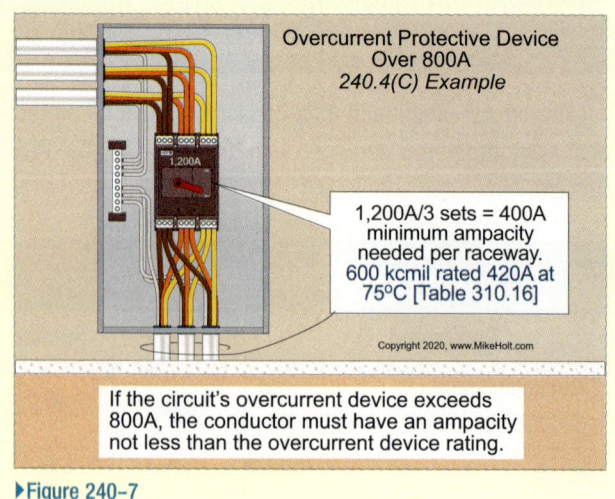
▶Figure 240-7

Overcurrent Protection | 240.4

Solution:

The total ampacity of the three parallel conductor sets must be equal to or greater than 1,200A [240.4(C)]. The ampacity for each conductor within the parallel set must be equal to or greater than 400A (1,200A/3 raceways).

Conductor Size = 600 kcmil conductors per phase rated 420A at 75°C [110.14(C)(1) and Table 310.16]

Total Conductor Ampacity = 420A × 3 conductors
Total Conductor Ampacity = 1,260A

Answer: *(c) 600 kcmil*

(D) Small Conductors. Unless specifically permitted in 240.4(E) or (G), overcurrent protection is not permitted to exceed the following: ▶Figure 240-8

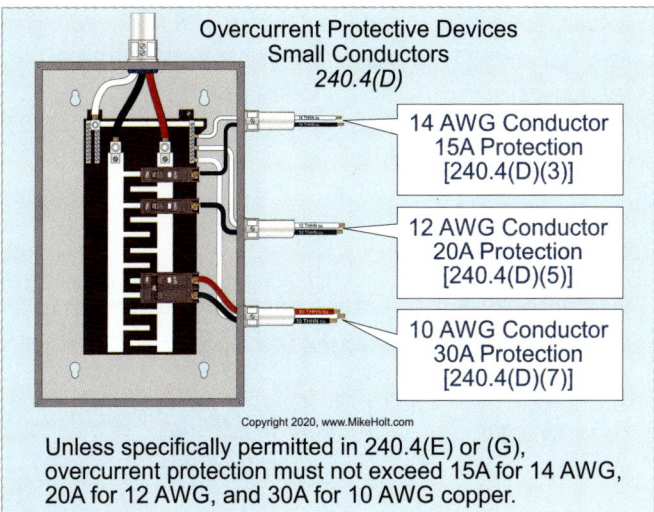

▶Figure 240-8

(1) 18 AWG Copper—7A.

(2) 16 AWG Copper—10A.

(3) 14 AWG Copper—15A.

(4) 12 AWG Aluminum and Copper-Clad Aluminum—15A.

(5) 12 AWG Copper—20A.

(6) 10 AWG Aluminum and Copper-Clad Aluminum—25A.

(7) 10 AWG Copper—30A.

(E) Tap Conductors. Tap conductors must have overcurrent protection in accordance with the following:

(1) Household Ranges, Cooking Appliances, and Other Loads [210.19(A)(3) and (4)].

(2) Fixture Wire [240.5(B)(2)].

(3) Location in Circuit [240.21].

(F) Transformer Secondary Conductors. For a 2-wire, single-voltage system and delta-delta, 3-wire systems, the primary overcurrent protective device sized in accordance with 450.3(B) is considered suitable to protect the secondary conductors, provided it does not exceed the value determined by multiplying the secondary conductor ampacity by the secondary-to-primary transformer voltage ratio.

▶ **Example**

Question: *What is the minimum size secondary conductor required for a single-phase, 1.50 kVA, 480V to 120V transformer that is protected with a 5A fuse?* ▶Figure 240-9

(a) 18 AWG (b) 16 AWG (c) 14 AWG (d) 12 AWG

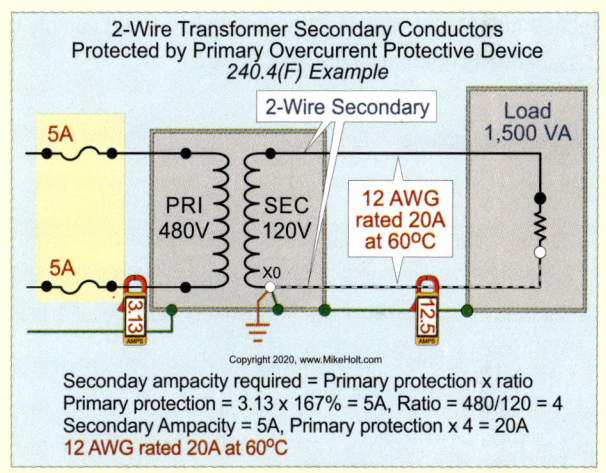

▶Figure 240-9

Solution:

Step 1: *Determine the primary current.*

VA/E
VA = 1,500 VA
E = 480V

Primary Current = 1,500 VA/480V
Primary Current = 3.13A

Step 2: *Determine the primary overcurrent protective device size [450.3(B)].*

Primary Overcurrent Protection = 3.13A × 167%
Primary Overcurrent Protection = 5.23A or a 5A Fuse

240.4 | Overcurrent Protection

Step 3: Determine the primary-to-secondary transformer winding voltage ratio.

Winding Voltage Ratio = Primary Volts/Secondary Volts

Winding Voltage Ratio = 480V/120V

Winding Voltage Ratio = 4 to 1

Step 4: Determine the secondary conductor minimum ampacity.

Secondary Ampacity = Primary Overcurrent Protection × Ratio

Secondary Ampacity = Primary of 5A × Winding Voltage Ratio of 4

Secondary Ampacity = 20A

Use a 12 AWG conductor rated 20A at 60°C [110.14(C)(1)(a)(2) and Table 310.16].

Answer: (d) 12 AWG

(G) Overcurrent Protection for Specific Applications. Overcurrent protection for specific equipment and conductors can comply with the requirements referenced in Table 240.4(G).

Author's Comment:

▸ Table 240.4(G) indicates that for overcurrent protection for specific applications like air-conditioning the overcurrent protection requirements of Article 440 may be applied; and for motors, the overcurrent protection requirements of Article 430 may be applied.

▶ **Air Conditioner Example**

Question: What size branch-circuit conductor and overcurrent protective device are required for an air conditioner when the nameplate indicates the minimum circuit ampacity is 23A and the maximum overcurrent protection is 40A? ▸Figure 240-10

(a) 10 AWG, 20A OCPD
(b) 10 AWG, 30A OCPD
(c) 10 AWG, 40A OCPD
(d) 10 AWG, 50A OCPD

Solution:

The nameplate values for listed air-conditioning and refrigeration equipment are used to size the branch-circuit conductors and short-circuit overcurrent protective device [440.4(A)]. No calculation is required.

Conductor: The air conditioner branch-circuit conductor is sized to the nameplate minimum circuit ampacity of 23A. A 10 AWG conductor is suitable since it has an ampacity of 30A at 60°C [110.14(C)(1) and Table 310.16].

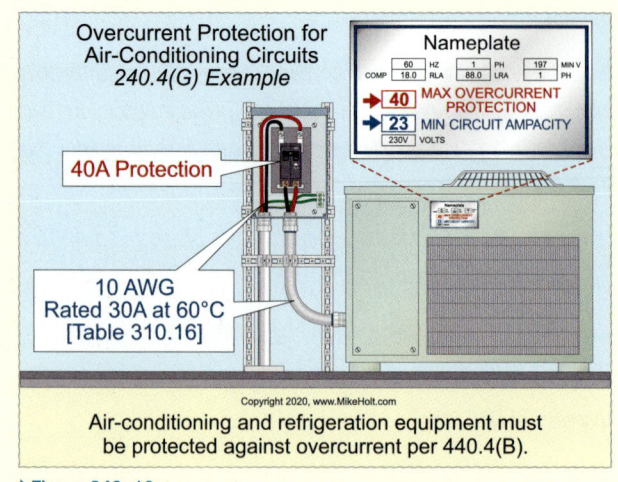

▸Figure 240-10

Protection: The air conditioner branch-circuit short-circuit protection is sized to the nameplate maximum value of 40A.

A 40A circuit breaker is permitted to protect a 10 AWG conductor rated 30A at 60°C in accordance with 110.14(C)(1)(a)(2), 240.4(G) and 440.4(A)

Answer: (c) 10 AWG, 40A

▶ **Motor Example**

Question: What size branch-circuit conductor and overcurrent protective device (circuit breaker) is required for a 7½ hp, 230V, three-phase motor? ▸Figure 240-11

(a) 10 AWG, 20A
(b) 10 AWG, 30A
(c) 10 AWG, 40A
(d) 10 AWG, 60A

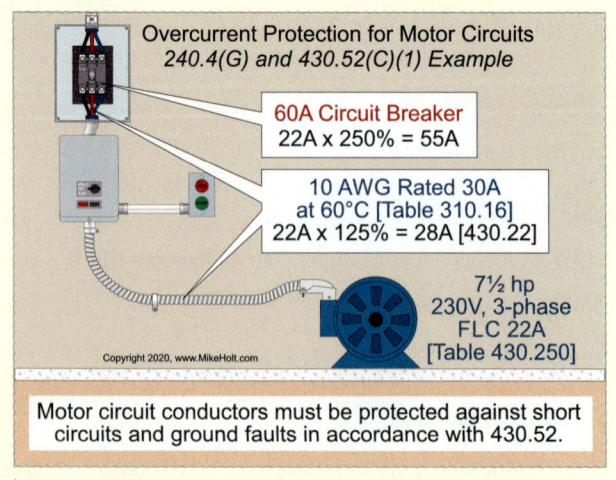

▸Figure 240-11

Solution:

Step 1: Determine the branch-circuit conductor size at 125% of the motor's FLC [430.22, and Table 430.250].

FLC = 22A [Table 430.250]

Conductor = 22A × 125% = 28A [430.22]
Conductor = 10 AWG which is rated 30A at 60°C [110.14(C)(1) and Table 310.16]

Step 2: Determine the branch-circuit overcurrent protection size at 250% of the motor's FLC [Table 430.52, 430.52(C)(1) Ex 1, and Table 430.250].

Inverse Time Circuit Breaker = 22A × 250%
Inverse Time Circuit Breaker = 55A

A 60A inverse time circuit breaker is permitted to protect the 10 AWG conductor rated 30A in accordance with 240.4(G), Table 430.52, and 430.52(C)(1) Ex 1.

Answer: (d) 10 AWG, 60A

Motor Control [Article 430]. Motor control circuit conductors are sized and protected in accordance with 430.72.

Remote-Control, Signaling, and Power-Limited Circuits [Article 725]. Remote-control, signaling, and power-limited circuit conductors are protected against overcurrent in accordance with 725.43.

240.5 Protection of Flexible Cords, Flexible Cables, and Fixture Wires

Flexible cord, including tinsel cord and extension cords, and fixture wires must be protected against overcurrent by either 240.5(A) or (B).

(A) Ampacities. Flexible cord must be protected by an overcurrent device in accordance with its ampacity as specified in Table 400.5(A)(1) and Table 400.5(A)(2). Fixture wire must be protected against overcurrent in accordance with its ampacity as specified in Table 402.5. Supplementary overcurrent protection, as covered in 240.10, is an acceptable means for providing this protection.

(B) Branch-Circuit Overcurrent Device. Flexible cord must be protected, where supplied by a branch circuit, in accordance with one of the methods described in 240.5(B)(1), (B)(3), or (B)(4). Fixture wire must be protected, where supplied by a branch circuit, in accordance with 240.5(B)(2).

(1) Supply Cord of Listed Appliance or Luminaire. Where flexible cord or tinsel cord is approved for (and used with) a specific listed appliance or luminaire, it is considered protected when applied within the appliance or luminaire listing requirements. For the purposes of this section, a luminaire may be either portable or permanent.

(2) Fixture Wire. Fixture wire is permitted to be tapped to the branch-circuit conductor of a branch circuit in accordance with the following:

(1) 15A or 20A circuits—18 AWG, up to 50 ft of run length
(2) 15A or 20A circuits—16 AWG, up to 100 ft of run length
(3) 20A circuits—14 AWG and larger
(4) 30A circuits—14 AWG and larger
(5) 40A circuits—12 AWG and larger
(6) 50A circuits—12 AWG and larger

(3) Extension Cord Sets. Flexible cord used in listed extension cord sets is considered protected when applied within the extension cord listing requirements.

(4) Field Assembled Extension Cord Sets. Flexible cord used in extension cords made with separately listed and installed components are permitted to be supplied by a branch circuit in accordance with the following: 20A circuits—16 AWG and larger

240.6 Standard Ampere Ratings

(A) Fuses and Fixed-Trip Circuit Breakers. The standard ratings in amperes for fuses and inverse time circuit breakers are shown in Table 240.6(A). The use of fuses and inverse time circuit breakers with nonstandard ampere ratings is permitted. ▶Figure 240–12

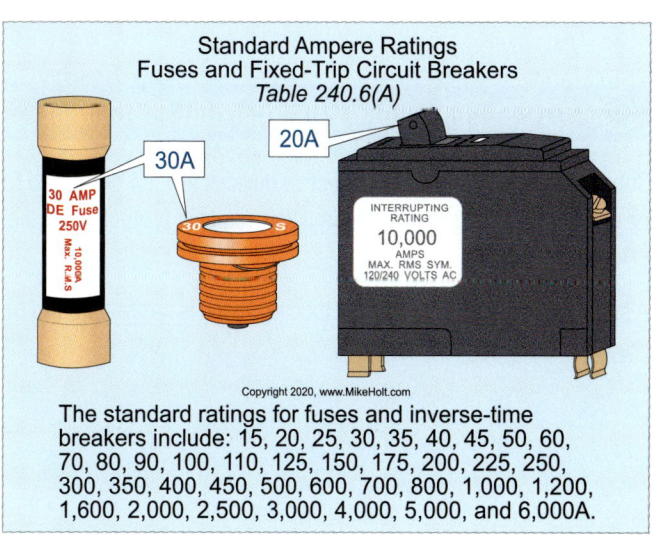

▶Figure 240–12

240.10 | Overcurrent Protection

Table 240.6(A) Standard Ampere Ratings for Fuses and Inverse Time Circuit Breakers Standard Ampere Ratings

15	20	25	30	35
40	45	50	60	70
80	90	100	110	125
150	175	200	225	250
300	350	400	450	500
600	700	800	1000	1200
1600	2000	2500	3000	4000

(B) Adjustable Trip Circuit Breakers, Without Restricted Access. The ampere rating of an adjustable trip circuit breaker without restricted access is equal to its maximum long-time pickup current setting.

(C) Adjustable Trip Circuit Breakers, Restricted Access. The ampere rating of adjustable trip circuit breakers with restricted access to the adjusting means is equal to the adjusted long-time pickup current settings. Restricted access is achieved by one of the following methods:

(1) Locating behind removable and sealable covers over the adjusting means

(2) Locating behind bolted equipment enclosure doors

(3) Locating behind locked doors accessible only to qualified personnel

(4) Being password protected with the password only accessible to qualified personnel

240.10 Supplementary Overcurrent Protection

Supplementary overcurrent protective devices are not permitted to be used as the required branch-circuit overcurrent protective device.
▶Figure 240–13

A supplementary overcurrent protective device is not required to be readily accessible [240.24(A)(2)].

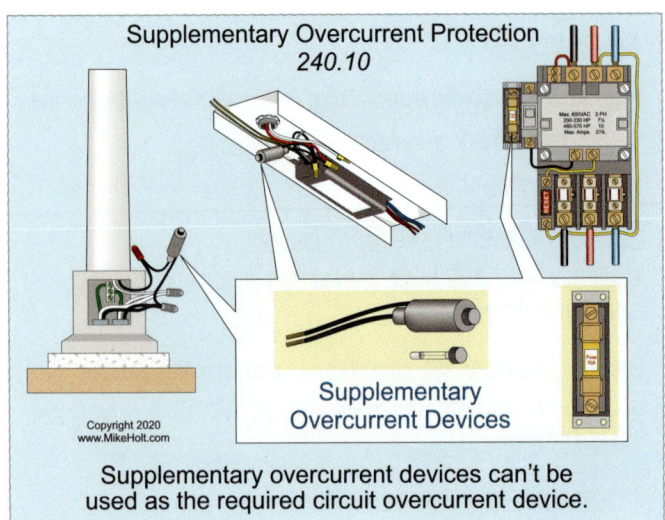
▶Figure 240–13

Author's Comment:

▸ Article 100 defines a "Supplementary Overcurrent Protective Device" as a device intended to provide limited overcurrent protection for specific applications and utilization equipment. This limited overcurrent protection is in addition to the overcurrent protection provided in the required branch circuit by the branch-circuit overcurrent protective device.

240.13 Ground-Fault Protection of Equipment

Ground-fault protection of equipment must be provided for service disconnects [230.95] and feeder disconnects [215.10] rated 1,000A or more supplied from a 4-wire, three-phase, 277/480V wye-connected system in accordance with 230.95.

Author's Comment:

▸ Article 100 defines "Ground-Fault Protection of Equipment" as a system intended to provide overcurrent protection of equipment from ground faults by opening the overcurrent protective device at current levels less than those required to protect conductors from damage. This type of protective system is not intended to protect people, only connected equipment.

▸ Ground-fault protection of equipment is not required for emergency power systems [700.31] or legally required standby power systems [701.31].

▸ Do not confuse ground-fault protection of equipment (GFPE) with ground-fault circuit interrupter (GFCI) protection for personnel.

Overcurrent Protection | 240.15

240.15 Phase Conductor Overcurrent Device

(B) Circuit Breaker. Circuit breakers protecting a circuit must automatically open all phase conductors of the circuit during an overcurrent condition, except as follows:

(1) Multiwire Branch Circuits. Individual single-pole breakers with handle ties identified for the purpose are permitted for each phase conductor of a multiwire branch circuit. ▶Figure 240–14

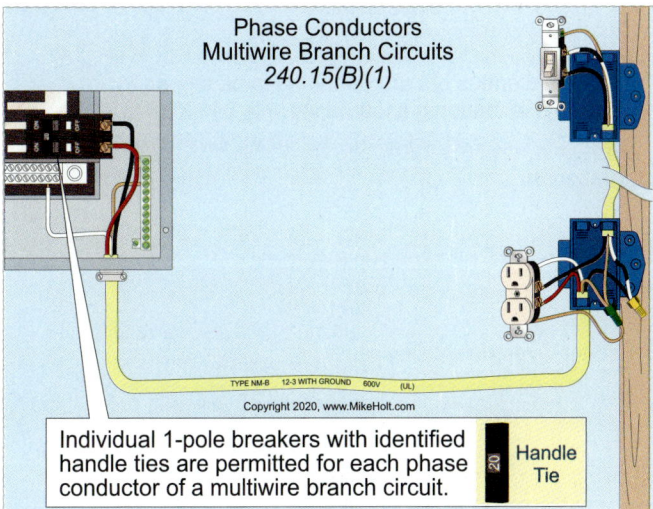
▶Figure 240–14

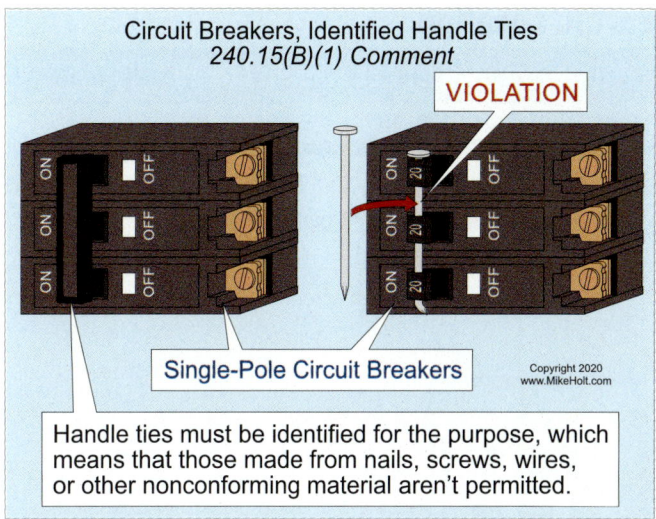
▶Figure 240–15

Author's Comment:

▸ According to Article 100, "Identified" means recognized as suitable for a specific purpose, function, or environment by listing, labeling, or other means approved by the authority having jurisdiction. This means handle ties made from nails, screws, wires, or other nonconforming materials are not permitted to serve as a handle tie. ▶Figure 240–15

(2) Line-to-Line Loads, Single-Phase. Individual single-pole circuit breakers rated 120/240V with handle ties identified for the purpose are permitted for each phase of a single-phase line-to-line load. ▶Figure 240–16

(3) Line-to-Line Loads, Three-Phase. Individual single-pole circuit breakers rated 120/240V with handle ties identified for the purpose are permitted for each phase of a three-phase line-to-line load. ▶Figure 240–17

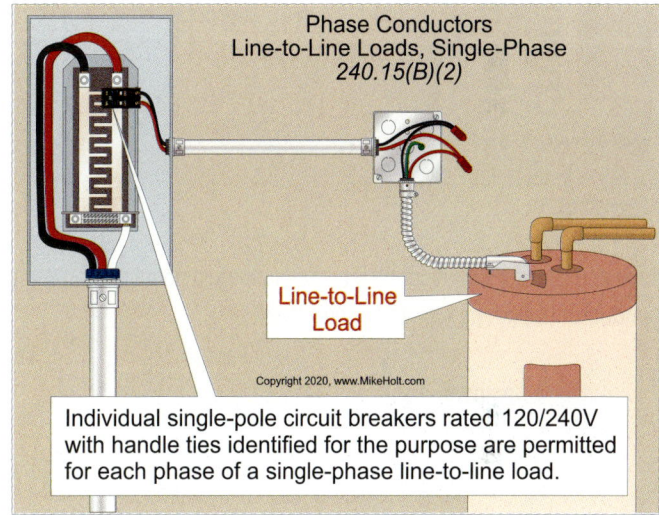
▶Figure 240–16

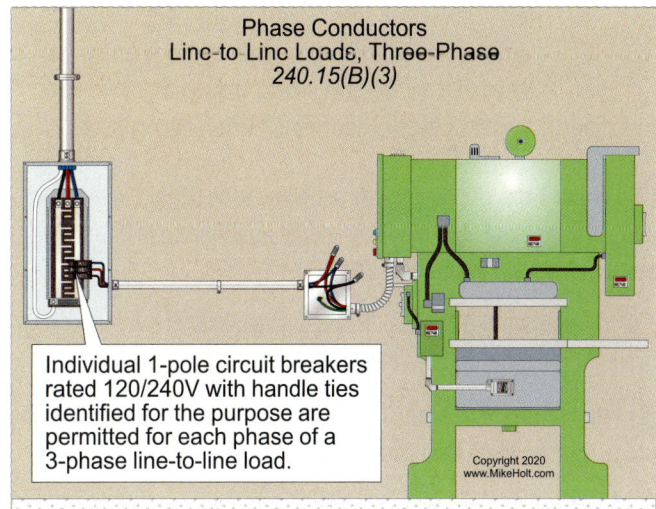
▶Figure 240–17

240.21 | Overcurrent Protection

Part II. Location

240.21 Location in Circuit

Overcurrent protection must be provided for each phase conductor at the point where the conductors receive their supply except as permitted by (A) through (H). ▶Figure 240-18

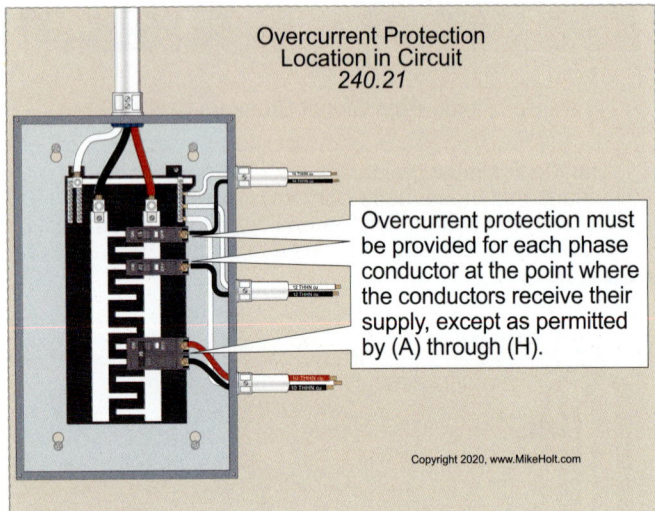
▶Figure 240-18

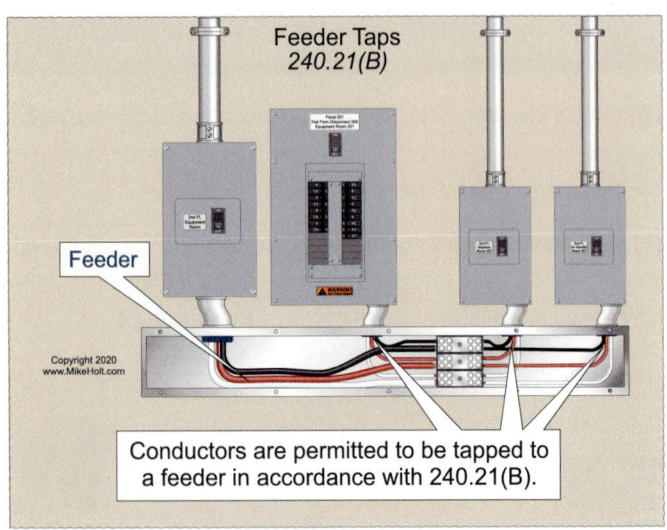
▶Figure 240-19

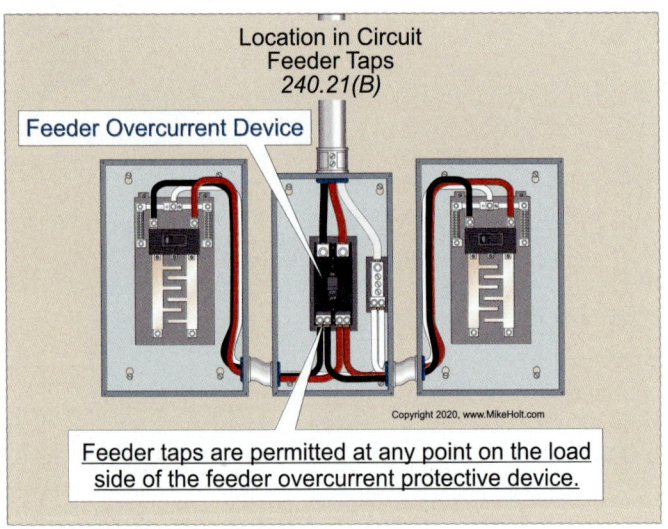
▶Figure 240-20

Taps and transformer secondary conductors must not supply another conductor (tapping a tap is not permitted).

Author's Comment:

▸ According to 240.2, a tap conductor is a conductor (other than a service conductor), that has overcurrent protection rated more than the ampacity of the conductor in accordance with 240.4. Instead of the conductors being protected at the point where they receive their supply, tap conductors are protected against an overload by the overcurrent protective device into which they feed, and against short circuit and ground fault by the feeder protective device from which they originate.

(B) Feeder Taps. Conductors are permitted to be tapped, without overcurrent protection at the tap, to a feeder as specified in 240.21(B)(1) through (B)(5). ▶Figure 240-19

The tap is permitted at any point on the load side of the feeder overcurrent protective device. ▶Figure 240-20

(1) Feeder Tap Not Over 10 Feet. Tap conductors up to 10 ft long are permitted when they comply with the following:

(1) Tap conductors have an ampacity equal to or greater than: ▶Figure 240-21

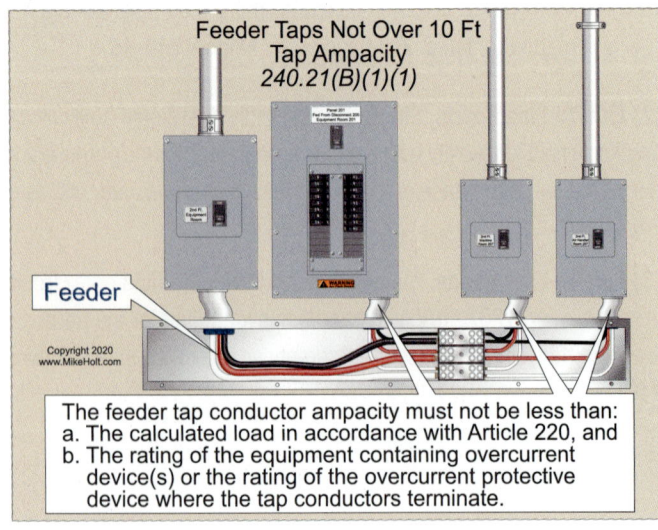
▶Figure 240-21

a. The calculated load in accordance with Article 220, and

b. The rating of the overcurrent device or the equipment supplied by the tap conductors.

(2) The tap conductors are not permitted to extend beyond the equipment they supply.

(3) The tap conductors are installed within a raceway.

(4) Tap conductors that leave the enclosure where the tap is made must have an ampacity of not less than 10 percent of the rating of the overcurrent device that protects the feeder. ▶Figure 240–22

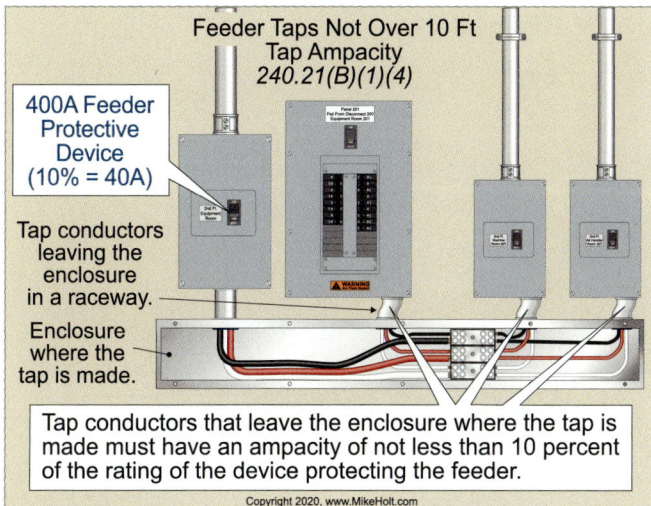

▶Figure 240–22

Note: If a tap supplies a panelboard, the tap conductors must terminate in an overcurrent device in accordance with 408.36.

10-Foot Tap Rule

▶ 10-Foot Tap Rule Example 1

Question: What size 10-ft tap conductor is needed from a 400A circuit breaker to supply a 200A panelboard if the terminals are rated 75°C? ▶Figure 240–23

(a) 1/0 AWG   (b) 2/0 AWG   (c) 3/0 AWG   (d) 4/0 AWG

Solution:

Ten Percent of 400A = 40A minimum conductor ampacity permitted

3/0 AWG is rated 200A at 75°C [110.14(C)(1) and Table 310.16] which is greater than 10 percent of the rating of the 400A overcurrent protective device.

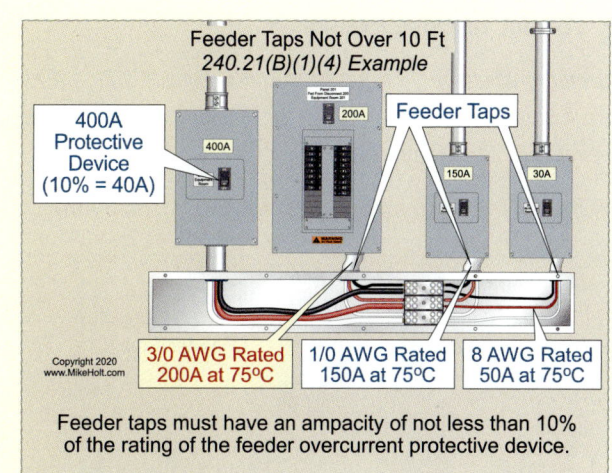

▶Figure 240–23

Answer: (c) 3/0 AWG

▶ 10-Foot Tap Rule Example 2

Question: What size 10-ft tap conductor is needed from a 400A circuit breaker to supply a 150A feeder disconnect if the terminals are rated 75°C? ▶Figure 240–24

(a) 1/0 AWG   (b) 2/0 AWG   (c) 3/0 AWG   (d) 4/0 AWG

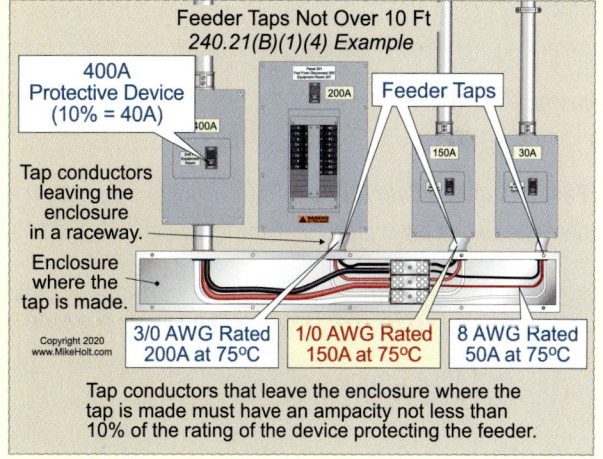

▶Figure 240–24

Solution:

Ten Percent of 400A = 40A minimum conductor ampacity permitted

1/0 AWG is rated 150A at 75°C [110.14(C)(1) and Table 310.16] which is greater than 10 percent of the rating of the 400A overcurrent protective device.

Answer: (a) 1/0 AWG

240.21 | Overcurrent Protection

▶ **10-Foot Tap Rule Example 3**

Question: What size 10-ft tap conductor is needed from a 400A circuit breaker to supply a 30A feeder disconnect if the terminals are rated 75°C? ▶Figure 240–25

(a) 8 AWG   (b) 6 AWG   (c) 4 AWG   (d) 3 AWG

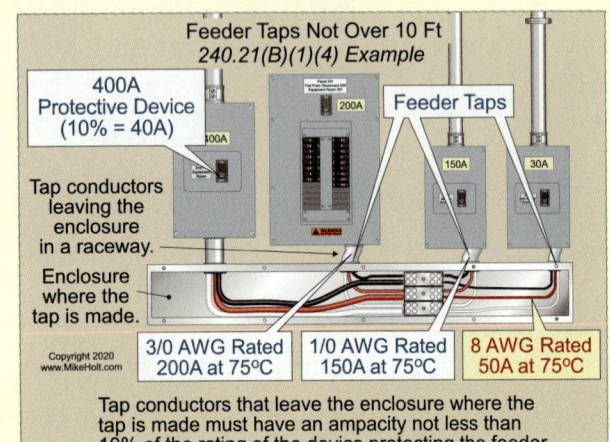

▶Figure 240–25

Solution:

Ten Percent of 400A = 40A minimum conductor ampacity permitted

8 AWG is rated 50A at 75°C [110.14(C)(1) and Table 310.16] which is greater than 10 percent of the rating of the 400A overcurrent device.

Answer: (a) 8 AWG

(2) Feeder Tap Not Over 25 Feet. Tap conductors up to 25 ft long are permitted when they comply with the following: ▶Figure 240–26

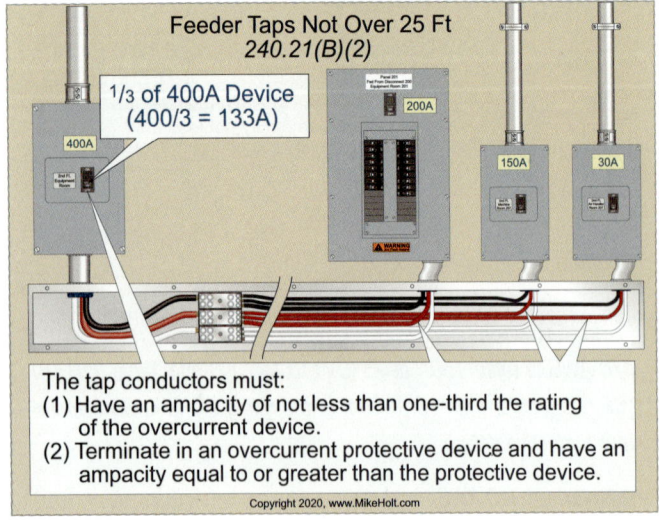

▶Figure 240–26

(1) The tap conductor has an ampacity not less than ⅓ the rating of the overcurrent protective device that protects the feeder.

(2) The tap conductors terminate in an overcurrent protective device and have an ampacity equal to or greater than the rating of the overcurrent protective device.

25-Foot Tap Rule

▶ **25-Foot Tap Example 1**

Question: What size 25-ft tap conductor is needed from a 400A circuit breaker to supply a 200A panelboard if the terminals are rated 75°C? ▶Figure 240–27

(a) 1/0 AWG   (b) 2/0 AWG   (c) 3/0 AWG   (d) 4/0 AWG

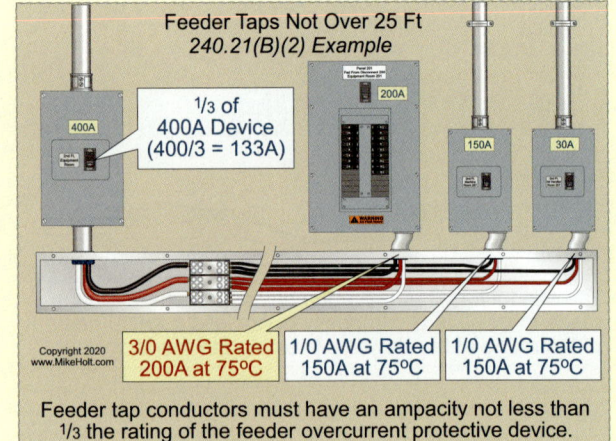

▶Figure 240–27

Solution:

The tap conductor must have a minimum rating of no less than 133A (⅓ the rating of the 400A overcurrent device). 3/0 AWG is rated 200A at 75°C [110.14(C)(1) and Table 310.16] which is greater than 133A (⅓ the rating of the 400A overcurrent device) and equal to the 200A disconnect.

Answer: (c) 3/0 AWG

Overcurrent Protection | **240.21**

▶ 25-Foot Tap Example 2

Question: What size 25-ft tap conductor is needed from a 400A circuit breaker to supply a 150A feeder disconnect if the terminals are rated 75°C? ▶Figure 240–28

(a) 1/0 AWG (b) 2/0 AWG (c) 3/0 AWG (d) 4/0 AWG

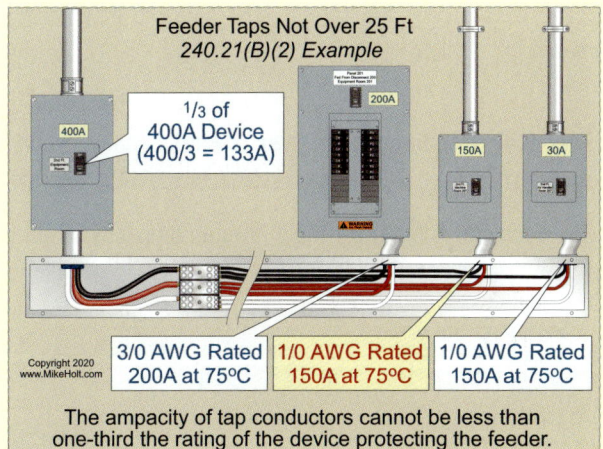

▶Figure 240–28

Solution:

The tap conductor must have a minimum rating of no less than 133A (⅓ the rating of the 400A overcurrent device).

1/0 AWG is rated 150A at 75°C [110.14(C)(1) and Table 310.16] which is greater than 133A (⅓ the rating of the 400A overcurrent device) and equal to the 150A disconnect.

Answer: (a) 1/0 AWG

▶ 25-Foot Tap Example 3

Question: What size 25-ft tap conductor is needed from a 400A circuit breaker to supply a 30A feeder disconnect if the terminals are rated 75°C? ▶Figure 240–29

(a) 3 AWG (b) 2 AWG (c) 1 AWG (d) 1/0 AWG

Solution:

The tap conductor must have a minimum rating of no less than 133A (⅓ the rating of the 400A overcurrent protective device). 1/0 AWG is rated 150A at 75°C [110.14(C)(1) and Table 310.16] which is greater than 133A (⅓ the rating of the 400A overcurrent device) and greater than the 30A disconnect.

Answer: (d) 1/0 AWG

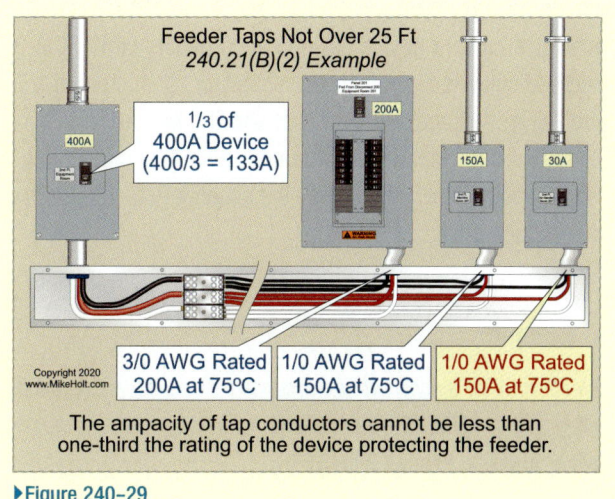

▶Figure 240–29

(5) Outside Feeder Taps. Outside tap conductors can be of unlimited length if they comply with all the following: ▶Figure 240–30

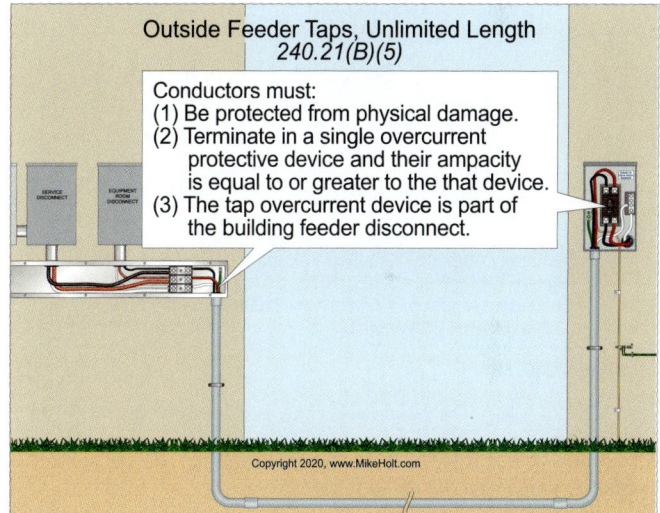

▶Figure 240–30

(1) The outside tap conductors are protected from physical damage.

(2) The outside tap conductors terminate in a circuit breaker or fuses that limits the load to the ampacity of the conductors.

(3) The tap's overcurrent device is part of the building feeder disconnect.

(C) Transformer Secondary Conductors. Secondary conductors must comply with the following:

240.21 | Overcurrent Protection

(1) Protection by Primary Overcurrent Protective Device. The primary overcurrent device sized in accordance with 450.3(B) is considered suitable to protect the secondary conductors of a 2- or 3-wire (single-voltage) system, provided the primary overcurrent device does not exceed the value determined by multiplying the secondary conductor ampacity by the secondary-to-primary transformer voltage ratio.

▶ **Example**

Question: What is minimum size secondary conductor required for a single-phase, 1.50 kVA, 480V-to-120V transformer that is protected with a 5A fuse? ▶Figure 240–31

(a) 14 AWG   (b) 12 AWG   (c) 10 AWG   (d) 8 AWG

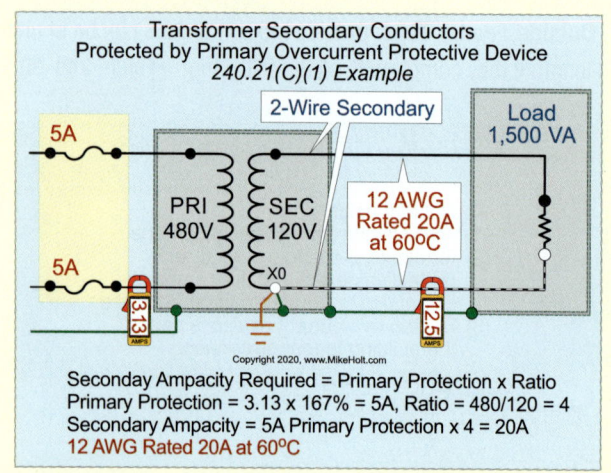

▶Figure 240–31

Solution:

Step 1: Determine the primary current.

VA/E

VA = 1,500 VA
E = 480V
Primary Current = 1,500 VA/480V
Primary Current = 3.13A

Step 2: Determine the primary overcurrent device [450.3(B)].

Primary Overcurrent Protection = 3.13A × 167%
Primary Overcurrent Protection = 5.23A; or 5A Fuse

Step 3: Determine the primary-to-secondary transformer winding voltage ratio.

Winding Voltage Ratio = Primary Volts/Secondary Volts
Winding Voltage Ratio = 480V/120V
Winding Voltage Ratio = 4 to 1

Step 4: Determine the secondary conductor minimum ampacity.

Secondary Ampacity = Primary Overcurrent Protection × Ratio
Secondary Ampacity = Primary of 5A × Winding Voltage Ratio of 4
Secondary Ampacity = 20A

Use a 12 AWG conductor rated 20A at 60°C [110.14(C)(1)(a)(2) and Table 310.16].

Answer: (b) 12 AWG

(2) Secondary Conductors Not Over 10 Feet. Secondary conductors up to 10 ft long are permitted when they comply with the following:

(1) The secondary conductor must have an ampacity of not less than: ▶Figure 240–32

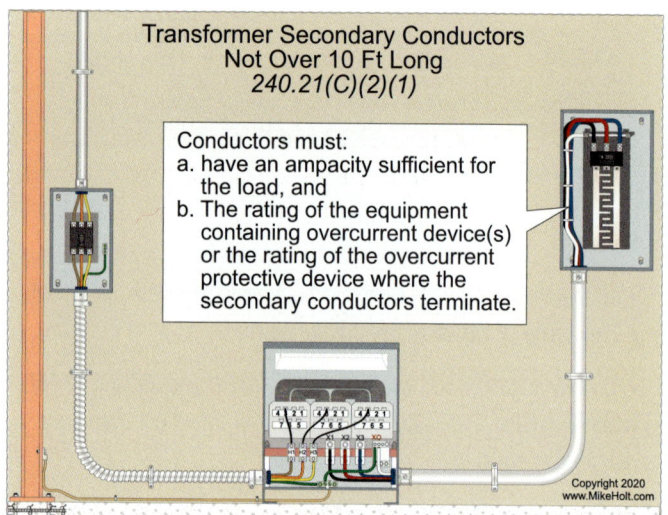

▶Figure 240–32

a. The calculated load in accordance with Article 220, and

b. The secondary conductor has an ampacity equal to or greater than the overcurrent device(s) or equipment supplied by the secondary conductors.

(4) Outside Secondary Conductors of Unlimited Length. Outside secondary conductors can be of unlimited length if they comply with all the following: ▶Figure 240–33

(1) The outside secondary conductors are protected from physical damage.

(2) The outside secondary conductors terminate in a single overcurrent device and their ampacity is equal to or greater than the overcurrent device in which they terminate.

Overcurrent Protection | 240.24

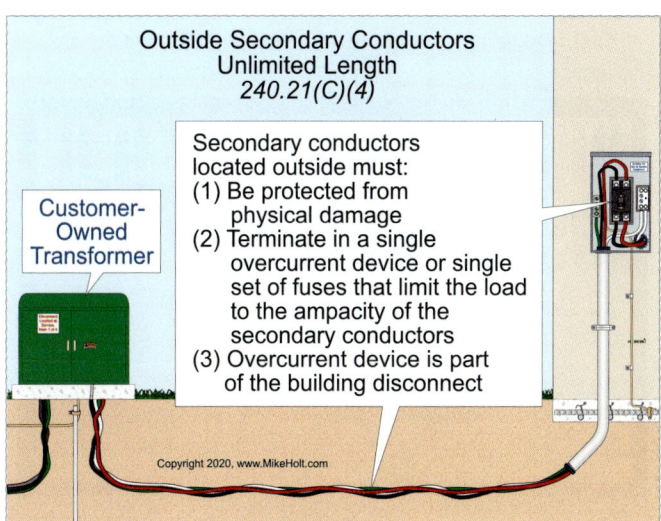
▶Figure 240-33

(3) The outside secondary overcurrent device is part of the building disconnect.

(6) Secondary Conductors Not Over 25 Feet. Secondary conductors up to 25 ft long are permitted when they comply with all the following:
▶Figure 240-34

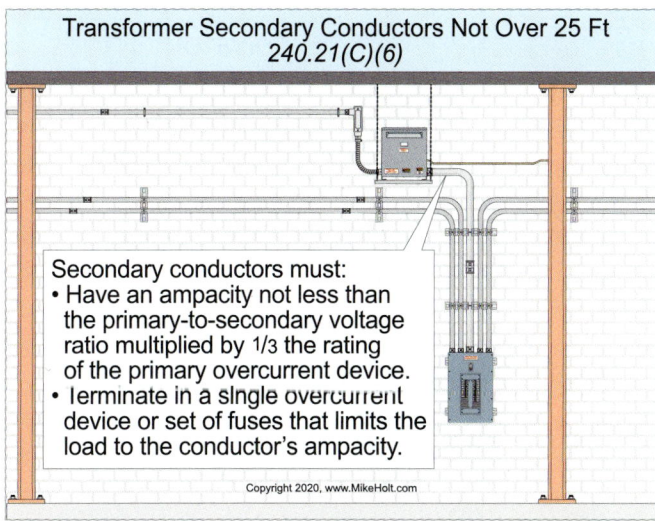
▶Figure 240-34

(1) The secondary has an ampacity not less than ⅓ the rating of the overcurrent device that protects the primary, multiplied by the primary-to-secondary voltage ratio.

(2) The secondary conductors terminate in an overcurrent device and have an ampacity rating not less than the rating of the overcurrent protective device.

240.24 Location of Overcurrent Protective Devices at Premises

(A) Readily Accessible. Circuit breakers and switches containing fuses must be readily accessible and be installed so the center of the grip of the operating handle of the circuit breaker or switch, when in its highest position, is not more than 6 ft 7 in. above the floor or working platform, except for the following: ▶Figure 240-35

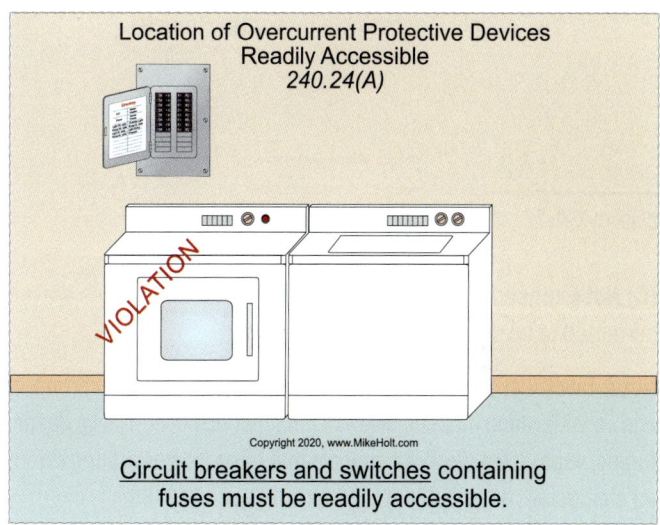
▶Figure 240-35

(2) Supplementary overcurrent protection, as described in 240.10 is not required to be readily accessible. ▶Figure 240-36

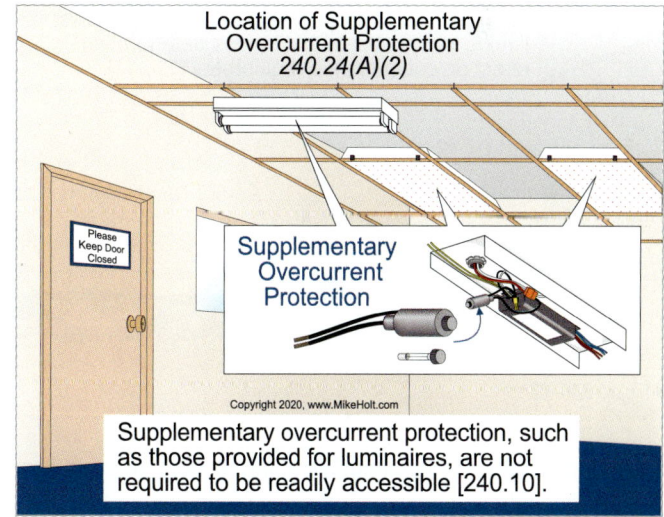
▶Figure 240-36

(4) Overcurrent devices are permitted to be above 6 ft 7 in. where located next to equipment they supply if accessible by portable means is not required to be readily accessible. ▶Figure 240-37

240.24 | Overcurrent Protection

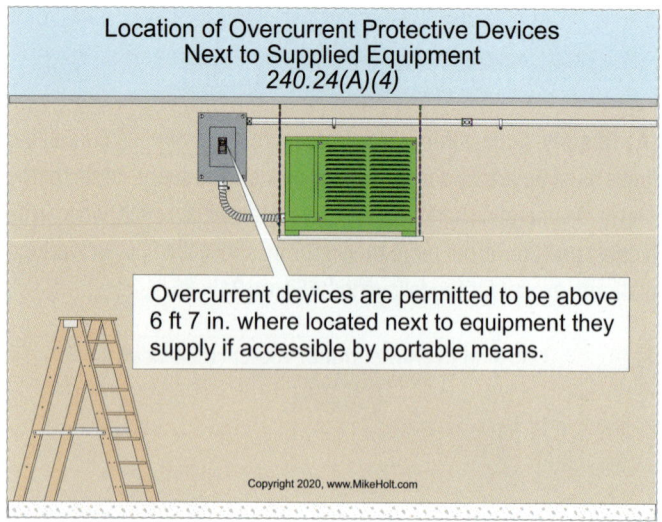
▶Figure 240–37

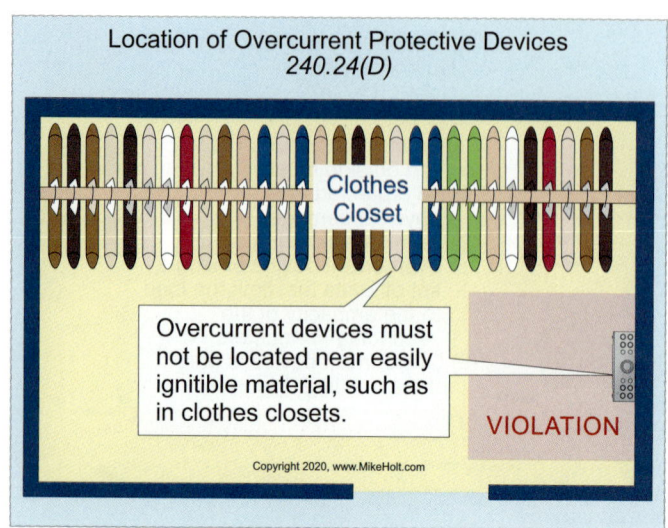
▶Figure 240–39

(C) Not Exposed to Physical Damage. Overcurrent devices are not permitted to be exposed to physical damage.

Note: Electrical equipment must be suitable for the environment, and consideration must be given to the presence of corrosive gases, fumes, vapors, liquids, or chemicals that have a deteriorating effect on conductors or equipment [110.11]. ▶Figure 240–38

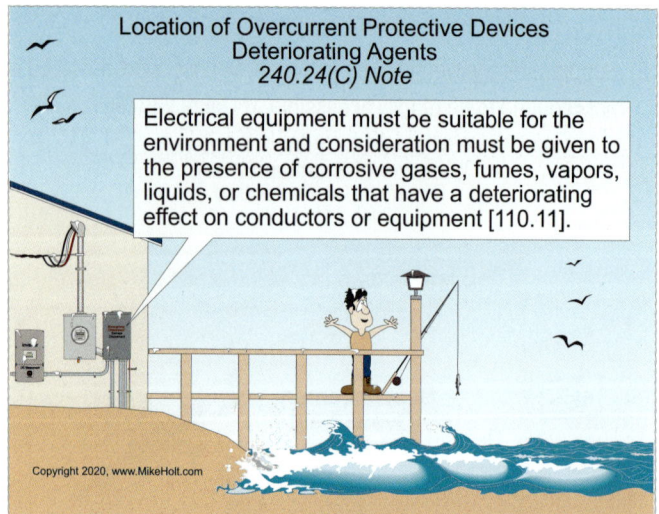
▶Figure 240–38

(D) Not in Vicinity of Easily Ignitible Material. Overcurrent devices cannot be located near easily ignitible material, such as in clothes closets. ▶Figure 240–39

(E) Not in Bathroom Areas. Overcurrent devices must not be installed in the bathroom areas of dwelling units, dormitory units, or guest rooms or guest suites of hotels or motels. ▶Figure 240–40

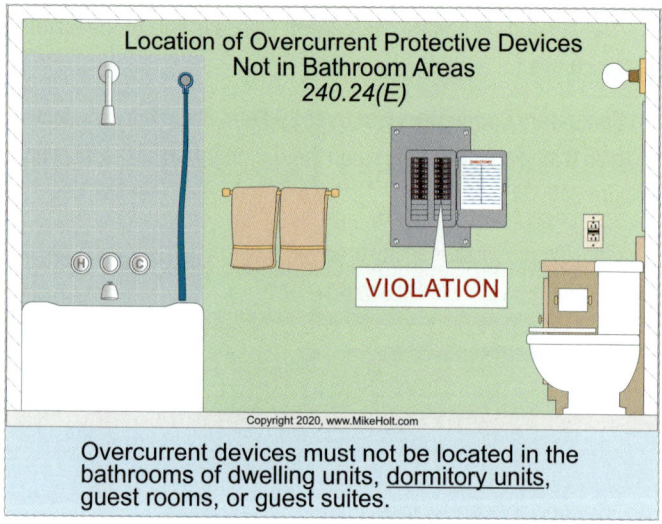
▶Figure 240–40

Author's Comment:

▸ The service disconnect switch is not permitted to be installed in a bathroom area, even in commercial or industrial facilities [230.70(A)(2)].

(F) Not Over Steps. Overcurrent devices are not permitted to be located over the steps of a stairway. ▶Figure 240–41

Author's Comment:

▸ Clearly, it is difficult for electricians to safely work on electrical equipment that is located on uneven surfaces such as over stairways.

Overcurrent Protection | 240.51

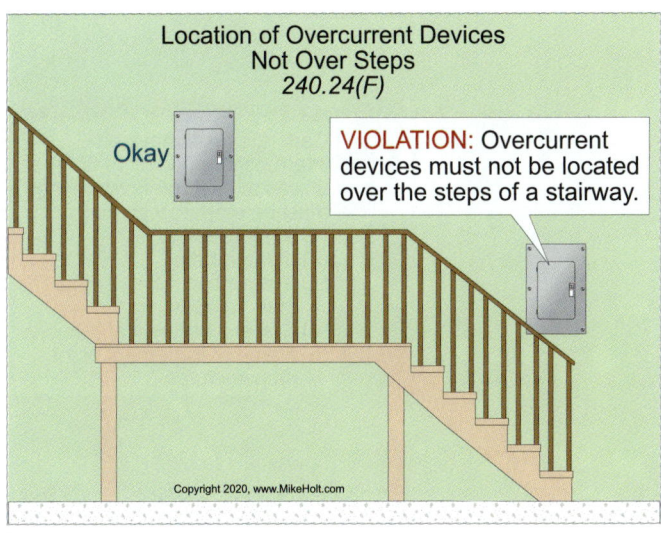
▶Figure 240-41

Part III. Enclosures

240.33 Vertical Position

Enclosures containing overcurrent devices must be mounted in a vertical position. Circuit-breaker enclosures can be mounted horizontally if the circuit breaker is installed in accordance with 240.81. ▶Figure 240-42

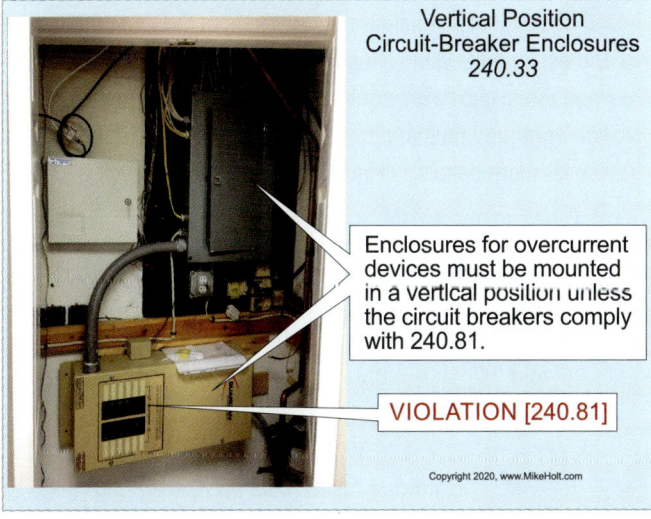
▶Figure 240-42

Author's Comment:

▸ Section 240.81 specifies that where circuit-breaker handles are operated vertically, the "up" position of the handle must be the "on" position. So, in effect, an enclosure that contains one row of circuit breakers can be mounted horizontally, but an enclosure that contains a panelboard with multiple circuit breakers on opposite sides of each other must be mounted vertically.

Part IV. Disconnecting and Guarding

240.40 Disconnecting Means for Fuses

Cartridge fuses and fuses in circuits over 150V to ground must be provided with a disconnecting means on their supply side so each circuit containing fuses can be independently disconnected from the source of power. ▶Figure 240-43

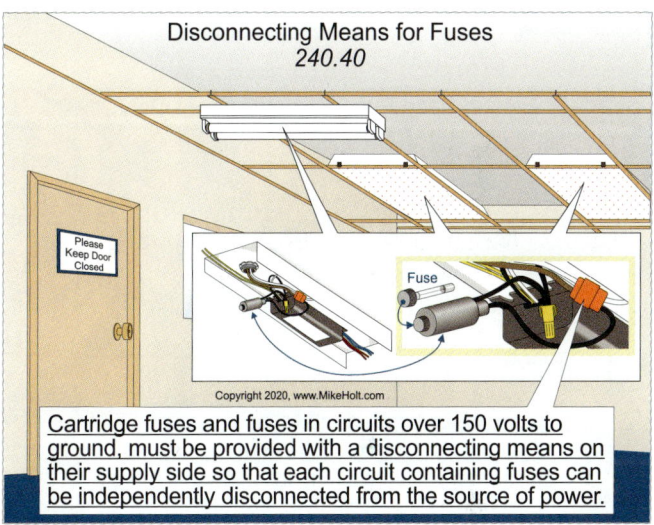
▶Figure 240-43

Part V. Plug Fuses, Fuseholders, and Adapters

240.51 Edison-Base Fuses

(A) Classification. Edison-base fuses are classified to operate at not more than 125V and have an ampere rating of not more than 30A. ▶Figure 240-44

(B) Replacement Only. Edison-base fuses are permitted only for replacement in an existing installation if there is no evidence of tampering or over fusing. ▶Figure 240-45

240.60 | Overcurrent Protection

▶Figure 240-44

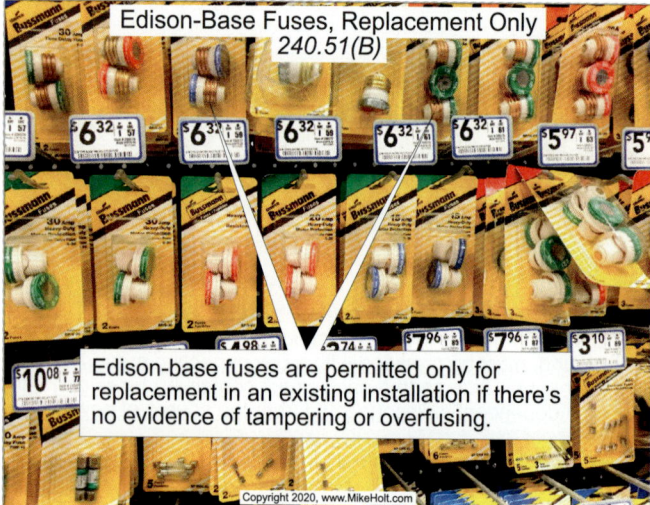
▶Figure 240-45

Part VI. Cartridge Fuses and Fuseholders

240.60 General

(B) Noninterchangeable—0A to 6,000A Cartridge Fuseholders. Fuseholders must be designed so it will be difficult to put a fuse of any given class into a fuseholder designed for a current lower, or voltage higher, than that of the class to which the fuse belongs. Fuseholders for current-limiting fuses must not permit insertion of fuses that are not current-limiting.

(C) Marking. Cartridge fuses have an interrupting rating of 10,000A, unless marked otherwise. They must be marked with the: ▶Figure 240-46

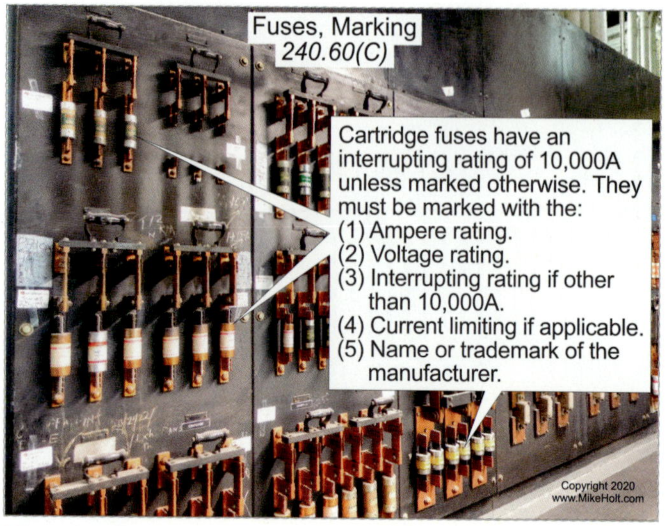

▶Figure 240-46

(1) Ampere rating.

(2) Voltage rating.

(3) Interrupting rating if other than 10,000A.

(4) Current limiting if applicable.

(5) Name or trademark of the manufacturer.

> **Warning**
> Fuses must have an interrupting rating sufficient for the short-circuit current available at the line terminals of the equipment. Using a fuse with an inadequate interrupting current rating can cause equipment to be destroyed from a line-to-line or ground fault and result in death or serious injury. See 110.9 for more details. ▶Figure 240-47

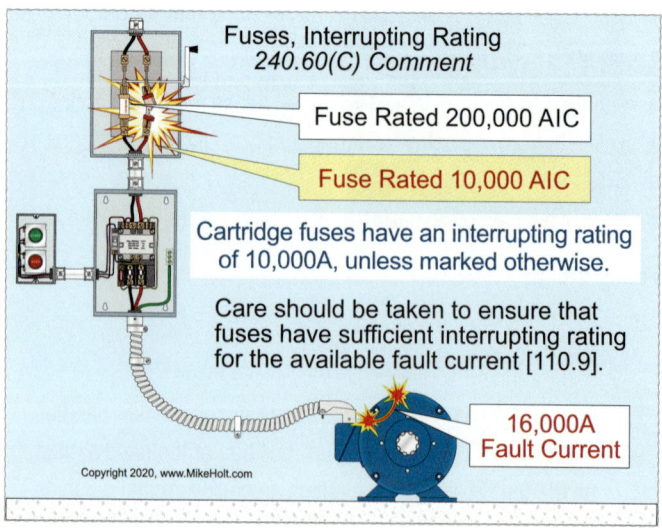
▶Figure 240-47

Author's Comment:

▸ There are two basic designs of cartridge fuses, the ferrule type with a maximum rating of 60A and the knife-blade type rated over 60A. The fuse length and diameter vary with the voltage and current rating. ▸Figure 240-48

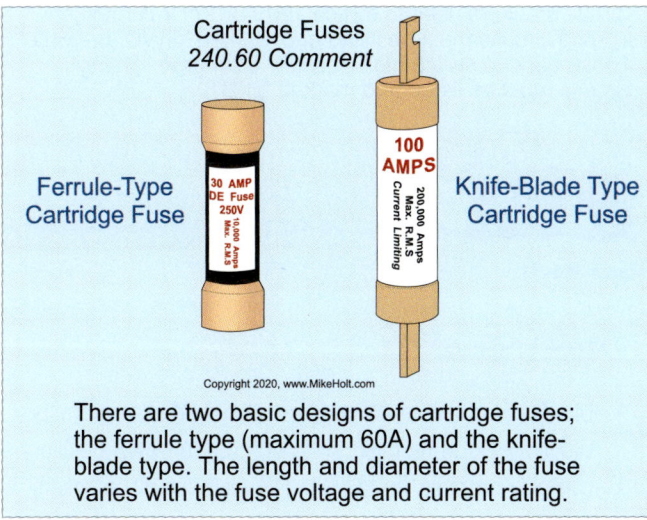

▸Figure 240-48

240.67 Arc Energy Reduction—Fuses

Where fuses rated 1,200A or greater are installed, 240.67(A) and (B) must be applied.

(A) Documentation. Documentation must be available to those authorized to design, install, operate, or inspect the installation as to the location of the fuses. Documentation must be provided to demonstrate that the method chosen to reduce clearing time is set to operate at a value below the available arcing current.

(B) Method to Reduce Clearing Time. A fuse must have a clearing time of 0.07 seconds or less at the available arcing current, or one of the following means must be provided and be set to operate at less than the available arcing current:

(1) Differential relaying.

(2) Energy-reducing maintenance switching with local status indicator.

(3) Energy-reducing active arc-flash mitigation system.

(4) Current-limiting, electronically actuated fuses.

(5) An approved equivalent means.

Note 1: An energy-reducing maintenance switch allows a worker to set a disconnect switch to reduce the clearing time while working within an arc-flash boundary as defined in NFPA 70E, *Standard for Electrical Safety in the Workplace*, and then to set the disconnect switch back to a normal setting after the potentially hazardous work is complete.

Note 2: An energy-reducing active arc-flash mitigation system helps in reducing arcing duration in the electrical distribution system. No change in the disconnect switch or the settings of other devices is required during maintenance when a worker is working within an arc-flash boundary as defined in NFPA 70E, *Standard for Electrical Safety in the Workplace*.

Note 3: IEEE 1584, *IEEE Guide for Performing Arc Flash Hazard Calculations*, is one of the available methods that provides guidance in determining arcing current.

(C) Performance Testing. Where a method to reduce clearing time is required in 240.67(B), the arc energy reduction system must be performance tested when installed. The testing must be conducted by a qualified person in accordance with the manufacturer's instructions.

Performance testing of an instantaneous element of the protective device must be conducted by a qualified person using a test process of primary current injection and the manufacturer's recommended test procedures. A written record of testing must be made available to the authority having jurisdiction.

Part VII. Circuit Breakers

240.81 Indicating

When the handle of a circuit breaker is operated vertically, the "up" position of the handle must be the "on" position. See 240.33 and 404.6(C).
▸Figure 240-49

240.83 Markings

(C) Interrupting Rating. Circuit breakers have an interrupting rating of 5,000A unless marked otherwise.

240.85 | Overcurrent Protection

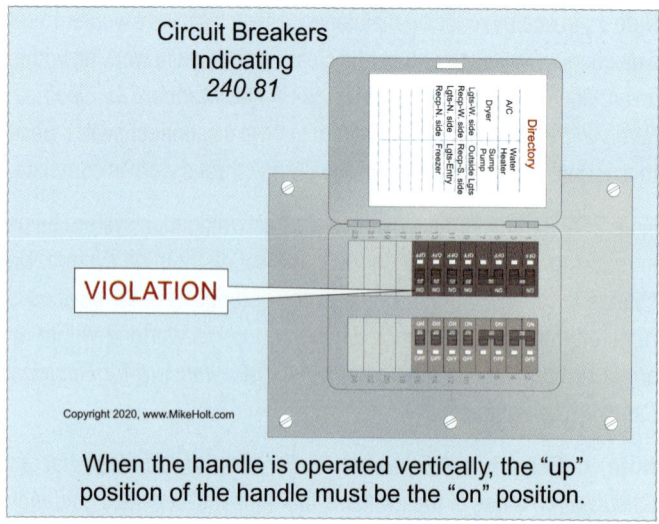
▶Figure 240–49

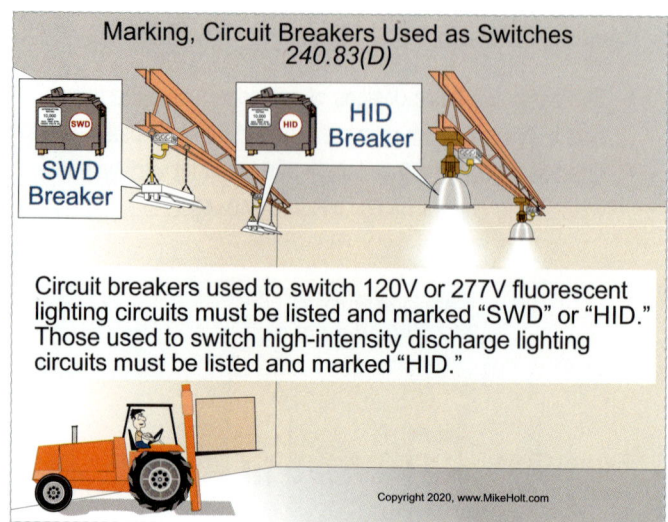
▶Figure 240–51

Author's Comment:

▸ Take care to ensure the circuit breaker has an interrupting rating sufficient for the short-circuit current available at the line terminals of the equipment. Using a circuit breaker with an inadequate interrupting current rating can cause equipment to be destroyed from a line-to-line or ground fault and result in death or serious injury. See 110.9 for more details. ▶Figure 240–50

Author's Comment:

▸ UL 489, *Standard for Molded Case Circuit Breakers*, permits HID breakers to be rated up to 50A, but an SWD breaker can only be rated up to 20A. The tests for HID breakers include an endurance test at 75 percent power factor, and SWD breakers are endurance-tested at 100 percent power factor. The contacts and the spring of an HID breaker are of a heavier duty material to dissipate the increased heat caused by the increased current flow in the circuit because the HID luminaire takes a minute or two to ignite the lamp.

240.85 Applications

Straight Voltage Rating Circuit Breaker. A circuit breaker with a straight voltage rating (such as 240V or 480V) is permitted on a circuit if the nominal voltage between any two conductors (line-to-neutral or line-to-line) does not exceed the circuit-breakers' voltage rating. ▶Figure 240–52 and ▶Figure 240–53

Slash Voltage Rating Circuit Breaker. A circuit breaker with a slash rating (such as 120/240V or 277/480V) is only permitted if the nominal voltage of any one conductor to ground does not exceed the lower of the two values, and the nominal voltage between any two conductors does not exceed the higher value. ▶Figure 240–54

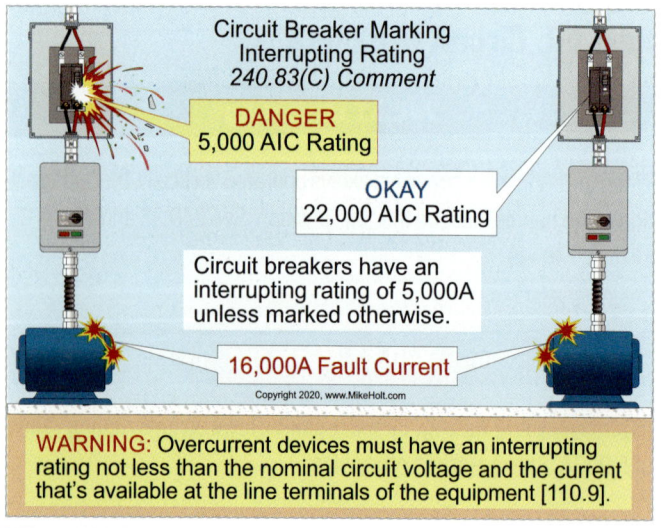
▶Figure 240–50

(D) Used as Switches. Circuit breakers used to switch 120V or 277V fluorescent lighting circuits must be listed and marked "SWD" or "HID." Circuit breakers used to switch high-intensity discharge lighting circuits must be listed and marked "HID." ▶Figure 240–51

Overcurrent Protection | 240.86

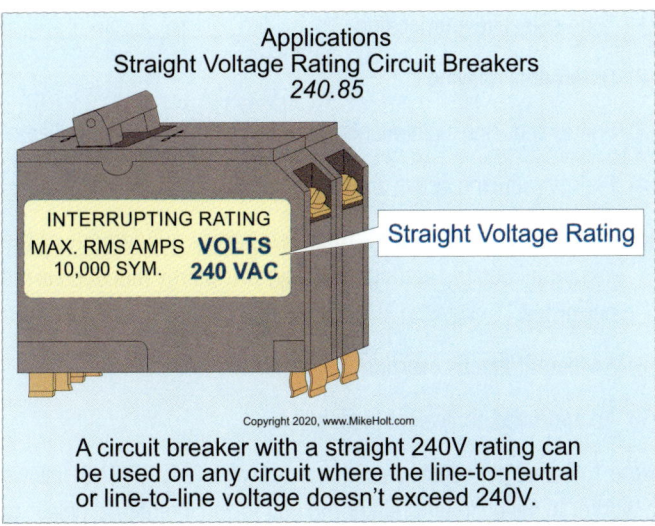

▶Figure 240-52

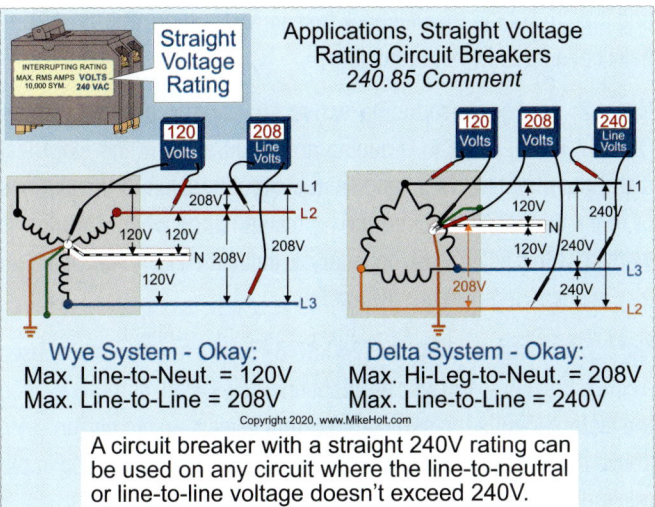

▶Figure 240-53

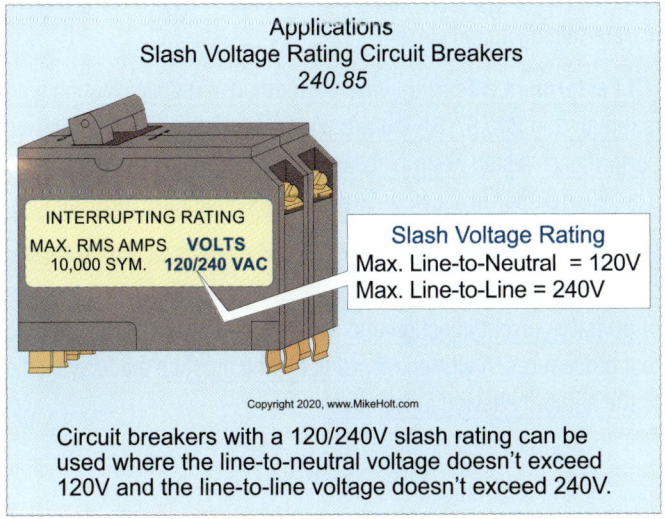

▶Figure 240-54

Author's Comment:

▸ A 120/240V slash circuit breaker is not permitted to be used on the high leg of a 4-wire, three-phase, 120/240V delta-connected system because the line-to-ground voltage of the high leg is 208V, which exceeds the 120V line-to-ground voltage rating of a 120/240V slash circuit breaker. ▶Figure 240-55

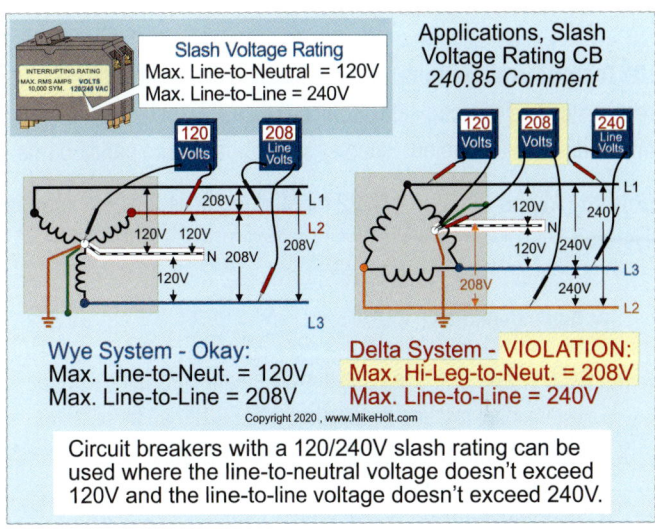

▶Figure 240-55

Note: When installing circuit breakers on corner-grounded delta systems, consideration needs to be given to the circuit breakers' individual pole-interrupting capability.

240.86 Series Ratings

Where a circuit breaker is used on a circuit having an available fault current higher than the marked interrupting rating by being connected on the load side of an approved overcurrent protective device having a higher rating, the circuit breaker must meet the requirements specified in 240.86 (A) or (B), and (C).

(A) Selected Under Engineering Supervision in Existing Installations. The series rated combination devices must be selected by a licensed professional engineer engaged primarily in the design or maintenance of electrical installations. The selection must be documented and stamped by the professional engineer. This documentation must be available to those authorized to design, install, inspect, maintain, and operate the system. This series combination rating, including identification of the upstream overcurrent protective device(s), must be field marked on the end use equipment. For calculated applications, the engineer must ensure the downstream circuit breakers that are part of the series combination remain passive during the interruption period of the line side fully rated, current-limiting device.

240.87 | Overcurrent Protection

Author's Comment:

▸ Upgrades or replacement of existing components in an electrical system, such as transformers and motors, can create an increase in the available fault current beyond that of the existing overcurrent protection system. An engineered series rated system can be less expensive than replacing the existing electrical system.

(B) Tested Combinations. The combination of the line-side overcurrent device and the load-side circuit breaker(s) is tested and marked on the end use equipment, such as switchboards and panelboards.

Note to (A) and (B): See 110.22 for marking of series combination systems.

Author's Comment:

▸ Section 240.86(A) is used for an engineered series rated system in an existing installation, 240.86(B) can be used for a tested combination system in a new or existing installation.

(C) Motor Contribution. Series ratings cannot be used where:

(1) Motor circuits are connected between the load side of the higher-rated overcurrent device of a series rated combination device and on the lower-rated circuit breaker, and

(2) The sum of the motor full-load currents exceeds one percent of the interrupting rating of the lower-rated circuit breaker.

240.87 Arc Energy Reduction—Circuit Breakers

Arc Energy Reduction. Where the highest continuous current trip setting for which the overcurrent device in a circuit breaker is rated or can be adjusted to 1,200A or higher, 240.87(A) and (B) apply.

(A) Documentation. Documentation must be available to those authorized to design, install, operate, or inspect the installation as to the location of the arc energy reduction circuit breaker(s). Documentation must be provided to demonstrate that the method chosen to reduce clearing time is set to operate at a value below the available arcing current.

(B) Method to Reduce Clearing Time. One of the following means must be provided and set to operate at less than the available arcing current:

(1) Zone-selective interlocking

(2) Differential relaying

(3) Energy-reducing maintenance switching with local status indicator

(4) Energy-reducing active arc-flash mitigation system

(5) An instantaneous trip setting. Temporary adjustment of the instantaneous trip setting to achieve arc energy reduction is not permitted.

(6) An instantaneous override

(7) An approved equivalent means

Note 1: An energy-reducing maintenance switch [240.87(B)(3)] allows a worker to set a circuit breaker trip unit to "no intentional delay" to reduce the clearing time while working within an arc-flash boundary as defined in NFPA 70E, *Standard for Electrical Safety in the Workplace*, and then to set the trip unit back to a normal setting after the potentially hazardous work is complete.

Note 2: An energy-reducing active arc-flash mitigation system [240.87(B)(4)] helps in reducing arcing duration in the electrical distribution system. No change in the circuit breaker or the settings of other devices is required during maintenance when a worker is working within an arc-flash boundary as defined in NFPA 70E, *Standard for Electrical Safety in the Workplace*.

Note 3: An instantaneous trip [240.87(B)(5)] is a function that causes a circuit breaker to trip with no intentional delay when currents exceed the instantaneous trip setting or current level. If arcing currents are above the instantaneous trip level, the circuit breaker will trip in the minimum possible time.

Note 4: IEEE 1584, *IEEE Guide for Performing Arc Flash Hazard Calculations*, is one of the available methods that provides guidance in determining arcing current.

(C) Performance Testing. Where a method to reduce clearing time is required in 240.67(B), the arc energy reduction system must be performance tested when installed. The testing must be conducted by a qualified person in accordance with the manufacturer's instructions.

Performance testing of an instantaneous element of the protective device must be conducted by a qualified person using a test process of primary current injection and the manufacturer's recommended test procedures. A written record of testing must be made available to the authority having jurisdiction.

240.88 Reconditioned Equipment

Reconditioned equipment must be listed as "reconditioned" and the original listing mark removed.

(A) Circuit Breakers. The use of reconditioned circuit breakers must comply with the following:

(1) Molded-case circuit breakers are not permitted to be reconditioned.

(2) Low- and medium-voltage power circuit breakers are permitted to be reconditioned.

(3) High-voltage circuit breakers are permitted to be reconditioned.

(B) Components. The use of reconditioned trip units, protective relays, and current transformers must comply with the following:

(1) Low-voltage power circuit breaker electronic trip units are not permitted to be reconditioned.

(2) Electromechanical protective relays and current transformers are permitted to be reconditioned.

Notes

ARTICLE 250
GROUNDING AND BONDING

Introduction to Article 250—Grounding and Bonding

No other article can match this one for misapplication, violation, and misinterpretation. The terminology used in Article 250 has been a source of much confusion but has been improved during the last few *NEC* revisions. It is very important for you to understand the difference between grounding and bonding in order to correctly apply the provisions of this article. Pay careful attention to the definitions of important terms located in Article 100 that apply to grounding and bonding. Article 250 covers the grounding requirements for providing a path to the Earth to reduce overvoltage from lightning strikes, and the bonding requirements that establish a low-impedance fault current path back to the source of the electrical supply to facilitate the operation of overcurrent protective devices in the event of a ground fault.

This article is arranged in a logical manner as illustrated in Figure 250.1 in the *NEC*. It may be a good idea for you to just read through the entire article first to get a big picture overview. Then, study Article 250 closely so you understand the details and remember to check Article 100 for the definitions of terms that may be new to you. The illustrations that accompany the text in this textbook will help you better understand the key points.

Part I. General

250.1 Scope

Article 250 covers the general requirements for the grounding and bonding of electrical installations. ▶Figure 250–1

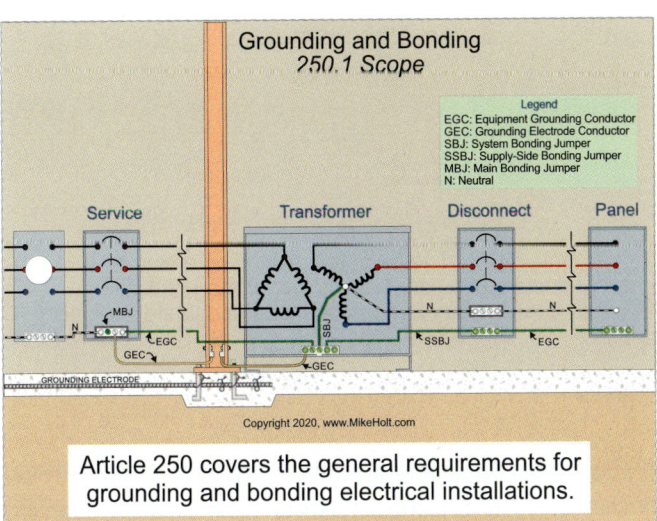

▶Figure 250–1

Author's Comment:

▸ There are two completely different concepts being covered in this article; "Grounding" which is the connection to the Earth, and "Bonding" which is mechanically connecting electrically conductive components together to ensure electrical conductivity between metal parts [Article 100]. While these two systems overlap each other, that portion of the electrical system that needs to be able to carry fault current to the source must be heartier and capable of handling excessive amounts of current. This is called the "Effective Ground-Fault Current Path." The effective ground-fault current path needs a low-impedance fault current path to the source so fault current can rise as quickly as possible to operate the overcurrent protective device as soon as possible. Since fault current can be thousands of amperes, the effective ground-fault current path must be designed to safely handle those high current levels. ▶Figure 250–2

250.4 | Grounding and Bonding

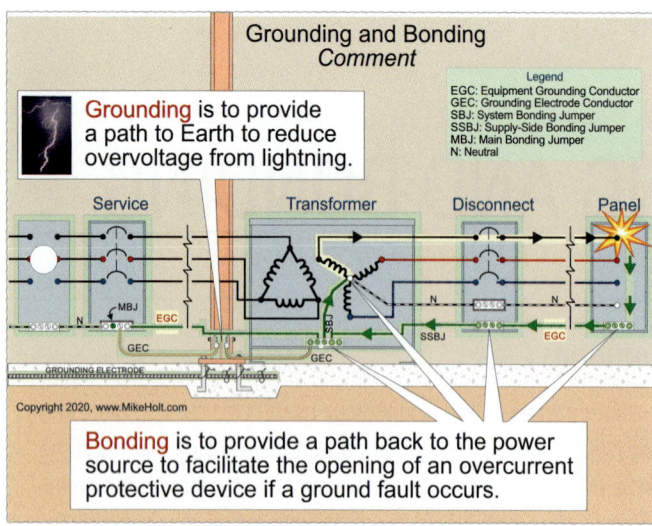

▶Figure 250-2

250.4 Performance Requirements for Grounding and Bonding

(A) Solidly Grounded Systems.

(1) Electrical System Grounding. Electrical power systems, such as the secondary winding of a transformer, are required to be connected to the Earth (grounded) in order to limit the voltage induced on the conductors by lightning strikes, line surges, or unintentional contact by higher-voltage lines, and to stabilize the secondary conductor's voltage to ground during normal operation. ▶Figure 250-3

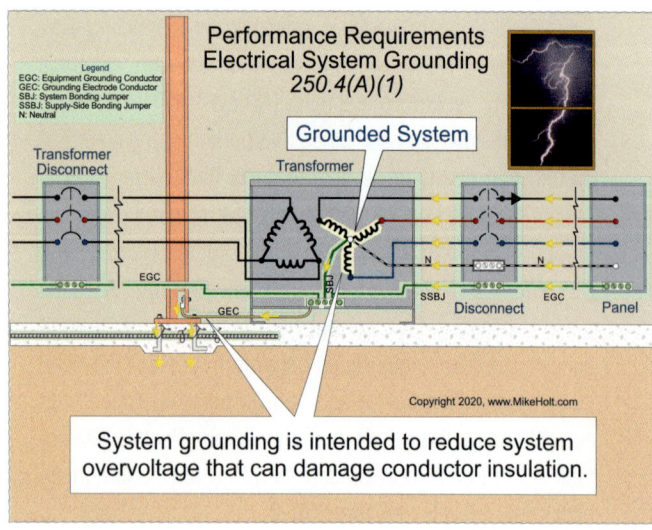

▶Figure 250-3

Author's Comment:

▸ System grounding helps reduce fires in buildings as well as voltage stress on electrical insulation, thereby ensuring longer insulation life for motors, transformers, and other system components. ▶Figure 250-4

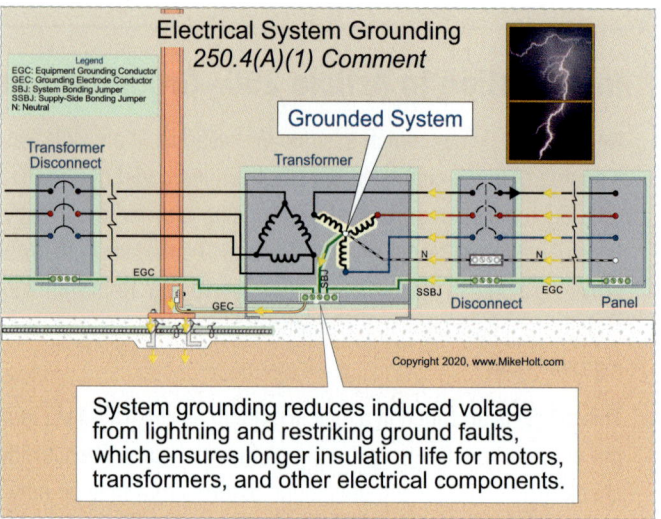

▶Figure 250-4

Note 1: To limit imposed voltage, the grounding electrode conductors should not be any longer than necessary and unnecessary bends and loops should be avoided. ▶Figure 250-5

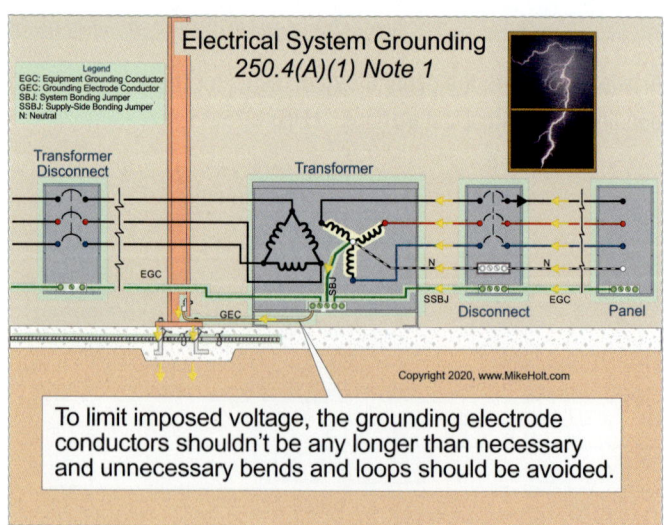

▶Figure 250-5

(2) Equipment Grounding. Metal parts of electrical equipment must be connected to other and to the Earth to reduce the voltage to ground on the metal parts from indirect lightning strikes. ▶Figure 250-6

Grounding and Bonding | 250.4

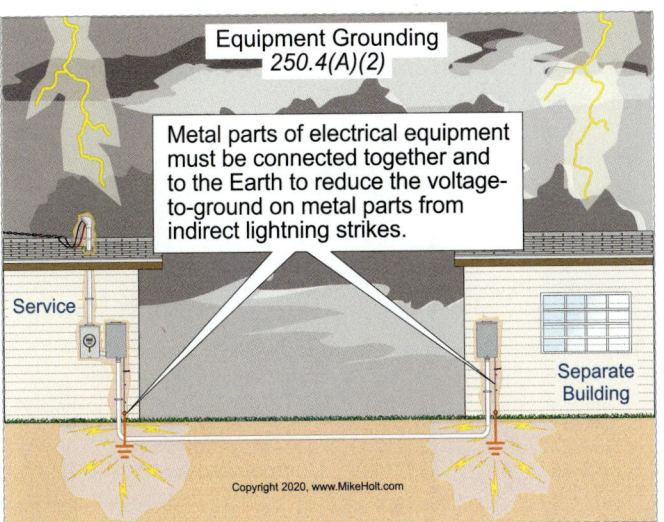
▶Figure 250-6

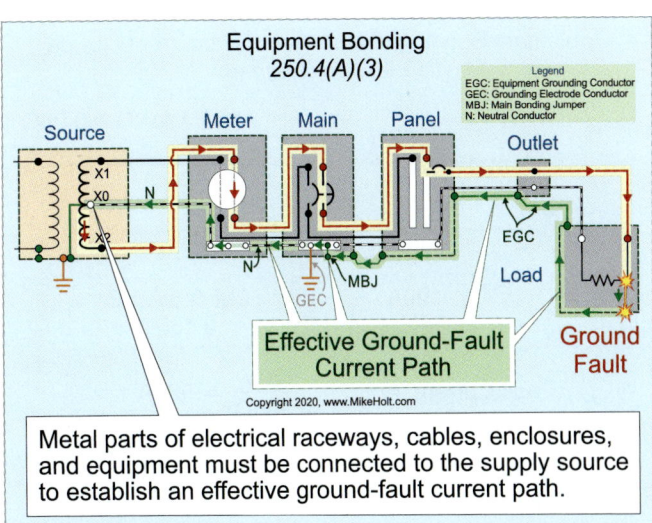
▶Figure 250-8

Danger

Failure to ground metal parts to earth can result in millions of volts of induced voltage on the metal parts of an electrical system generated by an indirect lightning strike. This energy seeks a path to the Earth within the building—possibly resulting in a fire and/or electric shock from a side flash. ▶Figure 250-7

Author's Comment:

▸ According to Article 100, an "Effective Ground-Fault Current Path" is an intentionally constructed low-impedance conductive path designed to carry fault current from the point of a ground fault to the source for the purpose of opening the circuit overcurrent protective device. ▶Figure 250-9

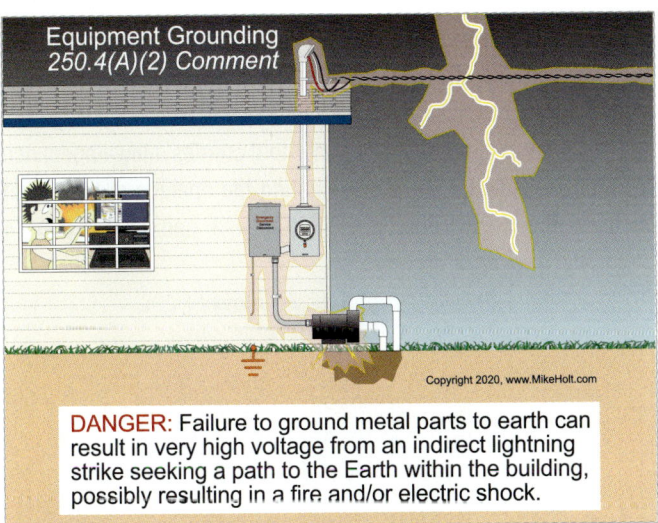
▶Figure 250-7

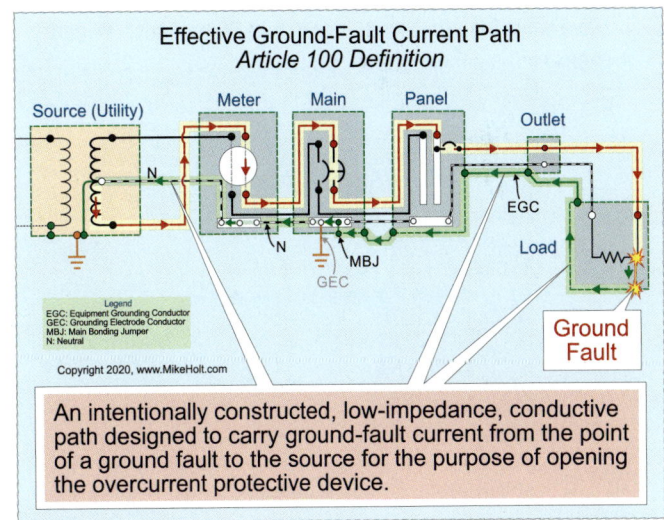
▶Figure 250-9

(3) Equipment Bonding. Metal parts of electrical raceways, cables, enclosures, and equipment must be connected together and to the supply system in a manner that establishes an effective ground-fault current path. See 250.4(A)(5). ▶Figure 250-8

Author's Comment:

▸ To quickly remove dangerous voltage on metal parts from a ground fault, the effective ground-fault current path must have sufficiently low impedance to the source so fault current will quickly rise to a level that will open the circuit overcurrent device. ▶Figure 250-10

250.4 | Grounding and Bonding

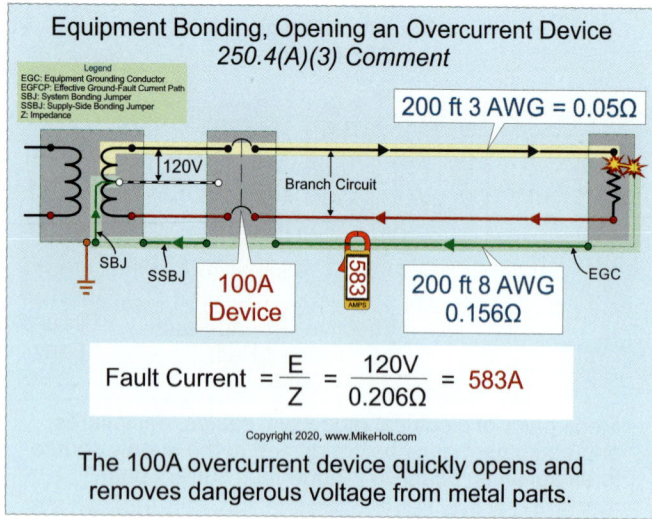

▶Figure 250–10

Author's Comment:

▸ The time it takes for an overcurrent device to open is dependent on the magnitude of the fault current. A higher fault current value will result in a shorter clearing time for the overcurrent protective device. For example, a 20A overcurrent device with an overload of 40A (two times the 20A rating) takes 25 to 150 seconds to open. The same device at 100A (five times the 20A rating) trips in 5 to 20 seconds. ▶Figure 250–11

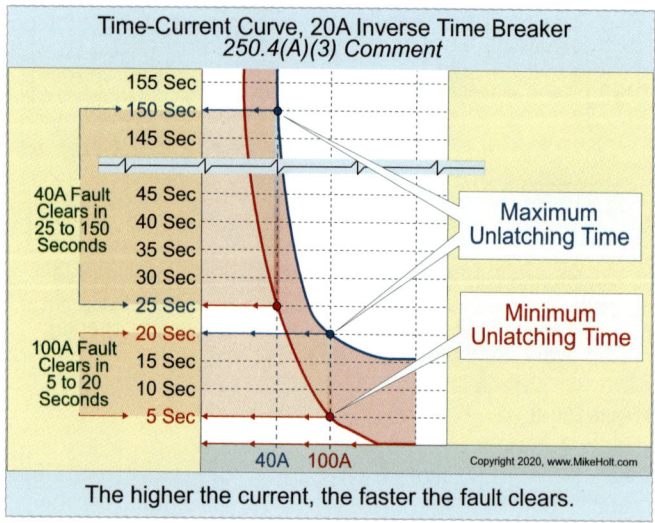

▶Figure 250–11

(4) Bonding Conductive Materials. Electrically conductive materials that are likely to become energized, such as metal water piping systems, metal sprinkler piping, metal gas piping, and other metal-piping systems, and exposed structural steel members must be connected (bonded) to the supply source via an effective ground-fault current path. ▶Figure 250–12

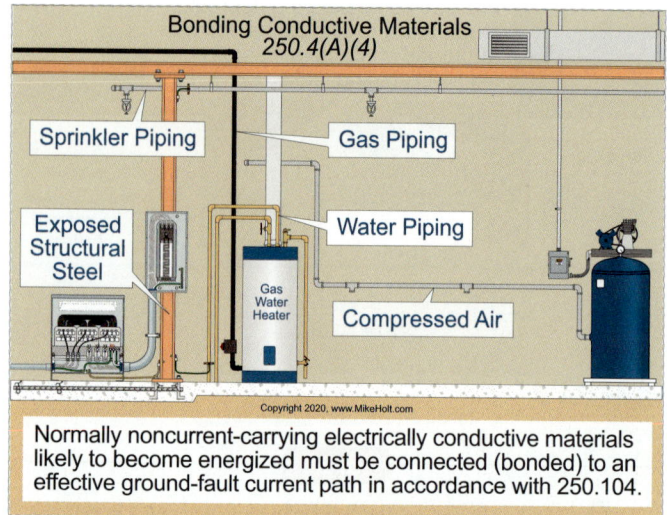

▶Figure 250–12

Author's Comment:

▸ According to the NFPA style manual, "Likely to Become Energized" means that an electrical conductor is present in some capacity.

(5) Effective Ground-Fault Current Path. Metal parts of electrical raceways, cables, enclosures, or equipment must be bonded together and to the supply source in a manner that creates a low-impedance path for ground-fault current facilitating the opening of the circuit overcurrent protective device. ▶Figure 250–13 and ▶Figure 250–14

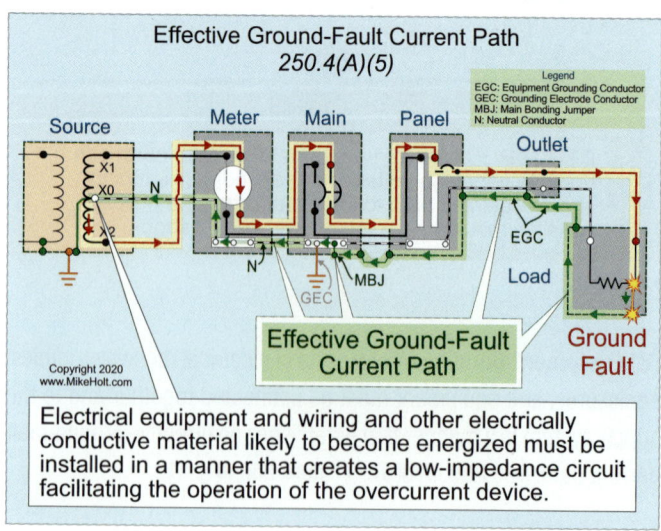

▶Figure 250–13

Grounding and Bonding | 250.4

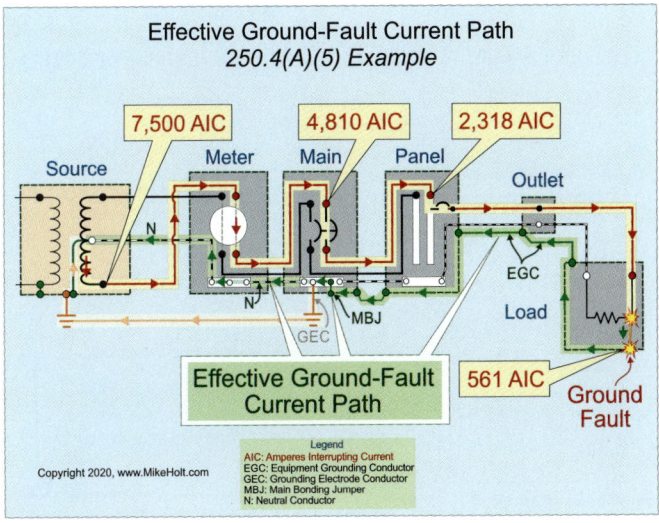
▶Figure 250-14

The effective ground-fault current path must be capable of safely carrying the maximum ground-fault current likely to be imposed on it from any point on the wiring system where a ground fault may occur to the electrical supply source.

The Earth is not permitted to serve as the required effective ground-fault current path, therefore an equipment grounding conductor of a type recognized in 250.118 is required to be installed with all circuits. ▶Figure 250-15

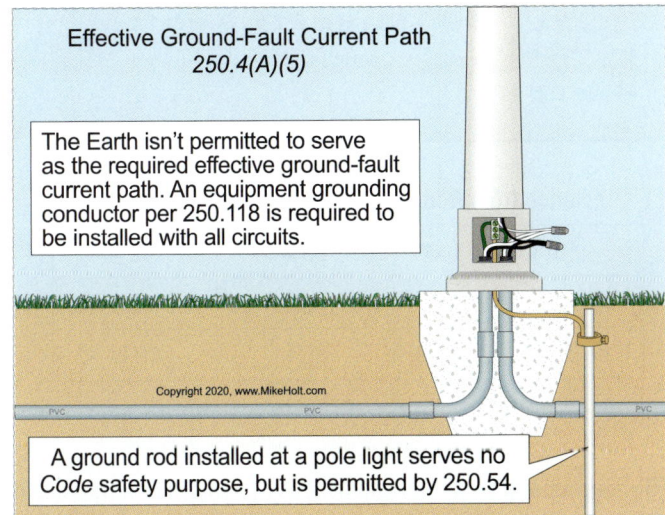
▶Figure 250-15

Danger

Earth grounding does not remove dangerous touch voltage. Because the contact resistance of a grounding electrode (like a ground rod) to the Earth is so high, very little fault current returns to the power supply. As a result, the circuit overcurrent protective device will not open, and all metal parts associated with the electrical installation, metal piping, and structural building steel will become and remain energized. ▶Figure 250-16

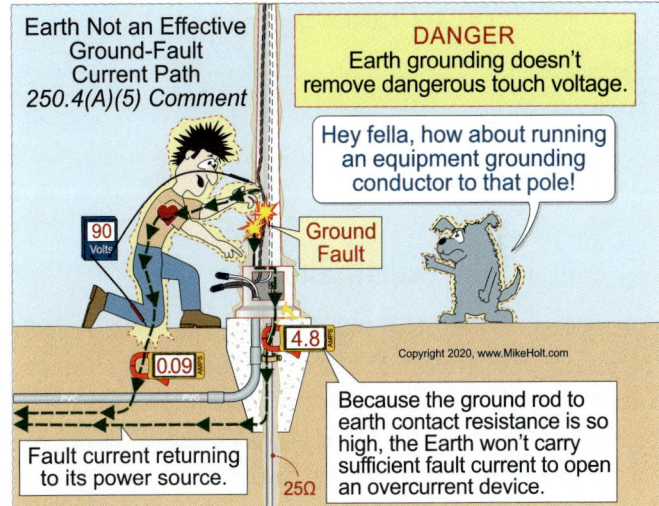
▶Figure 250-16

▶ **Example**

Question: What will the maximum fault current be when there is a 120V ground fault to the metal parts of a light pole that is grounded to a 25-ohm ground rod, but not bonded to an effective ground-fault current path? ▶Figure 250-17

(a) 3.70A (b) 4.80A (c) 5.20A (d) 6.40A

Solution:

I = Volts/Resistance

I = 120V/25 ohms

I = 4.80A

Answer: (b) 4.80A

250.4 | Grounding and Bonding

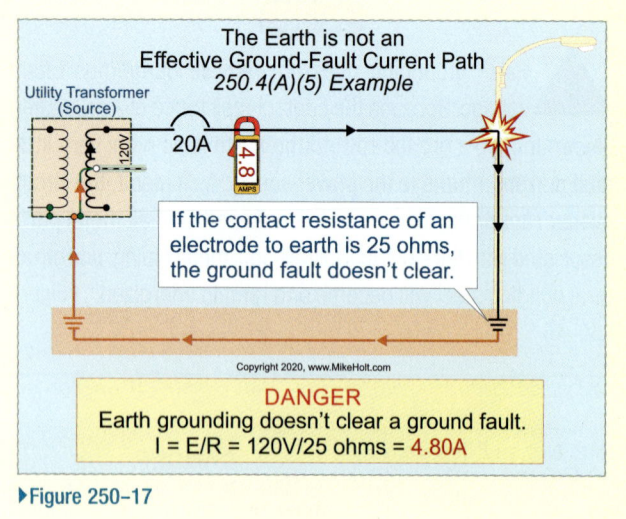
▶Figure 250–17

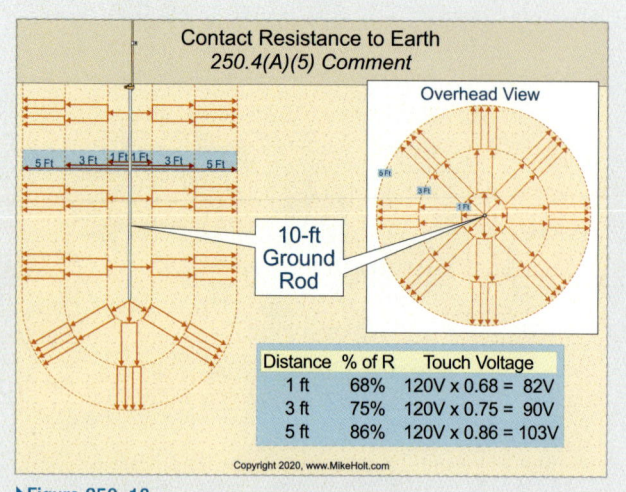
▶Figure 250–18

Earth Shells

According to ANSI/IEEE 142, *Recommended Practice for Grounding of Industrial and Commercial Power Systems* (Green Book) [4.1.1], the resistance of the soil outward from a 10-ft ground rod is equal to the sum of the series resistances of the Earth shells. The shell nearest the ground rod has the highest resistance and each successive shell has progressively larger areas and progressively lower resistances. Do not be concerned if you do not understand this statement; just review the table below.

Distance from Rod	Soil Contact Resistance
1 ft (Shell 1)	68% of total contact resistance
3 ft (Shells 1 and 2)	75% of total contact resistance
5 ft (Shells 1, 2, and 3)	86% of total contact resistance

Contact Resistance. The Earth is an excellent conductor due to an almost limitless number of parallel paths over which electrons can flow. However, the problem lies in the contact resistance between the grounding electrode and the Earth. The surface area of the electrode contacting the Earth is minimal compared to the Earth itself.

Since voltage is directly proportional to resistance, the voltage gradient of the Earth around an energized rod (assuming a 120V ground fault) will be as follows: ▶Figure 250–18 and ▶Figure 250–19

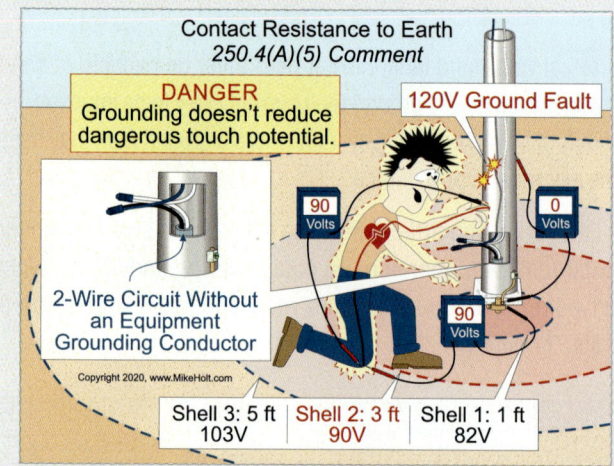
▶Figure 250–19

Distance from Rod	Soil Contact Resistance	Voltage Gradient
1 ft (Shell 1)	68%	82V
3 ft (Shells 1 and 2)	75%	90V
5 ft (Shells 1, 2, and 3)	86%	103V

(B) Ungrounded Systems. Ungrounded Systems must be grounded in accordance with 250.4(B)(1) through 250.4(B)(4).

Grounding and Bonding | 250.4

Author's Comment:

▸ According to Article 100, an ungrounded system is "a power-supply system not connected to earth (ground)," as demonstrated in the secondary winding of a transformer where there is no connection between the system winding and earth (ground) or to a conductive body that extends the Earth (ground) connection. ▸Figure 250–20

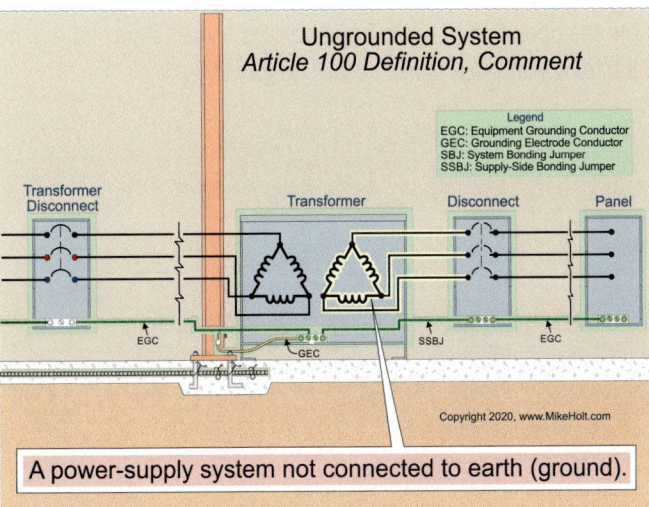

▸Figure 250–20

(1) Equipment Grounding. Metal parts of electrical equipment must be connected to each other and connected to the Earth to reduce the voltage to ground on the metal parts from indirect lightning strikes. ▸Figure 250–21

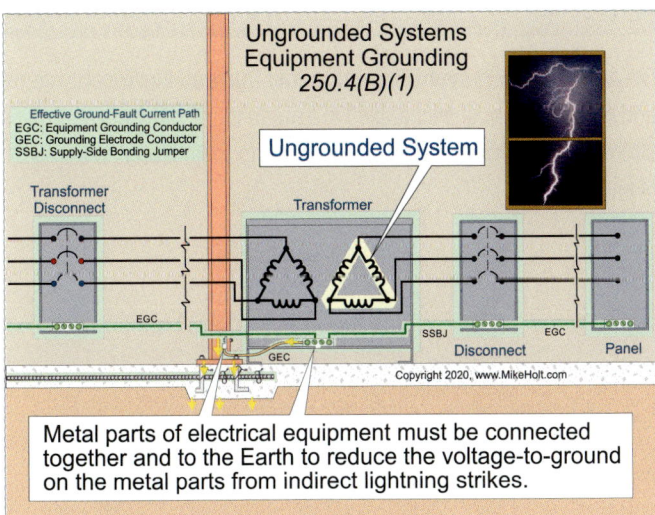

▸Figure 250–21

Danger

Failure to ground metal parts to earth can result in millions of volts of induced voltage on the metal parts of an electrical system from an indirect lightning strike. This energy seeks a path to the Earth within the building—possibly resulting in a fire and/or electric shock from a side flash.

(2) Equipment Bonding. Metal parts of electrical raceways, cables, enclosures, and equipment must be connected together and to the supply source in a manner that establishes an effective ground-fault current path. ▸Figure 250–22

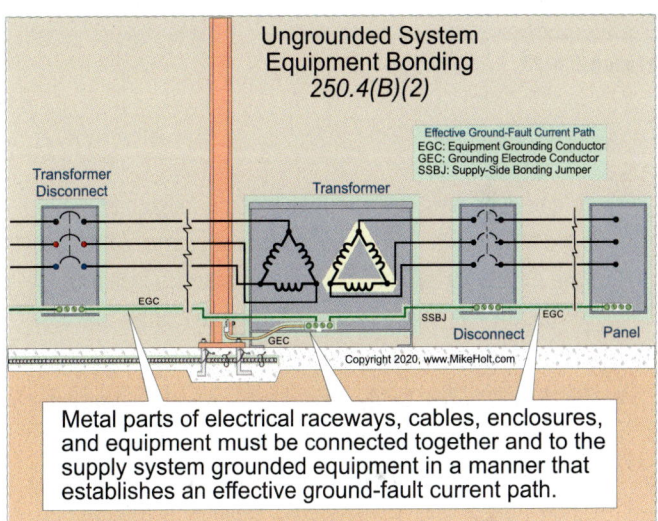

▸Figure 250–22

The effective ground-fault current path must be capable of safely carrying the maximum fault current likely to be imposed on it from any point on the wiring system should a ground fault occur at the electrical supply source.

Author's Comment:

▸ According to Article 100, an "Effective Ground-Fault Current Path" is an intentionally constructed low-impedance conductive path designed to carry fault current from the point of a ground fault to the source for the purpose of opening the circuit overcurrent protective device. ▸Figure 250–23

250.6 | Grounding and Bonding

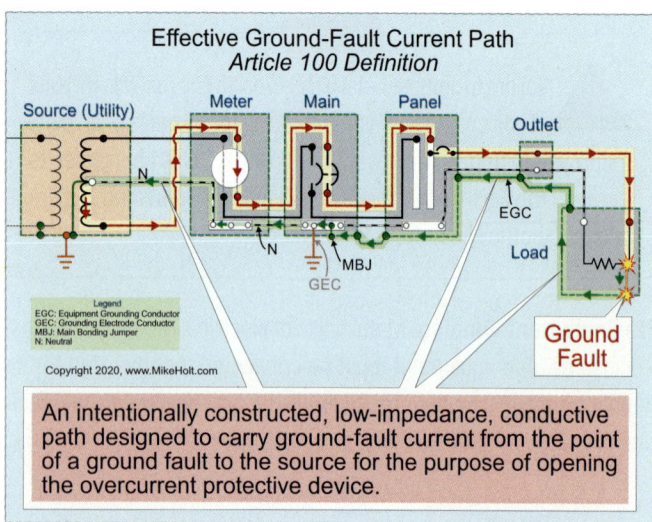
▶Figure 250–23

Author's Comment:

▸ To quickly remove dangerous voltage on metal parts from a ground fault, the effective ground-fault current path must have sufficiently low impedance to the source so fault current will quickly rise to a level that will open the circuit overcurrent protective device [250.4(A)(3)].

▸ The time it takes for an overcurrent protective device to open is dependent on the magnitude of the fault current. A higher fault current value will result in a shorter clearing time for the overcurrent device. For example, a 20A overcurrent protective device with an overload of 40A (two times the 20A rating) takes 25 to 150 seconds to open. The same device at 100A (five times the 20A rating) trips in 5 to 20 seconds. ▶Figure 250–24

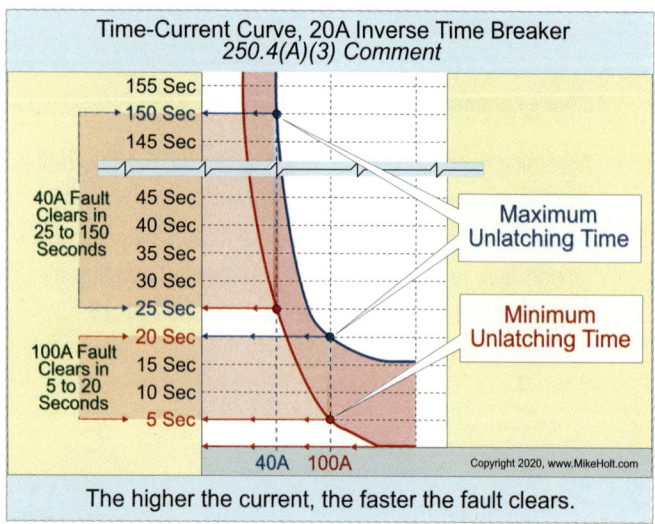
▶Figure 250–24

(3) Bonding Conductive Materials. Conductive materials such as metal water piping systems, metal sprinkler piping, metal gas piping, and other metal-piping systems, as well as exposed structural steel members likely to become energized must be bonded together in a manner that creates a low-impedance fault current path capable of carrying the maximum fault current likely to be imposed on it.

(4) Fault Current Path. Electrical equipment, wiring, and other electrically conductive material likely to become energized must be installed in a manner that creates a low-impedance fault current path to facilitate the operation of overcurrent devices should a second ground fault from a different phase occur. ▶Figure 250–25

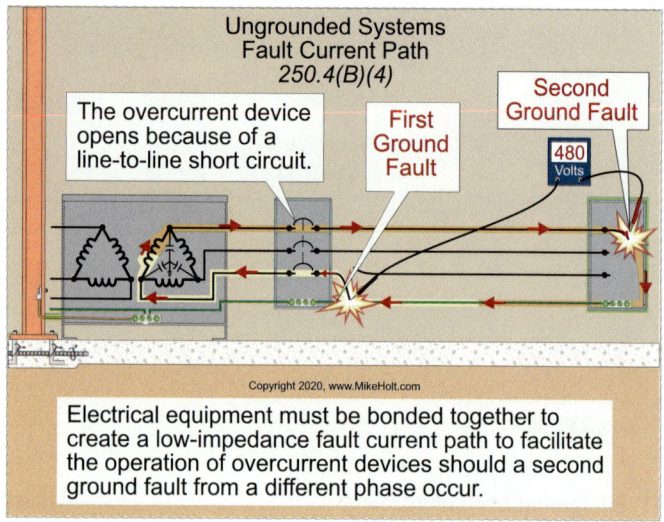
▶Figure 250–25

250.6 Objectionable Current

(A) Arranged to Prevent Objectionable Current. Electrical systems and equipment must be installed in a manner that prevents neutral or circuit current from flowing on metal parts (objectionable current).
▶Figure 250–26

Grounding and Bonding | 250.6

Arranged to Prevent Objectionable Current 250.6(A)

Electrical systems and equipment must be installed in a manner that prevents neutral or circuit current from flowing on metal parts.

▶Figure 250-26

Objectionable Current

Objectionable neutral current occurs because of improper neutral-to-case connections or wiring errors that violate 250.142(B).

Panelboards. Objectionable neutral current will flow on metal parts and the equipment grounding conductor when the neutral conductor is connected to the metal case of a panelboard on the load side of the service disconnect. ▶Figure 250-27

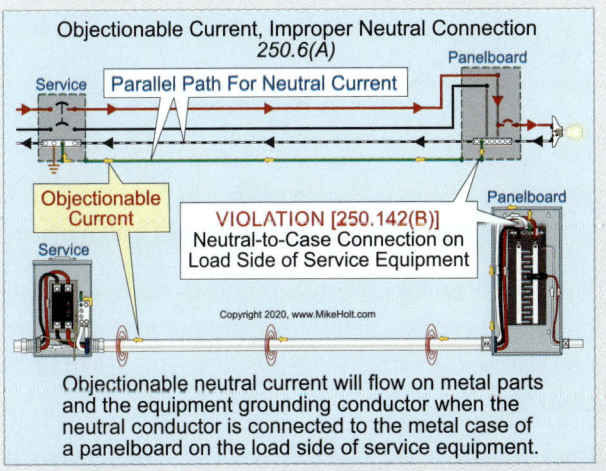

▶Figure 250-27

Transformers. Objectionable neutral current will flow on metal parts if the neutral conductor is connected to the circuit equipment grounding conductor at both the transformer and any other location on the load side of the system bonding jumper. ▶Figure 250-28

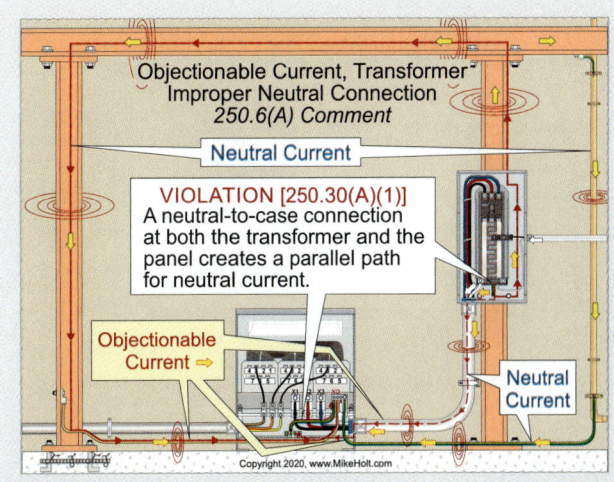

▶Figure 250-28

Generator. Objectionable neutral current will flow on metal parts and the equipment grounding conductor if a generator is connected to a transfer switch with a solidly connected neutral, and a neutral-to-case connection is made at the generator. ▶Figure 250-29

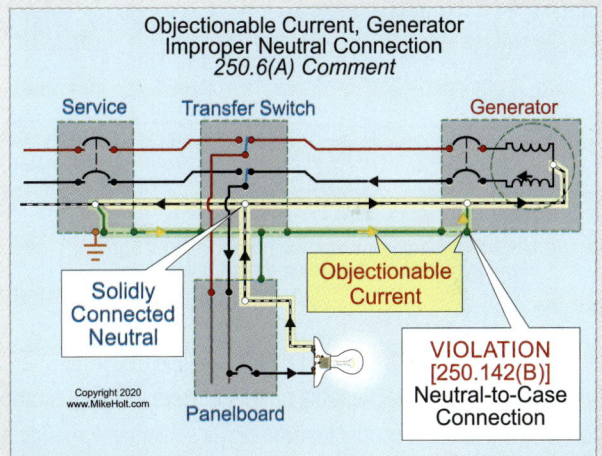

▶Figure 250-29

Disconnects. Objectionable neutral current will flow on metal parts and the equipment grounding conductor if the neutral conductor is connected to the metal case of a disconnect that is not part of the service disconnect. ▶Figure 250-30

Wiring Errors. Objectionable neutral current will flow on metal parts and equipment grounding conductors if the neutral conductor from one system is used as the neutral conductor for a different system. ▶Figure 250-31

250.6 | Grounding and Bonding

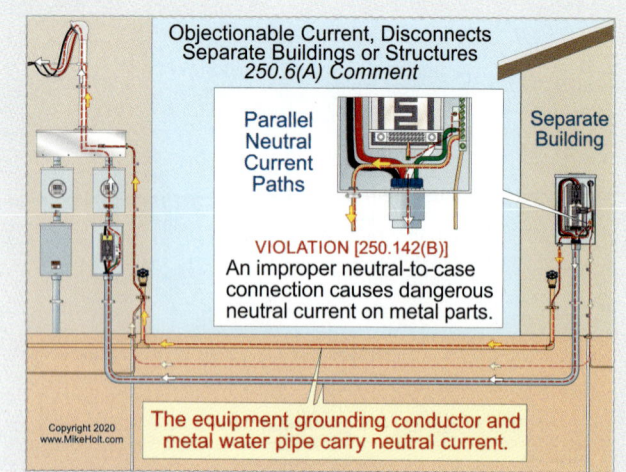
▶Figure 250-30

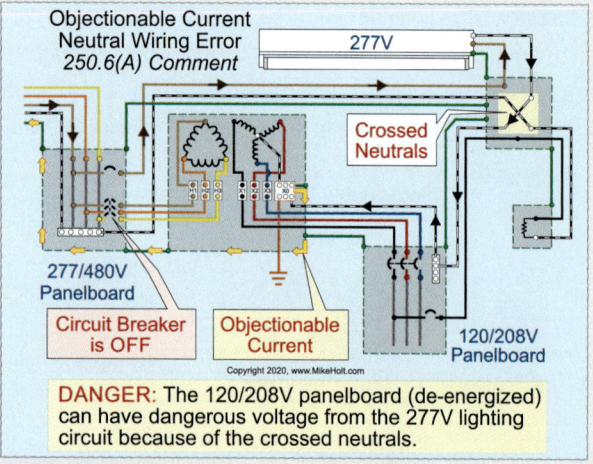
▶Figure 250-31

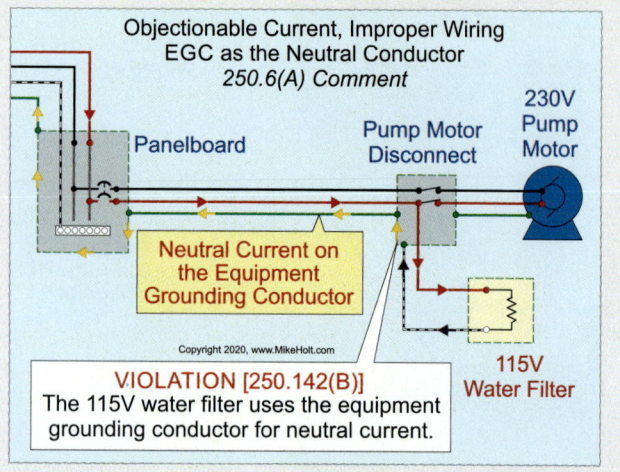
▶Figure 250-32

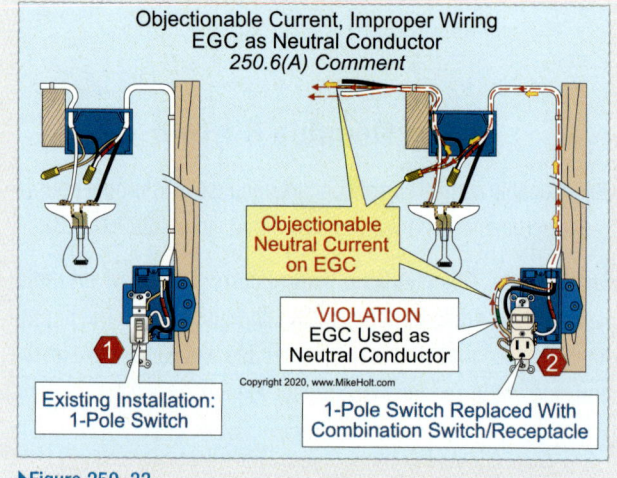
▶Figure 250-33

Improper Wiring. Objectionable neutral current will flow on the equipment grounding conductor if the circuit equipment grounding conductor is used as a neutral conductor, such as where:

- A 230V time-clock motor is replaced with a 115V time-clock motor, and the circuit equipment grounding conductor is used for neutral return current.
- A 115V water filter is wired to a 240V well-pump motor circuit, and the circuit equipment grounding conductor is used for neutral return current. ▶Figure 250-32
- The circuit equipment grounding conductor is used for neutral return current. ▶Figure 250-33

Dangers of Objectionable Current

Objectionable neutral current on metal parts can cause electric shock, fires, and the improper operation of electronic equipment and overcurrent protective devices such as GFPEs, GFCIs, and AFCIs.

Shock Hazard. When objectionable neutral current flows on metal parts or the equipment grounding conductor, electric shock and even death can occur from the elevated voltage. ▶Figure 250-34 and ▶Figure 250-35

Grounding and Bonding | 250.6

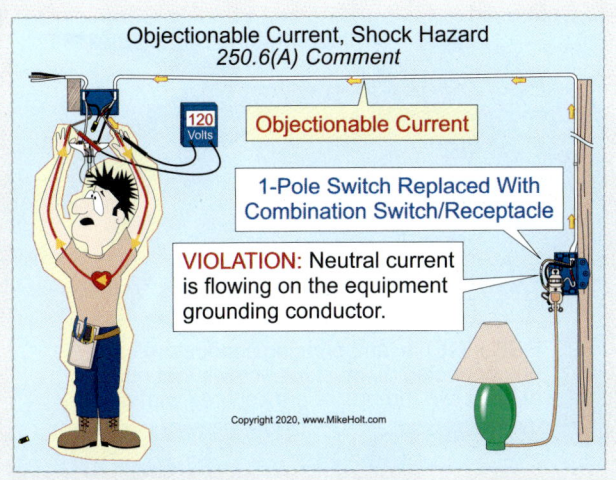
▶Figure 250-34

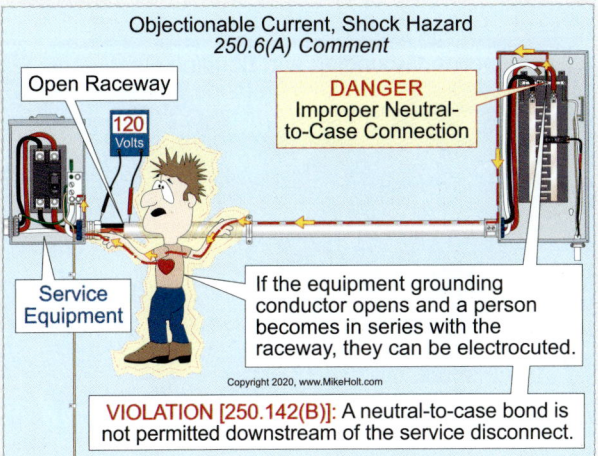
▶Figure 250-35

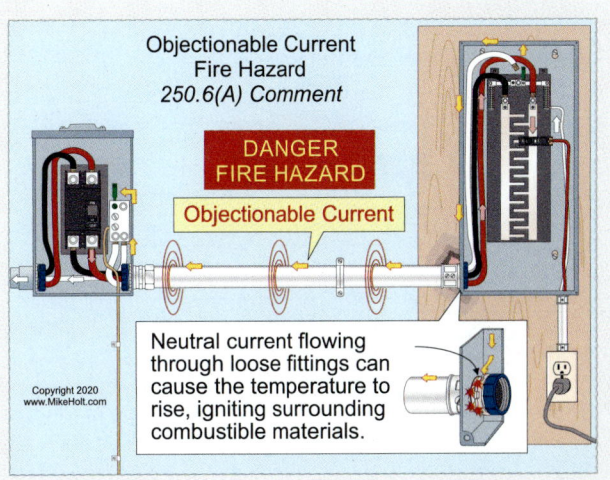
▶Figure 250-36

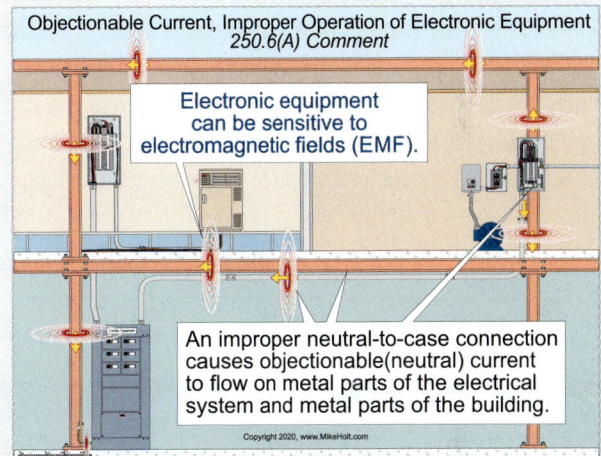
▶Figure 250-37

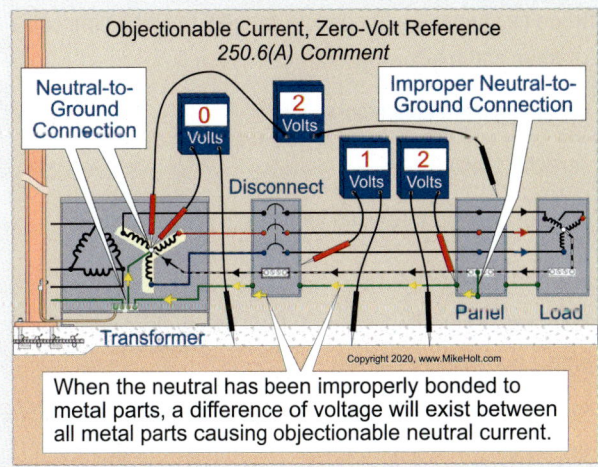
▶Figure 250-38

Fire Hazard. When objectionable neutral current flows on metal parts, a fire can ignite adjacent combustible material. Heat is generated whenever current flows, particularly over high-resistance parts. In addition, arcing at loose connections is especially dangerous in areas containing easily ignitible and explosive gases, vapors, or dust. ▶Figure 250-36

Improper Operation of Electronic Equipment. Objectionable neutral current flowing on metal parts of electrical equipment and building parts can create electromagnetic fields which negatively affect the performance of electronic devices; particularly medical equipment. ▶Figure 250-37

When objectionable neutral current travels on metal parts and equipment grounding conductors because the neutral has been improperly bonded to metal parts, a difference of voltage will exist between all metal parts. This situation can cause some electronic equipment to operate improperly. ▶Figure 250-38 and ▶Figure 250-39

2nd Printing | 2020 NEC Requirements for Solar PV and Energy Storage Systems | MikeHolt.com | **165**

250.8 | Grounding and Bonding

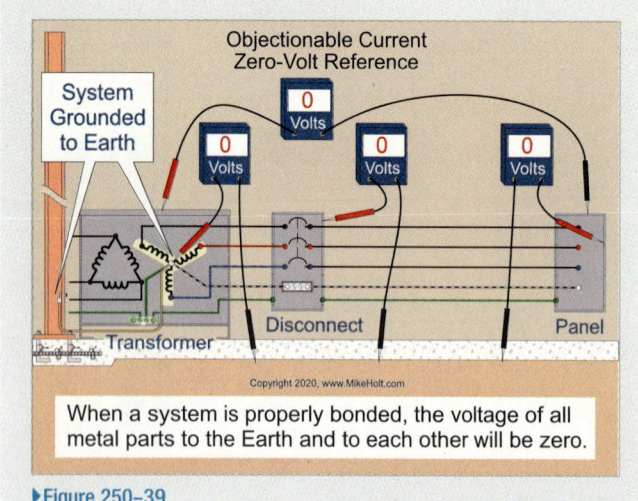

▶Figure 250–39

Operation of Overcurrent Protective Devices. When objectionable neutral current travels on metal parts, electronic overcurrent protective devices equipped with ground-fault protection can trip because some neutral current flows on the circuit equipment grounding conductor instead of on the neutral conductor.

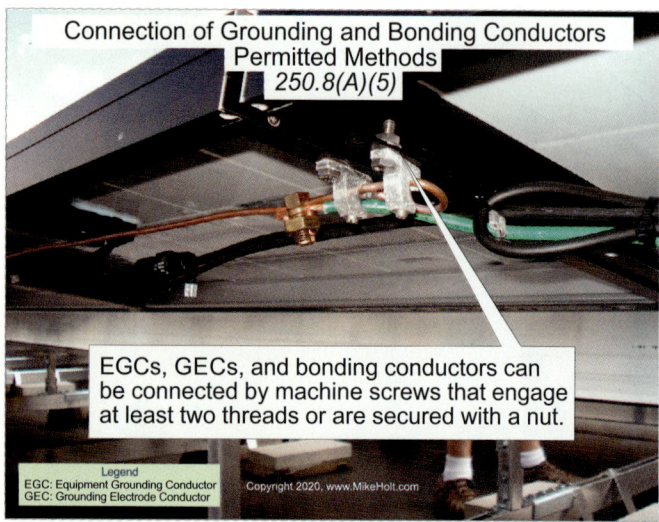

▶Figure 250–40

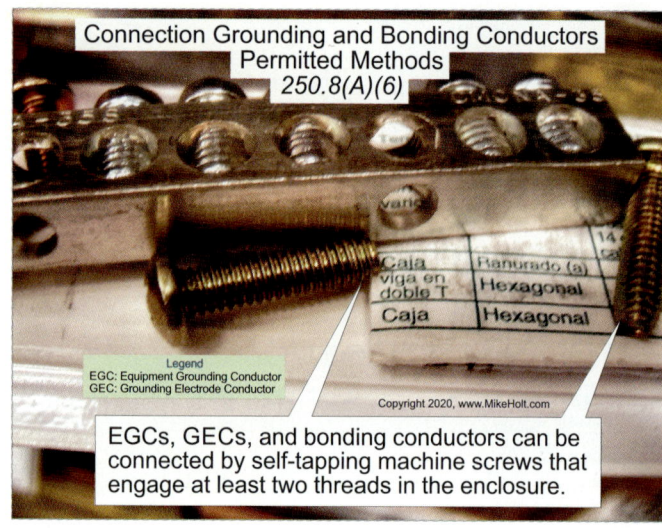

▶Figure 250–41

250.8 Connection of Grounding and Bonding Connectors

(A) Permitted Methods. Equipment grounding conductors, grounding electrode conductors, and bonding jumpers must be connected by one or more of the following methods:

(1) Listed pressure connectors

(2) Terminal bars

(3) Pressure connectors listed for grounding and bonding

(4) Exothermic welding

(5) Machine screws that engage at least two threads or are secured with a nut ▶Figure 250–40

(6) Self-tapping machine screws that engage at least two threads in the enclosure ▶Figure 250–41

(7) Connections that are part of a listed assembly

(8) Other listed means

250.10 Protection of Ground Clamps and Fittings

Ground clamps and fittings subject to physical damage must be protected. ▶Figure 250–42

250.12 Clean Surfaces

Nonconductive coatings (such as paint) on equipment to be grounded or bonded must be removed to ensure good electrical continuity, or the termination fittings must be designed so to make such removal unnecessary [250.53(A) and 250.96(A)].

Grounding and Bonding | 250.20

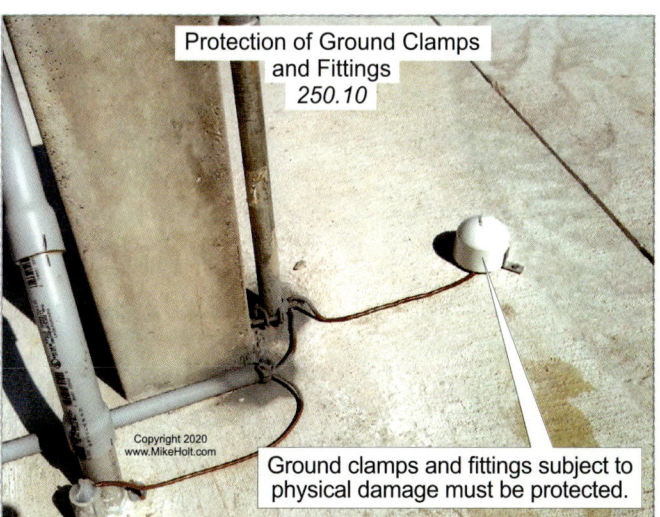
▶Figure 250-42

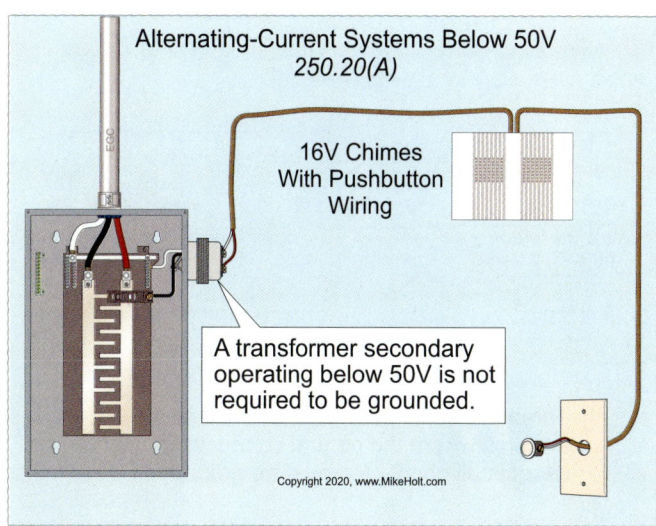
▶Figure 250-43

Author's Comment:

▸ Fittings such as locknuts are designed to cut through the nonconductive coating and establish the intended electrical continuity when they are properly tightened.

▸ Tarnish on copper water pipe need not be removed before making a termination.

Part II. System Grounding and Bonding

250.20 Systems Required to be Grounded

(A) Alternating-Current Systems Below 50V. The secondary of a transformer operating below 50V is not required to be grounded or bonded in accordance with 250.30 unless the transformer's primary supply is from: ▶Figure 250-43

(1) A 277V or 480V system

(2) An ungrounded system

(B) Alternating-Current Systems 50V to 1,000V. The following systems must be grounded (connected to a grounding electrode) where the neutral conductor is used as a circuit conductor:

(1) Single-phase systems. ▶Figure 250-44

(2) Three-phase, wye-connected systems. ▶Figure 250-45

(3) Three-phase, high-leg delta-connected systems. ▶Figure 250-46

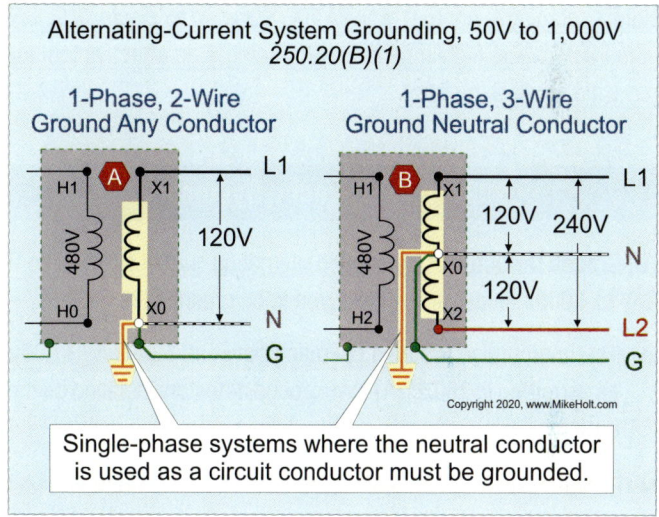
▶Figure 250-44

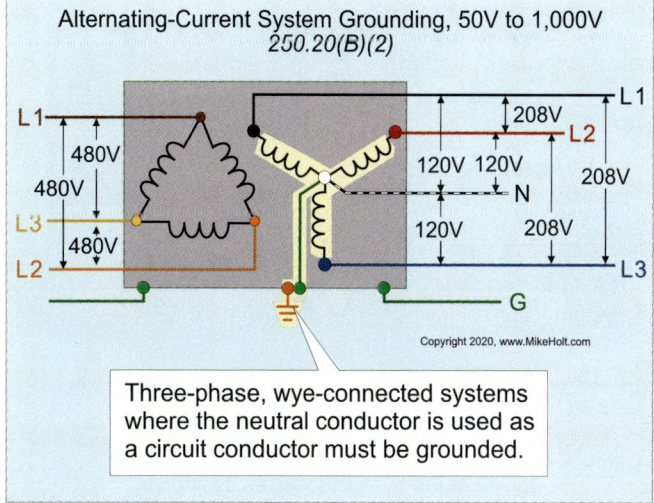
▶Figure 250-45

2020 NEC Requirements for Solar PV and Energy Storage Systems | MikeHolt.com | 167

250.21 | Grounding and Bonding

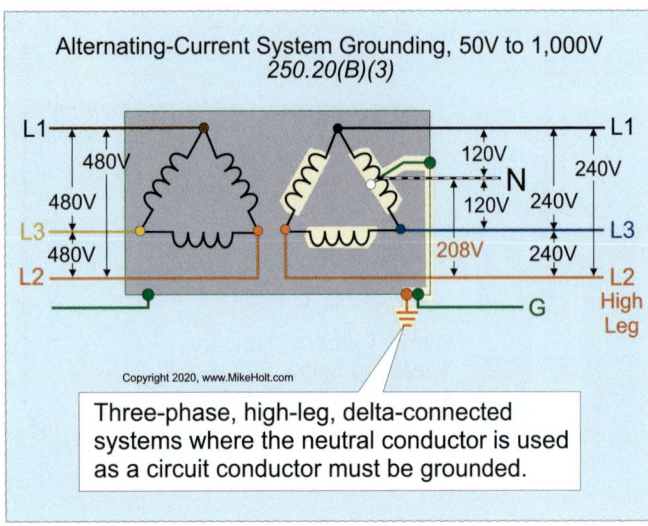

▶Figure 250–46

Note: According to Annex O of NFPA 70E, *Standard for Electrical Safety in the Workplace,* high-impedance grounding is an effective tool for reducing arc flash hazards.

250.21 Ungrounded Systems

(B) Ground Detectors. Ungrounded alternating-current systems from 50V to 1,000V or less are not required to be grounded if:

(1) The ungrounded systems operating between 120V and 1,000V as permitted in 250.21(A) have ground detectors installed on the system.

(2) The ground detection sensing equipment is connected as close as practicable to where the system receives its supply. ▶Figure 250–47

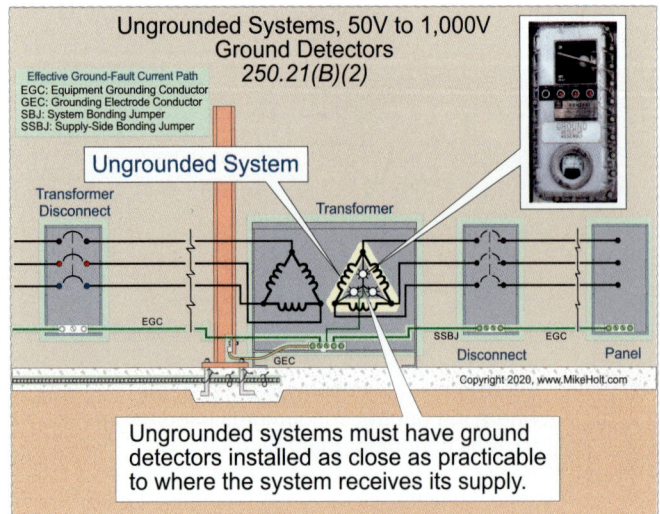

▶Figure 250–47

(C) Marking. Ungrounded systems must be legibly marked "**CAUTION UNGROUNDED SYSTEM OPERATING—_____ VOLTS BETWEEN CONDUCTORS**" with sufficient durability to withstand the environment involved at the source or first disconnect of the system. ▶Figure 250–48

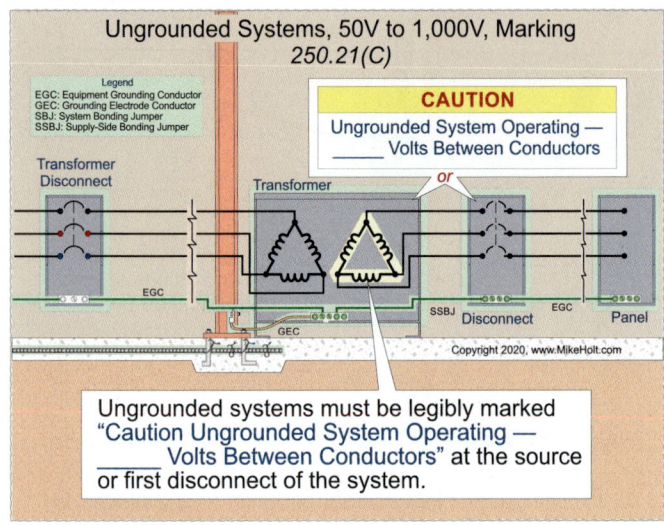

▶Figure 250–48

250.24 Grounding

(A) Grounded System. A premises wiring system supplied by a grounded alternating-current service must have a grounding electrode conductor connected to the service neutral conductor in accordance with the following:

(1) General. The grounding electrode conductor connection to the neutral conductor at service equipment must be made at any accessible point from the load end of the overhead service conductors, service drop, underground service conductors, or service lateral, including the terminal or bus to which the service neutral conductor is connected at the service disconnecting means. ▶Figure 250–49

Author's Comment:

▸ Some inspectors require the grounding electrode conductor connection to the service neutral conductor to be made at the meter socket enclosure, while others insist the connection be made only within the service disconnect. Grounding at either location complies with this rule but be sure you know the local utility company's policy on connections inside the meter socket as many do not permit access to it once it is sealed.

Grounding and Bonding | 250.24

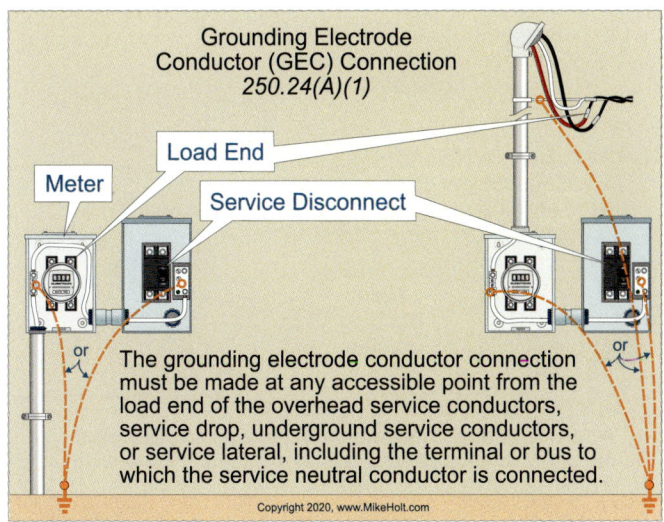
▶Figure 250-49

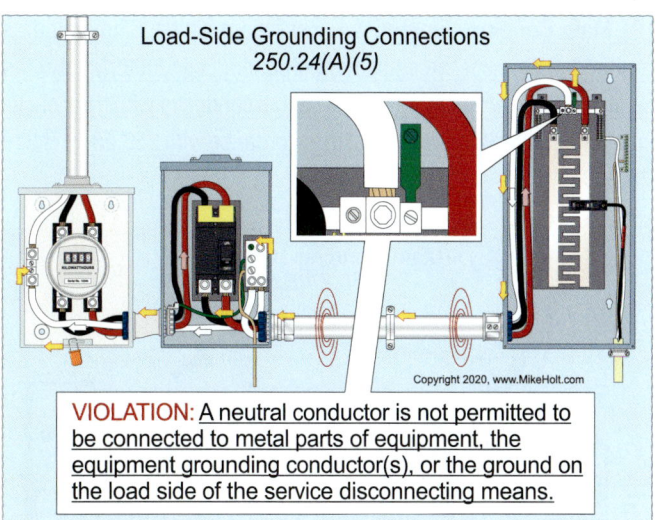
▶Figure 250-51

(4) Main Bonding Jumper as Wire or Busbar. Where the main bonding jumper specified in 250.28 is a wire or busbar and is installed from the service neutral conductor terminal bar or bus to the equipment grounding terminal bar or bus in the service equipment, the grounding electrode conductor is permitted to be connected to the equipment grounding terminal, bar, or bus to which the main bonding jumper is connected. ▶Figure 250-50

Author's Comment:

▶ If a neutral-to-case connection is made on the load side of the service disconnect, objectionable neutral current will flow on conductive metal parts of electrical equipment [250.6(A)]. Objectionable neutral current on metal parts of electrical equipment can be extremely dangerous. It does not take much current to cause electric shock or death (from ventricular fibrillation), as well as a fire. ▶Figure 250-52

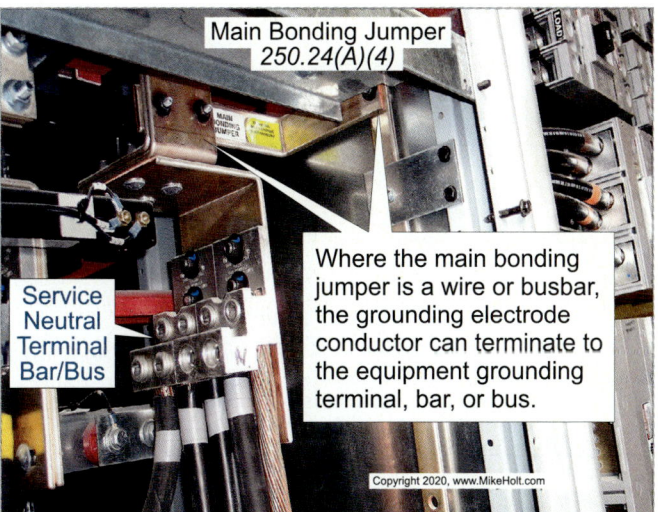
▶Figure 250-50

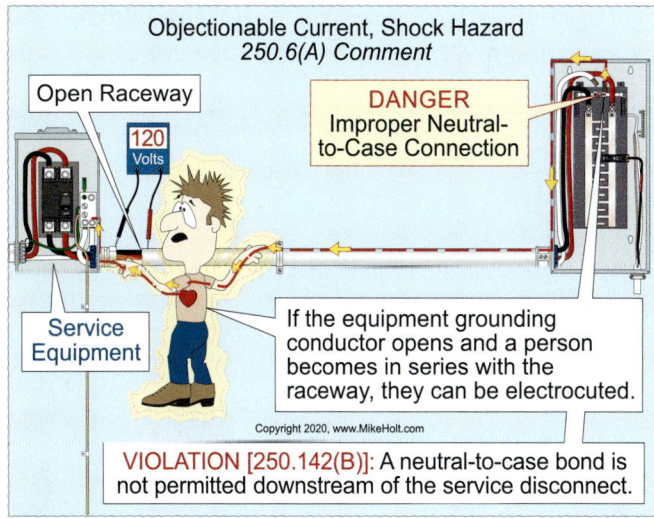
▶Figure 250-52

(5) Load-Side Grounding Connections. A neutral conductor is not permitted to be connected to metal parts of equipment, the equipment grounding conductor(s), or the ground on the load side of the service disconnecting means except as otherwise permitted in 250.142. ▶Figure 250-51

Note: See 250.30 for separately derived systems, 250.32 for connections at separate buildings, and 250.142 for where the neutral conductor is permitted to be connected to the equipment grounding conductor.

250.24 | Grounding and Bonding

(B) Main Bonding Jumper. An unspliced main bonding jumper is required to connect the equipment grounding conductor(s) and the service-disconnect enclosure to the neutral conductor within the enclosure for each service disconnect in accordance with 250.28. ▶Figure 250-53

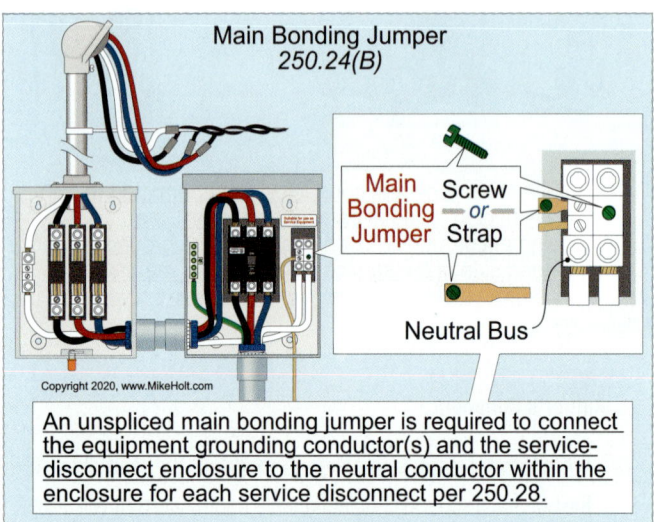
▶Figure 250-53

(C) Neutral Conductor Brought to Service Equipment. A neutral conductor(s) must be routed with the phase conductors to each service disconnecting means and be connected to each disconnecting mean's neutral conductor(s) terminal or bus. A main bonding jumper must connect the neutral conductor(s) to each service disconnecting means enclosure. ▶Figure 250-54 and ▶Figure 250-55

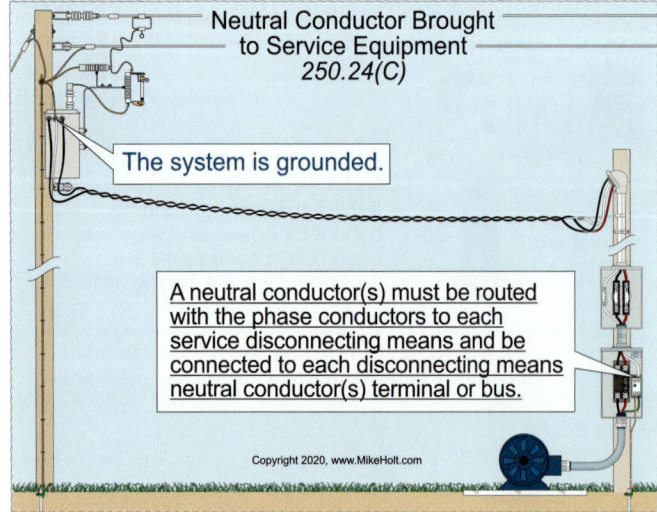
▶Figure 250-54

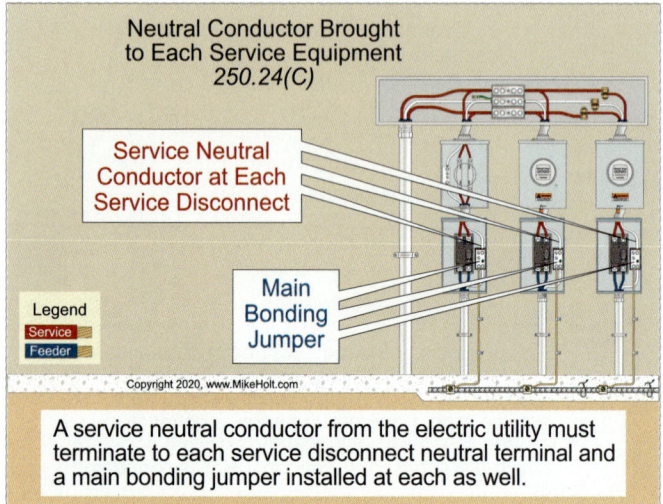
▶Figure 250-55

Author's Comment:

▶ The service neutral conductor provides the effective ground-fault current path to the power supply to ensure dangerous voltage from a ground fault will be quickly removed by the opening of the circuit overcurrent protective device [250.4(A)(3) and 250.4(A)(5)]. ▶Figure 250-56

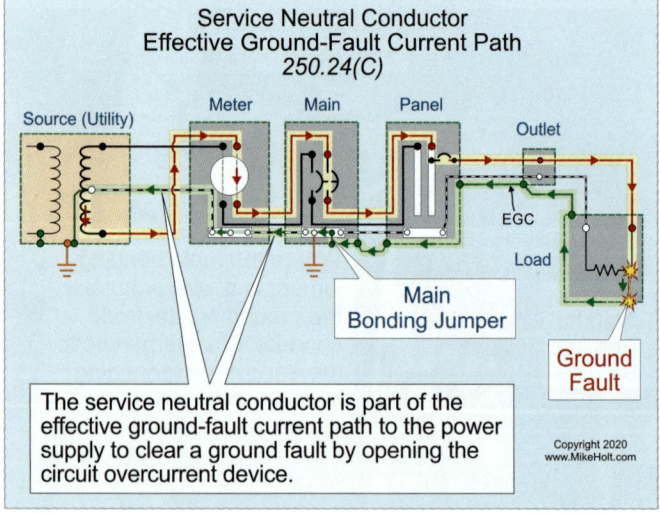
▶Figure 250-56

Author's Comment:

▶ The main bonding jumper is a vital component of bonding. It facilitates the operation of overcurrent protective devices and is a critical part of the grounding system since it bonds the neutral conductor, service enclosure, and the equipment grounding conductor to the grounding electrode system via the grounding electrode conductor.

Grounding and Bonding | 250.24

▸ If the neutral conductor is opened, dangerous voltage will be present on metal parts under normal conditions, providing the potential for electric shock. If the Earth's ground resistance is 25 ohms and the load's resistance is 25 ohms, the voltage drop across each of these resistances will be half of the voltage source. Since the neutral is connected to the service disconnect, all metal parts will be elevated 60V above the Earth's voltage for a 120/240V system. ▸Figure 250-57

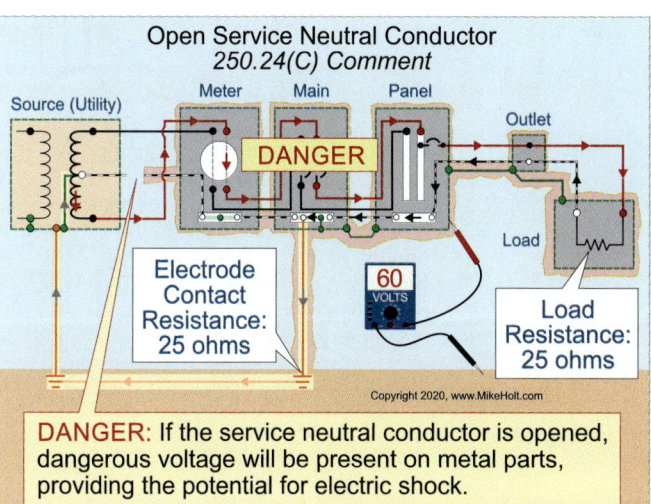

▸Figure 250-57

Danger

⚠ Dangerous voltage from a ground fault will not be removed from metal parts, metal piping, and structural steel if the service-disconnect enclosure is not connected to the service neutral conductor. This is because the contact resistance of a grounding electrode to the Earth is so great that insufficient ground-fault current returns to the power supply if that is the only ground-fault current return path available to open the circuit overcurrent device. ▸Figure 250-58

The neutral conductor(s) must be sized in accordance with the following:

(1) Sizing for a Single Raceway or Cable. The neutral conductor is not permitted to be smaller than specified in Table 250.102(C)(1). ▸Figure 250-59

Author's Comment:

▸ In addition, the neutral conductors must have the capacity to carry the maximum unbalanced neutral current in accordance with 220.61.

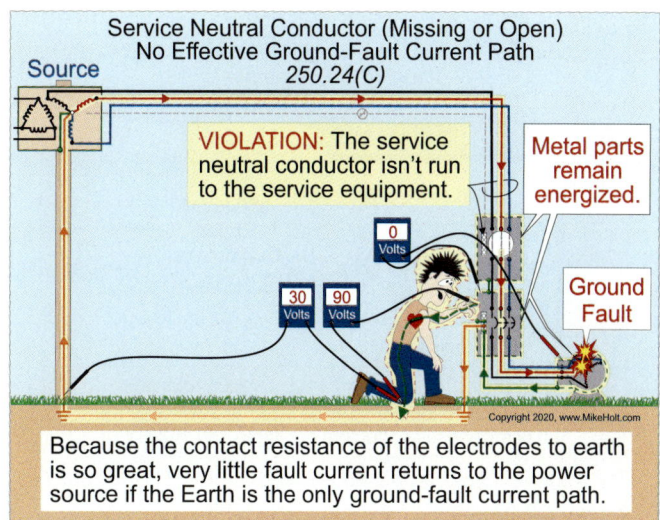

▸Figure 250-58

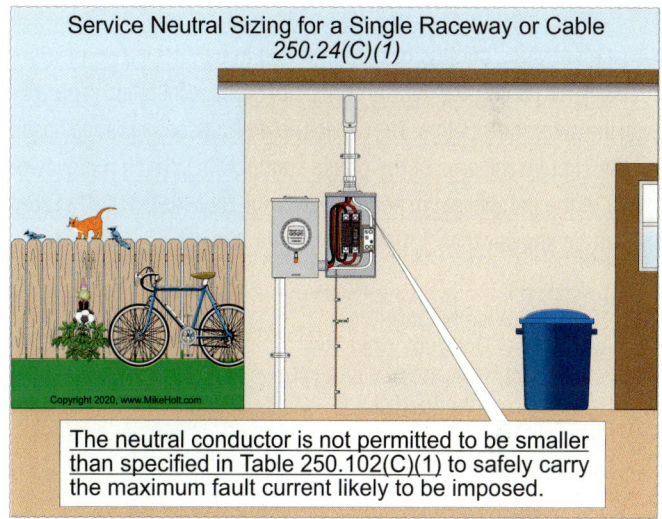

▸Figure 250-59

▸ **Example**

Question: What is the minimum size service neutral conductor required when the service phase conductors are 350 kcmil and the maximum unbalanced load is 100A? ▸Figure 250-60

(a) 3 AWG (b) 2 AWG (c) 1 AWG (d) 1/0 AWG

Solution:

The unbalanced load of 100A requires a 3 AWG service neutral conductor, which is rated 100A at 75°C in accordance with Table 310.16 [110.14(C)(1)(b)(2) and 220.61], but the neutral conductor cannot be smaller than 2 AWG to carry fault current based on the 350 kcmil phase conductors. Therefore, 2 AWG is the minimum size service neutral conductor required [Table 250.102(C)(1)].

Answer: (b) 2 AWG

250.25 | Grounding and Bonding

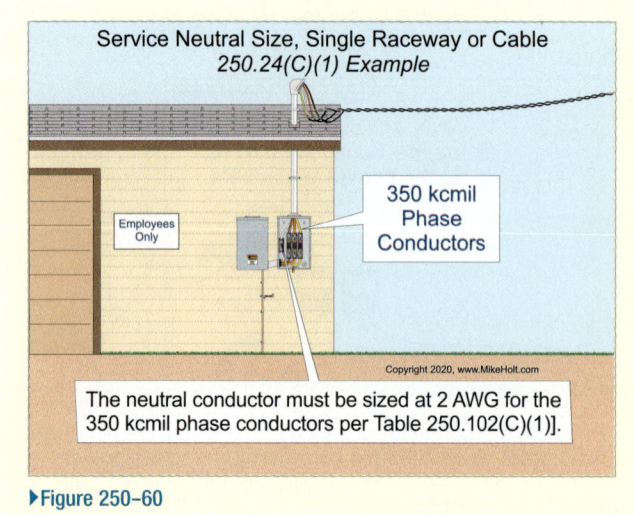

▶Figure 250–60

(2) Parallel Conductors in Two or More Raceways or Cables. If service-entrance conductors are installed in parallel in two or more raceways or cables, the neutral conductor must be installed in parallel with the phase conductors. The service neutral conductor is sized based on the circular mil area of the phase conductors in each raceway or cable of the parallel set in accordance with Table 250.102(C)(1) but cannot be smaller than 1/0 AWG. ▶Figure 250–61

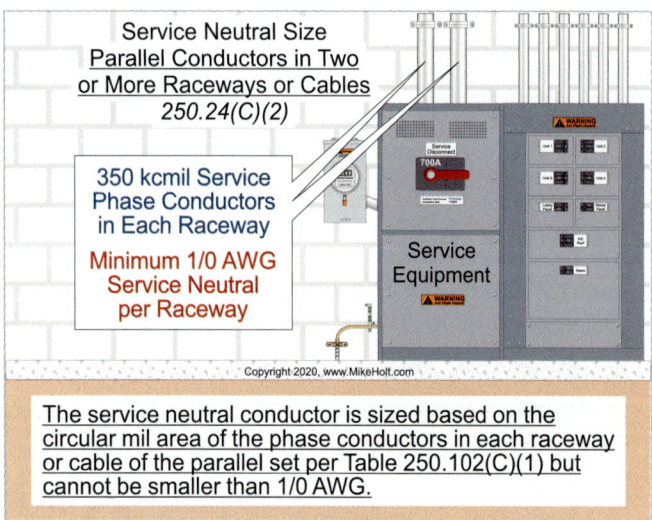

▶Figure 250–61

Note: See 310.10(G) for neutral conductors connected in parallel.

(3) Delta-Connected Service. The grounded conductor of a three-phase, 3-wire delta service must have an ampacity not less than that of the phase conductors.

(D) Grounding Electrode Conductor. A grounding electrode conductor must connect the equipment grounding conductors, the service-equipment enclosures, and the service neutral conductor to the grounding electrode system. This grounding electrode conductor is sized in accordance with 250.66. ▶Figure 250–62 and ▶Figure 250–63

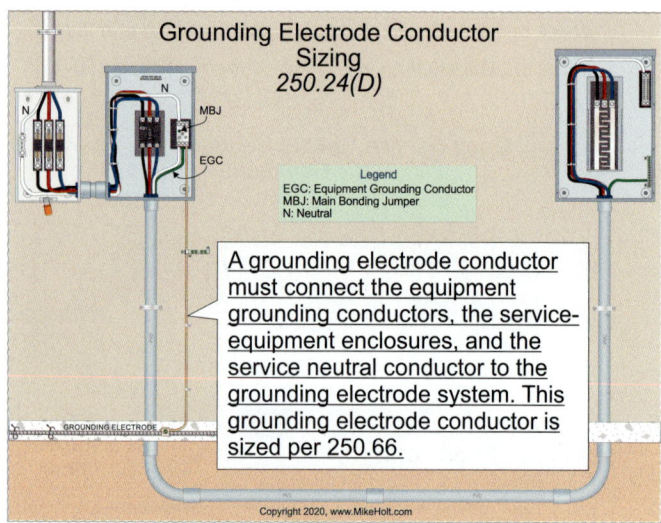

▶Figure 250–62

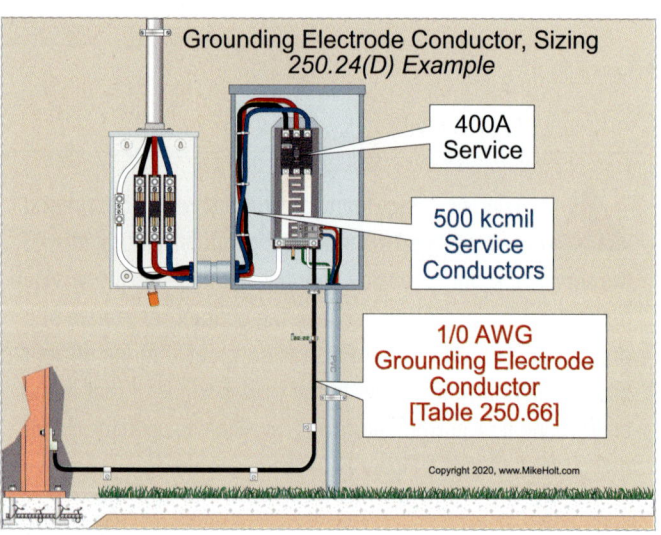

▶Figure 250–63

250.25 Grounding for Supply Side of the Service Disconnect

Electrical systems on the supply side of the service disconnect installed in accordance with 230.82 must be grounded and bonded in accordance with 250.24. ▶Figure 250–64

Grounding and Bonding | 250.28

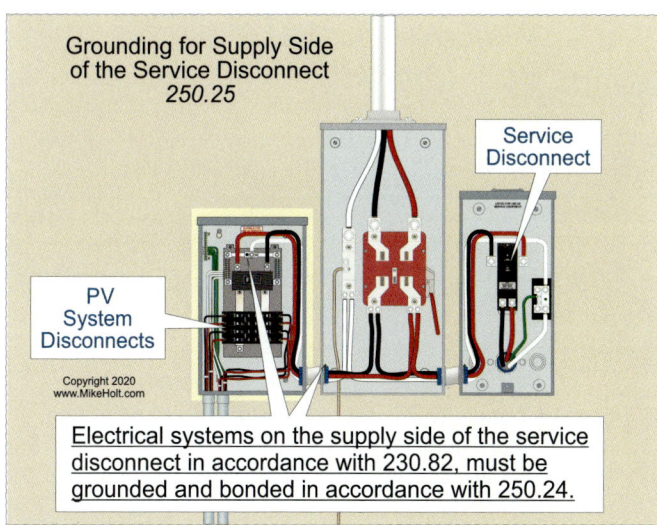
▶Figure 250-64

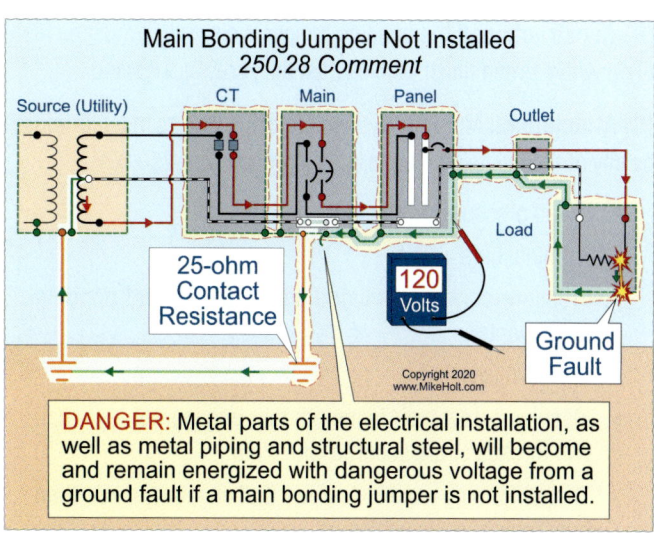
▶Figure 250-65

250.28 Main Bonding Jumper and System Bonding Jumper

Author's Comment:

▶ The primary purpose of the main and system bonding jumpers is to create a path for fault current to flow from a fault to the power supply to facilitate the opening of the circuit overcurrent protective device.

Danger

⚠ Metal parts of the electrical installation, as well as metal piping and structural steel, will become and remain energized with dangerous voltage from a ground fault if a main bonding jumper or system bonding jumper is not installed. A missing main or system bonding jumper causes an opening in the effective ground-fault current path back to the source and creates a condition where overcurrent devices will not open during a ground-fault condition. ▶Figure 250-65 and ▶Figure 250-66

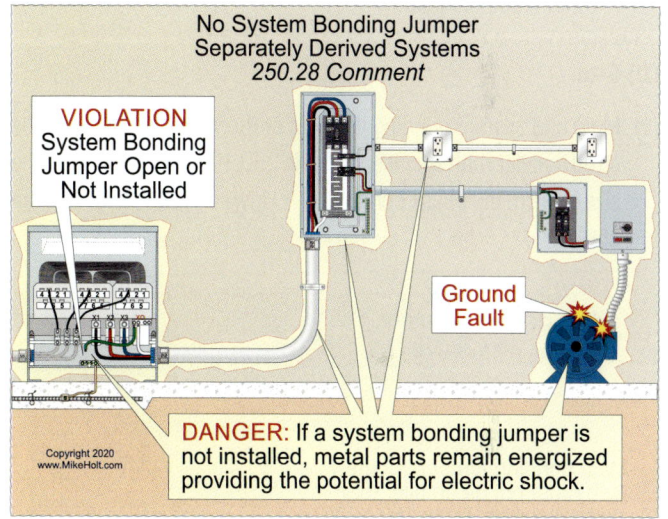
▶Figure 250-66

Main and system bonding jumpers must be installed as follows:

(A) Material. The bonding jumper can be a wire, bus, or screw and can be made of copper, copper-clad aluminum, or aluminum. ▶Figure 250-67

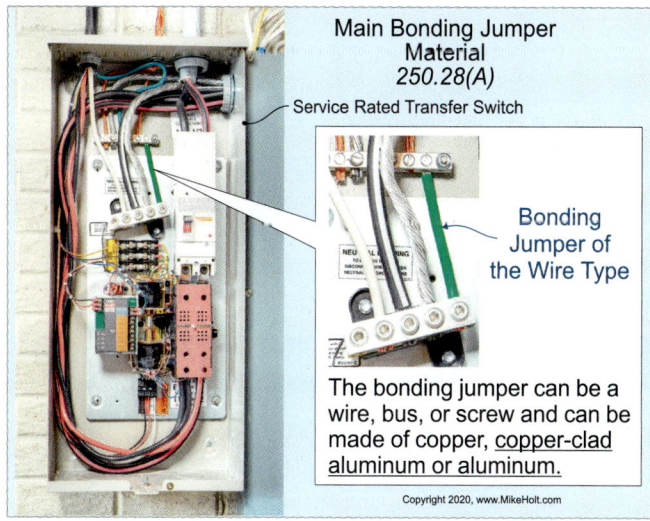
▶Figure 250-67

2nd Printing   2020 NEC Requirements for Solar PV and Energy Storage Systems | MikeHolt.com   173

250.30 | Grounding and Bonding

(B) Construction. If the bonding jumper is a screw, it must be identified with a green finish visible when the screw is installed.

(C) Attachment. Main and system bonding jumpers must terminate by any of the following means in accordance with 250.8(A):

- Listed pressure connectors
- Terminal bars
- Pressure connectors listed as grounding and bonding equipment
- Exothermic welding
- Machine screw-type fasteners that engage not less than two threads or are secured with a nut
- Thread-forming machine screws that engage not less than two threads in the enclosure
- Connections that are part of a listed assembly
- Other listed means

(D) Size.

(1) Main and system bonding jumpers of the wire type must not be sized smaller than specified in Table 250.102(C)(1), based on the size/area of the phase conductor. ▶Figure 250-68 and ▶Figure 250-69

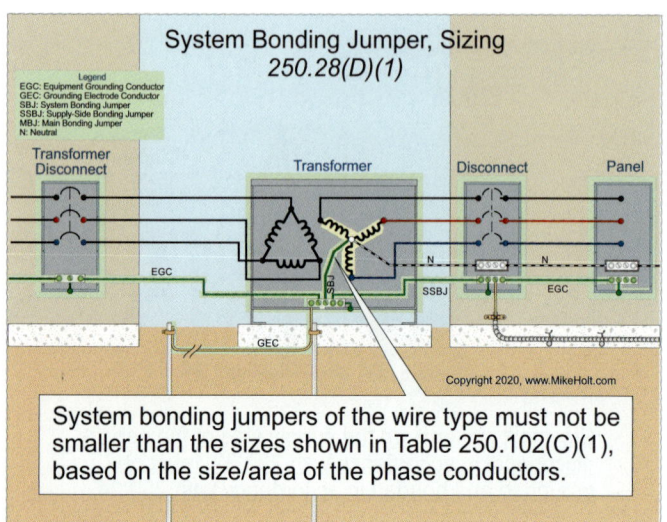

▶Figure 250-69

Note 1: An alternate alternating-current power source, such as an on-site generator, is not a separately derived system if the neutral conductor is solidly interconnected to a service-supplied system neutral conductor. An example of such a situation is where alternate source transfer equipment does not include a switching action in the neutral conductor and allows it to remain solidly connected to the service-supplied neutral conductor when the alternate source is operational and supplying the load served. ▶Figure 250-70 and ▶Figure 250-71

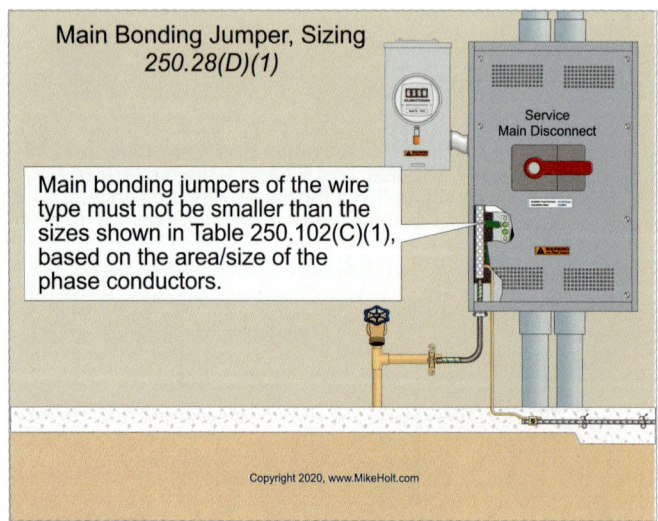

▶Figure 250-68

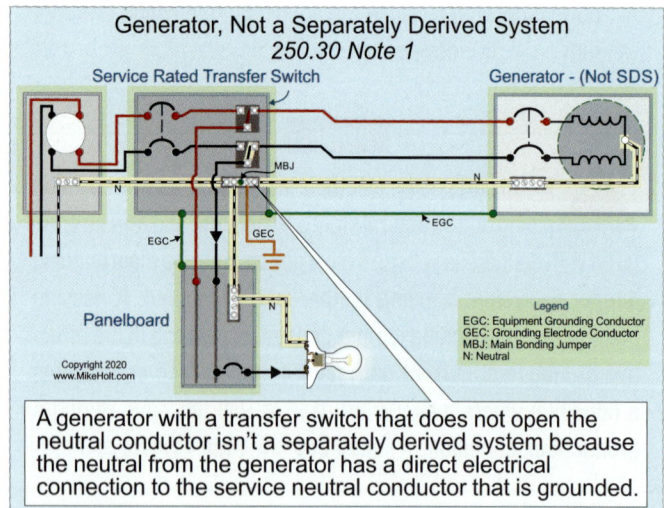

▶Figure 250-70

250.30 Separately Derived Systems

In addition to complying with 250.30(A) for grounded systems, or as provided in 250.30(B) for ungrounded systems, separately derived systems must comply with 250.20, 250.21, 250.22, or 250.26, as applicable.

Grounding and Bonding | 250.30

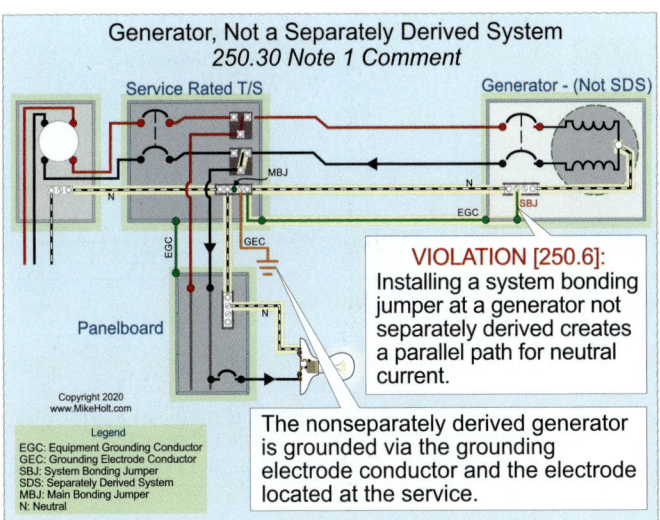

▶Figure 250-71

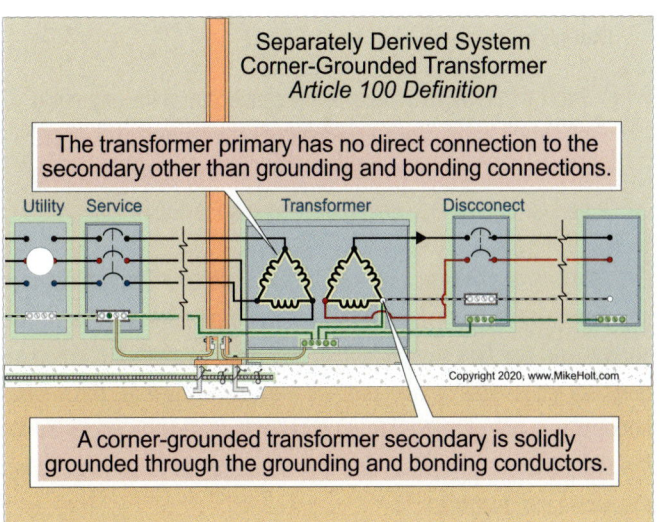

▶Figure 250-73

Author's Comment:

▶ According to Article 100, a "Separately Derived System" is a wiring system whose power is derived from a source, other than the serving electric utility, and where there is no direct electrical connection to the supply conductors of another system other than through grounding and bonding connections. ▶Figure 250-72

(A) Grounded Systems. Separately derived systems must be grounded and bonded in accordance with (A)(1) through (A)(8). A neutral-to-case connection is not permitted to be made on the load side of the system bonding jumper.

(1) System Bonding Jumper. A system bonding jumper must be installed at the same location where the grounding electrode conductor terminates to the neutral terminal of the separately derived system; either at the separately derived system or the secondary separately derived system disconnect, but not at both. ▶Figure 250-74

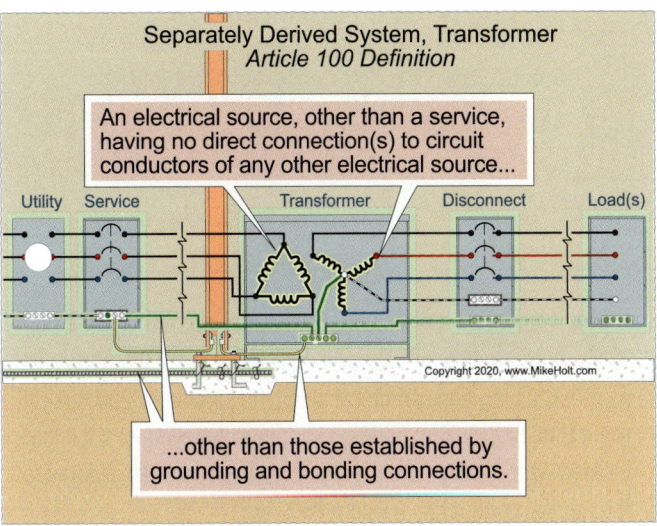

▶Figure 250-72

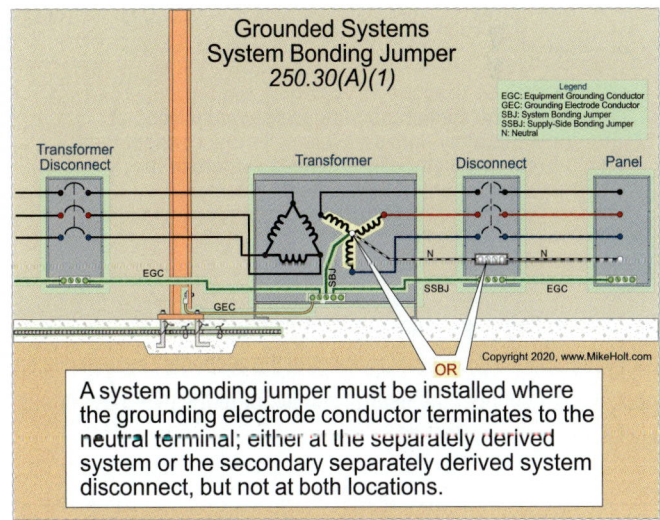

▶Figure 250-74

Author's Comment:

▶ Transformers are separately derived because the primary conductors have no direct electrical connection from the circuit conductors of one system to the circuit conductors of another. ▶Figure 250-73

250.30 | Grounding and Bonding

> **Author's Comment:**
> ▸ Section 250.30(A)(5) requires the connection of the grounding electrode conductor to be made at the same point where the neutral conductor is connected to the system bonding jumper in order to avoid parallel paths for neutral current.

Ex 2: If a building or structure is supplied by a feeder from an outdoor separately derived system, a system bonding jumper at both the source and the first disconnecting means is permitted if doing so does not establish a parallel path for the neutral current. The neutral conductor is not permitted to be smaller than the size specified for the system bonding jumper and it is not required to be larger than the phase conductor(s).

(a) System Bonding Jumper at Source. Where the system bonding jumper is installed at the separately derived system, it must connect the neutral conductor to the metal enclosure of the separately derived system. ▸Figure 250-75

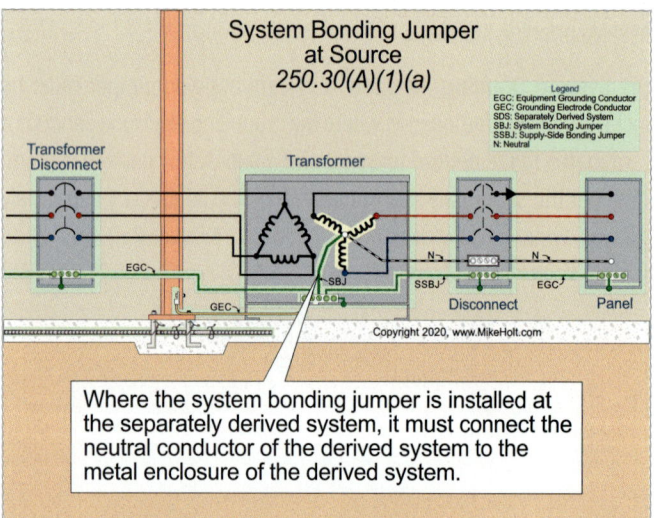

▸Figure 250-75

(b) System Bonding Jumper at First Disconnecting Means. Where the system bonding jumper is installed at the secondary system disconnect, it must connect the neutral conductor to the metal disconnect enclosure. ▸Figure 250-76

> **Danger**
> During a ground fault, metal parts of electrical equipment, as well as metal piping and structural steel, will become and remain energized providing the potential for electric shock and fire if the system bonding jumper is not installed. ▸Figure 250-77

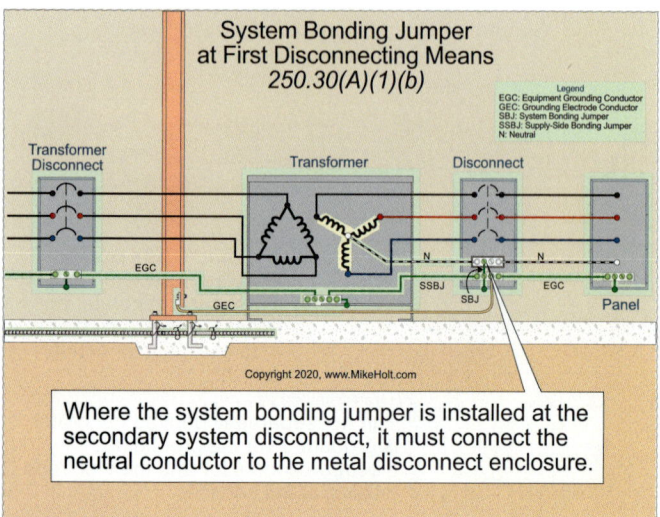

▸Figure 250-76

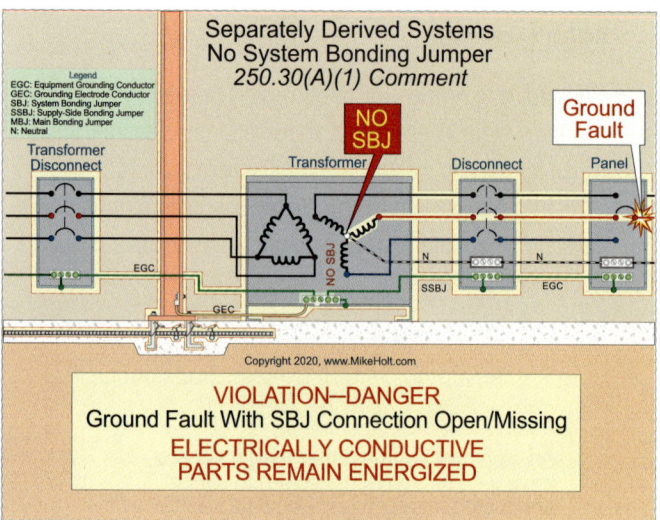

▸Figure 250-77

> **Caution**
> Dangerous objectionable neutral current will flow on conductive metal parts of electrical equipment as well as metal piping and structural steel, in violation of 250.6(A), if more than one system bonding jumper is installed, or if it is not located where the grounding electrode conductor terminates to the neutral conductor. ▸Figure 250-78

(2) Supply-Side Bonding Jumper to Disconnect. A supply-side bonding jumper must be installed at the first disconnecting means enclosure and it is not required to be larger than the derived phase conductors. The supply-side bonding jumper can be of a nonflexible metal raceway type or of the wire type.

Grounding and Bonding | 250.30

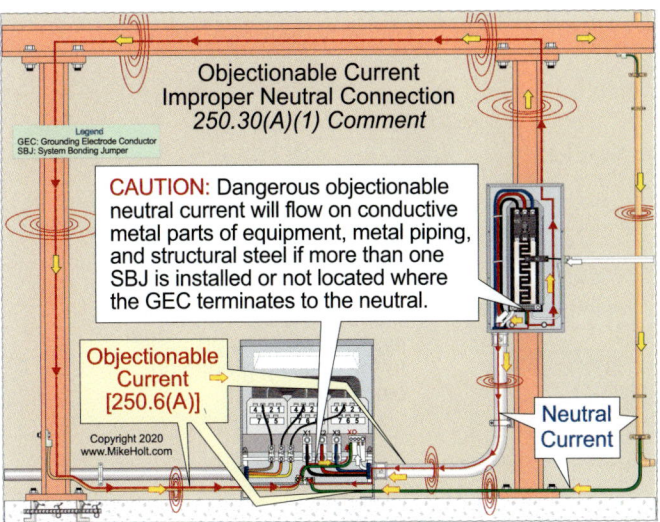
▶Figure 250-78

Author's Comment:

▸ The supply-side bonding jumper can be RMC, IMC, or EMT run between the separately derived system enclosure and the secondary system disconnect enclosure. A nonmetallic or flexible raceway must have a supply-side bonding jumper of the wire type.

(1) A supply-side bonding jumper of the wire type must be sized in accordance with 250.102(C) based on the size/area of the secondary phase conductor in the raceway or cable.

▶ **Example**

Question: What size supply-side bonding jumper is required for flexible metal conduit containing 300 kcmil secondary conductors? ▶Figure 250-79

(a) 4 AWG   (b) 2 AWG   (c) 1/0 AWG   (d) 3/0 AWG

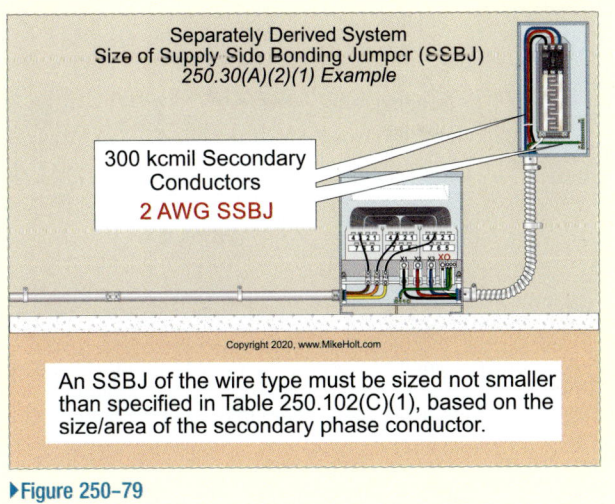
▶Figure 250-79

Answer: (b) 2 AWG [Table 250.102(C)(1)]

(3) Neutral Conductor Size. The neutral conductor between the separately derived system and the secondary system disconnect is not required to be larger than the derived phase conductors. If the system bonding jumper is installed at the secondary system disconnect instead of at the separately derived system, the following apply:

(a) Sizing for Single Raceway. A secondary neutral conductor must be run from the separately derived system to the secondary system disconnect and the secondary neutral conductor must be sized not smaller than specified in Table 250.102(C)(1), based on the size/area of the secondary phase conductor.

▶ **Example**

Question: What size neutral conductor is required for a 75 kVA transformer with 250 kcmil secondary conductors? ▶Figure 250-80

(a) 2 AWG   (b) 1/0 AWG   (c) 4/0 AWG   (d) 250 kcmil

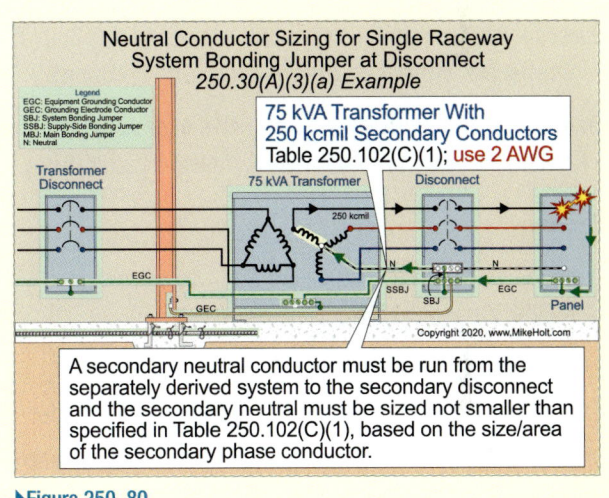
▶Figure 250-80

Answer: (a) 2 AWG [Table 250.102(C)(1)]

(b) Parallel Conductors in Two or More Raceways. A neutral conductor sized in accordance with 250.102(C)(1), but not smaller than 1/0 AWG must be installed in each raceway. ▶Figure 250-81

250.30 | Grounding and Bonding

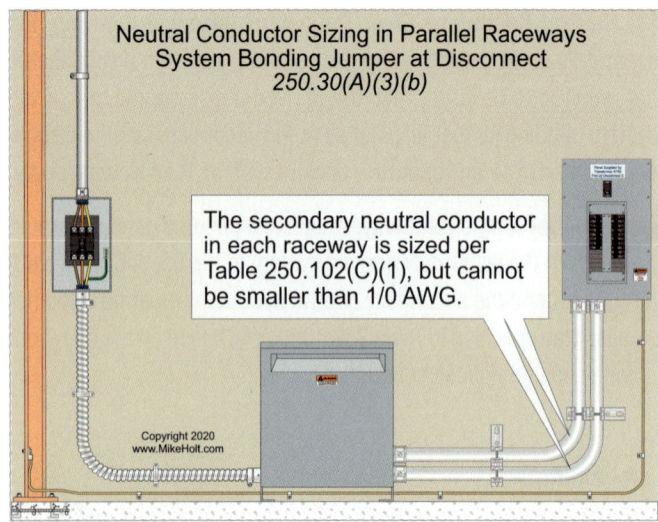

▶Figure 250–81

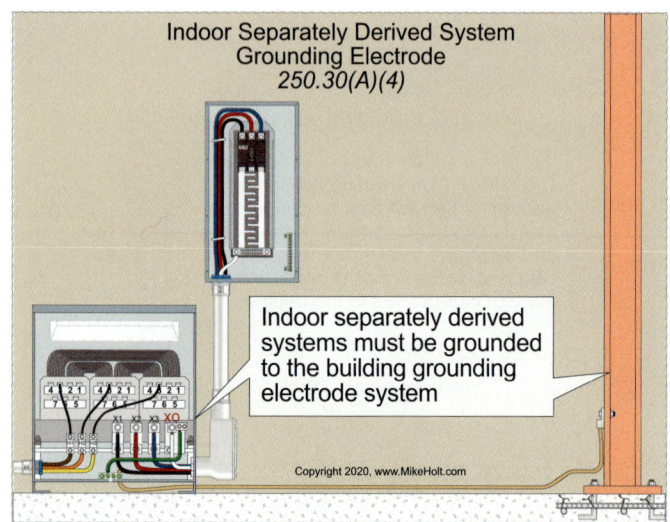

▶Figure 250–82

▶ Example

Question: What size neutral conductor is required for a 112.50 kVA transformer with two sets of 3/0 AWG secondary conductors?

(a) 4 AWG in each raceway (b) 2 AWG in each raceway
(c) 1/0 AWG in each raceway (d) 3/0 AWG in each raceway

Solution:

Determine the equivalent area for two 3/0 AWG conductors [250.102(C)(2) and Chapter 9, Table 8].

3/0 AWG = 167,800 circular mils
2 conductors × 167,800 cmil = 335,600 cmil [Table 250.102(C)(1)]

One 2 AWG supply-side bonding jumper (minimum) is needed to bond both raceways, but the minimum size neutral conductor in parallel is 1/0 AWG [310.10(G)(1)].

Answer: (c) 1/0 AWG in each raceway

(4) Grounding Electrode. Separately derived systems located indoors must be grounded to the building grounding electrode system. ▶Figure 250–82

Separately derived systems located outdoors must be grounded in accordance with 250.30(C).

Author's Comment:

▸ The metal structural frame of a building is itself not a grounding electrode, but when it is properly connected to the grounding electrodes [250.68(C)(2)] it can be used as a grounding electrode conductor.

Note 1: Interior metal water piping in the area served by separately derived systems must be bonded to the separately derived system in accordance with 250.104(D).

(5) Grounding Electrode Conductor, Single Separately Derived System. The grounding electrode conductor for a separately derived system must be sized in accordance with 250.66, based on the area of the largest secondary phase conductor. It must also terminate to the building grounding electrode in accordance with 250.30(A)(4), or to the building structural steel as permitted in 250.68(C).

The grounding electrode conductor is required to terminate to the neutral conductor at the same point on the separately derived system where the system bonding jumper is connected. ▶Figure 250–83

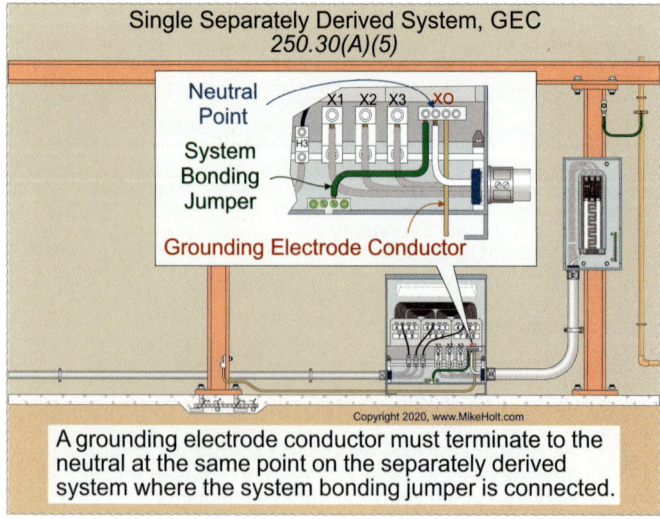

▶Figure 250–83

Grounding and Bonding | 250.30

Author's Comment:

▸ System grounding is intended to reduce overvoltage caused by induction from multiple indirect lightning strikes or intermittent ground faults. System grounding helps reduce fires in buildings as well as voltage stress on electrical insulation and therefore ensures longer insulation life for motors, separately derived systems, and other system components. ▸Figure 250-84

▸ To prevent objectionable neutral current from flowing onto metal parts [250.6], the grounding electrode conductor must originate at the same point on the separately derived system as where the system bonding jumper is connected [250.30(A)(1)].

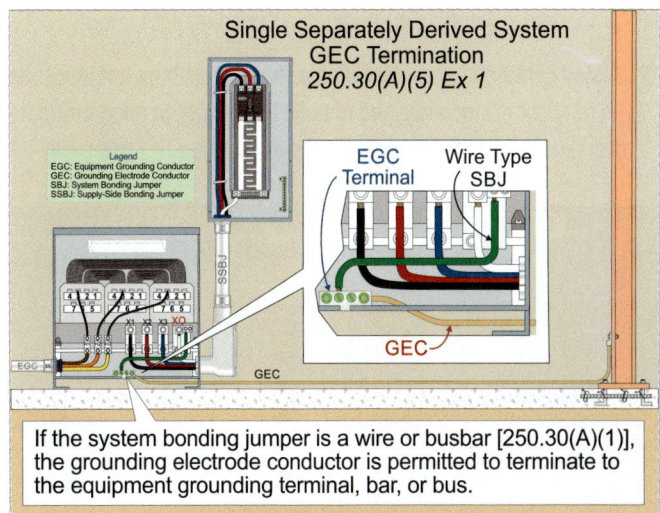

▸Figure 250-85

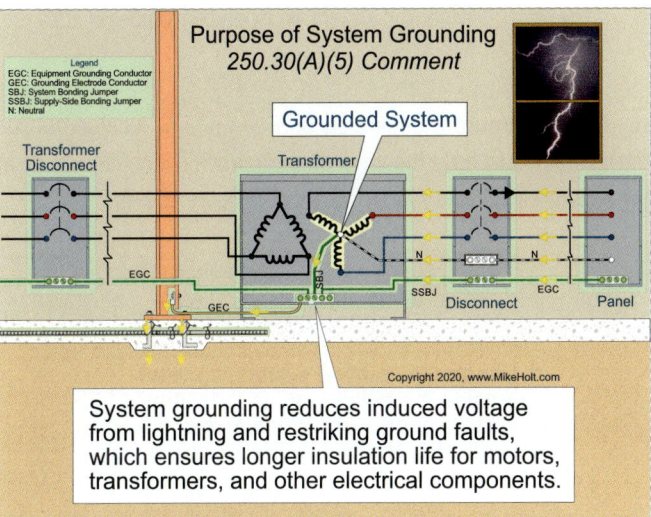

▸Figure 250-84

Ex 1: If the system bonding jumper is a wire or busbar [250.30(A)(1)], the grounding electrode conductor can terminate at the equipment grounding terminal, bar, or bus. ▸Figure 250-85

(6) Common Grounding Electrode Conductor, Multiple Separately Derived Systems. Where there are multiple separately derived systems, a grounding electrode conductor tap from each of them to a common grounding electrode conductor is permitted. This connection must be made at the same point on the separately derived system secondary as where the system bonding jumper is connected [250.30(A)(1)]. ▸Figure 250-86

(a) Common Grounding Electrode Conductor. The common grounding electrode conductor can be any of the following:

(1) An unspliced conductor not smaller than 3/0 AWG copper or 250 kcmil aluminum.

(2) Interior metal water pipe located not more than 5 ft from the point of entrance to the building [250.68(C)(1)].

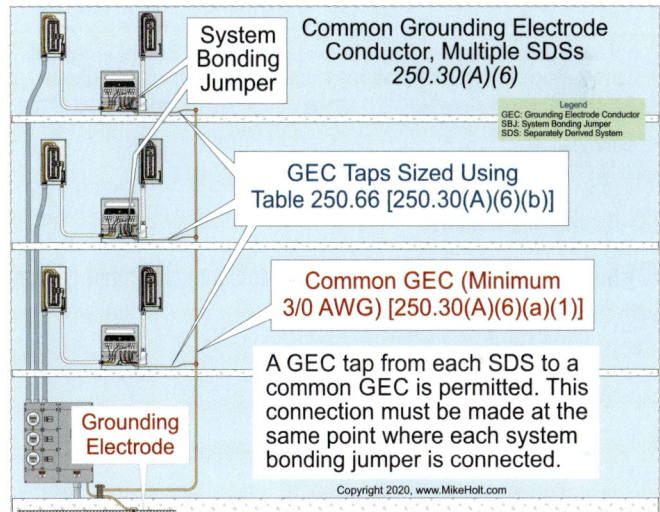

▸Figure 250-86

(3) The metal frame of the building that complies with 250.68(C)(2) or is connected to the grounding electrode system by a conductor not smaller than 3/0 AWG copper or 250 kcmil aluminum.

(b) Tap Conductor Size. Grounding electrode conductor taps must be sized in accordance with Table 250.66, based on the area of the largest secondary phase conductor.

Ex: If the only electrodes present are of the types specified in 250.66(A), (B), or (C), the size of the common grounding electrode conductor is not required to be larger than the largest conductor required by 250.66(A), (B), or (C) for the type of electrode that is present.

(c) Connections. Tap connections to the common grounding electrode conductor must be made at an accessible location by any of the following methods:

(1) A connector listed as grounding and bonding equipment.

(2) Listed connections to aluminum or copper busbars not less than ¼ in. thick × 2 in. wide, and of sufficient length to accommodate the terminations necessary for the installation. ▶Figure 250-87

▶Figure 250-87

(3) Exothermic welding.

(7) **Installation.** The grounding electrode conductor must comply with 250.64(A), (B), (C), and (E).

Author's Comment:

▶ According to 250.64, the grounding electrode conductor must be copper where within 18 in. of the surface of the Earth [250.64(A)], and:

▶ Be securely fastened to the surface on which it is carried [250.64(B)],

 ▶ Be adequately protected if exposed to physical damage [250.64(B)], and

 ▶ Ferrous metal enclosures enclosing a grounding electrode conductor must be made electrically continuous from the point of attachment to cabinets or equipment to the grounding electrode [250.64(E)].

(8) **Structural Steel and Metal Piping.** To ensure dangerous voltage on metal parts from a ground fault is removed quickly, structural steel and metal piping in the area served by a separately derived system must be bonded to the secondary neutral conductor in accordance with 250.104(D).

Author's Comment:

▶ If the structural steel of a building is connected to the Earth in accordance with 250.68(C)(2), it is part of the grounding electrode system, and an indoor separately derived system is required to be connected to the building steel [250.30(A)(4)]. If the structural steel of a building is not in compliance with 250.68(C)(2), it must be bonded to the neutral conductor of the separately derived system via a bonding jumper in accordance with 250.104(D).

(C) Outdoor Source. Separately derived systems located outside the building must have the grounding electrode connection made at the separately derived system location. ▶Figure 250-88

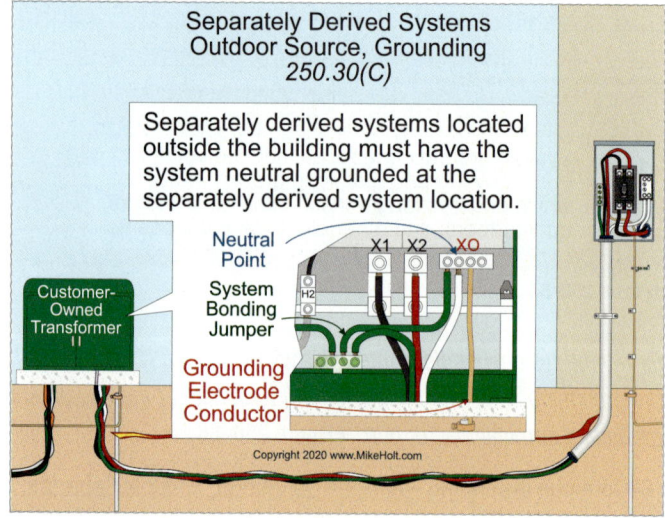

▶Figure 250-88

Author's Comment:

▶ A grounding electrode connection is required at the building disconnect supplied by the outdoor separately derived system [250.32(B)(2)].

Special Section 250.30
Separately Derived Systems

Outdoor Installations

Customer Transformer Outdoors. ▶Figure 250-89

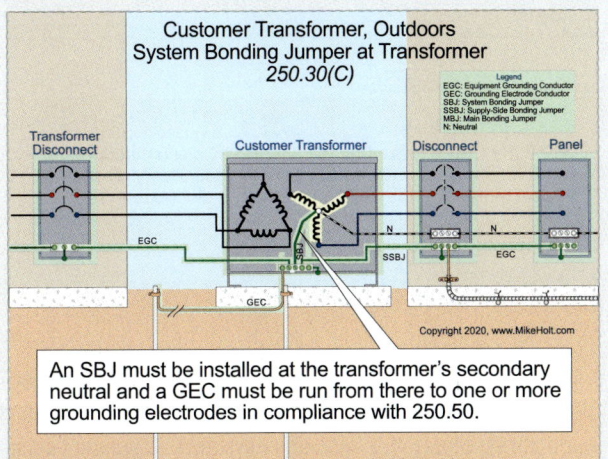

▶Figure 250-89

System Bonding Jumper. Where a separately derived system is installed outdoors, a system bonding jumper sized in accordance with Table 250.102(C)(1), if of the wire type, must be installed at the separately derived system's secondary neutral [250.30(A)(1)]. ▶Figure 250-90

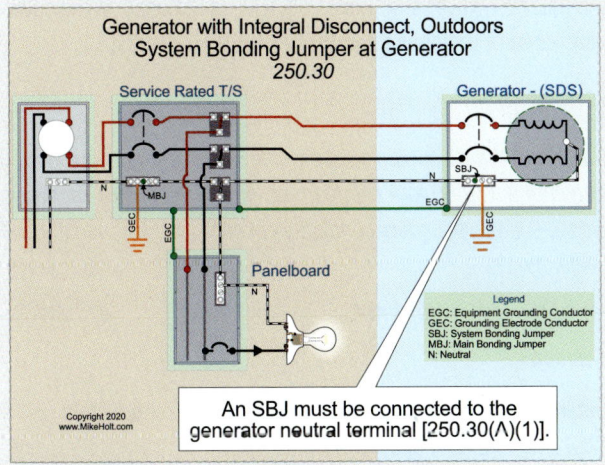

▶Figure 250-90

Grounding Electrode Conductor. A grounding electrode conductor sized in accordance with 250.66, based on the area of the largest secondary phase conductor [250.30(A)(5)], must be run from the separately derived system's neutral terminal to one or more grounding electrodes in compliance with 250.50 and in accordance with 250.30(C) [250.30(A)(4)].

Where the system bonding jumper is a wire or busbar, the grounding electrode conductor can originate at the generator's equipment grounding terminal, bar, or bus [250.30(A)(5) Ex 1].

Supply-Side Bonding Jumper. A supply-side bonding jumper must be run from the separately derived system's equipment grounding conductor terminal to the secondary system disconnect enclosure's equipment grounding conductor terminal.

Where the supply-side bonding jumper is of the wire type it must be sized in accordance with Table 250.102(C)(1), based on the size/area of the secondary phase conductor [250.30(A)(2)].

Indoor Installations

Indoor Separately Derived System, System Bonding Jumper at Separately Derived System. ▶Figure 250-91

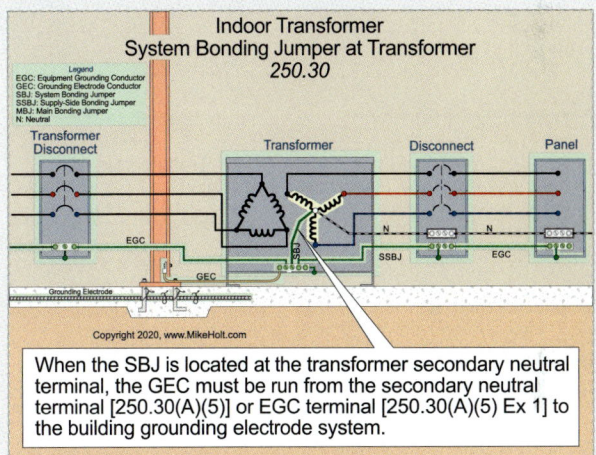

▶Figure 250-91

System Bonding Jumper. Where a separately derived system is installed indoors, the required system bonding jumper sized in accordance with Table 250.102(C)(1), if of the wire type, can be installed at the separately derived system's secondary neutral terminal [250.30(A)(1)(a)].

Grounding Electrode Conductor. A grounding electrode conductor sized in accordance with 250.66, based on the size/area of the secondary phase conductor, must be run from the separately derived system's neutral terminal to the building's grounding electrode system [250.30(A)(4)].

Where the system bonding jumper is a wire or busbar, the grounding electrode conductor can originate at the transformer's equipment grounding terminal, bar, or bus [250.30(A)(5) Ex 1].

250.30 | Grounding and Bonding

Supply-Side Bonding Jumper. A supply-side bonding jumper sized in accordance with Table 250.102(C)(1), if of the wire type, must be run from the separately derived system's equipment grounding conductor terminal to the secondary system disconnect enclosure's equipment grounding conductor terminal [250.30(A)(2)].

▶ **Example**

Question: What size supply-side bonding jumper is required between a 75 kVA transformer, with 250 kcmil secondary conductors in a single raceway, and the first disconnect? ▶Figure 250-92

(a) 4 AWG   (b) 3 AWG   (c) 2 AWG   (d) 1 AWG

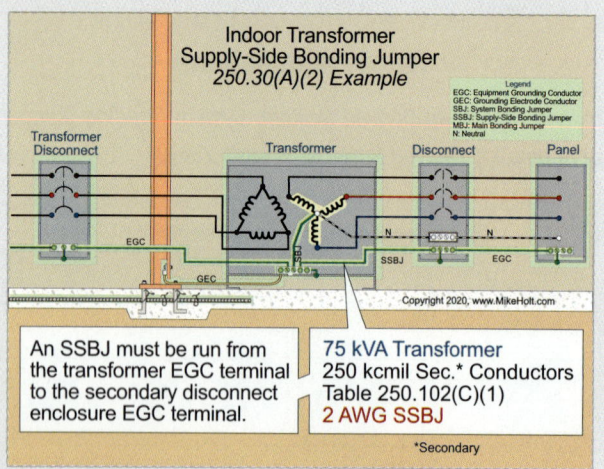

▶Figure 250-92

Answer: (c) 2 AWG; based on the 250 kcmil conductors [Table 250.102(C)(1)].

Separately Derived System Indoors, System Bonding Jumper at Secondary System Disconnect. ▶Figure 250-93

System Bonding Jumper. Where a separately derived system is installed indoors, the required system bonding jumper, sized in accordance with Table 250.102(C)(1), can be installed at the separately derived system's secondary system disconnect [250.30(A)(1)(b)].

Grounding Electrode Conductor. A grounding electrode conductor, sized in accordance with 250.66 based on the area of the largest secondary phase conductor, must be run from the separately derived system's disconnect neutral terminal to the building's grounding electrode system [250.30(A)(4)].

Where the system bonding jumper is a wire or busbar, the grounding electrode conductor can originate at the transformer's secondary disconned equipment grounding terminal, bar, or bus [250.30(A)(5) Ex 1].

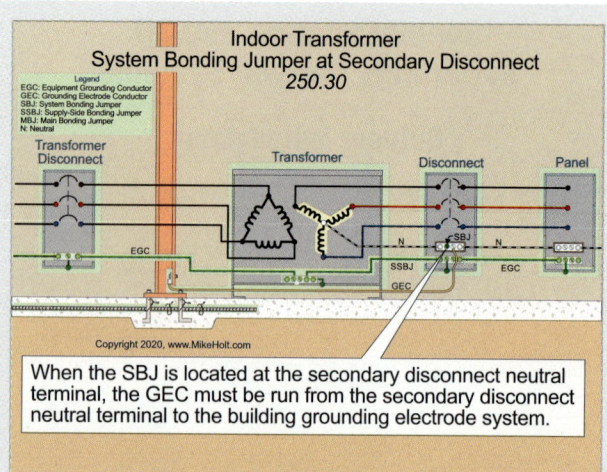

▶Figure 250-93

Supply-Side Bonding Jumper. A supply-side bonding jumper sized in accordance with Table 250.102(C)(1), if of the wire type, must be run from the separately derived system's equipment grounding conductor terminal to the secondary system's disconnect enclosure equipment grounding conductor terminal [250.30(A)(2)].

Sizing the Supply-Side Bonding Jumper for Parallel Raceways

Method 1. The supply-side bonding jumper can be run in each raceway and sized using Table 250.102(C)(1), based on the size/area of the phase conductors in each raceway [250.102(C)(2)].

Method 2. A single supply-side bonding jumper can be run for multiple raceways using Table 250.102(C)(1), based on the equivalent area of the phase conductors [250.102(C)(2)].

▶ **Example**

Question: What size single supply-side bonding jumper is required between a 112.60 kVA transformer, paralleled in two raceways with 3/0 AWG secondary conductors in each raceway, and the first disconnect?

(a) 4 AWG   (b) 3 AWG   (c) 2 AWG   (d) 1 AWG

Solution:

Determine the equivalent area for two 3/0 AWG conductors [250.102(C)(2) and Chapter 9, Table 8].

3/0 AWG = 167,800 circular mills

2 conductors × 167,800 cmil = 335,600 cmil [Table 250.102(C)(1)]

One 2 AWG supply-side bonding jumper (minimum) is needed to bond both raceways. The 1/0 AWG minimum conductor size for parallel conductors does not apply to supply-side bonding jumpers or equipment grounding conductors.

Answer: (c) 2 AWG

Author's Comment:

- A supply-side bonding jumper can also be run with each parallel raceway based on the size of the phase conductor in each raceway [250.102(C)(2)]. If the phase conductors in each raceway are 3/0 AWG, then a 4 AWG conductor must be installed in each raceway [250.102(C)(2)].

Neutral Conductor. When the system bonding jumper is installed at a secondary system disconnect, a secondary neutral conductor in each raceway, sized no smaller than specified in Table 250.102(C)(1), must be run from the separately derived system's secondary to the secondary system's disconnect enclosure.

▶ **Example**

Question: What size neutral conductor is required for a 112.50 kVA transformer paralleled in two raceways with 3/0 AWG secondary conductors in each raceway?

(a) 3 AWG (b) 2 AWG (c) 1 AWG (d) 1/0 AWG

Solution:

Determine the equivalent area for two 3/0 AWG conductors [250.102(C)(2) and Chapter 9, Table 8].

3/0 AWG = 167,800 circular mils
2 conductors x 167,800 cmil = 335,600 cmil [Table 250.102(C)(1)]

One 2 AWG supply-side bonding jumper (minimum) is needed to bond both raceways, but the minimum size neutral conductor in parallel is 1/0 AWG [310.10(G)(1)].

Answer: (d) 1/0 AWG

Author's Comment:

- Be sure the 1/0 AWG conductor is large enough to handle the maximum unbalanced load [220.61].
- When a system bonding jumper is installed at the secondary system's disconnect, the secondary neutral conductor will serve as part of the effective ground-fault current path.

250.32 Buildings Supplied by a Feeder

(A) Grounding Electrode. A building supplied by a feeder must have a grounding electrode system and a grounding electrode conductor installed in accordance with Part III of Article 250. ▶Figure 250-94

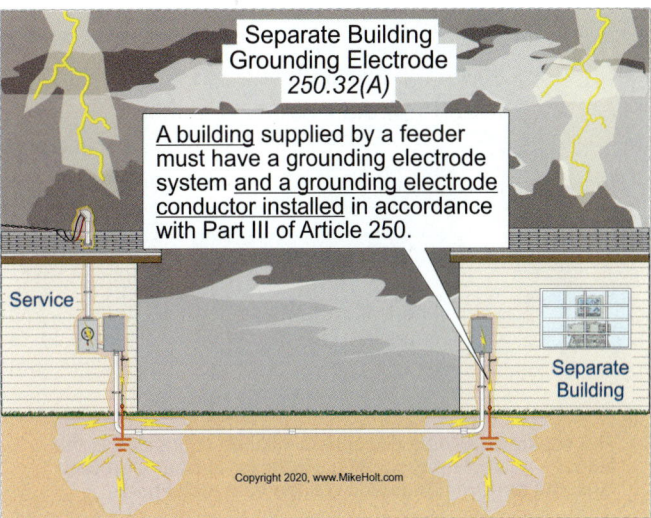
▶Figure 250-94

Ex: A grounding electrode is not required for a building if it is supplied by a single branch circuit or multiwire branch circuit. ▶Figure 250-95

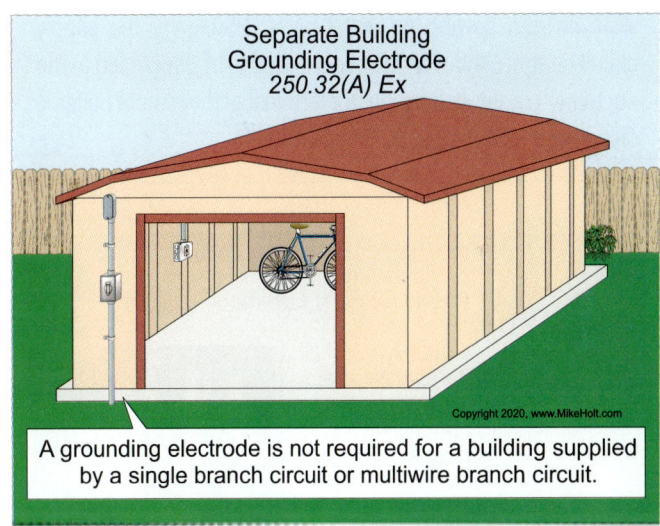
▶Figure 250-95

(B) Grounded Systems (Equipment Grounding Conductor).

(1) To clear a ground fault and remove dangerous voltage from metal parts due to a ground fault, the metal parts of the building disconnect must be connected to the feeder equipment grounding conductor of a type described in 250.118. ▶Figure 250-96

Where the supply circuit equipment grounding conductor is of the wire type, it must be sized in accordance with 250.122, based on the rating of the overcurrent protective device.

250.32 | Grounding and Bonding

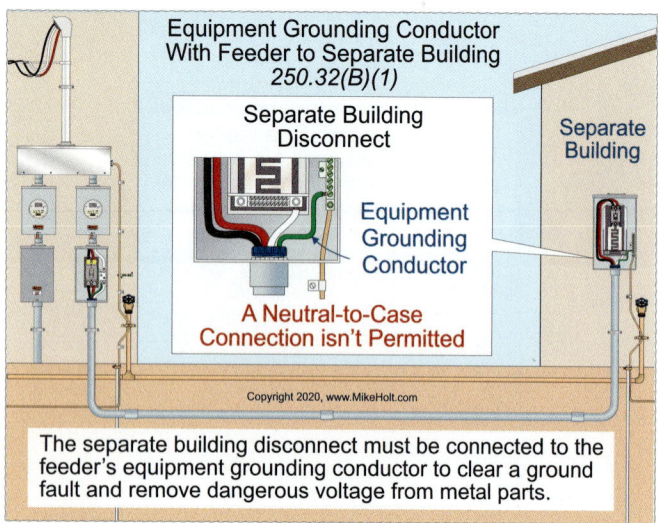

▶Figure 250–96

Caution: To prevent dangerous objectionable neutral current from flowing on metal parts [250.6(A)], the supply circuit neutral conductor is not permitted to be connected to the equipment grounding conductor terminal at the remote building disconnect [250.142(B)]. ▶Figure 250–97

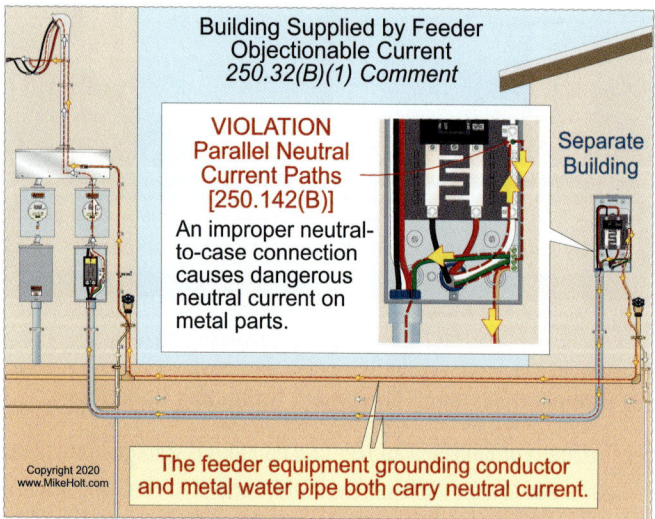

▶Figure 250–97

Ex 1: The neutral conductor can serve as the ground-fault return path for the building disconnect for existing installations where there are no continuous metallic paths between buildings and structures, ground-fault protection of equipment is not installed on the supply side of the circuit, and the neutral conductor is sized no smaller than the larger of:

(1) The maximum unbalanced neutral load in accordance with 220.61.

(2) The minimum equipment grounding conductor size in accordance with 250.122.

(2) Supplied by Separately Derived System.

(a) With Overcurrent Protection. If overcurrent protection is provided at the separately derived system, the installation must contain an equipment grounding conductor in accordance with 250.32(B)(1).

(b) Without Overcurrent Protection. If overcurrent protection is not provided at the separately derived system, the installation must comply with 250.30(A). ▶Figure 250–98

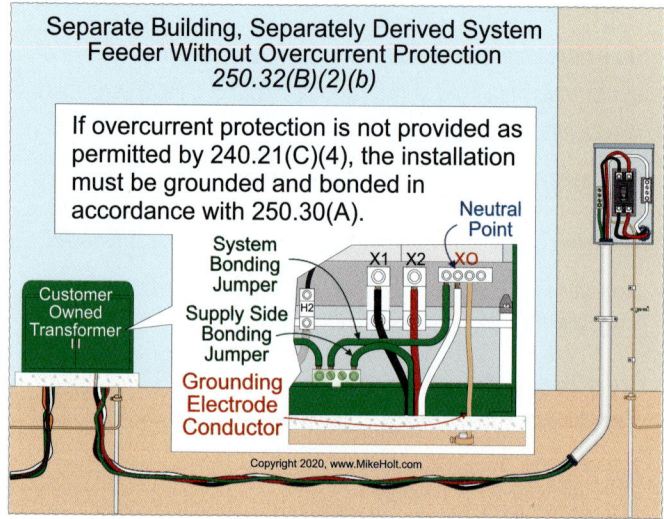

▶Figure 250–98

(E) Grounding Electrode Conductor Size. The grounding electrode conductor must terminate to the equipment grounding terminal of the disconnect (not the neutral terminal) and must be sized in accordance with 250.66 based, on the area of the largest phase conductor.

▶ **Example**

Question: What size grounding electrode conductor is required for a building disconnect supplied with a 3/0 AWG feeder with a concrete-encased electrode? ▶Figure 250–99

(a) 4 AWG   (b) 2 AWG   (c) 1 AWG   (d) 1/0 AWG

Answer: (a) 4 AWG [250.66(B) and Table 250.66]

Grounding and Bonding | 250.34

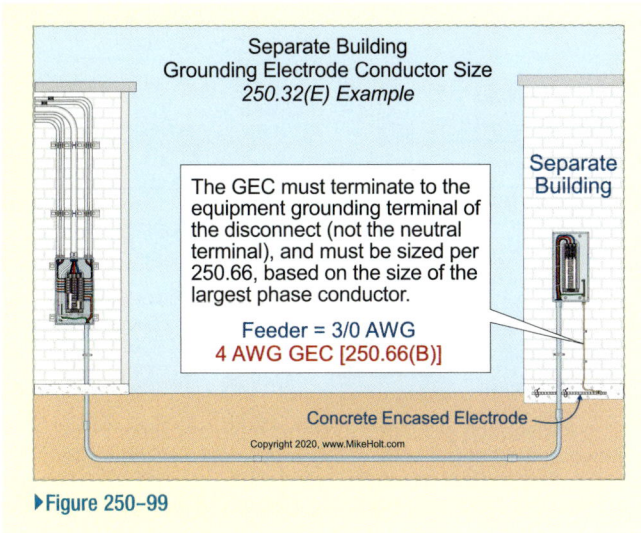
▶Figure 250-99

▶Figure 250-100

Author's Comment:

▸ If the grounding electrode conductor is connected to a rod(s), the portion of the conductor that connects only to the rod(s) is not required to be larger than 6 AWG copper [250.66(A)]. If the grounding electrode conductor is connected to a concrete-encased electrode(s), the portion of the conductor that connects only to the concrete-encased electrode(s) is not required to be larger than 4 AWG copper [250.66(B)].

250.34 Generators—Portable and Vehicle- or Trailer-Mounted

(A) Portable Generators. A portable generator is not required to be connected to a grounding electrode (grounded) where all the following conditions are met:

(1) The generator only supplies equipment and/or receptacles mounted on the generator. ▶Figure 250-100

(2) The normally noncurrent-carrying metal parts of equipment and the equipment grounding conductor terminals of the receptacles are connected to the generator frame.

(B) Vehicle- or Trailer-Mounted Generators. A vehicle- or trailer-mounted generator is not required to be connected to a grounding electrode where all the following conditions are met:

(1) The generator frame is bonded to the vehicle or trailer frame,

(2) The generator only supplies equipment or receptacles mounted on the vehicle, trailer, or generator, and ▶Figure 250-101

▶Figure 250-101

(3) The normally noncurrent-carrying metal parts of equipment and the equipment grounding conductor terminals of the receptacles are connected to the generator frame.

250.36 High-Impedance Grounded Systems

High-impedance grounded three-phase systems of 480V up to 1,000V are permitted where all the following conditions are met: ▶Figure 250-102

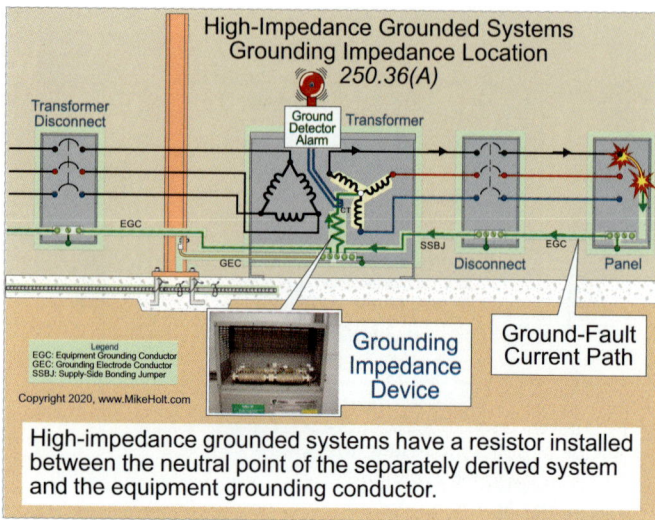

▶Figure 250-103

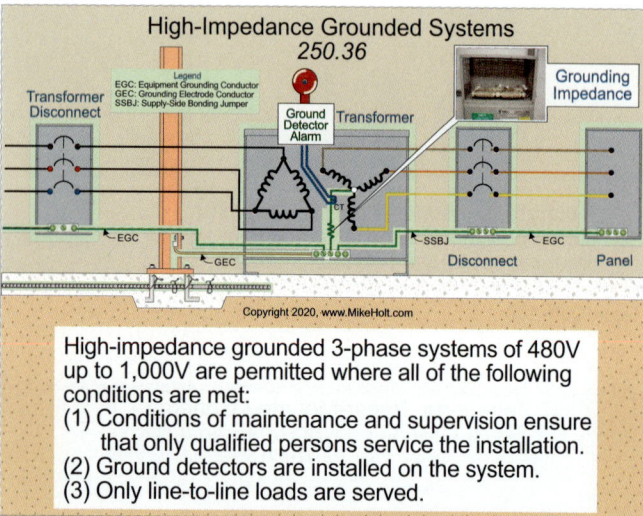

▶Figure 250-102

(1) Conditions of maintenance and supervision ensure that only qualified persons service the installation.

(2) Ground detectors are installed on the system.

(3) Only line-to-line loads are served.

Author's Comment:

▸ High-impedance grounded systems are generally referred to as "High-Resistance Grounded Systems" in the industry. They are generally used where sudden interruption of power will create increased hazards and where a reduction of incident energy is needed for worker safety.

(A) Grounding Impedance Location. To limit fault current to a very low value, high-impedance grounded systems must have a resistor installed between the neutral point of the separately derived system and the equipment grounding conductor. ▶Figure 250-103

Note: According to Annex O of NFPA 70E, *Standard for Electrical Safety in the Workplace*, high-impedance grounding is an effective tool for reducing arc flash hazards.

Part III. Grounding Electrode System and Grounding Electrode Conductor

250.50 Grounding Electrode System

A grounding electrode system is comprised of bonding together the grounding electrodes described in 250.52(A)(1) through (A)(7) that are present at a building or structure. ▶Figure 250-104

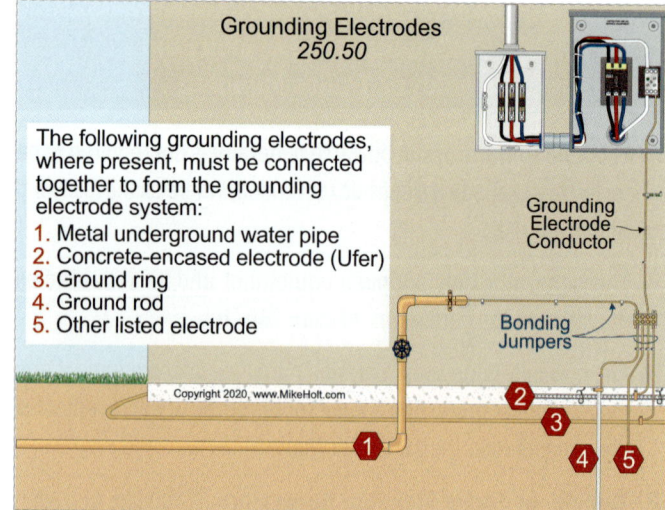

▶Figure 250-104

Ex: Concrete-encased electrodes are not required for existing buildings where the conductive steel reinforcing bars are not accessible without chipping up the concrete. ▶Figure 250-105

Grounding and Bonding | 250.52

▶Figure 250-105

250.52 Grounding Electrode Types

(A) Electrodes.

(1) Underground Metal Water Pipe Electrode. Underground metal water pipe in direct contact with the Earth for 10 ft or more can serve as a grounding electrode. ▶Figure 250-106

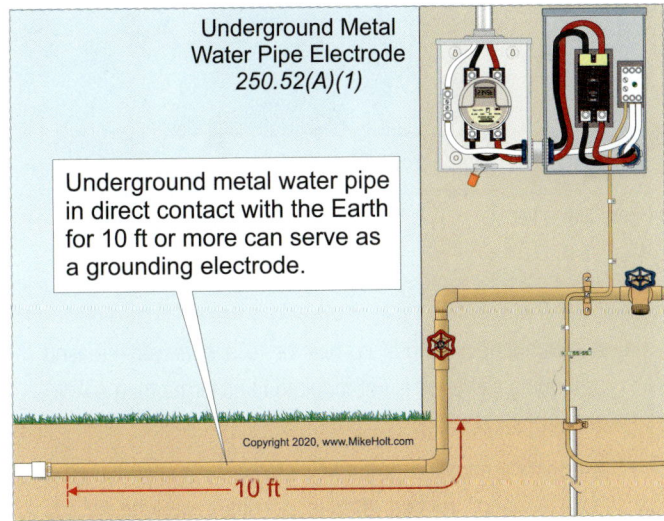

▶Figure 250-106

Author's Comment:

▸ Controversy about using metal underground water piping as a grounding electrode has existed since the early 1900s. The water industry believes that neutral current flowing on water piping corrodes the metal. For more information, contact the American Water Works Association about their report, *Effects of Electrical Grounding on Pipe Integrity and Shock Hazard*, Catalog No. 90702, 1.800.926.7337. ▶Figure 250-107

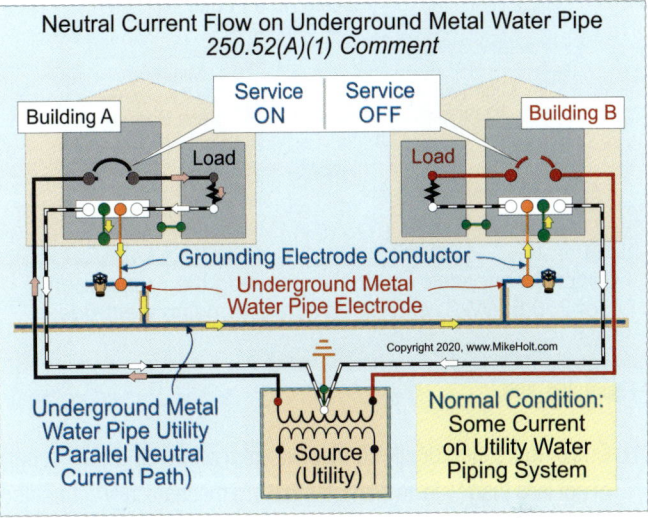

▶Figure 250-107

(2) Metal In-Ground Support Structure(s). Metal in-ground support structure(s) in direct contact with the Earth vertically for 10 ft or more can serve as a grounding electrode. ▶Figure 250-108

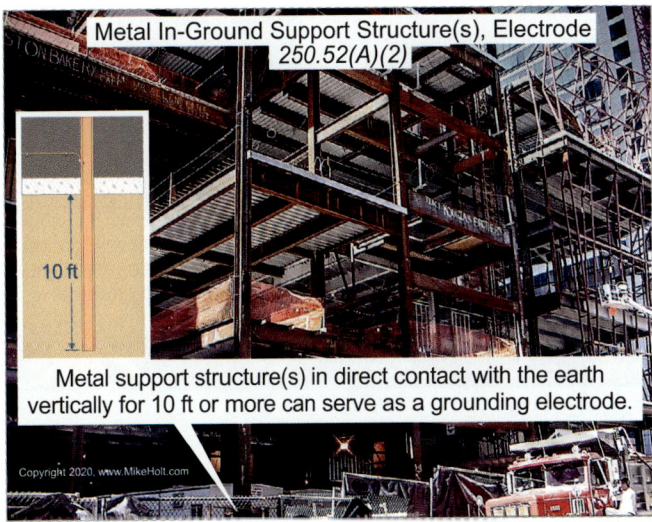

▶Figure 250-108

Note: Metal in-ground support structures include (but are not limited to) pilings, casings, and other structural metal.

(3) Concrete-Encased Electrode. Concrete-encased electrodes meeting the requirements of this subsection can serve as grounding electrodes. ▶Figure 250-109

250.52 | Grounding and Bonding

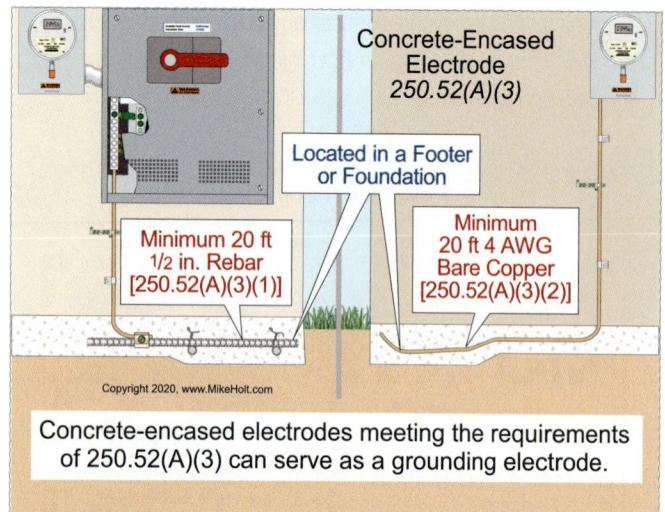

▶Figure 250–109

(1) One or more electrically conductive steel reinforcing bars (rebar) of not less than ½ in. diameter that are mechanically connected by steel tie wires to create a 20 ft or greater in length of steel can serve as a grounding electrode. ▶Figure 250–110

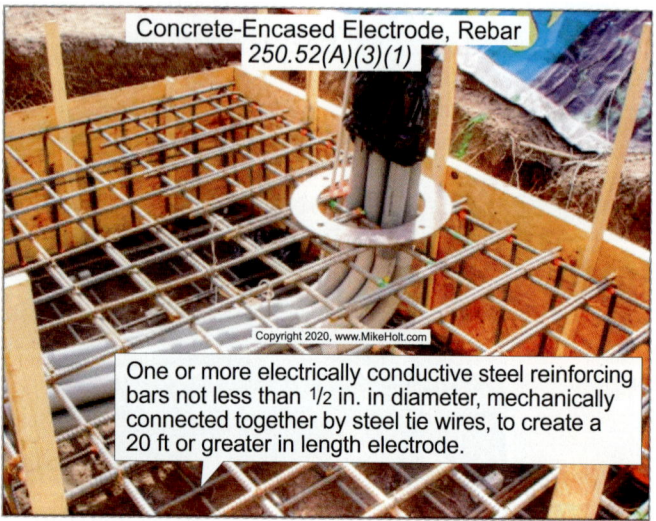

▶Figure 250–110

(2) A bare copper conductor not smaller than 4 AWG and 20 ft or greater in length can serve as a grounding electrode.

The rebar or bare copper conductor must be encased by at least 2 in. of concrete that is in direct contact with the Earth.

Where multiple concrete-encased electrodes are present at a building, only one is required to serve as a grounding electrode. ▶Figure 250–111

Note: Rebar in concrete that is not in direct contact with the Earth because of insulation, vapor barriers, or similar items is not considered to be a concrete-encased electrode. ▶Figure 250–112

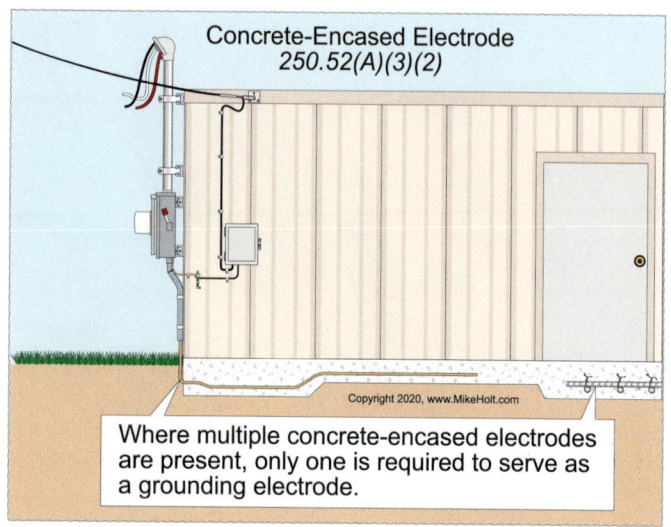

▶Figure 250–111

▶Figure 250–112

Author's Comment:

▸ A grounding electrode conductor to a concrete-encased grounding electrode is not required to be larger than 4 AWG copper [250.66(B)].

▸ A concrete-encased grounding electrode is also called a "Ufer Ground," named after a consultant working for the U.S. Army during World War II. The technique Herbert G. Ufer came up with was necessary because the site needing grounding had no underground water table and little rainfall. The desert site was a series of bomb storage vaults near of Flagstaff, Arizona. This type of grounding electrode generally offers the lowest ground resistance for the cost. In fact, Mr. Ufer's method is so effective that no other ground rods are necessary!

Grounding and Bonding | **250.52**

(4) Ground Ring. A direct buried bare copper conductor not smaller than 2 AWG encircling a building can serve as a grounding electrode. ▶Figure 250–113

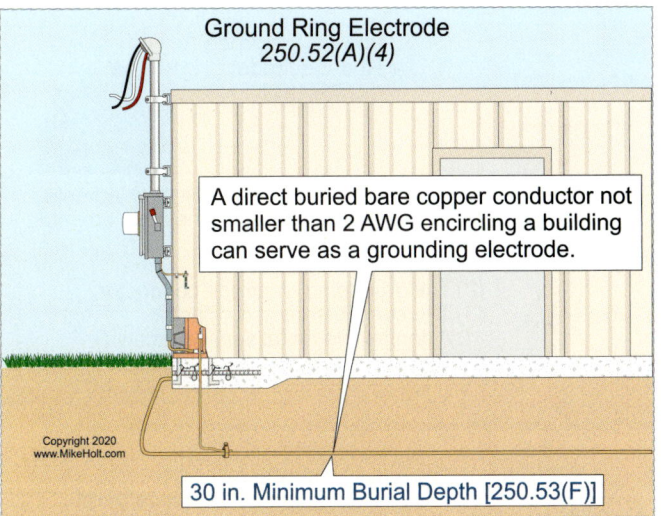
▶Figure 250–113

Author's Comment:

▸ A ground ring encircling a building must not be installed less than 30 in. below the surface of the Earth [250.53(F)].

(5) Ground Rod. Ground rods must have at least 8 ft in length in contact with the Earth [250.53(A)].

(b) Ground rods must have a diameter of at least ⅝ in., unless listed. ▶Figure 250–114

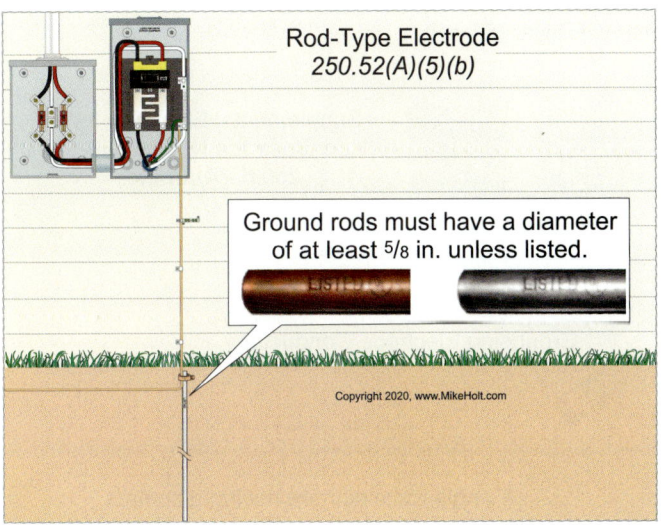
▶Figure 250–114

Author's Comment:

▸ The grounding electrode conductor, if it is the sole connection to the rod(s), is not required to be larger than 6 AWG copper [250.66(A)].

▸ The diameter of a ground rod has an insignificant effect on the contact resistance of a rod(s) to the Earth. However, larger diameter rods (¾ in. and 1 in.) are sometimes installed where mechanical strength is desired, or to compensate for the loss of the electrode's metal due to corrosion.

(6) Listed Electrode. Other listed grounding electrodes can serve as a grounding electrode.

(7) Plate Electrode. A bare or electrically conductive coated iron or a steel plate of not less than ¼ in. in thickness, or a solid uncoated copper metal plate not less than 0.06 in. in thickness, with an exposed surface area of not less than 2 sq ft can serve as a grounding electrode.

(8) Metal Underground Systems. Metal underground systems, piping, and well casings can serve as a grounding electrode. ▶Figure 250–115

▶Figure 250–115

Author's Comment:

▸ The grounding electrode conductor to the metal underground system must be sized in accordance with Table 250.66, based on the area of the largest phase conductor.

(B) Not Permitted for Use as a Grounding Electrode.

(1) Underground metal gas piping systems are not permitted to be used as a grounding electrode. ▶Figure 250–116

250.53 | Grounding and Bonding

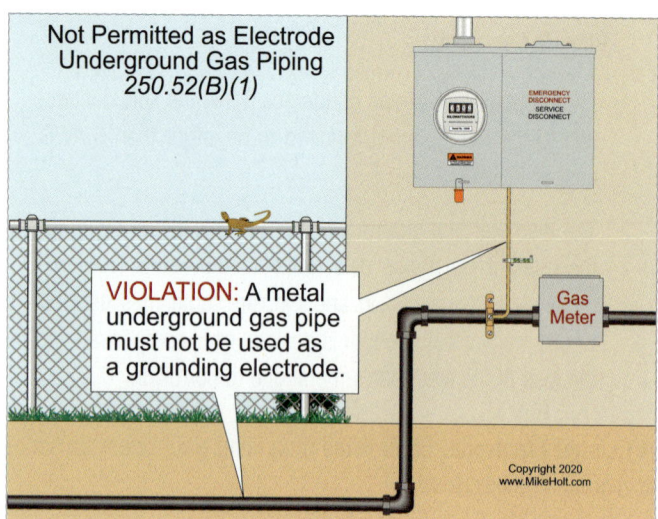

▶Figure 250–116

(2) Aluminum is not permitted to be used as a grounding electrode.

(3) The structures and structural reinforcing steel described in 680.26(B)(1) and (B)(2) are not permitted to be used as a grounding electrode. ▶Figure 250–117

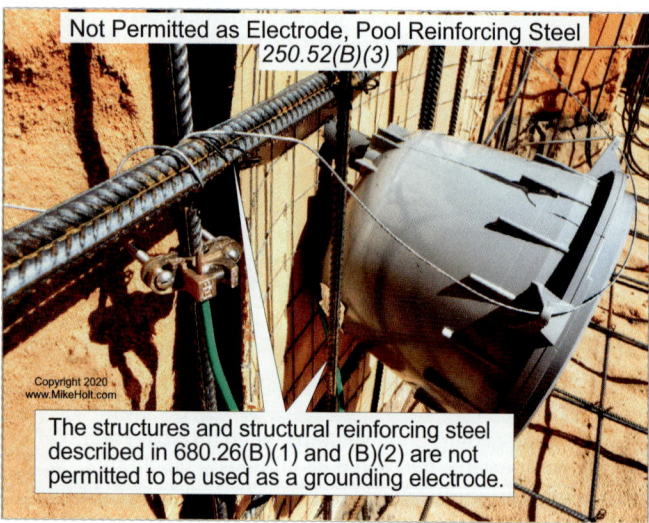

▶Figure 250–117

250.53 Grounding Electrode Installation Requirements

(A) Ground Rods.

(1) Below Permanent Moisture Level. If practicable, rod, pipe, and plate electrodes must be embedded below the permanent moisture level and must be free from nonconductive coatings such as paint or enamel.

(2) Supplemental Electrode. A single ground rod must be supplemented by an additional electrode. The supplemental electrode must be bonded to: ▶Figure 250–118

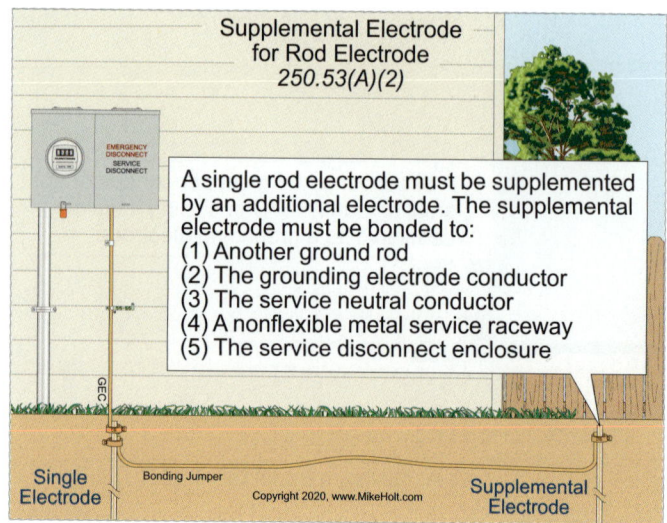

▶Figure 250–118

(1) Another ground rod
(2) The grounding electrode conductor
(3) The service neutral conductor
(4) A nonflexible metal service raceway
(5) The service-disconnect enclosure

Ex: A single ground rod electrode having a contact resistance to the Earth of 25 ohms or less is not required to have a supplemental electrode. ▶Figure 250–119

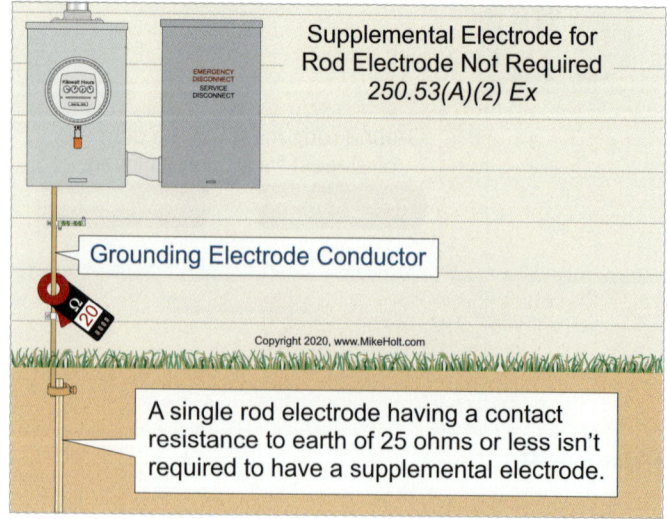

▶Figure 250–119

Grounding and Bonding | 250.53

(3) Supplemental Ground Rod, Spacing. The supplemental electrode must be installed not less than 6 ft from the ground rod. ▶Figure 250-120

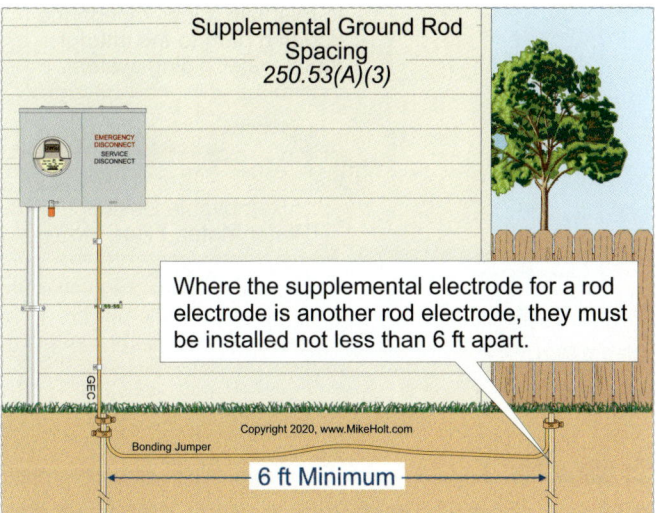
▶Figure 250-120

(4) Rod and Pipe Electrodes. The electrode must be installed such that at least 8 ft of length is in contact with the soil. It must be driven to a depth of not less than 8 ft except where rock bottom is encountered, the electrode must be driven at an oblique angle not to exceed 45 degrees from the vertical or, where rock bottom is encountered at an angle up to 45 degrees, the electrode is permitted to be buried in a trench that is at least 30 in. deep. ▶Figure 250-121

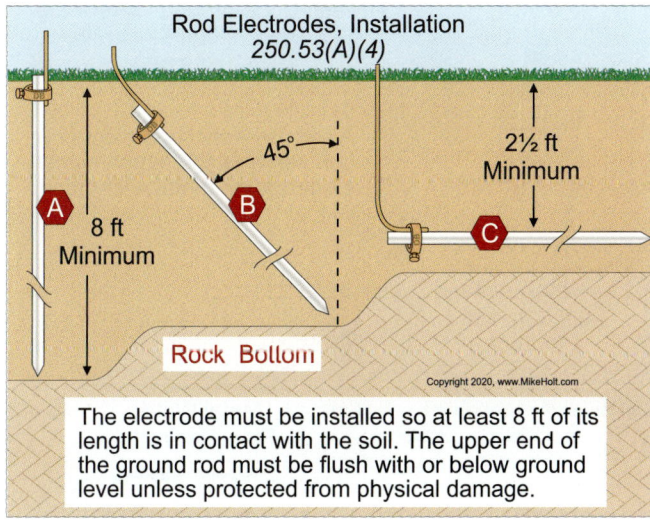
▶Figure 250-121

The upper end of the ground rod must be flush with or below ground level unless the grounding electrode conductor attachment is protected against physical damage as specified in 250.10. ▶Figure 250-122

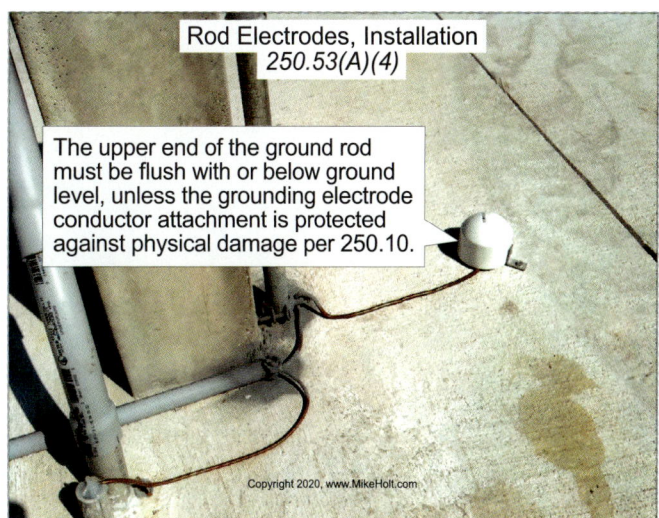
▶Figure 250-122

Author's Comment:

▶ When the grounding electrode attachment fitting is located underground (below ground level), it must be listed for direct soil burial [250.68(A) Ex 1 and 250.70].

(B) Electrode Spacing. Electrodes for premises systems must be located no closer than 6 ft from lightning protection system grounding electrodes.

Two or more grounding electrodes that are bonded together are considered a single grounding electrode system. ▶Figure 250-123

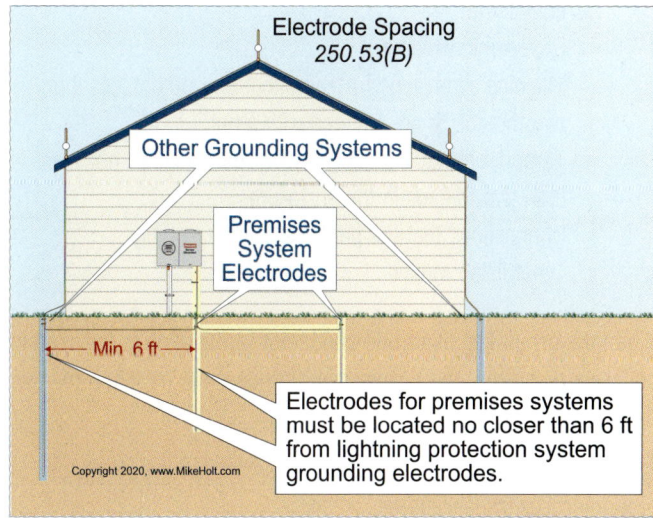
▶Figure 250-123

(C) Grounding Electrode Bonding Jumper. Grounding electrode bonding jumpers must be copper when within 18 in. of the Earth [250.64(A)]. Exposed grounding electrode bonding jumpers must be

250.53 | Grounding and Bonding

securely fastened to the surface and protected from physical damage [250.64(B)]. The bonding jumper to each electrode must be sized in accordance with 250.66, based on the area of the largest phase conductor. ▶Figure 250–124

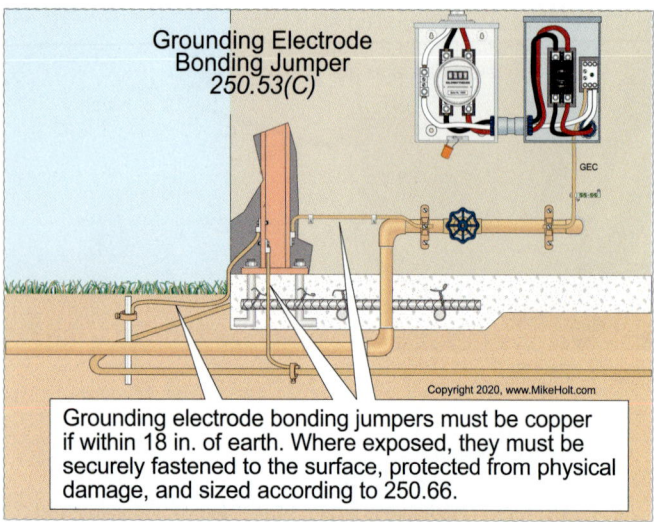

▶Figure 250–124

Author's Comment:

- Grounding electrode bonding jumpers must terminate by any of the following means in accordance with 250.8(A):
  - Listed pressure connectors
  - Terminal bars
  - Pressure connectors listed as grounding and bonding equipment
  - Exothermic welding
  - Machine screw-type fasteners that engage not less than two threads or are secured with a nut
  - Thread-forming machine screws that engage not less than two threads in the enclosure
  - Connections that are part of a listed assembly
  - Other listed means

When the grounding electrode conductor termination is encased in concrete or buried, the termination fittings must be listed for this purpose [250.70].

Rebar is not permitted to be used to interconnect the electrodes of grounding electrode systems.

(D) Underground Metal Water Pipe Electrode.

(1) Continuity. Continuity of the grounding path or the bonding connection to interior piping must not rely on water meters or filtering devices and similar equipment. ▶Figure 250–125

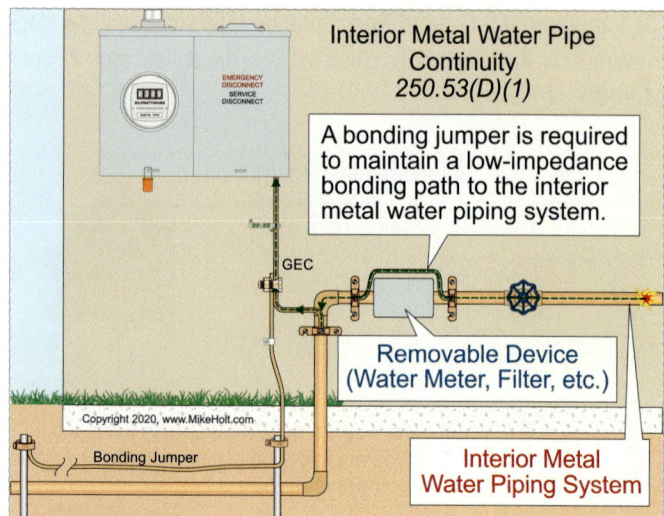

▶Figure 250–125

(2) Water Pipe Supplemental Electrode. When an underground metal water pipe grounding electrode is present, it must be supplemented by any of the following electrodes:

- Metal frame of the building electrode [250.52(A)(2)]
- Concrete-encased electrode [250.52(A)(3)] ▶Figure 250–126
- Rod electrode [250.52(A)(5)]
- Other type of listed electrode [250.52(A)(6)]
- Metal underground piping electrode [250.52(A)(8)]

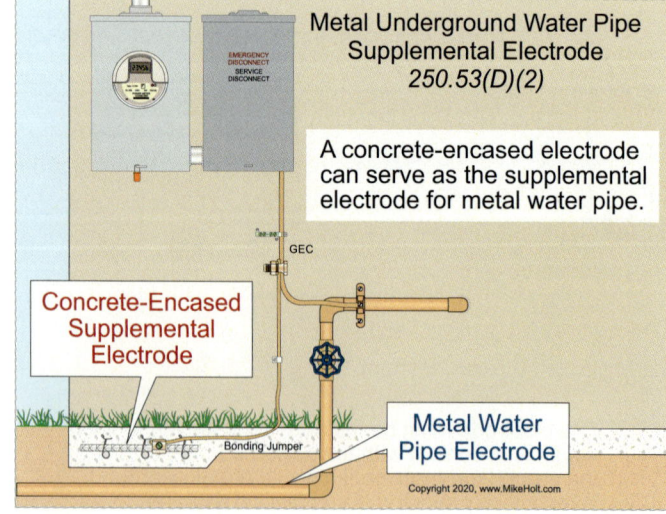

▶Figure 250–126

The grounding electrode conductor for the supplemental electrode must terminate to any of the following: ▶Figure 250–127

Grounding and Bonding | 250.53

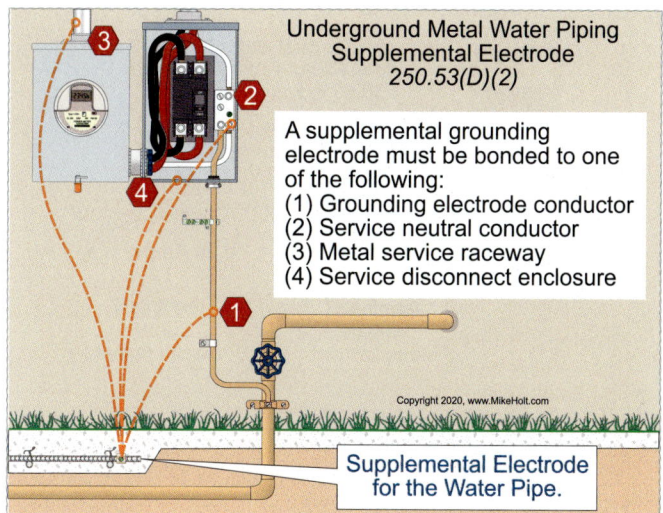
▶Figure 250-127

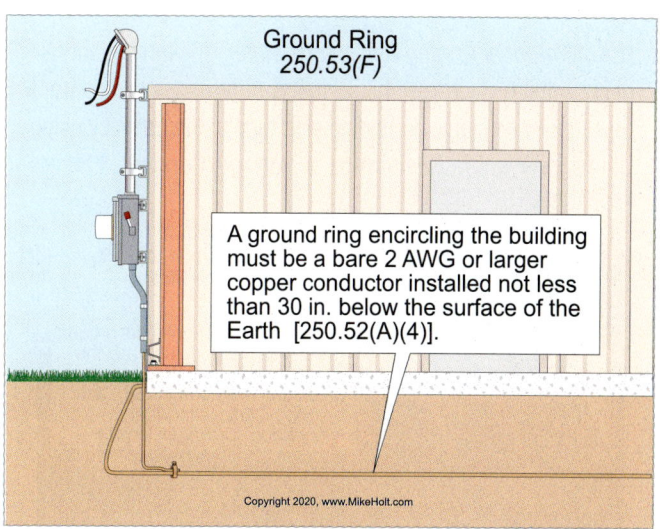
▶Figure 250-128

(1) Grounding electrode conductor

(2) Service neutral conductor

(3) Metal service raceway

(4) Service-disconnect enclosure

Author's Comment:

▸ Because a metal underground waterpipe electrode could be replaced by a plastic water pipe, the supplemental electrode must be installed as if it is the only electrode for the system.

Ex: The supplemental electrode can be bonded to interior metal water piping located not more than 5 ft from the point of entrance to the building [250.68(C)(1)].

(E) Supplemental Rod Electrode. The grounding electrode conductor to a ground rod that serves as a supplemental electrode is not required to be larger than 6 AWG copper.

(F) Ground Ring. A ground ring encircling a building must be a bare 2 AWG or larger copper conductor installed not less than 30 in. below the surface of the Earth [250.52(A)(4)]. ▶Figure 250-128

Measuring the Contact Resistance of Electrodes to Earth

A ground resistance clamp meter or a three-point fall-of-potential ground resistance meter can be used to measure the contact resistance of a grounding electrode to the Earth.

Ground Clamp Meter. The ground resistance clamp meter measures the contact resistance of the grounding electrode system to the Earth by injecting a high-frequency signal via the service neutral conductor to the serving electric utility's grounding system, and then measuring the strength of the return signal through the Earth to the grounding electrode being measured. ▶Figure 250-129

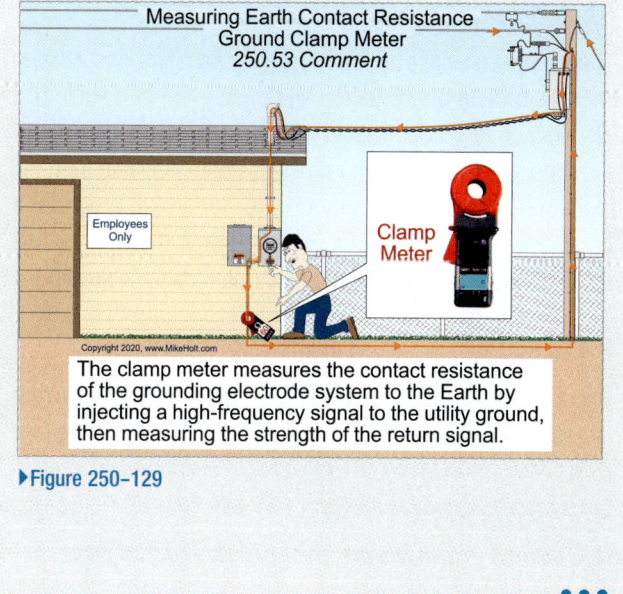
▶Figure 250-129

Fall-of-Potential Ground Resistance Meter. The three-point fall-of-potential ground resistance meter determines the contact resistance of a single grounding electrode to the Earth by using Ohm's Law where **Resistance = Voltage/Current**. ▶Figure 250–130

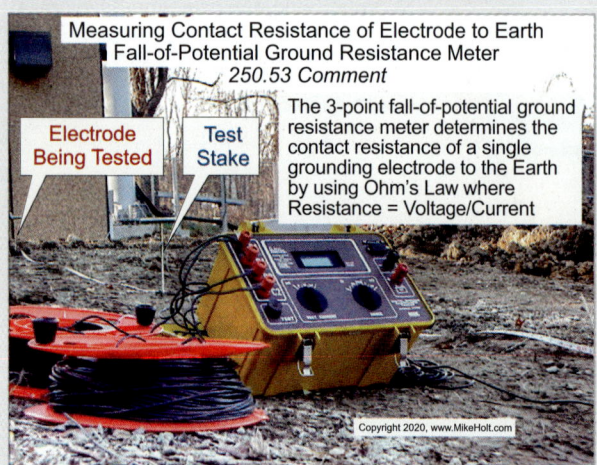

▶Figure 250–130

This meter divides the voltage difference between the electrode to be measured and a driven voltage test stake (P) by the current flowing between the electrode to be measured and a driven current test stake (C). The test stakes are typically made of ¼ in. diameter steel rods, 24 in. long, driven two-thirds of their length into the Earth.

The distance and alignment between the voltage and current test stakes, and the electrode, is extremely important to the validity of the Earth contact resistance measurements. For an 8-ft rod, the accepted practice is to space the current test stake (C) 80 ft from the electrode to be measured.

The voltage test stake (P) is positioned in a straight line between the electrode to be measured and the current test stake (C). The voltage test stake should be approximately 62 percent of the distance of where the current test stake is located from the electrode. If the current test stake (C) for an 8-ft ground rod is located 80 ft from the grounding electrode, the voltage test stake (P) will be about 50 ft from the electrode to be measured.

▶ **Example**

Question: If the voltage between the ground rod and the voltage test stake (P) is 3V, and the current between the ground rod and the current test stake (C) is 0.20A, what will be the Earth contact resistance of the electrode to the Earth? ▶Figure 250–131

(a) 3 ohms   (b) 5 ohms   (c) 10 ohms   (d) 15 ohms

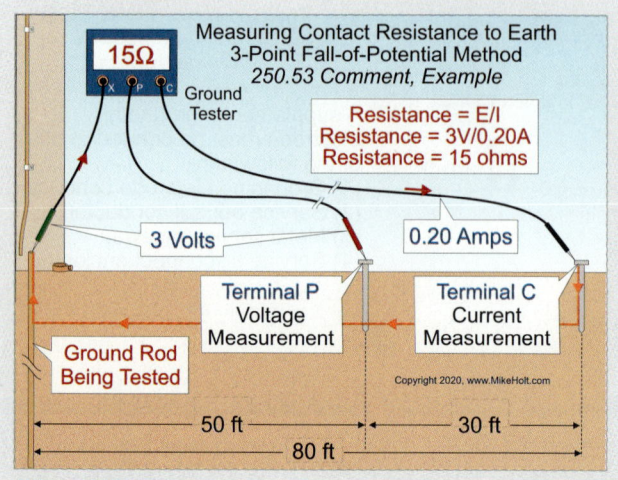

▶Figure 250–131

Solution:

Resistance = Voltage/Current

Voltage = 3V

Current = 0.20A

Resistance = 3V/0.20A
Resistance = 15 ohms

The Earth contact resistance of the electrode to the Earth will be 15 ohms.

Answer: (d) 15 ohms

Author's Comment:

▸ The three-point fall-of-potential meter should only be used to measure the contact resistance of one electrode to the Earth at a time, and that electrode must be independent and not connected to any part of the electrical system. The contact resistance of two electrodes bonded together cannot measured until they have been separated. The contact resistance of two separate electrodes to the Earth can be thought of as two resistors in parallel if they are outside each other's sphere of influence.

Soil Resistivity

The contact resistance of an electrode to the Earth is impacted by soil resistivity, which varies throughout the world. Soil resistivity is influenced by electrolytes, which consist of moisture, minerals, and dissolved salts. Because soil resistivity changes with moisture content, the contact resistance of a grounding system to the Earth varies with the seasons.

250.54 Auxiliary Grounding Electrodes

Grounding electrodes that are not required by the *NEC* are called "auxiliary electrodes" and can be connected to the equipment grounding conductors. Since they serve no purpose related to the electrical safety addressed by the *Code*, they have no *NEC* requirements. ▶Figure 250-132

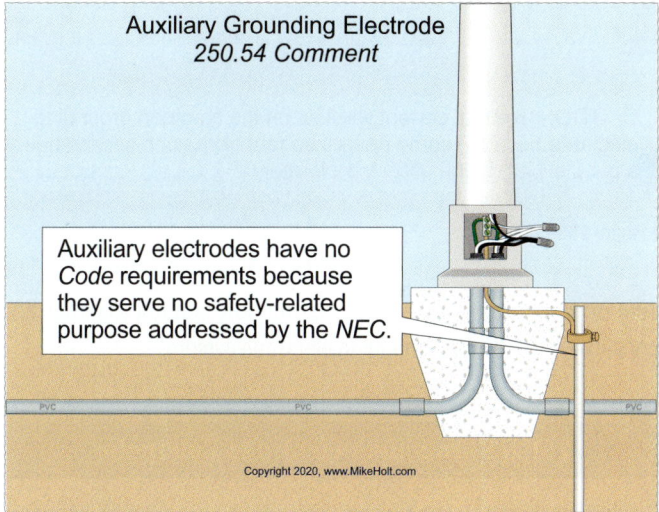
▶Figure 250-132

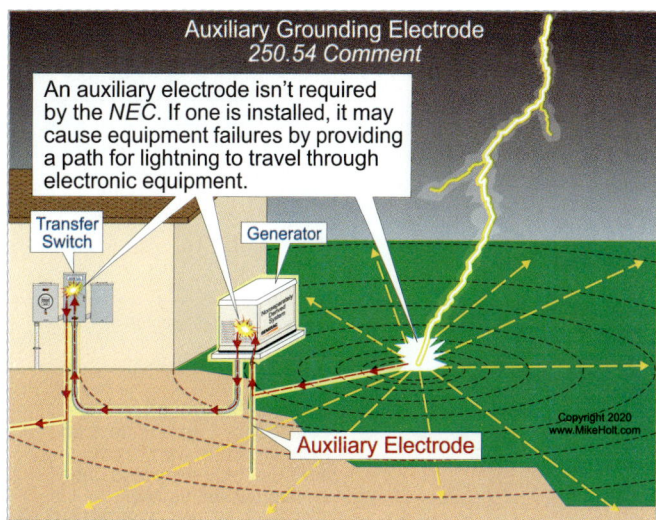
▶Figure 250-133

If an auxiliary electrode is installed, it is not required to be bonded to the building grounding electrode system, to have the grounding conductor sized to 250.66, nor must it comply with the 25-ohm single ground rod requirement of 250.53(A)(2) Ex.

> **Caution**
> An auxiliary electrode may cause equipment failures by providing a path for lightning to travel through electronic equipment. ▶Figure 250-133 and ▶Figure 250-134

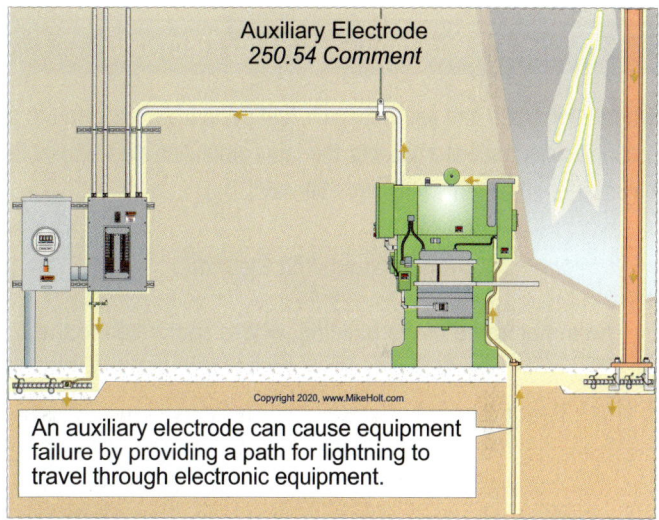
▶Figure 250-134

The Earth is not to be considered the effective ground-fault current path specified in 250.4(A)(5). ▶Figure 250-135

> **Danger**
> Because the contact resistance of an electrode to the Earth is so great, very little fault current returns to the power supply if the Earth is the only fault current return path. As a result, the circuit overcurrent protective device will not open and clear the ground fault, and all metal parts associated with the electrical installation, metal piping, and structural building steel will become and remain energized. ▶Figure 250-136

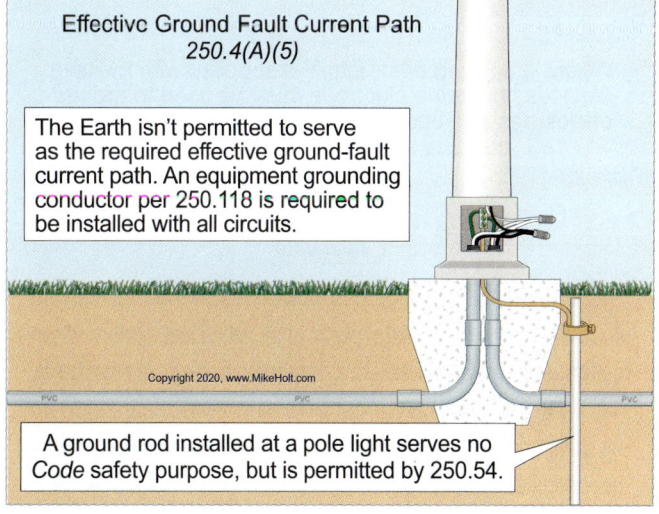
▶Figure 250-135

250.58 | Grounding and Bonding

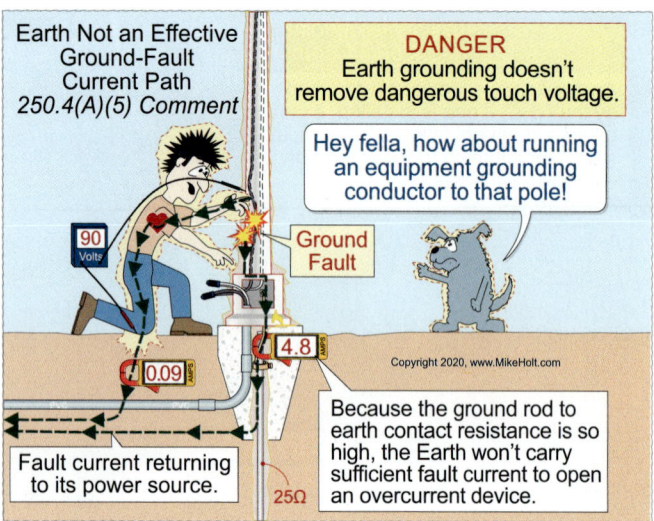
▶Figure 250-136

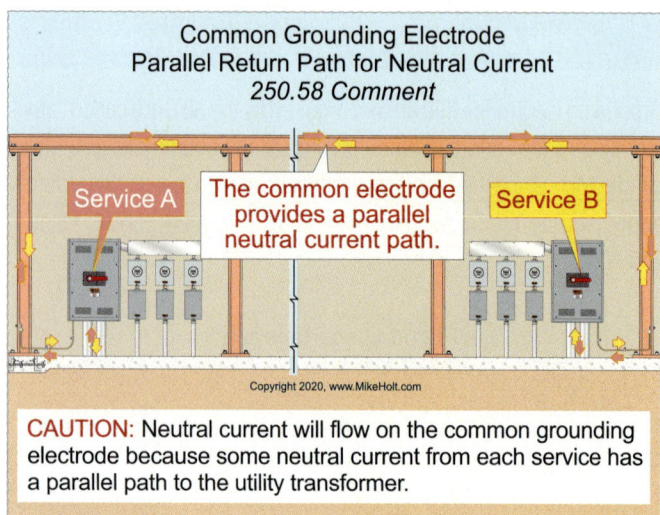
▶Figure 250-138

250.58 Common Grounding Electrode

Where more than one alternating-current system is connected to a grounding electrode at a building, the same grounding electrode must be used for all systems. ▶Figure 250-137

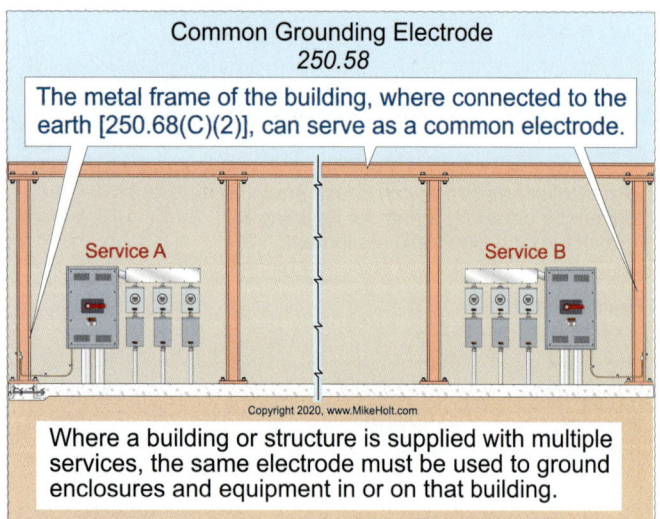
▶Figure 250-137

Caution

⚡ Potentially dangerous objectionable neutral current flows on the metal parts of an electrical system when multiple service disconnects are connected to the same electrode. This is because neutral current from each service can return to the utility via the common grounding electrode and its conductors and is especially a problem if a service neutral conductor is opened. ▶Figure 250-138

Two or more grounding electrodes that are bonded together are considered as a single grounding electrode system.

250.62 Grounding Electrode Conductor

Grounding electrode conductors of the wire type must be copper if within 18 in. of the Earth [250.64(A)]. ▶Figure 250-139

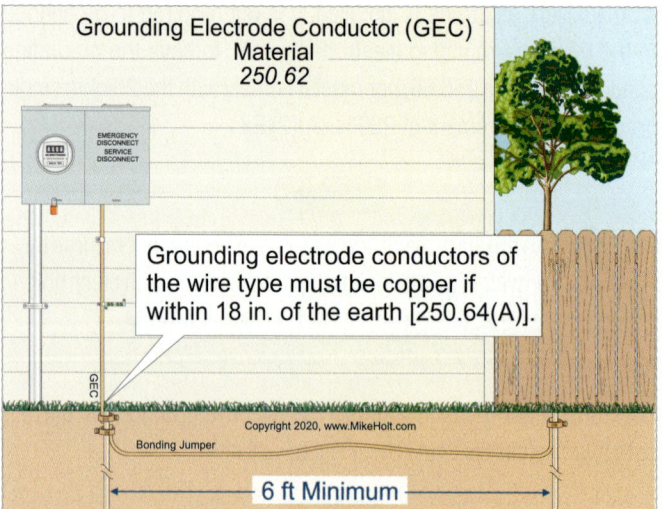
▶Figure 250-139

250.64 Grounding Electrode Conductor Installation

Grounding electrode conductors must be installed as specified in (A) through (F).

Grounding and Bonding | 250.64

(A) Aluminum Conductors. Bare, covered, or insulated aluminum grounding electrode conductors must comply with the following:

(1) Bare or covered conductors without an extruded polymeric covering are not permitted to be installed where subject to corrosive conditions or to be installed in direct contact with concrete.

(2) Terminations made within listed enclosures identified for outdoor use are permitted within 18 in. of the Earth. If open-bottom enclosures are installed on a concrete pad, the concrete is not considered earth.

(3) Aluminum conductors external to buildings or equipment enclosures are not permitted to be terminated within 18 in. of the Earth.

(B) Conductor Protection. Where exposed, a grounding electrode conductor must be securely fastened to the surface on which it is carried.

(1) Not Exposed to Physical Damage. Grounding electrode conductors 6 AWG and larger can be installed exposed along the surface of the building if securely fastened and not exposed to physical damage. ▶Figure 250-140

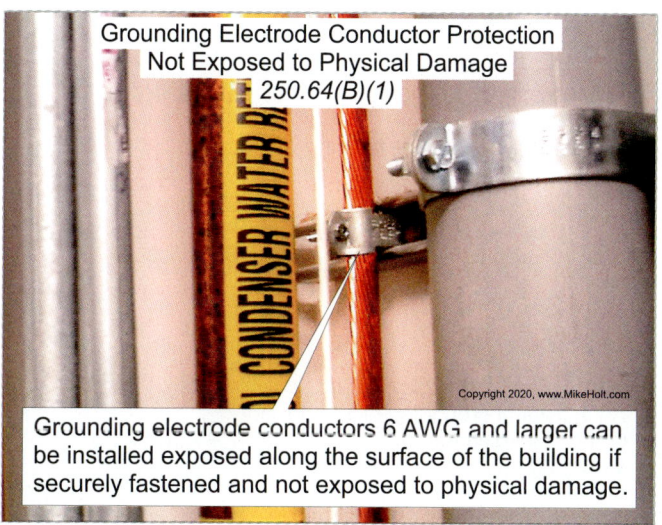
▶Figure 250-140

(2) Exposed to Physical Damage. Grounding electrode conductors 6 AWG and larger subject to physical damage must be protected in rigid metal conduit (RMC), intermediate metal conduit (IMC), Schedule 80 rigid polyvinyl chloride conduit (PVC), reinforced thermosetting resin conduit Type XW (RTRC-XW), electrical metallic tubing (EMT), or cable armor. ▶Figure 250-141

(3) Smaller Than 6 AWG. Grounding electrode conductors smaller than 6 AWG must be protected in RMC, IMC, Schedule 80 PVC, RTRC-XW, EMT, or cable armor.

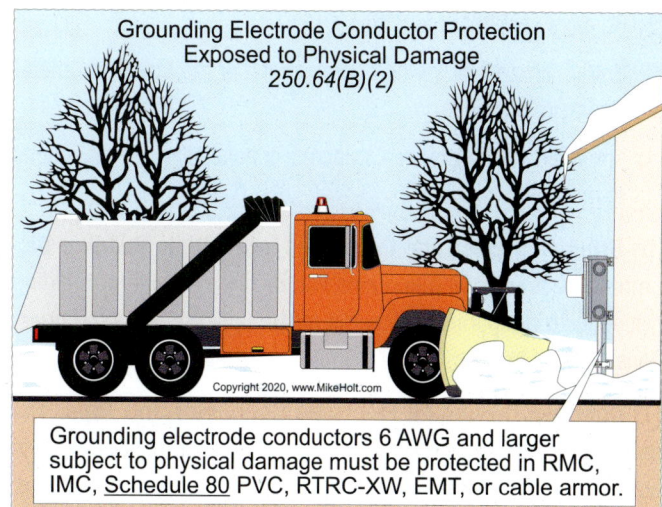
▶Figure 250-141

Author's Comment:

▸ While Table 250.66 permits the use of 8 AWG copper as the grounding electrode conductor for the phase conductor typically used for a 100A service, use of a GEC smaller than 6 AWG is not common.

(4) In Contact with the Earth. Grounding electrode conductors and bonding jumpers in contact with the Earth are not required to comply with the cover requirements of 300.5 but must be protected where subject to physical damage. ▶Figure 250-142

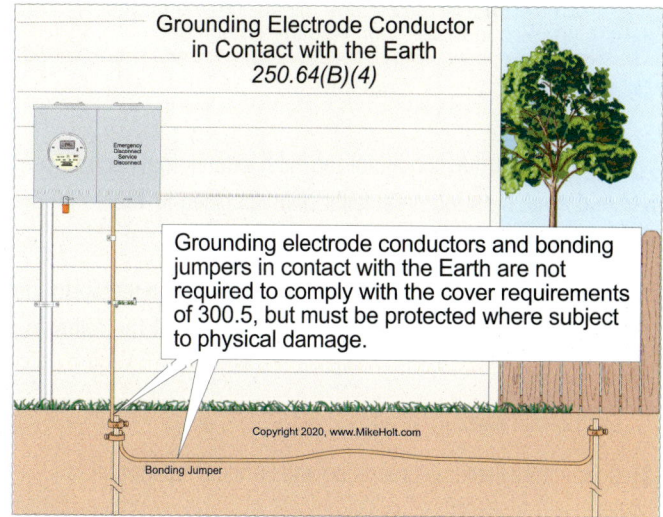
▶Figure 250-142

(C) Continuous. Grounding electrode conductor(s) must be installed without a splice or joint except by:

(1) Irreversible compression-type connectors or exothermic welding.

250.64 | Grounding and Bonding

(2) Busbars connected together.

(3) Bolted, riveted, or welded connections of the structural metal frames of buildings.

(4) Threaded, welded, brazed, soldered, or bolted-flange connections of metal water piping.

(D) Grounding Electrode Conductor for Multiple Building Disconnects. If a building contains two or more service or building disconnects in separate enclosures, the grounding electrode connections must be made by any of the following methods:

(1) Common Grounding Electrode Conductor and Taps. The unspliced common grounding electrode conductor must be sized in accordance with 250.66, based on the sum of the circular mil area of the largest phase conductor supplying the equipment. ▶Figure 250–143

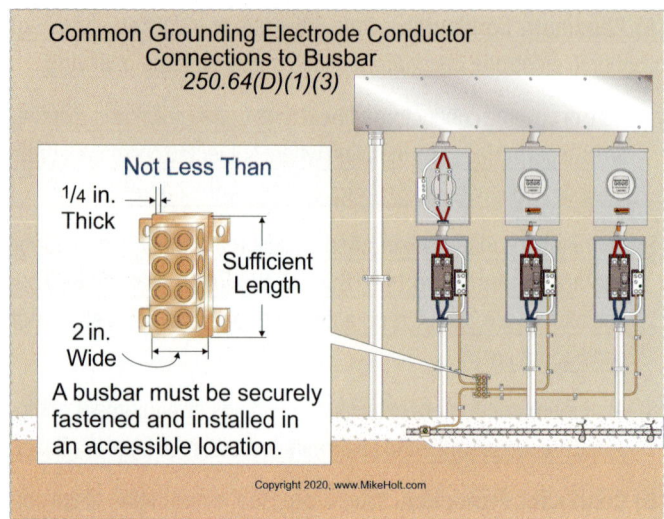
▶Figure 250–144

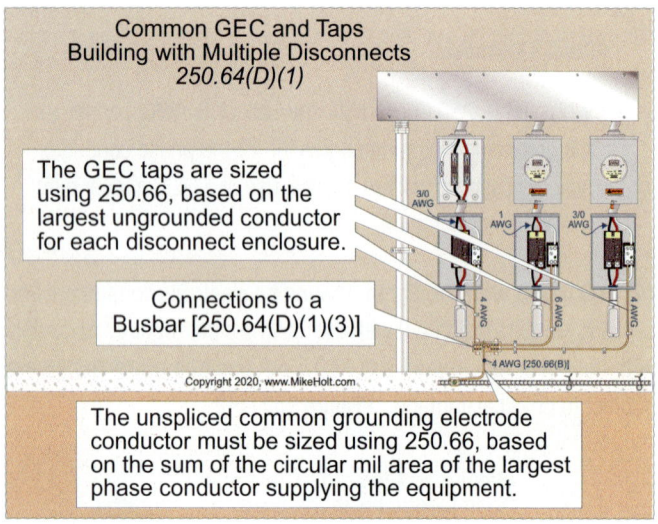
▶Figure 250–143

A grounding electrode conductor tap must extend from each disconnect and must be sized no smaller than specified in Table 250.66, based on the area of the largest phase conductor.

The grounding electrode conductor tap must be connected to the common grounding electrode conductor by any of the following methods:

(1) Exothermic welding.

(2) Connectors listed as grounding and bonding equipment.

(3) Connections to a busbar of sufficient length and not less than ¼ in. thick × 2 in. wide that is securely fastened and installed in an accessible location. ▶Figure 250–144

(2) Individual Grounding Electrode Conductors. An individual grounding electrode conductor from each disconnect sized in accordance with 250.66, based on the phase conductor(s) supplying the individual disconnect, must connect the grounding electrode system to one of the following:

(1) The service neutral conductor ▶Figure 250–145

(2) The equipment grounding conductor of the feeder circuit

(3) The service supply-side bonding jumper

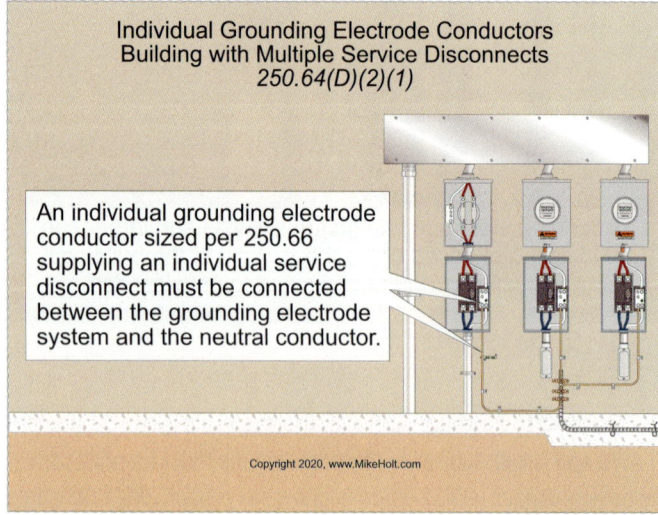
▶Figure 250–145

(3) Supply Side of Disconnects. A grounding electrode conductor from an accessible enclosure on the supply side of the disconnects, sized in accordance with 250.66 and based on the phase conductor(s) supplying the disconnect, must connect the grounding electrode system to one of the following:

(1) The service neutral conductor ▶Figure 250-146

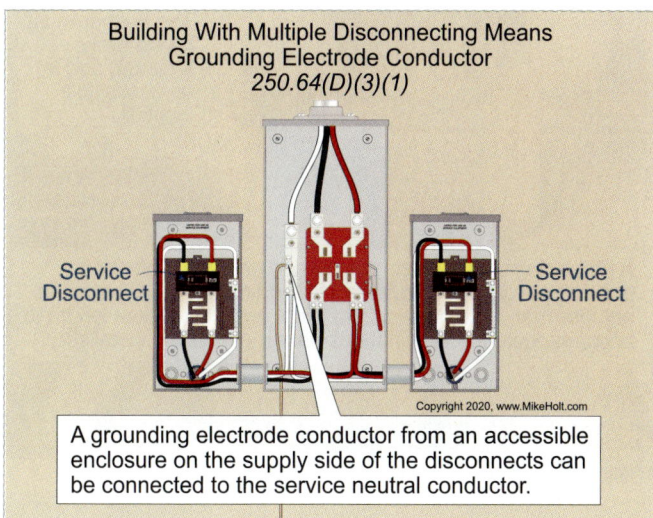

▶Figure 250-146

(2) The equipment grounding conductor of the feeder circuit

(3) The service supply-side bonding jumper

(E) Ferrous Raceways Containing Grounding Electrode Conductors.

(1) General. To prevent inductive choking of grounding electrode conductors, ferrous metal raceways, enclosures, and cable armor containing grounding electrode conductors must have each end of the raceway or enclosure bonded to the grounding electrode conductor. ▶Figure 250-147

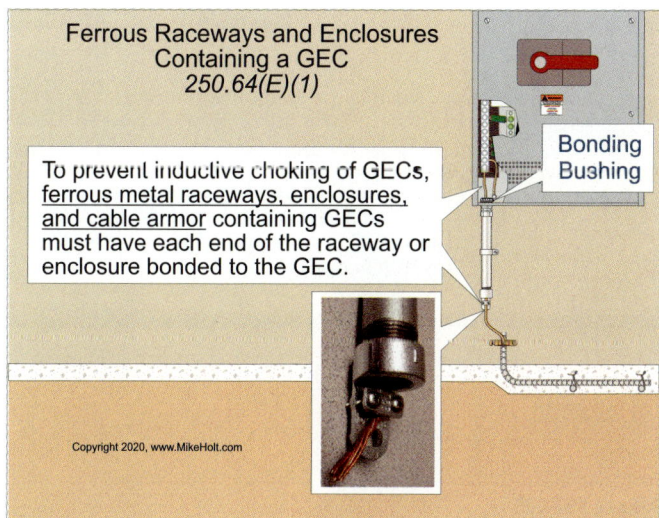

▶Figure 250-147

(2) Methods. Raceway bonding must be in accordance with 250.92(B)(2) through (B)(4).

(3) Size. Bonding jumpers must be the same size or larger than the largest grounding electrode conductor in the raceway or other enclosure. ▶Figure 250-148

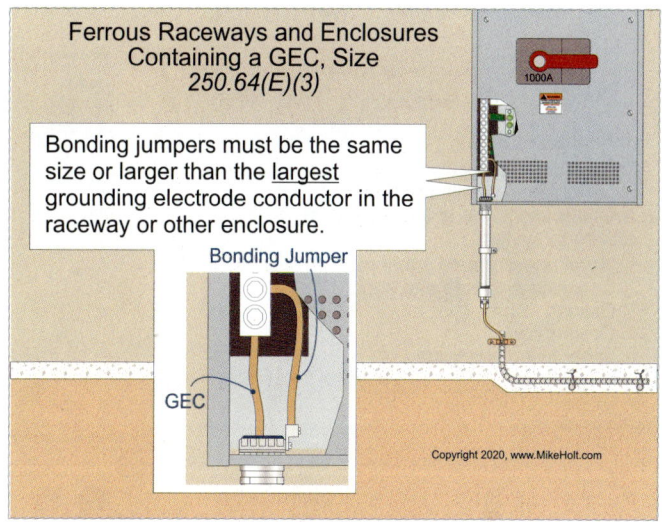

▶Figure 250-148

Author's Comment:

▸ Nonferrous metal raceways, such as aluminum rigid metal conduit, enclosing the grounding electrode conductor are not required to meet the "bonding each end of the raceway to the grounding electrode conductor" provisions of this section.

▸ To save of time and effort, install the grounding electrode conductor in a nonmetallic raceway suitable for the application [352.10(F)]. ▶Figure 250-149

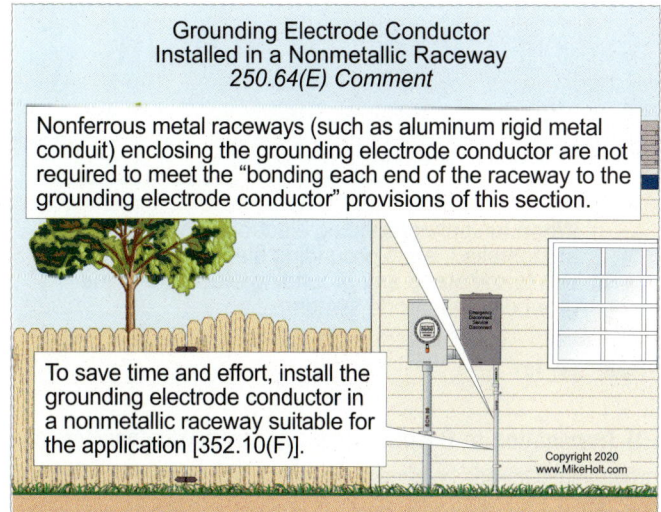

▶Figure 250-149

(F) Termination to Grounding Electrode.

(1) Single Grounding Electrode Conductor. A single grounding electrode conductor can terminate to any grounding electrode of the grounding electrode system. ▶Figure 250-150

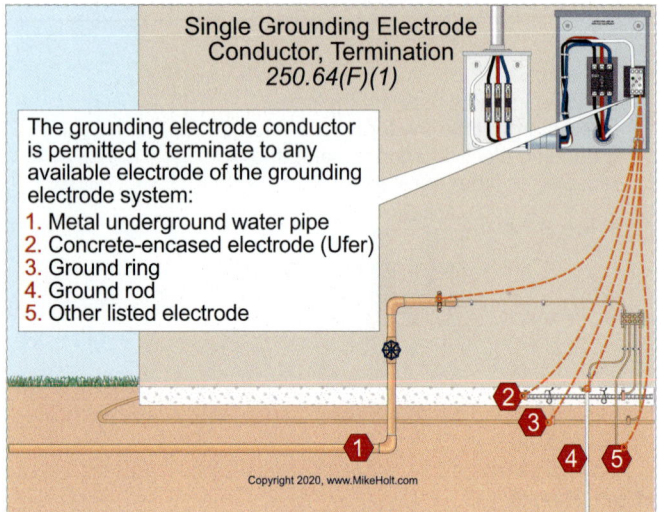

▶Figure 250-150

(2) Multiple Grounding Electrode Conductors. Where multiple grounding electrode conductors are installed [250.64(D)(2)], each one can terminate to any grounding electrode of the grounding electrode system. ▶Figure 250-151

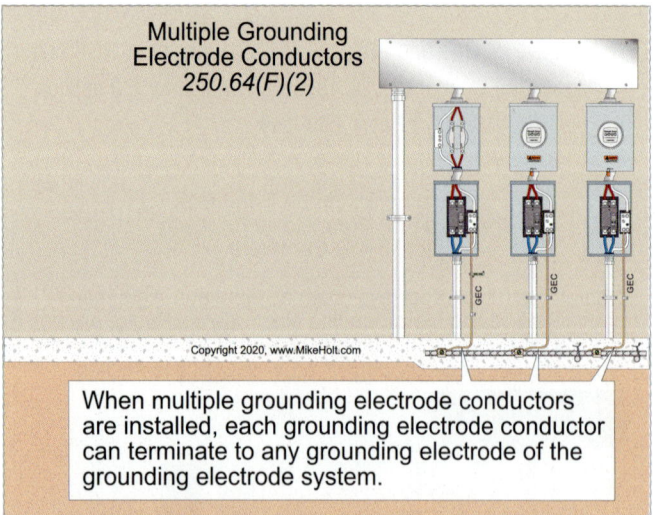

▶Figure 250-151

(3) Termination to Busbar. Grounding electrode conductors and grounding electrode bonding jumpers are permitted to terminate to a busbar not less than ¼ in. thick × 2 in. wide, and of sufficient length to accommodate the terminations necessary for the installation. The busbar must be securely fastened and installed in an accessible location. ▶Figure 250-152

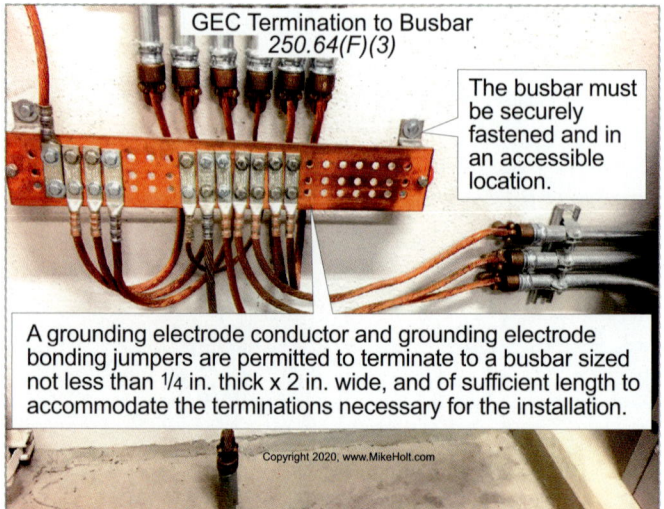

▶Figure 250-152

250.66 Sizing Grounding Electrode Conductor

Except as permitted in (A) through (C), grounding electrode conductors must be sized in accordance with Table 250.66, based on the area of the largest phase conductor.

(A) Ground Rods. If a grounding electrode conductor or bonding jumper only connects to a ground rod [250.52(A)(5)], the grounding electrode conductor is not required to be larger than 6 AWG copper. ▶Figure 250-153

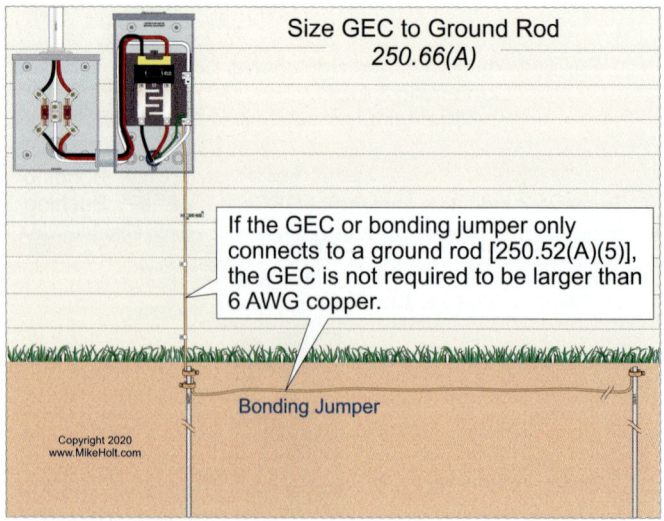

▶Figure 250-153

(B) Concrete-Encased Grounding Electrodes. If a grounding electrode conductor or bonding jumper only connects to a concrete-encased electrode [250.52(A)(3)], the grounding electrode conductor is not required to be larger than 4 AWG copper. ▶Figure 250-154

Grounding and Bonding | 250.68

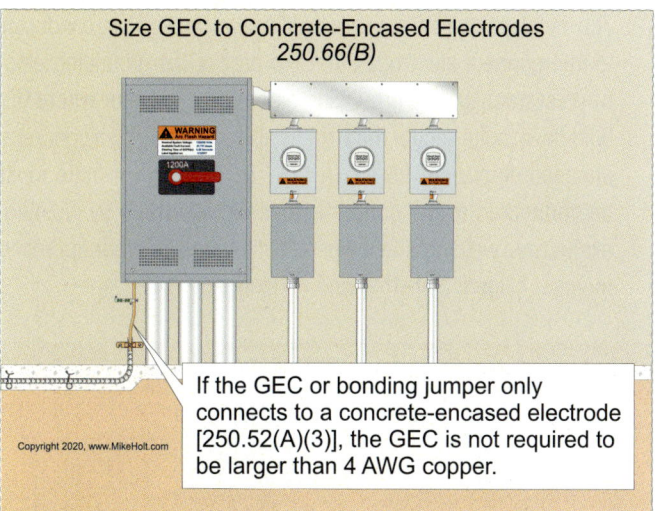
▶Figure 250–154

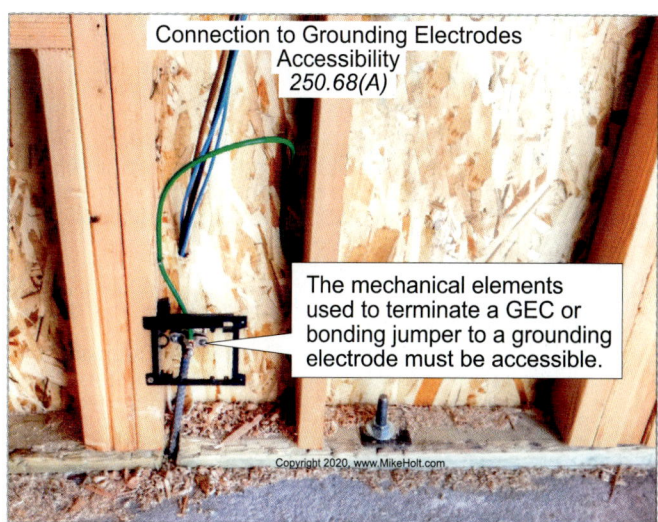
▶Figure 250–155

Table 250.66 Grounding Electrode Conductor	
AWG or Area of Parallel Copper Conductors	Copper Grounding Electrode Conductor
2 AWG or Smaller	8 AWG
1 or 1/0 AWG	6 AWG
2/0 or 3/0 AWG	4 AWG
Over 3/0 through 350 kcmil	2 AWG
Over 350 through 600 kcmil	1/0 AWG
Over 600 through 1,100 kcmil	2/0 AWG
Over 1,100 kcmil	3/0 AWG

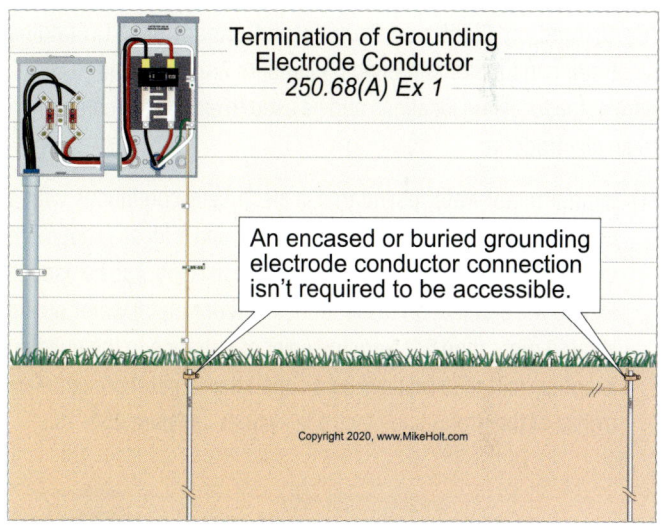
▶Figure 250–156

250.68 Grounding Electrode Conductor and Bonding Jumper Connection to Grounding Electrodes

(A) Accessibility. The mechanical elements used to terminate a grounding electrode conductor or bonding jumper to a grounding electrode must be accessible. ▶Figure 250–155

Ex 1: The termination is not required to be accessible if the termination to the electrode is encased in concrete or buried in the Earth. ▶Figure 250–156

Author's Comment:

▶ If the grounding electrode attachment fitting is encased in concrete or buried in the Earth, it must be listed for direct soil burial or concrete encasement [250.70].

Ex 2: Exothermic or irreversible compression connections, together with the mechanical means used to attach to fireproofed structural metal, are not required to be accessible.

(B) Integrity of Underground Metal Water Pipe Electrode. A bonding jumper must be installed around insulated joints and equipment likely to be disconnected for repairs or replacement for an underground metal water piping system used as a grounding electrode. The bonding jumper must be of sufficient length to allow the removal of such equipment while retaining the integrity of the grounding path. ▶Figure 250–157

250.68 | Grounding and Bonding

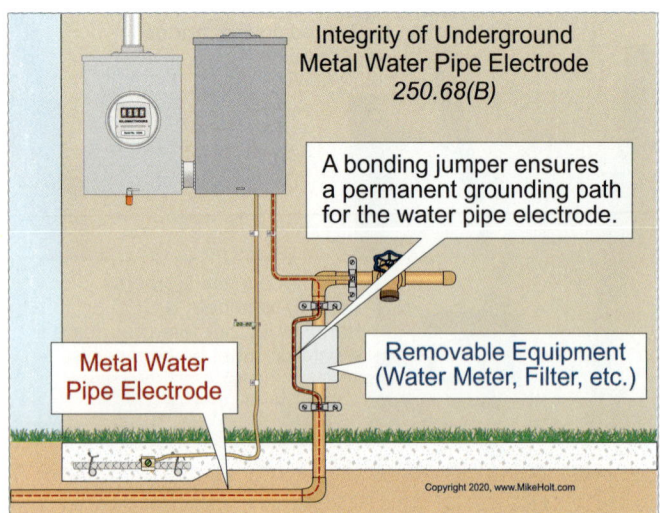
▶Figure 250–157

(C) Grounding Electrode Conductor Connections. Grounding electrode conductors and bonding jumpers are permitted to terminate at the following locations and be used to extend the connection to an electrode(s):

(1) Interior metal water piping that is electrically continuous with a metal underground water pipe electrode and is located not more than 5 ft from the point of entrance to the building, can be used to extend the connection to electrodes. Interior metal water piping located more than 5 ft from the point of entrance to the building is not permitted to be used as a conductor to interconnect electrodes of the grounding electrode system. ▶Figure 250–158

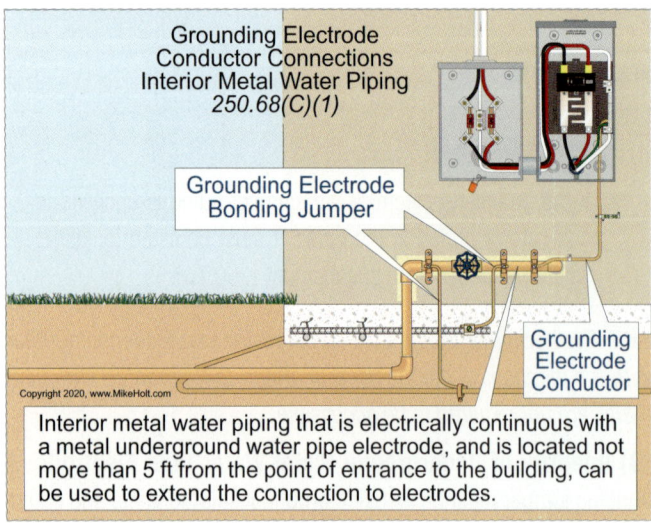
▶Figure 250–158

(2) The metal structural frame of a building can be used as a conductor to interconnect electrodes that are part of the grounding electrode system, or as a grounding electrode conductor where the hold-down bolts secure the structural steel column to a concrete-encased electrode [250.52(A)(3)]. The hold-down bolts must be connected to the concrete-encased electrode by welding, exothermic welding, the usual steel tie wires, or other approved means. ▶Figure 250–159 and ▶Figure 250–160

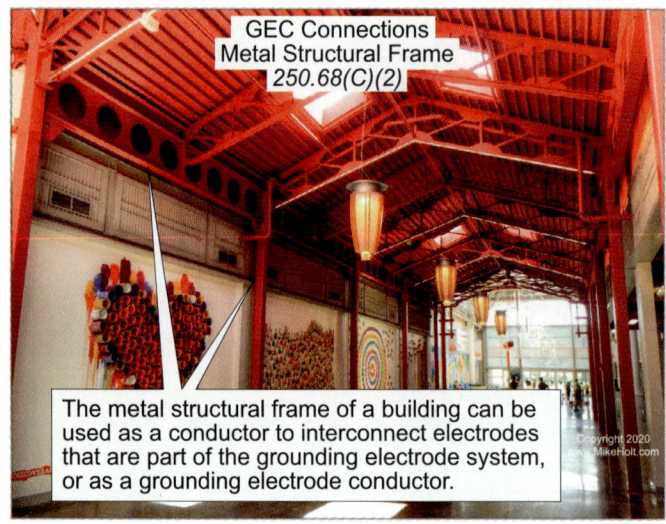
▶Figure 250–159

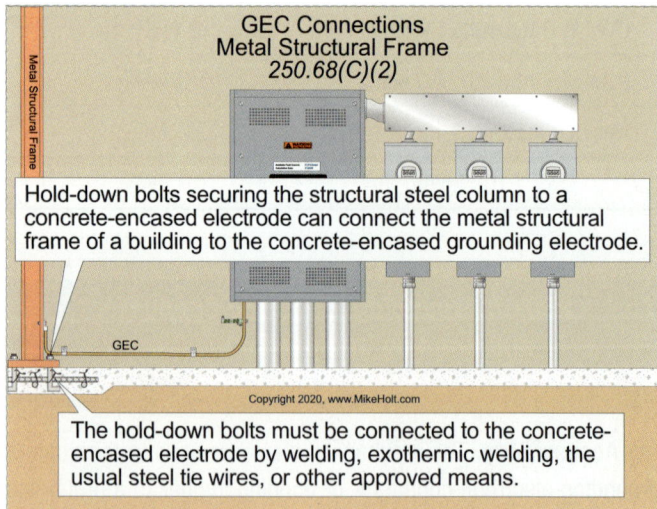
▶Figure 250–160

(3) A rebar-type concrete-encased electrode [250.52(A)(3)] with rebar extended to an accessible location above the concrete foundation or footing is permitted under the following conditions:

Grounding and Bonding | 250.70

(a) The additional rebar section must be continuous with the grounding electrode rebar or must be connected to the grounding electrode rebar and connected together by the usual steel tie wires, exothermic welding, welding, or other effective means. ▶Figure 250-161

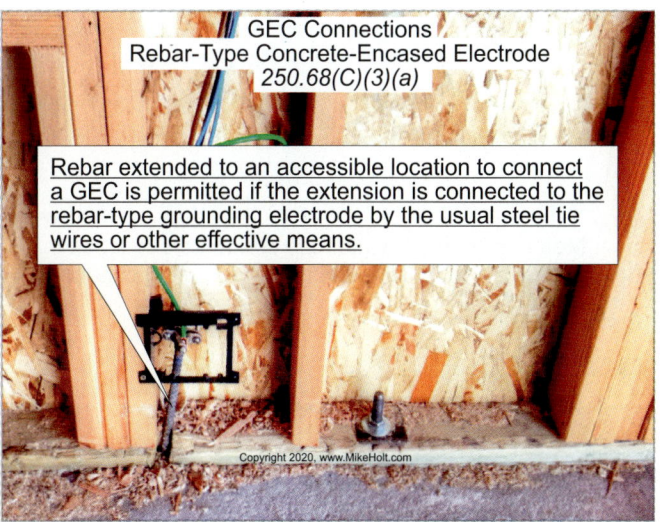

▶Figure 250-161

(b) The rebar extension is not permitted to be in contact with the Earth. ▶Figure 250-162

▶Figure 250-162

(c) The rebar extension is not permitted to be used as a conductor to interconnect the electrodes of grounding electrode systems.

250.70 Grounding Electrode Conductor Termination Fittings

The grounding electrode conductor must terminate to the grounding electrode by exothermic welding, listed lugs, listed pressure connectors, listed clamps, or other listed means. In addition, fittings terminating to a grounding electrode must be listed for the grounding electrode and the grounding electrode conductor. ▶Figure 250-163

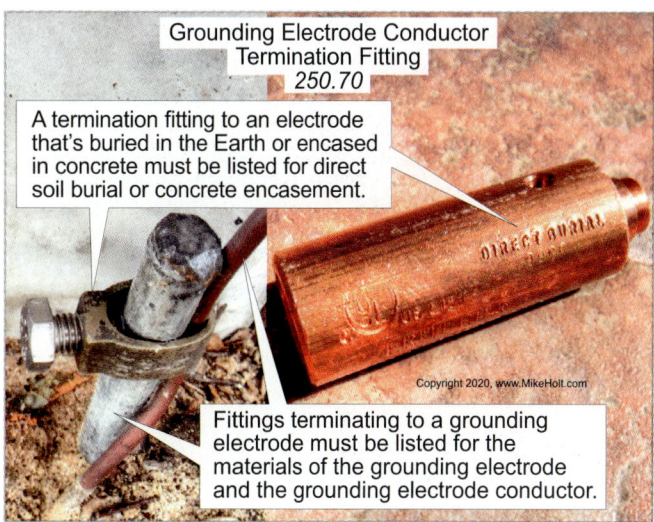

▶Figure 250-163

When the termination to a grounding electrode is buried in the Earth or encased in concrete, the termination fitting must be listed for direct soil burial or concrete encasement. ▶Figure 250-164

▶Figure 250-164

250.80 | Grounding and Bonding

No more than one conductor can terminate on a single clamp or fitting unless the clamp or fitting is listed for multiple connections. ▶Figure 250-165

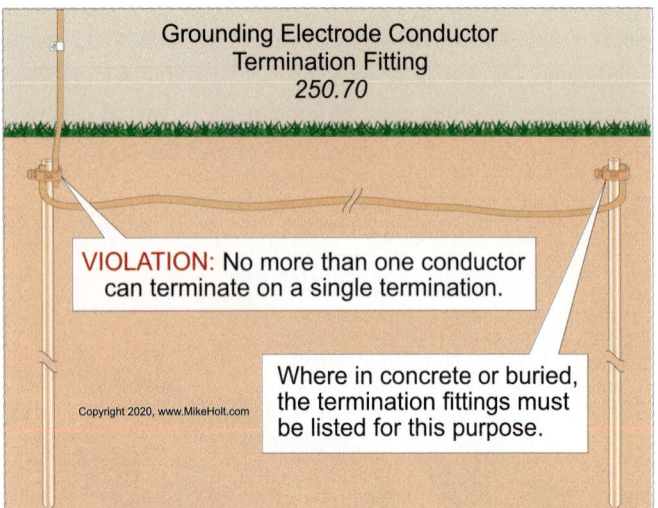

▶Figure 250-165

Part IV. Enclosure, Raceway, and Service Cable Connections

250.80 Service Raceways and Enclosures

Metal enclosures and raceways containing service conductors must be bonded to the service neutral conductor if the electrical system is grounded.

250.86 Other Enclosures

Metal raceways and enclosures containing conductors operating at 50V or more [250.20(A)] must be connected to the circuit equipment grounding conductor. ▶Figure 250-166

Author's Comment:

▸ Circuits described in 250.112(I) operating at less than 50V are not required to be grounded [250.20(A)].

Ex 2: Short sections of metal raceways used for the support or physical protection of cables are not required to be connected to the circuit equipment grounding conductor. ▶Figure 250-167

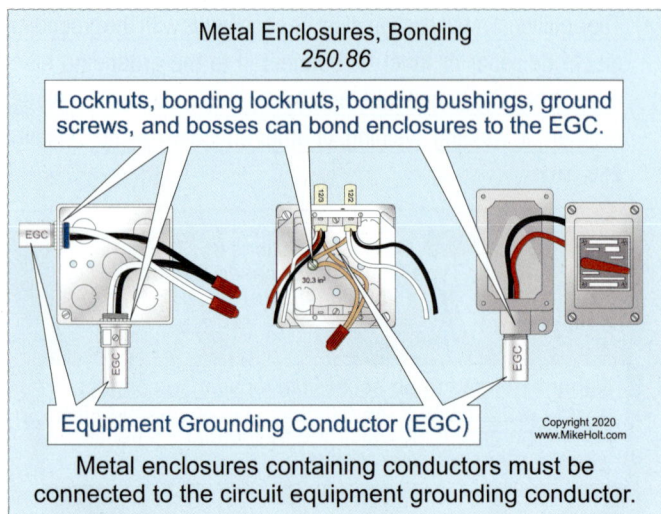

▶Figure 250-166

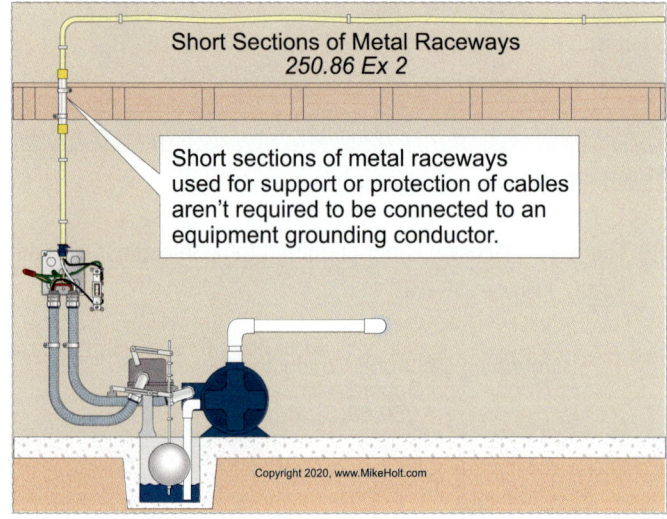

▶Figure 250-167

Part V. Bonding for Fault Current

250.90 General

Bonding must be provided where necessary to ensure electrical continuity and the capacity to conduct safely any fault current likely to be imposed

250.92 Bonding Equipment Containing Service Conductors

(A) Metal Raceways and Enclosures. The metal parts of equipment indicated below must be bonded together in accordance with 250.92(B). ▶Figure 250-168

Grounding and Bonding | 250.92

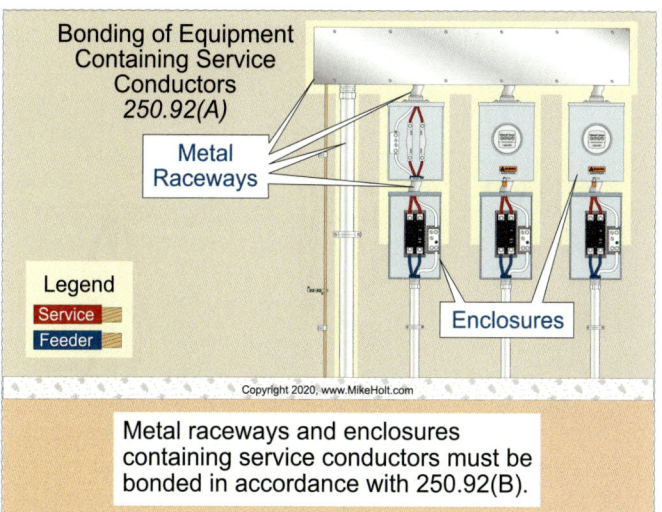
▶Figure 250-168

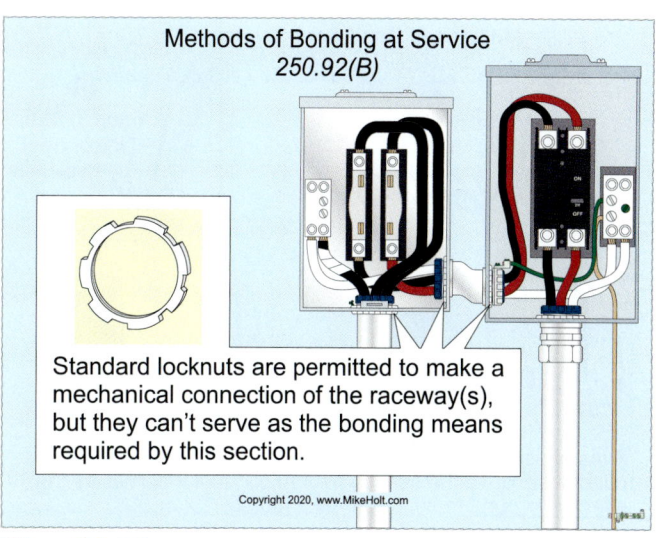
▶Figure 250-170

(1) Metal raceways containing service conductors.

(2) Metal enclosures containing service conductors.

(B) Methods of Bonding. Bonding jumpers are required around reducing washers or ringed knockouts. ▶Figure 250-169

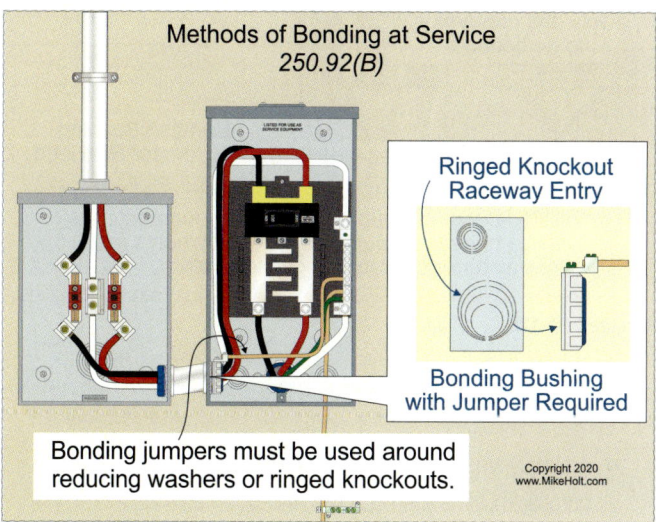
▶Figure 250-169

Standard locknuts are permitted to make a mechanical connection to the raceway(s), but they cannot serve as the bonding means required by this section. ▶Figure 250-170

Bonding must be ensured by one of the following methods:

(1) Bonding metal parts to the service neutral conductor. ▶Figure 250-171

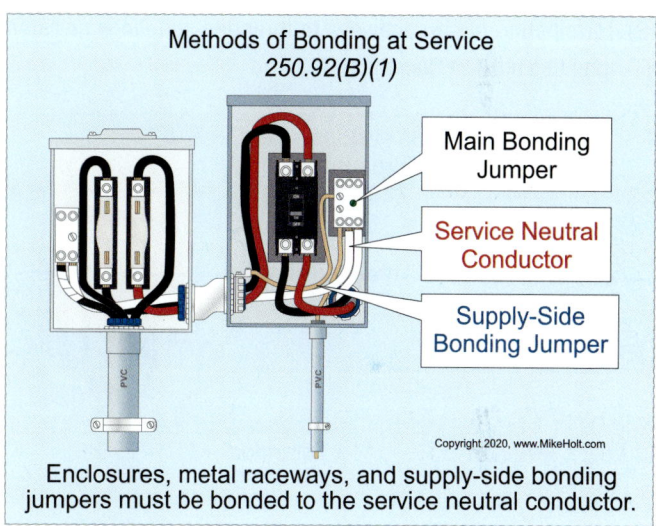
▶Figure 250-171

Author's Comment:

▸ A main bonding jumper is required to bond the service disconnect to the service neutral conductor [250.24(B) and 250.28].

▸ At the service disconnect, the service neutral conductor provides the effective ground-fault current path to the power supply [250.24(C)]; therefore, a supply-side bonding jumper is not required to be installed in PVC conduit containing service-entrance conductors [250.142(A)(1) and 352.60 Ex 2].
▶Figure 250-172

250.92 | Grounding and Bonding

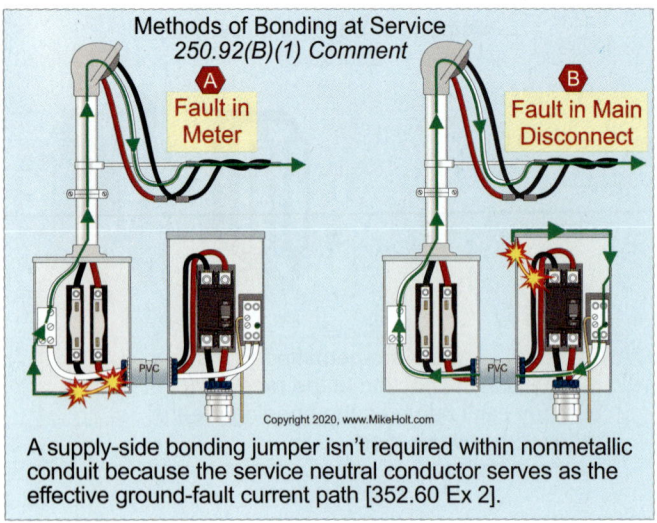
▶Figure 250–172

(2) Terminating metal raceways to threaded couplings or listed threaded hubs. ▶Figure 250–173

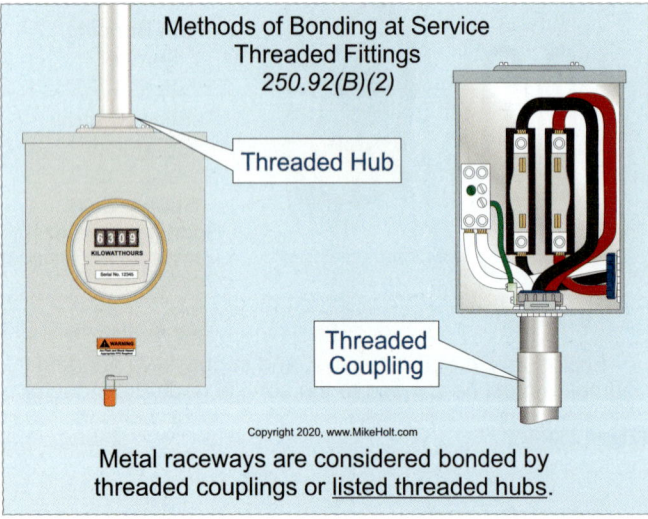
▶Figure 250–173

(3) Terminating metal raceways to threadless fittings. ▶Figure 250–174

(4) Using listed devices, such as bonding-type locknuts, bushings, wedges, or bushings with bonding jumpers to the service neutral conductor.

Author's Comment:

▶ A listed bonding wedge or bushing with a bonding jumper to the service neutral conductor is required when a metal raceway containing service conductors terminates to a ringed knockout. ▶Figure 250–175

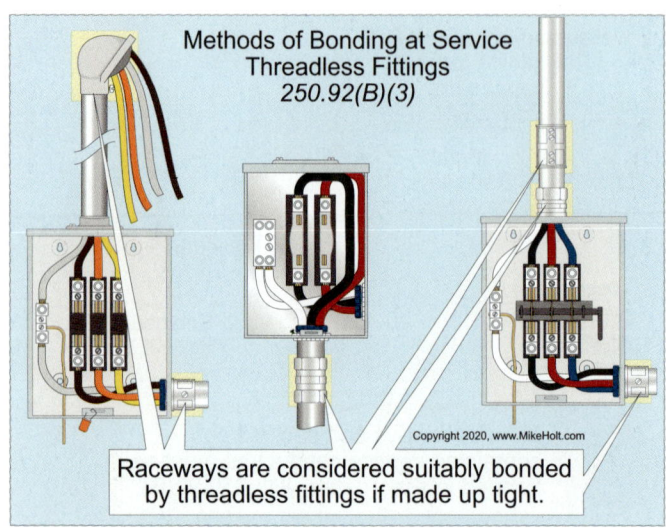
▶Figure 250–174

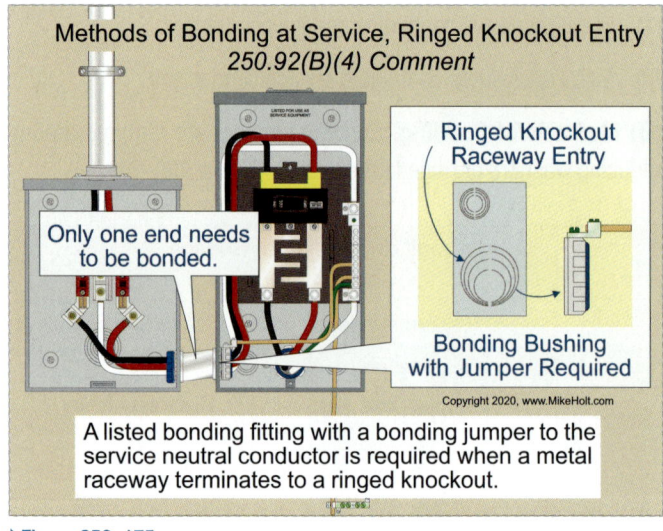
▶Figure 250–175

Author's Comment:

▶ A supply-side bonding jumper of the wire type used for this purpose must be sized in accordance with Table 250.102(C)(1), based on the size/area of the service phase conductors within the raceway [250.102(C)].

▶ A bonding-type locknut, bonding wedge, or bonding bushing with a bonding jumper can be used for a metal raceway that terminates to an enclosure without a ringed knockout. ▶Figure 250–176

Grounding and Bonding | 250.94

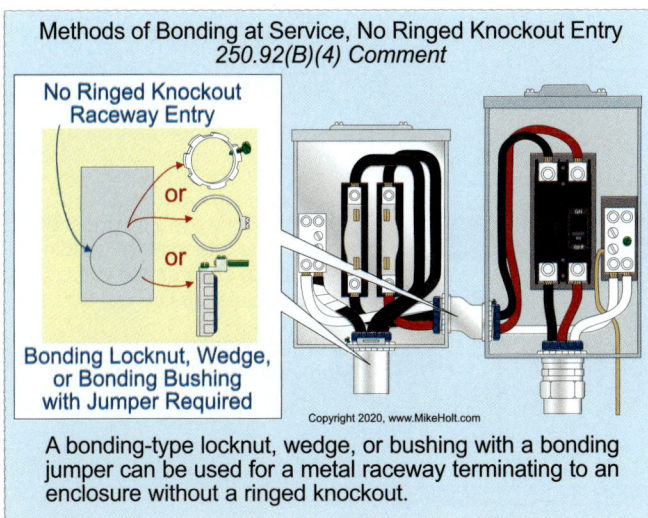

▶Figure 250-176

Author's Comment:

▸ A bonding locknut differs from a standard locknut in that it contains a bonding screw with a sharp point that drives into the metal enclosure to ensure a solid connection.

▸ Bonding one end of a service raceway to the service neutral provides the necessary low-impedance fault current path to the source required by this section. ▶Figure 250-177

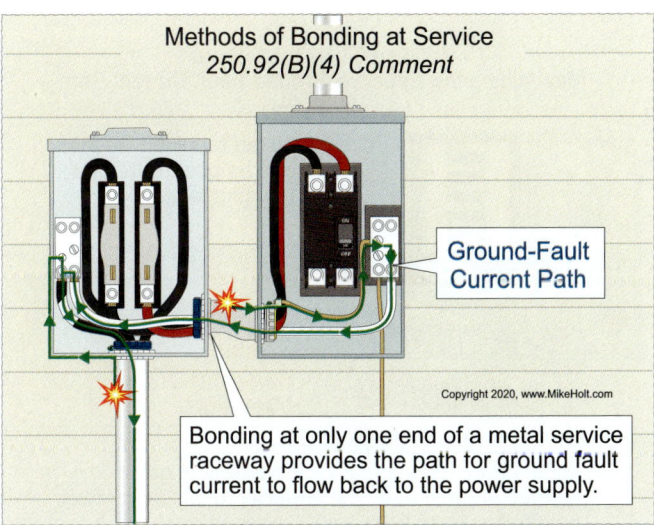

▶Figure 250-177

250.94 Bonding Communications Systems

A bonding termination device must be provided for communications systems in accordance with (A) and (B).

Author's Comment:

▸ These systems include communication systems (Article 805), radio and TV equipment (Article 810), and CATV (Article 820). Bonding communications systems together is intended to minimize damage from induced voltage differences between the systems that can be caused by lightning strikes. ▶Figure 250-178

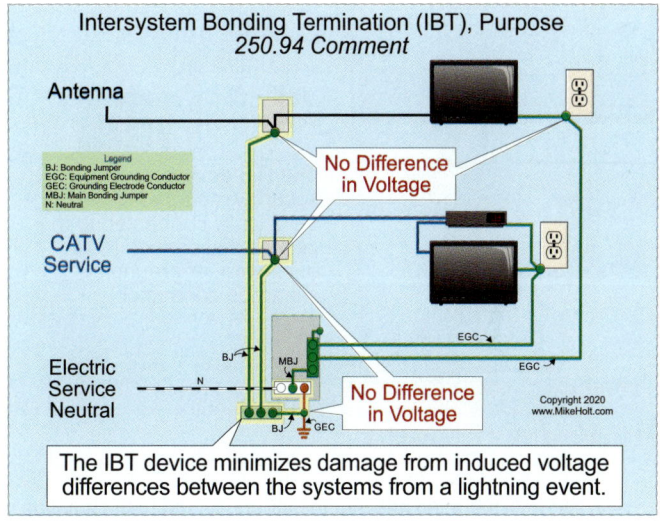

▶Figure 250-178

(A) Intersystem Bonding Termination Device. An intersystem bonding termination device must meet all of the following requirements:

(1) Be accessible. ▶Figure 250-179

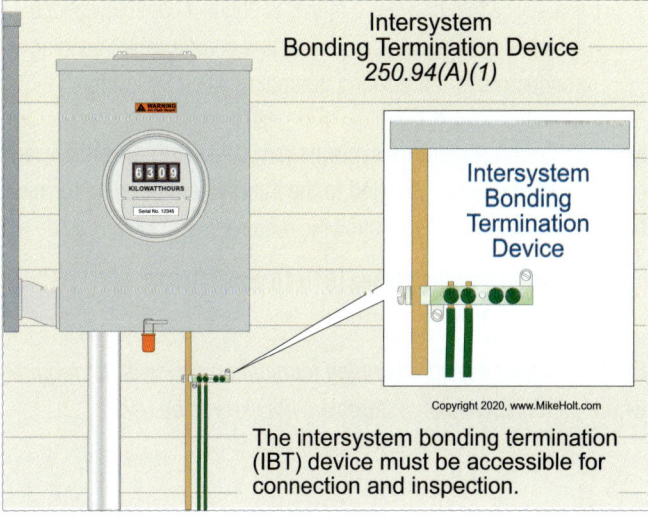

▶Figure 250-179

2nd Printing — 2020 NEC Requirements for Solar PV and Energy Storage Systems | MikeHolt.com | 207

250.96 | Grounding and Bonding

(2) Have a capacity for at least three intersystem bonding conductors.

(3) Be installed so it does not interfere with the opening of any enclosure.

(4) Be securely mounted and electrically connected to the service disconnect, meter enclosure, or grounding electrode conductor.
▶Figure 250–180

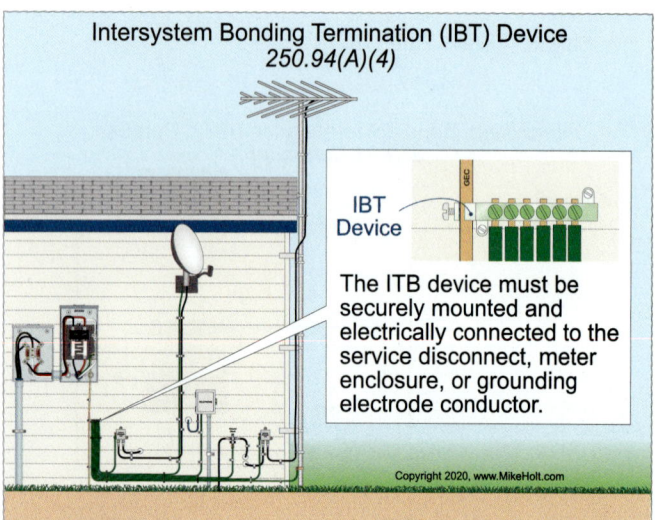

▶Figure 250–180

(5) Be securely mounted and electrically connected to the building's disconnect or grounding electrode conductor.

(6) Be listed as grounding and bonding equipment.

> **Author's Comment:**
> ▶ According to Article 100, an "Intersystem Bonding Termination" is a device that provides a means to connect communications systems' (twisted wire, antennas, and coaxial cable) bonding conductors to the building grounding electrode system.

Note 2: Communications systems (twisted wire, antennas, and coaxial cable) must be bonded to the intersystem bonding termination in accordance with the following requirements: ▶Figure 250–181

▶ Antennas/Satellite Dishes [810.15 and 810.21]
▶ CATV [820.100]

Ex to (A): An intersystem bonding termination device is not required where communications systems are not likely to be used.

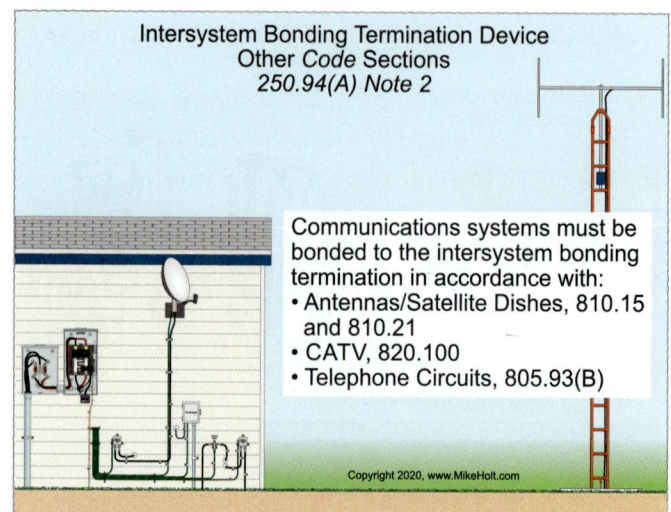

▶Figure 250–181

250.96 Bonding Other Enclosures

(A) Effective Ground-Fault Current Path. Metal parts intended to serve as equipment grounding conductors including raceways, cables, equipment, and enclosures must be bonded together to ensure they have the capacity to safely conduct any fault current likely to be imposed on them [110.10, 250.4(A)(5) and Table 250.122 Note].
▶Figure 250–182

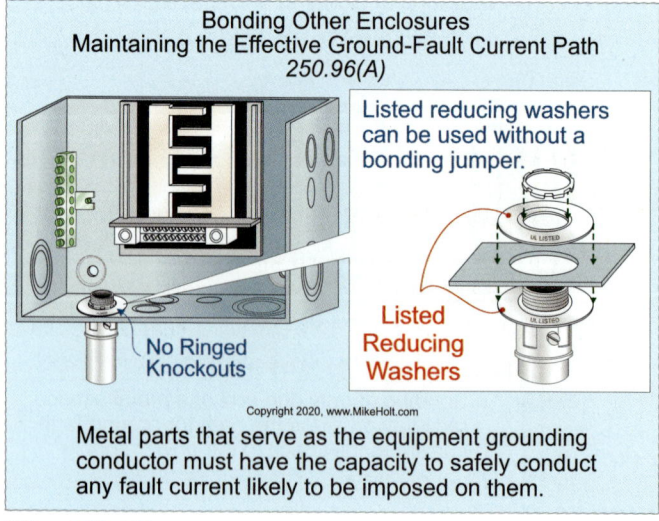

▶Figure 250–182

Nonconductive coatings such as paint, lacquer, and enamel on equipment must be removed to ensure an effective ground-fault current path, or the termination fittings must be designed so such removal is unnecessary [250.12].

Author's Comment:

▸ The practice of driving a locknut tight with a screwdriver and pliers is considered sufficient in removing paint and other nonconductive finishes to ensure an effective ground-fault current path.

250.97 Bonding Metal Parts Containing 277V and 480V Circuits

Metal raceways or cables containing 277V or 480V circuits terminating at ringed knockouts must be bonded to the metal enclosure with a bonding jumper. ▸Figure 250–183

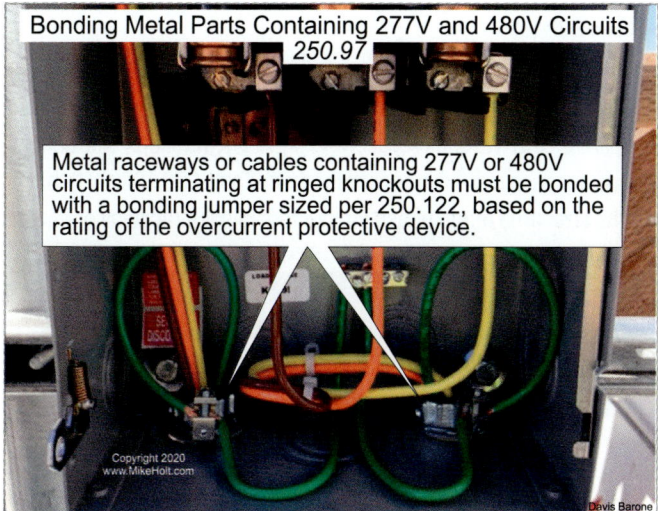
▸Figure 250–183

Author's Comment:

▸ Bonding jumpers for raceways and cables containing 277V or 480V circuits are required at ringed knockout terminations to ensure the ground-fault current path has the capacity to safely conduct the maximum ground-fault current likely to be imposed [110.10, 250.4(A)(5) and 250.96(A)]. Ringed knockouts are not listed to withstand the heat generated by a 277V ground fault, which generates five times as much heat as does a 120V ground fault. ▸Figure 250–184

Ex: Where oversized, concentric, or eccentric knockouts are not encountered, or where a box or enclosure with concentric or eccentric knockouts is listed to provide a reliable bonding connection, a bonding jumper is not required if the following methods are used: ▸Figure 250–185

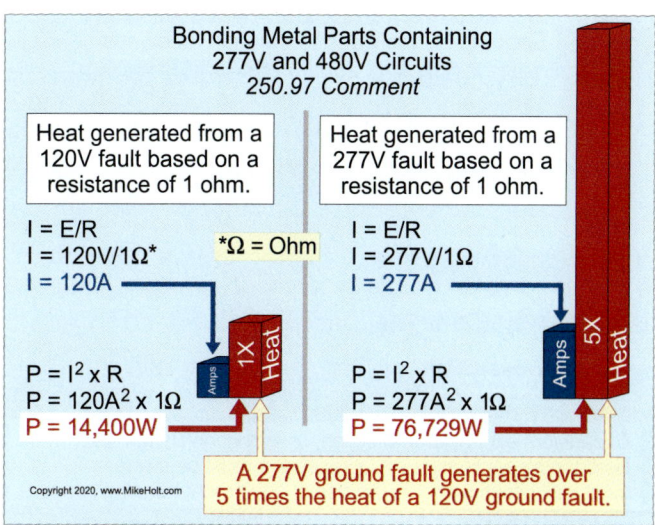
▸Figure 250–184

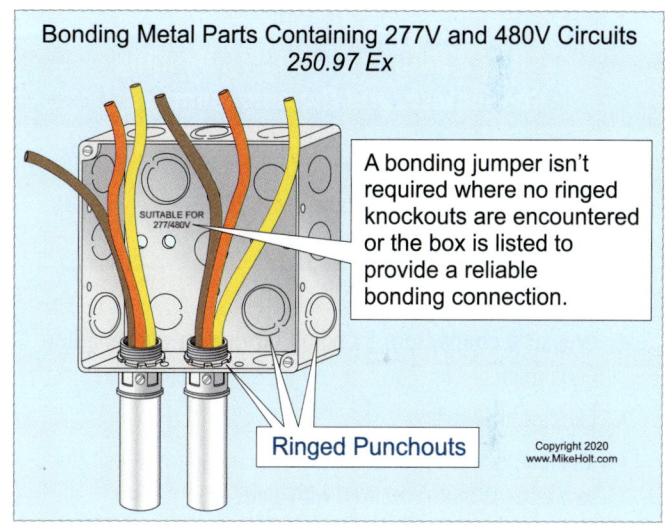
▸Figure 250–185

(1) Metal connectors for metal-sheathed cables
(2) Two locknuts, on rigid metal conduit or intermediate metal conduit, one inside and one outside of boxes and cabinets
(3) Electrical metallic tubing connectors, flexible metal conduit connectors, and cable connectors with one locknut on the inside of boxes and cabinets
(4) Listed fittings

250.98 Bonding Loosely Jointed Metal Raceways

Expansion, expansion-deflection, or deflection fittings and telescoping sections of metal raceways must be made electrically continuous using equipment bonding jumpers. ▸Figure 250–186

250.102 | Grounding and Bonding

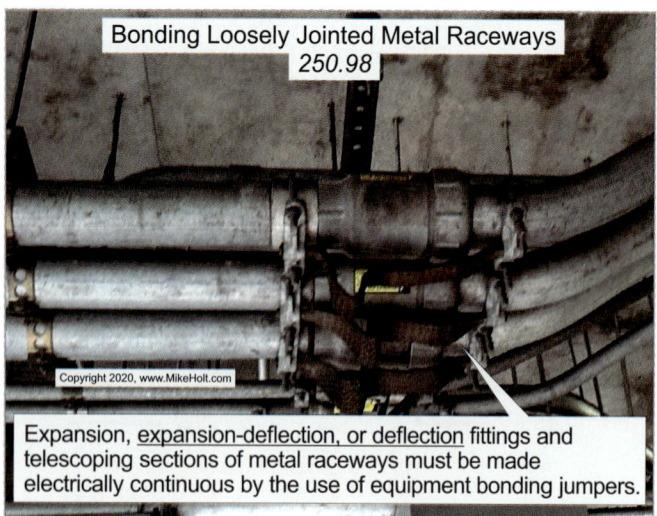

▶Figure 250–186

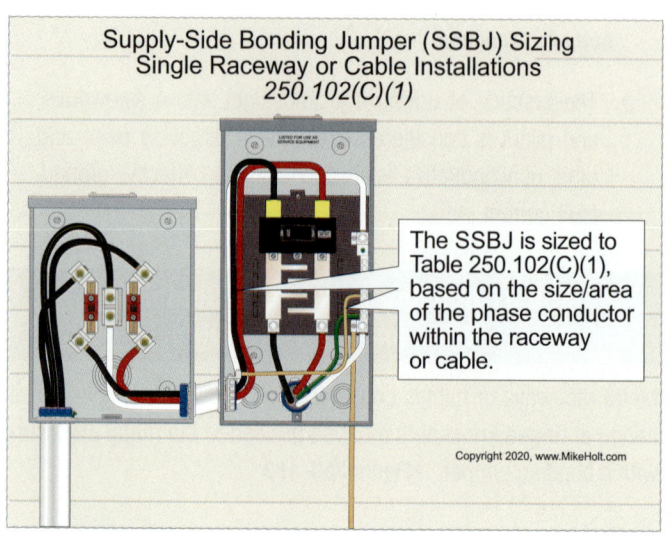

▶Figure 250–187

250.102 Neutral Conductor, Bonding Conductors, and Bonding Jumpers

(B) Termination. Equipment bonding jumpers must terminate by any of the following means in accordance with 250.8(A):

- Listed pressure connectors
- Terminal bars
- Pressure connectors listed as grounding and bonding equipment
- Exothermic welding
- Machine screw-type fasteners that engage not less than two threads or are secured with a nut
- Thread-forming machine screws that engage not less than two threads in the enclosure
- Connections that are part of a listed assembly
- Other listed means

(C) Supply-Side Bonding Jumper Sizing.

(1) Single Raceway or Cable Installations. Supply-side bonding jumpers must be sized in accordance with Table 250.102(C)(1), based on the size/area of the phase conductor within the raceway or cable. ▶Figure 250–187

(2) Parallel Conductor Installations. If the phase supply conductors are paralleled in two or more raceways or cables, the supply-side bonding jumper for each is sized in accordance with Table 250.102(C)(1), based on the size/area of the phase conductors in each raceway or cable.

Table 250.102(C)(1) Neutral Conductor, Main Bonding Jumper, System Bonding Jumper, and Supply-Side Bonding Jumper

Size of Largest Phase Conductor Per Raceway or Equivalent Area for Parallel Conductors		Size of Bonding Jumper or Neutral Conductor
Copper	Aluminum or Copper-Clad Aluminum	Copper-Aluminum
2 or smaller	1/0 or smaller	8 CU–6 AL
1 or 1/0	2/0 or 3/0	6 CU–4 AL
2/0 or 3/0	Over 3/0 250 kcmil	4 CU–2 AL
Over 3/0–350 kcmil	Over 250–500 kcmil	2 CU–1/0 AL
Over 350–600 kcmil	Over 500–900 kcmil	1/0 CU–3/0 AL
Over 600–1,100 kcmil	Over 900–1,750 kcmil	2/0 CU–4/0 AL
Over 1,100 kcmil	Over 1,750 kcmil	See Notes 1 and 2.

Grounding and Bonding | 250.102

▶ **Example**

Question: What size supply-side bonding jumper is required for each of three metal raceways, each of which contain 400 kcmil service conductors? ▶Figure 250–188

(a) 4 AWG (b) 2 AWG (c) 1 AWG (d) 1/0 AWG

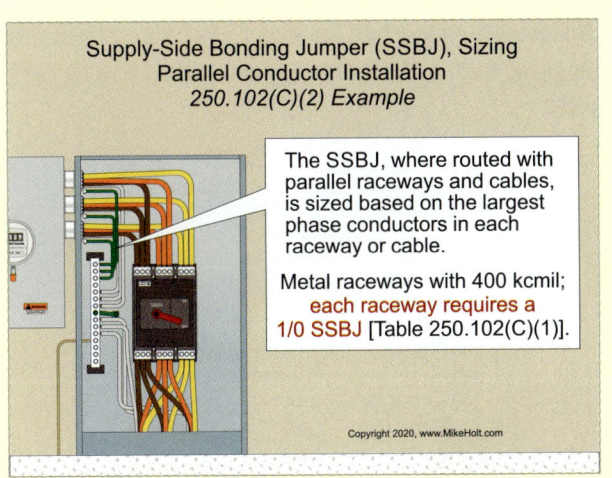

▶Figure 250–188

Solution:

A 1/0 AWG supply-side bonding jumper is required for each raceway. [250.102(C)(2) and Table 250.102(C)(1)]. A single supply-side bonding jumper is permitted for multiple raceways based on the equivalent area of the supply-side phase conductors.

Answer: (d) 1/0 AWG

▶ **Example**

Question: What size single supply-side bonding jumper is required for all three metal raceways, each of which contain 400 kcmil service conductors? ▶Figure 250–189

(a) 1/0 AWG (b) 2/0 AWG (c) 3/0 AWG (d) 4/0 AWG

Solution:

A singe 3/0 AWG supply-side bonding jumper is required if using one conductor for all three raceways.

400 kcmil × 3 Raceways = 1,200 kcmil which exceeds 1,100 kcmil [Table 250.102(C)(1) Note 1]

Conductor kcmil at 12½ % = 1,200 kcmil × 0.125

Convert kcmil to cmil = 150 kcmil × 1,000

Total bonding jumper cmil = 150,000 cmil

Use a 3/0 AWG supply-side bonding jumper [Chapter 9, Table 8].

Answer: (c) 3/0 AWG

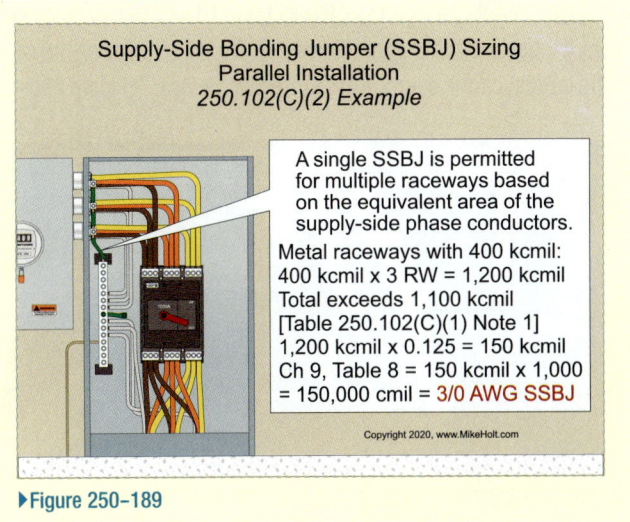

▶Figure 250–189

Note 1: The term "supply conductors" includes phase conductors that do not have overcurrent protection on their supply side and terminate at the service disconnect or the first disconnect of a separately derived system.

Note 2: See Chapter 9, Table 8 for the circular mil area of conductors 18 AWG through 4/0 AWG.

(D) Load-Side Bonding Jumper Sizing. Bonding jumpers on the load side of feeder and branch-circuit overcurrent devices are sized in accordance with 250.122.

▶ **Example**

Question: What size equipment bonding jumper is required for each metal raceway where the circuit conductors are protected by a 1,200A overcurrent protective device? ▶Figure 250–190

(a) 1/0 AWG (b) 2/0 AWG (c) 3/0 AWG (d) 4/0 AWG

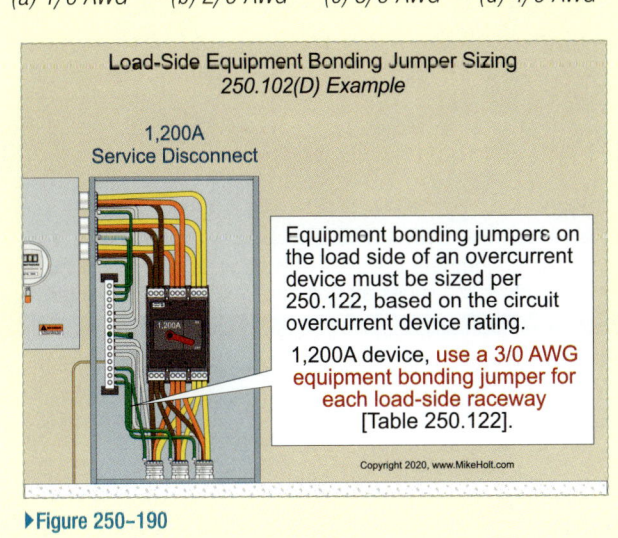

▶Figure 250–190

Answer: (c) 3/0 AWG [Table 250.122]

250.104 | Grounding and Bonding

If a single bonding jumper is used to bond two or more metal raceways, it must be sized in accordance with 250.122, based on the rating of the largest circuit overcurrent protective device. ▶Figure 250–191

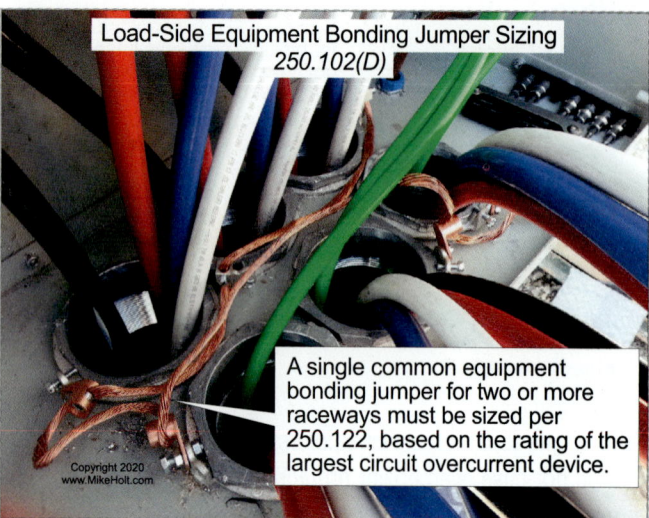

▶Figure 250–191

(E) Installation of Bonding Jumpers. Bonding jumpers can be installed inside or outside of a raceway or an enclosure.

(2) Outside a Raceway. Bonding jumpers installed outside a raceway must be routed with the raceway and the conductor cannot exceed 6 ft in length. ▶Figure 250–192

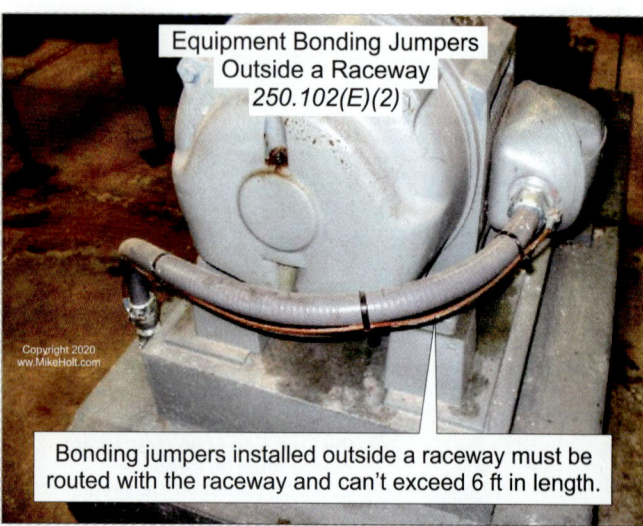

▶Figure 250–192

250.104 Bonding of Piping Systems and Exposed Structural Metal

(A) Metal Water Piping System. Electrically continuous metal water piping systems, including sprinkler piping, must be bonded in accordance with 250.104(A)(1), (A)(2), or (A)(3).

(1) Buildings Supplied by a Service. Electrically continuous metal water piping must be bonded to any one of the following: ▶Figure 250–193

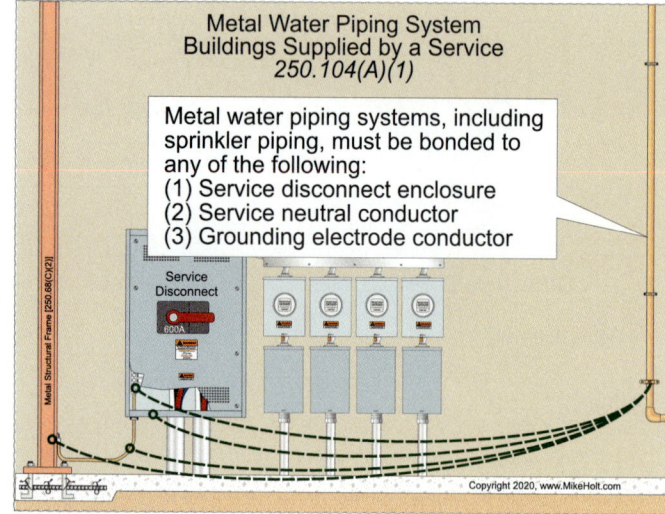

▶Figure 250–193

(1) Service-disconnect enclosure,

(2) Service neutral conductor,

(3) Grounding electrode conductor if of sufficient size, or

(4) One of the grounding electrodes of the grounding electrode system if the grounding electrode conductor or bonding jumper to the electrode is of sufficient size.

> **Author's Comment:**
>
> ▸ The intent of this rule is to remove dangerous voltage from a ground fault on metal parts from a ground fault to electrically conductive metal water piping systems and metal sprinkler piping. ▶Figure 250–194

The metal piping system bonding jumper must be copper where within 18 in. of the surface of earth [250.64(A)], must be adequately protected if exposed to physical damage [250.64(B)], and points of attachment must be accessible.

Grounding and Bonding | 250.104

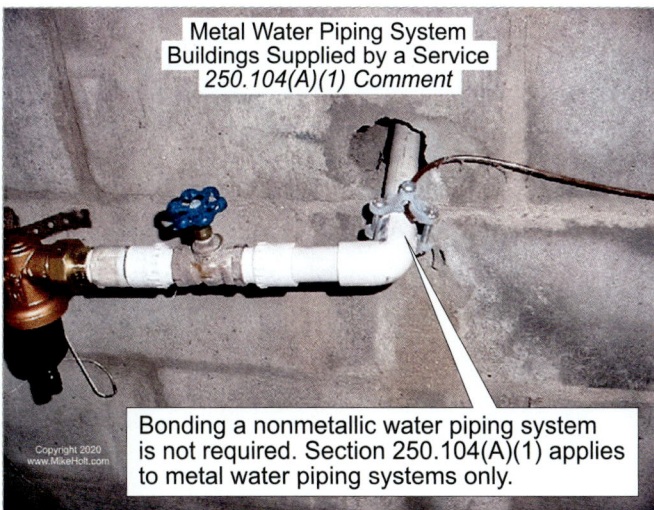

▶Figure 250-194

A ferrous metal raceway containing a grounding electrode conductor must be made electrically continuous by bonding each end of the raceway to the grounding electrode conductor [250.64(E)].

Metal water piping system bonding jumpers must be sized in accordance with Table 250.102(C)(1), based on the size/area of the service phase conductors and not required to be larger than 3/0 copper or 250 kcmil aluminum or copper-clad aluminum, except as permitted in 250.104(A)(2) and (A)(3).

▶ **Example**

Question: What size bonding jumper is required for a metal water piping system if the 300 kcmil service conductors are paralleled in two raceways? ▶Figure 250-195

(a) 1/0 AWG   (b) 2/0 AWG   (c) 3/0 AWG   (d) 4/0 AWG

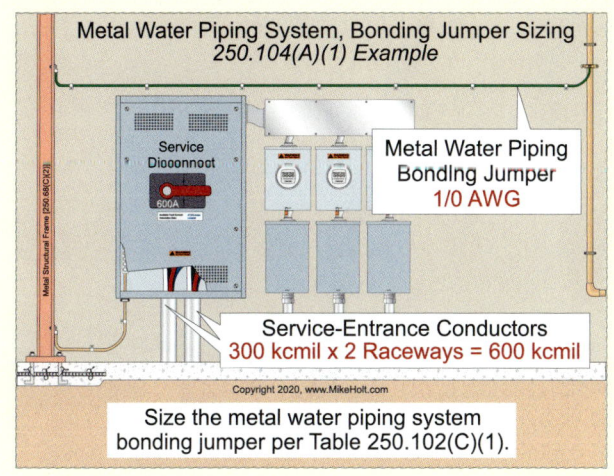

▶Figure 250-195

Solution:

A 1/0 AWG bonding jumper is required based on 600 kcmil conductors (300 kcmil × 2 raceways) [250.102(C)(1)].

Answer: (a) 1/0 AWG

Author's Comment:

▸ If hot and cold metal water pipes are electrically connected, only one bonding jumper is required, either to the cold or hot water pipe.

▸ Bonding is not required for isolated sections of metal water piping connected to a nonmetallic water piping system. In fact, these isolated sections of metal piping should not be bonded because they could become a shock hazard under certain conditions. ▶Figure 250-196

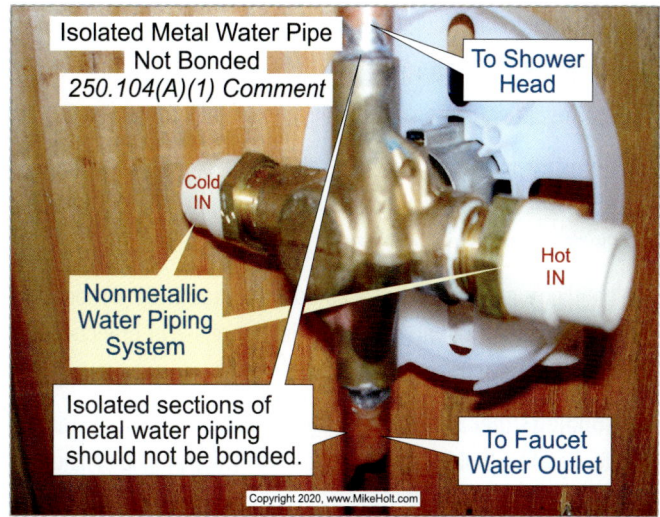

▶Figure 250-196

(2) Bonding Multiple Occupancy Buildings. When an electrically continuous metal water piping system in an individual occupancy is metallically isolated from other occupancies in a building, the metal water piping system for that occupancy can be bonded to the equipment grounding terminal of the occupancy's switchgear, switchboard, or panelboard. The bonding jumper must be sized based on the rating of the circuit overcurrent protective device in accordance with 250.122 [250.102(D)]. ▶Figure 250-197

250.104 | Grounding and Bonding

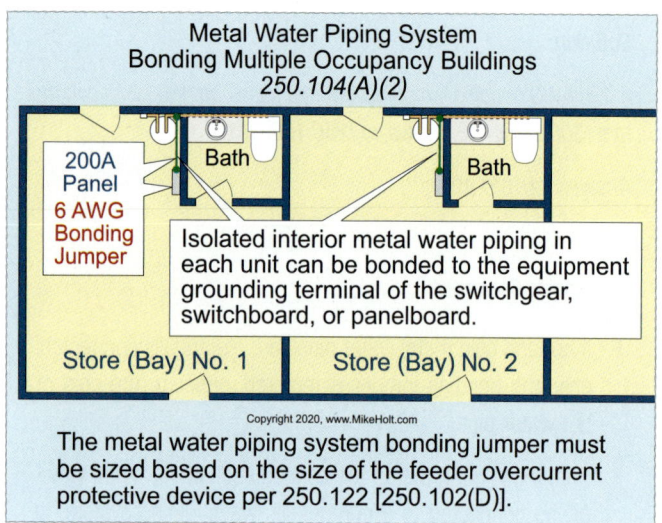
▶Figure 250–197

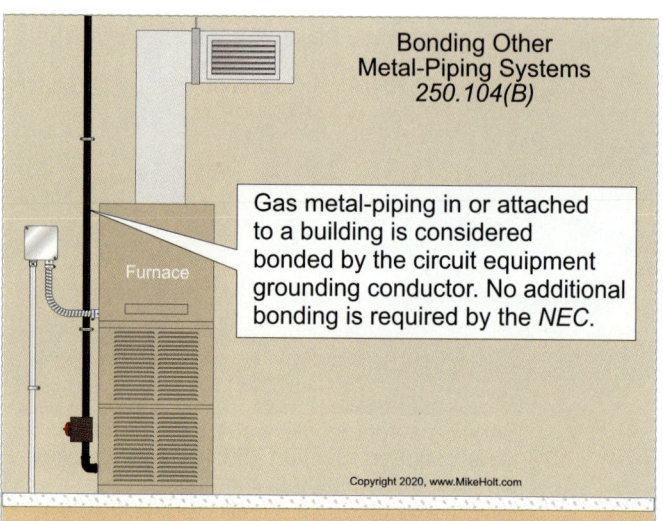
▶Figure 250–198

(3) Buildings Supplied by a Feeder. The metal water piping system of a building supplied by a feeder must be bonded to one of the following:

(1) The equipment grounding terminal of the building's disconnect enclosure,

(2) The feeder equipment grounding conductor, or

(3) One of the building's grounding electrodes of the grounding electrode system if the grounding electrode or bonding jumper to the electrode is of sufficient size.

The bonding jumper is sized in accordance with 250.102(D) and is not required to be larger than the largest feeder phase or branch-circuit conductor supplying the building.

(B) Bonding Other Metal-Piping Systems. Metal-piping systems in or attached to a building must be bonded. The piping is considered bonded when it is connected to an appliance that is connected to the circuit equipment grounding conductor. ▶Figure 250–198

Note 1: Bonding piping and metal air ducts within the premises will provide additional safety, but this is not required by the *NEC*. ▶Figure 250–199

Note 2: Additional information for gas piping systems can be found in NFPA 54, *National Fuel Gas Code,* and NFPA 780, *Standard for the Installation of Lightning Protection Systems*. ▶Figure 250–200

(C) Bonding Exposed Structural Metal. Exposed structural metal that is interconnected to form a metal building frame must be bonded to any of the following: ▶Figure 250–201

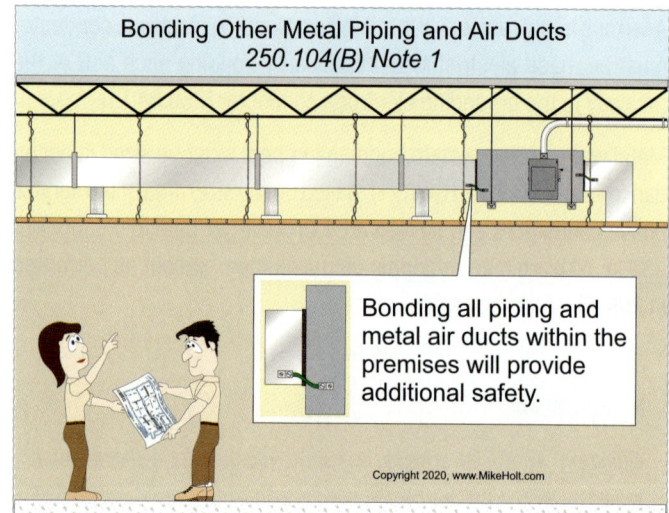
▶Figure 250–199

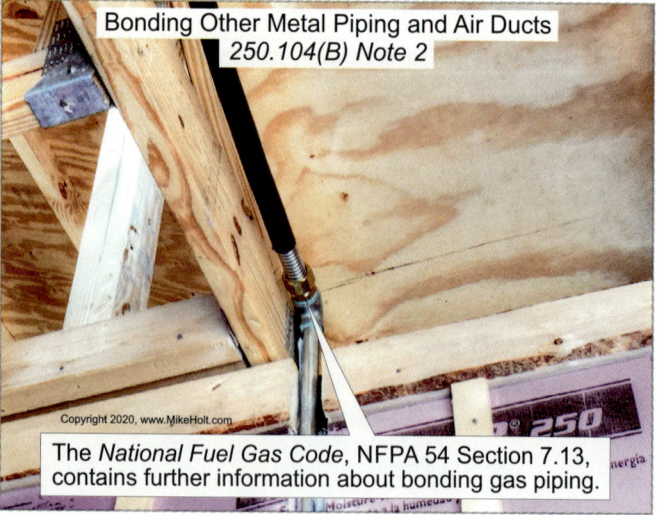
▶Figure 250–200

Grounding and Bonding | 250.104

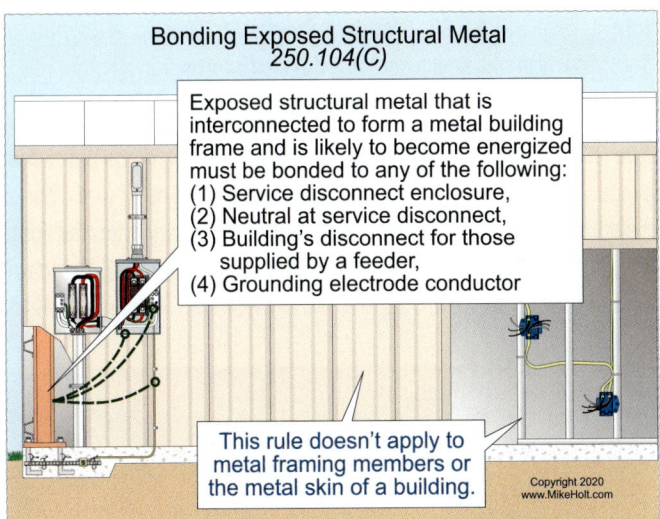
▶Figure 250–201

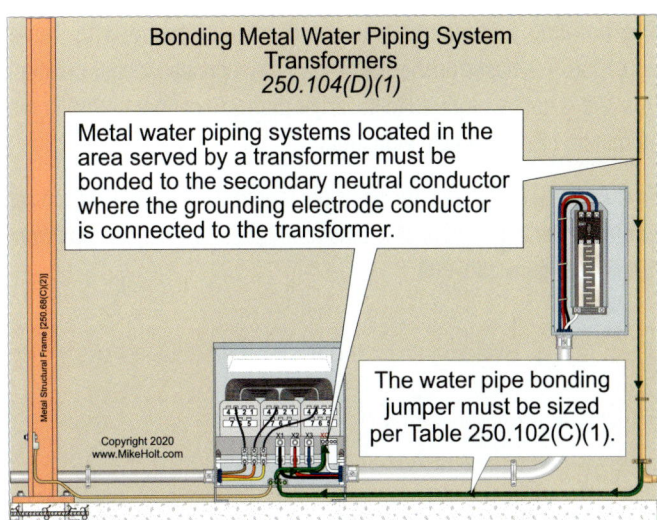
▶Figure 250–202

(1) The service-disconnect enclosure,

(2) The neutral at the service disconnect,

(3) The building's disconnect enclosure for those supplied by a feeder,

(4) The grounding electrode conductor where of sufficient size, or

(5) One of the grounding electrodes of the grounding electrode system if the grounding electrode conductor or bonding jumper to the electrode is of sufficient size.

The structural metal bonding conductor must be sized in accordance with Table 250.102(C)(1), based on the size/area of the supply phase conductors and is not required to be larger than 3/0 copper or 250 kcmil aluminum or copper-clad aluminum. The bonding jumper must be copper where within 18 in. of the surface of the Earth [250.64(A)], be securely fastened to the surface on which it is carried [250.64(B)] and be adequately protected if exposed to physical damage [250.64(B)]. In addition, all points of attachment must be accessible, except as permitted in 250.68(A) Ex 1 and 2.

(D) Transformers. Metal water piping systems and structural metal that is interconnected to form a building frame must be bonded to the transformer secondary winding in accordance with 250.104(D)(1) through (D)(3).

(1) Bonding Metal Water Pipe. Metal water piping systems located in the area served by a transformer must be bonded to the secondary neutral conductor where the grounding electrode conductor is connected at the transformer. ▶Figure 250–202

The bonding jumper must be sized in accordance with Table 250.102(C)(1), based on the size/area of the secondary phase conductors and is not be required to be larger than 3/0 copper or 250 kcmil aluminum or copper-clad aluminum.

Ex 2: The metal water piping system can be bonded to the metal structural building frame if it serves as the grounding electrode [250.52(A)(2)] for the transformer. ▶Figure 250–203

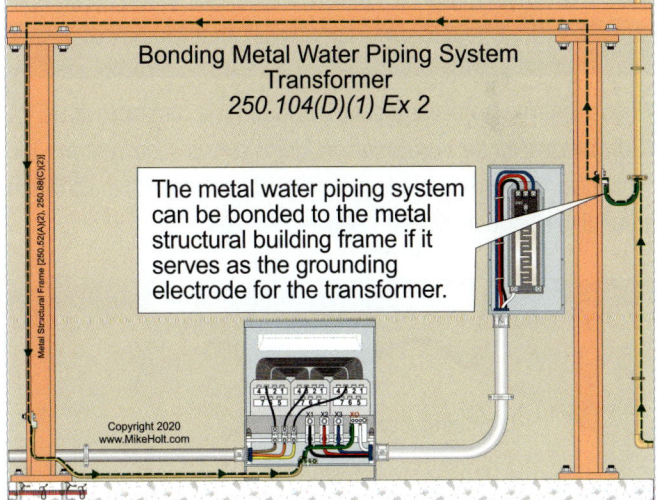
▶Figure 250–203

(2) Bonding Exposed Structural Metal. Exposed structural metal that is interconnected to form the building frame located in the area served by a transformer must be bonded to the secondary neutral conductor where the grounding electrode conductor is connected at the transformer.

250.106 | Grounding and Bonding

The bonding jumper must be sized in accordance with Table 250.102(C)(1), based on the size/area of the secondary phase conductors and is not be required to be larger than 3/0 copper or 250 kcmil aluminum or copper-clad aluminum.

Ex 1: Bonding to the transformer is not required if the metal structural frame serves as the grounding electrode [250.52(A)(2)] for the transformer. ▶Figure 250–204

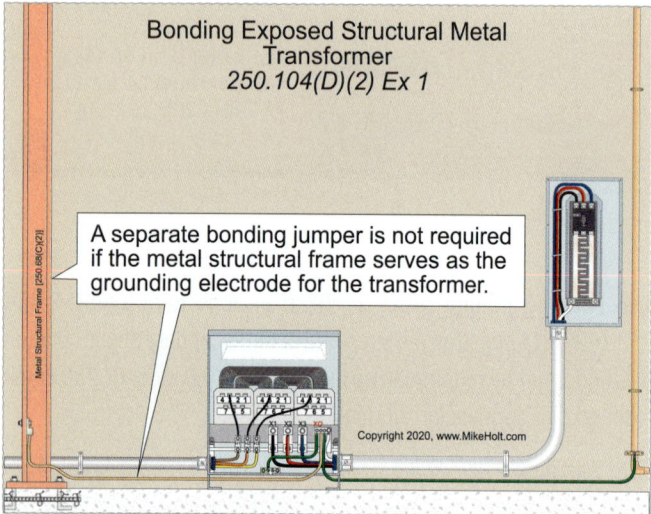

▶Figure 250–204

250.106 Lightning Protection Systems

When a lightning protection system is installed in accordance with NFPA 780, *Standard for the Installation of Lightning Protection Systems*, the lightning protection electrode system must be bonded to the building grounding electrode system. ▶Figure 250–205

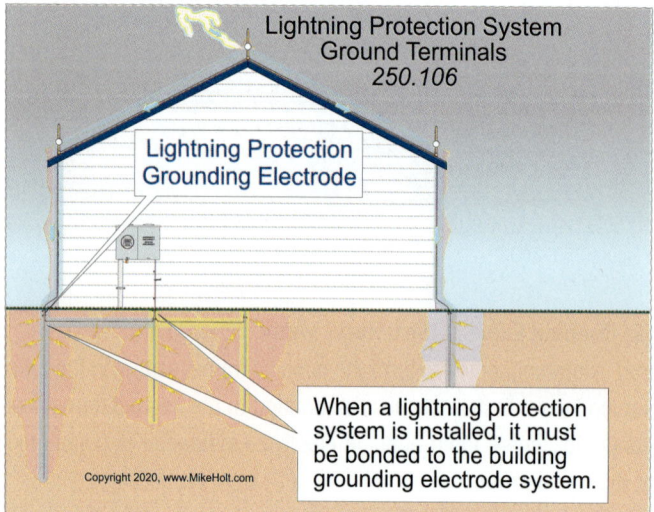

▶Figure 250–205

Note 1: See NFPA 780, *Standard for the Installation of Lightning Protection Systems*, which contains detailed information on grounding, bonding, and side-flash distances from lightning protection systems.

Note 2: To minimize the likelihood of arcing between metal parts due to induced voltage, metal raceways, enclosures, and other metal parts of electrical equipment may require bonding or spacing from the lightning protection conductors in accordance with NFPA 780, *Standard for the Installation of Lightning Protection Systems*. ▶Figure 250–206

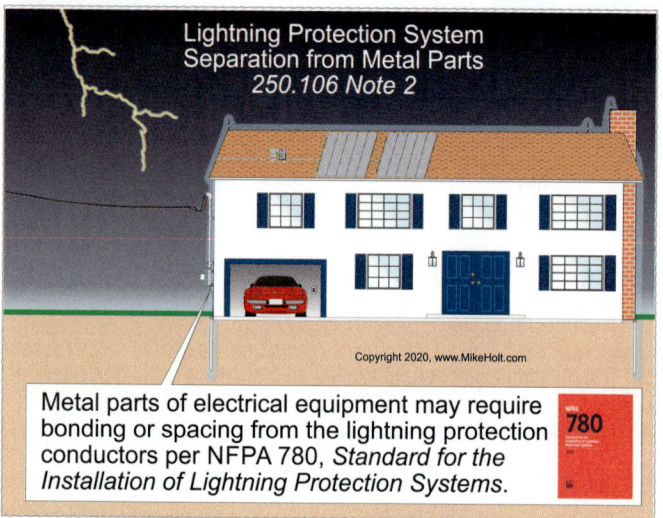

▶Figure 250–206

Part VI. Equipment Grounding and Equipment Grounding Conductors

250.109 Metal Enclosures

Metal enclosures can be used to connect bonding jumpers or equipment grounding conductors (or both) together to become part of an effective ground-fault current path. Metal covers and metal fittings attached to these metal enclosures are considered as being connected to bonding jumpers or equipment grounding conductors, or both. ▶Figure 250–207

250.114 Equipment Connected by Cord and Plug

Exposed, normally noncurrent-carrying metal parts of cord-and-plug-connected equipment must be connected to the equipment grounding conductor of the circuit suppling the equipment under any of the following conditions:

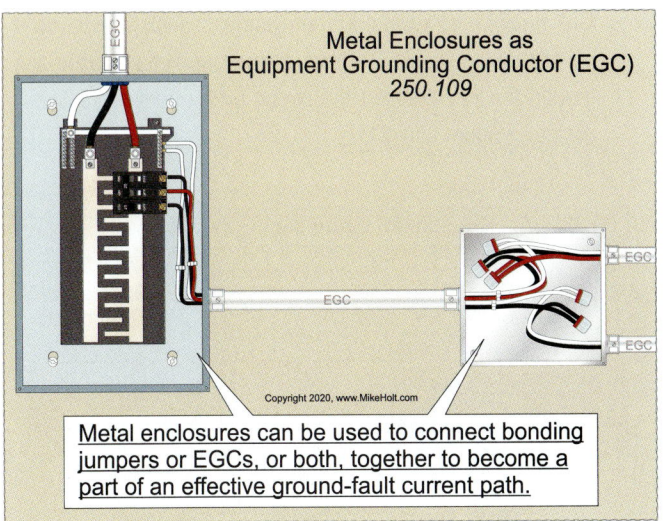
▶Figure 250-207

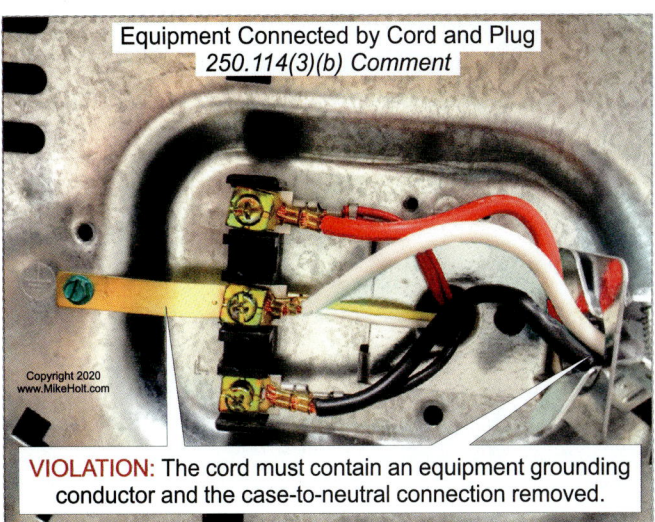
▶Figure 250-208

Ex: Listed tools, listed appliances, and listed equipment covered in 250.114(2) through (4) are not required to be connected to an equipment grounding conductor where protected by a system of double insulation or its equivalent. Double insulated equipment must be distinctively marked.

(1) In hazardous (classified) locations. [Articles 500 through 517].

(2) Where operated at over 150V to ground.

Ex 1 to (2): Motors that are guarded.

Ex 2 to (2): Metal frames of exempted electrically heated appliances.

(3) In residential occupancies:

 a. Refrigerators, freezers, and air conditioners.

 b. Clothes-washing, clothes-drying, and dish-washing machines; ranges; kitchen waste disposers; IT equipment; sump pumps; and electrical aquarium equipment.

 c. Hand-held, stationary or fixed, and light industrial motor-operated tools.

 d. Motor-operated hedge clippers, lawn mowers, snow-blowers, and wet scrubbers.

 e. Portable handlamps and portable luminaires.

(4) In other than residential occupancies:

 a. Refrigerators, freezers, and air conditioners.

 b. Clothes-washing, clothes-drying, and dish-washing machines; IT equipment; sump pumps; and electrical aquarium equipment.

 c. Hand-held, stationary or fixed, and light industrial motor-operated tools.

 d. Motor-operated hedge clippers, lawn mowers, snow-blowers, and wet scrubbers.

 e. Portable handlamps and portable luminaires.

 f. Appliances used in damp or wet locations or by persons standing on the ground, standing on metal floors, or working inside of metal tanks or boilers.

 g. Tools likely to be used in wet or conductive locations

Ex: Tools and portable handlamps and portable luminaires likely to be used in wet or conductive locations are not required to be connected to an equipment grounding conductor where supplied through an isolating transformer with an ungrounded secondary not over 50V.

Author's Comment:

▶ Electric ranges and clothes dryers are shipped from the factory with a bonding strap that bonds the metal frame of the appliance to the neutral termination of the cord connection terminal block. This bonding strap may or may not have to be removed! The *Code* requires an insulated neutral for these appliances using a 4-wire branch circuit and the bonding strap should be removed, but that was not always the case. If an existing 3-wire branch circuit is to supply a replacement appliance, the factory-installed bonding strap must remain in place [250.140 Ex]. ▶Figure 250-208

250.118 Types of Equipment Grounding Conductors

The equipment grounding conductor can be any one of the following types: ▶Figure 250–209

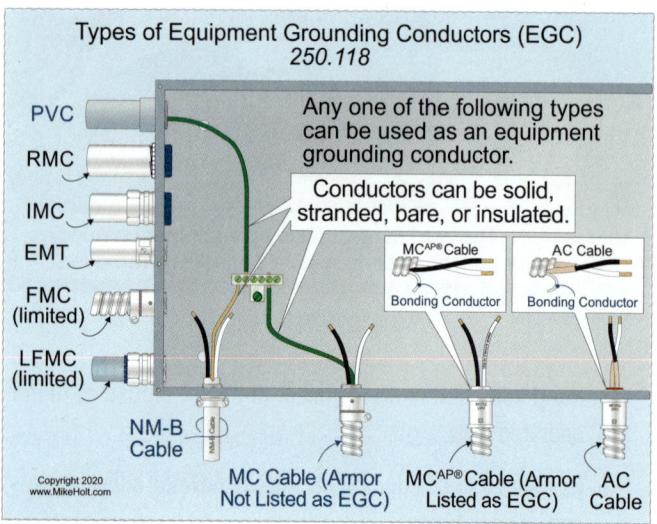

▶Figure 250–209

Note: The equipment grounding conductor is intended to serve as part of the effective ground-fault current path [Article 100]. ▶Figure 250–210

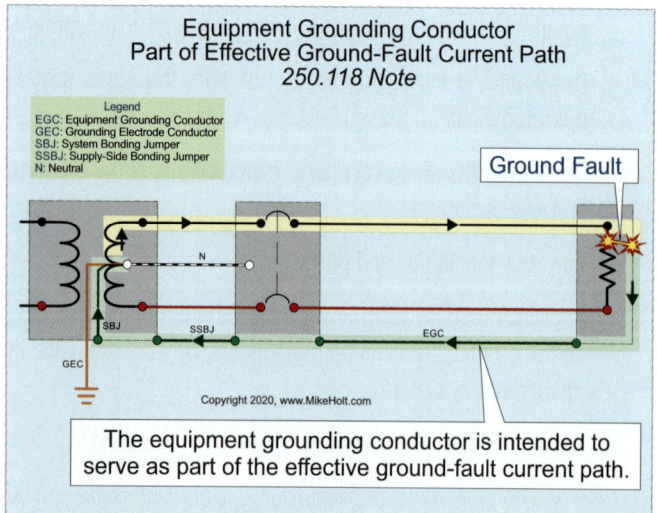

▶Figure 250–210

Author's Comment:

▸ The effective ground-fault current path [Article 100] is an intentionally constructed low-impedance conductive path designed to carry fault current from the point of a ground fault on a wiring system to the electrical supply source. Its purpose is to quickly remove dangerous voltage from a ground fault by opening the circuit overcurrent protective device. ▶Figure 250–211

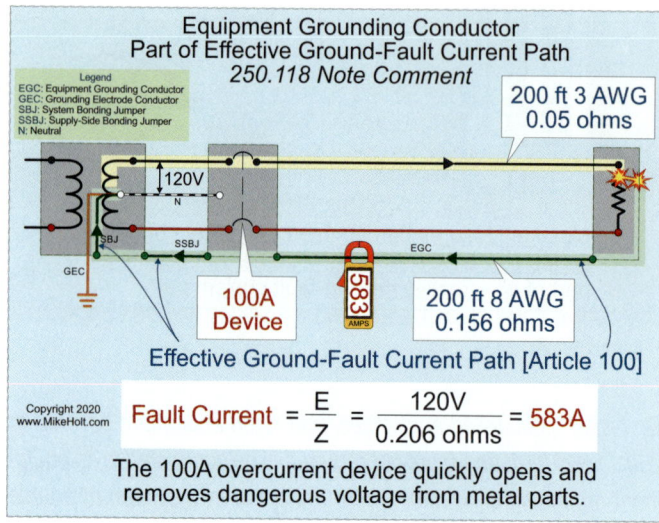

▶Figure 250–211

(1) A bare or insulated copper, aluminum, or copper-clad aluminum conductor sized in accordance with 250.122. ▶Figure 250–212

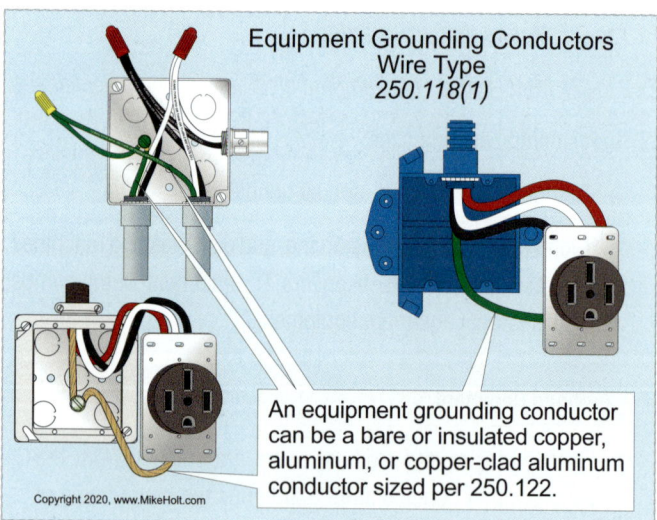

▶Figure 250–212

(2) Rigid metal conduit.

(3) Intermediate metal conduit.

(4) Electrical metallic tubing.

(5) Listed flexible metal conduit where: ▶Figure 250–213

Grounding and Bonding | 250.118

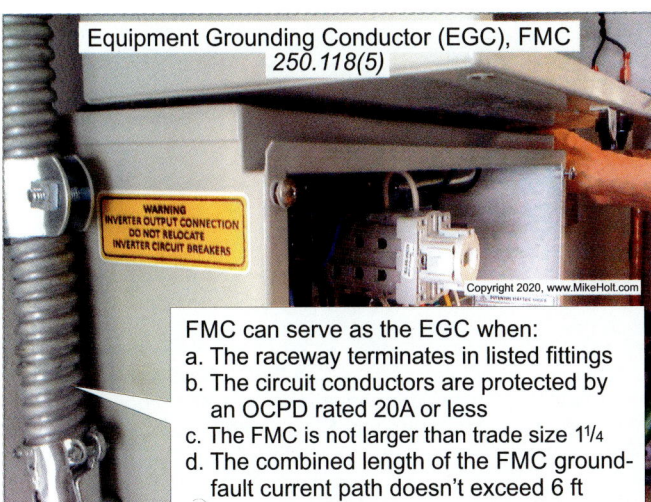
▶Figure 250-213

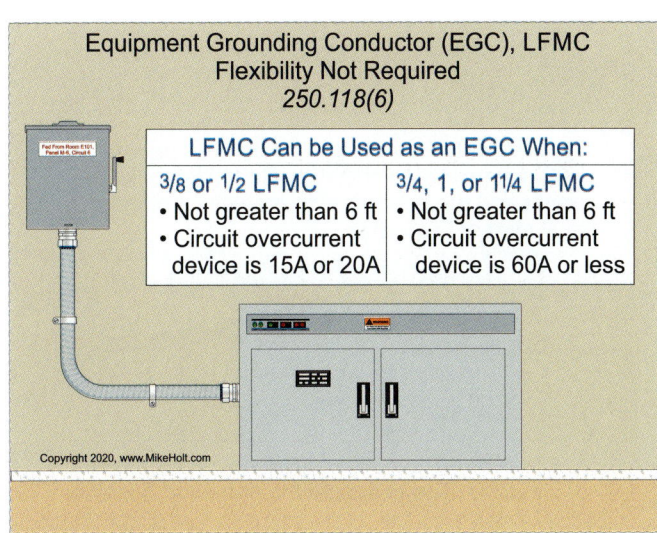
▶Figure 250-215

a. The raceway terminates in listed fittings.

b. The circuit conductors are protected by an overcurrent device rated 20A or less.

c. The size of the flexible metal conduit does not exceed 1¼.

d. The combined length of the flexible conduit in the same effective ground-fault current path does not exceed 6 ft.

e. If flexibility is required to minimize the transmission of vibration from equipment or to provide flexibility for equipment that requires movement after installation, an equipment grounding conductor of the wire type must be installed with the circuit conductors in accordance with 250.102(E). ▶Figure 250-214

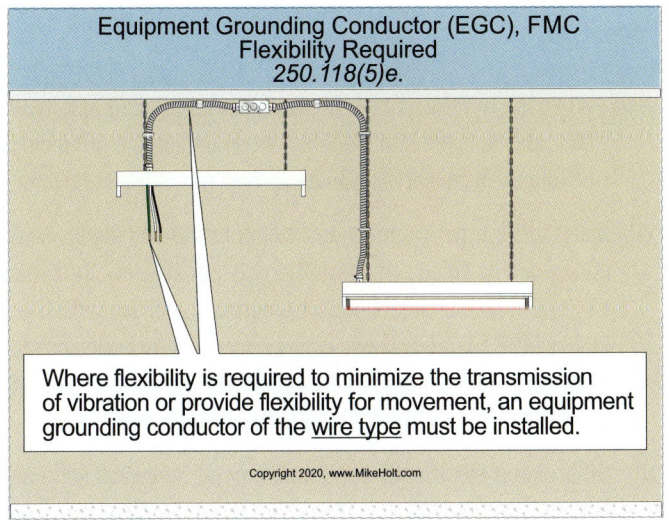
▶Figure 250-214

(6) Listed liquidtight flexible metal conduit where: ▶Figure 250-215

a. The raceway terminates in listed fittings.

b. For ⅜ in. through ½ in., the circuit conductors are protected by overcurrent protective devices rated 20A or less.

c. For ¾ in. through 1¼ in., the circuit conductors are protected by overcurrent protective devices rated 60A or less.

d. The combined length of the flexible metal conduit in the same effective ground-fault current path does not exceed 6 ft.

e. If flexibility is required to minimize the transmission of vibration from equipment or to provide flexibility for equipment that requires movement after installation, an equipment grounding conductor of the wire type must be installed with the circuit conductors in accordance with 250.102(E).

(8) The sheath of Type AC cable. ▶Figure 250-216

(9) The sheath of Type MI cable.

Author's Comment:

▶ The internal aluminum bonding strip is not an equipment grounding conductor, but it allows the interlocked armor of Type AC cable to serve as an equipment grounding conductor because it reduces the impedance of the armored spirals to ensure a ground fault will be cleared. It is the aluminum bonding strip in combination with the cable armor that creates the circuit equipment grounding conductor. Once the bonding strip exits the cable it can be cut off because it no longer serves any purpose.

250.118 | Grounding and Bonding

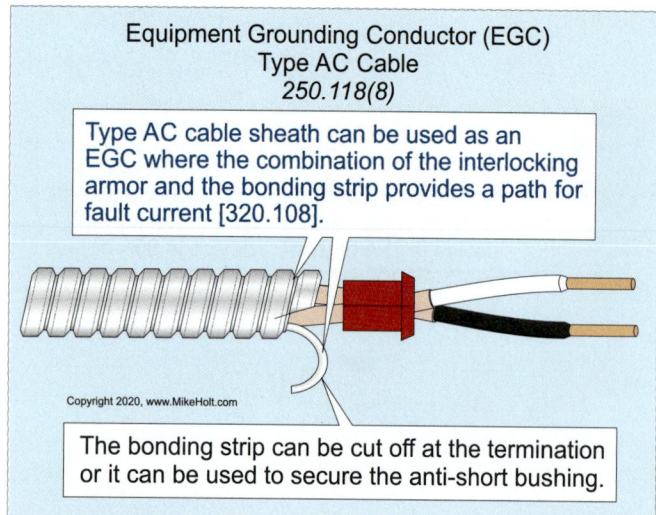
▶Figure 250–216

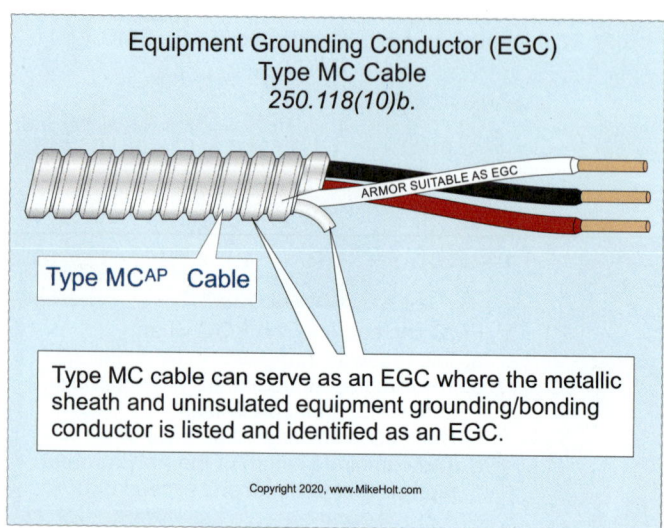
▶Figure 250–218

(10) Type MC cable:

   a. That contains an insulated or uninsulated equipment grounding conductor. ▶Figure 250–217

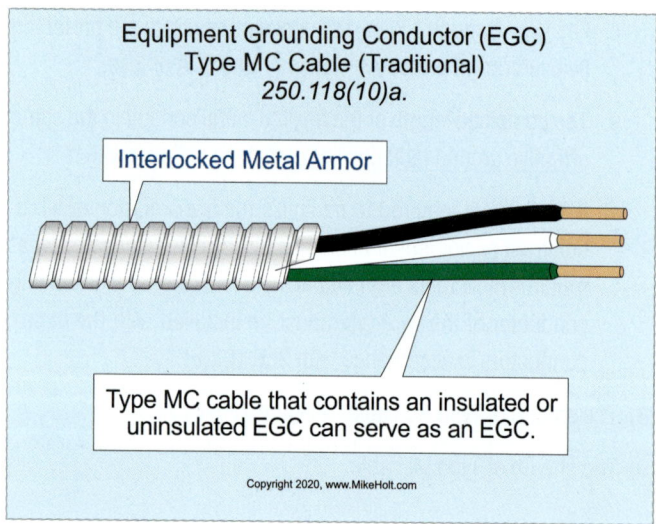
▶Figure 250–217

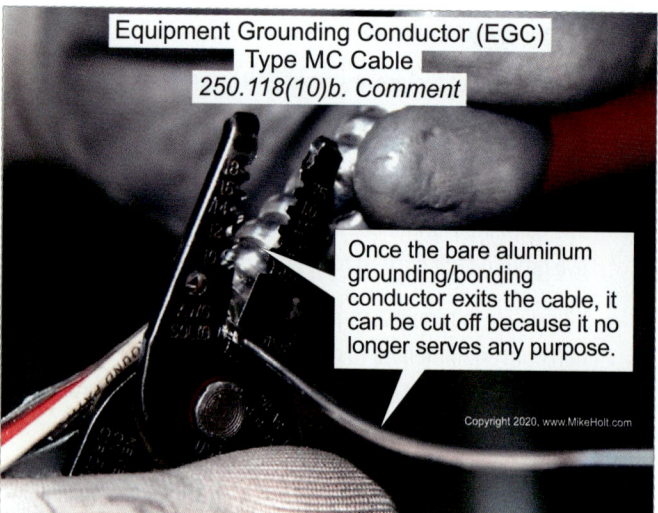
▶Figure 250–219

   b. Where the metallic sheath and uninsulated equipment grounding/bonding conductor is listed and identified as an equipment grounding conductor. ▶Figure 250–218

   Author's Comment:

   ▶ Once the bare aluminum grounding/bonding conductor of Type MC cable exits the cable it can be cut off because it no longer serves any purpose. The effective ground-fault current path must be maintained by the use of fittings specifically listed for Type MC$^{AP®}$ cable [330.6]. See 300.12, 300.15, and 330.108. ▶Figure 250–219

   c. When the metallic sheath of smooth or corrugated tube-type MC cable is listed and identified as an equipment grounding conductor it can serve as an equipment grounding conductor.

(11) Metal cable trays if continuous maintenance and supervision ensure only qualified persons will service the cable tray; the cable tray and fittings are identified for grounding; and the cable tray, fittings [392.10], and raceways are bonded together using bolted mechanical connectors or bonding jumpers sized and installed in accordance with 250.102 [392.60]. ▶Figure 250–220

(13) Other listed electrically continuous metal raceways such as metal wireways [Article 376] or strut-type channel raceways [384.60]. ▶Figure 250–221

Grounding and Bonding | 250.119

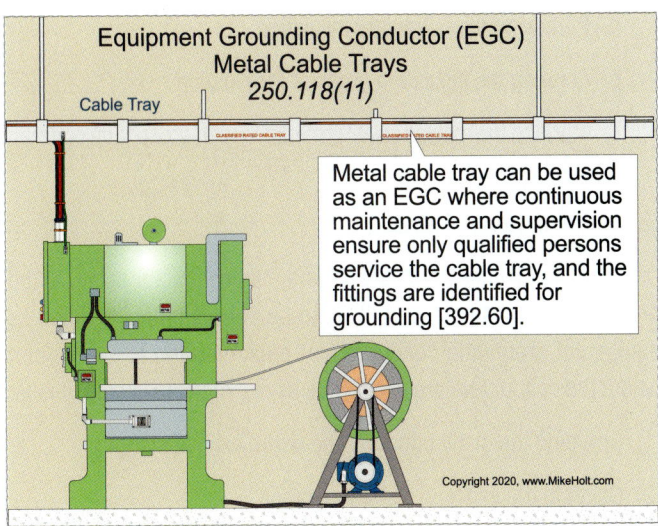
▶Figure 250-220

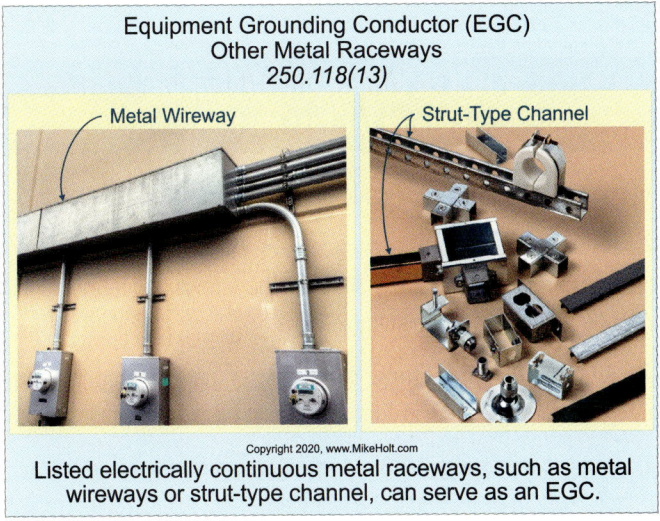
▶Figure 250-221

(14) Surface metal raceways listed for grounding [Article 386].

Note: For a definition of effective ground-fault current path, see Article 100.

Author's Comment:

▸ Listed offset nipples and metal fittings for metal cable, conduit, and tubing are considered suitable for grounding circuits where installed in accordance with the *NEC*, except as noted for flexible metal conduit fittings and liquid-tight flexible metal conduit fittings. See UL Product Spec™ *Guide, Information for "Conduit Fittings" (DWTT)*.

250.119 Identification of Equipment Grounding Conductors

Unless required to be insulated in this *Code*, equipment grounding conductors can be bare or covered.

Insulated equipment grounding conductors 6 AWG and smaller must have a continuous outer finish that is either green or green with one or more yellow stripes. ▶Figure 250-222

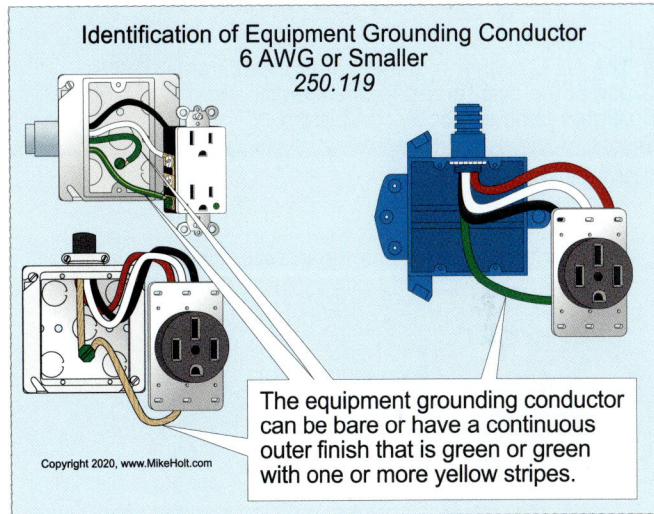
▶Figure 250-222

Conductors with insulation that is green, or green with one or more yellow stripes, are not permitted to be used for a phase or neutral conductor.

Author's Comment:

▸ The *NEC* neither requires nor prohibits the use of the color green for the identification of grounding electrode conductors. ▶Figure 250-223

(A) Conductors 4 AWG and Larger.

(1) Identified Where Accessible. Insulated equipment grounding conductors 4 AWG and larger can be reidentified at the time of installation where the conductor is accessible. ▶Figure 250-224

(2) Identification Methods. Identification must encircle the conductor and be accomplished by: ▶Figure 250-225

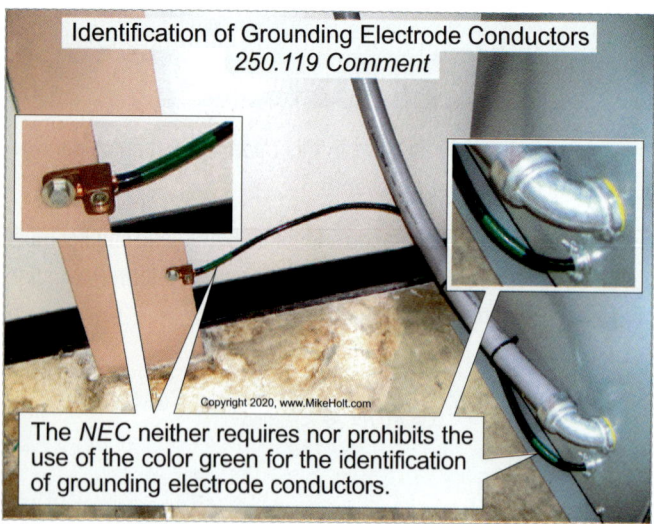
▶Figure 250-223

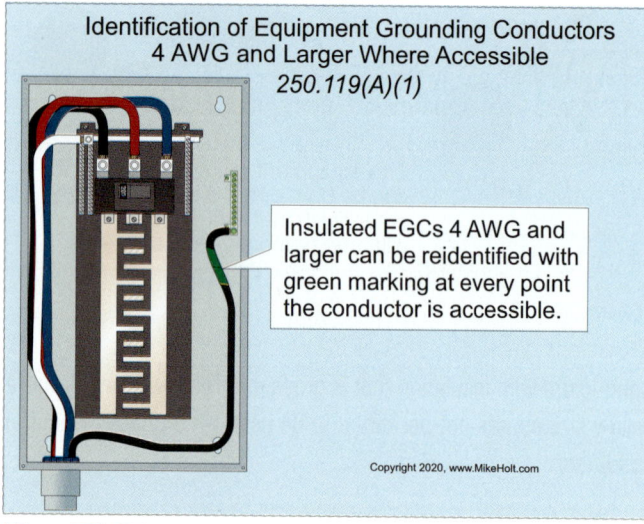
▶Figure 250-224

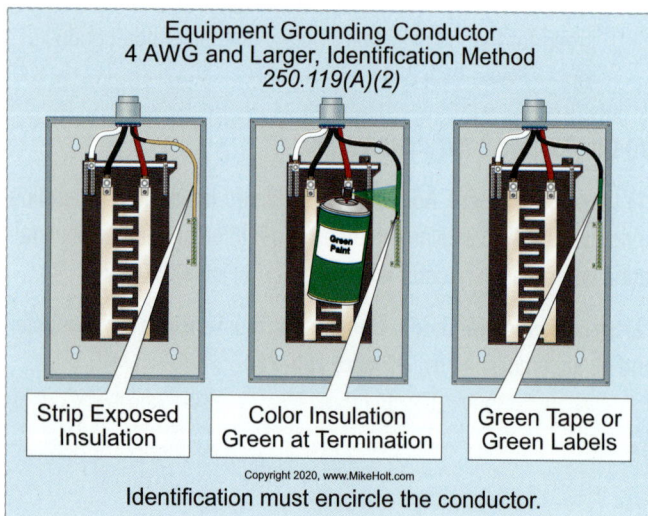
▶Figure 250-225

a. Removing the conductor insulation

b. Coloring the insulation green at termination

c. Marking the insulation at termination with green tape or green adhesive labels

(B) Multiconductor Cable.

One or more insulated conductors in a multiconductor cable, at the time of installation, are permitted to be permanently identified as equipment grounding conductors at each end and at every point where the conductors are accessible by one of the following means:

(1) Stripping the insulation from the entire exposed length.

(2) Coloring the exposed insulation green.

(3) Marking the exposed insulation with green tape or green adhesive labels. Identification must encircle the conductor.

250.120 Equipment Grounding Conductor Installation

An equipment grounding conductor must be installed as follows:

(A) Fittings Made Tight. For raceways, cable trays, cable armor, cablebus framework, or cable sheaths, the fittings and terminations must be made tight using suitable tools.

(B) Aluminum Conductors. Equipment grounding conductors of bare, covered, or insulated aluminum must be installed as follows:

(1) Unless part of a Chapter 3 wiring method, bare or covered conductors are not permitted to be installed where subject to corrosive conditions or in direct contact with concrete, masonry, or the Earth.

(2) Terminations made within outdoor enclosures that are listed and identified for the environment are permitted within 18 in. of the bottom of the enclosure.

(3) Aluminum conductors external to buildings or enclosures are not permitted to be terminated within 18 in. of the Earth, unless terminated within a listed wire connector system.

(C) Exposed. Exposed equipment grounding conductors 8 AWG and smaller for direct-current circuits [250.134(B) Ex.2], such as required by 690.45 for solar PV systems, are permitted to be run separately from the circuit conductors. 8 AWG or smaller exposed equipment grounding conductors must be protected from physical damage and must be installed within a raceway or cable.

Grounding and Bonding | 250.122

250.121 Restricted Use of Equipment Grounding Conductors

(A) Grounding Electrode Conductor. An equipment grounding conductor is not permitted to be used as a grounding electrode conductor. ▶Figure 250-226

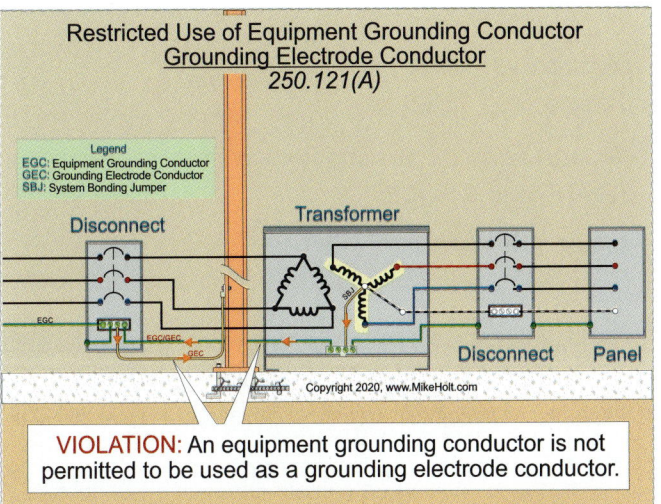

▶Figure 250-226

Ex: An equipment grounding conductor meeting the requirements for an equipment grounding conductor and grounding electrode conductor can be used as a grounding electrode conductor.

(B) Metal Frame of Building. The structural metal frame of a building must not be used as an equipment grounding conductor.

> **Author's Comment:**
> ▸ Here is a perfect example of why it is so important for you have a complete understanding of the terminology used throughout the *Code*. While the structural metal frame of a building is not permitted to be used as an "equipment grounding conductor," the metal structure of a building is permitted to be used as a "grounding electrode conductor." Knowing the difference, is what makes the difference!

250.122 Sizing Equipment Grounding Conductors

(A) General. Equipment grounding conductors must be sized not smaller than shown in Table 250.122; however, the equipment grounding conductor is not required to be larger than the phase conductors. ▶Figure 250-227

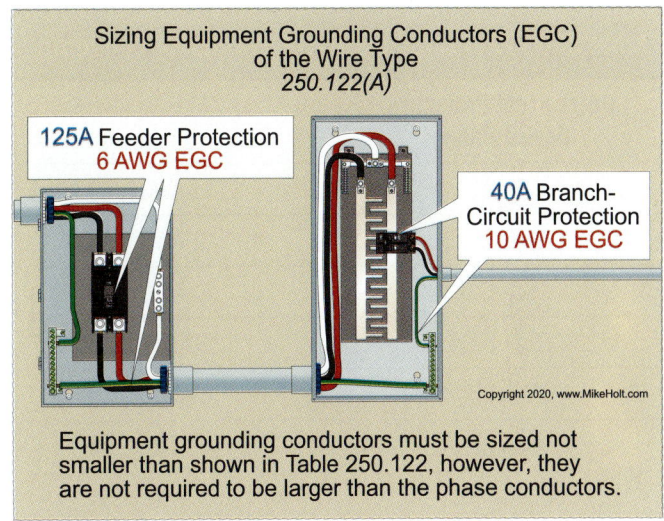

▶Figure 250-227

(B) Increased in Size. If phase conductors are increased in size for any reason other than as required in 310.15(B) or 310.15(C), wire-type equipment grounding conductors, if installed, must be increased in size proportionately to the increase in the circular mil area of the phase conductors. ▶Figure 250-228

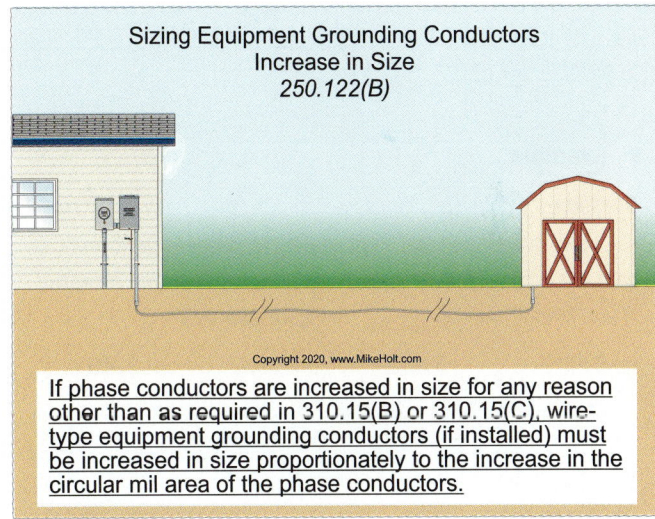

▶Figure 250-228

Ex: Equipment grounding conductors can be sized by a qualified person to provide an effective ground-fault current path in accordance with 250.4(A)(5) or (B)(4).

> **Author's Comment:**
> ▸ Phase conductors are sometimes increased in size to accommodate conductor voltage drop, short-circuit rating, or simply for future capacity.

250.122 | Grounding and Bonding

Table 250.122 Sizing Equipment Grounding Conductor

Overcurrent Protective Device Rating	Copper Conductor
15A	14 AWG
20A	12 AWG
25A–60A	10 AWG
70A–100A	8 AWG
110A–200A	6 AWG
225A–300A	4 AWG
350A–400A	3 AWG
450A–500A	2 AWG
600A	1 AWG
700A–800A	1/0 AWG
1,000A	2/0 AWG
1,200A	3/0 AWG

Note: Where necessary to comply with 250.4(A)(5) or (B)(4), the equipment grounding conductor might be required to be sized larger than given in this table.

▶ **Example**

Question: If the phase conductors for a 40A circuit (with 75°C terminals) are increased in size from 8 AWG to 6 AWG due to voltage drop, the circuit equipment grounding conductor must be increased in size from 10 AWG to _____. ▶Figure 250–229

(a) 8 AWG   (b) 6 AWG   (c) 4 AWG   (d) 3 AWG

Solution:

The circular mil area of 6 AWG is 59 percent more than 8 AWG (26,240 cmil/16,510 cmil) [Chapter 9, Table 8]. According to Table 250.122, the circuit equipment grounding conductor for a 40A overcurrent protective device will be 10 AWG (10,380 cmil), but the circuit equipment grounding conductor for this circuit must be increased in size by a multiplier of 159 percent.

Conductor Size = 10,380 cmil × 159%
Conductor Size = 16,504 cmil

The circuit equipment grounding conductor must be increased to 8 AWG [Chapter 9, Table 8].

Answer: (a) 8 AWG

(C) Multiple Circuits. A single equipment grounding conductor sized in accordance with Table 250.122 when multiple circuits are installed in the same raceway, cable, trench, or cable tray. ▶Figure 250–230

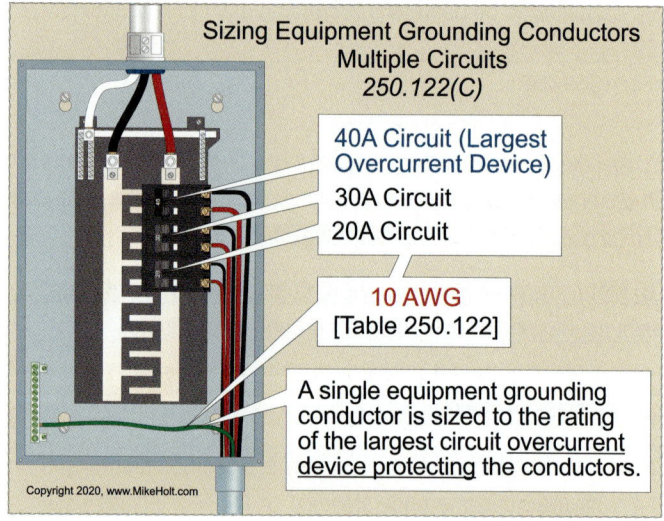

▶Figure 250–230

(D) Motor Branch Circuits. Equipment grounding conductors for motor circuits must be sized in accordance with 250.122(D)(1) or (D)(2).

(1) General. The equipment grounding conductor must not be smaller than determined by 250.122(A), based on the rating of the motor circuit branch-circuit short-circuit and ground-fault protective device sized in accordance with 430.52(C)(1) Ex 1.

Author's Comment:

▸ The equipment grounding conductor is not required to be larger than the motor circuit conductors. See 250.122(A).

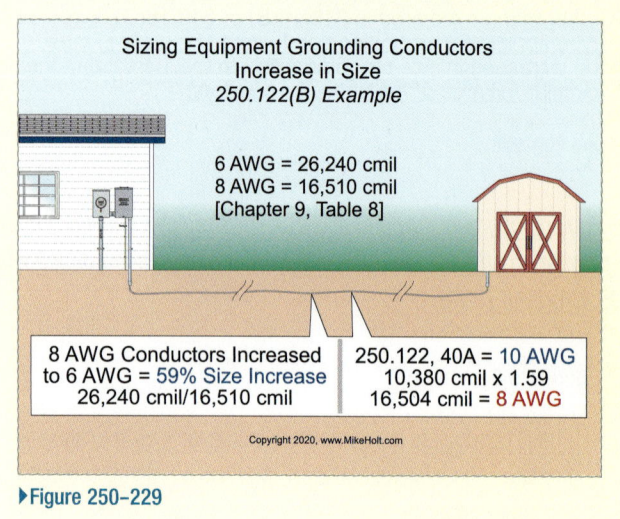

▶Figure 250–229

Grounding and Bonding | 250.122

▶ **Example**

Question: What size equipment grounding conductor of the wire type is required for a 14 AWG motor branch circuit [430.22], protected with a 2-pole, 30A circuit breaker in accordance with 430.22 and 430.52(C)(1)? ▶Figure 250-231

(a) 14 AWG   (b) 12 AWG   (c) 10 AWG   (d) 8 AWG

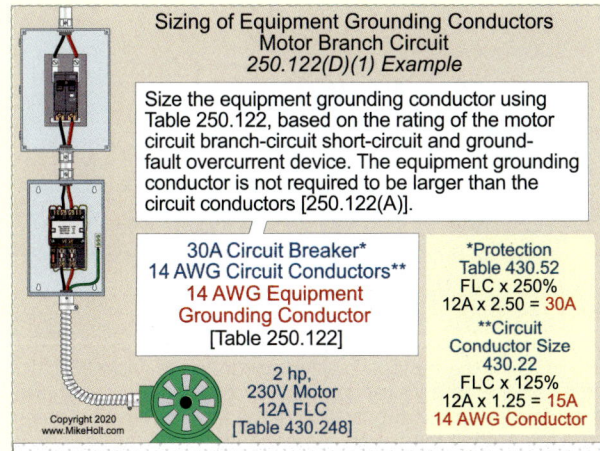

▶Figure 250-231

Solution:

The equipment grounding conductor is not required to be larger than the 14 AWG motor branch-circuit conductors [250.122(D)(1) and 250.122(A)].

Answer: (a) 14 AWG

(F) Parallel Conductors. Where circuit conductors are installed in parallel in accordance with 310.10(G), an equipment grounding conductor of the wire type must be installed in accordance with the following:

(1) Nonmetallic Raceways or Cable Trays

(a) Parallel Conductors in a Single Nonmetallic Raceway or Cable Tray. If parallel circuit conductors are installed in a single nonmetallic raceway or cable tray, a single wire-type equipment grounding conductor, sized in accordance with Table 250.122 based on the rating of the circuit overcurrent protective device, must be installed with the parallel circuit conductors.

(b) Parallel Conductors in Multiple Nonmetallic Raceways. If parallel circuit conductors are installed in multiple nonmetallic raceways, a wire-type equipment grounding conductor is required in each raceway. ▶Figure 250-232

The equipment grounding conductors in each raceway must be sized in accordance with Table 250.122. ▶Figure 250-233

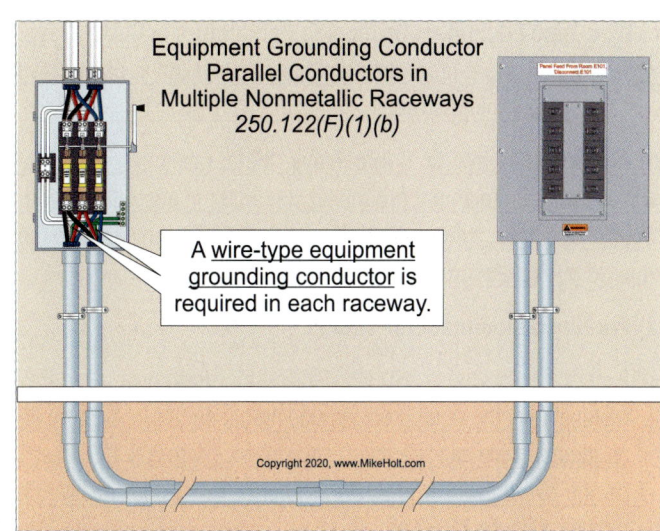

▶Figure 250-232

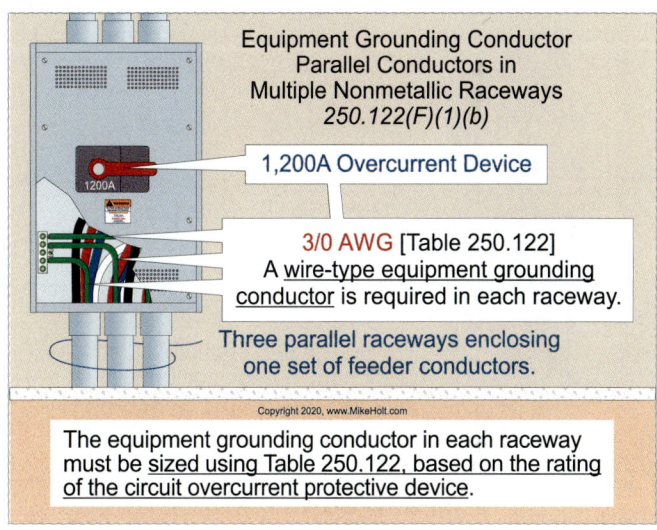

▶Figure 250-233

▶ **Example**

Question: What size copper equipment grounding conductor of the wire type is required for a 4,000A feeder containing thirteen parallel sets of 500 kcmil conductors per phase in PVC conduit?

(a) 250 kcmil   (b) 300 kcmil   (c) 400 kcmil   (d) 500 kcmil

Solution:

According to Table 250.122, the equipment grounding conductor in each raceway must not be smaller than 500 kcmil.

Answer: (d) 500 kcmil

250.134 | Grounding and Bonding

(c) Wire-Type Equipment Grounding Conductors in Cable Trays. Wire-type equipment grounding conductors installed in cable trays must meet the minimum requirements of 392.10(B)(1)(c).

(d) Metal Raceways or Cable Trays. Metal raceways can serve as the required equipment grounding conductor in accordance with 250.118 and cable trays complying with 392.60(B) can serve as the required equipment grounding conductor.

(2) Parallel Multiconductor Cables.

(a) Except as provided in 250.122(F)(2)(c) for raceway or cable tray installations, the equipment grounding conductor in each multiconductor cable must be sized in accordance with 250.122, based on the overcurrent protective device for the feeder or branch circuit. ▶Figure 250–234

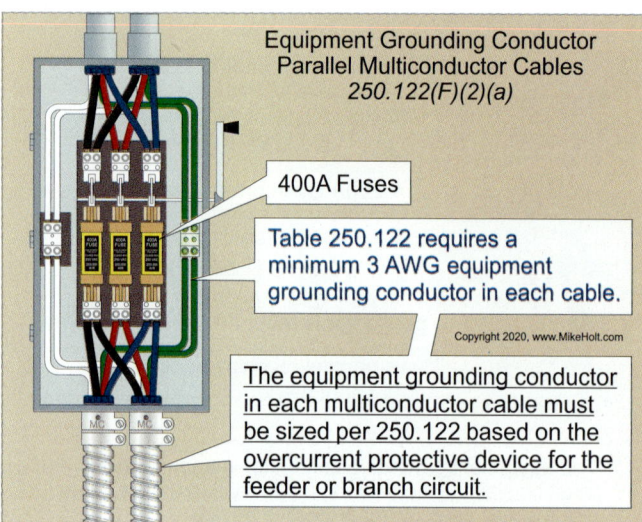

▶Figure 250–234

(b) If circuit conductors of multiconductor cables are connected in parallel, the equipment grounding conductor(s) in each cable must be connected in parallel.

(c) If multiconductor cables are paralleled in the same raceway or cable tray, a single equipment grounding conductor sized in accordance with 250.122 is permitted in combination with the equipment grounding conductors provided within the multiconductor cables and all equipment grounding conductors must be connected together.

(d) Equipment grounding conductors installed in cable trays must meet the requirements of 392.10(B)(1)(c).

Cable trays complying with 392.60(B) and metal raceways in accordance with 250.118 can be used as the required equipment grounding conductor.

(G) Feeder Tap Conductors. Equipment grounding conductors for feeder taps are not permitted to be smaller than shown in Table 250.122, based on the ampere rating of the overcurrent device ahead of the feeder on the supply side of the tap. The feeder equipment grounding conductor for the feeder tap is not be required to be larger than the tap conductors. ▶Figure 250–235

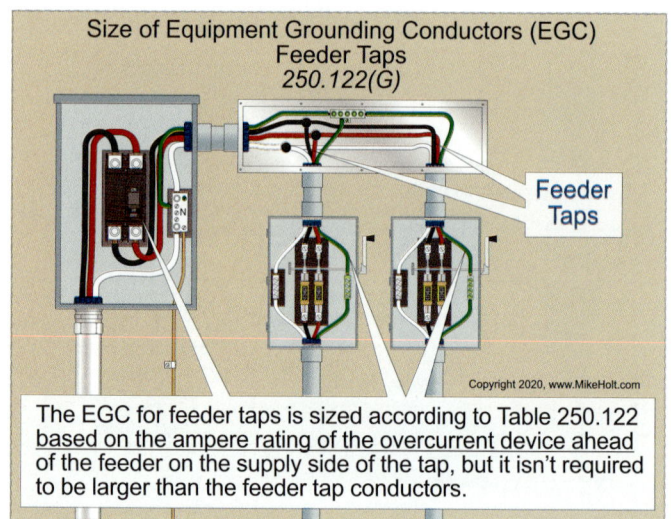

▶Figure 250–235

Part VII. Methods of Equipment Grounding Conductor Connections

250.134 Equipment Connected by Permanent Wiring Methods

Except as permitted for services or separately derived systems [250.142(A)], metal parts of equipment, raceways, and enclosures must be connected to an equipment grounding conductor by any of the following methods:

(1) Equipment Grounding Conductor. By connecting to one of the equipment grounding conductor types identified in 250.118(2) through (14).

(2) With Circuit Conductors. Where an equipment grounding conductor of the wire type is installed, it must be contained within the same raceway, cable tray, trench, cable, or flexible cord as the circuit conductors. ▶Figure 250–236

Ex 2: For direct-current circuits, the equipment grounding conductor is permitted to be run separately from the circuit conductors. ▶Figure 250–237

Grounding and Bonding | 250.140

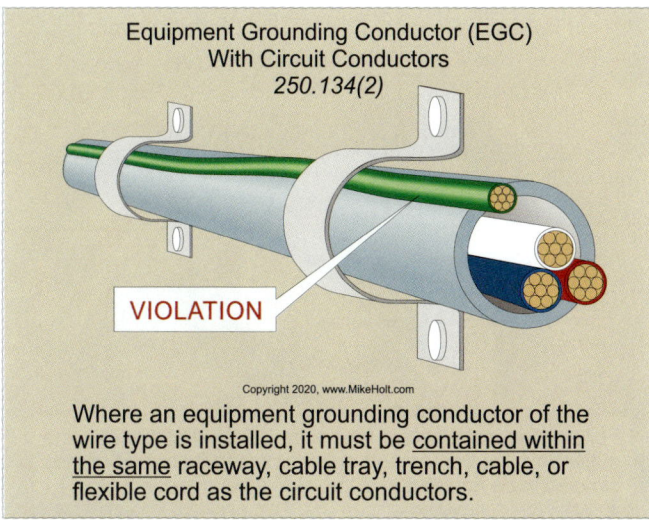
▶Figure 250–236

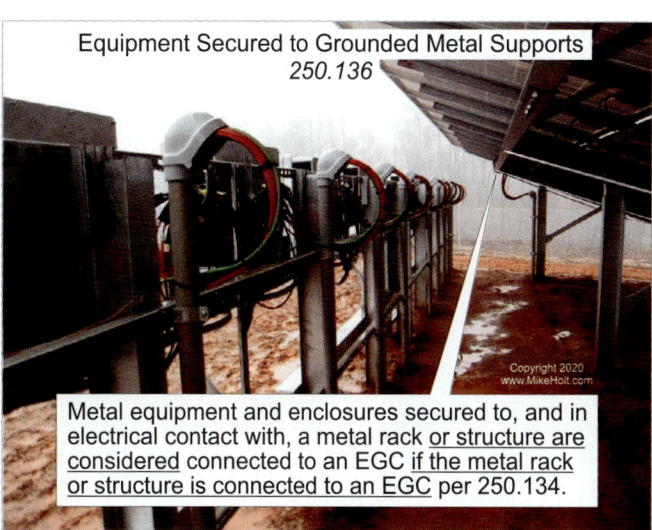
▶Figure 250–238

▶Figure 250–237

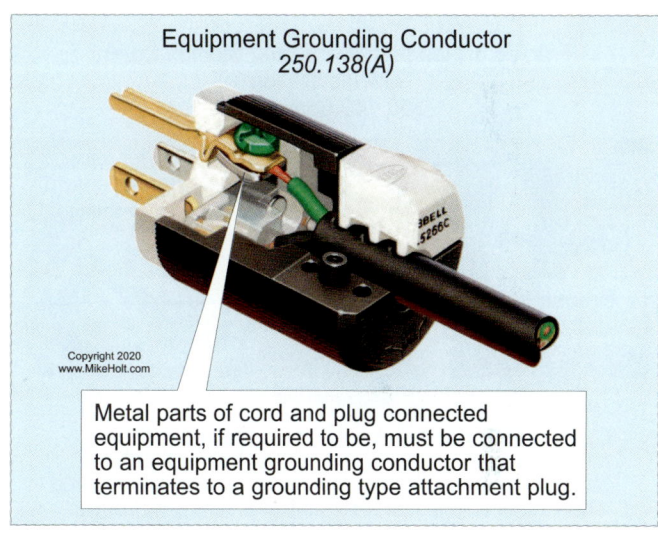
▶Figure 250–239

250.136 Equipment Secured to Grounded Metal Supports

Metal equipment and enclosures secured to and in electrical contact with a metal rack or structure are considered connected to an equipment grounding conductor if the metal rack or structure is connected to an equipment grounding conductor in accordance with 250.134. ▶Figure 250–238

250.138 Cord-and-Plug-Connected

(A) Equipment Grounding Conductor. Metal parts of cord-and-plug-connected equipment must be connected to an equipment grounding conductor that terminates to a grounding-type attachment plug. ▶Figure 250–239

250.140 Frames of Ranges, Ovens, and Clothes Dryers

The frames of electric ranges, wall-mounted ovens, counter-mounted cooking units, clothes dryers, and outlet boxes that are part of the circuit for these appliances must be connected to the circuit equipment grounding conductor in accordance with 250.134. ▶Figure 250–240

> **Caution**
>
> ⚡ Ranges, dryers, and ovens may have their metal cases connected to the neutral conductor at the factory. This neutral-to-case connection must be removed when these appliances are installed in new construction, and a 4-wire flexible cord and receptacle must be used [250.142(B)]. ▶Figure 250–241

250.142 | Grounding and Bonding

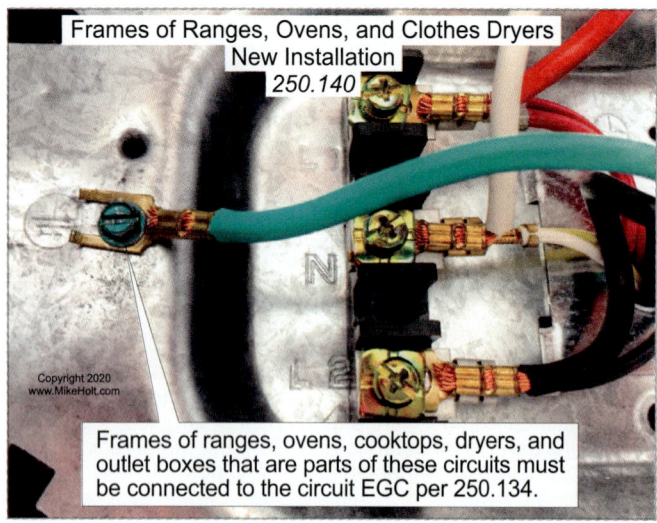
▶Figure 250–240

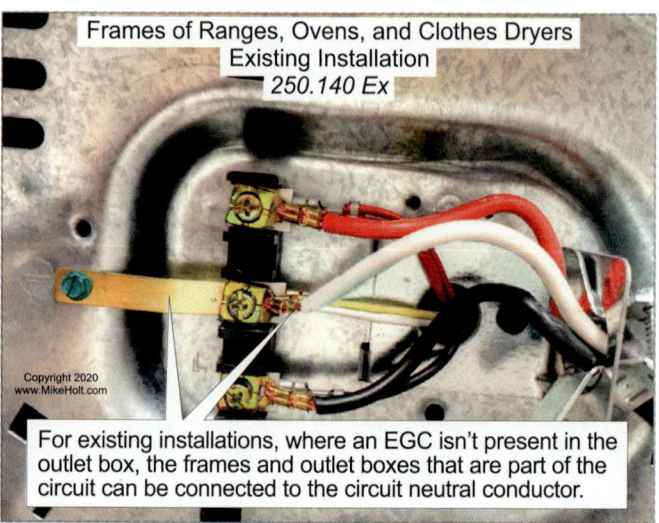
▶Figure 250–242

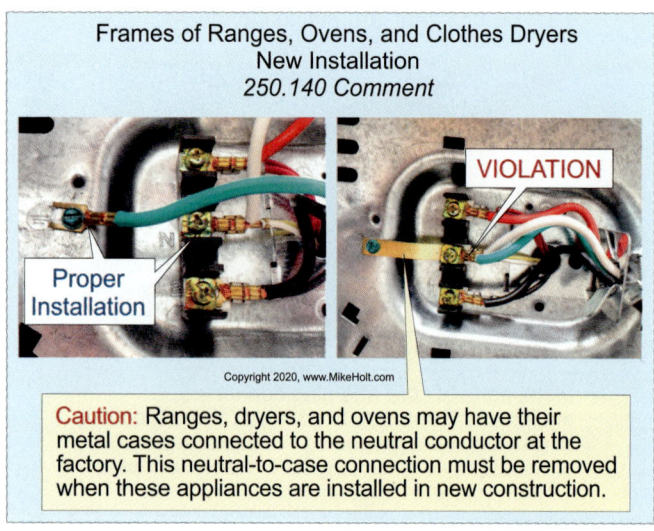
▶Figure 250–241

Ex: For existing installations, if an equipment grounding conductor is not present in the outlet box, the frames of electric ranges, wall-mounted ovens, counter-mounted cooking units, clothes dryers, and outlet boxes that are part of the circuit for these appliances may be connected to the circuit's neutral conductor. ▶Figure 250–242

250.142 Neutral Conductor for Effective Ground-Fault Current Path

(A) Services and Separately Derived Systems. The neutral conductor is permitted to be connected to metal parts of equipment, raceways, and enclosures for the purpose of serving as the effective ground-fault current path for fault current returning to the source at any of the following locations:

(1) Services. On the supply side of service disconnect in accordance with 250.24(A). ▶Figure 250–243

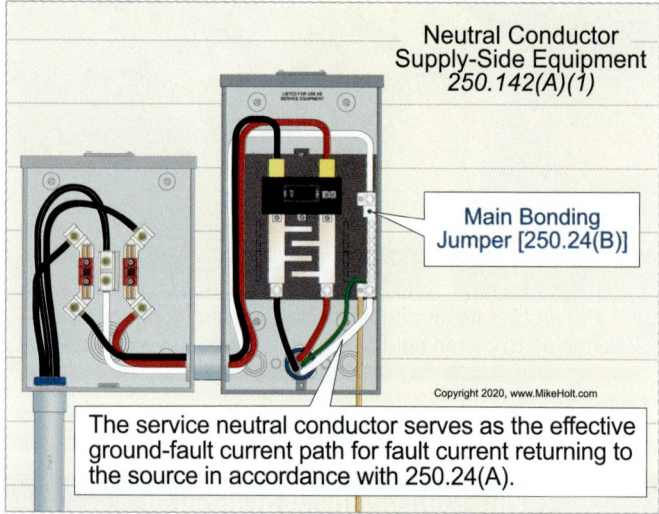
▶Figure 250–243

Author's Comment:

▶ The neutral-to-case connection between the service neutral conductor and the service-disconnect enclosure is accomplished by the required installation of the main bonding jumper in accordance with 250.24(B).

(2) Main Disconnect. On the supply side or within the enclosure of the main disconnecting means for separate buildings as provided in 250.32(B)(1) Ex 1.

(3) Separately Derived Systems. On the supply side or within the separately derived system disconnect in accordance with 250.30(A)(1).

Grounding and Bonding | 250.146

Author's Comment:

▸ The neutral-to-case connection between the separately derived system's secondary neutral conductor and the equipment grounding conductor is accomplished by the required installation of the system bonding jumper in accordance with 250.30(A)(1).

(B) Equipment on Load Side of Service Disconnect. Except as permitted in 250.142(A), the neutral conductor is not permitted to be connected to the equipment grounding conductor on the load side of the service disconnect [250.24] or separately derived system disconnect [250.30(A)]. ▸Figure 250–244

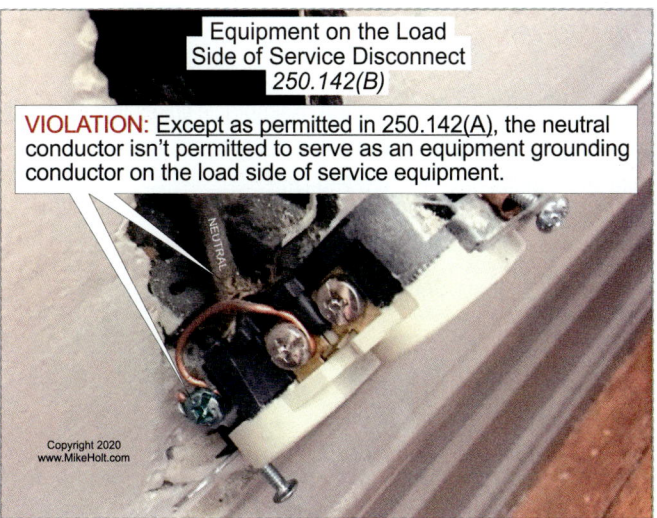
▸Figure 250–244

Ex 1: In existing installations, the frames of ranges, wall-mounted ovens, counter-mounted cooking units, and clothes dryers can be connected to the neutral conductor in accordance with 250.140 Ex.

Ex 2: The neutral conductor can be connected to meter socket enclosures on the load side of the service disconnect if: ▸Figure 250–245

(1) Ground-fault protection of equipment is not provided on service disconnect,

(2) Meter socket enclosures are immediately adjacent to the service disconnect, and

(3) The neutral conductor is sized in accordance with 250.122.

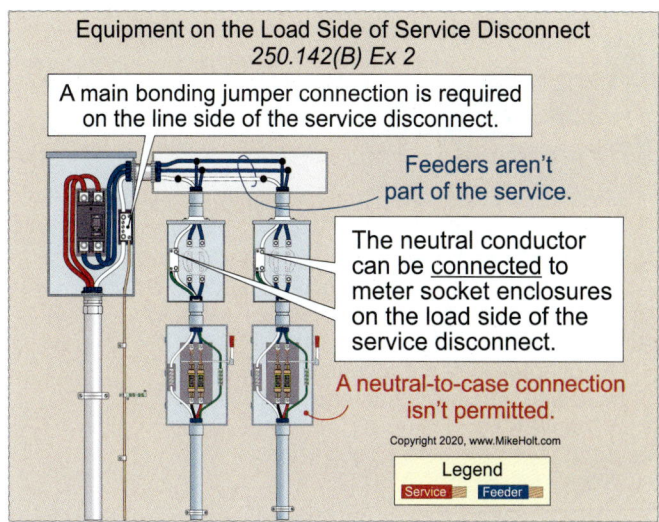
▸Figure 250–245

250.146 Connecting Receptacle Grounding Terminal to an Equipment Grounding Conductor

An equipment bonding jumper is required to connect the grounding contacts of a receptacle to a metal box connected to an equipment grounding conductor, except as permitted in (A) through (D). ▸Figure 250–246

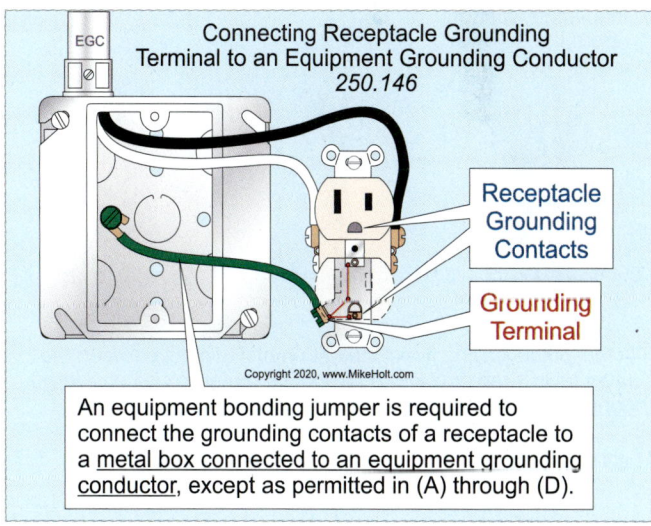
▸Figure 250–246

Author's Comment:

▸ The *NEC* does not restrict the position of the receptacle grounding terminal; it can be up, down, or sideways. *Code* proposals to specify the mounting position of receptacles have always been rejected. ▸Figure 250–247

250.146 | Grounding and Bonding

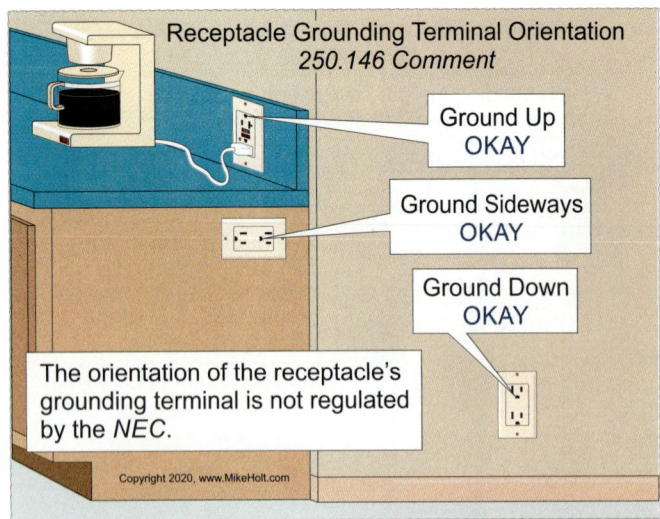
▶Figure 250–247

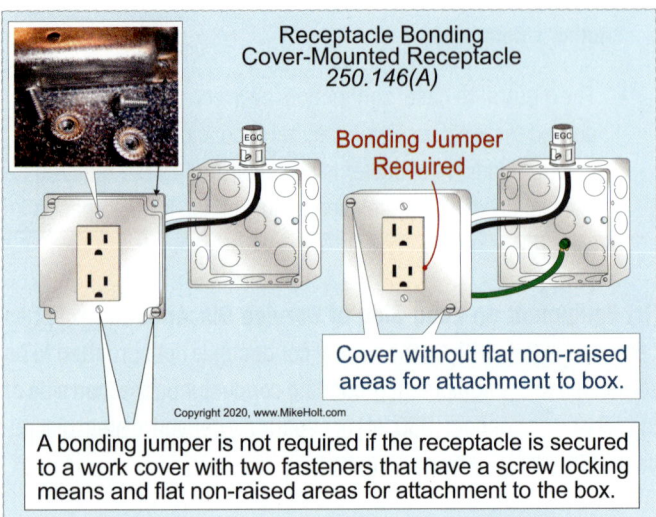
▶Figure 250–249

(A) Surface-Mounted Box. A receptacle having direct metal-to-metal contact between the receptacle strap or yoke and a surface metal box is considered to be connected to the required effective ground-fault current path. To ensure sufficient metal-to-metal contact, at least one of the insulating retaining washers on the yoke screw must be removed. ▶Figure 250–248

(B) Self-Grounding Receptacles. Receptacle yokes listed as self-grounding establish the equipment bonding between the receptacle yoke and a metal box. ▶Figure 250–250

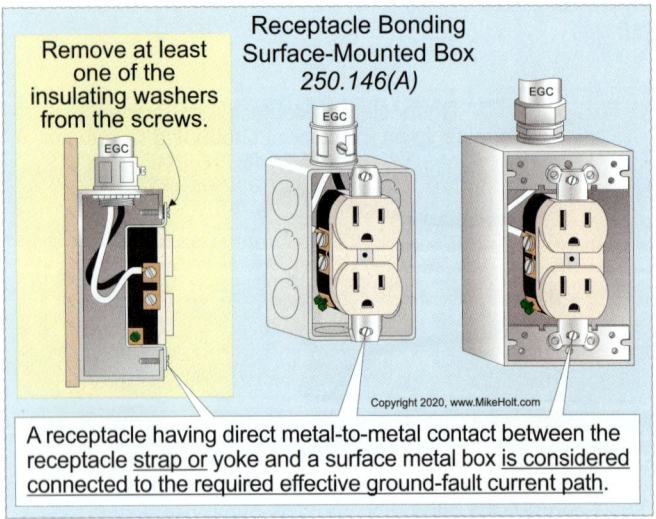
▶Figure 250–248

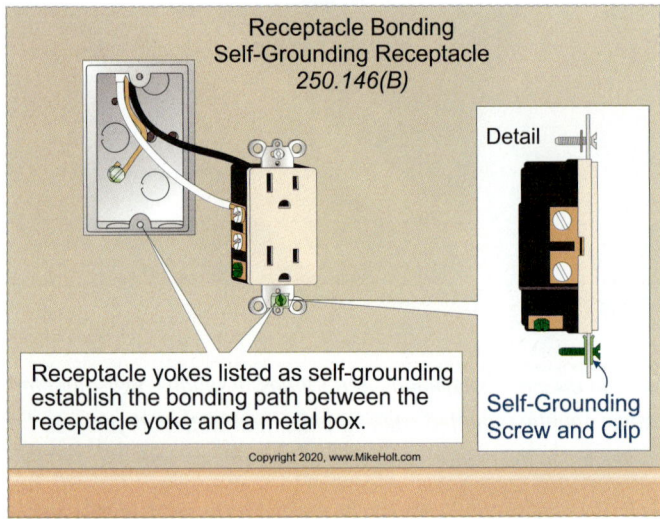
▶Figure 250–250

A receptacle installed on a cover is considered to be connected to the required effective ground-fault current path under both of the following conditions:

(1) The receptacle is attached to the metal cover with at least two fasteners that have a thread locking, or screw or nut locking means.

(2) The cover mounting holes are located on a flat non-raised portion of the cover. ▶Figure 250–249

(C) Floor Boxes. Listed metal floor boxes must establish the bonding path between the receptacle yoke and a metal box.

(D) Isolated Ground Receptacles. The grounding terminal of an isolated ground receptacle must be connected to an insulated equipment grounding conductor. ▶Figure 250–251

Note: Use of an isolated equipment grounding conductor does not relieve the requirement for connecting the raceway system and outlet box to an equipment grounding conductor. ▶Figure 250–252

Grounding and Bonding | 250.146

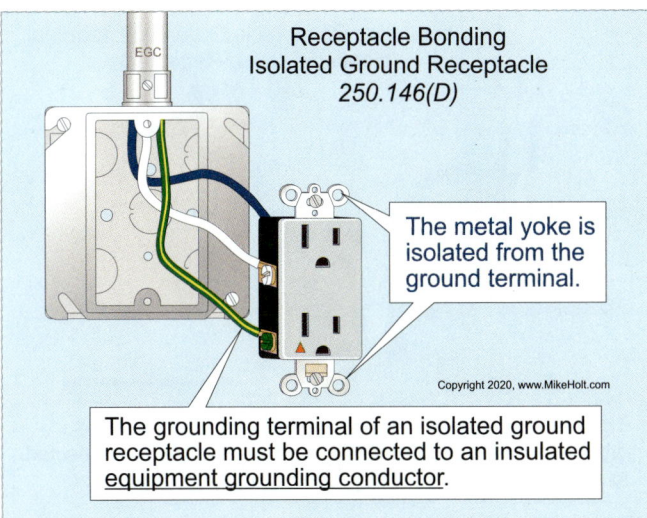
▶Figure 250–251

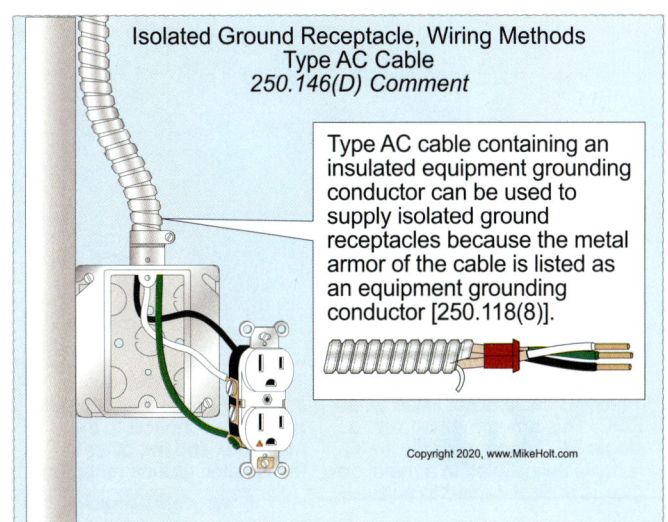
▶Figure 250–253

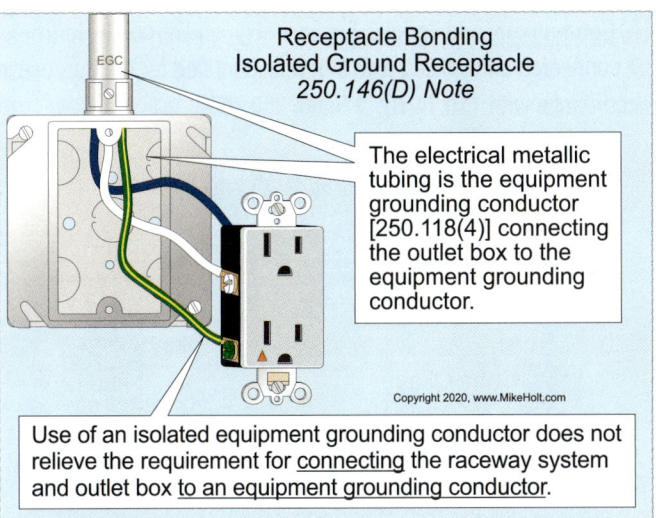
▶Figure 250–252

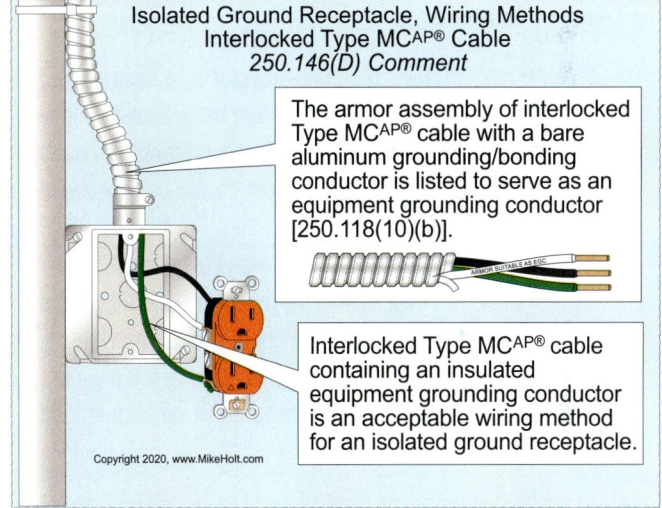
▶Figure 250–254

Author's Comment:

- Type AC cable containing an insulated equipment grounding conductor can be used to supply isolated ground receptacles because the metal armor of the cable is listed as an equipment grounding conductor [250.118(8)]. ▶Figure 250–253

- Interlocked Type MC$^{AP®}$ cable with a 10 AWG bare aluminum grounding/bonding conductor can be used to supply isolated ground receptacles because the combination of the metal armor and the 10 AWG bare aluminum conductor is listed as an equipment grounding conductor [250.118(10)(b)]. An interlocked Type MC$^{AP®}$ cable is an acceptable wiring method to use for an isolated ground receptacle. ▶Figure 250–254

Caution

⚡ *Type MC Cable.* The metal armor sheath of traditional interlocked Type MC cable containing an insulated equipment grounding conductor is not listed as an equipment grounding conductor. Therefore, this wiring method with a single equipment grounding conductor cannot supply an isolated ground receptacle. Type MC cable with two insulated equipment grounding conductors is acceptable, since one bonds to the metal box and the other one connects to the isolated ground receptacle. ▶Figure 250–255

250.148 | Grounding and Bonding

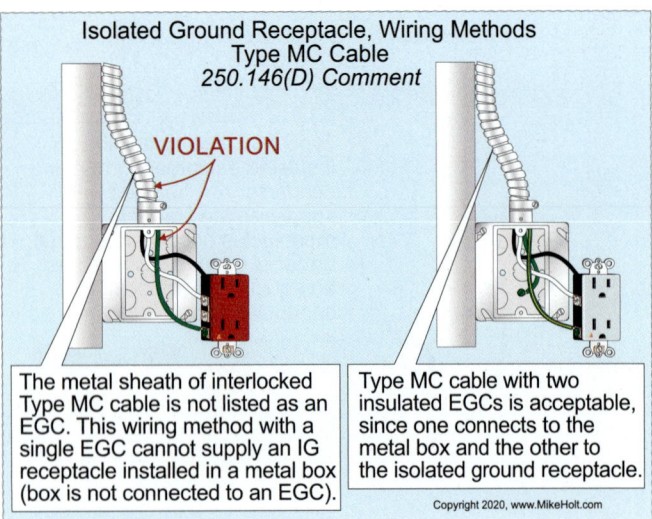

▶Figure 250–255

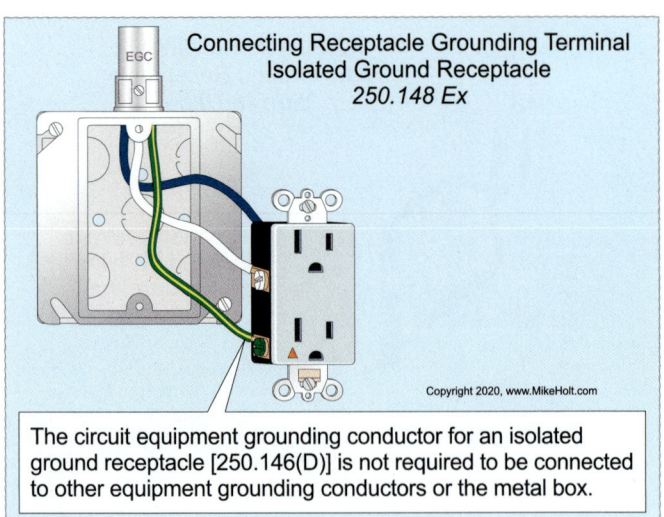

▶Figure 250–256

Author's Comment:

▸ When should an isolated ground receptacle be installed and how should the isolated ground system be designed? These questions are design issues and are not answered based on the *NEC* alone [90.1(A)]. In most cases, using isolated ground receptacles is a waste of money. For example, IEEE 1100, *Powering and Grounding Electronic Equipment (Emerald Book)* states, "The results from the use of the isolated ground method range from no observable effects, the desired effects, or worse noise conditions than when standard equipment bonding configurations are used to serve electronic load equipment [8.5.3.2]."

▸ In reality, few electrical installations truly require an isolated ground system. For those systems that can benefit from one, engineering opinions differ as to what is a proper design. Making matters worse—of those properly designed, few are correctly installed and even fewer are properly maintained.

250.148 Continuity and Attachment of Equipment Grounding Conductors in Boxes

Equipment grounding conductors associated with circuit conductors that are spliced or terminated on equipment within a box must be connected in, or to, the box in accordance with 250.8 and 250.148(A) through (D).

Ex: The circuit equipment grounding conductor for an isolated ground receptacle [250.146(D)] is not required to be connected to the other equipment grounding conductors or to the metal box. ▶Figure 250–256

(A) Connections and Splices. Equipment grounding conductors must be connected and spliced with a device identified for the purpose in accordance with 110.14(B). ▶Figure 250–257

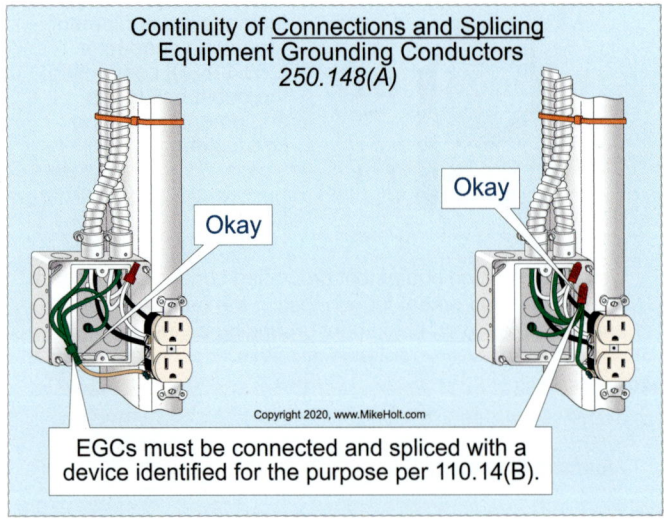

▶Figure 250–257

(B) Continuity of Equipment Grounding Conductors. Equipment grounding conductors must terminate in such a manner that the disconnection or removal of a receptacle, luminaire, or other device will not interrupt the electrical continuity of the equipment grounding conductor(s) providing an effective ground-fault current path. ▶Figure 250–258

(C) Metal Boxes. Equipment grounding conductors for circuit conductors that are spliced or terminated on equipment within a metal box must be spliced together [250.148] and have a connection to the metal box in accordance with 250.8. ▶Figure 250–259

Grounding and Bonding | 250.148

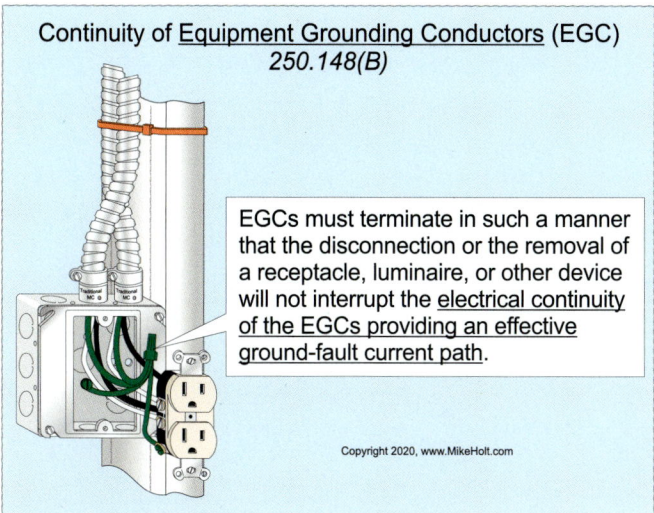

▶Figure 250-258

Author's Comment:

▸ Equipment grounding conductors are not permitted to terminate to a screw that secures a plaster ring. ▶Figure 250-260

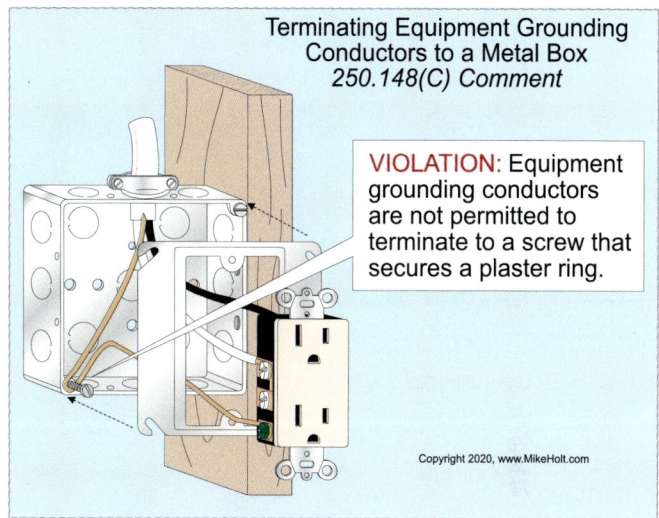

▶Figure 250-260

(D) Nonmetallic Boxes. Equipment grounding conductors in a nonmetallic outlet box must be arranged such that a connection can be made to any fitting or device in that box requiring connection to an equipment grounding conductor.

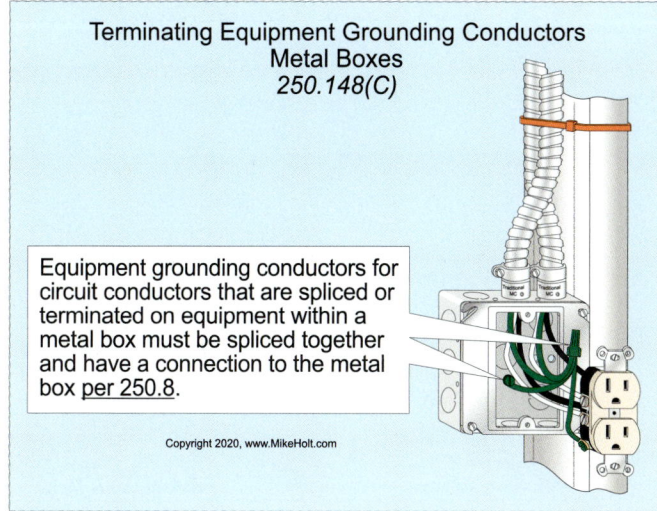

▶Figure 250-259

Notes

CHAPTER 3
WIRING METHODS AND MATERIALS

Introduction to Chapter 3—Wiring Methods and Materials

Chapter 3 focuses on wiring methods and materials, and provides some very specific installation requirements for conductors, cables, boxes, raceways, and fittings. This chapter includes detailed information about the installations and restrictions involved with wiring methods. Not fully understanding the information in this chapter may be the reason many people incorrectly apply these rules. Pay careful attention to each and every detail to be sure your installations comply with these requirements. Disregarding the rules for the wiring methods found in Chapter 3 can result in problems with power quality and can lead to fire, shock, and overall poor installations. The type of wiring method you will use depends on several factors; job specifications, *Code* requirements, the environment, need, the type of building construction, and cost effectiveness just to name a few.

Chapter 3 begins with rules that are common to most wiring methods [Article 300]. It then covers conductors [Article 310], cabinets, cutout boxes, and meter socket enclosures [Article 312], and boxes and conduit bodies [Article 314]. The articles that follow become more specific and deal more in-depth with individual wiring methods such as specific types of cables [Articles 320 through 340] and various raceways [Articles 342 through 390]. The chapter winds up with Article 392, a support system.

Notice as you read through the various wiring methods that the *Code* attempts to use similar section numbering for similar topics from one article to the next, using the same digits after the decimal point in the section number for the same topic. This makes it easier to locate the specific requirements of a particular article. For example, the rules for securing and supporting can be found in the section that ends with ".30" of each article.

Wiring Method Articles

▶ **Article 300—General Requirements for Wiring Methods and Materials.** Article 300 contains the general requirements for all wiring methods included in the *NEC*, except for signaling and communications systems (communications, antennas, and coaxial cable), which are covered in Chapters 7 and 8.

▶ **Article 310—Conductors for General Wiring.** This article contains the general requirements for conductors, such as insulation markings, ampacity ratings, and conductor use. There is also a section that addresses single family dwelling service and feeder conductors exclusively. Article 310 does not apply to conductors that are part of flexible cords, fixture wires, or conductors that are an integral part of equipment [90.7 and 310.1].

▶ **Article 312—Cabinets and Meter Socket Enclosures.** Article 312 covers the installation and construction specifications for cabinets and meter socket enclosures.

▶ **Article 314—Outlet, Device, Pull, and Junction Boxes; Conduit Bodies; Fittings; and Handhole Enclosures.** Installation requirements for outlet boxes, pull and junction boxes, as well as conduit bodies and handhole enclosures are contained in this article.

...

Chapter 3 | Wiring Methods and Materials

Cable Articles

Articles 320 through 340 address specific types of cables. If you take the time to become familiar with the various types of cables, you will be able to:

- Understand what is available for doing the work.
- Recognize cable types that have special *NEC* requirements.
- Avoid buying cable you cannot install due to *Code* requirements you cannot meet with that particular wiring method.

Here is a brief overview of those included in this book:

- **Article 320—Armored Cable (Type AC).** Armored cable is an assembly of insulated conductors, 14 AWG through 1 AWG, individually wrapped with wax paper. The conductors are contained within a flexible metal (steel or aluminum) spiral sheath that interlocks at the edges. Armored cable looks like flexible metal conduit. Many electricians call this metal cable "BX®."

- **Article 330—Metal-Clad Cable (Type MC).** Metal-clad cable encloses insulated conductors in a metal sheath of either corrugated or smooth copper or aluminum tubing, or spiral interlocked steel or aluminum. The physical characteristics of Type MC cable make it a versatile wiring method permitted in almost any location and for almost any application. The most commonly used Type MC cable is the interlocking kind, which looks similar to armored cable or flexible metal conduit.

- **Article 334—Nonmetallic-Sheathed Cable (Type NM).** Nonmetallic-sheathed cable is commonly referred to by its trade name "Romex®." It encloses two, three, or four insulated conductors, 14 AWG through 2 AWG, within a nonmetallic outer jacket. Because this cable is manufactured in this manner, it contains a separate (usually bare) equipment grounding conductor. Nonmetallic-sheathed cable is most commonly used for residential wiring applications but may sometimes be permitted for use in commercial occupancies.

- **Article 336—Power and Control Tray Cable (Type TC).** Power and control tray cable is flexible, inexpensive, and easily installed. It provides very limited physical protection for the conductors, so the installation restrictions are rigorous. Its low cost and relative ease of installation make it a common wiring method for industrial applications.

- **Article 338—Service-Entrance Cable (Types SE and USE).** Service-entrance and underground service-entrance cables can be a single conductor or a multiconductor assembly within an overall nonmetallic outer jacket or covering. These cables are most often used for services not over 1,000V, but are also permitted for feeders and branch circuits. When used as a service conductor(s) or a service-entrance conductor(s), pre-manufactured Type "SE" cable assemblies will typically contain two insulated phase conductors and a bare neutral conductor. When permitted for use as a feeder or branch circuit, Type SE cable is usually designated as Type "SER" and will contain the same three conductors as Type SE but a fourth conductor (which is insulated) will be added to serve as the neutral conductor.

- **Article 340—Underground Feeder and Branch-Circuit Cable (Type UF).** Underground feeder cable is a moisture-, fungus-, and corrosion-resistant cable suitable for direct burial in the earth, and it comes in sizes 14 AWG through 4/0 AWG [340.104]. Multiconductor UF cable is covered in molded plastic that surrounds the insulated conductors.

Raceway Articles

Articles 342 through 390 address specific types of raceways. Refer to Article 100 for the definition of a raceway. If you take the time to become familiar with the various types of raceways, you will be able to:

- Understand what is available for doing the work.
- Recognize raceway types that have special *Code* requirements.
- Avoid buying a raceway you cannot install due to *NEC* requirements you cannot meet with that particular wiring method.

Here is a brief overview of each those included in this book:

- **Article 342—Intermediate Metal Conduit (Type IMC).** Intermediate metal conduit is a circular metal raceway with the same outside diameter as rigid metal conduit. The wall thickness of intermediate metal conduit is less than that of rigid metal conduit, so it has a larger interior cross-sectional area for holding conductors. Intermediate metal conduit is lighter and less expensive than rigid metal conduit and is approved by the *NEC* for use in the same applications as rigid metal conduit. Intermediate metal conduit also uses a different steel alloy, which makes it stronger than rigid metal conduit, even though the walls are thinner.

- **Article 344—Rigid Metal Conduit (Type RMC).** Rigid metal conduit is similar to intermediate metal conduit, except the wall thickness is greater, so it has a smaller interior cross-sectional area. Rigid metal conduit is heavier than intermediate metal conduit and is permitted for use in the same applications as intermediate metal conduit (Type IMC).

- **Article 348—Flexible Metal Conduit (Type FMC).** Flexible metal conduit is a raceway of circular cross section made of a helically wound, interlocked metal strip of either steel or aluminum. It is commonly called "Greenfield" (after its inventor) or "Flex."

- **Article 350—Liquidtight Flexible Metal Conduit (Type LFMC).** Liquidtight flexible metal conduit is a raceway of circular cross section with an outer liquidtight, nonmetallic, sunlight-resistant jacket over an inner flexible metal core, with associated couplings, connectors, and fittings. It is listed for the installation of electrical conductors. Liquidtight flexible metal conduit is commonly called "Sealtite®" or simply "liquidtight." Liquidtight flexible metal conduit is similar in construction to flexible metal conduit, but it has an outer thermoplastic covering.

- **Article 352—Rigid Polyvinyl Chloride Conduit (Type PVC).** Rigid polyvinyl chloride conduit is a nonmetallic raceway of circular cross section with integral or associated couplings, connectors, and fittings. It is listed for the installation of electrical conductors.

- **Article 356—Liquidtight Flexible Nonmetallic Conduit (Type LFNC).** Liquidtight flexible nonmetallic conduit (most commonly referred to as "Carflex®") is a raceway of circular cross section with an outer liquidtight, nonmetallic, sunlight-resistant jacket over an inner flexible core, with associated couplings, connectors, and fittings.

- **Article 358—Electrical Metallic Tubing (EMT).** Electrical metallic tubing is a nonthreaded thinwall raceway of circular cross section designed for the physical protection and routing of conductors and cables. Compared to rigid metal conduit and intermediate metal conduit, electrical metallic tubing is relatively easy to bend, cut, and ream. EMT is not threaded, so all connectors and couplings are of the threadless type. It is available in a range of colors, such as red and blue.

- **Article 362—Electrical Nonmetallic Tubing (ENT).** Electrical nonmetallic tubing is a pliable, corrugated, circular raceway made of PVC. ENT resembles flexible tubing and is often referred to as "Smurf Pipe" or "Smurf Tube," because it was only available in blue when it first came out, and the nickname is a reference to the children's cartoon characters "The Smurfs." It is now available in additional colors such as red and yellow.

- **Article 376—Metal Wireways.** A metal wireway is a sheet metal trough with hinged or removable covers making the electrical conductors and cables housed and protected inside accessible. Metal wireways must be installed as a complete and contiguous system.

- **Article 380—Multioutlet Assemblies.** A multioutlet assembly is a surface, flush, or freestanding raceway designed to hold conductors and receptacles. It is assembled in the field or at the factory.

- **Article 386—Surface Metal Raceways.** A surface metal raceway is a metal raceway intended to be mounted to the surface with associated accessories, in which conductors are placed after the raceway has been installed as a complete system.

Cable Tray

- **Article 392—Cable Trays.** A cable tray system is a unit or assembly of units or sections with associated fittings that form a structural system used to securely fasten or support cables and raceways. A cable tray is not a raceway; it is a support system for raceways, cables, and enclosures.

Notes

ARTICLE 300 — GENERAL REQUIREMENTS FOR WIRING METHODS AND MATERIALS

Introduction to Article 300—General Requirements for Wiring Methods and Materials

Article 300 contains the general requirements for all wiring methods included in the *NEC*. However, it does not apply to twisted-pair cable and coaxial cable (which are covered in Chapters 7 and 8) unless Article 300 is specifically referenced.

This article is primarily concerned with how to install, route, splice, protect, and secure conductors and raceways. How well you understand and apply the requirements of Article 300 will usually be evident in the finished work. Many of its requirements will affect the appearance, longevity, and even the safety of the installation. Imagine your surprise if you are shoveling some soil onto a plant in the garden and your shovel hits an electrical service cable! After studying and learning the rules in this article, you will immediately realize that the burial depth requirements of 300.5 were possibly overlooked or ignored. Even worse, they might not even have been known at the time of installation.

A good understanding of this article will start you on the path to correctly and safely installing the wiring methods included in Chapter 3. Be sure to carefully consider the accompanying illustrations and refer to the definitions in Article 100 as needed.

Part I. General Requirements

300.1 Scope

(A) All Wiring Installations. Article 300 contains the general requirements for wiring methods and materials for power and lighting. ▶Figure 300–1

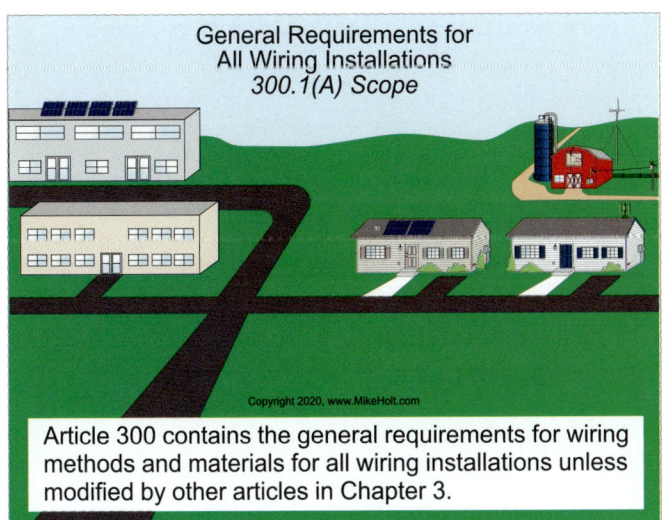

▶Figure 300–1

Author's Comment:

▶ The requirements contained in Article 300 do not apply to the wiring methods for Class 2 and 3 circuits, fire alarm circuits, and communications systems (twisted-pair conductors and coaxial cable). However, the chapters that contain the rules for such wiring methods (Chapters 7 and 8) may refer to Article 300 and those specific references will then apply.

(B) Integral Parts of Equipment. The requirements contained in Article 300 do not apply to the integral parts of electrical equipment. ▶Figure 300–2

Author's Comment:

▶ Integral wiring of equipment is covered by various product standards and not the *NEC*. It is the intent of this *Code* that the factory-installed internal wiring of equipment processed by a qualified testing laboratory does not need to be inspected [90.7].

(C) Trade Sizes. Designators for raceway trade sizes are given in Table 300.1(C).

300.3 | General Requirements for Wiring Methods and Materials

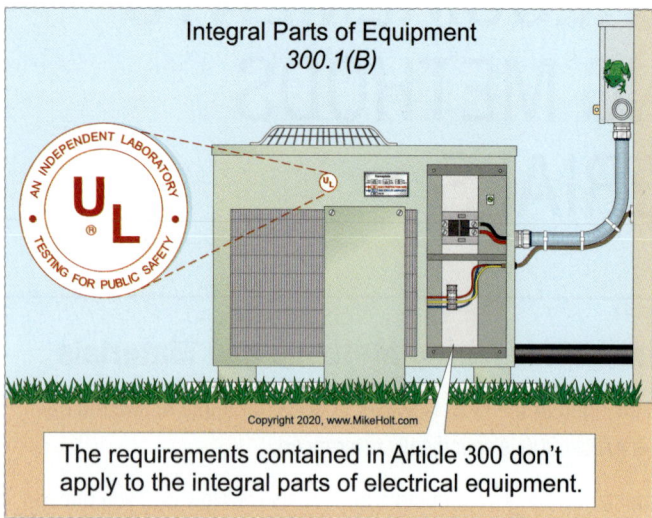

▶Figure 300–2

Author's Comment:

▸ Industry practice is to describe raceways using inch sizes, such as ½ in., 2 in., and so on; however, the proper reference is to use "Trade Size ½," or "Trade Size 2." In this textbook we use the proper reference and identify raceway sizes using the phrase "Trade Size."

300.3 Conductors

(A) Single Conductors. Conductors must be installed in a Chapter 3 wiring method such as in a raceway, cable, or enclosure. ▶Figure 300–3

▶Figure 300–3

(B) Circuit Conductors Grouped Together. All conductors of a circuit, including the neutral and equipment grounding conductors, must be installed together in the same raceway, cable, trench, cord, or cable tray; except as permitted by (1) through (4). ▶Figure 300–4 and ▶Figure 300–5

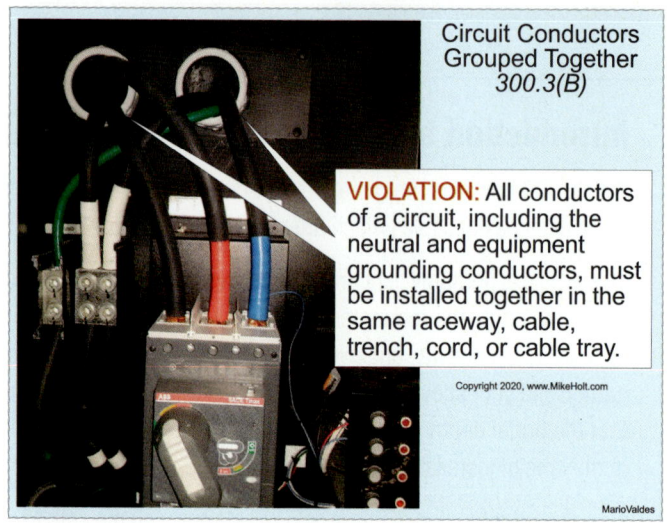

▶Figure 300–4

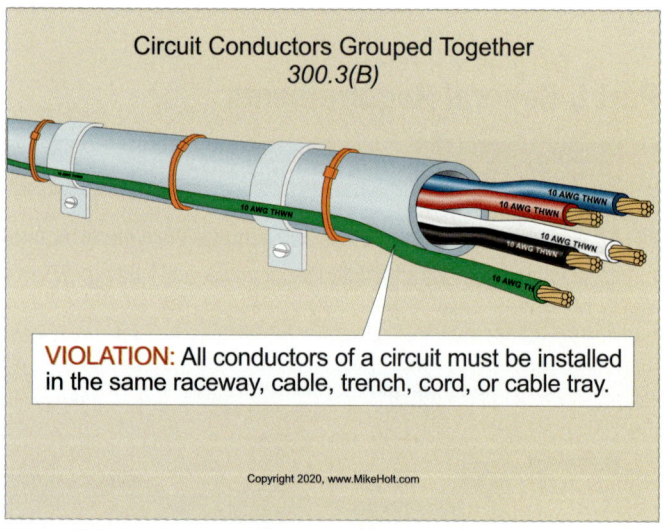

▶Figure 300–5

(1) Paralleled Installations. Conductors installed in parallel in accordance with 310.10(G) must have all circuit conductor sets grouped together within the same raceway, cable tray, trench, or cable. ▶Figure 300–6

General Requirements for Wiring Methods and Materials | **300.3**

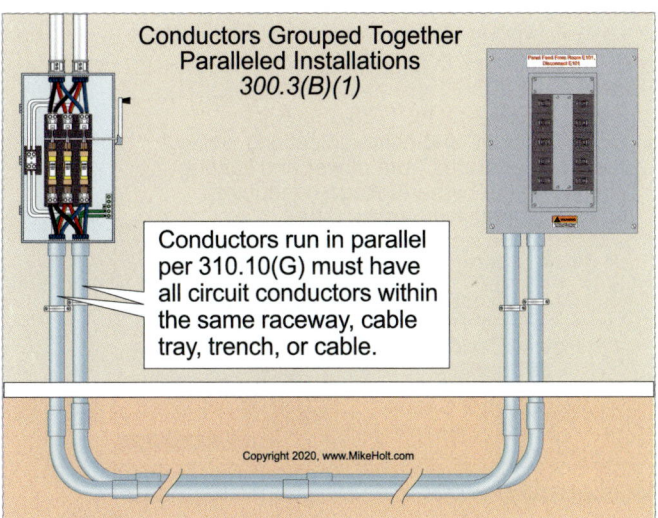
▶Figure 300–6

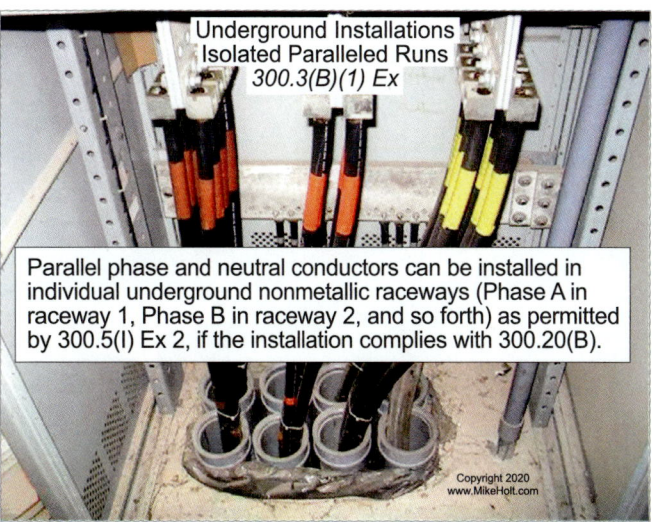
▶Figure 300–8

Author's Comment:

▸ Grouping of all conductors of the circuit is to minimize heating of surrounding ferrous metal raceways and enclosures by induction for alternating-current circuits. See 300.20(A). ▶Figure 300–7

(2) Outside a Raceway or an Enclosure. Equipment bonding jumpers can be located outside of a raceway if the bonding jumper is installed in accordance with 250.102(E)(2). ▶Figure 300–9

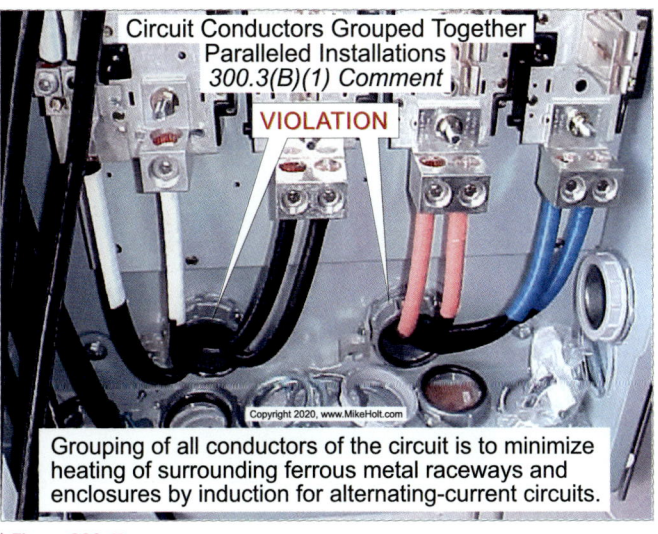
▶Figure 300–7

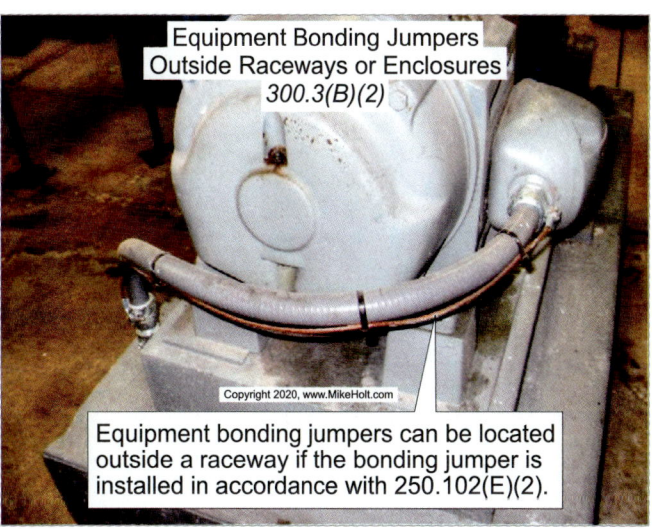
▶Figure 300–9

Connections, taps, or extensions made from paralleled conductors must connect to all conductors of the paralleled set.

Ex: Parallel phase and neutral conductors can be installed in individual underground nonmetallic raceways (Phase A in raceway 1, Phase B in raceway 2, and so forth) as permitted by 300.5(I) Ex 2 if the installation complies with 300.20(B). ▶Figure 300–8

For direct-current circuits, the equipment grounding conductor can be run separately from the circuit conductors in accordance with 250.134(2) Ex 2. ▶Figure 300–10

(C) Conductors of Different Systems.

(1) Mixing. Power conductors rated 1,000V or less can occupy the same raceway, cable, or enclosure if all conductors have an insulation voltage rating not less than the maximum circuit voltage. ▶Figure 300–11

300.3 | General Requirements for Wiring Methods and Materials

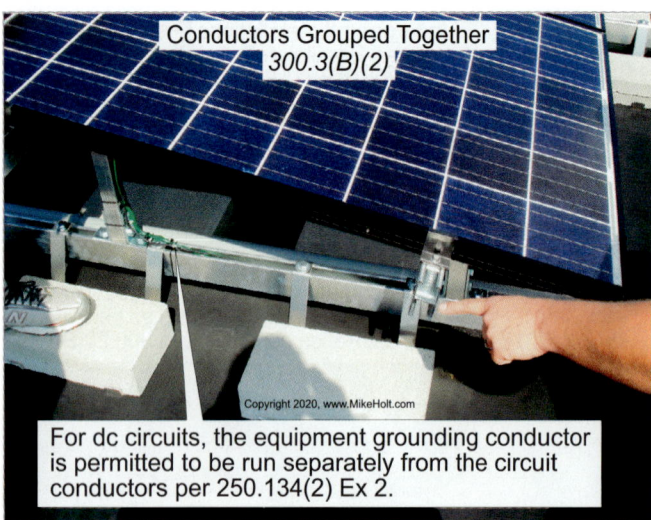

▶Figure 300-10

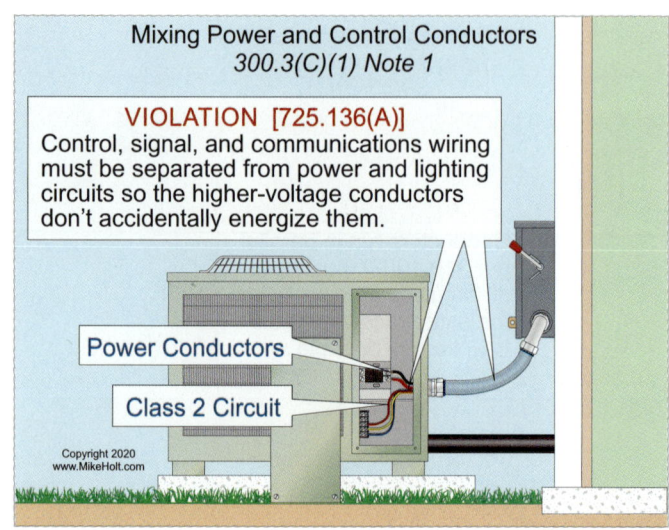

▶Figure 300-12

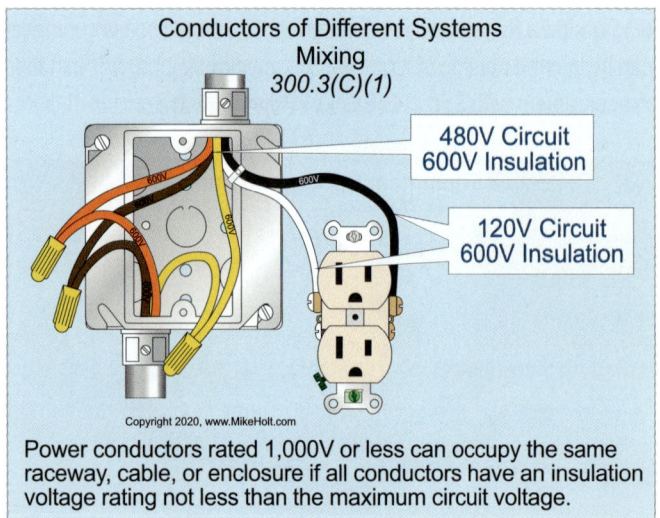

▶Figure 300-11

Author's Comment:

▶ Control, signaling, and communications wiring must be separated from power and lighting circuits so the higher-voltage conductors do not accidentally energize the control, signaling, or communications wiring: ▶Figure 300-12

　▶ Class 1 Control circuits, 725.48

　▶ Class 2 Control Circuits, 725.136(A)

　▶ Communications Circuits, 805.133(A)(1)(c)

　▶ Coaxial Cable, 820.133(A)

　▶ Fire Alarm Circuits, 760.136(A)

　▶ Sound Circuits, 640.9(C)

Author's Comment:

▶ Class 1 circuit conductors can be installed with associated power conductors [725.48(B)(1)] if all conductors have an insulation voltage rating not less than the maximum circuit voltage [300.3(C)(1)].

▶ A Class 2 circuit that has been reclassified as a Class 1 circuit [725.130(A) Ex 2] can be installed with associated power conductors [725.48(B)(1)] if all conductors have an insulation voltage rating not less than the maximum circuit voltage [300.3(C)(1)]. ▶Figure 300-13

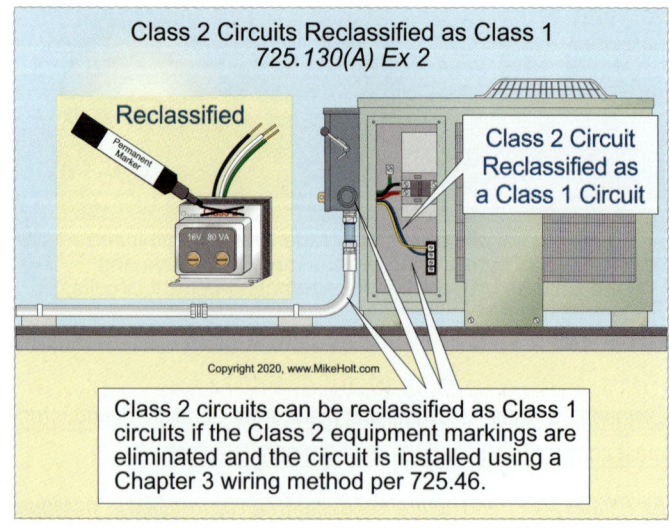

▶Figure 300-13

General Requirements for Wiring Methods and Materials | **300.4**

300.4 Protection Against Physical Damage

Where subject to physical damage, conductors, raceways, and cables must be protected in accordance with (A) through (H).

(A) Cables and Raceways Through Wood Members.

> **Author's Comment:**
>
> ▸ When the following wiring methods are installed through wood members, they must comply with 300.4(A)(1) or (2). ▸Figure 300–14
>
>   ▸ Armored Cable, Article 320
>   ▸ Electrical Nonmetallic Tubing, Article 362
>   ▸ Flexible Metal Conduit, Article 348
>   ▸ Liquidtight Flexible Metal Conduit, Article 350
>   ▸ Liquidtight Flexible Nonmetallic Conduit, Article 356
>   ▸ Metal-Clad Cable, Article 330
>   ▸ Nonmetallic-Sheathed Cable, Article 334
>   ▸ Service-Entrance Cable, Article 338
>   ▸ Underground Feeder and Branch-Circuit Cable, Article 340

▸Figure 300–15

(2) Notches in Wood Members. If notching of wood framing members for cables and raceways is permitted by the building code, a 1/16 in. thick steel plate of enough length and width must be installed to protect the wiring method laid in those wood notches from screws and nails. ▸Figure 300–16

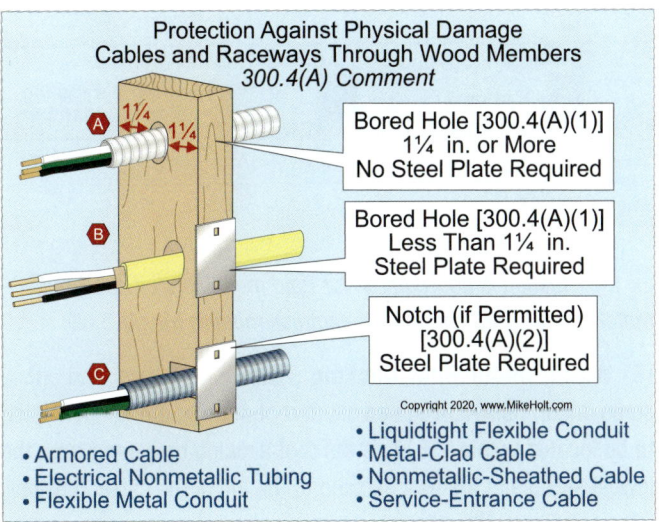
▸Figure 300–14

(1) Bored Holes in Wood Members. Holes through wood framing members for the above cables or raceways must be not less than 1¼ in. from the edge of the wood member. If the edge of a drilled hole in a wood framing member is less than 1¼ in. from the edge, a 1/16 in. thick steel plate of enough length and width must be installed to protect the wiring method from screws and nails. ▸Figure 300–15

Ex 1: A steel plate is not required to protect rigid metal conduit, intermediate metal conduit, PVC conduit, or electrical metallic tubing.

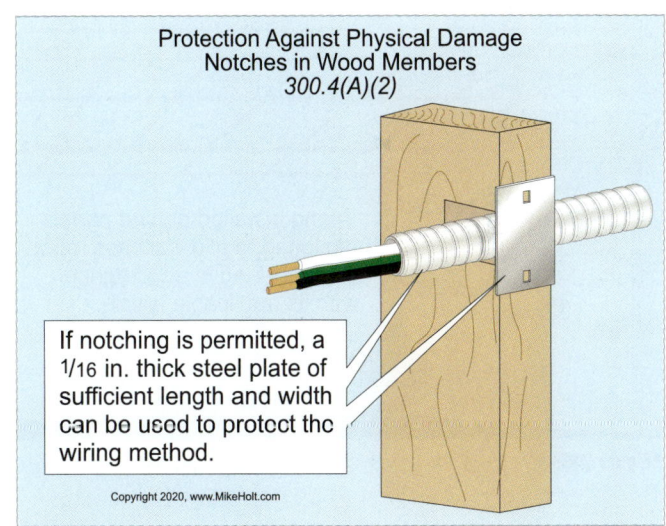
▸Figure 300–16

Ex 1: A steel plate is not required to protect rigid metal conduit, intermediate metal conduit, PVC conduit, or electrical metallic tubing.

> **Caution**
>
> ⚠ Many wood and metal framing members (especially joists and beams) have specific drilling and/or notching instructions meant to maintain structural integrity. Be sure to check with the building official for building code requirements.

300.4 | General Requirements for Wiring Methods and Materials

(B) Nonmetallic-Sheathed Cable and Electrical Nonmetallic Tubing Through Metal Framing Members.

(1) Type NM Cable, Metal Framing Members. If Type NM cables pass through factory or field-made openings in metal framing members, the cable must be protected by listed bushings or listed grommets that cover all metal edges. The protection fitting must be securely fastened in the opening before the installation of the cable.

(2) Type NM Cable and Electrical Nonmetallic Tubing. If nails or screws are likely to penetrate Type NM cable or electrical nonmetallic tubing, a steel sleeve, steel plate, or steel clip not less than 1/16 in. in thickness must be installed to protect the cable or tubing.

Ex: A listed and marked steel plate less than 1/16 in. thick that provides equal or better protection against nail or screw penetration is permitted.

(C) Behind Suspended Ceilings. Wiring methods such as boxes, enclosures, cables, or raceways, installed behind panels designed to allow access must be supported in accordance with its applicable article. ▶Figure 300–17

- Control and Signaling Cable, 725.21 and 725.24
- Fire Alarm Cable, 760.21 and 760.24
- Optical Fiber Cable, 770.21 and 770.24

(D) Cables and Raceways Parallel to Framing Members and Furring Strips. Cables or raceways run parallel to framing members or furring strips must be protected by installing the wiring method not less than 1¼ in. from the nearest edge of the framing member or furring strip. If the edge of the framing member or furring strip is less than 1¼ in. away, a 1/16 in. thick steel plate of enough length and width must be installed to protect the wiring method from screws and nails. ▶Figure 300–18

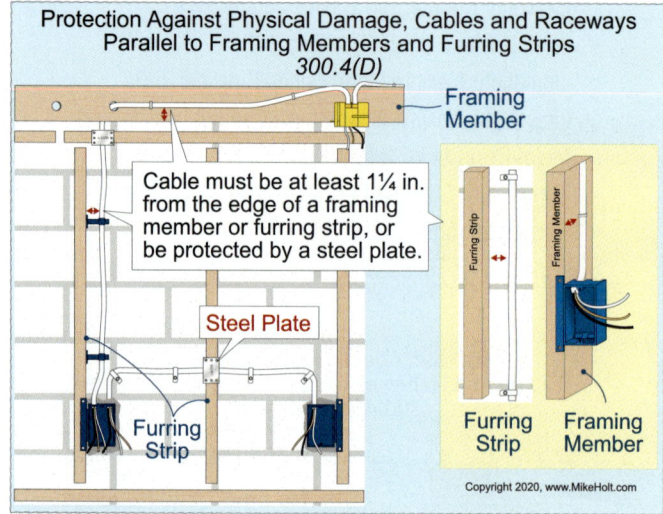

▶Figure 300–18

Ex 1: Protection is not required for rigid metal conduit, intermediate metal conduit, PVC conduit, or electrical metallic tubing.

(E) Wiring Under Roof Decking. Cables, raceways, and enclosures under metal-corrugated sheet roof decking are not permitted to be located within 1½ in. of the roof decking measured from the lowest surface of the roof decking to the top of the cable, raceway, or box. ▶Figure 300–19

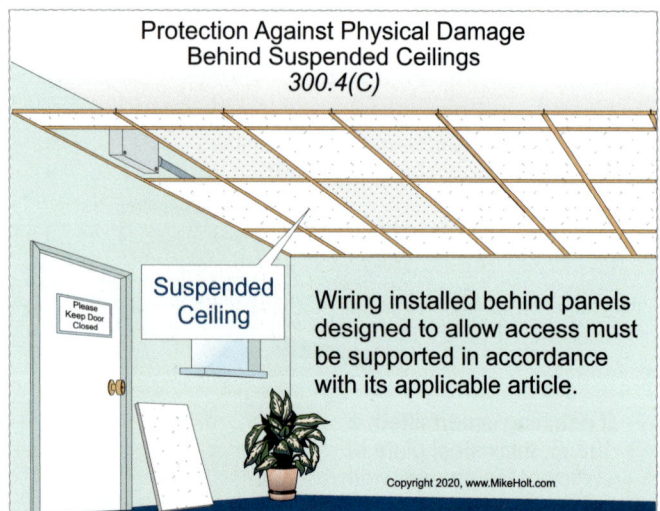

▶Figure 300–17

Author's Comment:

- Requirements for the support of various wiring methods in suspended ceilings can be found in 300.11(B). Check each applicable wiring method in Chapter 3 for additional support requirements.

- Similar support requirements are contained in Chapters 6, 7, and 8 as follows:

  - Audio Cable, 640.5 and 640.6(A)
  - Communications (twisted pair) Cable and Coaxial Cable, 800.21 and 800.24

Author's Comment:

- A similar requirement applies to luminaires installed in or under roof decking [410.10(F)].

Note: Raceways or cables installed under metal roof decking may be penetrated by screws or other mechanical devices designed to "hold down" the waterproof membrane or roof insulating material.

General Requirements for Wiring Methods and Materials | 300.4

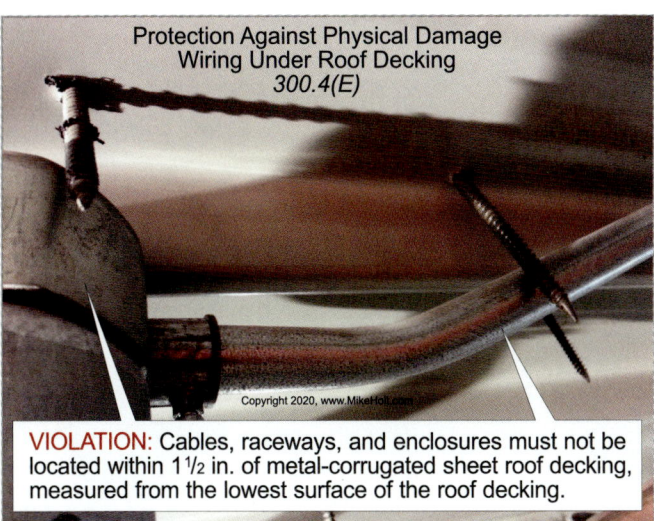

▶Figure 300-19

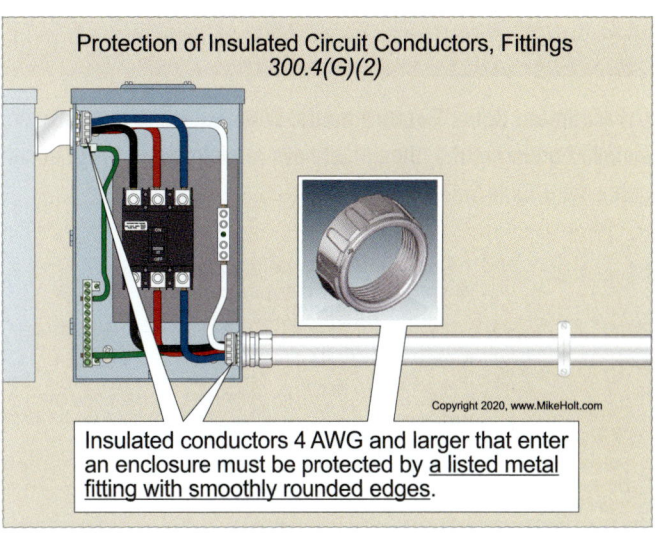

▶Figure 300-21

Ex: Spacing from roof decking does not apply to rigid metal conduit and intermediate metal conduit.

(G) Fittings. Raceways containing insulated circuit conductors 4 AWG and larger that enter a cabinet, box, enclosure, or raceway, must have the conductors protected as follows:

(1) A fitting providing a smoothly rounded insulating surface ▶Figure 300-20

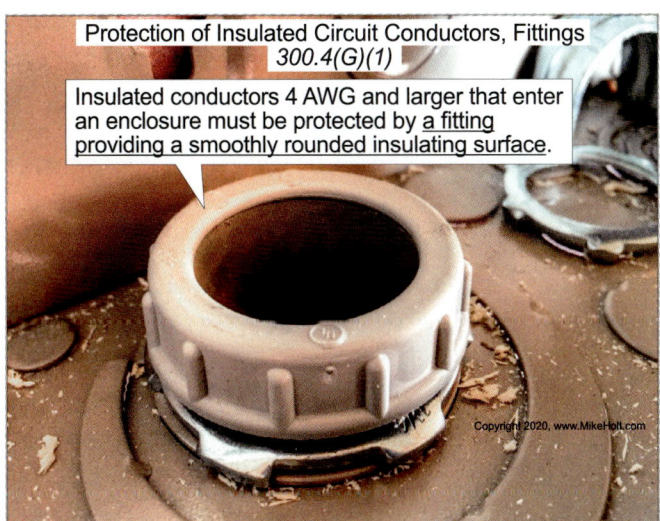

▶Figure 300-20

(2) A listed metal fitting that has smoothly rounded edges ▶Figure 300-21

(3) Separation from the fitting or raceway using an identified insulating material securely fastened in place

(4) Threaded hubs or bosses that are an integral part of a cabinet, box, enclosure, or raceway that provide a smoothly rounded or flared entry for conductors. ▶Figure 300-22

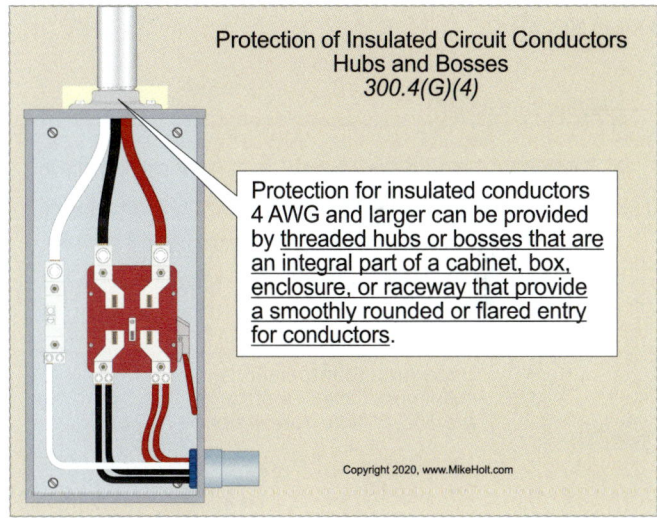

▶Figure 300-22

Author's Comment:

▶ If IMC or RMC enters an enclosure without a connector, a bushing must be provided regardless of the conductor size [342.46 and 344.46].

(H) Structural Joints. A listed expansion/deflection fitting, or other means approved by the authority having jurisdiction, must be used where a raceway crosses a structural joint intended for expansion, contraction, or deflection.

300.5 | General Requirements for Wiring Methods and Materials

300.5 Underground Installations

(A) Minimum Cover Requirements. When cables or raceways are installed underground, they must have a minimum cover in accordance with Table 300.5. ▶Figure 300–23

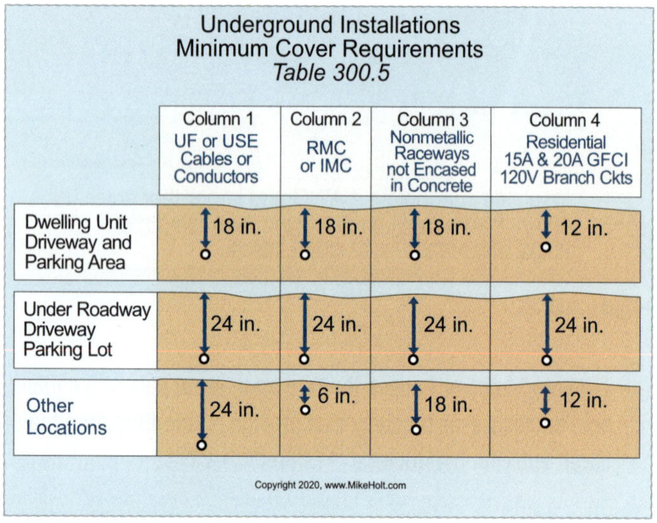

▶Figure 300–25

Table 300.5 Minimum Cover Requirements in Inches			
Location	Column 1 Buried Cables	Column 2 RMC or IMC	Column 3 Nonmetallic Raceways
Under Building	0	0	0
Dwelling Unit	24/12*	6	18/12*
Dwelling Unit Driveway	18/12*	18/12*	18/12*
Under Roadway	24	24	24
Other Locations	18/12*	6	18/12*

*Residential branch circuits rated 120V or less with GFCI protection and maximum protection of 20A.

See the table in the NEC for full details.

b. A depth of 6 in. is permitted for pool, spa, and fountain lighting wiring installed in a nonmetallic raceway, where part of a listed 30V or less lighting system. ▶Figure 300–26

Note 1 to Table 300.5: "Cover" is defined as the shortest distance from the top of the underground cable or raceway to the top surface of finished grade.

▶Figure 300–23

Author's Comment:

▶ Table 300.5 Note 1 defines "Cover" as the shortest distance in in. measured between the top of any direct-buried conductor, cable, or raceway to the surface of the finished grade, concrete, or similar cover. ▶Figure 300–24 and ▶Figure 300–25

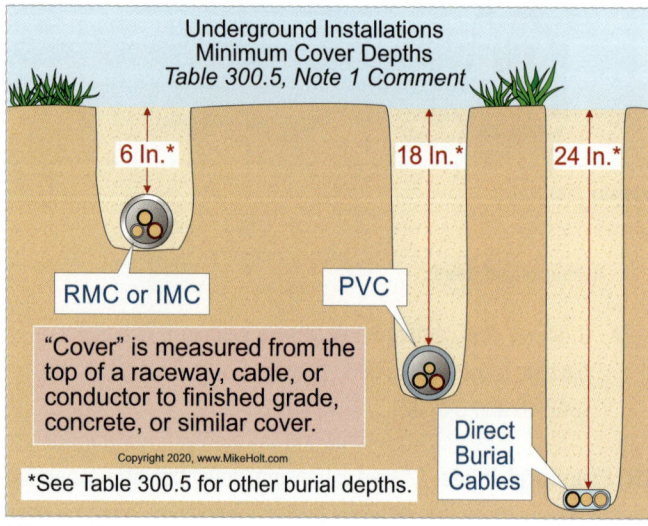

▶Figure 300–24

General Requirements for Wiring Methods and Materials | **300.5**

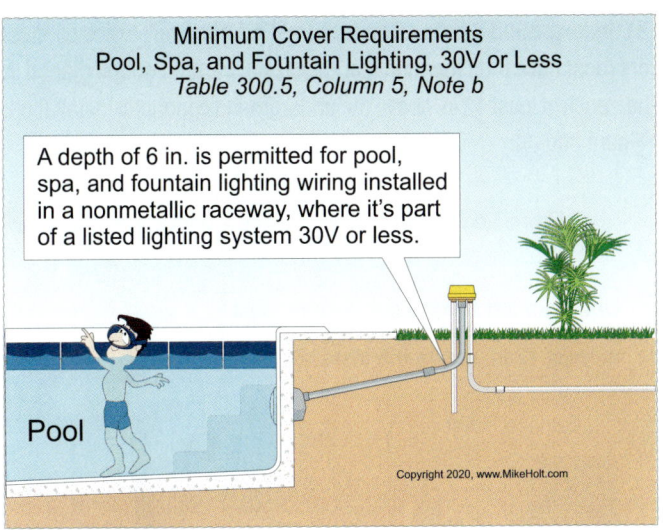
▶Figure 300-26

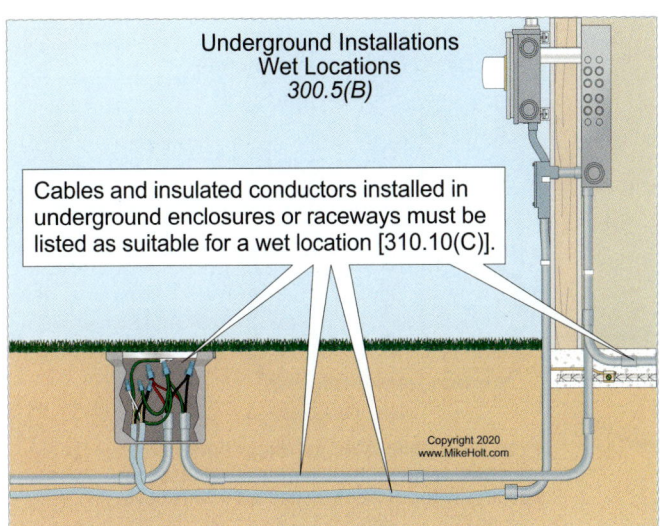
▶Figure 300-28

Author's Comment:

▸ The cover requirements contained in 300.5 do not apply to signaling, communications, and other power-limited wiring systems: ▶Figure 300-27

- Class 2 and 3 Circuits, 725.3
- Communications Cables and Raceways, 90.3
- Coaxial Cable, 90.3
- Fire Alarm Circuits, 760.3
- Optical Fiber Cables and Raceways, 770.3

Author's Comment:

▸ According to Article 100, a "Wet Location" includes installations underground, in concrete slabs in direct contact with the Earth, locations subject to saturation with water, and unprotected locations exposed to weather. See 300.9 for raceways in wet locations above ground.

(C) Cables and Conductors Under Buildings. Cables and conductors installed under a building must be installed within a raceway that extends past the outside walls of the building. ▶Figure 300-29

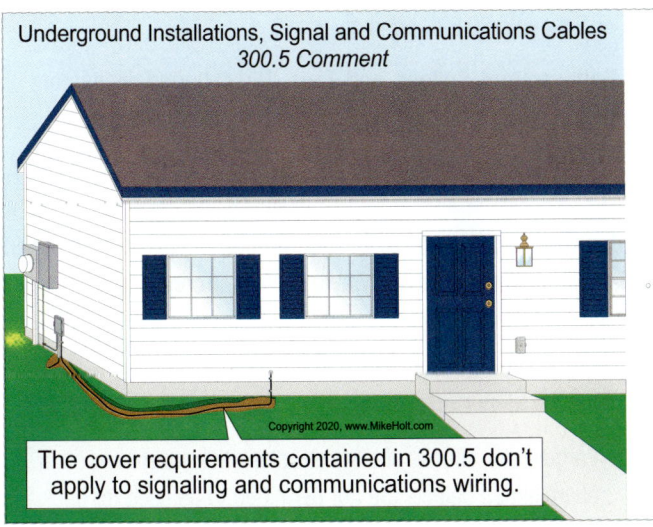
▶Figure 300-27

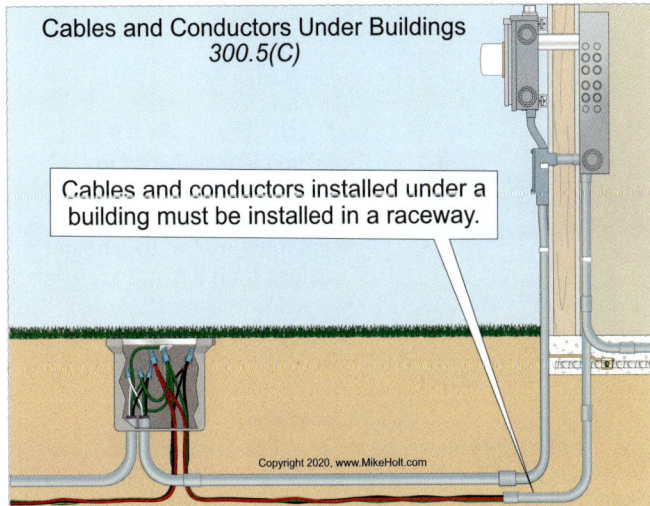
▶Figure 300-29

(B) Wet Locations. Cables and insulated conductors installed in underground enclosures or raceways must be listed as suitable for a wet location [310.10(C)]. ▶Figure 300-28

Ex 2: Type MC Cable listed for direct burial or concrete encasement is permitted under a building without installation within a raceway [330.10(A)(5) and 330.10(A)(11)]. ▶Figure 300-30

300.5 | General Requirements for Wiring Methods and Materials

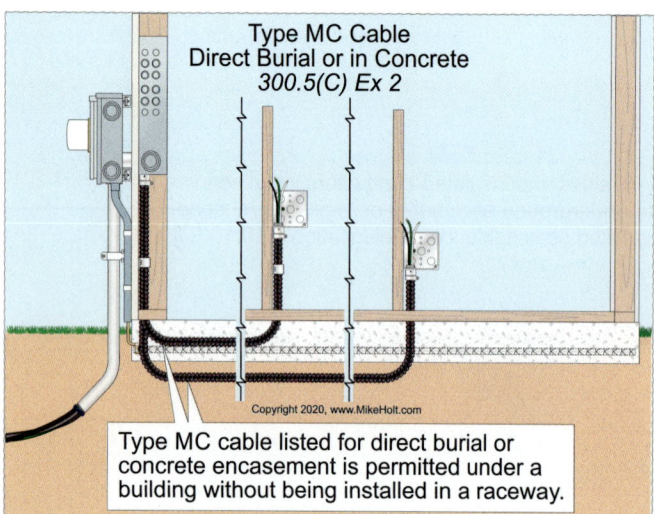

▶Figure 300–30

(D) Protecting Underground Cables and Conductors. Direct-buried conductors and cables such as Types MC, UF, and USE installed underground must be protected from damage in accordance with (1) through (4).

(1) Emerging from Grade. Direct-buried cables and conductors that emerge from grade must be protected against physical damage. Protection is not required to extend more than 18 in. below grade, and protection above ground must extend to a height of not less than 8 ft. ▶Figure 300–31

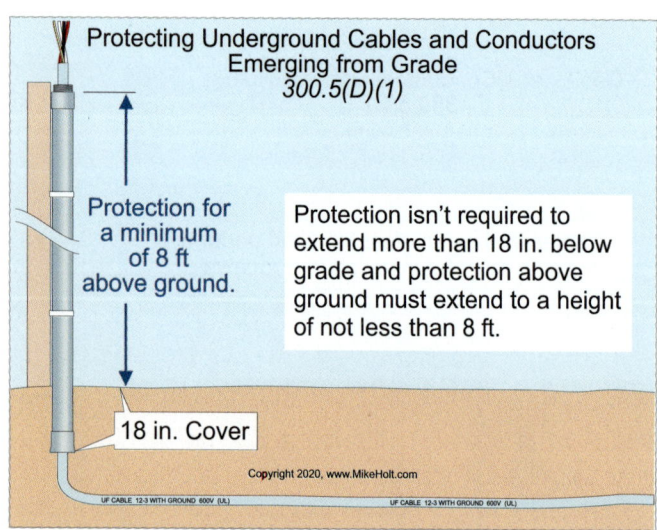

▶Figure 300–31

(2) Conductors Entering Buildings. Underground conductors and cables that enter a building must be protected to the point of entrance.

(3) Underground Service Conductors. Underground service conductors must have their location identified by a warning ribbon placed in the trench at least 12 in. above the underground conductor installation. ▶Figure 300–32

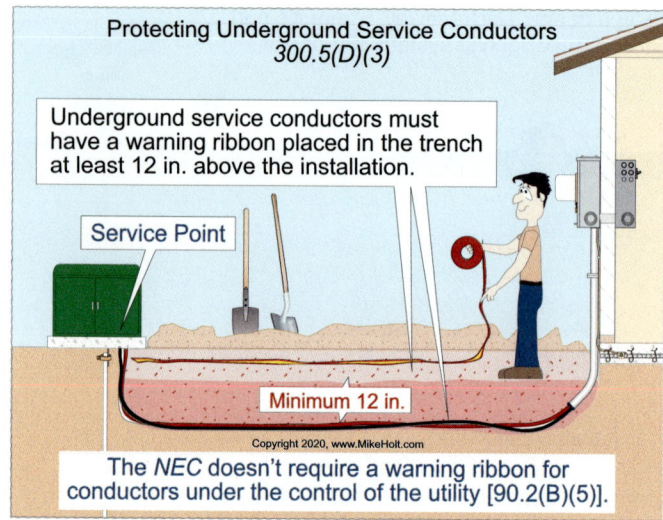

▶Figure 300–32

Author's Comment:

▸ The *NEC* does not require a warning ribbon for conductors under the exclusive control of the utility [90.2(B)(5)].

(4) Raceway Damage. Where a raceway is subject to physical damage, the conductors must be installed in EMT, RMC, IMC, RTRC-XW, or Schedule 80 PVC conduit.

(E) Underground Splices and Taps. Direct-buried conductors or cables can be spliced or tapped underground without a splice box [300.15(G)] if the splice or tap is made in accordance with 110.14(B). ▶Figure 300–33

(F) Backfill. Backfill material for underground wiring is not permitted to damage underground raceways, cables, or conductors. ▶Figure 300–34

Author's Comment:

▸ Large rocks, chunks of concrete, steel rods, mesh, and other sharp-edged objects are not permitted to be used for back-filling material because they can damage the underground conductors, cables, or raceways.

General Requirements for Wiring Methods and Materials | 300.5

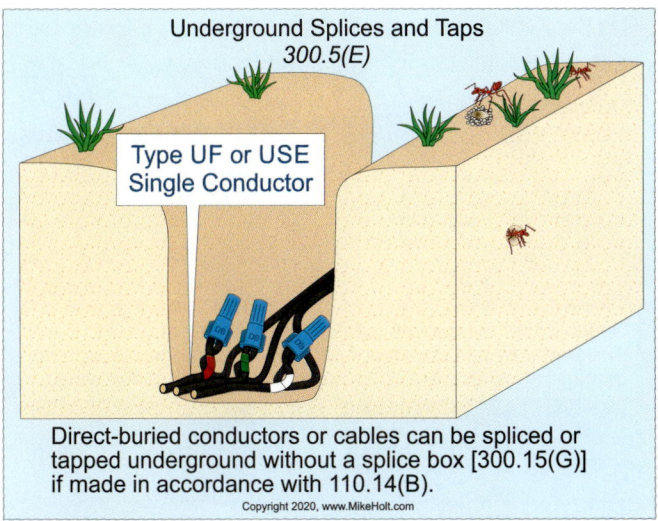
▶Figure 300-33

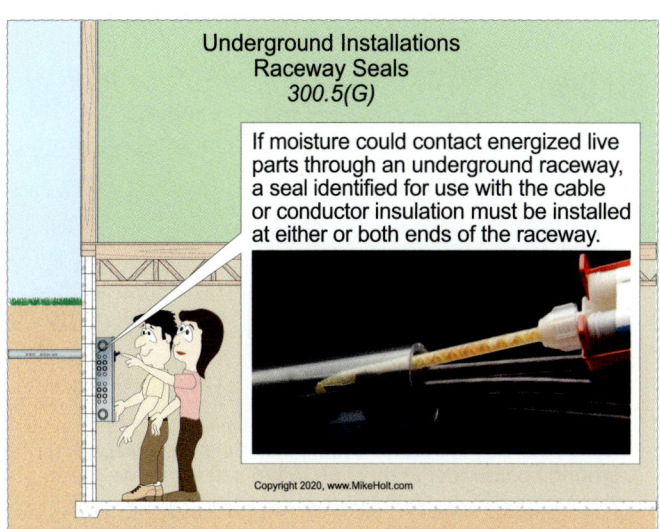
▶Figure 300-35

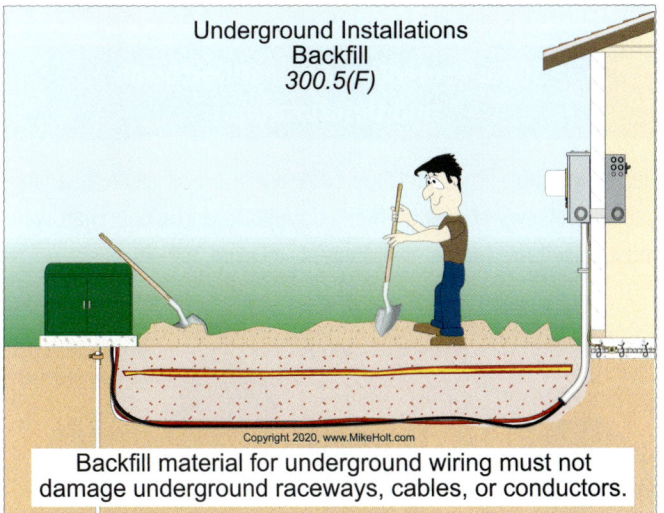
▶Figure 300-34

▶Figure 300-36

(G) Raceway Seals. If moisture could contact energized live parts through an underground raceway, a seal identified for use with the cable or conductor insulation must be installed at either or both ends of the raceway [225.27 and 230.8]. ▶Figure 300-35

Author's Comment:

▸ Moisture is a common problem for equipment located downhill from the supply, or in underground equipment rooms.

(H) Bushing. Raceways that terminate underground must have a bushing or fitting at the end of the raceway to protect emerging cables or conductors. ▶Figure 300-36

(I) Conductors of the Same Circuit. Underground conductors of the same circuit (including the equipment grounding conductor) must be installed inside the same raceway, multiconductor cable, or near each other in the same trench. See 300.3(B). ▶Figure 300-37

Ex 2: Underground parallel conductors can have the conductors of each phase or neutral installed in separate nonmetallic raceways where inductive heating at raceway terminations is reduced by the use of aluminum locknuts and by cutting a slot between the individual holes through which the conductors pass as required by 300.20(B). ▶Figure 300-38

300.6 | General Requirements for Wiring Methods and Materials

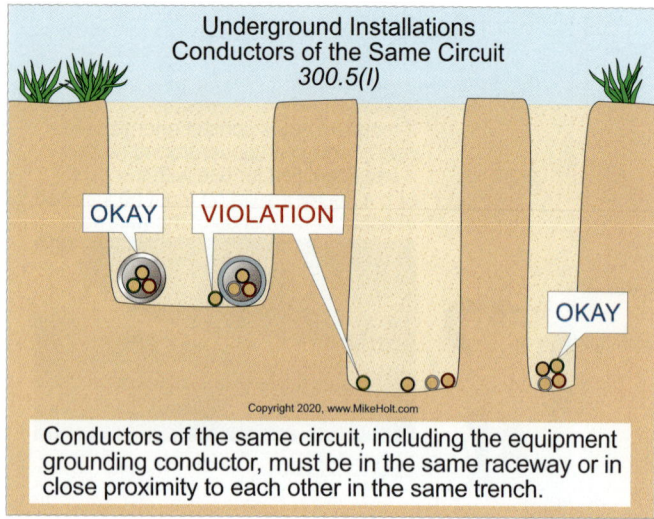

▶Figure 300-37

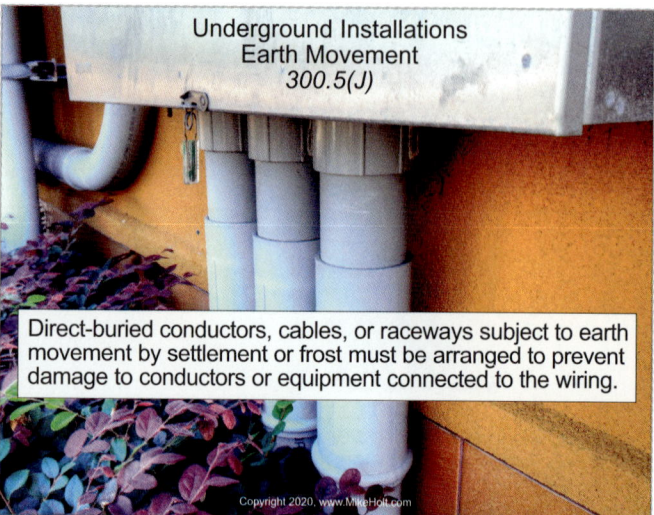

▶Figure 300-39

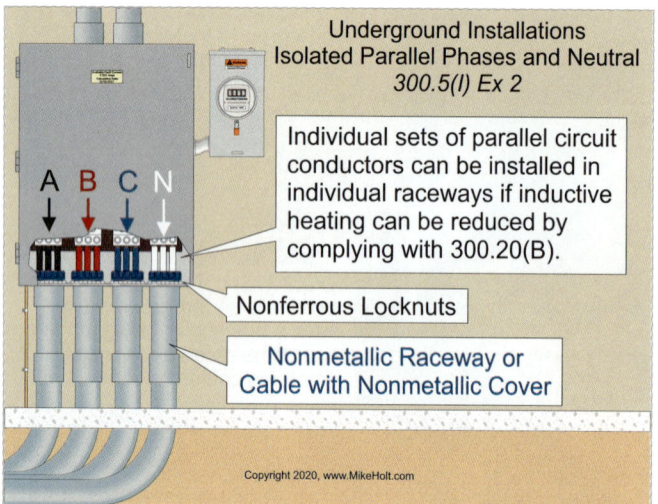

▶Figure 300-38

Author's Comment:

▸ Separating phase and neutral conductors in individual PVC conduits makes it easier to terminate larger parallel installations, but it also results in elevated electromagnetic fields (EMF). Keeping the phase and neutral conductors close to each other helps reduce circuit impedance.

(J) Earth Movement. Direct-buried conductors, cables, or raceways that are subject to movement by settlement or frost must be arranged to prevent damage to conductors or equipment connected to the wiring. ▶Figure 300-39

300.6 Protection Against Corrosion and Deterioration

Raceways, cable trays, cablebus, cable armor, boxes, cable sheathing, cabinets, elbows, couplings, fittings, supports, and support hardware must be suitable for the environment. ▶Figure 300-40

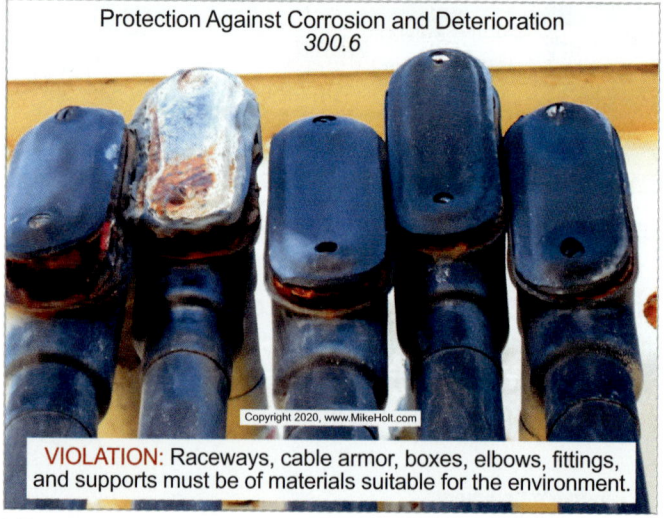

▶Figure 300-40

Author's Comment:

▸ Section 110.11 has similar requirements regarding deteriorating agents.

(A) Ferrous Metal Equipment. Ferrous metal raceways, enclosures, cables, cable trays, fittings, and support hardware must be protected against corrosion by a coating of listed corrosion-resistant material. Where conduit is threaded in the field, the threads must be coated with an approved electrically conductive, corrosion-resistant compound such as zinc galvanizing or KOPR-Shield®.

Note: Field-cut threads are those threads that are cut anywhere other than at the factory.

Author's Comment:

▸ Ferrous metals are those that are prone to higher degrees of oxidation or ferrous oxide; most commonly called "rust." The use of nonferrous materials is preferred in locations and environments that lead to this type of deterioration.

▸ Nonferrous metal raceways, such as aluminum rigid metal conduit, do not have to meet the provisions of this section. See 300.6(B).

300.7 Raceways Exposed to Different Temperatures

(A) Sealing. If a raceway is subjected to different temperatures, and where condensation is known to be a problem, the raceway must be filled with a material approved by the authority having jurisdiction that will prevent the circulation of warm air to a colder section of the raceway. Sealants must be identified for use with cable insulation, conductor insulation, a bare conductor, a shield, or other components. ▸Figure 300–41

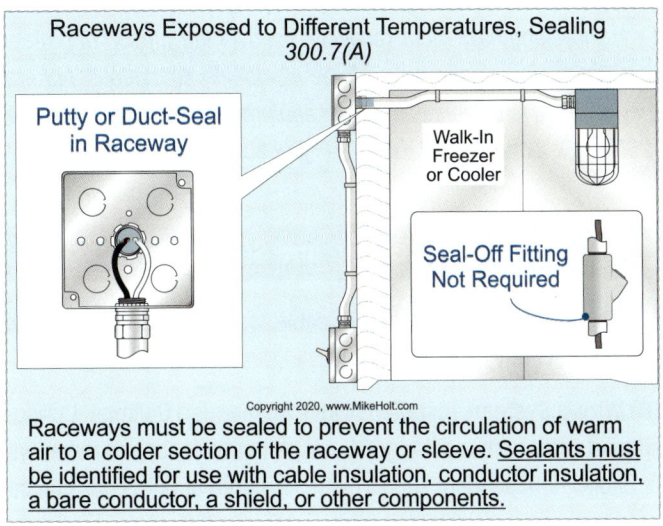
▸Figure 300–41

Author's Comment:

▸ One common product used for this is electrical duct seal and it is so identified. There are other identified products such as Polywater's FST Duct Sealant. Typical expanding foams used to seal buildings are not identified for this application.

(B) Expansion, Expansion-Deflection, and Deflection Fittings. Raceways must be provided with expansion, expansion-deflection, or deflection fittings where necessary to compensate for thermal expansion, deflection, and contraction. ▸Figure 300–42

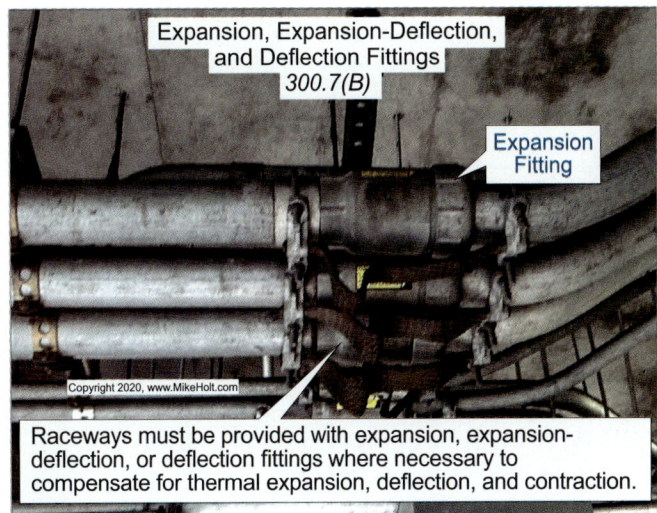
▸Figure 300–42

Note: Table 352.44 provides the expansion characteristics for PVC conduit. The expansion characteristics for steel conduit are determined by multiplying the values from Table 352.44 by 0.20, and those for aluminum raceways are determined by multiplying the values from Table 352.44 by 0.40. Table 355.44 provides the expansion characteristics for reinforced thermosetting resin conduit (RTRC). ▸Figure 300–43

300.9 Raceways in Wet Locations Above Grade

The interior of raceways installed in wet locations above ground is considered a wet location. Insulated conductors and cables installed in raceways in aboveground wet locations must be listed for use in wet locations in accordance with 310.10(C). ▸Figure 300–44

Author's Comment:

▸ In addition to 310.10(C), Table 310.4(A) can be used to find other insulation types permitted in wet locations.

300.10 | General Requirements for Wiring Methods and Materials

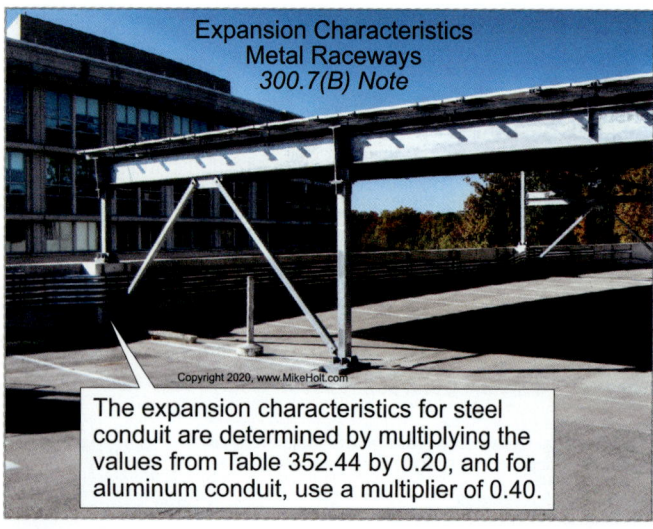

▶Figure 300–43

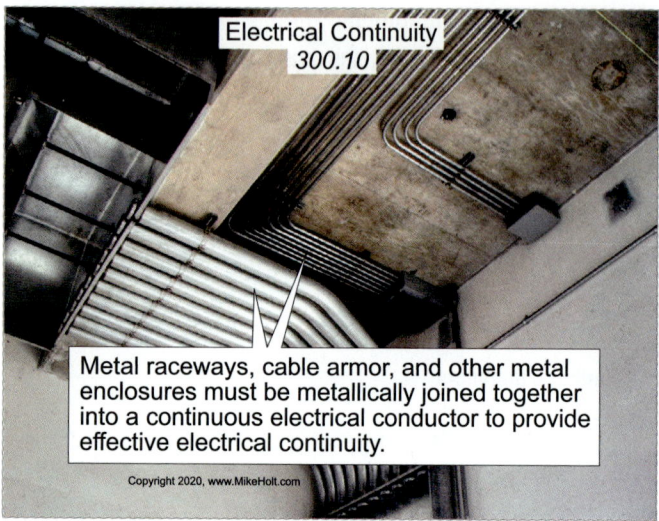

▶Figure 300–45

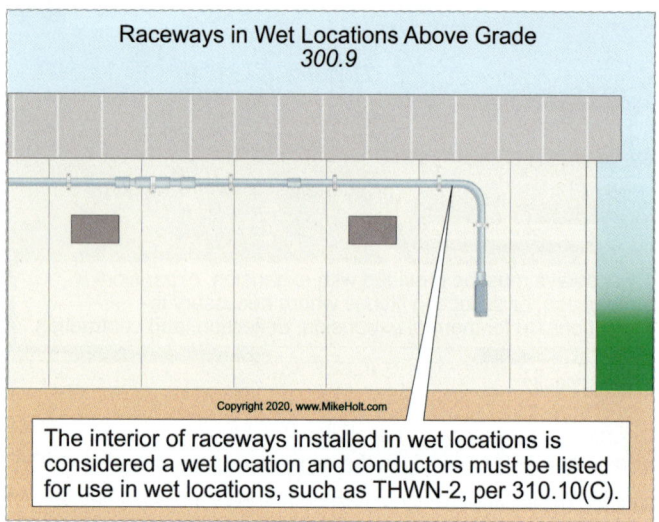

▶Figure 300–44

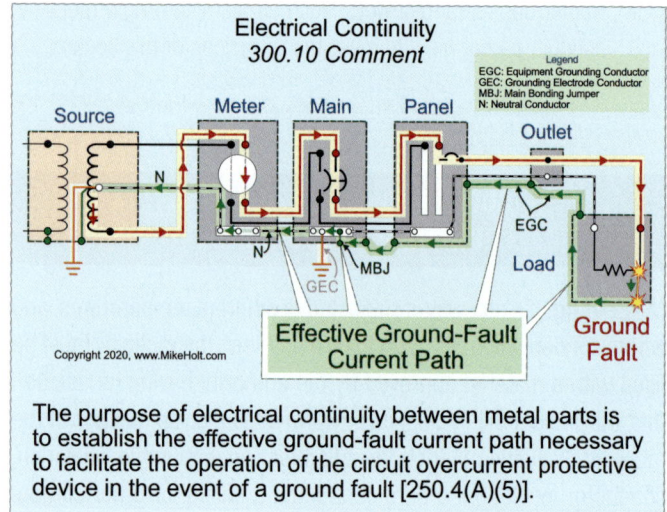

▶Figure 300–46

300.10 Electrical Continuity

Metal raceways, cable armor, and other metal enclosures must be metallically joined into a continuous electrical conductor to provide effective electrical continuity [110.10 and 250.4(A)]. ▶Figure 300–45

> **Author's Comment:**
>
> ▸ The purpose of electrical continuity between metal parts is to establish the effective ground-fault current path necessary to facilitate the operation of the circuit overcurrent protective device in the event of a ground fault [250.4(A)(5)]. ▶Figure 300–46

Ex 1: Short lengths of metal raceways used for the support or protection of cables are not required to be electrically continuous, nor are they required to be connected to an equipment grounding conductor [250.86 Ex 2 and 300.12 Ex 1]. ▶Figure 300–47

300.11 Securing and Supporting

(A) Secured in Place. Raceways, cable assemblies, and enclosures must be securely fastened in place.

(B) Wiring Systems Installed Above Suspended Ceilings. Ceiling-support wires or the ceiling grid is not permitted to support raceways or cables. Independent support wires secured at both ends can be used to support raceways or cables. ▶Figure 300–48

General Requirements for Wiring Methods and Materials | **300.11**

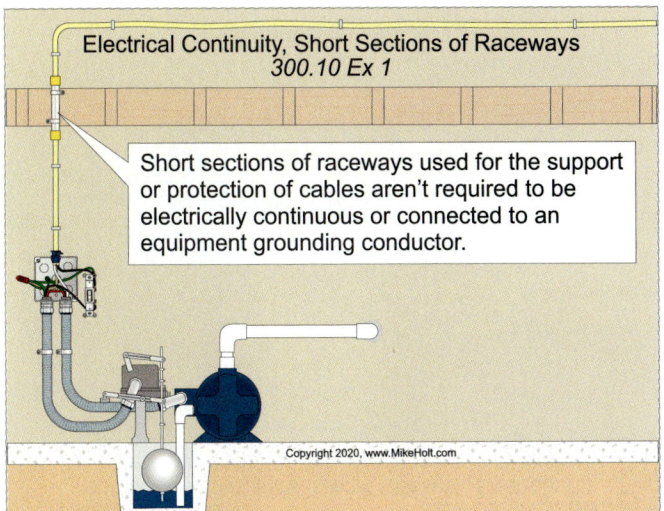

▶Figure 300–47

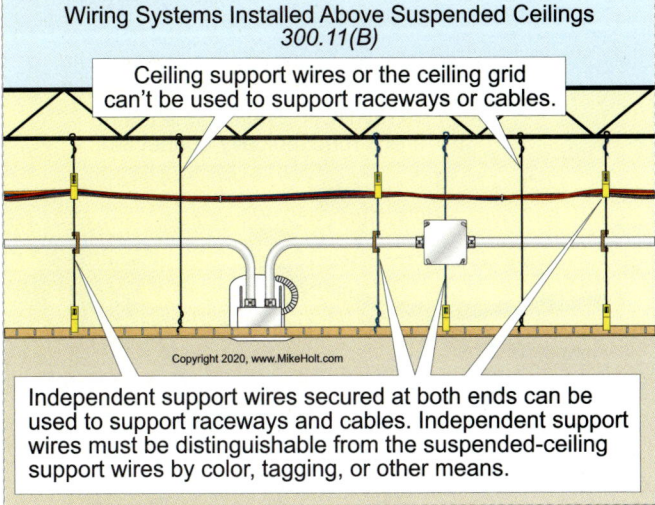

▶Figure 300–48

(1) Fire-Rated Assemblies. Electrical wiring within the cavity of a fire-rated ceiling assembly can be supported by independent support wires attached to the ceiling assembly. The independent support wires must be distinguishable from the suspended-ceiling support wires by color, tagging, or other effective means.

Author's Comment:

▸ Outlet boxes [314.23(D)] and luminaires can be secured to the suspended-ceiling grid if the luminaire is securely fastened to the ceiling-framing members by mechanical means such as bolts, screws, or rivets, or by the use of clips or other securing means identified for use with the type of ceiling-framing member(s) used [410.36(B)].

(C) Raceways Used for Support. Raceways are not permitted to support other wiring methods, except as follows: ▶Figure 300–49 and ▶Figure 300–50

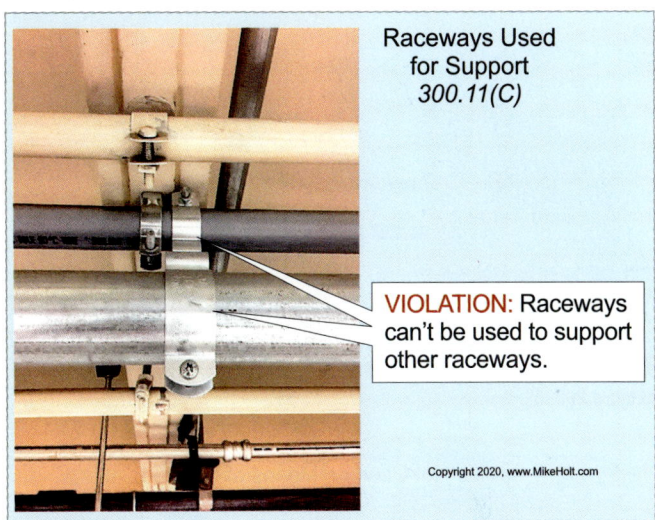

▶Figure 300–49

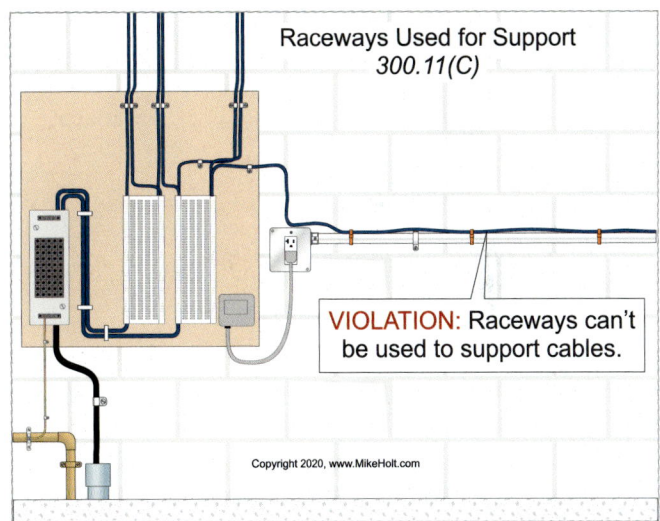

▶Figure 300–50

(1) Identified. If the raceway or means of support is identified as a means of support.

(2) Class 2 and 3 Circuits. Class 2 and 3 cables can be supported by the raceway that supplies power to the equipment controlled by the Class 2 or 3 circuit. ▶Figure 300–51

(D) Cables Not Used as Means of Support. Cables are not permitted to support other wiring methods. ▶Figure 300–52

300.12 | General Requirements for Wiring Methods and Materials

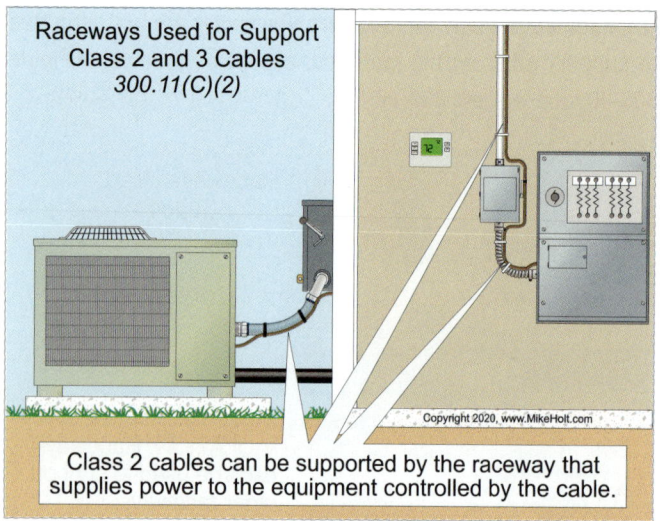
▶Figure 300–51

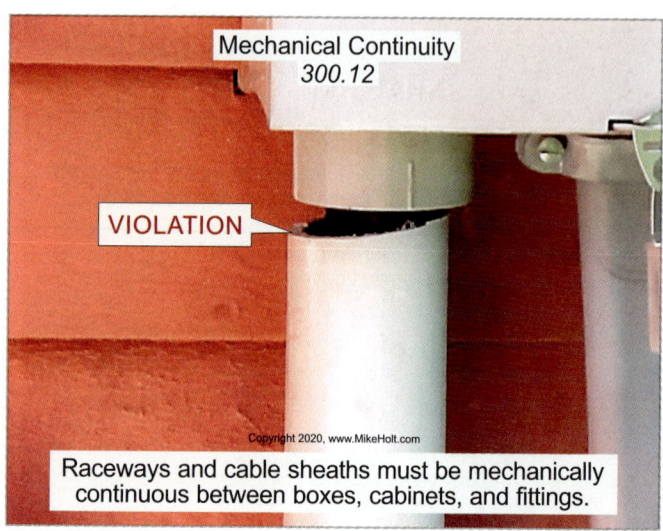
▶Figure 300–53

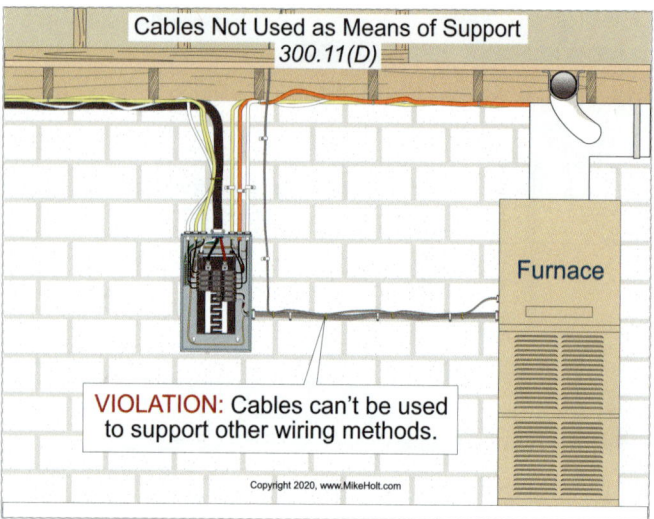
▶Figure 300–52

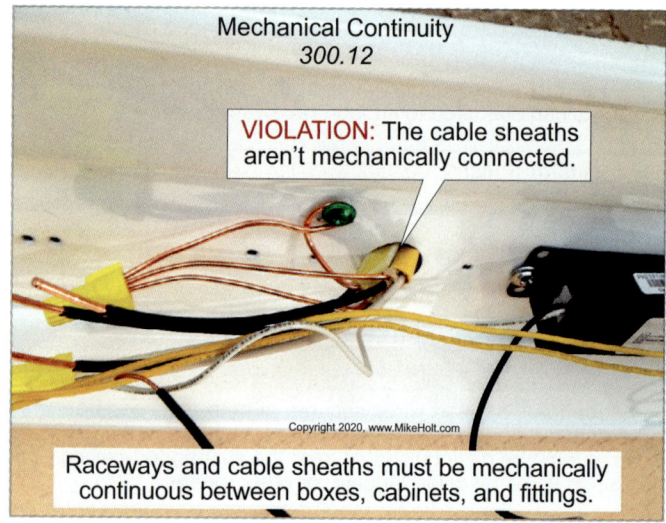
▶Figure 300–54

300.12 Mechanical Continuity

Raceways and cable sheaths must be mechanically continuous between boxes, cabinets, and fittings. ▶Figure 300–53 and ▶Figure 300–54

Ex 1: Short sections of raceways used to provide support or protection of cables from physical damage are not required to be mechanically continuous [250.86 Ex 2 and 300.10 Ex 1]. ▶Figure 300–55

Ex 2: Raceways and cables installed into the bottom of open-bottom equipment such as switchboards, motor control centers, and floor or pad-mounted transformers are not required to be mechanically secured to the equipment. ▶Figure 300–56

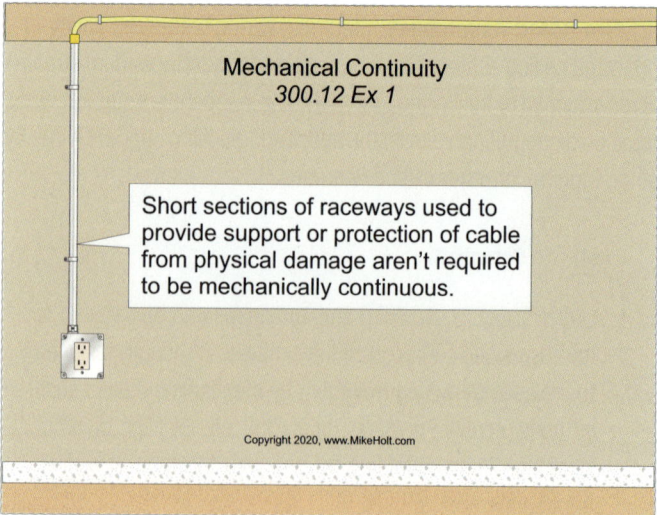
▶Figure 300–55

General Requirements for Wiring Methods and Materials | **300.13**

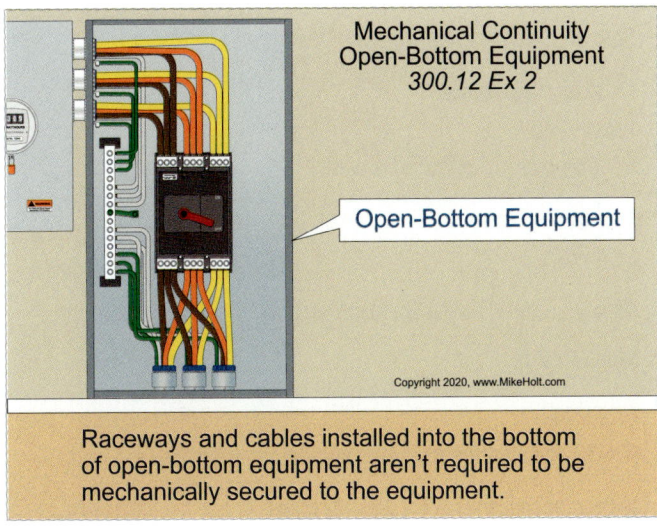

▶Figure 300-56

Author's Comment:

▸ This means that (for multiwire applications) the neutral conductors must be spliced together, and a pigtail must be provided for the wiring device. ▶Figure 300-58

▸ The opening of the phase conductors, or the neutral conductor of a 2-wire circuit while a device is replaced does not cause a safety hazard, so pigtailing these conductors is not required [110.14(B)].

300.13 Mechanical and Electrical Continuity of Conductors–Splices and Pigtails

(A) Conductor Splices. Conductor splices and taps must be made inside enclosures in accordance with 300.15. Splices are not permitted in raceways, except as permitted for wireways in 376.56. ▶Figure 300-57

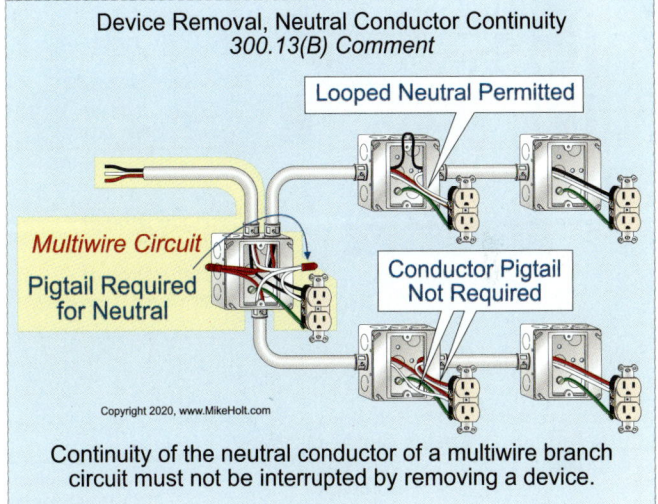

▶Figure 300-58

> **Caution**
> ⚠ If the continuity of the neutral conductor of a multiwire circuit is interrupted (opened), the resulting over- or undervoltage can cause a fire and/or destruction of electrical equipment.

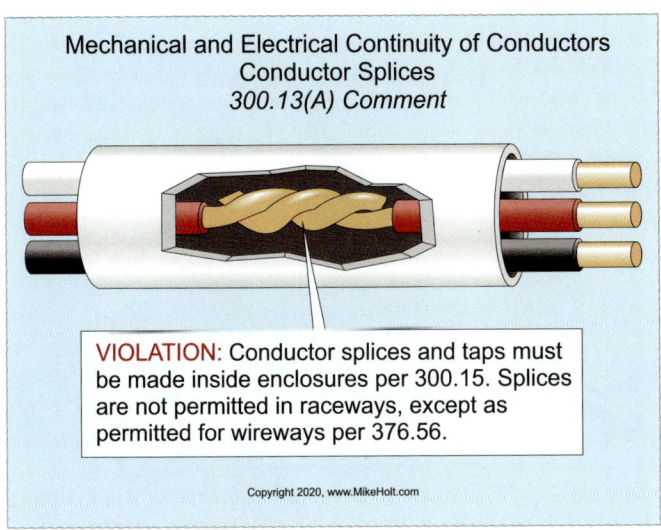

▶Figure 300-57

(B) Device Removal—Neutral Continuity. Continuity of the neutral conductor of a multiwire branch circuit is not permitted to be interrupted by the removal of a wiring device.

300.14 | General Requirements for Wiring Methods and Materials

▶ **Hazard of Open Neutral Example**

Example: If the neutral conductor is interrupted on a 3-wire, 120/240V multiwire circuit that supplies a 1,200W, 120V hair dryer and a 600W, 120V television, it will cause the 120V television to momentarily operate at 160V before it burns up. This can be determined as follows: ▶Figure 300-59 and ▶Figure 300-60

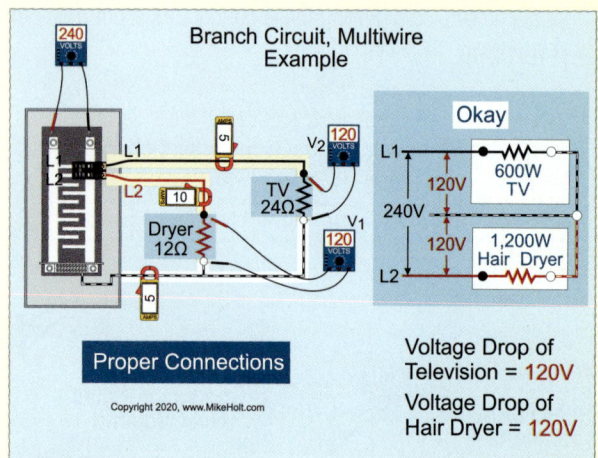

▶Figure 300-59

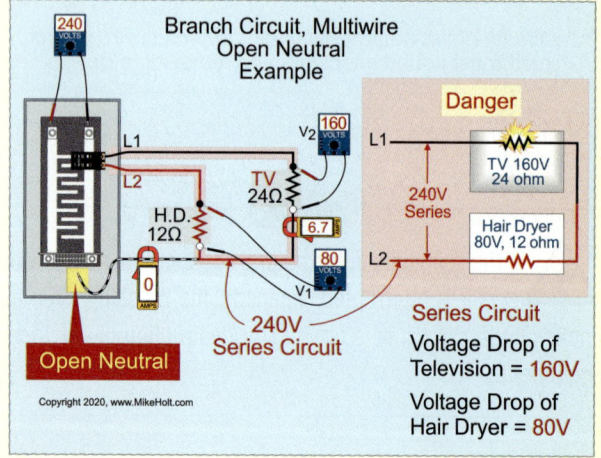

▶Figure 300-60

Step 1: Determine the resistance of each appliance.

$R = E^2/P$

R of the hair dryer = $120V^2/1,200W$
R of the hair dryer = 12 ohms

R of the television = $120V^2/600W$
R of the television = 24 ohms

Step 2: Determine the current of the circuit.

I = Volts/Resistance

Volts = 240V
R = 36 ohms (12 ohms + 24 ohms)

I = 240V/36 ohms
I = 6.70A

Step 3: Determine the operating voltage for each appliance.

Volts = I × R

I = 6.70A
R = 12 ohms for the hair dryer and 24 ohms for the TV.

Voltage of hair dryer = 6.70A × 12 ohms
Voltage of hair dryer = 80V

Voltage of television = 6.70A × 24 ohms
Voltage of television = 160V

300.14 Length of Free Conductors

At least 6 in. of conductor, measured from the point in the box where the conductors enter the enclosure, must be available at each point for conductor splices or terminations. ▶Figure 300-61

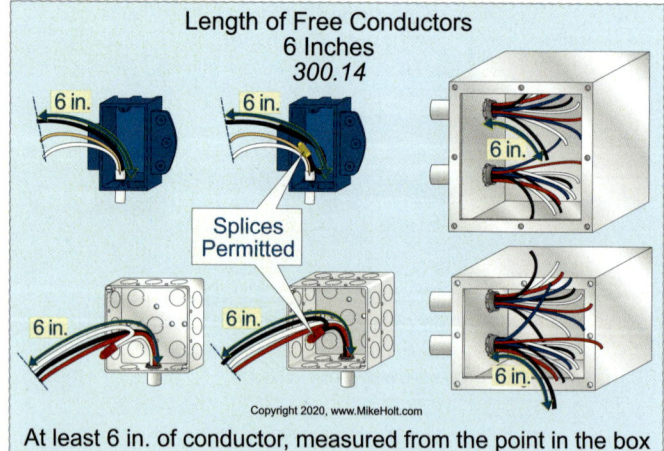

At least 6 in. of conductor, measured from the point in the box where the conductor enters the enclosure, must be available at each point for conductor splices or terminations.

▶Figure 300-61

Boxes with openings less than 8 in. at any dimension must have at least 6 in. of conductor, measured from the point where the conductors enter the box, and at least 3 in. of conductor outside the box. ▶Figure 300-62

General Requirements for Wiring Methods and Materials | 300.15

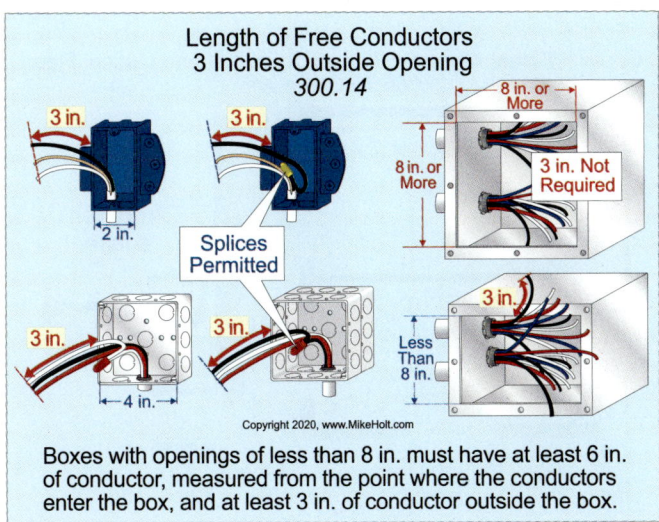
▶Figure 300-62

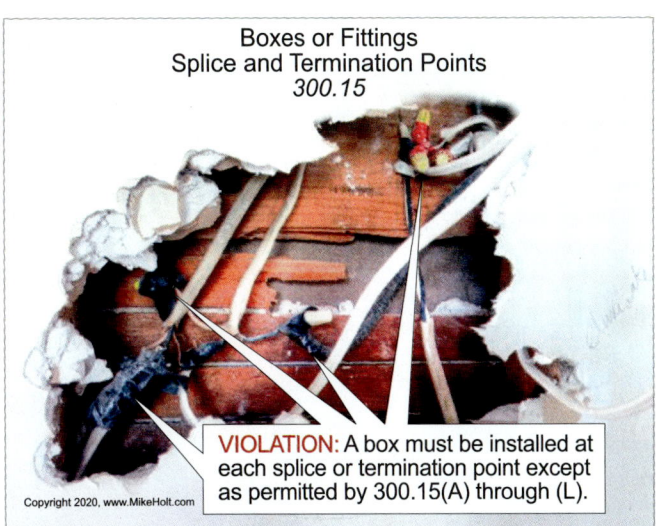
▶Figure 300-64

300.15 Boxes or Fittings

A box must be installed at each splice or termination point, except as permitted by 300.15(A) through (L): ▶Figure 300-63 and ▶Figure 300-64

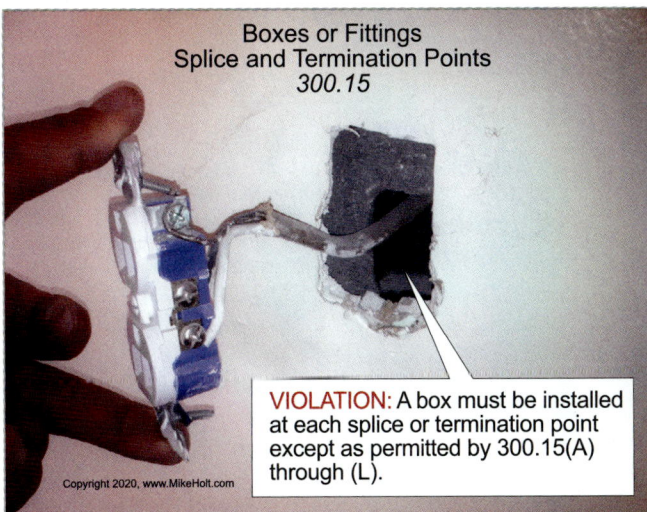
▶Figure 300-63

Author's Comment:

▶ Conductors can be spliced in a conduit body in accordance with 314.16(C). ▶Figure 300-65

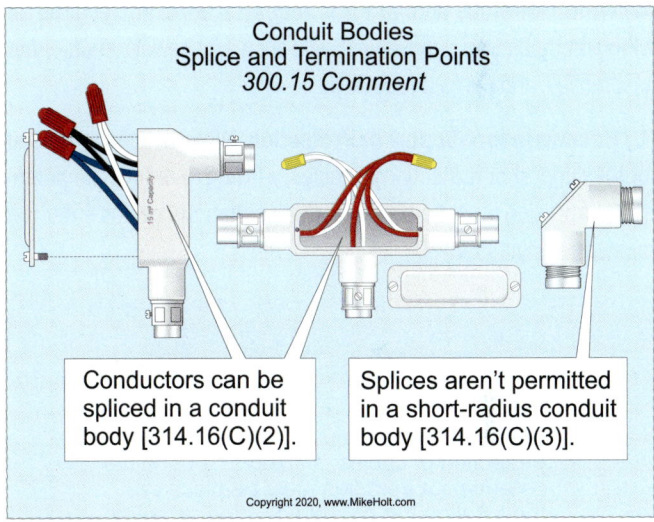
▶Figure 300-65

Fittings and connectors can only be used with the specific wiring methods for which they are designed and listed. ▶Figure 300-66

Author's Comment:

▶ Type NM cable connectors are not permitted to be used with Type AC cable, and electrical metallic tubing fittings are not permitted to be used with rigid metal conduit or intermediate metal conduit unless listed for the purpose

▶ PVC conduit couplings and connectors are permitted with electrical nonmetallic tubing if the proper glue is used in accordance with manufacturer's instructions [110.3(B)]. See 362.48.

300.15 | General Requirements for Wiring Methods and Materials

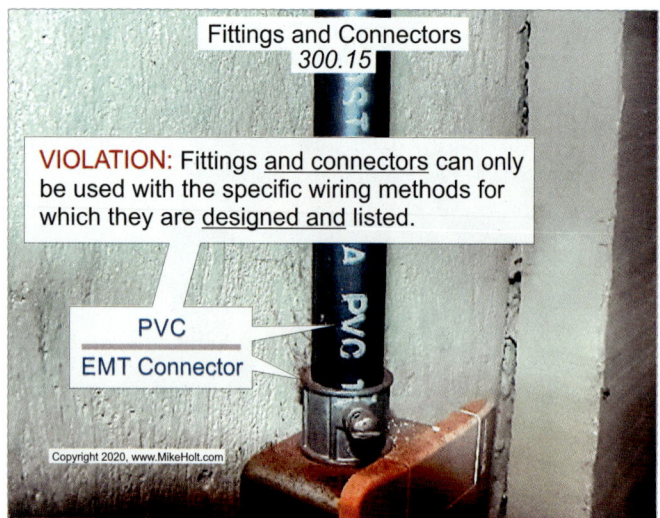

▶Figure 300-66

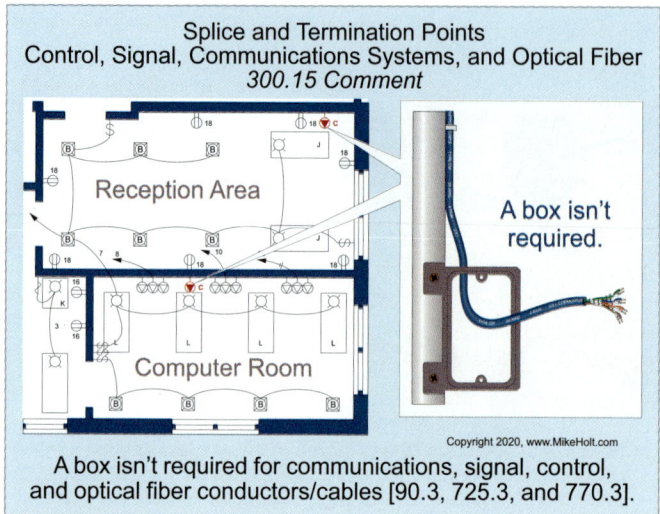

▶Figure 300-68

(A) Wiring Methods with Interior Access. A box is not required for wiring methods with removable covers such as wireways, multioutlet assemblies, and surface raceways.

(C) Raceways for Support or Protection. When a raceway is used for the support or protection of cables, a fitting to reduce the potential for abrasion must be placed at the location the cables enter the raceway. ▶Figure 300-67

(F) Fittings. A fitting identified for the use is permitted instead of a box or conduit body where conductors are not spliced or terminated within the fitting. The fitting must be accessible after installation, unless it is listed for concealed installation. ▶Figure 300-69

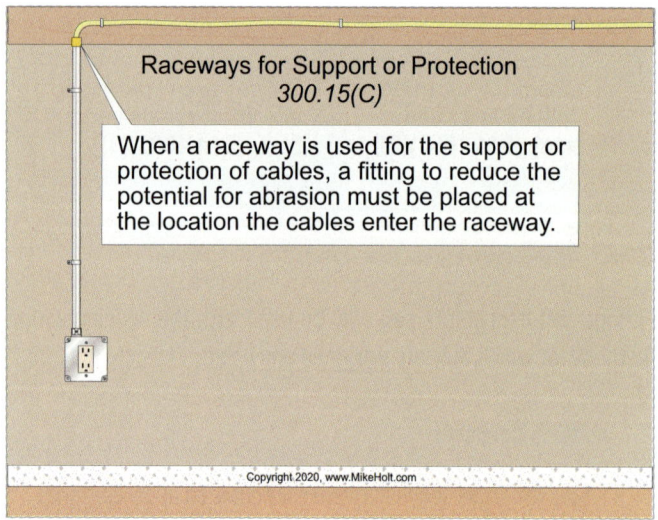

▶Figure 300-67

Author's Comment:

▶ Boxes are not required for the following signaling and communications cables or raceways: ▶Figure 300-68

- Class 2 and 3 Control and Signaling, 725.3
- Communications, 90.3
- Coaxial Cable, 90.3
- Optical Fiber, 770.3

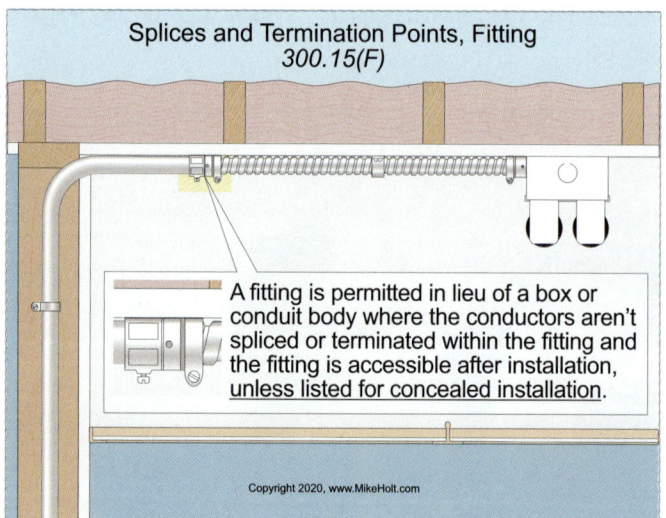

▶Figure 300-69

(G) Underground Splices. A box is not required where a splice is made underground if the conductors are spliced with a splicing device listed for direct burial. See 110.14(B) and 300.5(E).

(H) Type NM Cable Interconnector Device. A box is not required where a listed nonmetallic-sheathed cable interconnector device is used for exposed cable wiring or concealed repair wiring in an existing building in accordance with 334.40(B). ▶Figure 300-70

General Requirements for Wiring Methods and Materials | 300.17

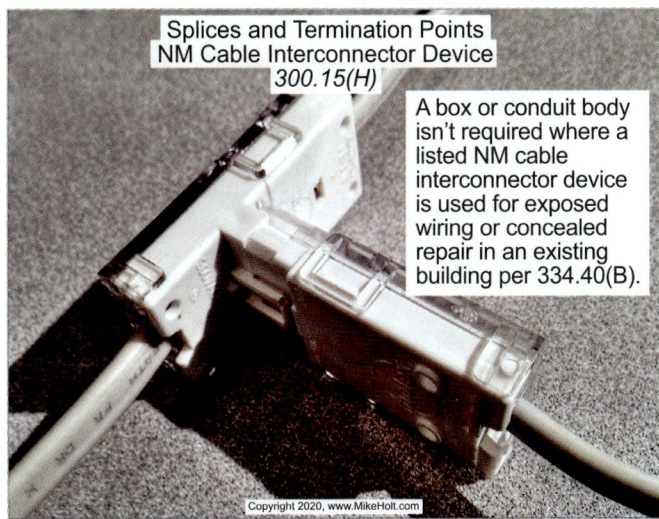
▶Figure 300-70

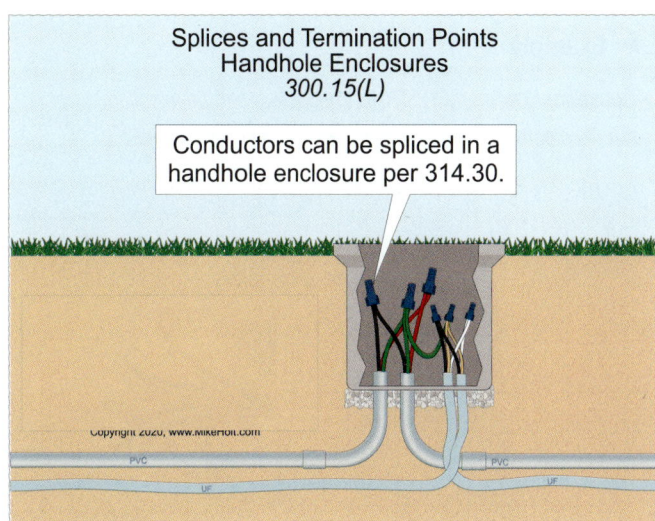
▶Figure 300-72

(I) Enclosures. A box or conduit body is not required where a splice is made in a cabinet containing switches or overcurrent protective devices if the splices or taps do not fill the wiring space at any cross section to more than 75 percent, and the wiring at any cross section does not exceed 40 percent. See 312.8 and 404.3(B). ▶Figure 300-71

Author's Comment:

▸ A handhole enclosure is used for underground wiring and designed to allow persons to reach into but not enter the enclosure [Article 100].

▸ Equipment used for splices or terminations in a handhole enclosure must be listed for wet locations [110.14(B) and 314.30(C)].

300.17 Number and Size of Conductors in a Raceway

Raceways must be large enough to permit the installation and removal of conductors without damaging the conductors' insulation.

Note: See the "xxx.22" section of the specific wiring method for more information about the number of conductors permitted.

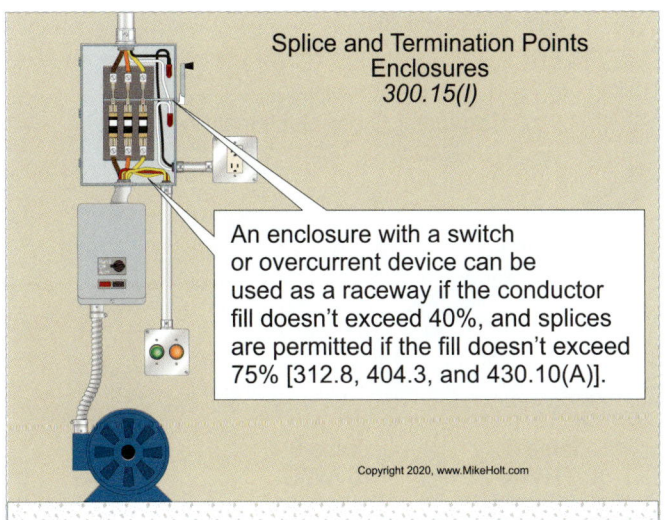
▶Figure 300-71

Author's Comment:

▸ When all conductors within a raceway are the same size and of the same insulation type, the number of conductors permitted, or the raceway size can be determined using Annex C.

(L) Handhole Enclosures. A box is not required for conductors installed in a handhole enclosure installed in accordance with 314.30. ▶Figure 300-72

300.17 | General Requirements for Wiring Methods and Materials

▶ **Example**

Question: How many 12 THHN conductors can be installed in trade size ¾ electrical metallic tubing (EMT)? ▶Figure 300–73

(a) 10 (b) 12 (c) 14 (d) 16

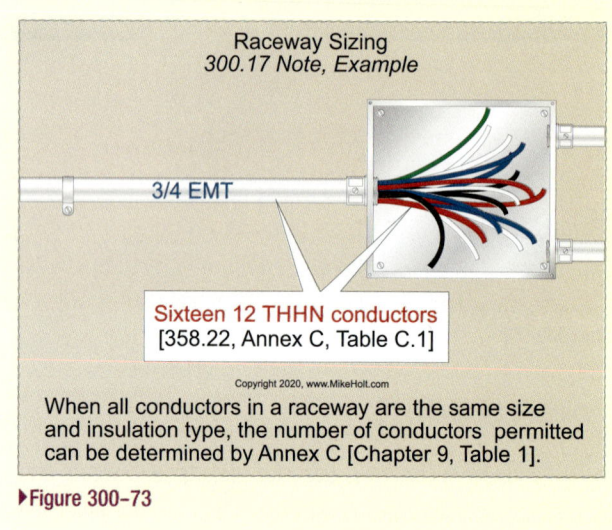

▶Figure 300–73

Answer: (d) 16 [Annex C, Table C.1]

Author's Comment:

▶ When different size conductors are installed in a raceway, conductor fill is limited to the percentages in Table 1 and Note (6) of Chapter 9. ▶Figure 300–74

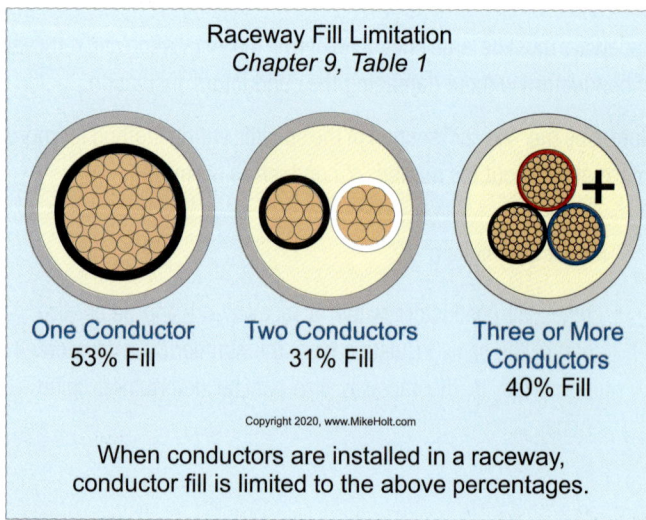

▶Figure 300–74

Chapter 9, Table 1	
Number	Percent Fill
1 Conductor	53%
2 Conductors	31%
3 or More	40%

The above percentages are based on conditions where the length of the conductor and number of raceway bends are within reasonable limits [Chapter 9, Table 1, Table Note 1].

Author's Comment:

▶ Follow these steps for sizing raceways:

  ▶ **Step 1:** When sizing a raceway, first determine the total area needed for the conductors (Chapter 9, Table 5 for insulated conductors and Chapter 9, Table 8 for bare conductors). ▶Figure 300–75

  ▶ **Step 2:** Select the raceway from Chapter 9, Table 4 in accordance with the percent fill listed in Chapter 9, Table 1. ▶Figure 300–76

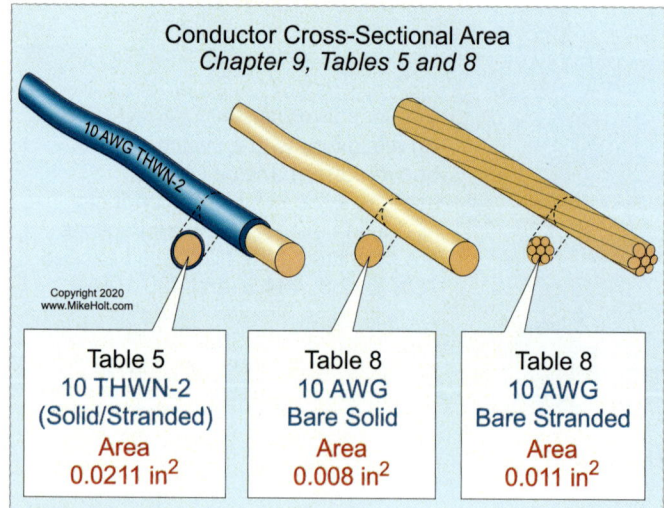

▶Figure 300–75

General Requirements for Wiring Methods and Materials | 300.19

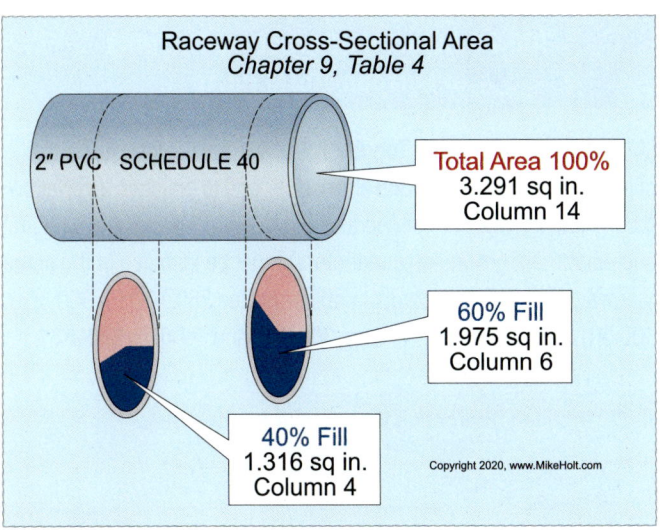
▶Figure 300-76

▶ **Example**

Question: What size Schedule 40 PVC conduit is required for the following conductors? ▶Figure 300-77

▶ 3–500 THHN
▶ 1–250 THHN
▶ 1–3 THHN

(a) Trade Size 1   (b) Trade Size 2   (c) Trade Size 3   (d) Trade Size 4

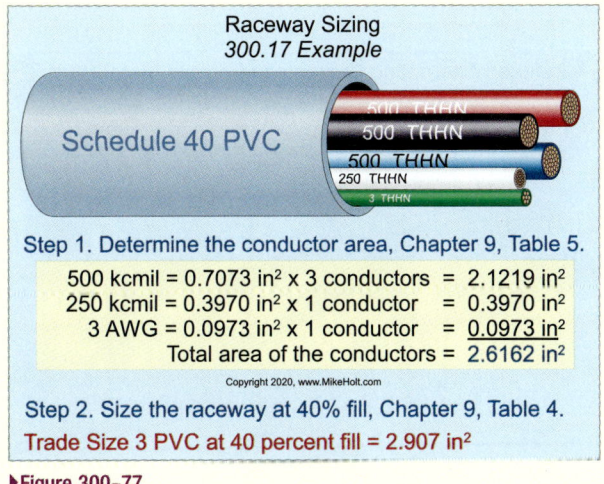
▶Figure 300-77

Solution:

Step 1: Determine the total area needed for the conductors [Chapter 9, Table 5].

500 THHN	0.7073 × 3 =	2.1219 in.²
250 THHN	0.3970 × 1 =	0.3970 in.²
3 THHN	0.0973 × 1 =	+ 0.0973 in.²
Total Area =		2.6162 in.²

Step 2: Select the raceway at 40 percent fill [Chapter 9, Table 1 and Table Note (6), and Table 4].

Use trade size 3 Schedule 40 PVC because there are 2.907 sq in. of conductor fill at 40 percent.

Answer: (c) Trade Size 3

300.18 Inserting Conductors in Raceways

(A) Complete Runs. To protect conductor insulation from abrasion during installation, raceways must be mechanically completed between the pulling points before conductors are installed. See 300.10 and 300.12. ▶Figure 300-78

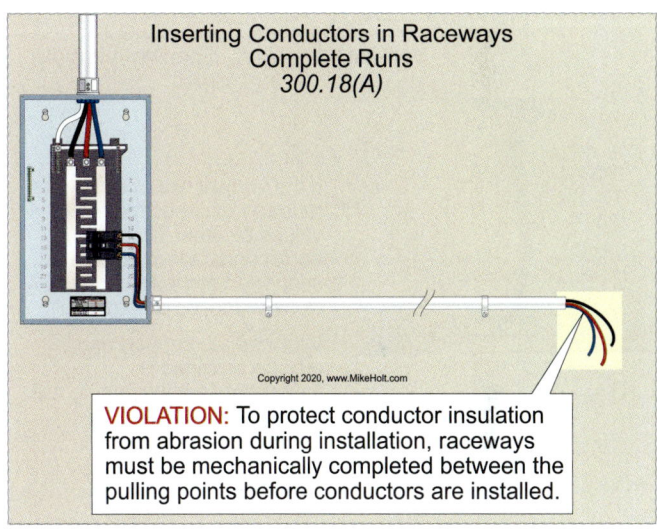
▶Figure 300-78

Ex: Short sections of raceways used for the protection of cables from physical damage are not required to be complete. ▶Figure 300-79

300.19 Supporting Conductors in Vertical Raceways

(A) Spacing Intervals. If the vertical rise of a raceway exceeds the values of Table 300.19(A), each conductor must be supported at the top or as close to the top as practical. Intermediate support must also be provided in increments not exceeding the values of Table 300.19(A). ▶Figure 300-80

300.20 | General Requirements for Wiring Methods and Materials

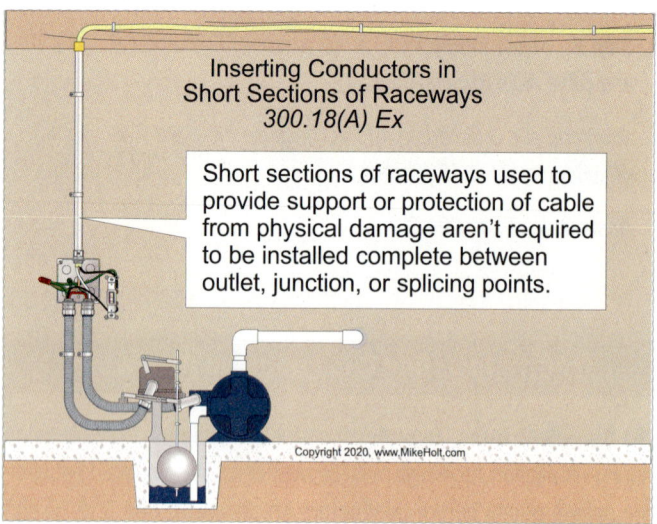

▶Figure 300-79

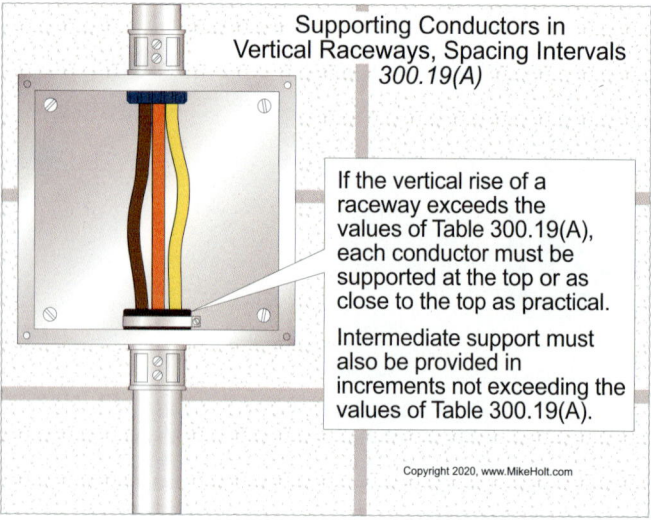

▶Figure 300-80

Author's Comment:

▶ A great deal of weight accumulates in long vertical runs of conductors and can cause them to drop out of the raceway (sometimes called a "runaway") if they are not properly secured. There have been many cases where conductors in a vertical raceway were released from the pulling "basket" or "grip" (at the top) without being secured. Sheer weight and gravity take over, accelerating the conductors down and out of the raceway and injuring those at the bottom of the installation.

300.20 Induced Alternating Currents in Ferrous Metal Parts

(A) Conductors Grouped Together. To minimize the induction heating of ferrous metal raceways and enclosures, and to maintain an effective ground-fault current path, all conductors of a circuit (including any neutral and equipment grounding conductors) must be installed in the same raceway, cable, trench, cord, or cable tray. See 250.102(E), 300.3(B), 300.5(I), and 392.20(C). ▶Figure 300-81 and ▶Figure 300-82

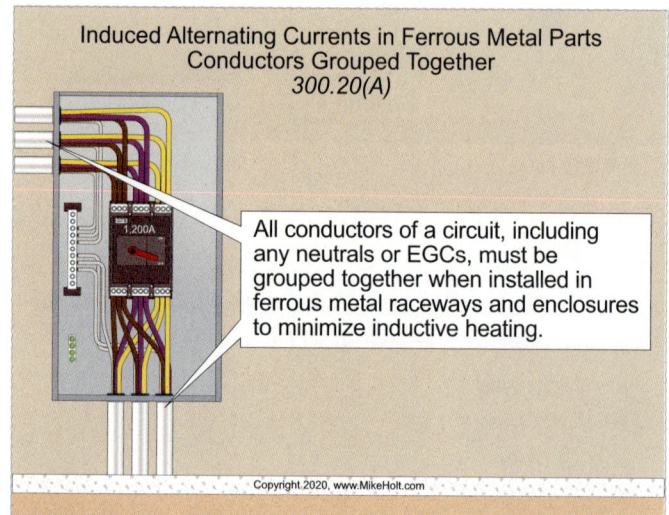

▶Figure 300-81

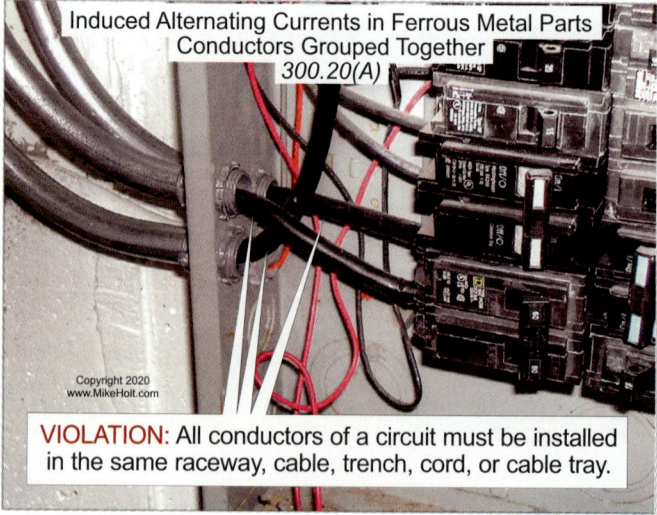

▶Figure 300-82

General Requirements for Wiring Methods and Materials | **300.20**

Author's Comment:

▸ When alternating current flows through a conductor, a pulsating or varying magnetic field is created around the conductor. This magnetic field is constantly expanding and contracting with the amplitude of the alternating current. In the United States, the frequency is 60 cycles per second (Hz). Since alternating current reverses polarity 120 times per second, the magnetic field that surrounds the conductor also reverses direction 120 times per second. This expanding and collapsing magnetic field induces eddy currents in the ferrous metal parts that surround the conductors, causing them to heat up due to hysteresis heating.

▸ Magnetic materials naturally resist rapidly changing magnetic fields. The resulting friction produces its own heat (hysteresis heating) in addition to eddy current heating. A metal which offers high resistance is said to have high magnetic "permeability." Permeability can vary on a scale of 100 to 500 for magnetic materials; nonmagnetic materials have a permeability of one.

▸ Simply put, the molecules of steel and iron align to the polarity of the magnetic field and when it reverses, the molecules reverse their polarity as well. This back-and-forth alignment of the molecules heats up the metal. The more the current flows, the more the heat increases in ferrous metal parts. ▸Figure 300–83

Author's Comment:

▸ When conductors of the same circuit are grouped together, the magnetic fields of the different conductors tend to cancel each other out, resulting in a reduced magnetic field around them. The smaller magnetic field reduces induced currents in ferrous metal raceways or enclosures, which reduces the hysteresis heating of the surrounding metal enclosure.

(B) Single Conductors. Where a single conductor carrying alternating current passes through metal with magnetic properties, the inductive effect must be minimized by either cutting slots in the metal between the individual holes through which the individual conductors pass, or passing all the conductors in the circuit through an insulating wall large enough for all the conductors of the circuit

Author's Comment:

▸ When single conductors are installed in nonmetallic raceways as permitted in 300.5(I) Ex 2, the inductive heating of the metal enclosure can be minimized by using aluminum locknuts and by cutting a slot between the individual holes through which the conductors pass. ▸Figure 300–84

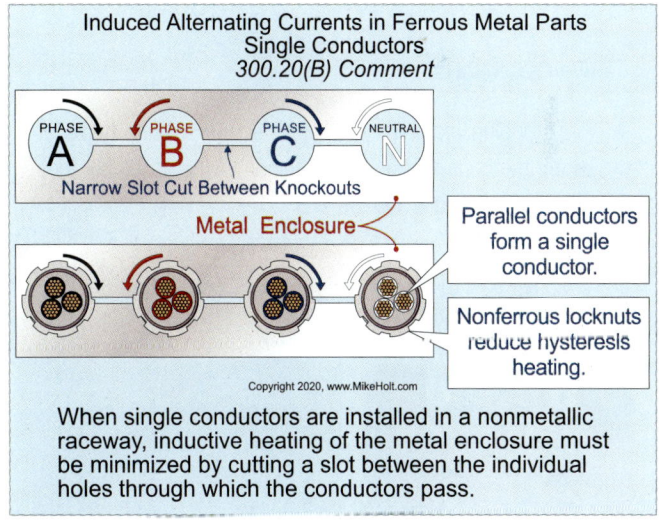

▸Figure 300–84

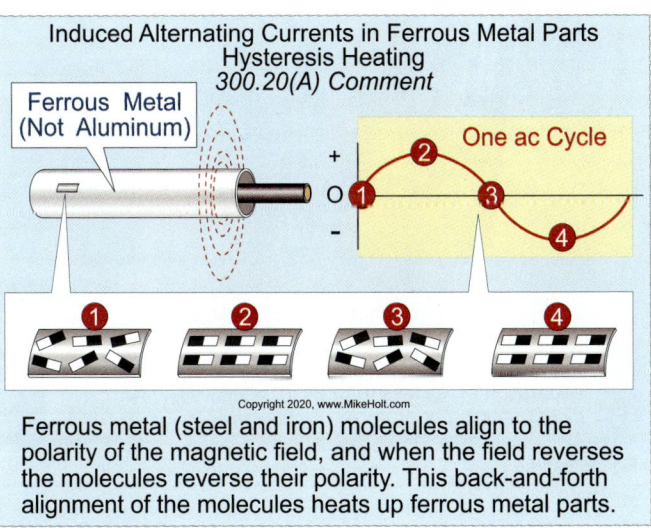

▸Figure 300–83

Note: Because aluminum is a nonmagnetic metal, aluminum parts do not heat up due to hysteresis heating.

300.21 Spread of Fire or Products of Combustion

Electrical circuits and equipment must be installed in such a way that the spread of fire or products of combustion will not be substantially increased. Openings around electrical penetrations into or through fire-resistant-rated walls, partitions, floors, or ceilings must be firestopped using approved methods to maintain the fire-resistance rating. ▶Figure 300–85

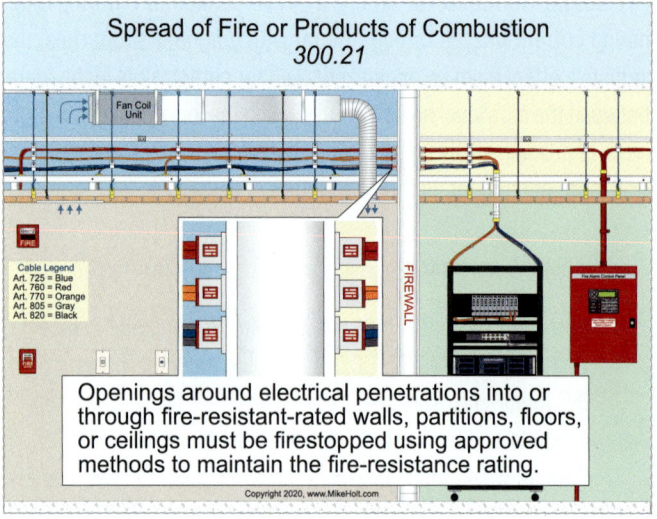

▶Figure 300–85

Author's Comment:

▸ Fire-stopping materials are listed for the specific types of wiring methods and the construction of the assembly they penetrate. ▶Figure 300–86

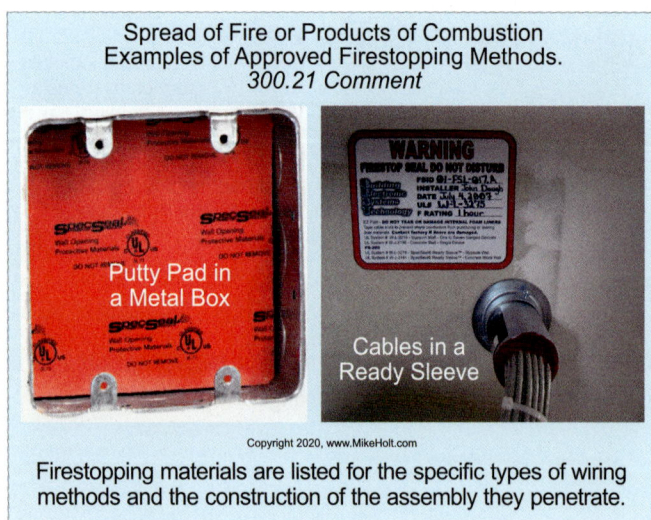

▶Figure 300–86

Note: Directories of electrical construction materials published by recognized testing laboratories contain listing and installation restrictions necessary to maintain the fire-resistive rating of assemblies. Building codes also have restrictions on penetrations on opposite sides of a fire-resistance rated wall. Outlet boxes must have a horizontal separation of not less than 24 in. when installed in a fire-rated assembly, unless an outlet box is listed for closer spacing or protected by fire-resistant "putty pads" in accordance with manufacturer's instructions. ▶Figure 300–87 and ▶Figure 300–88

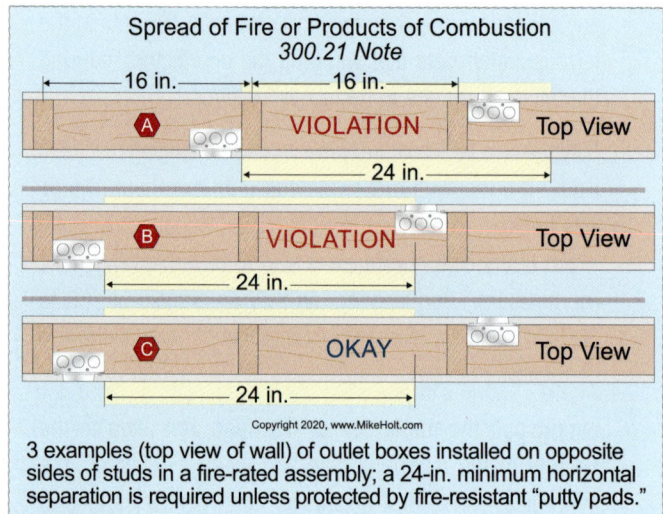

▶Figure 300–87

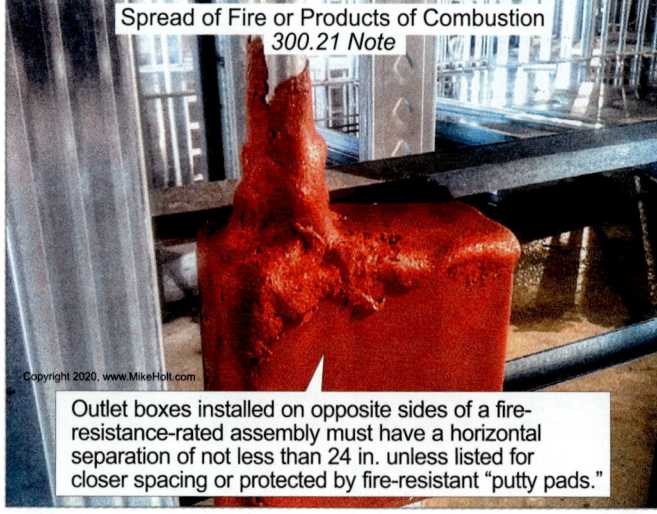

▶Figure 300–88

General Requirements for Wiring Methods and Materials | 300.22

Author's Comment:

▸ Boxes installed in fire-resistance rated assemblies must be listed for the purpose. If steel boxes are used, they must be secured to the framing member; cut-in type boxes are not permitted (UL White Book, *Guide Information for Electrical Equipment*).

▸ This requirement also applies to control, signaling, and communications cables or raceways.

  ▸ Communications and Coaxial Cable, 800.26
  ▸ Control and Signaling, 725.3(B)
  ▸ Fire Alarms, 760.3(A)
  ▸ Optical Fiber, 770.26
  ▸ Sound Systems, 640.3(A)

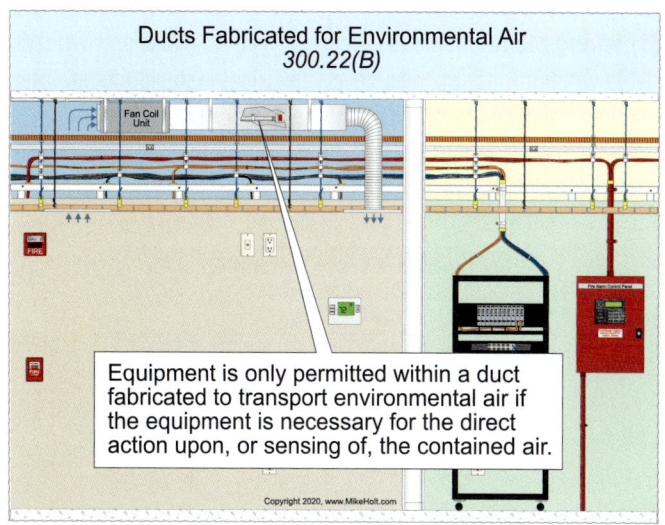

▸Figure 300-90

300.22 Wiring in Ducts and Plenum Spaces

This section applies to the installation and uses of electrical wiring and equipment in ducts used for dust, loose stock, or vapor removal; ducts specifically fabricated for environmental air; and plenum spaces used for environmental air.

(A) Ducts Used for Dust, Loose Stock, or Vapor. Wiring methods are not permitted to be installed in ducts that transport dust, loose stock, or flammable vapors. ▸Figure 300-89

▸Figure 300-89

(B) Ducts Fabricated for Environmental Air. Equipment is only permitted within a duct fabricated to transport environmental air if the equipment is necessary for the direct action upon, or sensing of, the contained air. ▸Figure 300-90

Type MC Cable without an overall nonmetallic covering and metal raceways can be installed in ducts fabricated to transport environmental air. Flexible metal conduit in lengths not exceeding 4 ft can be used to connect physically adjustable equipment and devices within the fabricated duct.

(C) Plenum Spaces for Environmental Air. This section applies only to the space above a suspended ceiling or below a raised floor used for environmental air. It does not apply to habitable rooms or areas of buildings, the prime purpose of which is not air handling.

Note 1: The spaces or cavities above a suspended ceiling and below a raised floor used for environmental air are examples of the type of plenum space to which this section applies. ▸Figure 300-91

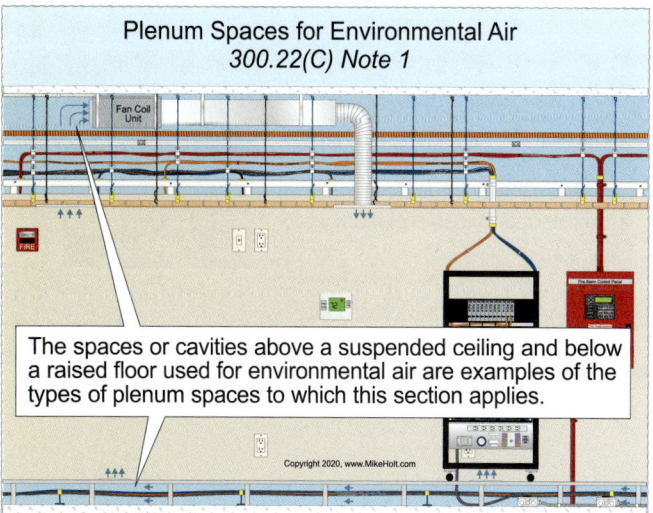

▸Figure 300-91

300.22 | General Requirements for Wiring Methods and Materials

(1) Wiring Methods. Metal raceways, Type AC cable, and Type MC cable without a nonmetallic cover, electrical metallic tubing, intermediate metal conduit, rigid metal conduit, flexible metal conduit, or (where accessible) surface metal raceways or metal wireways with metal covers. ▶Figure 300-92

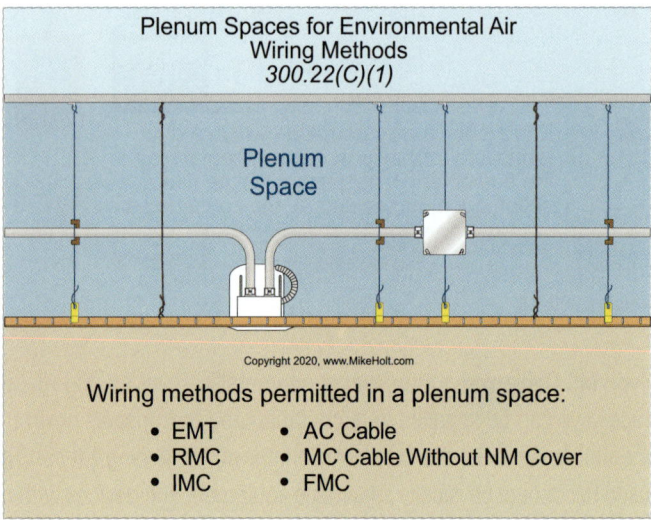

▶Figure 300-92

Cable ties for securing and supporting must be listed for use in a plenum space ▶Figure 300-93

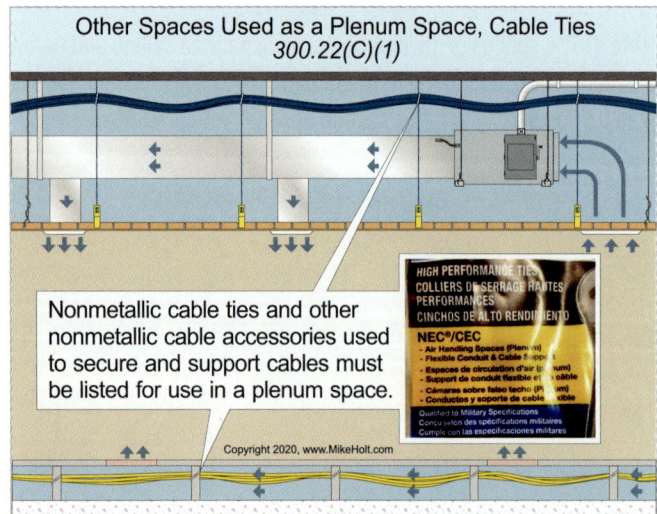

▶Figure 300-93

Author's Comment:

▸ Plenum-rated control, signaling, and communications cables and raceways are permitted in plenum spaces according to the following: ▶Figure 300-94

  ▸ Communications Cable and Coaxial Cable, 800.3(C) and Table 800.154(a)
  ▸ Control and Signaling, 725.3(C) Ex 2 and Table 725.154
  ▸ Fire Alarms, 760.3(B) Ex 2 and Table 760.154
  ▸ Optical Fiber Cables and Raceways, Table 770.154(a)
  ▸ Sound Systems, 640.9(C) and Table 725.154

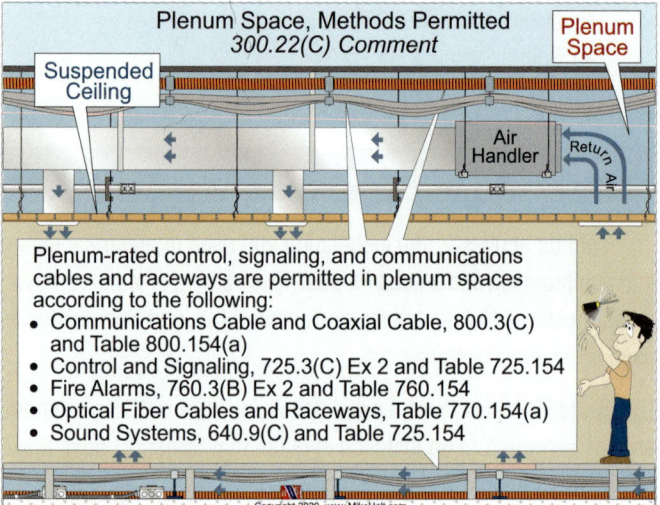

▶Figure 300-94

(2) Cable Tray Systems.

(a) Metal Cable Tray Systems. Metal cable tray systems can be installed to support the wiring methods and equipment permitted to be installed in a plenum space. ▶Figure 300-95

(3) Equipment. Electrical equipment with a metal enclosure or a nonmetallic enclosure listed for use in an air-handling space can be installed in a plenum space. ▶Figure 300-96

Author's Comment:

▸ Examples of electrical equipment permitted in plenum spaces are air handlers, junction boxes, and dry-type transformers; however, transformers are not permitted to be rated over 50 kVA when located in hollow spaces [450.13(B)].

General Requirements for Wiring Methods and Materials | 300.25

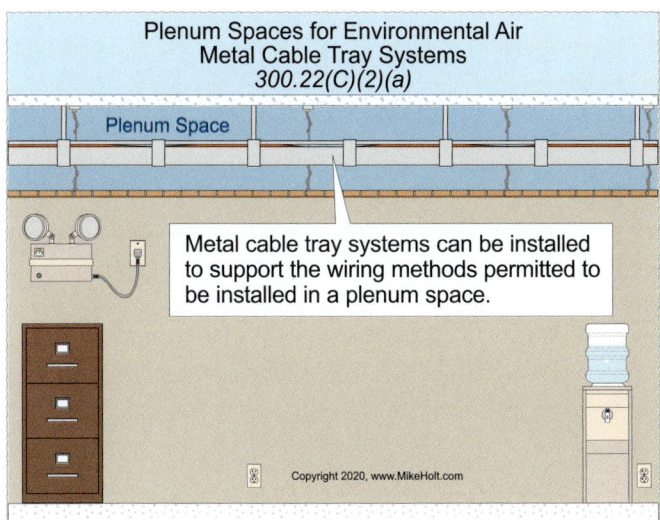
▶Figure 300-95

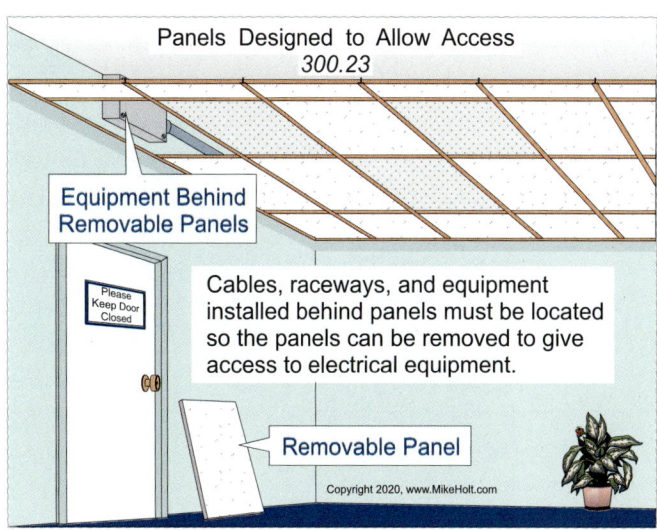
▶Figure 300-97

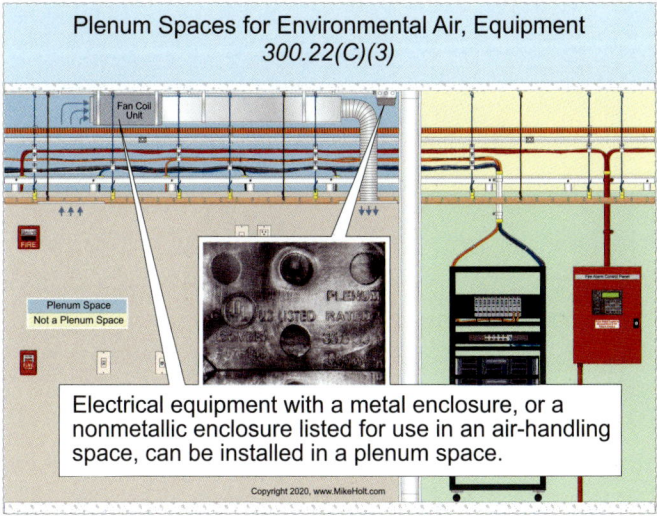
▶Figure 300-96

- Communications Cable and Coaxial Cable, 800.21
- Control and Signaling Cable, 725.21
- Fire Alarm Cable, 760.21
- Optical Fiber Cable, 770.21
- Audio Cable, 640.5

300.25 Exit Enclosures (Stair Towers)

Where an exit enclosure is required to be separated from the building, only the wiring methods serving equipment permitted by the authority having jurisdiction in the exit enclosure are permitted to be installed within the exit enclosure.

Author's Comment:

- As used here, "separated from the building" does not necessarily mean detached. Article 100 defines a "Building" as "a structure that stands alone or that is separated from adjoining structures by fire walls." The fire rating rules for walls surrounding a stair tower are much more stringent and serve to "separate" it from the main building. Typically, only lighting and heat are necessary to serve a stair tower. If a stair tower landing is the only place for a sub-panel (for example) to be installed, it will require documented special permission from the authority having jurisdiction.

Note: For more information, refer to NFPA 101, *Life Safety Code*, 7.1.3.2.1(10)(b).

300.23 Panels Designed to Allow Access

Cables, raceways, and equipment installed behind panels must be located so the panels can be removed to give access to electrical equipment. ▶Figure 300-97

Author's Comment:

- Access to equipment is not permitted to be hindered by an accumulation of cables that prevent the removal of suspended-ceiling panels. Control, signaling, and communications cables must be located and supported so the suspended-ceiling panels can be moved to provide access to electrical equipment.

Notes

ARTICLE 310 CONDUCTORS FOR GENERAL WIRING

Introduction to Article 310—Conductors for General Wiring

This article contains the general requirements for conductors such as their insulation markings, ampacity ratings, and conditions of use. It does not apply to conductors that are part of flexible cords, fixture wires, or to those that are an integral part of equipment [90.7 and 300.1(B)].

Why does Article 310 contain so many tables? Why does Table 310.17 list the ampacity of 6 THHN as 105A, while Table 310.16 lists the same conductor as having an ampacity of only 75A? To answer that, go back to Article 100, review the definition of "Ampacity" and notice the phrase "conditions of use." These tables set a maximum current value at which premature failure of the conductor insulation should not occur during normal use, under the conditions described in the tables. Tables throughout the *NEC* are accompanied by a section of text with information about that table. For example, section 310.16 says that Table 310.16 applies to conductors carrying voltages rated 0V through 2,000V. It can be easy to overlook that limitation if you are not careful! It is imperative for you to read the *Code* section pertaining to each table and any of the Table's footnotes before you decide what is necessary for your particular application.

THHN, THWN-2, RHH, and so on, are insulation types. Those containing a "W" are suitable for use in wet locations. Every type of insulation has a limit as to how much heat it can withstand. When current flows through a conductor, it creates heat. How well the insulation around a conductor can dissipate that heat depends on factors such as whether the conductor is in free air or not. Think about what happens when you put on a sweater, a jacket, and then a coat—all at the same time. You heat up. Your skin cannot dissipate heat with all that clothing on nearly as well as it can in free air. The same principle applies to conductors.

Conductor insulation degrades with age and is called "aging." Its failure takes decades under normal use and becomes a maintenance issue for the appropriate personnel to manage. However, if a conductor is forced to exceed the ampacity listed in the appropriate table (and as a result its design temperature is exceeded) insulation failure happens much sooner and is often catastrophic. Consequently, exceeding the ampacity of a conductor is a serious safety issue.

Part I. General

310.1 Scope

Article 310 contains the general requirements for conductors rated up to and including 2,000V, including their insulation markings, ampacity ratings, and use. ▶Figure 310–1

Note: For flexible cords and cable, see Article 400. For fixture wires, see Article 402.

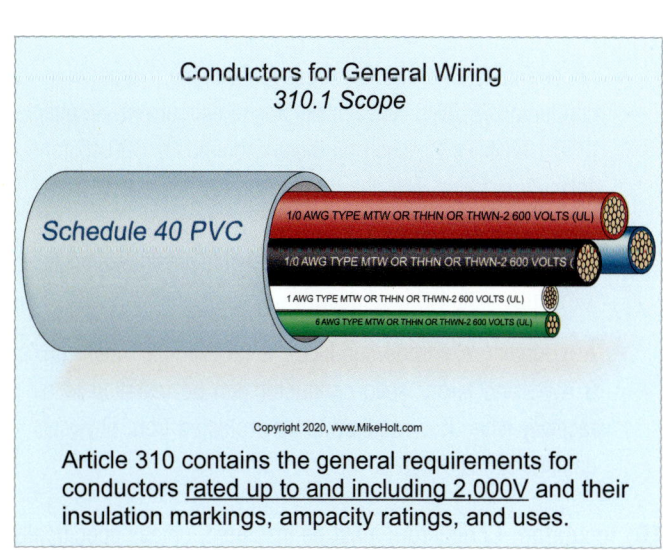
▶Figure 310–1

310.3 Conductors

(A) Minimum Size Conductors. The minimum sizes of conductors are 14 AWG copper or 12 AWG aluminum or copper-clad aluminum, except as permitted elsewhere in this *Code*.

310.4 | Conductors for General Wiring

Author's Comment:

- There is a misconception that 12 AWG copper is the smallest conductor permitted for commercial or industrial facilities. Although it is not true based on *NEC* rules, it might be a job specification or local code requirement.

- Conductors smaller than 14 AWG are permitted for Class 1 remote-control circuits [725.43], fixture wire [402.6], and motor control circuits [Table 430.72(B)].

(C) Stranded Conductors. Conductors 8 AWG and larger installed in a raceway must be stranded, unless specifically permitted or required elsewhere in this *Code* to be solid. ▶Figure 310–2

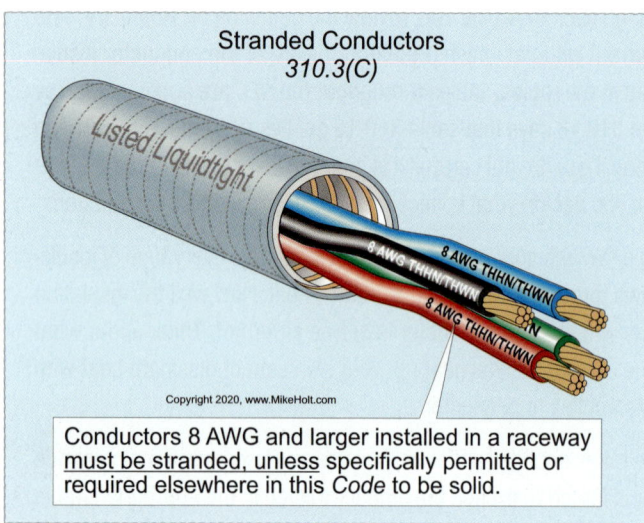

▶Figure 310–2

Author's Comment:

- According to 250.120(C), exposed equipment grounding conductors 8 AWG and smaller for direct-current circuits [250.134(2) Ex 2], such as those required by 690.45 for solar PV systems, are permitted to be run separately from the circuit conductors. Where an 8 AWG or smaller exposed equipment grounding conductor is subject to physical damage, it must be installed in a raceway or cable.

- A grounding electrode conductor is an example where an 8 AWG and larger solid conductor can be installed in a raceway when it is required to be protected from physical damage [250.64(B)].

(D) Insulated. Conductors must be insulated, unless specifically permitted to be bare. ▶Figure 310–3

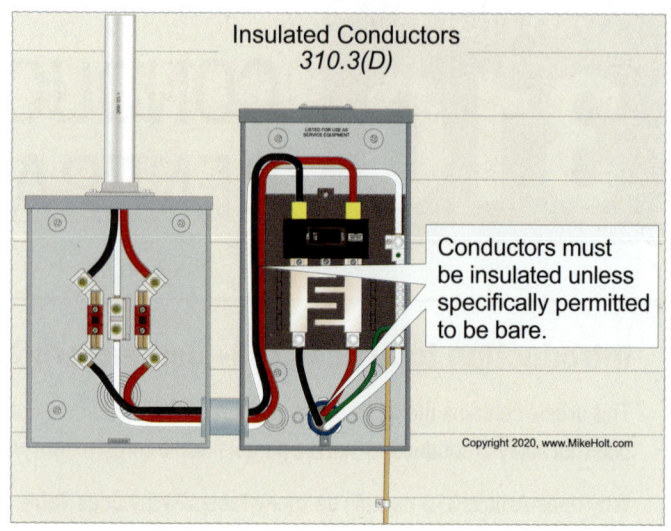

▶Figure 310–3

Part II. Construction Specifications

310.4 Conductor Construction and Application

Table 310.4(A) provides information on conductor insulation properties such as letter type, maximum operating temperature, application, insulation, and outer cover properties. Only conductors in Tables 310.4(A) can be installed for the application identified in the tables.

Author's Comment:

- The following explains the lettering on conductor insulation [Table 310.4(A)]: ▶Figure 310–4

    - No H   60°C insulation rating
    - H   75°C insulation rating
    - HH   90°C insulation rating permitted in dry locations
    - -2   90°C insulation rating permitted in wet locations
    - N   Nylon outer cover
    - T   Thermoplastic insulation
    - U   Underground
    - W   Permitted in wet or damp locations

Table 310.4(A) Conductor Applications and Insulations

Type Letter	Column 2 Insulation	Column 3 Max. Operating Temperature	Column 4 Application	Column 5 Sizes Available AWG or kcmil	Column 6 Outer Covering
RHH	Flame-retardant thermoset	90°C	Dry and damp locations	14 – 2,000	Moisture-resistant, flame-retardant, nonmetallic
RHW	Flame-retardant, moisture-resistant thermoset	75°C	Dry and wet locations	14 – 2,000	Moisture-resistant, flame-retardant, nonmetallic
RHW-2	Flame-retardant, moisture-resistant thermoset	90°C	Dry and wet locations	14 – 2,000	Moisture-resistant, flame-retardant, nonmetallic
THHN	Flame-retardant, heat-resistant thermoplastic	90°C	Dry and damp locations	14 – 1,000	Nylon jacket or equivalent
THHW	Flame-retardant, moisture- and heat-resistant thermoplastic	75°C 90°C	Wet locations Dry locations	14 – 1,000	None
THW	Flame-retardant, moisture- and heat-resistant thermoplastic	75°C	Dry, damp, and wet locations	14 – 2,000	None
THW-2	Flame-retardant, moisture- and heat-resistant thermoplastic	90°C	Dry, damp, and wet locations	14 – 1,000	None
THWN	Flame-retardant, moisture- and heat-resistant thermoplastic	75°C	Dry, damp, and wet locations	14 – 1,000	Nylon jacket or equivalent
THWN-2	Flame-retardant, moisture- and heat-resistant thermoplastic	90°C	Dry, damp, and wet locations	14 – 1,000	Nylon jacket or equivalent
TW	Flame-retardant, moisture-resistant thermoplastic	60°C	Dry, damp, and wet locations	14 – 2,000	None
USE	Heat- and moisture-resistant	75°C	See Article 338	14 – 2,000	Moisture-resistant nonmetallic
USE-2	Heat- and moisture-resistant	90°C	Dry, damp, and wet locations.	14 – 2,000	Moisture-resistant nonmetallic

310.4 | Conductors for General Wiring

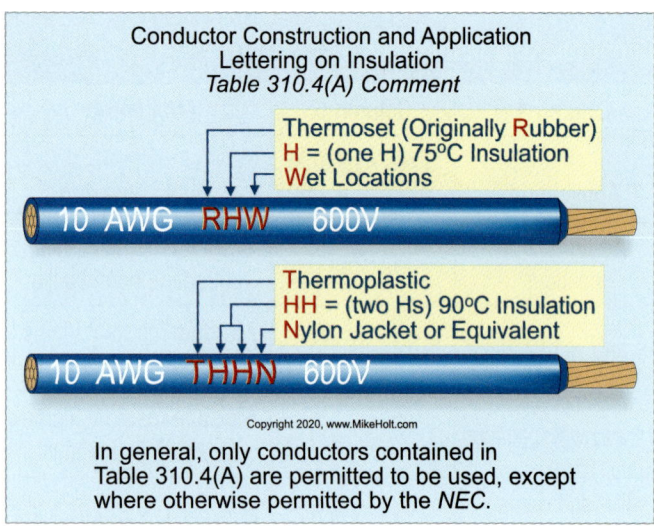
▶Figure 310–4

In general, only those conductors contained in Table 310.4(A) can be used, except where otherwise permitted in the *NEC*. Some examples are PV wire, PV cables, or DG cable [690.31(C)].

Author's Comment:

▸ It is common to see conductors with a multiple insulation rating, such as THHN/THWN. This type of conductor can be used in a dry location at the THHN 90°C ampacity. If it is used in a wet location, you must adhere to the THWN ampacity rating of the 75°C column of Table 310.16 for THWN insulation types. ▶Figure 310–5

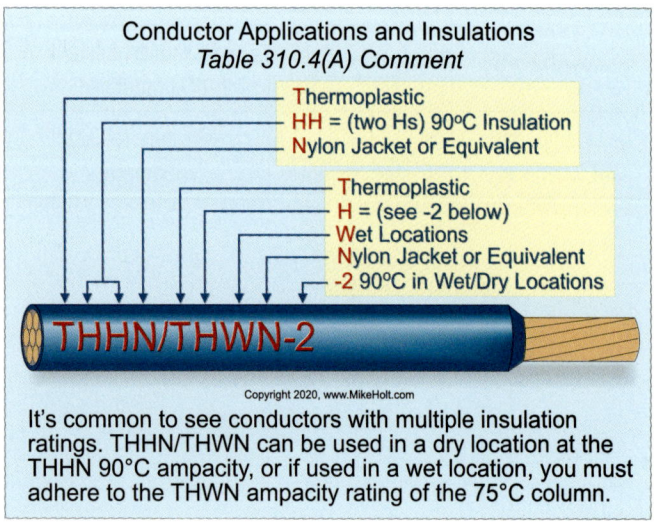
▶Figure 310–5

When a "-2" is added at the end of an insulation type (such as THWN-2), that means the conductor can be used in a wet or dry location at the 90°C ampacity rating. ▶Figure 310–6

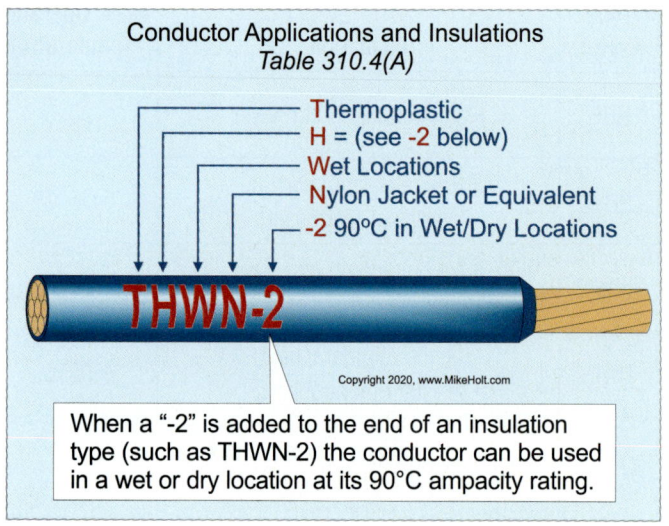
▶Figure 310–6

▶ **Table 310.4(A) Conductor Insulation Example**

Question: Which of the following describe(s) Type THHN insulation? ▶Figure 310–7

(a) Thermoplastic insulation.
(b) Suitable for dry or damp locations.
(c) A maximum operating temperature of 90°C.
(d) all of these

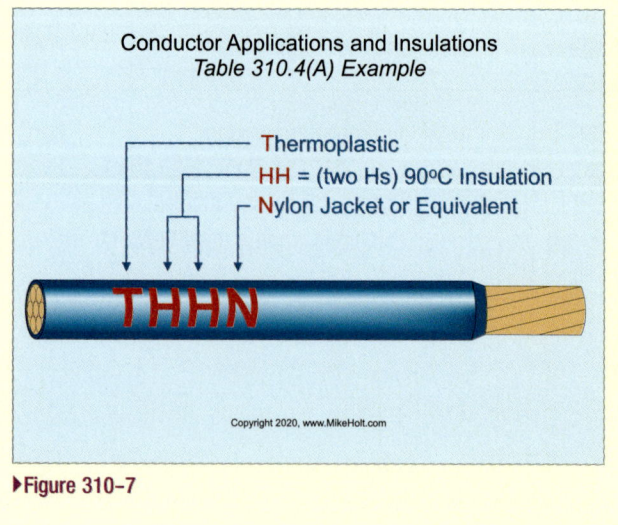
▶Figure 310–7

Answer: (d) all of these

Conductors for General Wiring | 310.10

310.6 Conductor Identification

(A) Neutral Conductor. The branch-circuit neutral conductors must be identified in accordance with 200.6.

(B) Equipment Grounding Conductor. Equipment grounding conductors can be bare, covered, or insulated. Insulated equipment grounding conductors 6 AWG and smaller must have a continuous outer finish either green, or green with one or more yellow stripes in accordance with 250.119.

Insulated equipment grounding conductors 4 AWG and larger can be permanently reidentified with green marking at the time of installation (where accessible) in accordance with 250.119(A).

(C) Identification of Phase Conductors. Circuit phase conductors must have a finish that is clearly distinguishable from the neutral and equipment grounding conductors. ▶Figure 310–8

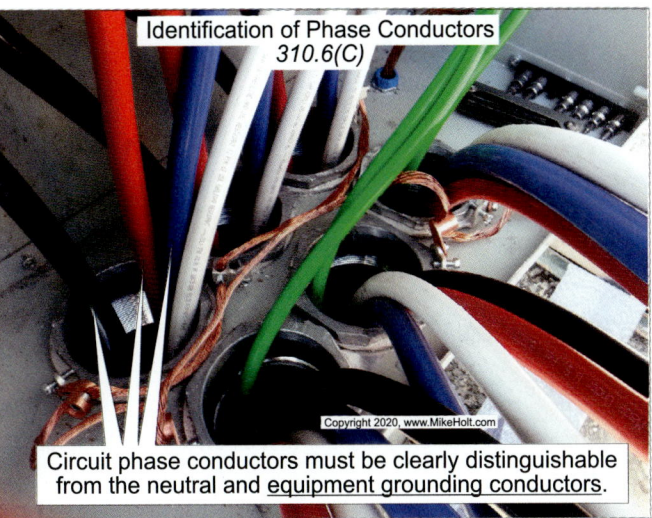

▶Figure 310–8

Where premises wiring is supplied from more than one nominal voltage system, branch-circuit phase conductors must be identified in accordance with 210.5(C) and feeders must be identified in accordance with 215.12(C).

Ex: Conductor identification is permitted in accordance with 200.7.

Author's Comment:

▶ Although the *NEC* does not require a specific color code for phase conductors, electricians often use the following color system: ▶Figure 310–9

▶Figure 310–9

▶ 120/240V, single-phase—black, red, and white

▶ 120/208V, three-phase—black, red, blue, and white

▶ 120/240V, three-phase—black, orange, blue, and white

▶ 277/480V, three-phase—brown, orange, yellow, and gray; or, brown, purple, yellow, and gray

Part III. Installation

310.10 Uses Permitted

Conductors described in Table 310.4(A) are permitted for use in any of the wiring methods covered in Chapter 3.

(B) Dry and Damp Locations. Insulated conductors typically used in dry and damp locations include THHN, THHW, THWN, THWN-2, XHHW, XHHN, XHWN, and XHWN-2.

(C) Wet Locations. Insulated conductors typically used in wet locations include THHW, THWN, THWN-2, XHHW, XHHW-2, XHWN, and XHWN-2.

Author's Comment:

▶ The letter "W" found on the insulation types indicate it is suitable for wet locations.

(D) Locations Exposed to Direct Sunlight. Insulated conductors or cables used where exposed to the direct rays of the sun must comply with the following:

(1) Conductors and cables must be listed as sunlight resistant, or listed and marked as being sunlight resistant. ▶Figure 310–10

310.10 | Conductors for General Wiring

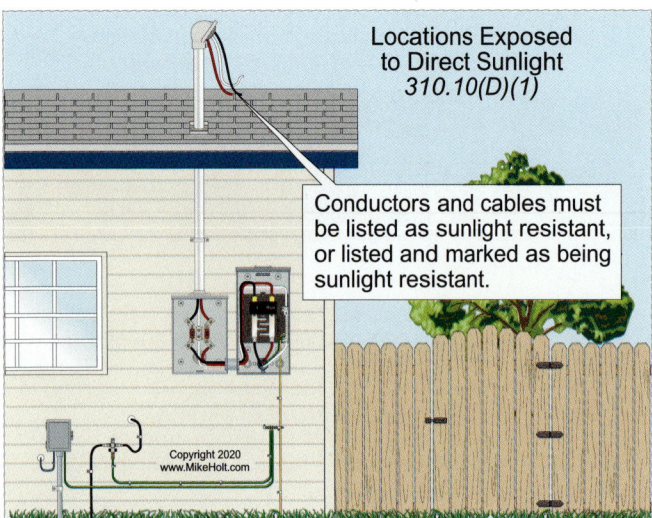

▶Figure 310–10

(2) Conductors and cables must be covered with insulating material (such as tape or sleeving) that is listed, or listed and marked, as being sunlight resistant

(E) Direct Burial Conductors. Conductors used for direct burial applications must be of a type identified for such use.

(F) Corrosive Conditions. Conductors exposed to oils, greases, vapors, gases, fumes, liquids, or other substances having a harmful effect on the conductor or insulation must be of a type suitable for the application.

(G) Conductors in Parallel.

(1) General. Phase and neutral conductors are permitted to be connected in parallel (electrically joined at both ends) for conductor sizes 1/0 AWG and larger in accordance with (G)(2) through (G)(6).
▶Figure 310–11

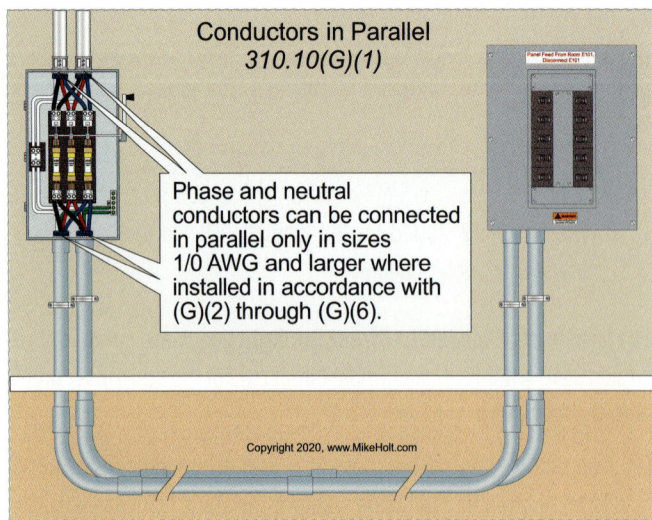

▶Figure 310–11

(2) Conductor and Installation Characteristics. When circuit conductors are installed in parallel, they must be connected so the current will be evenly distributed between the individual parallel conductors. This is accomplished by requiring all circuit conductors within each parallel set to: ▶Figure 310–12

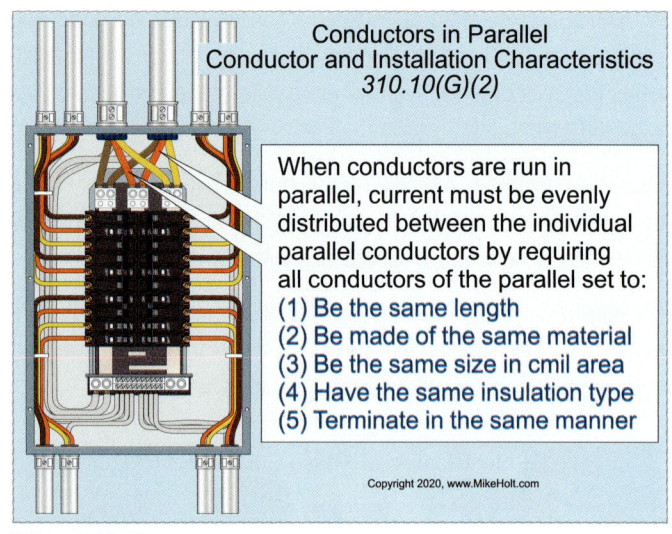

▶Figure 310–12

(1) Be the same length.

(2) Be of the same conductor material (copper, aluminum, or copper-clad aluminum).

(3) Be the same size in circular mil area (minimum 1/0 AWG).

(4) Have the same type of insulation.

(5) Terminate in the same manner (set screw versus compression fitting).

Parallel sets of conductors are not required to have the same physical characteristics as those of another set to achieve balance. Conductors of one phase, neutral, or equipment grounding conductor of a parallel set are not required to have the same physical characteristics as those of another phase, neutral, or equipment grounding conductor. ▶Figure 310–13

Conductors for General Wiring | 310.10

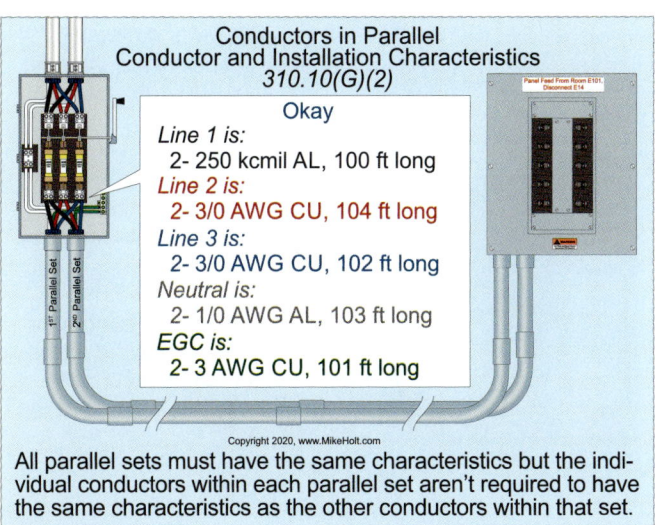

All parallel sets must have the same characteristics but the individual conductors within each parallel set aren't required to have the same characteristics as the other conductors within that set.

▶Figure 310-13

Author's Comment:

▸ When parallel circuit conductors are installed in different raceways, each raceway must include a phase A, B, C, a neutral (if used), and an equipment grounding conductor (if used). If all phase "A"s are grouped in one raceway, all phase "B"s in another raceway, and all phase "C"s are in a third raceway, the magnetic fields surrounding the conductors will not cancel and will result in inductive heating in violation of 300.20(A) unless appropriate steps are taken to minimize the inductive effect. ▶Figure 310-14

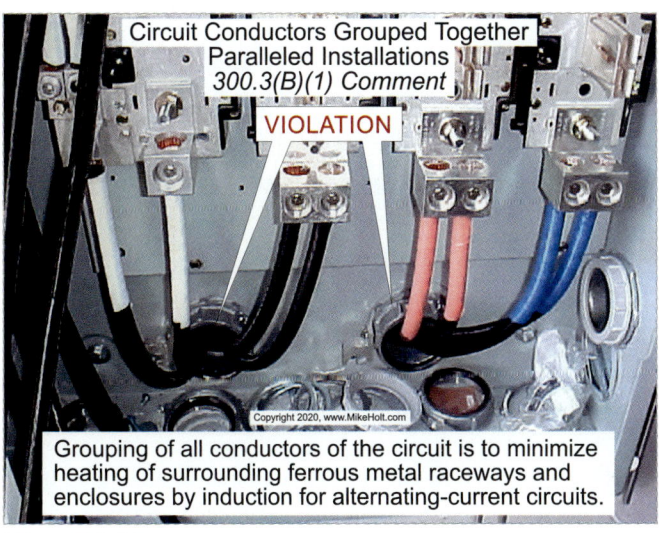

▶Figure 310-14

(3) Separate Raceways or Cables. Raceways or cables containing parallel conductors must have the same number of conductors and the same electrical characteristics. ▶Figure 310-15

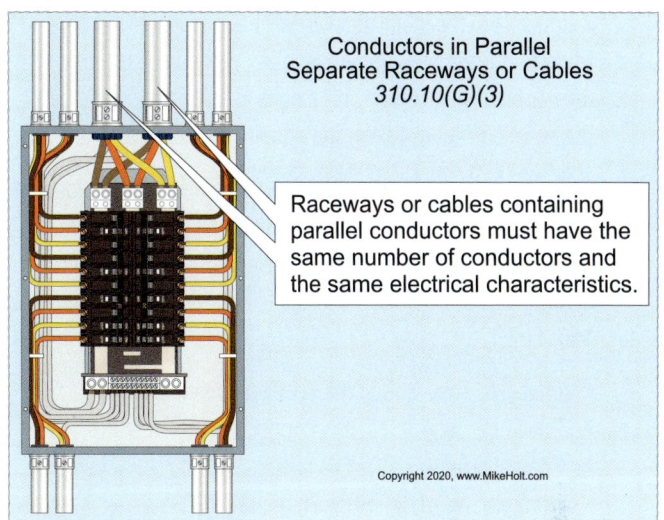

▶Figure 310-15

Author's Comment:

▸ Parallel conductor sets must have all circuit conductors in the same raceway [300.3(B)(1)]. ▶Figure 310-16

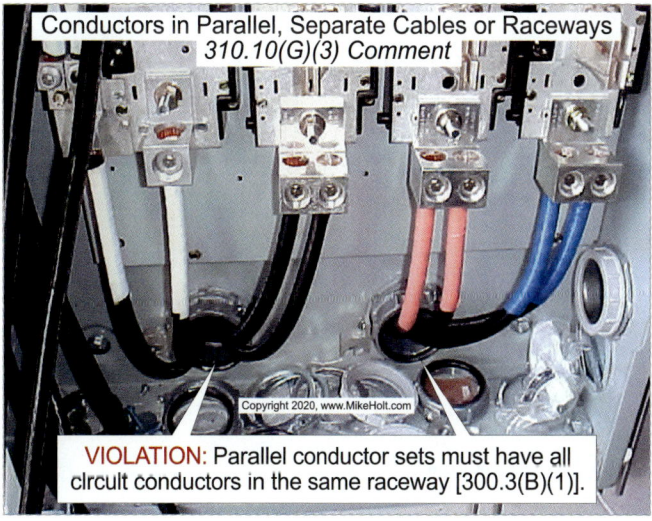

▶Figure 310-16

310.12 | Conductors for General Wiring

Author's Comment:

▸ If one set of parallel conductors is installed in a metal raceway and the other conductors are installed in PVC conduit, the conductors in the metal raceway will have an increased opposition to current flow (impedance) as compared to those in the nonmetallic raceway. This results in an unbalanced distribution of current between the parallel conductors.

▸ For current to be evenly distributed between the individual parallel conductors, each conductor (within a parallel set) must be identical to the other. For example, a 400A feeder with a neutral load of 240A can be paralleled as follows: ▸Figure 310–17

 ▸ Phase A; Two—250 kcmil THHN aluminum, 100 ft
 ▸ Phase B; Two—3/0 THHN copper, 104 ft
 ▸ Phase C; Two—3/0 THHN copper, 102 ft
 ▸ Neutral; Two—1/0 THHN aluminum, 103 ft
 ▸ Equipment grounding conductor; Two—3 AWG THHN copper, 101 ft

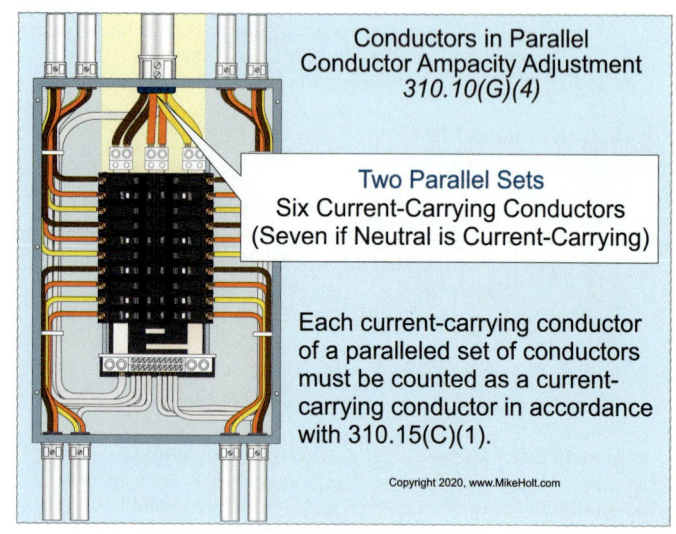

▸Figure 310–18

(5) Equipment Grounding Conductors. The equipment grounding conductors for parallel circuits must be sized in accordance with 250.122(F). ▸Figure 310–19

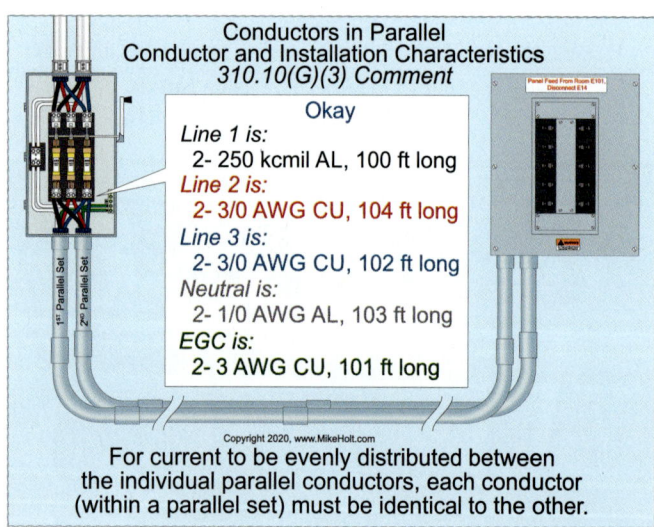

▸Figure 310–17

Author's Comment:

▸ The minimum 1/0 AWG conductor size for parallel does not apply to equipment grounding conductors [310.10(G)(5)].

(4) Conductor Ampacity Adjustment. Each current-carrying conductor of a paralleled set of conductors must be counted as a current-carrying conductor for the purpose of conductor ampacity adjustment, in accordance with 310.15(C)(1). ▸Figure 310–18

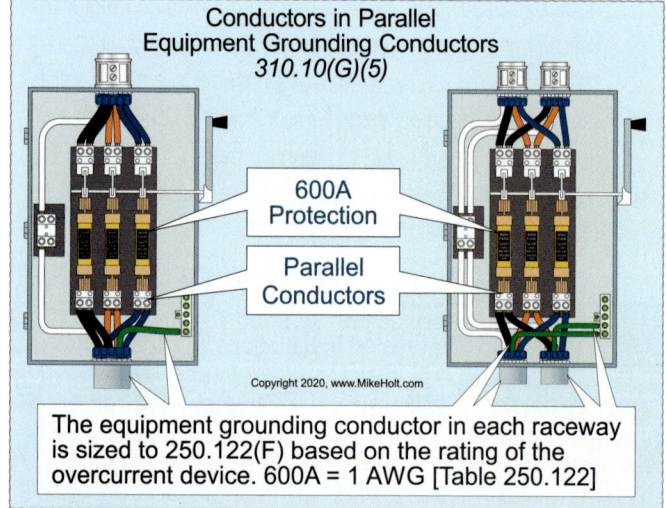

▸Figure 310–19

310.12 Single-Phase Dwelling Services and Feeders

Dwelling unit service conductors supplied by a single-phase, 120/240V system and dwelling unit feeder conductors supplied by a 120/240V or 120/208V system can be sized in accordance with the following: ▸Figure 310–20

Conductors for General Wiring | 310.12

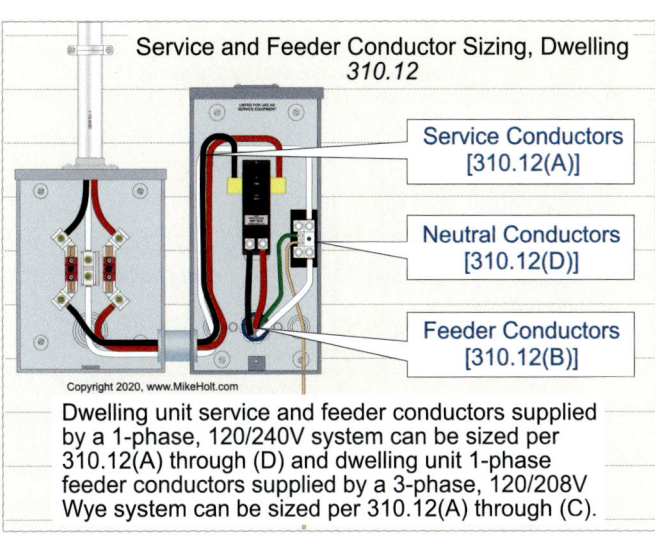
▶Figure 310–20

Author's Comment:

▶ Section 310.12 cannot be used for service conductors for two-family or multifamily dwelling buildings. ▶Figure 310–22

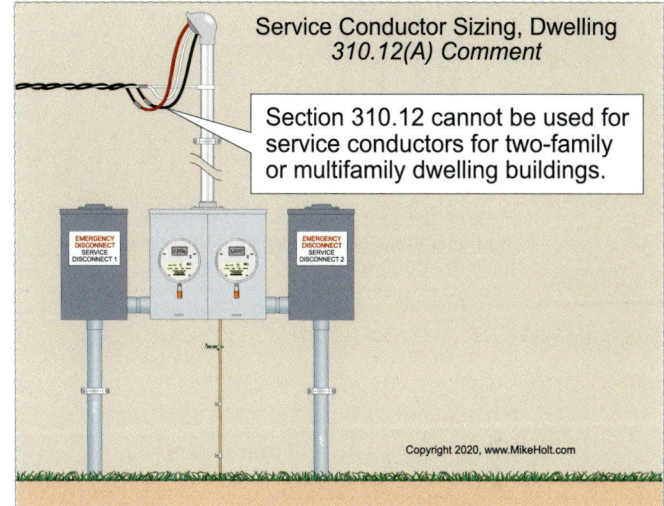
▶Figure 310–22

(A) Services. Single-phase, 120/240V service conductors supplying the entire load associated with a dwelling unit can be sized in accordance with Table 310.12 where there is no conductor ampacity adjustment or correction as required by 310.14.

Service conductors supplying the entire load associated with a dwelling unit can be sized to 83 percent of the service rating where conductor ampacity adjustment or correction is required by 310.14. ▶Figure 310–23

▶ **Example**

Question: What size service conductors are required if the calculated load for a dwelling unit requires a service disconnect rated 200A? ▶Figure 310–21

(a) 1/0 AWG (b) 2/0 AWG (c) 3/0 AWG (d) 4/0 AWG

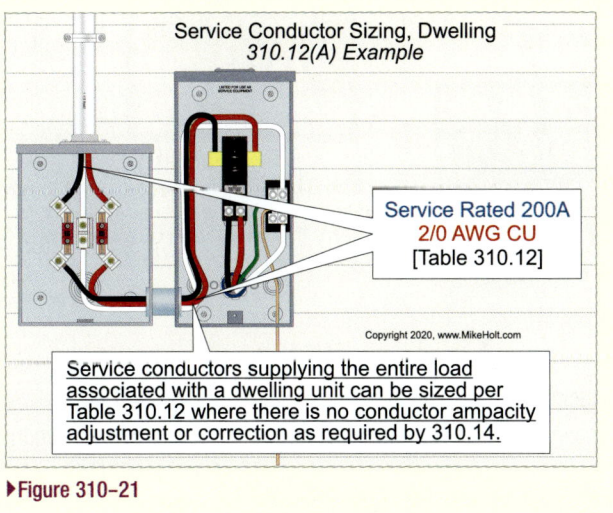
▶Figure 310–21

Answer: (b) 2/0 AWG [Table 310.12]

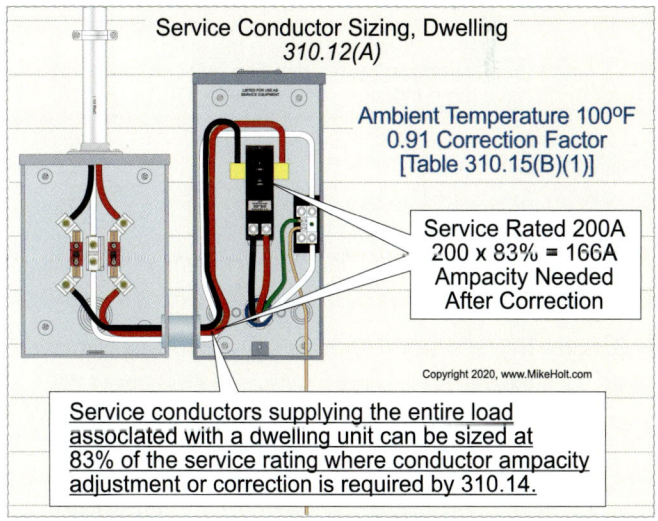
▶Figure 310–23

(B) Feeders. Single-phase, 120/240V or 120/208V feeder conductors supplying the entire load associated with a dwelling unit can be sized in accordance with Table 310.12 where there is no conductor ampacity adjustment or correction as required by 310.14. ▶Figure 310–24 and ▶Figure 310–25

310.12 | Conductors for General Wiring

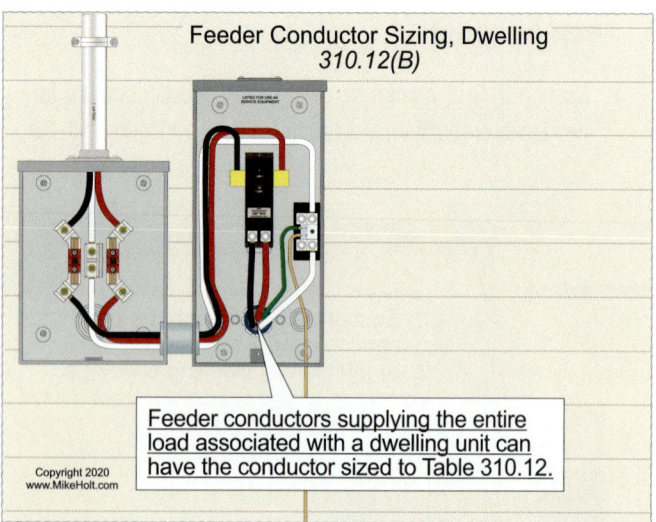
▶Figure 310-24

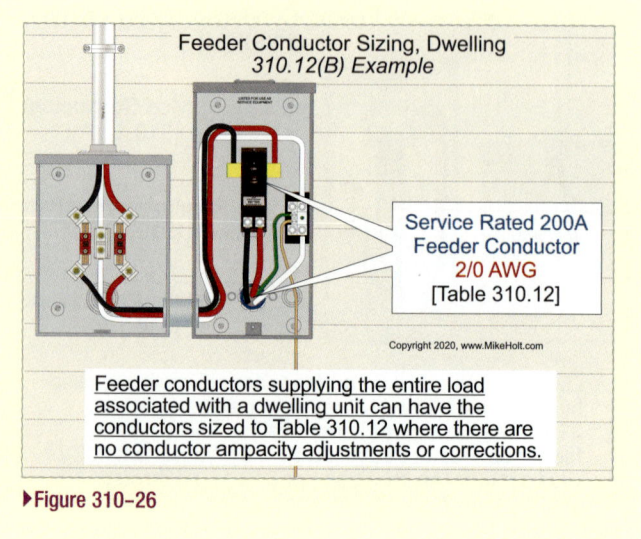
▶Figure 310-26

Author's Comment:

▸ Table 310.12 cannot be used to size feeder conductors where a feeder does not carry the entire load of the dwelling unit, except as permitted in 310.12(C). ▶Figure 310-27

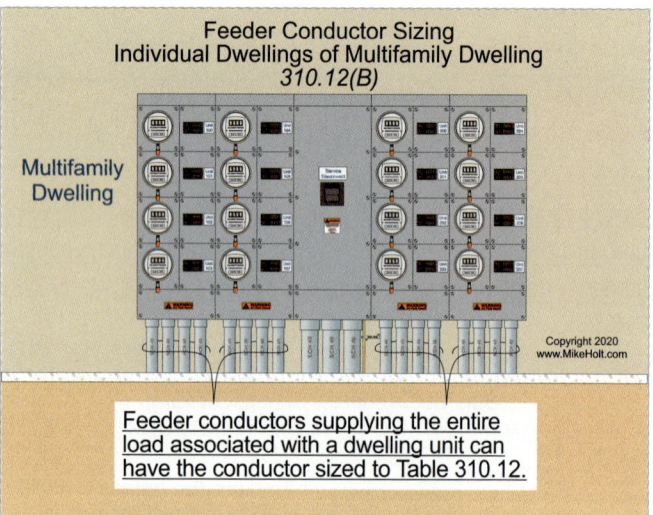
▶Figure 310-25

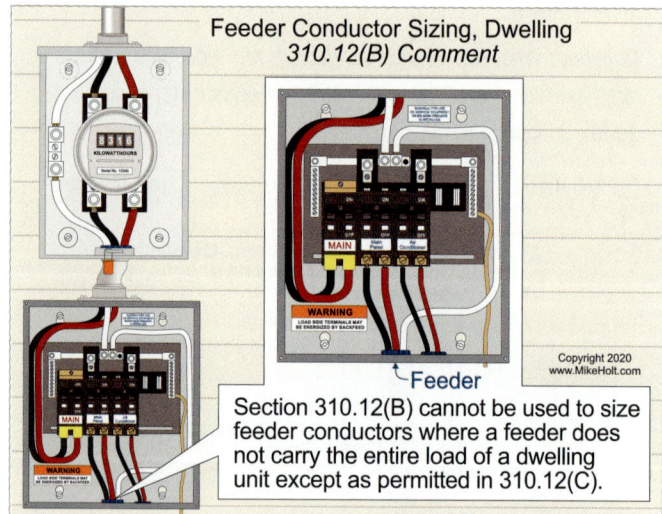
▶Figure 310-27

▶ **Example**

Question: What size feeder conductors are required if the calculated load for a dwelling unit requires a service disconnect rated 200A, and the feeder conductors carry the entire load of the dwelling unit? ▶Figure 310-26

(a) 1/0 AWG (b) 2/0 AWG (c) 3/0 AWG (d) 4/0 AWG

Answer: (b) 2/0 AWG [Table 310.12]

Feeder conductors supplying the entire load associated with a dwelling unit can be sized to 83 percent of the service where there is conductor ampacity adjustment or correction as required by 310.14. ▶Figure 310-28

Conductors for General Wiring | 310.14

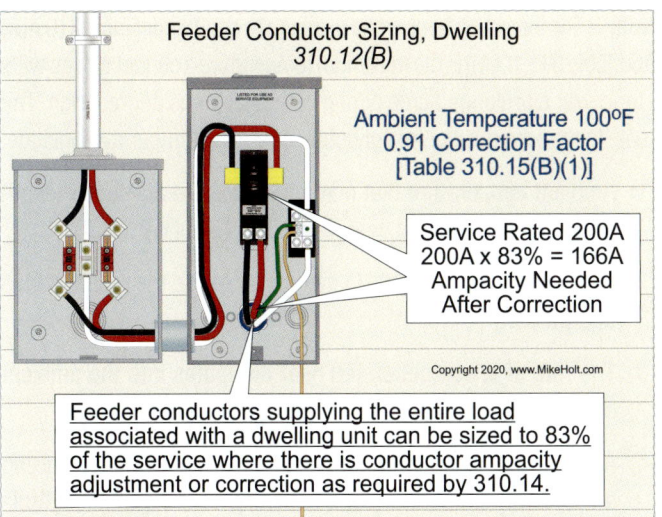
▶Figure 310–28

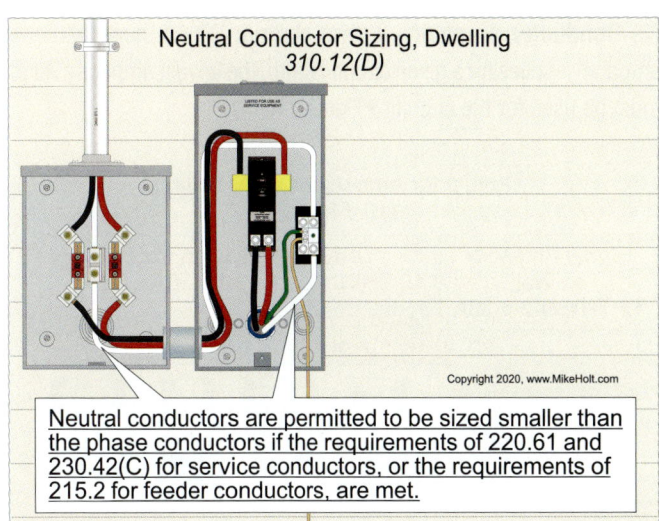
▶Figure 310–30

(C) Feeder Conductors Not Greater Than Service Conductors. Feeder conductors for an individual dwelling unit sized to Table 310.12 are not required to be larger than the service conductors sized to Table 310.12. ▶Figure 310–29

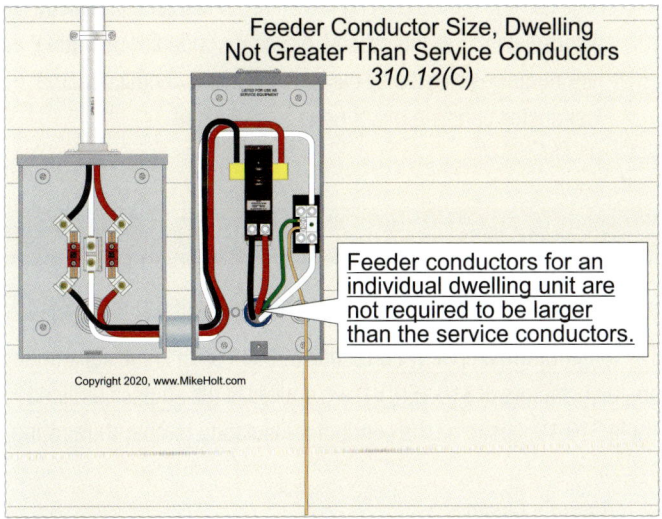
▶Figure 310–29

(D) Neutral Conductors. Neutral conductors are permitted to be sized smaller than the phase conductors in accordance with 220.61 and 230.42 for service conductors, and 215.2 and 220.61 for feeder conductors. ▶Figure 310–30

Table 310.12 Single-Phase Dwelling Services and Feeders

Service or Feeder Rating	Copper	Aluminum or Copper-Clad Aluminum
100A	4 AWG	2 AWG
110A	3 AWG	1 AWG
125A	2 AWG	1/0 AWG
150A	1 AWG	2/0 AWG
175A	1/0 AWG	3/0 AWG
200A	2/0 AWG	4/0 AWG
225A	3/0 AWG	250 kcmil
250A	4/0 AWG	300 kcmil
300A	250 kcmil	350 kcmil
350A	350 kcmil	500 kcmil
400A	400 kcmil	600 kcmil

310.14 Ampacities for Conductors Rated 0V to 2,000V

(A) General Requirements

(1) Tables or Engineering Supervision. The ampacity of a conductor can be determined either by using the tables contained in the *NEC* as corrected and adjusted in accordance with 310.15, or under engineering supervision as provided in 310.14(B).

310.15 | Conductors for General Wiring

(2) Conductor Ampacity—Lower Rating. Where more than one ampacity applies for a given circuit length, the lowest ampacity value must be used for the circuit. ▶Figure 310–31

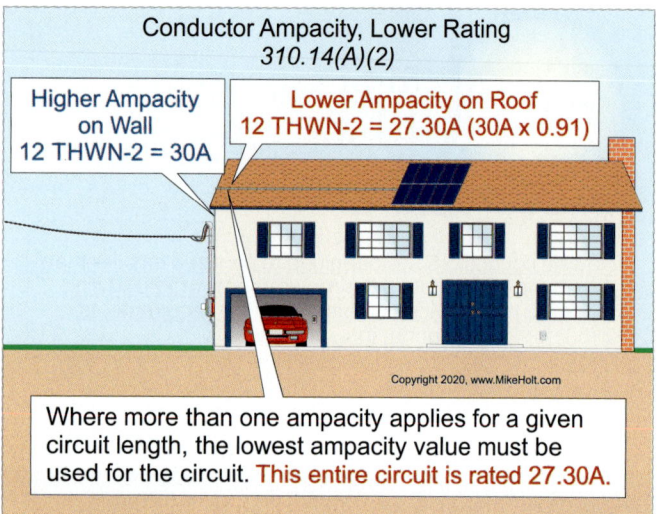

▶Figure 310–31

Ex: When different ampacities apply to parts of a circuit because of temperature correction [310.15(B)(1)] or conductor bundling [Table 310.15(C)(1)], the higher ampacity can apply for the entire circuit if the length of the lower ampacity does not exceed the lesser of 10 ft or 10 percent of the length of the total circuit. ▶Figure 310–32

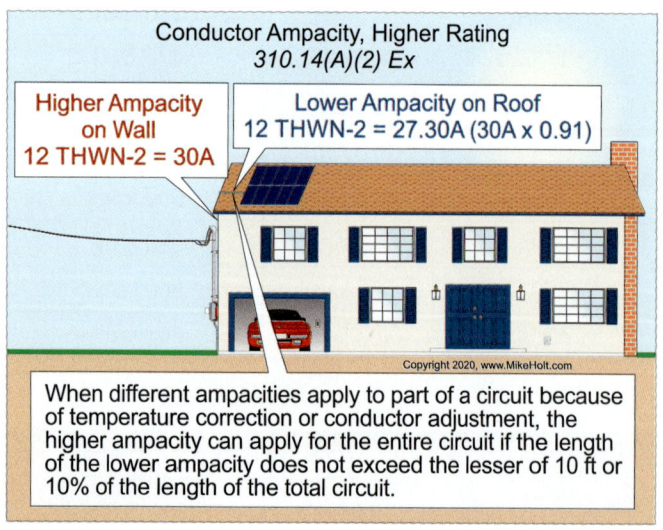

▶Figure 310–32

(3) Insulation Temperature Limitation. Conductors are not permitted to be used where the operating temperature exceeds that designated for the type of insulated conductor involved.

Note 1: The insulation temperature rating of a conductor [Table 310.4(A) and Table 311.10(A)] is the maximum temperature a conductor can withstand over a prolonged time period without serious degradation. The main factors to consider for conductor operating temperature include:

(1) Ambient temperature that may vary along the conductor length as well as from time to time [Table 310.15(B)(1)].

(2) Heat generated internally in the conductor as the result of load current flow.

(3) The rate at which generated heat dissipates into the ambient medium.

(4) Adjacent load-carrying conductors that have the effect of raising the ambient temperature and impeding heat dissipation [Table 310.15(C)(1)].

Author's Comment:

▸ The insulation temperature rating of a conductor must be limited to an operating temperature that prevents damage to the conductor's insulation. If the conductor carries excessive current, the I^2R heating within the conductor can destroy its insulation. For this reason, elevated conductor operating temperatures created by current flow in the conductors and conductor bundling might need to be limited.

310.15 Ampacity Tables

(A) General. Ampacities for conductors are contained in Table 310.16.

The temperature ampacity correction of 310.15(B)(1) and adjustment ampacity factors of 310.15(C)(1) are applied to the ampacities listed in Table 310.16, based on the conductor insulation temperature rating.

Author's Comment:

▸ The Table 310.16 ampacity must be corrected when the ambient temperature is not between 78°F and 86°F and must be adjusted when more than three current-carrying conductors are bundled together. The temperature correction multiplier [310.15(B)(1)] and adjustment multiplier [310.15(C)(1)] are applied to the conductor ampacity, based on the temperature rating of the conductor insulation as contained in Table 310.16, typically in the 90°C column. ▶Figure 310–33

Conductors for General Wiring | 310.15

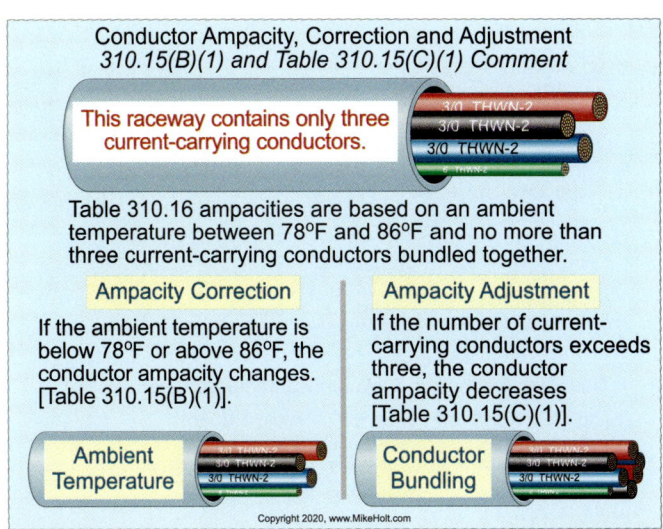

▶Figure 310-33

Author's Comment:

▸ When correcting or adjusting conductor ampacity, the ampacity is based on the conductor material and its insulation temperature rating as listed in the appropriate column of Table 310.16; not the temperature rating of the terminal [110.14(C)].

▸ According to Article 100, the ampacity of a conductor is the maximum current a conductor can carry continuously, under the conditions of use, without exceeding its temperature rating. ▶Figure 310-34

▸ The neutral conductor might be a current-carrying conductor, but only under the conditions specified in 310.15(E). Equipment grounding conductors are never considered current carrying [310.15(F)].

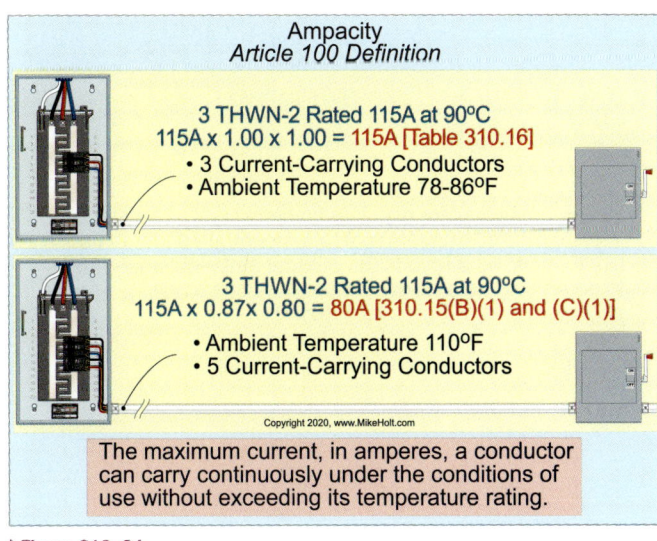

▶Figure 310-34

(B) Ambient Temperature Correction Factors.

(1) General. Ampacities for ambient temperatures other than those shown in the ampacity tables must be corrected in accordance with Table 310.15(B)(1). ▶Figure 310-35

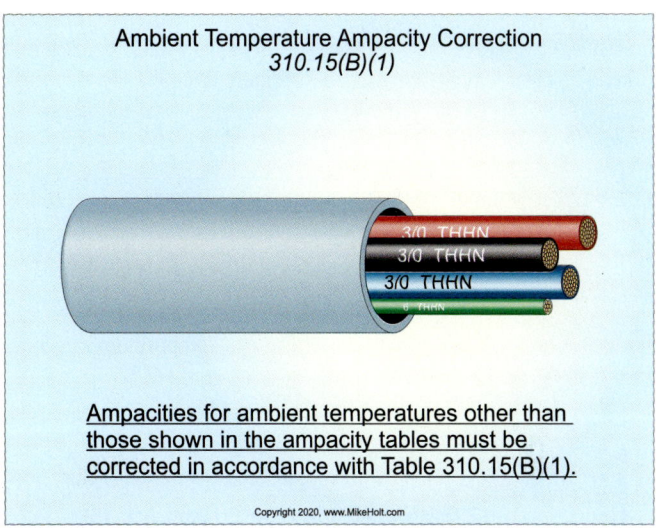

▶Figure 310-35

Table 310.15(B)(1) Ambient Temperature Correction Factors Based on 30°C (86°F) and 90°C Insulation		
Ambient Temperature °F	Ambient Temperature °C	Correction Factor 90°C Conductors
50°F or less	10°C or less	1.15
51–59°F	11–15°C	1.12
60–68°F	16–20°C	1.08
69–77°F	21–25°C	1.04
78–86°F	26–30°C	1.00
87–95°F	31–35°C	0.96
96–104°F	36–40°C	0.91
105–113°F	41–45°C	0.87
114–122°F	46–50°C	0.82
123–131°F	51–55°C	0.76
132–140°F	56–60°C	0.71
141–149°F	61–65°C	0.65
150–158°F	66–70°C	0.58
159–167°F	71–75°C	0.50

310.15 | Conductors for General Wiring

Corrected Conductor Ampacity—Ambient Temperature Correction
Formula: Corrected Ampacity = Table 310.16 Ampacity × Ambient Correction Factor

▶ **Ambient Temperature Below 86°F Example**

Question: What is the ampacity of a 12 THHN conductor when installed in an ambient temperature of 50°F? ▶Figure 310-36

(a) 20A (b) 25A (c) 31A (d) 35A

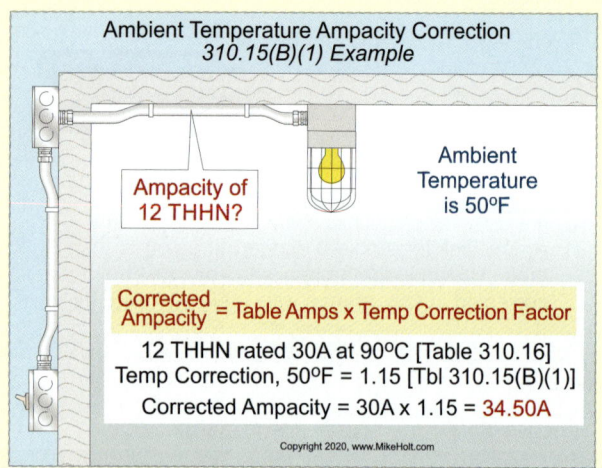

▶Figure 310-36

Solution:

The conductor ampacity for 12 THHN is 30A at 90°C [Table 310.16].

The correction factor for a 90°C conductor installed in an ambient temperature of 50°F is 1.15 [Table 310.15(B)(1)].

Corrected Ampacity = 30A × 115%
Corrected Ampacity = 34.50A; round to 35A

Note: Ampacity increases when the ambient temperature is less than 86°F.

Answer: (d) 35A

▶ **Ambient Temperature Above 86°F Example**

Question: What is the ampacity of a 6 THWN-2 conductor installed in an ambient temperature of 122°F? ▶Figure 310-37

(a) 35A (b) 53A (c) 62A (d) 75A

Solution:

The conductor ampacity for 6 THWN-2 is 75A at 90°C [Table 310.16].

The correction factor for a 90°C conductor installed in an ambient temperature of 122°F is 0.82 [Table 310.15(B)(1)].

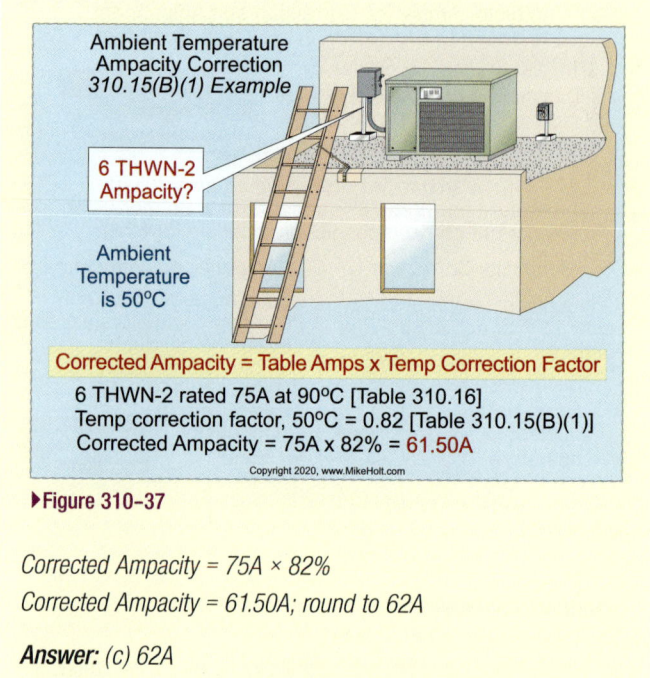

▶Figure 310-37

Corrected Ampacity = 75A × 82%
Corrected Ampacity = 61.50A; round to 62A

Answer: (c) 62A

(2) Raceways and Cables Exposed to Sunlight on Rooftops. Where raceways or cables are exposed to direct sunlight and located less than ⅞ in. above the roof, a temperature adder of 60°F (33°C) must be added to the outdoor ambient temperature to determine the ambient temperature correction in accordance with Table 310.15(B)(1). ▶Figure 310-38

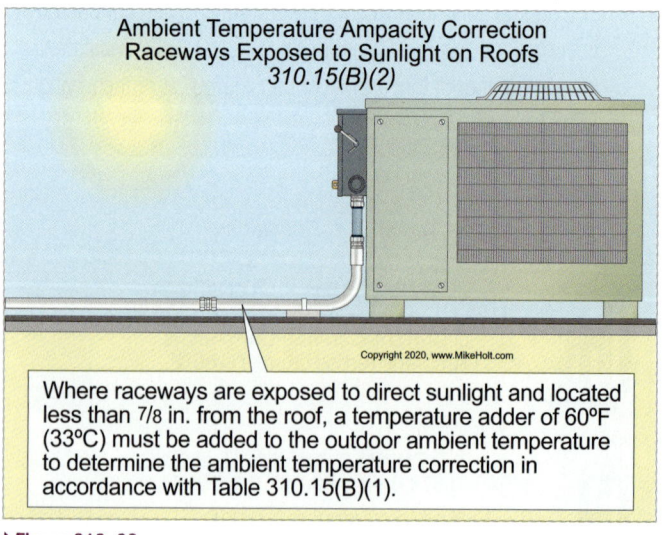

▶Figure 310-38

Author's Comment:

▸ The reason for the temperature adder is because the air inside raceways and cables that are in direct sunlight is significantly hotter than the surrounding air.

▶ Example

Question: What is the ampacity of a 6 THWN-2 in a raceway located ½ in. above the roof, where the ambient temperature is 90°F? ▶Figure 310-39

(a) 40A (b) 41A (c) 42A (d) 44A

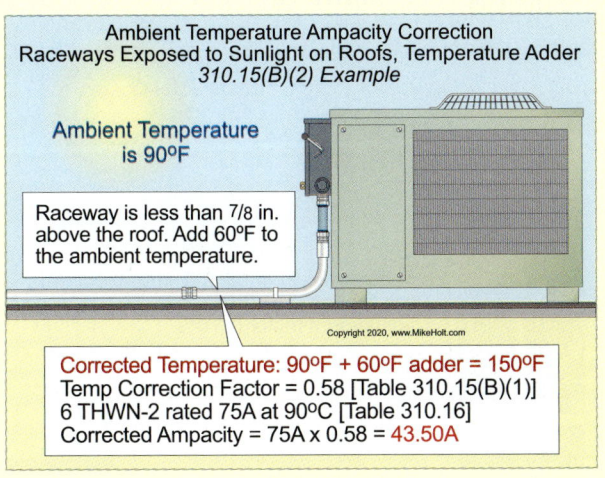

▶Figure 310-39

Solution:

Corrected Temperature = 90°F + 60°F adder

Corrected Temperature = 150°F

The temperature correction factor for 150°F = 0.58 [Table 310.15(B)(1)]

6 THWN-2 is rated 75A at 90°C [Table 310.16]

Corrected Ampacity = 75A × 58%

Corrected Ampacity = 43.50A; round to 44A

Answer: (d) 44A

Ex: Type XHHW-2 insulated conductors are not subject to the rooftop temperature adder.

Note 1: See the ASHRAE Handbook—Fundamentals (www.ashrae.org) as a source for the ambient temperatures in various locations.

(C) Conductor Bundle Adjustment.

(1) Four or More Current-Carrying Conductors. Where four or more current-carrying conductors are contained in a raceway that is longer than 24 in., the ampacities contained in Table 310.16 must be reduced in accordance with Table 310.15(C)(1).

Where multiconductor cables are installed without maintaining spacing for a continuous length longer than 24 in., the ampacities contained in Table 310.16 must be reduced in accordance with Table 310.15(C)(1). ▶Figure 310-40

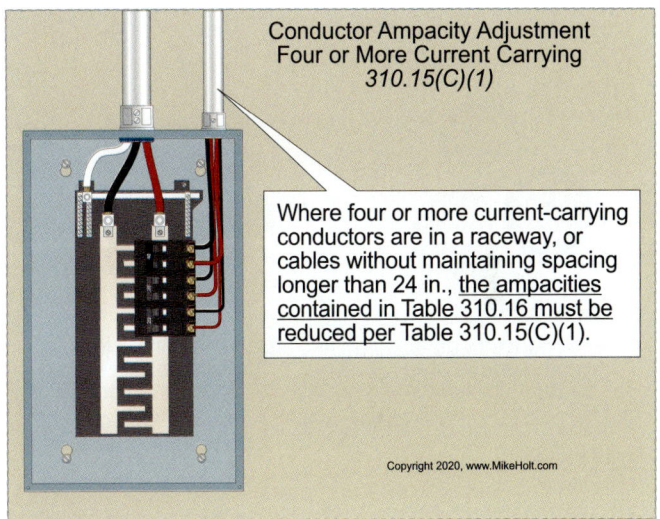

▶Figure 310-40

Author's Comment:

▸ The neutral conductor might be a current-carrying conductor, but only under the conditions specified in 310.15(E). Equipment grounding conductors are never considered current carrying [310.15(F)].

Table 310.15(C)(1) Conductor Ampacity Adjustment for More Than Three Current–Carrying Conductors	
Number of Conductors[1]	Adjustment
4–6	80%
7–9	70%
10–20	50%
21–30	45%
31–40	40%
41 and above	35%

[1] *Does not include conductors that cannot be energized at the same time.*

310.15 | Conductors for General Wiring

Author's Comment:

▸ Conductor ampacity reduction is required when four or more current-carrying conductors are bundled together because heat generated by current flow is not able to dissipate as quickly as when there are fewer current-carrying conductors. ▸Figure 310–41

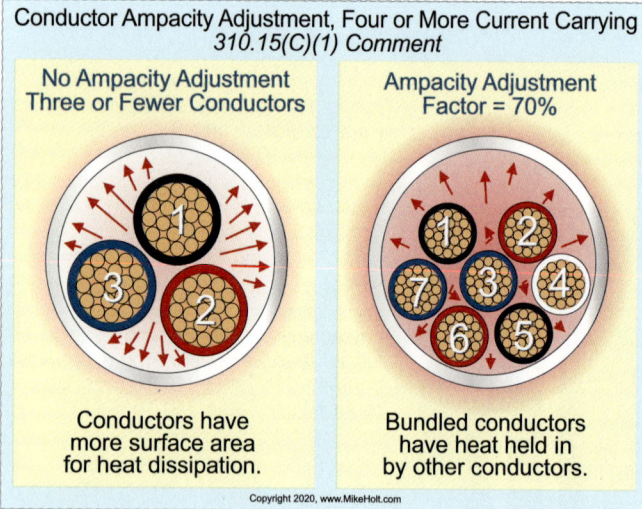

▸Figure 310–41

▸ **Ampacity Adjustment Example 1**

Question: What is the adjusted ampacity of four current-carrying 12 THWN-2 conductors in a raceway? ▸Figure 310–42

(a) 20A (b) 24A (c) 29A (d) 32A

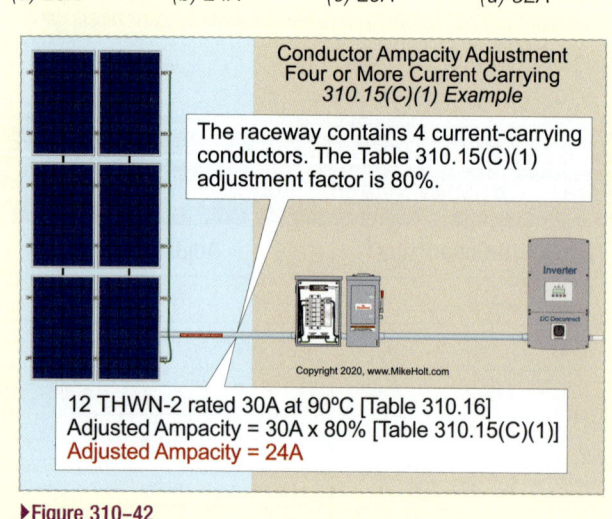

▸Figure 310–42

Solution:

Adjusted Ampacity = Table 310.16 Ampacity × Bundled Ampacity Adjustment Factor from Table 310.15(C)(1)

12 THWN-2 is rated 30A at 90°C [Table 310.16].

The adjustment factor for four current-carrying conductors is 80 percent [Table 310.15(C)(1)].

Adjusted Ampacity = 30A × 80%
Adjusted Ampacity = 24A

Answer: (b) 24A

▸ **Ampacity Adjustment Example 2**

Question: What is the adjusted ampacity of eight current-carrying 12 THWN-2 conductors in a raceway? ▸Figure 310–43

(a) 16A (b) 21A (c) 35A (d) 43A

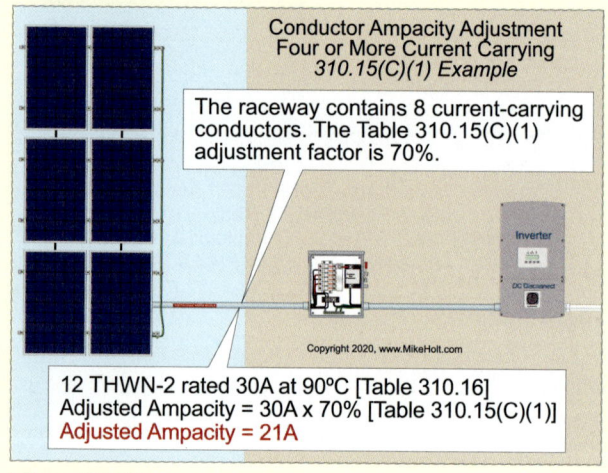

▸Figure 310–43

Solution:

Adjusted Ampacity = Table 310.16 Ampacity × Bundled Ampacity Adjustment Factor from Table 310.15(C)(1)

12 THWN-2 is rated 30A at 90°C [Table 310.16].

The adjustment factor for eight current-carrying conductors is 70 percent [Table 310.15(C)(1)].

Adjusted Ampacity = 30A × 70%
Adjusted Ampacity = 21A

Answer: (b) 21A

(a) Where conductors are installed in cable trays, the provisions of 392.80 apply.

(b) Conductor ampacity adjustment from Table 310.15(C)(1) does not apply to conductors in raceways having a length not exceeding 24 in. ▶Figure 310-44

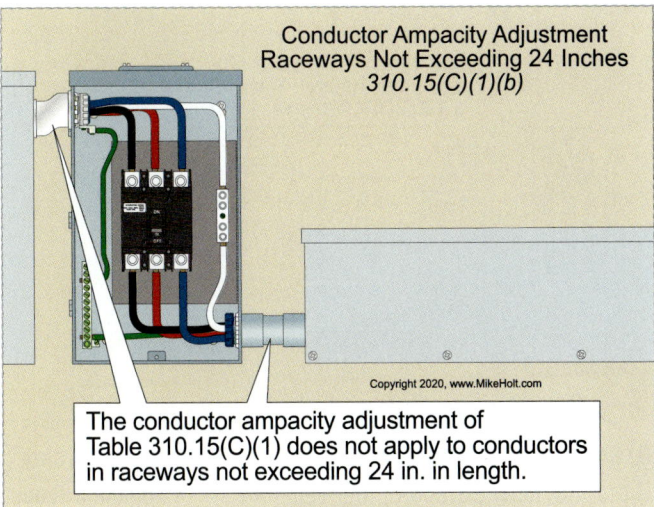

▶Figure 310-44

(d) The conductor ampacity adjustment of Table 310.15(C)(1) does not apply to conductors in Type AC or Type MC cable under the following conditions: ▶Figure 310-46

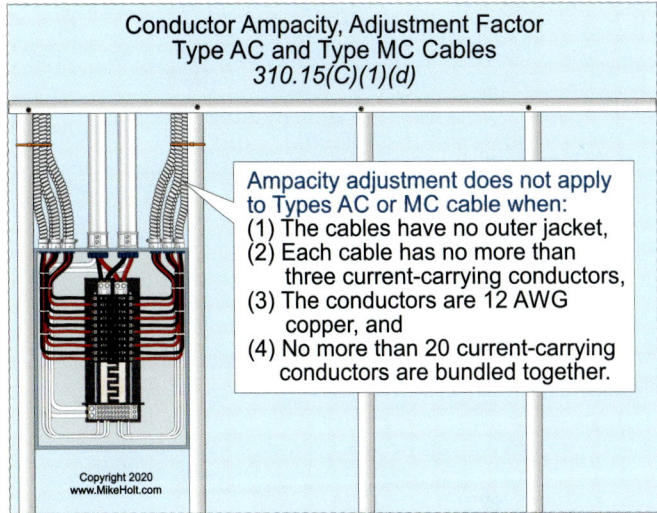

▶Figure 310-46

(1) The cables do not have an outer jacket,

(2) Each cable has no more than three current-carrying conductors,

(3) The conductors are 12 AWG copper, and

(4) No more than twenty current-carrying conductors (ten 2-wire cables or six 3-wire cables) are bundled together.

Ex: A 60 percent adjustment factor can be applied if more than twenty current-carrying conductors in these cables are bundled together.

(E) Neutral Conductor. Neutral conductors must be considered current carrying in accordance with the following:

(1) Not Considered Current Carrying. The neutral conductor of a 3-wire, single-phase, 120/240V system, or a 4-wire, three-phase, 120/208V or 277/480V wye-connected system, is not considered a current-carrying conductor for the application of conductor ampacity adjustments in accordance with Table 310.15(C)(1). ▶Figure 310-47

(2) Considered Current Carrying. The neutral conductor of a 3-wire circuit from a 4-wire, three-phase, wye-connected system carries approximately the same current as the line-to-neutral load currents of the other conductors and is considered a current-carrying conductor for conductor ampacity adjustments in accordance with Table 310.15(C)(1). ▶Figure 310-48

Unbalanced 3-Wire Wye Secondary Neutral Current Formula:
$$I_{Neutral} = \sqrt{(I_{Line1}^2 + I_{Line2}^2) - (I_{Line1} \times I_{Line2})}$$

▶ **Ampacity Adjustment—Raceway Not Exceeding 24 In. Example**

Question: What is the ampacity of five 3/0 THWN-2 conductors in a raceway that does not exceed 24 in. in length? ▶Figure 310-45

(a) 150A   (b) 195A   (c) 205A   (d) 225A

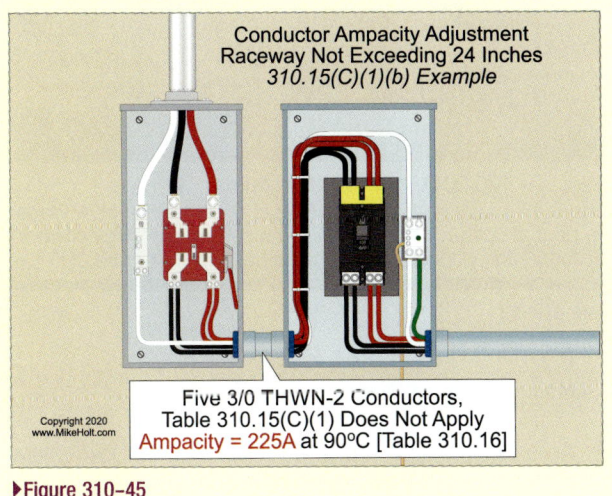

▶Figure 310-45

Solution:

3/0 THWN-2 is rated 225A at 90°C [Table 310.16].

Answer: (d) 225A

310.15 | Conductors for General Wiring

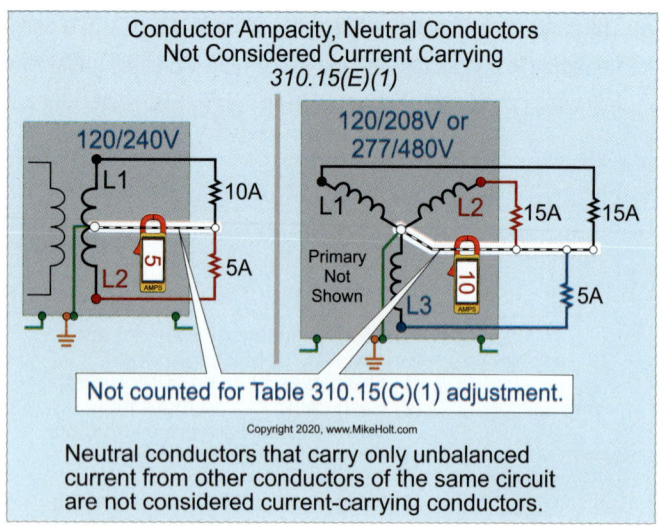
▶Figure 310–47

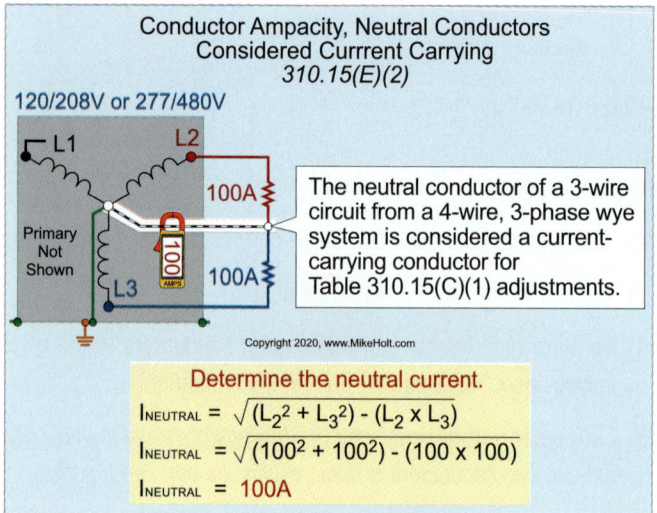
▶Figure 310–48

▶ Neutral Conductor Current Example

Question: What is the neutral current for two 16A, 120V circuits? The system is a 120/208V, three-phase, 4-wire, wye-connected system. ▶Figure 310–49

(a) 8A   (b) 16A   (c) 32A   (d) 40A

Solution:

$I_{Neutral} = \sqrt{(I_{Line1}^2 + I_{Line2}^2) - (I_{Line1} \times I_{Line2})}$

$I_{Neutral} = \sqrt{(16^2 + 16^2) - (16 \times 16)}$

$I_{Neutral} = \sqrt{(512 - 256)}$

$I_{Neutral} = \sqrt{256}$

$I_{Neutral} = 16A$

Answer: (b) 16A

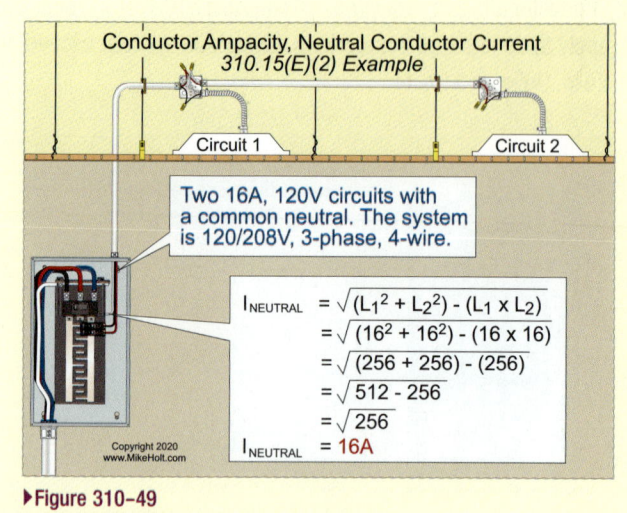
▶Figure 310–49

(3) Considered Current Carrying. On a 4-wire, 3-phase, wye circuit where the major portion of the load consists of nonlinear loads, the neutral conductor is considered a current-carrying conductor for conductor ampacity adjustments in accordance with Table 310.15(C)(1). ▶Figure 310–50

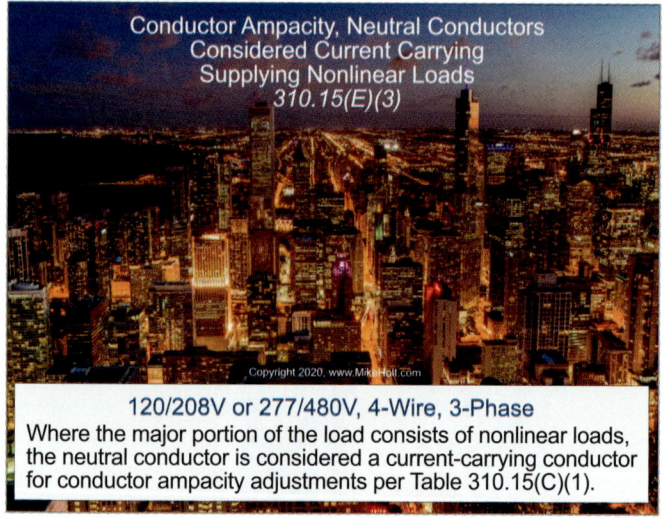
▶Figure 310–50

Author's Comment:

▸ According to Article 100, a "Nonlinear Load" is a load where the current waveform does not follow the applied sinusoidal voltage waveform.

Conductors for General Wiring | **310.16**

(F) Equipment Grounding and Bonding Conductor. Equipment grounding and bonding conductors are not considered current carrying for conductor ampacity adjustments in accordance with Table 310.15(C)(1).
▶Figure 310–51

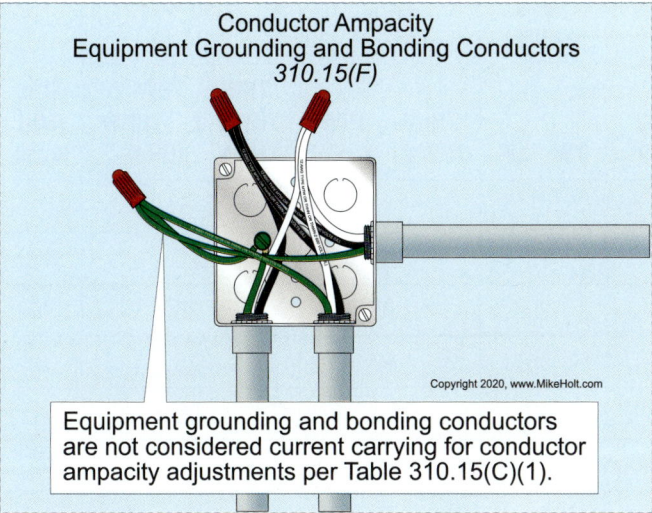

▶Figure 310–51

310.16 Ampacities of Insulated Conductors in Raceways, Cables, or Buried

The conductor ampacities specified in Table 310.16 are based on the following conditions: ▶Figure 310–52

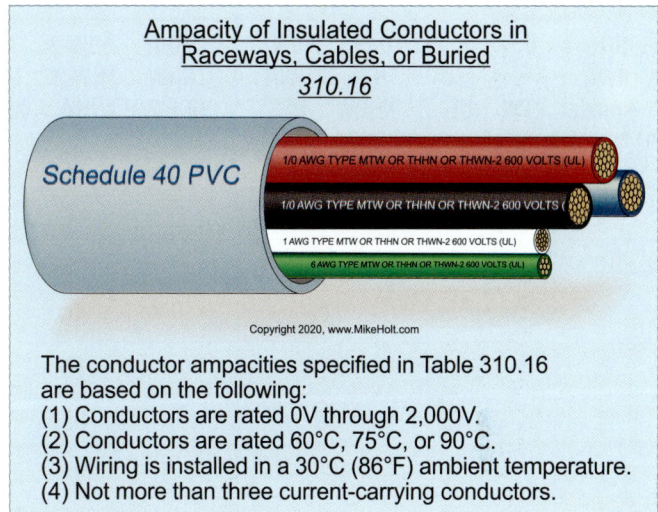

▶Figure 310–52

(1) Conductors are rated 0V through 2,000V.

(2) Conductors are rated 60°C (140°F), 75°C (167°F), or 90°C (194°F).

(3) Wiring is installed in a 30°C (86°F) ambient temperature.

(4) There are not more than three current-carrying conductors.

310.16 | Conductors for General Wiring

Table 310.16 Ampacities of Insulated Conductors Not More Than Three Current-Carrying Conductors in Raceway, Cable, or Earth (Directly Buried)

	Copper			Aluminum			
	60°C (140°F)	75°C (167°F)	90°C (194°F)	60°C (140°F)	75°C (167°F)	90°C (194°F)	
Size AWG kcmil	TW UF	RHW THHW THW THWN XHHW USE	RHH RHW-2 THHN THHW THW-2 THWN-2 USE-2 XHHW XHHW-2	TW UF	THHW THW THWN XHHW	THHN THW-2 THWN-2 THHW XHHW XHHW-2	Size AWG kcmil
14	15	20	25				
12	20	25	30	15	20	25	12
10	30	35	40	25	30	35	10
8	40	50	55	35	40	45	8
6	55	65	75	40	50	55	6
4	70	85	95	55	65	75	4
3	85	100	115	65	75	85	3
2	95	115	130	75	90	100	2
1	110	130	145	85	100	115	1
1/0	125	150	170	100	120	135	1/0
2/0	145	175	195	115	135	150	2/0
3/0	165	200	225	130	155	175	3/0
4/0	195	230	260	150	180	205	4/0
250	215	255	290	170	205	230	250
300	240	285	320	195	230	260	300
350	260	310	350	210	250	280	350
400	280	335	380	225	270	305	400
500	320	380	430	260	310	350	500

Notes:

1. Section 310.15(B) must be referenced for the ampacity correction factors where the ambient temperature is other than 30°C (86°F).
2. Section 310.15(C)(1) must be referenced for more than three current-carrying conductors.
3. Section 310.16 must be referenced for conditions of use.

ARTICLE 312 CABINETS

Introduction to Article 312—Cabinets

Conditions of use affect the selection and application of cabinets. For example, you cannot use just any enclosure in a wet or a hazardous location. The conditions of use impose special requirements for these situations.

For all such enclosures, certain requirements apply—regardless of the use. For example, you must cover any openings, protect conductors from abrasion, and allow sufficient bending room for conductors.

Notice that Article 408 covers switchboards, switchgear, and panelboards, with the primary emphasis on the interior (or "guts") while the cabinet used to enclose a panelboard is covered here in Article 312. Therefore, you will find that some important considerations such as wire-bending space at the terminals of panelboards are included in this article.

Part I. Scope and Installation

312.1 Scope

Article 312 covers the installation and construction specifications for cabinets used to enclose a panelboard, cutout boxes and meter cans. ▶Figure 312–1

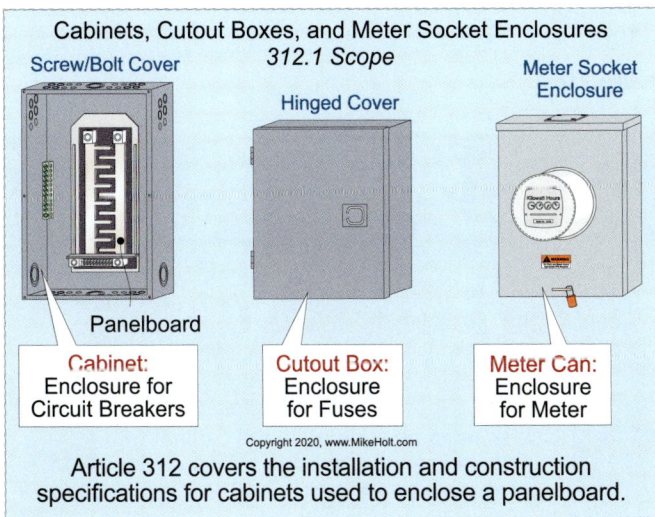

▶Figure 312–1

312.2 Damp or Wet Locations

Cabinets installed in damp or wet locations must be weatherproof.

Raceways or cables entering weatherproof enclosures above the level of uninsulated live parts must use fittings listed for wet locations. ▶Figure 312–2

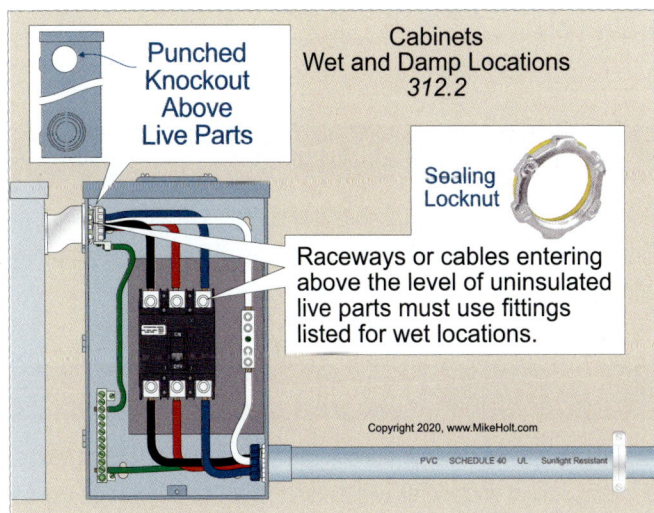

▶Figure 312–2

312.3 | Cabinets

Author's Comment:

▸ "Weatherproof" means constructed or protected so exposure to the weather will not interfere with successful operation [Article 100].

312.3 Position in Walls

Cabinets installed in walls of noncombustible material must be installed so the front edge of the cabinet is set back no more than ¼ in. from the finished surface. In walls constructed of wood or other combustible material, cabinets must be flush with the finished surface or project outward. ▸Figure 312–3

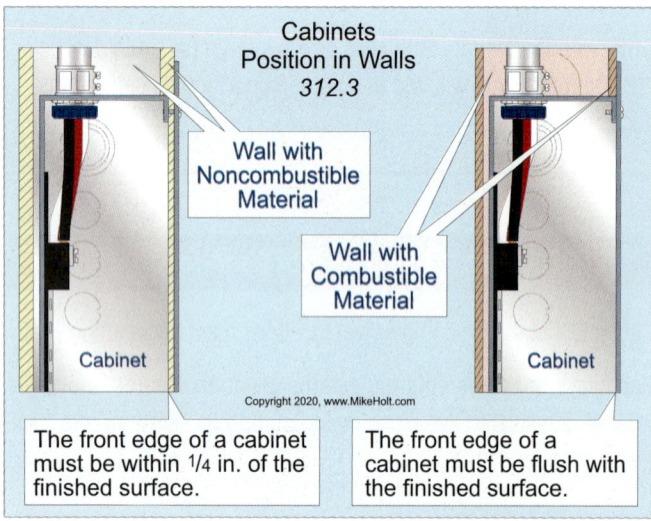

▸Figure 312–3

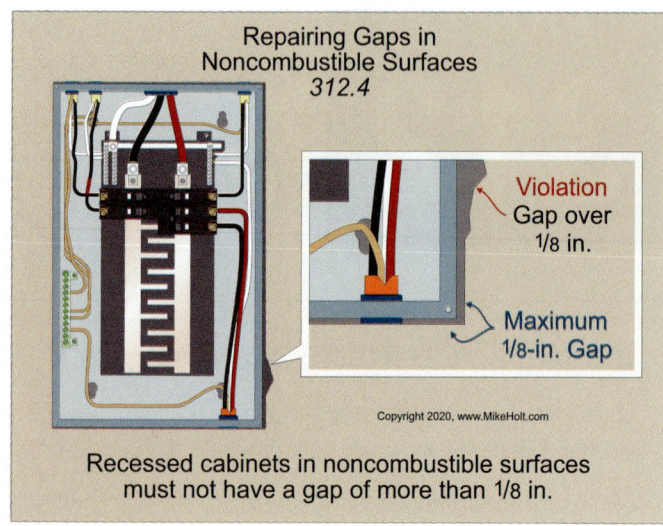

▸Figure 312–4

312.4 Repairing Gaps in Noncombustible Surfaces

Recessed cabinets in noncombustible surfaces (plaster, drywall, or plasterboard) must not have a gap of more than ⅛ in. around any edge of the cabinet. ▸Figure 312–4

312.5 Enclosures

(A) Opening to be Closed. Openings through cabinets, cutout boxes, or meter socket enclosures which conductors enter must be closed in an approved manner. ▸Figure 312–5

(C) Cable Termination. Cables must be secured to the cabinet, cutout box, or meter socket enclosures with fittings designed and listed for the cable. See 300.12 and 300.15. ▸Figure 312–6 and ▸Figure 312–7

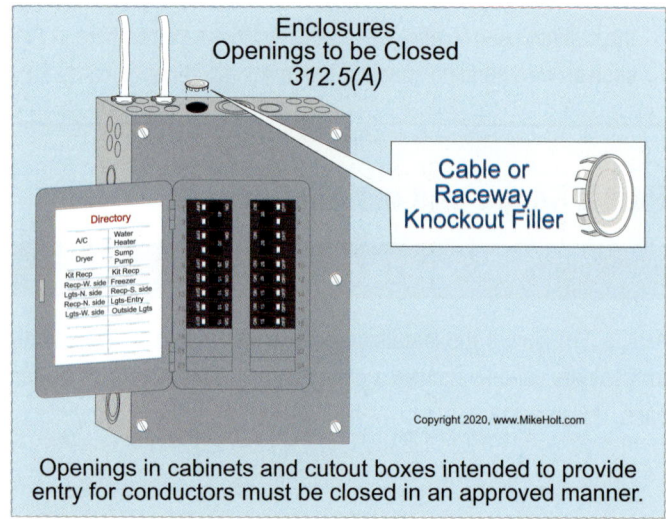

▸Figure 312–5

▸Figure 312–6

Cabinets | **312.5**

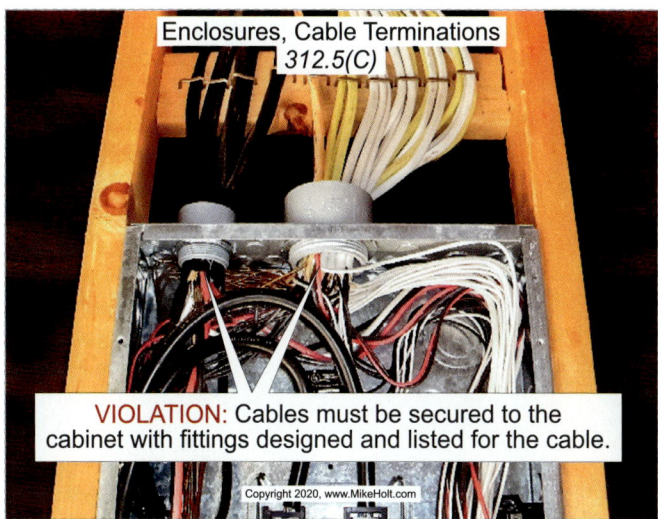
▶Figure 312-7

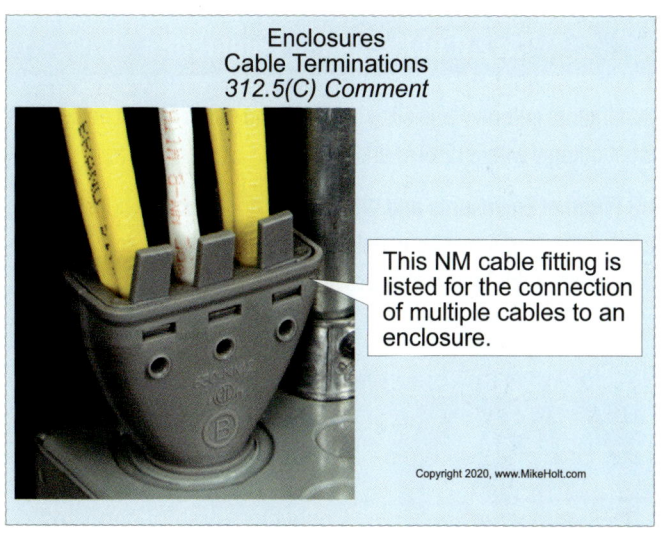
▶Figure 312-9

Author's Comment:

▸ Cable clamps or cable connectors must only be used with one cable, unless that clamp or fitting is identified for more than one. Some Type NM cable clamps are listed for two or more Type NM cables within a single fitting (UL White Book, *Guide Information for Electrical Equipment*). ▶Figure 312-8 and ▶Figure 312-9

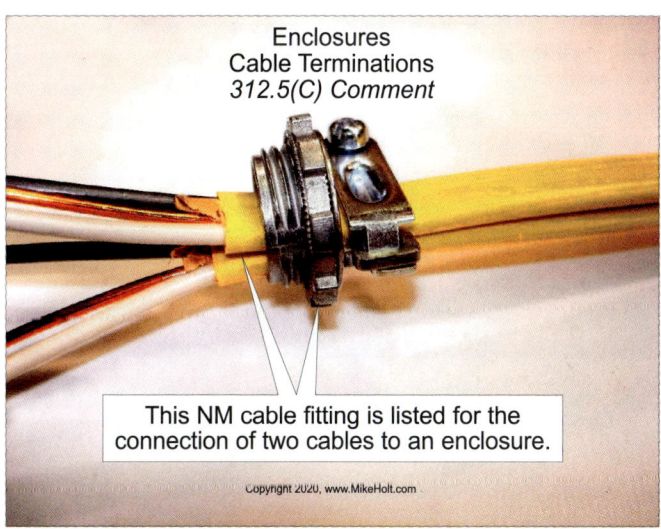
▶Figure 312-8

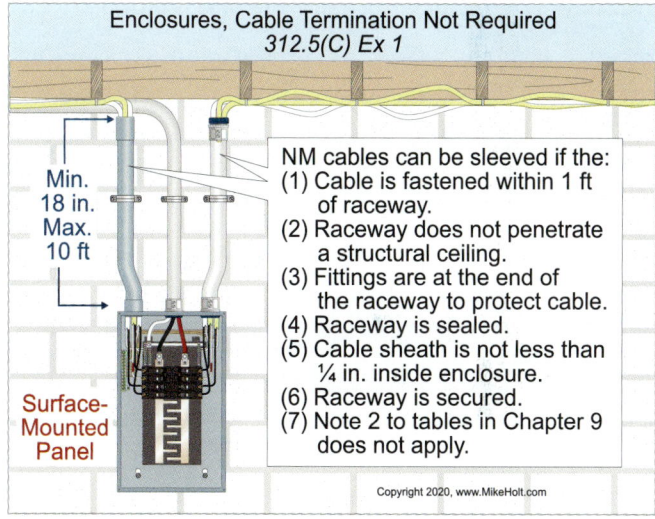
▶Figure 312-10

(1) Each cable is fastened within 12 in. from the raceway.

(2) The raceway does not penetrate a structural ceiling.

(3) Fittings are provided on the raceway to protect the cables from abrasion.

(4) The raceway is sealed.

(5) Each cable sheath extends not less than ¼ in. into the enclosure.

(6) The raceway is properly secured.

(7) Where installed as conduit or tubing so Chapter 9, Table 1 may be used; Note 2 to the tables in Chapter 9 does not apply to this condition.

Ex 1: Cables with nonmetallic sheaths are not required to be secured to the cabinet, cutout box, and meter socket enclosure if the cables enter the top of a surface-mounted enclosure through a nonflexible raceway not less than 18 in. or more than 10 ft long, if all the following conditions are met: ▶Figure 312-10

312.6 | Cabinets

312.6 Deflection of Conductors

Conductors entering or leaving cabinets and meter socket enclosures must comply with 312.6(A) and 312.6(B).

(A) Width of Enclosures and Wireways. Conductors are not permitted to be deflected in a cabinet unless a space having a width in accordance with Table 312.6(A) is provided. ▶Figure 312-11

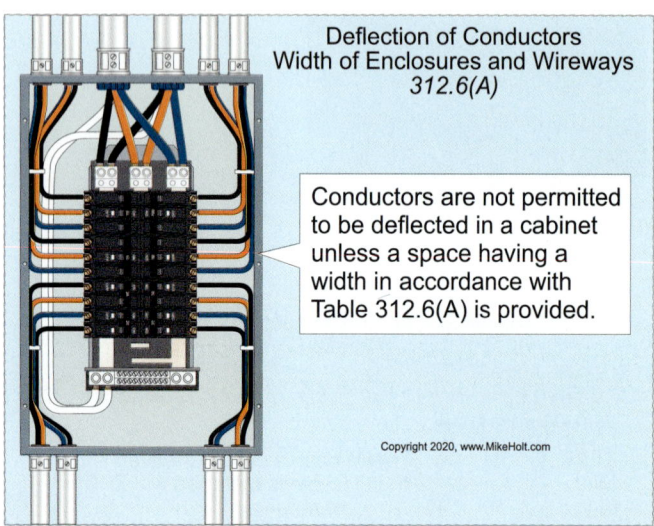

▶Figure 312-11

Table 312.6(A) Minimum Wire-Bending Space

Wire Size (AWG or kcmil)	Inches
8-6	1½
4-3	2
2	2½
1	3
1/0-2/0	3½
3/0-4/0	4
250	4½
300-350	5
400-500	6
600-700	8

(B) Wire-Bending Space at Terminals.

(2) Conductors Entering or Leaving Opposite Wall. Table 312.6(B) applies where the conductor enters or leaves the cabinet through the wall opposite its terminal. ▶Figure 312-12

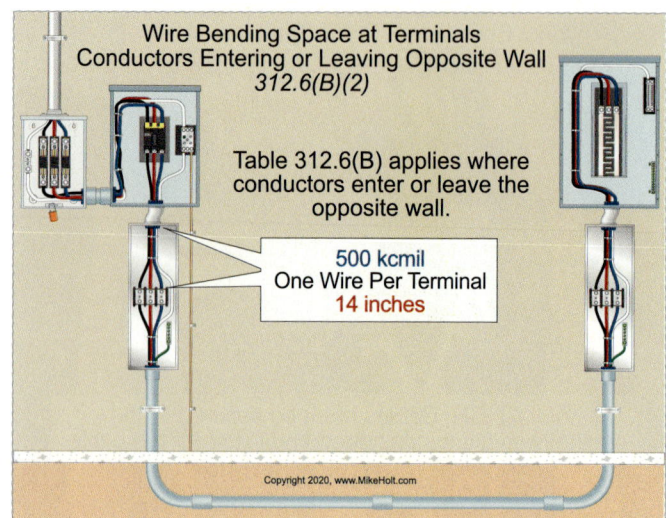

▶Figure 312-12

Table 312.6(B) Minimum Wire-Bending Space

Wire Size (AWG or kcmil)	Inches
2	3½
1	4½
1/0	5½
3/0	6½
250	8½
350	12
500	14
600	15

312.8 Overcurrent Device Enclosures

Cabinets are permitted to contain wiring as provided in 312.8 (A) and (B).

(A) Splices, Taps, and Feed-Through Conductors. The wiring space within cabinets can be used for conductors feeding through, spliced, or tapped where all the following conditions are met:

(1) The area of all conductors at any cross section does not exceed 40 percent of the cross-sectional area of that space. ▶Figure 312-13

(2) The area of all conductors, splices, and taps installed at any cross section does not exceed 75 percent of the cross-sectional area of that space. ▶Figure 312-14

Cabinets | 312.8

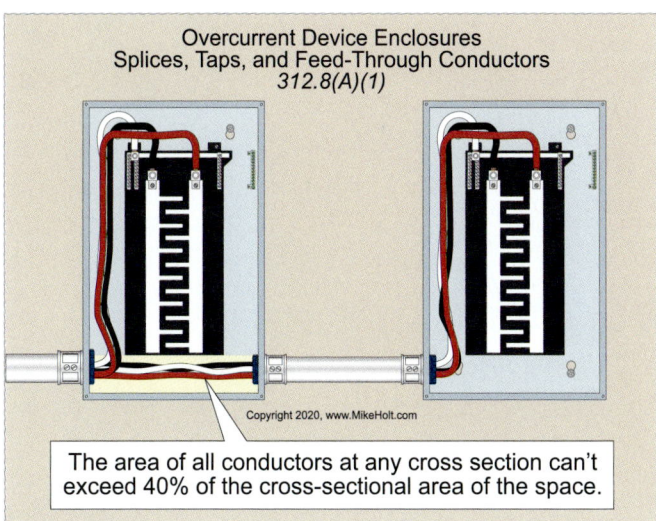

▶Figure 312–13

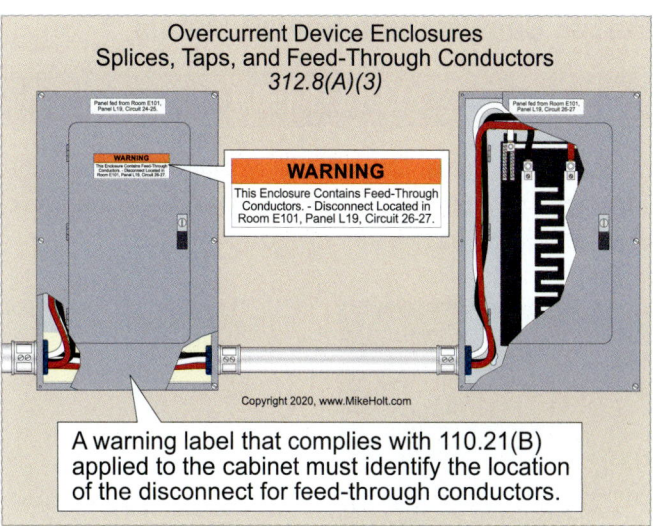

▶Figure 312–15

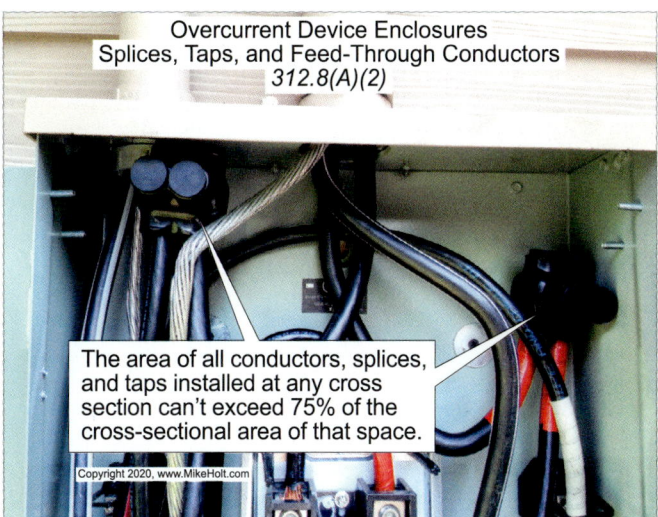

▶Figure 312–14

Author's Comment:

▶ The 40 and 75 percent requirements apply to all conductors, all splices, and all taps within the cross-sectional area; not just conductors, splice(s), or tap(s) being added.

(3) Where conductors feed through the cabinet, a permanently affixed warning label sufficiently durable to withstand the environment involved, and complying with 110.21(B), must be applied on the cabinet to identify the location of the disconnect for the feed-through conductors. ▶Figure 312–15

(B) Power Monitoring or Energy Management Equipment. The wiring space of enclosures for switches or overcurrent devices are permitted to contain power monitoring or energy management equipment where all the following conditions are met:

(1) Identification. The power monitoring or energy management equipment is identified as a field installable accessory as part of the listed equipment or is a listed kit evaluated for field installation in switch or overcurrent device enclosures.

(2) Area. The total area of all conductors, splices, taps, and equipment at any cross section of the wiring space does not exceed 75 percent of the cross-sectional area of that space.

(3) Conductors. Conductors used exclusively for control or instrumentation circuits must comply with either 312.8(B)(3)(a) or (b).

(a) Conductors must comply with 725.49.

(b) Conductors smaller than 18 AWG, but not smaller than 22 AWG for a single conductor and 26 AWG for a multiconductor cable, are permitted where the conductors and cable assemblies meet all of the following conditions:

(1) Conductors or cables are within raceways or routed along one or more walls of the enclosure and secured at intervals not exceeding 10 in.

(2) Are secured within 10 in. of terminations.

(3) Are secured to prevent contact with current-carrying components within the enclosure

(4) Are rated for the system voltage and not less than 600V

(5) Have a minimum insulation temperature rating of 90°C

312.10 | Cabinets

Part II. Construction Specifications

312.10 Material

(A) Metal Enclosures. Metal enclosures within the scope of this article must be protected both inside and outside against corrosion. ▶Figure 312–16

▶Figure 312–16

ARTICLE 314 — OUTLET, PULL, AND JUNCTION BOXES; CONDUIT BODIES; AND HANDHOLE ENCLOSURES

Introduction to Article 314—Outlet, Pull, and Junction Boxes; Conduit Bodies; and Handhole Enclosures

Article 314 contains the installation requirements for outlet boxes, pull and junction boxes, conduit bodies, and handhole enclosures. As with the cabinets covered in Article 312, the conditions of use have a bearing on the type of material and equipment selected for the installation.

The information contained in this article will help you size an outlet box using the proper cubic-inch capacity as well as calculating the minimum dimensions for pull boxes. There are limits on the amount of weight that can be supported by an outlet box, and rules on how to support a device or outlet box to various surfaces. Article 314 will help you understand these rules so your installation will be compliant with the *NEC*. As always, the clear illustrations will help you visualize the finished installation.

Part I. Scope and General

314.1 Scope

Article 314 contains the installation requirements for outlet boxes, pull and junction boxes, conduit bodies, and handhole enclosures. ▶Figure 314–1

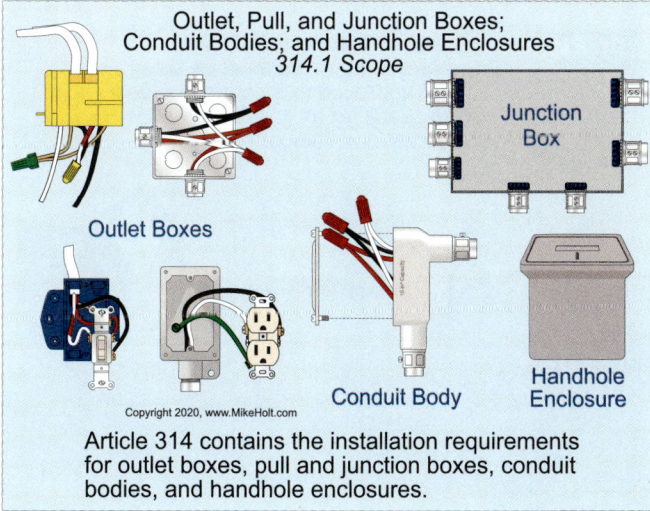

▶Figure 314–1

314.3 Nonmetallic Boxes

Nonmetallic boxes can only be used with nonmetallic cables and raceways.

Ex 1: Metal raceways and cables can be used with nonmetallic boxes if the raceways and cables are bonded together in the nonmetallic box. ▶Figure 314–2

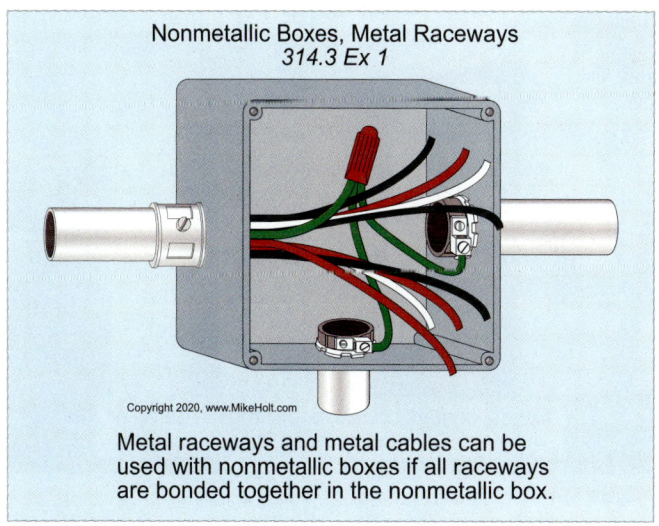

▶Figure 314–2

2nd Printing — 2020 NEC Requirements for Solar PV and Energy Storage Systems | MikeHolt.com | 295

314.4 Metal Boxes

Metal boxes must be connected to an equipment grounding conductor in accordance with 250.148. ▶Figure 314–3

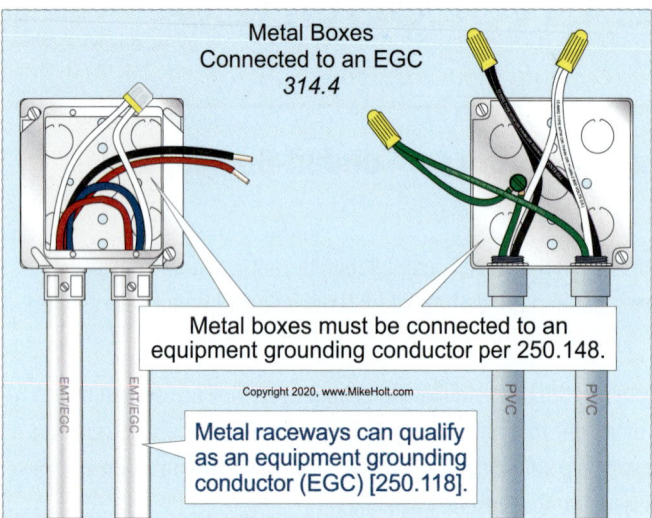

▶Figure 314–3

Part II. Installation

314.15 Damp or Wet Locations

Boxes, conduit bodies, and fittings in damp or wet locations must be listed for use in wet locations. ▶Figure 314–4 and ▶Figure 314–5

▶Figure 314–4

▶Figure 314–5

314.16 Sizing Outlet Boxes

Boxes containing 6 AWG and smaller conductors must be sized in an approved manner to provide free space for all conductors, devices, and fittings. In no case can the volume of the box, as calculated in 314.16(A), be less than the volume requirement as calculated in 314.16(B). ▶Figure 314–6 and ▶Figure 314–7

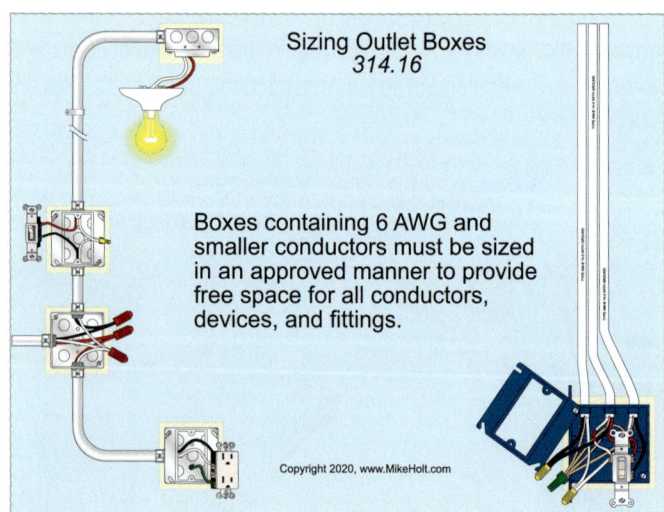

▶Figure 314–6

Outlet, Pull, and Junction Boxes; Conduit Bodies; and Handhole Enclosures | 314.16

▶Figure 314-7

Author's Comment:

▶ The requirements for sizing boxes and conduit bodies containing conductors 4 AWG and larger are in 314.28, and those for sizing handhole enclosures are contained in 314.30(A). An outlet box is generally used for the attachment of devices and luminaires and has a specific amount of space (volume) for conductors, devices, and fittings. The volume taken up by conductors, devices, and fittings in a box must not exceed the box fill capacity.

Boxes and conduit bodies enclosing conductors 4 AWG or larger must also comply with the provisions of 314.28.

(A) Box Volume Calculations. The volume of a box is the total volume of its assembled parts including plaster rings, raised covers, and extension rings. The total volume includes only those parts marked with their volumes in cubic inches (cu in.) [314.16(A)] or included in Table 314.16(A). ▶Figure 314-8

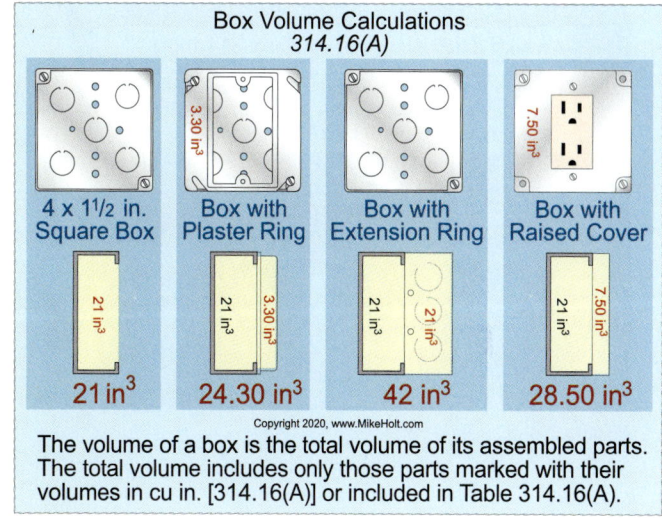

▶Figure 314-8

Table 314.16(A) Metal Boxes							
Box Trade Size		Minimum Volume	Maximum Number of Conductors (arranged by AWG size)					
in.	Box Shape	In³	18	16	14	12	10	8
(4 × 1¼)	round/octagonal	12.50	8	7	6	5	5	5
(4 × 1½)	round/octagonal	15.50	10	8	7	6	6	5
(4 × 2⅛)	round/octagonal	21.50	14	12	10	9	8	7
(4 × 1¼)	square	18.00	12	10	9	8	7	6
(4 × 1½)	square	21.00	14	12	10	9	8	7
(4 × 2⅛)	square	30.30	20	17	15	13	12	10
(4¹¹⁄₁₆ × 1¼)	square	25.50	17	14	12	11	10	8
(4¹¹⁄₁₆ × 1½)	square	29.50	19	16	14	13	11	9
(4¹¹⁄₁₆ × 2⅛)	square	42.00	28	24	21	18	16	14

314.16 | Outlet, Pull, and Junction Boxes; Conduit Bodies; and Handhole Enclosures

▶ **Example**

Question: What is the total box volume for a 4 × 4 × 1½ outlet box and a 4 × 4 × 1½ extension box with a domed cover marked with a 7.50 cu in. volume? ▶Figure 314–9

(a) 44.50 cu in. (b) 46.50 cu in. (c) 47.50 cu in. (d) 49.50 cu in.

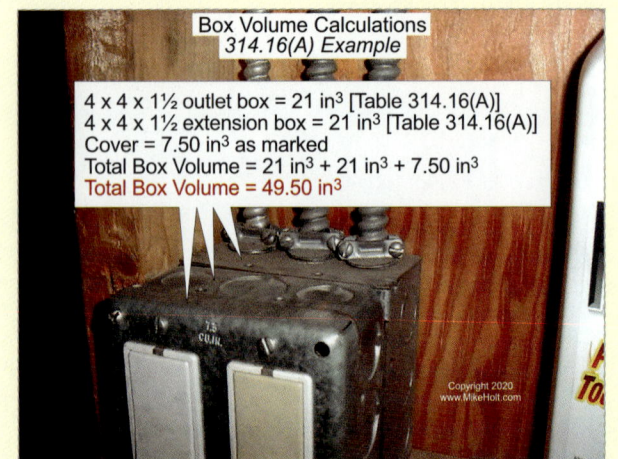

▶Figure 314–9

Solution:

Volume of 4 × 4 × 1½ outlet box = 21 cu in. [Table 314.16(A)]
Volume of 4 × 4 × 1½ extension box = 21 cu in. [Table 314.16(A)]

Cover Volume = 7.50 cu in. as marked

Total Volume = 21 cu in. + 21 cu in. + 7.50 cu in.
Total Volume = 49.50 cu in.

Do not calculate the actual volume of a box contained in Table 314.16(A) since the table volume is based on the inside dimensions of the box, not the outside dimensions.

Answer: (d) 49.50 cu in.

Where a box is provided with barriers, the volume is apportioned to each of the resulting spaces. Each barrier, if not marked with its volume, is considered to take up ½ cu in. if metal and 1 cu in. if nonmetallic. ▶Figure 314–10

Author's Comment:

▸ When all the conductors in an outlet box are the same size (insulation does not matter), Table 314.16(A) can be used to determine the number of conductors permitted in the outlet box, or to determine the required outlet box size for the given number of conductors.

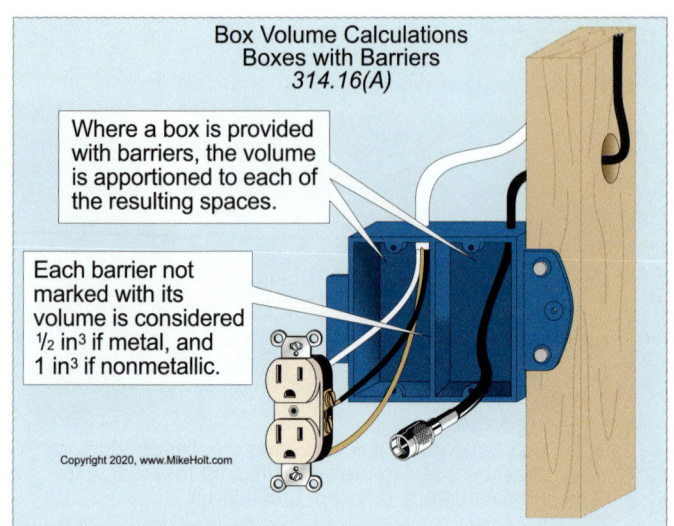

▶Figure 314–10

▸ If the outlet box contains switches, receptacles, luminaire studs, luminaire hickeys, cable clamps, or equipment grounding conductors, then allowance must be made for these items which are not reflected in Table 314.16(A).

▶ **Table 314.16(A) Example**

Question: Which 4-in. square outlet box will be required for three 12 THW and six 12 THHN conductors? ▶Figure 314–11

(a) 4 × 1¼ in. square   (b) 4 × 1½ in. square
(c) 4 × 2⅛ in. square   (d) 4 × 2⅛ in. with extension

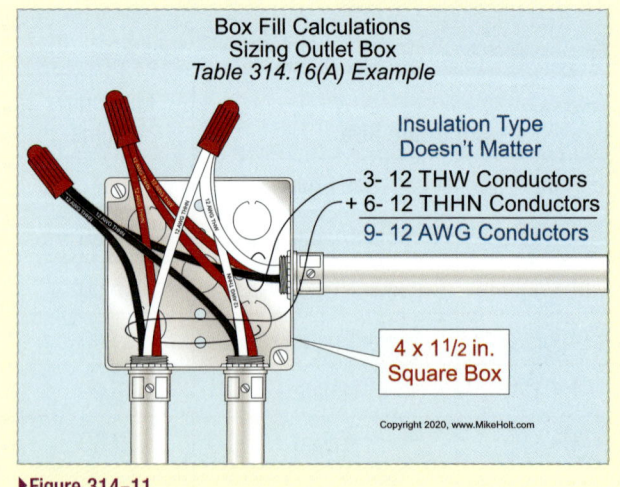

▶Figure 314–11

Answer: (b) 4 × 1½ in. square

Outlet, Pull, and Junction Boxes; Conduit Bodies; and Handhole Enclosures | 314.16

(B) Box Fill Calculations. Table 314.16(A) does not consider switches, receptacles, luminaire studs, luminaire hickeys, cable clamps, or equipment grounding conductors. The calculated conductor volumes determined by 314.16(B)(1) through (B)(5) are added together to determine the total volume of the conductors, devices, and fittings. ▶Figure 314–12

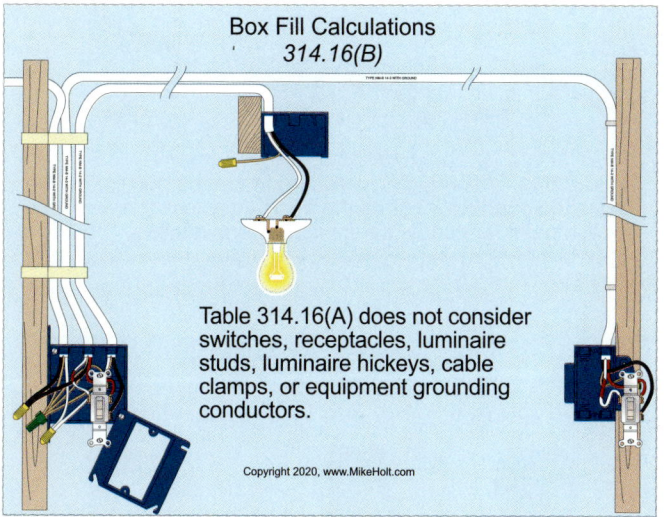
▶Figure 314–12

Raceway and cable fittings, including locknuts and bushings, are not counted for box fill calculations. ▶Figure 314–13

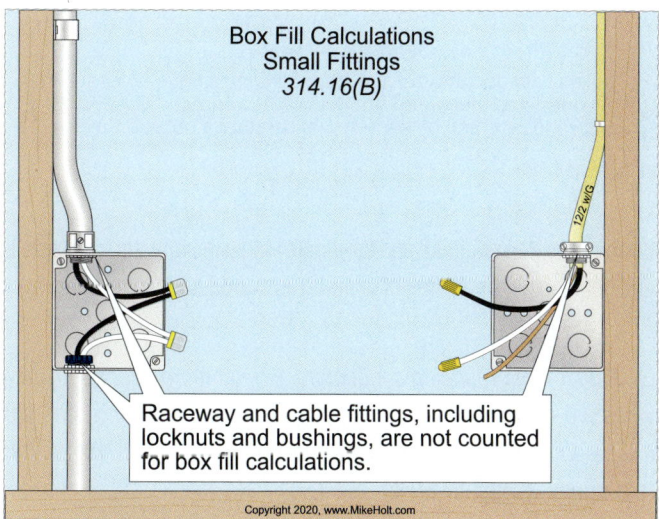
▶Figure 314–13

Each space within a box with a barrier must be calculated separately. ▶Figure 314–14

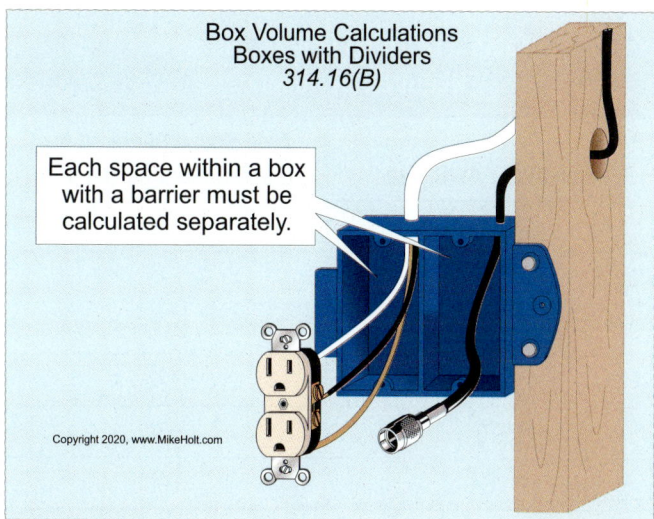
▶Figure 314–14

(1) Conductor Volume. Each conductor that originates outside the box and terminates or is spliced inside the box counts as a single conductor volume as shown in Table 314.16(B). ▶Figure 314–15

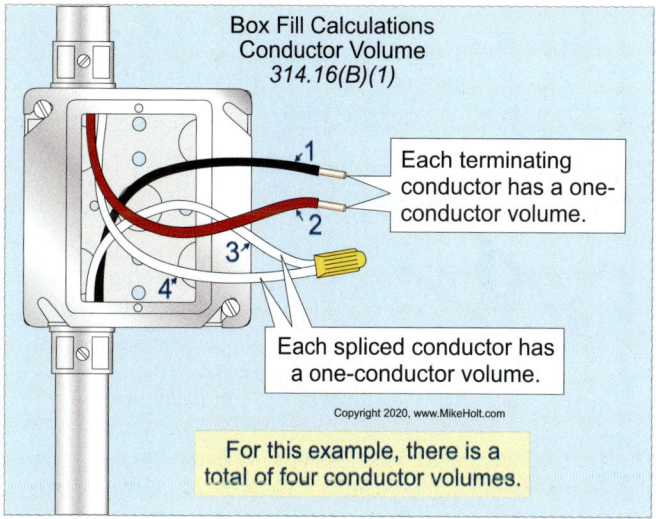
▶Figure 314–15

Author's Comment:

▸ Table 314.16(B) lists the conductor cu in. volumes for 18 AWG through 6 AWG. For example, one 14 AWG conductor has a volume of 2 cu in. If a box has four 14 AWG conductors, the conductor volume is 8 cu in.

▸ Conductor insulation is not a factor for box fill calculations.

314.16 | Outlet, Pull, and Junction Boxes; Conduit Bodies; and Handhole Enclosures

Table 314.16(B) Volume Allowance Required per Conductor	
Conductor AWG Size	Free Space Required for Each Conductor (cu in.)
18	1.50
16	1.75
14	2.00
12	2.25
10	2.50
8	3.00
6	5.00

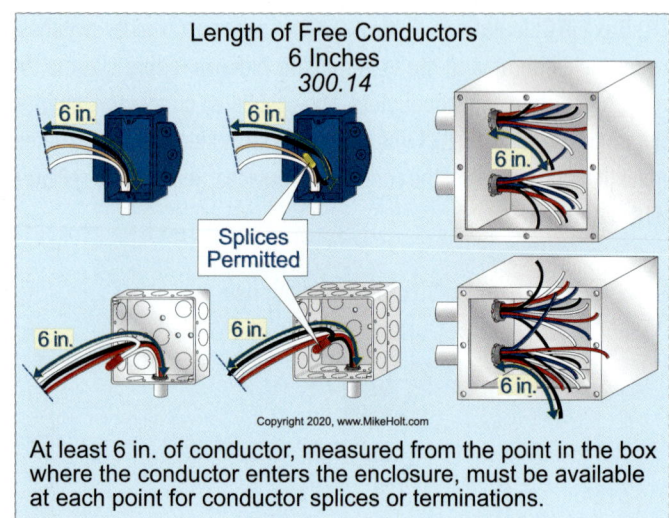

At least 6 in. of conductor, measured from the point in the box where the conductor enters the enclosure, must be available at each point for conductor splices or terminations.

▶Figure 314–17

Each conductor loop having a total length of less than 12 in. is considered a single conductor volume, and each conductor loop having a length of at least 12 in. is considered as two conductor volumes in accordance with Table 314.16(B) [300.14]. ▶Figure 314–16

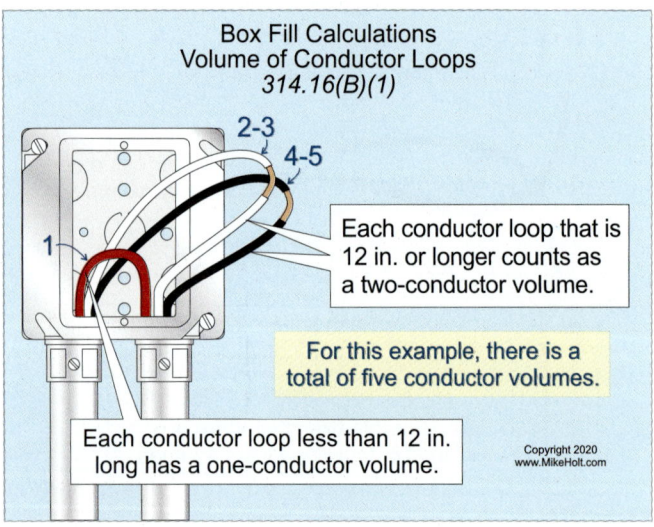

▶Figure 314–16

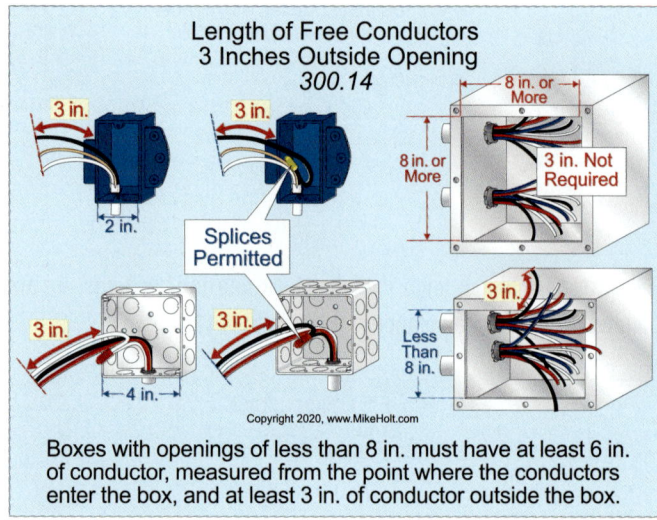

Boxes with openings of less than 8 in. must have at least 6 in. of conductor, measured from the point where the conductors enter the box, and at least 3 in. of conductor outside the box.

▶Figure 314–18

Conductors that originate and terminate within the box, such as pigtails and bonding jumpers, are not counted as a conductor volume. ▶Figure 314–19

Ex: Equipment grounding conductors and not more than four fixture wires are not counted as a conductor volume if they enter the box from a domed luminaire or similar canopy, such as a ceiling paddle fan canopy. ▶Figure 314–20

(2) Cable Clamp Volume. Cable clamps that are part of the outlet box are counted as a single conductor volume based on the largest conductor in the box in accordance with Table 314.16(B). ▶Figure 314–21

Author's Comment:

▸ At least 6 in. of conductor, measured from the point in the box where the conductor enters the enclosure, must be available at each point for conductor splices or terminations. ▶Figure 314–17

▸ Boxes that have openings of less than 8 in. in any dimension must have at least 6 in. of conductor, measured from the point where the conductor enters the box, and at least 3 in. of conductor outside the box. ▶Figure 314–18

Outlet, Pull, and Junction Boxes; Conduit Bodies; and Handhole Enclosures | **314.16**

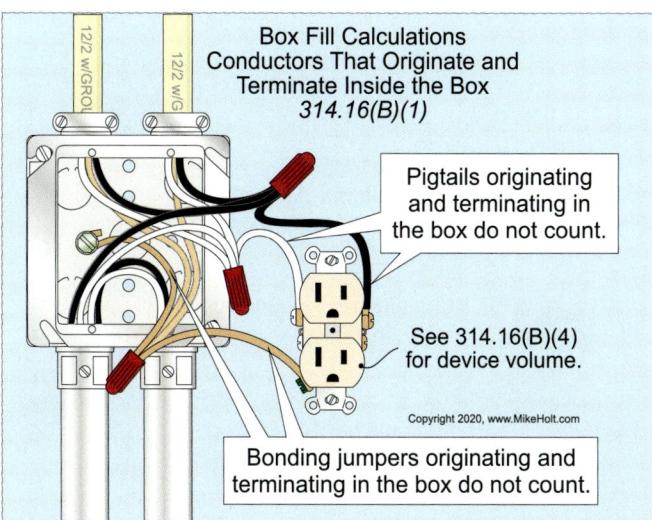
▶Figure 314-19

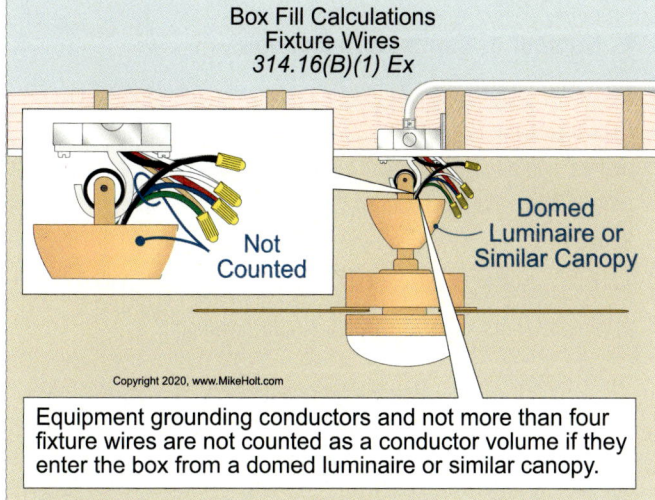
▶Figure 314-20

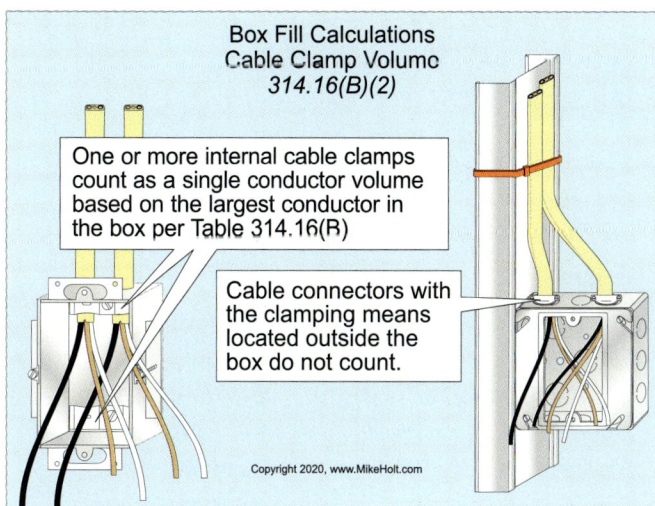
▶Figure 314-21

(3) Support Fitting Volume. Each luminaire stud or luminaire hickey counts as a single conductor volume based on the largest conductor that enters the box in accordance with Table 314.16(B). ▶Figure 314-22

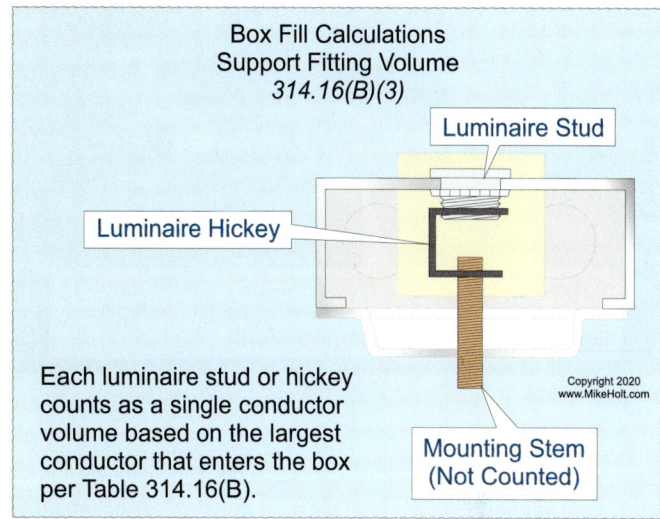
▶Figure 314-22

(4) Device Yoke Volume. Each single-gang device yoke counts as two conductor volumes based on the largest conductor that terminates on the device in accordance with Table 314.16(B). ▶Figure 314-23

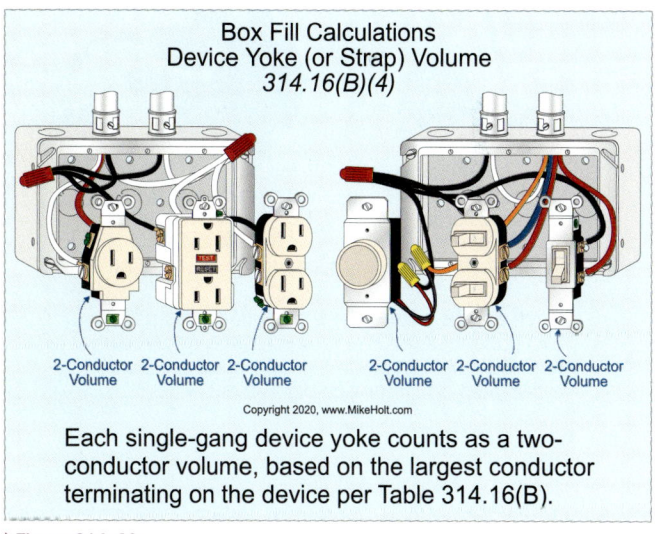
▶Figure 314-23

Author's Comment:

▸ A device yoke (also called a "strap") is the mounting structure for a receptacle, switch, switch with pilot light, switch/receptacle, and so forth. ▶Figure 314-24

| 314.16 | Outlet, Pull, and Junction Boxes; Conduit Bodies; and Handhole Enclosures |

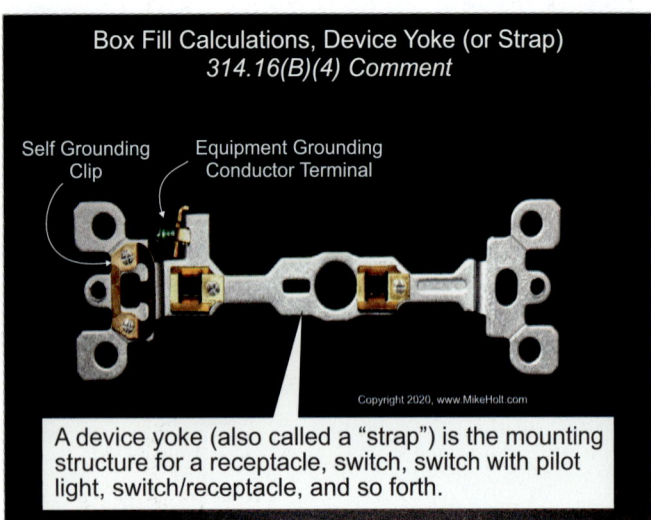

▶Figure 314–24

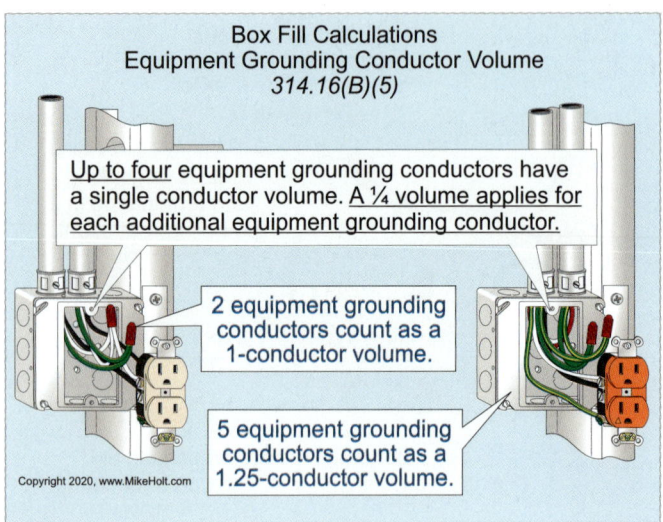

▶Figure 314–26

Each device yoke wider than 2 in. counts as a two-conductor volume for each gang required for mounting, based on the largest conductor that terminates on the device in accordance with Table 314.16(B). ▶Figure 314–25

▶ **Number of Conductors Example**

Question: What is the total number of conductors used for box fill calculations in a 4-in. square × 2⅛ in. deep box with two internal cable clamps, one single-pole switch, one duplex receptacle, one 14/3 with ground NM cable, and one 14/2 with ground NM cable? ▶Figure 314–27

(a) 5 conductors (b) 7 conductors
(c) 9 conductors (d) 11 conductors

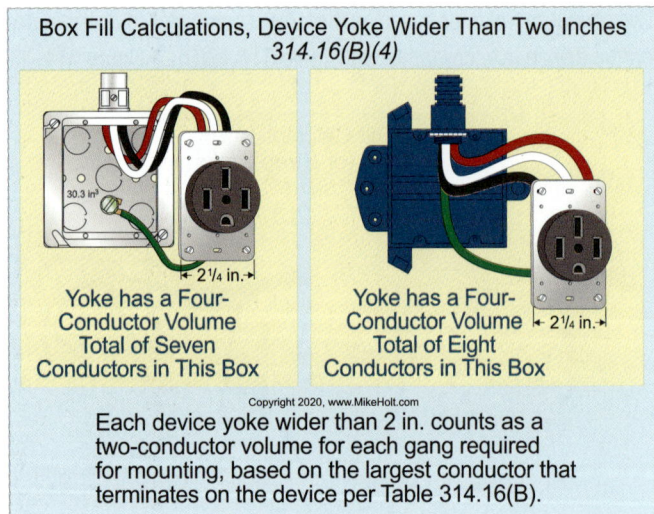

▶Figure 314–25

(5) Equipment Grounding Conductor Volume. Up to four equipment grounding conductors count as a single conductor volume, based on the largest equipment grounding conductor that enters the box in accordance with Table 314.16(B).

A ¼ volume allowance applies for each additional equipment grounding conductor or equipment bonding jumper that enters the box, based on the largest equipment grounding or bonding conductor. ▶Figure 314–26

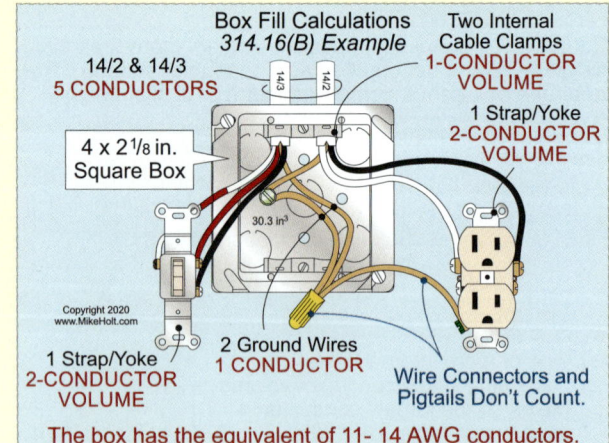

▶Figure 314–27

Solution:

Switch and Conductors	5–14 AWG conductors †
Receptacles and Conductors	4–14 AWG conductors ††
Equipment Grounding Conductor	1–14 AWG conductor
Cable Clamps	+ 1–14 AWG conductor
Total	11–14 AWG conductors

†Two conductors for the device and three conductors terminating
††Two conductors for the device and two conductors terminating

Each 14 AWG conductor counts as 2 cu in. [Table 314.16(B)]. 11 conductors × 2 cu in. = 22 cu in.

If the cubic-inch volume of the plaster ring is not stamped on it, or given in the problem, it cannot be included in the box volume. Without knowing the plaster ring volume, a 4 in. square by 2⅛ in. deep box is the minimum required for this example.

Answer: (d) 11 conductors

▶ Box Fill Example

Question: How many 14 AWG conductors can be pulled through a 4-in. square × 2⅛ in. deep box with a plaster ring with a marking of 3.60 cu in.? The box contains two receptacles, five 12 AWG conductors, and two 12 AWG equipment grounding conductors. ▶Figure 314–28

(a) 4 conductors (b) 5 conductors
(c) 6 conductors (d) 7 conductors

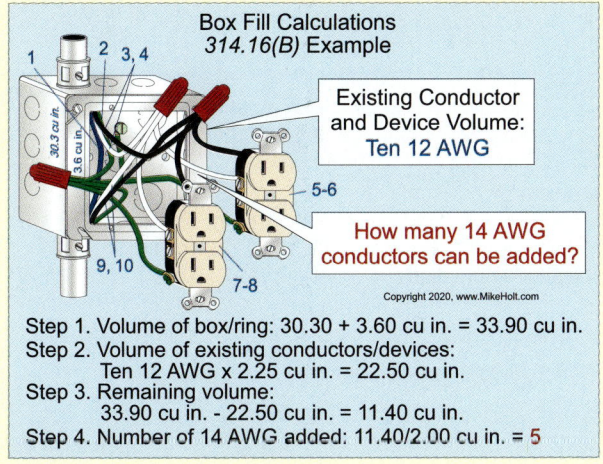

▶Figure 314–28

Solution:

Step 1: Determine the volume of the box assembly [314.16(A)].

Box Assembly Volume = Box 30.30 cu in. + 3.60 cu in. plaster ring
Box Assembly Volume = 33.90 cu in.

Step 2: Determine the volume of the devices and conductors in the box:

Two–receptacles	4–12 AWG
Five–12 AWG conductors	5–12 AWG
Two–12 AWG equipment grounding conductors	1–12 AWG

Total Device Volume and Conductors = Ten–12 AWG × 2.25 cu in.
Total Device Volume and Conductors = 22.50 cu in.

Step 3: Determine the remaining volume permitted for the 14 AWG conductors (volume of the box minus the volume of the conductors).

Remaining Volume = 33.90 cu in. – 22.50 cu in.
Remaining Volume = 11.40 cu in.

Step 4: Determine the number of 14 AWG conductors (at 2.00 cu in. each) permitted in the remaining volume of 11.40 cu in.:

14 AWG = 2.00 cu in. each [Table 314.16(B)]
11.40 cu in./2.00 cu in. = 5 conductors

Five 14 AWG conductors can be pulled through.

Answer: (b) 5 conductors

(C) Conduit Bodies

(2) Splices. Splices are permitted in conduit bodies that are legibly marked by the manufacturer with their volume. The maximum number of conductors permitted in a conduit body is limited in accordance with 314.16(B).

▶ Number of Conductors in Conduit Body Example

Example: How many 12 AWG conductors can be spliced in an 11.80 cu in. conduit body? ▶Figure 314–29

(a) four conductors (b) five conductors
(c) six conductors   (d) seven conductors

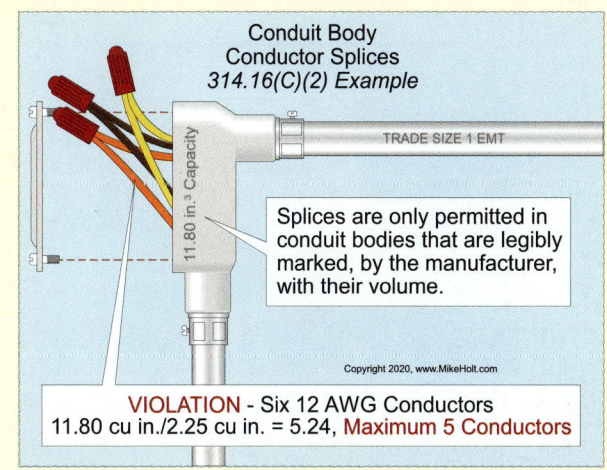

▶Figure 314–29

Solution:

12 AWG = 2.25 cu in. [Table 314.16(B)]
11.80 cu in./2.25 cu in. = 5.24 conductors

Answer: (b) five conductors

314.17 | Outlet, Pull, and Junction Boxes; Conduit Bodies; and Handhole Enclosures

(3) Short Radius Conduit Bodies. Capped elbows, handy ells, and service-entrance elbows are not permitted to contain any splices. ▶Figure 314–30

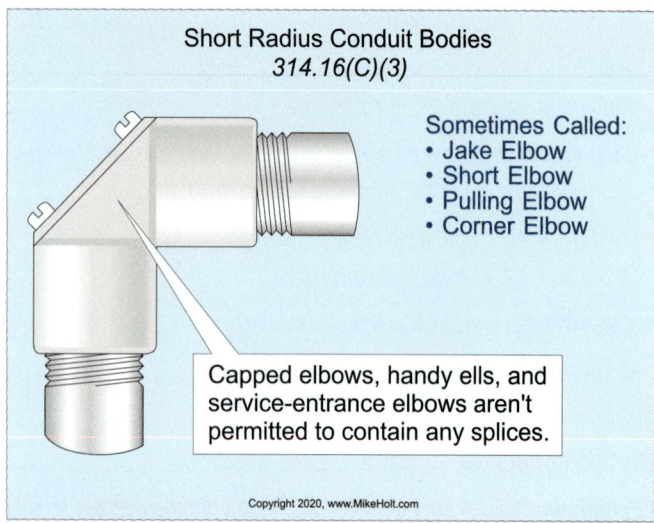
▶Figure 314–30

314.17 Conductors That Enter Boxes or Conduit Bodies

(A) Openings to be Closed. Unused openings through which conductors enter a box must be closed in an approved manner identified for the application. ▶Figure 314–31

▶Figure 314–31

Author's Comment:

▸ Unused cable or raceway openings must be effectively closed by fittings that provide protection substantially equivalent to the wall of the equipment [110.12(A)].

(B) Boxes. The installation of the conductors in boxes must comply with the following:

(2) Conductors Entering Through Cable Clamps. Where cable assemblies (Type NM or UF) are used, the sheath must extend not less than ¼ in. inside the box and beyond any cable clamp. ▶Figure 314–32

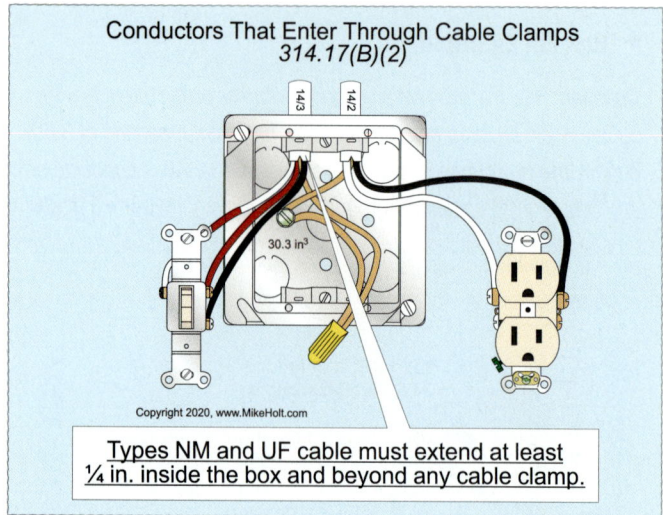
▶Figure 314–32

Author's Comment:

▸ Two Type NM cables can terminate in a single cable clamp if it is listed for this purpose [UL White Book].

Ex: Type NM cable terminating to a single-gang nonmetallic box is not required to be secured to the box if the cable is securely fastened within 8 in. of the box and the sheath extends at least ¼ in. inside the box. ▶Figure 314–33

314.20 Flush-Mounted Box Installations

Installation within walls or ceilings constructed of noncombustible material must have the front edge of the box, plaster ring, extension ring, or listed extender set back no more than ¼ in. from the finished surface. ▶Figure 314–34

Outlet, Pull, and Junction Boxes; Conduit Bodies; and Handhole Enclosures | 314.21

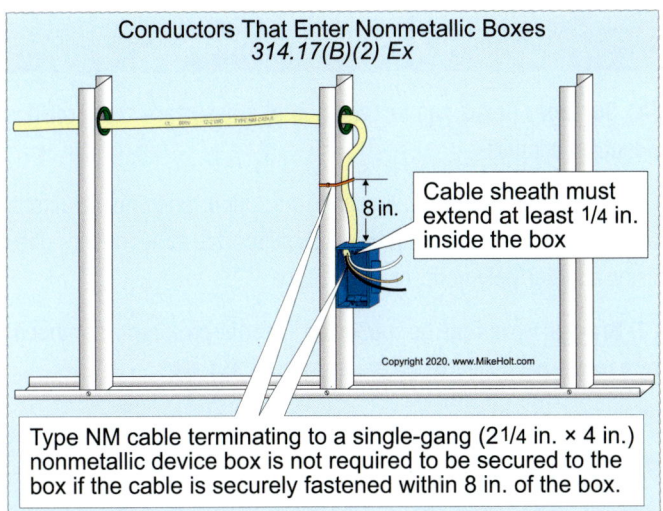
▶Figure 314-33

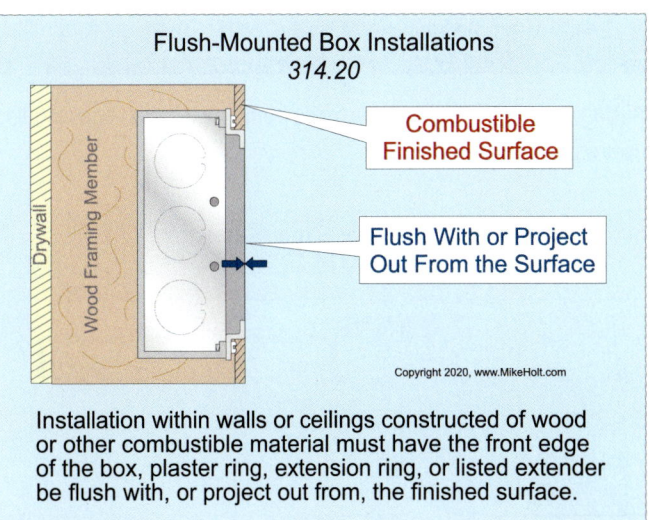
▶Figure 314-35

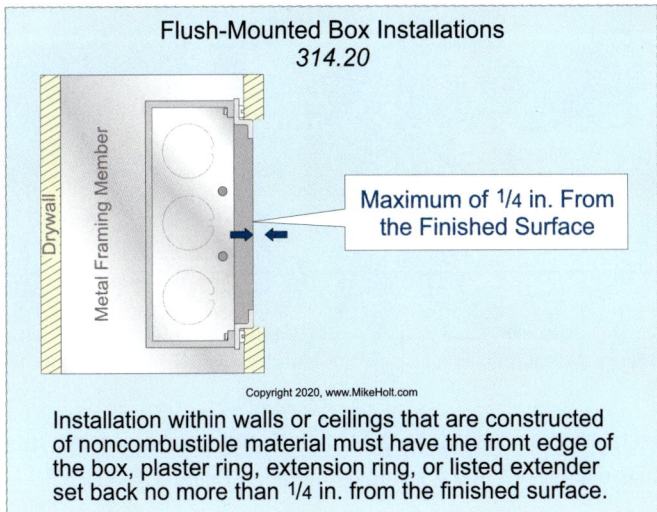
▶Figure 314-34

Installation within walls or ceilings constructed of wood or other combustible material must have the front edge of the box, plaster ring, extension ring, or listed extender extend to or project out from the finished surface. ▶Figure 314-35

Author's Comment:

- Plaster rings and extension rings are available in a variety of depths to meet the above requirements.

- Final finished surfaces such as backsplashes and tile may need to be considered in order to meet the requirements of this section.

314.21 Repairing Noncombustible Surfaces

Gaps around boxes that are recessed in noncombustible surfaces (such as plaster, drywall, or plasterboard) must be repaired so there will be no gap more than 1/8 in. at the edge of the box. ▶Figure 314-36

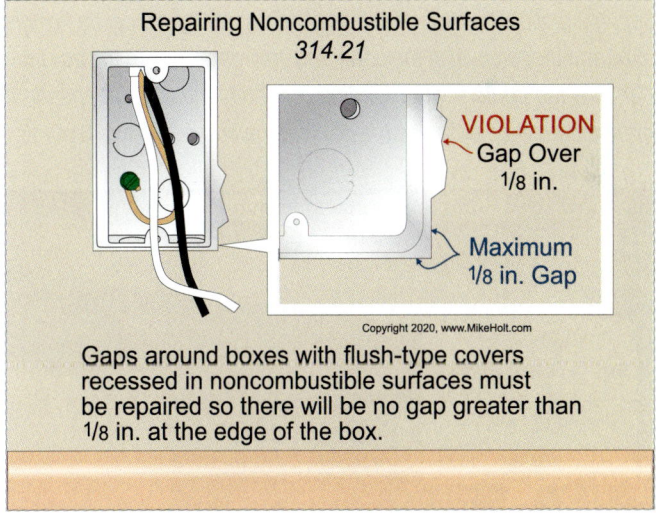
▶Figure 314-36

Author's Comment:

- Other examples of noncombustible surfaces include ceramic wall tile, ceramic or marble floor tile, brick, cinder block, and other types of masonry or stone; all of which are subject to the requirements of 314.20 and 314.21.

314.22 | Outlet, Pull, and Junction Boxes; Conduit Bodies; and Handhole Enclosures

314.22 Surface Extensions

Surface extensions can only be made from an extension ring installed over a box. ▶Figure 314–37

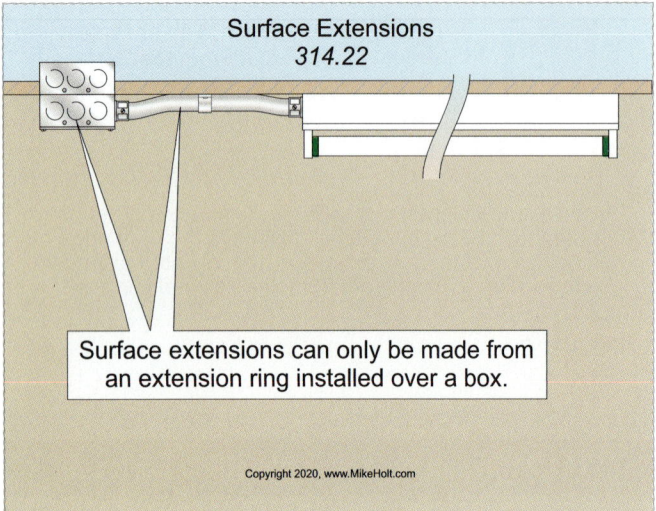

▶Figure 314–37

Ex: A surface extension can be made from the cover of a box if the cover is designed so it is unlikely to fall off if the mounting screws become loose. The surface extension wiring method must be flexible to permit the removal of the cover and provide access to the box interior, and the equipment grounding continuity must be independent of the connection between the box and the cover. ▶Figure 314–38

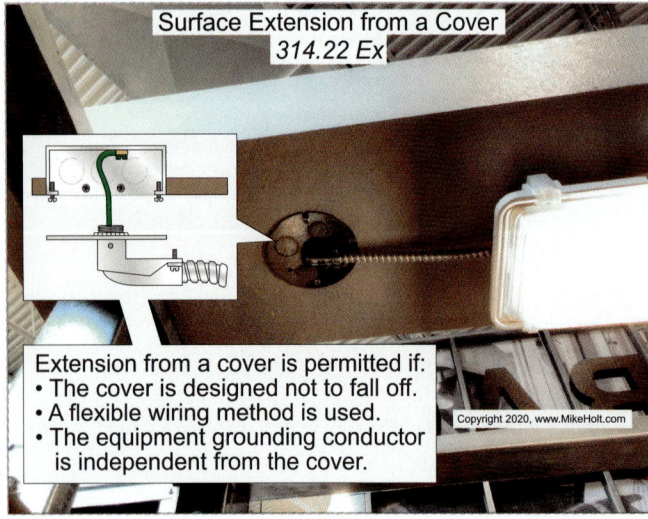

▶Figure 314–38

314.23 Support of Boxes

(A) Surface. Boxes can be fastened to any surface that provides adequate support.

(B) Structural Mounting. An enclosure supported from a structural member or from grade must be rigidly supported either directly or by using a metal, polymeric, or wood brace.

(2) Braces. Boxes can be supported from any structural member or by a metal, plastic, or wood brace. ▶Figure 314–39

▶Figure 314–39

Metal braces no less than 0.02 in. thick and wood braces not less than a nominal 1 in. × 2 in. are permitted. ▶Figure 314–40

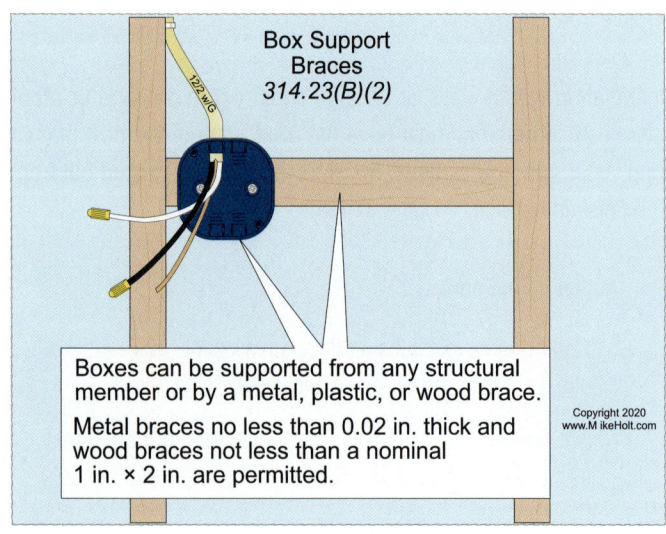

▶Figure 314–40

Outlet, Pull, and Junction Boxes; Conduit Bodies; and Handhole Enclosures | 314.23

(C) Finished Surface Support. Boxes can be secured to a finished surface (drywall, plaster walls, or ceilings) by clamps or fittings identified for the purpose. ▶Figure 314–41

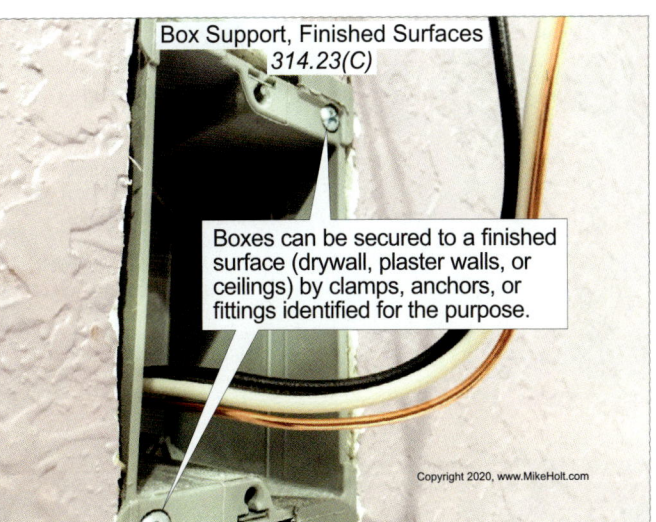

▶Figure 314–41

(D) Suspended-Ceiling Support. Outlet boxes can be supported to the structural or supporting elements of a suspended ceiling, if they are securely fastened by any of the following methods:

(1) Ceiling Framing Members. An outlet box can be secured to suspended-ceiling framing members by bolts, screws, rivets, clips, or other means identified for the suspended-ceiling framing member(s). ▶Figure 314–42

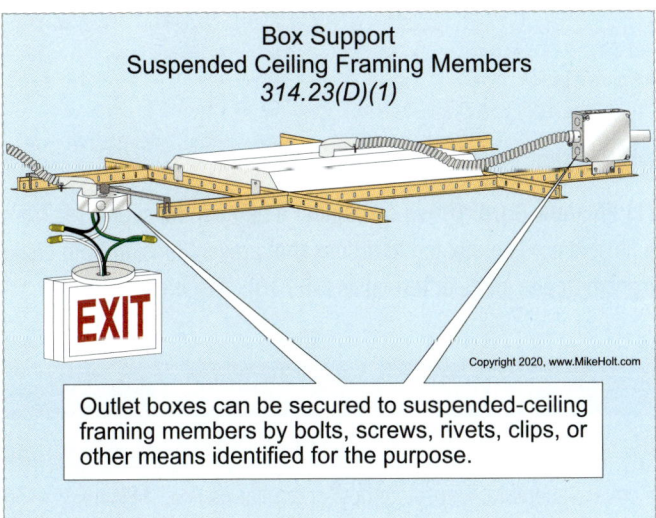

▶Figure 314–42

(2) Independent Support Wires. Outlet boxes can be secured with identified fittings to independent support wires in accordance with 300.11(B). ▶Figure 314–43

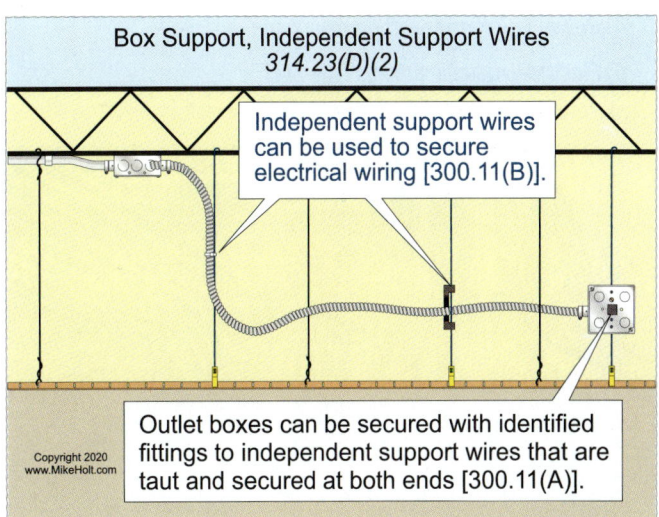

▶Figure 314–43

(E) Threaded Raceway-Supported Boxes Without Devices or Luminaires. Two intermediate metal or rigid metal conduits, threaded wrenchtight into the enclosure, can be used to support an outlet box that does not contain a device or luminaire if each raceway is supported within 36 in. of the box, or within 18 in. of the box if all conduit entries are on the same side. ▶Figure 314–44

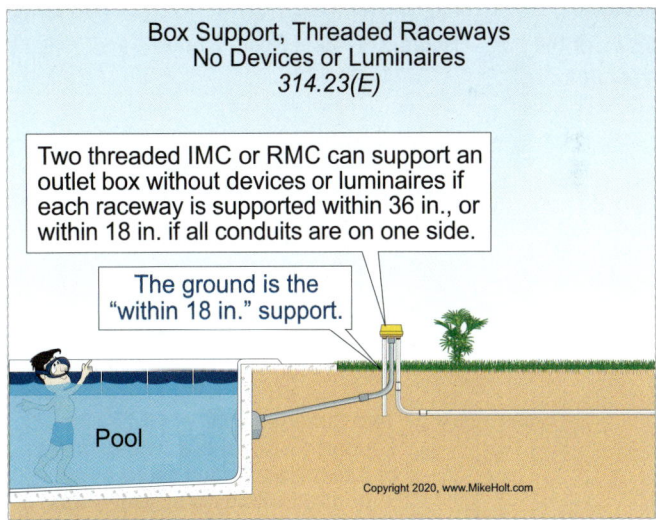

▶Figure 314–44

Ex: The following wiring methods are permitted to support a conduit body of any size, including a conduit body constructed with only one conduit entry, provided the trade size of the conduit body is not larger than the largest trade size of the conduit or tubing: ▶Figure 314–45

(1) Intermediate metal conduit, Type IMC

(2) Rigid metal conduit, Type RMC

(3) Rigid polyvinyl chloride conduit, Type PVC

314.25 | Outlet, Pull, and Junction Boxes; Conduit Bodies; and Handhole Enclosures

(4) Reinforced thermosetting resin conduit, Type RTRC

(5) Electrical metallic tubing, Type EMT

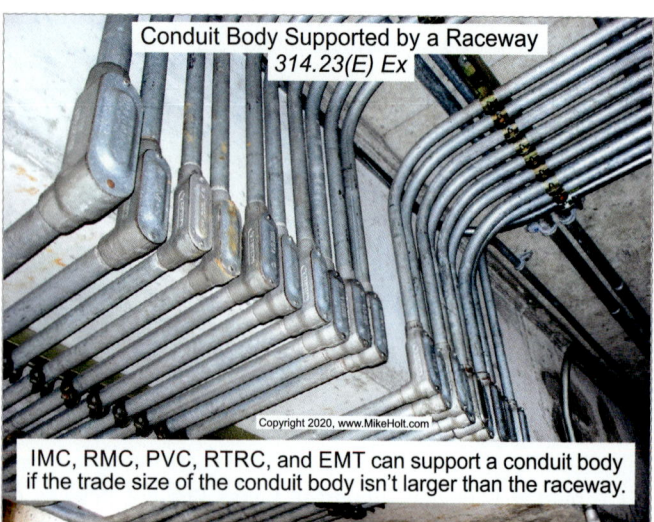

▶Figure 314–45

▶Figure 314–47

(F) Threaded Raceway-Supported Boxes with Devices or Luminaires. Two intermediate metal or rigid metal conduits, threaded wrenchtight into the enclosure, can be used to support an outlet box containing devices or luminaires if each raceway is supported within 18 in. of the box. ▶Figure 314–46, ▶Figure 314–47, and ▶Figure 314–48

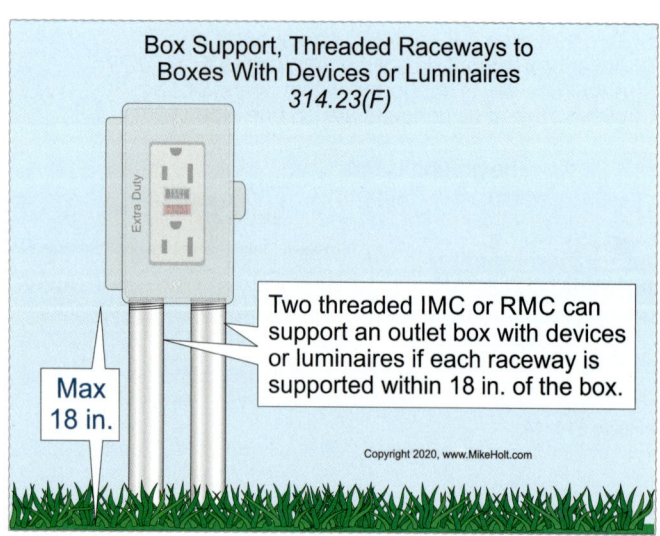

▶Figure 314–46

(G) Boxes in Concrete or Masonry. Boxes must be identified as suitably protected from corrosion and be securely embedded in concrete or masonry.

▶Figure 314–48

(H) Pendant Boxes.

(1) Flexible Cord. Boxes containing a hub can be supported from a flexible cord connected to fittings that prevent tension from being transmitted to joints or terminals [400.10]. ▶Figure 314–49

314.25 Covers and Canopies

When the installation is complete, each outlet box must be provided with a cover, faceplate, fixture canopy, or similar device. ▶Figure 314–50

Screws used for attaching covers to the box must be machine screws that match the thread gage and size of the screw holes in the box. ▶Figure 314–51

Outlet, Pull, and Junction Boxes; Conduit Bodies; and Handhole Enclosures | 314.27

▶Figure 314-49

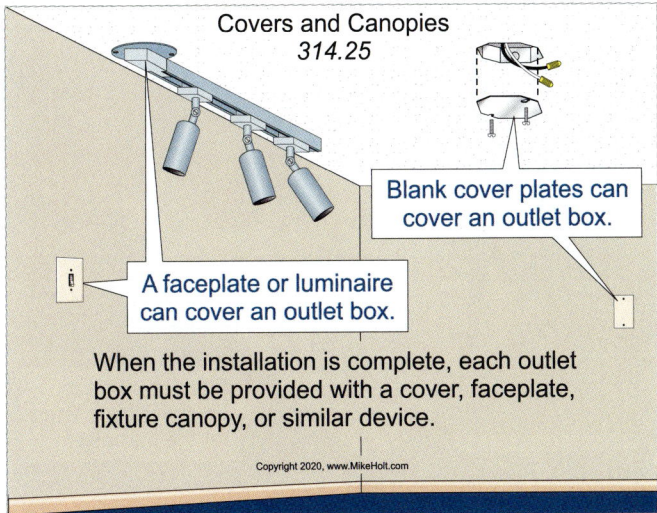

▶Figure 314-50

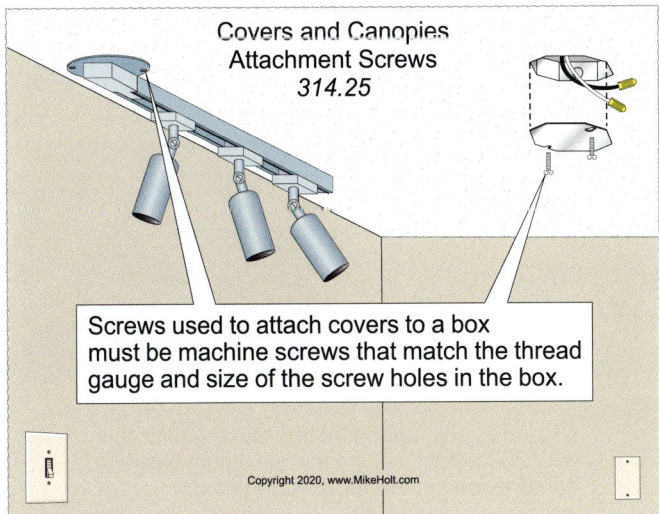

▶Figure 314-51

(A) Metal Covers. Metal covers are only permitted if they can be connected to the circuit equipment grounding conductor [250.110]. ▶Figure 314-52

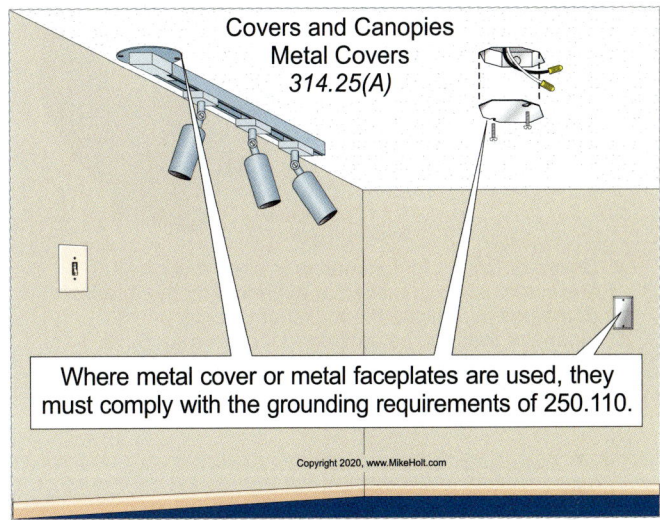

▶Figure 314-52

Author's Comment:

▸ Metal switch cover plates are connected to the circuit equipment grounding conductor in accordance with 404.9(B), and metal receptacle cover plates are connected to the circuit equipment grounding conductor in accordance with 406.6(B).

314.27 Outlet Box Requirements

(A) Boxes at Luminaire Outlets.

(1) Luminaire Outlets in or on Vertical Surfaces. Boxes or fittings designed for the support of luminaires in or on a wall or other vertical surface must be identified and marked on the interior of the box to indicate the maximum weight of the luminaire that can be supported by the box if other than 50 lb. ▶Figure 314-53

Ex: A vertically mounted luminaire weighing no more than 6 lb can be supported to a device box or plaster ring secured to a device box, provided the luminaire or its supporting yoke is secured to the box with no fewer than two No. 6 or larger screws. ▶Figure 314-54

314.27 | Outlet, Pull, and Junction Boxes; Conduit Bodies; and Handhole Enclosures

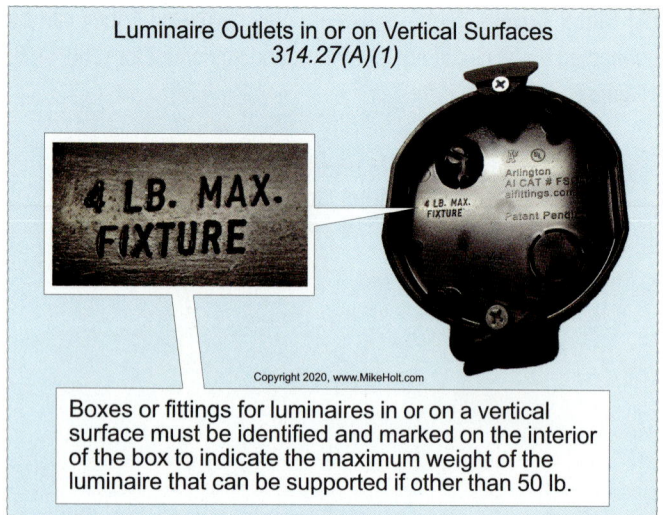
▶Figure 314–53

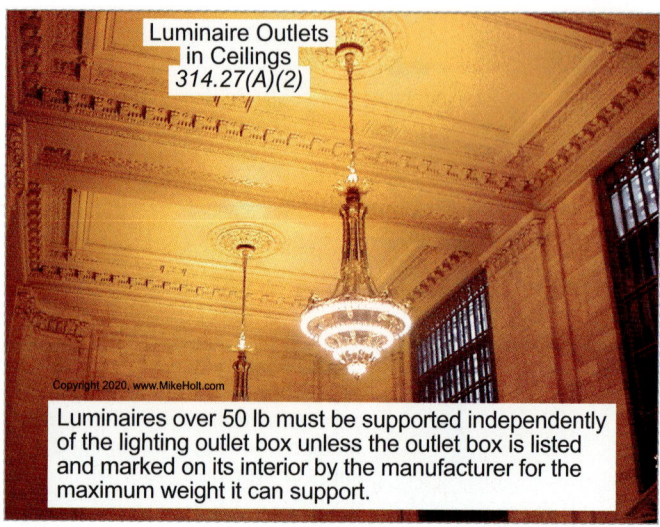
▶Figure 314–55

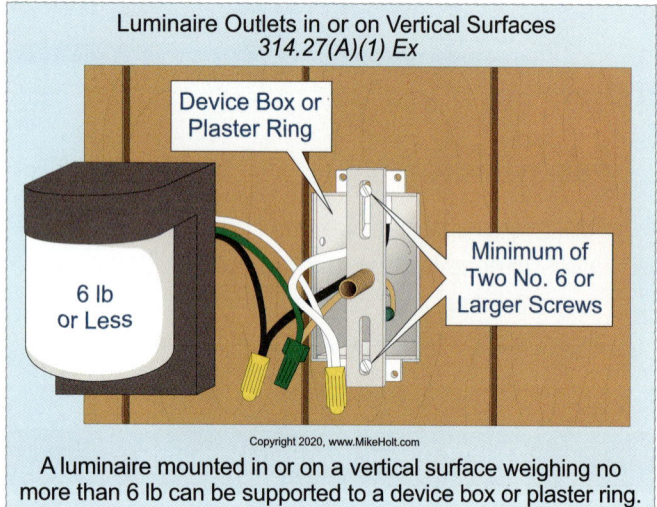
▶Figure 314–54

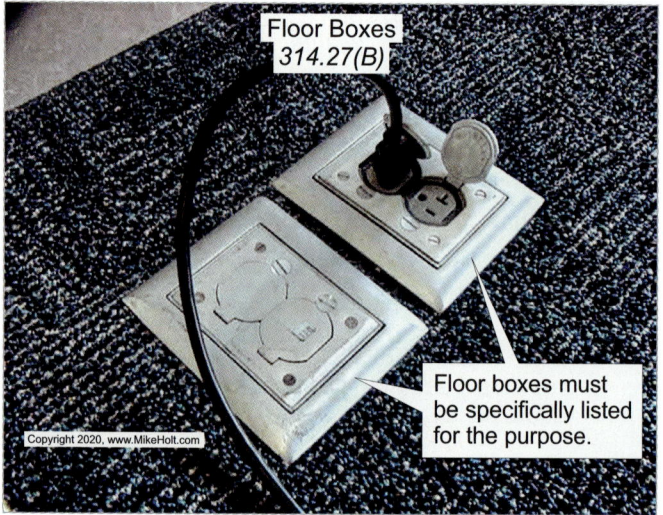
▶Figure 314–56

(2) Luminaire Outlets in a Ceiling. Boxes for ceiling luminaires must be listed and marked to support a luminaire weighing a minimum of 50 lb. Luminaires weighing more than 50 lb must be supported independently of the outlet box unless it is listed and marked on the interior of the box by the manufacturer for the maximum weight it can support. ▶Figure 314–55

(B) Floor Box. Floor boxes must be specifically listed for the purpose. ▶Figure 314–56

(C) Ceiling Paddle Fan Box. Outlet boxes for a ceiling paddle fan must be listed and marked as suitable for the purpose and are not permitted to support a fan weighing more than 70 lb. Outlet boxes for a ceiling paddle fan that weighs more than 35 lb must include the maximum weight to be supported in the required marking. ▶Figure 314–57

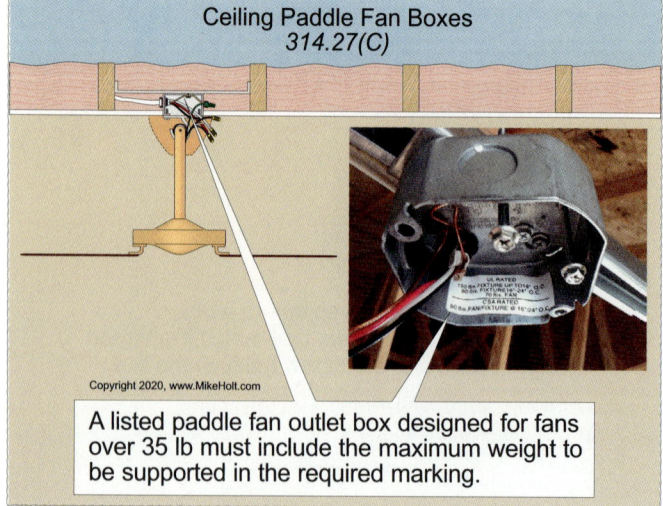
▶Figure 314–57

Ceiling-mounted outlet boxes in a habitable room of a dwelling unit where a ceiling-suspended (paddle) fan could be installed must comply with one of the following: ▶Figure 314-58

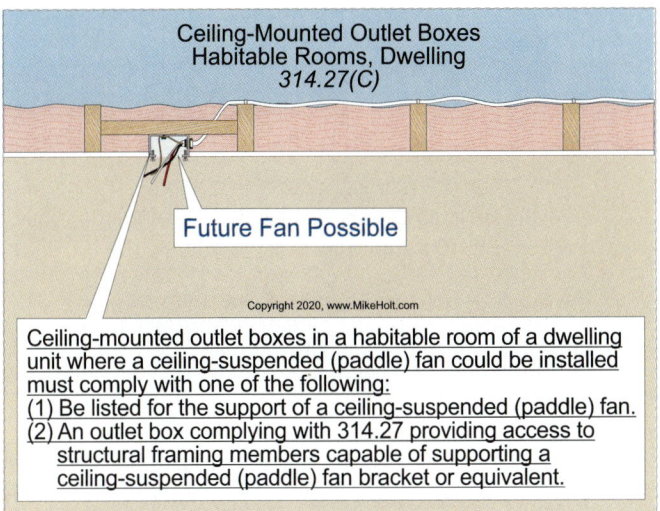
▶Figure 314-58

(1) Be listed for the support of a ceiling-suspended (paddle) fan.

(2) An outlet box complying with 314.27 providing access to structural framing members capable of supporting a ceiling-suspended (paddle) fan bracket or equivalent.

(D) Utilization Equipment. Boxes used for the support of utilization equipment must be designed to support equipment that weighs a minimum of 50 lb [314.27(A)].

Ex: Utilization equipment weighing 6 lb or less can be supported by any box or plaster ring secured to a box, provided the equipment is secured with no fewer than two No. 6 or larger screws. ▶Figure 314-59

(E) Separable Attachment Fittings. Outlet boxes required in 314.27 are permitted to support listed locking support and mounting receptacles used in combination with compatible attachment fittings. The combination must be identified for the support of equipment within the weight and mounting orientation limits of the listing. Where the supporting receptacle is installed within a box, it must be included in the fill calculation in accordance with 314.16(B)(4). ▶Figure 314-60

314.28 Sizing Pull and Junction Boxes

Boxes containing conductors 4 AWG and larger must be sized so the conductor insulation will not be damaged. ▶Figure 314-61 and ▶Figure 314-62

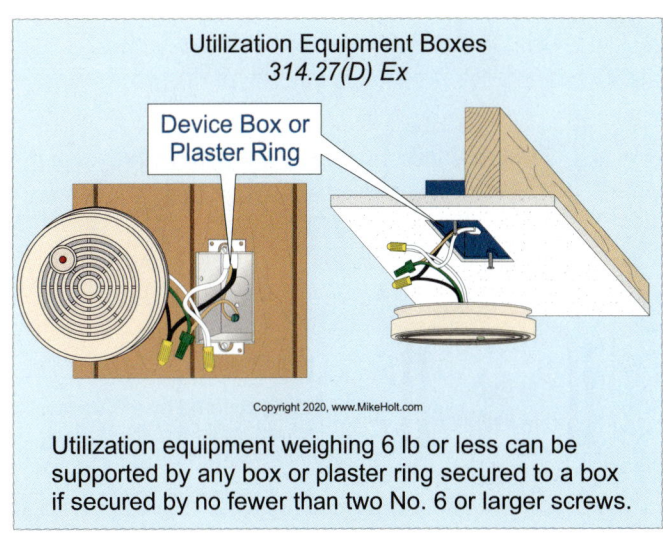
▶Figure 314-59

▶Figure 314-60

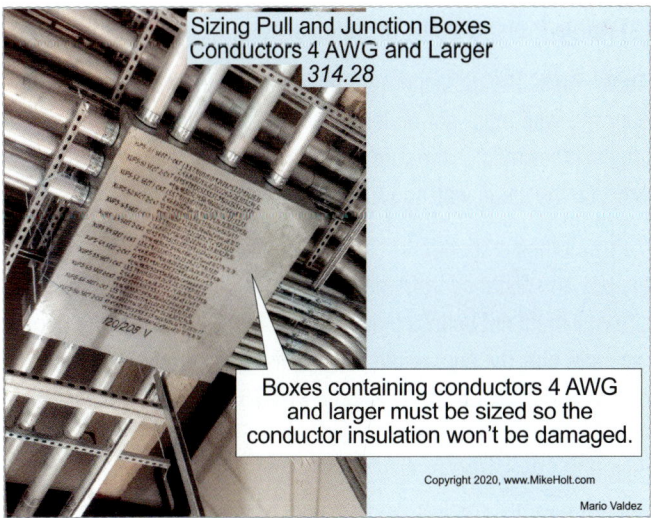
▶Figure 314-61

314.28 | Outlet, Pull, and Junction Boxes; Conduit Bodies; and Handhole Enclosures

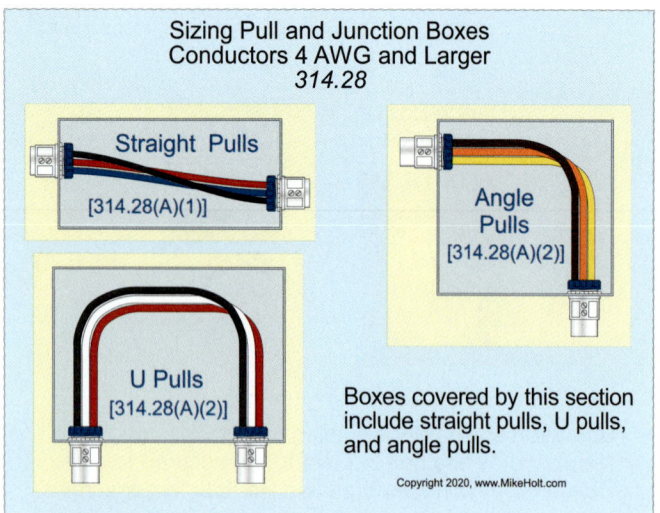
▶Figure 314-62

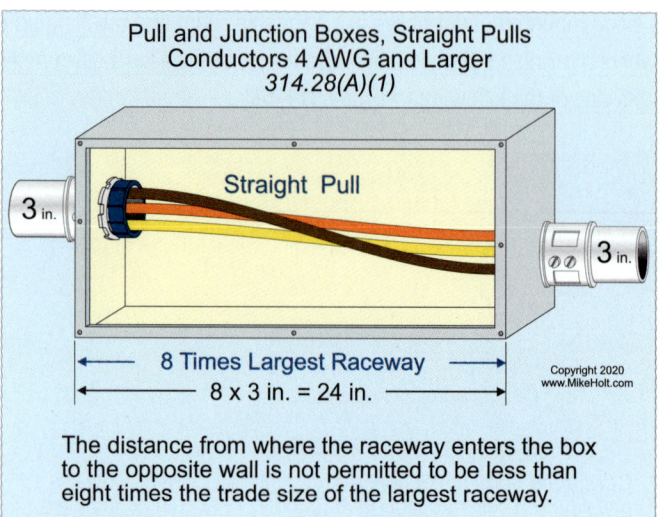
▶Figure 314-63

Author's Comment:

▸ The requirements for sizing boxes containing conductors 6 AWG and smaller are contained in 314.16.

▸ If conductors 4 AWG and larger enter a box or other enclosure, a fitting that provides a smooth, rounded, insulating surface (such as a bushing or adapter) is required to protect them from abrasion during and after installation [300.4(G)].

(A) Minimum Size. For raceways containing conductors 4 AWG and larger, the minimum dimensions of boxes must comply with the following:

(1) Straight Pulls. The distance from where the raceway enters the box to the opposite wall must not be less than eight times the trade size of the largest raceway. ▶Figure 314-63

(2) Angle Pulls, U Pulls, or Splices

Angle Pulls. The distance from the raceway entry of the box to the opposite wall must not be less than six times the trade size of the largest raceway, plus the sum of the trade sizes of the remaining raceways on the same wall and row. ▶Figure 314-64

U Pulls. When a conductor enters and leaves from the same wall of the box, the distance from the raceway entry of the box to the opposite wall must not be less than six times the trade size of the largest raceway, plus the sum of the trade sizes of the remaining raceways on the same wall and row. ▶Figure 314-65

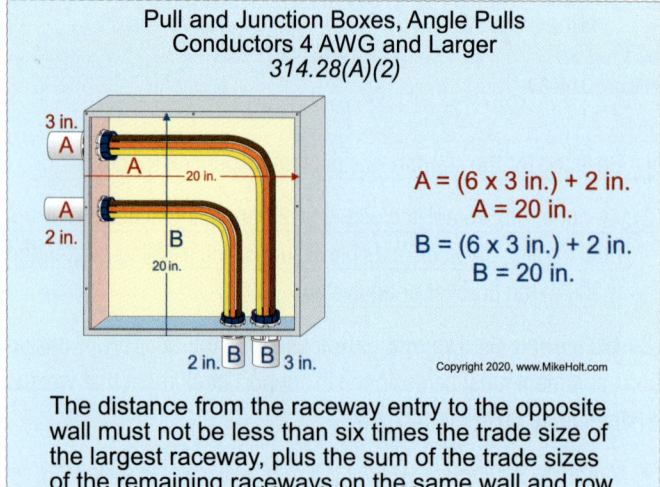
▶Figure 314-64

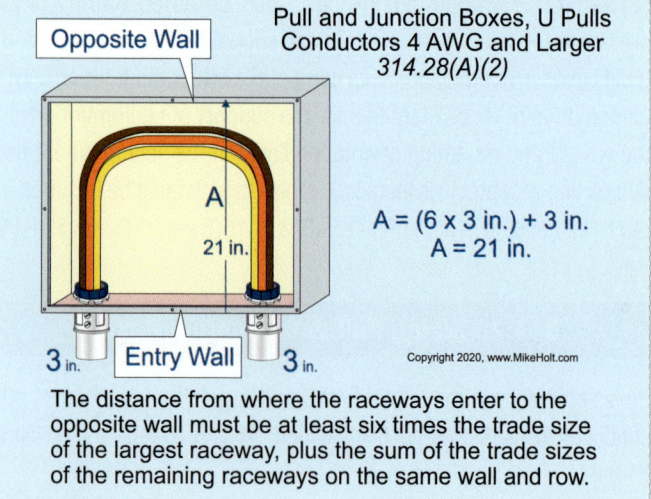
▶Figure 314-65

Splices. When conductors are spliced, the distance from the raceways' entry of the box to the opposite wall must not be less than six times the trade size of the largest raceway, plus the sum of the trade sizes of the remaining raceways on the same wall and row. ▶Figure 314–66

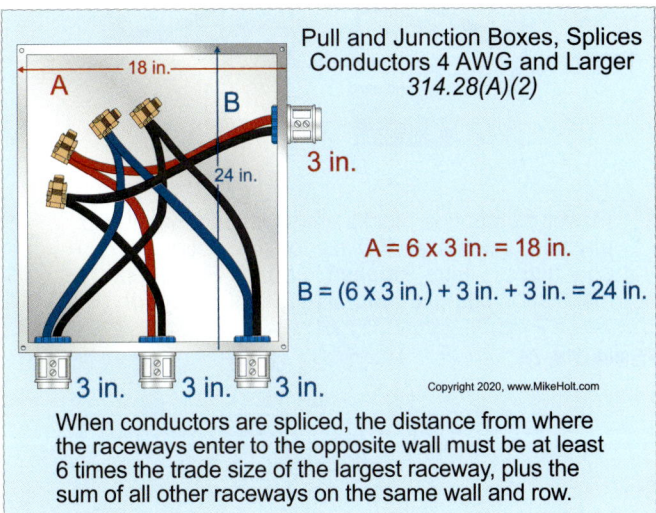

When conductors are spliced, the distance from where the raceways enter to the opposite wall must be at least 6 times the trade size of the largest raceway, plus the sum of all other raceways on the same wall and row.

▶Figure 314–66

Rows. If there are multiple rows of raceway entries, each row is calculated individually and the row with the largest distance must be used. ▶Figure 314–67

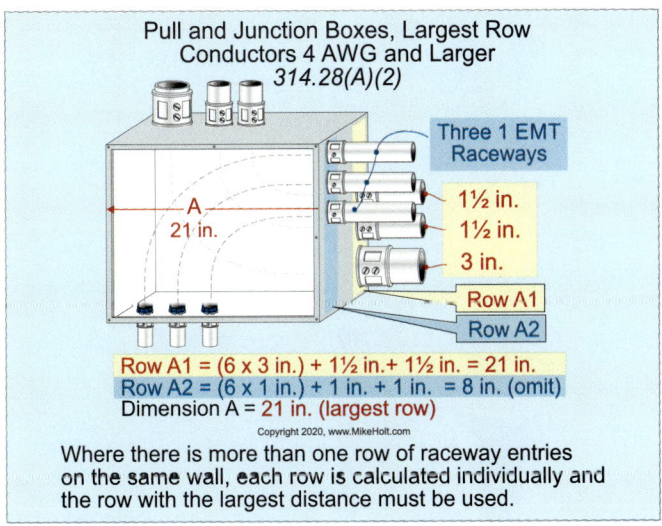

Where there is more than one row of raceway entries on the same wall, each row is calculated individually and the row with the largest distance must be used.

▶Figure 314–67

Distance Between Raceways. The distance between raceway entries enclosing the same conductor must not be less than six times the trade size of the largest raceway, measured between the raceway entry openings. ▶Figure 314–68 and ▶Figure 314–69

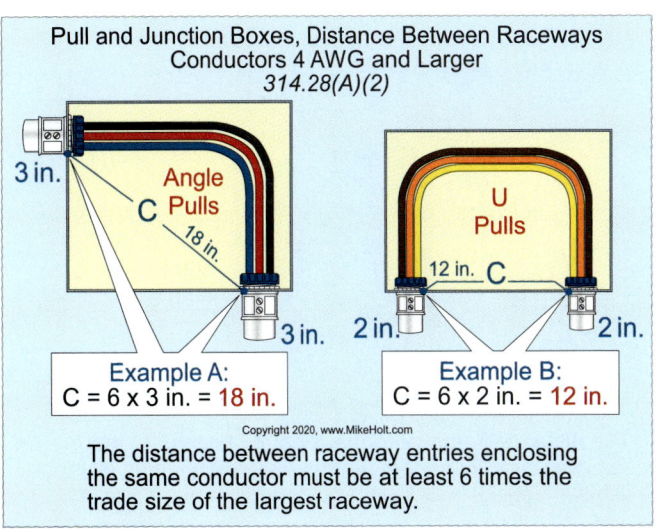

The distance between raceway entries enclosing the same conductor must be at least 6 times the trade size of the largest raceway.

▶Figure 314–68

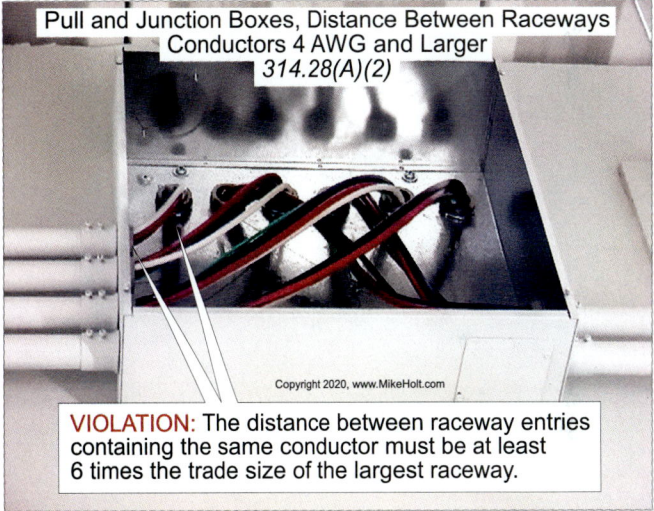

VIOLATION: The distance between raceway entries containing the same conductor must be at least 6 times the trade size of the largest raceway.

▶Figure 314–69

Ex: When conductors enter an enclosure with a removable cover, the distance from where the conductors enter to the removable cover is not permitted to be less than the bending distance as contained in Table 312.6(A) for one conductor per terminal. ▶Figure 314–70

(B) Conductors in Pull or Junction Boxes. Pull boxes or junction boxes with any dimension over 6 ft must have all conductors cabled or racked in an approved manner.

(C) Covers. Metal covers must be connected to an equipment grounding conductor of a type recognized in 250.118, in accordance with 250.110 [250.4(A)(3)]. ▶Figure 314–71

314.29 | Outlet, Pull, and Junction Boxes; Conduit Bodies; and Handhole Enclosures

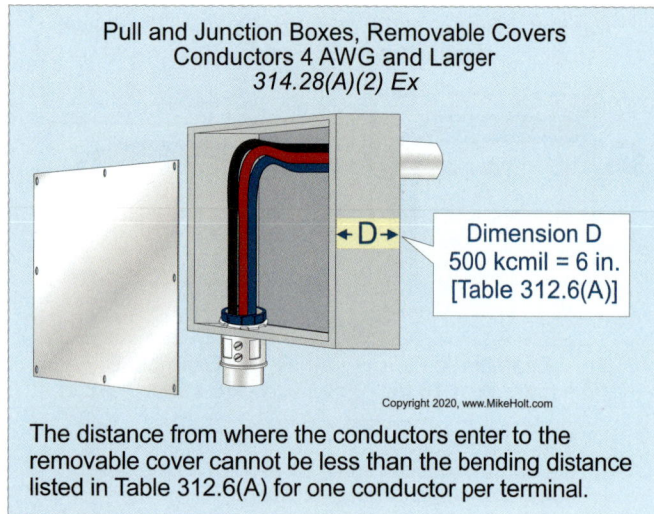

▶Figure 314-70

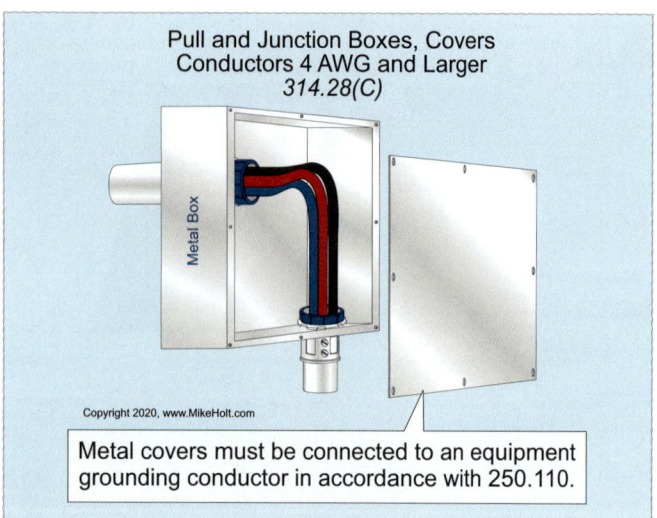

▶Figure 314-71

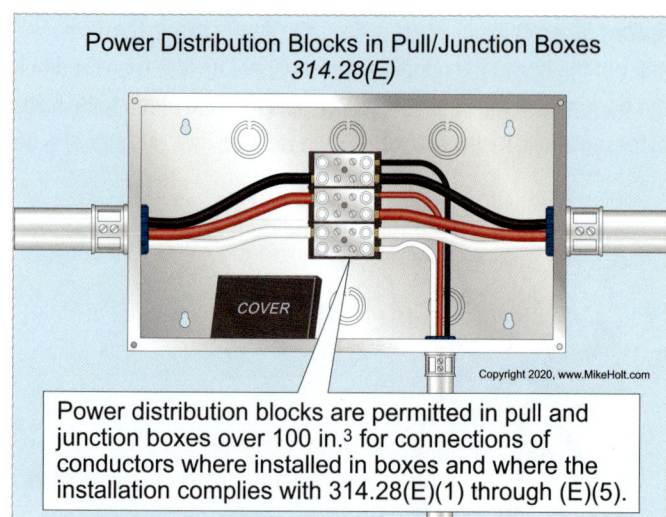

▶Figure 314-72

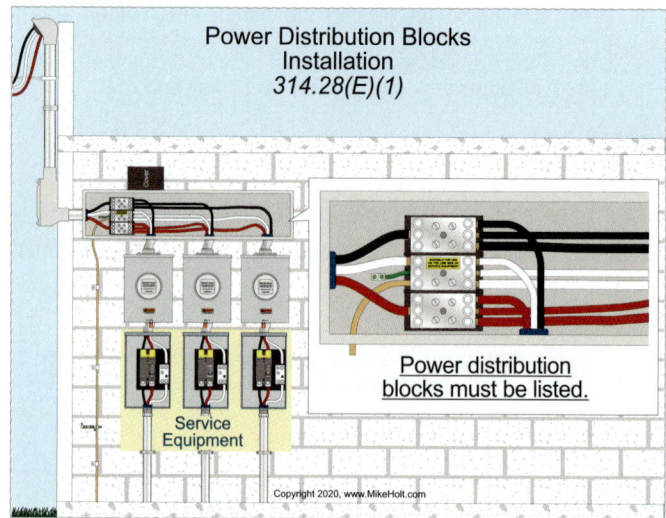

▶Figure 314-73

(E) Power Distribution Blocks. Power distribution blocks are permitted in pull and junction boxes over 100 in.³ for connections of conductors where installed in boxes and where the installation complies with 314.28(E)(1) through (E)(5). ▶Figure 314-72

Ex: Equipment grounding terminal bars are permitted in smaller enclosures.

(1) Installation. Power distribution blocks installed in boxes must be listed. ▶Figure 314-73

314.29 Wiring to be Accessible

(A) In Buildings and Other Structures. Boxes and conduit bodies must be installed so the wiring contained within is accessible without removing any part of the building or structure. ▶Figure 314-74

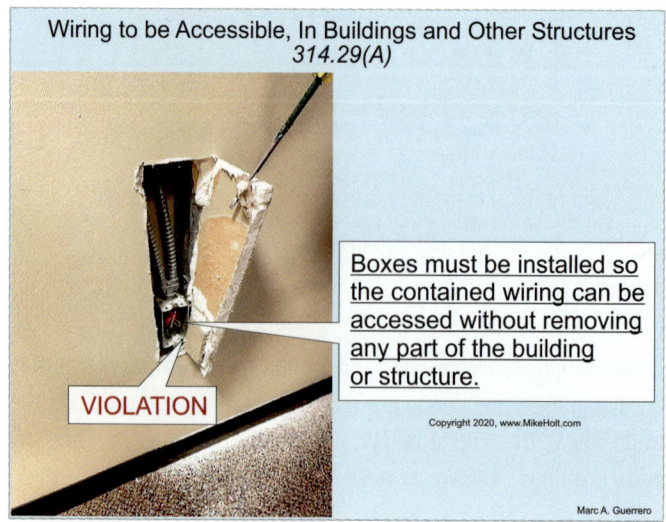

▶Figure 314-74

(B) Underground. Underground boxes, conduit bodies, and handhole enclosures must be installed so the wiring contained within is accessible without removing any part of the excavating, sidewalks, paving, earth, or other substance used to establish the finished grade.

314.30 Handhole Enclosures

Handhole enclosures must be identified for underground use and be designed and installed to withstand all loads likely to be imposed on them. ▶Figure 314–75

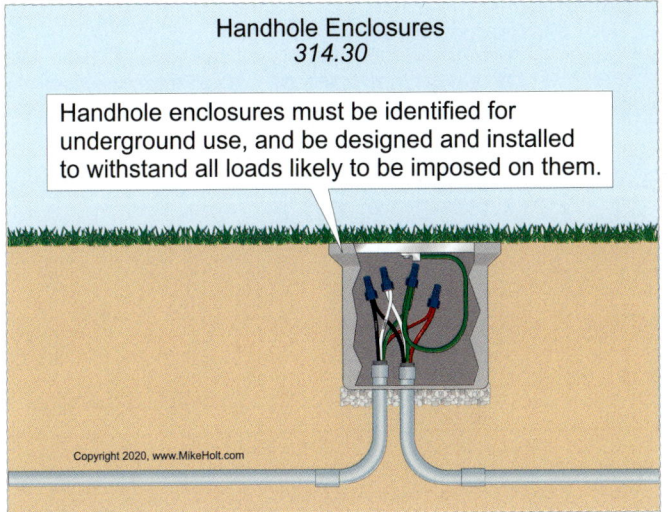

▶Figure 314–75

(B) Wiring Entries. Underground raceways and cables entering a handhole are not required to be mechanically connected to the handhole. ▶Figure 314–76

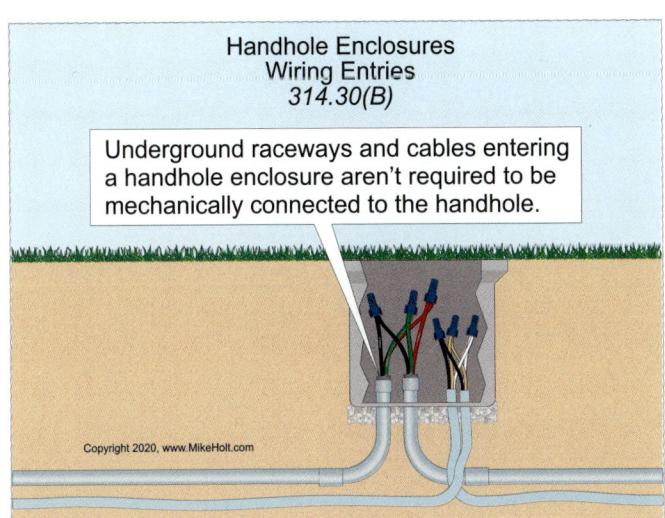

▶Figure 314–76

(C) Enclosure Wiring. Splices or terminations within a handhole must be listed for wet locations [110.14(B)].

(D) Covers. Handhole covers must have an identifying mark or logo that prominently identifies the function of the handhole, such as "electric." Handhole covers must require the use of tools to open, or they must weigh over 100 lb. ▶Figure 314–77

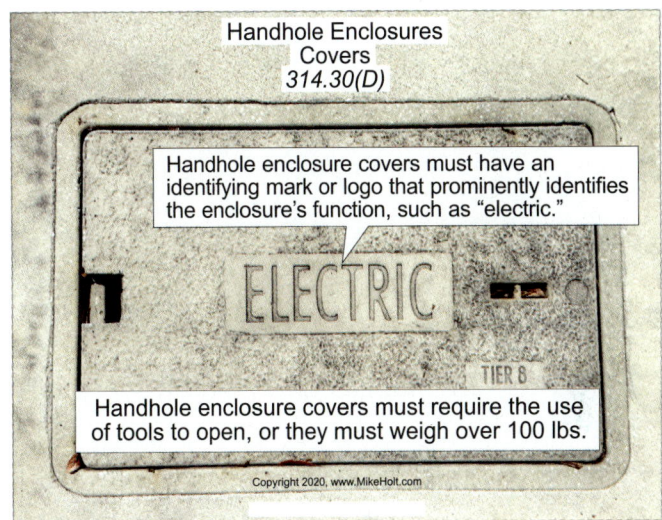

▶Figure 314–77

Metal covers and exposed conductive surfaces of handhole enclosures must be connected to an equipment grounding conductor sized in accordance with 250.122, based on the rating of the overcurrent protective device [250.102(D)]. ▶Figure 314–78

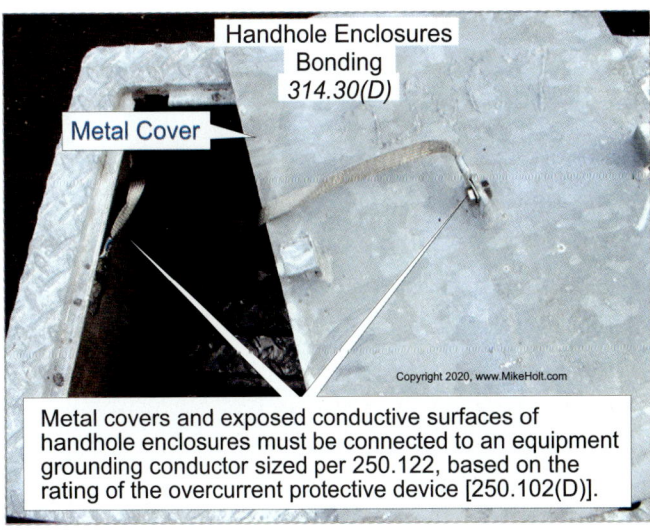

▶Figure 314–78

Notes

ARTICLE 320 — ARMORED CABLE (TYPE AC)

Introduction to Article 320—Armored Cable (Type AC)

Armored cable (Type AC) is an assembly of insulated conductors, 14 AWG through 1 AWG, individually wrapped in wax paper (jute) and contained within a flexible spiral metal sheath. To the casual observer the outside appearance of armored cable is like flexible metal conduit and metal-clad cable (Type MC). Type AC cable has been referred to as "BX®" cable over the years.

Part I. General

320.1 Scope

This article covers the use, installation, and construction specifications of armored cable, Type AC. ▶Figure 320–1

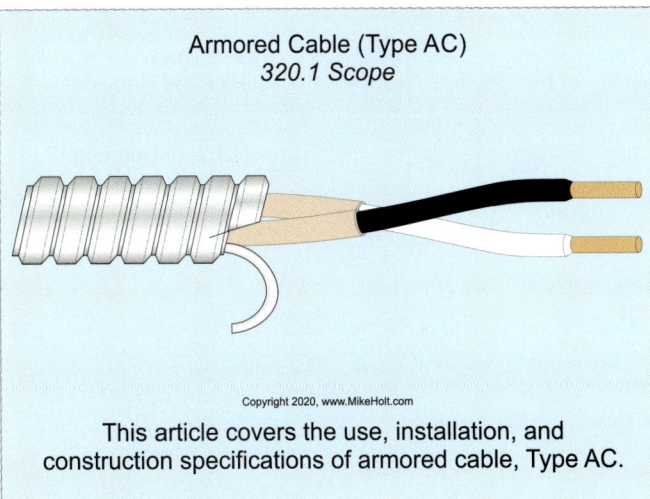

▶Figure 320–1

320.2 Definition

The definition in this section applies within this article and throughout the *Code*.

Armored Cable (Type AC). A fabricated assembly of conductors in a flexible interlocked metal armor with an internal bonding strip in intimate contact with the armor for its entire length. ▶Figure 320–2

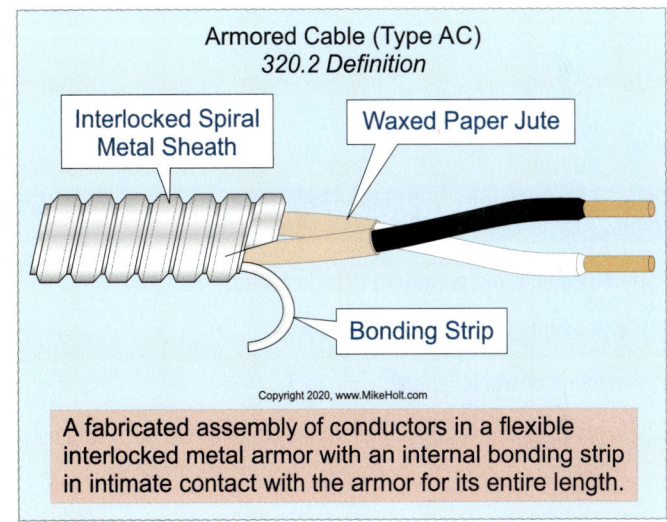

▶Figure 320–2

Author's Comment:

▶ Type AC cable conductors are contained within a flexible metal sheath that interlocks at the edges with an internal aluminum bonding strip, giving the cable an outside appearance of flexible metal conduit. The advantages of any flexible cable, as compared to raceway wiring methods, are that there is no limit to the number of bends between terminations and the cable can be quickly installed.

320.6 Listing Requirements

Type AC cable and associated fittings must be listed.

320.10 | Armored Cable (Type AC)

Part II. Installation

320.10 Uses Permitted

Type AC cable can be used or installed as follows:

(1) For feeders and branch circuits in both exposed and concealed installations.

(2) In cable trays.

(3) In dry locations.

(4) Embedded in plaster in dry locations.

(5) In air voids where not exposed to excessive moisture or dampness.

Note: The "Uses Permitted" is not an all-inclusive list, which indicates other suitable uses are permitted if approved by the authority having jurisdiction.

> **Author's Comment:**
> ▸ Type AC cable can also be installed in a plenum space in accordance with 300.22(C)(1).

320.12 Uses Not Permitted

Type AC cable is not permitted to be installed:

(1) Where subject to physical damage.

(2) In damp or wet locations.

(3) In air voids of masonry block or tile walls where such walls are exposed or subject to excessive moisture or dampness.

(4) Where exposed to corrosive conditions.

320.15 Exposed Work

Exposed Type AC cable, except as provided in 300.11(B), must closely follow the surface of the building finish or running boards. If installed on the bottom of floor or ceiling joists it must be secured at every joist and must not be subject to physical damage. ▸Figure 320-3

320.17 Through or Parallel to Framing Members

Type AC cable installed through, or parallel to, framing members or furring strips must be protected against physical damage from penetration by screws or nails by maintaining 1¼ in. of separation between the cable and the nearest edge of a framing member or furring strip, or by a suitable metal plate in accordance with 300.4(A), (C), and (D). ▸Figure 320-4 and ▸Figure 320-5

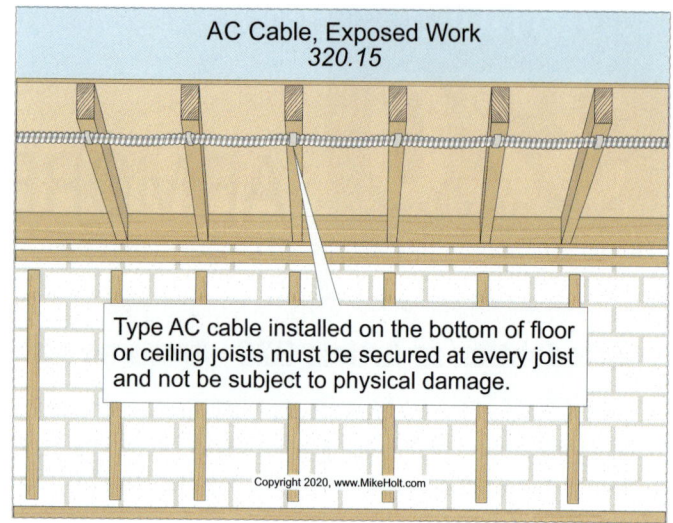
▸Figure 320-3

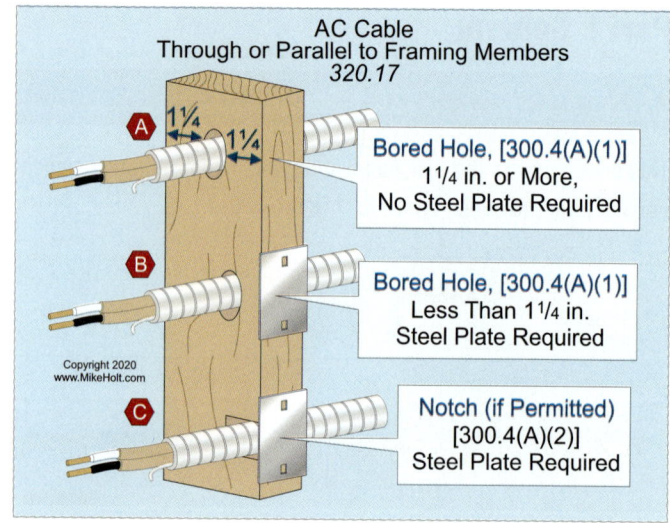
▸Figure 320-4

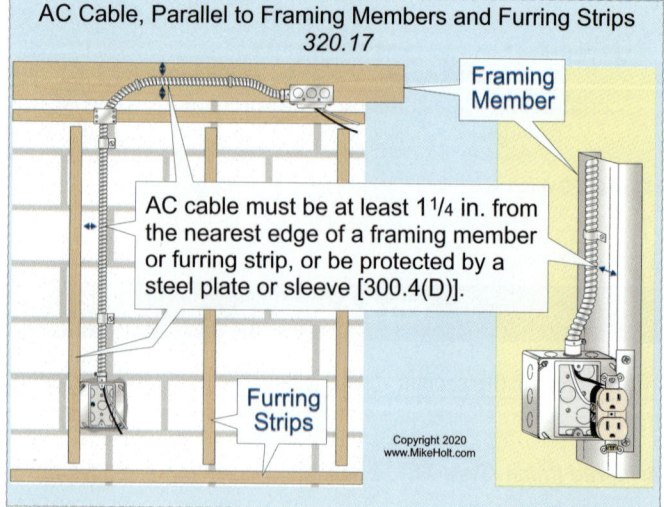
▸Figure 320-5

320.23 In Accessible Attics or Roof Spaces

(A) Cables Run Across the Top of Floor Joists. Where run across the top of floor joists, or across the face of rafters or studding within 7 ft of the floor or floor joists, Type AC cable must be protected by guard strips that are at least as high as the cable.

If this space is not accessible by permanently installed stairs or ladders, protection is required only within 6 ft of the nearest edge of the scuttle hole or attic entrance. ▶Figure 320-6

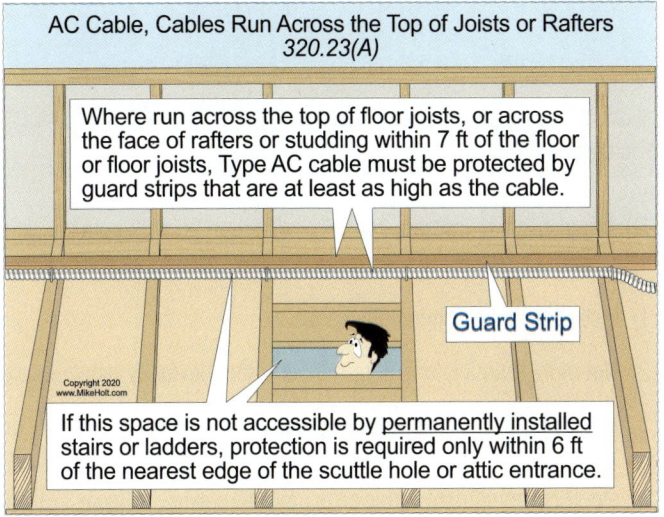

▶Figure 320-6

(B) Cable Installed Parallel to Framing Members. Where Type AC cable is installed on the side of rafters, studs, ceiling joists, or floor joists, no protection is required if the nearest outside surface of the cable is at least 1¼ in. from the nearest edge of the framing member [300.4(D)]. ▶Figure 320-7

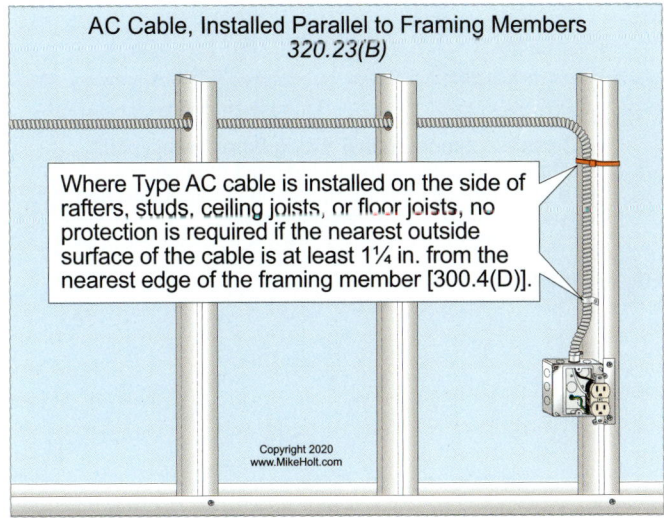

▶Figure 320-7

320.24 Bending Radius

Type AC cable is not permitted to be bent in a manner that will damage the cable. This is accomplished by limiting bending of the inner edge of the cable to a radius of not less than five times the diameter of the cable. ▶Figure 320-8

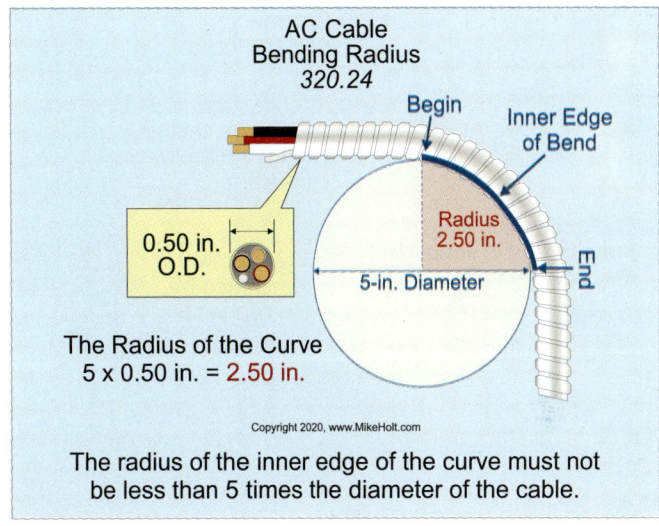

▶Figure 320-8

320.30 Securing and Supporting

(A) General. Type AC cable must be supported and secured by staples; cable ties listed and identified for securing and supporting; straps, hangers, or similar fittings; or other approved means designed and installed so the cable is not damaged. ▶Figure 320-9

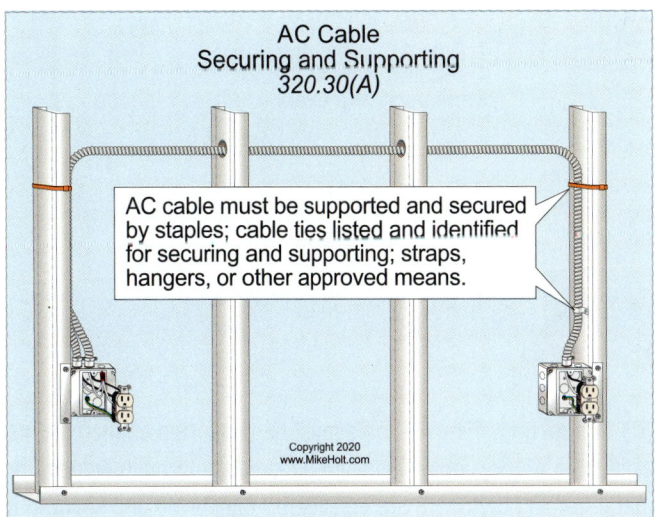

▶Figure 320-9

320.30 | Armored Cable (Type AC)

Author's Comment:

▸ Secured means "Fastened" such as with a strap or tie wrap; supported means "Held" such as with a hanger or run through a hole in a stud, joist, or rafter. ▸Figure 320-10

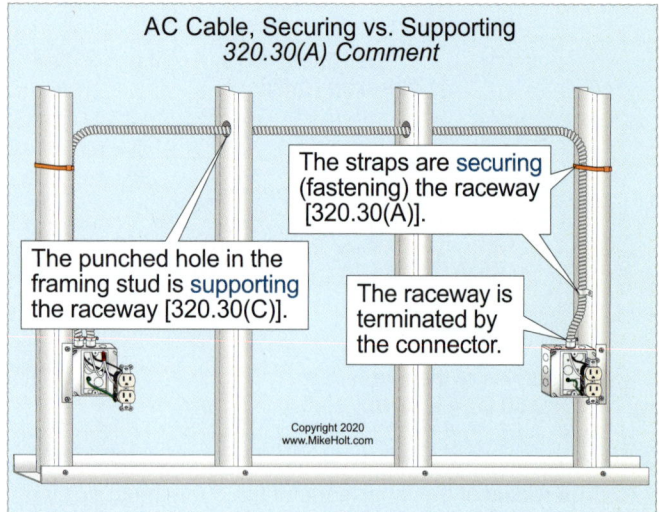

▸Figure 320-10

(B) Securing. Type AC cable must be secured within 12 in. of every outlet box, junction box, cabinet, or fitting and at intervals not exceeding 4½ ft. ▸Figure 320-11

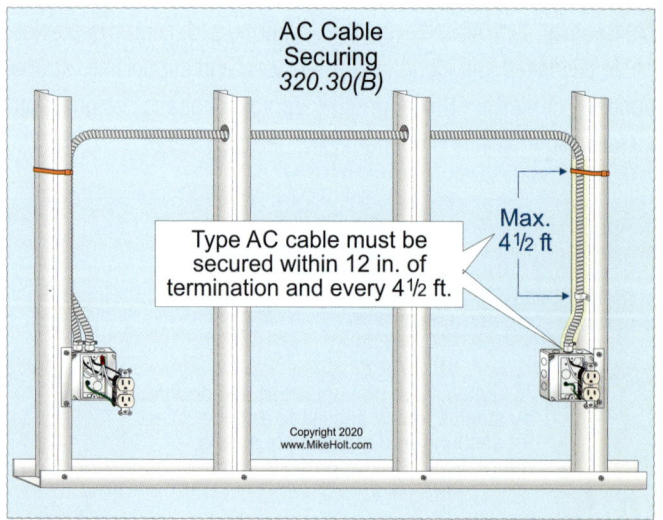

▸Figure 320-11

(C) Supporting. Type AC cable must be supported at intervals not exceeding 4½ ft. Cables installed horizontally through wooden or metal framing members are considered supported and secured if such support does not exceed 4½-ft intervals. ▸Figure 320-12

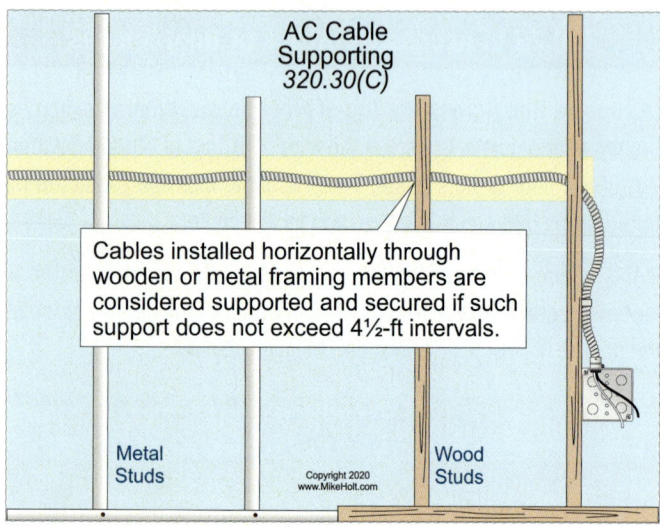

▸Figure 320-12

(D) Unsupported Cables. Type AC cable can be unsupported and unsecured where:

(1) Fished through concealed spaces

(2) Not more than 2 ft long at terminals where flexibility is necessary

(3) Not more than 6 ft long from the last point of cable support or Type AC cable fitting to the point of connection to a luminaire or electrical equipment within an accessible ceiling. ▸Figure 320-13

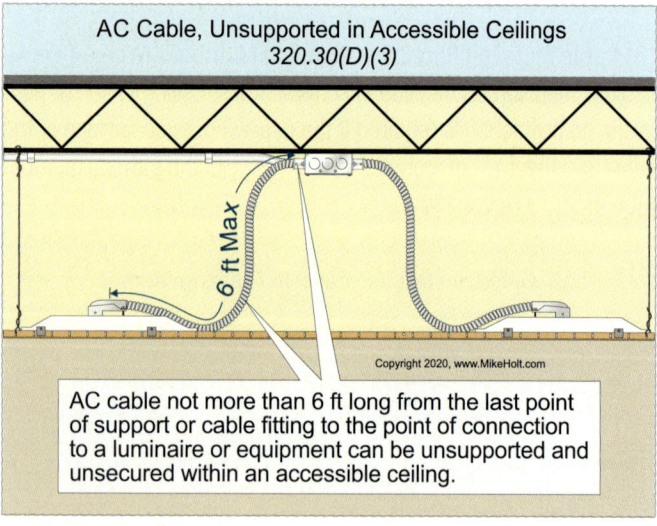

▸Figure 320-13

320.40 Boxes and Fittings

Unless the design of the termination fitting provides protection, an insulating anti-short bushing (sometimes called a "redhead") must be installed at all Type AC cable terminations. The termination fitting must permit the visual inspection of the anti-short bushing once the cable has been installed. ▶Figure 320–14

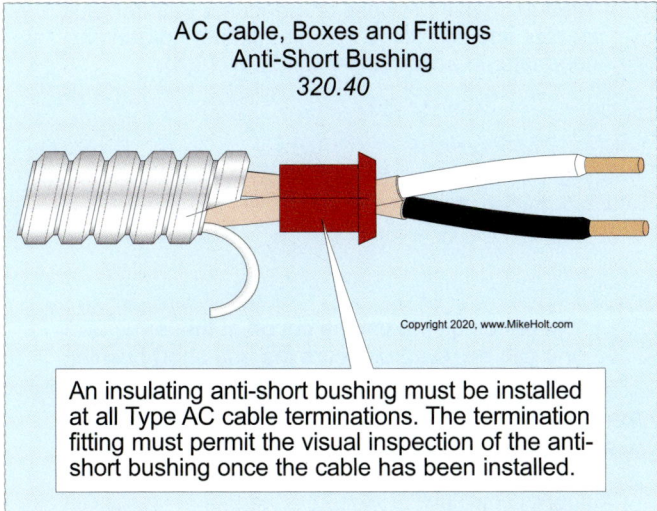

▶Figure 320–14

Author's Comment:

▶ To protect the conductors from abrasion, Type AC cable must terminate in boxes or fittings specifically listed for Type AC cable [300.15]. ▶Figure 320–15

▶ The internal aluminum bonding strip within the cable serves no electrical purpose once it is outside the cable and can be cut off, but many electricians use it to secure the anti-short bushing to the cable. See 320.108.

320.80 Conductor Ampacity

The ampacity of Type AC cable must be determined in accordance with 310.14.

(A) Thermal Insulation. Type AC cable installed in thermal insulation is permitted to have its conductor ampacity adjustment and correction based on 90°C rated conductors in accordance with 310.15(B), but the conductor selected must be based on the 60°C column of Table 310.16. ▶Figure 320–16

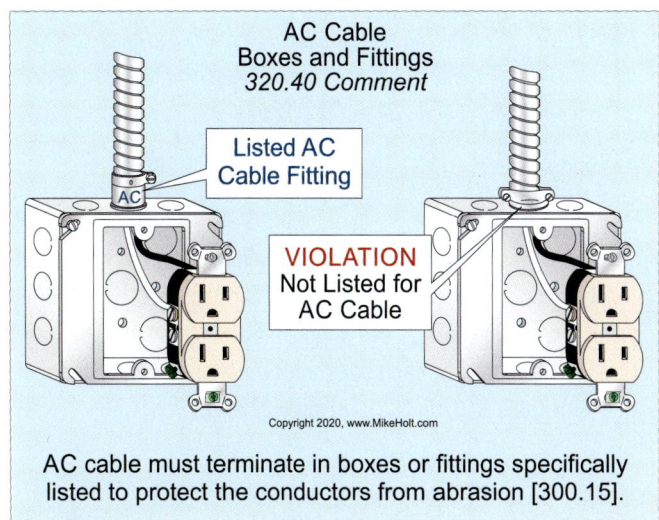

▶Figure 320–15

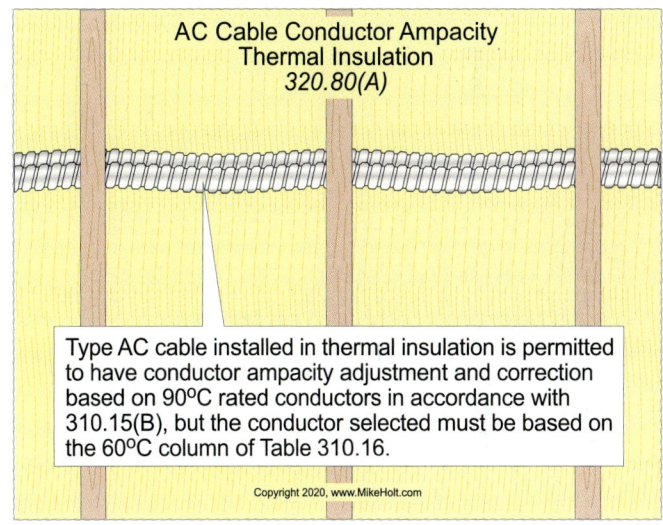

▶Figure 320–16

▶ Example

Question: Is Type AC cable containing four 12 AWG current-carrying conductors suitable to be protected by a 20A circuit breaker?

(a) Yes   (b) No

Solution:

Step 1: Determine the ampacity of the circuit conductors in accordance with 310.16 and Table 310.15(C)(1). 12 AWG is rated 30A at 90°C [Table 310.16]

Conductor Adjustment = 80% [Table 310.15(C)(1)]
Conductor Adjusted Ampacity = 30A × 80%
Conductor Adjusted Ampacity = 24A

•••

320.100 | Armored Cable (Type AC)

Step 2: Verify that the adjusted conductor ampacity can be protected by the 20A circuit breaker. In this case, 12 AWG is rated 24A after adjustment at 90°C and 20A at 60°C [240.4(D)].

Answer: (a) Yes

Where more than two Type AC cables containing two or more current-carrying conductors in each cable are installed in contact with thermal insulation, caulk, or sealing foam without maintaining spacing between cables, the ampacity of each conductor must be adjusted in accordance with Table 310.15(C)(1). ▶Figure 320–17

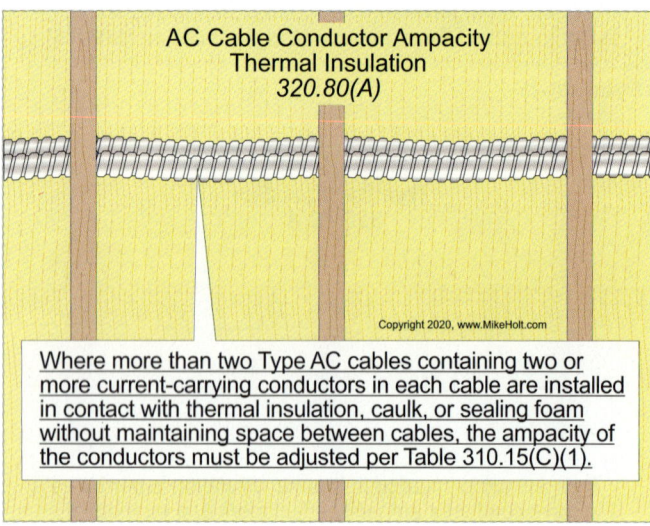

▶Figure 320–17

Part III. Construction Specifications

320.100 Construction

Type AC cable must have an armor of flexible metal tape with an internal aluminum bonding strip in intimate contact with the armor for its entire length.

Author's Comment:

▸ The best method of cutting Type AC cable is to use a tool specifically designed for the purpose, such as a rotary armor cutter.

▸ When cutting Type AC cable with a hacksaw, be sure to cut only one spiral of the cable and be careful not to nick the conductors; this is done by cutting the cable at an angle. Breaking the cable spiral (bending the cable very sharply), then cutting the cable with a pair of dikes is not a good practice.

320.108 Equipment Grounding Conductor

Type AC cable provides an adequate path for fault current and can serve as an equipment grounding conductor [250.118(8)]. ▶Figure 320–18

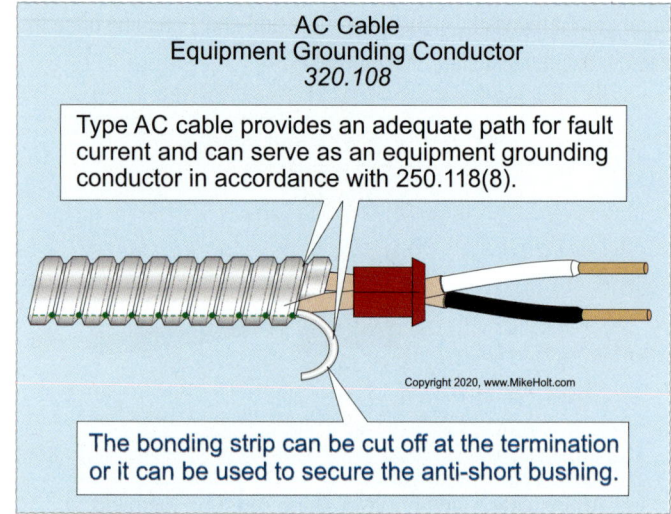

▶Figure 320–18

Author's Comment:

▸ The internal aluminum bonding strip is not an equipment grounding conductor, but it allows the interlocked armor to serve as one because it reduces the impedance of the armored spirals to ensure a ground fault will be cleared. It is the combination of the aluminum bonding strip and the cable armor that creates the equipment grounding conductor. Once the bonding strip exits the cable, it can be cut off because it no longer serves any purpose. The effective ground-fault current path must be maintained by using fittings specifically listed for Type AC cable [320.40]. See 300.12, 300.15, and 300.10.

ARTICLE 330 METAL-CLAD CABLE (TYPE MC)

Introduction to Article 330—Metal-Clad Cable (Type MC)

Metal-clad cable (Type MC) is probably the most often used metal-protected wiring method. Type MC cable encloses insulated conductors in a metal sheath of either corrugated or smooth copper or aluminum tubing, or in spiral interlocked steel or aluminum. The physical characteristics of Type MC cable make it a versatile wiring method that can be used in almost any location, and for almost any application. The most commonly used Type MC cable is the interlocking kind, which looks like armored cable or flexible metal conduit. Traditional interlocked Type MC cable is not permitted to serve as an equipment grounding conductor; therefore, this cable must contain an equipment grounding conductor in accordance with 250.118(1). Another type of Type MC cable is called interlocked Type MC$^{AP®}$ cable. It contains a bare aluminum grounding/bonding conductor running just below the metal armor, which allows the sheath to serve as an equipment grounding conductor [250.118(10)(b)].

Part I. General

330.1 Scope

Article 330 covers the use, installation, and construction specifications of metal-clad cable, Type MC. ▶Figure 330-1

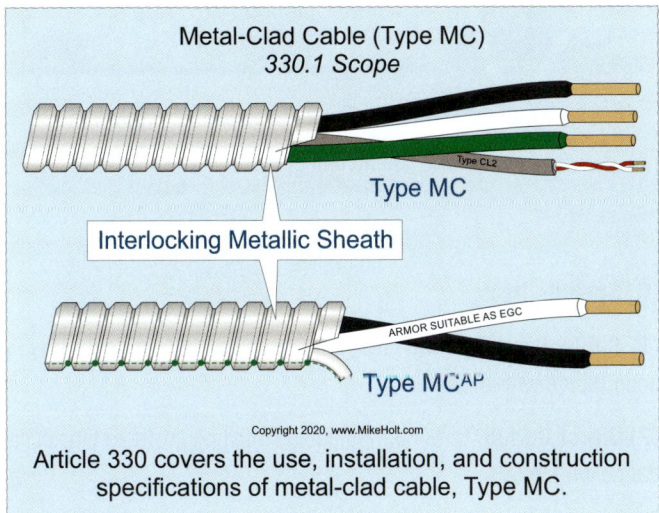

▶Figure 330-1

330.2 Definition

The definition in this section applies within this article and throughout the *NEC*.

Metal-Clad Cable (Type MC). A factory assembly of insulated circuit conductors, with or without optical fiber members, enclosed in an armor of interlocking metal tape; or a smooth or corrugated metallic sheath. ▶Figure 330-2

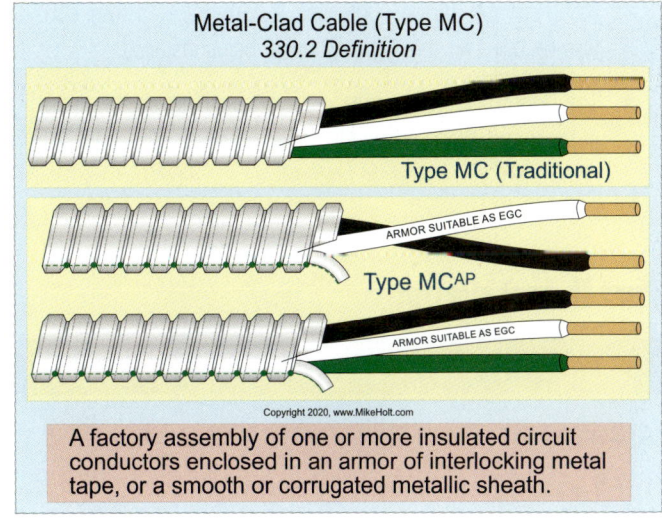

▶Figure 330-2

330.6 | Metal-Clad Cable (Type MC)

330.6 Listing Requirements

Type MC cable must be listed, and its fittings must be listed and identified for the use. ▶Figure 330–3

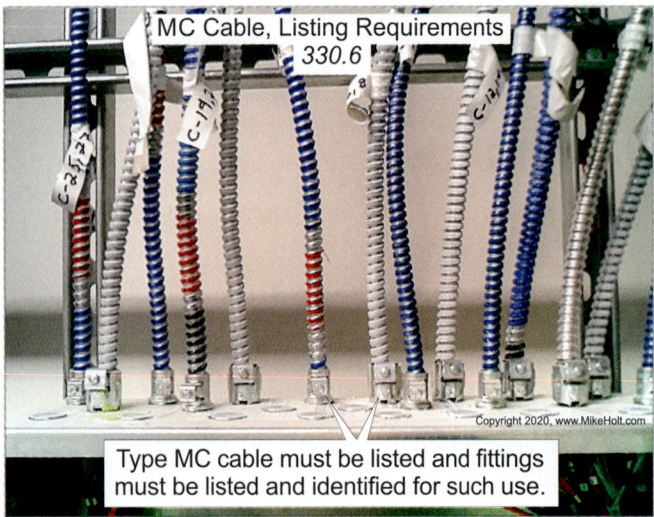

▶Figure 330–3

Author's Comment:

▸ Type MC cable is made with several types of metal sheaths. Steel and aluminum are the most common, but it is also available with a corrugated copper sheath or with a PVC outer jacket for use in environments requiring such protection. Fittings must be listed and identified for the specific type of MC cable being installed [300.15].

▸ Type AC cable connectors can sometimes be used if the fitting (or the carton containing them) indicates they can also be used for the Type MC cable being installed.

▸ The *Code* does not require anti-short bushings (red heads) at the termination of Type MC cable, but if they are supplied, using them is a matter of preference.

Part II. Installation

330.10 Uses Permitted

(A) General Uses. Type MC cable can be used:

(1) For branch circuits, feeders, and services.

(2) For power, lighting, control, and signaling circuits.

(3) For indoor or outdoor locations.

(4) Exposed or concealed.

(5) To be directly buried (if identified for the purpose).

(6) In a cable tray (if identified for the purpose).

(7) In a raceway.

(8) As aerial cable on a messenger.

(9) In hazardous (classified) locations as permitted in 501.10(B), 502.10(B), and 503.10.

(10) Embedded in plaster in dry locations.

(11) In wet locations, where a corrosion-resistant jacket is provided over the metallic sheath and any of the following conditions are met:

    a. The metallic covering is impervious to moisture.

    b. A jacket is provided under the metal covering that is moisture resistant. ▶Figure 330–4

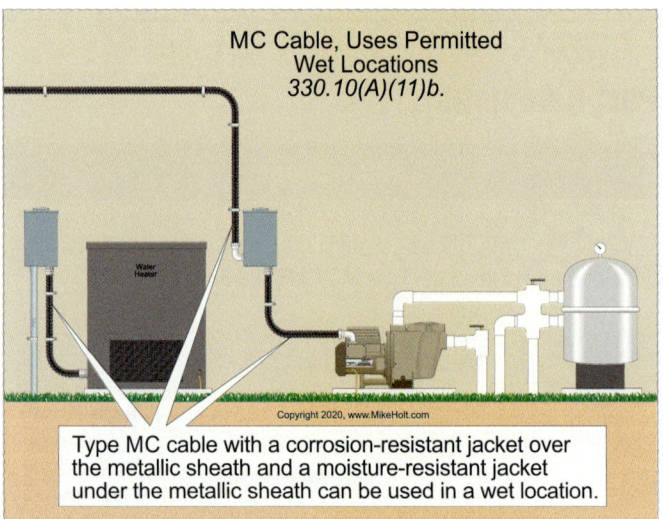

▶Figure 330–4

(B) Specific Uses.

(1) Cable Tray. Type MC cable can be installed in a cable tray in accordance with Article 392.

(2) Direct Buried. Direct-buried cables must be protected in accordance with 300.5.

(3) Installed as Service-Entrance Cable. Type MC cable is permitted to be used as service-entrance cable when installed in accordance with 230.43.

(4) Installed Outside Buildings. Type MC cable installed outside buildings must comply with 225.10, 396.10, and 396.12.

Note: The "Uses Permitted" is not an all-inclusive list, which indicates other suitable uses are permitted if approved by the authority having jurisdiction.

330.12 Uses Not Permitted

Type MC cable is not permitted to be used where:

(1) Subject to physical damage.

(2) Exposed to the destructive corrosive conditions in (a) or (b), unless the metallic sheath or armor is resistant to the conditions or protected by material resistant to the conditions:

   a. Direct burial in the earth or embedded in concrete unless identified for the application.

   b. Exposed to cinder fills, strong chlorides, caustic alkalis, or vapors of chlorine or hydrochloric acids.

330.15 Exposed Work

Exposed runs of Type MC cable, except as provided in 300.11(B), must closely follow the surface of the building finish or running boards. Type MC cable installed on the bottom of floor or ceiling joists must be secured at every joist and not be subject to physical damage. ▶Figure 330-5

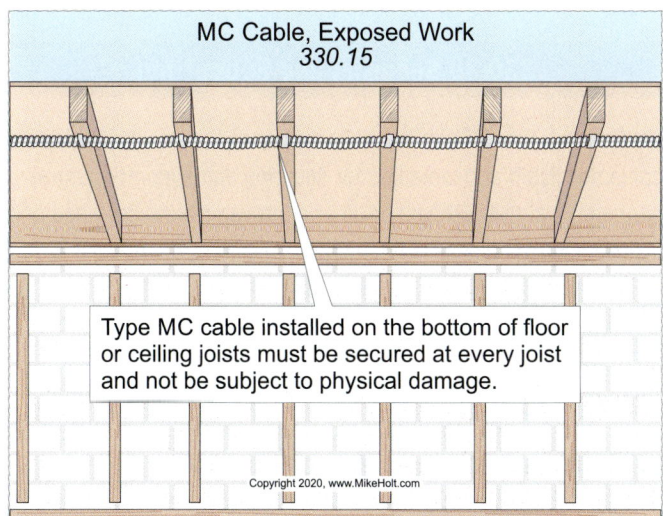
▶Figure 330-5

330.17 Through or Parallel to Framing Members

Type MC cable installed through or parallel to framing members or furring strips must be protected against physical damage from the penetration of screws or nails by maintaining a 1¼ in. separation from the nearest edge of a framing member or furring strip, or by installing a suitable metal plate in accordance with 300.4(A), (C), and (D) ▶Figure 330-6 and ▶Figure 330-7

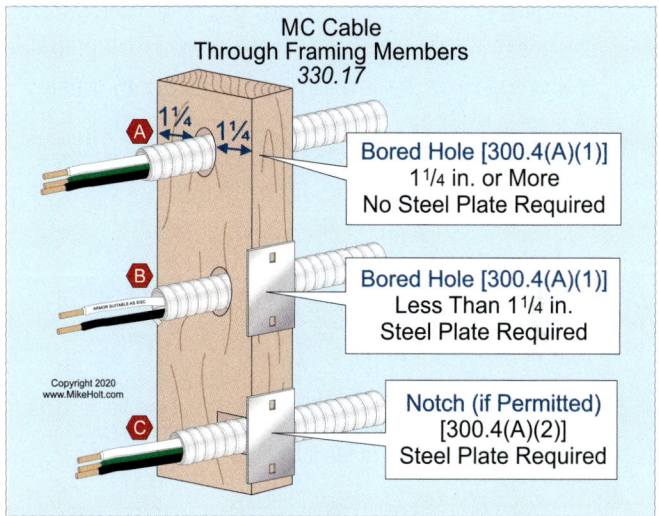
▶Figure 330-6

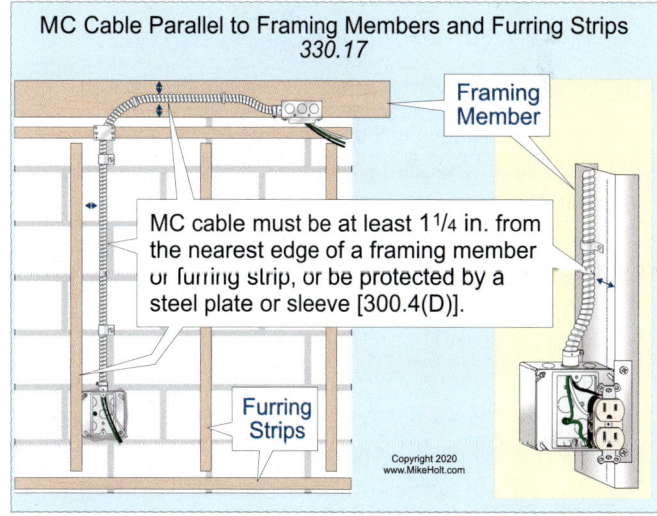
▶Figure 330-7

330.23 In Accessible Attics or Roof Spaces

Type MC cable installed in accessible attics or roof spaces must comply with 320.23.

> **Author's Comment:**
>
> ▸ On the Surface of Floor Joists, Rafters, or Studs. In attics and roof spaces that are accessible, substantial guards must protect cables installed across the top of floor joists, or across the face of rafters or studding within 7 ft of the floor or floor joists. If this space is not accessible by permanent stairs or ladders, protection is required only within 6 ft of the nearest edge of the scuttle hole or attic entrance [320.23(A)]. ▸Figure 330–8

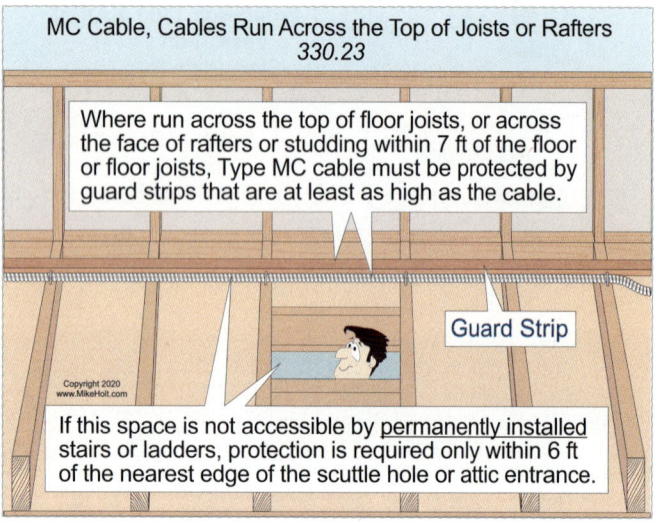

▸Figure 330–8

> **Author's Comment:**
>
> ▸ Along the Side of Framing Members [320.23(B)]. When Type MC cable is installed on the side of rafters, studs, or floor joists, no protection is required if the cable is installed at least 1¼ in. from the nearest edge of the framing member where nails or screws are likely to penetrate [300.4(D)].

330.24 Bending Radius

Bends must be made so the cable will not be damaged, and the radius of the curve of any bend at the inner edge of the cable must not be less than that dictated in each of the following instances:

(A) Smooth-Sheath Cables

(1) Smooth-sheath Type MC cables are not permitted to be bent so the bending radius of the inner edge of the cable is less than 10 times the external diameter of the metallic sheath for cable up to ¾ in. in external diameter.

(B) Interlocked- or Corrugated-Sheath Armor. Interlocked- or corrugated-sheath Type MC cable is not permitted to be bent so the bending radius of the inner edge of the cable is less than seven times the external diameter of the cable. ▸Figure 330–9

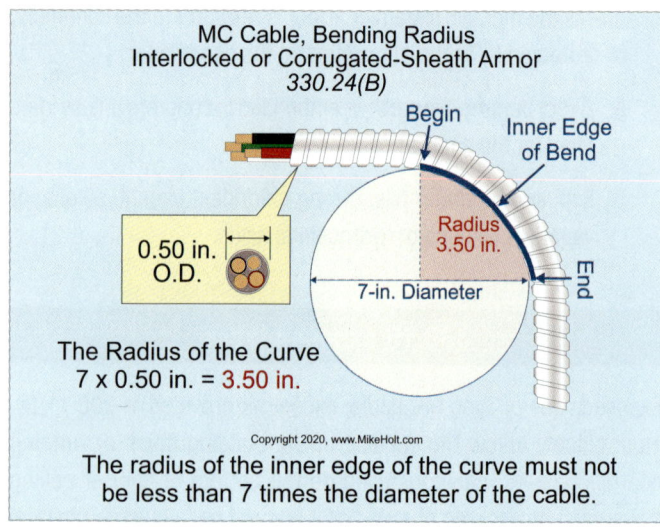

▸Figure 330–9

330.30 Securing and Supporting

(A) General. Type MC cable must be supported and secured by staples; cable ties listed and identified for securing and supporting; straps, hangers, or similar fittings; or other approved means designed and installed so the cable is not damaged. ▸Figure 330–10

> **Author's Comment:**
>
> ▸ Secured means "Fastened" such as with a strap or tie wrap; supported means "Held" such as with a hanger or run through a hole in a stud, joist, or rafter. ▸Figure 330–11

(B) Securing. Type MC cable with four or fewer conductors sized no larger than 10 AWG must be secured within 12 in. of every outlet box, junction box, cabinet, or fitting and at intervals not exceeding 6 ft. ▸Figure 330–12

Metal-Clad Cable (Type MC) | 330.30

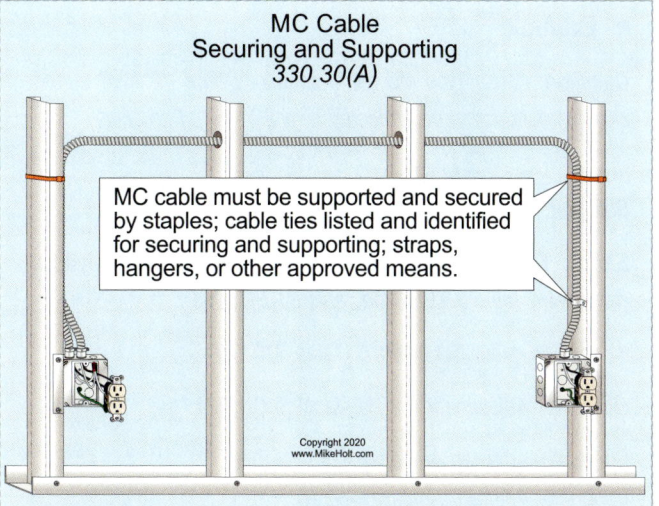
▶Figure 330-10

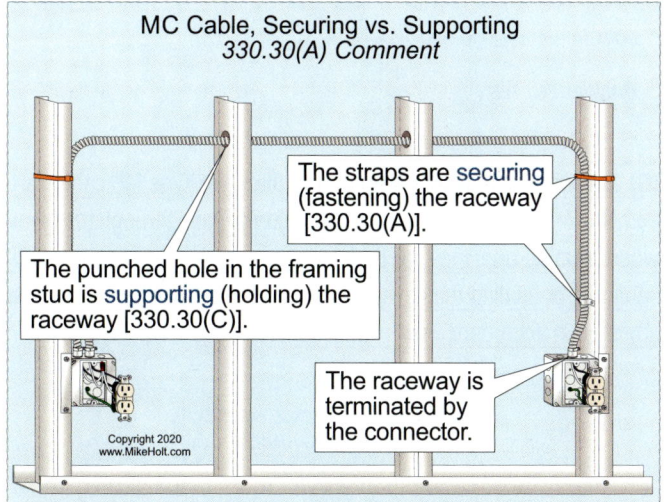
▶Figure 330-11

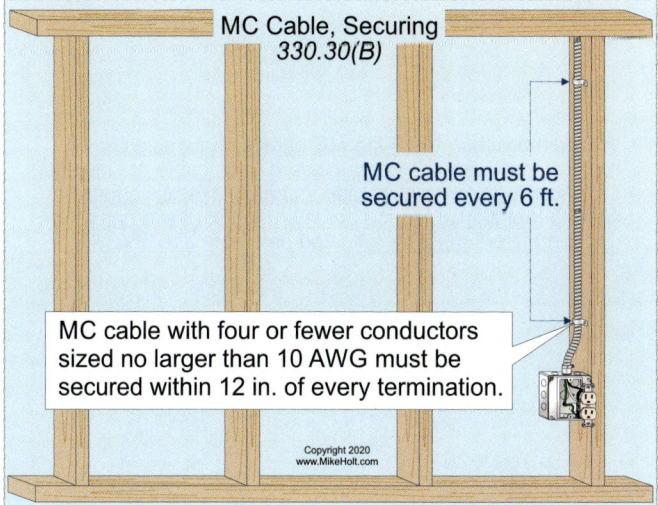
▶Figure 330-12

(C) Supporting. Type MC cable must be supported at intervals not exceeding 6 ft. Cables installed horizontally through wooden or metal framing members are considered secured and supported if such support does not exceed 6-ft intervals. ▶Figure 330-13

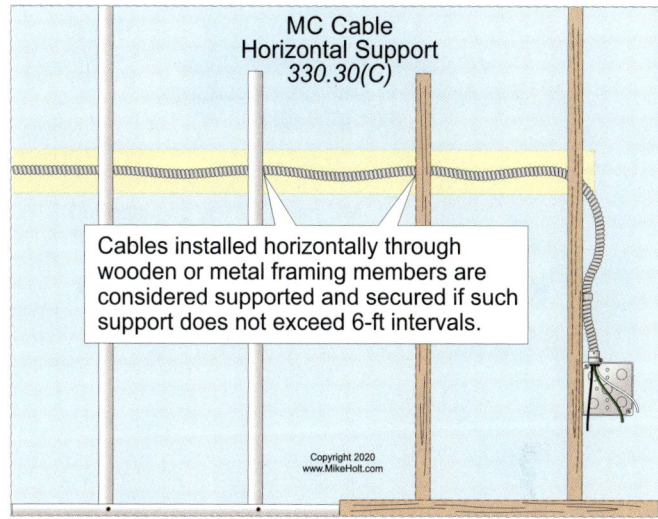
▶Figure 330-13

(D) Unsupported Cables. Type MC cable can be unsupported and unsecured where:

(1) Fished through concealed spaces in a finished building and support is impractical.

(2) Not more than 6 ft long from the last point of cable support to the point of connection to a luminaire or electrical equipment within an accessible ceiling. For the purposes of this section, Type MC cable fittings are permitted as a means of cable support. ▶Figure 330-14

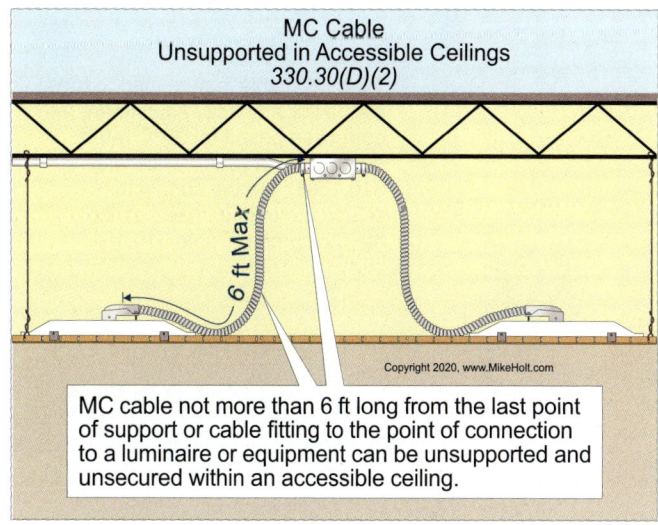
▶Figure 330-14

330.80 | Metal-Clad Cable (Type MC)

(3) Not more than 3 ft from the last point where it is securely fastened to provide flexibility for equipment that requires movement after installation, or to connect equipment where flexibility is necessary to minimize the transmission of vibration from the equipment. ▶Figure 330–15

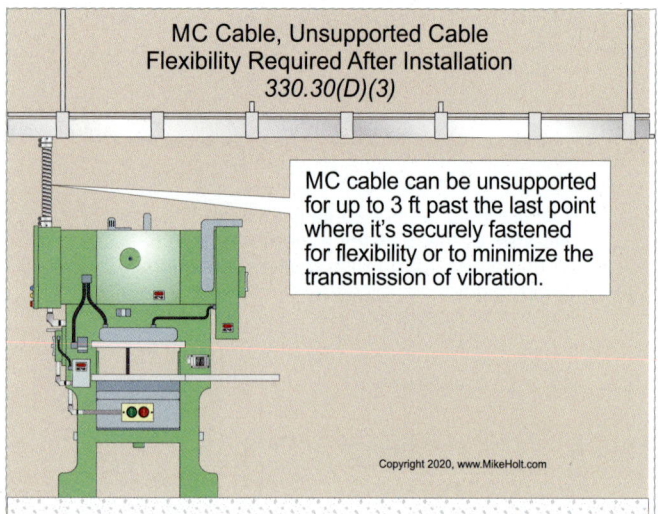

▶Figure 330–15

▶ Example

Question: Can a Type MC cable containing four 12 AWG current-carrying conductors be protected by a 20A circuit breaker?

(a) Yes   (b) No

Solution:

Step 1: Determine the ampacity of the circuit conductors in accordance with Table 310.16 and Table 310.15(C)(1).

12 AWG is rated 30A at 90°C [Table 310.16]

Conductor Adjustment = 80% [Table 310.15(C)(1)]

Conductor Adjusted Ampacity = 30A × 80%
Conductor Adjusted Ampacity = 24A

Step 2: Verify that the adjusted conductor ampacity can be protected by the 20A circuit breaker. In this case, 12 AWG is rated 24A after adjustment at 90°C and 20A at 60°C [240.4(D)].

Answer: (a) Yes

(C) Thermal Insulation. Where more than two Type MC cables are installed in contact with thermal insulation or pass through the same wood framing opening that is to be sealed with thermal insulation, caulking, or sealing foam, the ampacity of each conductor must be adjusted in accordance with Table 310.15(C)(1). ▶Figure 330–17

330.80 Conductor Ampacities

Type MC cable is permitted to have its conductor ampacity adjustment and correction based on 90°C rated conductors in accordance with 310.15, but the conductor selected must be based on the 60°C column of Table 310.16. ▶Figure 330–16

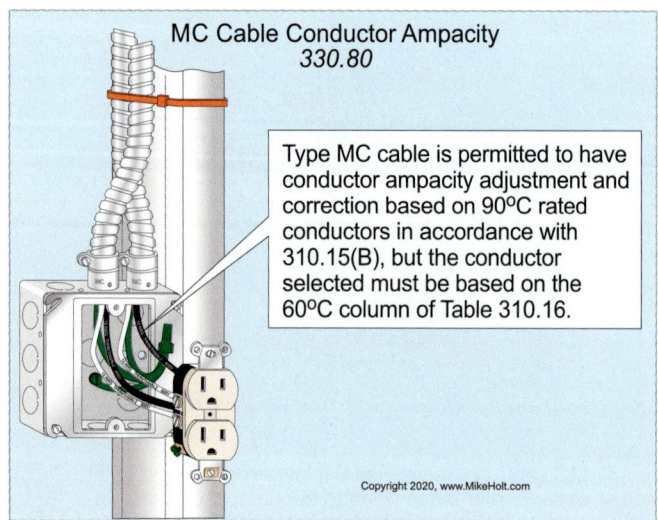

▶Figure 330–16

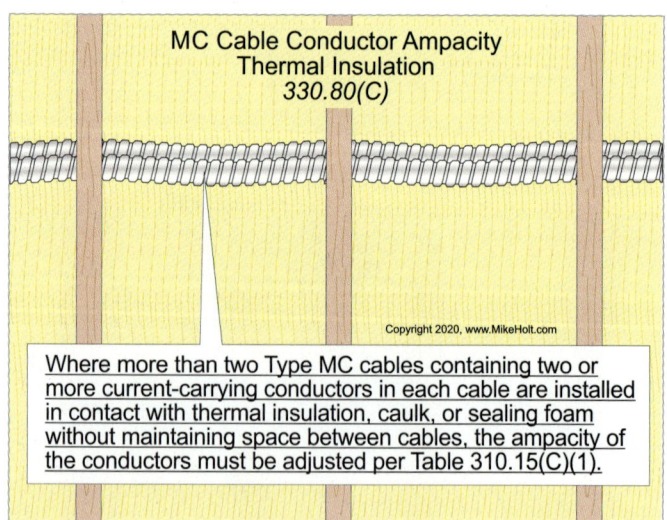

▶Figure 330–17

Part III. Construction Specifications

330.108 Equipment Grounding Conductor

If Type MC cable is to serve as an equipment grounding conductor, it must comply with 250.118(10)(a) and 250.122.

Author's Comment:

- The outer sheath of:
  - Traditional interlocked Type MC cable is not permitted to serve as an equipment grounding conductor; therefore, this cable must contain an equipment grounding conductor in accordance with 250.118(10)(a) [250.118(1)]. ▶Figure 330-18
  - Interlocked Type MC^AP cable combines the metallic sheath with an uninsulated aluminum grounding/bonding conductor and is listed and identified as an equipment grounding conductor [250.118(10)(b)]. ▶Figure 330-19

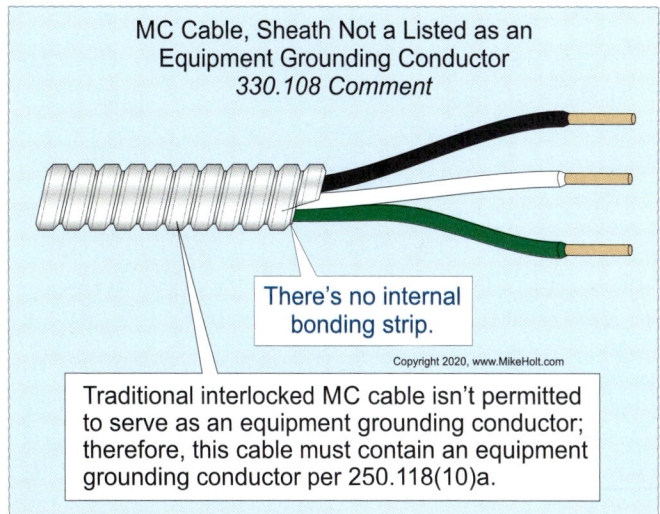

▶Figure 330-18

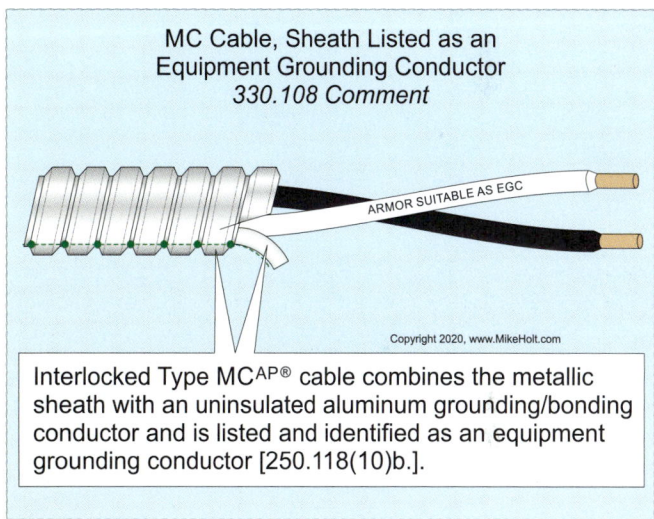

▶Figure 330-19

Notes

ARTICLE 334
NONMETALLIC-SHEATHED CABLE (TYPE NM)

Introduction to Article 334—Nonmetallic-Sheathed Cable (Type NM)

Nonmetallic-sheathed cable (Type NM) provides very limited physical protection for the conductors inside, so the installation restrictions are stringent. Its low cost and relative ease of installation make it a common wiring method for residential and commercial branch circuits.

Part I. General

334.1 Scope

Article 334 covers the use, installation, and construction specifications of nonmetallic-sheathed cable, Type NM. ▶Figure 334–1

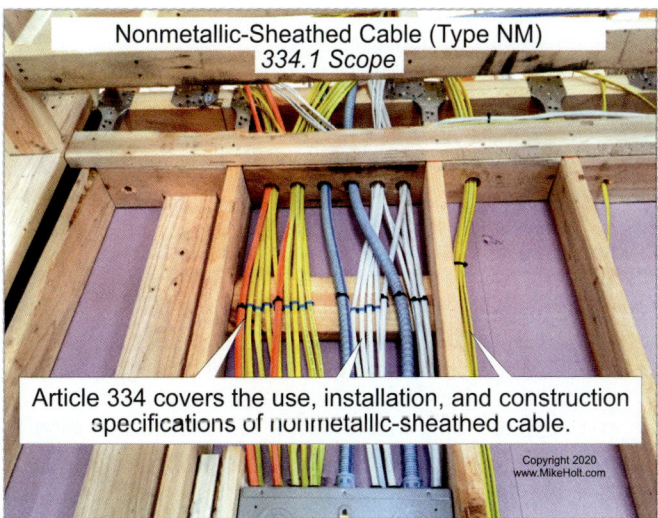

▶Figure 334–1

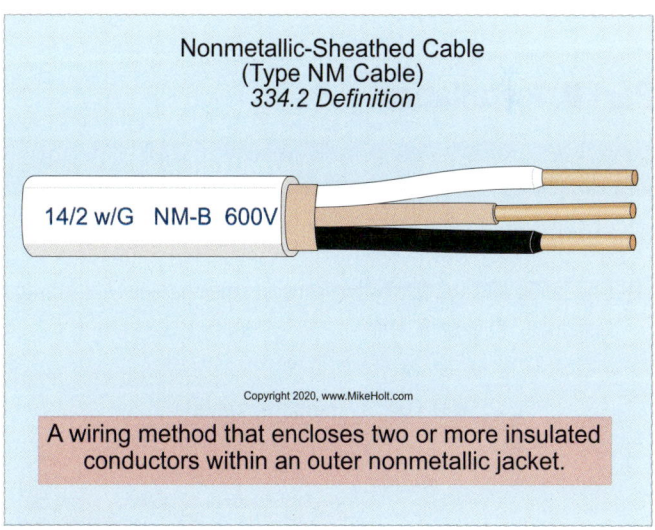

▶Figure 334–2

334.2 Definition

Nonmetallic-Sheathed Cable (Type NM). A wiring method that encloses two or more insulated conductors within a nonmetallic jacket. ▶Figure 334–2

Author's Comment:

▶ It is the generally accepted practice in the electrical industry to call Type NM cable "Romex®," a registered trademark of the Southwire Company.

334.6 Listing Requirements

Type NM cable and associated fittings must be listed. ▶Figure 334–3

334.10 | Nonmetallic-Sheathed Cable (Type NM)

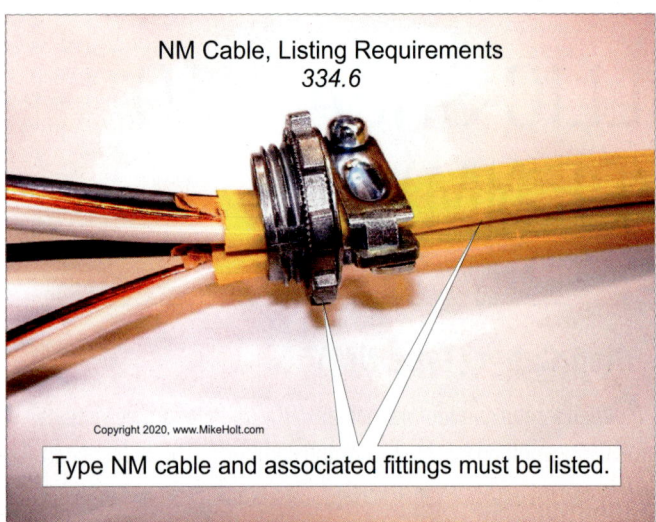
▶Figure 334-3

Part II. Installation

334.10 Uses Permitted

Type NM cables can be used in:

(1) One-family and two-family dwellings and their garages and storage buildings. ▶Figure 334-4

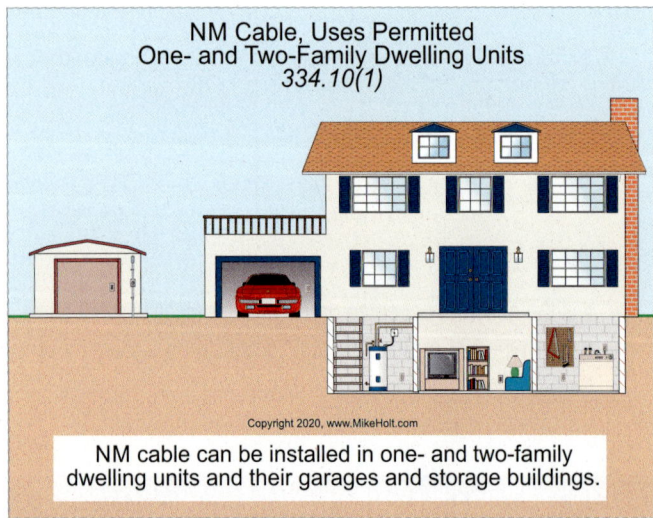
▶Figure 334-4

(2) Multifamily dwellings of Types III, IV, and V construction. ▶Figure 334-5

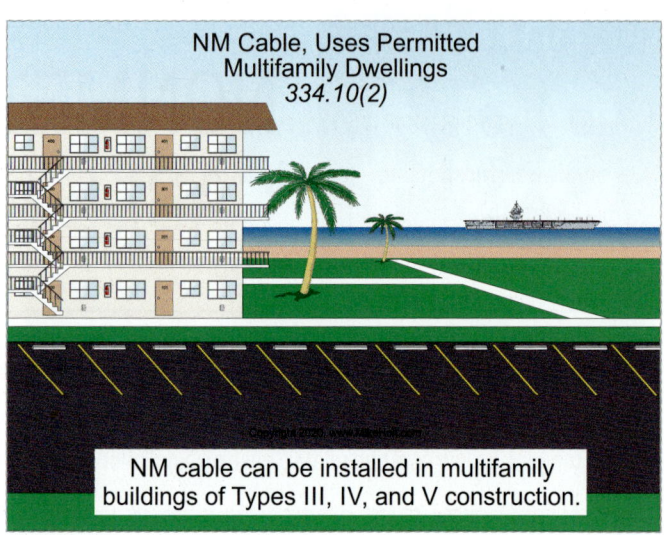
▶Figure 334-5

(3) Other buildings of Types III, IV, and V construction where the cable must be concealed within walls, floors, or ceilings that provide a thermal barrier of material with at least a 15-minute finish rating, as identified in listings of fire-rated assemblies. ▶Figure 334-6

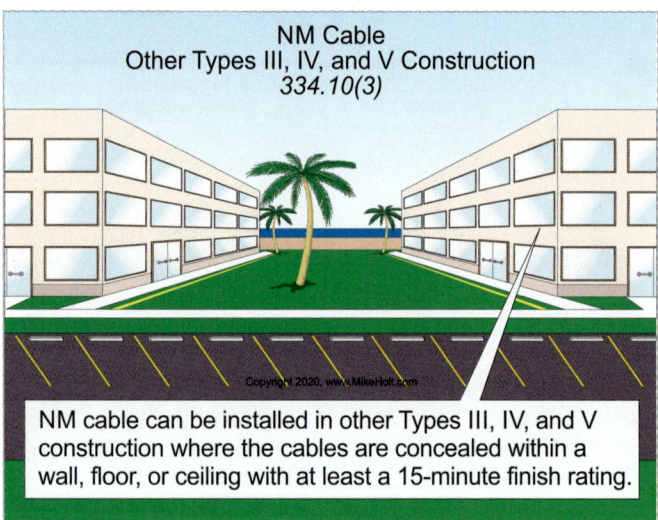
▶Figure 334-6

Author's Comment:

▸ See the definition of "Concealed" in Article 100.

Note 1: Building constructions are defined in NFPA 220, *Standard on Types of Building Construction*.

Note 2: See Annex E of the *NEC* for the determination of building types [NFPA 220, Table 4.1.1].

334.12 Uses Not Permitted

(A) Type NM. Type NM cable is not permitted:

(1) In any dwelling or structure not specifically permitted in 334.10(1), (2), (3), and (5).

(2) Exposed within a dropped or suspended ceiling in other than dwelling units. ▶Figure 334-7

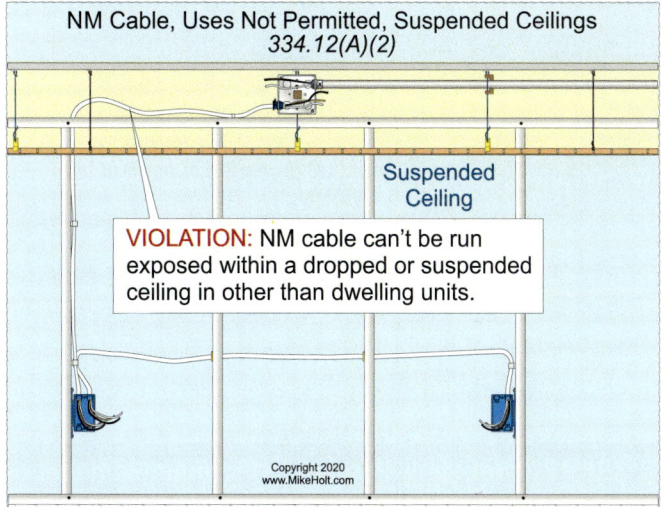

▶Figure 334-7

(3) As service-entrance cable.

(4) In commercial garages having hazardous (classified) locations, as defined in 511.3.

(5) In theaters and similar locations, except where permitted in 518.4(B).

(6) In motion picture studios.

(7) In storage battery rooms.

(8) In hoistways, or on elevators or escalators.

(9) Embedded in poured cement, concrete, or aggregate.

(10) In any hazardous (classified) location, except where permitted by other sections in this *Code*.

(B) Type NM. Type NM cable is not permitted to be used under the following conditions, or in the following locations:

(1) If exposed to corrosive fumes or vapors.

(2) If embedded in masonry, concrete, adobe, fill, or plaster.

(3) In a shallow chase in masonry, concrete, or adobe and covered with plaster, adobe, or similar finish.

(4) In wet or damp locations. ▶Figure 334-8

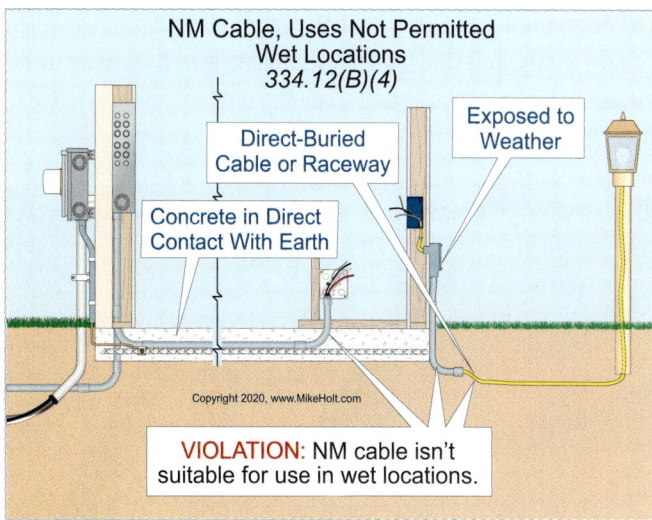

▶Figure 334-8

Author's Comment:

▸ A raceway in a ground floor slab is considered a wet location [Article 100]. ▶Figure 334-9

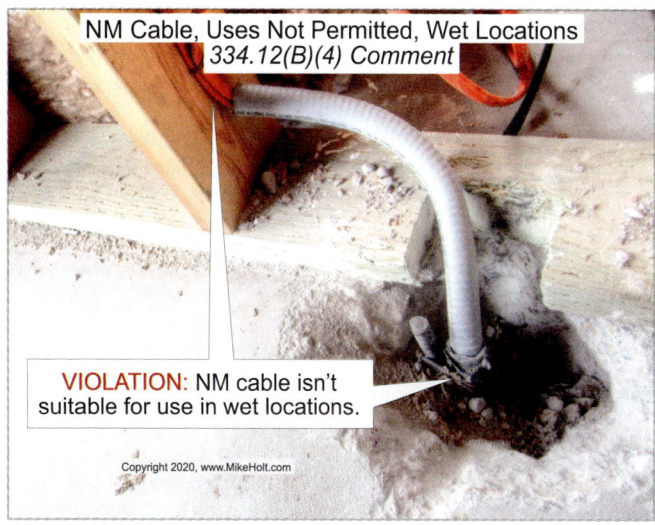

▶Figure 334-9

334.15 Exposed Work

Except as provided in 300.11(B), exposed Type NM can be installed as follows:

(A) Surface of the Building. Exposed NM cable must closely follow the surface of the building.

334.17 | Nonmetallic-Sheathed Cable (Type NM)

(B) Protected from Physical Damage. Nonmetallic-sheathed cable must be protected from physical damage by a raceway, guard strips, or other means approved by the authority having jurisdiction. ▶Figure 334–10

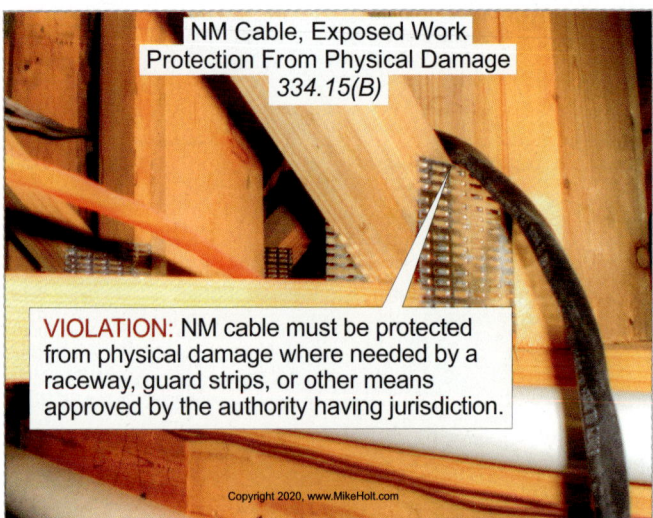

▶Figure 334–10

(C) In Unfinished Basements and Crawl Spaces. If Type NM cable is installed at angles with joists in unfinished basements and crawl spaces, cables containing conductors not smaller than two 6 AWG or three 8 AWG can be secured directly to the lower edges of the joists. Smaller cables must be installed through bored holes in joists or on running boards. ▶Figure 334–11

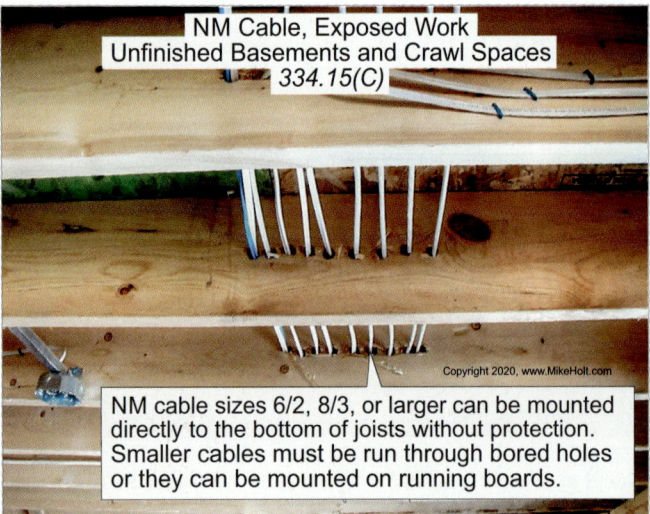

▶Figure 334–11

Type NM cable installed on a wall of an unfinished basement or crawl space subject to physical damage must be protected in accordance with 300.4 or be installed within a raceway with a nonmetallic bushing or adapter at the point where the cable enters the raceway. The cable must be secured within 12 in. of the point where it enters the raceway. ▶Figure 334–12

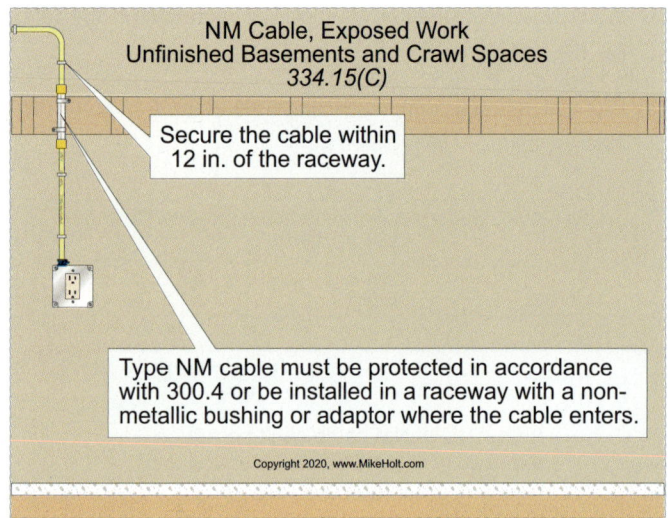

▶Figure 334–12

334.17 Through or Parallel to Framing Members

Type NM cable installed through, or parallel to, framing members or furring strips must be protected against physical damage from penetration by screws or nails by maintaining 1¼ in. of separation between the cable and the nearest edge of a framing member or furring strip, or by a suitable metal plate in accordance with 300.4(A), (C), and (D) ▶Figure 334–13 and ▶Figure 334–14

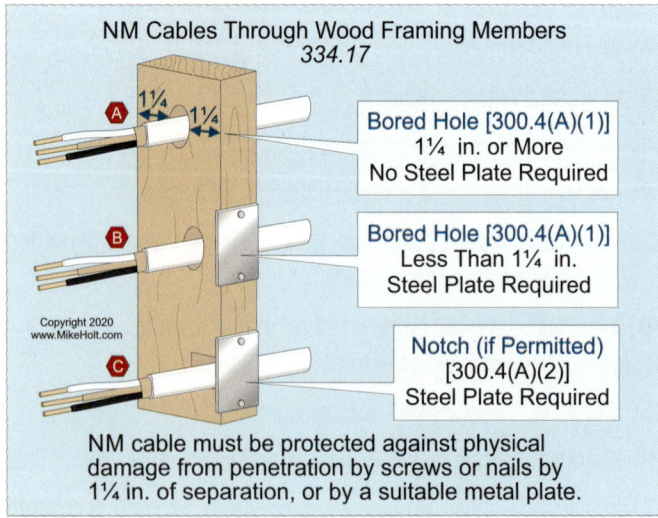

▶Figure 334–13

Nonmetallic-Sheathed Cable (Type NM) | **334.24**

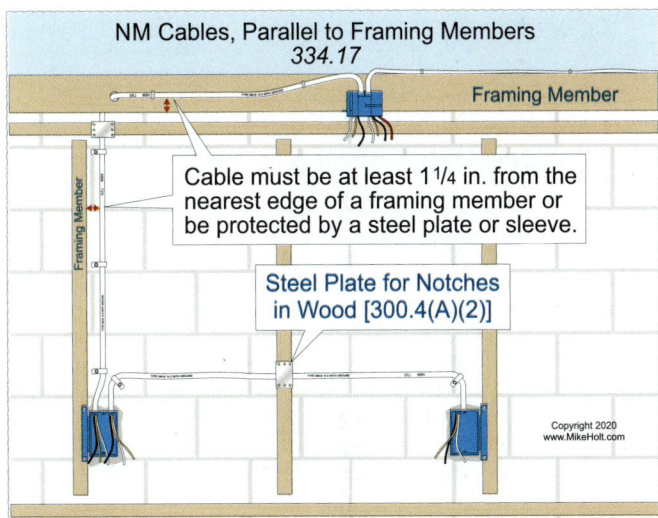

▶Figure 334-14

Author's Comment:

▸ On the Surface of Floor Joists, Rafters, or Studs. In attics and roof spaces that are accessible, substantial guards must protect cables installed across the top of floor joists, or across the face of rafters or studding within 7 ft of the floor or floor joists. If this space is not accessible by permanent stairs or ladders, protection is required only within 6 ft of the nearest edge of the scuttle hole or attic entrance [320.23(A)] ▶Figure 334-16

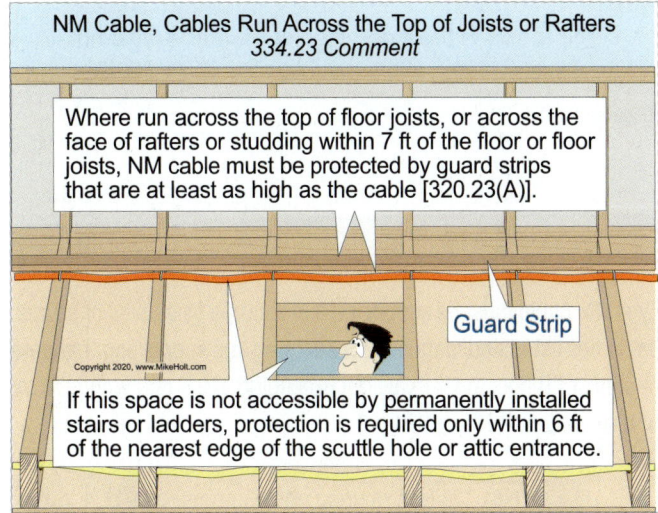

▶Figure 334-16

If Type NM cable passes through factory or field openings in metal framing members, the cable must be protected by listed bushings or grommets that cover all metal edges [300.4(B)(1)]. The protection fitting must be securely fastened in the opening before installing the cable. ▶Figure 334-15

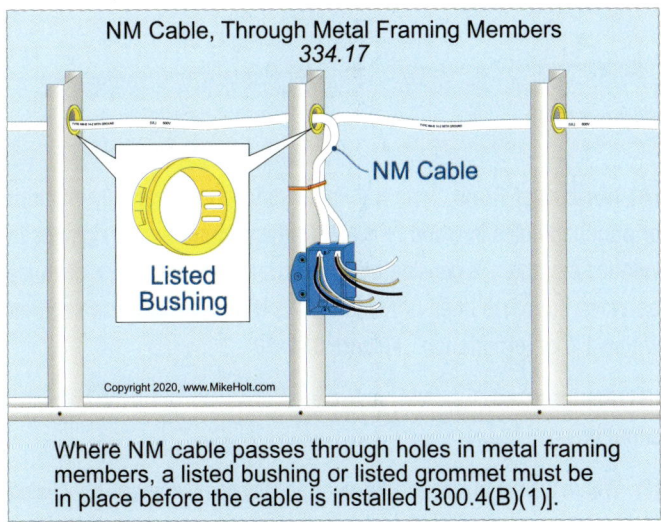

▶Figure 334-15

Author's Comment:

▸ Along the Side of Framing Members [320.23(B)]. When Type NM cable is installed on the side of rafters, studs, or floor joists, no protection is required if the cable is installed so the nearest outside surface of the cable or raceway is at least 1¼ in. from the nearest edge of the framing member if nails or screws are likely to penetrate [300.4(D)].

334.23 Accessible Attics and Roof Spaces

Type NM cable installed in accessible attics or roof spaces must comply with 320.23.

334.24 Bending Radius

When Type NM cable is bent, it is not permitted to be damaged and the radius of the curve of the inner edge of any bend must not be less than five times the diameter of the cable. ▶Figure 334-17

334.30 | Nonmetallic-Sheathed Cable (Type NM)

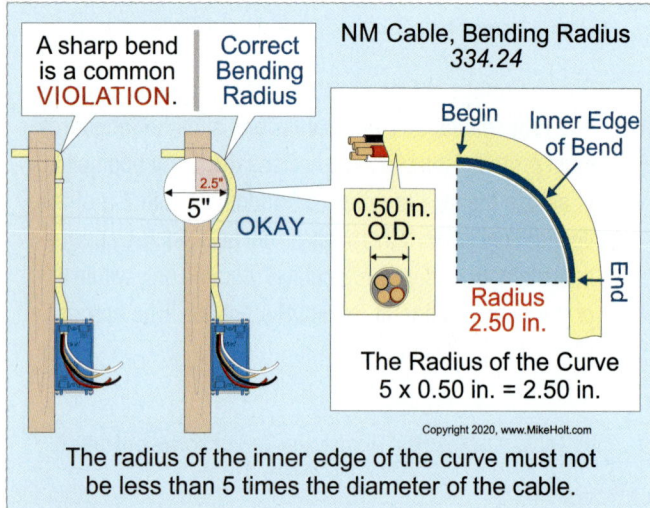

▶Figure 334-17

334.30 Securing and Supporting

Type NM cable must be supported and secured by staples or straps; cable ties listed and identified for securing and supporting; hangers or similar fittings, at intervals not exceeding 4½ ft and within 12 in. of termination. ▶Figure 334-18

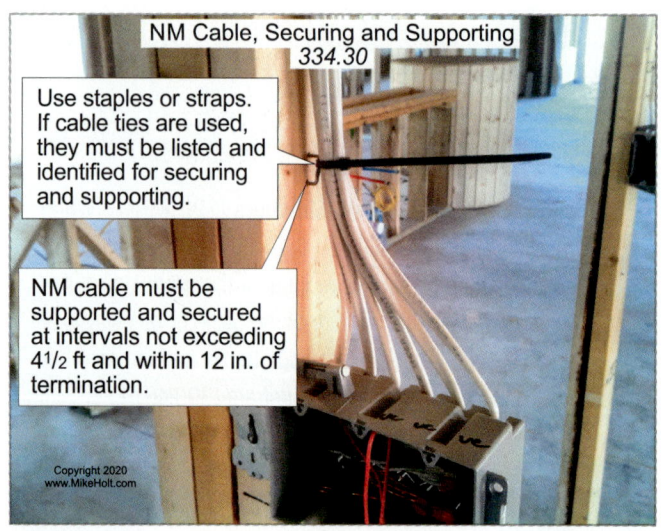

▶Figure 334-18

The cable length between the cable entry into cabinets and enclosures, and the closest cable support, must not exceed 18 in.

Author's Comment:

▸ Many times there is a tendency to leave a length of sheathed NM cable in a box or enclosure (such as a panelboard) just to have "extra" cable. While this practice is not prohibited, the length of such sheathed cable cannot exceed 18 in. as measured in a straight line.

Two-wire (flat) Type NM cable is not permitted to be stapled on edge. ▶Figure 334-19

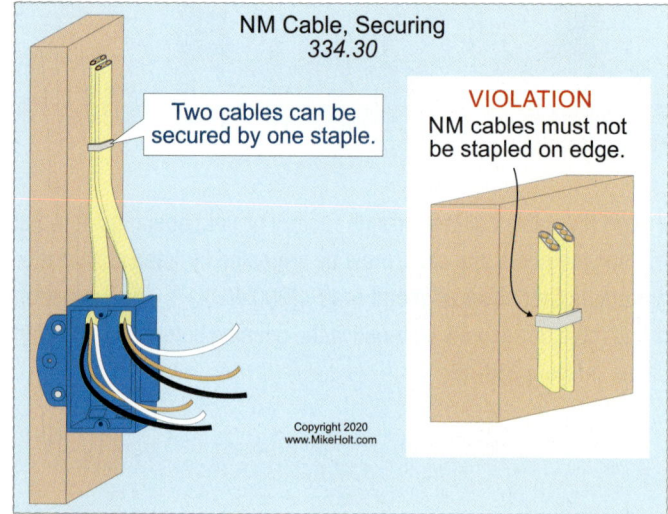

▶Figure 334-19

(A) Horizontal Runs. Type NM cable installed horizontally in bored or punched holes in wood or metal framing members, or notches in wooden members, is considered secured and supported if the distance between supports does not exceed 4½ ft and the cable is secured within 1 ft of termination. ▶Figure 334-20

(B) Unsupported. Type NM cable can be unsupported in the following situations:

(1) Where the cable is fished between access points through concealed spaces in finished buildings, and support is impractical.

(2) Not more than 4½ ft of unsupported cable is permitted from the last point of support within an accessible ceiling for the connection of luminaires or equipment in a dwelling unit. ▶Figure 334-21

Nonmetallic-Sheathed Cable (Type NM) | 334.80

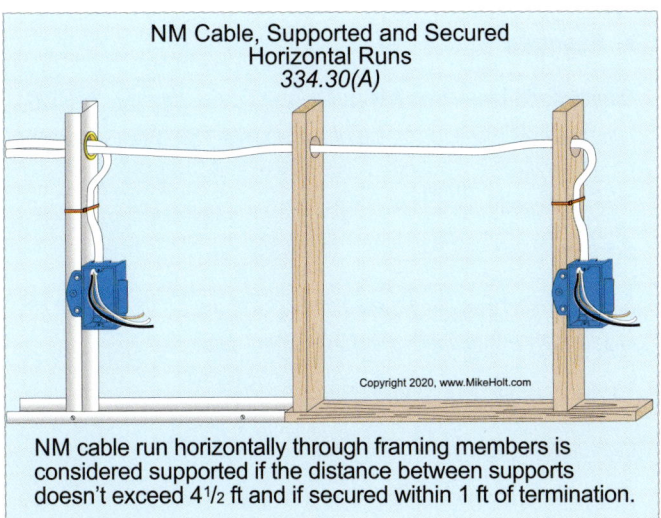

▶Figure 334-20

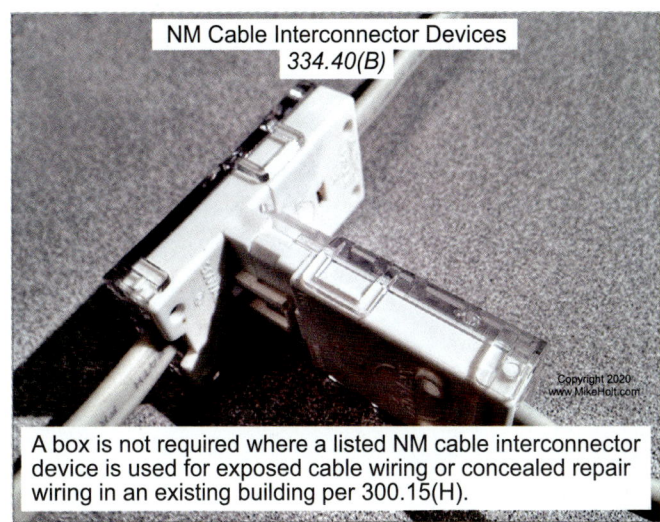

▶Figure 334-22

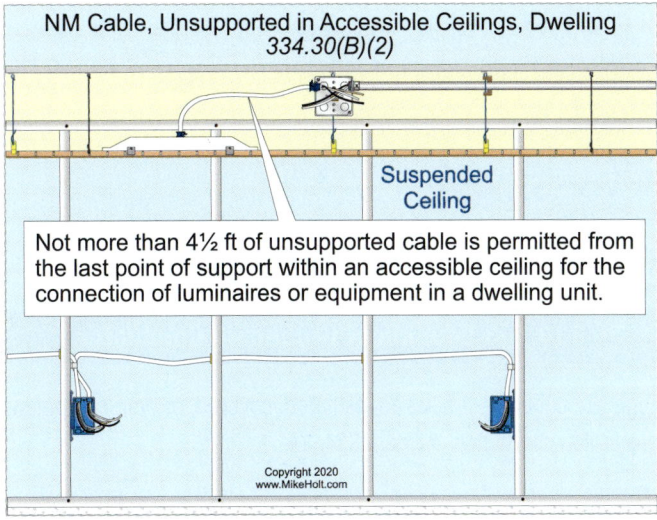

▶Figure 334-21

334.40 Boxes and Fittings

(B) NM Cable Interconnector Devices. A box is not required where a listed nonmetallic-sheathed cable interconnector device is used for exposed cable wiring, or for concealed repair wiring in an existing building in accordance with 300.15(H). ▶Figure 334-22

Author's Comment:

▸ According to UL, interconnector devices have been investigated for equivalency to Type NM cable in insulation and temperature rise, and for their capability to withstand fault currents, and vibration.

334.80 Conductor Ampacity

Adjusted and corrected conductor ampacity for Type NM cable is based on the 90°C insulation rating in accordance with Table 310.16; however, conductors must be sized in accordance with the 60°C termination temperature rating in accordance with Table 310.16.

▶ Example

Question: What size conductor and overcurrent device are required for a 9,600W, 240V fixed electric space heater that has a 3A, 240V blower motor? ▶Figure 334-23

(a) 10 AWG/30A (b) 8 AWG/40A
(c) 6 AWG/50A   (d) 6 AWG/60A

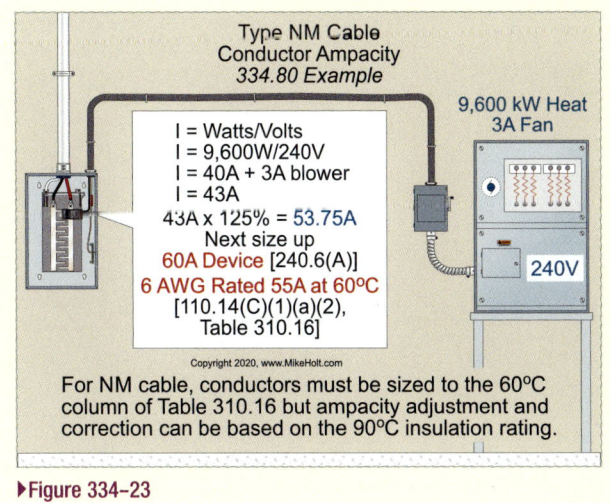

▶Figure 334-23

334.108 | Nonmetallic-Sheathed Cable (Type NM)

Solution:

Step 1: Determine the total load.

$I = Watts/Volts$

I = 9,600W/240V

I = 40A

Total Amperes = 40A (heat) + 3A (blower)
Total Amperes = 43A

Step 2: Size the conductors at 125 percent of the total current load [110.14(C)(1), 210.19(A)(1), 424.3(B), and Table 310.16].

Conductor = 43A × 125%
Conductor = 53.75A; round to 54A
Conductor = 6 AWG rated 55A at 60°C

Step 3: Size the overcurrent device at 125 percent of the total current load [210.20(A), 240.4(B), and 240.6(A)].

Overcurrent protection = 43A × 125%
Overcurrent protection = 53.75A, use next size up: 60A [240.6(A)]

Use a 6 AWG conductor with 60A overcurrent device.

Answer: (d) 6 AWG/60A

If multiple Type NM cables pass through the same wood framing opening that is to be sealed with thermal insulation, caulking, or sealing foam, the ampacity of each conductor must be adjusted in accordance with Table 310.15(C)(1).

▶ **Example**

Question: Can four Type NM cables, each containing two 14 AWG current-carrying conductors be protected by a 15A circuit breaker?

(a) Yes   (b) No

Solution:

Step 1: Determine the adjusted ampacity of the circuit conductors in accordance with Table 310.15(C)(1) and Table 310.16.

14 AWG is rated 25A at 90°C [Table 310.16]

Conductor Adjustment = 70% [Table 310.15(C)(1)]

Conductor Adjusted Ampacity = 25A × 70%
Conductor Adjusted Ampacity = 17.50A

Step 2: Verify that the adjusted conductor ampacity can be protected by the 15A circuit breaker. In this case, 14 AWG is rated 17.50A after adjustment at 90°C and 15A at 60°C [210.19(A)(1) and 240.4(D)].

Answer: (a) Yes

Part III. Construction Specifications

334.108 Equipment Grounding Conductor

Type NM cable must have an insulated, covered, or bare equipment grounding conductor. ▶Figure 334–24

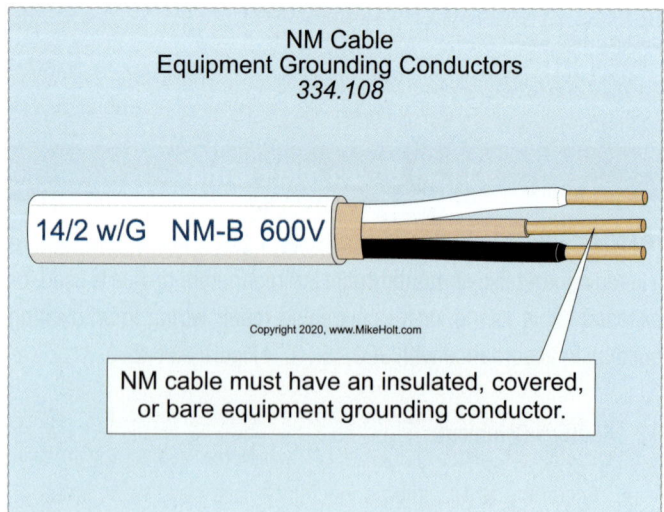

▶Figure 334–24

ARTICLE 336 — POWER AND CONTROL TRAY CABLE (TYPE TC)

Introduction to Article 336—Power and Control Tray Cable (Type TC)

Power and control tray cable (Type TC) is flexible, inexpensive, and easily installed. It provides very limited physical protection for the conductors, so the installation restrictions are stringent. Its low cost and relative ease of installation make it a common wiring method for industrial applications.

Part I. General

336.1 Scope

This article covers the use and installation for power and control tray cable, Type TC. ▶Figure 336–1

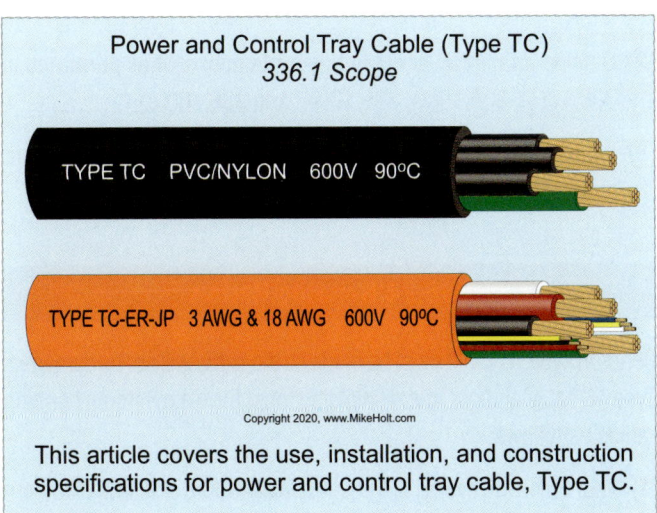

▶Figure 336–1

336.2 Definition

Power and Control Tray Cable (Type TC). A factory assembly of two or more insulated conductors, with or without associated bare or covered equipment grounding conductors, under a nonmetallic jacket. ▶Figure 336–2

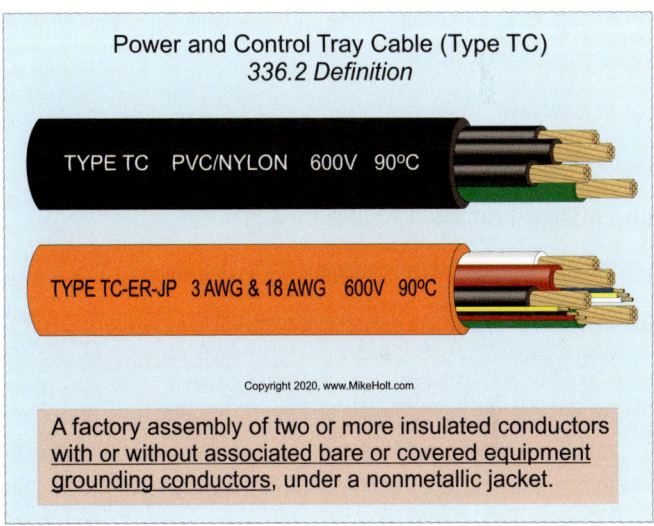

▶Figure 336–2

336.6 Listing Requirements

Type TC cable and associated fittings must be listed. ▶Figure 336–3

Part II. Installation

336.10 Uses Permitted

Type TC cable is permitted to be used:

(1) For power, lighting, control, and signaling circuits.

336.12 | Power and Control Tray Cable (Type TC)

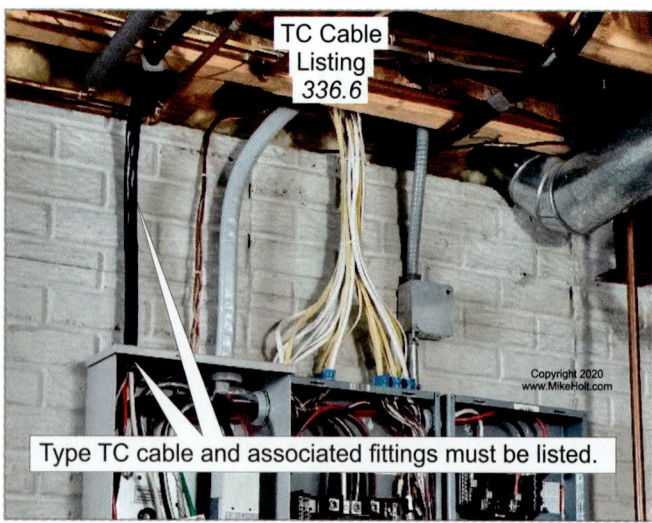

▶Figure 336–3

(2) In cable trays including those with mechanically discontinuous segments up to 1 ft.

(3) In raceways.

(4) In outdoor locations supported by a messenger wire.

(5) For Class 1 circuits in accordance with Article 725.

(7) Between a cable tray and equipment if it complies with 336(10)(7).

(8) In wet locations where the cable is resistant to moisture and corrosive agents.

(9) In one- and two-family dwellings, Type TC-ER-JP cable is permitted for branch circuits and feeders where installed in accordance with Part II of Article 334 for interior wiring, and Part II of Article 340 for exterior wiring. ▶Figure 336–4

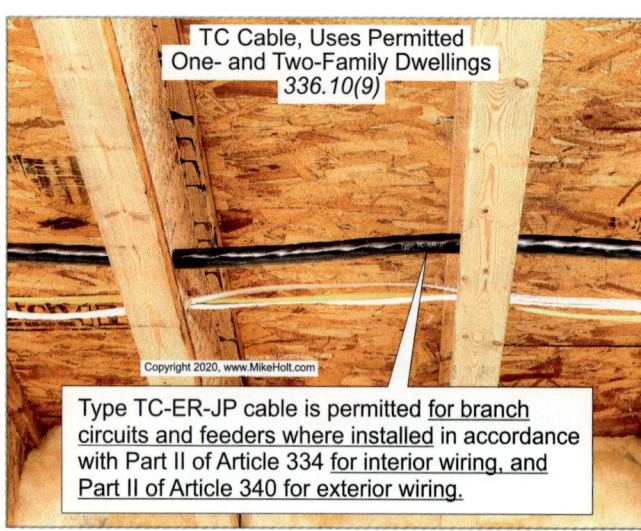

▶Figure 336–4

Author's Comment:

▸ The "ER" marking on Type TC-ER cable identifies it as suitable for exposed run use in accordance with UL and the suffix "-JP identifies it as being suitable for pulling through wood framing members.

Ex: Where Type TC-ER-JP cable is used to connect a generator and its associated equipment, the cable ampacity limitations of 334.80 and 340.80 do not apply.

Author's Comment:

▸ The "JP" marking on Type TC-ER-JP cable identifies it as suitable to be pulled through wood framing members because the cable has met the joist pull testing requirements of UL.

(10) Direct buried where identified for direct burial.

336.12 Uses Not Permitted

Type TC cables are not permitted:

(1) Where exposed to physical damage.

(2) Outside a raceway or cable tray system, except as permitted in 336.10(4), 336.10(7), 336.10(9), and 336.10(10).

(3) Exposed to the direct rays of the sun, unless identified as sunlight resistant.

336.24 Bending Radius

Bends in Type TC cable must be made so the cable will not be damaged. Type TC cable without metal shielding must have a minimum bending radius as follows:

(1) Four times the overall diameter for cables 1 in. or less in diameter.

(2) Five times the overall diameter for cables larger than 1 in. but not more than 2 in. in diameter.

ARTICLE 338 — SERVICE-ENTRANCE CABLE (TYPES SE AND USE)

Introduction to Article 338—Service-Entrance Cable (Types SE and USE)

Service-entrance (SE) and underground service-entrance (USE) cables, can be a single conductor or a multiconductor assembly within an overall nonmetallic outer jacket or covering. This cable is used primarily for services but is permitted for feeders and branch circuits. When used as a service conductor(s) or service entrance conductor(s), Type SE cable assemblies will contain insulated phase conductors and a bare neutral conductor. For feeders or branch circuits, you must use Type SE cable that contains insulated phase and neutral conductors with an uninsulated equipment grounding conductor.

Part I. General

338.1 Scope

Article 338 covers the use, installation, and construction specifications of service-entrance cable, Types SE and USE. ▶Figure 338–1

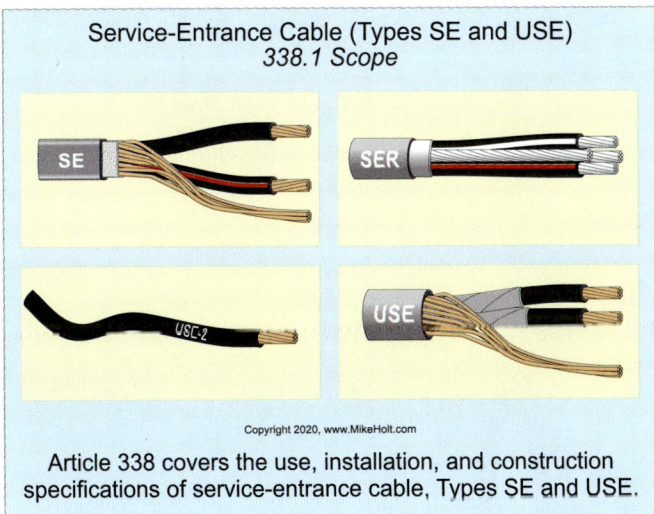

▶Figure 338–1

338.2 Definitions

Service-Entrance Cable (Types SE and USE). Service-entrance cable is a single or multiconductor cable with an overall covering. ▶Figure 338–2

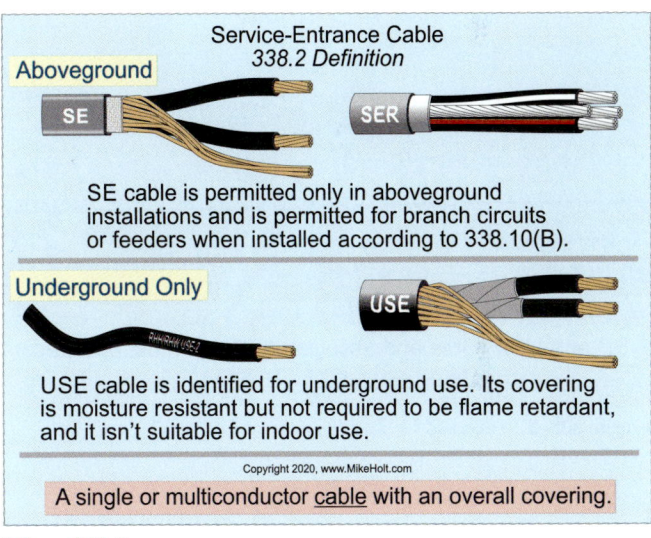

▶Figure 338–2

Service-Entrance Conductor Assembly. Multiple single-insulated conductors twisted together without an overall covering, other than an optional binder intended only to keep the conductors together.

Author's Comment:

▸ "Triplex" and "Quadruplex" with an outer wire wrapped around them are examples of an SE conductor assembly.

Type SE. Type SE cables have a flame-retardant, moisture-resistant covering and are permitted only in aboveground installations. These cables are permitted for branch circuits or feeders when installed in accordance with 338.10(B).

338.6 | Service-Entrance Cable (Types SE and USE)

Type USE. USE cable is identified as a wiring method permitted for underground use; its covering is moisture resistant, but not flame retardant.

> **Author's Comment:**
> ▸ Type USE cable is not permitted to be installed indoors [338.12(B)].

338.6 Listing Requirements

Types SE and USE cables and associated fittings must be listed. ▸Figure 338-3

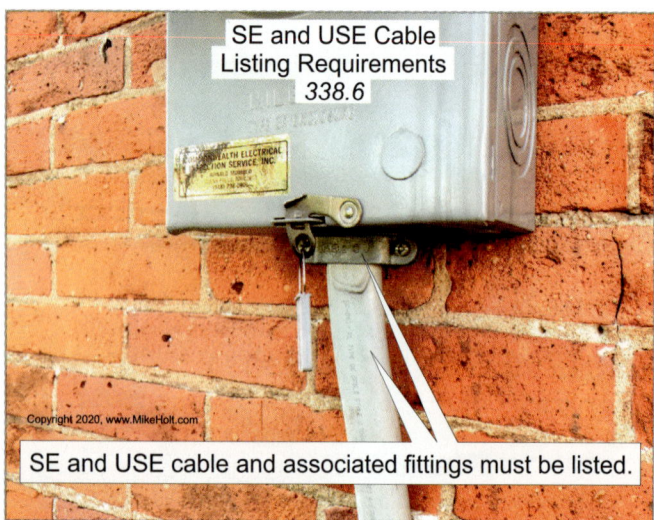

▸Figure 338-3

Part II. Installation

338.10 Uses Permitted

(A) Service-Entrance Conductors. Types SE and USE cable can be used as service-entrance conductors in accordance with Article 230.

(B) Branch Circuits or Feeders.

(2) Insulated Conductor. Type SE service-entrance cable is permitted for branch circuits and feeders where the neutral conductor is insulated, and the uninsulated conductor is only used for equipment grounding. ▸Figure 338-4

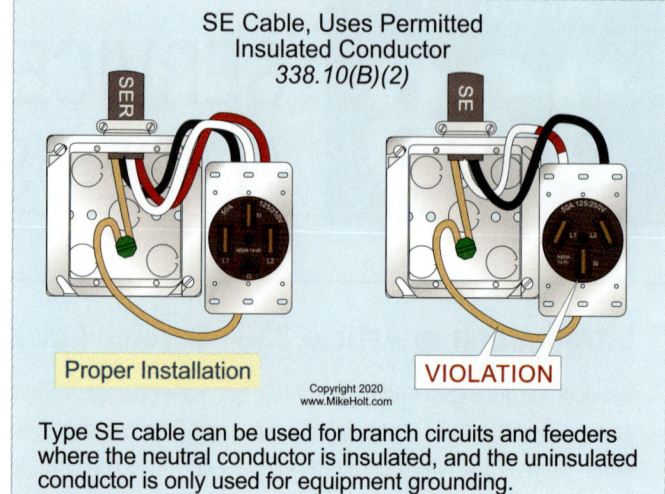

▸Figure 338-4

(3) Temperature Limitations. SE cable is not permitted to be subjected to conductor temperatures exceeding its insulation rating.

(4) Installation Methods for Branch Circuits and Feeders. SE cable used for branch circuits or feeders must comply with (a) and (b).

(a) Interior Installations.

(1) SE cable used for interior branch-circuit or feeder wiring must be installed in accordance with the same requirements as Type NM cable in Part II of Article 334, excluding 334.80. ▸Figure 338-5

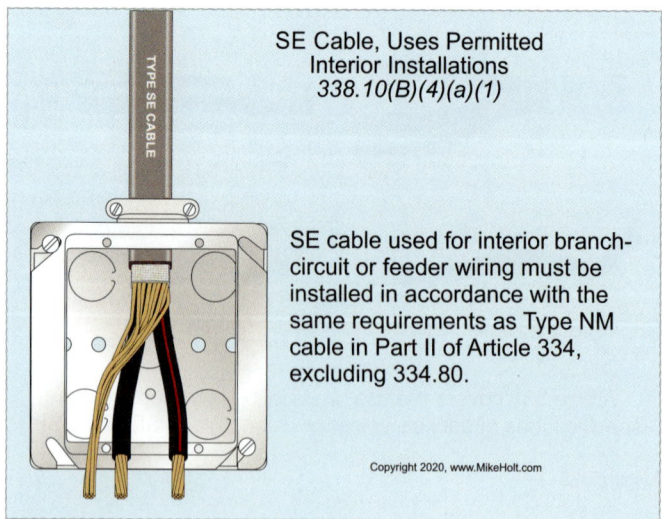

▸Figure 338-5

(2) If multiple cables pass through the same wood framing opening that is to be sealed with thermal insulation, caulking, or sealing foam, the ampacity of each conductor must be adjusted in accordance with Table 310.15(C)(1). ▸Figure 338-6

Service-Entrance Cable (Types SE and USE) | 338.24

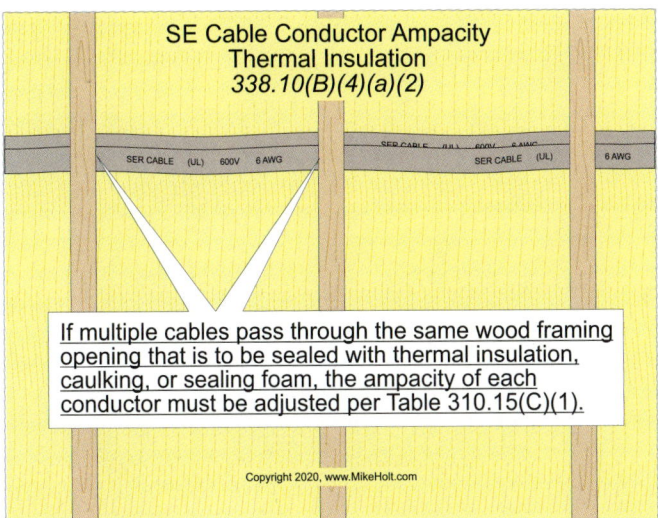

▶Figure 338-6

(3) The ampacity of conductors 10 AWG and smaller, where installed in contact with thermal insulation, must be sized in accordance with 60°C (140°F) conductor temperature rating. For conductor ampacity correction and/or adjustment, the conductor temperature rating ampacity must be used.

(b) Exterior Installations.

(1) The cable must be installed in accordance with Part I of Article 225 and supported in accordance with 334.30. Where it is run underground, the cable must comply with Part II of Article 340.

338.12 Uses Not Permitted

(A) Service-Entrance Cable. Type SE cable is not permitted under the following conditions or locations:

(1) Where subject to physical damage.

(2) Underground with or without a raceway.

(B) Underground Service-Entrance Cable. Type USE cable is not permitted:

(1) For interior wiring.

(2) Above ground, except where protected against physical damage in accordance with 300.5(D).

338.24 Bending Radius

Bends in cable must be made so the protective coverings of the cable are not damaged, and the radius of the curve of the inner edge is at least five times the diameter of the cable. ▶Figure 338-7 and ▶Figure 338-8

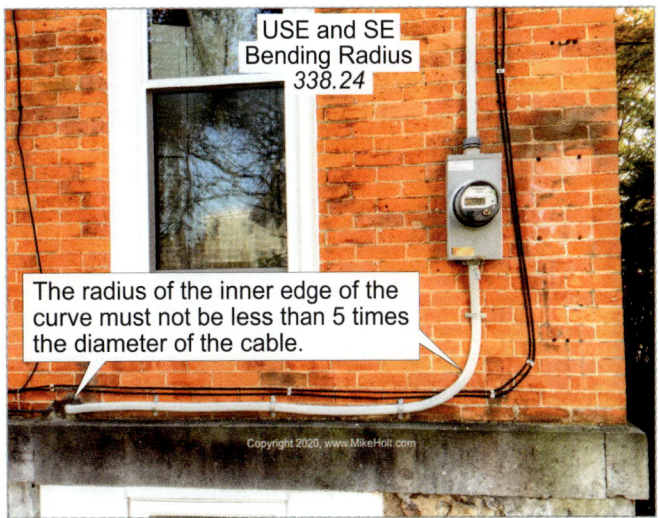

▶Figure 338-7

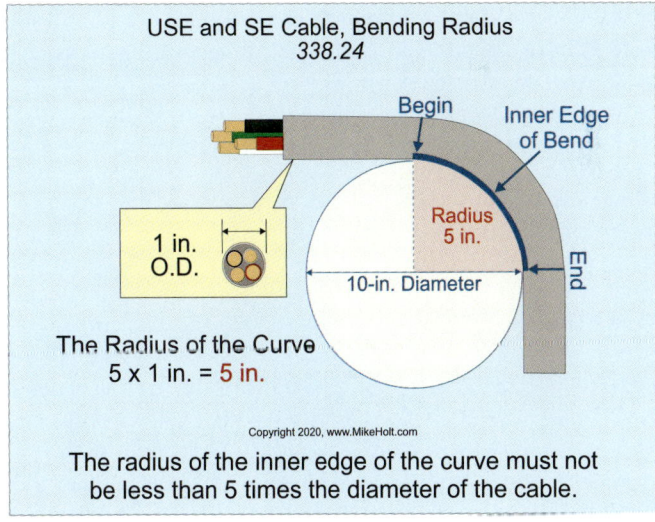

▶Figure 338-8

Notes

ARTICLE 340

UNDERGROUND FEEDER AND BRANCH-CIRCUIT CABLE (TYPE UF)

Introduction to Article 340—Underground Feeder and Branch-Circuit Cable (Type UF)

UF cable (Type UF) is a moisture-, fungus-, and corrosion-resistant cable suitable for direct burial in the Earth. It comes in sizes 14 AWG through 4/0 AWG [340.104]. The covering of multiconductor Type UF cable is molded plastic that encases the insulated conductors. Because the covering of Type UF cable encloses the insulated conductors, it is difficult to strip off the outer jacket to gain access to them, but this covering provides excellent corrosion protection. Be careful not to damage the conductor insulation or cut yourself when you remove the outer cover.

Part I. General

340.1 Scope

Article 340 covers the use, installation, and construction specifications of underground feeder and branch-circuit cable, Type UF. ▶Figure 340–1

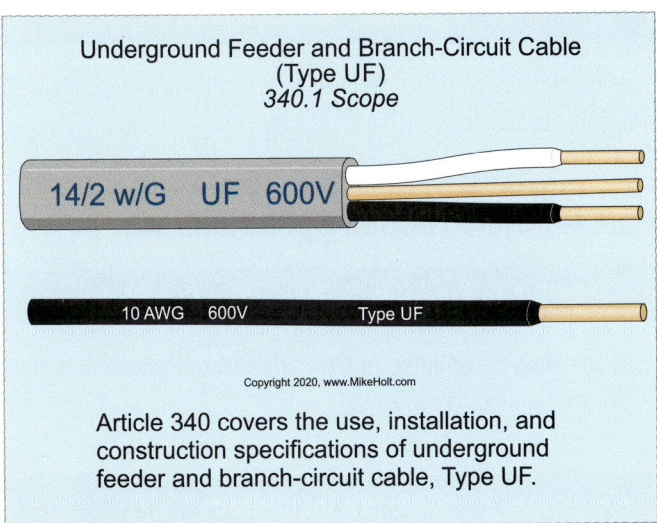

▶Figure 340–1

340.2 Definition

Underground Feeder and Branch-Circuit Cable (Type UF). A factory assembly of insulated conductors with an integral or an overall covering of nonmetallic material suitable for direct burial in the Earth. ▶Figure 340–2

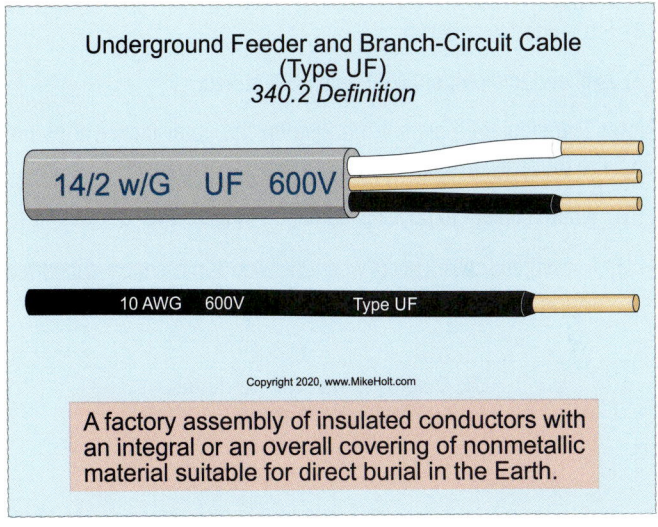

▶Figure 340–2

340.6 Listing Requirements

Type UF cable and associated fittings must be listed.

Part II. Installation

340.10 Uses Permitted

Type UF cable is permitted:

(1) Underground in accordance with 300.5.

(2) As a single conductor in a trench or raceway with circuit conductors.

340.12 | Underground Feeder and Branch-Circuit Cable (Type UF)

(3) For wiring in wet, dry, or corrosive locations.

(4) Where installed as nonmetallic-sheathed cable, the installation must comply with Parts II and III of Article 334.

340.12 Uses Not Permitted

Type UF cable is not permitted to be used:

(1) As service-entrance cable [230.43].

(2) In commercial garages [511.3].

(3) In theaters [520.5].

(4) In motion picture studios [530.11].

(5) In storage battery rooms [Article 480].

(6) In hoistways [Article 620].

(7) In hazardous (classified) locations, except as specifically permitted by other articles in this *Code*.

(8) Embedded in concrete.

(9) Exposed to direct sunlight unless identified.

Note: The sunlight-resistant marking on the outer jacket does not apply to the individual conductors.

(10) Where subject to physical damage. ▶Figure 340-3

(11) As overhead cable, except where installed as messenger-supported wiring in accordance with Part II of Article 396.

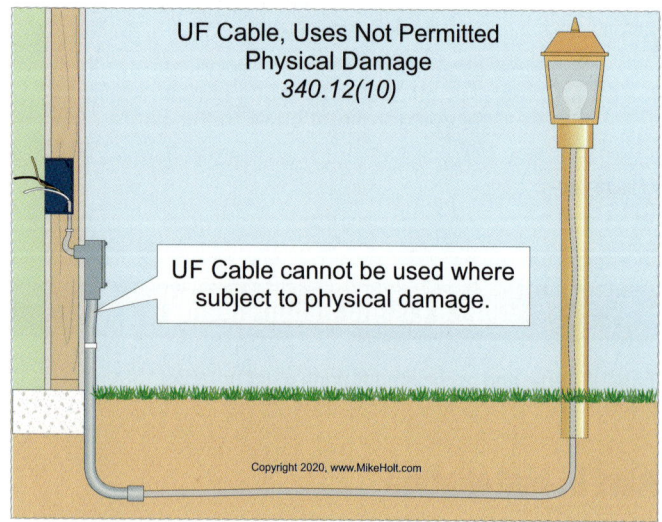

▶Figure 340-3

Author's Comment:

▸ UF cable is not permitted in ducts or plenum spaces [300.22], or in patient care spaces of health care facilities [517.13].

340.24 Bends

Bends in cables must be made so the protective coverings of the cable are not damaged, and the radius of the curve of the inner edge must not be less than five times the diameter of the cable. ▶Figure 340-4

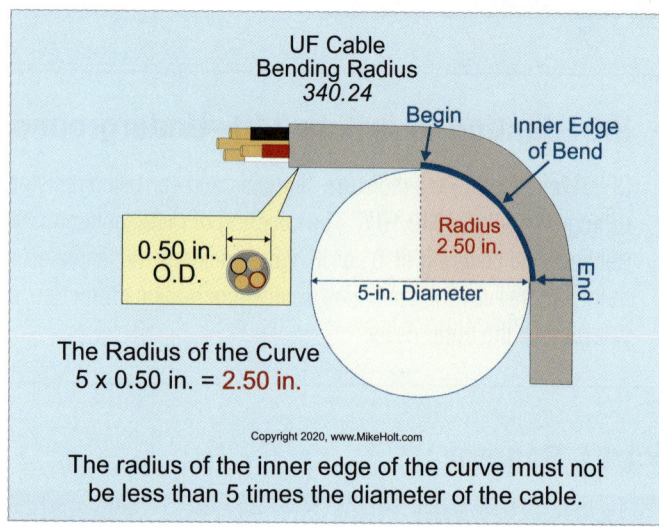

▶Figure 340-4

340.80 Ampacity

Type UF cable is permitted to have an insulated or bare equipment grounding conductor.

Part III. Construction Specifications

340.108 Equipment Grounding Conductor

Type UF cable is permitted to have an insulated, covered, or bare equipment grounding conductor.

340.112 Insulation

The conductors of UF cable must be one of the moisture-resistant types listed in Table 310.4(A) that is suitable for branch-circuit wiring. If installed as a substitute wiring method for Type NM cable, the conductor insulation must be rated 90°C (194°F).

ARTICLE 342 — INTERMEDIATE METAL CONDUIT (TYPE IMC)

Introduction to Article 342—Intermediate Metal Conduit (Type IMC)

Intermediate metal conduit is a circular metal raceway with the same outside diameter as rigid metal conduit (Type RMC). The wall thickness of IMC is less than that of rigid metal conduit, so it has a larger interior cross-sectional area for holding conductors. IMC is lighter and less expensive than RMC and is approved by the *NEC* for use in the same applications. IMC also uses a different steel alloy, which makes it stronger than RMC even though the walls are thinner. Intermediate metal conduit is manufactured in both galvanized steel and aluminum; the steel type is much more common.

Part I. General

342.1 Scope

Article 342 covers the use, installation, and construction specifications of intermediate metal conduit (Type IMC) and associated fittings. ▶Figure 342–1

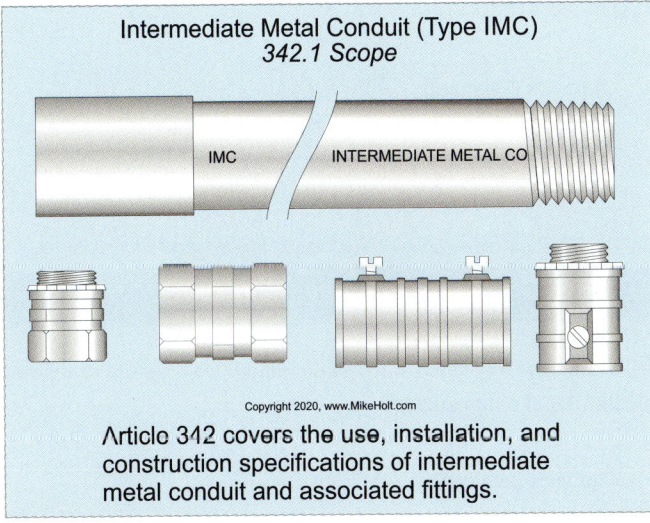

▶Figure 342–1

342.2 Definition

Intermediate Metal Conduit (Type IMC). A steel raceway of circular cross section that can be threaded with integral or associated couplings listed for the installation of electrical conductors. ▶Figure 342–2

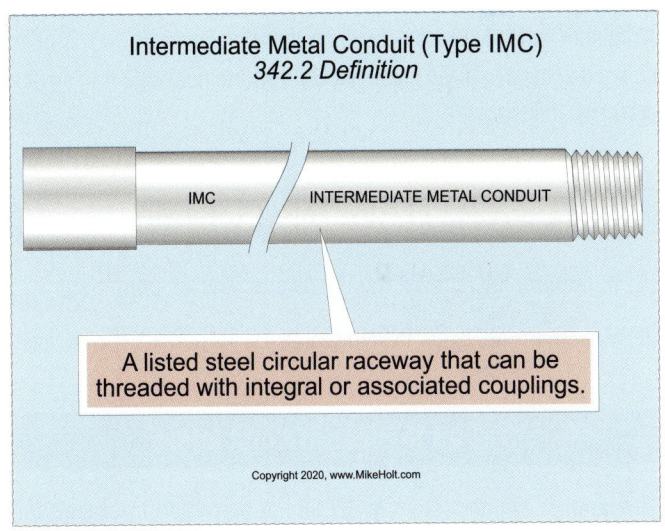

▶Figure 342–2

Author's Comment:

▶ The type of steel from which intermediate metal conduit is manufactured, the process by which it is made, and the corrosion protection applied are all equal (or superior) to that of rigid metal conduit.

342.6 Listing Requirements

Intermediate metal conduit and its associated fittings must be listed.

342.10 | Intermediate Metal Conduit (Type IMC)

Part II. Installation

342.10 Uses Permitted

(A) Atmospheric Conditions and Occupancies. IMC is permitted in all atmospheric conditions and occupancies.

(B) Corrosive Environments. IMC, elbows, couplings, and fittings can be installed in concrete, in direct contact with the Earth, or in areas subject to severe corrosive influences if provided with supplementary corrosion protection approved for the condition.

(E) Severe Physical Damage. IMC is permitted where subject to severe physical damage.

342.14 Dissimilar Metals

Where practical, contact of IMC with dissimilar metals should be avoided to prevent the deterioration of the metal because of galvanic action. Aluminum and stainless steel fittings and enclosures are permitted to be used with galvanized steel Type IMC where not subject to severe corrosive influences.

342.20 Trade Size

(A) Minimum. IMC smaller than trade size ½ is not permitted.

(B) Maximum. IMC larger than trade size 4 is not permitted to be used.

342.22 Number of Conductors

The number of conductors in IMC is not permitted to exceed the percentage fill specified in Chapter 9, Table 1. Raceways must be large enough to permit the installation and removal of conductors without damaging the conductors' insulation.

Author's Comment:

▸ See 300.17 for examples on how to size raceways when conductors are not all the same size.

342.24 Bends

Raceway bends are not permitted to be made in any manner that will damage the raceway or significantly change its internal diameter (no kinks).

Author's Comment:

▸ This is not a problem if you use a bender in accordance with the manufacturer's instructions.

342.26 Number of Bends (360°)

To reduce the stress and friction on conductor insulation, the total bends (including offsets) between pull points are not permitted to exceed 360°. ▸Figure 342–3

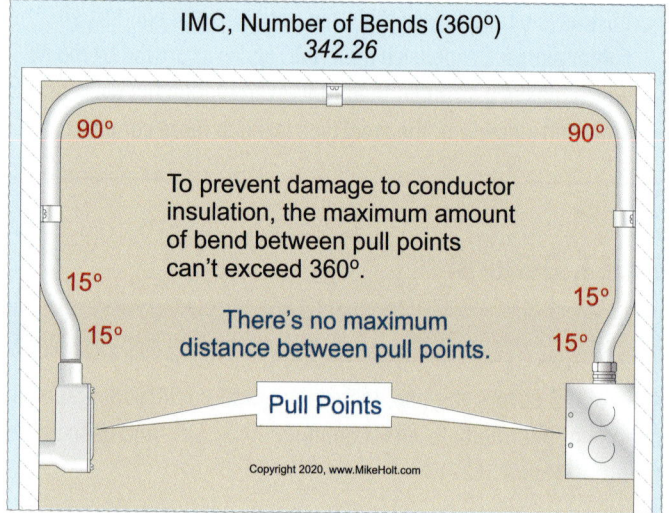

▸Figure 342–3

Author's Comment:

▸ There is no maximum distance between pull boxes because this is a design issue rather than a safety issue.

342.28 Reaming

When the raceway is cut in the field, reaming is required to remove the burrs and rough edges.

Author's Comment:

▸ It is a commonly accepted practice to ream small raceways with a screwdriver or the backside of pliers. However, when the raceway is cut with a three-wheel pipe cutter, a reaming tool is required to remove the sharp edge or burr of the indented raceway. When conduits are threaded in the field, the threads must be coated with an electrically conductive, corrosion-resistant compound approved by the authority having jurisdiction in accordance with 300.6(A).

Intermediate Metal Conduit (Type IMC) | 342.30

342.30 Securing and Supporting

IMC must be securely fastened in place and supported in accordance with (A) and (B).

(A) Securely Fastened. IMC must be secured in accordance with any of the following:

(1) Fastened within 3 ft of each outlet box, junction box, device box, cabinet, conduit body, or other conduit termination. ▶Figure 342–4

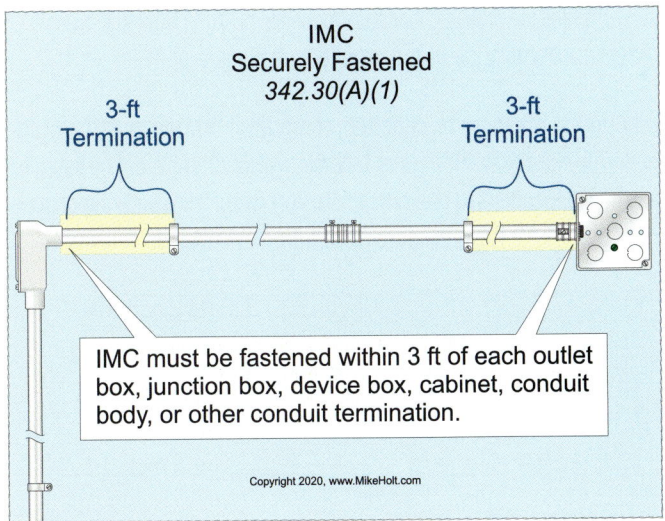

▶Figure 342–4

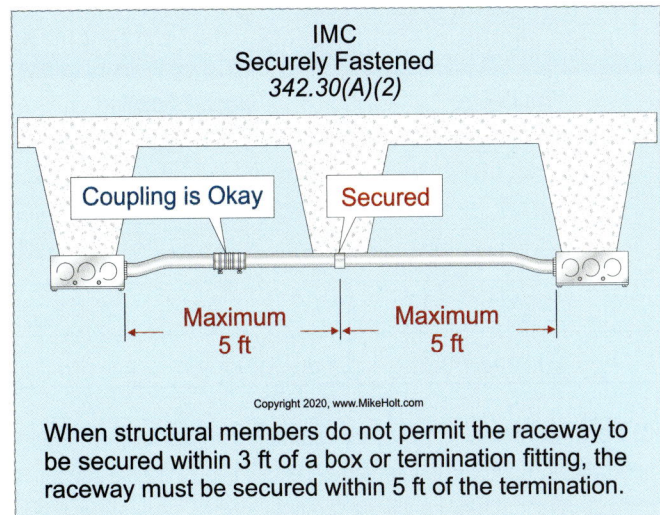

▶Figure 342–5

Author's Comment:

▸ Fastening is required within of terminations, not within 3 ft of each coupling.

(2) When structural members do not permit the raceway to be secured within 3 ft of a box or termination fitting, the raceway must be secured within 5 ft of the termination. ▶Figure 342–5

(3) Where approved, IMC is not required to be securely fastened within 3 ft of the service head for an above-the-roof termination of a mast. ▶Figure 342–6

(B) Supports.

(1) General. IMC must be supported at intervals not exceeding 10 ft.

(2) Straight Runs. Straight runs with threaded couplings can be supported in accordance with the distances contained in Table 344.30(B)(2). ▶Figure 342–7

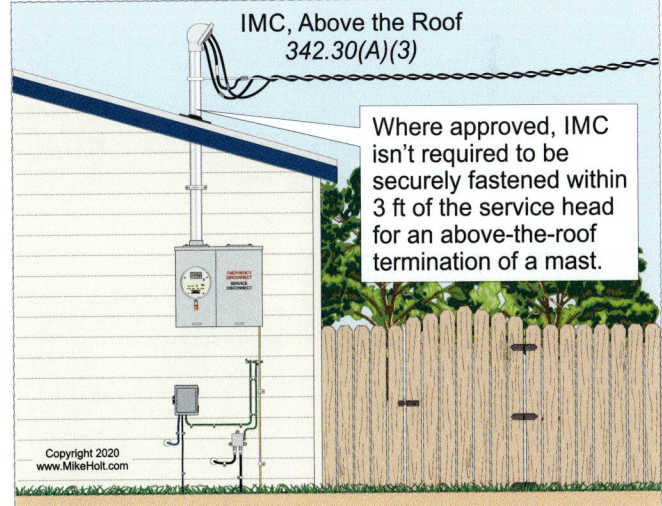

▶Figure 342–6

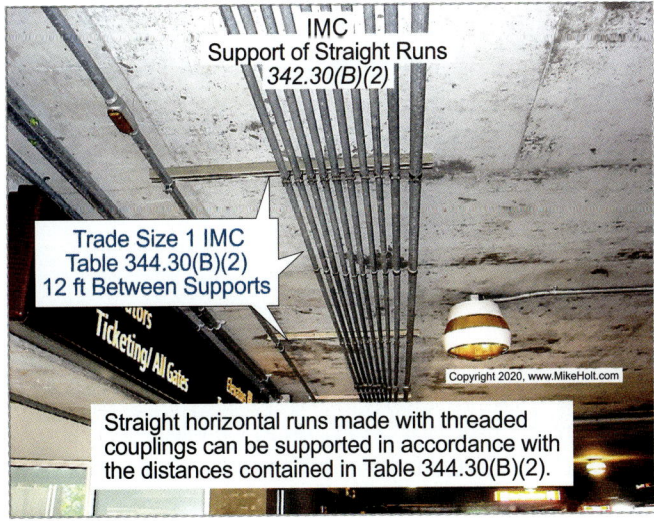

▶Figure 342–7

342.42 | Intermediate Metal Conduit (Type IMC)

Table 344.30(B)(2) Supports for Rigid Metal Conduit	
Trade Size	Support Spacing
½–¾	10 ft
1	12 ft
1¼–1½	14 ft
2–2½	16 ft
3 and larger	20 ft

(3) Vertical Risers. Exposed vertical risers of IMC for fixed equipment can be supported at intervals not exceeding 20 ft if the conduit is made up with threaded couplings, firmly supported, securely fastened at the top and bottom of the riser, and if no other means of support is available. ▶Figure 342–8

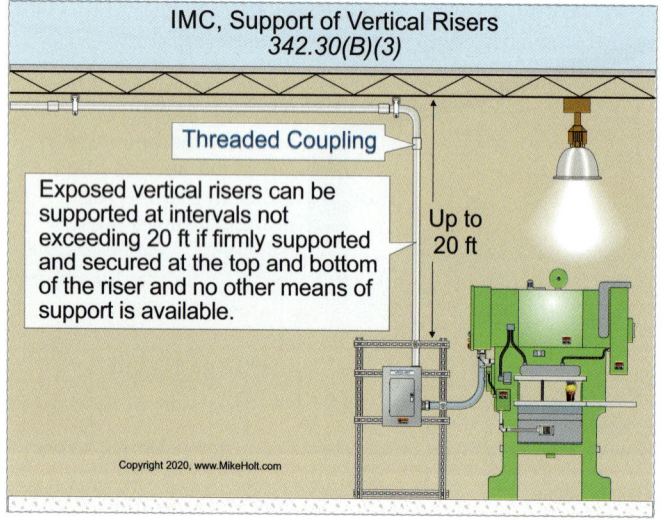
▶Figure 342–8

(4) Horizontal Runs. IMC installed horizontally in bored or punched holes in wood or metal framing members, or notches in wooden members are considered supported, but the raceway must be secured within 3 ft of termination.

> **Author's Comment:**
> ▸ IMC must be provided with expansion fittings where necessary to compensate for thermal expansion and contraction [300.7(B)]. The expansion characteristics for metal raceways are determined by multiplying the values from Table 352.44 by 0.20, and those for aluminum raceways are determined by multiplying the values from Table 352.44 by 0.40 [300.7 Note].

342.42 Couplings and Connectors

(A) Installation. Threadless couplings and connectors must be made up tight to maintain an effective ground-fault current path to safely conduct fault current in accordance with 250.4(A)(5), 250.96(A), and 300.10.

> **Author's Comment:**
> ▸ Loose locknuts have been found to nearly disintegrate before a fault was cleared because loose termination fittings increase the impedance of the ground-fault current path.

If buried in masonry or concrete, threadless fittings must be of the concrete-tight type. Fittings installed in wet locations must be listed for use in wet locations to prevent moisture or water from entering or accumulating within the enclosure as required by 314.15. ▶Figure 342–9

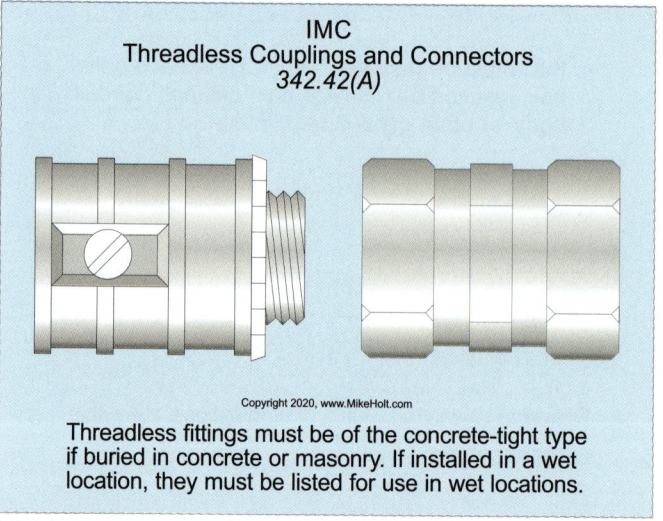
▶Figure 342–9

(B) Running Threads. Running threads are not permitted for the connection of couplings, but they are permitted at other locations. ▶Figure 342–10

342.46 Bushings

To protect conductors from abrasion, a metal or plastic bushing must be installed on conduit termination threads (regardless of conductor size) unless the box, fitting, or enclosure is designed to provide this protection.

Intermediate Metal Conduit (Type IMC) | 342.60

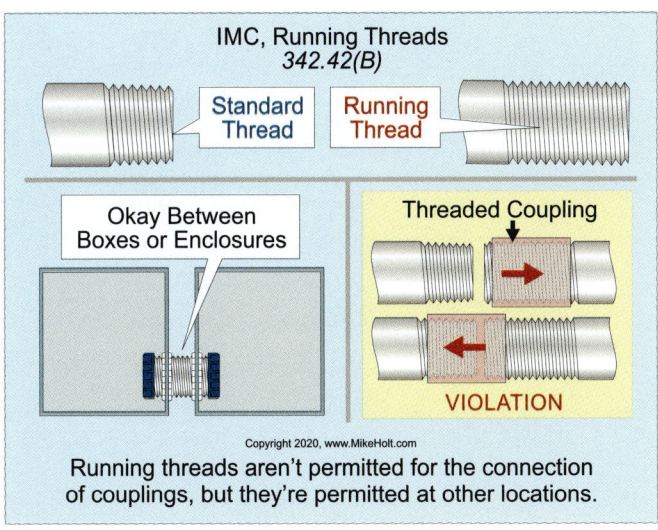
▶Figure 342–10

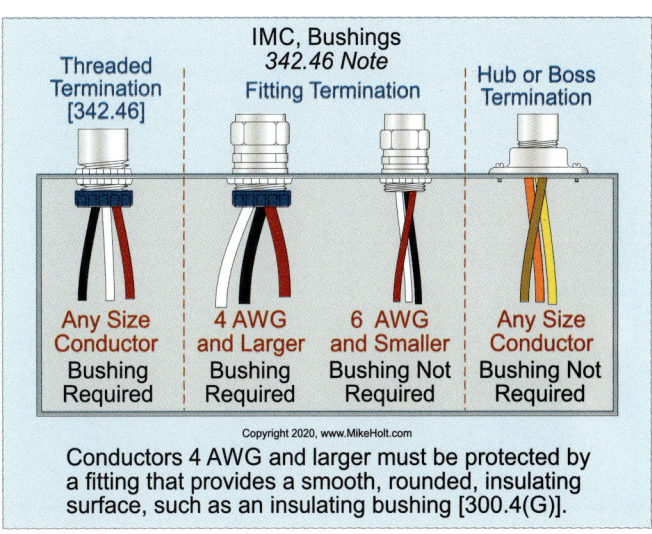
▶Figure 342–11

Author's Comment:

▸ According to UL 514B, section 5.4.1.1 reads: "Other than a coupling or a locknut, a conduit fitting shall be provided with a positive end stop for the conduit and a smooth rounded throat to protect against abrasion of insulation on conductors entering the conduit from the fitting from the conduit."

Note: Conductors 4 AWG and larger that enter an enclosure must be protected from abrasion, during and after installation, by a fitting that provides a smooth, rounded, insulating surface (such as an insulating bushing) unless the design of the box, fitting, or enclosure provides equivalent protection in accordance with 300.4(G). ▶Figure 342–11

342.60 Equipment Grounding Conductor

IMC can be used as an equipment grounding conductor.

Notes

ARTICLE 344 RIGID METAL CONDUIT (TYPE RMC)

Introduction to Article 344—Rigid Metal Conduit (Type RMC)

Rigid metal conduit (Type RMC), commonly called "rigid," has long been the standard raceway used to protect conductors from physical damage and from difficult environments. The outside diameter of rigid metal conduit is the same as intermediate metal conduit. However, the wall thickness is greater than IMC so the interior cross-sectional area is smaller. RMC is heavier and more expensive than intermediate metal conduit, and it can be used in any location. It is manufactured in both galvanized steel and aluminum; the steel type is much more common.

Part I. General

344.1 Scope

Article 344 covers the use, installation, and construction specifications of rigid metal conduit (Type RMC) and associated fittings. ▶Figure 344-1

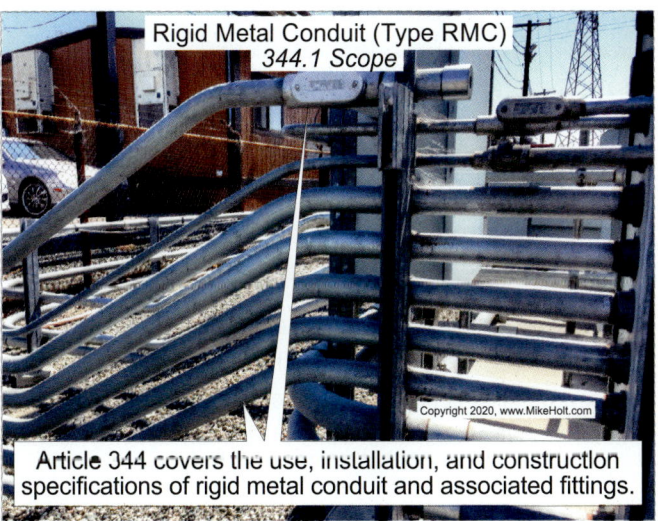
▶Figure 344-1

344.2 Definition

Rigid Metal Conduit (Type RMC). A listed metal raceway of circular cross section with integral or associated couplings listed for the installation of electrical conductors. ▶Figure 344-2

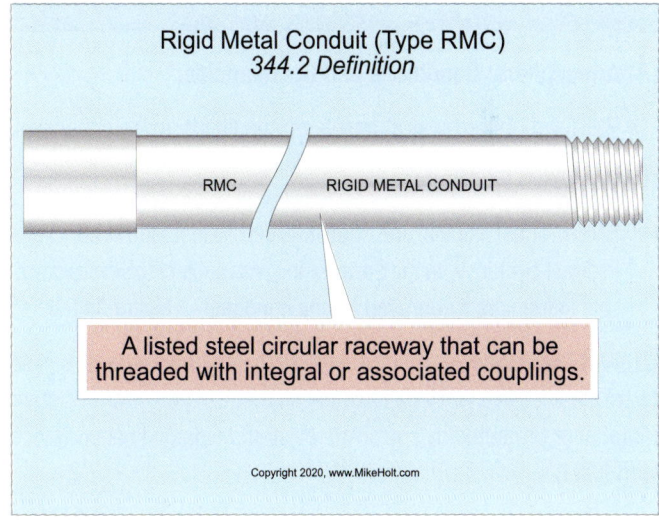
▶Figure 344-2

344.6 | Rigid Metal Conduit (Type RMC)

Author's Comment:

▸ When the mechanical and physical characteristics of rigid metal conduit are necessary, but the installation will be in an environment detrimental to the metal, a PVC-coated raceway system is commonly used. This variation of RMC is frequently used in the petrochemical industry. The common trade name of this coated raceway is "Plasti-Bond®," and is commonly referred to as "Rob Roy." The benefits of the improved corrosion protection can be achieved only when the system is properly installed. Joints must be sealed in accordance with the manufacturer's instructions and coated to prevent corrosion where damaged with tools such as benders, pliers, and pipe wrenches. Couplings are available with an extended skirt that can be properly sealed after installation.

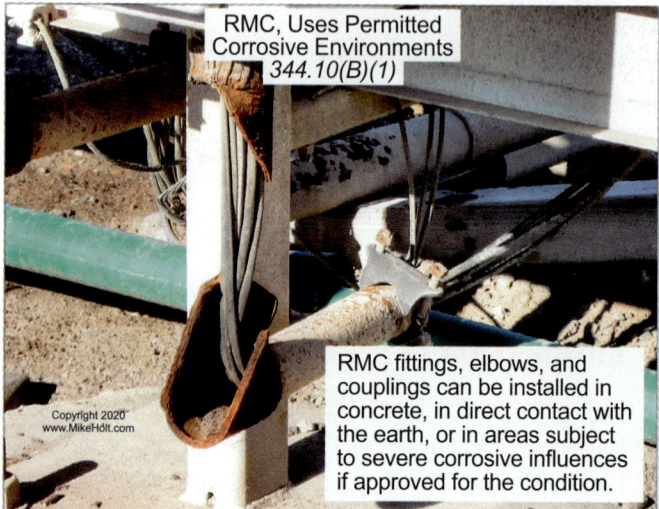

▸Figure 344–3

344.6 Listing Requirements

RMC and associated fittings must be listed.

Part II. Installation

344.10 Uses Permitted

(A) Atmospheric Conditions and Occupancies.

(1) RMC is permitted in all atmospheric conditions and occupancies.

(B) Corrosive Environments.

(1) RMC fittings, elbows, and couplings can be installed in concrete, in direct contact with the Earth, or in areas subject to severe corrosive influences if approved for the condition. ▸Figure 344–3

(D) Wet Locations. Support fittings (such as screws, straps, and so forth) installed in a wet location must be made of corrosion-resistant material or protected by corrosion-resistant coatings in accordance with 300.6.

(E) Severe Physical Damage. RMC is permitted where subject to severe physical damage.

344.14 Dissimilar Metals

If practical, contact of RMC with dissimilar metals should be avoided to prevent the deterioration of the metal because of galvanic action. Aluminum and stainless steel fittings and enclosures are permitted to be used with galvanized steel rigid metal conduit where not subject to severe corrosive influences.

344.20 Trade Size

(A) Minimum. RMC smaller than trade size ½ is not permitted.

(B) Maximum. RMC larger than trade size 6 is not permitted to be used.

344.22 Number of Conductors

For complete systems, the number of conductors in RMC is not permitted to exceed the percentage fill specified in Chapter 9, Table 1. Raceways must be large enough to permit the installation and removal of conductors without damaging the conductors' insulation.

Author's Comment:

▸ See 300.17 for examples on how to size raceways when conductors are not all the same size.

Rigid Metal Conduit (Type RMC) | **344.30**

344.24 Bends

Raceway bends are not permitted to be made in any manner that will damage the raceway or significantly change its internal diameter (no kinks). The radius of the curve of any field bend to the centerline of the conduit is not permitted to be less than indicated in Chapter 9, Table 2.

Author's Comment:

▸ This is not a problem if you use a bender in accordance with the manufacturer's instructions.

344.26 Number of Bends (360°)

To reduce stress and friction on conductor insulation, the total bends (including offsets) between pull points are not permitted to exceed 360°. ▸Figure 344–4 and ▸Figure 344–5

▸Figure 344–4

Author's Comment:

▸ There is no maximum distance between pull boxes because this is a design issue, not a safety issue.

344.28 Reaming

When the raceway is cut in the field, reaming is required to remove the burrs and rough edges.

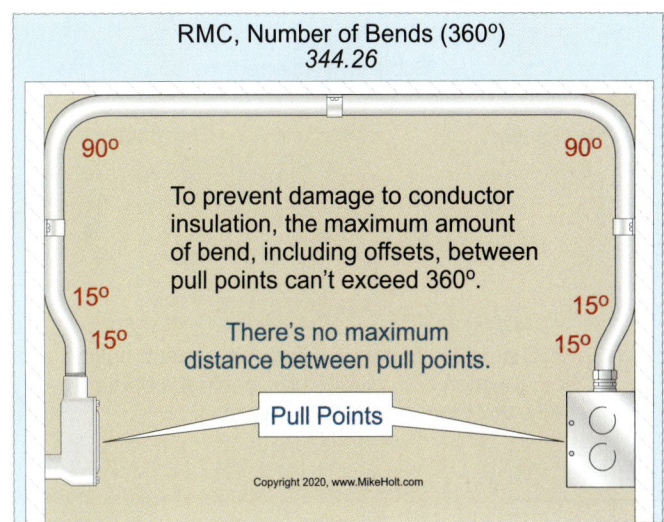

▸Figure 344–5

Author's Comment:

▸ It is a commonly accepted practice to ream small raceways with a screwdriver or the backside of pliers. However, when the raceway is cut with a three-wheel pipe cutter, a reaming tool is required to remove the sharp edge of the indented raceway. When conduit is threaded in the field, the threads must be coated with an electrically conductive, corrosion-resistant compound approved by the authority having jurisdiction in accordance with 300.6(A).

344.30 Securing and Supporting

RMC must be securely fastened in place and supported in accordance with (A) and (B).

(A) Securely Fastened. RMC must be secured in accordance with any of the following:

(1) Fastened within 3 ft of each outlet box, junction box, device box, cabinet, conduit body, or other conduit termination. ▸Figure 344–6

Author's Comment:

▸ Fastening is required within **3 ft** of terminations, not within **3 ft** of each coupling.

(2) When structural members do not permit the raceway to be secured within 3 ft of a box or termination fitting, the raceway must be secured within 5 ft of the termination. ▸Figure 344–7

344.30 | Rigid Metal Conduit (Type RMC)

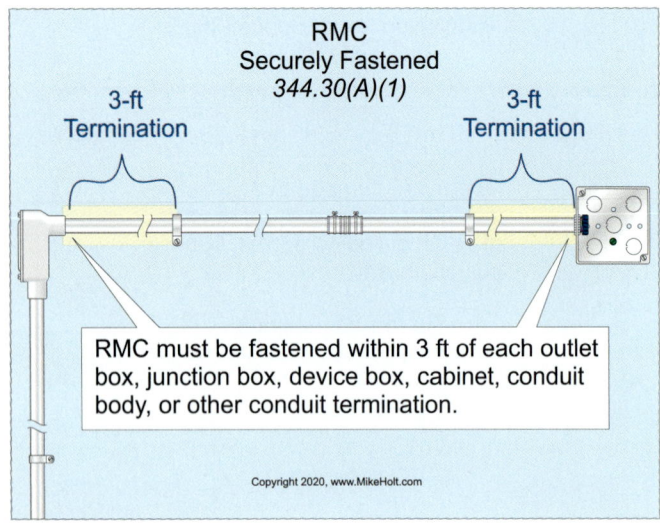

▶Figure 344-6

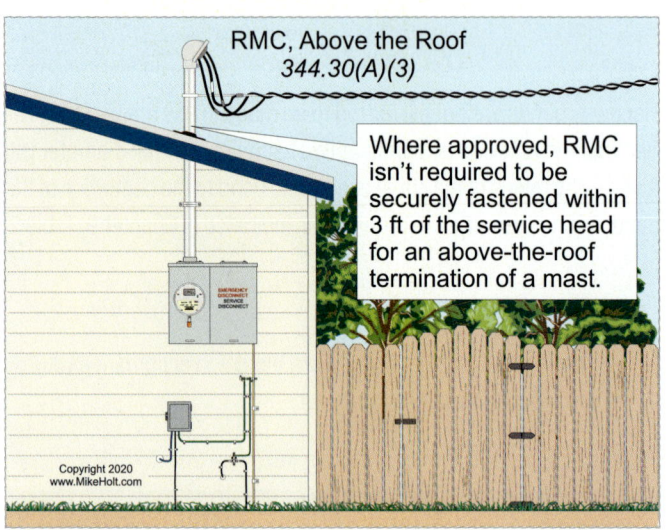

▶Figure 344-8

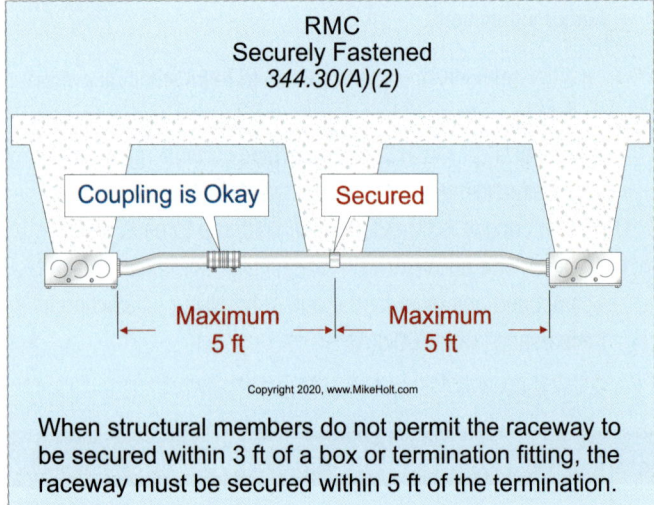

▶Figure 344-7

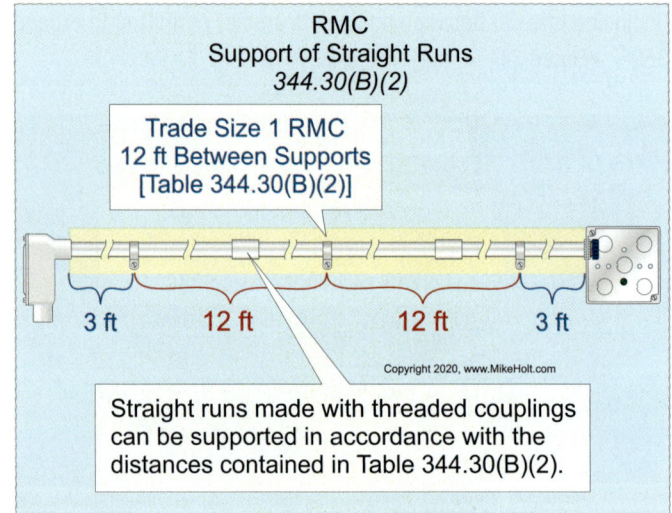

▶Figure 344-9

(3) Where approved, RMC is not required to be securely fastened within 3 ft of the service head for an above-the-roof termination of a mast. ▶Figure 344-8

(B) Supports.

(1) General. RMC must be supported at intervals not exceeding 10 ft.

(2) Straight Runs. Straight runs made with threaded couplings can be supported in accordance with the distances contained in Table 344.30(B)(2). ▶Figure 344-9

Table 344.30(B)(2) Supports for Rigid Metal Conduit

Trade Size	Support Spacing
½–¾	10 ft
1	12 ft
1¼–1½	14 ft
2–2½	16 ft
3 and larger	20 ft

Rigid Metal Conduit (Type RMC) | 344.42

(3) Vertical Risers. Exposed vertical risers for fixed equipment can be supported at intervals not exceeding 20 ft if the conduit is made up with threaded couplings, firmly supported, securely fastened at the top and bottom of the riser, and if no other means of support is available. ▶Figure 344-10

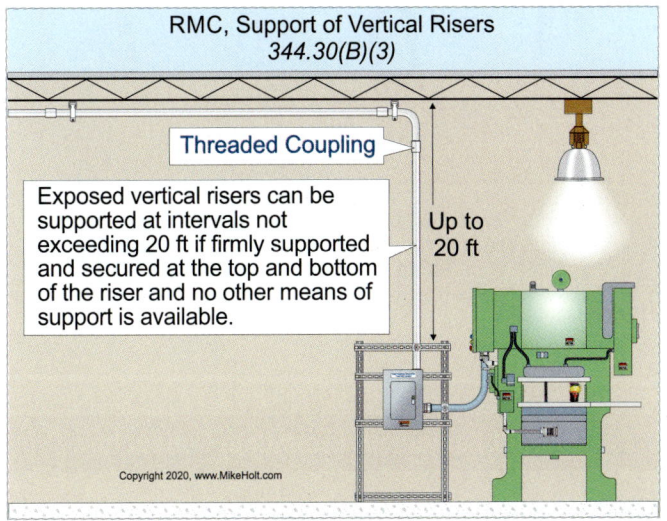

▶Figure 344-10

(4) Horizontal Runs. Conduits installed horizontally in bored or punched holes in wood or metal framing members, or notches in wooden members are considered supported, but the raceway must be secured within 3 ft of termination.

Author's Comment:

▸ RMC must be provided with expansion fittings where necessary to compensate for thermal expansion and contraction [300.7(B)]. The expansion characteristics for metal raceways are determined by multiplying the values from Table 352.44 by 0.20, and those for aluminum raceways are determined by multiplying the values from Table 352.44 by 0.40 [300.7 Note].

344.42 Couplings and Connectors

(A) Installation. Threadless couplings and connectors must be made up tight to maintain an effective ground-fault current path to safely conduct fault current in accordance with 250.4(A)(5), 250.96(A), and 300.10.

Author's Comment:

▸ Loose locknuts have been found to burn away before a fault was cleared because loose connections increase the impedance of the ground-fault current path.

If buried in masonry or concrete, threadless fittings must be of the concrete-tight type. ▶Figure 344-11

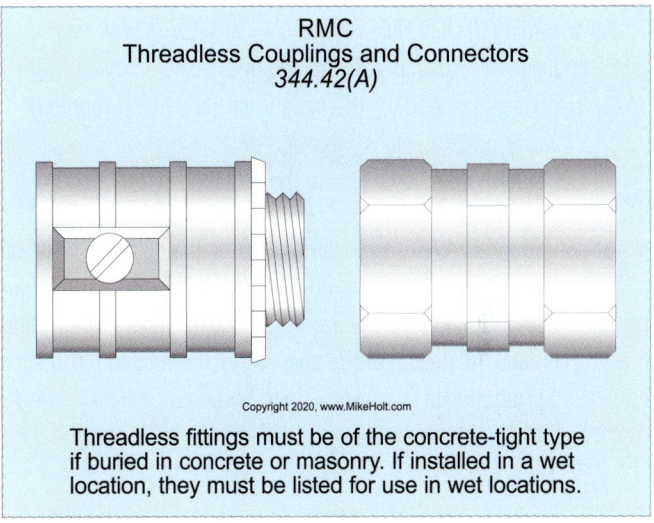

▶Figure 344-11

If installed in wet locations, fittings must be listed for use in wet locations and prevent moisture or water from entering or accumulating within the enclosure in accordance with 314.15.

(B) Running Threads. Running threads are not permitted for the connection of couplings, but they are permitted at other locations. ▶Figure 344-12

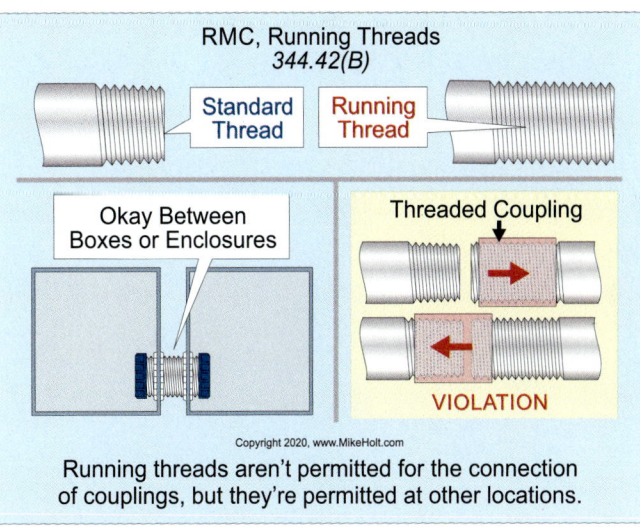

▶Figure 344-12

344.46 | Rigid Metal Conduit (Type RMC)

344.46 Bushings

To protect conductors from abrasion, a metal or plastic bushing must be installed on conduit threads at terminations (regardless of conductor size) unless the box, fitting, or enclosure is designed to provide this protection.

Author's Comment:

▸ According to UL 514B, section 5.4.1.1 reads: "Other than a coupling or a locknut, a conduit fitting shall be provided with a positive end stop for the conduit and a smooth rounded throat to protect against abrasion of insulation on conductors entering the conduit from the fitting from the conduit."

Note: Conductors 4 AWG and larger that enter an enclosure must be protected from abrasion, during and after installation, by a fitting that provides a smooth, rounded, insulating surface (such as an insulating bushing) unless the design of the box, fitting, or enclosure provides equivalent protection in accordance with 300.4(G). ▸Figure 344–13

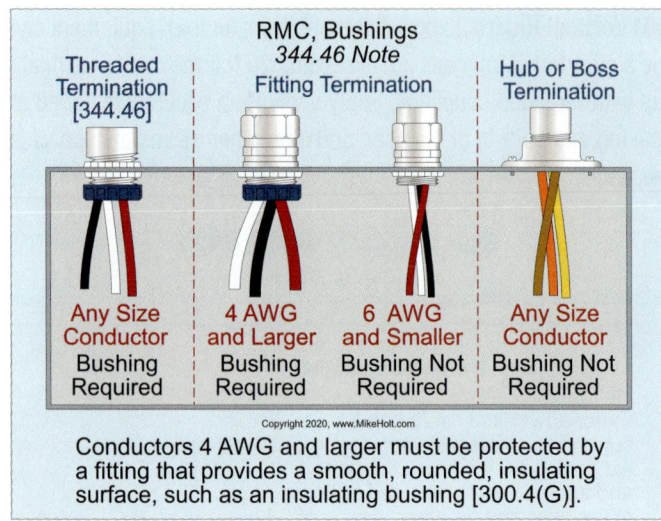

▸Figure 344–13

344.60 Equipment Grounding Conductor

RMC can be used as an equipment grounding conductor.

ARTICLE 348 — FLEXIBLE METAL CONDUIT (TYPE FMC)

Introduction to Article 348—Flexible Metal Conduit (Type FMC)

Flexible metal conduit (Type FMC), commonly called "Greenfield" (after its inventor) or "flex," is an interlocked metal strip type of raceway made of either steel or aluminum. It is primarily used where flexibility is necessary or where equipment moves, shakes, or vibrates.

Part I. General

348.1 Scope

Article 348 covers the use, installation, and construction specifications for flexible metal conduit (FMC) and associated fittings. ▶Figure 348–1

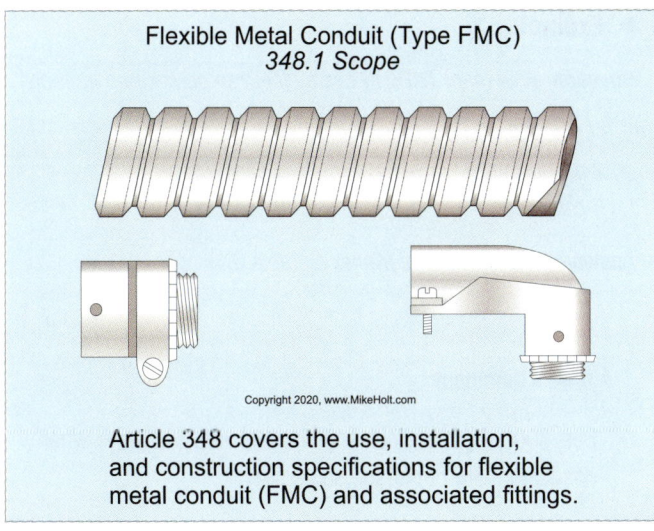

▶Figure 348–1

348.2 Definition

Flexible Metal Conduit (Type FMC). A raceway of circular cross section made of a helically wound, formed, interlocked metal strip, listed for the installation of electrical conductors. ▶Figure 348–2

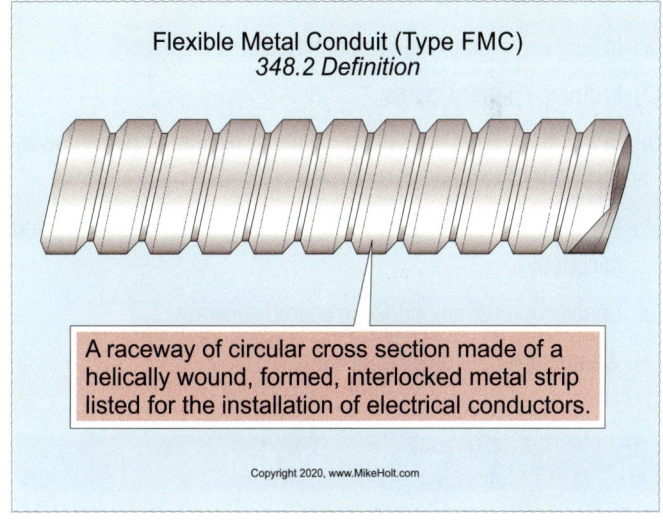

▶Figure 348–2

348.6 Listing Requirements

Flexible metal conduit and associated fittings must be listed.

Part II. Installation

348.10 Uses Permitted

FMC is permitted to be installed exposed or concealed.

348.12 Uses Not Permitted

FMC is not permitted:

(1) In wet locations. ▶Figure 348–3

348.20 | Flexible Metal Conduit (Type FMC)

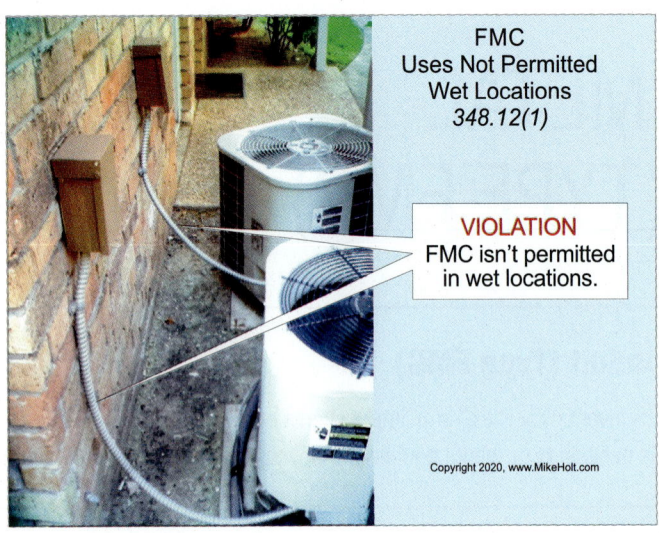
▶Figure 348–3

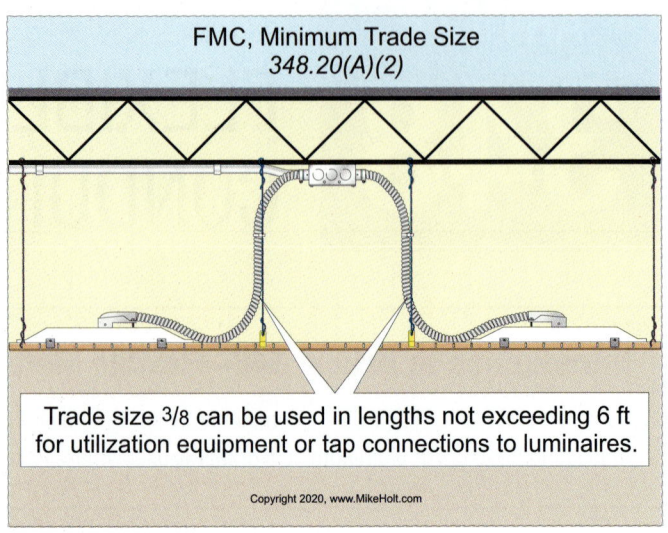
▶Figure 348–4

(2) In hoistways, other than as permitted in 620.21(A)(1).

(3) In storage battery rooms.

(4) In any hazardous (classified) location, except as permitted by 501.10(B).

(5) Exposed to material having a deteriorating effect on the installed conductors.

(6) Underground or embedded in poured concrete.

(7) Where subject to physical damage.

348.20 Trade Size

(A) Minimum. Trade size ½, except trade size ⅜ is permitted for the following applications:

(1) For enclosing the leads of motors.

(2) Not exceeding 6 ft in length: ▶Figure 348–4

  a. For utilization equipment,

  b. As part of a listed assembly, or

  c. For luminaire tap connections in accordance with 410.117(C).

(B) Maximum. Trade size 4.

348.22 Number of Conductors

FMC trade size ½ in. and larger must be large enough to permit the installation and removal of conductors without damaging the conductors' insulation. When all conductors within a raceway are the same size and insulation, the number of conductors permitted can be found in Annex C for the raceway type.

The number of conductors in FMC is not permitted to exceed the percentage fill specified in Chapter 9, Table 1. Raceways must be large enough to permit the installation and removal of conductors without damaging the conductor insulation.

▶ **Example**

Question: How many 6 THHN conductors can be installed in trade size 1 FMC?

(a) 2 conductors   (b) 4 conductors
(c) 6 conductors   (d) 8 conductors

Answer: (c) 6 conductors [Annex C, Table C.3]

Author's Comment:

▸ See 300.17 for examples on how to size raceways when conductors are not all the same size.

Trade Size ⅜. The number and size of conductors in ⅜ FMC must comply with Table 348.22.

▶ **Example**

Question: How many 12 THHN conductors can be installed in trade size ⅜ Type FMC that uses outside fittings?

(a) 2 conductors   (b) 3 conductors
(c) 4 conductors   (d) 5 conductors

Solution:

One insulated, covered, or bare equipment grounding conductor of the same size is permitted with the circuit conductors. See the "" note at the bottom of Table 348.22.*

Answer: *(b) 3 conductors [Table 348.22]*

Cables can be installed in FMC if the total area of cables does not exceed the allowable percentage fill specified in Chapter 9, Table 1.

348.24 Bends

Bends must be made so the conduit will not be damaged, and its internal diameter will not be effectively reduced. The radius of the curve of the inner edge of any field bend is not permitted to be less than shown in Chapter 9, Table 2 using the column "Other Bends."

348.26 Number of Bends (360°)

To reduce the stress and friction on conductor insulation, the total bends (including offsets) between pull points are not permitted to exceed 360°.

348.28 Trimming

The cut ends of FMC must be trimmed to remove the rough edges but is not necessary if fittings are threaded into the convolutions.

348.30 Securing and Supporting

(A) Securely Fastened. FMC must be securely fastened by a means approved by the authority having jurisdiction within 1 ft of termination, and it must be secured and supported at intervals not exceeding 4½ ft. ▶Figure 348-5

Where cable ties are to be used to secure and support Type FMC, they must be listed and identified for securing and supporting.

Ex 1: Type FMC is not required to be securely fastened or supported where fished between access points through concealed spaces and supporting is impractical.

Ex 2: If flexibility is necessary after installation, unsecured lengths from the last point the raceway is securely fastened are not permitted to exceed: ▶Figure 348-6

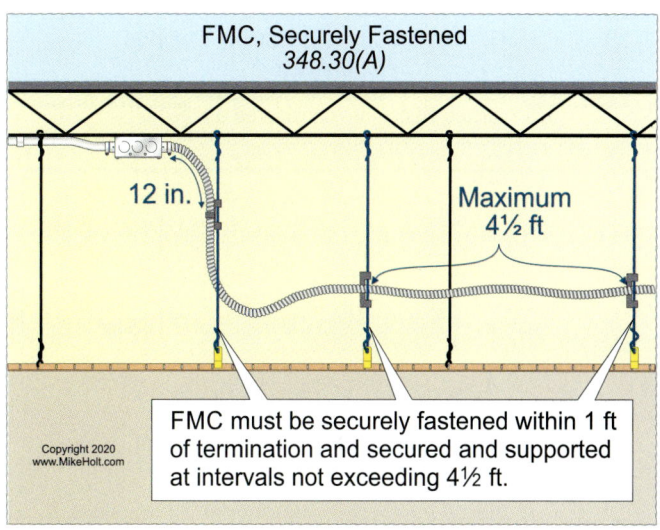
▶Figure 348-5

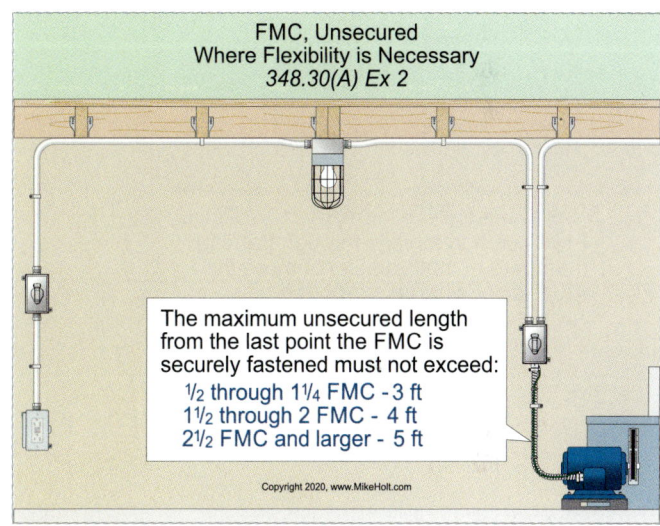
▶Figure 348-6

(1) 3 ft for trade sizes ½ through 1¼

(2) 4 ft for trade sizes 1½ through 2

(3) 5 ft for trade sizes 2½ and larger

Ex 4: Lengths not exceeding 6 ft from the last point where the raceway is securely fastened can be unsecured within an accessible ceiling for a luminaire(s) or other equipment. Listed fittings are considered a means of securement and support. ▶Figure 348-7

(B) Horizontal Runs. FMC installed horizontally in bored or punched holes in wood or metal framing members, or notches in wooden members, at intervals not more than 4½ ft is considered supported, but the raceway must be secured within 1 ft of terminations. ▶Figure 348-8

348.60 | Flexible Metal Conduit (Type FMC)

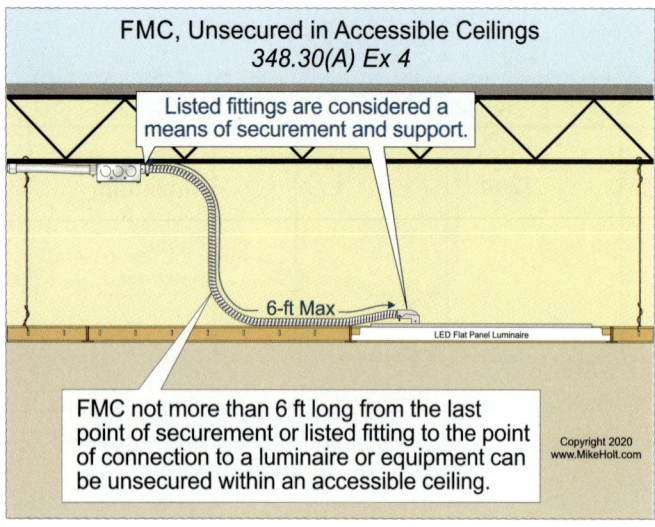
▶Figure 348-7

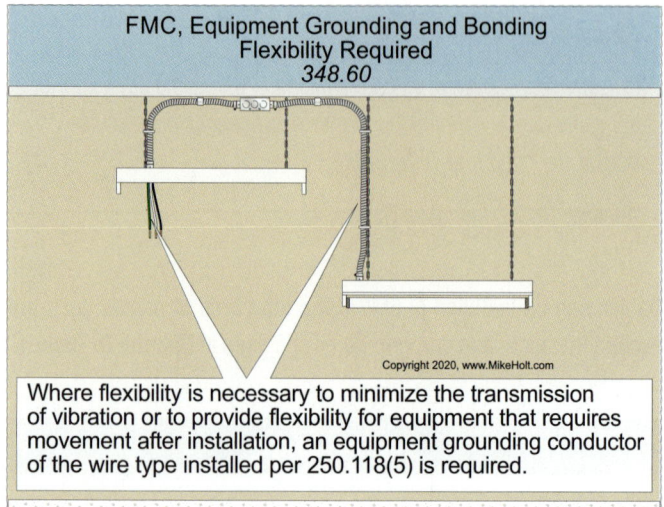
▶Figure 348-9

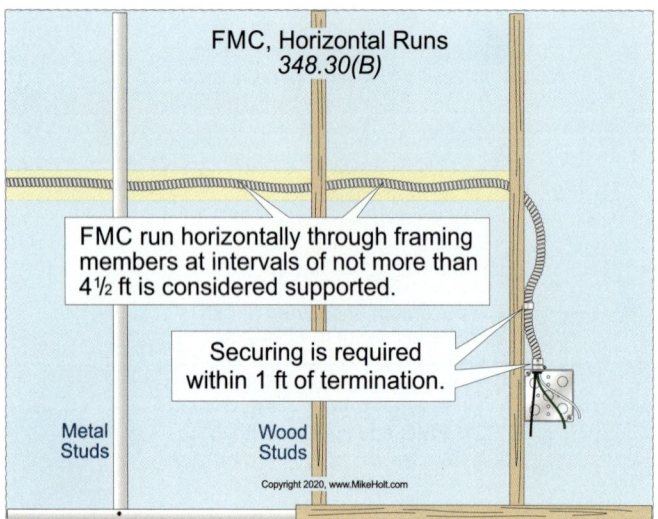
▶Figure 348-8

If flexibility is not necessary after installation, and vibration is not a concern, the metal armor of FMC can serve as an equipment grounding conductor if the circuit conductors contained in the raceway are protected by an overcurrent protective device rated 20A or less, and the combined length of the raceway in the same ground-fault return path does not exceed 6 ft [250.118(5)]. ▶Figure 348-10

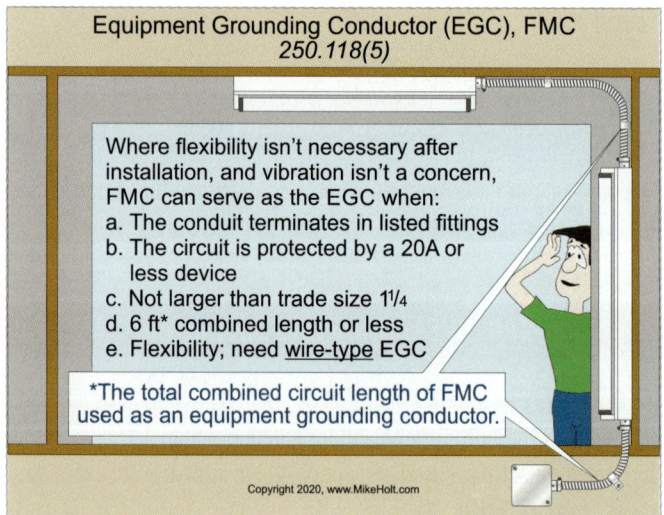
▶Figure 348-10

348.60 Equipment Grounding and Bonding Conductors

If flexibility is necessary to minimize the transmission of vibration from equipment, or to provide flexibility for equipment that requires movement after installation, an equipment grounding conductor of the wire type must be installed with the circuit conductors in accordance with 250.118(5). ▶Figure 348-9

The equipment bonding jumper can be installed inside or outside the flexible metal conduit. Where installed outside the FMC, the length of the equipment bonding jumper is not permitted to exceed 6 ft and it must be routed with the flexible metal conduit in accordance with 250.102(E)(2).

ARTICLE 350 LIQUIDTIGHT FLEXIBLE METAL CONDUIT (TYPE LFMC)

Introduction to Article 350—Liquidtight Flexible Metal Conduit (Type LFMC)

Liquidtight flexible metal conduit (Type LFMC), with its associated connectors and fittings, is a flexible raceway commonly used for connections to equipment that vibrates or must be occasionally moved. Liquidtight flexible metal conduit is commonly called "Sealtite®" or "liquidtight." It is similar in construction to flexible metal conduit, but it has an outer liquidtight thermoplastic covering. LFMC has the same primary purpose as flexible metal conduit, but also provides protection from liquids and some corrosive effects.

Part I. General

350.1 Scope

Article 350 covers the use, installation, and construction specifications of liquidtight flexible metal conduit (Type LFMC) and associated fittings. ▶Figure 350–1

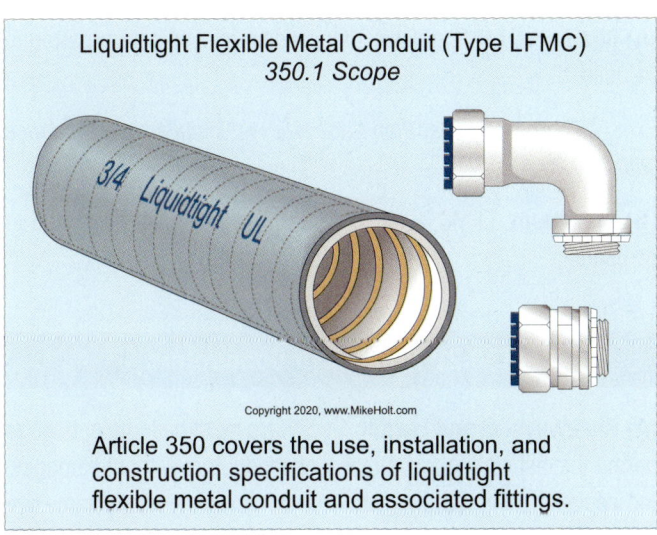

▶Figure 350–1

▶Figure 350–2

350.6 Listing Requirements

LFMC and its associated fittings must be listed.

Part II. Installation

350.10 Uses Permitted

Listed LFMC is permitted, either exposed or concealed, at any of the following locations: ▶Figure 350–3

350.2 Definition

Liquidtight Flexible Metal Conduit (Type LFMC). A raceway of circular cross section, having an outer liquidtight, nonmetallic, sunlight-resistant jacket over an inner flexible metal core, with associated connectors and fittings, listed for the installation of electrical conductors. ▶Figure 350–2

350.12 | Liquidtight Flexible Metal Conduit (Type LFMC)

▶Figure 350–3

(1) If flexibility or protection from machine oils, liquids, vapors, or solids is required.

(2) In hazardous (classified) locations as permitted in Chapter 5.

(3) For direct burial if listed and marked for this purpose. ▶Figure 350–4

▶Figure 350–4

(4) Conductors or cables rated at a temperature higher than the listed temperature rating of LFMC conduit may be installed in LFMC, provided the conductors or cables are not operated at a temperature higher than the listed temperature rating of the LFMC per 110.14(C).

350.12 Uses Not Permitted

LFMC must not be used where subject to physical damage. ▶Figure 350–5

▶Figure 350–5

350.20 Trade Size

(A) Minimum. LFMC smaller than trade size ½ is not permitted to be used.

Ex: LFMC can be smaller than trade size ½ if installed in accordance with 348.20(A).

(B) Maximum. LFMC larger than trade size 4 is not permitted to be used.

350.22 Number of Conductors

(A) Raceways ½ and Larger. Raceways must be large enough to permit the installation and removal of conductors without damaging the insulation. When all conductors within a raceway are the same size and insulation, the number of conductors permitted can be found in Annex C for the raceway type. The number of cables must not exceed the allowable percentage fill specified in Chapter 9, Table 1.

Liquidtight Flexible Metal Conduit (Type LFMC) | 350.30

▶ **Example**

Question: How many 6 THHN conductors can be installed in trade size 1 LFMC? ▶Figure 350–6

(a) 2 conductors (b) 4 conductors
(c) 6 conductors (d) 7 conductors

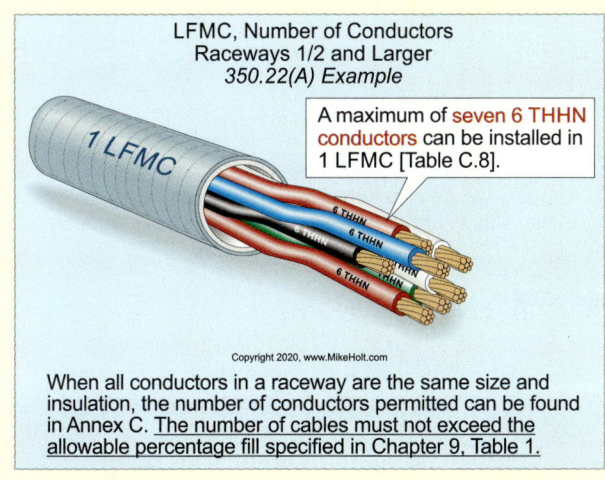

▶Figure 350–6

Answer: (d) 7 conductors [Annex C, Table C.8]

Author's Comment:

▸ See 300.17 for examples on how to size raceways when conductors are not all the same size.

Cables can be installed in LFMC if the number of cables does not exceed the allowable percentage fill specified in Chapter 9, Table 1.

(B) Raceways Trade Size ⅜. The number and size of conductors in trade size ⅜ LFMC must comply with Table 348.22.

▶ **Example**

Question: How many 12 THHN conductors can be installed in trade size ⅜ LFMC that uses outside fittings?

(a) 2 conductors (b) 3 conductors
(c) 4 conductors (d) 5 conductors

Solution:

One insulated, covered, or bare equipment grounding conductor of the same size is permitted with the circuit conductors. See the "*" note at the bottom of Table 348.22.

Answer: (b) 3 conductors [Table 348.22]

350.24 Bends

Bends must be made so the conduit will not be damaged, and the internal diameter will not be effectively reduced.

350.26 Number of Bends (360°)

To reduce the stress and friction on conductor insulation, the total bends (including offsets) between pull points are not permitted to exceed 360°.

350.28 Trimming

Cut ends of LFMC must be trimmed both inside and outside the raceway to remove rough edges.

350.30 Securing and Supporting

LFMC must be securely fastened in place and supported in accordance with (A) and (B).

(A) Securely Fastened. LFMC must be securely fastened by a means approved by the authority having jurisdiction within 1 ft of termination and must be secured and supported at intervals not exceeding 4½ ft. ▶Figure 350–7

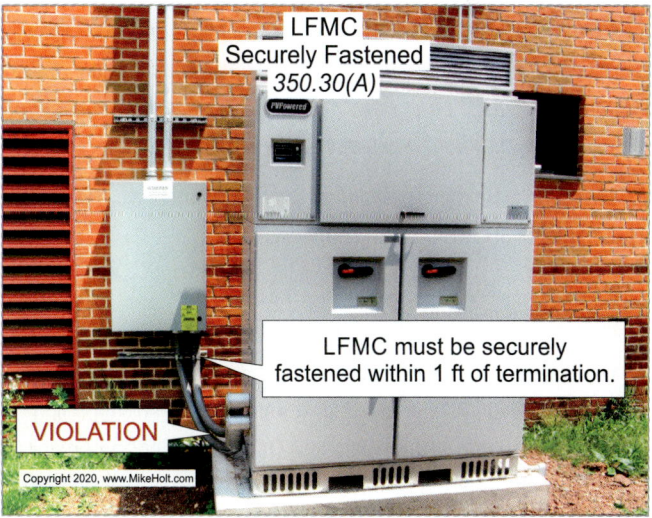

▶Figure 350–7

Where cable ties are used for securing LFMC they must be listed and identified for securement and support.

350.60 | Liquidtight Flexible Metal Conduit (Type LFMC)

Ex 1: LFMC is not required to be securely fastened or supported where fished between access points through concealed spaces and supporting is impractical.

Ex 2: If flexibility is necessary after installation, unsecured lengths from the last point where the raceway is securely fastened are not permitted to exceed: ▶Figure 350-8

(1) 3 ft for trade sizes ½ through 1¼

(2) 4 ft for trade sizes 1½ through 2

(3) 5 ft for trade sizes 2½ and larger

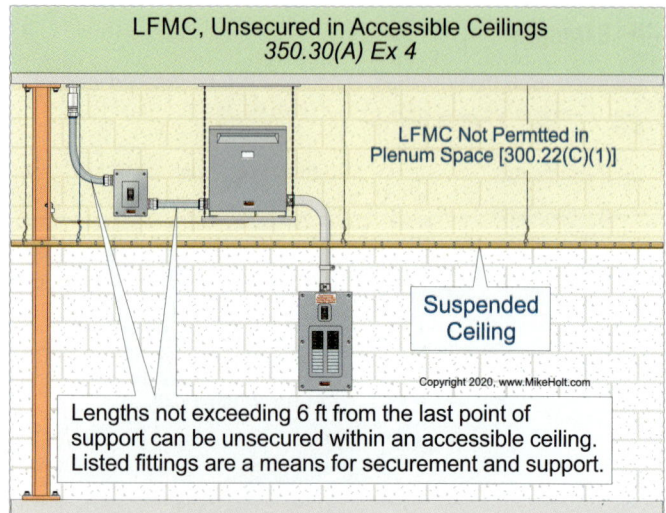

▶Figure 350-9

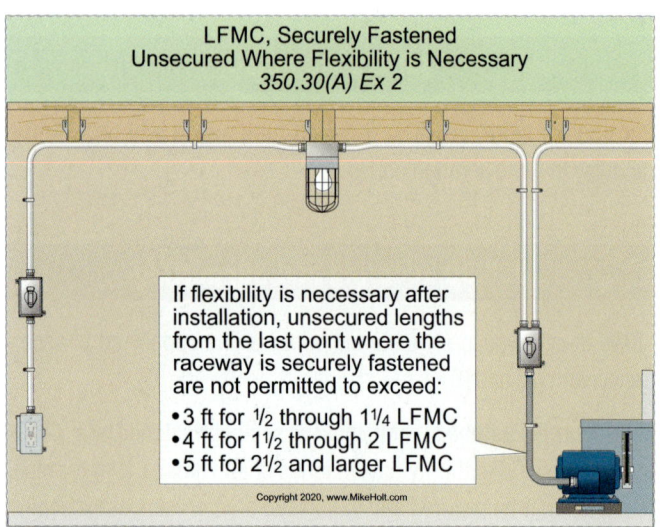

▶Figure 350-8

Ex 4: Lengths not exceeding 6 ft from the last point where the raceway is securely fastened can be unsecured within an accessible ceiling for a luminaire(s) or other equipment. Listed fittings are considered a means of securement and support. ▶Figure 350-9

For the purposes of these exceptions, listed LFMC fittings are permitted as a means of securement and support.

> **Author's Comment:**
>
> ▶ This last sentence following the four exceptions means that the use of LFMC fittings as the means of securing and supporting only applies to installations made using one of the four exceptions. It should not be interpreted as permission to use these fittings to secure and support LFMC in all applications.

(B) Horizontal Runs. LFMC installed horizontally in bored or punched holes in wood or metal framing members, or notches in wooden members, is considered supported, but the raceway must be secured within 1 ft of termination.

350.60 Equipment Grounding and Bonding Conductors

If flexibility is necessary to minimize the transmission of vibration from equipment, or to provide flexibility for equipment that requires movement after installation, an equipment grounding conductor of the wire type must be installed with the circuit conductors in accordance with 250.118(6). ▶Figure 350-10

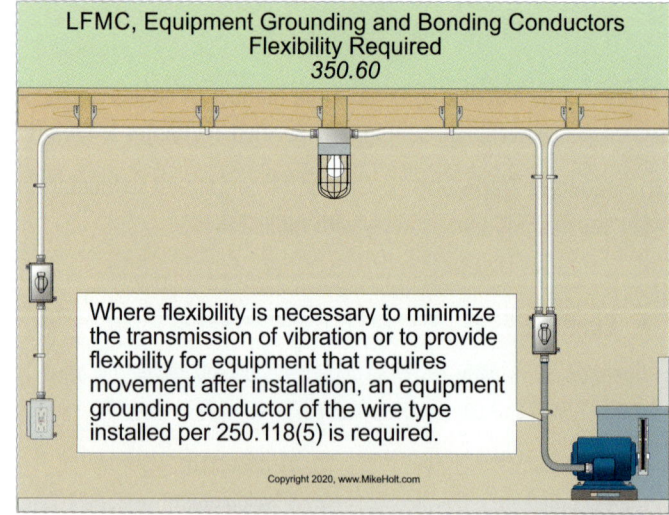

▶Figure 350-10

If flexibility is not necessary after installation, and vibration is not a concern, the metal armor of liquidtight flexible metal conduit can serve as an equipment grounding conductor if the circuit conductors contained in the raceway are protected by an overcurrent protective device rated 20A or less, and the combined length of the raceway in the same ground-fault return path does not exceed 6 ft in accordance with 250.118(6). ▶Figure 350–11

The equipment bonding jumper can be installed inside or outside the liquidtight flexible metal conduit. Where the bonding jumper is installed outside the LFMC, the length of the equipment bonding jumper cannot exceed 6 ft, and it must be routed with the liquidtight flexible metal conduit in accordance with 250.102(E)(2). ▶Figure 350-12

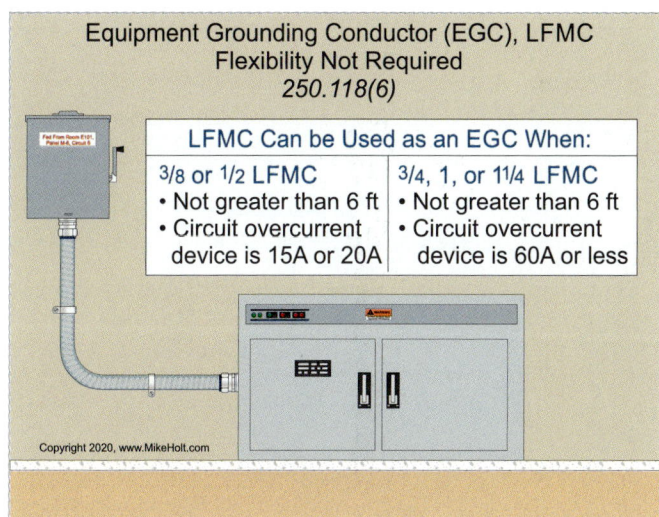

▶Figure 350–11

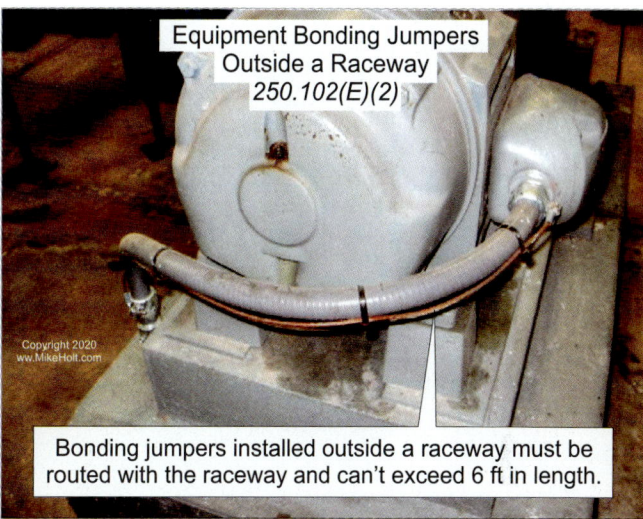

▶Figure 350-12

Notes

ARTICLE 352 — RIGID POLYVINYL CHLORIDE CONDUIT (TYPE PVC)

Introduction to Article 352—Rigid Polyvinyl Chloride Conduit (Type PVC)

Rigid polyvinyl chloride conduit (Type PVC) is a rigid nonmetallic conduit that provides many of the advantages of rigid metal conduit, while allowing installation in wet or corrosive areas. It is an inexpensive raceway and easily installed, lightweight, easily cut and glued together, and relatively strong. However, rigid polyvinyl chloride (PVC) is brittle when cold and will sag when hot. This type of conduit is commonly used as an underground raceway because of its low cost, ease of installation, and resistance to corrosion and decay.

Part I. General

352.1 Scope

Article 352 covers the use, installation, and construction specifications of polyvinyl chloride conduit (Type PVC) and associated fittings. ▶Figure 352–1

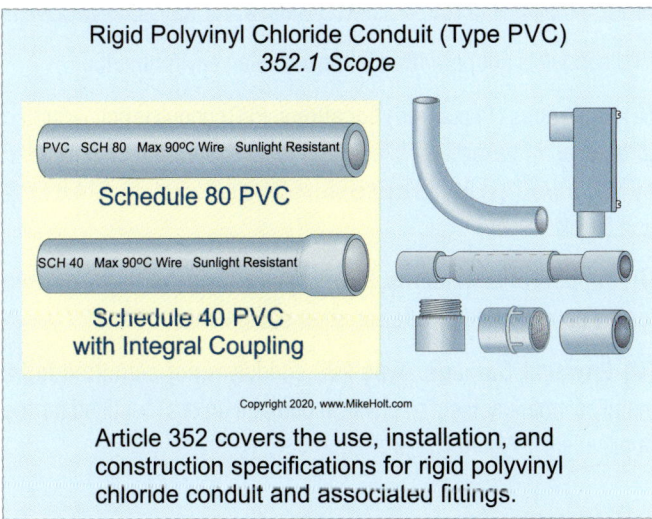

▶Figure 352–1

352.2 Definition

Rigid Polyvinyl Chloride Conduit (Type PVC). A rigid nonmetallic raceway of circular cross section with integral or associated couplings, listed for the installation of electrical conductors. ▶Figure 352–2

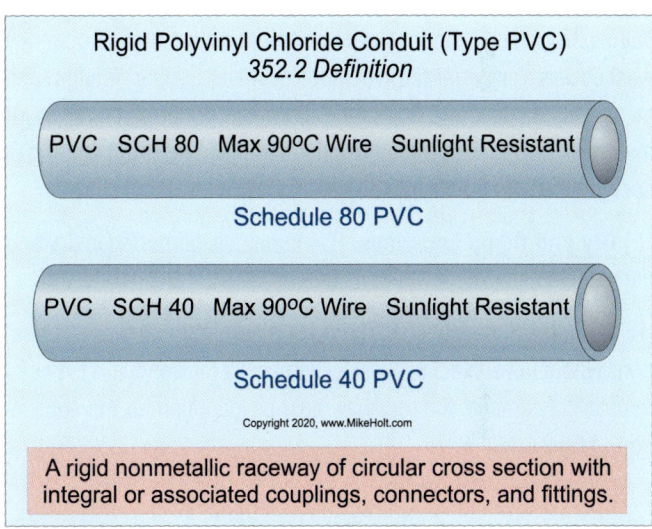

▶Figure 352–2

Part II. Installation

352.10 Uses Permitted

Type PVC conduit is permitted in the following applications:

Note: In extreme cold, PVC conduit can become brittle and is more susceptible to physical damage.

(A) Concealed. PVC conduit can be concealed within walls, floors, or ceilings. ▶Figure 352–3

(B) Corrosive Influences. PVC conduit is permitted in areas subject to severe corrosion for which the material is specifically approved by the authority having jurisdiction.

352.12 | Rigid Polyvinyl Chloride Conduit (Type PVC)

▶Figure 352–3

(D) Wet Locations. PVC conduit is permitted in wet locations such as dairies, laundries, canneries, car washes, and other areas frequently washed. It is also permitted in outdoor locations. Support fittings such as straps, screws, and bolts must be made of corrosion-resistant materials or must be protected with a corrosion-resistant coating in accordance with 300.6(A).

(E) Dry and Damp Locations. PVC conduit is permitted in dry and damp locations except where limited in 352.12.

(F) Exposed. Schedule 40 PVC conduit is permitted for exposed locations where not subject to physical damage. If the conduit is exposed to physical damage, the raceway must be identified for the application. ▶Figure 352–4

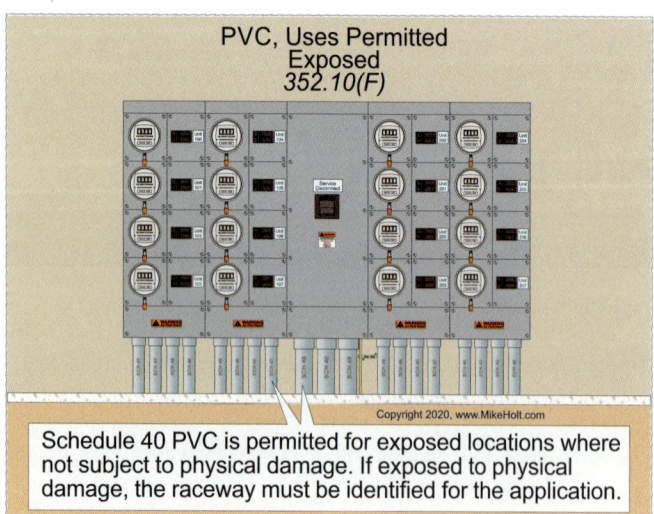

▶Figure 352–4

Note: PVC Schedule 80 conduit is identified for use in areas subject to physical damage. ▶Figure 352–5

▶Figure 352–5

(G) Underground. PVC conduit is permitted to be installed underground and in concrete and must comply with the burial requirements of 300.5.

352.12 Uses Not Permitted

PVC conduit is not permitted in the following environments:

(A) Hazardous (Classified) Locations. PVC conduit is not permitted to be used in hazardous (classified) locations except as permitted by 501.10(A)(1)(1) Ex, 501.10(B)(6), 503.10(A), 504.20, 514.8 Ex 2, and 515.8.

(B) Support of Luminaires. PVC conduit is not permitted to be used for the support of luminaires or other equipment.

(C) Physical Damage. Type PVC conduit is not permitted to be installed where subject to physical damage unless identified for the application. ▶Figure 352–6

> **Author's Comment:**
> ▸ PVC Schedule 40 conduit is not identified for use where subject to physical damage, but PVC Schedule 80 conduit is [352.10(F) Note].

(D) Ambient Temperature. PVC conduit is not permitted to be installed if the ambient temperature exceeds 50°C (122°F).

Rigid Polyvinyl Chloride Conduit (Type PVC) | 352.22

▶Figure 352–6

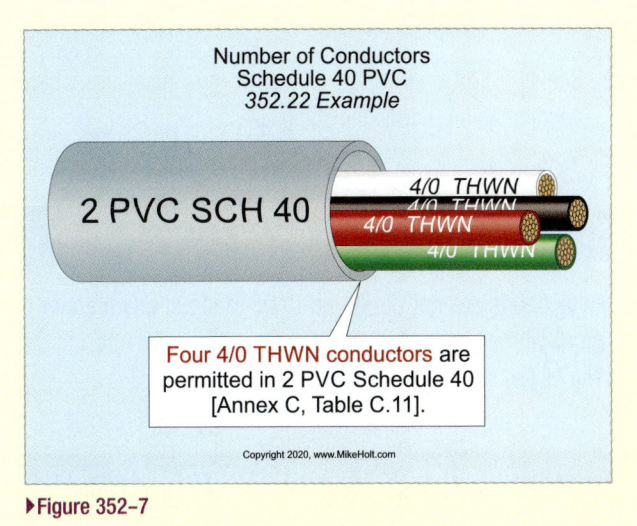
▶Figure 352–7

Author's Comment:

▸ PVC conduit and fittings are not permitted to be installed in environmental air spaces (plenums) [300.22(C)].

Author's Comment:

▸ Schedule 80 PVC conduit has the same outside diameter as Schedule 40, but the wall thickness is greater which results in a reduced interior area for conductor fill.

352.20 Trade Size

(A) Minimum. PVC conduit smaller than trade size ½ is not permitted to be used.

(B) Maximum. PVC conduit larger than trade size 6 is not permitted to be used.

▶ Example

Question: How many 4/0 THWN conductors can be installed in trade size 2 Schedule 80 PVC conduit? ▶Figure 352–8

(a) 2 conductors (b) 3 conductors
(c) 4 conductors (d) 5 conductors

352.22 Number of Conductors

Raceways must be large enough to permit the installation and removal of conductors without damaging the conductors' insulation, and the number of conductors is not permitted to exceed the percentage fill specified in Chapter 9, Table 1.

When all conductors within a raceway are the same size and insulation, the number of conductors permitted can be found in Annex C for the raceway type.

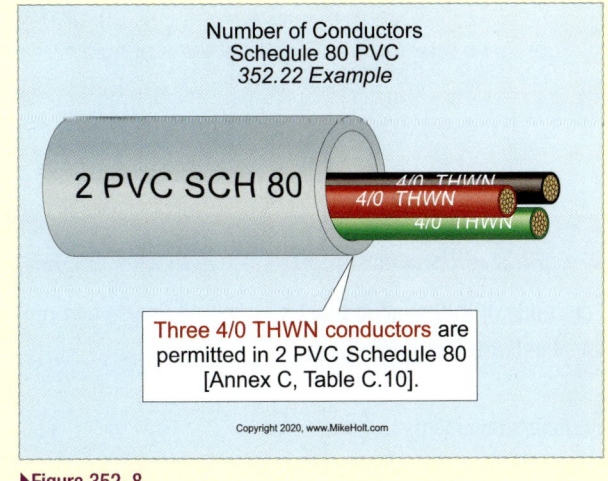
▶Figure 352–8

Answer: (b) 3 conductors [Annex C, Table C.10]

▶ Example

Question: How many 4/0 THWN conductors can be installed in trade size 2 Schedule 40 PVC conduit? ▶Figure 352–7

(a) 2 conductors (b) 4 conductors
(c) 6 conductors (d) 8 conductors

Answer: (b) 4 conductors [Annex C, Table C.11]

352.24 | Rigid Polyvinyl Chloride Conduit (Type PVC)

Author's Comment:

▸ See 300.17 for examples on how to size raceways when conductors are not all the same size.

352.24 Bends

Raceway bends are not permitted to be made in any manner that will damage the raceway or significantly change its internal diameter (no kinks).

352.26 Number of Bends (360°)

To reduce the stress and friction on conductor insulation, the total bends (including offsets) between pull points are not permitted to exceed 360°. ▸Figure 352–9

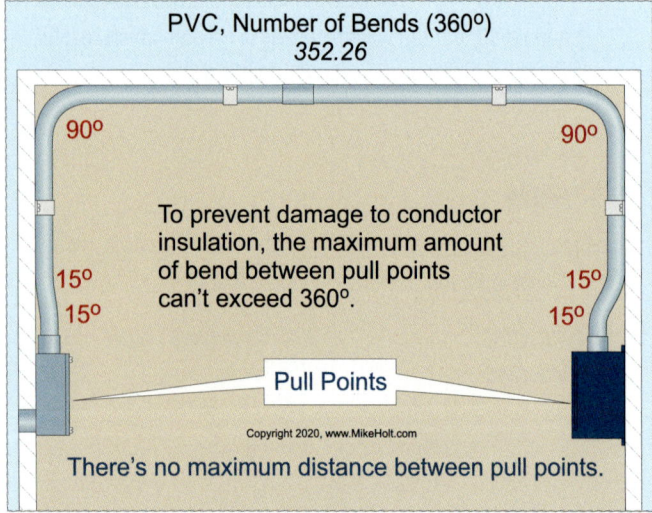

▸Figure 352–9

352.28 Trimming

The cut ends of PVC conduit must be trimmed (inside and out) to remove the burrs and rough edges.

Author's Comment:

▸ Trimming PVC conduit is very easy; most of the burrs will rub off with your fingers, and a knife will smooth the rough edges.

352.30 Securing and Supporting

PVC conduit must be fastened and supported in accordance with (A) and (B) so movement from thermal expansion and contraction is permitted.

(A) Securely Fastened. PVC conduit must be secured within 3 ft of every box, cabinet, or termination fitting, such as a conduit body. ▸Figure 352–10

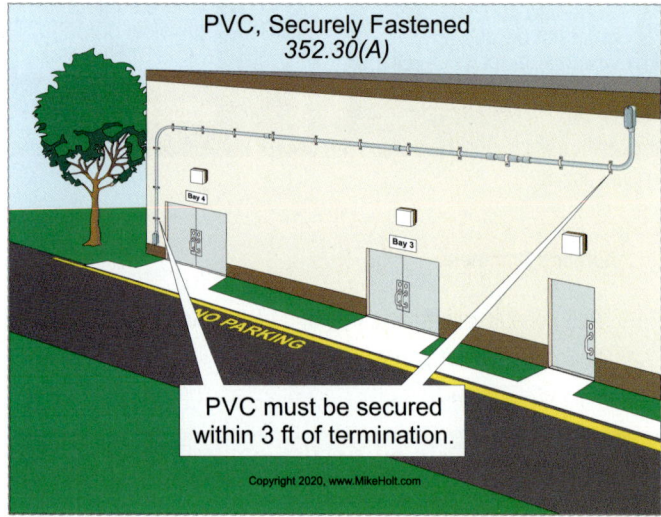

▸Figure 352–10

(B) Supports. PVC conduit must be supported at intervals not exceeding the values in Table 352.30, and the raceway must be fastened in a manner that permits movement from thermal expansion or contraction. ▸Figure 352–11

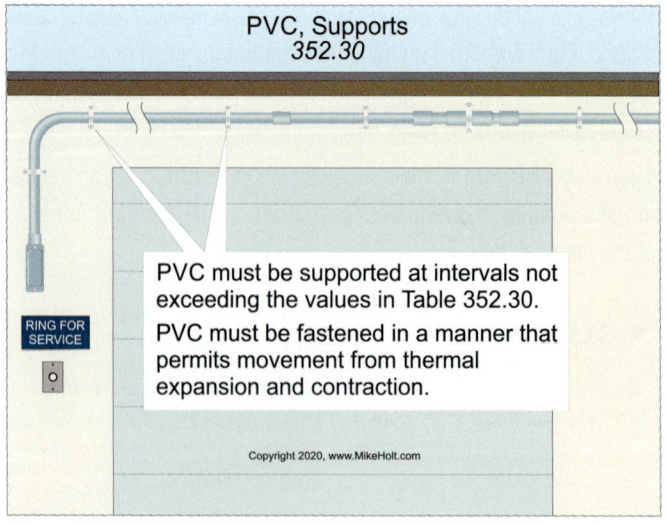

▸Figure 352–11

Rigid Polyvinyl Chloride Conduit (Type PVC) | 352.46

Table 352.30 Support of Rigid PVC	
Trade Size	Support Spacing
½–1	3 ft
1¼–2	5 ft
2½–3	6 ft
3½–5	7 ft
6	8 ft

PVC conduit installed horizontally in bored or punched holes in wood or metal framing members, or notches in wooden members, is considered supported, but the raceway must be secured within 3 ft of termination.

352.44 Expansion Fittings

If PVC conduit is installed in a straight run between securely mounted items such as boxes, cabinets, elbows, or other conduit terminations, expansion fittings must be provided if the expansion or contraction length change (in accordance with Table 352.44) is expected to be ¼ in. or greater. ▶Figure 352-12

Table 352.44 Expansion Characteristics of PVC Rigid Nonmetallic Conduit Coefficient of Thermal Expansion			
Temperature Change (°C)	Length of Change of PVC Conduit (mm/m)	Temperature Change (°F)	Length Change of PVC Conduit (in./100 ft)
5	0.30	5	0.20
10	0.61	10	0.41
15	0.91	15	0.61
20	1.22	20	0.81
25	1.52	25	1.01
30	1.83	30	1.22
35	2.13	35	1.42
40	2.43	40	1.62
45	2.74	45	1.83
50	3.04	50	2.03
55	3.35	55	2.23
60	3.65	60	2.43
65	3.95	65	2.64
70	4.26	70	2.84
75	4.56	75	3.04
80	4.87	80	3.24
85	5.17	85	3.45
90	5.48	90	3.65
95	5.78	95	3.85
100	6.08	100	4.06

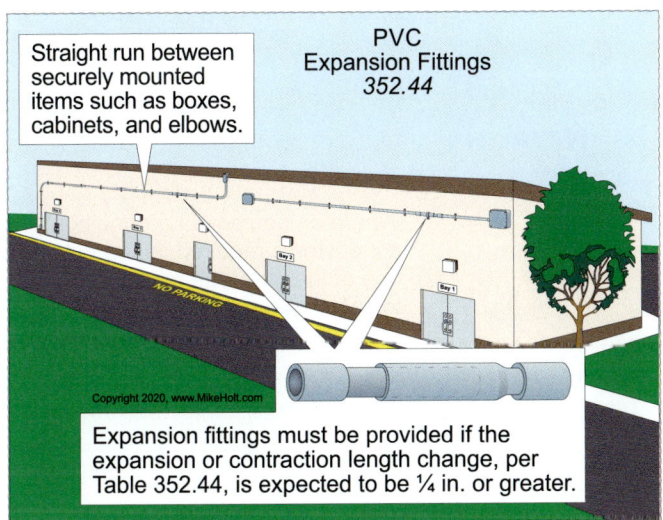

▶Figure 352-12

Author's Comment:

▸ When determining the number and setting of expansion fittings, you must read the manufacturer's documentation. For example, instructions for Carlon® expansion fittings for PVC conduit say that when it has sunlight exposure, 30°F must be added to the high ambient temperature.

352.46 Bushings

Where PVC conduit enters a box, fitting, or other enclosure, conductors 4 AWG and larger must be protected from abrasion during and after installation by a fitting that provides a smooth, rounded insulating surface [300.4(G)]. ▶Figure 352-13

352.48 | Rigid Polyvinyl Chloride Conduit (Type PVC)

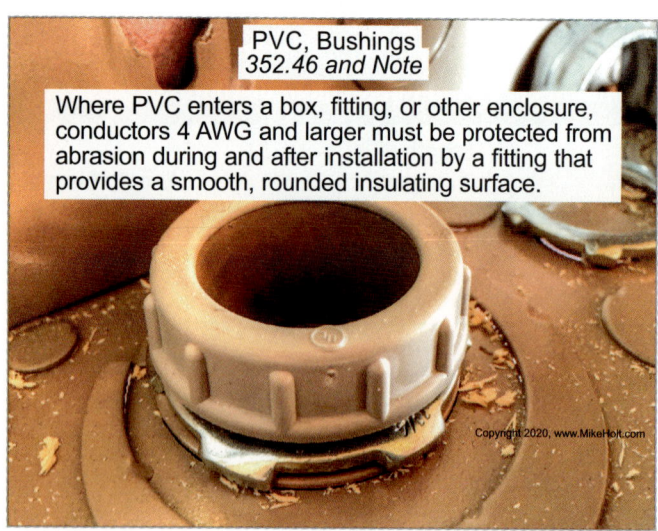
▶Figure 352–13

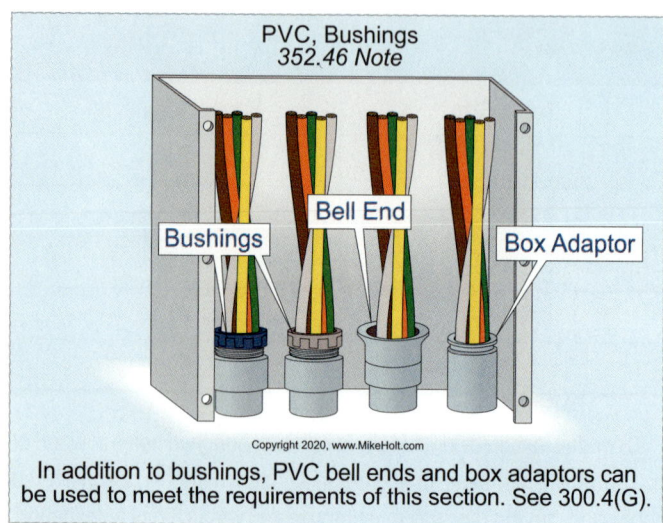
▶Figure 352–14

Author's Comment:

▸ According to UL 651, section 5.1.2 reads: "The inner and outer surfaces of a fitting shall not be subject to peeling, scaling, or flaking and shall be smooth and free from blisters, cracks, or other defects. The fitting shall have a smooth, rounded inlet hole to afford protection to the conductors. In the case of a molded product, excess flashing shall be removed from the mold line of all interior surfaces so that there are no sharp edges or obstructions to the passage of wiring or mating products in the intended use of the product."

Note: Conductors 4 AWG and larger that enter an enclosure must be protected from abrasion (during and after installation) by a fitting that provides a smooth, rounded insulating surface such as an insulating bushing, unless the design of the box, fitting, or enclosure provides equivalent protection in accordance with 300.4(G). ▶Figure 352–14

352.48 Joints

Joints, such as couplings and connectors, must be made in a manner approved by the authority having jurisdiction.

Author's Comment:

▸ Follow the manufacturers' instructions for the raceway, fittings, and glue. Some glue requires the raceway surface to be cleaned with a solvent before it is applied. After applying glue to both surfaces, a quarter turn of the fitting is required.

352.60 Equipment Grounding Conductor

If equipment is required to be connected to an equipment grounding conductor, a separate one of the wire type must be installed inside the raceway [300.2(B)]. ▶Figure 352–15

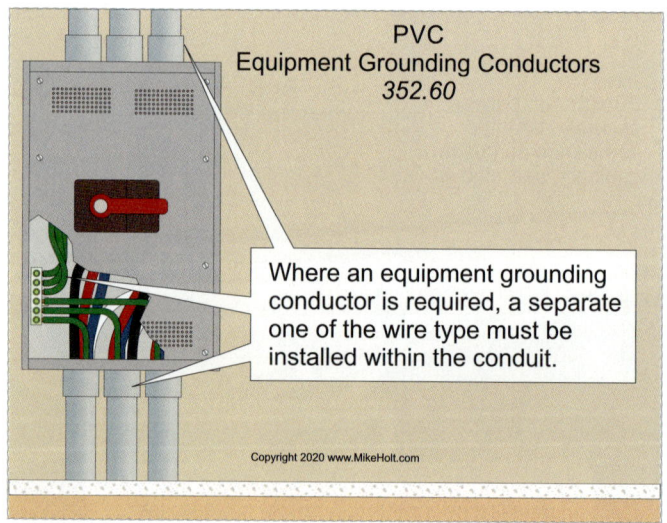
▶Figure 352–15

Ex 2: An equipment grounding conductor is not required in PVC conduit if the neutral conductor is used for equipment grounding at the service disconnect in accordance with 250.142(A) [250.24(C)]. ▶Figure 352–16

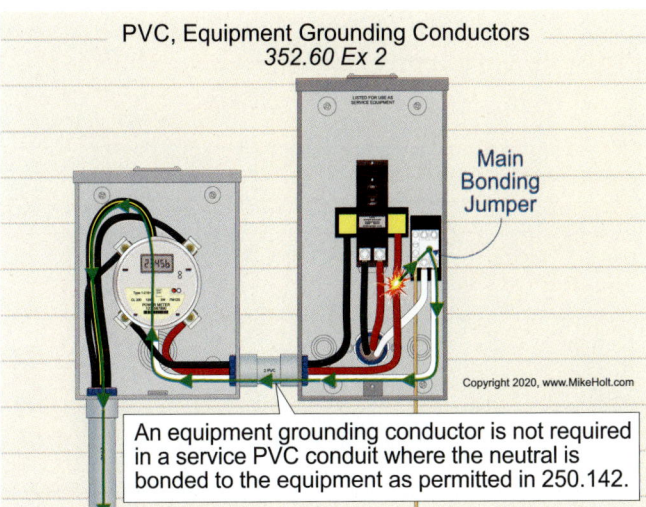

Figure 352–16

Notes

ARTICLE 356 — LIQUIDTIGHT FLEXIBLE NONMETALLIC CONDUIT (TYPE LFNC)

Introduction to Article 356—Liquidtight Flexible Nonmetallic Conduit (Type LFNC)

Liquidtight flexible nonmetallic conduit (Type LFNC) is a listed raceway of circular cross section with an outer liquidtight, nonmetallic, sunlight-resistant jacket over an inner flexible core with associated couplings, connectors, and fittings. It is commonly referred to as "Carflex®."

Part I. General

356.1 Scope

Article 356 covers the use, installation, and construction specifications of liquidtight flexible nonmetallic conduit (Type LFNC) and associated fittings. ▶Figure 356–1

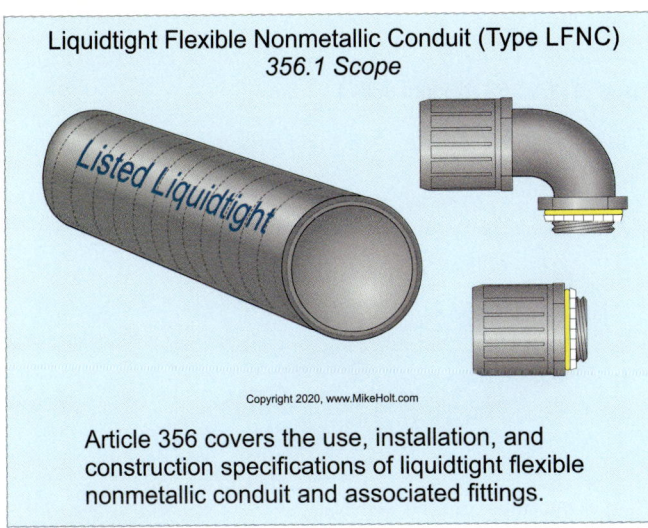

▶Figure 356–1

356.2 Definition

Liquidtight Flexible Nonmetallic Conduit (Type LFNC). A raceway of circular cross section, with an outer liquidtight, nonmetallic, sunlight-resistant jacket over a flexible inner core, with associated couplings, connectors, and fittings, listed for the installation of electrical conductors. ▶Figure 356–2

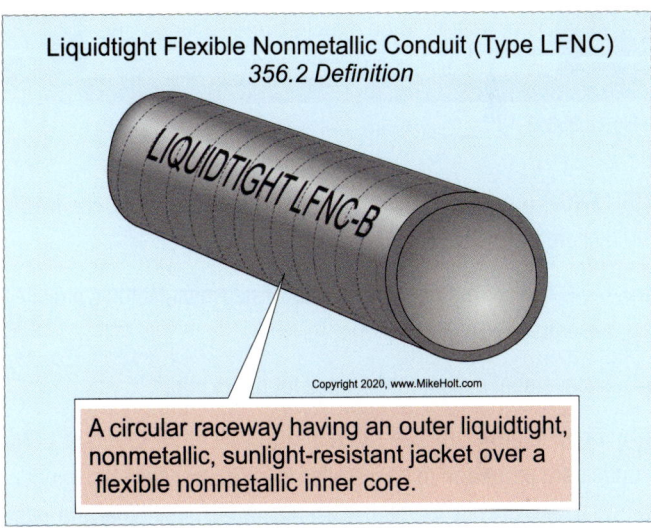

▶Figure 356–2

356.6 Listing Requirements

LFNC and its associated fittings must be listed.

Part II. Installation

356.10 Uses Permitted

Listed LFNC is permitted, either exposed or concealed, at any of the following locations:

(1) If flexibility is required.

(2) If protection from liquids, vapors, machine oils, and solids is required.

356.12 | Liquidtight Flexible Nonmetallic Conduit (Type LFNC)

(3) Outdoors, if listed and marked for this purpose.

(4) Directly buried in the Earth if listed and marked for this purpose.
▶Figure 356–3

▶Figure 356–3

(5) LFNC-B (gray color) is permitted in lengths over 6 ft if secured in accordance with 356.30.

(6) LFNC-C (black color) is permitted as a listed manufactured prewired assembly.

(7) Encasement in concrete if listed for direct burial.

(8) Conductors or cables rated at a temperature rating of LFNC conduit are permitted to be installed in LFNC, provided the conductors or cables are not operated at a temperature higher than the listed temperature rating of the LFNC.

Note: Extreme cold can cause some types of nonmetallic conduits to become brittle and therefore more susceptible to damage from physical contact.

356.12 Uses Not Permitted

(1) Where subject to physical damage.

(2) If the ambient temperature and/or conductor temperature is in excess of its listing.

(3) Longer than 6 ft, except if approved by the authority having jurisdiction as essential for a required degree of flexibility.

(4) In any hazardous (classified) location except as permitted by 501.10(B), 502.10(A) and (B), and 504.20.

356.20 Trade Size

(A) Minimum. LFNC smaller than trade size ½ is not permitted, except as in the following applications:

(1) Enclosing the leads of motors [430.245(B)].

(2) For tap connections to lighting fixtures in accordance with 410.117(C) for trade size ⅜.

(B) Maximum. LFNC larger than trade size 4 is not permitted.

356.22 Number of Conductors

Raceways must be large enough to permit the installation and removal of conductors without damaging the conductors' insulation, and the number of conductors is not permitted to exceed the percentage fill specified in Chapter 9, Table 1.

When all conductors within a raceway are the same size and insulation, the number of conductors permitted can be found in Annex C for the raceway type.

▶ **Example**

Question: How many 8 THHN conductors can be installed in trade size ¾ LFNC-B? ▶Figure 356–4

(a) 2 conductors (b) 4 conductors
(c) 6 conductors (d) 8 conductors

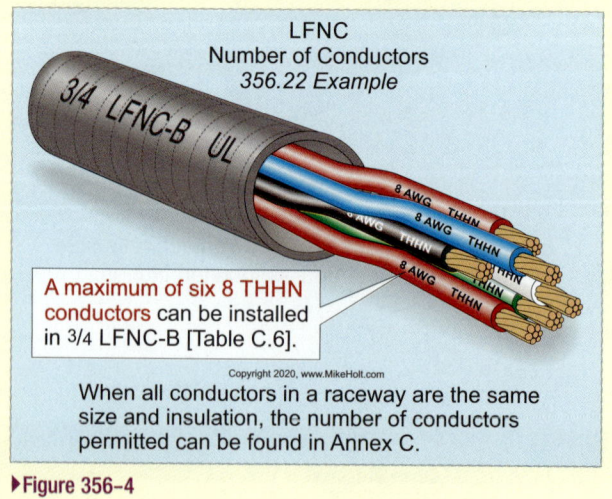

▶Figure 356–4

Answer: (c) 6 conductors [Annex C, Table C.6]

Liquidtight Flexible Nonmetallic Conduit (Type LFNC) | **356.60**

Author's Comment:

▸ See 300.17 for examples on how to size raceways when conductors are not all the same size.

Cables can be installed in LFNC if the number of cables does not exceed the allowable percentage fill specified in Chapter 9, Table 1.

356.24 Bends

Raceway bends are not permitted to be made in any manner that will damage the raceway or significantly change its internal diameter (no kinks).

356.26 Number of Bends (360°)

To reduce the stress and friction on conductor insulation, the total bends (including offsets) between pull points are not permitted to exceed 360°.

356.30 Securing and Supporting

LFNC must be securely fastened and supported in accordance with any of the following:

(1) The conduit must be securely fastened at intervals not exceeding 3 ft, and within 1 ft of termination when installed in lengths longer than 6 ft. ▸Figure 356–5

Where cable ties are to be used to secure and support LFNC, they must be listed for the application and for securing and supporting.

(2) Securing or supporting is not required if LFNC is fished or installed in lengths not exceeding 3 ft at terminals if flexibility is required.

(3) Runs of LFNC installed horizontally in bored or punched holes in wood or metal framing members, or notches in wooden members, are considered supported, but the raceway must be secured within 1 ft of termination.

(4) Securing or supporting LFNC is not required if installed in lengths not exceeding 6 ft from the last point where the raceway is securely fastened for connections within an accessible ceiling to a luminaire(s) or other equipment. For the purposes of this allowance, listed fittings are considered support. ▸Figure 356–6

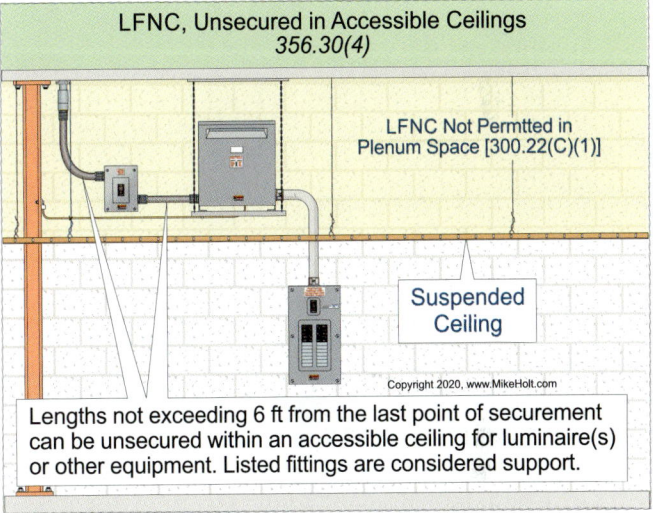

▸Figure 356–6

356.42 Fittings

Only fittings that are listed for use with LFNC can be used [300.15]. Straight LFNC fittings are permitted for direct burial or encasement in concrete. ▸Figure 356–7

356.60 Equipment Grounding Conductor

If equipment grounding is required, a separate equipment grounding conductor of the wire type must be installed inside the conduit [250.134(2)].

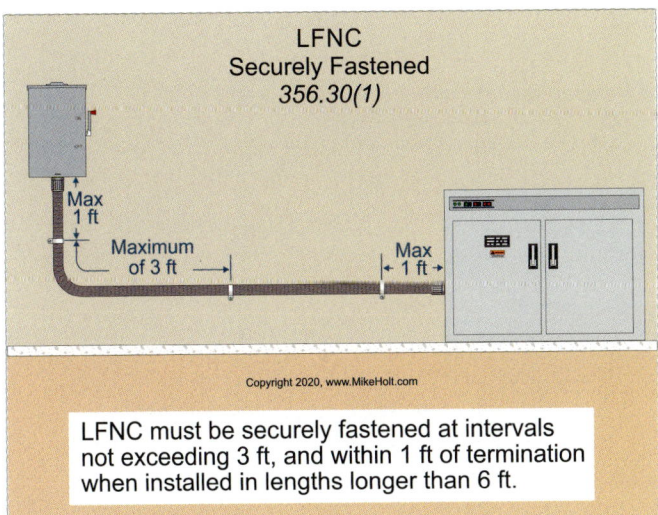

▸Figure 356–5

356.60 | Liquidtight Flexible Nonmetallic Conduit (Type LFNC)

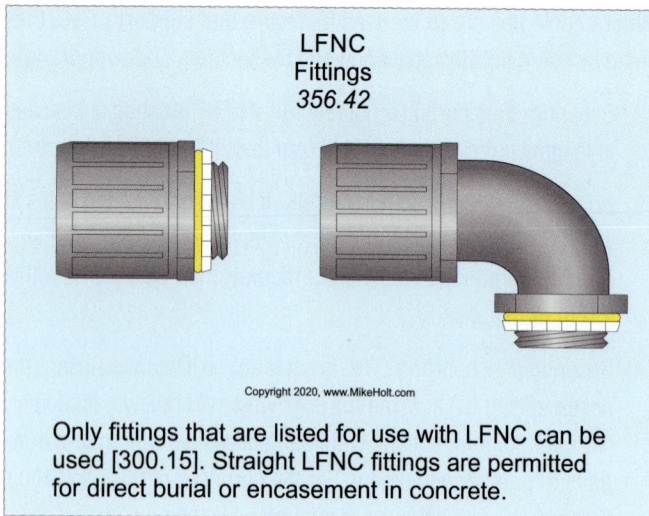

Only fittings that are listed for use with LFNC can be used [300.15]. Straight LFNC fittings are permitted for direct burial or encasement in concrete.

▶Figure 356–7

Author's Comment:

▶ An equipment grounding conductor is not required to be installed in a nonmetallic raceway supplying nonmetallic equipment because there is nothing in the nonmetallic box that requires a connection to an equipment grounding conductor. ▶Figure 356–8

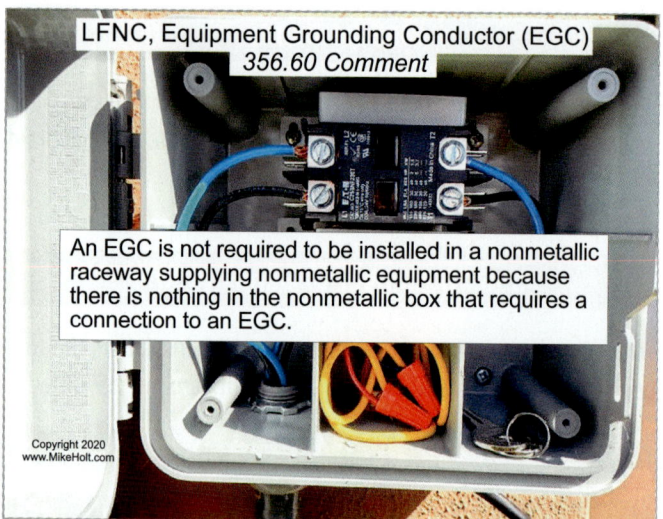

▶Figure 356–8

ARTICLE 358 ELECTRICAL METALLIC TUBING (TYPE EMT)

Introduction to Article 358—Electrical Metallic Tubing (Type EMT)

Electrical metallic tubing (Type EMT) is perhaps the most commonly used raceway in commercial and industrial installations. It is a lightweight raceway that is relatively easy to bend, cut, and ream. Because EMT is not threaded, all connectors and couplings are of the threadless type (either set screw or compression) and provide for quick, easy, and inexpensive installations as compared to other metallic raceway systems; all of which make it very popular. Electrical metallic tubing is manufactured in both galvanized steel and aluminum; the steel type is used most often.

Part I. General

358.1 Scope

Article 358 covers the use, installation, and construction specifications of electrical metallic tubing (Type EMT) and associated fittings. ▶Figure 358–1

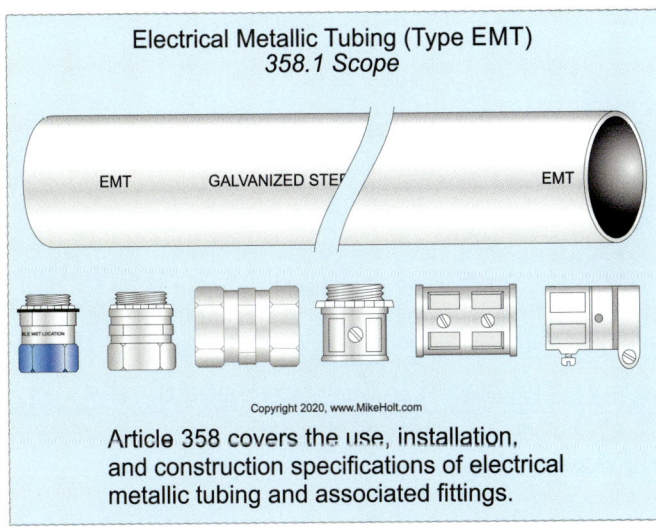

▶Figure 358–1

When joined together with listed fittings and enclosures as a complete system, it is a reliable wiring method providing both physical protection for conductors as well an effective ground-fault current path. ▶Figure 358–2

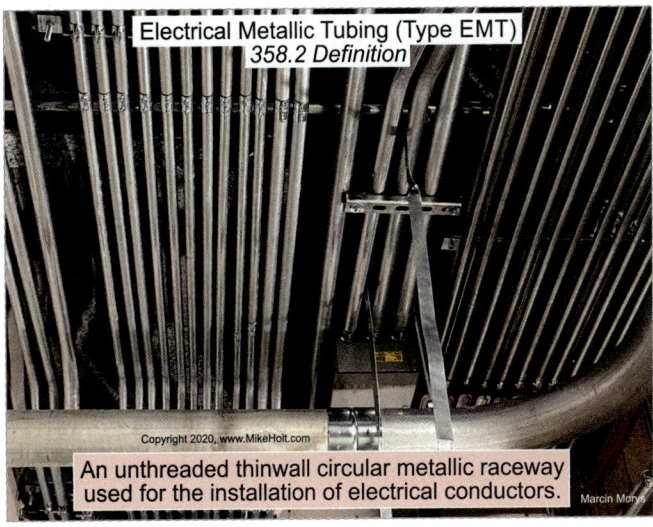

▶Figure 358–2

358.6 Listing Requirements

EMT and associated fittings must be listed.

358.2 Definition

Electrical Metallic Tubing (Type EMT). An unthreaded thinwall circular metallic raceway used for the installation of electrical conductors.

358.10 | Electrical Metallic Tubing (Type EMT)

Part II. Installation

358.10 Uses Permitted

(A) Exposed and Concealed. EMT is permitted to be used exposed and concealed for the following applications: ▶Figure 358-3

▶Figure 358-3

(1) In concrete in direct contact with the earth in accordance with 358.10(B).

(2) In dry, damp, or wet locations.

(3) In any hazardous (classified) location as permitted by other articles in this *Code*.

(B) Corrosive Environments.

(1) Galvanized Steel. Galvanized steel EMT, elbows, and fittings can be installed in concrete, in direct contact with the Earth, or in areas subject to severe corrosive influences if protected by corrosion protection and approved as suitable for the condition [300.6(A)].

(D) Wet Locations. Support fittings such as screws, straps, and so on, installed in a wet location must be made of corrosion-resistant material.

Author's Comment:

▸ If installed in wet locations, fittings for EMT must be listed for use in wet locations and prevent moisture or water from entering or accumulating within the enclosure in accordance with 314.15 [358.42].

358.12 Uses Not Permitted

EMT is not permitted to be used under the following conditions:

(1) Where subject to severe physical damage. ▶Figure 358-4

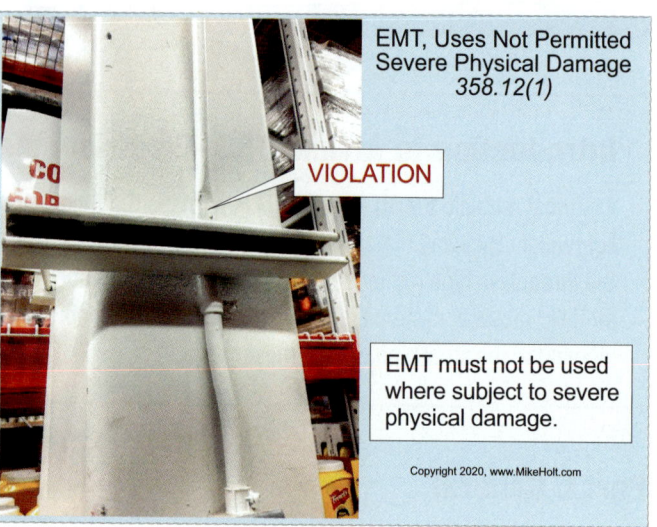
▶Figure 358-4

(2) For the support of luminaires or other equipment. ▶Figure 358-5

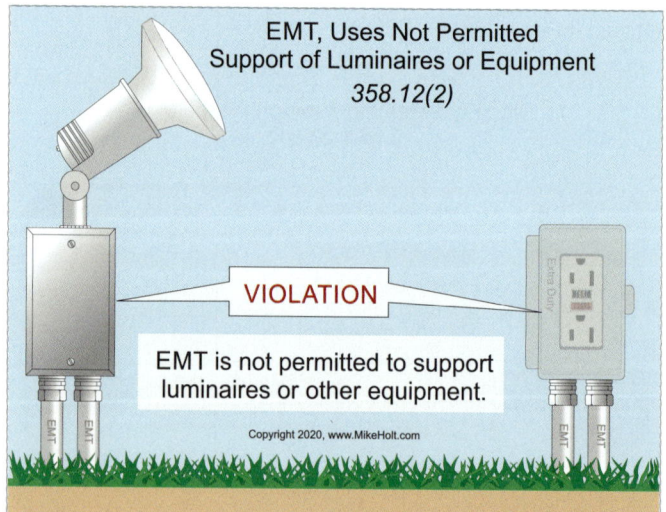
▶Figure 358-5

358.20 Trade Size

(A) Minimum. EMT smaller than trade size ½ is not permitted.

(B) Maximum. EMT larger than trade size 4 is not permitted.

358.22 Number of Conductors

Raceways must be large enough to permit the installation and removal of conductors without damaging the conductors' insulation, and the number of conductors is not permitted to exceed the percentage fill specified in Chapter 9, Table 1.

When all conductors within a raceway are the same size and insulation, the number of conductors permitted can be found in Annex C for the raceway type.

▶ **Example**

Question: How many 12 THHN conductors can be installed in trade size 1 EMT? ▶Figure 358-6

(a) 23 conductors
(b) 24 conductors
(c) 25 conductors
(d) 26 conductors

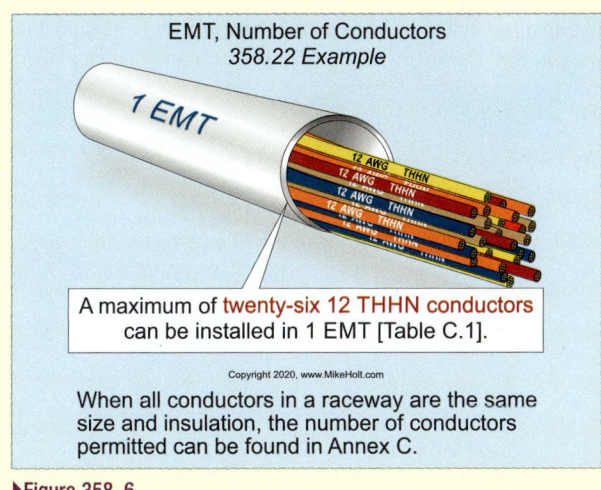

▶Figure 358-6

Answer: (d) 26 conductors [Annex C, Table C.1]

Author's Comment:

▸ See 300.17 for examples on how to size raceways when conductors are not all the same size.

358.24 Bends

Raceway bends are not permitted to be made in any manner that will damage the raceway or significantly change its internal diameter (no kinks).

Author's Comment:

▸ This is generally not a problem, because typical EMT benders are made to comply with this requirement.

358.26 Number of Bends (360°)

To reduce the stress and friction on conductor insulation, the total bends (including offsets) between pull points cannot exceed 360°. ▶Figure 358-7

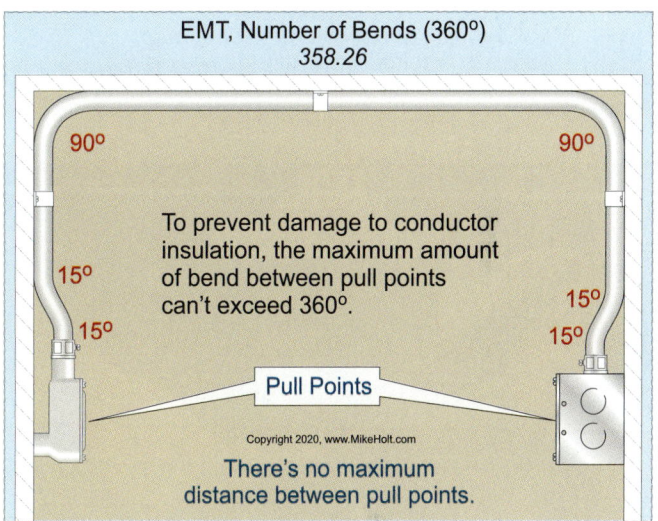

▶Figure 358-7

Author's Comment:

▸ There is no maximum distance between pull boxes because this is a design issue, not a safety issue.

358.28 Reaming

(A) Reaming. Reaming to remove the burrs and rough edges is required when the raceway is cut. ▶Figure 358-8

Author's Comment:

▸ It is considered an accepted practice to ream small raceways with a screwdriver or lineman's pliers. ▶Figure 358-9

358.30 | Electrical Metallic Tubing (Type EMT)

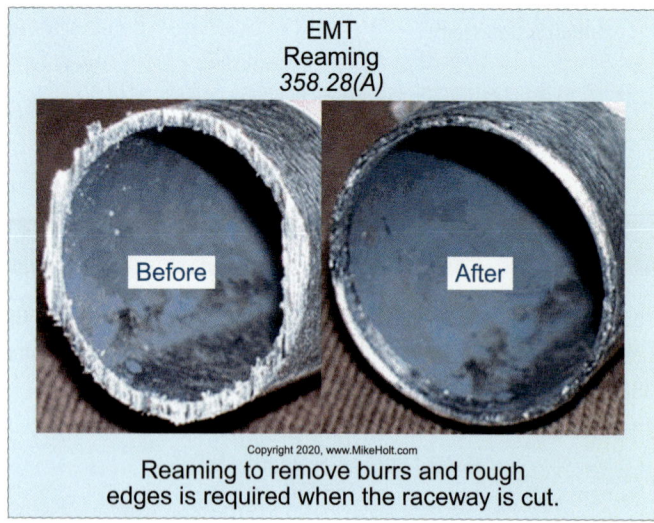
▶Figure 358-8

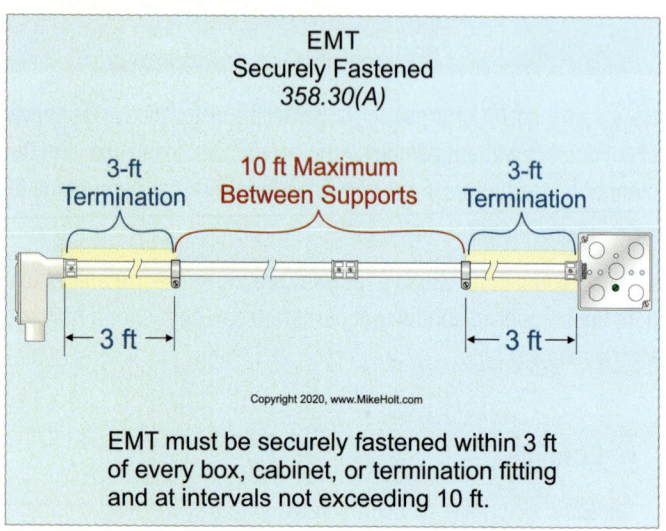
▶Figure 358-10

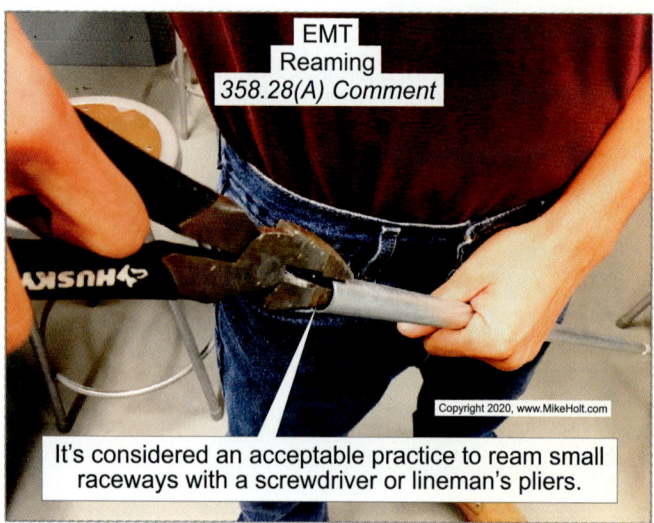
▶Figure 358-9

Ex 1: When structural members do not permit the raceway to be secured within of a box or termination fitting, an unbroken raceway can be secured within of a box or termination fitting. ▶Figure 358-11

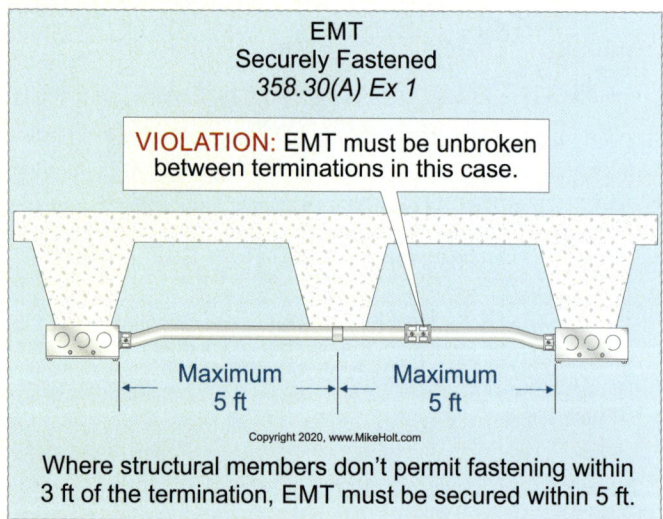
▶Figure 358-11

358.30 Securing and Supporting

EMT must be securely fastened in place and supported in accordance with (A) and (B).

(A) Securely Fastened. EMT must be securely fastened within 3 ft of every box, cabinet, or termination fitting, and at intervals not exceeding 10 ft. ▶Figure 358-10

Author's Comment:

▶ Fastening is required within of termination, not within of a coupling.

(B) Horizontal Runs. EMT installed horizontally in bored or punched holes in wood or metal framing members, or notches in wooden members at intervals not greater than 3 ft, is considered supported, but the raceway must be secured within 3 ft of termination. ▶Figure 358-12

Electrical Metallic Tubing (Type EMT) | **358.60**

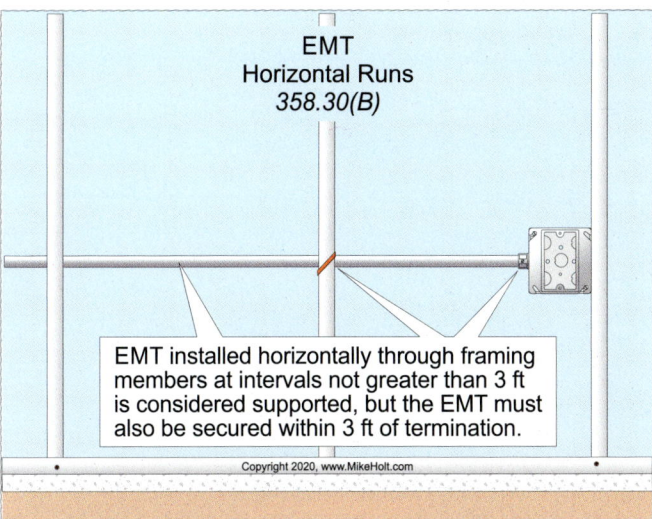
▶Figure 358–12

358.42 Couplings and Connectors

Couplings and connectors must be made up tight to maintain an effective ground-fault current path to safely conduct fault current in accordance with 250.4(A)(5), 250.96(A), and 300.10.

If buried in masonry or concrete, threadless EMT fittings must be of the concrete-tight type. If installed in wet locations, they must be listed for use in wet locations and prevent moisture or water from entering or accumulating inside the enclosure in accordance with 314.15.
▶Figure 358–13

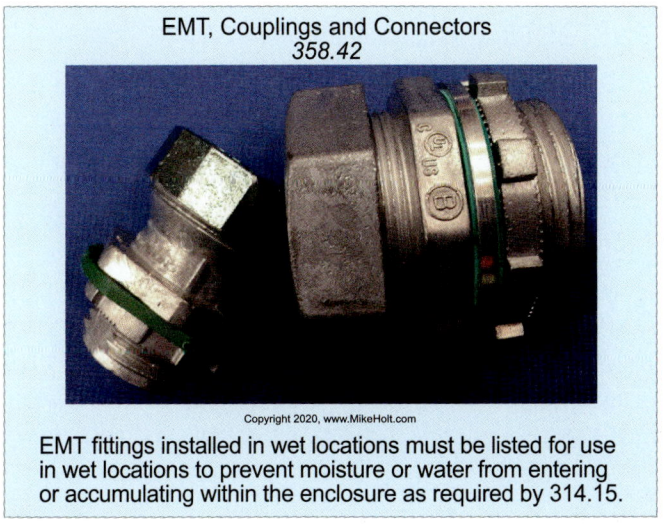
▶Figure 358–13

358.60 Equipment Grounding Conductor

EMT can serve as an equipment grounding conductor [250.118(4)].
▶Figure 358–14

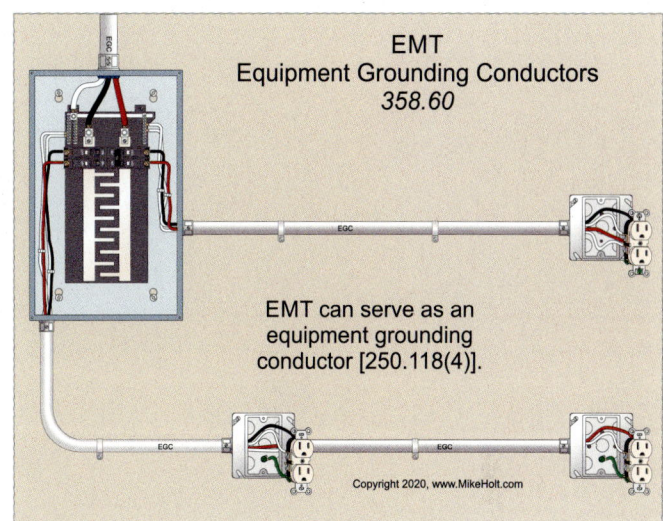
▶Figure 358–14

Notes

ARTICLE 362 — ELECTRICAL NONMETALLIC TUBING (TYPE ENT)

Introduction to Article 362—Electrical Nonmetallic Tubing (Type ENT)

Electrical nonmetallic tubing is a pliable, corrugated, circular raceway. It resembles the flexible tubing you might see used at swimming pools and is often referred to as "Smurf Pipe" or "Smurf Tube" (as a reference to the children's cartoon characters "The Smurfs") because it was only available in blue when it first came out. It can now be purchased in additional colors such as red and yellow.

Part I. General

362.1 Scope

Article 362 covers the use, installation, and construction specifications of electrical nonmetallic tubing (Type ENT) and associated fittings. ▶Figure 362–1

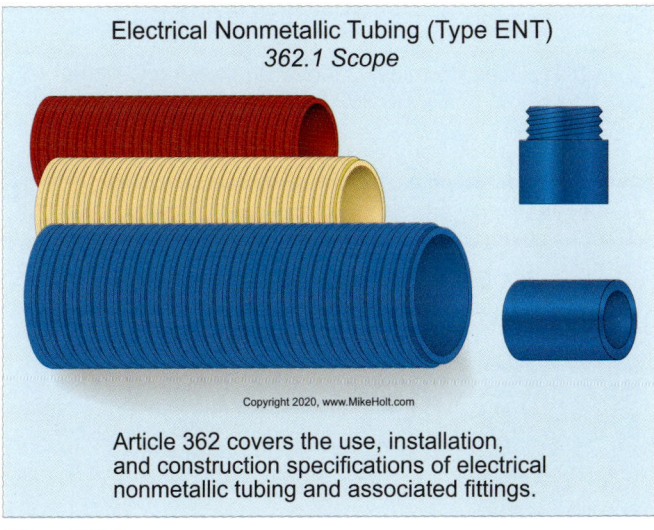

▶Figure 362–1

362.2 Definition

Electrical Nonmetallic Tubing (Type ENT). A pliable corrugated raceway of circular cross section, with integral or associated couplings, connectors, and fittings that are listed for the installation of electrical conductors. It is composed of a material that is resistant to moisture and chemical atmospheres and is flame retardant. ▶Figure 362–2

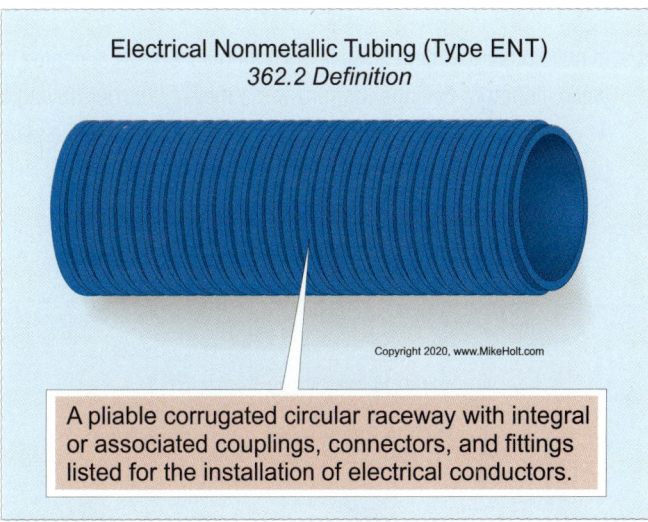

▶Figure 362–2

Electrical nonmetallic tubing can be bent by hand with reasonable force but without other assistance.

362.6 Listing

ENT and its associated fittings must be listed.

Part II. Installation

362.10 Uses Permitted

Electrical nonmetallic tubing is permitted as follows:

(1) In buildings not exceeding three floors. ▶Figure 362–3

    a. Exposed, where not prohibited by 362.12.

    b. Concealed within walls, floors, and ceilings.

362.10 | Electrical Nonmetallic Tubing (Type ENT)

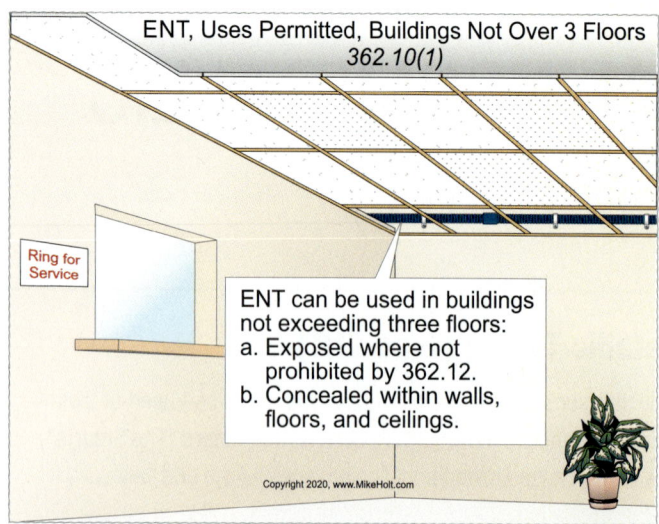
▶ Figure 362-3

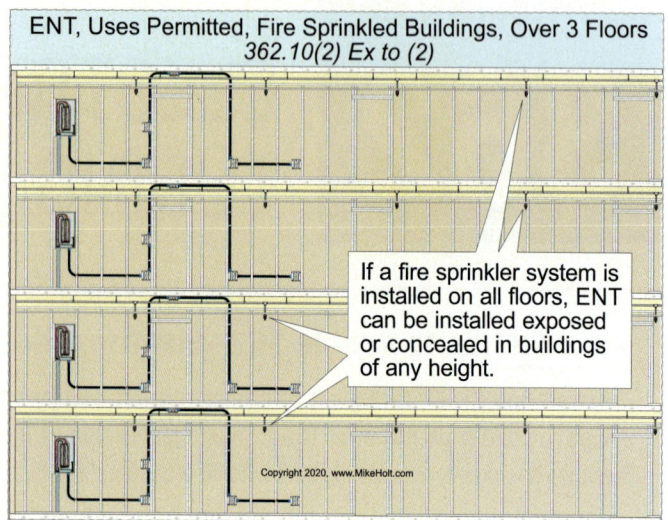
▶ Figure 362-5

(2) In buildings exceeding three floors, where installed concealed in walls, floors, or ceilings that provide a thermal barrier having a 15-minute finish rating, as identified in listings of fire-rated assemblies. ▶Figure 362-4

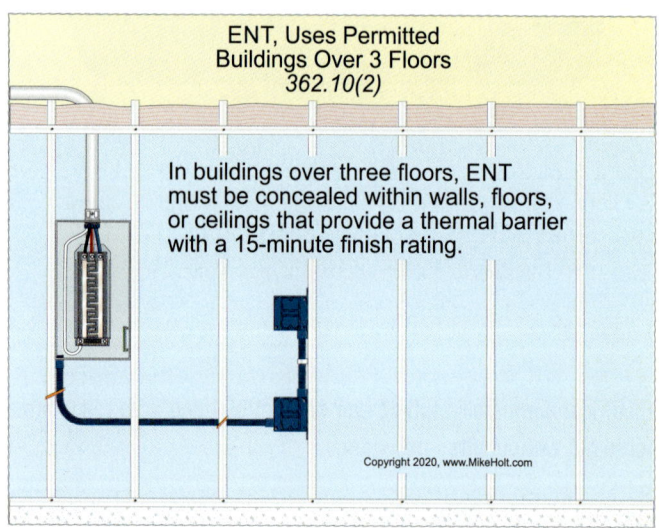
▶ Figure 362-4

Ex to (2): If a fire sprinkler system is installed on all floors in accordance with NFPA 13, Standard for the Installation of Sprinkler Systems, electrical nonmetallic tubing is permitted exposed or concealed in buildings of any height. ▶Figure 362-5

Author's Comment:

▸ ENT is not permitted above a suspended ceiling used as a plenum space [300.22(C)].

(3) In severe corrosive and chemical locations when identified for this use.

(4) In dry and damp concealed locations if not prohibited by 362.12.

(5) Above a suspended ceiling if the suspended ceiling provides a thermal barrier having a 15-minute finish rating, as identified in listings of fire-rated assemblies. ▶Figure 362-6

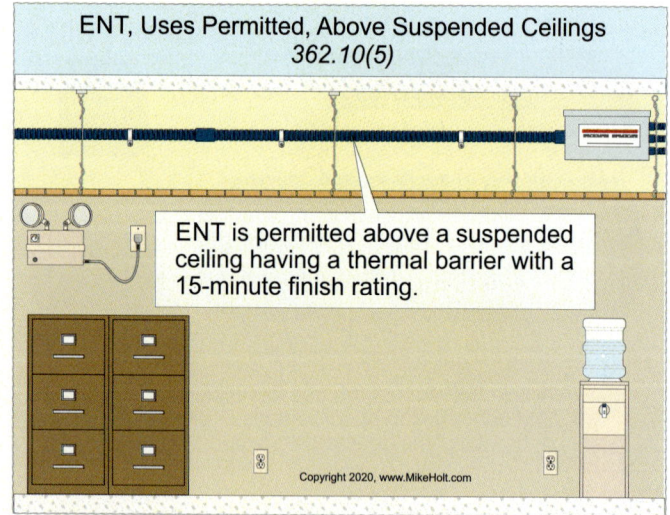
▶ Figure 362-6

Ex to (5): If a fire sprinkler system is installed on all floors in accordance with NFPA 13, Standard for the Installation of Sprinkler Systems, ENT is permitted above a suspended ceiling that does not have a 15-minute finish rated thermal barrier. ▶Figure 362-7

Electrical Nonmetallic Tubing (Type ENT) | 362.22

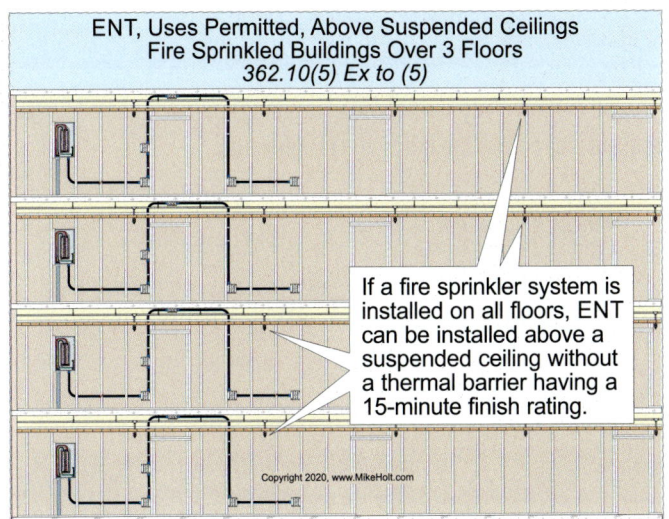
▶Figure 362–7

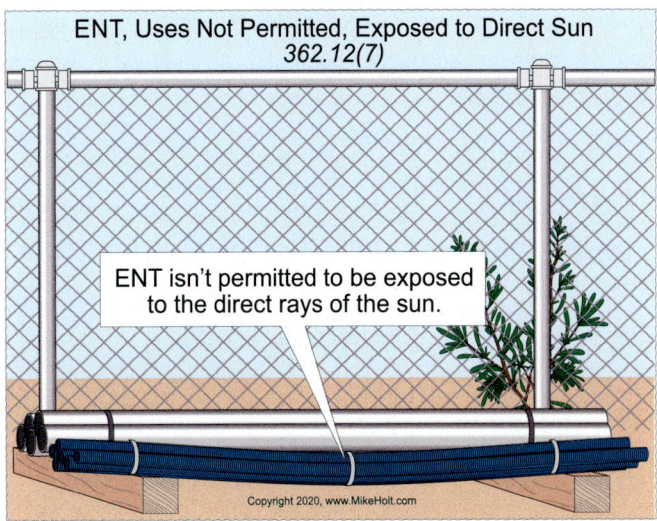
▶Figure 362–8

(6) Encased or embedded in a concrete slab provided fittings identified for the purpose are used.

(7) In wet locations indoors, or in a concrete slab on or below grade, with fittings that are listed for the purpose.

362.12 Uses Not Permitted

ENT is not permitted to be used in the following applications:

(1) In any hazardous (classified) location, except as permitted by 504.20 and 505.15(A)(1).

(2) For the support of luminaires or equipment. See 314.23.

(3) If the ambient temperature exceeds 50°C (122°F).

(4) For direct Earth burial.

Author's Comment:

▸ Electrical nonmetallic tubing is permitted to be encased in concrete [362.10(6)].

(5) Exposed in buildings over three floors, except as permitted by 362.10(1) and (5) Ex.

(6) In assembly occupancies or theaters, except as permitted by 518.4 and 520.5.

(7) Exposed to the direct rays of the sun. ▶Figure 362–8

Author's Comment:

▸ Exposing electrical nonmetallic tubing to the direct rays of the sun for an extended time may result in the product becoming brittle, unless it is listed to resist the effects of ultraviolet (UV) radiation.

(8) Where subject to physical damage.

Author's Comment:

▸ Electrical nonmetallic tubing is prohibited in ducts, plenum spaces [300.22(C)], and patient care space circuits in health care facilities [517.13(A)].

362.20 Trade Sizes

(A) Minimum. Electrical nonmetallic tubing smaller than trade size ½ is not permitted.

(B) Maximum. Electrical nonmetallic tubing larger than trade size 2½ is not permitted.

362.22 Number of Conductors

Raceways must be large enough to permit the installation and removal of conductors without damaging the conductors' insulation, and the number of conductors is not permitted to exceed the percentage fill specified in Chapter 9, Table 1.

362.24 | Electrical Nonmetallic Tubing (Type ENT)

When all conductors within a raceway are the same size and insulation, the number of conductors permitted can be found in Annex C for the raceway type.

▶ **Example**

Question: How many 12 THHN conductors can be installed in trade size ½ ENT? ▶Figure 362–9

(a) 2 conductors
(b) 4 conductors
(c) 6 conductors
(d) 8 conductors

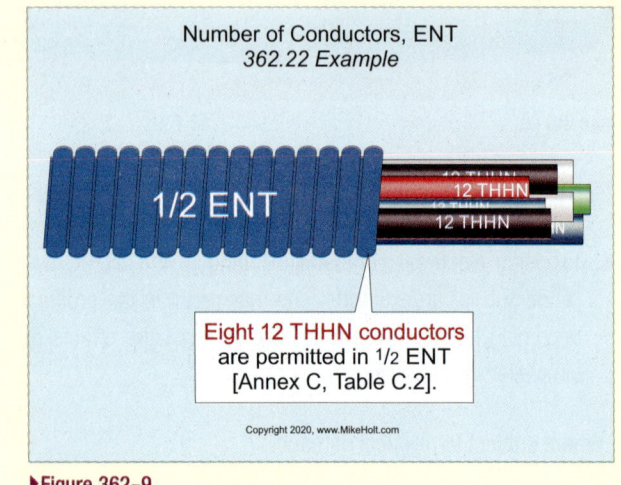

▶Figure 362–9

Answer: (d) 8 conductors [Annex C, Table C.2]

Author's Comment:

▸ See 300.17 for examples on how to size raceways when conductors are not all the same size.

362.24 Bends

Raceway bends are not permitted to be made in any manner that will damage the raceway or significantly change its internal diameter (no kinks).

362.26 Number of Bends (360°)

To reduce the stress and friction on conductor insulation, the total bends (including offsets) between pull points cannot exceed 360°.

362.28 Trimming

The cut ends of electrical nonmetallic tubing must be trimmed (inside and out) to remove the burrs and rough edges.

Author's Comment:

▸ Trimming electrical nonmetallic tubing is very easy; most of the burrs will rub off with your fingers, and a knife will smooth the rough edges.

362.30 Securing and Supporting

ENT must be securely fastened in place by an approved means and supported in accordance with (A) and (B).

(A) Securely Fastened. ENT must be secured within 3 ft of every box, cabinet, or termination fitting (such as a conduit body) and at intervals not exceeding 3 ft. ▶Figure 362–10

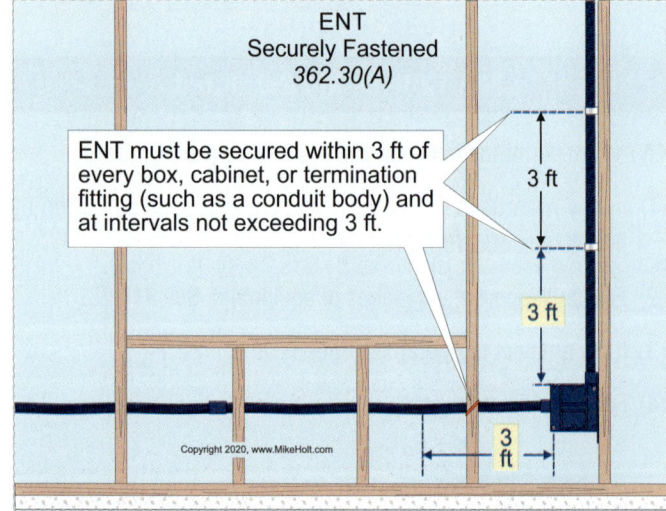

▶Figure 362–10

Where cable ties are to be used to secure and support electrical nonmetallic tubing, they must be listed as suitable for the application and for securing and supporting.

Ex 2: Lengths not exceeding 6 ft from the last point of support, if the raceway is securely fastened within an accessible ceiling to a luminaire(s) or other equipment.

Ex 3: If fished between access points through concealed spaces and securing is impractical.

(B) Horizontal Runs. ENT installed horizontally in bored or punched holes in wood or metal framing members, or notches in wooden members, is considered supported, but the raceway must be secured within 3 ft of terminations. ▶Figure 362–11

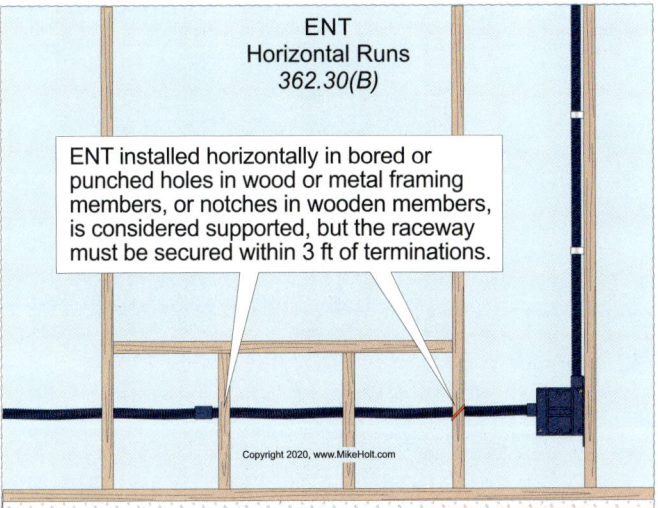

▶Figure 362–11

362.46 Bushings

Conductors 4 AWG and larger that enter an enclosure from a fitting must be protected from abrasion during and after installation by a fitting that provides a smooth, rounded, insulating surface (such as an insulating bushing) unless the design of the box, fitting, or enclosure provides equivalent protection in accordance with 300.4(G). ▶Figure 362–12

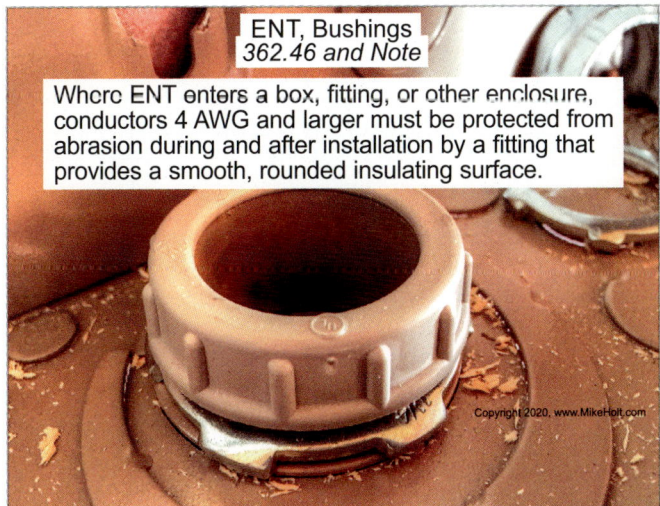

▶Figure 362–12

362.48 Joints

Joints such as couplings and connectors, must be made in a manner approved by the authority having jurisdiction.

Author's Comment:

▸ Follow the manufacturers' instructions for the raceway, fittings, and glue. According to product listings, Type PVC conduit fittings are permitted to be used with electrical nonmetallic tubing.

Caution

⚡ Glue used with electrical nonmetallic tubing must be listed for ENT. Glue for Type PVC is not permitted to be used with electrical nonmetallic tubing because it damages the plastic from which ENT is manufactured.

362.60 Equipment Grounding Conductor

If equipment grounding is required, a separate equipment grounding conductor of the wire type must be installed inside the raceway. ▶Figure 362–13

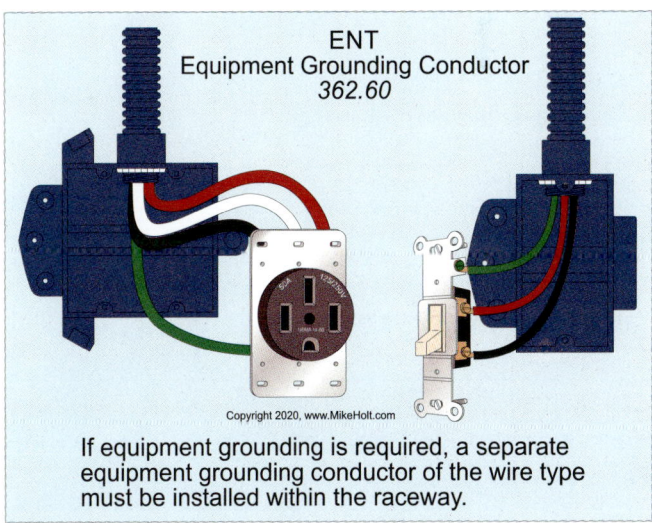

▶Figure 362–13

Notes

ARTICLE 376 — METAL WIREWAYS

Introduction to Article 376—Metal Wireways

Metal wireways are commonly used where access to conductors inside a raceway is required to make terminations, splices, or taps to several devices at a single location. High cost precludes their use for other than short distances, except in some commercial or industrial occupancies where the wiring is frequently revised. They are often incorrectly called "troughs," "auxiliary gutters," "auxiliary wireways," or "gutters" in the field. Wireways and auxiliary gutters are similar in design but one of the main differences is in the application. A wireway is a raceway (Article 100) while an auxiliary gutter [Article 366] is a supplemental enclosure for wiring and is not considered a raceway.

Part I. General

376.1 Scope

Article 376 covers the use, installation, and construction specifications of metal wireways and associated fittings. ▶Figure 376–1

▶Figure 376–1

376.2 Definition

Metal Wireway. A sheet metal trough with hinged or removable covers for housing and protecting electrical conductors and cable, and in which conductors are placed after the raceway has been installed.
▶Figure 376–2

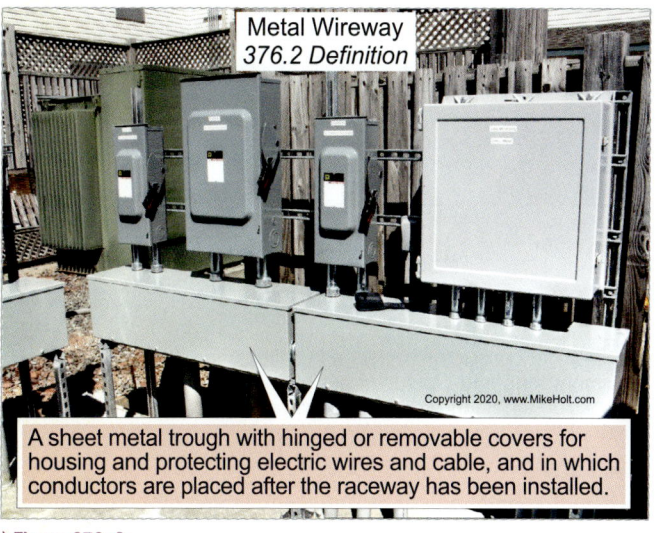

▶Figure 376–2

Part II. Installation

376.10 Uses Permitted

Wireways are permitted to be used in the following manners:

(1) Exposed.

(2) In any hazardous (classified) location as permitted by other articles in the *Code*.

(3) In wet locations where listed for the purpose.

(4) Unbroken through walls, partitions, and floors.

376.12 | Metal Wireways

376.12 Uses Not Permitted

Wireways are not permitted to be used:

(1) Where subject to severe physical damage.

(2) Where subject to severe corrosive environments.

376.20 Conductors Connected in Parallel

Where conductors are installed in parallel as permitted in 310.10(G), the parallel conductors must be installed in groups consisting of not more than one conductor per phase or neutral conductor to prevent current imbalance in the paralleled conductors due to inductive reactance. ▶Figure 376–3

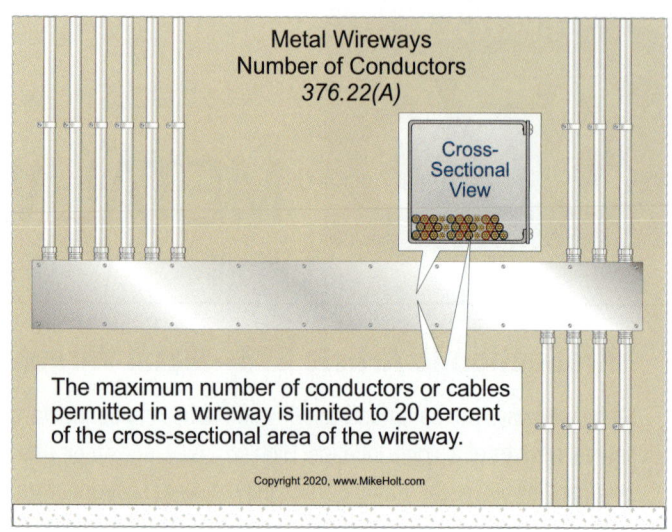

▶Figure 376–4

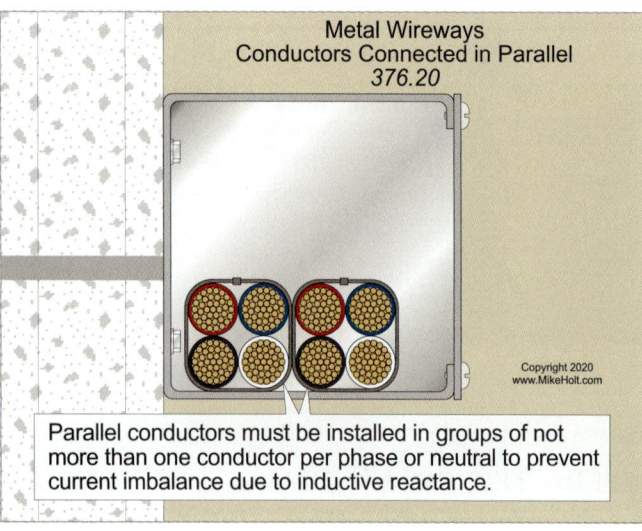

▶Figure 376–3

Note: The purpose of having all parallel conductor sets within the same group is to prevent current imbalance in the paralleled conductors due to inductive reactance.

376.22 Number of Conductors and Ampacity

(A) Number of Conductors. The maximum number of conductors permitted in a wireway is limited to 20 percent of the cross-sectional area of the wireway. ▶Figure 376–4

Author's Comment:

▶ Splices and taps, including conductors, are not permitted to fill more than 75 percent of the wiring space at any cross section [376.56(A)].

▶ **Wireway Conductor Fill Example 1**

Question: What is the maximum conductor fill permitted for a 6 in. × 6 in. wireway? ▶Figure 376–5

(a) 7.20 sq in.   (b) 15 sq in.   (c) 21.5 sq in.   (d) 36 sq in.

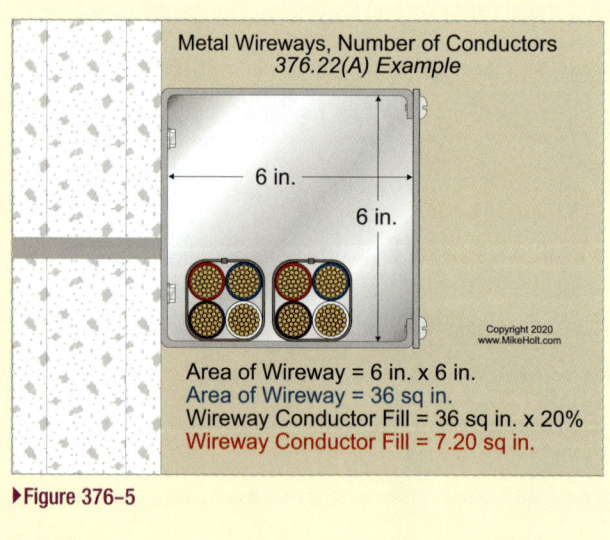

▶Figure 376–5

Solution:

36 sq in. × 20% = 7.20 sq in.

Answer: (a) 7.20 sq in.

▶ Wireway Conductor Fill Example 2

Question: What is the minimum size wireway suitable for three 500 kcmil THHN, one 250 kcmil THHN, and four 4/0 THHN conductors?

(a) 4 in. × 4 in. (16 sq in.) (b) 6 in. × 6 in. (36 sq in.)
(c) 8 in. × 8 in. (64 sq in.) (d) 10 in. × 10 in. (100 sq in.)

Solution:

Find the conductor area [Chapter 9, Table 5].

500 kcmil THHN = 0.7073 sq in. × 3 conductors
500 kcmil THHN = 2.1219 sq in.

250 kcmil THHN = 0.3970 sq in.

4/0 THHN = 0.3237 sq in. × 4 conductors
4/0 THHN = 1.2948 sq in.

Total Conductor Area = 3.8137 sq in.

The wireway must not be filled to over 20 percent of its cross-sectional area [376.22(A)]. Twenty percent is equal to one-fifth, so we can multiply the required conductor area by five to find the minimum square inch area required.

Conductor Area × 5 = Required Wireway Minimum Area

3.8137 sq in. × 5 = 19.07 sq in. (less than 36 sq in.)

A 6 in. × 6 in. wireway has a cross-sectional area of 36 sq in. and will be large enough.

Answer: (b) 6 in. × 6 in. (36 sq in.)

(B) Conductor Ampacity Adjustment. When more than thirty current-carrying conductors are installed in any cross-sectional area of the wireway, the conductor ampacity, as contained in Table 310.16, must be adjusted in accordance with Table 310.15(C)(1). ▶Figure 376–6

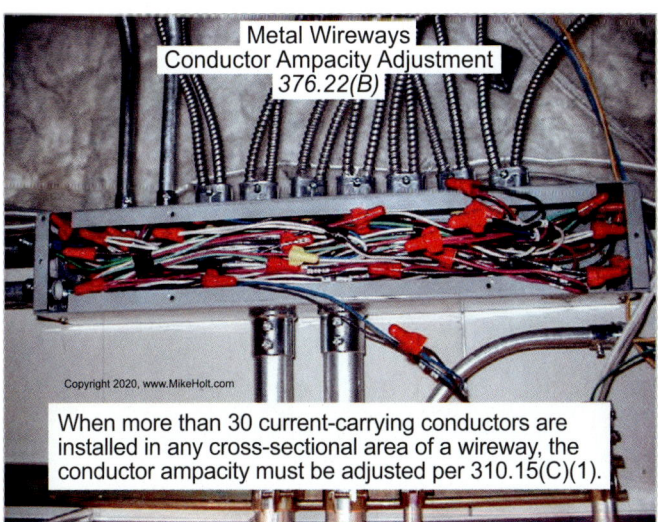

▶Figure 376–6

▶ Wireway—Conductor Ampacity Adjustment Example

Question: What is the ampacity of 8 THHN conductors if there are thirty-one conductors in a cross-sectional area of a wireway? ▶Figure 376–7

(a) 20A (b) 22A (c) 29A (d) 32A

Solution:

Adjusted Ampacity = Table 310.16 Ampacity × Bundled Ampacity Adjustment Factor from Table 310.15(C)(1)

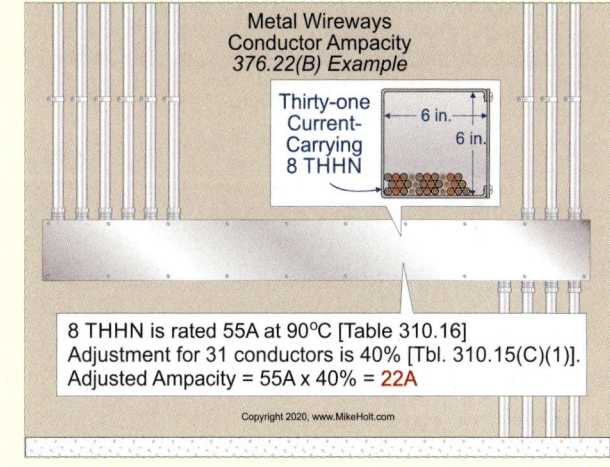

▶Figure 376–7

8 THHN is rated 55A at 90°C [Table 310.16].

The adjustment factor for thirty-one current-carrying conductors is 40 percent [Table 310.15(C)(1)].

Adjusted Ampacity = 55A × 40%
Adjusted Ampacity = 22A

Answer: (b) 22A

376.23 Wireway Sizing

(A) Sizing for Conductor Bending Radius. Where conductors are deflected more than 30 degrees in a wireway, they must be sized to the conductor bending space requirements contained in Table 312.6(A), based on one wire per terminal. ▶Figure 376–8

376.30 | Metal Wireways

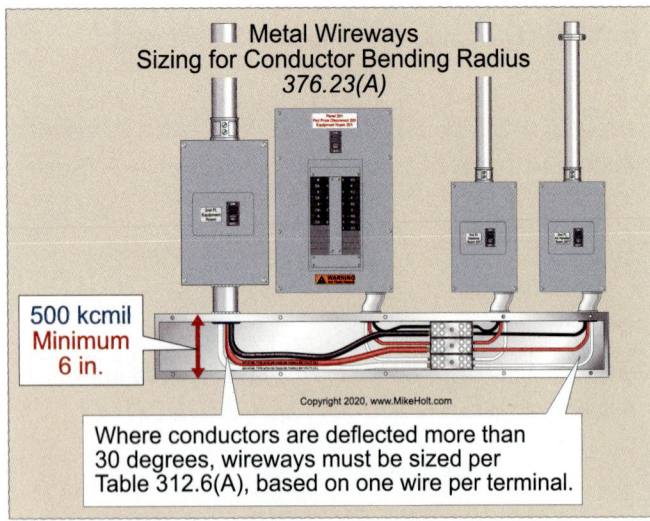
▶Figure 376-8

Solution:

According to Table 312.6(A), based on one wire per terminal, the wireway must be large enough to accommodate the bending space required for the largest conductor. In this application, it is based on the 500 kcmil conductors [376.23(A)].

Answer: (b) 6 in.

376.30 Supports

Wireways must be supported in accordance with (A) and (B).

(A) Horizontal Support. If installed horizontally, metal wireways must be supported at each end and at intervals not exceeding 5 ft. The distance between supports must not exceed 10 ft. ▶Figure 376-10

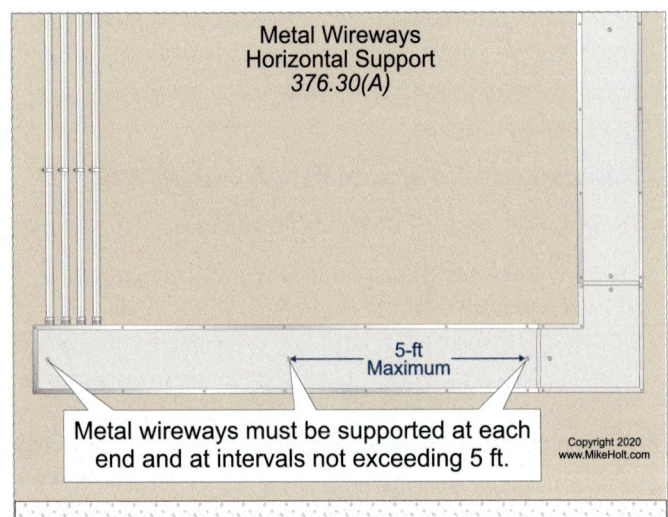
▶Figure 376-10

▶ **Wireway Bending Space Example**

Question: What minimum size wireway is suitable for three 500 kcmil THHN conductors from the first disconnect, three 3/0 AWG THHN conductors from the panelboard, and three 1/0 AWG THHN conductors from the other disconnect? ▶Figure 376-9

(a) 4 in.　　(b) 6 in.　　(c) 8 in.　　(d) 10 in.

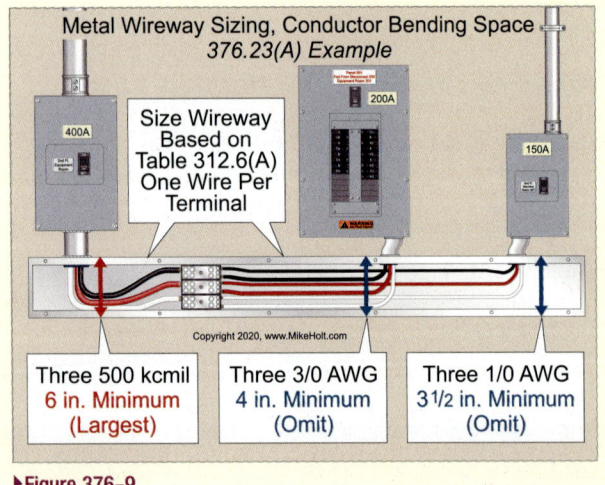
▶Figure 376-9

(B) Vertical Support. If installed vertically, metal wireways must be securely supported at intervals not exceeding 15 ft and with no more than one joint between supports. ▶Figure 376–11

▶Figure 376–11

376.56 Splices, Taps, and Power Distribution Blocks

(A) Splices and Taps. Splices and taps in metal wireways must be accessible, and they are not permitted to fill the wireway to more than 75 percent of the wireway's cross-sectional area. ▶Figure 376–12

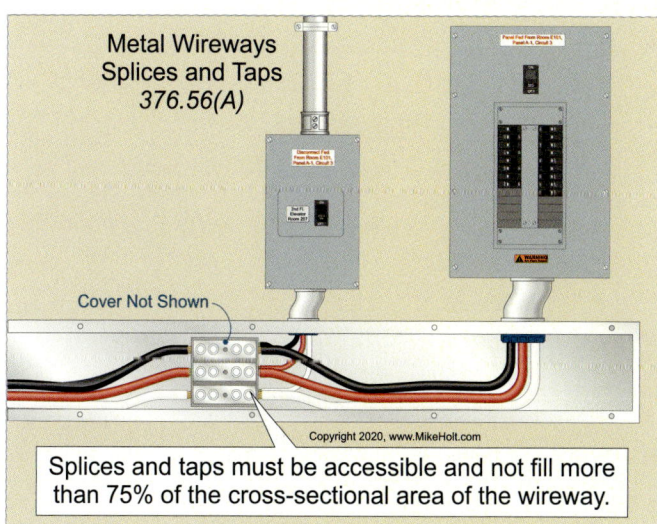
▶Figure 376–12

(B) Power Distribution Blocks.

(1) Installation. Power distribution blocks installed in wireways must be listed; if installed on the supply side of the service disconnect, they must be marked "suitable for use on the line side of service disconnect" or equivalent. ▶Figure 376–13

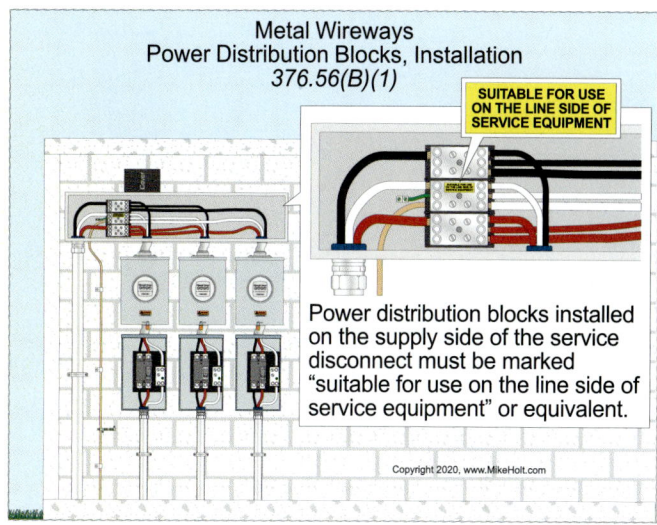
▶Figure 376–13

(2) Size of Enclosure. In addition to the wiring space requirements [376.56(A)], the power distribution block must be installed in a metal wireway not smaller than specified in the installation instructions of the power distribution block.

(3) Wire-Bending Space. Wire-bending space at the terminals of power distribution blocks must comply with 312.6(B).

(4) Live Parts. Power distribution blocks are not permitted to have uninsulated exposed live parts in the metal wireway after installation, whether the wireway cover is installed or not. ▶Figure 376–14

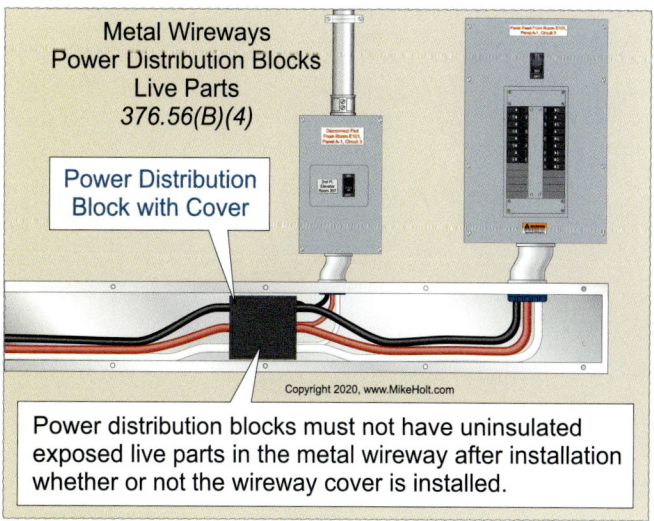
▶Figure 376–14

376.100 | Metal Wireways

(5) Conductors. Conductors must be installed so the terminals of the power distribution block are not obstructed. ▶Figure 376–15

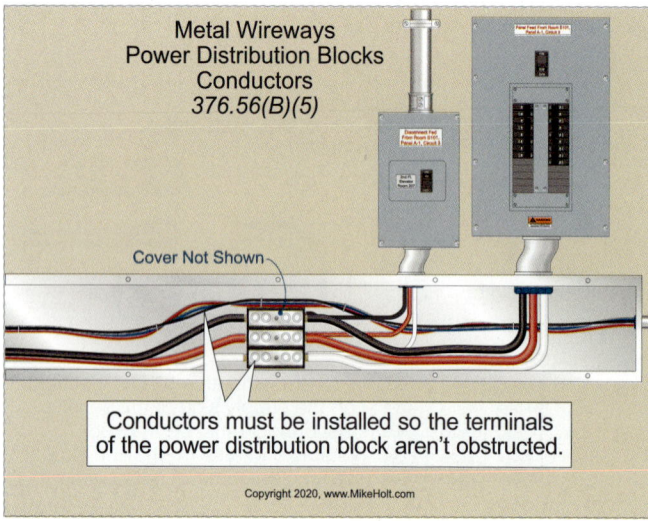

▶Figure 376–15

Part III. Construction Specifications

376.100 Construction

(A) Electrical and Mechanical Continuity. Wireways must be constructed and installed so the electrical and mechanical continuity of the complete system are assured. ▶Figure 376–16

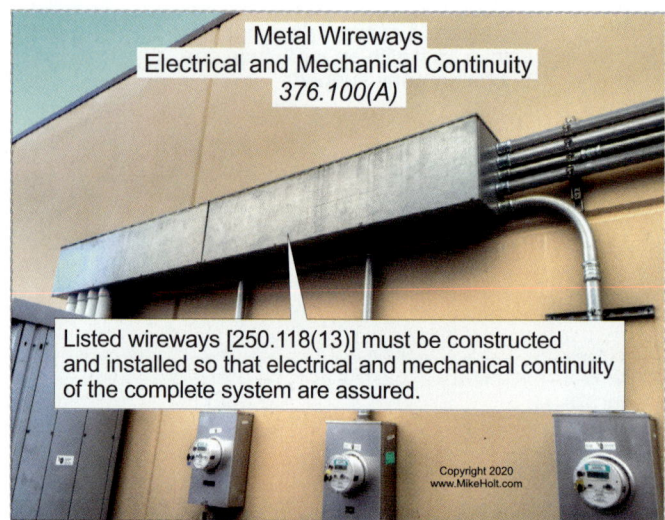

▶Figure 376–16

ARTICLE 380
MULTIOUTLET ASSEMBLIES

Introduction to Article 380—Multioutlet Assemblies

A multioutlet assembly is a surface, flush, or freestanding raceway designed to hold conductors and receptacles, and is assembled in the field or at the factory [Article 100]. It is not limited to systems commonly referred to by the trade names "Plugtrak®" or "Plugmold®."

Part I. General

380.1 Scope

Article 380 covers the use and installation requirements for multioutlet assemblies ▶Figure 380–1

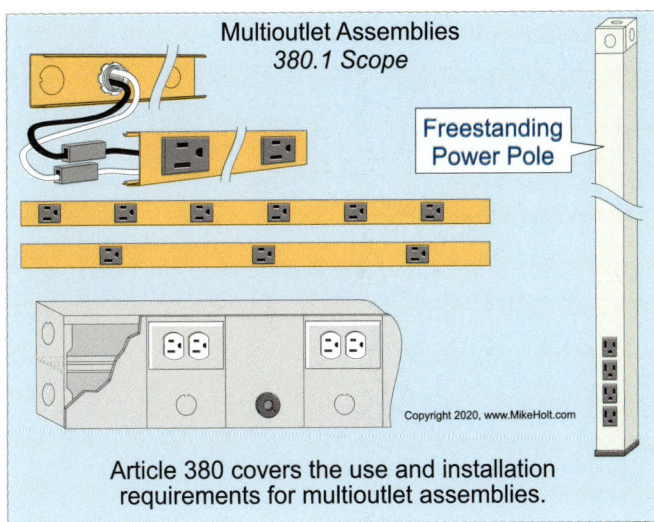

▶Figure 380–1

Part II. Installation

380.10 Uses Permitted

Multioutlet assemblies are only permitted in dry locations.

380.12 Uses Not Permitted

A multioutlet assembly must not be installed as follows:

(1) Concealed.

(2) Where subject to severe physical damage.

(3) If the voltage is 300V or more between conductors, unless the metal has a thickness not less than 0.04 in.

(4) Where subject to corrosive vapors.

(5) In hoistways.

(6) In any hazardous (classified) location except as permitted by 501.10(B).

(7) Where cord-and-plug-connected.

380.76 Through Partitions

Metal multioutlet assemblies can pass through a dry partition provided no receptacle is concealed in the wall, and the cover of the exposed portion of the system can be removed.

Notes

ARTICLE 386 SURFACE METAL RACEWAYS

Introduction to Article 386—Surface Metal Raceways

Using a surface metal raceway is a common method of adding a raceway when exposed traditional raceway systems are not acceptable, and concealing the raceway is not economically feasible. They come in several colors and are available with colored or real wood inserts designed to make them look like molding rather than raceways. A surface metal raceway is commonly known as "Wiremold®" in the field.

Part I. General

386.1 Scope

This article covers the use, installation, and construction specifications of surface metal raceways and associated fittings. ▶Figure 386–1

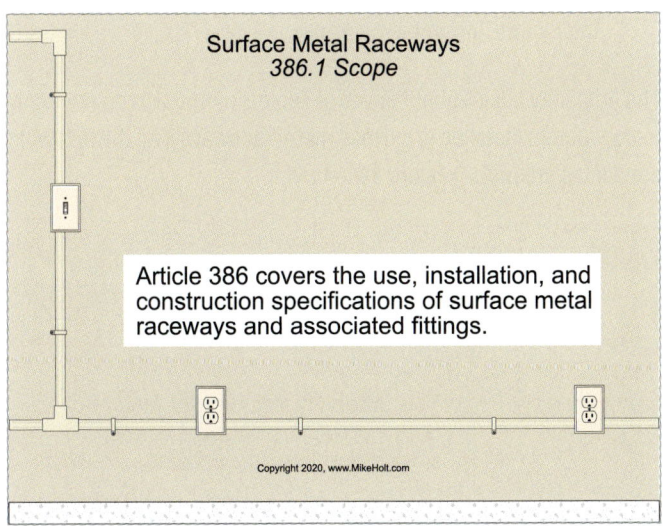

▶Figure 386–1

386.2 Definition

Surface Metal Raceway. A metal raceway with associated fittings in which conductors are placed after the raceway has been installed as a complete system [300.18(A)]. ▶Figure 386–2

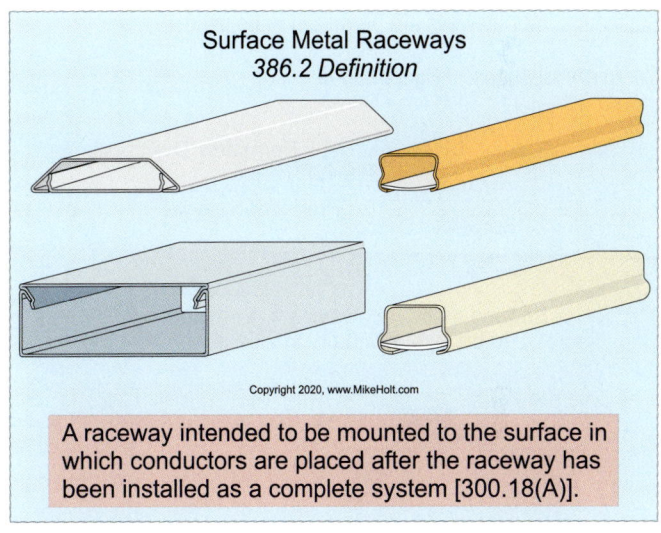

▶Figure 386–2

Author's Comment:

▸ Surface metal raceways are available in different shapes and sizes and can be mounted on walls, ceilings, or floors. Some of them have two or more separate compartments which permit the separation of power and lighting conductors from low-voltage or limited-energy conductors or cables (control, signaling, and communications cables and conductors) [386.70].

386.6 Listing Requirements

Surface metal raceways and associated fittings must be listed.

> **Author's Comment:**
> - Enclosures for switches, receptacles, luminaires, and other devices are identified by the markings on their packaging, which specify the type of surface metal raceway that can be used with the enclosure.

Part II. Installation

386.10 Uses Permitted

Surface metal raceways are permitted to be used:

(1) In dry locations. ▶Figure 386-3

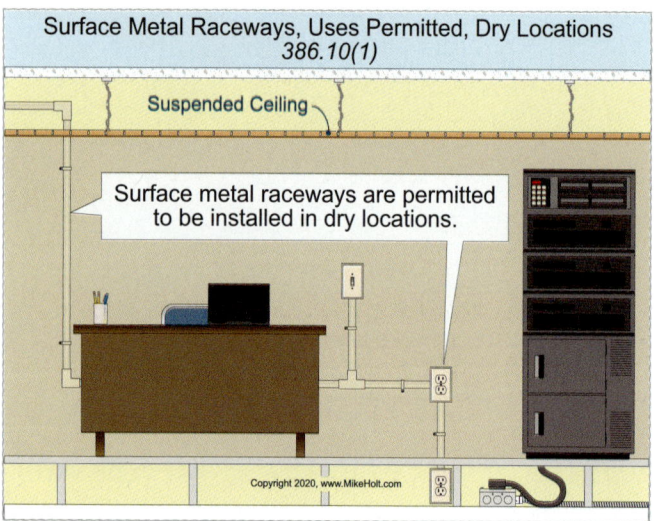

▶Figure 386-3

(2) In Class I, Division 2 locations, as permitted in 501.10(B)(3).

(3) Under raised floors, as permitted in 645.5(E)(2).

(4) Through walls and floors, if access to the conductors is maintained on both sides of the wall, partition, or floor.

386.12 Uses Not Permitted

Surface metal raceways are not permitted to be used:

(1) Where subject to severe physical damage unless approved by the authority having jurisdiction.

(2) If the voltage is 300V or more between conductors, unless the metal has a thickness not less than 0.04 in.

(3) Where subject to corrosive vapors.

(4) In hoistways.

(5) If concealed, except as permitted in 386.10.

386.21 Size of Conductors

The maximum size conductor permitted in a surface metal raceway is not permitted to be larger than that for which the raceway is designed.

386.22 Number of Conductors

The number of conductors installed in a surface metal raceway must not be more than the number for which the raceway is designed.

> **Author's Comment:**
> - The size and number of conductors permitted is marked on the raceway or on the package.

The ampacity adjustment factors of Table 310.15(C)(1) do not apply to conductors installed in surface metal raceways if all the following conditions are met: ▶Figure 386-4

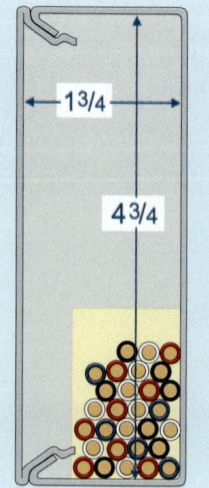

▶Figure 386-4

(1) The cross-sectional area of the raceway exceeds 4 sq in.,

(2) The number of current-carrying conductors does not exceed 30, and

(3) The sum of the cross-sectional areas of all contained conductors does not exceed 20 percent of the interior cross-sectional area of the raceway.

386.30 Securing and Supporting

Surface metal raceways and fittings must be supported in accordance with the manufacturer's installation instructions. ▶Figure 386-5

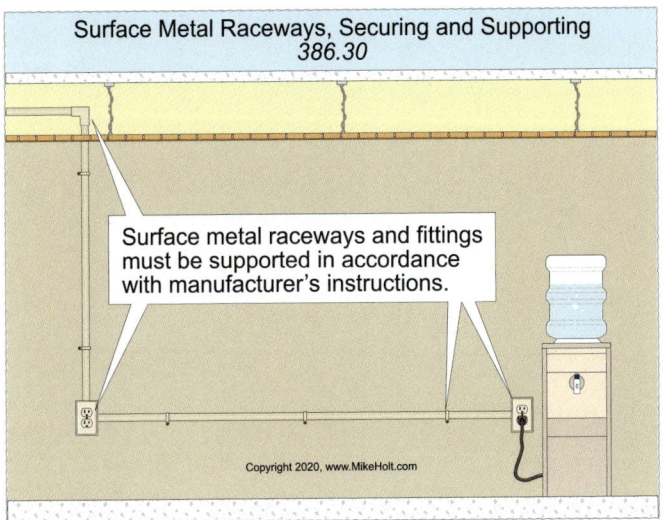

▶Figure 386-5

386.56 Splices and Taps

Splices and taps must be accessible and they, along with any conductors, must not fill the raceway to more than 75 percent of its cross-sectional area.

386.60 Equipment Grounding Conductor

Surface metal raceway fittings must be mechanically and electrically joined together in a manner that does not subject the conductors to abrasion. Surface metal raceways that allow a transition to another wiring method, such as knockouts for connecting raceways, must have a means for the termination of an equipment grounding conductor.

A surface metal raceway is suitable as an equipment grounding conductor in accordance with 250.118(14). ▶Figure 386-6

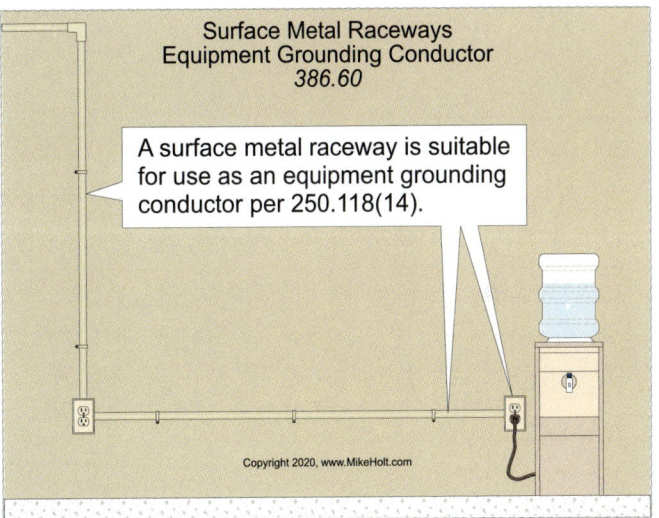

▶Figure 386-6

386.70 Separate Compartments

Where surface metal raceways have separate compartments, power and lighting conductors can occupy one compartment and the other one may contain control, signaling, or communications wiring. Stamping, imprinting, or color coding of the interior finish must identify the separate compartments, and the same relative position of compartments must be maintained throughout the premises.

Notes

ARTICLE 392 CABLE TRAYS

Introduction to Article 392—Cable Trays

A cable tray system is a unit or an assembly of units or sections with associated fittings that forms a structural system used to securely fasten or support cables and raceways. Cable tray systems include ladder, ventilated trough, ventilated channel, solid bottom, and other similar structures. They are manufactured in many forms—from a simple hanger or wire mesh to a substantial, rigid, steel support system. Cable trays are designed and manufactured to support specific wiring methods, as identified in 392.10(A).

Part I. General

392.1 Scope

Article 392 covers cable tray systems, including ladder, ventilated trough, ventilated channel, solid bottom, and other similar structures. ▶Figure 392–1

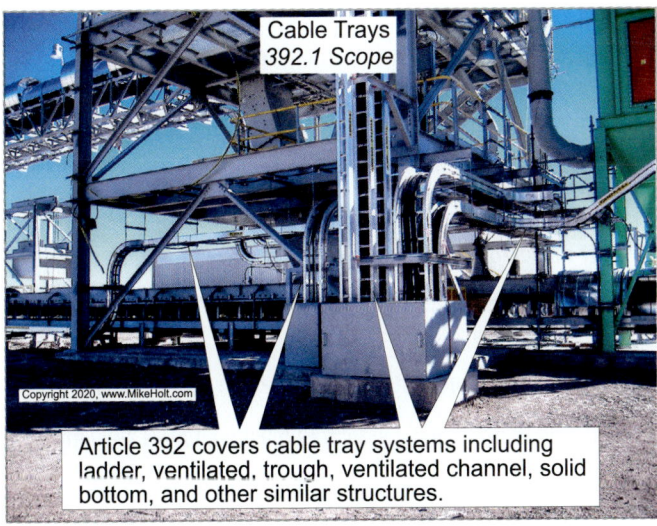

▶Figure 392–1

392.2 Definition

Cable Tray System. A unit or assembly of units or sections with associated fittings forming a rigid structural system used to securely fasten or support cables and raceways. ▶Figure 392–2

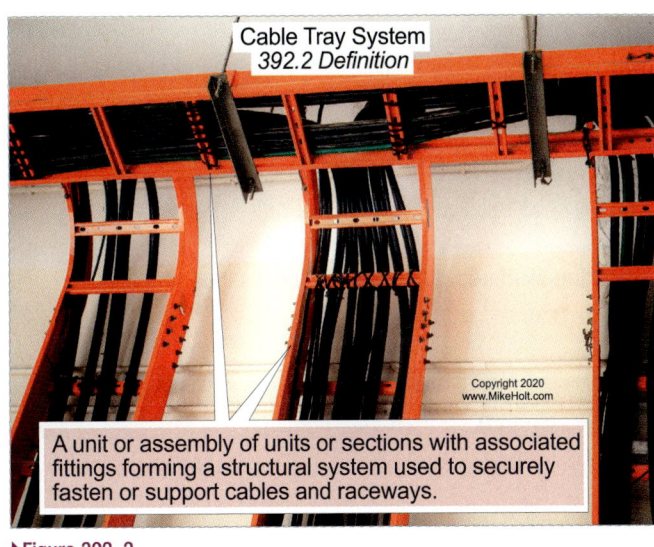

▶Figure 392–2

Author's Comment:

▶ A cable tray is not a raceway, it is a support system for cables and raceways.

Part II. Installation

392.10 Uses Permitted

Cable trays can be used as a support system for wiring methods containing service, feeder, branch circuits, communications circuits, control circuits, and signaling circuits. ▶Figure 392–3

392.10 | Cable Trays

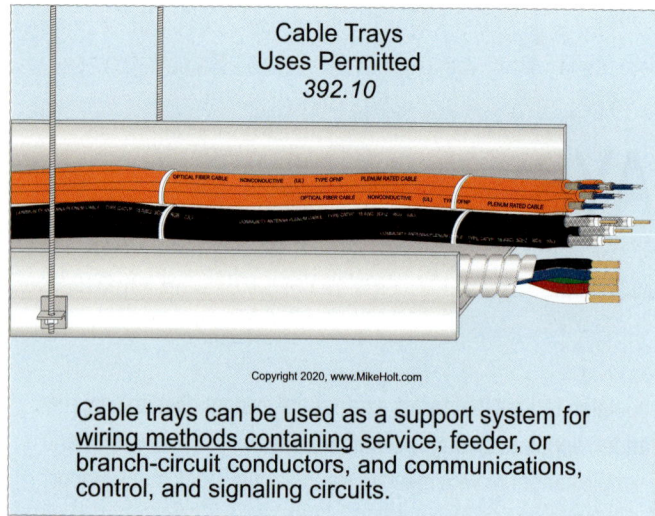

Cable trays can be used as a support system for wiring methods containing service, feeder, or branch-circuit conductors, and communications, control, and signaling circuits.

▶Figure 392–3

Single insulated conductors are only permitted in cable trays when installed in accordance with 392.10(B)(1).

Author's Comment:

▶ Cable trays used to support service-entrance conductors must be installed in accordance with 230.44.

(A) Wiring Methods. Any of the wiring methods contained in Table 392.10(A) can be installed in a cable tray.

Table 392.10(A) Wiring Methods

Wiring Method	Article/Section
Armored cable	320
Coaxial cables	820
Class 2 & 3 cables	725
Communications cables	800
Communications raceways	725, 770, and 800
Electrical metallic tubing	358
Electrical nonmetallic tubing	362
Fire alarm cables	760
Flexible metal conduit	348
Instrumentation tray cable	727
Intermediate metal conduit	342
Liquidtight flexible metal conduit	350
Liquidtight flexible nonmetallic conduit	356
Metal-clad cable	330
Nonmetallic-sheathed cable	334
Polyvinyl chloride (PVC) conduit	352
Power and control tray cable	336
Power-limited fire alarm cable	760
Power-limited tray cable	Table 725.154 and 725.179(E) and 725.135(H)
Rigid metal conduit	344
Service-entrance cable	338
Signaling raceway	725
Underground feeder and branch-circuit cable	340

Author's Comment:

▶ Metal cable trays can be used in environmental air spaces (plenums) only when the wiring methods it supports are permitted in accordance with 300.22(C).

(B) In Industrial Establishments.

(1) Where conditions of maintenance and supervision ensure that only qualified persons service the installed cable tray system, single-conductor cables can be installed in accordance with the following: ▶Figure 392–4

(a) 1/0 AWG and larger listed and marked for use in cable trays.

(c) Equipment grounding conductors must be 4 AWG and larger.

(C) Hazardous (Classified) Locations. Cable trays in hazardous (classified) locations must contain only the cable types and raceways permitted by this *Code* for the application.

Author's Comment:

▶ For permitted cable types in hazardous (classified) locations, see 501.10, 502.10, 503.10, 504.20, and 505.15.

Cable Trays | 392.18

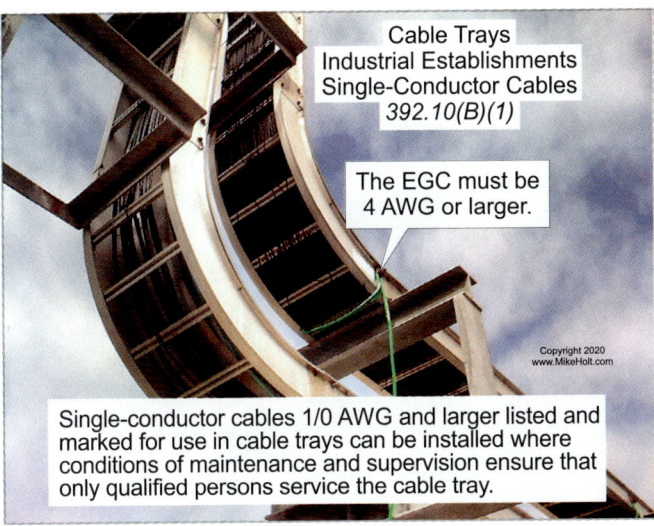
▶Figure 392-4

392.12 Uses Not Permitted

Cable tray systems are not permitted in hoistways or where subject to severe physical damage.

392.18 Cable Tray Installations

(A) Complete System. Cable trays must be installed as a complete system, except that mechanically discontinuous segments between cable tray runs, or between cable tray runs and equipment are permitted. The system must provide for the support of the cables and raceways in accordance with their corresponding articles. ▶Figure 392-5

▶Figure 392-5

A bonding jumper, sized in accordance with 250.102 and installed in accordance with 250.96, must bond the sections of metal cable tray, or the cable tray and the raceway or equipment.

(B) Completed Before Installation. Each run of cable tray must be completed before the installation of cables or conductors.

(D) Through Partitions and Walls. Cable trays can extend through partitions and walls, or vertically through platforms and floors, if the installation is made in accordance with the firestopping requirements of 300.21.

(E) Exposed and Accessible. Cable trays must be exposed and accessible, except as permitted by 392.18(D).

(F) Adequate Access. Sufficient space must be provided and maintained about cable trays to permit adequate access for installing and maintaining the cables.

(G) Raceways, Cables, and Boxes Supported from Cable Trays. In industrial facilities where conditions of maintenance and supervision ensure only qualified persons will service the installation, cable tray systems can support raceways, cables, boxes, and conduit bodies.
▶Figure 392-6

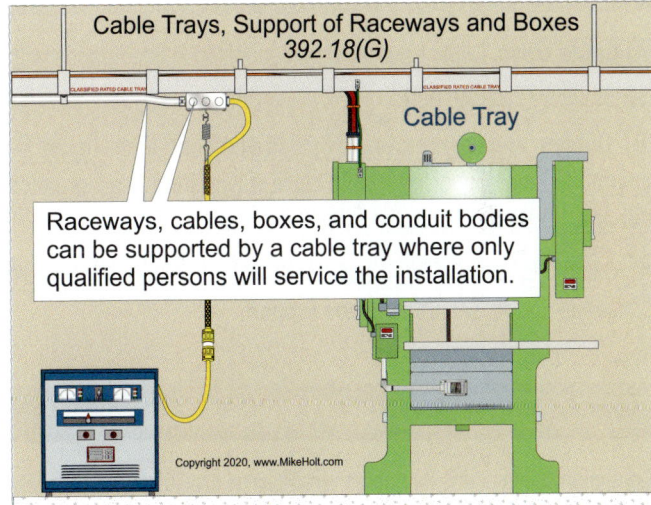
▶Figure 392-6

For raceways terminating at a cable tray, a listed cable tray clamp or adapter must be used to securely fasten the raceway to the cable tray system. The raceway must be supported and secured in accordance with the appropriate raceway article.

Raceways or cables running parallel to a cable tray system can be attached to the bottom or side of the cable tray system. The raceway or cable must be fastened and supported in accordance with the appropriate raceway or cable article.

392.20 | Cable Trays

Boxes and conduit bodies attached to the bottom or side of a cable tray system must be fastened and supported in accordance with 314.23.

(H) Marking. Cable trays containing conductors operating over 600 volts must have a permanent, legible warning notice carrying the wording, **"DANGER—HIGH VOLTAGE—KEEP AWAY"** placed in a readily visible position on all cable trays, with the spacing of warning notices not to exceed 10 ft. The danger marking(s) or labels must comply with 110.21(B).

392.20 Cable and Conductor Installation

(C) Connected in Parallel. To prevent unbalanced current in the parallel conductors due to inductive reactance, all circuit conductors of a parallel set (phase and neutral [310.10(G)]) must be bundled together and secured to prevent excessive movement due to fault-current magnetic forces.

(D) Single Conductors. Conductors not connected in parallel must be installed in a single layer, unless the conductors are bound together.

392.30 Securing and Supporting

(A) Cable Trays. Cable trays must be supported in accordance with the installation instructions.

(B) Cables and Conductors. Cables and conductors must be secured to, and supported by, the cable tray system in accordance with 392.30(B)(1), (2), (3), and (4).

(4) Cable ties must be listed and identified as suitable for the application and for securement and support.

392.44 Expansion Splice Plates

Expansion splice plates for cable trays must be provided where necessary to compensate for thermal expansion and contraction.

392.46 Bushed Conduit and Tubing

A box is not required where cables or conductors are installed in a bushed raceway used for support, protection against physical damage, or where conductors or cables transition to a raceway from the cable tray. ▶Figure 392–7

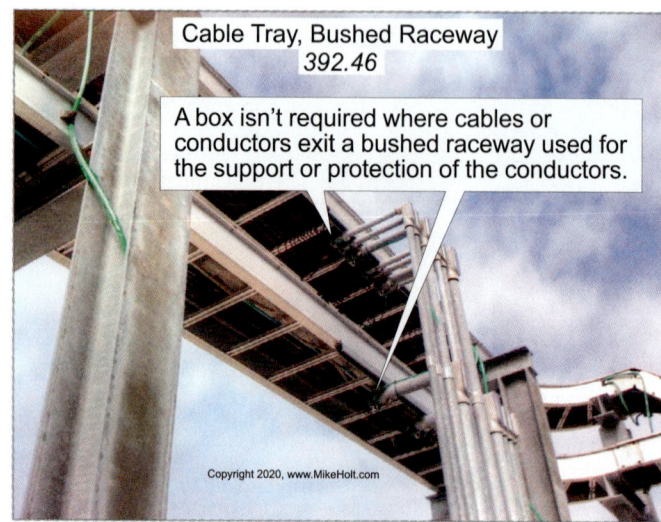

▶Figure 392–7

(A) Through Bushed Conduit or Tubing. Individual conductors or multiconductor cables with entirely nonmetallic sheaths, can enter enclosures where they are terminated through nonflexible bushed conduit or tubing installed for their protection, provided they are secured at the point of transition from the cable tray and the raceway is sealed at the outer end using an approved means so debris is prevented debris from entering the equipment through the raceway.

(B) Flanged Connections. Individual conductors or multiconductor cables with entirely nonmetallic sheaths can enter enclosures through openings associated with flanges from cable trays where the cable tray is attached to the flange and the flange is mounted directly to the equipment. The openings must be made so the conductors are protected from abrasion and must be sealed or covered to prevent debris from entering the enclosure through them.

Note: One method of preventing debris from entering the enclosure is to seal the outer end of the raceway or the opening with duct seal.

392.56 Cable Splices

Splices are permitted in a cable tray if the splice is accessible and insulated by a method approved by the authority having jurisdiction. Splices can project above the side rails of the cable tray if not subject to physical damage. ▶Figure 392–8

Cable Trays | 392.60

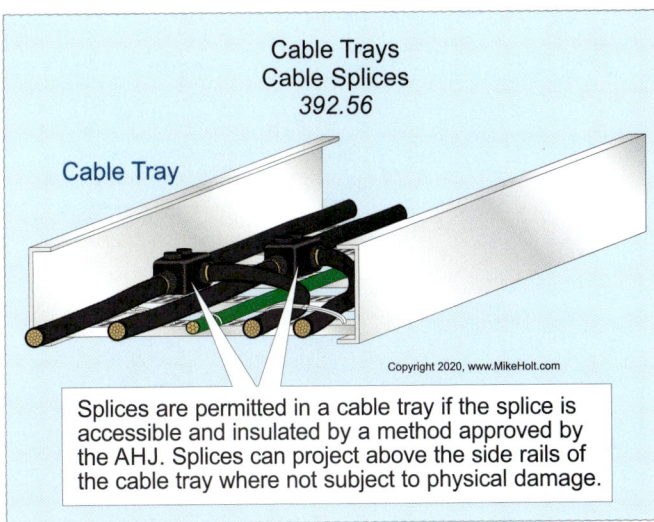
▶Figure 392–8

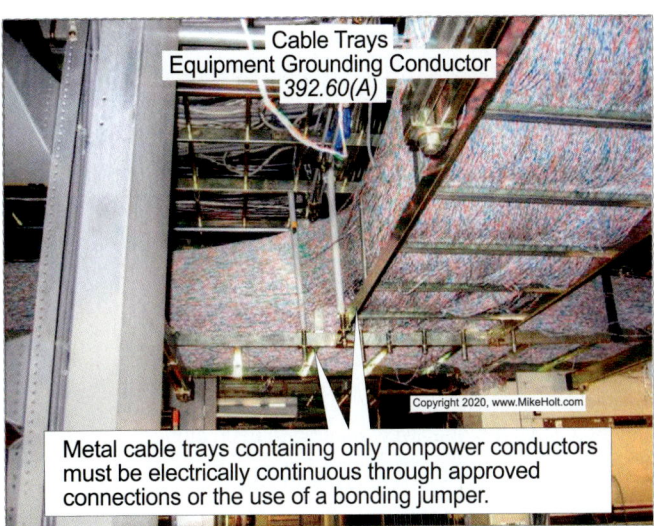
▶Figure 392–10

392.60 Equipment Grounding Conductor

(A) Used as an Equipment Grounding Conductor. Metal cable trays can be used as equipment grounding conductors where continuous maintenance and supervision ensure that only qualified persons will service the cable tray system. ▶Figure 392–9

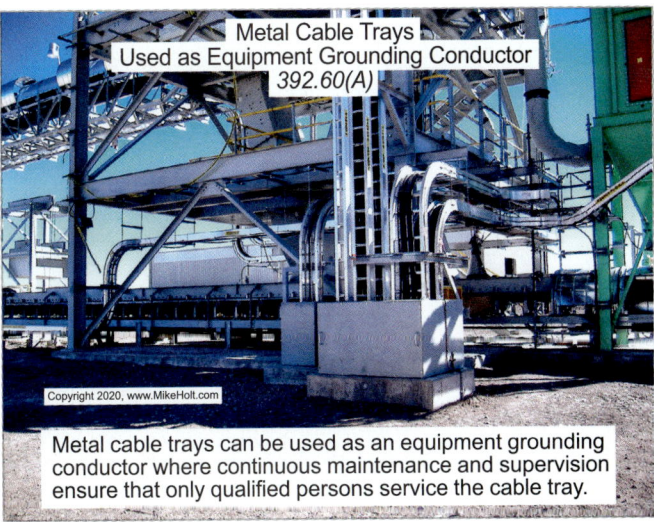
▶Figure 392–9

Metal cable trays containing single conductors must be bonded together to ensure they have the capacity to conduct safely any fault current likely to be imposed, in accordance with 250.96(A).

Metal cable trays containing communications, data, and signaling conductors and cables must be electrically continuous through approved connections or the use of a bonding jumper. ▶Figure 392–10

(B) Serve as an Equipment Grounding Conductor. Metal cable trays can serve as equipment grounding conductors where the following requirements have been met [392.10(C)]:

(1) Metal cable trays and fittings are identified as an equipment grounding conductor. ▶Figure 392–11

▶Figure 392–11

(4) Cable tray sections, fittings, and connected raceways are effectively bonded to each other to ensure electrical continuity and the capacity to conduct safely any fault current likely to be imposed on them [250.96(A)]. This is accomplished by using bolted mechanical connectors or bonding jumpers sized in accordance with 250.102. ▶Figure 392–12

392.60 | Cable Trays

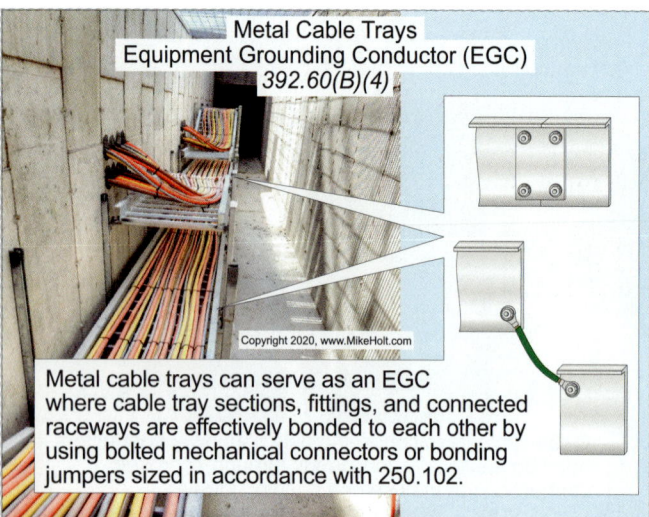

▶Figure 392–12

CHAPTER 4

EQUIPMENT FOR GENERAL USE

Introduction to Chapter 4—Equipment for General Use

With the first three chapters of the *NEC* behind you, this fourth one is necessary for building a solid foundation in general equipment installations. It helps you apply the first three chapters to installations involving general equipment. You need to understand the first four chapters of the *Code* to properly apply the requirements to Chapters 5, 6, and 7, and at times to Chapter 8.

Chapter 4 is arranged in the following manner:

- **Article 400—Flexible Cords and Flexible Cables.** Article 400 covers the general requirements, applications, and construction specifications for flexible cords and flexible cables.
- **Article 404—Switches.** The requirements of Article 404 apply to switches of all types. These include snap (toggle) switches, dimmer switches, fan switches, knife switches, circuit breakers, and automatic switches such as time clocks, timers, and switches and circuit breakers used for a disconnecting means.
- **Article 408—Switchboards and Panelboards.** Article 408 covers specific requirements for switchboards, panelboards, and distribution boards that supply lighting and power circuits.

   Author's Comment:
   - See Article 100 for the definitions of "Panelboard" and "Switchboard."

- **Article 445—Generators.** Article 445 contains the electrical installation requirements for generators and other requirements, such as where they can be installed, nameplate markings, conductor ampacity, and disconnecting means.
- **Article 450—Transformers.** This article covers the installation of transformers.
- **Article 480—Storage Batteries.** Article 480 covers stationary installations of storage batteries.

Notes

ARTICLE 400 — FLEXIBLE CORDS AND FLEXIBLE CABLES

Introduction to Article 400—Flexible Cords and Flexible Cables

This article covers the general requirements, applications, and construction specifications for flexible cords and flexible cables. The *NEC* does not consider flexible cords to be a wiring method like those addressed in Chapter 3.

Always use a flexible cord (and fittings) identified for the application. Table 400.4 will help you in that regard. For example, use cords listed for a wet location if you are using them outdoors. The jacket material of any flexible cord is tested to maintain its insulation properties and other characteristics in the environments for which it has been listed. Tables 400.5(A)(1) and 400.5(A)(2) are also important tables to turn to when looking for the ampacity of flexible cords and flexible cables. Flexible cords and flexible cables may include the various types of wire which are used for lamps, appliances, extension cords, drop and pendant lights, pool pumps, and so on.

400.1 Scope

Article 400 covers the general requirements, applications, and construction specifications for flexible cords and flexible cables as contained in Table 400.4. ▶Figure 400-1

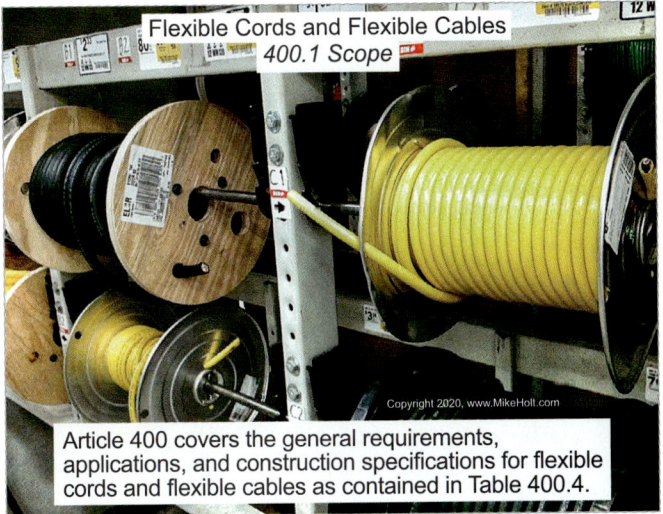

▶Figure 400-1

400.3 Suitability

Flexible cords and flexible cables, as well as their fittings, must be suitable for the use and location. ▶Figure 400-2

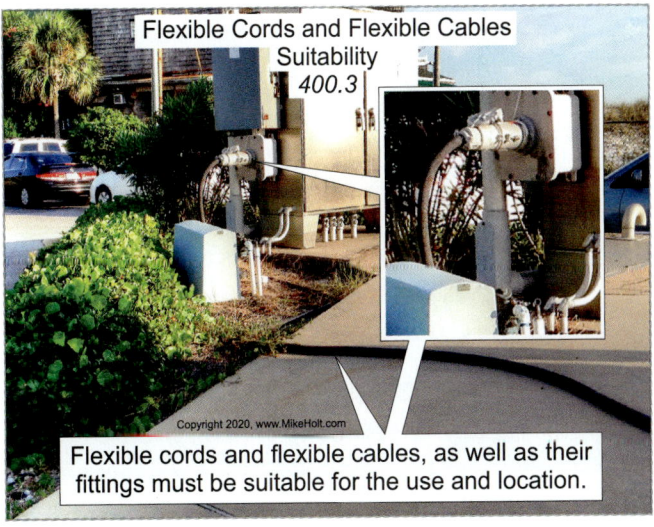

▶Figure 400-2

400.4 Types of Flexible Cords and Flexible Cables

The use of flexible cords and flexible cables must conform to the descriptions contained in Table 400.4. ▶Figure 400–3

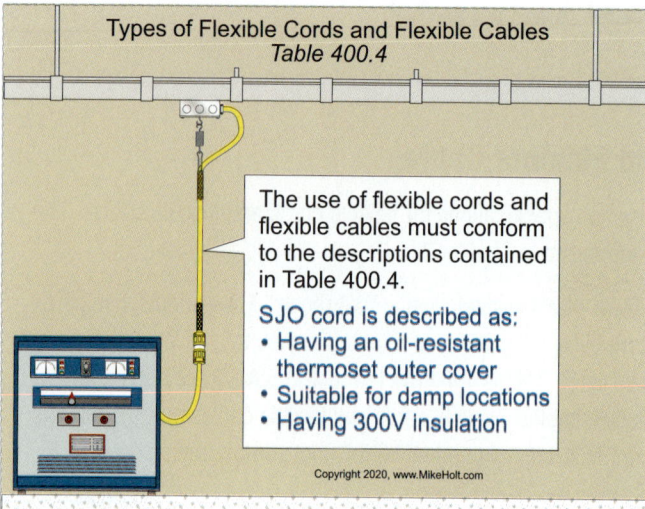

▶Figure 400–3

Author's Comment:

▸ The suffix "W" at the end of a flexible cord type designates that it is water and sunlight resistant [Table 400.4, Note 9].

▸ When ordering cord, be sure you are specific! Unlike Romex®, when you order cord, what you ask for is exactly what you get. For example, 14/2 Romex® will have a black, white, and equipment grounding conductor. Not so with Type SJ flexible cord; 14/2 SJ will only have two conductors and no equipment grounding conductor while 14/3 SJ has three conductors including an equipment grounding conductor. Be sure to order by the total number of conductors needed for your installation.

400.5 Ampacity of Flexible Cords and Flexible Cables

(A) Ampacity Tables. Table 400.5(A)(1) lists the ampacity for the individual conductors inside manufactured flexible cords while Table 400.5(A)(2) lists the ampacity for overall cord assemblies with not more than three current-carrying conductors in an ambient temperature of not more than 86°F.

400.10 Uses Permitted

(A) Uses Permitted. Flexible cords and flexible cables within the scope of this article can be used for:

(1) Pendants [receptacles—210.50(A) and boxes—314.23(H)].

(2) Wiring of luminaires [410.24(A) and 410.62(B)].

(3) Connection of portable luminaires, portable and mobile signs, or appliances [422.16]. ▶Figure 400–4

▶Figure 400–4

(4) Elevator cables.

(5) Wiring of cranes and hoists.

(6) Connection of utilization equipment to facilitate frequent interchange [422.16]. ▶Figure 400–5

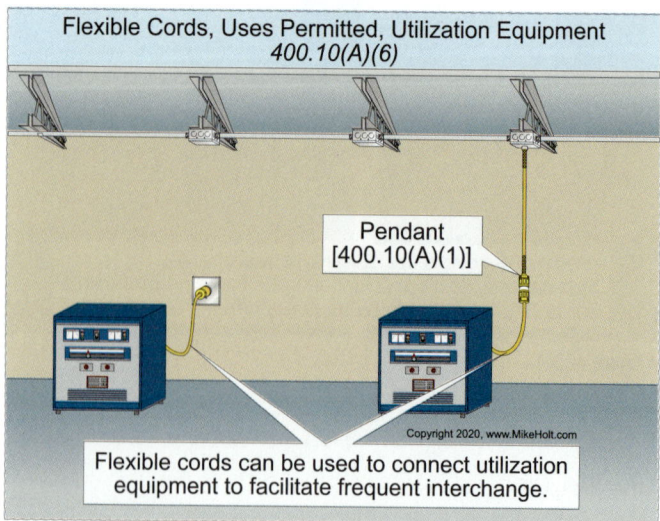

▶Figure 400–5

(7) Prevention of the transmission of noise or vibration [422.16].

(8) Appliances where the fastening means and mechanical connections are specifically designed to permit ready removal for maintenance and repair, and the appliance is intended or identified for flexible cord connections [422.16]. ▶Figure 400-6

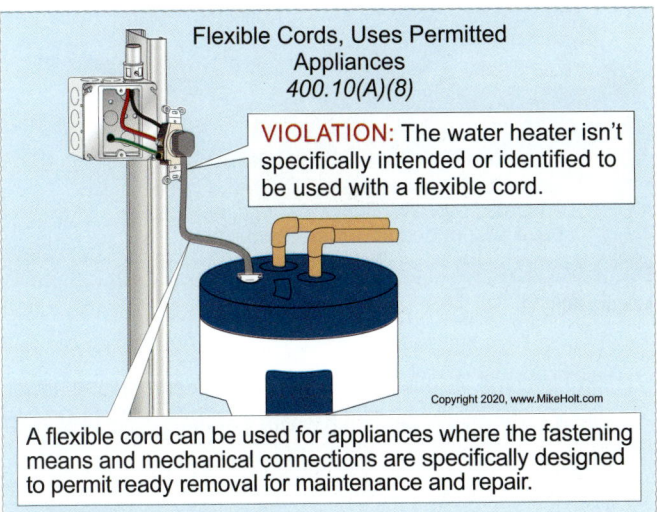
▶Figure 400-6

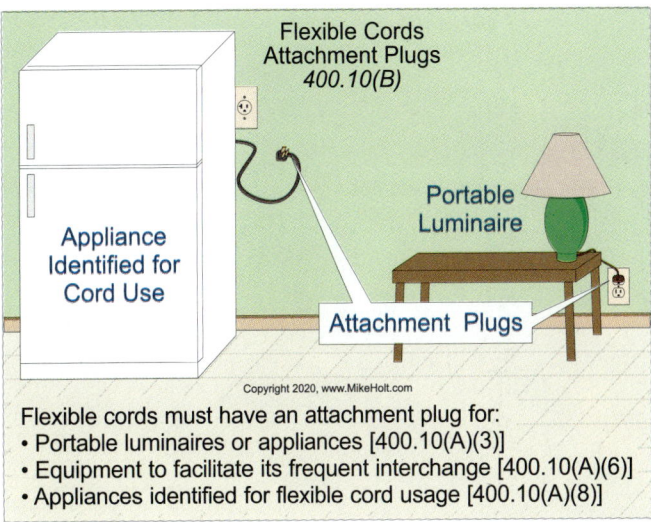
▶Figure 400-7

Author's Comment:

▸ Water heaters, furnaces, and other appliances fastened in place cannot be connected by a flexible cord unless the appliances are specifically identified to be used with a flexible cord [422.16].

(9) Connection of moving parts.

(B) Attachment Plugs. Attachment plugs are required for flexible cords used in any of the following applications: ▶Figure 400-7

- Portable luminaires, portable and mobile signs, or appliances [400.10(A)(3)].
- Stationary equipment to facilitate its frequent interchange [400.10(A)(6) and 422.16].
- Appliances specifically designed to permit ready removal for maintenance and repair and identified for flexible cord connection [400.10(A)(8)].

400.12 Uses Not Permitted

Unless specifically permitted in 400.10, flexible cords, flexible cables, cord sets (extension cords), and power-supply cords are not permitted for the following:

(1) Flexible cords, flexible cables, cord sets (extension cords), and power-supply cords are not permitted to be a substitute for the fixed wiring. ▶Figure 400-8

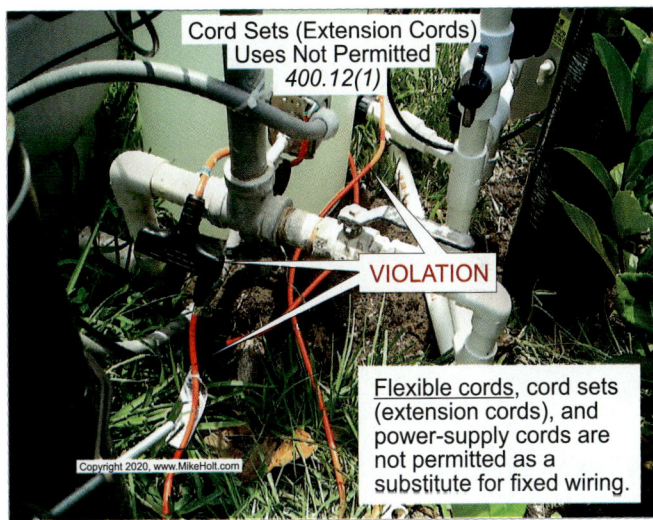
▶Figure 400-8

(2) Flexible cords, flexible cables, cord sets (extension cords), and power-supply cords must not be run through holes in walls, ceilings, or floors. ▶Figure 400-9 and ▶Figure 400-10

(3) Flexible cords, flexible cables, cord sets (extension cords), and power-supply cords are not permitted to be run through doorways, windows, or similar openings.

(4) Flexible cords, flexible cables, cord sets (extension cords), and power-supply cords must not be attached to building surfaces.

400.14 | Flexible Cords and Flexible Cables

▶Figure 400-9

▶Figure 400-11

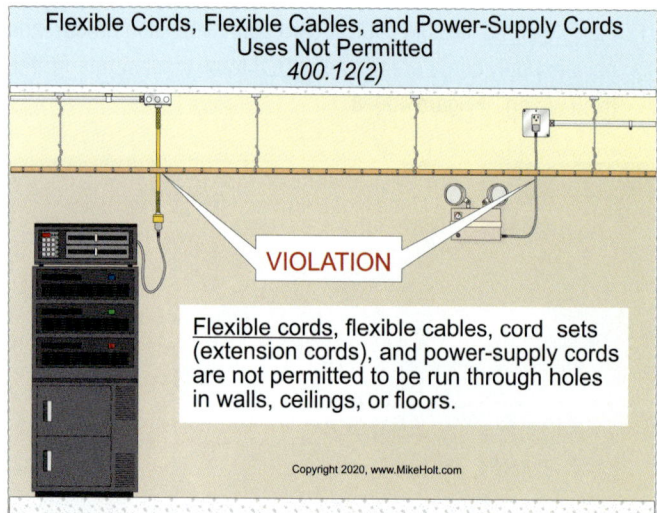
▶Figure 400-10

(5) Flexible cords, flexible cables, cord sets (extension cords), and power-supply cords are not permitted to be concealed by walls, floors, or ceilings, or located above suspended or dropped ceilings. ▶Figure 400-11

Ex to (5): Flexible cords, flexible cables, and power-supply cords are permitted if contained within an enclosure for use in other spaces used for environmental air as permitted by [300.22(C)(3)].

(6) Flexible cords, flexible cord sets (extension cords), and power-supply cords must not be installed in raceways, except as permitted by 400.17 for industrial establishments where the conditions of maintenance and supervision ensure that only qualified persons will service the installation.

(7) Flexible cords, flexible cord sets (extension cords), and power-supply cords are not permitted where they are subject to physical damage.

400.14 Pull at Joints and Terminals

Flexible cords must be installed so tension will not be transmitted to the conductor terminals. ▶Figure 400-12

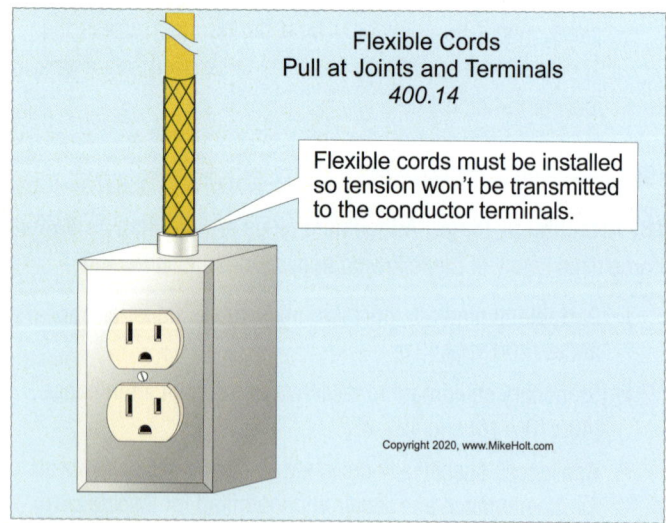
▶Figure 400-12

Note: This can be accomplished by knotting the cord, winding it with tape, or by using support or strain-relief fittings. ▶Figure 400-13

Flexible Cords and Flexible Cables | 400.17

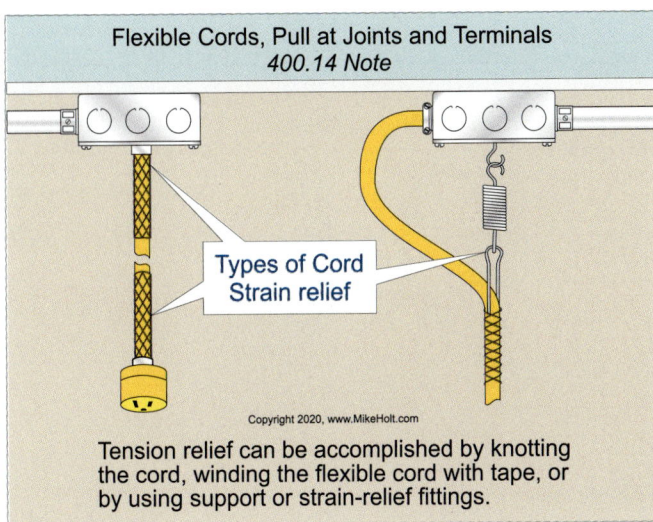
▶Figure 400-13

400.17 Protection from Damage

Flexible cords must be protected by bushings or fittings where passing through holes in covers, outlet boxes, or similar enclosures.

Notes

ARTICLE 404 SWITCHES

Introduction to Article 404—Switches

The requirements of Article 404 address switches of all types including snap (toggle) switches, dimmer switches, fan switches, knife switches, circuit breakers, and automatic switches such as time clocks and timers.

Part I. Installation

404.1 Scope

The requirements of Article 404 apply to all types of switches, switching devices, and circuit breakers. ▶Figure 404-1

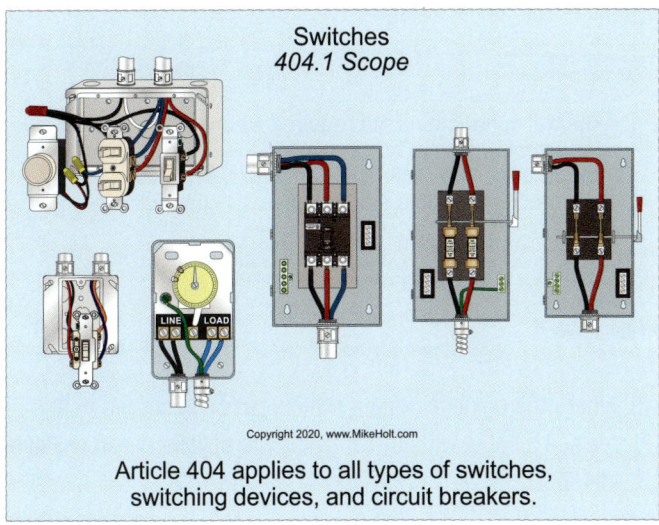

▶Figure 404-1

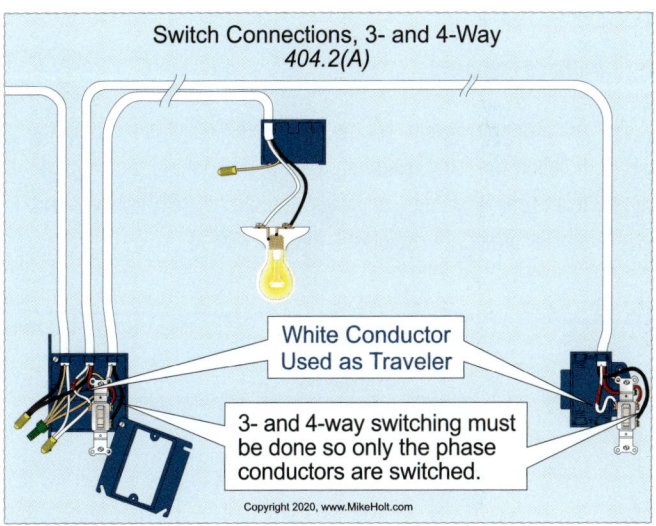

▶Figure 404-2

404.2 Switch Connections

(A) Three-Way and Four-Way Switches. Wiring for 3-way and 4-way switching must be done so only the phase conductors are switched. ▶Figure 404-2

(B) Switching Neutral Conductors. Neutral conductors are not permitted to be switched.

Author's Comment:

▶ A permanently reidentified white conductor within a cable can be used as a phase conductor for switching purposes [200.7(C)(1)].

(C) Switches Controlling Lighting Loads. Switches controlling line-to-neutral lighting loads must have a neutral conductor installed at all switches serving bathroom areas, hallways, stairways, and habitable rooms or occupiable spaces as defined in the building code. ▶Figure 404-3

404.2 | Switches

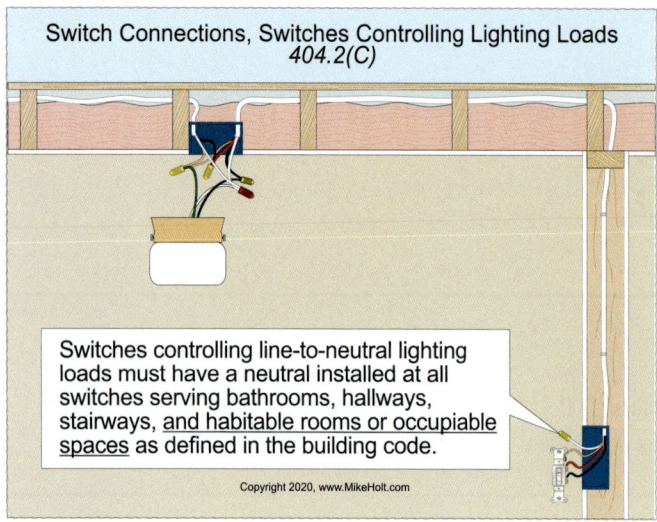
▶Figure 404–3

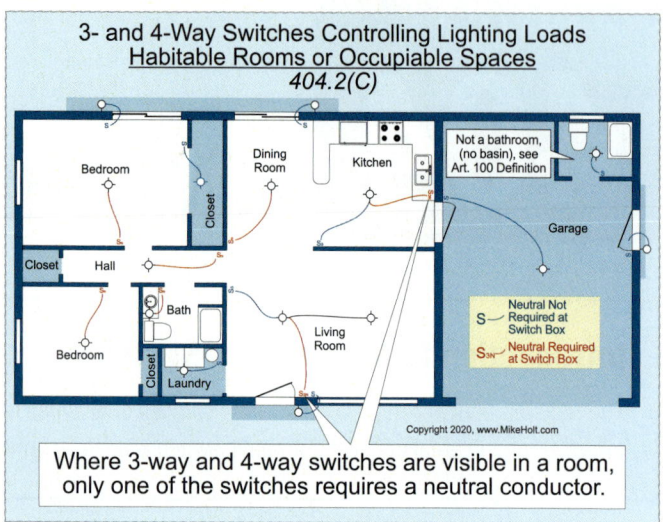
▶Figure 404–5

Author's Comment:

▸ According to Article 100, a "Habitable Room" is a room in a building for living, sleeping, eating, or cooking. Bathrooms, toilet rooms, closets, hallways, storage or utility spaces, and similar areas are excluded. ▶Figure 404–4

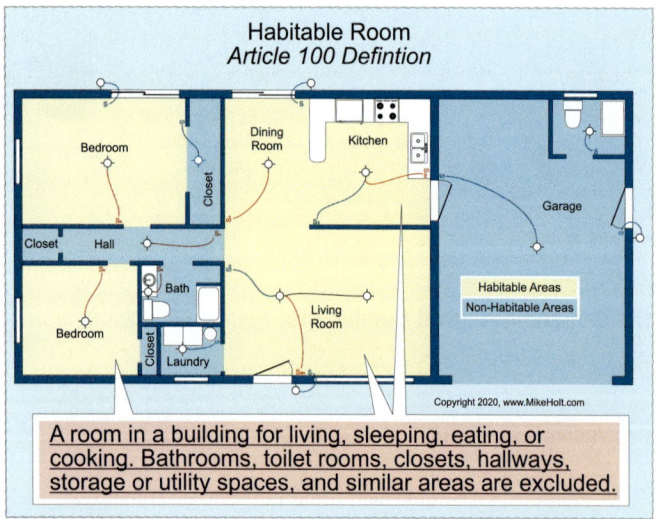
▶Figure 404–4

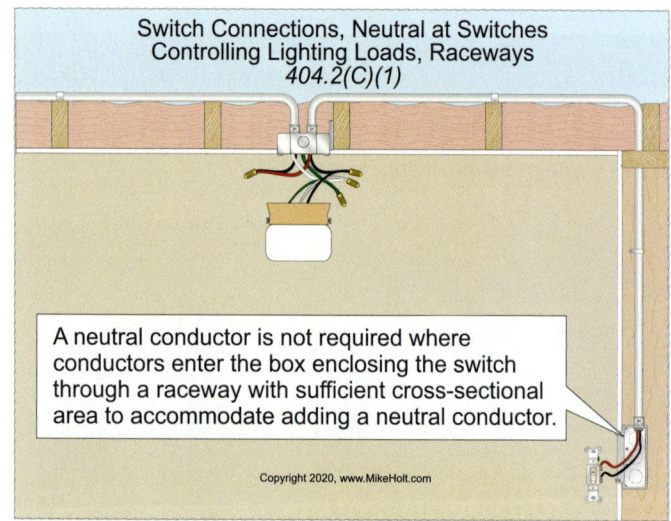
▶Figure 404–6

Where 3-way and 4-way switches are visible in a room, only one of the switches requires a neutral conductor. ▶Figure 404–5

A neutral conductor is not required to be installed at lighting switch locations under any of the following conditions:

(1) Where conductors enter the box enclosing the switch through a raceway with enough cross-sectional area to accommodate a neutral conductor. ▶Figure 404–6

(2) Where the box enclosing a switch can be accessed to add or replace a cable without damaging the building finish. ▶Figure 404–7

(3) Where snap switches with integral enclosures comply with 300.15(E).

(4) Where the lighting is controlled by automatic means.

(5) Where switches control receptacles. ▶Figure 404–8

If not already present, a neutral conductor must be installed for any replacement switch that requires line-to-neutral voltage [404.22] to operate the electronics of the switch in the standby mode. ▶Figure 404–9

Switches | 404.3

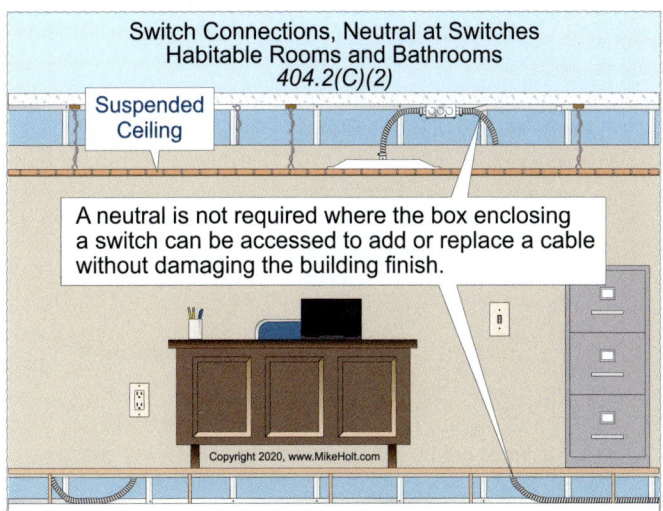

▶Figure 404-7

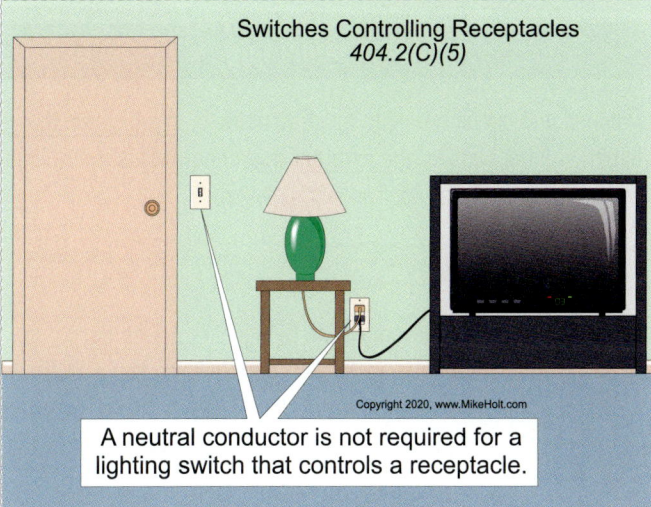

▶Figure 404-8

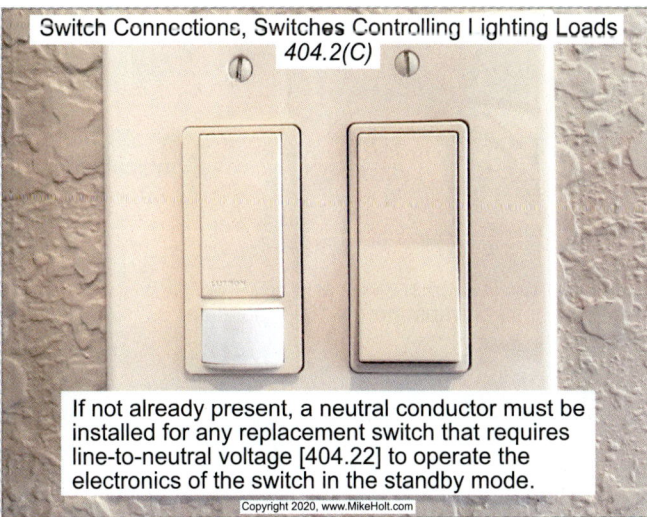

▶Figure 404-9

Ex: A neutral conductor is not required for replacement switches installed in locations wired prior to the adoption of 404.2(C) where the neutral conductor cannot be extended without removing finish materials. The number of electronic lighting control switches without a neutral conductor on a branch circuit is not permitted to exceed five, and the number of switches connected to any feeder is not permitted to exceed 25.

Author's Comment:

▸ The purpose of the neutral conductor at a switch is to complete a circuit path for electronic lighting control devices that require a neutral conductor.

404.3 Switch Enclosures

(A) General. Switches and circuit breakers must be mounted in an enclosure listed for the intended use.

(B) Used as a Raceway, Taps, or Splices. Switch or circuit-breaker enclosures can contain splices and taps if the conductors, splices, and/or taps do not fill the wiring space at any cross section to more than 75 percent. Switch or circuit-breaker enclosures can have conductors feed through them if the wiring does not fill the wiring space at any cross section to more than 40 percent in accordance with 312.8. ▶Figure 404-10

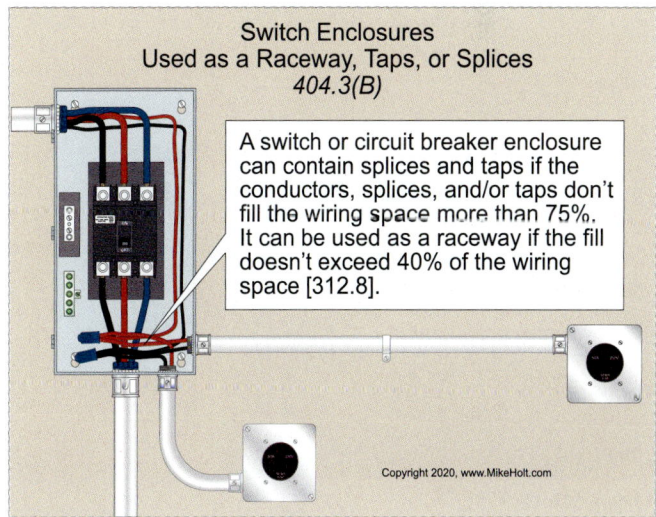

▶Figure 404-10

404.4 | Switches

404.4 Damp or Wet Locations

(A) Surface-Mounted Switches or Circuit Breakers. Surface-mounted switches and circuit breakers in a damp or wet location must be installed in a weatherproof enclosure. ▶Figure 404–11

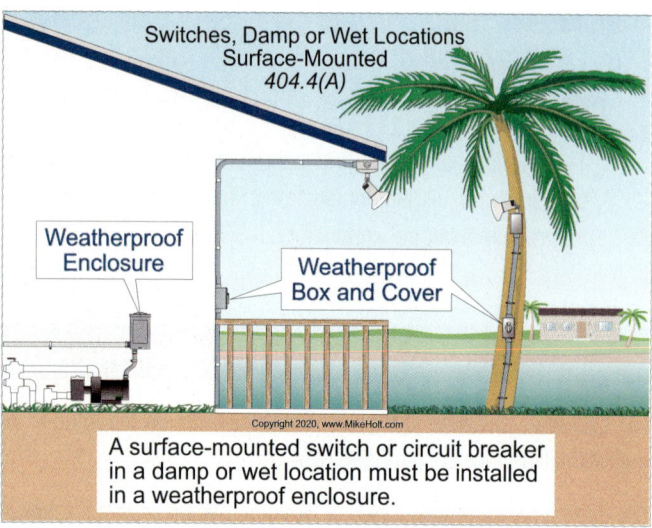

▶Figure 404–11

(B) Flush-Mounted Switches or Circuit Breakers. A flush-mounted switch or circuit breaker in a damp or wet location must have a weatherproof cover. ▶Figure 404–12

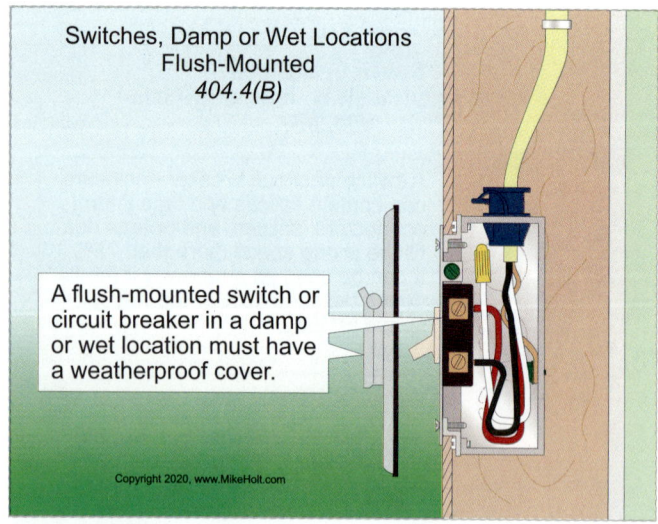

▶Figure 404–12

(C) Switches Within Tub or Shower Spaces. Switches must not be installed within tub or shower spaces unless installed as part of a listed tub or shower assembly. ▶Figure 404–13

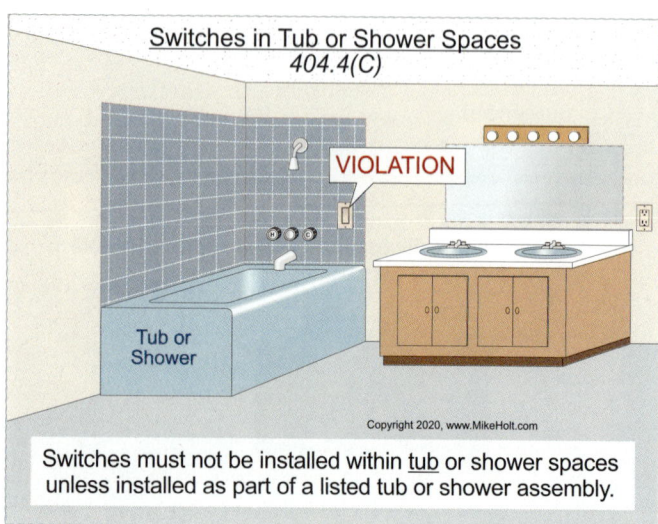

▶Figure 404–13

404.7 Indicating

Switches and circuit breakers must be marked, in a location that is visible when accessing the external operating means, to indicate whether they are in the "on" or "off" position.

Author's Comment:

▸ This is typically accomplished by marking on the toggle of the switch itself or by indicative labeling. If you find a switch not so marked, chances are it is a 3-way or 4-way switch which can be on or off in either the up or down position.

When the switch is operated vertically, it must be installed so the "up" position is the "on" position [240.81]. ▶Figure 404–14

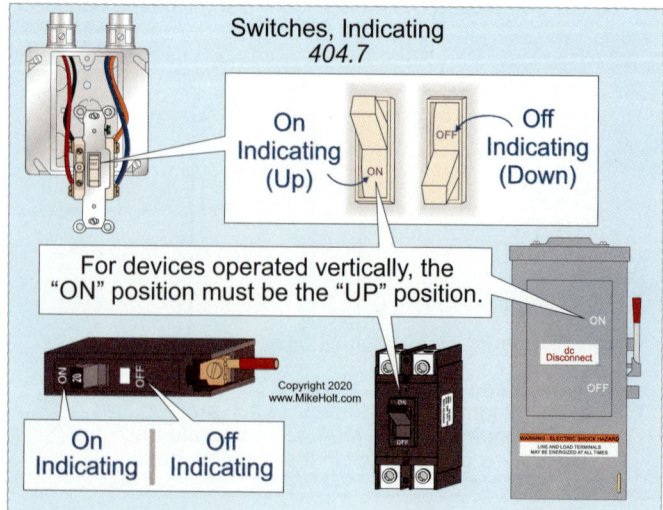

▶Figure 404–14

Ex 1: Double-throw switches, such as 3-way and 4-way switches, are not required to be marked "on" or "off."

Author's Comment:

▸ Circuit breakers used to switch fluorescent lighting must be listed and marked "SWD" or "HID." Circuit breakers used to switch high-intensity discharge lighting must be listed and must be marked "HID" [240.83(D)]. ▸**Figure 404-15**

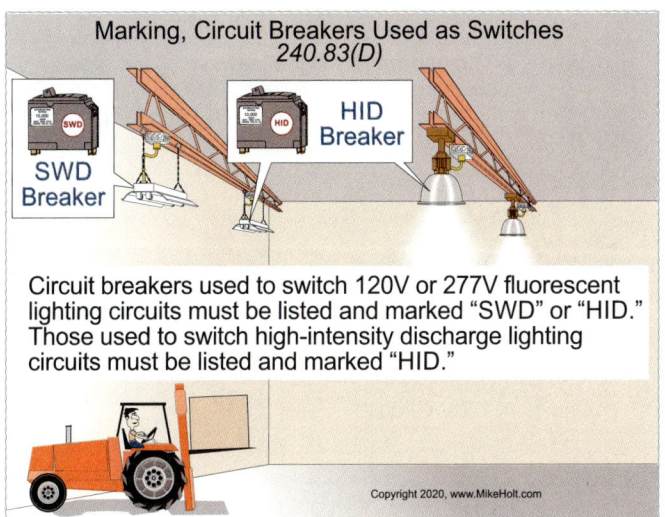

▸Figure 404-15

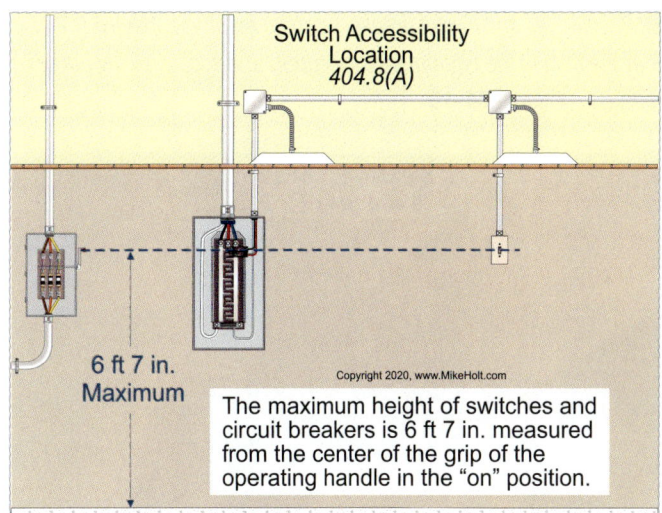

▸Figure 404-16

404.8 Accessibility and Grouping

(A) Location. Switches and circuit breakers must be capable of being operated from a readily accessible location with the center of the grip of the operating handle, when in its highest position, not more than 6 ft 7 in. above the floor or working platform [240.24(A)]. ▸**Figure 404-16**

Author's Comment:

▸ There are no requirements for a minimum height above the floor or working platform for switches or circuit breakers. ▸**Figure 404-17**

Ex 1: On busways, fusible switches and circuit breakers can be located at the same level as the busway where suitable means is provided to operate the handle of the device from the floor. ▸**Figure 404-18**

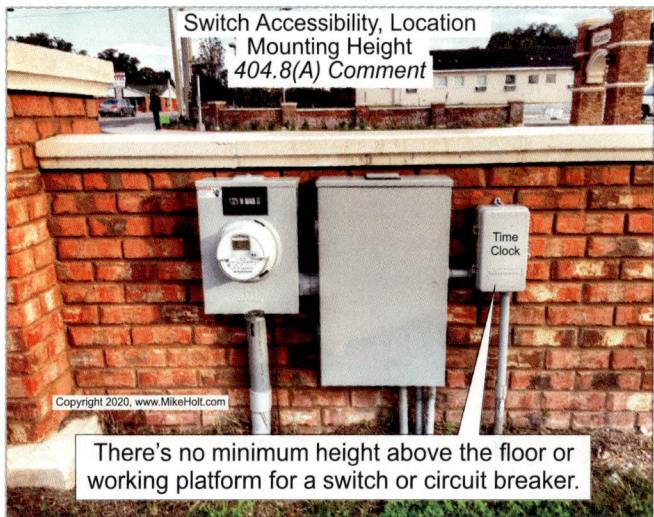

▸Figure 404-17

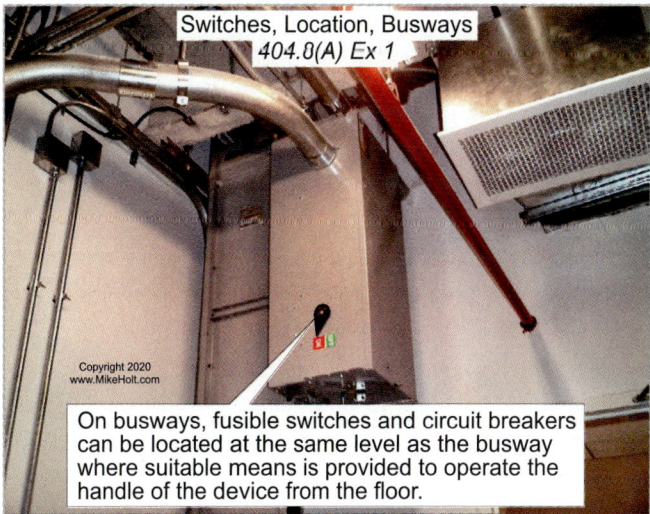

▸Figure 404-18

404.8 | Switches

Ex 2: Switches and circuit breakers can be mounted above 6 ft 7 in. if they are next to the equipment they supply and accessible by portable means. ▶Figure 404–19

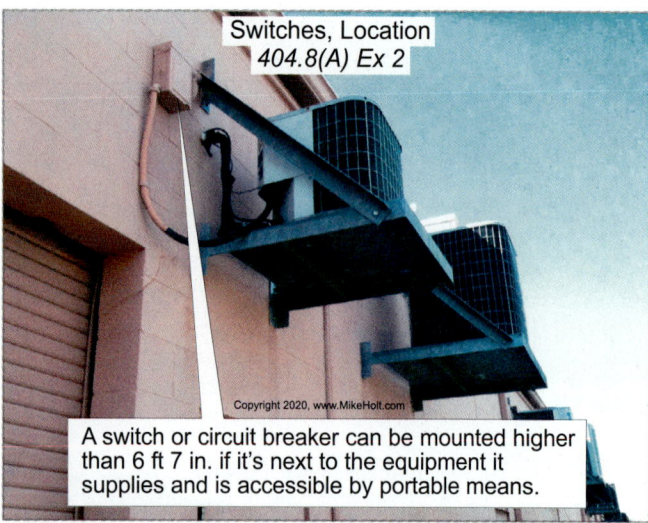

▶Figure 404–19

(B) Voltage Between Devices. Snap switches are not permitted to be in enclosures with other switches or receptacles if the voltage between adjacent devices exceeds 300V, unless the devices are installed in enclosures equipped with barriers identified for the purpose that are securely installed between adjacent devices. ▶Figure 404–20

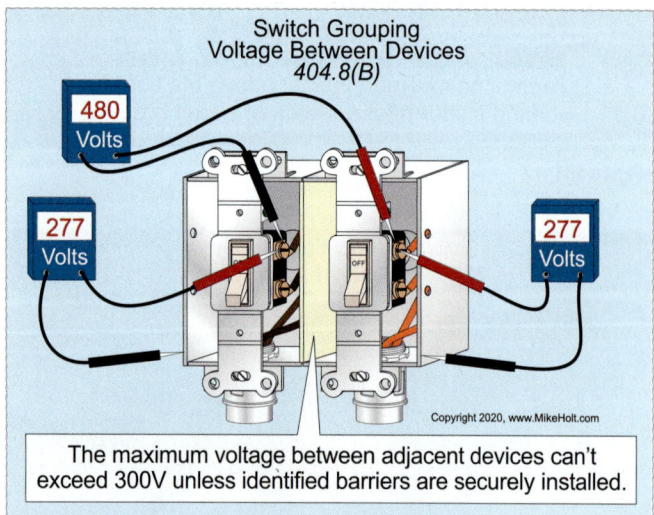

▶Figure 404–20

Author's Comment:

▸ The voltage between devices is a function of the difference in voltage between the conductors. When adjacent devices are connected to different systems (such as 120/208V and 277/480V), the voltage difference between the devices can be as much as 381V. ▶Figure 404–21 and ▶Figure 404–22

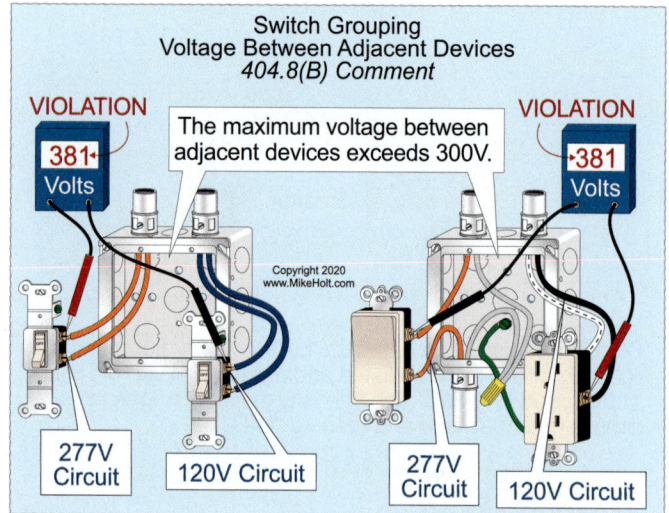

▶Figure 404–21

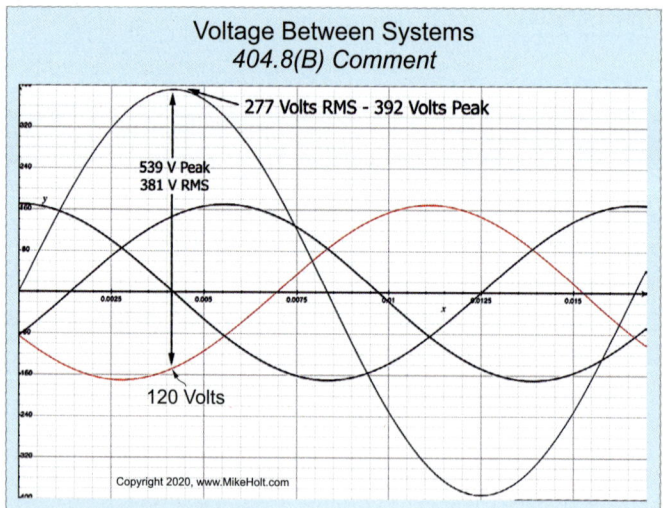

▶Figure 404–22

404.9 General-Use Snap Switches, Dimmers, and Control Switches

(A) Faceplates. Faceplates for switches, dimmers, and control switches must completely cover the outlet box opening and, where flush mounted, the faceplate must seat against the wall surface. ▶Figure 404–23

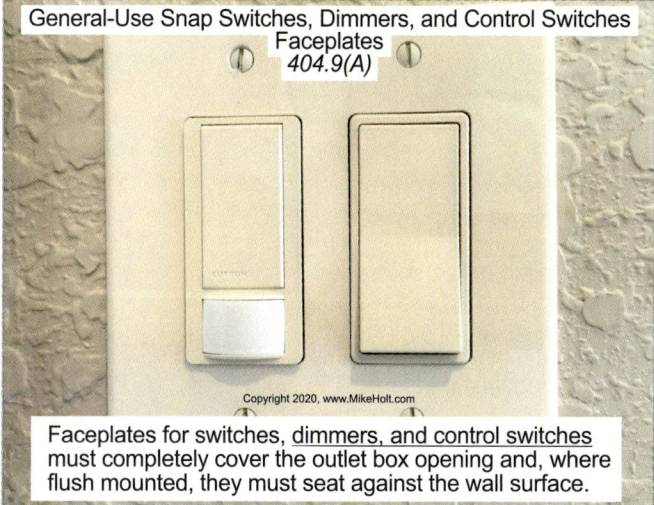

▶Figure 404–23

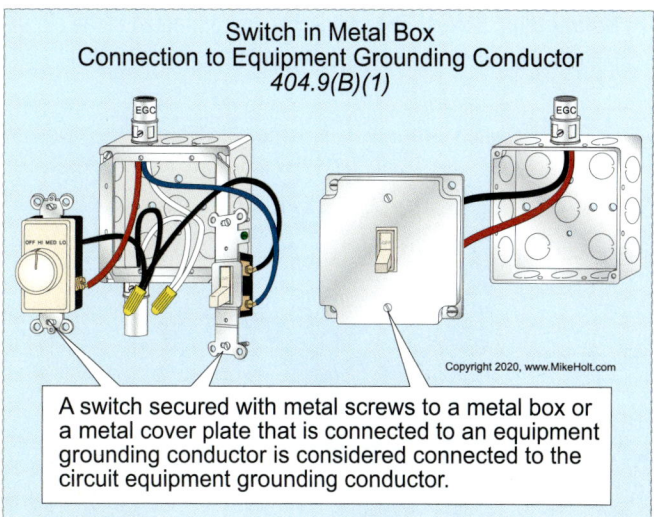

▶Figure 404–24

(B) Equipment Grounding Conductor. The metal mounting yokes for switches, dimmers, and control switches and metal faceplates must be connected to the circuit equipment grounding conductor using either of the following methods:

(1) Metal Boxes. The switch yoke is secured with metal screws to a metal box or a metal cover that is connected to an equipment grounding conductor [250.109]. ▶Figure 404–24

The metal faceplate is secured with metal screws to a switch that is connected to an equipment grounding conductor [250.109]. ▶Figure 404–25

Author's Comment:

▸ Direct metal-to-metal contact between the device yoke of a switch and the box is not required. The switch is connected to the effective ground-fault current path when the yoke is mounted with metal screws to a metal box. ▶Figure 404–26

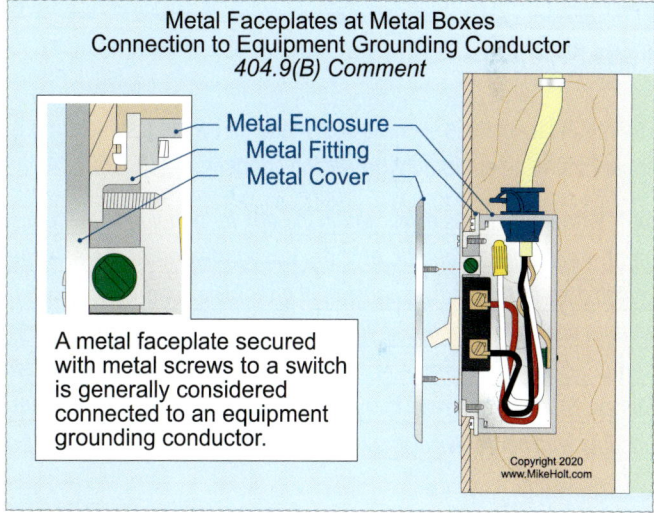

▶Figure 404–25

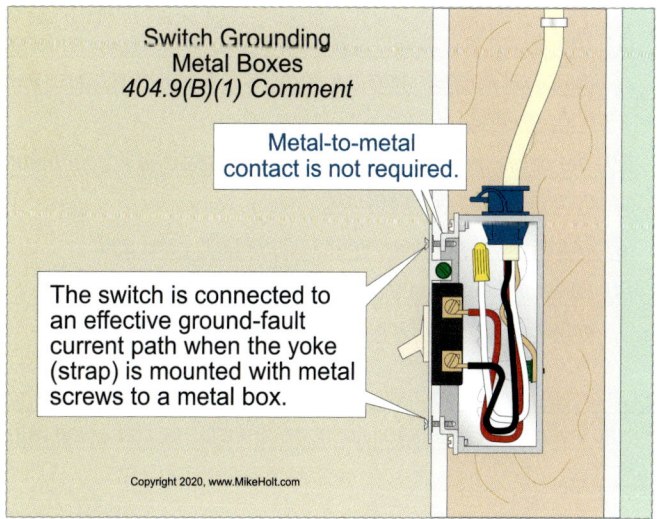

▶Figure 404–26

404.10 | Switches

(2) Nonmetallic Boxes. The switch yoke is connected to the circuit equipment grounding conductor. ▶Figure 404–27

▶Figure 404–27

The metal faceplate is secured with metal screws to a switch that is connected to an equipment grounding conductor [250.109].

Ex 1: Where no means exists within the box for bonding to an equipment grounding conductor, or if the wiring method at the existing switch does not contain an equipment grounding conductor, a switch without such a connection to the equipment grounding conductor is permitted for replacement purposes only. A switch installed under this exception must have a faceplate that is nonmetallic and noncombustible with nonmetallic screws, or the replacement switch must be GFCI protected.

Ex 2: Listed assemblies are not required to be bonded to an equipment grounding conductor if all the following conditions are met:

(1) The device is provided with a nonmetallic faceplate and the device is designed such that no metallic faceplate replaces the one provided,

(2) The device does not have a mounting means to accept other configurations of faceplates,

(3) The device is equipped with a nonmetallic yoke, and

(4) Parts of the device that are accessible after the faceplate is installed are manufactured of nonmetallic material.

Ex 3: An equipment grounding conductor is not required for bonding a snap switch with an integral nonmetallic enclosure complying with 300.15(E).

404.10 Mounting of Snap Switches, Dimmers, and Control Switches

(B) Box Mounted.

General-use snap switches, dimmers, and control switches mounted in boxes that are set back from the finished surface must be installed so the extension plaster ears are seated against the surface. ▶Figure 404–28

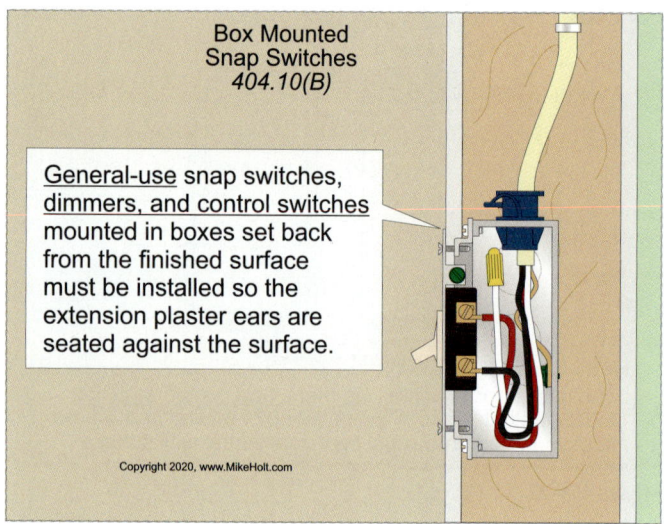

▶Figure 404–28

Screws used for the purpose of attaching a device to a box must be of the type provided with a listed device or be machine screws having 32 threads per in. or part of listed assemblies or systems, in accordance with the manufacturer's instructions. ▶Figure 404–29

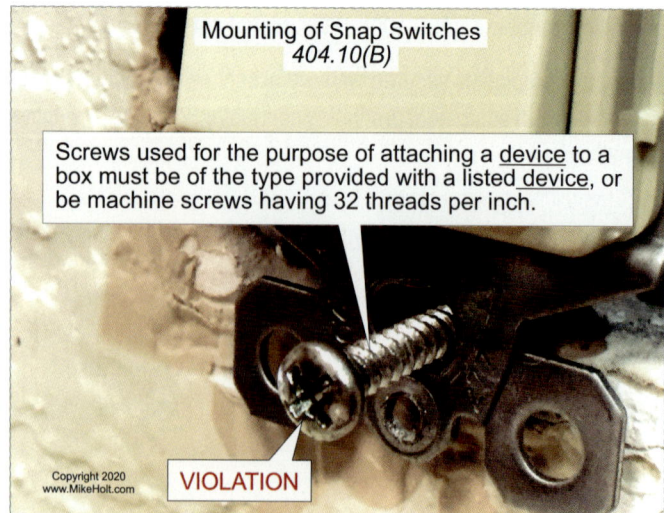

▶Figure 404–29

Switches | **404.20**

Author's Comment:

▶ In walls or ceilings of noncombustible material (such as drywall) boxes are not permitted to be set back more than ¼ in. from the finished surface. In combustible walls or ceilings, boxes must be flush with, or project slightly from, the finished surface [314.20]. There must not be any gaps more than ⅛ in. at the edge of the box [314.21].

404.12 Grounding of Enclosures

Metal enclosures for switches and circuit breakers must be connected to an equipment grounding conductor of a type recognized in 250.118 [250.4(A)(3)]. Where nonmetallic enclosures are used with metal raceways or metal-armored cables, they must comply with 314.3 Ex 1 or Ex 2.

404.14 Rating and Use of Snap Switches

General-Use Snap Switches. General-use snap switches must be listed and used within their ratings as indicated.

(A) Alternating-Current General-Use Snap Switches. General-use snap switches are permitted to control:

(4) Motor loads not exceeding 80 percent of the ampere rating of the switch at its rated voltage [430.109(C)].

(5) Electronic ballasts, self-ballasted lamps, compact fluorescent lamps, and LED lamp loads with their associated drivers, not exceeding 20A and not exceeding the ampere rating of the switch at the voltage applied.

(E) Dimmer and Electronic Control Switches. General-use dimmer switches are only permitted to control permanently installed incandescent luminaires unless listed for control of other loads. ▶Figure 404–30

Other electronic control switches, such as timing switches and occupancy sensors, can only be used to control permanently connected loads. Such switches must be marked by the manufacturer with their current and voltage ratings and used for loads that do not exceed their ampere rating at the voltage applied.

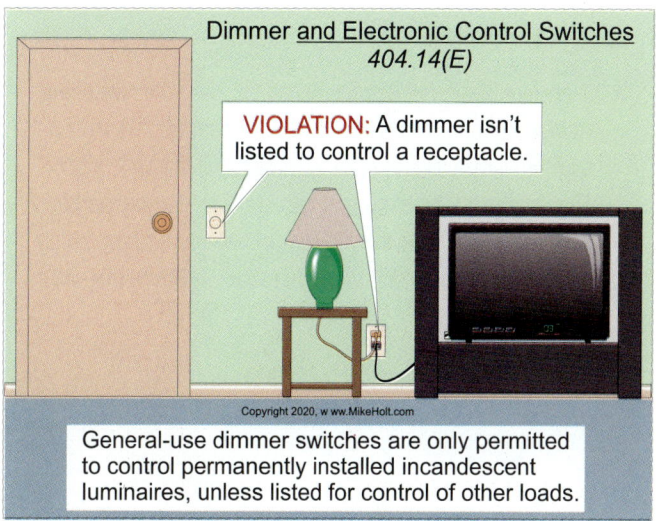

▶Figure 404–30

Part II. Construction Specifications

404.20 Switch Marking

(A) Markings. Switches must be marked with the current, voltage, and if horsepower rated, the maximum rating for which they are designed.
▶Figure 404–31

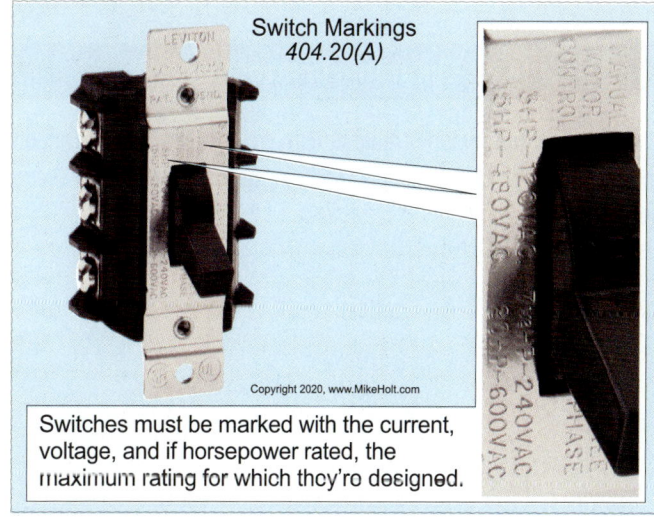

▶Figure 404–31

(B) Off Indication. If in the off position, a switching device with a marked "off" position must completely disconnect all phase conductors of the load it controls.

404.22 | Switches

Author's Comment:

▸ If an electronic occupancy sensor is used for switching, voltage will be present and a small current of 0.05 mA can flow through the circuit when the switch is in the "off" position. This small amount of current can startle a person, perhaps causing a fall. To solve this problem, manufacturers have simply removed the word "off" from the switch. ▸Figure 404-32

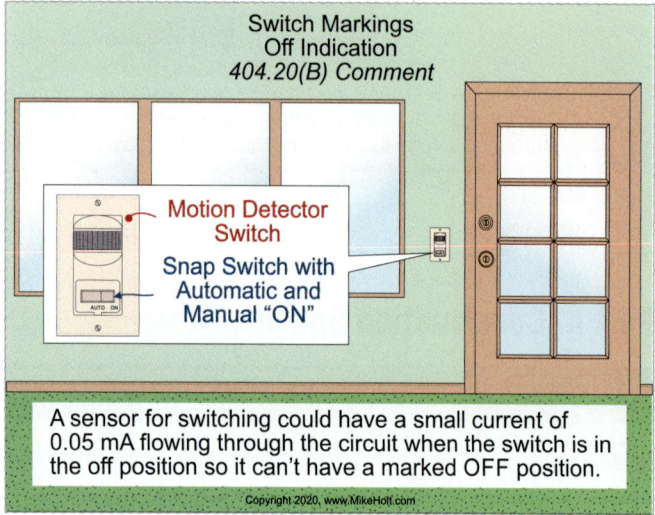

▸Figure 404-32

404.22 Electronic Control Switches

Electronic control switches must be listed to not introduce current on the equipment grounding conductor during normal operation. ▸Figure 404-33

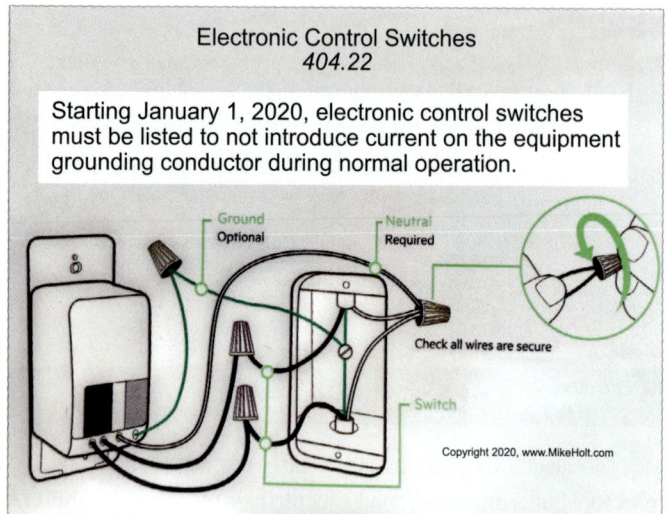

▸Figure 404-33

Author's Comment:

▸ If an electronic occupancy sensor is used for switching, voltage will be present and a small current of 0.05 mA can flow through the circuit when the switch is in the "off" position. This small amount of current can startle a person, perhaps causing a fall. To solve this problem, manufacturers have simply removed the word "off" from the switch.

Ex: Electronic control switches that put current on the equipment grounding conductor [404.2(C) Ex] must be listed and marked for use only for replacement or retrofit applications.

ARTICLE 408 — SWITCHBOARDS AND PANELBOARDS

Introduction to Article 408—Switchboards and Panelboards

Article 408 covers the specific requirements for switchboards and panelboards that control power and lighting circuits. As you study this article, keep these key points in mind:

- Perhaps the most important objective of Article 408 is to ensure that the installation will prevent contact between current-carrying conductors and people or equipment.
- The circuit directory of a panelboard must clearly identify the purpose or use of each circuit that originates in the panelboard.
- You must understand the detailed grounding and overcurrent protection requirements for panelboards.

Part I. General

408.1 Scope

Article 408 covers the requirements for switchboards and panelboards that control power and lighting circuits. ▶Figure 408-1

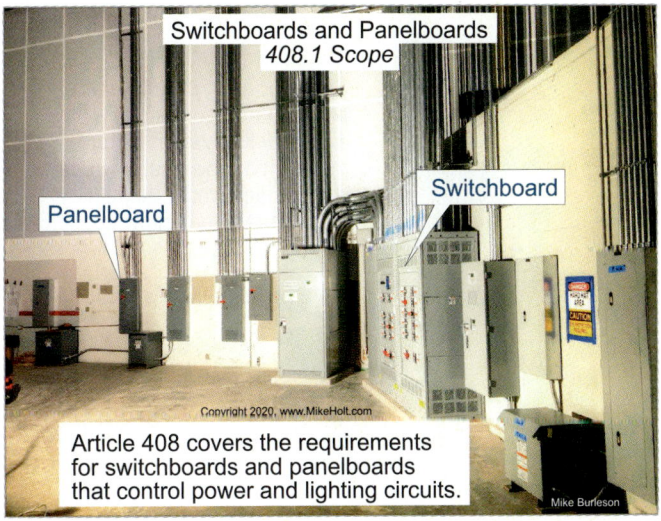

▶Figure 408-1

Author's Comment:

- See Article 100 for the definitions for "Switchboard" and "Panelboard."

408.3 Arrangement of Busbars and Conductors

(E) Bus Arrangement.

(1) Alternating-Current Phase Arrangement. Panelboards supplied by a 4-wire, delta-connected, three-phase (high-leg) system must have the high-leg conductor (which operates at 208V to ground) terminate to the "B" phase of the panelboard. ▶Figure 408-2

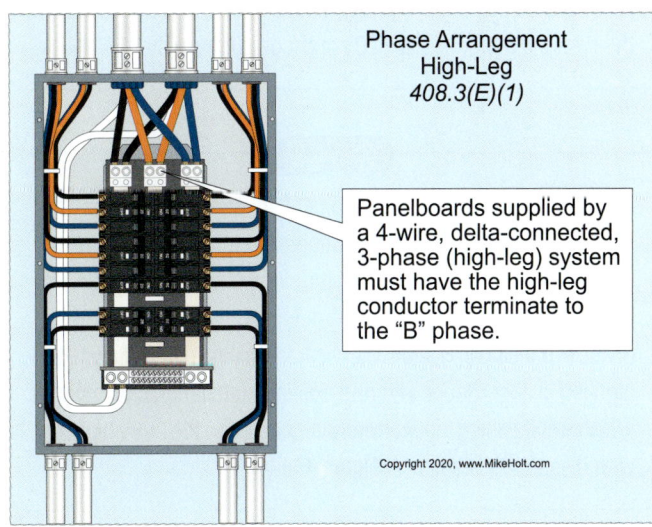

▶Figure 408-2

408.4 | Switchboards and Panelboards

Note: On a 4-wire, delta-connected, three-phase system, where the midpoint of one phase winding of the secondary is grounded, the conductor with the resulting 208V to ground (high-leg) must be durably and permanently marked by an outer finish (insulation) that is orange in color or other effective means. Such identification must be placed at each point where a connection is made if the neutral conductor is present [230.56]. ▶Figure 408-3

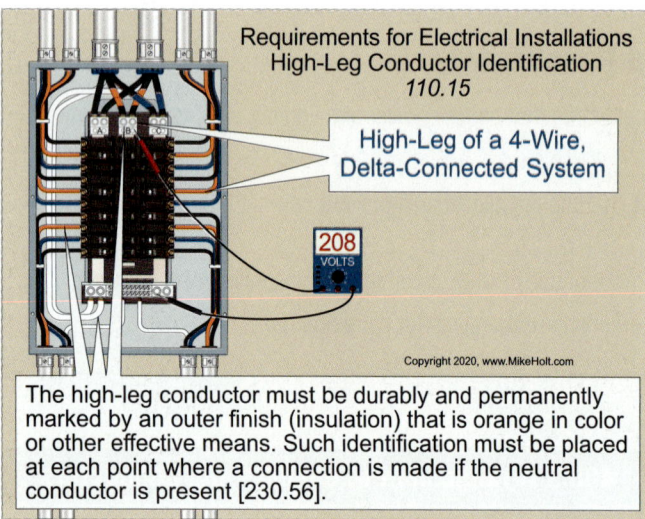

▶Figure 408-3

Warning

The ANSI standard for meter equipment requires the high-leg conductor (208V to neutral) to terminate on the "C" (right) phase of the meter socket enclosure. This is because the demand meter needs 120V and it gets it from the "B" phase.

Warning

When replacing equipment in existing facilities that contain a high-leg conductor, use care to ensure the high-leg conductor is replaced in the same phase position. Prior to 1975, the high-leg conductor was required to terminate on the "C" phase of panelboards and switchboards. Failure to re-terminate the high-leg in accordance with the existing installation can result in 120V circuits being inadvertently connected to the 208V high-leg, with disastrous results. ▶Figure 408-4

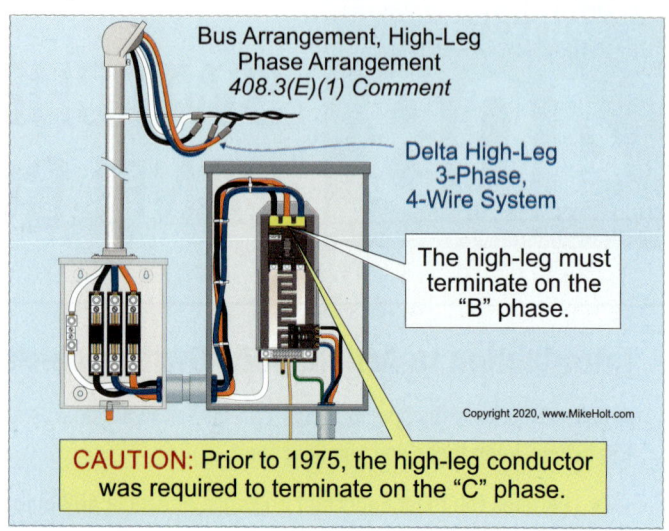

▶Figure 408-4

(F) Switchboard and Panelboard Identification.

(1) High-Leg Identification. A switchboard or panelboard containing a 4-wire, delta-connected system where the midpoint of one phase winding is grounded, must have a label that is legibly and permanently field marked as follows: **"CAUTION _____ PHASE HAS _____ VOLTS TO GROUND"** ▶Figure 408-5

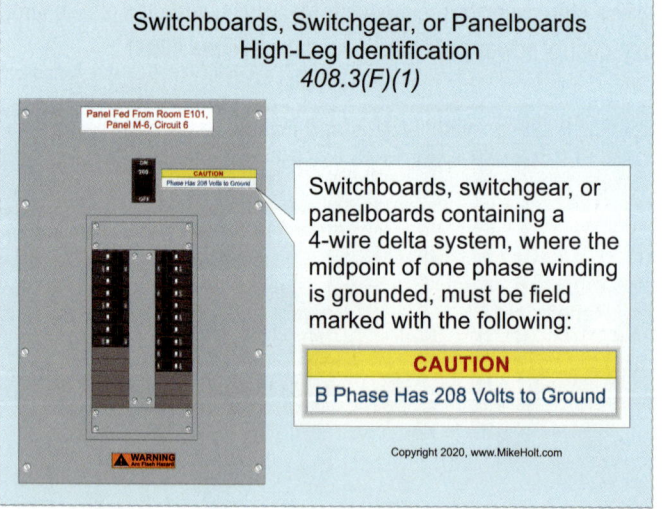

▶Figure 408-5

408.4 Field Identification

(A) Circuit Directory or Circuit Identification. Circuits and circuit modifications must be legibly identified as to their clear, evident, and specific purpose. Spare positions that contain unused overcurrent devices must be described accordingly. ▶Figure 408-6

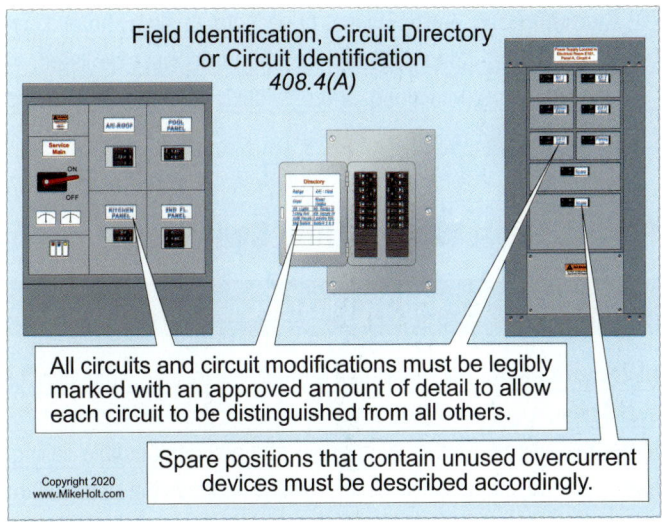

▶Figure 408–6

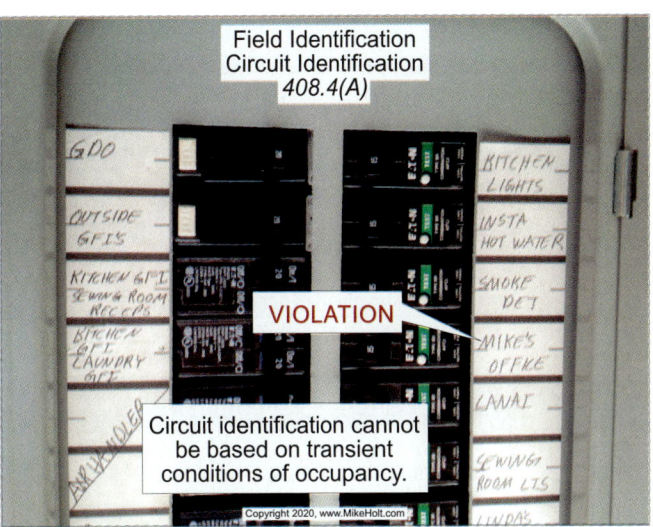

▶Figure 408–8

Identification must include an approved amount of detail to allow each circuit to be distinguished from all others, and the identification must be on a circuit directory located on the face of, inside of, or in an approved location adjacent to, the door of the panelboard. See 110.22. ▶Figure 408–7

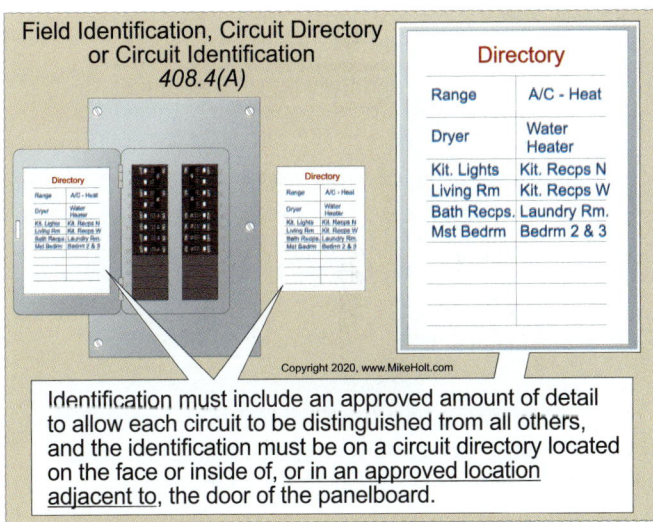

▶Figure 408–7

Circuit identification must not be based on transient conditions of occupancy such as "Dad's Office." ▶Figure 408–8

(B) Source of Supply. Switchboards and panelboards supplied by a feeder, in other than one- or two-family dwellings must be marked with a permanent (not handwritten) label that withstands the environment indicating where the power supply originates. ▶Figure 408–9

▶Figure 408–9

408.5 Clearance for Conductors Entering Bus Enclosures

If raceways enter a switchboard, floor-standing panelboard, or similar enclosure, the raceways (including end fittings) are not permitted to rise more than 3 in. above the bottom of the enclosure.

408.6 Short-Circuit Current Rating

Switchboards and panelboards must have a short-circuit current rating of not less than the available fault current. In other than one- and two-family dwellings, the available fault current and the date the calculation was performed must be field marked on the enclosure at the point of supply. The marking must be of sufficient durability to withstand the environment involved in accordance with 110.21(B)(3).

408.7 Unused Openings

Unused openings for circuit breakers must be closed using identified closures, or other approved means, that provide protection substantially equivalent to the wall of the enclosure. ▶Figure 408–10

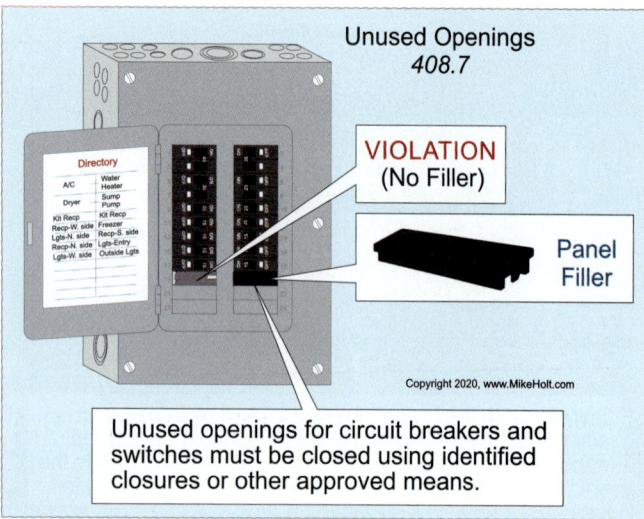

▶Figure 408–10

408.8 Reconditioning of Equipment

The reconditioning process must use design qualified parts verified under applicable standards and be performed in accordance with any instructions provided by the manufacturer. If equipment has been damaged by fire, products of combustion, or water, it must be specifically evaluated by its manufacturer or a qualified testing laboratory prior to being returned to service.

(A) Panelboards. Panelboards are not permitted to be reconditioned, but replacement of a panelboard within an enclosure is. In the event the replacement panelboard has not been listed for the specific enclosure and the available fault current is greater than 10,000A, the completed work must be field labeled and previously applied listing marks on the cabinet must be removed.

(B) Switchboards. Switchboards or sections of switchboards can be reconditioned. Reconditioned switchboards must be listed, or field labeled as reconditioned, and previously applied listing marks must be removed.

Part II. Switchboards and Switchgear

408.18 Clearances

(A) From Ceiling. For other than a totally enclosed switchboard or switchgear, a space not less than 3 ft must be provided between the top of the switchboard or switchgear and any combustible ceiling, unless a noncombustible shield is provided between the switchboard or switchgear and the ceiling.

(B) Around Switchboards and Switchgear. Clearances around switchboards and switchgear must comply with 110.26.

(C) Connections. Each section of equipment that requires rear or side access to make field connections must be so marked by the manufacturer on the front of the equipment. Section openings requiring rear or side access must comply with the workspace and access to workspace requirements of 110.26. ▶Figure 408–11

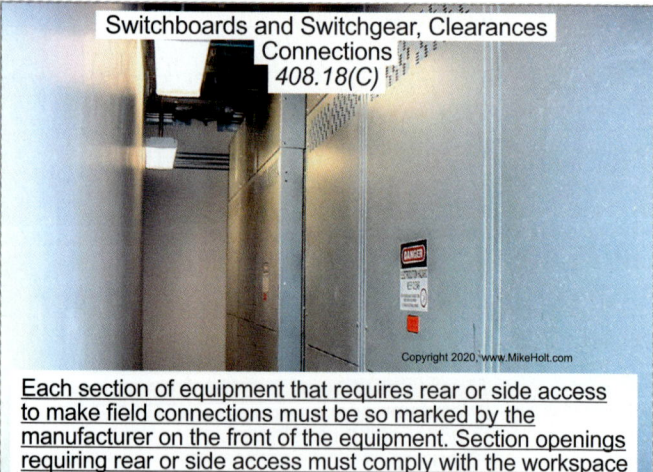

▶Figure 408–11

Part III. Panelboards

408.36 Overcurrent Protection

Panelboards must be provided with overcurrent protection located within or at any point on the supply side of the panelboard with a rating not greater than that of the panelboard. ▶Figure 408–12

Switchboards and Panelboards | 408.40

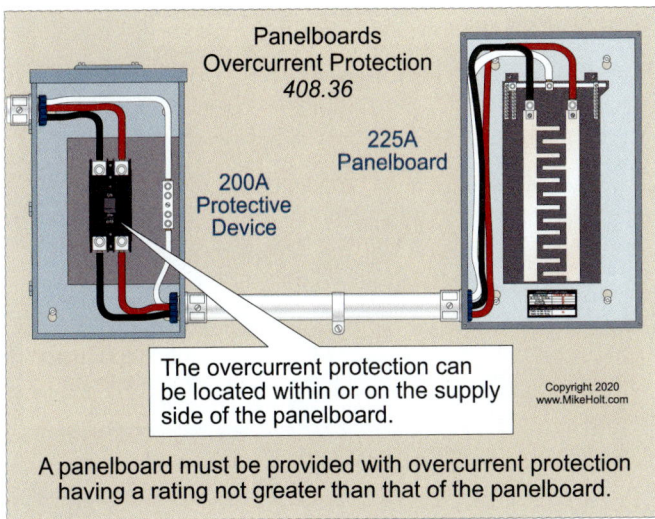
▶Figure 408-12

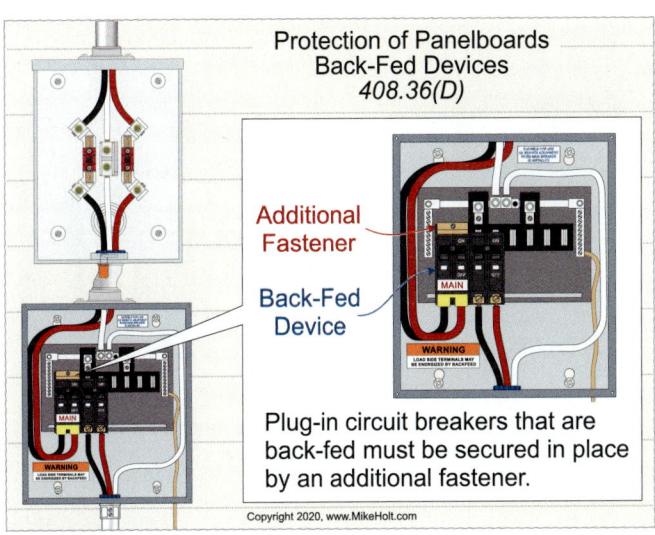
▶Figure 408-14

(B) Panelboards Supplied by a Transformer. When a panelboard is supplied from a transformer, as permitted in 240.21(C), the overcurrent protection for the panelboard must be on the secondary side of the transformer. The overcurrent protection can be in an enclosure ahead of the panelboard or within the panelboard. ▶Figure 408-13

> **Caution**
> Circuit breakers marked "Line" and "Load" must be installed in accordance with listing or labeling instructions [110.3(B)]; therefore, these types of devices are not permitted to be backfed.

408.37 Panelboards in Damp or Wet Locations

Cabinets for panelboards installed in damp or wet locations must be weatherproof in accordance with 312.2.

408.40 Equipment Grounding Conductor

Metal cabinets containing panelboards must be connected to an equipment grounding conductor of a type recognized in 250.118 [215.6 and 250.4(A)(3)]. Where a panelboard cabinet contains equipment grounding conductors of the wire type, a terminal bar for them must be installed and bonded to the metal cabinet. ▶Figure 408-15

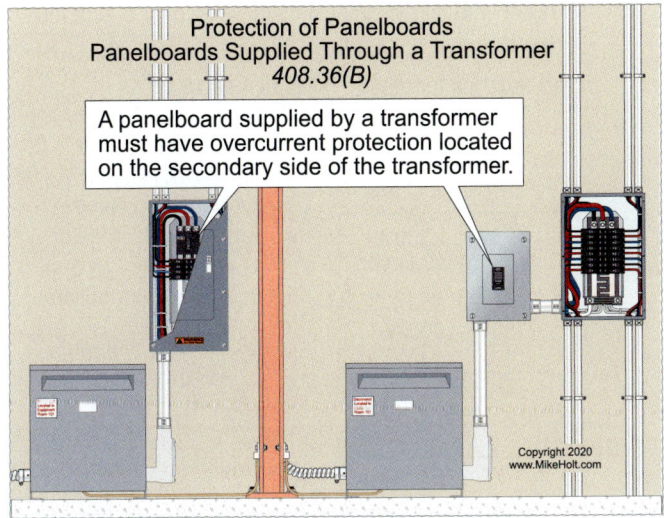
▶Figure 408-13

(D) Back-Fed Devices. Plug-in circuit breakers that are backfed must be secured in place by a fastener that requires other than a pull to release the breaker from the panelboard. ▶Figure 408-14

Equipment grounding conductors are not permitted to terminate on the neutral terminal bar except as permitted by 250.142(A) for services and separately derived systems. ▶Figure 408-16

Author's Comment:

▶ The purpose of the breaker fastener is to prevent the circuit breaker from being accidentally removed from the panelboard while energized, thereby exposing someone to dangerous voltage.

2nd Printing | 2020 NEC Requirements for Solar PV and Energy Storage Systems | MikeHolt.com | 433

408.41 | Switchboards and Panelboards

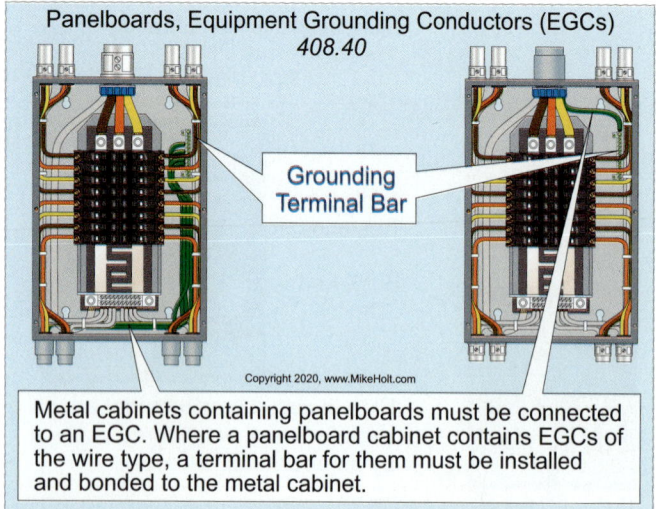
▶Figure 408–15

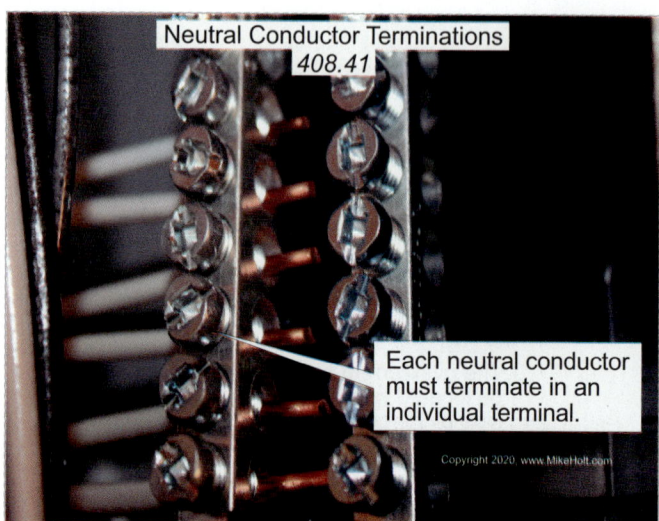
▶Figure 408–17

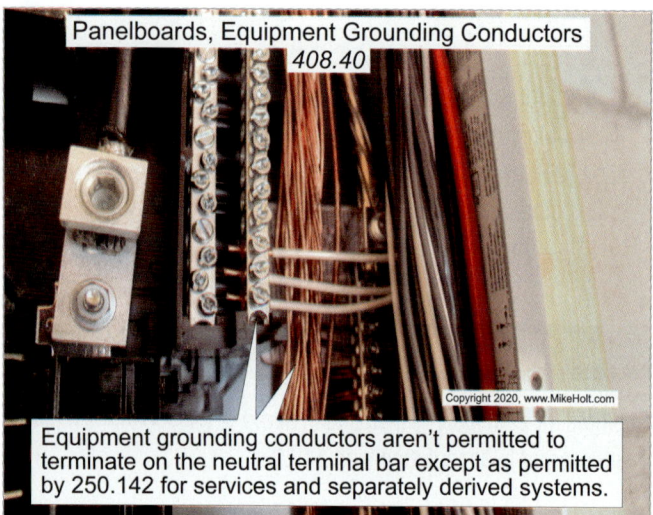
▶Figure 408–16

Author's Comment:

▶ If two neutral conductors are connected to the same terminal, and someone removes one of them, the other neutral conductor might unintentionally be removed as well. If that happens to the neutral conductor of a multiwire circuit, it can result in excessive line-to-neutral voltage for one of the circuits, as well as undervoltage for the other. See 300.13(B) of this textbook for details. ▶Figure 408–18

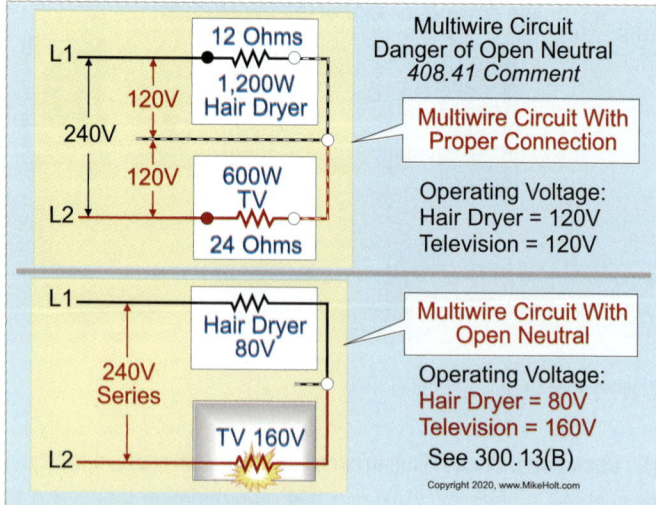
▶Figure 408–18

Caution: Many panelboards are rated for use as service disconnects, which means they are supplied with a main bonding jumper [250.28]. This screw or strap is not permitted to be installed except when the panelboard is used for a service disconnect [250.24(A)(5)] or a separately derived system [250.30(A)(1)].

408.41 Neutral Conductor Terminations

Each neutral conductor within a panelboard must terminate in an individual terminal. ▶Figure 408–17

408.43 Panelboard Orientation

Panelboards are not permitted to be installed in the face-up position.

ARTICLE 445 GENERATORS

Introduction to Article 445—Generators

This article contains the electrical installation and other requirements for generators. These rules include such things as where generators can be installed, nameplate markings, conductor ampacity, transference of power, and disconnect requirements.

445.1 Scope

Article 445 contains the installation and other requirements for generators. ▶Figure 445–1

▶Figure 445–1

Author's Comment:

- Generators, associated wiring, and equipment must be installed in accordance with the following requirements depending on their use:
  - Fire Pumps, Article 695
  - Emergency Systems, Article 700
  - Legally Required Standby Systems, Article 701
  - Optional Standby Systems, Article 702
  - Interconnected Electric Power Production Sources, Article 705

445.6 Listing

Stationary generators rated 600V and less must be listed.

Ex: One-of-a-kind or custom manufactured generators are permitted to be field labeled by a field evaluation body.

445.11 Marking

Generators must have a nameplate giving the manufacturer's name, the rated frequency, number of phases, rating in kilowatts or kilovolt-amperes, power factor, and the volts and amperes corresponding to the rating. ▶Figure 445–2

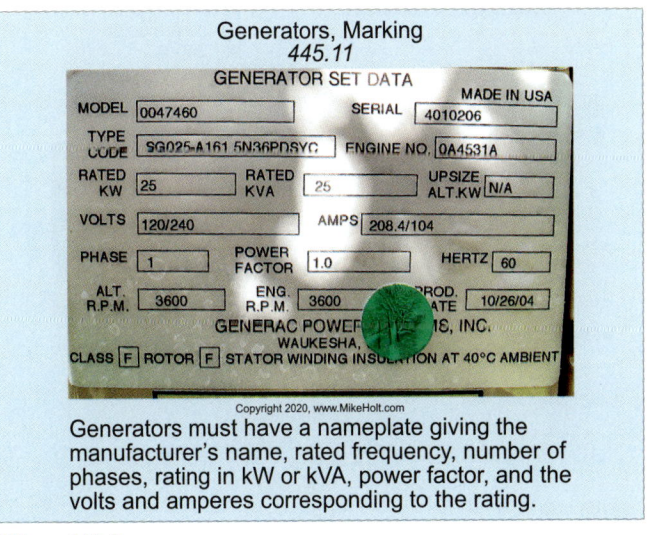

▶Figure 445–2

445.13 | Generators

445.13 Ampacity of Conductors

(A) General. The ampacity of the conductors from the generator winding output terminals to the first overcurrent protective device must be not less than 115 percent of the nameplate current rating of the generator.

> **Author's Comment:**
> - Since the overcurrent protective device is typically part of the generator, this 115-percent rule applies to the generator manufacturer, not the field installer.
> - Conductors from the load side of the generator are called feeder conductors and are sized to the generator's overcurrent protective device rating in accordance with 240.4.

▶ **Example**

Question: What size feeder conductor is required from a 100A overcurrent protective device on a 20 kW, 120/240V, single-phase generator to the transfer switch if the generator and transfer switch terminals are rated 75°C? ▶Figure 445-3

(a) 4 AWG   (b) 3 AWG   (c) 2 AWG   (d) 1 AWG

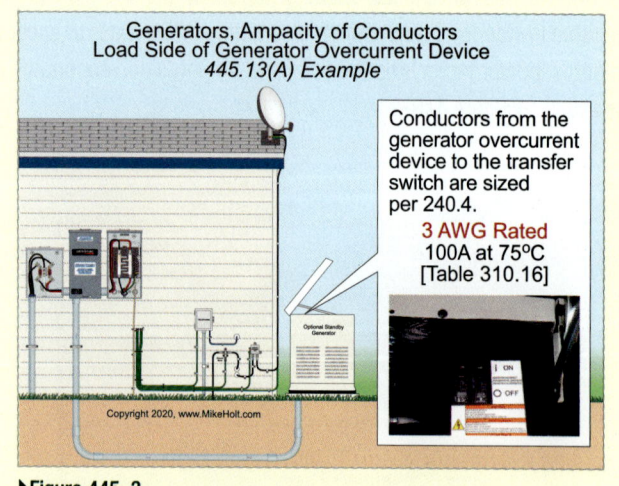

▶Figure 445-3

Solution:

3 AWG is rated 100A at 75°C [110.14(C)(1) and Table 310.16].

Answer: (b) 3 AWG

The generator's feeder neutral must be sized to carry the maximum unbalanced current as determined by 220.61. ▶Figure 445-4

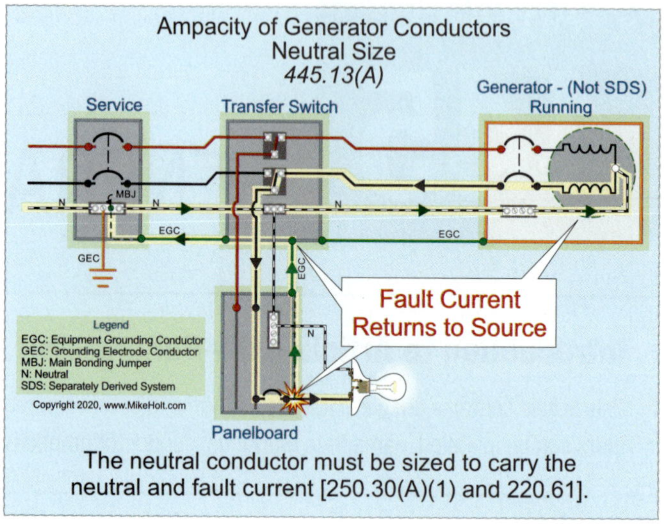

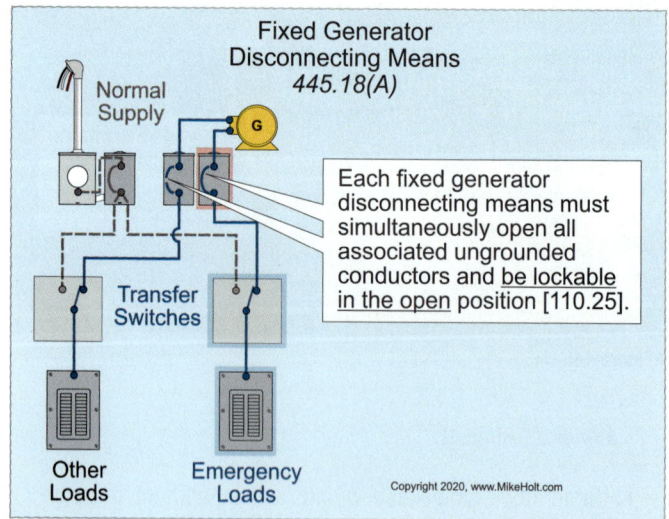

▶Figure 445-4

445.18 Disconnecting Means and Emergency Shutdown

(A) Disconnecting Means. Generators, other than cord-and-plug-connected portable generators, must have one or more disconnecting means and must be capable lockable in accordance with 110.25. ▶Figure 445-5

▶Figure 445-5

(B) Emergency Shutdown of Prime Mover. Generators must have provisions to shut down the prime mover. The means of shutdown must comply with all the following:

(1) Be equipped with provisions to disable all prime mover start control circuits to render the prime mover incapable of starting

(2) Initiate a shutdown mechanism that requires a mechanical reset.

The provisions to shut down the prime mover is permitted to satisfy the requirements of 445.18(A) where the shutdown device is capable of being locked in the open position in accordance with 110.25.

(C) Remote Emergency Shutdown. Generators with a rating greater than 15 kW must be provided with a remote emergency stop switch to shut down the prime mover. The remote emergency stop switch must be located outside the equipment room or generator enclosure and must also meet the requirements of 445.18(B)(1) and (B)(2).

(D) Emergency Shutdown in One- and Two-Family Dwelling Units. For other than cord-and-plug-connected portable generators, an emergency shutdown device must be located outside the dwelling unit at a readily accessible location.

Notes

ARTICLE 450 TRANSFORMERS

Introduction to Article 450—Transformers

Article 450 opens by saying, "This article covers the installation of all transformers." Then it lists eight exceptions. So, what does it really cover? Essentially, this article covers transformers supplying power and lighting loads. For the purposes of Article 450 only, a transformer is an individual power transformer, single- or poly-phase, identified by a single nameplate—unless otherwise indicated.

A major concern with transformers is preventing overheating. The *Code* does not completely address this issue. Article 90 explains that the *NEC* is not a design manual, and it assumes that anyone using the *Code* has a certain level of expertise. Proper transformer selection is an important part of preventing them from overheating. The *NEC* assumes you have already selected a transformer suitable for the load characteristics. For the *Code* to tell you how to do that would push it into the realm of a design manual. Article 450 then takes you to the next logical step—providing overcurrent protection and the proper connections. But this article does not stop there; 450.9 provides ventilation requirements, and 450.13 contains accessibility requirements.

Part I contains the general requirements such as guarding, marking, and accessibility; Part II contains those for different types of transformers; and Part III covers transformer vaults.

450.1 Scope

Article 450 covers the installation requirements of all transformers.
▶Figure 450–1

Article 450 covers the installation of transformers.
▶Figure 450–1

Ex 4: Class 2 and 3 transformers that comply with Article 725.

Ex 5: Sign and outline transformers complying with Article 600.

Ex 6: Electric-discharge lighting transformers that comply with Article 410.

Ex 7: Transformers for power-limited fire alarm circuits complying with Article 760 Part III.

450.3 Overcurrent Protection

(B) Overcurrent Protection for Transformers Not Over 1,000V. Transformers having a secondary voltage not exceeding 1,000V, with primary overcurrent protection only, must have the primary overcurrent protective device sized in accordance with the percentages contained in Table 450.3(B) and its applicable notes.

Table 450.3(B) Primary Only Protection	
Primary Current Rating	**Maximum Protection**
9A or More	125%, see Table Note 1
Less Than 9A	167%
Less Than 2A	300%

450.9 | Transformers

Note 1 of Table 450.3(B): If 125 percent of the primary current does not correspond to a standard rating of an overcurrent protective device [240.6(A)], the next higher rating is permitted [240.6(A)]. ▶Figure 450–2

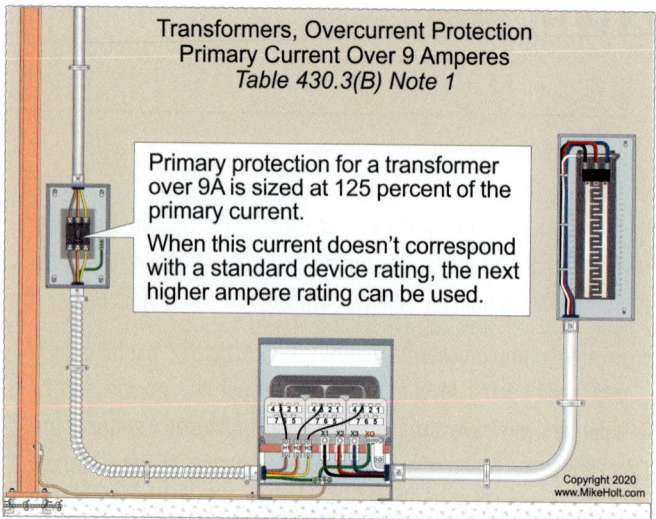

▶Figure 450–2

▶ **Example**

Question: What is the primary overcurrent protection rating and conductor size required for a 45 kVA, three-phase, 480V transformer that is fully loaded? The terminals are rated 75°C. ▶Figure 450–3

(a) 70A breaker, 6 AWG conductor
(b) 100A breaker, 3 AWG conductor
(c) 110A breaker, 2 AWG conductor
(d) 125A breaker, 1 AWG conductor

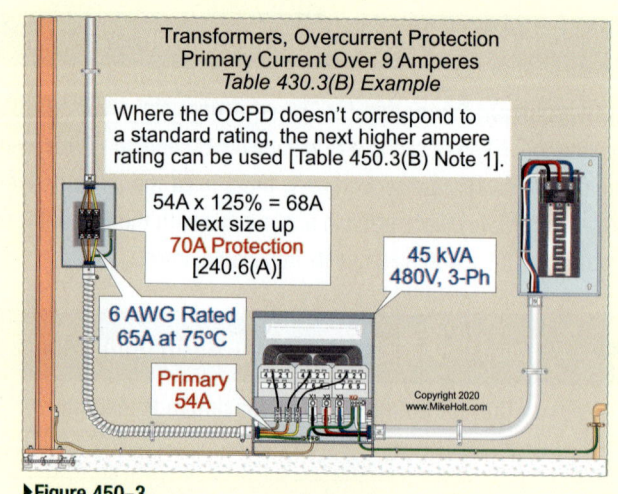

▶Figure 450–3

Solution:

Step 1: Determine the primary current.

$I = VA/(E \times 1.732)$

$I = 45,000 \text{ VA}/(480V \times 1.732)$

$I = 54A$

Step 2: Determine the primary overcurrent protection rating [240.6(A)].

Primary Overcurrent Protection = 54A × 125%
Primary Overcurrent Protection = 68A; use the next size up, 70A [240.6(A) and Table 450.3(B) Note 1]

Step 3: Determine the conductor size.

The conductor must be sized to accommodate the 70A primary overcurrent protection in accordance with 240.4(B).

Primary Conductor = 6 AWG conductor rated 65A at 75°C [110.14(C)(1) and Table 310.16]

Answer: (a) 70A breaker, 6 AWG conductor

450.9 Ventilation

Transformers must be installed in accordance with the manufacturer's instructions and their ventilating openings are not permitted to be blocked [110.3(B)].

Transformer top surfaces that are horizontal and readily accessible must be marked to prohibit storage.

450.10 Grounding and Bonding

(A) Dry-Type Transformer Enclosures. A terminal bar for equipment grounding conductors, system bonding jumpers, supply-side bonding jumpers, and grounding electrode conductors must be installed and bonded inside the transformer enclosure. ▶Figure 450–4

450.13 Transformer Accessibility

Transformers must be readily accessible to qualified personnel for inspection and maintenance except as permitted by (A) or (B).

(A) Open Installations. Dry-type transformers having a secondary voltage of 1,000V or less are not required to be readily accessible. ▶Figure 450–5

Transformers | 450.14

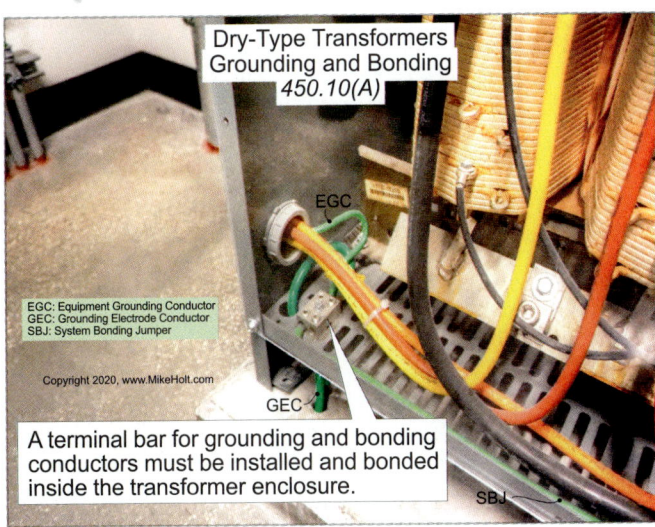
▶Figure 450-4

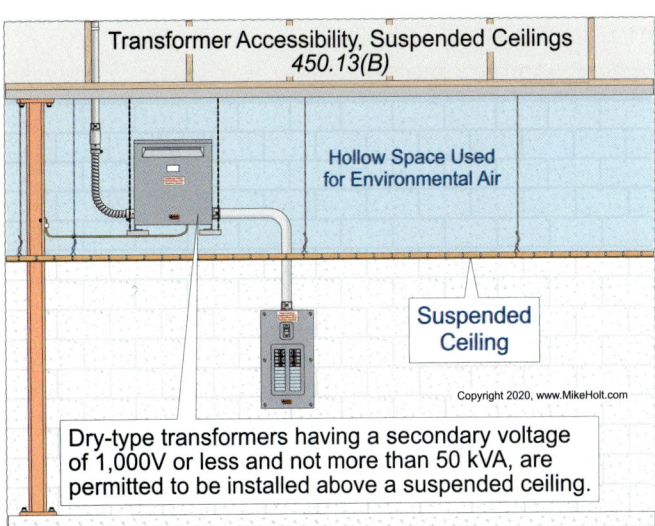
▶Figure 450-6

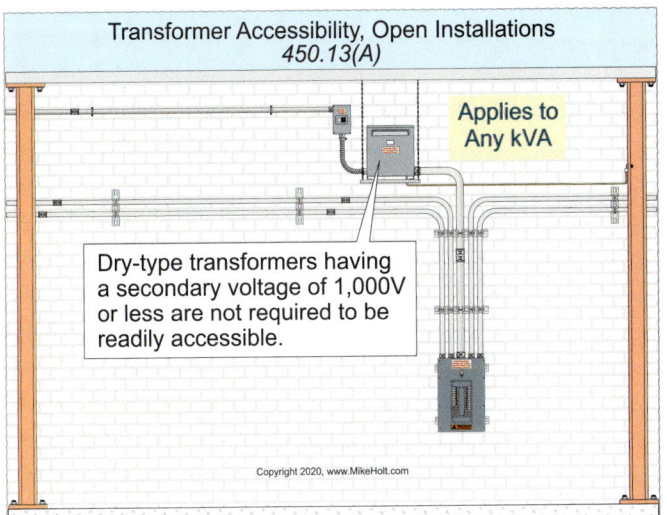
▶Figure 450-5

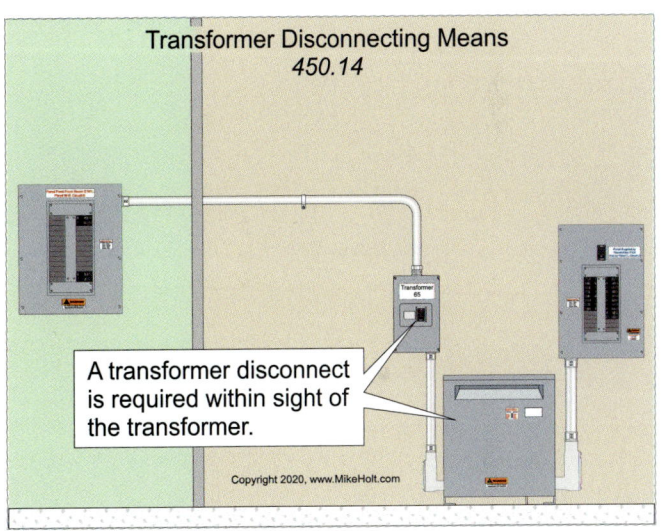
▶Figure 450-7

(B) Suspended Ceilings. Dry-type transformers having a secondary voltage of 1,000V or less and not more than 50 kVA are permitted to be installed above a suspended ceiling. ▶Figure 450-6

450.14 Disconnecting Means

A transformer must have a disconnect located within sight of the transformer unless the disconnect location is field marked on the transformer and the disconnect is capable of being locked in the open position in accordance with 110.25. ▶Figure 450-7 and ▶Figure 450-8

Author's Comment:

▸ "Within Sight" means it is visible and not more than 50 ft from the location of the equipment [Article 100].

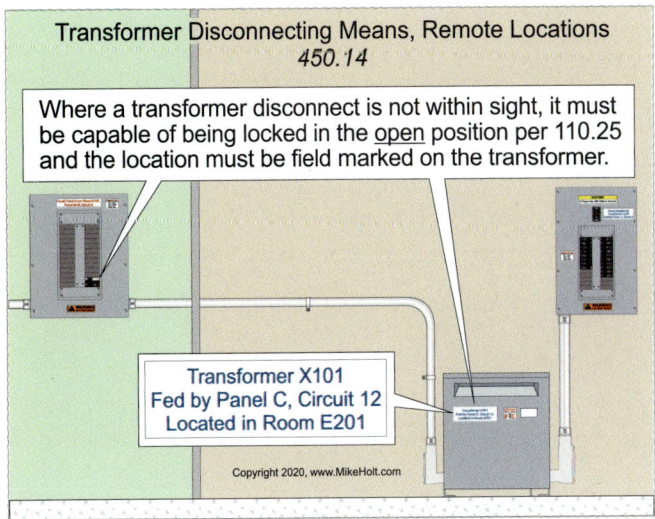
▶Figure 450-8

2nd Printing | 2020 NEC Requirements for Solar PV and Energy Storage Systems | MikeHolt.com | 441

Notes

ARTICLE 480 STORAGE BATTERIES

Introduction to Article 480—Storage Batteries

The stationary battery is the heart of any uninterruptible power supply. Article 480 addresses stationary batteries for commercial and industrial grade power supplies; not the small, "point of use," UPS boxes.

Stationary batteries are also used in other applications, such as emergency power systems. Regardless of the application, if it uses stationary batteries, this article applies.

Lead-acid stationary batteries fall into two general categories; flooded and valve regulated (VRLA). These differ markedly in such ways as maintainability, total cost of ownership, and scalability. The *NEC* does not address these differences since they are engineering issues rather than fire safety or electrical safety matters [90.1].

The *Code* does not address such design issues as optimum tier height, distance between tiers, determination of charging voltage, or string configuration. Nor does it address battery testing, monitoring, or maintenance. All of these involve highly specialized areas of knowledge and are required for optimizing operational efficiency. Standards other than the *NEC* address these topics.

What the *Code* does address in Article 480, are issues related to preventing electrocution and the ignition of the gases that all stationary batteries (even "sealed" ones) emit.

480.1 Scope

The provisions of Article 480 apply to stationary storage battery installations. ▶Figure 480–1

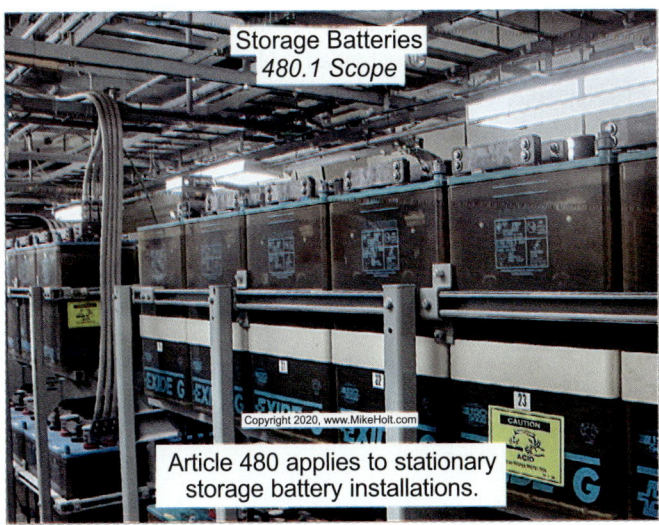

▶Figure 480–1

480.2 Definitions

The definitions in this section apply only within this article.

Cell. The basic electrochemical unit (consisting of an anode and a cathode) which receives, stores, and delivers electrical energy.

Author's Comment:

▸ A battery is made up of one or more cells.

Container. An object that holds the elements of a single unit in a battery.

Note: Containers can be single-cell or multi-cell and are often called "jars."

Electrolyte. The medium that provides the ion transport mechanism between the positive and negative electrodes of a cell.

Intercell Connector. A conductive bar or cable that connects adjacent cells.

480.4 | Storage Batteries

Intertier Connector. An electrical conductor that connects two cells on different tiers of the same rack, or different shelves of the same rack.

Nominal Voltage (Battery or Cell). The value assigned to a cell or battery for conveniently designating the voltage class. The operating voltage of the cell or battery can be higher or lower than the nominal voltage.

Note: The most common nominal cell voltages are 2V per cell for lead-acid, 1.20V per cell for alkali, and 3.60V to 3.80V per cell for lithium-ion. ▶Figure 480–2

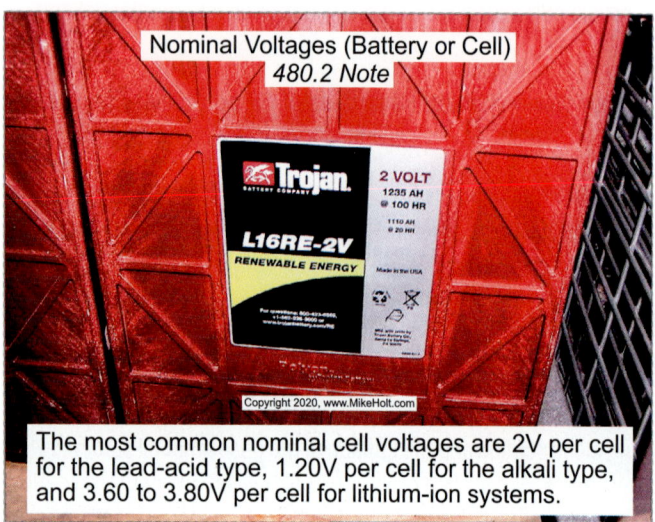

▶Figure 480–2

Author's Comment:

- The voltage of a battery will decrease below the nominal voltage while it is being used (discharged) and the actual voltage will often be higher than nominal when the battery is fully charged.

Sealed Cell or Battery. A cell or battery with no provision for the routine addition of water or electrolytes.

Storage Battery. A single or group of rechargeable cells connected together electrically in series, in parallel, or a combination of both, and comprised of lead-acid, nickel-cadmium, or other rechargeable electrochemical types.

480.4 Battery and Cell Terminations

(A) Dissimilar Metals. Where connections between dissimilar metals occur, antioxidant material must be used. ▶Figure 480–3

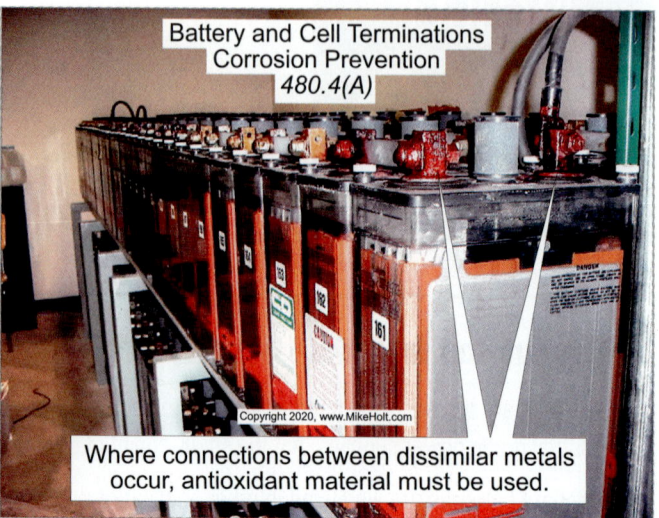

▶Figure 480–3

Note: The manufacturer's instructions may have guidance for acceptable materials.

(B) Intercell and Intertier Conductors and Connections. The ampacity of field-assembled intercell and intertier connectors and conductors must be sized so that the temperature rise under maximum load conditions, and at maximum ambient temperature, does not exceed the safe operating temperature of the conductor insulation.

Note: IEEE 1375, *Guide for the Protection of Stationary Battery Systems*, provides guidance for overcurrent protection and associated cable sizing. Typical voltage-drop considerations for alternating-current circuits might not be adequate for battery systems.

(C) Battery Terminals. Electrical connections to the battery, and the cable(s) between cells on separate levels or racks, must not put mechanical strain on the battery terminals.

Note: Conductors are commonly pre-formed to eliminate stress on battery terminations. Fine-stranded cables may also eliminate the stress on battery terminations. See the manufacturer's instructions for guidance.

(D) Accessibility. The terminals of all cells or multicell units must be readily accessible for readings, inspections, and cleaning where required by the equipment design. One side of transparent battery containers must be readily accessible for inspection of the internal components.

480.5 Wiring and Equipment Supplied from Batteries

Wiring and equipment supplied from storage batteries must be in accordance with Chapters 1 through 4 unless otherwise permitted by 480.6.

480.7 Direct-Current Disconnect Methods

(A) Disconnecting Means. A disconnect is required to open all phase conductors derived from a stationary battery system with a voltage over 60V dc. The disconnecting means must be readily accessible and located within sight of the battery system.

(B) Emergency Disconnect. For one- and two-family dwellings, a disconnecting means or its remote control for a stationary battery system must be located at a readily accessible location outside the building for emergency use. The disconnect must be labeled "EMERGENCY DISCONNECT."

(D) Remote Actuation. Where a disconnecting means, located in accordance with 480.7(A), is provided with remote controls to activate the disconnecting means, and the controls for the disconnecting means are not located within sight of the stationary battery system, the disconnecting means must be capable of being locked in the open position in accordance with 110.25 with the location of the controls field marked on the disconnecting means.

(F) Notification. The disconnecting means must be legibly marked in the field. A label with the marking must be placed in a conspicuous location near the battery if a disconnecting means is not provided. The marking must be of sufficient durability to withstand the environment involved and must include the following:

(1) Nominal battery voltage

(2) Available fault current derived from the stationary battery system

Note: Battery equipment suppliers can provide information about available fault current on any particular battery model.

(3) An arc flash label in accordance with acceptable industry practice

Note: NFPA 70E, *Standard for Electrical Safety in the Workplace*, aids in determining the severity of potential exposure, planning safe work practices, arc flash labeling, and selecting personal protective equipment.

(4) Date the available fault current calculation was performed

Ex: List items (2), (3), and (4) do not apply to one- and two-family dwellings.

(G) Identification of Power Sources. Battery systems must be indicated by 480.7(G)(1) and (G)(2).

(1) Facilities with Utility Services and Battery Systems. Plaques or directories must be installed in accordance with 705.10 and 712.10(A).

Ex: This requirement does not apply where a disconnect in 480.7(A) is not required.

(2) Facilities with Stand-Alone Systems. A permanent plaque or directory must be installed in accordance with 710.10.

Ex: This requirement does not apply where a disconnect in 480.7(A) is not required.

480.8 Insulation of Batteries

Batteries constructed of an electrically conductive container must have insulating support if a voltage is present between the container and ground.

480.9 Battery Support Systems

Structures that support batteries must be able to resist the corrosion inherent in this type of environment. Therefore, the structures must be provided with nonconducting support members or be made with a continuous insulating material. Paint alone is not considered an insulating material. ▶Figure 480–4

▶Figure 480–4

480.10 Battery Locations

Battery locations must conform with the following:

(A) Ventilation. Provisions must permit sufficient diffusion and ventilation of battery gases to prevent the accumulation of an explosive mixture. ▶Figure 480–5

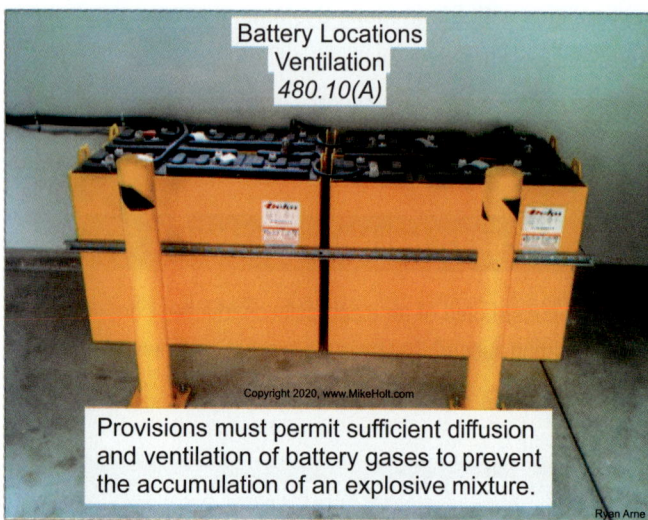

▶Figure 480–5

(B) Live Parts. Live parts of battery systems must be protected in accordance with 110.27.

> **Author's Comment:**
>
> ▸ According to 110.27, electrical equipment must not be installed where subject to physical damage unless enclosures or guards are arranged and of such strength as to prevent damage [110.27(B)]. In addition, entrances to rooms and other guarded locations containing exposed live parts must be marked with conspicuous signs forbidding unqualified persons to enter [110.27(C)].

(C) Working Space for Battery Racks. A minimum clearance of 1 in. is required between a cell container and any wall or structure on the side not requiring access for maintenance. Battery stands can contact adjacent walls or structures, provided that the battery shelf has a free air space for not less than 90 percent of its length.

Note: Additional space is often needed to accommodate battery hoisting equipment, tray removal, or spill containment.

(D) Top Terminal Batteries. Where top terminal batteries are installed on tiered racks, working space in accordance with the battery manufacturer's instructions must be provided between the highest point on a cell and the row or ceiling above that point.

Note: Battery manufacturers' installation instructions typically define how much top working space is necessary for a particular battery model.

(E) Egress. Personnel doors intended for entrance to, and egress from, rooms designated as battery rooms must open in the direction of egress and be equipped with listed panic or listed fire exit hardware.

(F) Piping in Battery Rooms. Gas piping is not permitted in a dedicated battery room.

(G) Illumination. The working space must have illumination that is not controlled only by automatic means and that does not:

(1) Expose personnel to energized battery components while performing maintenance on the luminaires, or

(2) Create a hazard to the battery upon failure of the luminaire.

480.12 Battery Interconnections

Flexible cables, as identified in Article 400, in sizes 2/0 AWG and larger are permitted within the battery enclosure from battery terminals to a nearby junction box where they must be connected to an approved wiring method. Flexible battery cables are also permitted between batteries and cells within the battery enclosure. Such cables must be listed and identified for the environmental conditions. Flexible, fine-stranded cables may only be used with terminals, lugs, devices, or connectors in accordance with 110.14.

480.13 Ground-Fault Detection

Battery circuits exceeding 100V between the conductors or to ground are permitted to operate with phase conductors provided a ground-fault detector and indicator is installed to monitor for ground faults.

CHAPTER 6

SPECIAL EQUIPMENT

Introduction to Chapter 6—Special Equipment

Chapter 6, which covers special equipment, is the second of the four *NEC* chapters that deal with special topics. Chapters 5 and 7 focus on special occupancies and special conditions respectively, while Chapter 8 covers communications systems. Remember, the first four chapters of the *Code* are sequential and form a foundation for each of the subsequent four.

What exactly is "Special Equipment"? It is equipment that, by the nature of its use, construction, or by its unique nature creates a need for additional measures to ensure the "safeguarding of people and property" mission of the *NEC*, as stated in Article 90. The *Code* groups the articles in this chapter logically, as you might expect.

- **Article 690—Solar Photovoltaic (PV) Systems.** This article focuses on reducing the electrical hazards that may arise from installing and operating a solar PV system, to the point where it can be considered safe for property and people. The requirements of the *NEC* Chapters 1 through 4 apply to these installations, except as specifically modified here.

- **Article 691—Large-Scale Solar Photovoltaic (PV) Electric Power Production Facility.** Article 691 covers large-scale PV power production facilities with a generating capacity of 5,000 kW or more and not under exclusive utility control.

Notes

ARTICLE 690 — SOLAR PHOTOVOLTAIC (PV) SYSTEMS

Introduction to Article 690—Solar Photovoltaic (PV) Systems

You have seen, or maybe own, devices powered by photovoltaic cells, such as night lights, car coolers, and toys. These generally consist of a small solar module powering a small device running on a few volts and a fraction of an ampere. A solar PV system that powers a building or interconnects with an electric utility operates on the same principals but on a much larger scale.

Solar PV systems that provide electrical power to an electrical system are complex. There are many issues that require expert knowledge in electrical, structural, and architectural issues.

The purpose of the *NEC* is to safeguard persons and property from the hazards arising from the use of electricity [90.1(A)]. Article 690 is focused on the electrical hazards that may arise from installing and operating a PV system. It consists of eight parts.

The general *Code* requirements of Chapters 1 through 4 also apply to these installations, except as specifically modified by this article [90.3].

Part I. General

690.1 Scope

 Scan this QR code for a video of Mike explaining this topic; it's a sample from the videos that accompany this textbook. www.MikeHolt.com/20PVvideos

The requirements contained in Article 690 apply to solar photovoltaic systems other than those covered by Article 691. ▶Figure 690–1

This article includes those PV systems that are interactive (operate in parallel with the electric utility), that are stand-alone systems, or are a combination of the two. PV systems can provide either ac or dc power.

Author's Comment:

▸ Energy storage systems are covered in Article 706 and are permitted to be connected to, but are not a part of, PV systems.

Review the details in ▶Figure 690–2, ▶Figure 690–3, ▶Figure 690–4, ▶Figure 690–5, and ▶Figure 690–6.

Note 2: Article 691 covers the installation of large-scale PV electric supply stations with an inverter generating capacity of not less than 5,000 kW, and not under the electric utility control. These facilities have specific design and safety features unique to large-scale PV supply stations and are for the sole purpose of providing electric supply to a system operated by a regulated utility. ▶Figure 690–7

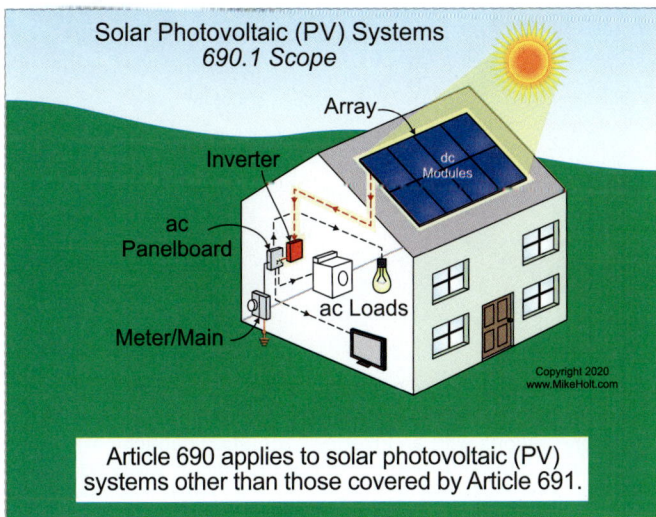

▶Figure 690–1

690.1 | Solar Photovoltaic (PV) Systems

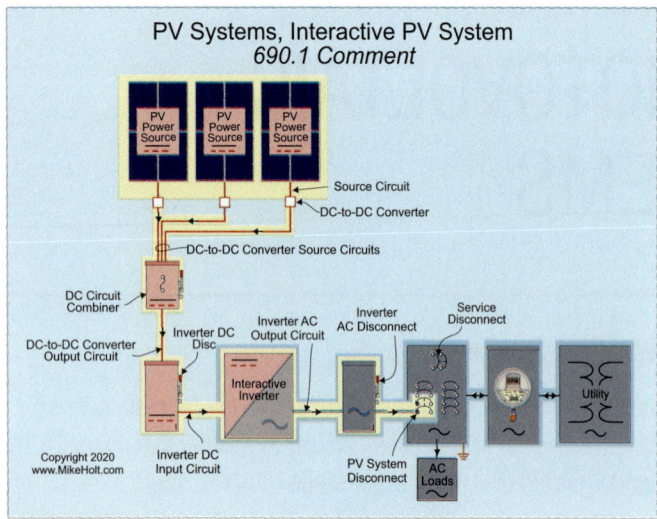
▶Figure 690-2

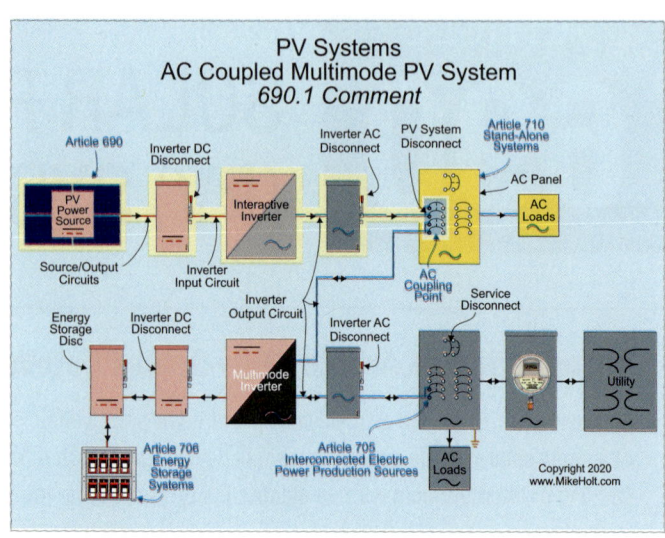
▶Figure 690-5

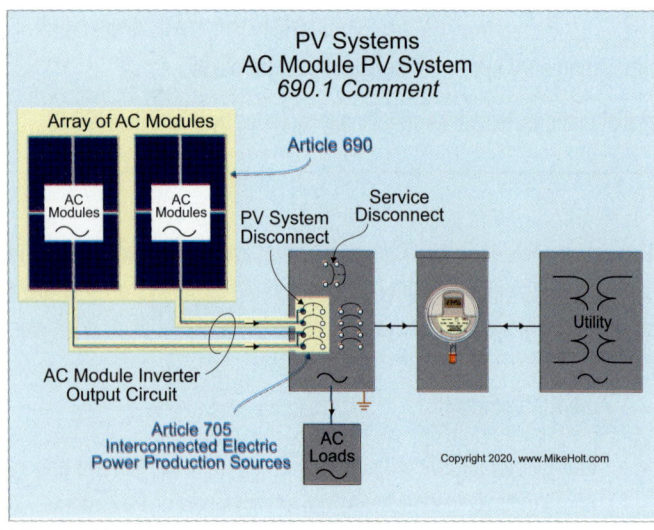
▶Figure 690-3

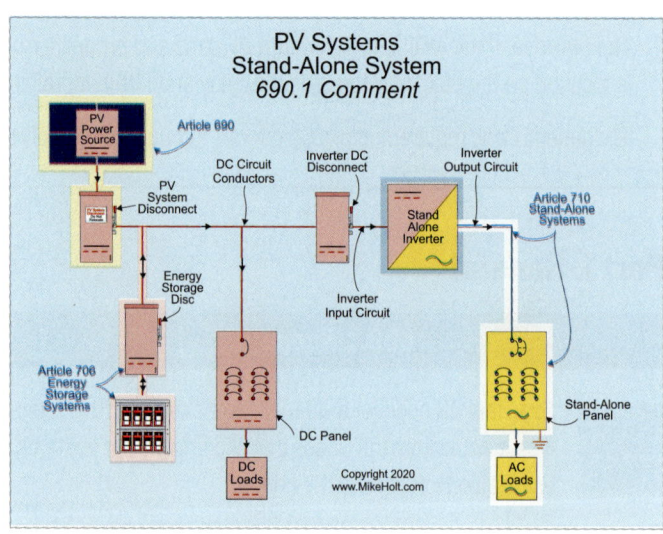
▶Figure 690-6

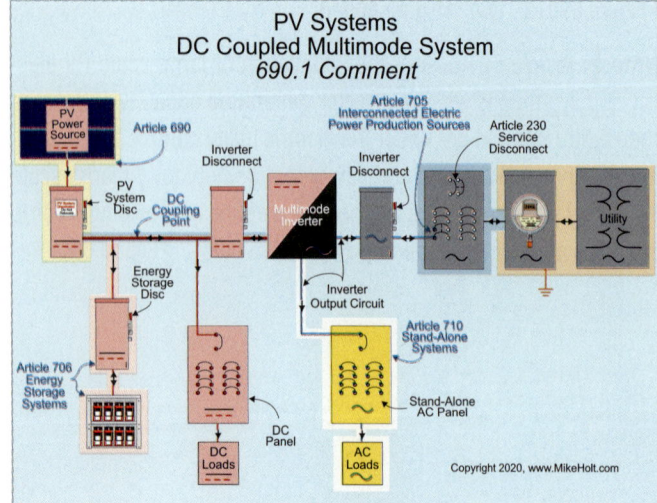
▶Figure 690-4

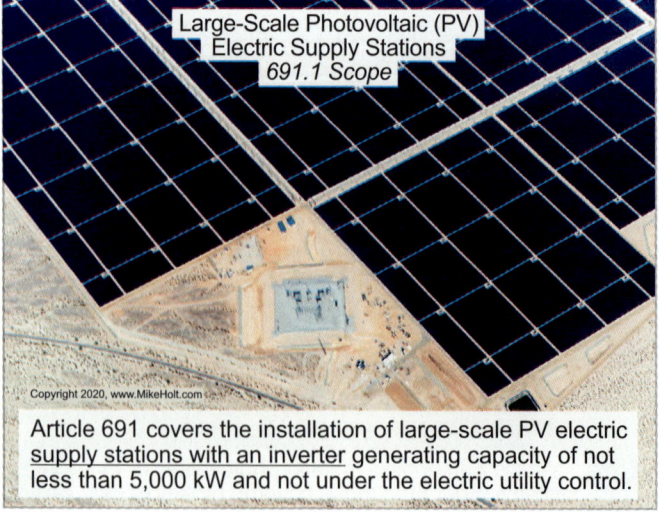
▶Figure 690-7

Solar Photovoltaic (PV) Systems | **690.2**

690.2 Definitions

The definitions in this section only apply within this article.

Alternating-Current Module System. An assembly of ac modules, wiring methods, materials, and subassemblies that are evaluated, identified, and defined as a system.

Alternating-Current Module. An ac module is a complete, environmentally protected unit consisting of solar cells, inverter, and other components designed to produce alternating-current power. ▶Figure 690-8

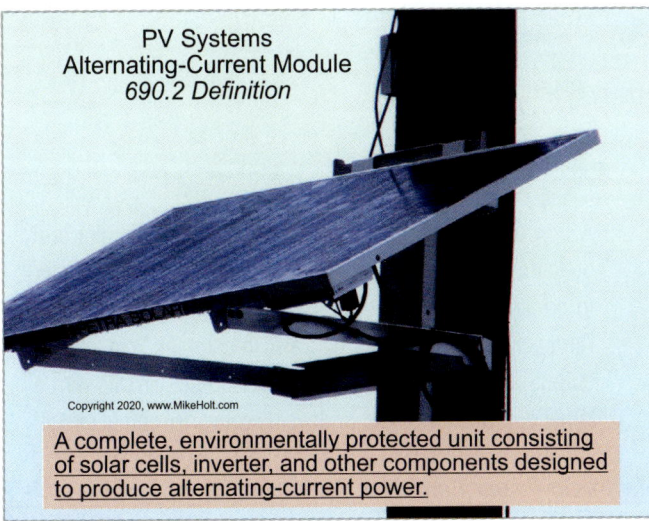

▶Figure 690-8

Author's Comment:

▸ Alternating-current modules are connected in parallel with each other and in parallel with the electric utility in an interactive mode. These modules operate interactively with the electric utility meaning that the ac output current from the ac module will cease exporting power upon sensing the loss of voltage from the electric utility.

▸ Manufacturers' instructions for ac modules will specify the size of the dedicated branch circuit on which they are to be connected and the maximum number of ac modules permitted on the branch circuit.

Array. An array is a mechanically and electrically integrated grouping of modules with a support system, including any attached system components such as inverter(s), dc-to-dc converter(s), and associated wiring. ▶Figure 690-9

▶Figure 690-9

DC-to-DC Converter Output Circuit. A dc-to-dc converter output circuit consists of the dc circuit conductors connected to the output of a dc combiner containing multiple dc-to-dc converter source circuits. ▶Figure 690-10

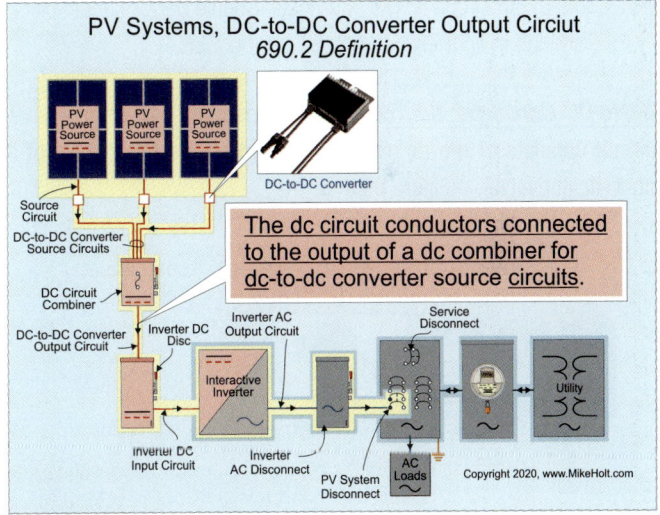

▶Figure 690-10

Author's Comment:

▸ According to Article 100, a "DC-to-DC Converter" is a device that can provide an output dc voltage and current at a higher or lower value than the input dc voltage and current. ▶Figure 690-11

▸ DC-to-DC converters are intended to maximize the power output of independent modules and reduce losses due to variances between the modules' outputs.

690.2 | Solar Photovoltaic (PV) Systems

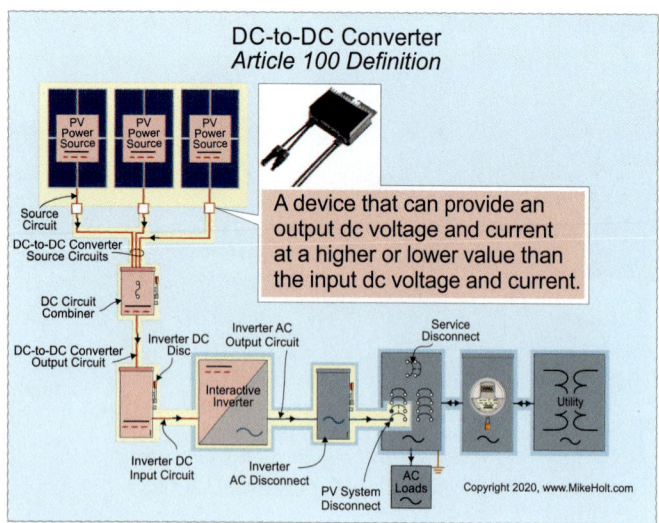
▶Figure 690–11

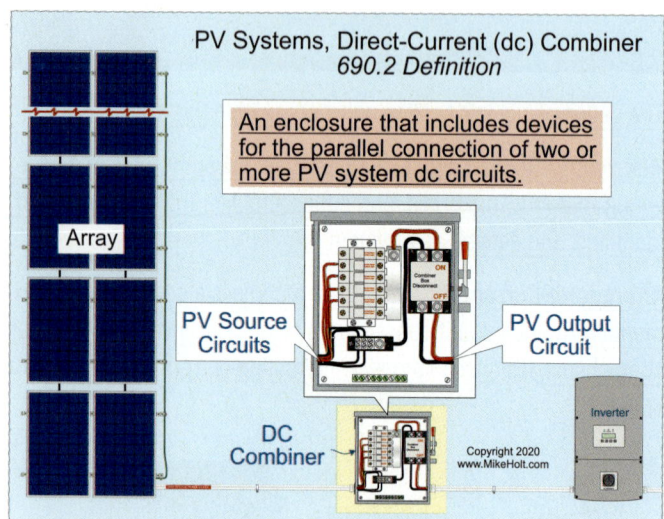
▶Figure 690–13

Author's Comment:

▸ A dc-to-dc converter enables the inverter to receive the circuit voltage that is maximized for direct-current and/or alternating-current power production by the inverter regardless of the circuit length, individual module performance, or variance in light exposure between modules.

DC-to-DC Converter Source Circuit. A dc-to-dc converter source circuit consists of the dc circuit conductors from the output of a dc-to-dc converter. ▶Figure 690–12

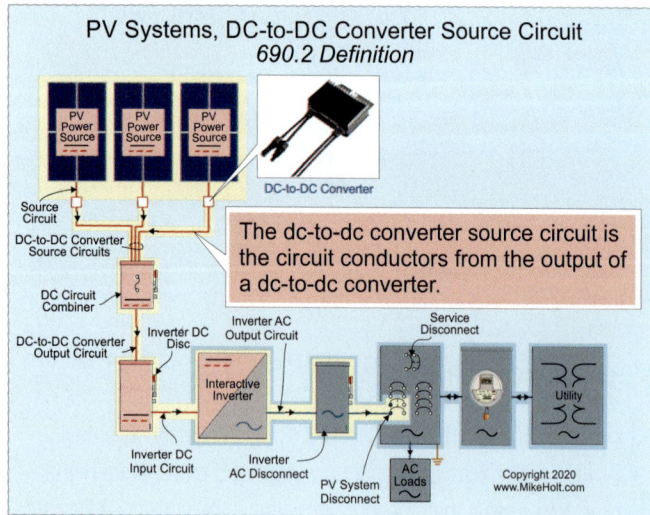
▶Figure 690–12

Direct-Current (dc) Combiner. A dc combiner is an enclosure that includes devices for the parallel connection of two or more PV system dc circuits. ▶Figure 690–13

Author's Comment:

▸ A dc combiner connects multiple PV source circuits and dc-to-dc converter source circuits in parallel with each other to create a PV output or dc-to-dc converter output circuit. Direct-current combiners can also recombine multiple PV output circuits and dc-to-dc converter output circuits with a larger two-wire PV output or dc-to-dc converter output circuit.

Electronic Power Converter. An electronic power converter is a device that uses electronics to convert one form of electrical power into another.

Note: Examples of electronic power converters include (but are not limited to) inverters, dc-to-dc converters, and electronic charge controllers. These devices have limited current capabilities based on the device ratings at continuous rated power.

Grounded, Functionally. A functionally grounded PV system is one that has an electrical ground reference for operational purposes that is not solidly grounded. ▶Figure 690–14

Note: A functionally grounded PV system is often connected to ground through an electronic means that is internal to an inverter or charge controller that provides ground-fault protection. Examples of operational purposes for functionally grounded systems include ground-fault detection and protection, as well as performance-related issues for some power sources.

Module. A PV module is a unit of environmentally protected solar cells and components designed to produce dc power. ▶Figure 690–15

Solar Photovoltaic (PV) Systems | 690.2

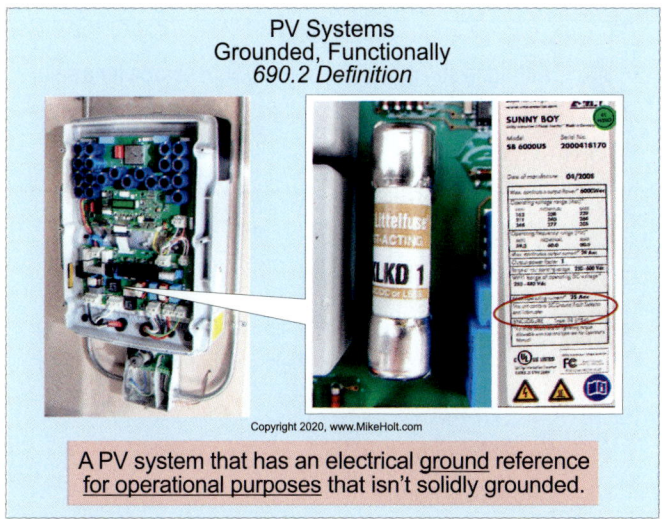

▶Figure 690–14

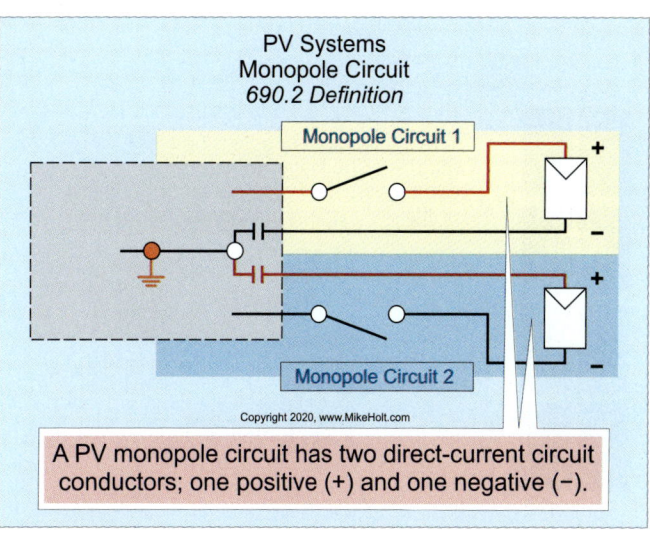

▶Figure 690–16

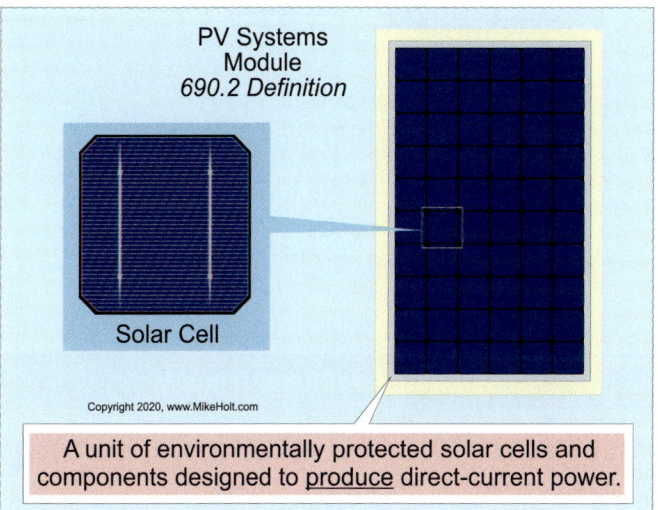

▶Figure 690–15

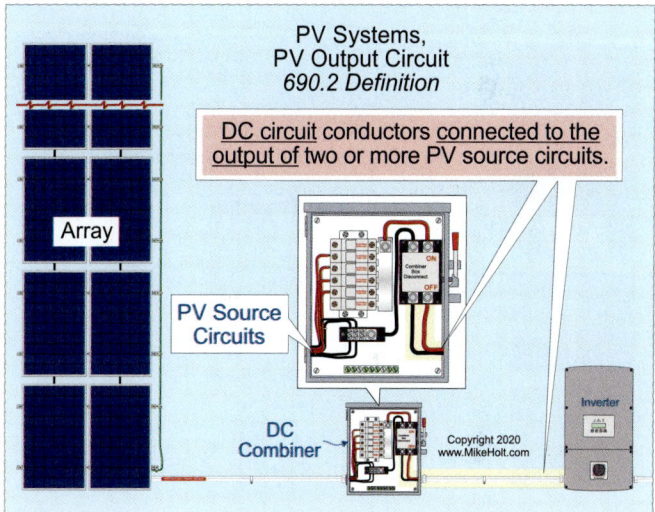

▶Figure 690–17

Author's Comment:

▶ PV modules use sunlight to generate direct-current (dc) electricity by using light (photons) to move electrons in a semiconductor. This is known as the "photovoltaic effect."

Monopole Circuit. A PV monopole circuit has two dc circuit conductors: one positive (+) and one negative (−). ▶Figure 690–16

PV Output Circuit. A PV output circuit consists of dc circuit conductors connected to the output of two or more PV source circuits. ▶Figure 690–17

PV Source Circuit. The PV source circuit consists of the dc circuit conductors between modules and from modules to dc combiners, electronic power converters, or the PV System disconnecting means. ▶Figure 690–18 and ▶Figure 690–19

PV System DC Circuit. The PV system dc circuit consists of any dc conductor in PV source circuits, PV output circuits, dc-to-dc converter source circuits, and dc-to-dc converter output circuits.

Solar Cell. The building block of a PV module that generates dc power when exposed to light. ▶Figure 690–20

690.4 | Solar Photovoltaic (PV) Systems

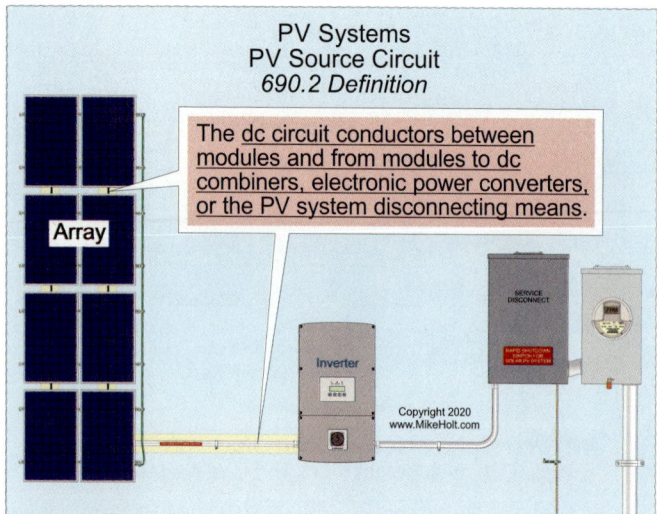
▶Figure 690–18

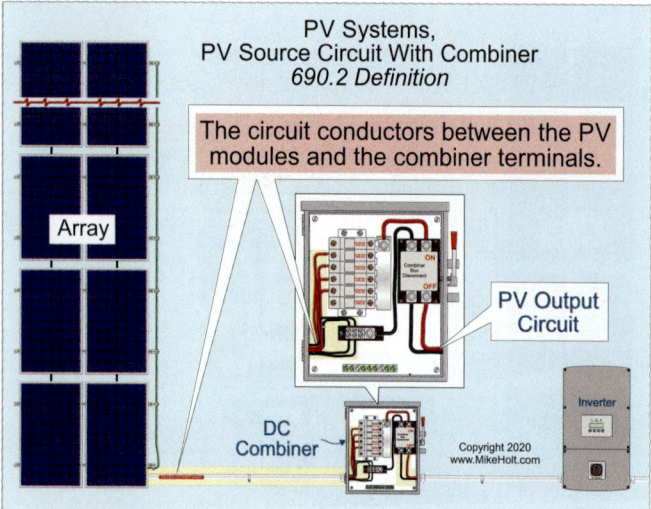
▶Figure 690–19

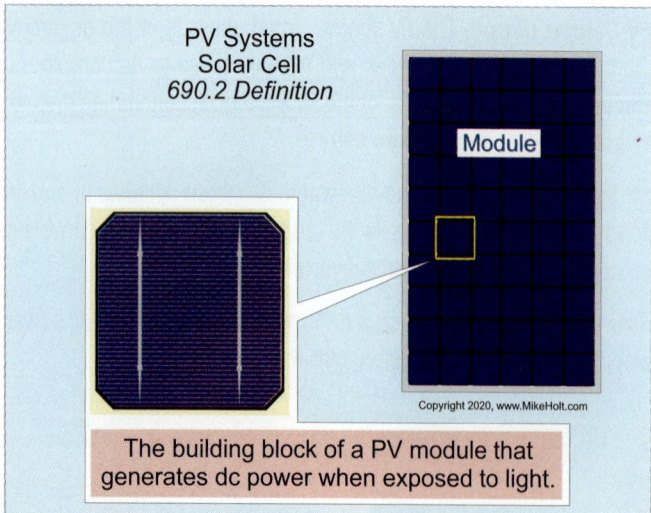
▶Figure 690–20

> **Caution**
>
> Although sunlight is the primary light source for a solar cell, other light sources such as moonlight can generate dc power.

Author's Comment:

▸ All Article 100 definitions are important, but the following definitions located there are often components commonly found in PV systems:

- Charge Controller
- DC-to-DC Converter
- DC-to-DC Output Circuit
- Hybrid System
- Interactive Inverter
- Interactive System
- Inverter, Multimode
- Inverter Output Circuit
- Power Production System
- Photovoltaic (PV) System
- Stand-Alone System

690.4 General Requirements

(A) PV Systems. A PV system is permitted to supply electric power to buildings or other electrical supply systems.

(B) Listed or Field Labeled Equipment. Components of the PV system including inverters, PV modules, ac modules, ac module systems, dc combiners, dc-to-dc converters, rapid shutdown equipment, dc circuit controllers, and charge controllers must be listed or be evaluated for the application and have a field label applied. ▶Figure 690–21

Author's Comment:

▸ "Listing" means the equipment is included in a list published by a testing laboratory acceptable to the authority having jurisdiction [Article 100].

▸ "Field Labeled" means the equipment or materials which have a label, symbol, or other identifying mark of a field evaluation body (FEB) indicates the equipment or material was evaluated and found to comply with the requirements described in the field body evaluation report [Article 100].

Solar Photovoltaic (PV) Systems | **690.6**

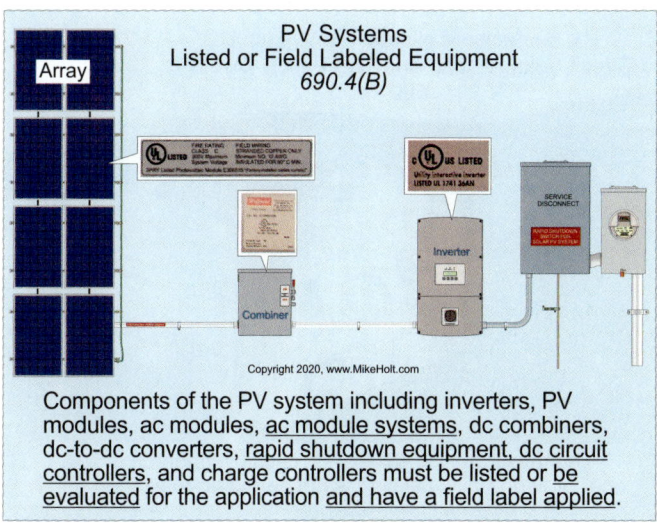
▶Figure 690–21

(C) Qualified Persons. The installation of PV systems must be performed by a qualified person.

Note: A qualified person has the knowledge related to the construction and operation of PV equipment and installations; along with safety training to recognize and avoid hazards to persons and property [Article 100]. ▶Figure 690–22

▶Figure 690–22

Author's Comment:

▸ NFPA 70E, *Standard for Electrical Safety in the Workplace*, provides information on the safety training requirements expected of a "qualified person."

▸ Examples of this safety training include (but are not limited to) training in the use of special precautionary techniques, personal protective equipment (PPE), insulating and shielding materials, and in the use of insulated tools and test equipment when working on or near exposed conductors or circuit parts that can become energized.

▸ In many parts of the United States, electricians, electrical contractors, electrical inspectors, and electrical engineers must complete an *NEC* review course each year as a requirement to maintain licensing. This, in and of itself, does not make one qualified to deal with the specific hazards involved with PV systems.

(D) Multiple PV Systems. Multiple PV systems are permitted on or in a building. Where PV systems are remotely located from each other a directory must be provided at each PV disconnect in accordance with 705.10.

(E) Where Not Permitted. No part of a PV system is permitted to be installed within a bathroom.

(F) Electronic Power Converters Not Readily Accessible. Electronic power converters (inverters and dc-to-dc converters) are not required to be readily accessible.

690.6 Alternating-Current Modules and Systems

(A) PV Source Circuits. The requirements of Article 690 do not apply to the source circuits for an ac module or ac module system. The source circuit, conductors, and the inverter(s) are considered internal components of a listed product. ▶Figure 690–23

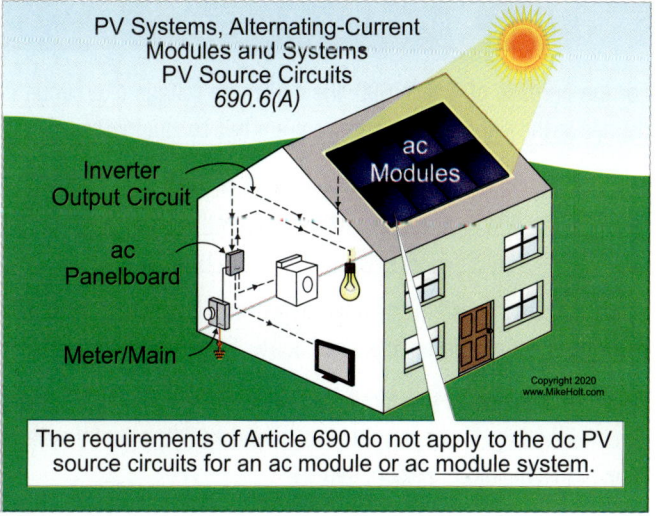
▶Figure 690–23

690.7 | Solar Photovoltaic (PV) Systems

Author's Comment:

▸ PV source circuits and inverters for ac modules or ac module systems are covered by the listing of the product. Listed factory-installed internal wiring of equipment that has been evaluated by a qualified testing laboratory does not require inspecting for *NEC* compliance [90.7].

(B) Output Circuit. The ac output circuit conductors for an ac module or ac module system are considered to be the "Inverter Output Circuit" as defined in Article 100. ▸Figure 690-24

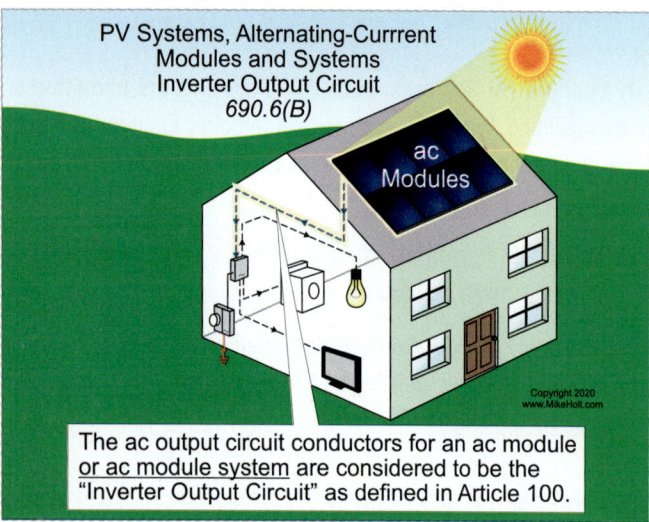

▸Figure 690-24

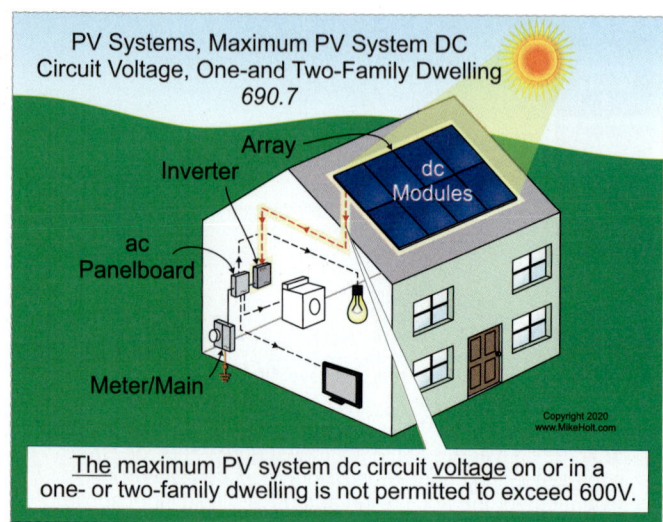

▸Figure 690-25

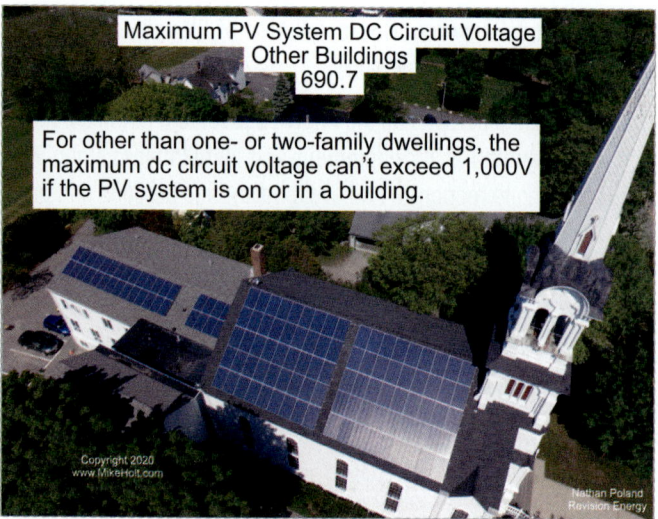

▸Figure 690-26

Part II. Circuit Requirements

690.7 Maximum PV System Direct-Current Circuit Voltage

For the purpose of Article 690, the maximum voltage of a circuit is defined as the highest voltage between any two conductors of a circuit.

The maximum voltage of a circuit value is used when selecting conductors, cables, equipment, determining working space, and other applications where circuit voltage ratings are used.

The maximum PV system dc circuit voltage on or in a one- or two-family dwelling is not permitted to exceed 600V. ▸Figure 690-25

For other than one- or two-family dwellings, the maximum PV system dc circuit voltage is not permitted to exceed 1,000V if the PV system is on or in a building. ▸Figure 690-26

PV systems not located on or in buildings with a maximum dc circuit voltage of not over 1,500V are not required to comply with Parts II and III of Article 490. ▸Figure 690-27

Author's Comment:

▸ The PV system dc circuit consists of PV source circuits, PV output circuits, dc-to-dc converter source circuits, and dc-to-dc converter output circuits [690.2].

(A) PV Source and Output Circuit Volts. The maximum PV source and output circuit dc voltage is determined by one of the following methods:

Solar Photovoltaic (PV) Systems | 690.7

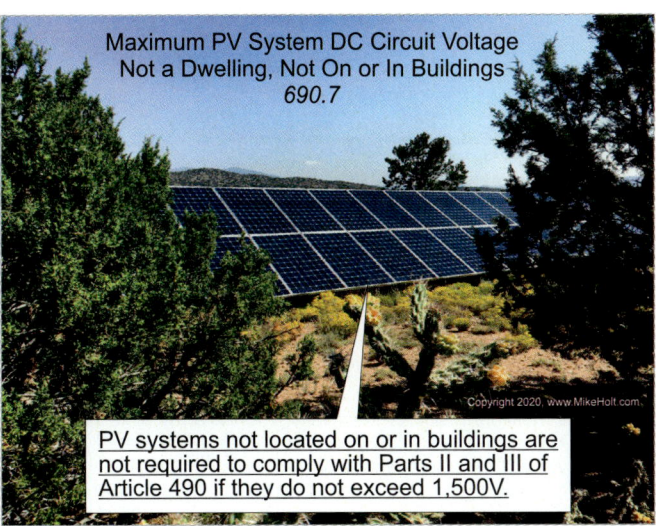
▶Figure 690-27

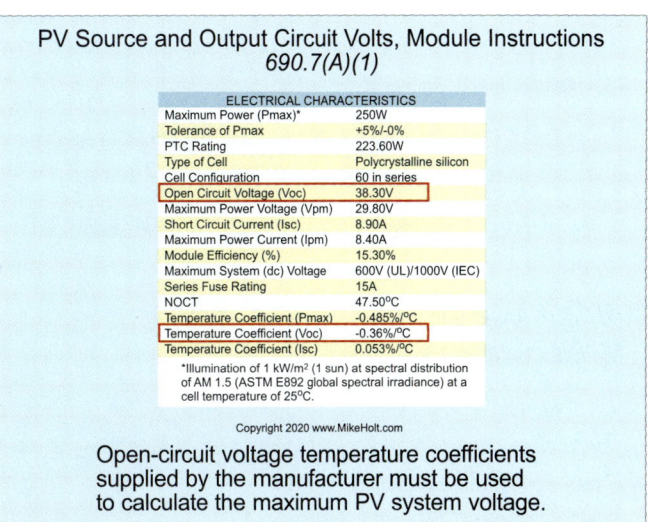
▶Figure 690-29

(1) Module Instructions. The maximum PV source and output circuit dc voltage is equal to the sum of the dc module open-circuit voltage (Voc) of the series-connected modules as corrected for the lowest expected ambient temperature using the manufacturer's voltage temperature coefficient correction. ▶Figure 690-28 and ▶Figure 690-29

▶ **Maximum PV System Voltage, Based on Manufacturer Temperature Coefficient, %/°C Example**

Question: Using the manufacturer's temperature coefficient of –0.36%/°C, what is the maximum PV system source and output circuit dc voltage for twelve modules each rated Voc 38.30 at a temperature of –7°C? ▶Figure 690-30

(a) 493V (b) 513V (c) 529V (d) 541V

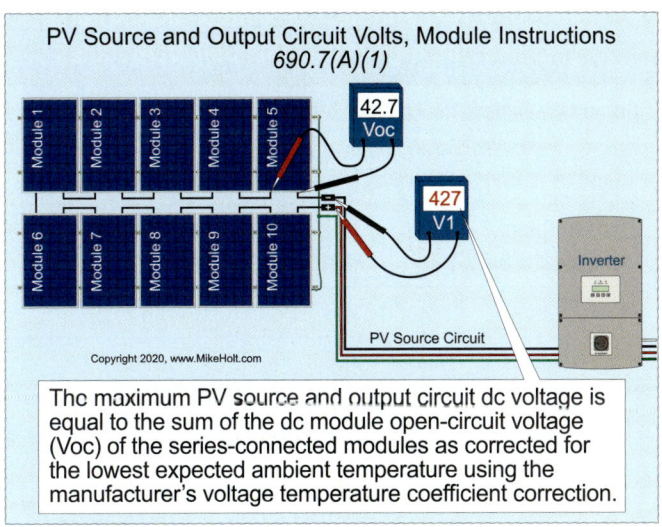
▶Figure 690-28

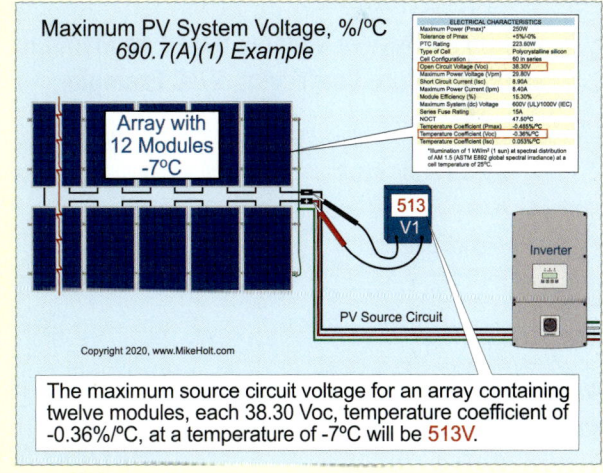
▶Figure 690-30

Author's Comment:

▶ A PV module's dc voltage has an inverse relationship with temperature, which means that at lower ambient temperatures, the module's dc output voltage increases and at higher ambient temperatures, the modules' dc voltage output decreases.

Solution:

Four things are needed to calculate the maximum PV system circuit voltage:

1. The module Voc (open-circuit voltage) found on the manufacturer's label or datasheet.

•••

690.7 | Solar Photovoltaic (PV) Systems

2. The module temperature coefficient of the Voc which is found on the manufacturer's label or datasheet.

3. The lowest expected ambient temperature. See the Solar America Board for Codes and Standards website (www.solarabcs.org).

4. The number of modules that are connected in series with each other.

PV Voc = Rated Voc × {1 + [(Temp. °C – 25°C) × Module Coefficient %/°C]} × # Modules

Voc of Module = 38.30 Voc
Temperature Coefficient of Voc of Module = –0.36%/°C
Lowest Temperature Expected = –7°C
Number of Series-Connected Modules = 12

PV Circuit Voltage = 38.30 Voc × {1+ [(–7°C – 25°C) × –0.36%/°C]} × 12 modules
PV Circuit Voltage = 38.30 Voc × [(1 + (-32°C × –0.36%/°C)] × 12 modules
PV Circuit Voltage = 38.30 Voc × (1 + 11.52%) × 12 modules
PV Circuit Voltage = 38.30 Voc × 111.52% × 12 modules
PV Circuit Voltage = 42.71V × 12 modules
PV Circuit Voltage = 513V

Answer: (b) 513V

▶ **Maximum PV System Voltage, Based on Manufacturer Temperature Coefficient, V/°C Example**

Question: Using the manufacturer's temperature coefficient of –0.137V/°C, what is the maximum PV source and output circuit dc voltage for twelve modules each rated Voc 38.30 at a temperature of –7°C? ▶Figure 690–31

(a) 493V (b) 512V (c) 524V (d) 541V

Solution:

PV Voc (V/°C) = Rated Voc + [(Temp. °C – 25°C) × Module Coefficient V/°C] × # Modules

PV Circuit Voltage = {38.30V + [(–7°C – 25°C) × -0.137V/°C]} × 12 modules
PV Circuit Voltage = [38.30V + (-32°C × -0.137V/°C)] × 12 modules
PV Circuit Voltage = (38.30V + 4.384V) × 12 modules
PV Circuit Voltage = 42.684V × 12 modules
PV Circuit Voltage = 512V

Answer: (b) 512V

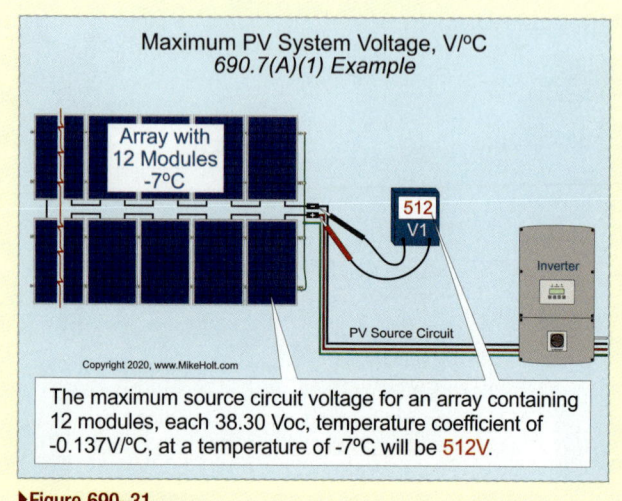

▶Figure 690–31

(2) Table of Crystalline and Multicrystalline Modules. The maximum PV source and output circuit voltage is equal to the sum of the dc module-rated open-circuit voltage (Voc) of the series-connected modules as corrected for the lowest expected ambient temperature in accordance with Table 690.7(A).

Table 690.7(A) Voltage Correction Factors for Crystalline and Multicrystalline Silicon Modules

Correction Factors for Ambient Temperatures Below 25°C (77°F).
(Multiply the rated open-circuit voltage by the appropriate correction factor shown below.)

Ambient Temperature (°C)	Factor	Ambient Temperature (°F)
24 to 20	1.02	76 to 68
19 to 15	1.04	67 to 59
14 to 10	1.06	58 to 50
9 to 5	1.08	49 to 41
4 to 0	1.10	40 to 32
–1 to –5	1.12	31 to 23
–6 to –10	1.14	22 to 14
–11 to –15	1.16	13 to 5
–16 to –20	1.18	4 to -4
–21 to –25	1.20	–5 to –13
–26 to -30	1.21	–14 to –22
–31 to –35	1.23	–23 to –31
–36 to –40	1.25	–32 to –40

> **Caution:** Illumination at dawn, dusk, when there is heavy overcast, and even on rainy days is sufficient to produce dangerous dc voltage. ▶Figure 690–32

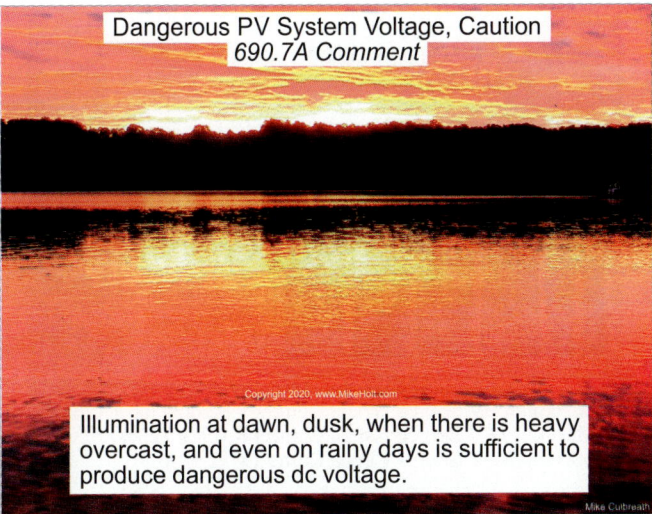

▶Figure 690–32

▶ **Maximum PV System Voltage, Based on Table 690.7(A) Temperature Correction [690.7(A)(2)] Example**

Question: Using Table 690.7(A), what is the maximum PV system source and output circuit dc voltage for twelve crystalline modules each rated Voc 38.30 at a temperature of -7°C? ▶Figure 690–33

(a) 493V (b) 513V (c) 524V (d) 541V

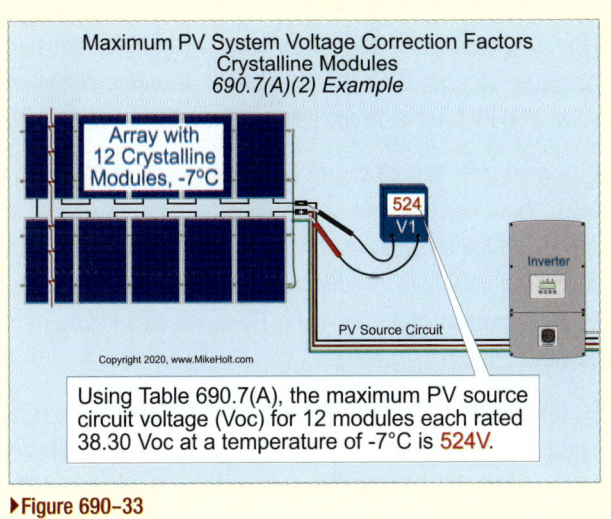

▶Figure 690–33

Solution:

PV Voc = Module Voc ×
Table 690.7 Correction Factor × # Modules
PV Circuit Voltage = 38.30 Voc × 1.14 × 12 modules
PV Circuit Voltage = 524V

Answer: (c) 524V

(3) Engineered Industry Standard Method. For PV systems with an inverter generating capacity of 100 kW or greater, the maximum PV source and output circuit dc voltage is permitted to be determined by a licensed professional electrical engineer providing documented and stamped PV system design using an industry standard method maximum dc voltage calculation.

Note 1: One source for lowest-expected, ambient temperature design data for various locations is the chapter titled "Extreme Annual Mean Minimum Design Dry Bulb Temperature" found in the *ASHRAE Handbook—Fundamentals.* This temperature data can be used to calculate maximum voltage.

Note 2: One industry standard method for calculating the maximum PV source and output circuit dc voltage is published by Sandia National Laboratories, reference SAND 2004-3535, *Photovoltaic Array Performance Model.*

(B) DC-to-DC Converter Source and Output Circuit Voltage. The maximum dc-to-dc converter dc voltage is determined by one of the following methods:

(1) Single DC-to-DC Converter. The maximum output dc voltage for a single dc-to-dc converter is based on the manufacturer's instructions for the dc-to-dc converter.

If the instructions do not provide a method to determine the maximum dc-to-dc converter output dc voltage, the maximum dc-to-dc output dc voltage will be equal to the rated output dc voltage of the dc-to-dc converter.

(2) Two or More Series-Connected DC-to-DC Converters. The maximum output circuit dc voltage for series-connected dc-to-dc converters is based on the manufacturer's instructions for the dc-to-dc converter.

If the instructions do not provide a method to determine the dc-to-dc converters' maximum output dc voltage, the maximum dc-to-dc output dc voltage for the series-connected dc-to-dc converters will be equal to the sum of the maximum rated output dc voltage of the dc-to-dc converters connected in series.

690.8 Circuit Current and Conductor Sizing

(A) Calculation of Maximum PV Circuit Current. The maximum PV system current is calculated in accordance with 690.8(A)(1) or (2):

(1) PV System Circuit Current. The maximum PV system dc circuit current is calculated in accordance with 690.8(A)(1)(a) through (e).

(a) PV Source Circuit Current Calculation.

(1) PV Systems Rated Less Than 100 kW. The maximum PV source circuit dc current is equal to the short-circuit current ratings marked on the modules connected in parallel multiplied by 125 percent. ▶Figure 690-34

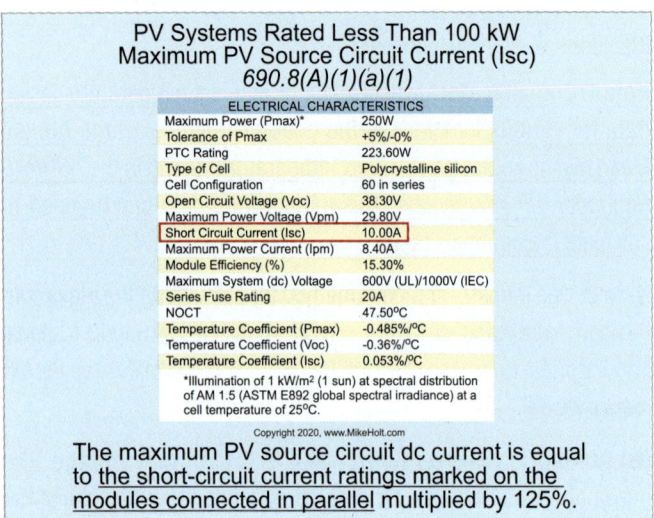

▶Figure 690-34

Author's Comment:

▶ The PV source circuit is defined as the two dc circuit conductors between modules, dc circuit conductors from the modules to dc-to-dc converters, dc circuit conductors from modules to dc combiners, and dc circuit conductors from modules to inverters [690.2].

▶ A module can produce more than the rated current when the intensity of the sunlight is greater than the standard used to determine the module's short-circuit rating. This happens when sunlight intensity is affected by altitude, reflection due to snow, refraction through clouds, or low humidity. For this reason, the PV system circuit current is calculated at 125 percent of the module's short-circuit current rating marked on the module's nameplate. This is commonly referred to as an "irradiance factor."

▶ **Maximum PV Source Circuit Current Example**

Question: What is the maximum PV source circuit dc current for 12 series-connected modules having a nameplate short-circuit current (Isc) of 10A? ▶Figure 690-35

(a) 12.50A   (b) 15A   (c) 20A   (d) 25A

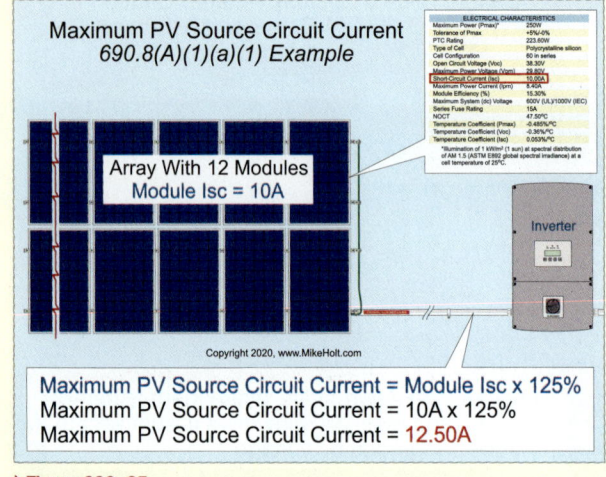

▶Figure 690-35

Solution:

Source Circuit Current = Module Isc × 125%

Source Circuit Current = 10A × 125%

Source Circuit Current = 12.50A

Answer: (a) 12.50A

(2) PV System Rated 100 kW or Greater. The maximum PV source circuit dc current calculations for PV systems with an inverter with a generating capacity of 100 kW or greater can be determined by a licensed professional electrical engineer providing documented and stamped PV system design using an industry standard method.

The maximum PV source circuit dc current value is based on the highest 3-hour current average resulting from the simulated local irradiance on the array accounting for elevation and orientation. In no case is the maximum PV source circuit dc current permitted to be less than 70 percent of the maximum PV source circuit dc current as calculated in 690.8(A)(1)(a)(1).

Note: One industry standard method for calculating the maximum PV source current is available from Sandia National Laboratories, reference SAND 2004-3535, *Photovoltaic Array Performance Model.* This model is used by the System Advisor Model simulation program provided by the National Renewable Energy Laboratory.

(b) PV Output Circuit Current Calculation. The maximum PV output circuit dc current is equal to the sum of parallel PV source circuit dc currents as calculated in 690.8(A)(1)(a).

Author's Comment:

▸ The PV output circuit consists of the two dc circuit conductors connected to the output of a dc combiner.

▶ **Maximum PV Output Circuit Current Example**

Question: What is the maximum PV output circuit dc current for four source circuits where each source circuit contains 12 dc modules, each having a nameplate Isc of 10A? ▶Figure 690-36

(a) 25A   (b) 35A   (c) 40A   (d) 50A

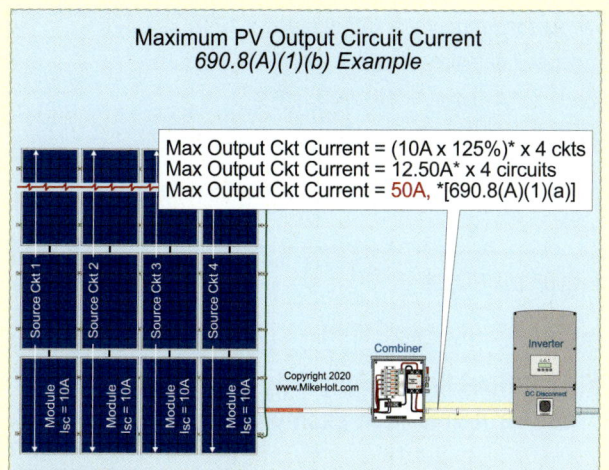

▶Figure 690-36

Solution:

PV Output Circuit Current = (Module Isc × 125%)* × Number of Source Circuits

PV Output Circuit Current = (10A × 125%)* × 4 circuits
PV Output Circuit Current = 12.50A × 4 circuits
PV Output Circuit Current = 50A
*[690.8(A)(1)(a)]

Answer: *(d) 50A*

(c) DC-to-DC Converter Source Circuit Current. The maximum dc-to-dc converter source circuit dc current is equal to the dc-to-dc converter's continuous output current rating marked on the converter.
▶Figure 690-37

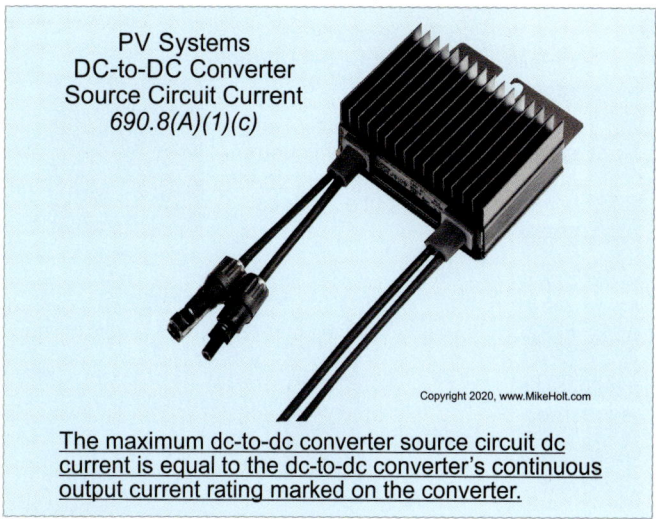

▶Figure 690-37

Author's Comment:

▸ A dc-to-dc converter source circuit is the two dc circuit conductors from the output of a dc-to-dc converter [690.2].

(d) DC-to-DC Converter Output Circuit Current. The maximum dc-to-dc output circuit dc current is equal to the sum of the parallel-connected dc-to-dc converter source circuit dc currents as calculated in 690.8(A)(1)(c).

Author's Comment:

▸ A dc-to-dc converter output circuit is the two dc circuit conductors connected to the output of the dc combiner containing multiple dc-to-dc converter source circuits [690.2].

(e) Inverter Output Circuit Current. The maximum inverter output circuit dc current is equal to the continuous output current rating marked on the inverter for the output ac voltage. ▶Figure 690-38

Author's Comment:

▸ The inverter output circuit is the circuit conductors connected to the alternating-current output of an inverter [Article 100].

(2) Input of Electronic Power Converters. Where a circuit is protected with an overcurrent device not exceeding the conductor ampacity, the maximum current can be the rated input current of the electronic power converter.

(B) Conductor Sizing. PV circuit conductors must be sized to carry the larger of 690.8(B)(1) or (B)(2).

690.8 | Solar Photovoltaic (PV) Systems

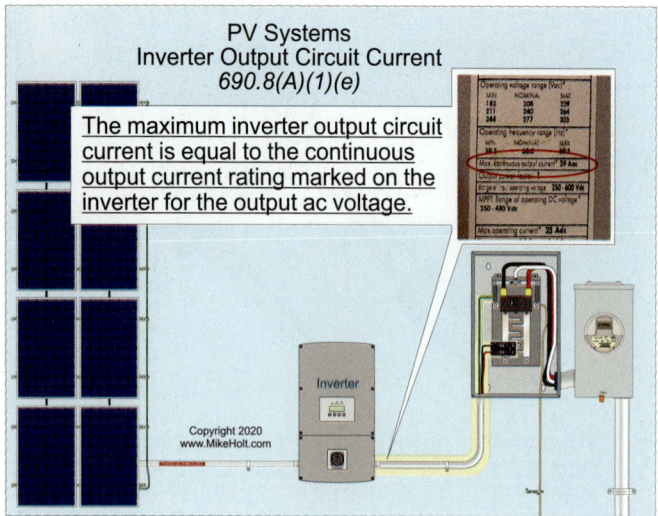

▶Figure 690-38

(1) Conductor Sizing, Without Ampacity Correction and/or Adjustment. PV circuit conductors within the scope of 690.8(A) must have an ampacity of not less than 125 percent of the current as determined by 690.8(A), without ampacity correction and/or adjustment.
▶Figure 690-39

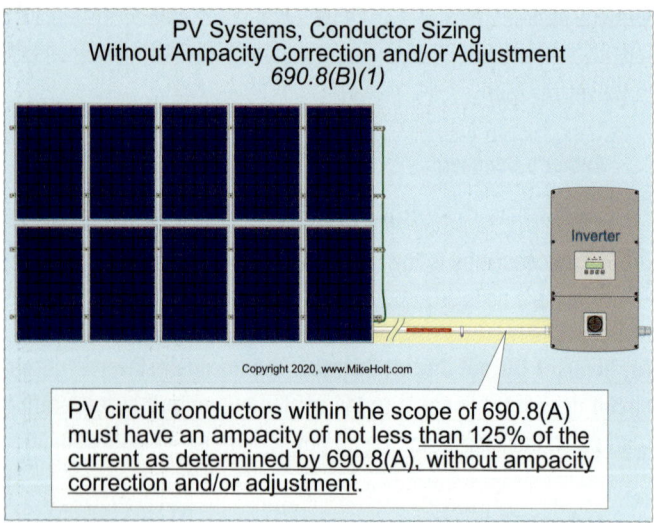

▶Figure 690-39

▶ PV Source Circuit Without Ampacity Correction and/or Adjustment Example

Question: What is the minimum dc source circuit conductor ampacity, without the application of conductor correction or adjustment, for source circuit conductors having a short-circuit current rating of 10A? ▶Figure 690-40

(a) 12.50A (b) 15.62A (c) 20.41A (d) 25.56A

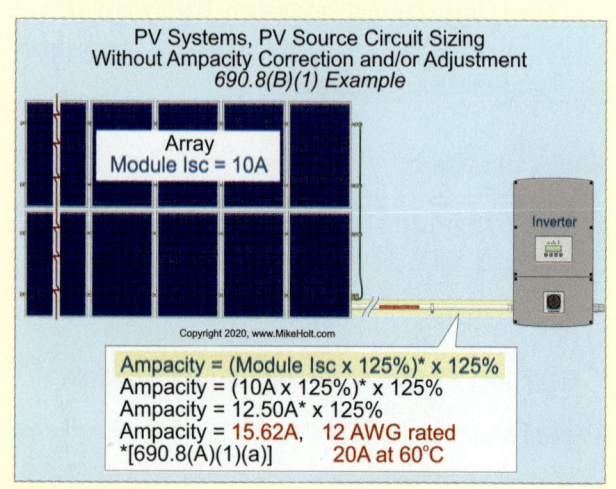

▶Figure 690-40

Solution:

Conductor Ampacity = (Module Isc × 125%)* × 125%
Conductor Ampacity = (10A × 125%)* × 125%
Conductor Ampacity = 12.50A × 125%
Conductor Ampacity = 15.62A

Use 12 AWG rated 20A at 60°C [110.14(C)(1)(a) and Table 310.16].
*[690.8(A)(1)(a)]

Answer: (b) 15.62A

▶ PV Output Circuit Ampacity Without Correction and/or Adjustment Example

Question: What is the minimum dc PV output circuit conductor ampacity, without the application of conductor correction or adjustment, supplied by four source circuits each with a short-circuit current rating of 10A where the terminals are rated 75°C? ▶Figure 690-41

(a) 33A (b) 32A (c) 43A (d) 63A

Solution:

Conductor Ampacity = (Module Isc × 125% × Number of Source Circuits)* × 125%
Conductor Ampacity = (10A × 125% × 4 circuits)* × 125%
Conductor Ampacity = 50A × 125%
Conductor Ampacity = 62.50A

Use 6 AWG rated 65A at 75°C [110.14(C)(1)(a)(3) and Table 310.16].
*[690.8(A)(1)(a)]

Answer: (d) 63A

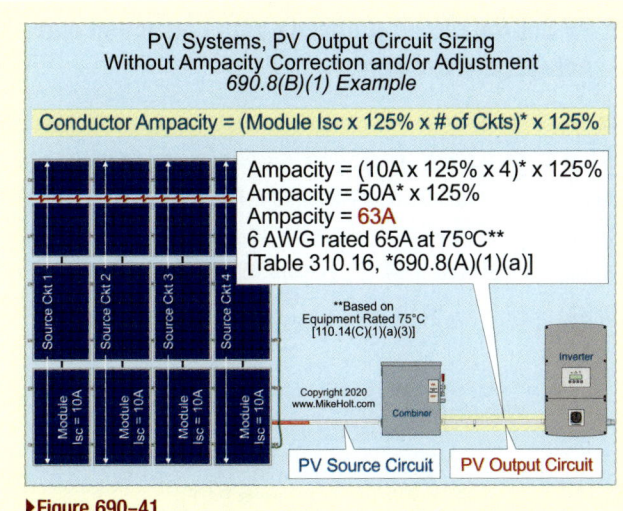

▶Figure 690-41

Ex: Where the assembly, including the overcurrent devices protecting the circuit(s), is listed for operation at 100 percent of its rating, the ampere rating of the overcurrent device can be sized to 100 percent of the continuous and noncontinuous loads.

(2) Conductor Sizing, With Ampacity Correction and/or Adjustment. PV circuit conductors within the scope of 690.8(A) must have an ampacity of not less than 100 percent of the current as determined by 690.8(A) after the application of conductor ampacity correction and adjustment in accordance with Table 310.15(B)(1) and Table 310.15(C)(1). ▶Figure 690-43

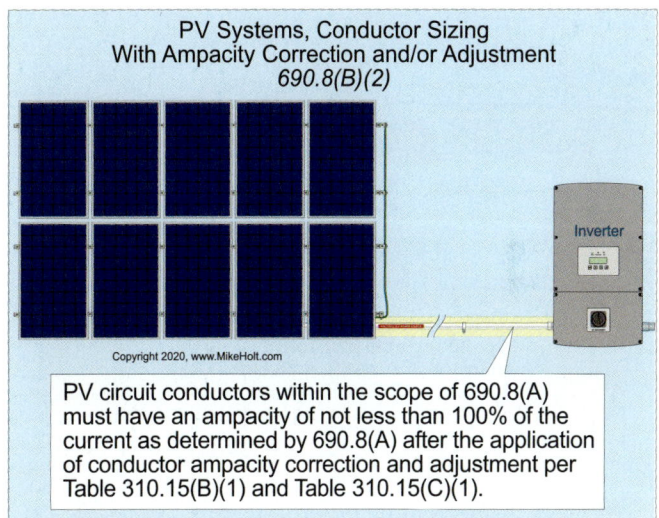

▶Figure 690-43

Author's Comment:

▶ The Table 310.16 ampacity must be corrected when the ambient temperature is less than 77°F or greater than 86°F and adjusted when more than three current-carrying conductors are bundled together. The temperature correction [Table 310.15(B)(1)] and conductor bundling adjustment [Table 310.15(C)(1)] are applied to the conductor ampacity based on the temperature rating of the conductor insulation as contained in Table 310.16, typically in the 90°C column [310.15].

▶ **Inverter Output Circuit Ampacity Without Correction and/or Adjustment Example**

Question: What is the minimum inverter ac output circuit conductor ampacity, without the application of conductor ampacity correction and/or adjustment factors, if the maximum continuous nameplate rating of the inverter is 24A where the terminals are rated 75°C? ▶Figure 690-42

(a) 20A   (b) 25A   (c) 30A   (d) 35A

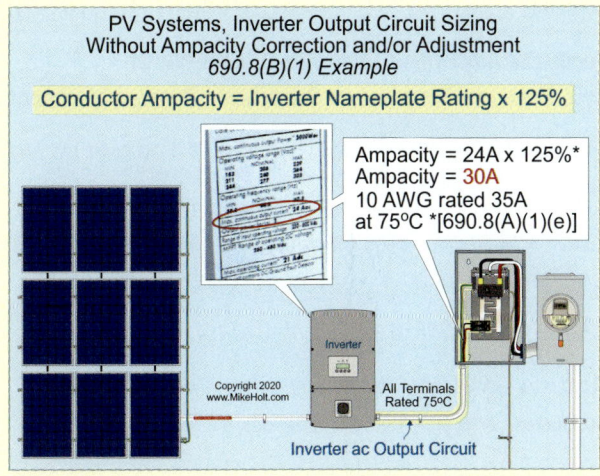

▶Figure 690-42

Solution:

Conductor Ampacity = Inverter Nameplate Rating [690.8(A)(1)(e)] × 125%

Conductor Ampacity = 24A × 125%

Conductor Ampacity = 30A

Use 10 AWG rated 35A at 75°C [310.16].

Answer: *(c) 30A*

690.8 | Solar Photovoltaic (PV) Systems

▶ **PV Source Circuit Ampacity with Correction and Adjustment Example 1**

Question: What is the conductor ampacity with temperature correction for two current-carrying 12 AWG USE-2 or PV conductors rated 90°C within a raceway or cable located 1 in. above a roof where the ambient temperature is 94°F in accordance with 310.15(B)(1)? The modules have an Isc rating of 10A. ▶Figure 690–44

(a) 19A (b) 29A (c) 39A (d) 49A

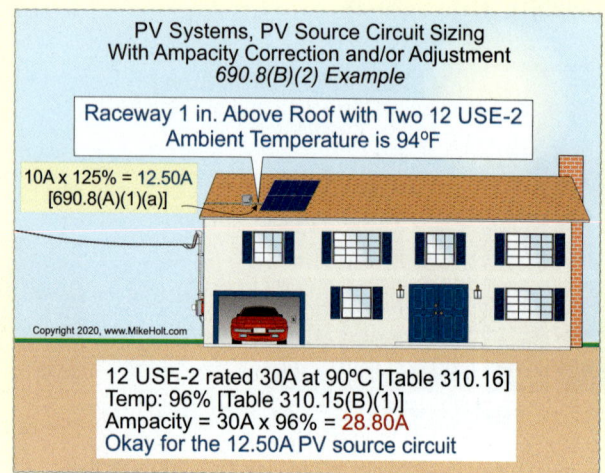

▶Figure 690–44

Solution:

Conductor Ampacity = Table 310.16 Ampacity at 90°C Column x Temperature Correction.

Temperature Correction = 0.96 based on a 94°F ambient temperature [Table 310.15(B)(1)].

12 AWG is rated 30A at 90°C [Table 310.16].

Conductor Corrected Ampacity = 30A x 96%
Conductor Corrected Ampacity = 28.80A

Note: 12 AWG with ampacity correction has sufficient ampacity to supply the source circuit dc current of 12.50A (10A x 125%) [690.8(A)(1)(a)].

Answer: (b) 29A

▶ **PV Source Circuit Ampacity with Correction and Adjustment Example 2**

Question: For an array with modules having a nameplate Isc rating of 10A for each source circuit, what is the conductor ampacity with temperature correction and adjustment for four current-carrying 12 AWG USE-2 conductors located 1 in. above a roof where the ambient temperature is 94°F? ▶Figure 690–45

(a) 23A (b) 24A (c) 25A (d) 26A

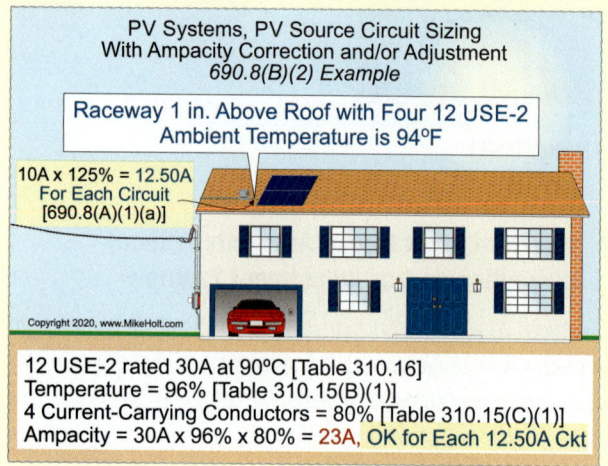

▶Figure 690–45

Solution:

Conductor Ampacity = Table 310.16 Ampacity at 90°C Column x Temperature Correction x Bundle Adjustment

Temperature Correction = 0.96 based on a 94°F ambient temperature [Table 310.15(B)(1)].

Bundle Adjustment = 80% based on four current-carrying conductors [Table 310.15(C)(1)].

12 AWG is rated 30A at 90°C [Table 310.16].

Conductor Corrected/Adjusted Ampacity = 30A x 96% x 80%
Conductor Corrected/Adjusted Ampacity = 23A

Note: 12 AWG has sufficient ampacity with correction and adjustment to supply the dc source circuits each with a current of 12.50A (10A × 125%) [690.8(A)(1)(a)].

Answer: (a) 23A

▶ PV Output Circuit Ampacity with Correction Example

Question: What is the dc PV output circuit conductor ampacity with conductor temperature correction for two 6 AWG USE-2 or PV output circuit conductors located 1 in. above a roof where the PV output circuit dc current is 40A and the ambient temperature is 94°F? ▶Figure 690-46

(a) 59A (b) 69A (c) 72A (d) 89A

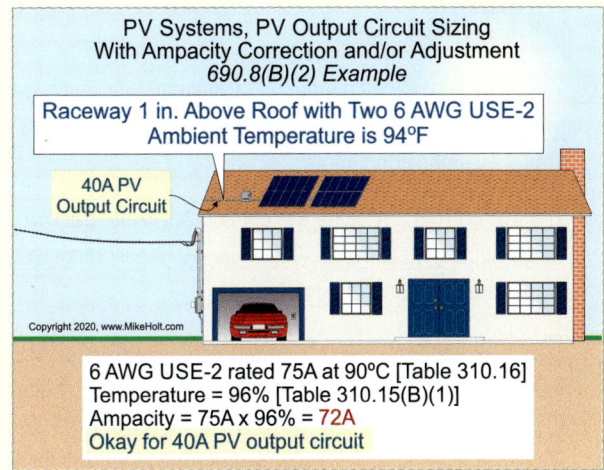

▶Figure 690-46

Solution:

Conductor Ampacity = Table 310.16 Ampacity at 90°C Column x Temperature Correction

Temperature Correction = 0.96 based on 94°F ambient temperature [Table 310.15(B)(1)].

6 AWG is rated 75A at 90°C [Table 310.16].

Conductor Corrected Ampacity = 75A x 96%
Conductor Corrected Ampacity = 72A

Note: 6 AWG with correction has sufficient ampacity to supply the PV output circuit dc current of 40A.

Answer: (c) 72A

▶ Inverter Output Circuit Ampacity with Correction and Adjustment Example

Question: What is the conductor ampacity with temperature correction for two current-carrying 10 AWG RHH/RHW-2/USE-2 or PV conductors rated 90°C supplying a 24A inverter output circuit and installed in a location where the ambient temperature is 94°F? ▶Figure 690-47

(a) 18.40A (b) 29.40A (c) 38.40A (d) 49.40A

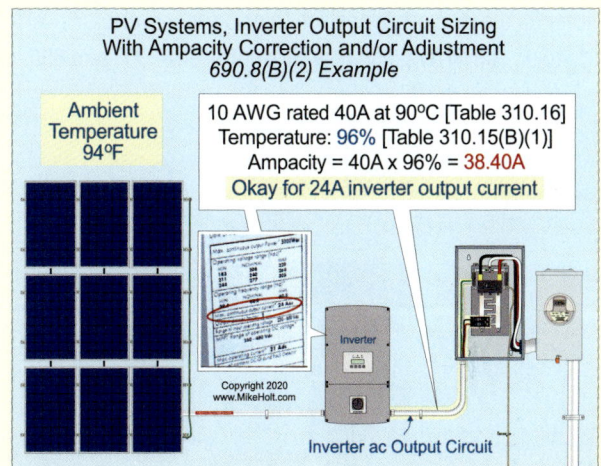

▶Figure 690-47

Solution:

Conductor Ampacity = Ampacity at 90°C Column [Table 310.16] x Temperature Correction.

Temperature Correction = 0.96 based on a 94°F ambient temperature [Table 310.15(B)(1)].

10 AWG is rated 40A at 90°C [Table 310.16].

Conductor Ampacity = 40A x 96%
Conductor Ampacity = 38.40A

Note: 10 AWG has sufficient ampacity with correction to supply the inverter output circuit dc current of 24A [690.8(A)(1)(e)].

Answer: (c) 38.40A

690.9 Overcurrent Protection

(A) General. PV system dc circuit and inverter output conductors and equipment must be protected against overcurrent. PV system dc circuit conductors sized in accordance with 690.8(A)(2) are required to be protected against overcurrent by one of the methods in 690.9(A)(1) through (A)(3).

(1) Circuits Without Overcurrent Protective Device. Overcurrent protective devices are not required where both of the following conditions are met:

(1) The PV system dc circuit conductors have an ampacity equal to or greater than the maximum dc current calculated in accordance with 690.8(A).

(2) Where the currents from all PV sources do not exceed the maximum overcurrent protective device rating specified by the manufacturer for the PV module or electronic power converters (inverters, dc-to-dc converters, and charger controllers). ▶Figure 690–48

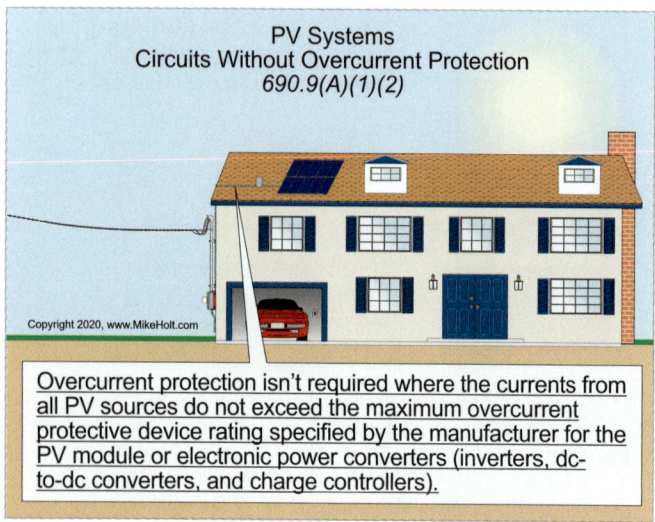

▶Figure 690–48

(2) Overcurrent Protection Required on One End. PV system circuit conductors connected to sources having an available maximum circuit current greater than the ampacity of the conductor must have overcurrent protection at the point of connection to the higher current source for circuit conductors connected at one end to a current-limited supply (PV modules, inverters, and dc-to-dc converters).

Note: PV system dc circuits and electronic power converter (inverters, dc-to-dc converters, and charge controllers) outputs are current-limited and in some cases do not need overcurrent protection. When these circuits are connected to higher current sources, such as parallel-connected PV system dc circuits or energy storage systems, the overcurrent device is often installed at the higher current source end of the circuit conductor.

(3) Other Circuits. PV circuits conductors that do not comply with 690.9(A)(1) or (A)(2) must be protected by one of the following methods:

(1) PV circuit conductors on (but not within) a building must not be longer than 10 ft in length and must have overcurrent protection at one end of the circuit.

(2) PV system circuit conductors within a building must not be longer than 10 ft in length, be within a raceway or metal-clad cable, and have overcurrent protection at on one end of the circuit.

(3) PV circuit conductors protected from overcurrent on both ends.

(4) PV circuit conductors not installed on or within buildings having overcurrent protection at one end of the circuit must comply with all of the following conditions:

  a. The PV system circuit conductors are in metal raceways, metal-clad cables, enclosed metal cable trays, underground, or in pad-mounted enclosures.

  b. The PV system circuit conductors terminate to a single circuit breaker or a single set of fuses that limit the current to the ampacity of the conductors.

  c. The overcurrent device for the conductors is integral with the disconnecting means or located within 10 ft (conductor length) of the disconnecting means.

  d. The disconnecting means is located outside the building or at a readily accessible location nearest the point of entrance of the conductors inside the building. PV circuit conductors are considered outside of a building where they are encased or installed under not less than 2 in. of concrete or brick in accordance with 230.6.

(B) Overcurrent Device Ratings. Overcurrent devices for PV dc circuits must be listed for PV systems. ▶Figure 690–49

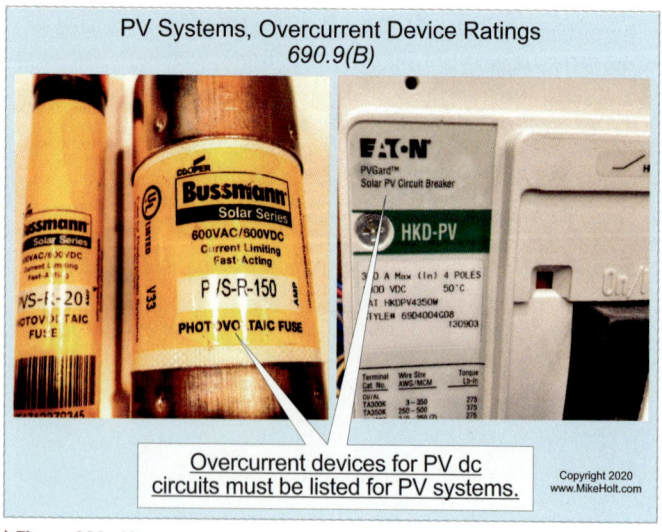

▶Figure 690–49

Electronic devices that are listed to prevent backfeed in PV dc circuits are permitted to prevent overcurrent of conductors on the PV array side of the electronic device.

Overcurrent protective devices required by 690.9(A)(2) must comply with one of the following. The next higher standard size overcurrent device in accordance with 240.4(B) is permitted.

(1) The overcurrent protective device must have a rating of not less than 125 percent of the maximum currents as calculated in 690.8(A).
▶Figure 690-50

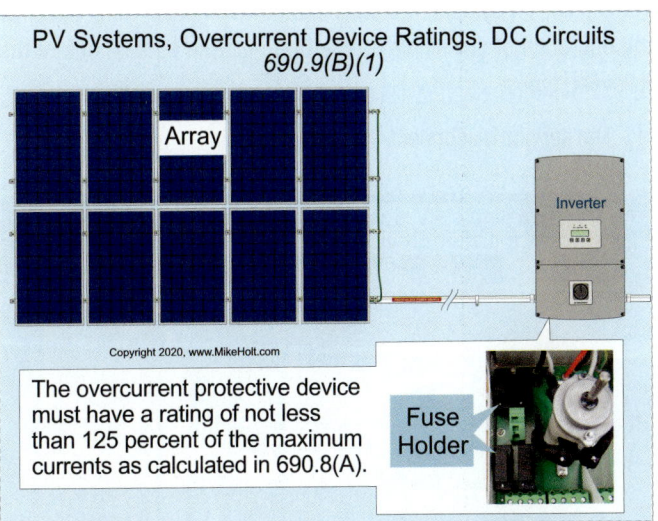

▶Figure 690-50

(2) Where the assembly, together with its overcurrent device(s), is listed for continuous operation at 100 percent of its rating, the overcurrent protective device can be sized at 100 percent of the maximum currents as calculated in 690.8(A).

Note: Some electronic devices prevent backfeed current, which in some cases is the only source of overcurrent in PV system dc circuits.

(C) Source and Output Circuits. A single overcurrent protective device can be used to protect PV modules, dc-to-dc converters, and source circuit and output circuit conductors. Where a single overcurrent protective device is used to protect source circuits or output circuits, it must be placed in the same polarity for all circuits within the PV system.

Note: A single overcurrent protective device in either the positive or negative conductors of a functionally grounded PV system provides adequate overcurrent protection.

690.10 Stand-Alone Systems

Wiring for stand-alone PV systems must be in accordance with 710.15.
▶Figure 690-51

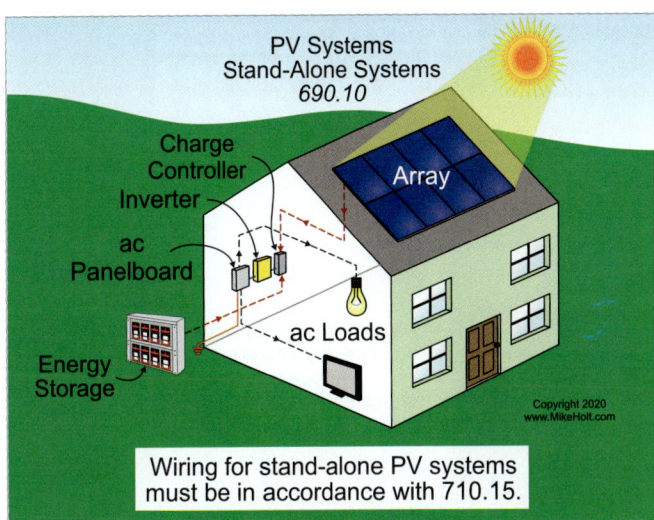

▶Figure 690-51

690.11 Arc-Fault Circuit Protection

PV system dc circuits operating at 80V dc or greater must be protected by a listed PV arc-fault circuit interrupter or other component listed to provide equivalent protection.

Ex: PV dc AFCI protection is not required for PV circuits not installed on or in buildings if the circuits are within metal raceways, metal-clad cables, enclosed cable trays, or underground. PV dc AFCI protection is not required for PV circuits installed in a detached building whose sole purpose is to house PV system equipment.

690.12 Rapid Shutdown

 Scan this QR code for a video of Mike explaining this topic; it's a sample from the videos that accompany this textbook. www.MikeHolt.com/20PVvideos

PV system conductors on or in a building must be controlled by a rapid shutdown system to reduce shock hazard for firefighters in accordance with 690.12(A) through (D). ▶Figure 690-52

Ex: A rapid shutdown system is not required for ground-mounted PV system conductors that enter buildings whose sole purpose is to house PV system equipment.

(A) Controlled Conductors. PV system conductors controlled by the rapid shutdown system include:

(1) PV system dc circuit conductors.

(2) Inverter output ac circuits originating from inverters located within the array boundary.

690.12 | Solar Photovoltaic (PV) Systems

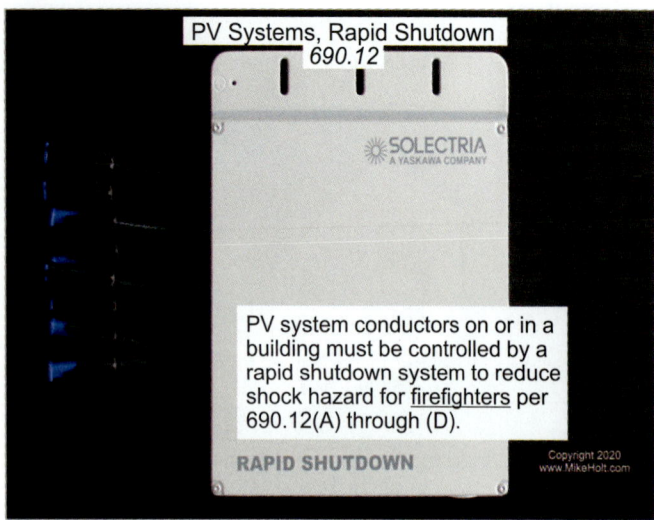

▶Figure 690–52

Note: The ac output conductors from PV systems will be either de-energized after shutdown initiation or remain energized if supplied by a utility service. To prevent PV systems with ac output conductors from remaining energized, they must be controlled by the rapid shutdown system after shutdown initiation.

(B) Controlled Limits. For the purpose of rapid shutdown, the array boundary is defined as the area 1 ft outside the perimeter of the PV array.

(1) Outside the Array Boundary. PV system circuit conductors located outside the PV array boundary or more than 3 ft from the point of entry inside a building must be limited to 30V within 30 seconds of rapid shutdown initiation.

(2) Inside the Array Boundary. The PV system rapid shutdown system must comply with one of the following:

(1) A PV hazard control system listed for the purpose must be installed in accordance with the manufacturer's installation instructions. Where a hazard control system requires initiation to transition to a controlled state, the rapid shutdown initiation device [690.12(C)] must perform this initiation.

Note: A listed or field-labeled hazard PV control system is comprised of either an individual piece of equipment that fulfills the necessary functions, or multiple pieces of equipment coordinated to perform the functions as described in the manufacturer's installation instructions.

(2) PV system circuit conductors located inside the PV array boundary must be limited to 80V within 30 seconds of rapid shutdown initiation.

(3) PV arrays must have no exposed wiring methods or exposed conductive parts and be installed more than 8 ft from exposed conductive parts.

(C) Initiation Device. A rapid shutdown initiation device is required to initiate the rapid shutdown function of the PV system. When the rapid shutdown initiation device is placed in the "off" position, this indicates that the rapid shutdown function has been initiated.

For one- and two-family dwellings, the rapid shutdown initiation device must be located outside the building at a readily accessible location.

For a single PV system, the rapid shutdown initiation must occur by the operation of any single device that must be at least one of the following types:

(1) The service disconnect. ▶Figure 690–53

▶Figure 690–53

(2) The PV system disconnect. ▶Figure 690–54

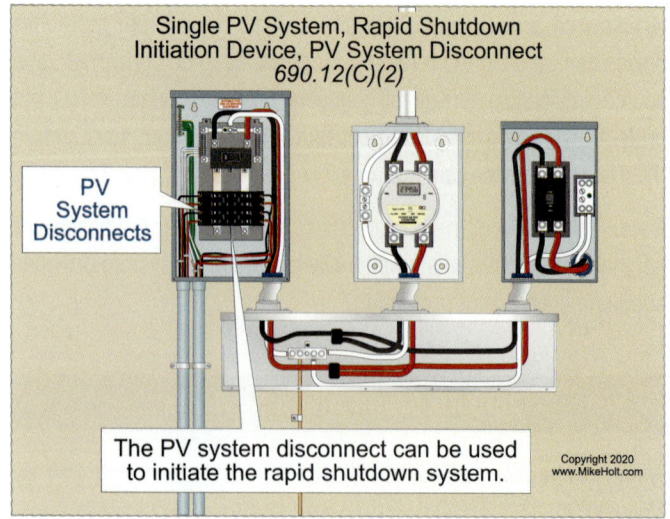

▶Figure 690–54

(3) A readily accessible switch that plainly indicates whether it is in the "off" or "on" position.

Note: An example of where a rapid shutdown initiation device that complies with 690.12(C)(3) would be used is where a PV system is connected to an optional standby or stand-alone system.

Where multiple PV systems are on a single service, the rapid shutdown initiation device(s) for the multiple PV systems must consist of not more than six switches or six sets of circuit breakers, or a combination of not more than six switches and sets of circuit breakers.

(D) Equipment. Equipment that performs the rapid shutdown function, other than initiation devices, must be listed for providing rapid shutdown protection.

Part III. Disconnect

690.13 PV System Disconnect

Means must be provided to disconnect the PV system conductors from power systems, energy storage systems, utilization equipment, and associated premises wiring.

(A) Location. The PV system disconnect must be readily accessible.

The door or hinged cover for the PV system disconnecting means must be locked or require a tool to open.

Note: Rapid shutdown systems installed in accordance with 690.12 address the concerns related to energized conductors entering a building.

(B) Marking. The PV system disconnect must indicate if it is in the open (off) or closed (on) position and be marked "PV SYSTEM DISCONNECT" or equivalent. ▶Figure 690–55

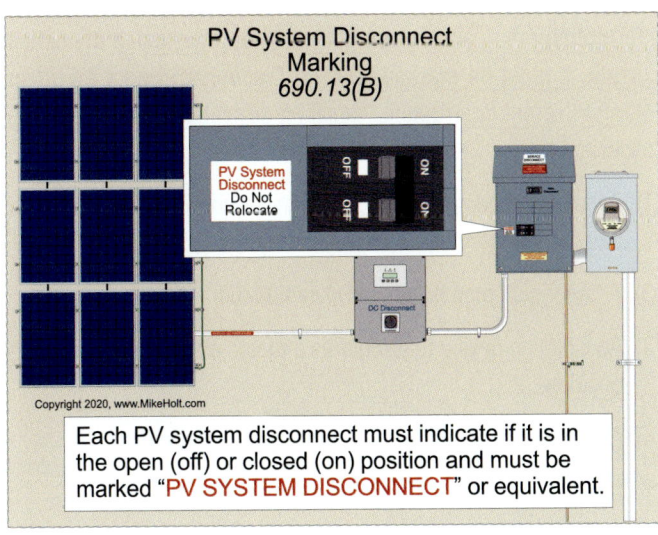

Each PV system disconnect must indicate if it is in the open (off) or closed (on) position and must be marked "PV SYSTEM DISCONNECT" or equivalent.

▶Figure 690–55

Where the line and load terminals of the PV system disconnect may be energized when the disconnect is in the open (off) position, the disconnect must be marked with the following or equivalent:

**WARNING—ELECTRIC SHOCK HAZARD
TERMINALS ON THE LINE AND LOAD SIDES
MAY BE ENERGIZED IN THE OPEN POSITION**

The warning markings on the disconnect must be permanently affixed and have sufficient durability to withstand the environment involved [110.21(B)].

(C) Maximum Number of Disconnects. The disconnecting means for a PV system must consist of not more than six switches or six sets of circuit breakers, or a combination of not more than six switches and sets of circuit breakers. ▶Figure 690–56

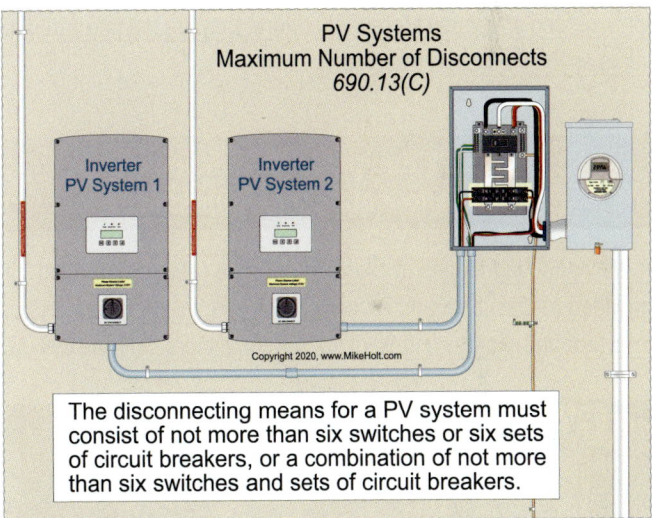

The disconnecting means for a PV system must consist of not more than six switches or six sets of circuit breakers, or a combination of not more than six switches and sets of circuit breakers.

▶Figure 690–56

A single PV system disconnect is permitted for the combined ac output of one or more inverters or ac modules in an interactive system.

Note: This requirement of a maximum of six PV system disconnects does not limit the number of PV systems on a premises [690.4(D)]. The dedicated circuit breaker for an interactive inverter in accordance with 705.12(A) is an example of a single PV system disconnect.

(D) Ratings. The PV system disconnect must have a rating sufficient for the maximum circuit current, the available fault current, and the voltage at the terminals of the PV system disconnect.

690.15 | Solar Photovoltaic (PV) Systems

(E) Type of Disconnect. The PV system disconnect must simultaneously disconnect all PV system circuit conductors. The PV system disconnect, its remote operating device, or the enclosure providing access to the disconnect must be capable of being locked in the open position in accordance with 110.25. The PV system disconnect must be one of the following types:

(1) A manually operable switch or circuit breaker.

(2) A mating connector meeting the requirements of 690.33(D)(1) or (D)(3).

(3) A pull-out switch with sufficient interrupting rating.

(4) A remote-controlled switch or circuit breaker that is operable manually and is opened automatically when control power is interrupted.

(5) A device listed or approved for the intended application.

Note: Circuit breakers marked "line" and "load" may not be suitable for backfeed or reverse current; therefore, they are not permitted to serve as the PV system disconnect.

690.15 PV Equipment Disconnecting Means to Isolate PV Equipment

A disconnecting means of the required type [690.15(D)] must be provided to disconnect ac PV modules, fuses, dc-to-dc converters, inverters, and charge controllers from all conductors. ▶Figure 690–57

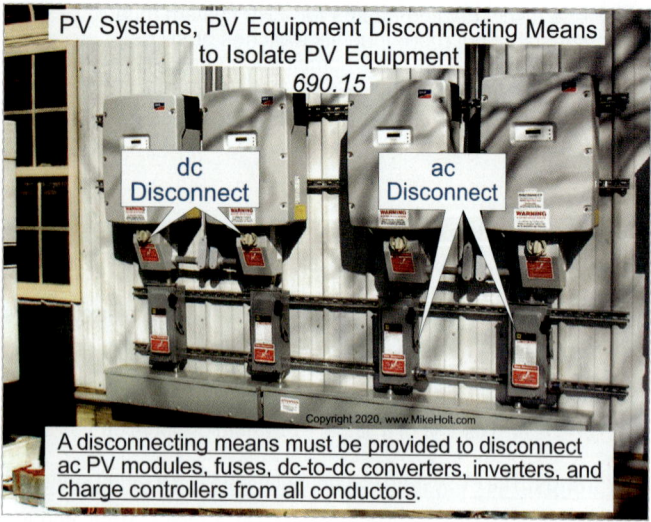

▶Figure 690–57

Author's Comment:

▸ The purpose of the PV disconnecting means is to ensure the safe and convenient replacement or maintenance of PV equipment without exposing qualified persons to energized conductors.

(A) Location. Isolating devices or disconnecting means must be placed either within the PV equipment or within sight and within 10 ft of the PV equipment. The PV equipment disconnect can be located further than 10 ft from the equipment if it can be remotely operated from within 10 ft of the equipment. ▶Figure 690–58

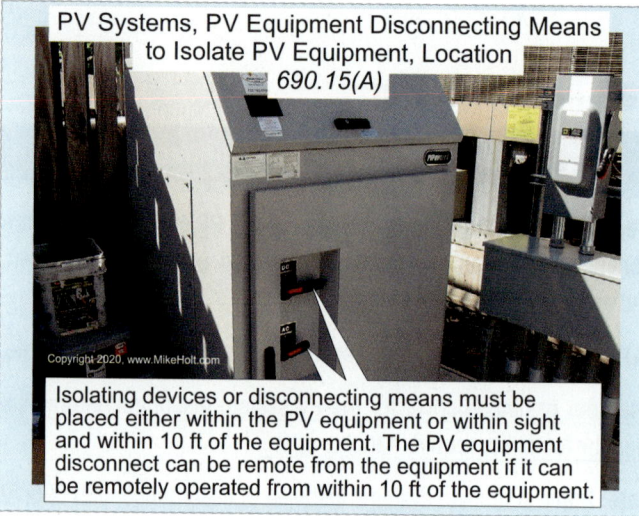

▶Figure 690–58

The door or hinged cover for the PV equipment disconnect must be locked or require a tool to open.

(B) Isolating Device. An isolating device is not required to have an interrupting rating and, where not rated for interrupting the circuit current, it must be marked "Do Not Disconnect Under Load" or "Not for Current Interrupting." Isolating devices must be one of the following types:

(1) A mating connector meeting the requirements of 690.33 and listed and identified for use with specific equipment. ▶Figure 690–59

(2) A finger-safe fuse holder. ▶Figure 690–60

(3) An isolating device that requires a tool to place in the open (off) position.

(4) An isolating device listed for the intended application.

Solar Photovoltaic (PV) Systems | **690.15**

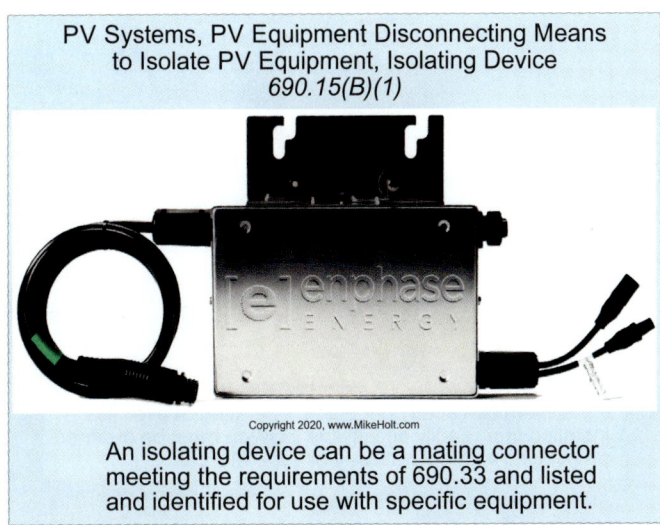
▶Figure 690–59

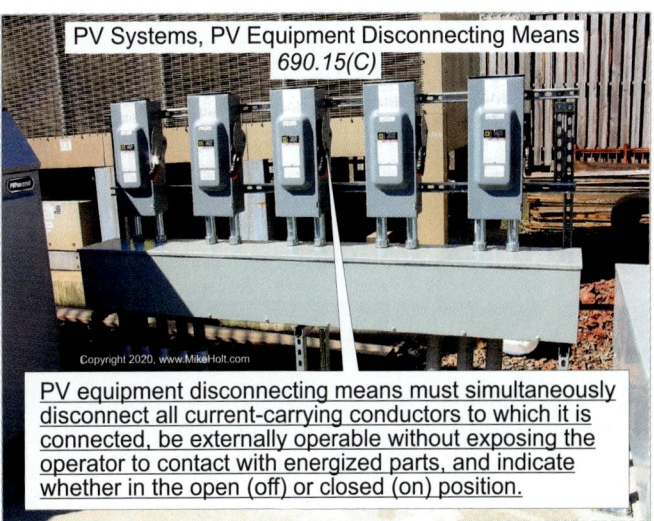
▶Figure 690–61

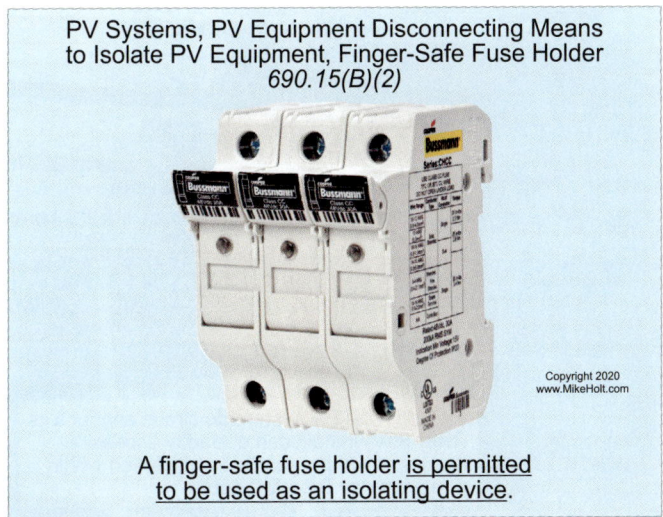
▶Figure 690–60

(C) Equipment Disconnecting Means. The PV equipment disconnecting means must have a rating sufficient for the maximum circuit current, available fault current, and the voltage at the terminals of the disconnect.

The PV equipment disconnecting means must simultaneously disconnect all current-carrying circuit conductors to which it is connected, must be externally operable without exposing the operator to contact with energized parts, and indicate whether it is in the open (off) or closed (on) position. ▶Figure 690–61

Where the PV equipment disconnect is not within sight and within 10 ft of the equipment, the PV equipment disconnect must be capable of being locked in the open position in accordance with 110.25.

The equipment disconnecting means must be of the same type as required in 690.13(E).

An equipment disconnecting means, other than those complying with 690.33, must be marked in accordance with the warning in 690.13(B) if the line and load terminals can be energized in the open position.

Author's Comment:

▸ According to 690.13(B), each PV system disconnect must indicate if it is in the open (off) or closed (on) position and the disconnect must be permanently marked "PV SYSTEM DISCONNECT" or equivalent. Where the line and load terminals of the PV system disconnect may be energized when the disconnect is in the open (off) position, the disconnect must be marked with the following words or equivalent:

> **WARNING—ELECTRIC SHOCK HAZARD**
> **TERMINALS ON THE LINE AND LOAD SIDES**
> **MAY BE ENERGIZED IN THE OPEN POSITION**

The warning markings on the disconnect must be permanently affixed and have sufficient durability to withstand the environment involved [110.21(B)].

Note: A common installation practice is to terminate circuit conductors on the line side of a disconnect which will de-energize load-side terminals, blades, and fuses when the disconnect is in the open position.

(D) Type of Disconnecting Means. Where disconnects are required to isolate equipment, the disconnecting means must be one of the following types:

690.31 | Solar Photovoltaic (PV) Systems

(1) Over 30A Circuit. A disconnecting means in accordance with 690.15(C).

(2) Not over 30A Circuit. An isolating device in accordance with 690.15(B).

Part IV. Wiring Methods

690.31 Wiring Methods

(A) Wiring Systems. Permitted methods include Chapter 3 wiring methods, wiring systems and fittings listed for PV arrays, and wiring that is part of a listed PV system. ▶Figure 690-62

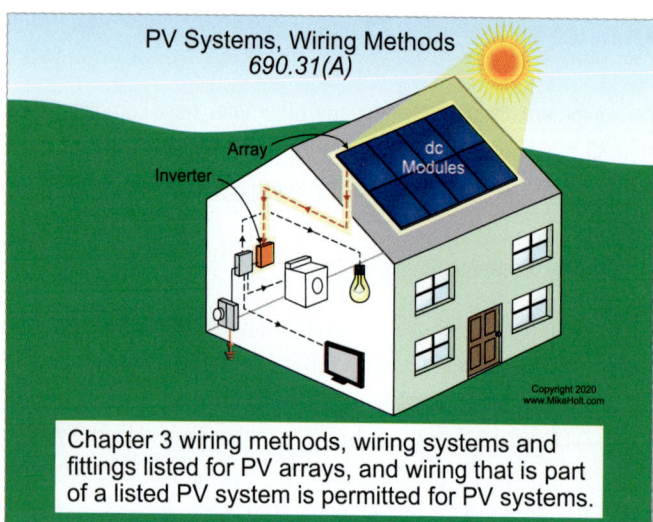
▶Figure 690-62

PV system dc circuit conductors operating at over 30V installed in a readily accessible location must be guarded or installed within a raceway or Type MC cable. ▶Figure 690-63 and ▶Figure 690-64

PV circuit conductors with insulation rated at 105°C and 125°C must have their ampacity [690.31(A)(b)] corrected by Table 690.31(A)(a).

Note: See 110.14(C) for conductor temperature limitations due to termination provisions.

(B) Identification and Grouping. PV system circuits are permitted in the same enclosure, cable, or raceway with each other and with Class 1 circuits associated with the PV system [725.48(B)(1)].

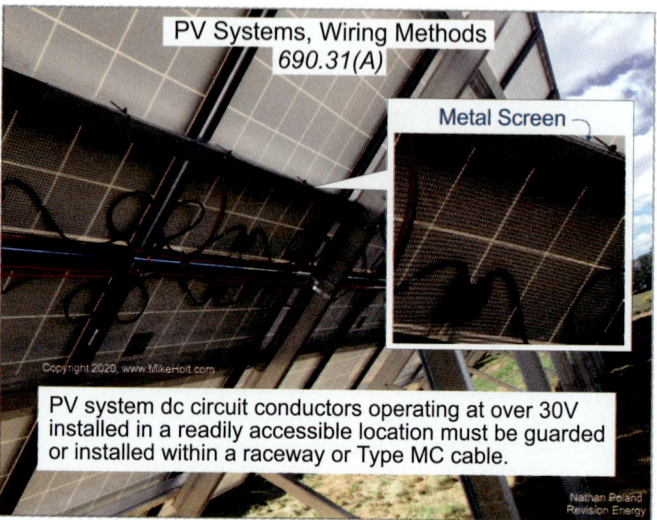
▶Figure 690-63

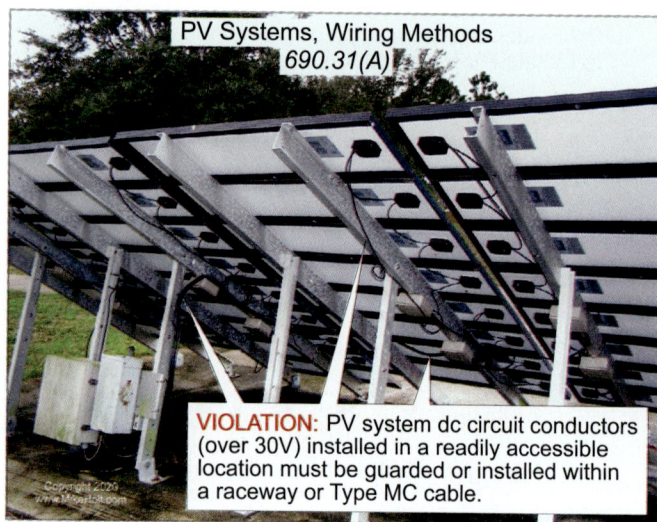
▶Figure 690-64

Table 690.31(A)(a) Correction Factors

Ambient Temperature (°C)	Temperature Rating of Conductor		Ambient Temperature (°F)
	105°C (221°F)	125°C (257°F)	
31–35	0.97	0.97	87–95
36–40	0.93	0.95	96–104
41–45	0.89	0.92	105–113
46–50	0.86	0.89	114–122
51–55	0.82	0.86	123–131
56–60	0.77	0.83	132–140

Table 690.31(A)(a) Correction Factors (continued)

Ambient Temperature (°C)	Temperature Rating of Conductor		Ambient Temperature (°F)
	105°C (221°F)	125°C (257°F)	
61–65	0.73	0.79	141–149
66–70	0.68	0.76	150–158
71–75	0.63	0.73	159–167
76–80	0.58	0.69	168–176
81–85	0.52	0.65	177–185
86–90	0.45	0.61	186–194
91–95	0.37	0.56	195–203
96–100	0.26	0.51	204–212
101–105	–	0.46	213–221
106–110	–	0.4	222–230
111–115	–	0.32	231–239
116–120	–	0.23	240–248

Table 690.31(A)(b) Conductor Ampacity, Not More Than Three Current-Carrying Conductors in Raceway, Cable, or Earth, with Ambient Temperature of 30°C (86°F)

Wire Size AWG	PVC, CPE, XLPE 105°C	XLPE, EPDM 125°C
18	15	16
16	19	20
14	29	31
12	36	39
10	46	50
8	64	69
6	81	87
4	109	118
3	129	139
2	143	154
1	168	181
1/0	193	208
2/0	229	247
3/0	263	284
4/0	301	325

PV system dc circuit conductors are not permitted to be installed in the same enclosure, cable, or raceway with non-PV system circuit conductors or inverter output circuit conductors unless separated by a barrier or partition. ▶Figure 690–65

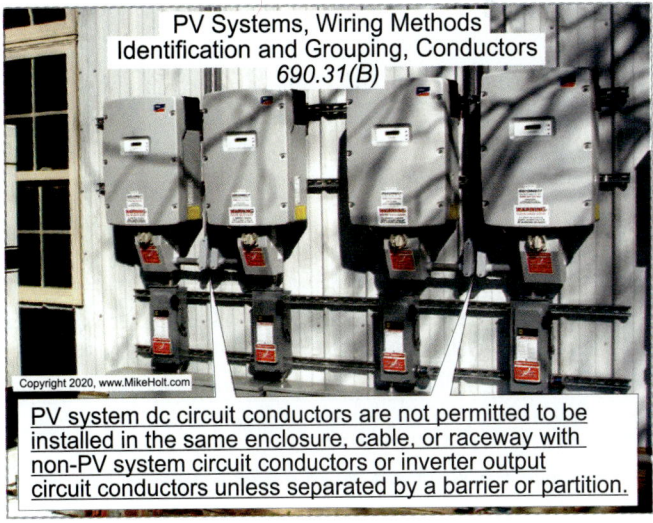

▶Figure 690–65

Ex: PV system dc circuits within multiconductor jacketed cable, Type MC cable, or listed wiring harnesses identified for the application can be installed in the same enclosure, cable, or raceway with non-PV system circuits. All conductors, harnesses, or assemblies must have an insulation rating equal to at least the maximum circuit dc voltage applied to any conductor within the enclosure, cable, or raceway.

PV system dc circuits must be identified and grouped as required by 690.31(B)(1) and (B)(2).

690.31 | Solar Photovoltaic (PV) Systems

(1) Identification. PV system dc circuit conductors must have all termination, connection, and splice points permanently identified for polarity by color coding, marking tape, tagging, or other approved means. ▶Figure 690–66

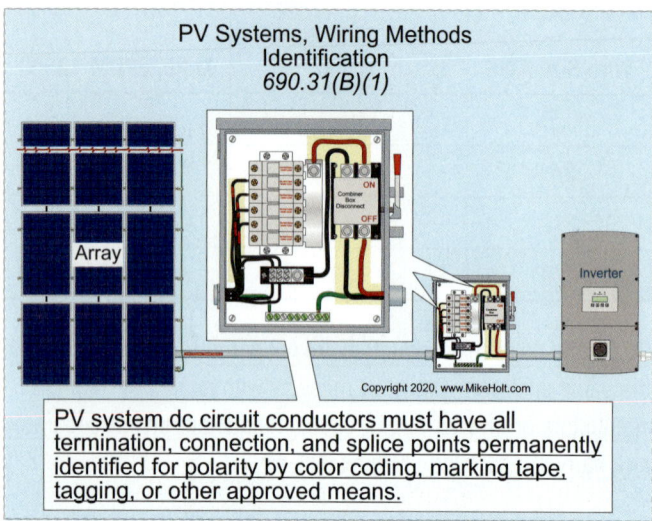

▶Figure 690–66

Conductors relying on marking tape, tagging, or other approved means for polarity identification must be by an approved permanent marking means such as labeling, sleeving, or shrink-tubing that is suitable for the conductor size.

The marking tape, tagging, or other approved means for polarity identification must include the positive sign (+) or the word "POSITIVE" or "POS" for the positive conductor, and the negative sign (–) or the word "NEGATIVE" or "NEG" for the negative conductor. Marking must be durable and be of a color other than green, white, gray, or red.

Ex: Identification is not required where the identification of the conductors is evident by spacing or arrangement.

(2) Grouping. Where PV system dc circuit conductors are in the same enclosure or wireway with other PV system dc circuit conductors, the PV system dc circuit conductors of each system must be grouped together by the use of cable ties or similar means at least once and at intervals not to exceed 6 ft.

Ex: Grouping is not required if the dc circuit enters from a cable or raceway unique to the circuit that makes the grouping obvious.

(C) Cables. Type PV wire, Type PV cable, and Type DG cable must be listed.

(1) Single-Conductor Cable. Single-conductor cable within the PV array must be one of the following types: ▶Figure 690–67

(1) Type PV wire or Type PV Cable.

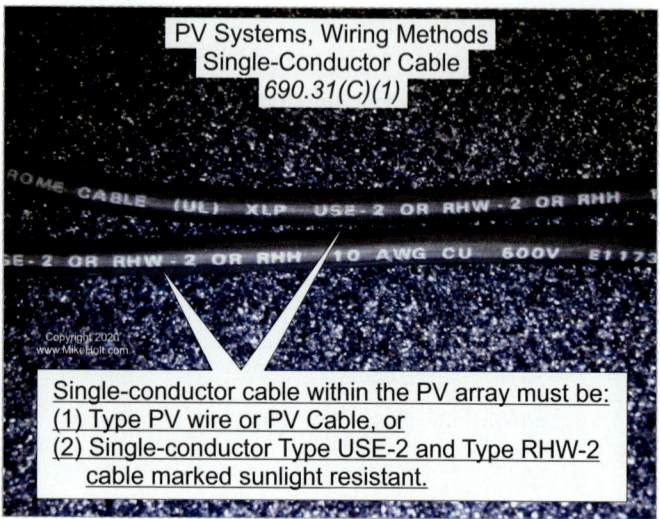

▶Figure 690–67

(2) Single-conductor Type USE-2 and Type RHW-2 cable marked sunlight resistant.

Exposed single-conductor cables must be supported and secured at intervals not to exceed 24 in. by cable ties, straps, hangers, or similar fittings listed and identified for securement and support in outdoor locations.

Type PV wire or Type PV cable is permitted to be installed in all locations where RHW-2 is permitted.

(2) Cable Tray. Single-conductor Type PV wire, Type PV cable, or Type DG cable can be installed in cable trays in outdoor locations, provided the cables are supported at intervals not to exceed 12 in. and secured at intervals not to exceed 4½ ft.

Note: Type PV wire, Type PV cable, and Type DG cable have nonstandard outer diameters. Chapter 9, Table 1 contains the allowable percent of cross section of conduit and tubing for conductors and cables. ▶Figure 690–68

(3) Multiconductor Jacketed Cable. Where a multiconductor jacketed cable is part of a listed PV assembly, the cable must be installed in accordance with the manufacturer's instructions.

Multiconductor jacketed cable that is not part of a listed assembly or not covered in this *Code* must be installed in accordance with the product listing instructions.

Multiconductor jacketed cable must be installed in accordance with the following requirements:

(1) In Raceways. Multiconductor jacketed cable on or in buildings must be installed in a raceway, except for rooftop installations.

Solar Photovoltaic (PV) Systems | 690.31

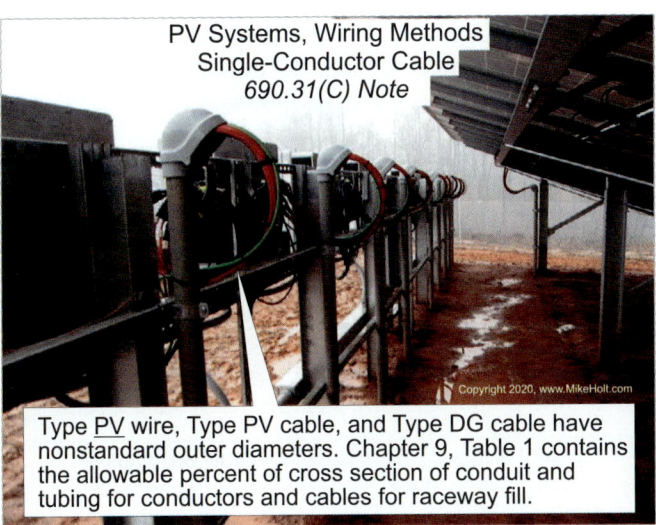

Type PV wire, Type PV cable, and Type DG cable have nonstandard outer diameters. Chapter 9, Table 1 contains the allowable percent of cross section of conduit and tubing for conductors and cables for raceway fill.

▶Figure 690-68

(2) Not Within Raceway. Where multiconductor jacketed cable is not installed within a raceway, the cable must:

a. Be marked "Sunlight Resistant" in exposed outdoor locations.

b. Be protected or guarded where subject to physical damage.
▶Figure 690-69

▶Figure 690-69

c. Closely follow the surface of support structures.

d. Be secured at intervals not exceeding 6 ft.

e. Be secured within 24 in. of mating connectors or entering enclosures.

f. Be marked "Direct Burial" where buried in the earth.

(4) Flexible Cords and Cables for Tracking PV Arrays. Flexible cords connected to moving parts of tracking PV arrays must be installed in accordance with Article 400, be identified as hard-service cord or portable power cable, be suitable for extra-hard usage, and be listed for outdoor use, water resistant, and sunlight resistant.

Stranded copper Type PV wire used for moving parts of tracking PV arrays must have a minimum number of strands as specified in Table 690.31(C)(4).

Table 690.31(C)(4) Minimum PV Wire Strands for Moving Parts of Tracking PV Arrays	
PV Wire AWG	Minimum Strands
18	17
16–10	19
8–4	49
2	130
1 AWG–1,000 MCM	259

(5) Flexible, Fine-Stranded Cables. Flexible, fine-stranded cables must terminate on terminals, lugs, devices, or connectors identified for the use of finely stranded conductors in accordance with 110.14. ▶Figure 690-70

(D) PV System Direct-Current Circuits On or In Buildings. When the PV system dc circuit is located inside a building, the PV system's dc circuit conductors must be installed in a metal raceway, Type MC cable, or a metal enclosure. ▶Figure 690-71

690.31 | Solar Photovoltaic (PV) Systems

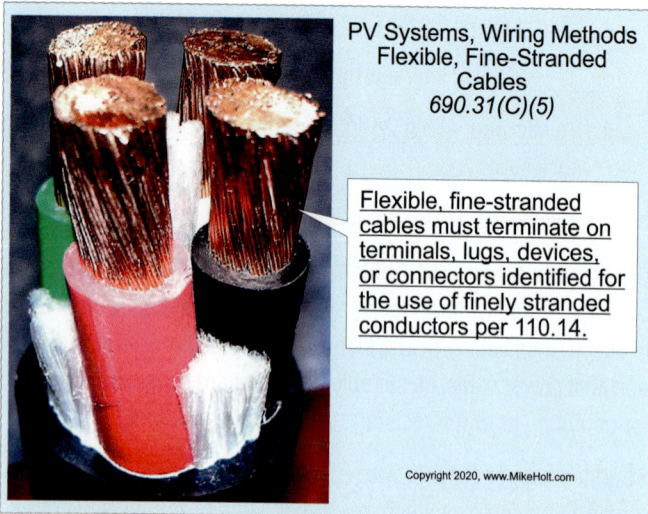

▶Figure 690–70

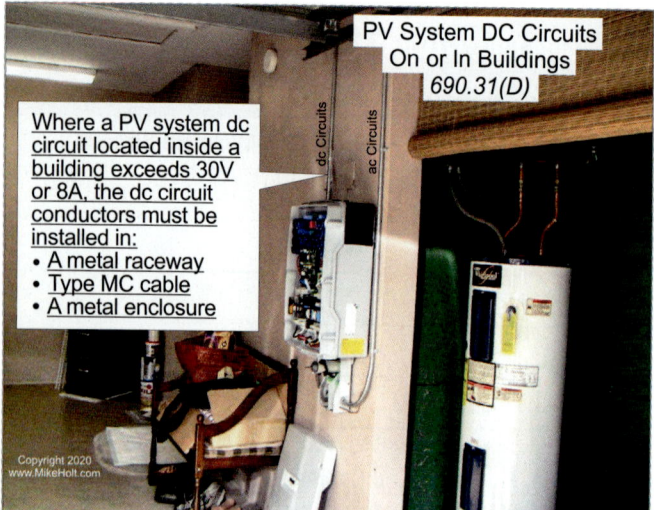

▶Figure 690–71

Where flexible metal conduit or Type MC cable containing PV system dc circuit conductors is run exposed further than 6 ft from their connection to equipment, the flexible metal conduit or Type MC cable must closely follow the building surface or be protected from physical damage by an approved means.

(2) Marking and Labeling. Unless located and arranged so the purpose is evident, the following wiring methods and enclosures containing PV system dc circuit conductors must be marked with a permanent label containing the words "PHOTOVOLTAIC POWER SOURCE" or "SOLAR PV DC CIRCUIT." ▶Figure 690–72

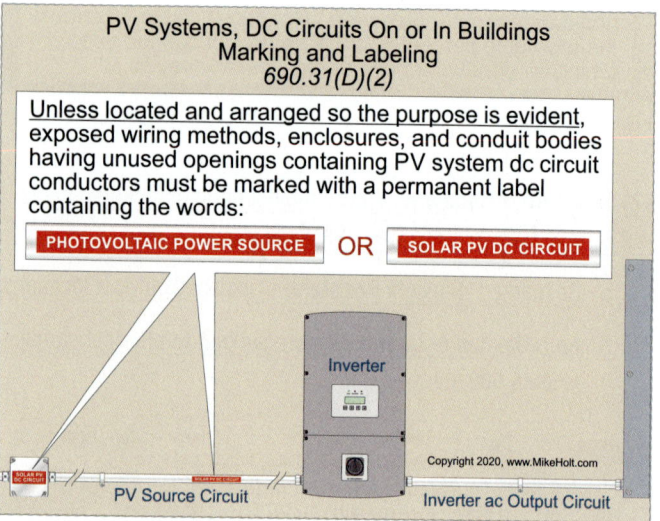

▶Figure 690–72

(1) Exposed raceways, cable trays, and other wiring methods.

(2) Covers or enclosures of pull boxes and junction boxes.

(3) Conduit bodies having unused openings.

The label must be visible after installation. The letters must be capitalized and be a minimum height of ⅜ in. in white on a red background. ▶Figure 690–73

Labels must appear on every section of the wiring system that is separated by enclosures, walls, partitions, ceilings, or floors. Spacing between labels must not be more than 10 ft, and the label must be suitable for the environment. ▶Figure 690–74

(F) Wiring Methods and Mounting Systems. Roof-mounted PV array mounting systems are permitted to be held in place with an approved means other than those required by 110.13. The wiring methods must allow any expected movement of the array.

Note: Expected movement of unattached PV arrays is often included in structural calculations.

Ex: PV hazard control system conductors that are installed for a rapid shutdown application in accordance with 690.12(B)(2)(1) can be provided with (or listed for use with) nonmetallic enclosures, nonmetallic raceways, and permitted cable types other than Type MC cable, at the point of penetration of the building to the PV hazard control actuator.

Wiring methods for PV system dc circuits on or in buildings must comply with the following additional requirements:

(1) Flexible Wiring Methods. Where flexible metal conduit smaller than trade size ¾ or Type MC cable smaller than 1 in. in diameter containing PV system dc circuit conductors is run across ceilings or floor joists, the flexible metal conduit or Type MC cable must be protected by substantial guard strips that are at least as high as the flexible metal conduit or Type MC cable.

Solar Photovoltaic (PV) Systems | 690.33

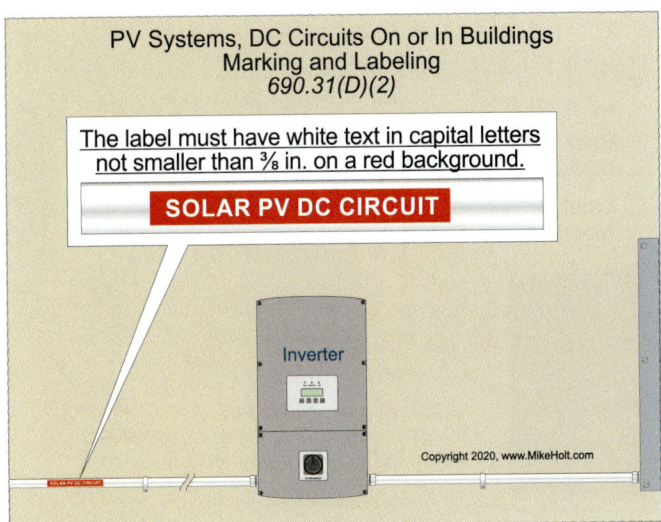
▶Figure 690–73

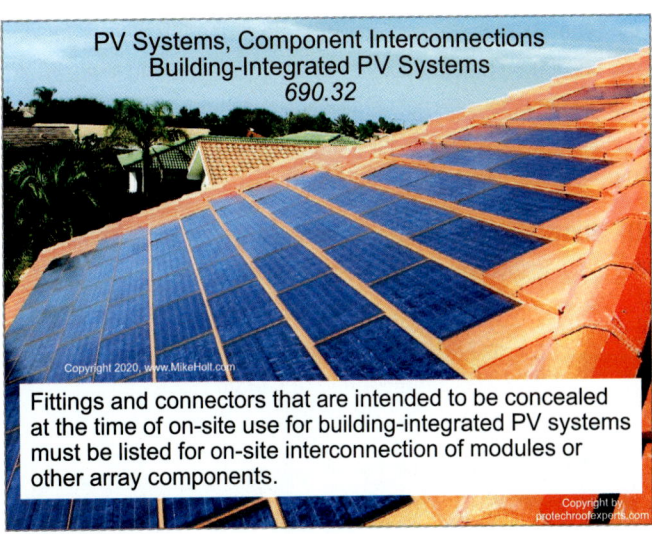
▶Figure 690–75

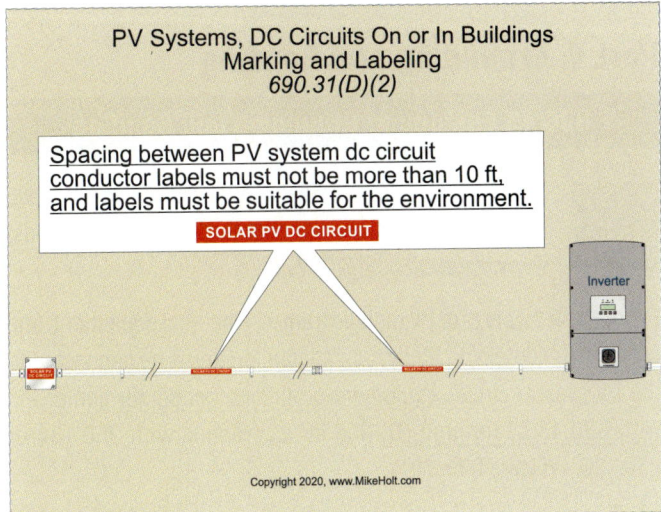
▶Figure 690–74

690.32 Component Interconnections

Fittings and connectors that are intended to be concealed at the time of on-site use for building-integrated PV systems must be listed for on-site interconnection of modules or other array components. ▶Figure 690–75

Author's Comment:

▸ Building-integrated PV systems have PV system dc circuit conductors embedded in built-up, laminate, or membrane roofing materials on roofs.

690.33 Connectors (Mating)

Mating connectors, other than listed connectors for building-integrated PV systems as covered in 690.32, must comply with the following:
▶Figure 690–76

▶Figure 690–76

(A) Configuration. The mating connectors must be polarized and be noninterchangeable with other electrical systems on the premises.

(B) Guarding. The mating connectors must be constructed and installed so as to guard against inadvertent contact with live parts by persons.

(C) Type. Mating connectors must be of the latching or locking type and where readily accessible require a tool for opening. Where mating connectors are not of the identical type and brand, they must be listed and identified for intermatability as described in the manufacturer's instructions.

(D) Interruption of Circuit. Mating connectors must comply with one of the following requirements. ▶Figure 690-77

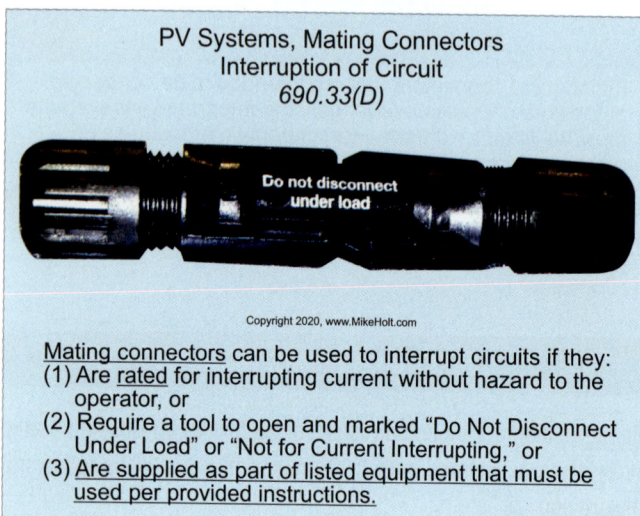
▶Figure 690-77

(1) Mating connectors must be rated to interrupt current without hazard to the operator.

(2) A tool must be required to open the mating connector and the mating connectors must be marked "Do Not Disconnect Under Load" or "Not for Current Interrupting."

(3) Mating connectors supplied as part of listed equipment must be used in accordance with instructions provided with the listed connected equipment.

Note: Some listed equipment, such as micro inverters, are evaluated to make use of mating connectors as disconnect devices even though the mating connectors are marked as "Do Not Disconnect Under Load" or "Not for Current Interrupting."

690.34 Access to Boxes

Junction, pull, and outlet boxes are permitted to be located behind PV modules. ▶Figure 690-78

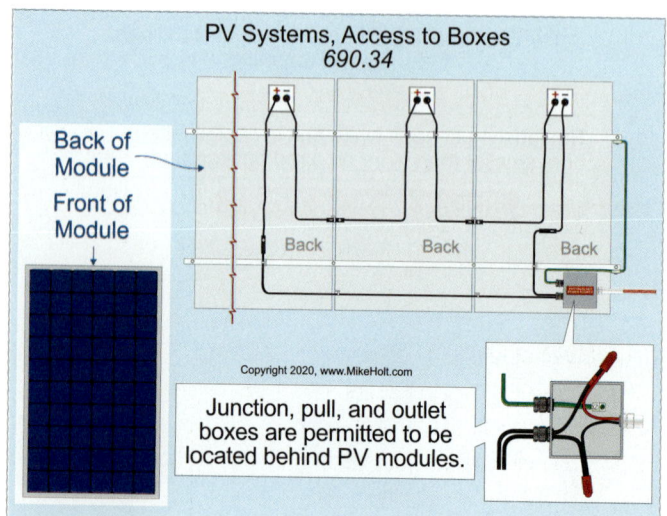
▶Figure 690-78

Part V. Grounding and Bonding

690.43 Equipment Grounding and Bonding

 Scan this QR code for a video of Mike explaining this topic; it's a sample from the videos that accompany this textbook. www.MikeHolt.com/20PVvideos

Exposed metal parts of PV module frames, electrical equipment, and enclosures containing PV system conductors must be connected to the PV system circuit equipment grounding conductor complying with 690.43(A) through (D) and in accordance with 250.134 or 250.136. ▶Figure 690-79

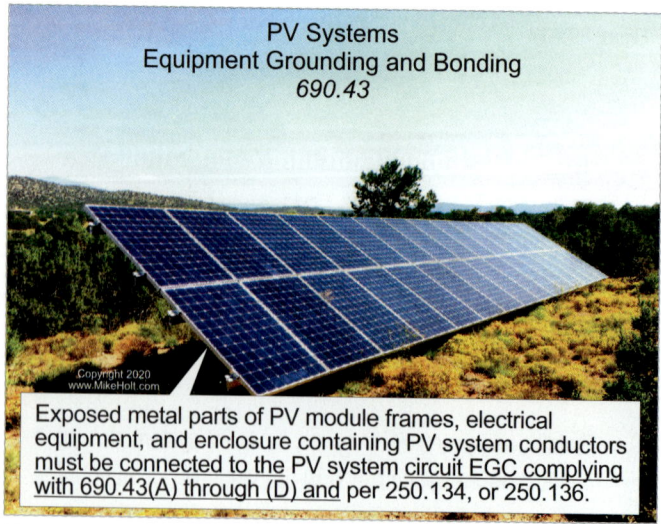
▶Figure 690-79

Author's Comment:

▸ According to 250.134, metal parts of equipment, raceways, and enclosures must be connected to one of the equipment grounding conductor types identified in 250.118. An equipment grounding conductor of the wire type for a dc circuit can be run separately from the circuit conductors when it is within the array [250.134 Ex 2].

(A) Photovoltaic Module Mounting Systems and Devices. Devices used to secure and bond PV module frames to metal support structures and adjacent PV modules must be listed, labeled, and identified for bonding. Devices that mount adjacent PV modules are permitted to bond adjacent PV modules.

(B) Equipment Secured to Grounded Metal Support Structure. Metallic support structures listed, labeled, and identified for bonding and grounding metal parts of PV systems can be used to bond PV equipment to the metal support structure.

Metallic support structures used as equipment grounding conductors must have identified bonding jumpers installed between separate metallic sections of the support structure or the support structure must be identified for equipment bonding purposes. The metallic support structure must be connected to the PV circuit equipment grounding conductor as required by 690.43. ▸Figure 690-80

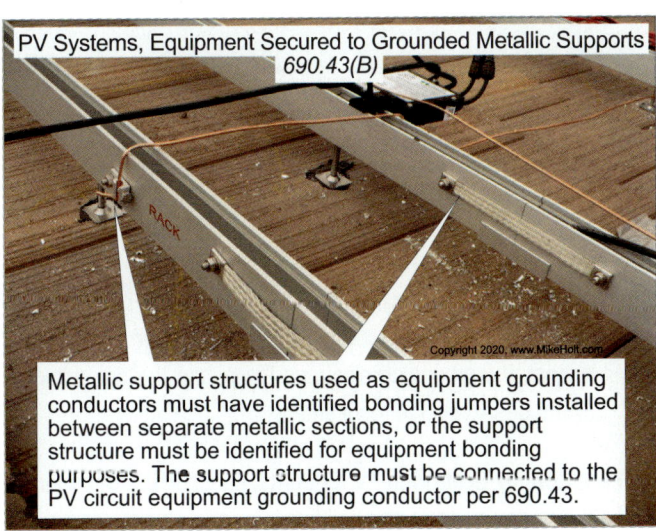

▸Figure 690-80

(C) With Circuit Conductors. When PV system circuit conductors leave the vicinity of the PV array, the equipment grounding conductors for the PV system and metal support structure must be contained within the same raceway, cable, or otherwise run with the PV circuit conductor. ▸Figure 690-81 and ▸Figure 690-82

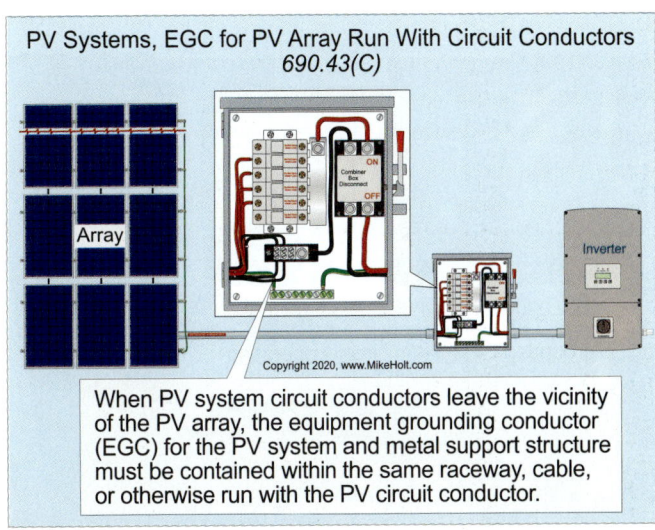

▸Figure 690-81

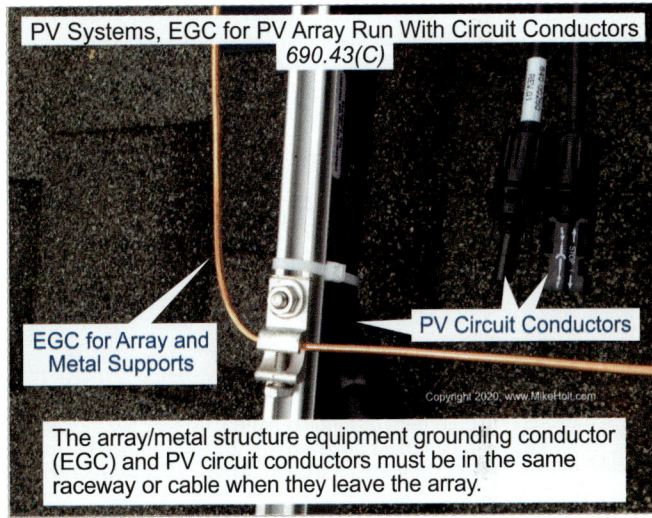

▸Figure 690-82

Author's Comment:

▸ Exposed equipment grounding conductors 8 AWG and smaller for dc circuits [250.134 Ex 2] are permitted to be run separately from the circuit conductors where not subject to physical damage [250.120(C)].

(D) Bonding Over 250V. The bonding requirements contained in 250.97 do not apply to functionally grounded PV system circuits operating at over 250V to ground. ▸Figure 690-83

690.45 Size of Equipment Grounding Conductors

Equipment grounding conductors for PV system circuits must be sized in accordance with 250.122 based on the rating of the circuit overcurrent protective device. ▸Figure 690-84

690.47 | Solar Photovoltaic (PV) Systems

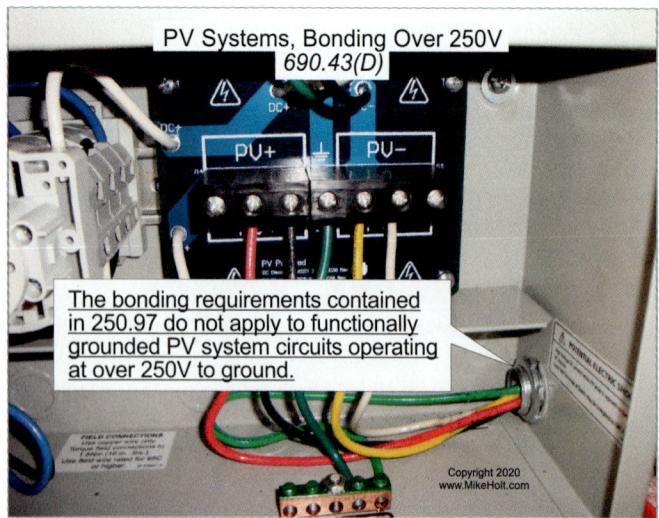

▶Figure 690–83

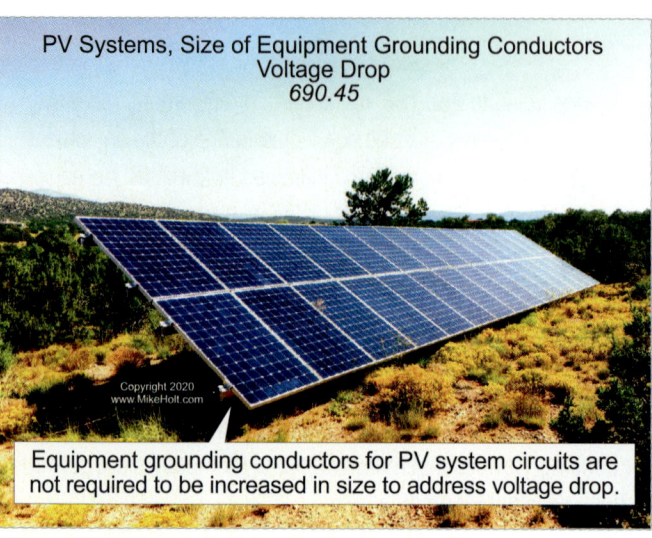

▶Figure 690–85

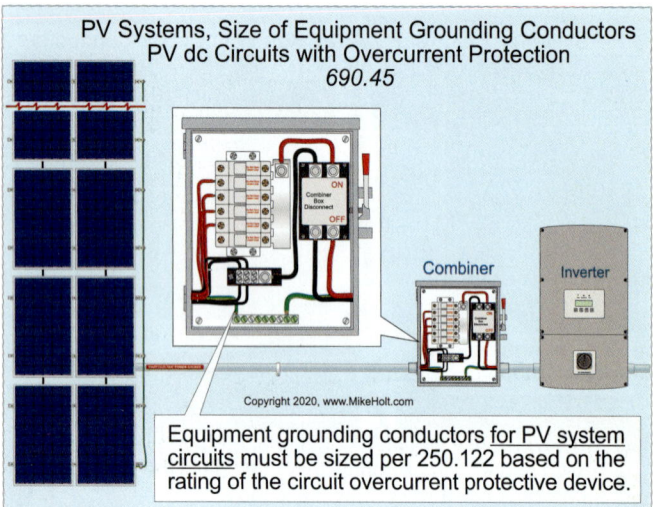

▶Figure 690–84

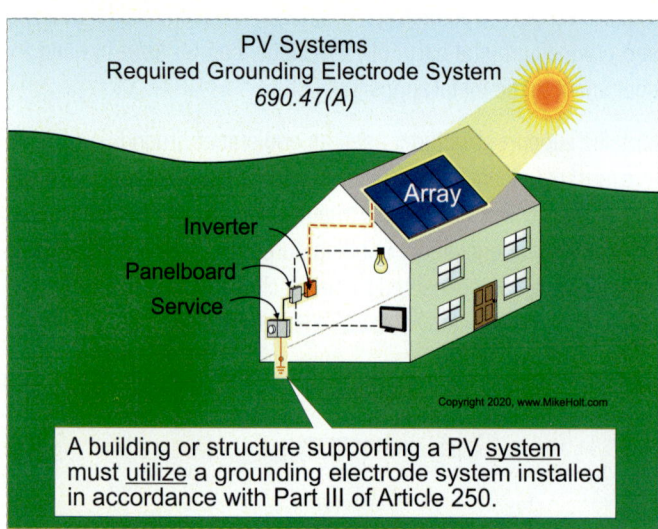

▶Figure 690–86

Where no overcurrent protective device is required [690.9(A)(1)], the equipment grounding conductor for the PV system dc circuit must be sized in accordance with Table 250.122 based on an assumed overcurrent device for the circuit sized in accordance with 690.9(B). Equipment grounding conductors are not required to be increased in size to address voltage-drop considerations. ▶Figure 690–85

690.47 Grounding Electrode System

 Scan this QR code for a video of Mike explaining this topic; it's a sample from the videos that accompany this textbook. www.MikeHolt.com/20PVvideos

(A) Required Grounding Electrode System. A building or structure supporting a PV system must utilize a grounding electrode system installed in accordance with Part III of Article 250. ▶Figure 690–86

Author's Comment:

▶ Part III of Article 250 addresses the grounding electrode system, the grounding electrode types, and the grounding electrode installation requirements.

(1) Functionally Grounded PV Systems. Functionally grounded PV systems are grounded to the building grounding electrode system when the PV output ac circuit equipment grounding conductor terminates to distribution equipment. ▶Figure 690–87

The use of the PV output circuit equipment grounding conductor to serve as the required PV equipment grounding conductor connection to ground is the only connection to ground required for the functionally grounded PV system. ▶Figure 690–88

Solar Photovoltaic (PV) Systems | 690.53

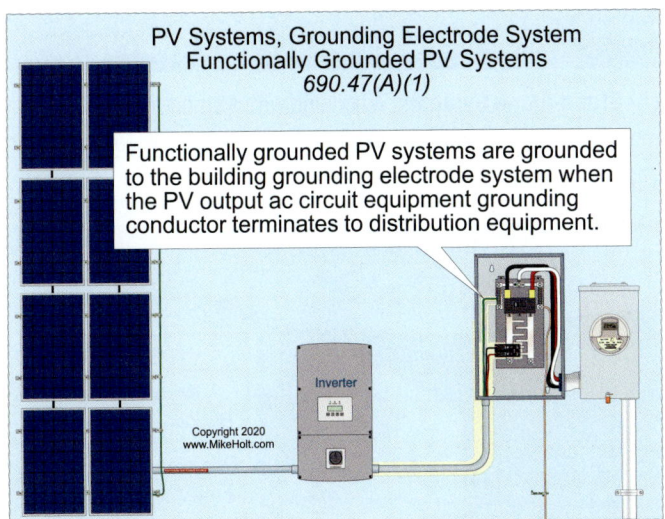
▶Figure 690-87

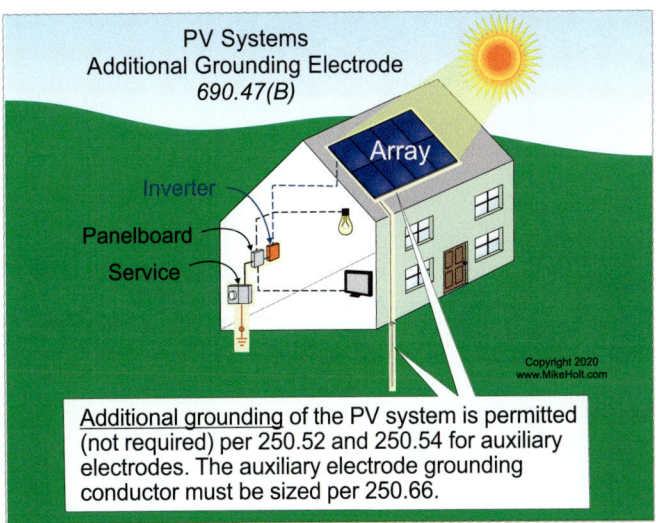
▶Figure 690-89

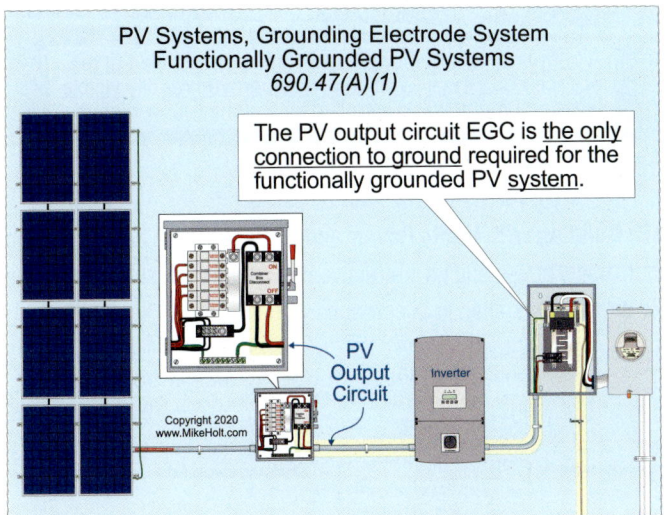
▶Figure 690-88

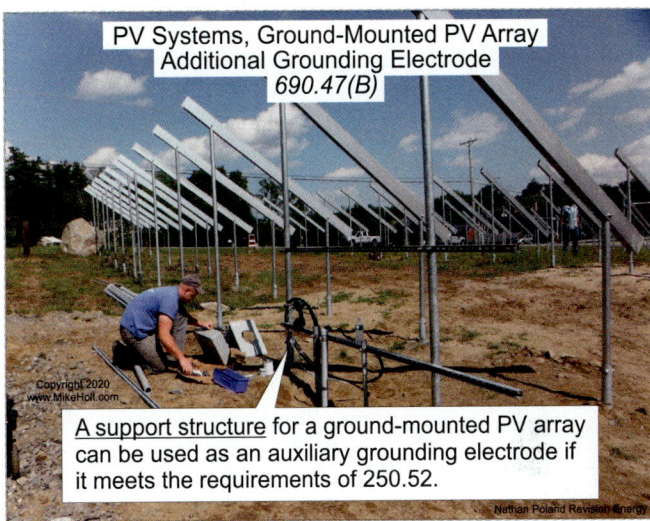
▶Figure 690-90

Note. Most PV systems are functionally grounded rather than solidly grounded. For functionally grounded systems, the inverter equipment grounding conductor is connected to the grounded distribution equipment. This connection is used for the ground-fault protection and equipment grounding of the PV array.

(B) Additional Grounding Electrode. Additional grounding of the PV system is permitted (but not required) in accordance with 250.52 and 250.54 for auxiliary electrodes. The auxiliary electrode grounding conductor must be sized in accordance with 250.66. ▶Figure 690-89

A support structure for a ground-mounted PV array can be used as an auxiliary grounding electrode if it meets the requirements of 250.52.
▶Figure 690-90

PV arrays mounted to buildings can use the metal frame of the building structure as a grounding electrode conductor where the requirements of 250.68(C)(2) are met.

Part VI. Markings and Labels

690.53 Direct-Current PV Circuit Label

A permanent readily visible label indicating the maximum PV system dc voltage as calculated in accordance with 690.7 must be installed at one of the following locations: ▶Figure 690-91

(1) PV system dc disconnect

(2) PV system electronic power conversion equipment

(3) Distribution equipment associated with the PV system

690.54 | Solar Photovoltaic (PV) Systems

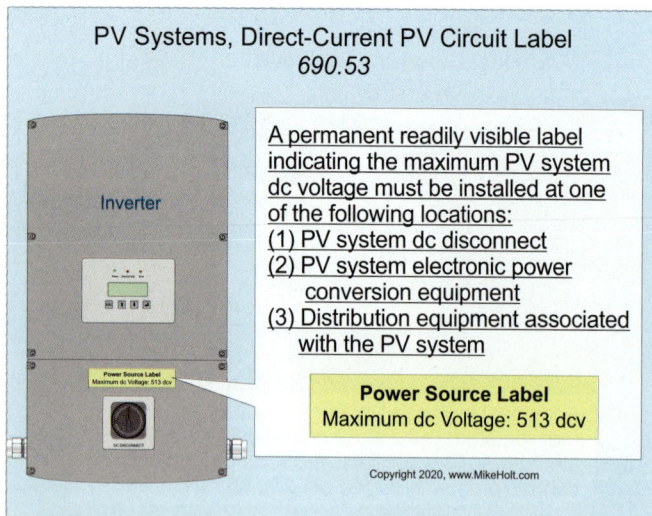
▶Figure 690-91

690.54 Interactive System Point of Interconnection

The point of interactive system interconnection with the electric utility must be marked at the PV system disconnecting means with the rated inverter ac output current and nominal ac voltage. ▶Figure 690-92

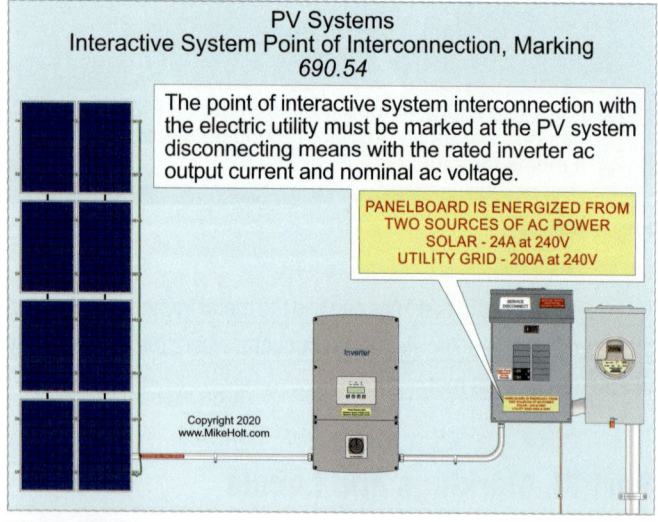
▶Figure 690-92

690.55 Energy Storage

PV system dc circuit conductors connected to energy storage systems must be marked for polarity in accordance with 690.31(B)(1).

690.56 Identification of Power Sources

(A) Stand-Alone Systems. A building with a stand-alone PV system must have a permanent plaque or directory installed in accordance with 710.10. ▶Figure 690-93

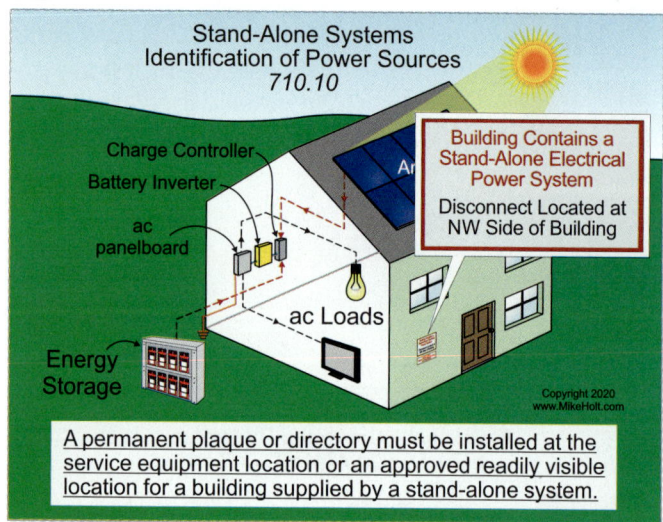
▶Figure 690-93

(B) Building with Utility Power and PV Systems. A building having both utility power and an interactive PV system(s) must have a plaque or directory installed in accordance with 705.10. ▶Figure 690-94

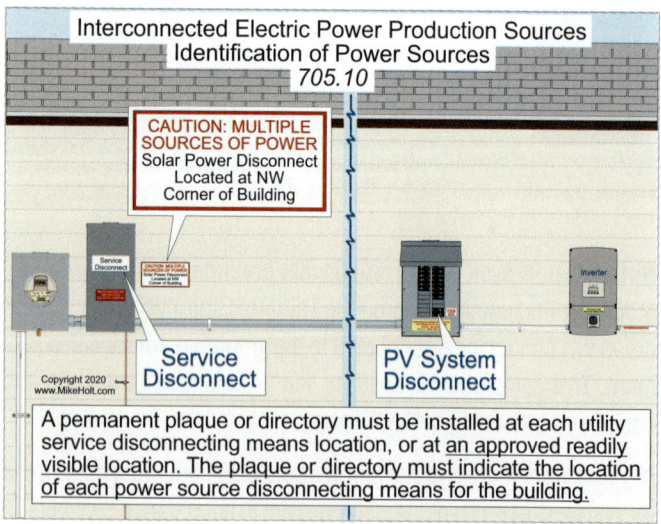
▶Figure 690-94

(C) Building with Rapid Shutdown System(s). A building with a rapid shutdown system [690.12] must have a permanent label indicating the location of all rapid shutdown initiation devices. The label must be located at each service equipment location or at an approved readily visible location and the label must include a diagram of a building with a roof with the following words: ▶Figure 690-95

Solar Photovoltaic (PV) Systems | 690.71

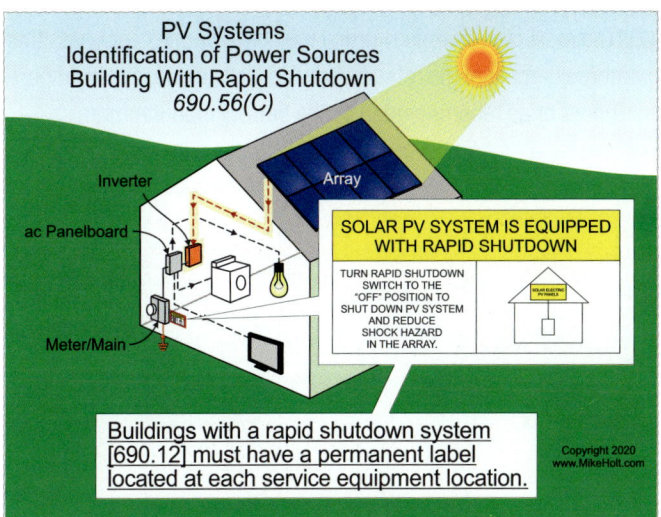

▶Figure 690-95

The title "SOLAR PV SYSTEM IS EQUIPPED WITH RAPID SHUTDOWN" must have capitalized characters with a minimum height of ⅜ in. in black on a yellow background. The remaining characters must be capitalized with a minimum height of 3/16 in. in black on white background.
▶Figure 690-96

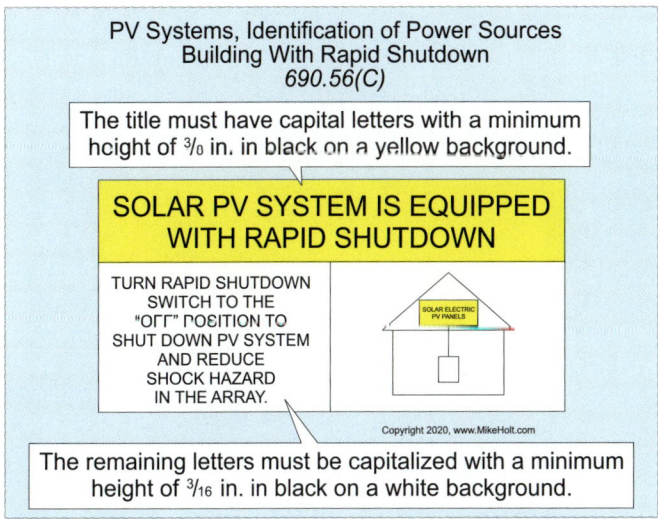

▶Figure 690-96

Note: See Note Figure 690.56(C) in the *NEC* for an example.

(1) Buildings with More Than One Rapid Shutdown Type. A building having more than one rapid shutdown system or a building without a rapid shutdown system must have a label with a detailed plan view diagram of the roof showing each PV system with a dotted line around areas that remain energized after the rapid shutdown has been initiated.

(2) Rapid Shutdown Switch. A rapid shutdown switch must have a label that includes the following wording located on or no more than 3 ft from the switch: "RAPID SHUTDOWN SWITCH FOR SOLAR PV SYSTEM." The rapid shutdown label must be reflective with all letters capitalized and having a minimum height of ⅜ in. in white on a red background. ▶Figure 690-97

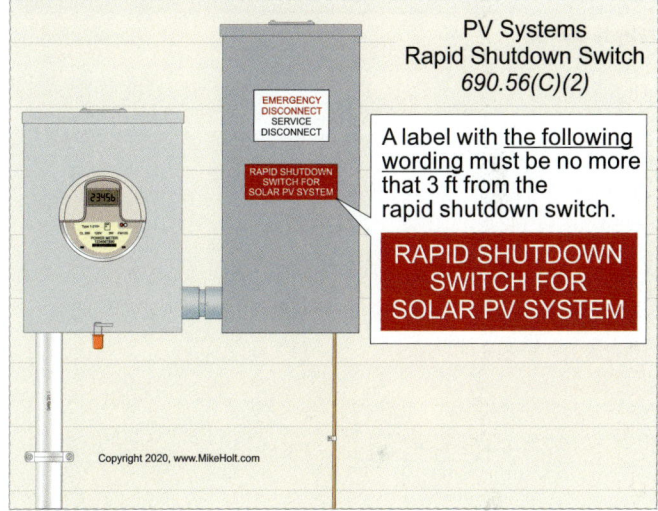

▶Figure 690-97

Part VII. Connections to Other Sources

690.59 Connection to Other Power Sources

PV systems connected in parallel with the electric utility must have the interconnection made in accordance with Parts I and II of Article 705 for the interconnection of electric utility and PV systems. ▶Figure 690-98

Part VIII. Energy Storage Systems

690.71 Energy Storage Systems

Energy storage systems connected to a PV system must be installed in accordance with Article 706.

690.72 | Solar Photovoltaic (PV) Systems

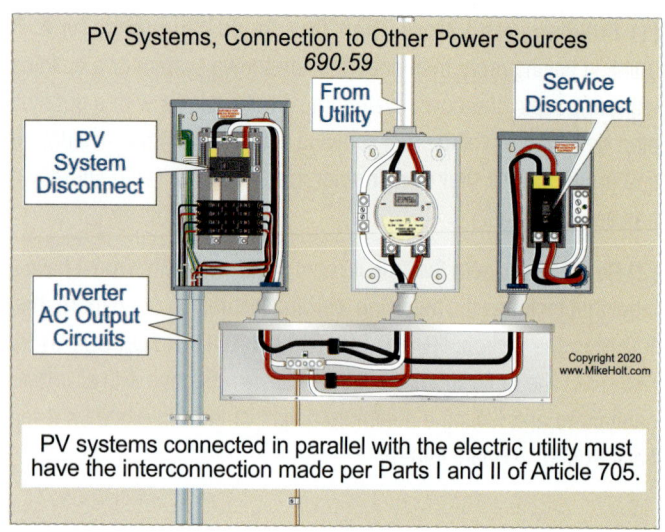

▶Figure 690–98

690.72 Self-Regulated PV Charge Control

The PV dc charge controller source circuit is considered to comply with 706.33 if:

(1) The PV source circuit is matched to the dc voltage rating and charge current requirements of the interconnected battery cells, and

(2) The maximum charging current multiplied by one hour is less than three percent of the rated battery capacity expressed in ampere-hours or as recommended by the battery manufacturer.

ARTICLE 691 — LARGE-SCALE PHOTOVOLTAIC (PV) ELECTRIC SUPPLY STATIONS

Introduction to Article 691—Large-Scale Photovoltaic (PV) Electric Supply Stations

The general requirements for solar photovoltaic (PV) systems are covered by Article 690. When a system is 5,000kW or larger, it becomes a large-scale PV electric supply station and is then covered by the requirements of Article 691.

This article defines what a large-scale photovoltaic system is and the additional requirements that must be met to take advantage of the alternative design and safety features unique to large systems.

Large-scale PV systems are privately owned PV systems that are operated solely to provide electricity to a regulated utility as compared to Article 690 systems that may be operated to provide power to the end user, utility, or a combination of both. They require a careful documented review of the design by an engineer to ensure safe operation and compliance with the applicable electrical standards and industry practices.

691.1 Scope

Article 691 covers the installation of large-scale PV electric supply stations with an inverter generating capacity of not less than 5,000 kW and not under the electric utility control. ▶Figure 691–1

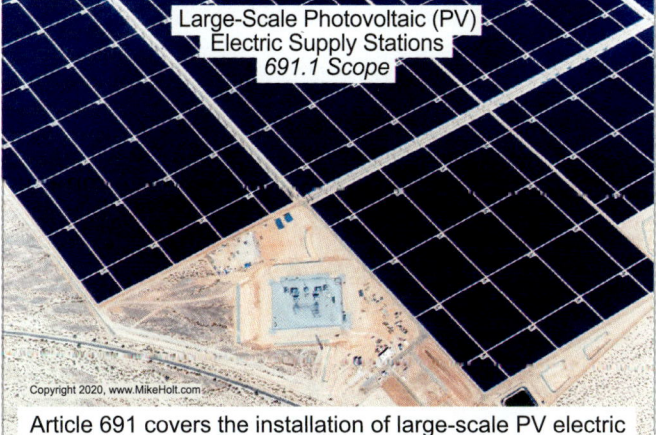

Article 691 covers the installation of large-scale PV electric supply stations with an inverter generating capacity of not less than 5,000 kW and not under the electric utility control.

▶Figure 691–1

Note 1: Facilities covered by this article have specific design and safety features unique to large-scale PV facilities and are operated for the sole purpose of providing electric supply to a system operated by a regulated utility for the transfer of electric energy.

691.2 Definitions

The definitions in this section apply only within this article.

691.4 Special Requirements for Large-Scale PV Electric Supply Stations

Large-scale PV electric supply stations are only permitted to be accessible to authorized personnel and must comply with the following requirements:

(1) Electrical circuits and equipment must be maintained and operated by qualified personnel.

(2) PV electric supply stations must be restricted by fencing or other means in accordance with 110.31 and have field-applied hazard markings that are permanently affixed and have sufficient durability to withstand the environment involved [110.21(B)].

(3) The connection between the PV electric supply and the utility system must be through medium- or high-voltage switch gear, substation, switchyard, or similar methods whose sole purpose is to safely and effectively interconnect the two systems.

(4) Loads within the PV electric supply station must only be used to power auxiliary equipment for the generation of the PV power.

(5) Large-scale PV electric supply stations must not be installed on buildings.

691.5 | Large-Scale Photovoltaic (PV) Electric Supply Stations

691.5 Equipment

All electrical equipment must be approved for installation by one of the following:

(1) Listing and labeling.

(2) Be evaluated for the application and have a field label applied.

(3) Where products complying with 691.5(1) or (2) are not available, by engineering review validating that the electrical equipment is evaluated and tested to relevant standards or industry practice.

691.6 Engineered Design

Documentation of the electric supply station must be stamped by a licensed professional electrical engineer and provided upon request of the authority having jurisdiction. Additional stamped independent engineering reports by a licensed professional electrical engineer detailing compliance of the design with applicable electrical standards and industry practice must be provided upon request of the authority having jurisdiction.

This documentation must include details of the conformance of the design with Article 690 and any alternative methods to Article 690, or other articles of the *NEC*.

691.7 Conformance of Construction to Engineered Design

Documentation by a licensed professional electrical engineer that the construction of the electric supply station conforms to the electrical engineered design must be provided upon request of the authority having jurisdiction. Additional stamped independent engineering reports by a licensed professional electrical engineer detailing that the construction conforms with this *Code*, applicable standards, and industry practice must be provided upon request of the authority having jurisdiction. This independent engineer must be retained by the system owner or installer.

691.8 Direct-Current Operating Voltage

Large-scale PV electric supply station calculations must be included in the documentation required in 691.6.

691.9 Disconnect for Isolating Photovoltaic Equipment

Isolating devices are not required to be located within sight of equipment and may be located remotely from the equipment.

The engineered design required by 691.6 must document disconnection procedures and means of isolating equipment.

Note: For information on electrical system maintenance, see NFPA 70B, *Recommended Practice for Electrical Equipment Maintenance*. For information on written procedures and conditions of maintenance, including lockout/tagout procedures, see NFPA 70E, *Standard for Electrical Safety in the Workplace*.

Buildings whose sole purpose is to house and protect supply station equipment are not required to include a rapid shutdown function to reduce shock hazard for firefighters [690.12]. Written standard operating procedures must be available at the site detailing necessary shutdown procedures in the event of an emergency.

691.10 Arc-Fault Mitigation

PV systems that do not provide arc-fault protection as required by 690.11 must include details of fire mitigation plans to address dc arc faults in the documentation required in 691.6.

691.11 Fence Bonding and Grounding

Fence grounding requirements and details must be included in the documentation required in 691.6.

Note: See 250.194 for fence bonding and grounding requirements for PV systems that operate at more than 1,000V between conductors. Grounding requirements for other portions of electric supply station fencing are assessed based on the presence of overhead conductors, proximity to generation and distribution equipment, and associated step and touch potential.

SPECIAL CONDITIONS

Introduction to Chapter 7—Special Conditions

Chapter 7, which covers special conditions, is the third of the *NEC* chapters that deal with special topics. Chapters 5 and 6 cover special occupancies, and special equipment, respectively. Remember, the first four chapters of the *Code* are sequential and form a foundation for each of the subsequent three. Chapter 8 covers communications systems (twisted pair and coaxial cable) and is not subject to the requirements of Chapters 1 through 7 except where the requirements are specifically referenced there.

What exactly is a "Special Condition"? It is a situation that does not fall under the category of special occupancies or special equipment but creates a need for additional measures to ensure the "safeguarding of people and property" mission of the *NEC*, as stated in 90.1(A).

▶ **Article 705—Interconnected Electric Power Production Sources.** It used to be that a premises having more than one electric power source was a unique situation, but as more and more facilities supplement their utility electric supply with alternate sources of energy it's become more commonplace. Alternate power sources such as solar or wind turbine that run in parallel with a primary utility source require particular consideration an requirements. Article 705 provides the guidance necessary to ensure a safe installation.

▶ **Article 706—Energy Storage Systems.** Energy storage systems can be (and usually are) connected to other energy sources, such as the local utility distribution system. There can be more than one source of power connected to an ESS and the connection to other energy sources is required to comply with the requirements of Article 705 which covers installation of one or more electric power production sources operating in parallel with a utility source of electricity. It might also be a good idea to be mindful of how this article correlates with other articles in the *Code* such as Articles 480, 690, 692, and 694.

▶ **Article 710—Stand Alone Systems.** A "stand alone system" is an electrical system that is self-sufficient and a completely "off the grid" source of electrical energy such as solar or wind. However, it still may be connected to a utility supply as part of an interconnected system but the fact that it can be self-sustaining is why Article 710 specifically addresses these systems.

Notes

ARTICLE 705 — INTERCONNECTED ELECTRIC POWER PRODUCTION SOURCES

Introduction to Article 705—Interconnected Electric Power Production Sources

Anytime there is more than one source of power supplying a building, safety concerns arise. In cases where a source such as a generator is used strictly for backup power, Articles 700, 701, or 702 require transfer switches and other safety measures to be implemented. When interconnected electrical power production sources, such as wind powered generators, solar PV systems, or fuel cells are connected in parallel with utility power, there is no transfer switch. In fact, there will often be multiple sources of electrical supply connected simultaneously.

Article 705 covers the requirements for the interconnection of electric power sources that operate in parallel with a primary source. The primary source is typically the electric utility power source, but it can be an on-site source.

Part I. General

705.1 Scope

 Scan this QR code for a video of Mike explaining this topic; it's a sample from the videos that accompany this textbook. www.MikeHolt.com/20PVvideos

This article covers the installation of electric power production sources operating in parallel with the primary source of electricity. ▶Figure 705-1

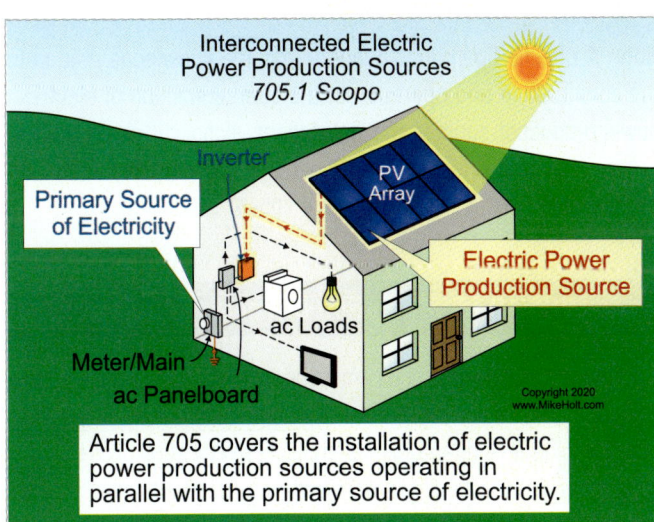

▶Figure 705-1

Note: The primary source of electricity typically includes the electric utility or it can be an on-site power source(s).

Author's Comment:

▶ Other on-site sources include:

  ▶ Energy storage systems, Article 706.
  ▶ Fuel cells, Article 692.
  ▶ Generators, Article 445.
  ▶ Solar PV systems, Article 690.
  ▶ Large-scale PV electric power production facilities, Article 691.
  ▶ Storage batteries, Article 480.
  ▶ Wind electric systems, Article 694.

705.2 Definitions

The definitions in this section apply within this article and throughout the *Code*.

Microgrid Interconnect Device. A device that enables a microgrid system to separate from and reconnect to operate in parallel with a primary power source. ▶Figure 705-2

Note: Microgrid controllers typically are used to measure and evaluate electrical parameters and provide the logic for the signal to initiate and complete transition processes.

705.6 | Interconnected Electric Power Production Sources

▶Figure 705-2

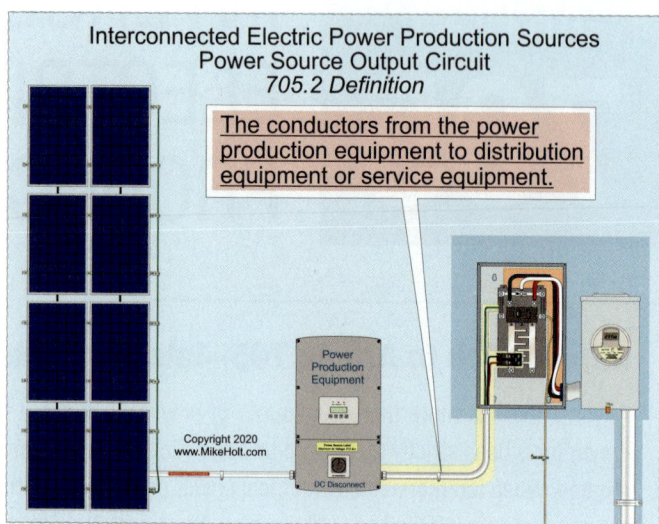

▶Figure 705-4

Microgrid System. A premises wiring system that has generation, energy storage, and load(s), or any combination of them, that includes the ability to disconnect from and operate in parallel with the primary source. ▶Figure 705-3

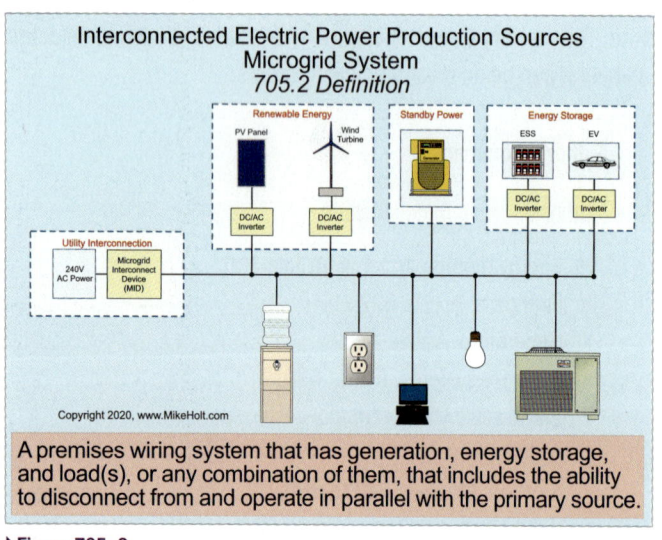

▶Figure 705-3

Power Source Output Circuit. The conductors from the power production equipment to distribution equipment or service equipment. ▶Figure 705-4

705.6 Equipment Approval

Interactive equipment intended to operate in parallel with electric power production sources including (but not limited to) interactive inverters, engine generators, energy storage equipment, and wind turbines must be approved for interactive function and be listed or be evaluated for interactive function and have a field label applied, or both.

705.8 System Installation

The installation of electrical power production sources operating in parallel with a primary source of electricity (electric utility) must be performed by a qualified person.

Note: A qualified person is one who has the knowledge related to the construction and operation of the interconnection of electrical power production sources and installations; along with safety training to recognize and avoid hazards to persons and property relating to those systems [Article 100]. ▶Figure 705-5

705.10 Identification of Power Sources

A permanent plaque or directory must be installed at each utility service disconnecting means location, or at an approved readily visible location. The plaque or directory must indicate the location of all building power source disconnecting means and be grouped with other plaques or directories for other on-site sources of power. ▶Figure 705-6

Interconnected Electric Power Production Sources | **705.11**

▶Figure 705–5

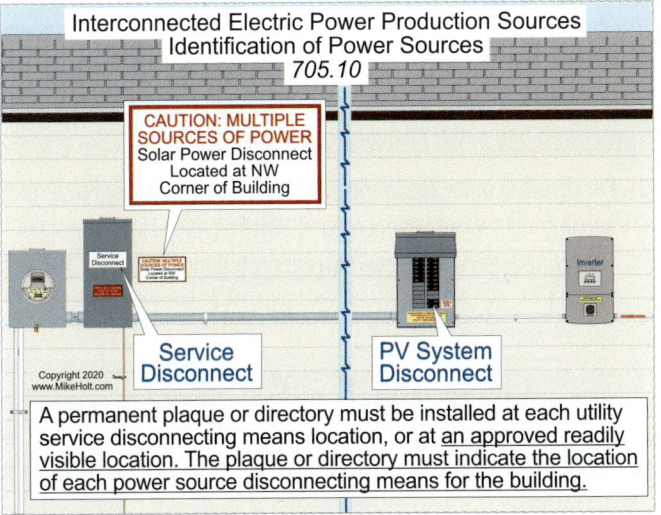

▶Figure 705–6

The plaque or directory must be marked with the wording "CAUTION: MULTIPLE SOURCES OF POWER." Any posted diagrams must be correctly oriented with respect to the diagram's location.

The marking must be permanently affixed and have sufficient durability to withstand the environment involved [110.21(B)].

Ex: Plaques or directories for installations having multiple co-located power production sources are permitted to be identified as a group(s). A plaque or directory is not required for each power source.

Author's Comment:

▸ The exception to 705.10 infers that since there is typically only one utility supply location that if there are other alternative power sources at remote locations, only one plaque or directory is required at the utility source indicating the location of the other remote power sources.

705.11 Supply-Side Source Connections

 Scan this QR code for a video of Mike explaining this topic; it's a sample from the videos that accompany this textbook. www.MikeHolt.com/20PVvideos

An electric power production source connected on the supply side of the electric utility service disconnecting means as permitted in 230.82(6) must comply with (A) through (E): ▶Figure 705–7

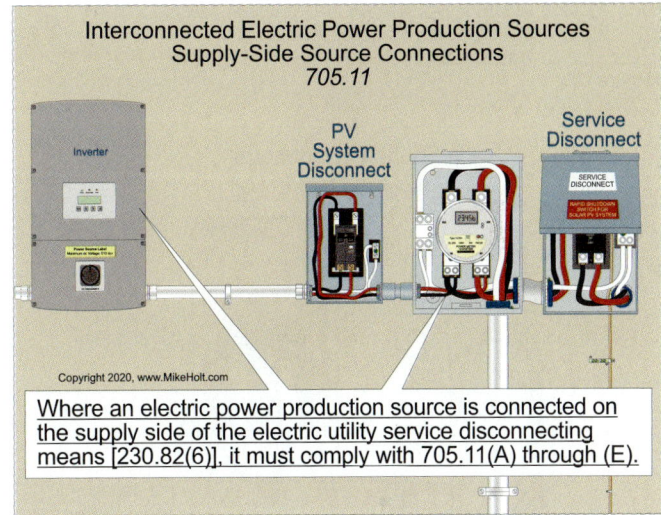

▶Figure 705–7

(A) Output Rating. The sum of the supply-side power source output current ratings, other than those controlled by a power control system in accordance with 705.13, are not permitted to exceed the ampacity of the service conductors. ▶Figure 705–8

Note: See Article 100 for the definition of "Service Conductors."

Author's Comment:

▸ Service conductors are the conductors from the load side of the electric utility service point to the service disconnect [Article 100]. ▶Figure 705–9

▸ Service conductors (load side of service point) include overhead service conductors, overhead service-entrance conductors, and underground service conductors. These conductors are not under the exclusive control of the serving electric utility, which means they are owned by the customer and fall within the requirements of Article 230.

705.11 | Interconnected Electric Power Production Sources

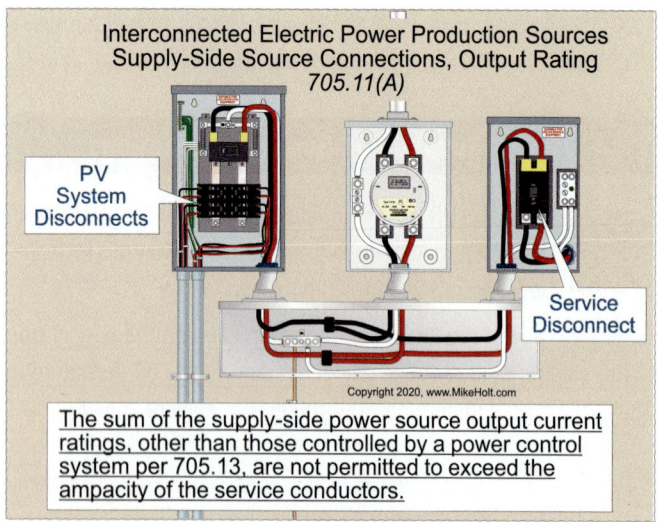
▶Figure 705-8

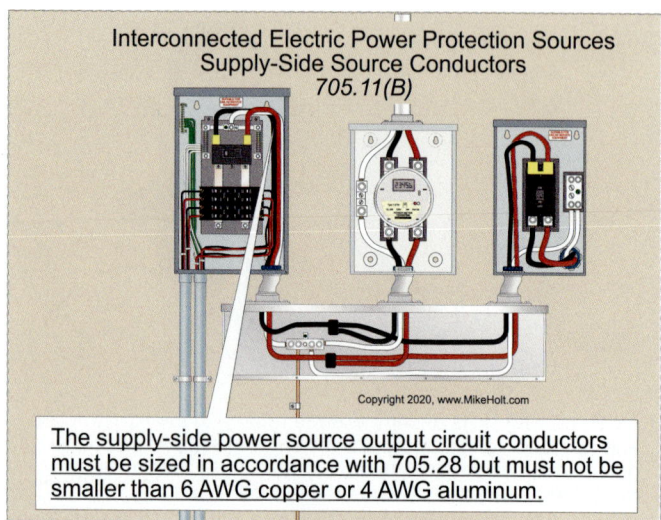
▶Figure 705-10

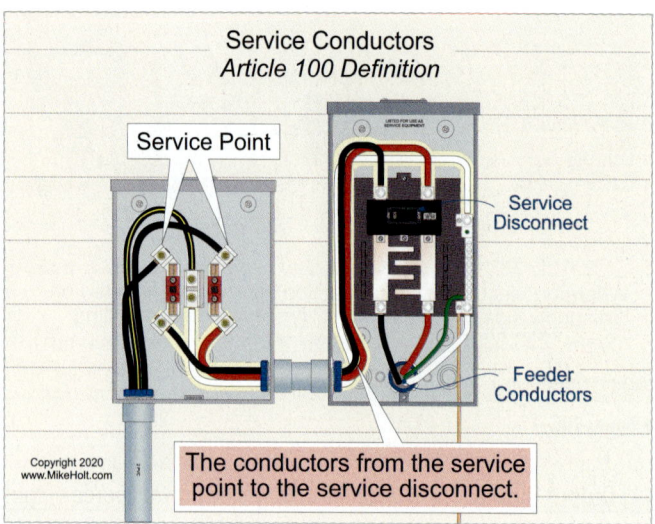
▶Figure 705-9

(B) Conductors. The supply-side power source output circuit conductors must be sized in accordance with 705.28 but must not be smaller than 6 AWG copper or 4 AWG aluminum. ▶Figure 705-10

Supply-side power source output circuit conductors must be installed within a wiring method in accordance with 230.30 for underground installations and 230.43 for aboveground installations.

(C) Overcurrent Protection. Supply-side power source output circuit conductors must have overcurrent protection in accordance with 705.30.

Outside. Where supply-side power source output circuit conductors make their supply-side connection to service conductors outside a building, the overcurrent protective device for the supply-side power source output circuit conductors must be located at a readily accessible location outside the building or at the first readily accessible location where the supply-side power source output circuit conductors enter the building.

Inside. Where the supply-side power source output circuit conductors make their connection to service conductors inside a building, the length of supply-side power source output circuit conductors must comply with one of the following requirements:

(1) For dwelling units, the length of supply-side power source output circuit conductors must not exceed 10 ft from the point of the supply-side connection to the overcurrent protection [705.30]. ▶Figure 705-11

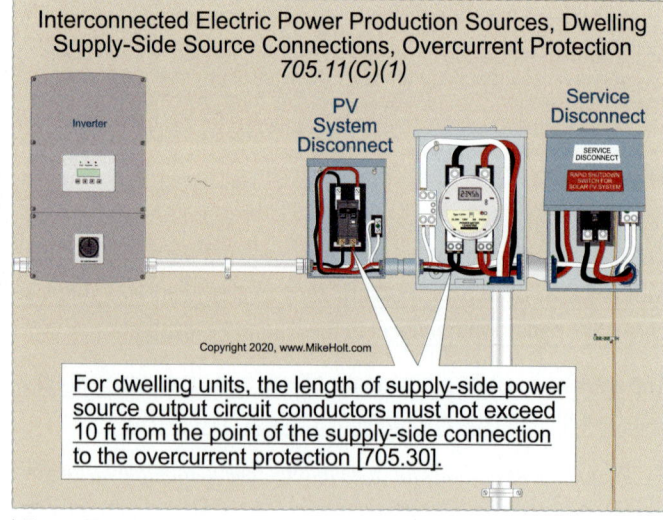
▶Figure 705-11

For other than dwelling units, the length of the supply-side power source output circuit conductors must not exceed 16.50 ft from the point of the supply-side connection to the overcurrent protection [705.30].

(2) In other than dwelling units, where cable limiters are located within 16.50 ft from the point of the supply-side connection, overcurrent protection of supply-side conductors is required within 71 ft from the point of the supply-side connection [705.30].

(D) Connections. Supply-side connections must be made with listed connectors that comply with 110.14.

Modifications to equipment to accommodate the supply-side connection must be in accordance with the manufacturer's instructions or the equipment modification must be evaluated for the application and have a field label applied.

Supply-side connections within meter socket enclosures under the exclusive control of the electric utility are only permitted where approved by the electric utility.

(E) Ground-Fault Protection. Ground-fault protection of equipment meeting the requirements of 230.95 must be provided for power source output circuit current rated 1,000A or more from a solidly grounded wye system where the voltage-to-ground exceeds 150V and the phase-to-phase voltage does not exceed 1,000V.

705.12 Load-Side Source Connections

Electric power source output circuit conductors are permitted to be connected to the load side of service equipment. ▶Figure 705-12

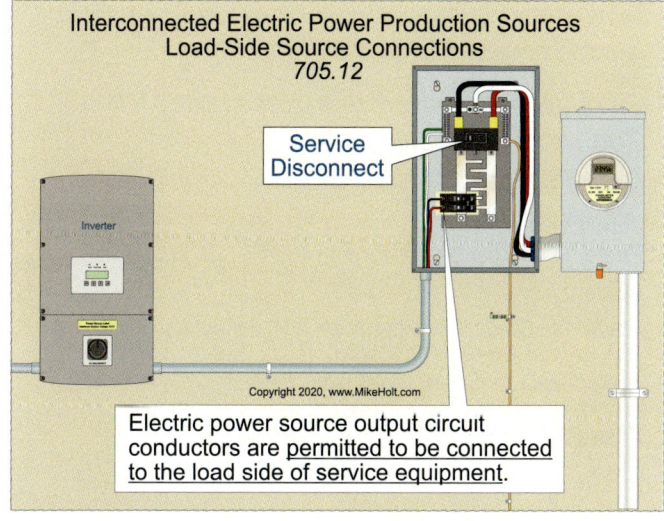

▶Figure 705-12

Where distribution equipment or feeders are capable of supplying branch circuits and/or feeders, or are supplied with a primary source of electricity and other power production sources, the interconnection of power production source equipment to the primary source of electricity must be in accordance with one of the following methods:

(A) Dedicated Overcurrent and Disconnect. The power production source terminates to a dedicated circuit breaker or fusible disconnect.

(B) Bus or Conductor Ampere Rating. The interconnection of each power production source to a bus or conductor must be in accordance with one of the following methods:

(1) Feeder Ampacity. Where a power source connection is made to the feeder primary source overcurrent device, the feeder conductor must have an ampacity of no less than 125 percent of the source output circuit current.

Where a power source output connection is made to a feeder at a location that is not at the opposite end of the feeder primary source overcurrent device, the feeder ampacity on the load side of the power source output connection must be as follows:

(a) The feeder ampacity on the load side of the power source connection must not be less than the sum of the rating of the primary source overcurrent device plus 125 percent of the power source output circuit current rating. ▶Figure 705-13

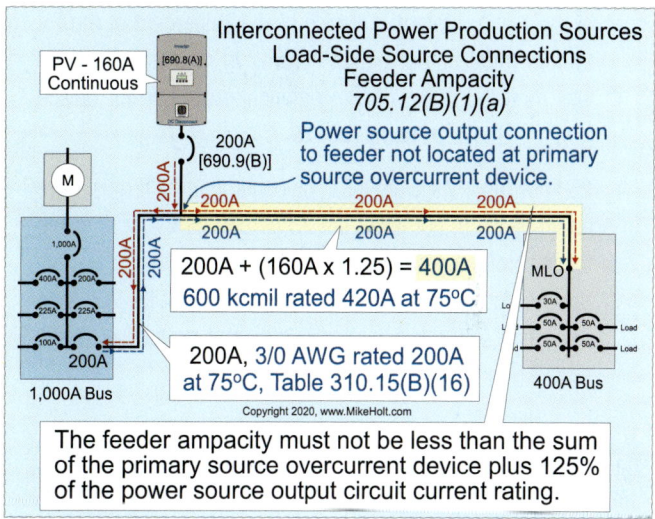

▶Figure 705-13

(b) Where an overcurrent protective device is placed at the load side of the power source connection to the feeder conductor, the feeder ampacity must not be less than the rating of the overcurrent protective device. ▶Figure 705-14

(2) Taps. Where a tap connection is made to a feeder that is supplied with both a primary source of power and an additional power source, the tap conductors in accordance with 240.21(B) must be sized based on the sum of the feeder protective device plus 125 percent of the PV system rated output circuit current.

705.12 | Interconnected Electric Power Production Sources

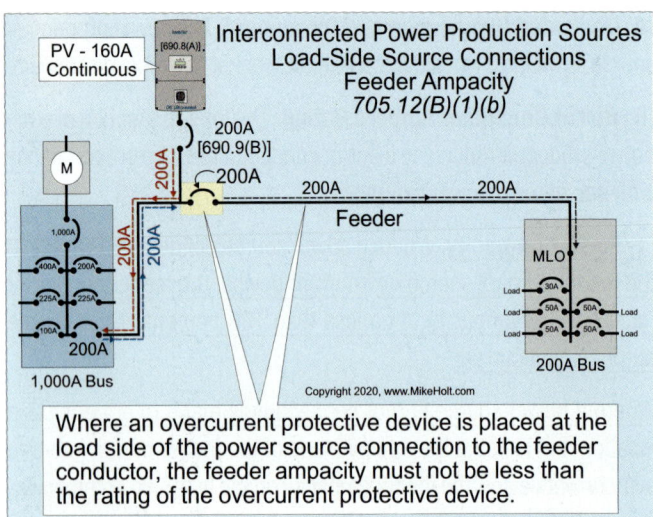
▶Figure 705-14

Author's Comment:

▶ **10-Foot Tap.** PV system taps not longer than 10 ft must have an ampacity of not less than ten percent of the sum of the feeder protective device plus 125 percent of the PV system rated output circuit current. In no case can it be less than the rating of the terminating overcurrent device [240.21(B)(1)]. ▶Figure 705-15

▶ **25-Foot Tap.** PV system taps not longer than 25 ft must have an ampacity of not less than 33 percent of the sum of the feeder protective device plus 125 percent of the PV system rated output circuit current. In no case can it be less than the rating of the terminating overcurrent protective device [240.21(B)(2)].

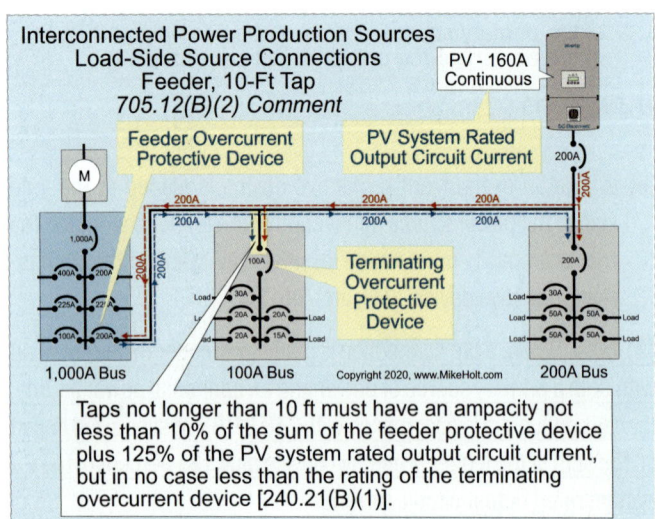
▶Figure 705-15

▶ **Feeder Tap—10-Foot Example**

Question: What size tap conductor (not over 10 ft long) made from a 200A-protected feeder supplied with an inverter having an ac output current rating of 160A is required to a 100A overcurrent protective device? ▶Figure 705-16

(a) 3 AWG   (b) 2 AWG   (c) 1 AWG   (d) 3/0 AWG

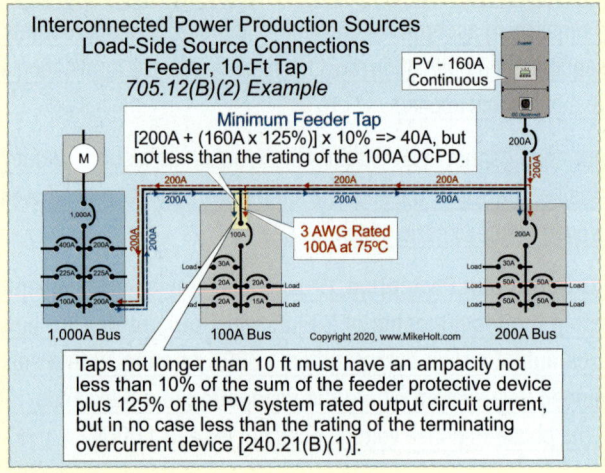
▶Figure 705-16

Solution:

PV system taps not longer than 10 ft must have an ampacity of not less than ten percent of the sum of the feeder protective device (200A) plus 125 percent of the PV system rated output circuit current (160A); but, in no case can the tap be less than the rating of the terminating overcurrent protective device (100A) [240.21(B)(1)].

Feeder Tap Conductor Ampacity => [200A + (160A x 125%)] x 10%, but not less than 100A

Feeder Tap Conductor Ampacity => (200A + 200A) x 10%, but not less than 100A

Feeder Tap Conductor Ampacity => 400A x 10%, but not less than 100A

Feeder Tap Conductor Ampacity => 40A, but not less than 100A

Feeder Contactor Size = 3 AWG rated 100A at 75°C [Table 310.16]

Answer: (a) 3 AWG

▶ **Feeder Tap—25-Foot Example**

Question: What size tap conductor, more than 10 ft but not more than 25 ft long made from a 200A-protected feeder supplied with an inverter having an ac output current rating of 160A is required to a 100A overcurrent protective device? ▶Figure 705-17

(a) 3 AWG   (b) 2 AWG   (c) 1 AWG   (d) 1/0 AWG

Interconnected Electric Power Production Sources | 705.12

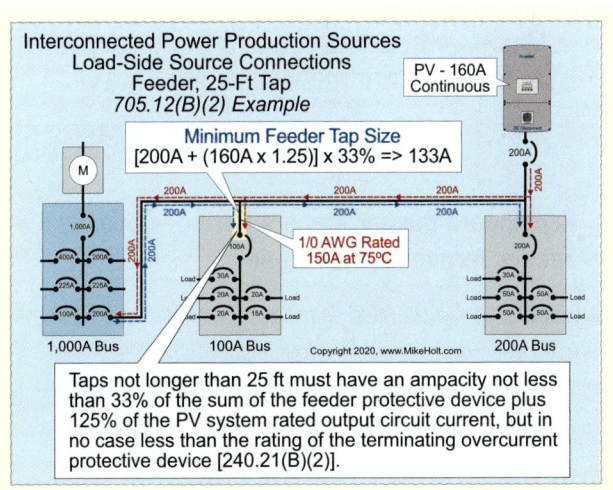
▶Figure 705-17

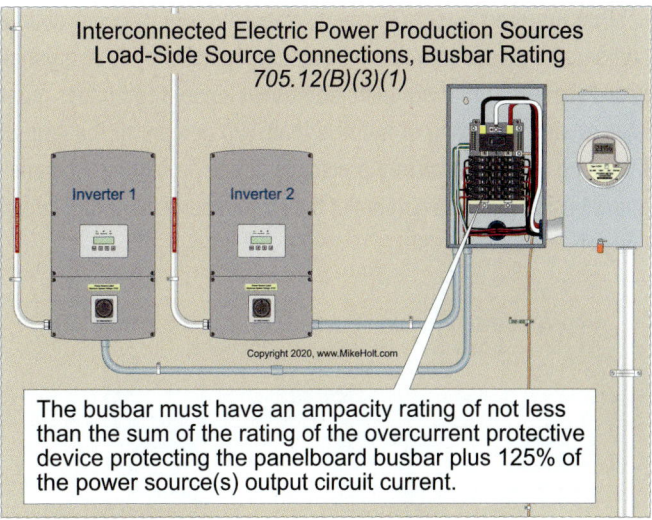
▶Figure 705-18

Solution:

PV system taps not longer than 25 ft must have an ampacity of not less than 33 percent of the sum of the feeder protective device (200A) plus 125 percent of the PV system rated output circuit current (160A); but, in no case less than the rating of the terminating overcurrent protective device (100A) [240.21(B)(2)].

Feeder Tap Conductor Ampacity => [200A + (160A x 125%)] x 33%, but not less than 100A

Feeder Tap Conductor Ampacity => (200A + 200A) x 33%, but not less than 100A

Feeder Tap Conductor Ampacity => 400A x 33%, but not less than 100A

Feeder Tap Conductor Ampacity => 133A, but no less than 100A

Feeder Contactor Size = 1/0 AWG rated 150A at 75°C [Table 310.16]

Answer: *(d) 1/0 AWG*

(3) Busbars. Power source connections to panelboard busbars must be by one of the following methods:

(1) Busbars at 100%. Termination of power source conductors to an overcurrent protective device placed at any point of the panelboard requires the busbar to have an ampere rating of not less than the sum of the rating of the overcurrent protective device protecting the panelboard busbar plus 125 percent of the power source(s) output circuit current. ▶Figure 705-18

▶ **Panelboard Busbar Ampere Rating—Example**

Question: *What is the minimum busbar ampere rating for a panelboard protected by a 150A overcurrent protective device if it is supplied by two interactive inverters each having an output ac current rating of 20A?* ▶Figure 705-19

(a) 200A (b) 250A (c) 260A (d) 300A

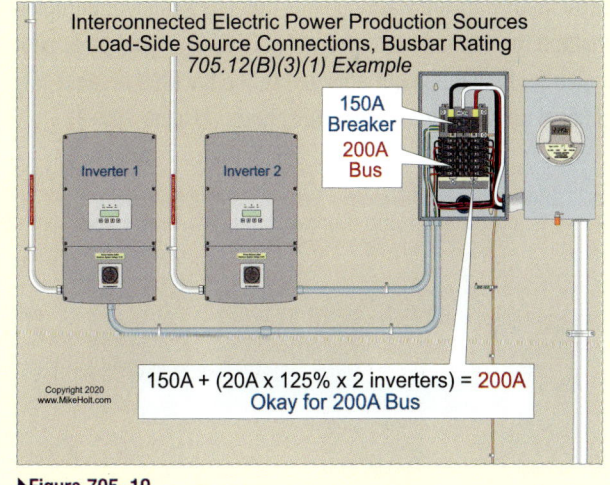
▶Figure 705-19

Solution:

Minimum Busbar Ampere Rating => 150A + (20A x 125% x 2 interactive inverters)
Minimum Busbar Ampere Rating => 150A + 50A
Minimum Busbar Ampere Rating => 200A

Answer: *(a) 200A*

705.12 | Interconnected Electric Power Production Sources

(2) One Hundred Twenty Percent. Where the primary power source and another power source are located at opposite ends of a panelboard (backfed) that contains additional loads, the busbar must have an ampere rating of not less than 120 percent of the sum of the rating of the overcurrent protective device protecting the panelboard busbar plus 125 percent of the power source(s) output circuit current. ▶Figure 705-20

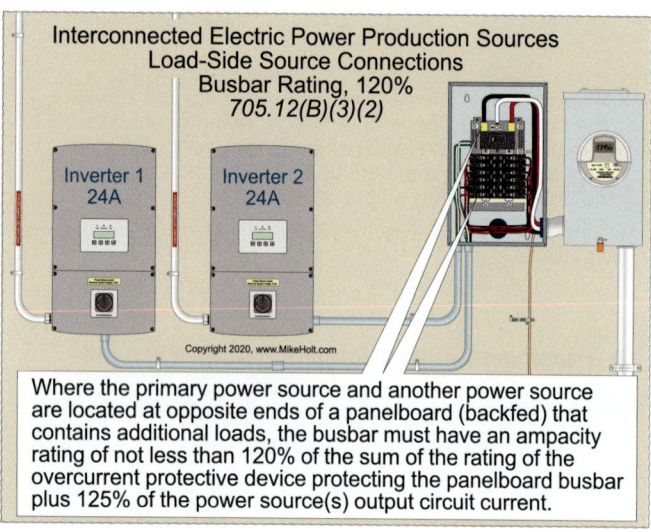

▶Figure 705-20

A permanently affixed warning label that has sufficient durability to withstand the environment involved [110.21(B)] must be applied to the distribution equipment adjacent to the backfed breaker for the additional power source(s) and must read: ▶Figure 705-21

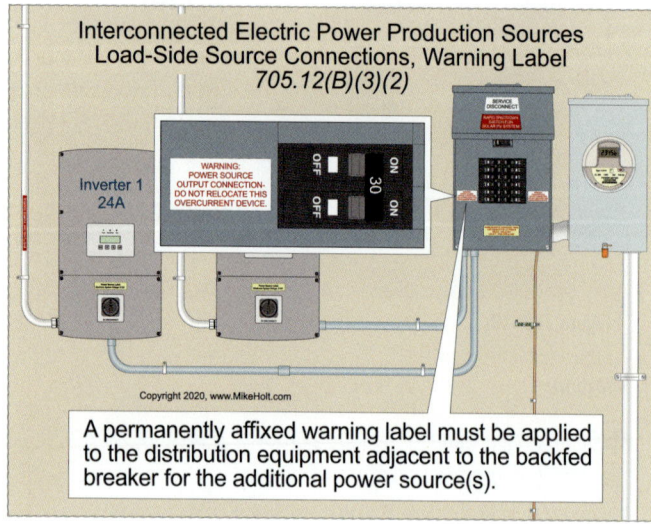

▶Figure 705-21

**WARNING—POWER SOURCE OUTPUT CONNECTION
DO NOT RELOCATE THIS OVERCURRENT DEVICE**

▶ **Panelboard Busbar Ampere Rating—Opposite Feeder Termination Example**

Question: Can a 200A rated panelboard protected by a 175A overcurrent device be supplied by two interactive inverters where each has an output ac current rating of 24A and are located opposite the feeder termination? ▶Figure 705-22

(a) Yes (b) No

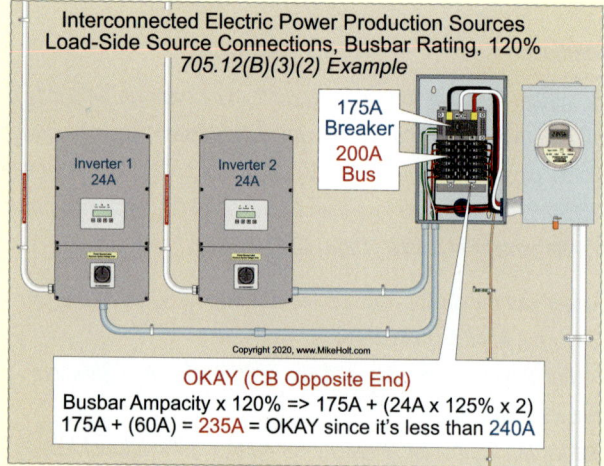

▶Figure 705-22

Solution:

The panelboard busbar ampacity must have an ampacity of not less than 120 percent of the sum of the rating of the overcurrent protective device protecting the panelboard busbar plus 125 percent of the power source(s) output circuit current.

Panelboard Ampacity x 120% => 175A + (24A x 125% x 2 interactive inverters)
200A x 120% => 175A + 60A
240A =>235A

Answer: (a) Yes

(3) Sum of Breakers. Where the primary power source and another power source are not located at opposite ends of a panelboard, the busbar must have an ampere rating of not less than the sum of the ampere ratings of all the overcurrent protective devices, exclusive of the overcurrent device protecting the panelboard busbar. ▶Figure 705-23

Interconnected Electric Power Production Sources | 705.12

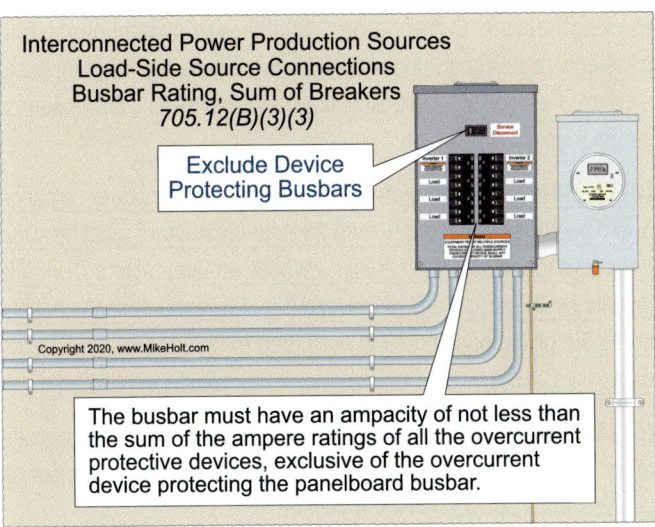
▶Figure 705-23

▶ **Panelboard Busbar Ampere Rating—Sum of Breakers Not to Exceed Busbar Ampere Rating Example 1**

Question: What is the minimum busbar ampere rating for a panelboard containing two 30A, two-pole circuit breakers and six 20A, two-pole circuit breakers? ▶Figure 705-24

(a) 12A   (b) 140A   (c) 180A   (d) 210A

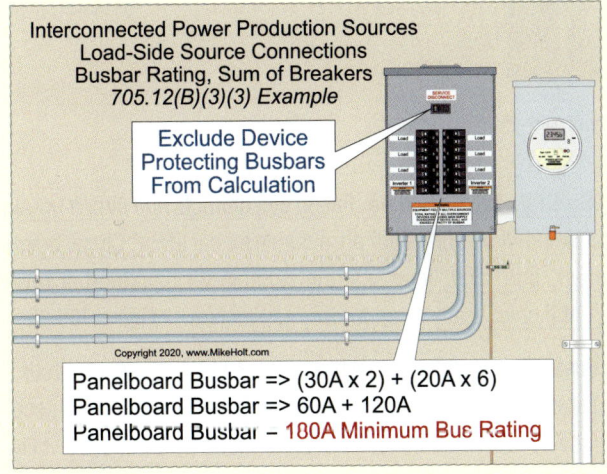
▶Figure 705-24

Solution:

The panelboard busbar ampacity must have an ampacity of not less than the sum of the ampere ratings of all the overcurrent protective devices, exclusive of the overcurrent device protecting the panelboard busbar.

Panelboard Busbar = >(30A x 2) + (20A x 6)
Panelboard Busbar = >60A + 120A
Panelboard Busbar = 180A

Answer: (c) 180A

▶ **Panelboard Busbar Ampere Rating—Sum of Breakers Not to Exceed Busbar Ampere Rating Example 2**

Question: What is the minimum busbar ampere rating for a panelboard containing six 30A, two-pole circuit breakers and one 20A, one-pole circuit breaker? ▶Figure 705-25

(a) 125A   (b) 150A   (c) 175A   (d) 200A

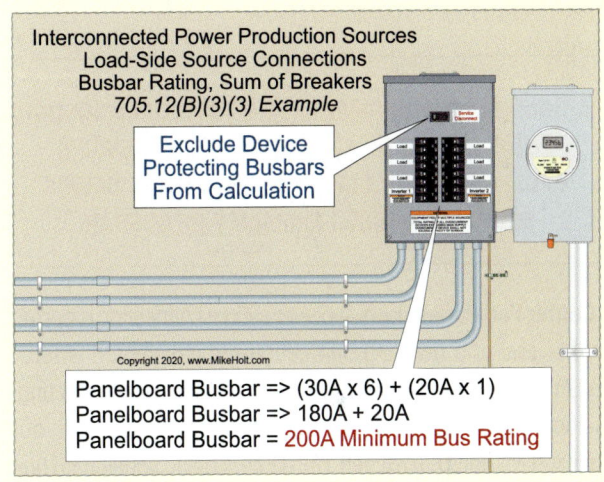
▶Figure 705-25

Solution:

The panelboard busbar ampacity must be equal to or greater than the sum of the ampere ratings of all the overcurrent protective devices on the panelboard busbar.

Panelboard Busbar = >(30A x 6) + (20A x 1)
Panelboard Busbar = >180A + 20A
Panelboard Busbar = 200A

Answer: (d) 200A

A permanently affixed warning label that has sufficient durability to withstand the environment involved [110.21(B)] must be applied to the distribution equipment and read: ▶Figure 705-26

705.12 | Interconnected Electric Power Production Sources

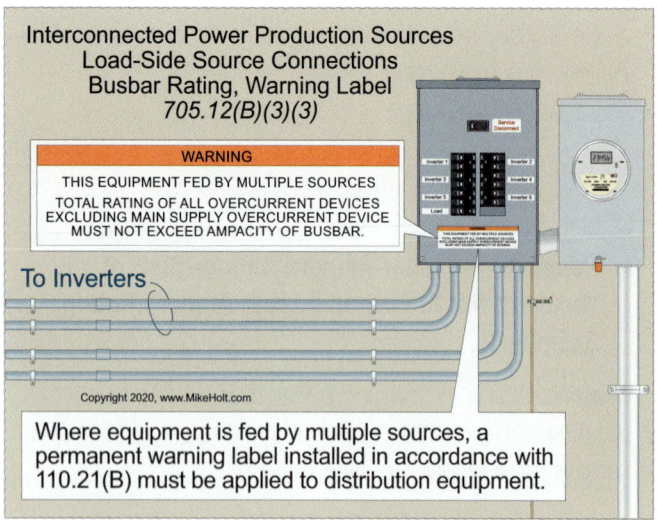
▶Figure 705-26

WARNING—THIS EQUIPMENT FED BY MULTIPLE SOURCES. TOTAL RATING OF ALL OVERCURRENT DEVICES EXCLUDING MAIN SUPPLY OVERCURRENT DEVICE MUST NOT EXCEED AMPACITY OF BUSBAR.

(4) Center-Fed Panelboard. A power source connection is permitted at either end of a dwelling unit center-fed panelboard where the sum of the rating of the overcurrent protective device protecting the panelboard busbar plus 125 percent of the power source(s) output circuit current does not exceed 120 percent of the panelboard busbar ampacity. ▶Figure 705-27

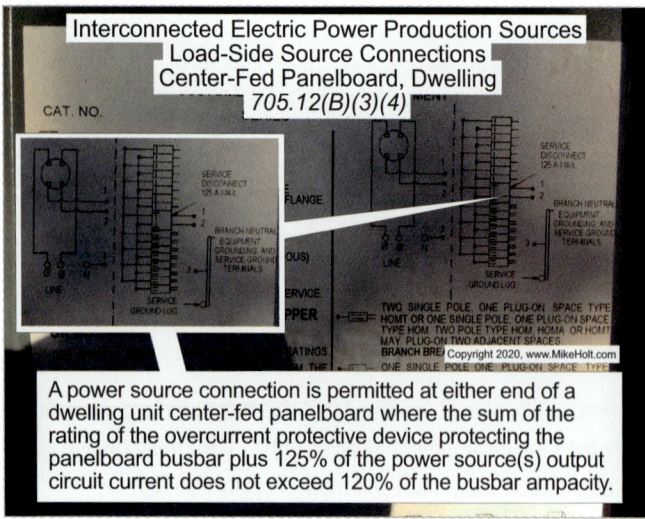
▶Figure 705-27

(5) Engineering Supervisions. Switchgear, switchboards, and panelboards designed under engineering supervision that includes available fault current and busbar load calculations for a power source connection.

(6) Feed-Through Connection. Power source connections on panelboard busbars connected to feed-through conductors must be sized in accordance with 705.12(B)(1). Where an overcurrent device is installed at the supply end of the feed-through conductors, the busbar in the supplying panelboard is permitted to be sized in accordance with 705.12(B)(3).

(C) Marking. Panelboards containing multiple power source circuits must be field marked to indicate the presence of all sources of all power source circuits. ▶Figure 705-28

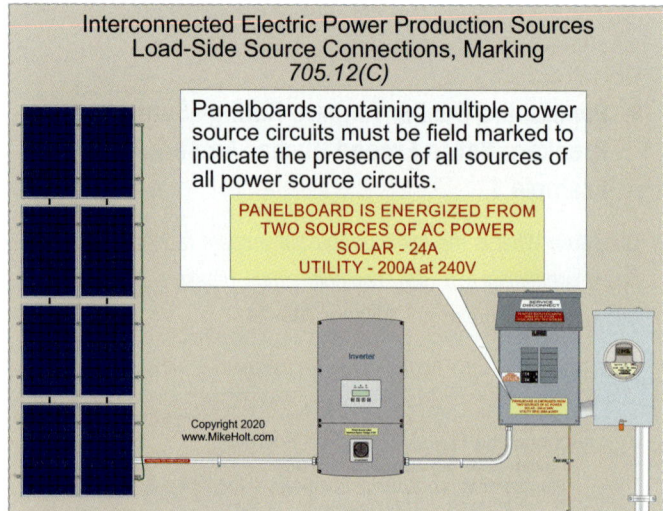
▶Figure 705-28

(D) Suitable for Backfeed. Fused disconnects and circuit breakers not marked "line" and "load" are suitable for backfeed. Circuit breakers marked "line" and "load" can be suitable for backfeed or reverse current if specifically rated for this application. ▶Figure 705-29

(E) Fastening. Backfed circuit breakers for electric power sources that are listed and identified as interactive are not required to be secured in place by an additional fastener as required by 408.36(D). ▶Figure 705-30

> **Author's Comment:**
>
> ▶ PV ac inverter circuit breakers are not required to be fastened in place because the PV interactive inverter automatically ceases to export ac current when the breaker is removed.

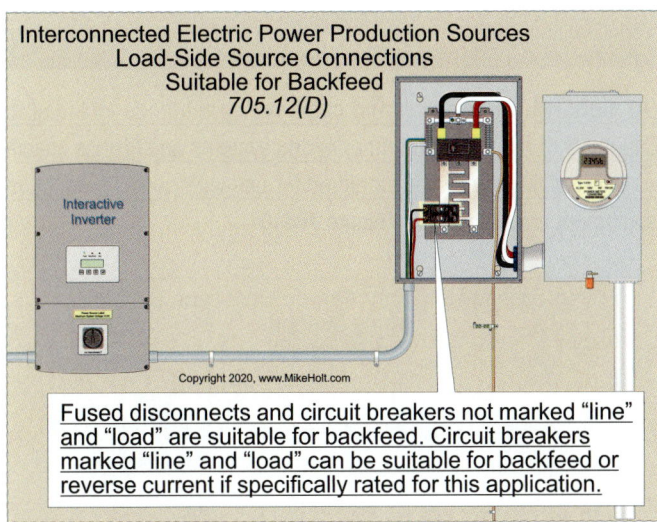

▶ Figure 705-29

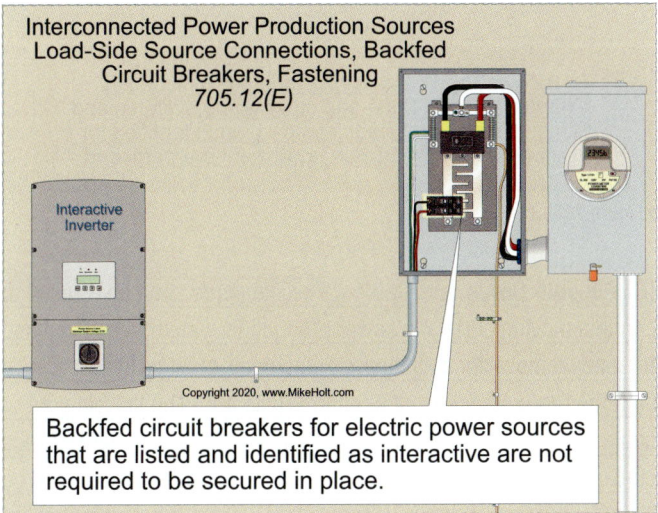

▶ Figure 705-30

705.13 Power Control Systems

 Scan this QR code for a video of Mike explaining this topic; it's a sample from the videos that accompany this textbook. www.MikeHolt.com/20PVvideos

Power control systems that control the output of power production sources, energy storage systems, and other equipment must be listed. The power control system must limit the current to the ampacity of the conductors or the ratings of the busbars to which it is connected in accordance with 705.13(A) through (E).

(A) Monitoring. The power control system controller must monitor all current within the power control system.

A busbar or conductor on the load side of the service disconnect that is not monitored by the power control system must be sized in accordance with 705.12.

Where the power control system is connected to the supply side of service equipment as permitted by 705.11, the power control system must monitor the current on the service conductors and prevent overload of those conductors.

(B) Settings. The sum of the power control system currents plus all monitored currents from other sources of supply must not exceed the ampacity of any busbar or conductor ampacity supplied by the power production sources.

Where the power control system is connected to an overcurrent device protecting busbars or conductors not monitored by the power control system, the setting of the power control system must be set to the ratings of that overcurrent device.

(C) Overcurrent Protection. The power control system must provide overcurrent protection either by overcurrent devices or the functionality as an overcurrent device in the product listing.

Note: Some power control systems are listed to provide overcurrent protection.

(D) Single Power Source Rating. The rating of the overcurrent device for any single power source controlled by the power control system is not permitted to exceed the rating of the busbar or the ampacity of the conductors to which it is connected.

(E) Access to Settings. The access to settings of the power control system must be restricted to qualified personnel in accordance with the requirements of 240.6(C).

Author's Comment:

- According to 240.6(C), restricted access is achieved by one of the following methods:
  - Locating behind removable and sealable covers over the adjusting means.
  - Locating behind bolted equipment enclosure doors.
  - Locating behind locked doors accessible only to qualified personnel.
  - Password protection, with the password accessible only to qualified personnel.

705.16 Interrupting and Short-Circuit Current Rating

Consideration should be given to the contribution of fault currents from all interconnected power sources for the interrupting and short-circuit current ratings of equipment on interactive systems.

705.20 Disconnect

Means must be provided to disconnect the power source output circuit conductors from conductors of other systems. The supply-side power source disconnecting means must comply with the following:

(1) The disconnect must be one of the following types:

(a) A manually operable switch or circuit breaker.

(b) A load-break-rated pull-out switch.

(c) A remote-controlled switch or circuit breaker that is capable of being operated manually and can be opened automatically when control power is interrupted.

(d) A device listed or approved for the intended application.

(2) The disconnect must simultaneously disconnect all phase conductors of the circuit.

(3) The disconnect must be readily accessible from a readily accessible location.

(4) The disconnect must be externally operable without exposed live parts.

(5) Enclosures with doors or hinged covers with exposed live parts when open must require a tool to open or must be lockable where readily accessible to unqualified persons.

(6) The disconnect must indicate if it is in the open (off) or closed (on) position.

(7) The disconnect must have a rating that is sufficient for the maximum circuit current, available fault current, and voltage at the terminals.

(8) The disconnect must be marked in accordance with the warning in 690.13(B) where the line and load terminals are capable of being energized in the open position.

Note: With interconnected power sources, some switches and fuses are likely to be energized from both directions. See 240.40.

705.25 Wiring Methods

(A) General. All raceway and cable wiring methods included in Chapter 3 of this *Code* and other wiring systems and fittings specifically listed, intended, and identified for use with power production equipment are permitted. ▶Figure 705-31

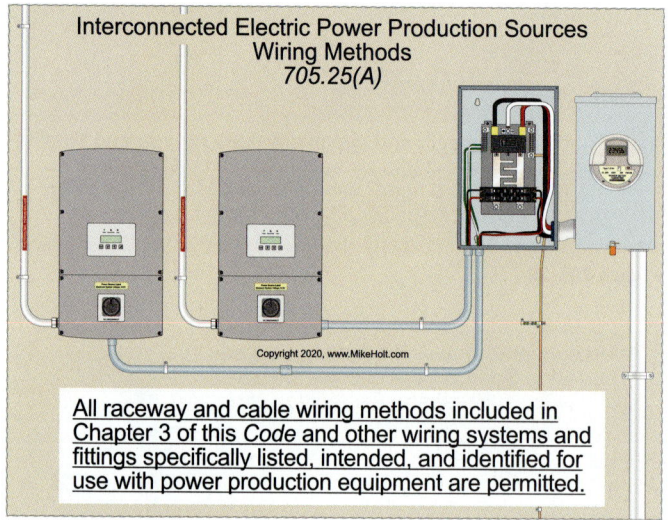

▶Figure 705-31

(B) Flexible Cords and Cables. Flexible cords and cables used to connect moving parts of a power production system, or where used for ready removal for maintenance and repair, must be in accordance with the requirements contained in Article 400. The flexible cord or cable must be listed and identified as Type DG cable, hard service cord or portable power cable, be suitable for extra-hard usage, and be listed for outdoor use and water resistant. Cables exposed to sunlight must be sunlight resistant. Flexible, fine-stranded cables must terminate on terminals, lugs, devices, or connectors identified for the use of finely stranded conductors in accordance with 110.14(A).

(C) Multiconductor Cable Assemblies. Multiconductor cable assemblies used in accordance with their listings are permitted.

Note: An ac module harness is one example of a multiconductor cable assembly.

705.28 Circuit Sizing and Current

(A) Calculation of Maximum Circuit Current. The maximum power source output circuit current is equal to the continuous output current rating of the power production equipment. ▶Figure 705-32

Interconnected Electric Power Production Sources | 705.30

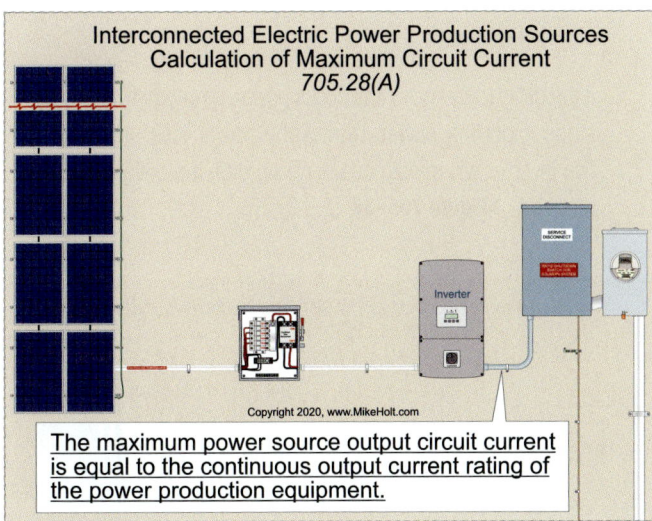
▶Figure 705-32

(B) Conductor Ampacity. Circuit conductors must be sized to the largest of the following:

(1) One hundred twenty-five percent of the maximum continuous output current rating of the power production equipment [705.28(A)] without conductor ampacity correction and/or adjustment.

(2) One hundred percent of the maximum continuous output current rating of the power production equipment [705.28(A)] after conductor ampacity correction and/or adjustment.

(3) Where circuit conductors are tapped to feeders, the tap conductors must have an ampacity as calculated in accordance with 240.21(B) [705.12(B)(2)]. ▶Figure 705-33

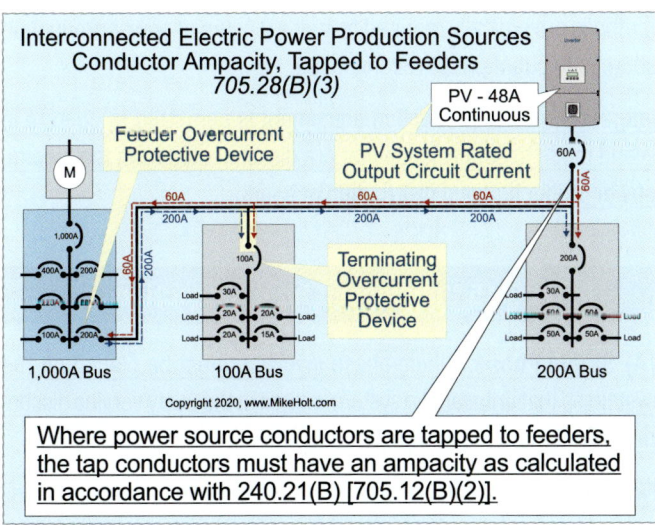
▶Figure 705-33

(C) Neutral Conductors. Neutral conductors may be sized in accordance with either of the following:

(1) Single-Phase Line-to-Neutral Power Sources. The ampacity of a neutral conductor to which a single-phase line-to-neutral power source is connected is not permitted to be less than the ampacity calculation in accordance with 705.28(B).

(2) Neutral Conductor for Instrumentation, Voltage Detection, or Phase Detection. A neutral conductor to power production equipment that is used solely for instrumentation, voltage detection, or phase detection is permitted to be sized in accordance with Table 250.102(C)(1).

705.30 Overcurrent Protection

(A) Circuits and Equipment. Power source output circuit conductors must be provided with overcurrent protection. Circuits connected to more than one electrical power source must have overcurrent protection located so as to provide overcurrent protection from all sources of power. ▶Figure 705-34

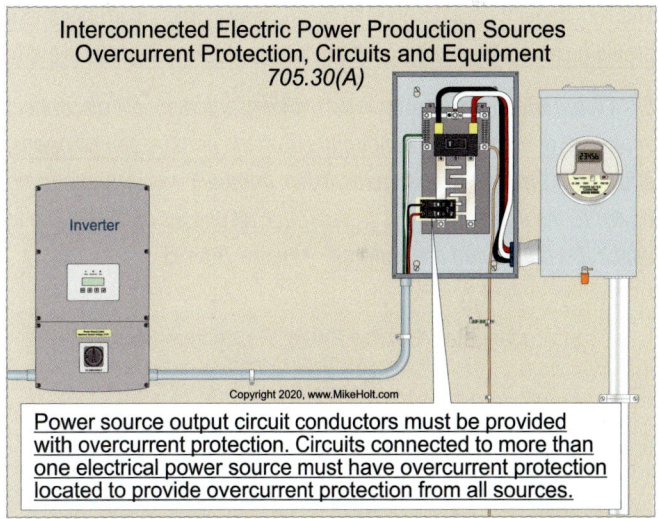
▶Figure 705-34

(B) Overcurrent Device Ratings. The overcurrent protective device must have an ampere rating of not less than 125 percent of the maximum current as calculated in 705.28(A).

Ex: Where the assembly, together with its overcurrent device(s) is listed for continuous operation at 100 percent of its rating, the overcurrent device is permitted to be sized at 100 percent of the maximum current calculated in 705.28(A).

(C) Power Transformers. Transformers with a source of power on each side (inverter and utility) are required to have overcurrent protection in accordance with 450.3(B) by considering the utility-powered side of the transformer as the primary.

705.32 | Interconnected Electric Power Production Sources

705.32 Ground-Fault Protection

Where a ground-fault protection of equipment (GFPE) device is installed in accordance with 230.95, the output of an interactive system must be connected to the supply side of the GFPE device.

Ex: The output connection of an interactive system is permitted to be made to the load side of the ground-fault protection, if ground-fault protection for equipment from all ground-fault current sources is provided.

705.40 Loss of Utility Power

The output of power production equipment must automatically disconnect from all phase conductors of the interconnected systems when one or more of the primary source (utility) phases opens. The power production equipment cannot be reconnected to the primary source of power until all the phases of the interconnected system to which it's connected are restored.

This requirement does not apply to electric power production equipment providing power to an emergency or legally required standby system.

Ex: A listed interactive inverter is permitted to automatically disconnect when one or more phase conductors from the primary source opens, and it is permitted to automatically or manually resume exporting power to the interconnected system once all phases of the source to which it is connected are restored. ▶Figure 705-35

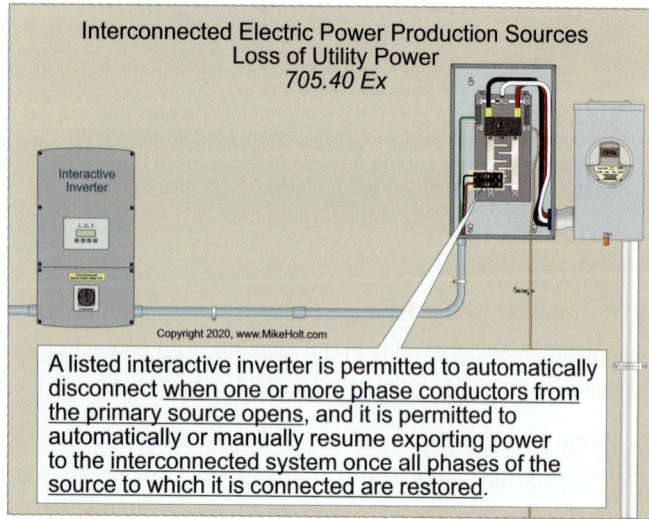

▶Figure 705-35

Author's Comment:

▶ If the utility (primary source) loses power, an interactive inverter stops exporting power. During the power loss, an interactive inverter will remain de-energized until the utility power is restored. ▶Figure 705-36

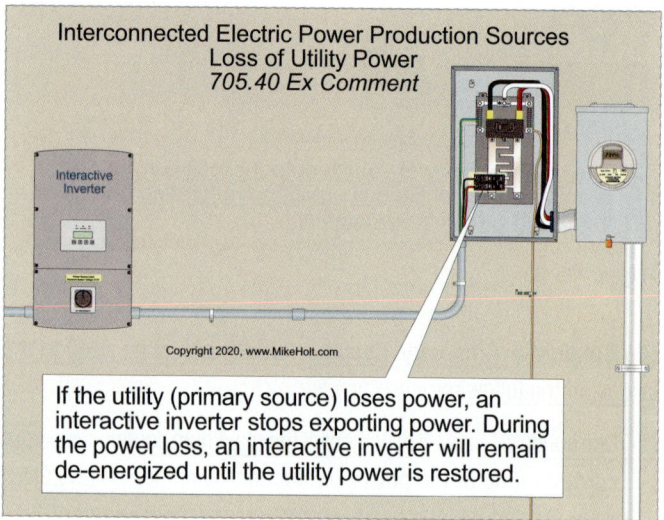

▶Figure 705-36

Note 1: Risks to personnel and equipment associated with the primary source could occur if an interactive electric power production source is set to operate as an intentional island. Special detection methods are required to determine that a primary source supply system outage has occurred and whether there should be automatic disconnection. When the primary source supply system is restored, special detection methods are typically required to limit exposure of power production sources to out-of-phase reconnection.

Interactive power production equipment is permitted to operate in island mode to supply loads that are disconnected from the electric power production and distribution network.

705.45 Unbalanced Interconnections

(A) Single-Phase. Single-phase inverters must be placed on the system so that unbalanced system voltage at the utility service disconnect is not more than three percent.

Note: For interactive power sources, unbalanced voltages can be minimized by the same methods that are used for single-phase loads on a three-phase power system. See ANSI/C84.1, *Electric Power Systems and Equipment—Voltage Ratings (60 Hertz).*

Interconnected Electric Power Production Sources | 705.45

Author's Comment:

▸ ANSI C84.1, *Electric Power Systems and Equipment—Voltage Ratings (60 Hertz)* recommends that "electric supply systems should be designed to limit the maximum voltage unbalance to three percent when measured at the electric-utility revenue meter under no-load conditions." Connecting multiple single-phase inverters to a three-phase system can result in an increase in unbalanced system voltage.

▸ The formula to determine the maximum unbalanced voltage is: **Maximum Unbalanced Voltage = Maximum Deviation from Average Voltage/Average Voltage x 100%**.

▸ Existing Installation Example

Question: If two single-phase PV systems are connected to lines B-C and this causes the B-C voltage to increase from 200V to 202V because of a decrease in loading, the maximum unbalanced system voltage for the following line voltages: A-B 206V, B-C 202V, and A-C 204V will be _____ percent.

(a) 1 (b) 1.50 (c) 2.04 (d) 3

Solution:

Maximum Unbalanced Voltage = Maximum Deviation Volts from Average Voltage/Average Voltage x 100%

Average Voltage = (206V + 202V + 204V)/3 lines
Average Voltage = 612V/3 lines
Average Voltage = 204V

Maximum Deviation from Average = 206V–204V
Maximum Deviation from Average = 2V

Maximum Unbalanced Voltage = 2V/204V x 100%
Maximum Unbalancod Voltage = .0098 x 100%
Maximum Unbalanced Voltage = 1%

Answer: (a) 1

▸ Unbalanced System Voltage—Two Inverters Example 1

Question: If two single-phase PV systems are connected to lines B-C and this results in the B-C voltage increasing from 200V to 201V because of a decrease in loading, the maximum unbalanced system voltage for the following line voltages: A-B 206V, B-C 201V, and A-C 204V will be _____ percent.

(a) 1 (b) 1.15 (c) 1.50 (d) 2.06

Solution:

Maximum Unbalanced Voltage = Maximum Deviation from Average Voltage/Average Voltage x 100%.

Average Voltage = (206V + 201V + 204V)/3 lines
Average Voltage = 611V/3 lines
Average Voltage = 203.67V

Maximum Deviation from Average = 206V–203.67V
Maximum Deviation from Average = 2.33V

Maximum Unbalanced Voltage = 2.33V/203.66V x 100%
Maximum Unbalanced Voltage = .0114 x 100%
Maximum Unbalanced Voltage = 1.15%

Answer: (b) 1.15

▸ Unbalanced System Voltage—Two Inverters Example 2

Question: If two single-phase PV systems are connected to lines A-B and this causes the A-B voltage to increase from 206V to 208V because of a decrease in loading, the maximum unbalanced system voltage for the following line voltages: A-B 208V, B-C 200V, and A-C 204V will be _____ percent.

(a) 1 (b) 1.15 (c) 1.50 (d) 1.96

Solution:

Maximum Unbalanced Voltage = Maximum Deviation from Average Voltage/Average Voltage x 100% (for Percent).

Average Voltage = (208V + 200V + 204V)/3 lines
Average Voltage = 612V/3 lines
Average Voltage = 204V

Maximum Deviation from Average = 208V–204V
Maximum Deviation from Average = 4V

Maximum Unbalanced Voltage = 4V/204V x 100%
Maximum Unbalanced Voltage = .0196 x 100%
Maximum Unbalanced Voltage = 1.96%

Answer: (d) 1.96

(B) Three-Phase. Three-phase inverters must have all phases automatically de-energized upon loss of, or unbalanced voltage in one or more phases unless the inverter is designed so that significant unbalanced voltages will not result.

705.50 | Interconnected Electric Power Production Sources

Part II. Microgrid Systems

705.50 System Operation

Microgrid systems are permitted to disconnect from the primary source of power or other interconnected electric power production sources and operate as an isolated microgrid system operating in island mode.

705.60 Primary Power Source Connection

Connections to primary power sources that are external to the microgrid system must comply with the requirements of 705.11, 705.12, or 705.13.

Power source conductors connecting to a microgrid system, including conductors supplying distribution equipment, are considered power source output conductors.

ARTICLE 706 — ENERGY STORAGE SYSTEMS

Introduction to Article 706—Energy Storage Systems

The addition of Article 706 to the *Code* during the 2017 revision cycle recognized the important role that energy storage would play to manage the massive amounts of grid-connected energy production from alternative sources such as wind and solar. Because of the need to store this energy, the *NEC* Correlating Committee formed a 79-member task group (along with input from many other sources) to develop the requirements contained within this article.

It is important to understand what Article 706 does and does not apply to. The scope says it applies to all permanently installed energy storage systems (ESS) "having a capacity greater than 1 kWh." They may be stand-alone or interactive with other electric power production sources. Although much of the original language used to create Article 706 came from deleted sections of Article 690 Solar Photovoltaic (PV) Systems, an ESS can store energy from any power source; there are no restrictions.

An energy storage system consists of one or more components that (when assembled together) is capable of storing electrical energy for future use. An energy storage system (ESS) might include (but is not limited to) batteries, capacitors, and kinetic energy devices (such as flywheels and compressed air). Some of these systems will have either ac or dc output available. They may also include inverters and converters to change stored energy into electrical energy. An ESS might directly power loads such as in a stand-alone system, or it might provide another energy management function like buffering energy produced by an intermittent source such as a wind or PV system.

Energy storage systems can be (and usually are) connected to other energy sources, such as the local utility distribution system. There can be more than one source of power connected to these systems and their connection to other energy sources must comply with the requirements of Article 705 which provides the rules for installations of one or more electric power production source operating in parallel with a primary source of electricity, such as a utility.

It is important to note that Article 480 (Storage Batteries) has not been removed. While this may create confusion for some struggling to understand the difference between an ESS and a battery system, the easiest way to identify the two at this point is to look for the system listing. Updates to the 2020 *NEC* now require that any ESS be listed as a system and will most often be based on the requirements of UL 9540, Standard for Energy Storage Systems and Equipment. There is no system listing requirement for battery systems in 480, and all lead-acid batteries are exempt from any listing. Unlike battery systems, an ESS often also includes other equipment such as inverters or other electronic power converters.

Part I. General

706.1 Scope

Scan this QR code for a video of Mike explaining this topic; it's a sample from the videos that accompany this textbook.
www.MikeHolt.com/20PVvideos

This article applies to all energy storage systems having a capacity greater than 1 kWh that may be stand-alone or interactive with the electric utility supply. Energy storage systems are primarily intended to store and provide energy during normal operating conditions. ▶Figure 706–1

Note 1: For batteries rated in ampere hours, kWh is equal to the battery nominal rated voltage times the battery ampere-hour rating, divided by 1,000.

706.2 | Energy Storage Systems

▶Figure 706–1

▶Figure 706–2

Author's Comment:

▸ To better understand ampere hours relative to kilo-watt hours think of your cellphone. Many cellphone batteries are rated at 3,000 mAh (milli-amp hours) which, when divided by 1,000, equal be 3 ampere hours. Lithium-ion batteries, prominent in cell phones, have a voltage of 3.70V so when multiplied by 3 ampere hours result in 11.10 watt-hours. As you probably now realize, calculating the amount of power available in a battery is simply an exercise in Ohm's Law but on a larger scale.

706.2 Definitions

The definitions in this section only apply to this article.

Energy Storage System (ESS). One or more components assembled together capable of storing energy and providing electrical energy into the premises wiring system or the electric utility supply. Figure 706–2

Note 1: Energy storage systems can include (but are not limited to) batteries, capacitors, and kinetic energy devices such as flywheels and compressed air. Energy storage systems can include inverters or converters to change voltage levels or to make a change between an alternating-current or a direct-current system.

Note 2: Energy storage systems differ from other storage systems such as a UPS system, which is a power supply that provides alternating-current power for loads for some period of time in the event of a power failure.

Flow Battery. An energy storage component similar to a fuel cell that stores its active materials in the form of two electrolytes external to the reactor interface.

Note: Two commercially available flow battery technologies are zinc bromine and vanadium redox, sometimes referred to as a pumped electrolyte energy storage system.

706.3 Qualified Personnel

The installation and maintenance of energy storage system equipment and all associated wiring and interconnections must be performed only by qualified persons.

Note: See Article 100 for the definition of "Qualified Person."

706.4 System Requirements

Each energy storage system must have a nameplate plainly visible after installation and marked with the following:

(1) Manufacturer's name, trademark, or other descriptive marking by which the organization responsible for supplying the energy storage system can be identified.

(2) Rated frequency.

(3) Number of phases if alternating current.

(4) Rating (kW or kVA).

(5) Available fault current derived by the energy storage system (ESS) at the output terminals.

(6) Maximum output and input current of the energy storage system (ESS) at the output terminals.

(7) Maximum output and input voltage of the energy storage system (ESS) at the output terminals.

(8) Utility-interactive capability if applicable.

706.5 Listing

Energy storage systems must be listed.

Author's Comment:

▸ Although the *Code* does not specify the specific standard used to list ESSs, updated building and fire codes are more specific and now increasingly require a UL 9540, *Standard for Energy Storage Systems and Equipment* listing for these systems. Annex A of the *NEC* provides references to product safety standards that the Code-Making Panels believe are generally relevant to each article.

706.6 Multiple Systems

Multiple energy storage systems are permitted in or on a single building.

Author's Comment:

▸ As with PV systems, energy storage systems may be multiple pieces of equipment assembled into a single system, or each piece of equipment may be considered an ESS on its own. The best way to identify an ESS is to look for a nameplate and review the instructions, both of which are part of the equipment's listing.

706.8 Storage Batteries

Storage batteries not associated with an energy storage system (ESS) must comply with Article 480.

Author's Comment:

▸ The difference between a storage battery as addressed in Article 480 and an ESS covered in Article 706 is not completely clear in the *NEC*. We expect this differentiation will improve in future *Code* revisions. From a practical perspective, storage batteries in Article 480 will be more limited to commercial or industrial applications for purposes such as starting generators or backing up exit lighting. The popularity of packaged and listed ESS systems utilizing new battery chemistries such as lithium-ion will continue to rise so Article 706 will be increasingly utilized for future battery storage applications. Also note that unlike Article 480, Article 706 is not just limited to battery-based energy storage.

706.9 Maximum Voltage

The maximum voltage of an energy storage system must be the rated energy storage system input and output voltage(s) indicated on the energy storage system nameplate(s) or system listing.

Part II. Disconnect

706.15 Disconnect

(A) ESS Disconnecting Means. A disconnecting means must be provided for all phase conductors derived from an energy storage system (ESS) and is permitted to be integral to listed ESS equipment. The disconnecting means must be readily accessible and located within sight of the ESS. The disconnecting means must comply with all of the following:

(1) The disconnecting means must be readily accessible.

(2) The disconnecting means must be located within sight of the ESS. Where it is impractical to install the disconnecting means within sight of the ESS, the disconnect is permitted to be installed as close as practicable, and the location of the disconnecting means must be field marked on (or immediately adjacent to) the ESS. The marking must be of sufficient durability to withstand the environment involved and must not be handwritten.

(3) The disconnecting means must be lockable in the open position in accordance with 110.25. For dwelling unit(s) the disconnect must be located at a readily accessible locations outside the building.

706.20 | Energy Storage Systems

> **Author's Comment:**
>
> ▸ It is important to note that the requirements in 706.15(A) can be met with disconnects that are integral to the listed ESS equipment. Since an ESS application may have multiple individual ESS units, each may require a disconnecting means, but this does not necessarily mean each will require a separate disconnect switch adjacent to the units. Many ESS manufacturers will choose to incorporate a means of disconnect into their ESS units. These disconnects will be evaluated during the system's listing.

(B) Remote Actuation. Where controls to activate the disconnect of an energy storage system are not located within sight of the system, the location of the controls must be field marked on the disconnect.

(C) Notification and Marking. Each energy storage system disconnect must plainly indicate whether it is in the open (off) or closed (on) position and be permanently marked:

> **ENERGY STORAGE SYSTEM DISCONNECT**

The disconnect must be legibly marked in the field to indicate the following:

(1) The nominal energy storage system alternating-current voltage and maximum energy storage system direct-current voltage.

(2) The available fault current derived from the energy storage system.

(3) An arc-flash label applied in accordance with acceptable industry practice.

(4) The date the available fault current calculation was performed.

Ex: List items (2), (3), and (4) do not apply to one- and two-family dwellings.

Note 1: Industry practices for equipment labeling are described in NFPA 70E, *Standard for Electrical Safety in the Workplace*. This standard provides specific criteria for developing arc-flash labels for equipment that provides nominal system voltage, incident energy levels, arc-flash boundaries, minimum required levels of personal protective equipment, and so forth.

Note 2: Battery equipment suppliers can provide available fault current on any particular battery model.

Where the line and load terminals within the energy storage system disconnect may be energized in the open position, the disconnect must be marked with the following words or equivalent:

> **WARNING ELECTRIC SHOCK HAZARD**
> **TERMINALS ON THE LINE AND LOAD**
> **SIDES MAY BE ENERGIZED IN THE OPEN POSITION**

The notification(s) and marking(s) must be permanently affixed and have sufficient durability to withstand the environment involved [110.21(B)].

(D) Partitions Between Components. Where circuits from the input or output terminals of energy storage components pass through a wall, floor, or ceiling, a readily accessible disconnect must be provided within sight of the energy storage component. Fused disconnects or circuit breakers are permitted to serve as the required disconnect.

> **Author's Comment:**
>
> ▸ It is important to note that 706.15(D) will not apply to every ESS application where circuit conductors travel through walls, floors, or ceilings. This section is for those applications (typically large ones) where the battery is in one room and other equipment that is part of the ESS is in another. In those cases, a disconnect must be located in the room containing the battery. This does not apply to situations where the entire ESS is in one room and the output circuit from the ESS connects to other systems in other rooms. In those cases, the disconnect location requirements in 706.15(A) are all that apply.

Part III. Installation Requirements

706.20 General

(A) Ventilation. Provisions appropriate to the energy storage technology must be made for sufficient diffusion and ventilation of any possible gases from the storage device (if present) to prevent the accumulation of an explosive mixture. A pre-engineered or self-contained energy storage system is permitted to provide ventilation in accordance with the manufacturer's recommendations and listing for the system.

Note 1: See NFPA 1, *Fire Code*, Chapter 52, for ventilation considerations for specific battery chemistries.

Note 2: Some storage technologies do not require ventilation.

Note 3: Sources for the design of ventilation of battery systems are IEEE 1635-2012/ASHRAE Guideline 21, *Guide for the Ventilation and Thermal Management of Batteries for Stationary Applications*, and the UBC.

Note 4: Fire protection considerations are addressed in NFPA 1, *Fire Code*.

Author's Comment:

▸ To meet unique requirements such as ventilation of an ESS, the manufacturer's instructions included in the product's listing must be used. Requiring energy storage systems to be listed means installers will not be asked to calculate things such as proper ventilation. They will simply comply with the installation instructions, much like they do with other electrical equipment.

(B) Dwelling Units. Energy storage systems for one- and two-family dwelling units are not permitted to have a direct-current voltage greater than 100V between conductors or to ground.

Ex: Where live parts are not accessible during routine energy storage system maintenance, a maximum energy storage system voltage of 600V dc is permitted.

Author's Comment:

▸ Since an ESS may have alternating-current output, there will be many cases where the voltage limits in 706.20(B) will not even be considered by installers or inspectors since the dc voltages will be internal to the equipment and therefore covered under the equipment's listing.

(C) Spaces About Energy Storage System Components.

(1) General. Working spaces for energy storage systems must be in accordance with 110.26.

(2) Space Between Components. Energy storage systems are permitted to have space between components in accordance with the manufacturer's instructions and listing.

Note: Additional space may be needed to accommodate energy storage system hoisting equipment, tray removal, or spill containment.

706.21 Directory (Identification of Power Sources)

Energy storage systems must be identified by markings or labels that are permanently affixed with sufficient durability to withstand the environment involved [110.21(B)].

(A) Facilities with Utility Services and Energy Storage Systems. Plaques or directories must be installed in accordance with 705.10.

Part IV. Circuit Requirements

706.30 Circuit Sizing and Current

(A) Maximum Rated Current for a Specific Circuit. The maximum current for a specific circuit must be calculated in accordance with the following.

(1) Nameplate-Rated Circuit Current. Circuit current must be the rated current indicated on the energy storage system nameplate(s) or system listing. Where the energy storage system has separate input (charge) and output (discharge) circuits or ratings, they must be considered individually. Where the same terminals on the energy storage system are used for charging and discharging, the rated current must be the greater of the two.

(2) Inverter Output Circuit Current. The maximum current must be the inverter's continuous output current rating.

(3) Inverter Input Circuit Current. The maximum current must be the continuous inverter input current rating when the inverter is producing its rated power at the lowest input voltage.

(4) Inverter Utilization Output Circuit Current. The maximum current must be the continuous alternating-current output current rating of the inverter when the inverter is producing its rated power.

(5) DC-to-DC Converter Output Current. The maximum current must be the dc-to-dc converter's continuous output current rating.

(B) Conductor Ampacity. The ampacity of the feeder circuit conductors from the energy storage system(s) to the wiring system serving the loads to be serviced by the system must not be less than the greater of the (1) nameplate(s)-rated circuit current as determined in accordance with 706.30(A)(1), or (2) the rating of the energy storage system's overcurrent protective device(s).

(C) Ampacity of Grounded or Neutral Conductor. If the output of a single-phase, 2-wire energy storage system output(s) is connected to the grounded or neutral conductor and a single-phase conductor of a 3-wire system or of a three-phase, 4-wire, wye-connected system, the maximum unbalanced neutral load current plus the energy storage system(s) output rating must not exceed the ampacity of the grounded or neutral conductor.

706.31 | Energy Storage Systems

706.31 Overcurrent Protection

(A) Circuits and Equipment. Energy storage system circuit conductors must be protected in accordance with the requirements of Article 240. Protective devices for energy storage system circuits must be in accordance with the requirements of 706.31(B) through (F), and circuits must be protected at the source from overcurrent.

(B) Overcurrent Device Ampere Ratings. Overcurrent protective devices, where required, must be rated in accordance with Article 240 and the rating provided on systems serving the energy storage system and must be not less than 125 percent of the maximum currents calculated in 706.30(A).

Ex: Where the assembly (including the overcurrent protective devices) is listed for operation at 100 percent of its rating, the ampere rating of the overcurrent devices is permitted to be not less than the maximum currents calculated in 706.30(B).

(C) Direct-Current Rating. Overcurrent protective devices, either fuses or circuit breakers, used in any direct-current portion of an energy storage system must be listed for direct current and have the appropriate voltage, current, and interrupting ratings for the application.

(D) Current Limiting. A listed and labeled current-limiting overcurrent protective device must be installed adjacent to the energy storage system for each direct-current output circuit.

Ex: Where current-limiting overcurrent protection is provided for the direct-current output circuits of a listed energy storage system, additional current-limiting overcurrent devices are not required.

(E) Fuses. Means must be provided to disconnect any fuses associated with energy storage system equipment and components when the fuse is energized from both directions and is accessible to other than qualified persons. Switches, pullouts, or similar devices that are rated for the application are permitted to serve as a means to disconnect fuses from all sources of supply.

(F) Location. Where circuits from the input or output terminals of energy storage components in an energy storage system pass through a wall, floor, or ceiling, overcurrent protection must be provided at the energy storage component of the circuit.

> **Author's Comment:**
>
> ▸ As with 706.15(D), this one will not apply to every ESS application where circuit conductors travel through walls, floors, or ceilings. This section is for those applications (typically large ones) where the battery is in one room and other equipment that is part of that ESS system is located in another.

706.33 Charge Control

(A) General. Provisions must be provided to control the charging process of the energy storage system. All adjustable means for control of the charging process must be accessible only to qualified persons.

(B) Diversion Charge Controller.

(1) Sole Means of Regulating Charging. An energy storage system employing a diversion charge controller as the sole means of regulating charging must be equipped with a second independent means to prevent overcharging of the storage device.

(2) Circuits with Diversion Charge Controller and Diversion Load. Circuits containing a diversion charge controller and a diversion load must comply with the following:

(1) The current rating of the diversion load must be less than or equal to the current rating of the diversion load charge controller. The voltage rating of the diversion load must be greater than the maximum energy storage system voltage. The power rating of the diversion load must be at least 150 percent of the power rating of the charging source.

(2) The conductor ampacity and the rating of the overcurrent device for this circuit must be at least 150 percent of the maximum current rating of the diversion charge controller.

(3) Energy Storage System Using Interactive Inverters. Systems using interactive inverters to control energy storage state-of-charge by diverting excess power into an alternate electric power production and distribution system, such as utility, must comply with 706.33(B)(3)(a) and (b).

(a) These systems are not required to comply with 706.33(B)(2).

(b) These systems must have a second, independent means of controlling the energy storage system charging process for use when the alternate system is not available, or when the primary charge controller fails or is disabled.

(C) Charge Controllers and DC-to-DC Converters. Where charge controllers and other dc-to-dc power converters that increase or decrease the output current or output voltage with respect to the input current or input voltage are installed, all of the following apply:

(1) The ampacity of the conductors in output circuits must be based on the maximum rated continuous output current of the charge controller or converter for the selected output voltage range.

(2) The voltage rating of the output circuits must be based on the maximum voltage output of the charge controller or converter for the selected output voltage range.

Part V. Flow Battery Energy Storage Systems

Part V applies to energy storage systems composed of, or containing, flow batteries.

Note: Due to the unique design features and difference in operating characteristics of flow batteries as compared with that of storage batteries such as lead acid or lithium ion batteries, the requirements for flow batteries have been included here rather than in Article 480.

Notes

ARTICLE 710 — STAND-ALONE SYSTEMS

Introduction to Article 710—Stand-Alone Systems

Stand-alone power production sources are what the name implies; they are not connected to the utility power grid or any other power production/distribution network.

The wiring for stand-alone systems must comply with Chapters 1 through 4 of the *NEC*. Depending on the purpose and design of a particular stand-alone source, the wiring might need to comply with Chapter 6 and other articles in Chapter 7.

Occupying about half a page, this article is one of the shortest in the *Code*, but its brevity does not imply insignificance. In fact, it will take on increasing significance as the growth in stand-alone system installations continues. Many of these are systems that use solar or other "alternative energy" sources, but fossil fuel sources are also in the mix.

710.1 Scope

This article covers electric power production systems that operate in island mode and are not connected to an electric utility supply. ▶Figure 710–1

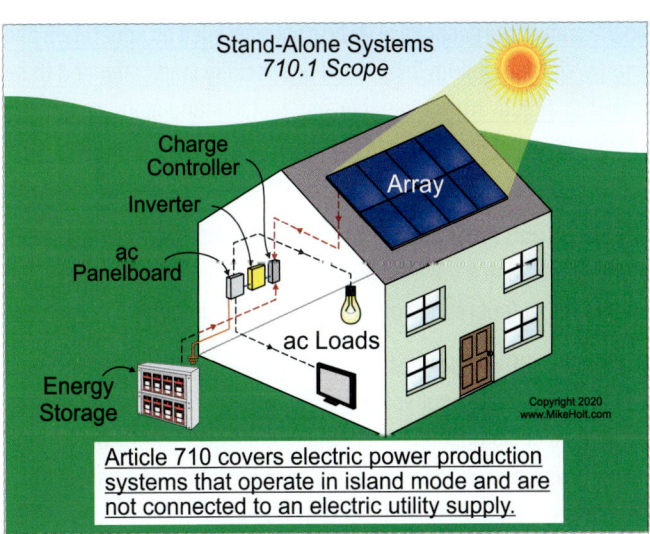

▶Figure 710–1

Note: Stand-alone systems are capable of operating in island mode, independent from the electric utility, and include isolated microgrid systems or they can be interactive with other power sources. Stand-alone systems often include a single or a compatible interconnection of sources such as engine generators, solar PV, wind, an energy storage system, or batteries.

Author's Comment:

▶ According to Article 100, "Island Mode" is the operational mode for stand-alone power production equipment, an isolated microgrid, multimode inverter, or an interconnected microgrid that is disconnected from the electric utility supply.

710.6 Equipment Approval

Stand-alone equipment must be approved for the intended use in accordance with one of the following: ▶Figure 710–2

(1) Be listed for the application.

(2) Be evaluated for the application and have a field label applied.

Note: Inverters identified as "multimode" and "stand-alone" are specifically identified and certified to operate in this application. Stand-alone inverters operate only in island mode. Multimode inverters operate in either island mode or interactive mode setting. A multimode inverter operates in island mode when it is not connected to an electric utility supply. Stand-alone inverters are not evaluated and are not intended for connection to export power in parallel with an electric utility.

710.10 | Stand-Alone Systems

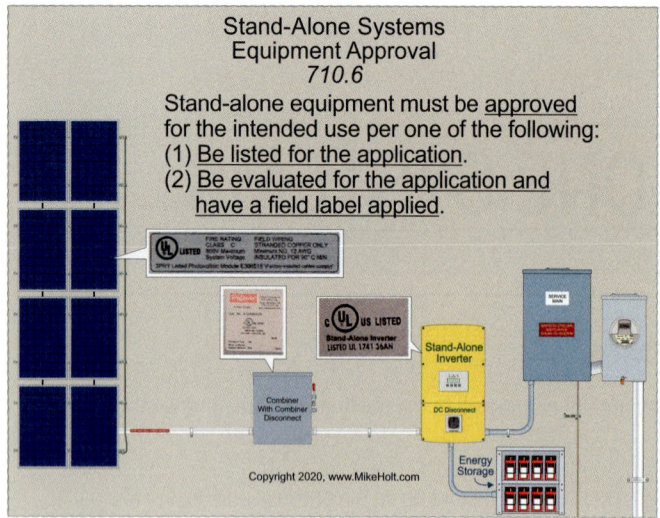
▶Figure 710–2

Where multiple sources supply the building, the plaque or directory must be marked with the wording "CAUTION: MULTIPLE SOURCES OF POWER." The marking must be permanently affixed with sufficient durability to withstand the environment involved [110.21(B)].

Ex: Installations with multiple co-located power production sources can be identified as a group(s). The plaque or directory is not required to identify each power source individually.

710.12 Stand-Alone Inverter Input Circuit Current

The maximum inverter input current is the continuous inverter input current rating when the inverter is producing its rated power at the lowest input voltage.

710.15 General

The wiring on the supply side of the building disconnect must comply with the following:

(A) Supply Output. The power supply to premises wiring systems fed by stand-alone or isolated microgrid power sources can have a capacity that is less than the calculated load, but it must not be less than the largest single utilization equipment connected to the stand-alone system.

Note: For general-use loads, the stand-alone system capacity is based on the sum of the capacity of all firm sources such as generators and energy storage system inverters. For specialty loads intended to be powered directly from a variable source, the stand-alone capacity is calculated using the sum of the variable sources, such as PV or wind inverters, or the combined capacity of both firm and variable sources.

(B) Sizing and Protection. The circuit conductors between a stand-alone source and a building disconnect must be sized based on the sum of the output ratings of the stand-alone source(s).

(C) Single 120V Supply. Stand-alone and isolated microgrid systems can supply 2-wire, single-phase, 120V or 3-wire, 120/240V service equipment or distribution panels where there are no 240V outlets and no multiwire circuits. Service equipment or distribution panels must be marked with the following words or equivalent:

> **WARNING: SINGLE 120-VOLT SUPPLY. DO NOT CONNECT MULTIWIRE BRANCH CIRCUITS!**

Author's Comment:

▶ According to Article 100, a "Multimode Inverter" is equipment having the capabilities of both interactive and stand-alone inverters. ▶Figure 710–3

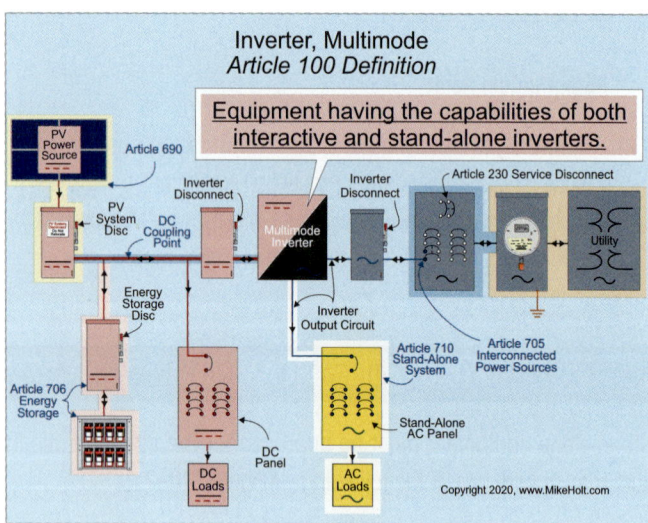
▶Figure 710–3

710.10 Identification of Power Sources

A permanent plaque or directory must be installed at the service equipment location or an approved readily visible location for a building supplied by a stand-alone system. The plaque or directory must identify the location of each power source disconnect or be grouped with other plaques or directories for other on-site sources.

Stand-Alone Systems | **710.15**

(E) Energy Storage or Backup Power System Requirements. Stand-alone system are not required to have energy storage or backup power.

(F) Backfed Circuit Breakers. Plug-in type backfed circuit breakers must be secured in accordance with 408.36(D). **Figure 710–4**

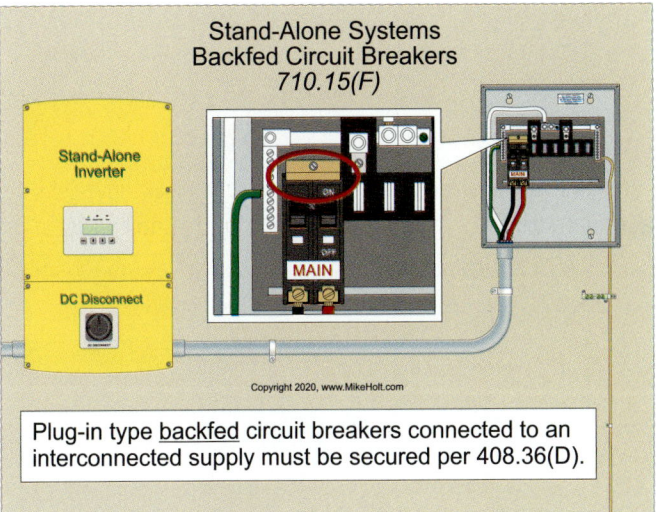

▶Figure 710–4

Notes

PRACTICE QUESTIONS

Please use the 2020 *Code* book to answer the following questions.

Article 90—Introduction to the *National Electrical Code*

1. The *NEC* is _____.
   (a) intended to be a design manual
   (b) meant to be used as an instruction guide for untrained persons
   (c) for the practical safeguarding of persons and property
   (d) published by the Bureau of Standards

2. Compliance with the provisions of the *NEC* will result in _____.
   (a) good electrical service
   (b) an efficient electrical system
   (c) an electrical system essentially free from hazard
   (d) all of these

3. Electrical hazards often occur because the initial _____ did not provide for increases in the use of electricity and therefore wiring systems become overloaded.
   (a) inspection
   (b) owner
   (c) wiring
   (d) builder

4. Which of the following systems shall be installed and removed in accordance with the *NEC* requirements?
   (a) Signaling conductors, equipment, and raceways
   (b) Communications conductors, equipment, and raceway
   (c) Electrical conductors, equipment, and raceways
   (d) all of these

5. This *Code* covers the installation of _____ for public and private premises including buildings, structures, mobile homes, recreational vehicles, and floating buildings.
   (a) optical fiber cables
   (b) electrical equipment
   (c) raceways
   (d) all of these

6. Installations used to export electric power from vehicles to premises wiring or for _____ current flow are covered by the *NEC*.
   (a) emergency
   (b) primary
   (c) bidirectional
   (d) secondary

7. The *NEC* does not cover electrical installations in ships, watercraft, railway rolling stock, aircraft, or automotive vehicles.
   (a) True
   (b) False

8. Installations of communications equipment that are under the exclusive control of communications utilities and located outdoors or in building spaces used exclusively for such installations _____ covered by the *NEC*.
   (a) are
   (b) are sometimes
   (c) are not
   (d) may be

Article 100 | Practice Questions

9. Chapters 1 through 4 of the *NEC* apply _____.

    (a) generally to all electrical installations
    (b) only to special occupancies and conditions
    (c) only to special equipment and material
    (d) all of these

10. Chapters 5, 6, and 7 of the *NEC* apply to _____.

    (a) special occupancies
    (b) special equipment
    (c) special conditions
    (d) all of these

11. The authority having jurisdiction has the responsibility for _____.

    (a) making interpretations of rules
    (b) deciding upon the approval of equipment and materials
    (c) waiving specific requirements in the *Code* and permitting alternate methods and material if safety is maintained
    (d) all of these

12. If the *NEC* requires new products that are not yet available at the time a new edition is adopted, the _____ may permit the use of the products that comply with the most recent previous edition of the *Code* adopted by that jurisdiction.

    (a) electrical engineer
    (b) master electrician
    (c) authority having jurisdiction
    (d) permit holder

13. When the *Code* uses "_____," it means the identified actions are allowed but not required, and they may be options or alternative methods.

    (a) shall
    (b) shall not
    (c) shall be permitted
    (d) shall or shall not

14. Explanatory material, such as references to other standards, references to related sections of the *NEC*, or information related to a *Code* rule, are included in the form of Informational Notes.

    (a) True
    (b) False

15. It is the intent of the *NEC* that factory-installed _____ wiring of listed equipment need not be inspected at the time of installation of the equipment, except to detect alterations or damage.

    (a) external
    (b) associated
    (c) internal
    (d) all of these

CHAPTER 1—GENERAL RULES

Article 100—Definitions

1. Article 100 contains only those definitions essential to the application of the *Code*. Definitions are also found in _____.

    (a) the index
    (b) the annex
    (c) the xxx.2 sections of other articles
    (d) the scope of each article

2. The maximum current, in amperes, that a conductor can carry continuously under the conditions of use, where the temperature will not be raised in excess of the conductor's insulation temperature rating is called its "_____."

    (a) short-circuit rating
    (b) ground-fault rating
    (c) ampacity
    (d) all of these

3. A "_____" is an area that includes a sink (basin) with a toilet, urinal, tub, shower, bidet, or similar plumbing fixtures.

    (a) bath area
    (b) bathroom
    (c) rest area
    (d) master suite

4. The connection between the grounded circuit conductor and the supply-side bonding jumper or equipment grounding conductor, or both, at a _____ is called a "system bonding jumper."

    (a) service disconnect
    (b) separately derived system
    (c) motor control center
    (d) separate building or structure disconnect

5. A circuit breaker is a device designed to open and close a circuit by nonautomatic means and to _____ the circuit automatically on a predetermined overcurrent without damage to itself when properly applied within its rating.

   (a) energize
   (b) reset
   (c) connect
   (d) open

6. A unit of an electrical system, other than a conductor, that carries or controls electric energy as its principal function is a(n) "_____."

   (a) raceway
   (b) fitting
   (c) device
   (d) enclosure

7. Surrounded by a case, housing, fence, or wall(s) that prevents persons from accidentally contacting energized parts is called "_____."

   (a) guarded
   (b) covered
   (c) protection
   (d) enclosed

8. A(n) _____ that performs field evaluations of electrical or other equipment is known as a "Field Evaluation Body (FEB)."

   (a) home inspector
   (b) field installer
   (c) organization or part of an organization
   (d) insurance underwriter

9. The word "Earth" best describes what *NEC* term?

   (a) Bonded
   (b) Ground
   (c) Effective ground-fault current path
   (d) Guarded

10. A(n) "_____" is a conductive path(s) that is part of an effective ground-fault current path and connects normally noncurrent-carrying metal parts of equipment together and to the system grounded conductor or to the grounding electrode conductor, or both.

    (a) grounding electrode conductor
    (b) main bonding jumper
    (c) system bonding jumper
    (d) equipment grounding conductor

11. A "_____" is an accommodation that combines living, sleeping, sanitary, and storage facilities within a compartment.

    (a) guest room
    (b) guest suite
    (c) dwelling unit
    (d) single-family dwelling

12. An electric power production system that is operating in parallel with and capable of delivering energy to an electric primary source supply system defines a(n) "_____ system."

    (a) hybrid
    (b) inverted
    (c) interactive
    (d) internal

13. The operational mode for stand-alone power production equipment defines the term "_____ mode."

    (a) island
    (b) isolation
    (c) isolated
    (d) standby

14. Conduit installed underground or encased in concrete slabs that are in direct contact with the earth is considered a _____ location.

    (a) dry
    (b) damp
    (c) wet
    (d) moist

15. An overload is the same as a short circuit or ground fault.

    (a) True
    (b) False

Article 110 | Practice Questions

16. Premises wiring includes _____ wiring from the service point or power source to the outlets.

    (a) interior
    (b) exterior
    (c) underground
    (d) interior and exterior

17. A raintight enclosure is constructed or protected so that exposure to a beating rain will not result in the entrance of water under specified test conditions.

    (a) True
    (b) False

18. "Underground service conductors" are the underground conductors between the service point and the first point of connection to the service-entrance conductors in a terminal box, meter, or other enclosure, _____ the building wall.

    (a) inside or outside
    (b) concealed within
    (c) above
    (d) below

19. A "service drop" is defined as the overhead conductors between the utility electric supply system and the _____.

    (a) service equipment
    (b) service point
    (c) grounding electrode
    (d) equipment grounding conductor

20. The "_____" is the necessary equipment, usually consisting of a circuit breaker(s) or switch(es) and fuse(s) and their accessories, connected to the load end of service conductors, and intended to constitute the main control and cutoff of the supply.

    (a) service equipment
    (b) service
    (c) service disconnect
    (d) service overcurrent device

21. The "_____" is the point of connection between the facilities of the serving utility and the premises wiring.

    (a) service entrance
    (b) service point
    (c) overcurrent protection
    (d) beginning of the wiring system

22. The "voltage of a circuit" is defined by the *Code* as the _____ root-mean-square (effective) difference of potential between any two conductors of the circuit concerned.

    (a) lowest
    (b) greatest
    (c) average
    (d) nominal

23. A(n) "_____" enclosure is constructed or protected so that exposure to the weather will not interfere with successful operation.

    (a) weatherproof
    (b) weathertight
    (c) weather-resistant
    (d) all weather

Article 110—Requirements for Electrical Installations

24. General requirements for the examination and approval, installation and use, access to and spaces about electrical conductors and equipment; enclosures intended for personnel entry; and tunnel installations are within the scope of _____.

    (a) Article 800
    (b) Article 300
    (c) Article 110
    (d) Annex J

25. Listed or labeled equipment shall be installed and used in accordance with any instructions included in the listing or labeling.

    (a) True
    (b) False

26. Conductor sizes are expressed in American Wire Gage (AWG) or in _____.

    (a) inches
    (b) circular mils
    (c) square inches
    (d) cubic inches

27. Equipment intended to interrupt current at fault levels shall have an interrupting rating at nominal circuit voltage at least equal to the current that is available at the line terminals of the equipment.

    (a) True
    (b) False

28. Equipment not _____ for outdoor use and equipment identified only for indoor use such, as "dry locations" or "indoor use only," shall be protected against damage from the weather during construction.

    (a) listed
    (b) identified
    (c) suitable
    (d) marked

29. The NEC requires that electrical equipment be _____.

    (a) installed in a neat and workmanlike manner
    (b) installed under the supervision of a licensed person
    (c) completed before being inspected
    (d) all of these

30. Cables and conductors installed exposed on the surfaces of ceilings and sidewalls shall be secured by hardware including straps, staples, cable ties, hangers, or _____ fittings designed and installed so as not to damage the cable.

    (a) approved
    (b) identified
    (c) listed
    (d) similar

31. Connectors and terminals for conductors more finely stranded than Class B and Class C, as shown in Table 10 of Chapter 9, shall be _____ for the specific conductor class or classes.

    (a) listed
    (b) approved
    (c) identified
    (d) all of these

32. All _____ shall be covered with an insulation equivalent to that of the conductors or with an identified insulating device.

    (a) splices
    (b) joints
    (c) free ends of conductors
    (d) all of these

33. Conductors shall have their ampacity determined using the _____ column of Table 310.16 for circuits rated over 100A, or marked for conductors larger than 1 AWG, unless the equipment terminals are listed for use with higher temperature-rated conductors.

    (a) 30°C
    (b) 60°C
    (c) 75°C
    (d) 90°C

34. Tightening torque values for terminal connections shall be as indicated on equipment or in installation instructions provided by the manufacturer. An approved means shall be used to achieve the _____ torque value.

    (a) indicated
    (b) identified
    (c) maximum
    (d) minimum

Article 110 | Practice Questions

35. Electrical equipment such as switchboards, switchgear, panelboards, industrial control panels, meter socket enclosures, and motor control centers, that are in other than dwelling units, and are likely to require _____ while energized, shall be field or factory marked to warn qualified persons of potential electric arc-flash hazards.

    (a) examination
    (b) adjustment
    (c) servicing or maintenance
    (d) any of these

36. NFPA 70E, *Standard for Electrical Safety in the Workplace*, provides guidance, such as determining severity of potential exposure, planning safe work practices, arc-flash labeling, and selecting _____.

    (a) personal protective equipment
    (b) coordinated overcurrent protective devices
    (c) emergency egress plans
    (d) fire suppression systems

37. Reconditioned equipment shall be marked with the _____ by which the organization responsible for reconditioning the electrical equipment can be identified, along with the date of the reconditioning.

    (a) name
    (b) trademark
    (c) descriptive marking
    (d) any of these

38. Reconditioned equipment's original listing mark may include the mark of the certifying body and not the entire equipment label.

    (a) True
    (b) False

39. The *NEC* requires tested series-rated installations of circuit breakers or fuses to be legibly marked in the field to indicate the equipment has been applied with a series combination rating.

    (a) True
    (b) False

40. When modifications to the electrical installation occur that affect the maximum available fault current at the service, the maximum available fault current shall be verified or _____ as necessary to ensure the service equipment ratings are sufficient for the maximum available fault current at the line terminals of the equipment.

    (a) recalculated
    (b) increased
    (c) decreased
    (d) adjusted

41. Access and _____ shall be provided and maintained about all electrical equipment to permit ready and safe operation and maintenance of such equipment.

    (a) ventilation
    (b) cleanliness
    (c) circulation
    (d) working space

42. Working space distances for enclosed live parts shall be measured from the _____ of equipment or apparatus, if the live parts are enclosed.

    (a) enclosure or opening
    (b) front or back
    (c) mounting pad
    (d) footprint

43. Concrete, brick, or tile walls are considered _____, as applied to working space requirements.

    (a) inconsequential
    (b) in the way
    (c) grounded
    (d) free from hazards

44. The required working space for access to live parts of equipment operating at 300 volts-to-ground, where there are exposed live parts on both sides of the workspace is _____ ft.

    (a) 3
    (b) 3½
    (c) 4
    (d) 4½

45. Where equipment operating at 1,000 volts, nominal, or less to ground and likely to require examination, adjustment, servicing, or maintenance while energized is required by installation instructions or function to be located in a space with limited access, and where equipment is installed above a lay-in ceiling, there shall be an opening not smaller than _____.

    (a) 6 in. × 6 in.
    (b) 12 in. × 12 in.
    (c) 22 in. × 22 in.
    (d) 22 in. × 30 in.

46. Where equipment operating at 1,000 volts, nominal, or less to ground and likely to require examination, adjustment, servicing, or maintenance while energized is required by installation instructions or function to be located in a space with limited access, the space in front of the enclosure shall comply with the depth requirements of Table 110.26(A)(1).

    (a) True
    (b) False

47. For large equipment that contains overcurrent devices, switching devices, or control devices, there shall be one entrance to and egress from the required working space not less than _____ in. wide.

    (a) 24
    (b) 30
    (c) 36
    (d) 42

48. For equipment rated 800A or more that contains overcurrent devices, switching devices, or control devices; and where the entrance to the working space has a personnel door(s) less than 25 ft from the nearest edge of the working space, the door shall _____.

    (a) open either in or out with simple pressure and shall not have any lock
    (b) open in the direction of egress and be equipped with listed panic hardware
    (c) be equipped with a locking means
    (d) be equipped with an electronic opener

49. The minimum height of dedicated equipment space for motor control centers installed indoors is _____ ft above the enclosure, or to the structural ceiling, whichever is lower.

    (a) 3
    (b) 5
    (c) 6
    (d) 6½

50. All switchboards, switchgear, panelboards, and motor control centers shall be located in dedicated spaces and protected from damage, and outdoor installations shall be _____.

    (a) installed in identified enclosures
    (b) protected from accidental contact by unauthorized personnel or by vehicular traffic
    (c) protected from accidental spillage or leakage from piping systems
    (d) all of these

CHAPTER 2—WIRING AND PROTECTION

Article 230—Services

1. Service conductors and equipment for control and protection of services and their installation requirements are covered in Article _____.

    (a) 210
    (b) 220
    (c) 230
    (d) 240

2. Where a building or structure is supplied by more than one service, a permanent plaque or directory shall be installed at each service disconnect location denoting all other services supplying that building or structure and the area served by each.

    (a) True
    (b) False

Article 230 | Practice Questions

3. Service conductors shall be considered outside of a building or other structure where installed under not less than _____ in. of concrete beneath a building or other structure.

    (a) 2
    (b) 4
    (c) 5
    (d) 6

4. Service conductors installed as unjacketed multiconductor cable shall have a minimum clearance of _____ ft from windows that are designed to be opened, doors, porches, balconies, ladders, stairs, fire escapes, or similar locations.

    (a) 3
    (b) 4
    (c) 6
    (d) 10

5. The requirement to maintain a 3-foot vertical clearance from the edge of a roof does not apply to the final conductor span where the service drop is attached to _____.

    (a) a service pole
    (b) the side of a building
    (c) an antenna
    (d) the base of a building

6. Underground service conductors shall be protected from damage in accordance with _____ including minimum cover requirements.

    (a) 240.6(A)
    (b) 300.5
    (c) 310.16
    (d) 430.52

7. Wiring methods permitted for service-entrance conductors include _____.

    (a) rigid metal conduit
    (b) electrical metallic tubing
    (c) PVC conduit
    (d) all of these

8. Underground service-entrance conductors shall be protected against physical damage.

    (a) True
    (b) False

9. Overhead service-entrance cables shall be equipped with a _____.

    (a) raceway
    (b) service head
    (c) cover
    (d) all of these

10. Service heads on raceways or service-entrance cables and goosenecks in service-entrance cables shall be located _____ the point of attachment, unless impracticable.

    (a) above
    (b) below
    (c) even with
    (d) any of these

11. Barriers shall be placed in service equipment such that no uninsulated, ungrounded service busbar or service _____ is exposed to inadvertent contact by persons or maintenance equipment while servicing load terminations.

    (a) phase conductor
    (b) neutral conductor
    (c) terminal
    (d) disconnect

12. Individual meter socket enclosures shall not be considered service equipment but shall be _____ for the voltage and ampacity of the service.

    (a) listed and rated
    (b) labeled and approved
    (c) inspected and rated
    (d) suitable

13. The surge protective device (SPD) required for a dwelling unit service shall be _____.

    (a) Type 1 or 2
    (b) Type 2 or 3
    (c) Type 3
    (d) Type 4

14. A service disconnecting means shall be installed at a(n) _____ location.

    (a) dry
    (b) readily accessible
    (c) outdoor
    (d) indoor

15. There shall be no more than _____ disconnects installed for each service or for each set of service-entrance conductors as permitted in 230.2 and 230.40.

    (a) two
    (b) four
    (c) six
    (d) eight

16. The additional service disconnecting means for fire pumps, emergency systems, legally required standby, or optional standby services shall be installed remote from the one to six service disconnecting means for normal service to minimize the possibility of _____ interruption of supply.

    (a) intentional
    (b) accidental
    (c) simultaneous
    (d) prolonged

Article 240—Overcurrent Protection

17. Overcurrent protection for conductors and equipment is provided to _____ the circuit if the current reaches a value that will cause an excessive or dangerous temperature in conductors or conductor insulation.

    (a) open
    (b) close
    (c) monitor
    (d) record

18. Overcurrent protection shall not exceed _____.

    (a) 15A for 14 AWG copper
    (b) 20A for 12 AWG copper
    (c) 30A for 10 AWG copper
    (d) all of these

19. Supplementary overcurrent protection _____.

    (a) shall not be used in luminaires
    (b) may be used as a substitute for a branch-circuit overcurrent device
    (c) may be used to protect internal circuits of equipment
    (d) shall be readily accessible

20. Feeder taps are permitted to be located at any point on the load side of the feeder overcurrent protective device.

    (a) True
    (b) False

21. Outside feeder tap conductors can be of unlimited length without overcurrent protection at the point they receive their supply if the tap conductors _____.

    (a) are protected from physical damage
    (b) terminate at a single circuit breaker or a single set of fuses that limits the load to the ampacity of the tap conductors
    (c) the overcurrent device is part of the building feeder disconnect
    (d) all of these

22. Circuit breaker enclosures shall be permitted to be installed _____ where the circuit breaker is installed in accordance with 240.81.

    (a) vertically
    (b) horizontally
    (c) face up
    (d) face down

23. Plug fuses of the Edison-base type shall be used only _____.

    (a) where over fusing is necessary
    (b) as a replacement in existing installations
    (c) as a replacement for Type S fuses
    (d) if rated 50A and above

24. Circuit breakers used to switch 120V and 277V fluorescent lighting circuits shall be listed and marked _____.

    (a) UL
    (b) SWD or HID
    (c) Amps
    (d) VA

Article 250 | Practice Questions

25. A circuit breaker with a _____ rating, such as 120/240V or 277/480V can be used on a solidly grounded circuit where the nominal voltage of any conductor to ground does not exceed the lower of the two values, and the nominal voltage between any two conductors does not exceed the higher value.

    (a) straight
    (b) slash
    (c) high
    (d) low

Article 250—Grounding and Bonding

26. Grounded electrical systems shall be connected to earth in a manner that will _____.

    (a) limit voltages due to lightning, line surges, or unintentional contact with higher-voltage lines
    (b) stabilize the voltage-to-ground during normal operation
    (c) facilitate overcurrent device operation in case of ground faults
    (d) limit voltages due to lightning, line surges, or unintentional contact with higher-voltage lines and stabilize the voltage-to-ground during normal operation

27. For ungrounded systems, noncurrent-carrying conductive materials enclosing electrical conductors or equipment, or forming part of such equipment, shall be connected together and to the supply system grounded equipment in a manner that creates a low-impedance path for ground-fault current that is capable of carrying _____.

    (a) the maximum branch-circuit current
    (b) at least twice the maximum ground-fault current
    (c) the maximum fault current likely to be imposed on it
    (d) the equivalent of the main service rating

28. Equipment grounding conductors, grounding electrode conductors, and bonding jumpers shall be connected by _____.

    (a) listed pressure connectors
    (b) terminal bars
    (c) exothermic welding
    (d) any of these

29. Ungrounded alternating-current systems from 50V to less than 1,000V shall be legibly marked "Caution: Ungrounded System Operating — _____ Volts Between Conductors" at _____ of the system, with sufficient durability to withstand the environment involved.

    (a) the source
    (b) the first disconnecting means
    (c) every junction box
    (d) the source or the first disconnecting means

30. Where an alternating-current system operating at 1,000V or less is grounded at any point, the _____ conductor(s) shall be routed with the ungrounded conductors to each service disconnecting means and shall be connected to each disconnecting means grounded conductor(s) terminal or bus.

    (a) ungrounded
    (b) grounded
    (c) grounding
    (d) paralleled

31. Where a main bonding jumper is a screw only, the screw shall be identified with a(n) _____ that shall be visible with the screw installed.

    (a) silver or white finish
    (b) etched ground symbol
    (c) hexagonal head
    (d) green finish

32. The connection of the system bonding jumper for a separately derived system shall be made _____ on the separately derived system from the source to the first system disconnecting means or overcurrent device.

    (a) in at least two locations
    (b) in every location where the grounded conductor is present
    (c) at any single point
    (d) effectively

33. The common grounding electrode conductor installed for multiple separately derived systems shall not be smaller than _____ AWG copper when using a wire-type conductor.

    (a) 1/0
    (b) 2/0
    (c) 3/0
    (d) 4/0

34. A grounding electrode shall be required if a building or structure is supplied by a feeder.

    (a) True
    (b) False

35. The size of the grounding electrode conductor for a building or structure supplied by a feeder shall not be smaller than that identified in _____, based on the largest ungrounded supply conductor.

    (a) 250.66
    (b) 250.102
    (c) 250.122
    (d) Table 310.16

36. A bare 4 AWG copper conductor installed horizontally near the bottom or vertically, and within that portion of a concrete foundation or footing that is in direct contact with the earth, can be used as a grounding electrode when the conductor is at least _____ ft in length.

    (a) 10
    (b) 15
    (c) 20
    (d) 25

37. Local metal underground systems or structures such as underground tanks are permitted to serve as grounding electrodes.

    (a) True
    (b) False

38. Where the supplemental electrode is a rod, that portion of the bonding jumper that is the sole connection to the supplemental grounding electrode shall not be required to be larger than _____ AWG copper wire.

    (a) 8
    (b) 6
    (c) 4
    (d) 1

39. Bare or covered aluminum or copper-clad aluminum grounding electrode conductors without an extruded polymeric covering shall not be installed where subject to corrosive conditions or be installed in direct contact with _____.

    (a) concrete
    (b) bare copper conductors
    (c) wooden framing members
    (d) all of these

40. Grounding electrode conductors and grounding electrode bonding jumpers in contact with _____ shall not be required to comply with 300.5 but shall be buried or otherwise protected if subject to physical damage.

    (a) water
    (b) the earth
    (c) metal
    (d) all of these

41. A grounding electrode conductor shall be permitted to be run to any convenient grounding electrode available in the grounding electrode system where the other electrode(s), if any, is connected by bonding jumpers that are installed in accordance with 250.53(C).

    (a) True
    (b) False

Article 250 | Practice Questions

42. In an ac system, if the size of the grounding electrode conductor or bonding jumper connected to a concrete-encased electrode does not extend on to other types of electrodes that require a larger size of conductor, the grounding electrode conductor shall not be required to be larger than _____ AWG copper.

    (a) 10
    (b) 8
    (c) 6
    (d) 4

43. A rebar-type concrete-encased electrode installed in accordance with 250.52(A)(3) with an additional rebar section extended from its location within the concrete foundation or footing to an accessible location that is not subject to _____ shall be permitted for connection of grounding electrode conductors and bonding jumpers in accordance with 250.68(C)(3)(a), (b), and (c).

    (a) physical damage
    (b) moisture
    (c) corrosion
    (d) any of these

44. Bonding shall be provided where necessary to ensure _____ and the capacity to conduct safely any fault current likely to be imposed.

    (a) electrical continuity
    (b) fiduciary responsibility
    (c) listing requirements are met
    (d) sufficient electrical demand

45. The intersystem bonding termination shall _____.

    (a) be accessible for connection and inspection
    (b) consist of a set of terminals with the capacity for connection of not less than three intersystem bonding conductors
    (c) not interfere with opening the enclosure for a service, building/structure disconnecting means, or metering equipment
    (d) all of these

46. Supply-side bonding jumpers shall be no smaller than the sizes specified in _____.

    (a) Table 250.102(C)(1)
    (b) Table 250.122
    (c) Table 310.16
    (d) Table 250.66

47. An equipment bonding jumper can be installed on the outside of a raceway, providing the length of the equipment bonding jumper is not more than _____ in. and the equipment bonding jumper is routed with the raceway.

    (a) 12
    (b) 24
    (c) 36
    (d) 72

48. The bonding jumper(s) required for the metal water piping system(s) installed in or attached to a building or structure supplied by a feeder(s) or branch circuit(s) shall be sized in accordance with _____.

    (a) 250.66
    (b) 250.102(D)
    (c) 250.122
    (d) 310.16

49. A separate bonding jumper to the building structural metal shall not be required if the metal frame of a building or structure is used as the _____ for the separately derived system.

    (a) bonding jumper
    (b) ground-fault current path
    (c) grounding electrode
    (d) lightning protection

50. Listed liquidtight flexible metal conduit (LFMC) is acceptable as an equipment grounding conductor when it terminates in listed fittings and is protected by an overcurrent device rated 60A or less for trade sizes ⅜ through ½.

    (a) True
    (b) False

CHAPTER 3—WIRING METHODS AND MATERIALS

Article 300—General Requirements for Wiring Methods and Materials

1. The provisions of Article 300 apply to the conductors that form an integral part of equipment or listed utilization equipment.

    (a) True
    (b) False

2. The requirement to run all paralleled circuit conductors within the same _____ applies separately to each portion of the paralleled installation.

    (a) raceway or auxiliary gutter
    (b) cable tray or trench
    (c) cable or cord
    (d) all of these

3. Where nails or screws are likely to penetrate nonmetallic-sheathed cable or ENT installed through metal framing members, a steel sleeve, steel plate, or steel clip not less than _____ in. in thickness shall be used to protect the cable or tubing.

    (a) 1/16
    (b) 1/8
    (c) 1/2
    (d) 3/4

4. What is the minimum cover requirement for direct burial Type UF cable installed outdoors that supplies a 120V, 30A circuit?

    (a) 6 in.
    (b) 12 in.
    (c) 18 in.
    (d) 24 in.

5. Underground cable and conductors installed under a building shall be _____.

    (a) in the same trench
    (b) in a raceway
    (c) encased in concrete
    (d) under at least 2 in. of concrete

6. A(n) _____ with an integral bushed opening shall be used at the end of a conduit or other raceway that terminates underground where the conductors or cables emerge as a direct burial wiring method.

    (a) splice kit
    (b) connector
    (c) adapter
    (d) bushing or terminal fitting

7. Where portions of a cable raceway or sleeve are subjected to different temperatures and condensation is known to be a problem, the _____ shall be sealed to prevent the circulation of warm air to a colder section of the raceway or sleeve.

    (a) opening
    (b) cable
    (c) space
    (d) raceway or sleeve

8. Raceways can be used as a means of support of Class 2 circuit conductors or cables that connect to the same equipment.

    (a) True
    (b) False

9. In multiwire branch circuits, the continuity of the _____ shall not be dependent upon the device connections.

    (a) ungrounded conductor
    (b) grounded conductor
    (c) grounding electrode
    (d) raceway

10. A box or conduit body shall not be required for splices and taps in direct-buried conductors and cables as long as the splice is made with a splicing device that is identified for the purpose.

    (a) True
    (b) False

Article 310 | Practice Questions

11. Conductors in ferrous metal raceways or enclosures shall be arranged so as to avoid heating the surrounding ferrous metal by alternating-current induction. To accomplish this, the _____ conductor(s) shall be grouped together.

    (a) phase
    (b) grounded
    (c) equipment grounding
    (d) all of these

12. Electrical installations in hollow spaces shall be made so as not to increase the spread of fire. An example is boxes installed in a wall cavity on opposite sides of a fire-resistance-rated wall where a minimum horizontal separation of _____ in. usually applies between boxes.

    (a) 6
    (b) 12
    (c) 18
    (d) 24

13. Wiring methods permitted in the ceiling areas used for environmental air include _____.

    (a) electrical metallic tubing
    (b) FMC of any length
    (c) RMC without an overall nonmetallic covering
    (d) all of these

14. Where an exit enclosure is required to be separated from the building, only electrical wiring methods serving equipment permitted by the _____ in the exit enclosure shall be installed within the exit enclosure.

    (a) fire *code* official
    (b) building *code* official
    (c) authority having jurisdiction
    (d) electrical engineer

Article 310—Conductors for General Wiring

15. Where installed in raceways, conductors _____ AWG and larger shall be stranded, unless specifically permitted or required elsewhere in the *NEC*.

    (a) 10
    (b) 8
    (c) 6
    (d) 4

16. Where conductors in parallel are run in separate raceways, the raceways shall have the same electrical characteristics.

    (a) True
    (b) False

17. Where correction or adjustment factors are required by 310.15(B) or (C) for single-phase feeder conductors installed for _____ dwellings, they shall be permitted to be applied to the ampacity associated with the temperature rating of the conductor.

    (a) one-family
    (b) the individual dwelling units of two-family
    (c) the individual dwelling units of multifamily
    (d) all of these

18. Each current-carrying conductor of a paralleled set of conductors shall be counted as a current-carrying conductor for the purpose of applying the adjustment factors of 310.15(C)(1).

    (a) True
    (b) False

19. In a 3-wire circuit consisting of two phase conductors and the neutral conductor of a 4-wire, 3-phase, _____ system, the common conductor is a current-carrying conductor and subject to the adjustment provisions of 310.15(C)(1).

    (a) delta-connected
    (b) delta-wye connected
    (c) delta-delta connected
    (d) wye-connected

Article 312—Cabinets

20. In walls constructed of wood or other _____ material, electrical cabinets shall be flush with the finished surface or project therefrom.

    (a) nonconductive
    (b) porous
    (c) fibrous
    (d) combustible

Article 314—Outlet, Pull, and Junction Boxes; Conduit Bodies; and Handhole Enclosures

21. The installation and use of all boxes and conduit bodies used as outlet, device, junction, or pull boxes, depending on their use, and handhole enclosures, are covered within Article _____.

    (a) 110
    (b) 200
    (c) 300
    (d) 314

22. Boxes, conduit bodies, and fittings installed in wet locations shall be listed for use in wet locations.

    (a) True
    (b) False

23. Metal handhole enclosure covers and other exposed conductive surfaces shall be _____.

    (a) listed
    (b) bonded to the equipment grounding conductor
    (c) grounded
    (d) installed

Article 330—Metal-Clad Cable (Type MC)

24. The use, installation, and construction specifications of metal-clad cable, Type MC are covered within Article _____.

    (a) 300
    (b) 310
    (c) 320
    (d) 330

25. Type MC cable installed through, or parallel to, framing members shall be protected against physical damage from penetration by screws or nails by 1¼ in. separation or protected by a suitable metal plate.

    (a) True
    (b) False

26. Type MC cable installed horizontally through wooden or metal framing members is considered secured and supported where such support does not exceed _____-ft intervals.

    (a) 3
    (b) 4
    (c) 6
    (d) 8

Article 348—Flexible Metal Conduit (Type FMC)

27. Article 348 covers the use, installation, and construction specifications for flexible metal conduit (FMC) and associated _____.

    (a) fittings
    (b) connections
    (c) terminations
    (d) ratings

28. FMC can be installed exposed or concealed where not subject to physical damage.

    (a) True
    (b) False

29. Bends in FMC _____ between pull points.

    (a) shall not be made
    (b) need not be limited (in degrees)
    (c) shall not exceed 360 degrees
    (d) shall not exceed 180 degrees

30. Cable ties used to securely fasten flexible metal conduit shall be _____ for securement and support.

    (a) identified
    (b) labeled
    (c) marked
    (d) listed and identified

31. Flexible metal conduit shall not be required to be _____ where fished between access points through concealed spaces in finished buildings or structures and supporting is impracticable.

    (a) secured
    (b) supported
    (c) complete
    (d) secured and supported

32. When FMC is used where flexibility is necessary to minimize the transmission of vibration from equipment or to provide flexibility for equipment that requires movement after installation, _____ shall be installed.

    (a) an equipment grounding conductor
    (b) an expansion fitting
    (c) flexible nonmetallic connectors
    (d) adjustable supports

Article 350—Liquidtight Flexible Metal Conduit (Type LFMC)

33. The use, installation, and construction specifications for liquidtight flexible metal conduit (LFMC) and associated fittings are covered within Article _____.

    (a) 300
    (b) 334
    (c) 350
    (d) 410

34. The use of LFMC shall be permitted for direct burial where listed and marked for the purpose.

    (a) True
    (b) False

35. LFMC shall be supported and secured _____.

    (a) at intervals not exceeding 4½ ft
    (b) within 8 in. on each side of a box where fished
    (c) where fished
    (d) at intervals not exceeding 6 ft

36. For liquidtight flexible metal conduit, if flexibility is necessary after installation, unsecured lengths from the last point the raceway is securely fastened shall not exceed _____.

    (a) 3 ft for trade sizes ½ through 1¼
    (b) 4 ft for trade sizes 1½ through 2
    (c) 5 ft for trade sizes 2½ and larger
    (d) all of these

37. When LFMC is used to connect equipment where flexibility is necessary to minimize the transmission of vibration from equipment or for equipment requiring movement after installation, a(n) _____ conductor shall be installed.

    (a) main bonding
    (b) grounded
    (c) equipment grounding
    (d) grounding electrode

38. Where flexibility is not required after installation, liquidtight flexible metal conduit shall be permitted to be used as an equipment grounding conductor when installed in accordance with _____.

    (a) 250.102
    (b) 250.118(5)
    (c) 250.118(6)
    (d) 348.60

Article 352—Rigid Polyvinyl Chloride Conduit (Type PVC)

39. A rigid nonmetallic raceway of circular cross section, with integral or associated couplings, connectors, and fittings for the installation of electrical conductors and cables describes _____.

    (a) ENT
    (b) RMC
    (c) IMC
    (d) PVC

40. PVC conduit is permitted in locations subject to severe corrosive influences and where subject to chemicals for which the materials are specifically _____.

    (a) approved
    (b) identified
    (c) listed
    (d) nonhazardous

41. PVC conduit shall not be used _____, unless specifically permitted.

    (a) in hazardous (classified) locations
    (b) for the support of luminaires or other equipment
    (c) where subject to physical damage unless identified for such use
    (d) all of these

42. Field bends in PVC conduit shall be made only _____.

    (a) by hand forming the bend
    (b) with bending equipment identified for the purpose
    (c) with a truck exhaust pipe
    (d) by use of an open flame torch

43. The cut ends of PVC conduit shall be trimmed to remove the burrs and rough edges.

    (a) True
    (b) False

44. PVC conduit in trade sizes of 1¼ in. to 2 in. shall be supported at intervals not greater than _____ ft between supports.

    (a) 3
    (b) 4
    (c) 5
    (d) 6

45. Where a PVC conduit enters a box, fitting, or other enclosure, a bushing or adapter shall be provided to protect the wire from abrasion unless the box, fitting, or enclosure design provides equivalent protection.

    (a) True
    (b) False

Article 358—Electrical Metallic Tubing (Type EMT)

46. Article _____ covers the use, installation, and construction specifications for electrical metallic tubing (EMT) and associated fittings.

    (a) 334
    (b) 350
    (c) 356
    (d) 358

47. The use of EMT shall be permitted for both exposed and concealed work in _____.

    (a) concrete, in direct contact with the earth, or in areas subject to severe corrosive influences where installed in accordance with 358.10(B)
    (b) dry, damp, and wet locations
    (c) any hazardous (classified) location as permitted by other articles in this *Code*
    (d) all of these

48. When EMT is installed in wet locations, all supports, bolts, straps, and screws shall be _____.

    (a) made of aluminum
    (b) protected against corrosion
    (c) made of stainless steel
    (d) of nonmetallic materials only

49. EMT shall be securely fastened in place at intervals not to exceed _____ ft.

    (a) 4
    (b) 5
    (c) 8
    (d) 10

50. EMT run in unbroken lengths between termination points is permitted to be securely fastened within _____ ft of each outlet box, junction box, device box, cabinet, conduit body, or other tubing termination where structural members do not readily permit fastening.

    (a) 1
    (b) 3
    (c) 5
    (d) 10

CHAPTER 4—EQUIPMENT FOR GENERAL USE

Article 400—Flexible Cords and Flexible Cables

1. Article 400 covers general requirements, applications, and construction specifications for flexible cords and flexible cables.

    (a) True
    (b) False

2. The ampacities of flexible cords and flexible cables are found in _____.

    (a) Table 310.16
    (b) Tables 400.5(A)(1) and (A)(2)
    (c) Chapter 9, Table 1
    (d) Table 430.52

3. Flexible cords and flexible cables can be used for _____.

    (a) wiring of luminaires
    (b) connection of portable luminaires or appliances
    (c) connection of utilization equipment to facilitate frequent interchange
    (d) all of these

4. Flexible cord sets and power-supply cords shall not be used as a substitute for _____ wiring of a structure.

    (a) temporary
    (b) fixed
    (c) concealed
    (d) permanent

5. Flexible cords and power-supply cords shall not be concealed behind building _____, or run through doorways, windows, or similar openings.

    (a) structural ceilings
    (b) suspended or dropped ceilings
    (c) floors or walls
    (d) all of these

6. Flexible cords and flexible cables shall be protected by _____ where passing through holes in covers, outlet boxes, or similar enclosures.

    (a) sleeves
    (b) grommets
    (c) raceways
    (d) bushings or fittings

Article 404—Switches

7. Article 404 covers all _____ used as switches operating at 1,000V and below, unless specifically referenced elsewhere in this *Code* for higher voltages.

    (a) switches
    (b) switching devices
    (c) circuit breakers
    (d) all of these

8. The grounded circuit conductor for the controlled lighting circuit shall be installed at the location where switches control lighting loads that are supplied by a grounded general-purpose branch circuit serving _____.

    (a) habitable rooms or occupiable spaces
    (b) attics
    (c) crawlspaces
    (d) basements

9. Switch enclosures shall not be used as _____ for conductors feeding through or tapping off to other switches or overcurrent devices, unless the enclosure complies with 312.8.

    (a) junction boxes
    (b) raceways
    (c) auxiliary gutters
    (d) any of these

10. Switches shall not be installed within tubs or shower spaces unless installed as part of a listed tub or shower assembly.

    (a) True
    (b) False

11. Switches and circuit breakers used as switches shall be installed so that they may be operated from a readily accessible place.

    (a) True
    (b) False

12. Snap switches shall not be grouped or ganged in enclosures unless the voltage between adjacent devices does not exceed _____.

    (a) 100V
    (b) 200V
    (c) 300V
    (d) 400V

13. Snap switches, dimmers, and control switches are considered to be part of the effective ground-fault current path when _____.

    (a) the switch is connected to the intersystem bonding termination
    (b) the switch is mounted with metal screws to a metal box or a metal cover that is connected to an equipment grounding conductor
    (c) an equipment grounding conductor or equipment bonding jumper is connected to the equipment grounding termination of the snap switch
    (d) the switch is mounted with metal screws to a metal box or a metal cover that is connected to an equipment grounding conductor, or when an equipment grounding conductor or equipment bonding jumper is connected to the equipment grounding termination of the snap switch

14. The metal mounting yoke of a replacement switch is not required to be connected to an equipment grounding conductor if the wiring at the existing switch does not contain an equipment grounding conductor, and the _____.

    (a) switch faceplate is metallic and installed with nonmetallic screws
    (b) circuit is GFCI protected
    (c) the switch is mounted to a nonmetallic box
    (d) circuit is AFCI protected

15. A snap switch with an integral nonmetallic enclosure complying with 300.15(E) is required to be connected to an equipment grounding conductor.

    (a) True
    (b) False

16. Metal enclosures for switches or circuit breakers shall be connected to the circuit _____ conductor.

    (a) grounded
    (b) grounding
    (c) equipment grounding
    (d) any of these

17. General-use _____ switches shall be used only to control permanently installed incandescent luminaires unless listed for control of other loads and installed accordingly.

    (a) dimmer
    (b) fan speed control
    (c) timer
    (d) all of these

18. Where in the off position, a switching device with a marked OFF position shall completely disconnect all _____ conductors of the load it controls.

    (a) grounded
    (b) ungrounded
    (c) grounding
    (d) all of these

Article 408—Switchboards and Panelboards

19. Article 408 covers _____.

    (a) switchboards
    (b) switchgear
    (c) panelboards
    (d) all of these

Article 408 | Practice Questions

20. A switchboard, switchgear, or panelboard containing a 4-wire, _____ system where the midpoint of one phase winding is grounded, shall be legibly and permanently field-marked to caution that one phase has a higher voltage-to-ground.

    (a) wye-connected
    (b) delta-connected
    (c) solidly grounded
    (d) ungrounded

21. Panelboard circuit directories can include labels that depend on transient conditions of occupancy.

    (a) True
    (b) False

22. The label required for switchboards, switchgear, and panelboards [408.4(B)] shall be permanently affixed, of sufficient durability to withstand the environment involved, and handwritten.

    (a) True
    (b) False

23. Panelboards for one- and two-family dwellings shall have a short-circuit current rating not less than the _____ current.

    (a) equipment rated
    (b) available fault
    (c) overcurrent protection rated
    (d) ground-fault protection

24. Reconditioned switchboards and switchgear that have been damaged by fire, products of combustion, or water, shall be specifically evaluated by _____ prior to being returned to service.

    (a) the installer
    (b) its manufacturer
    (c) a qualified testing laboratory
    (d) its manufacturer or a qualified testing laboratory

25. Switchboards and switchgear, or sections of switchboards or switchgear, shall be permitted to be reconditioned. Reconditioned switchgear shall be listed or field labeled as _____.

    (a) used
    (b) repurposed
    (c) redesigned
    (d) reconditioned

26. A panelboard shall be protected by an overcurrent device within the panelboard, or at any point on the _____ side of the panelboard.

    (a) load
    (b) supply
    (c) branch circuit
    (d) any of these

27. Where a panelboard is supplied through a transformer, the overcurrent protection shall be located _____.

    (a) at the main distribution panel
    (b) on the primary side of the transformer
    (c) on the secondary side of the transformer
    (d) on either the primary or secondary side of the transformer

28. Plug-in-type back-fed circuit breakers used to terminate field-installed ungrounded supply conductors shall be _____ by an additional fastener that requires more than a pull to release.

    (a) grounded
    (b) secured in place
    (c) shunt tripped
    (d) current-limited

29. Panelboard cabinets and panelboard frames, if of metal, shall be in physical contact with each other and shall be connected to a(n) _____.

    (a) equipment grounding conductor
    (b) grounding electrode conductor
    (c) steel building structure
    (d) separate ground rod

30. Panelboards _____ be installed in the face-up position.

    (a) shall not
    (b) are permitted to
    (c) listed for such purpose may
    (d) approved for such use may

Article 445—Generators

31. Article 445 contains installation and other requirements for generators.

    (a) True
    (b) False

32. Stationary generators _____ and less shall be listed.

    (a) 250V
    (b) 300V
    (c) 600V
    (d) 1,000V

33. Generators shall have the _____ conductor sized not smaller than required to carry the maximum unbalanced current as determined by 220.61.

    (a) neutral
    (b) grounding
    (c) bonding
    (d) all of these

34. Generators with greater than _____ rating shall be provided with a remote emergency stop switch to shut down the prime mover.

    (a) 12.50 kW
    (b) 15 kW
    (c) 25 kW
    (d) 35 kW

35. For other than cord-and-plug-connected portable generators, an emergency shutdown device for a dwelling unit shall be located _____ at a readily accessible location.

    (a) inside the dwelling unit
    (b) outside the dwelling unit
    (c) within sight of the generator
    (d) inside or outside the dwelling unit

Article 450—Transformers

36. Transformers with ventilating openings shall be installed so that the ventilating openings are _____.

    (a) a minimum 18 in. above the floor
    (b) not blocked by walls or obstructions
    (c) aesthetically located
    (d) vented to the exterior of the building

37. Transformer top surfaces that are horizontal and readily accessible shall be marked _____.

    (a) to warn of high surface temperature(s)
    (b) with an arc-flash boundary warning
    (c) to prohibit storage
    (d) all of these

38. The equipment grounding conductor terminal bar of a dry-type transformer shall be bonded to the enclosure in accordance with 250.12 and shall not be installed on or over any _____.

    (a) ungrounded conductor terminations
    (b) transformer coils or windings
    (c) vented portion of the enclosure
    (d) all of these

39. Dry-type transformers 1,000V, nominal, or less and not exceeding _____ kVA that are installed in hollow spaces of buildings and not permanently closed in by the structure, shall not be required to be readily accessible.

    (a) 10
    (b) 25
    (c) 50
    (d) 112.50

40. For transformers, other than Class 2 and Class 3, a means is required to disconnect all transformer ungrounded primary conductors. The disconnecting means shall be located within sight of the transformer unless the disconnect _____.

    (a) location is field marked on the transformer
    (b) is lockable open in accordance with 110.25
    (c) is nonfusible
    (d) location is field marked on the transformer and is lockable open in accordance with 110.25

Article 480—Storage Batteries

41. The provisions of Article _____ apply to stationary installations of storage battery installations.

    (a) 450
    (b) 460
    (c) 470
    (d) 480

42. Nominal battery voltage, as it relates to storage batteries, is the value of a(n) _____ of a given voltage class for convenient designation.

    (a) cell or battery
    (b) container
    (c) electrolyte
    (d) intertier connector

43. A storage battery is a single or group of _____ cells connected together electrically in series, in parallel, or a combination of both, and comprised of lead-acid, nickel-cadmium, or other rechargeable electrochemical types.

    (a) disposable
    (b) reusable
    (c) rechargeable
    (d) recyclable

44. Electrical _____ to a storage battery, and the cable(s) between cells on separate levels or racks, shall not put mechanical strain on the battery terminals.

    (a) connections
    (b) continuity
    (c) conductivity
    (d) accessibility

45. The terminals of all storage battery cells or multicell units shall be readily accessible for _____ where required by the equipment design.

    (a) readings
    (b) inspections
    (c) cleaning
    (d) all of these

46. A disconnecting means is required within sight of the storage battery for all ungrounded stationary battery system conductors operating at over _____ dc.

    (a) 30V
    (b) 40V
    (c) 50V
    (d) 60V

47. For one-family and two-family dwellings, a disconnecting means or its remote control for a stationary battery system shall be located at a readily accessible location _____ the building for emergency use.

    (a) outside
    (b) inside
    (c) within sight of
    (d) outside or inside

48. Metallic structures for the support of storage batteries shall be provided with nonconducting support members for the cells or shall be constructed with a continuous insulating material; paint alone shall not be considered as an insulating material.

    (a) True
    (b) False

49. For battery racks, there shall be a minimum clearance of _____ in. between a cell container and any wall or structure on the side not requiring access for maintenance.

    (a) 1
    (b) 6
    (c) 12
    (d) 24

50. Battery stands are permitted to contact adjacent walls or structures, provided that the battery shelf has a free air space for not less than _____ percent of its length.

    (a) 50
    (b) 75
    (c) 90
    (d) 100

CHAPTER 6—SPECIAL EQUIPMENT

Article 690—Solar Photovoltaic (PV) Systems

1. Article 690 applies to solar PV systems, including _____.

    (a) array circuit(s), inverter(s), and controller(s) for such PV systems
    (b) those interactive with other electrical power production sources or stand-alone, or both
    (c) PV systems with ac or dc output for utilization
    (d) all of these

2. In accordance with Article 690, an "ac module system" is an assembly or subassembly of _____ that are evaluated, identified, and defined as a system.

    (a) ac modules
    (b) wiring methods
    (c) material
    (d) all of these

3. In accordance with Article 690, a "dc-to-dc _____ circuit" is the dc circuit conductors connected to the output of a dc combiner for dc-to-dc converter source circuits.

    (a) converter output
    (b) converter control
    (c) inverter output
    (d) inverter control

4. In accordance with Article 690, a "dc combiner" is an enclosure that includes devices used to connect two or more PV system dc circuits in _____.

    (a) series
    (b) series-parallel
    (c) parallel
    (d) parallel-series

5. In accordance with Article 690, a solidly grounded PV system is often connected to ground through an electronic means internal to an inverter or charge controller that provides ground-fault protection.

    (a) True
    (b) False

6. In PV systems, a "_____ circuit" is an electrical subset of a PV system that has two conductors in the output circuit, one positive (+) and one negative (-).

    (a) bipolar
    (b) monopole
    (c) double-pole
    (d) module

7. In accordance with Article 690, a "PV system dc circuit" includes any dc conductor(s) in PV source circuits, PV output circuits, _____ converter source circuits, and dc-to-dc converter output circuits.

    (a) ac-to-dc
    (b) dc-to-ac
    (c) dc-to-dc
    (d) any of these

8. PV systems are permitted to supply a building or other structure in addition to any other _____ supply system(s).

    (a) electrical
    (b) telephone
    (c) data
    (d) communications

9. The installation of PV equipment and all associated wiring and interconnections shall be performed only by _____.

    (a) licensed electricians
    (b) qualified personnel
    (c) master electricians
    (d) journeyman electricians

10. PV system equipment and disconnecting means are permitted to be installed in a bathroom when listed for the application.

    (a) True
    (b) False

11. Article 690 requirements pertaining to dc PV source circuits do not apply to ac PV modules since the PV source circuit, conductors, and inverters are considered as internal wiring of the ac module.

    (a) True
    (b) False

Article 690 | Practice Questions

12. For one- and two-family dwellings, the maximum voltage for PV system dc circuits is limited to _____.

    (a) 30V
    (b) 50V
    (c) 600V
    (d) 1,000V

13. In a dc PV source circuit or output circuit, the maximum voltage, corrected for the lowest expected ambient temperature for that circuit, is permitted to be calculated in accordance with the listing or labelling instructions of the module.

    (a) True
    (b) False

14. For PV system source circuit or output circuits with a generating capacity of _____ kW or greater, the maximum voltage may be calculated using a documented and stamped PV system design, using an industry standard method maximum voltage calculation provided by a licensed professional electrical engineer.

    (a) 25
    (b) 50
    (c) 75
    (d) 100

15. For PV dc circuits connected to the output of a single dc-to-dc converter, the _____ shall be determined in accordance with the instructions included in the listing or labeling of the dc-to-dc converter.

    (a) minimum voltage
    (b) minimum current
    (c) maximum voltage
    (d) maximum current

16. To prevent PV system overvoltage of bipolar circuits in the event of a ground fault or arc fault, each monopole subarray circuit shall be _____ from ground.

    (a) grounded
    (b) connected to earth
    (c) isolated
    (d) shielded

17. The PV maximum output circuit current shall be the sum of parallel PV source circuit maximum currents as calculated in _____.

    (a) 690.8(A)(1)(a)
    (b) 690.8(A)(2)
    (c) 690.8(A)(3)
    (d) Article 220

18. In PV systems, where a single overcurrent device is used to protect a set of two or more parallel-connected module circuits, the ampacity of each of the module interconnection conductors shall not be less than the sum of the rating of the single overcurrent device plus _____ percent of the short-circuit current from the other parallel-connected modules.

    (a) 100
    (b) 115
    (c) 125
    (d) 150

19. In PV systems, when a circuit conductor is connected to a current-limited supply at one end, and also connected to a source having an available maximum current greater than the ampacity of the circuit conductor, the circuit conductors shall be protected from overcurrent at the point of connection to _____ current source(s).

    (a) the lower
    (b) the higher
    (c) either
    (d) both

20. Fuses or circuit breakers for PV dc circuits shall be _____ for use in PV systems.

    (a) identified
    (b) approved
    (c) recognized
    (d) listed

21. Overcurrent devices for PV source and output circuits shall be readily accessible.

    (a) True
    (b) False

22. Ground mounted PV system circuits that enter buildings, of which the sole purpose is to house PV system equipment, shall include a rapid shutdown function to reduce shock hazard for firefighters.

    (a) True
    (b) False

23. PV system circuits installed on or in buildings shall include a rapid shutdown function to reduce the risk of electrical shock for _____.

    (a) personnel
    (b) employees
    (c) firefighters
    (d) installers

24. For PV system rapid shutdown systems, controlled conductors located outside the array boundary or more than 3 ft from the point of entry inside a building shall be limited to not more than _____ within 30 seconds of rapid shutdown initiation.

    (a) 15V
    (b) 30V
    (c) 50V
    (d) 80V

25. For a single PV system, the rapid shutdown initiation shall occur by the operation of _____.

    (a) the service disconnecting means
    (b) the PV system disconnecting means
    (c) a readily accessible switch that plainly indicates whether it is in the "off" or "on" position
    (d) any of these

26. A means is required to disconnect the PV system from all wiring systems including power systems, energy storage systems, and utilization equipment and its associated premises wiring.

    (a) True
    (b) False

27. Where PV system disconnecting means of systems above _____ are readily accessible to unqualified persons, any enclosure door or hinged cover that exposes live parts when open shall be locked or require a tool to open.

    (a) 30V
    (b) 120V
    (c) 240V
    (d) 600V

28. The maximum number of disconnects for each PV system shall consist of not more than _____ switches or _____ sets of circuit breakers, or a combination of not more than _____ switches and sets of circuit breakers, mounted in a single enclosure, or in a group of separate enclosures.

    (a) one
    (b) six
    (c) eight
    (d) twelve

29. The PV system equipment disconnecting means shall have ratings sufficient for the _____ that is available at the terminals.

    (a) maximum circuit current
    (b) available fault current
    (c) voltage
    (d) all of these

30. Isolating devices or equipment disconnecting means for PV system equipment shall be installed within the equipment or within sight and within _____ ft of the equipment.

    (a) 3
    (b) 10
    (c) 25
    (d) 50

31. An isolating device for PV system equipment shall be a(an) _____.

    (a) mating connector meeting the requirements of 690.33 and listed and identified for use with specific equipment
    (b) finger-safe fuse holder or an isolating switch that requires a tool to place the device in the open (off) position
    (c) isolating device listed for the intended application
    (d) any of these

Article 690 | Practice Questions

32. The conductors of PV output circuits and inverter input and output circuits shall be identified at all points of termination, connection, and splices.

    (a) True
    (b) False

33. Where the conductors of more than one PV system occupy the same junction box or raceway with removable cover(s), the ac and dc conductors of each system shall be grouped separately by cable ties or similar means at least once, and then shall be grouped at intervals not to exceed _____ ft.

    (a) 1
    (b) 3
    (c) 6
    (d) 10

34. Single-conductor cable _____ sunlight resistant and Type USE-2 and RHW-2 cable can be run exposed at outdoor locations for PV source circuits within the PV array.

    (a) approved
    (b) listed or labeled
    (c) marked
    (d) manufacturer certified

35. Where inside buildings, PV system dc circuits that exceed 30V or 8A where Type MC cable smaller than _____ in. in diameter containing PV power circuit conductors is installed across ceilings or floor joists, the raceway or cable shall be protected by substantial guard strips that are at least as high as the raceway or cable.

    (a) 3/8
    (b) 1/2
    (c) 3/4
    (d) 1

36. Labels or markings of PV system raceways and enclosures shall be suitable for the environment and be placed with a maximum of _____ ft of spacing.

    (a) 5
    (b) 10
    (c) 20
    (d) 25

37. Fittings and connectors that are intended to be concealed at the time of on-site assembly, where _____ for such use, shall be permitted for on-site interconnection of modules or other array components.

    (a) approved
    (b) identified
    (c) marked
    (d) listed

38. PV systems that exceed 30V or 8A shall be provided with direct-current _____ to reduce fire hazards.

    (a) arc-fault protection
    (b) rectifier protection
    (c) ground-fault monitors
    (d) ground-fault protection

39. Ground-fault protection of PV system equipment shall provide indication of ground faults at a readily accessible location. Examples of indication include but are not limited to _____.

    (a) a remote indicator light
    (b) alarm system monitoring
    (c) web-based services
    (d) any of these

40. Devices and systems used for mounting PV modules that are also used for bonding module frames shall be _____ for bonding PV modules. Devices that mount adjacent PV modules shall be permitted for bonding adjacent PV modules.

    (a) listed
    (b) labeled
    (c) identified
    (d) all of these

41. Where no overcurrent protection is provided for the PV circuit, an assumed overcurrent device rated in accordance with 690.9(B) shall be used to size the equipment grounding conductor in accordance with _____.

    (a) 250.66
    (b) 250.102(C)(1)
    (c) 250.122
    (d) Table 250.122

42. For PV systems that are not solidly grounded, the equipment grounding conductor for the output of the PV system, where connected to associated distribution equipment connected to a grounding electrode system, shall be permitted to be the only connection to ground for the system.

    (a) True
    (b) False

43. Facilities with stand-alone systems shall have _____ installed in accordance with 710.10.

    (a) plaques
    (b) directories
    (c) directions
    (d) plaques or directories

44. Buildings with PV systems shall have a permanent label located at each _____ location to which the PV systems are connected or at an approved readily visible location and shall indicate the location of rapid shutdown initiation devices.

    (a) service equipment
    (b) PV system disconnect
    (c) PV equipment disconnect
    (d) all of these

45. For buildings with rapid shutdown, the rapid shutdown switch shall have a label that reads "RAPID SHUTDOWN SWITCH FOR SOLAR PV SYSTEM" installed within _____ ft of the switch.

    (a) 3
    (b) 6
    (c) 10
    (d) 25

Article 691—Large-Scale Photovoltaic (PV) Electric Supply Stations

46. Article _____ covers the installation of large-scale PV electric supply stations with a generating capacity of not less than 5,000 kW and not under the electric utility control.

    (a) 690
    (b) 691
    (c) 705
    (d) 711

47. Facilities covered by Article 691 have specific design and safety features unique to large-scale _____ facilities and are operated for the sole purpose of providing electric supply to a system operated by a regulated utility for the transfer of electric energy.

    (a) industrial
    (b) electrical
    (c) distribution
    (d) PV

48. Large-scale PV electric supply stations are only permitted to be accessible to authorized personnel and, electrical circuits and equipment shall be maintained and operated by qualified personnel.

    (a) True
    (b) False

49. Electrical equipment for large-scale PV electric supply stations shall only be approved for installation by _____.

    (a) listing and labeling
    (b) being evaluated for the application and having a field label applied
    (c) qualified personnel
    (d) listing and labeling, or being evaluated for the application and having a field label applied

50. Engineering documentation of large-scale electric supply stations shall include details of conformance of the design with Article _____.

    (a) 250
    (b) 690
    (c) 702
    (d) 710

Article 705 | Practice Questions

CHAPTER 7—SPECIAL CONDITIONS

Article 705—Interconnected Electric Power Production Sources

1. Article 705 covers installations of one or more electric power production sources operating in parallel with a _____ source(s) of electricity.

    (a) secondary
    (b) alternate
    (c) primary
    (d) stand-alone

2. The definitions in Article 705 shall apply only within Article 705.

    (a) True
    (b) False

3. In accordance with Article 705, a premises wiring system that has generation, energy storage, and load(s), or any combination thereof, that includes the ability to disconnect from and parallel with the primary source is known as a "_____ system."

    (a) tandem
    (b) primary
    (c) microgrid
    (d) dual function

4. Interactive equipment intended to operate in parallel with electric power production sources shall be listed for interactive function or be _____ for interactive function and have a field label applied, or both.

    (a) tested
    (b) evaluated
    (c) approved
    (d) licensed

5. For interconnected power production source(s), installation of one or more electrical power production sources operating in parallel with a primary source(s) of electricity shall be performed only by _____.

    (a) qualified persons
    (b) utility company persons
    (c) the authority having jurisdiction
    (d) utility company persons or the authority having jurisdiction

6. Interconnected power production installations with multiple co-located power production sources shall be permitted to be identified as a group(s).

    (a) True
    (b) False

7. Interconnected power production source(s) are permitted to be connected to the supply side of the service disconnecting means when in compliance with 705.11.

    (a) True
    (b) False

8. For supply-side connected interconnected power production source(s), the sum of the interconnected power source continuous current output ratings on a service, other than those controlled in accordance with 705.13, shall not exceed the ampacity of the _____.

    (a) service conductors
    (b) power production source output current
    (c) service disconnect rating
    (d) sum of all overcurrent protective devices

9. Where supply-side power source output circuit conductors make their connection to the service outside of a building, they shall be protected by overcurrent devices in a(an) _____ outside the building or at the first readily accessible location where the power source conductors enter the building.

    (a) location
    (b) readily accessible location
    (c) accessible location
    (d) secured location

10. For supply-side connected interconnected power production source(s), the connection of power source output circuit conductors to the _____ conductors shall be made using listed connectors as described in 110.14.

    (a) service
    (b) grounded
    (c) bonded
    (d) feeder

11. For meter socket enclosures or other equipment under the exclusive control of the electric utility for supply-side connected interconnected power production source(s), only connections approved by the _____ shall be permitted.

    (a) electric utility
    (b) general contractor
    (c) electrical engineer
    (d) fire marshal

12. For supply-side connected interconnected power production source(s), if the power production equipment requires a grounded conductor, a connection shall be made between the supply-side bonding jumper and the grounded conductor at the supply-side disconnecting means in accordance with 705.11(F).

    (a) True
    (b) False

13. For supply-side connected interconnected power production source(s), the connection of power source output circuit conductors to the service conductors shall be made using _____ connectors as described in 110.14 and comply with all enclosure fill requirements.

    (a) listed
    (b) marked
    (c) identified
    (d) all of these

14. Interconnected power production source(s) are permitted to be connected to the load side of the service disconnecting means at any distribution equipment on the premises.

    (a) True
    (b) False

15. Where an interconnected power source connection is made to a feeder, the feeder shall have an ampacity _____ percent of the power source output circuit current.

    (a) equal to 125
    (b) greater than 125
    (c) not greater than 125
    (d) equal to 125 percent of the power source output circuit current, or greater than 125

16. Where interconnected power production source output connections are made at feeders, all taps shall be sized based on the sum of _____ percent of all power source(s) output circuit current(s) and the rating of the overcurrent device protecting the feeder conductors for sizing tap conductors using the calculations in 240.21(B).

    (a) 100
    (b) 115
    (c) 125
    (d) 175

17. Where interconnected power production source output connections are made at busbars, and there are two sources (one a primary power source and the other another power source) located at opposite ends of a busbar that contains loads, the sum of 125 percent of the power source(s) output circuit current and the rating of the overcurrent device protecting the busbar shall not exceed _____ percent of the ampacity of the busbar.

    (a) 110
    (b) 120
    (c) 125
    (d) 150

18. When determining the ampere rating of busbars associated with load-side source connections of interconnected power production sources, one can use the sum of the ampere ratings of all overcurrent devices on _____, both load and supply devices, excluding the rating of the overcurrent device protecting the busbar, but shall not exceed the ampacity of the busbar.

    (a) metering equipment
    (b) panelboards
    (c) switchgear
    (d) all of these

Article 705 | Practice Questions

19. Where interconnected power production source output connections are made at either end of busbars of a center-fed panelboard in a dwelling unit, the sum of 125 percent of the power source(s) output circuit current and the rating of the overcurrent device protecting the busbar shall not exceed _____ percent of the current rating of the busbar.

    (a) 110
    (b) 115
    (c) 120
    (d) 125

20. Where interconnected power production source output connections are made to circuit breakers not marked "line" and "load," the circuit breaker is considered suitable for backfeed.

    (a) True
    (b) False

21. Where interconnected power production source output connections are made to circuit breakers _____ "line" and "load," the circuit breaker is considered suitable for backfeed.

    (a) not marked
    (b) labeled
    (c) identified as
    (d) listed for

22. Listed plug-in-type circuit breakers backfed for interconnected power production sources that are listed and identified as _____ shall not require a fastener as required by 408.36(D).

    (a) interactive
    (b) active
    (c) reactive
    (d) interactive or active

23. In accordance with Article 705, the sum of all PCS-controlled currents, plus all monitored _____ from other sources of supply, shall not exceed the ampacity of any busbar or conductor supplied by the power production sources.

    (a) currents
    (b) receptacles
    (c) feeders
    (d) protective devices

24. In accordance with Article 705, consideration shall be given to contribution of _____ currents from all interconnected power production source(s) for the interrupting and short-circuit current ratings of equipment on interactive systems.

    (a) demand
    (b) load
    (c) fault
    (d) limited

25. Means shall be provided to disconnect power source output circuit conductors of interconnected electric power production equipment from conductors of other systems. The disconnecting means shall be a _____.

    (a) manually operable switch or circuit breaker
    (b) load-break-rated pull-out switch
    (c) device listed or approved for the intended application
    (d) any of these

26. All raceway and cable wiring methods included in _____ of this *Code* and other wiring systems and fittings specifically listed, intended, and identified for used with interconnected electric power production systems and equipment shall be permitted.

    (a) Chapter 1
    (b) Chapter 2
    (c) Chapter 3
    (d) Chapter 4

27. Circuit conductors for interconnected power production systems shall _____.

    (a) be sized to carry the maximum currents in 705.28(A) multiplied by 125 percent without adjustment or correction factors
    (b) be sized to carry the maximum currents in 705.28(A) with adjustment and correction factors
    (c) where connected to feeders if smaller than the feeder conductors (feeder tap), the conductor ampacity shall be calculated in accordance with 240.21(B) based on the overcurrent device protecting the feeder
    (d) all of these

28. Neutral conductors for interconnected power production systems used solely for instrumentation, voltage detection, or phase detection can be sized in accordance with _____.

    (a) 250.66
    (b) 250.102
    (c) 250.122
    (d) 310.16

29. In accordance with Article 705, transformers with power sources on each side (primary and secondary) of the transformer shall be provided with primary overcurrent protection in accordance with 450.3. The primary shall be the side of the transformer connected to the largest source of _____ current.

    (a) available fault
    (b) short-circuit
    (c) output power source
    (d) available fault current or short-circuit

30. For interconnected power production systems, risks to personnel and equipment associated with the _____ could occur if an interactive electric power production source can operate as an intentional island.

    (a) primary source of power
    (b) power production system
    (c) primary source of power or power production system
    (d) possibility of a lightning strike

31. For interconnected power production systems, when the primary source supply system is restored, special detection methods are typically required to limit exposure of power production sources to _____ reconnection.

    (a) out-of-phase
    (b) primary power
    (c) secondary power
    (d) utility

32. For interconnected power production systems, single-phase power sources in interactive systems shall be connected to three-phase power systems in order to limit unbalanced voltages at the point of interconnection to not more than _____ percent.

    (a) 2
    (b) 3
    (c) 5
    (d) 10

33. In accordance with Article 705, microgrid systems shall be permitted to disconnect from the primary source of power or other interconnected power production source(s) and operate as an isolated microgrid system operating in _____ mode.

    (a) isolated
    (b) island
    (c) standby
    (d) shutdown

34. In accordance with Article 705, microgrid interconnect devices shall _____.

    (a) be required for any connection between a microgrid system and a primary power source
    (b) be listed or field labeled for the application
    (c) have a sufficient number of overcurrent devices located to provide protection from all sources
    (d) all of these

Article 706—Energy Storage Systems

35. Energy storage systems can include inverters or converters to change current levels, or to make a change between an alternating-current or a direct-current system.

    (a) True
    (b) False

36. A disconnecting means must be provided for all _____ derived from an energy storage system (ESS).

    (a) branch circuits
    (b) phase conductors
    (c) supply circuits
    (d) combiners

Article 710 | Practice Questions

37. Provisions appropriate to the energy storage technology must be made for sufficient diffusion and ventilation of any possible gases from the storage device (if present) to prevent the accumulation of _____.

    (a) noxious gases
    (b) toxic gases
    (c) an explosive mixture
    (d) fumes

38. Energy storage systems for one- and two-family dwelling units are not permitted to have a direct-current voltage greater than _____ between conductors or to ground.

    (a) 100V
    (b) 120V
    (c) 240V
    (d) 300V

Article 710—Stand-Alone Systems

39. Article 710 covers electric power production systems that operate in _____ mode and installations not connected to an electric power production and distribution network.

    (a) island
    (b) standby
    (c) tandem
    (d) generating

40. Stand-alone systems are capable of operating in _____ with other power sources.

    (a) island mode, independent from the electric utility
    (b) isolated microgrid systems
    (c) interactive mode
    (d) all of these

41. All stand-alone system equipment shall be approved for the intended use by being _____.

    (a) listed for the application
    (b) evaluated for the application and having a field label applied
    (c) listed for the application, or being evaluated for the application and having a field label applied
    (d) listed for the application, and being evaluated for the application and having a field label applied

42. A permanent _____ shall be installed at a building supplied by a stand-alone system at each service equipment location or at an approved readily visible location. The _____ shall denote the location of each power source disconnect for the building or be grouped with other plaques or directories for other on-site sources.

    (a) plaque
    (b) directory
    (c) marking
    (d) plaque or directory

43. For stand-alone systems, where multiple sources supply the building, the plaque or directory shall be marked with the wording "_____."

    (a) CAUTION: INDIVIDUAL POWER SOURCE
    (b) DANGER: HYBRID SOURCES OF POWER ONLY
    (c) DANGER: UTILITY-SUPPLIED SOURCES OF POWER
    (d) CAUTION: MULTIPLE SOURCES OF POWER

44. The supply output of the power supply to premises wiring systems fed by stand-alone or isolated microgrid power sources shall be permitted to have less capacity than the calculated load.

    (a) True
    (b) False

45. The capacity of the sum of all sources of the stand-alone supply shall be _____ the load posed by the largest single utilization equipment connected to the stand-alone system.

    (a) less than
    (b) the lowest demand on
    (c) equal to or greater than
    (d) the highest demand on

46. In consideration of the supply output for general-use loads, the stand-alone system capacity can be calculated using the sum of the capacity of the firm sources, such as _____.

    (a) generators
    (b) energy storage system inverters
    (c) generators and energy storage system inverters
    (d) PV combiners

47. The sizing and protection of the circuit conductors between a stand-alone system source and a building or structure disconnecting means shall be based on the sum of the output ratings of the stand-alone source(s).

    (a) True
    (b) False

48. Stand-alone and isolated microgrid systems can supply 120V to single-phase, 3-wire, 120/240V service disconnects of distribution panels if there are no 240V outlets and no multiwire circuits.

    (a) True
    (b) False

49. Stand-alone systems require either energy storage or backup power supplies.

    (a) True
    (b) False

50. Stand-alone system plug-in type backfed circuit breakers connected to an interconnected supply shall be secured in accordance with 408.36(D).

    (a) True
    (b) False

Notes

FINAL EXAM A
STRAIGHT ORDER

1. Installations supplying _____ power to ships and watercraft in marinas and boatyards are covered by the *NEC*.

    (a) shore
    (b) primary
    (c) secondary
    (d) auxiliary

2. The *NEC* does apply to installations in _____.

    (a) floating buildings
    (b) mobile homes
    (c) recreational vehicles
    (d) all of these

3. If the *NEC* requires new products that are not yet available at the time a new edition is adopted, the _____ may permit the use of the products that comply with the most recent previous edition of the *Code* adopted by that jurisdiction.

    (a) electrical engineer
    (b) master electrician
    (c) authority having jurisdiction
    (d) permit holder

4. A device that, when inserted in a receptacle, establishes a connection between the conductors of the attached flexible cord and the conductors connected permanently to the receptacle is called a(n) "_____."

    (a) attachment plug
    (b) plug cap
    (c) plug
    (d) any of these

5. A "battery system" includes storage batteries and battery chargers, and can include inverters, converters, and associated electrical equipment.

    (a) True
    (b) False

6. A "dc-to-dc converter" is a device that can provide an output _____ voltage and current at a higher or lower value than the input _____ voltage and current.

    (a) ac, dc
    (b) ac, ac
    (c) dc, dc
    (d) dc, ac

7. A _____ is a single unit that provides complete and independent living facilities for one or more persons, including permanent provisions for living, sleeping, cooking, and sanitation.

    (a) one-family dwelling
    (b) two-family dwelling
    (c) dwelling unit
    (d) multifamily dwelling

8. "Generating capacity, inverter" is defined as the sum of parallel-connected inverter maximum continuous output power at 40°C in _____.

    (a) amperes or kVA
    (b) volts or kV
    (c) watts or kW
    (d) a 24-hour period

Straight Order | Final Exam A—Straight Order

9. Connected (connecting) to ground or to a conductive body that extends the ground connection is called "_____."

    (a) equipment grounding
    (b) bonded
    (c) grounded
    (d) all of these

10. An interactive inverter is an inverter intended for use in parallel with power source(s) such as a(an) _____ to supply common loads and capable of delivering power to the utility.

    (a) electric utility
    (b) photovoltaic (PV) system
    (c) battery
    (d) generator

11. Conduit installed underground or encased in concrete slabs that are in direct contact with the earth is considered a _____ location.

    (a) dry
    (b) damp
    (c) wet
    (d) moist

12. Any current in excess of the rated current of equipment or the ampacity of a conductor is called "_____."

    (a) trip current
    (b) fault current
    (c) overcurrent
    (d) a short circuit

13. An overload is the same as a short circuit or ground fault.

    (a) True
    (b) False

14. The "voltage of a circuit" is defined by the Code as the _____ root-mean-square (effective) difference of potential between any two conductors of the circuit concerned.

    (a) lowest
    (b) greatest
    (c) average
    (d) nominal

15. The conductors and equipment required or permitted by this Code shall be acceptable only if _____.

    (a) labeled
    (b) listed
    (c) approved
    (d) identified

16. Unless identified for use in the operating environment, no conductors or equipment shall be _____ having a deteriorating effect on the conductors or equipment.

    (a) located in damp or wet locations
    (b) exposed to fumes, vapors, liquids, or gases
    (c) exposed to excessive temperatures
    (d) all of these

17. The temperature rating associated with the ampacity of a _____ shall be selected and coordinated so as not to exceed the lowest temperature rating of any connected termination, conductor, or device.

    (a) terminal
    (b) conductor
    (c) device
    (d) all of these

18. Examples of approved means of achieving terminal connection torque values include torque tools or an experienced qualified person who can demonstrate that the proper torque has been applied.

    (a) True
    (b) False

19. For equipment rated 800A or more that contains overcurrent devices, switching devices, or control devices; and where the entrance to the working space has a personnel door(s) less than 25 ft from the nearest edge of the working space, the door shall _____.

    (a) open either in or out with simple pressure and shall not have any lock
    (b) open in the direction of egress and be equipped with listed panic hardware
    (c) be equipped with a locking means
    (d) be equipped with an electronic opener

20. Where grounded conductors of different systems are installed in the same raceway, cable, or enclosure, each neutral conductor shall be identified to distinguish the systems by _____.

    (a) a continuous white or gray outer finish for one system
    (b) a neutral conductor with a different continuous white or gray outer finish or white or gray with a stripe for one system
    (c) other identification allowed by 200.6(a) or (b) that distinguishes each system from other systems
    (d) any of these

21. A building or structure shall be supplied by a maximum of _____ feeder(s) or branch circuit(s), unless specifically permitted otherwise.

    (a) one
    (b) two
    (c) three
    (d) four

22. The disconnecting means for a building supplied by a feeder shall be installed at a(n) _____ location.

    (a) accessible
    (b) readily accessible
    (c) outdoor
    (d) indoor

23. Where dwelling unit service equipment is replaced, a surge protective device (SPD) shall be installed.

    (a) True
    (b) False

24. Supplementary overcurrent protection _____.

    (a) shall not be used in luminaires
    (b) may be used as a substitute for a branch-circuit overcurrent device
    (c) may be used to protect internal circuits of equipment
    (d) shall be readily accessible

25. Fuses shall be marked with their _____.

    (a) ampere and voltage rating
    (b) interrupting rating where other than 10,000A
    (c) name or trademark of the manufacturer
    (d) all of these

26. Where a method to reduce clearing time for fuses rated 1,200A or greater is required in accordance with 240.67(B), the _____ reduction system shall be performance tested when first installed on site.

    (a) ground-fault
    (b) short-circuit
    (c) arc-fault
    (d) arc-energy

27. For ungrounded systems, noncurrent-carrying conductive materials enclosing electrical conductors or equipment shall be connected to the _____ in a manner that will limit the voltage imposed by lightning or unintentional contact with higher-voltage lines.

    (a) ground
    (b) earth
    (c) electrical supply source
    (d) enclosure

28. Electrically conductive materials that are likely to _____ in ungrounded systems shall be connected together and to the supply system grounded equipment in a manner that creates a low-impedance path for ground-fault current that is capable of carrying the maximum fault current likely to be imposed on it.

    (a) become energized
    (b) require servicing
    (c) be removed
    (d) be coated with paint or nonconductive materials

29. Where an ac system operating at 1,000V or less is grounded at any point, a(n) _____ jumper shall connect the grounded conductor(s) to each service disconnecting means enclosure.

    (a) system bonding
    (b) supply-side bonding
    (c) main bonding
    (d) equipment bonding

30. The building or structure grounding electrode system shall be used as the _____ electrode for the separately derived system.

    (a) grounding
    (b) bonding
    (c) grounded
    (d) bonded

31. An electrode encased by at least 2 in. of concrete, located horizontally near the bottom or vertically and within that portion of a concrete foundation or footing that is in direct contact with the earth, shall be permitted as a grounding electrode when it consists of a bare copper conductor not smaller than _____ AWG.

    (a) 8
    (b) 6
    (c) 4
    (d) 1/0

32. A ground ring encircling the building or structure can be used as a grounding electrode when the _____.

    (a) ring is in direct contact with the earth
    (b) ring consists of at least 20 ft of bare copper conductor
    (c) bare copper conductor is not smaller than 2 AWG
    (d) all of these

33. Local metal underground systems or structures such as underground tanks are permitted to serve as grounding electrodes.

    (a) True
    (b) False

34. When a ground ring is used as a grounding electrode, it shall be installed at a depth below the earth's surface of not less than _____.

    (a) 18 in.
    (b) 24 in.
    (c) 30 in.
    (d) 8 ft

35. Where _____, a grounding electrode conductor or its enclosure shall be securely fastened to the surface on which it is carried.

    (a) exposed
    (b) exposed to physical damage
    (c) encased in concrete
    (d) installed on a roof

36. If a building or structure is supplied by a service or feeder with _____ or more disconnecting means in separate enclosures, the grounding electrode connections shall be made in accordance with 250.64(D)(1), 250.64(D)(2), or 250.64(D)(3).

    (a) one
    (b) two
    (c) three
    (d) four

37. Ferrous metal raceways and enclosures for grounding electrode conductors shall be bonded at each end of the raceway or enclosure to the grounding electrode or grounding electrode conductor to create a(n) _____ parallel path.

    (a) mechanically
    (b) electrically
    (c) physically
    (d) effective

38. A grounding electrode conductor shall be permitted to be run to any convenient grounding electrode available in the grounding electrode system where the other electrode(s), if any, is connected by bonding jumpers that are installed in accordance with 250.53(C).

    (a) True
    (b) False

39. Exothermic or irreversible compression connections used at terminations of grounding electrode conductors, together with the mechanical means used to attach to fireproofed structural metal, shall not be required to be accessible.

    (a) True
    (b) False

40. A rebar-type concrete-encased electrode installed in accordance with 250.52(A)(3) with an additional rebar section extended from its location within the concrete foundation or footing to an accessible location that is not subject to _____ shall be permitted for connection of grounding electrode conductors and bonding jumpers in accordance with 250.68(C)(3)(a), (b), and (c).

    (a) physical damage
    (b) moisture
    (c) corrosion
    (d) any of these

41. At existing buildings or structures, an intersystem bonding termination is not required if other acceptable means of bonding exists. An external accessible means for bonding communications systems together can be by the use of a(n) _____.

    (a) nonflexible metallic raceway
    (b) exposed grounding electrode conductor
    (c) connection to a grounded raceway or equipment approved by the authority having jurisdiction
    (d) any of these

42. Listed FMC can be used as the equipment grounding conductor if the conduit does not exceed trade size _____.

    (a) 1¼
    (b) 1½
    (c) 2
    (d) 2¼

43. If circuit conductors are installed in parallel in the same raceway, auxiliary gutter, or cable tray, a single wire-type conductor shall be permitted as the equipment grounding conductor and sized in accordance with 250.122, based on the overcurrent protective device for the _____.

    (a) feeder
    (b) branch circuit
    (c) feeder or branch circuit
    (d) service conductors

44. The arrangement of grounding connections shall ensure that the disconnection or the removal of a luminaire, receptacle, or other device fed from the box does not interrupt the electrical continuity of the _____ providing an effective ground-fault current path.

    (a) grounded conductor(s)
    (b) ungrounded conductor(s)
    (c) equipment grounding conductor(s)
    (d) all of these

45. Where Type NM cables pass through cut or drilled slots or holes in metal members, the cable shall be protected by _____ which are installed in the opening prior to the installation of the cable and which securely cover all metal edges.

    (a) anti-shorts
    (b) sleeves
    (c) plates
    (d) listed bushings or grommets

46. A cable, raceway, or box installed under metal-corrugated sheet roof decking shall be supported so the top of the cable, raceway, or box is not less than _____ in. from the lowest surface of the roof decking to the top of the cable, raceway, or box.

    (a) ½
    (b) 1
    (c) 1½
    (d) 2

47. What is the minimum cover requirement for Type UF cable supplying power to a 120V, 15A, GFCI-protected circuit outdoors under a driveway of a one-family dwelling?

    (a) 6 in.
    (b) 12 in.
    (c) 16 in.
    (d) 24 in.

48. All conductors of the same circuit shall be _____, unless otherwise specifically permitted in the *Code*.

    (a) bonded
    (b) grounded
    (c) the same size
    (d) in the same raceway or cable or be in close proximity in the same trench

49. A vertical run of 4/0 AWG copper shall be supported at intervals not exceeding _____ ft.

    (a) 40
    (b) 80
    (c) 100
    (d) 120

50. The space above a hung ceiling used for environmental air-handling purposes is an example of _____, and the wiring limitations of _____ apply.

    (a) a specifically fabricated duct used for environmental air [300.22(B)]
    (b) other space used for environmental air (plenum) [300.22(C)]
    (c) a supply duct used for environmental air [300.22(B)]
    (d) a supplemental return duct used for environmental air [300.22(C)]

51. In general, where installed in raceways, conductors _____ AWG and larger shall be stranded.

    (a) 2
    (b) 4
    (c) 6
    (d) 8

52. Where installed in raceways, conductors _____ AWG and larger shall be stranded, unless specifically permitted or required elsewhere in the *NEC*.

    (a) 10
    (b) 8
    (c) 6
    (d) 4

53. Where correction or adjustment factors are required by 310.15(B) or (C), for single-phase feeder conductors installed for _____ dwellings, they shall be permitted to be applied to the ampacity associated with the temperature rating of the conductor.

    (a) one-family
    (b) the individual dwelling units of two-family
    (c) the individual dwelling units of multifamily
    (d) all of these

54. Type _____ insulated conductors shall not be subject to ampacity adjustment where installed exposed to direct sunlight on a rooftop.

    (a) THW-2
    (b) XHHW-2
    (c) THWN-2
    (d) RHW-2

55. The installation and use of all boxes and conduit bodies used as outlet, device, junction, or pull boxes, depending on their use, and handhole enclosures, are covered within Article _____.

    (a) 110
    (b) 200
    (c) 300
    (d) 314

56. In installations within or behind noncombustible walls or ceilings, the front edge of a box, plaster ring, extension ring, or listed extender employing a flush-type cover, shall be set back not more than _____ in. from the finished surface.

    (a) ⅛
    (b) ¼
    (c) ⅜
    (d) ½

57. Conductors, splices, or terminations in a handhole enclosure shall be listed as suitable for _____.

    (a) wet locations
    (b) damp locations
    (c) direct burial in the earth
    (d) exterior use

58. Type NM cables shall not be used in one- and two-family dwellings exceeding three floors above grade.

    (a) True
    (b) False

59. Type NM cable can be supported and secured by _____.

    (a) staples
    (b) cable ties listed and identified for securement and support
    (c) straps
    (d) any of these

60. Where Type TC cable is installed in one- and two-family dwelling units, 725.136 provides rules for limitations on Class 2 or 3 circuits contained within the same cable with conductors of electric light, power, or Class 1 circuits.

    (a) True
    (b) False

61. The minimum radius of a field bend on trade size 1¼ RMC is _____ in.

    (a) 7
    (b) 8
    (c) 10
    (d) 14

62. A run of RMC shall not contain more than the equivalent of _____ quarter bend(s) between pull points such as conduit bodies and boxes.

    (a) one
    (b) two
    (c) three
    (d) four

63. Rigid metal conduit (RMC) shall be securely fastened within _____ ft of each outlet box, junction box, device box, cabinet, conduit body, or other conduit termination.

    (a) 3
    (b) 4
    (c) 5
    (d) 6

64. Where framing members do not readily permit fastening, rigid metal conduit (RMC) may be fastened within _____ ft of each outlet box, junction box, device box, cabinet, conduit body, or other conduit termination.

    (a) 3
    (b) 4
    (c) 5
    (d) 6

65. FMC can be installed exposed or concealed where not subject to physical damage.

    (a) True
    (b) False

66. For flexible metal conduit, if flexibility is necessary after installation, unsecured lengths from the last point the raceway is securely fastened shall not exceed _____.

    (a) 3 ft for trade sizes ½ through 1¼
    (b) 4 ft for trade sizes 1½ through 2
    (c) 5 ft for trade sizes 2½ and larger
    (d) all of these

67. LFMC shall be supported and secured _____.

    (a) at intervals not exceeding 4½ ft
    (b) within 8 in. on each side of a box where fished
    (c) where fished
    (d) at intervals not exceeding 6 ft

68. When a building is supplied with a fire sprinkler system, ENT can be installed above any suspended ceiling.

    (a) True
    (b) False

69. ENT shall not be used where exposed to the direct rays of the sun, unless identified as _____.

    (a) high-temperature rated
    (b) sunlight resistant
    (c) Schedule 80
    (d) suitable

70. Where ENT is the wiring method and equipment grounding is required, a separate equipment grounding conductor shall be installed in the raceway.

    (a) True
    (b) False

Straight Order | Final Exam A—Straight Order

71. Where a metal wireway houses and protects conductors, and where single conductor cables comprising each phase, neutral, or grounded conductor of an alternating-current circuit are connected in parallel as permitted in 310.10(G), the conductors shall be installed in groups consisting of not more than _____ conductor(s) per phase, neutral, or grounded conductor to prevent current imbalance in the paralleled conductors due to inductive reactance.

    (a) one
    (b) two
    (c) three
    (d) four

72. Cable trays can be used as a support system for _____.

    (a) service conductors, feeders, and branch circuits
    (b) communications circuits
    (c) control and signaling circuits
    (d) all of these

73. Panelboards supplied by a three-phase, 4-wire, delta-connected system shall have the phase with the higher voltage-to-ground (high-leg) connected to the _____ phase.

    (a) A
    (b) B
    (c) C
    (d) any of these

74. Reconditioned switchboards and switchgear that have been damaged by fire, products of combustion, or water, shall be specifically evaluated by _____ prior to being returned to service.

    (a) the installer
    (b) its manufacturer
    (c) a qualified testing laboratory
    (d) its manufacturer or a qualified testing laboratory

75. Plug-in-type back-fed circuit breakers used to terminate field-installed ungrounded supply conductors shall be _____ by an additional fastener that requires more than a pull to release.

    (a) grounded
    (b) secured in place
    (c) shunt tripped
    (d) current-limited

76. Panelboard cabinets and panelboard frames, if of metal, shall be in physical contact with each other and shall be connected to a(n) _____.

    (a) equipment grounding conductor
    (b) grounding electrode conductor
    (c) steel building structure
    (d) separate ground rod

77. Panelboards are permitted to be installed in the face-up position.

    (a) True
    (b) False

78. Transformers with ventilating openings shall be installed so that the ventilating openings are _____.

    (a) a minimum 18 in. above the floor
    (b) not blocked by walls or obstructions
    (c) aesthetically located
    (d) vented to the exterior of the building

79. Wiring and equipment supplied from storage batteries shall be in accordance with Chapters 1 through 4 of the *NEC* unless otherwise permitted by 480.6.

    (a) True
    (b) False

80. Article 690 applies to solar PV systems, including _____.

    (a) array circuit(s), inverter(s), and controller(s) for such PV systems
    (b) those interactive with other electrical power production sources or stand-alone, or both
    (c) PV systems with ac or dc output for utilization
    (d) all of these

81. A dc circuit that is comprised of two monopole circuits, each having an opposite polarity connected to a common reference point is known as a "_____."

    (a) bipolar circuit
    (b) polar photovoltaic array
    (c) bipolar circuit or polar photovoltaic array
    (d) bidirectional circuit

82. In accordance with Article 690, a "dc combiner" is an enclosure that includes devices used to connect two or more PV system dc circuits in _____.

    (a) series
    (b) series-parallel
    (c) parallel
    (d) parallel-series

83. In accordance with Article 690, a "PV system dc circuit" includes any dc conductor(s) in PV source circuits, PV output circuits, _____ converter source circuits, and dc-to-dc converter output circuits.

    (a) ac-to-dc
    (b) dc-to-ac
    (c) dc-to-dc
    (d) any of these

84. In PV systems, when a circuit conductor is connected to a current-limited supply at one end, and also connected to a source having an available maximum current greater than the ampacity of the circuit conductor, the circuit conductors shall be protected from overcurrent at the point of connection to _____ current source(s).

    (a) the lower
    (b) the higher
    (c) either
    (d) both

85. For PV systems, overcurrent protection for a transformer with a source(s) on each side shall be provided in accordance with 450.3 by considering first one side of the transformer, then the other side of the transformer, as the primary.

    (a) True
    (b) False

86. When not installed in or on buildings, PV output circuits and dc-to-dc converter output circuits do not require arc-fault protection if they are installed _____.

    (a) in metal raceways or metal-clad cables
    (b) in enclosed metal cable trays
    (c) underground
    (d) any of these

87. A means is required to disconnect the PV system from all wiring systems including power systems, energy storage systems, and utilization equipment and its associated premises wiring.

    (a) True
    (b) False

88. Where PV system disconnecting means of systems above _____ are readily accessible to unqualified persons, any enclosure door or hinged cover that exposes live parts when open shall be locked or require a tool to open.

    (a) 30V
    (b) 120V
    (c) 240V
    (d) 600V

89. The maximum number of disconnects for each PV system shall consist of not more than _____ switches or _____ sets of circuit breakers, or a combination of not more than _____ switches and sets of circuit breakers, mounted in a single enclosure, or in a group of separate enclosures.

    (a) one
    (b) six
    (c) eight
    (d) twelve

90. The PV system disconnecting means or the enclosure providing access to the disconnecting means shall be capable of being locked in accordance with 110.25.

    (a) True
    (b) False

91. The PV system equipment disconnecting means shall have ratings sufficient for the _____ that is available at the terminals of the PV system disconnect.

    (a) maximum circuit current
    (b) available fault current
    (c) voltage
    (d) all of these

92. Where PV source and output circuits operating at over 30V are installed in readily accessible locations, circuit conductors shall be guarded or installed in _____.

    (a) Type MC cable
    (b) a cable
    (c) a raceway
    (d) Type MC cable or a raceway

93. Flexible cords and flexible cables, where connected to moving parts of tracking PV arrays, shall be exempt from the provisions of Article 400.

    (a) True
    (b) False

94. All PV system circuit conductors, including the equipment grounding conductor, shall be _____ when they leave the vicinity of the PV array.

    (a) installed in the same raceway
    (b) installed in the same cable
    (c) run with PV array circuit conductors
    (d) any of these

95. Electrical equipment for large-scale PV electric supply stations shall only be approved for installation by _____.

    (a) listing and labeling
    (b) being evaluated for the application and having a field label applied
    (c) qualified personnel
    (d) listing and labeling, or being evaluated for the application and having a field label applied

96. Documentation of the electrical portion of the engineered design of the electric supply station shall be stamped by a licensed professional electrical engineer and provided upon request of the _____.

    (a) authority having jurisdiction
    (b) utility company
    (c) owner of the facility
    (d) all of these

97. Engineering documentation of large-scale electric supply stations shall include details of conformance of the design with Article _____.

    (a) 250
    (b) 690
    (c) 702
    (d) 710

98. In accordance with Article 705, a premises wiring system that has generation, energy storage, and load(s), or any combination thereof, that includes the ability to disconnect from and parallel with the primary source is known as a "_____ system."

    (a) tandem
    (b) primary
    (c) microgrid
    (d) dual function

99. Where interconnected power production source output connections are made at feeders, all taps shall be sized based on the sum of _____ percent of all power source(s) output circuit current(s) and the rating of the overcurrent device protecting the feeder conductors for sizing tap conductors using the calculations in 240.21(B).

    (a) 100
    (b) 115
    (c) 125
    (d) 175

100. Means shall be provided to disconnect power source output circuit conductors of interconnected electric power production equipment from conductors of other systems. The disconnecting means shall _____.

    (a) be readily accessible
    (b) be externally operable without exposed live parts
    (c) plainly indicate whether in the open (off) or closed (on) position
    (d) all of these

Notes

FINAL EXAM B

RANDOM ORDER

1. The sizing and protection of the circuit conductors between a stand-alone system source and a building or structure disconnecting means shall be based on the sum of the output ratings of the stand-alone source(s).

    (a) True
    (b) False

2. LFMC shall not be required to be secured or supported where fished between access points through _____ spaces in finished buildings or structures and supporting is impractical.

    (a) concealed
    (b) exposed
    (c) hazardous
    (d) completed

3. All _____ shall be covered with an insulation equivalent to that of the conductors or with an identified insulating device.

    (a) splices
    (b) joints
    (c) free ends of conductors
    (d) all of these

4. Openings around electrical penetrations into or through fire-resistant-rated walls, partitions, floors, or ceilings shall _____ to maintain the fire-resistance rating.

    (a) be documented
    (b) not be permitted
    (c) be firestopped using approved methods
    (d) be enlarged

5. Electrical continuity at service equipment, service raceways, and service conductor enclosures shall be ensured by _____.

    (a) bonding equipment to the grounded service conductor
    (b) connections utilizing threaded couplings on enclosures, if made up wrenchtight
    (c) other listed bonding devices, such as bonding-type locknuts, bushings, or bushings with bonding jumpers
    (d) any of these

6. Working space shall not be used for _____.

    (a) storage
    (b) raceways
    (c) lighting
    (d) accessibility

7. A branch circuit that supplies only one utilization equipment is a(n) "_____" branch circuit.

    (a) individual
    (b) general-purpose
    (c) isolated
    (d) special-purpose

8. In a 3-wire circuit consisting of two phase conductors and the neutral conductor of a 4-wire, 3-phase, wye-connected system, the common conductor _____ a current-carrying conductor.

    (a) shall be counted as
    (b) is not
    (c) shall be considered to be
    (d) shall not be considered

Random Order | Final Exam B—Random Order

9. Nonmandatory Informative Annexes contained in the back of the *Code* book are _____.

    (a) for information only
    (b) not enforceable as a requirement of the *Code*
    (c) enforceable as a requirement of the *Code*
    (d) for information only and not enforceable as a requirement of the *Code*

10. Where RMC enters a box, fitting, or other enclosure, _____ shall be provided to protect the wire from abrasion, unless the design of the box, fitting, or enclosure affords equivalent protection.

    (a) a bushing
    (b) duct seal
    (c) electrical tape
    (d) seal fittings

11. Switches controlling line-to-neutral lighting loads shall not be required to have a grounded conductor provided at the switch location where a switch controls a _____.

    (a) ceiling fan
    (b) bathroom exhaust fan
    (c) lighting load that consists of all fluorescent fixtures with integral disconnects for the ballasts
    (d) receptacle load

12. A device designed to open and close a circuit by nonautomatic means and to _____ the circuit automatically on a predetermined overcurrent without damage to itself when properly applied within its rating.

    (a) energize
    (b) reset
    (c) connect
    (d) open

13. The minimum clearance for overhead feeder conductors not exceeding 1,000V that pass over commercial areas subject to truck traffic is _____ ft.

    (a) 10
    (b) 12
    (c) 15
    (d) 18

14. For buildings that have a PV system with more than one type of rapid shutdown or no rapid shutdown, a(n) _____ is required.

    (a) diagram indicating what remains energized after rapid shutdown is initiated
    (b) monitoring system with lights indicating what remains energized
    (c) audible alarm that goes silent when shutdown is complete
    (d) readily accessible actual voltage display for each system

15. "_____" means acceptable to the authority having jurisdiction.

    (a) Identified
    (b) Listed
    (c) Approved
    (d) Labeled

16. Documentation by a licensed professional _____ that the construction of the large-scale PV electric supply station conforms to the electrical engineered design shall be provided upon request of the authority having jurisdiction

    (a) PV installer
    (b) electrician
    (c) electrical engineer
    (d) electrical inspector

17. The dedicated space above a panelboard extends to a dropped or suspended ceiling, which is considered a structural ceiling.

    (a) True
    (b) False

18. Running threads shall not be used on IMC for connection at couplings.

    (a) True
    (b) False

19. When armored cable is run parallel to the sides of rafters, studs, or floor joists in an accessible attic, the cable shall be protected with running boards.

    (a) True
    (b) False

20. Where raceways or cables enter above the level of uninsulated live parts of cabinets, cutout boxes, and meter socket enclosures in a wet location, a(n) _____ shall be used.

    (a) fitting listed for wet locations
    (b) explosionproof seal
    (c) fitting listed for damp locations
    (d) insulated fitting

21. A box is not required where conductors or cables in a cable tray transition to a raceway wiring method from a cable tray.

    (a) True
    (b) False

22. Plug fuses of the Edison-base type shall have a maximum rating of _____.

    (a) 20A
    (b) 30A
    (c) 40A
    (d) 50A

23. Underground service conductors shall be protected from damage in accordance with _____ including minimum cover requirements.

    (a) 240.6(A)
    (b) 300.5
    (c) 310.16
    (d) 430.52

24. Where a box is provided with _____ or more securely installed barriers, the volume shall be apportioned to each of the resulting spaces; each barrier, if not marked with its volume, shall be considered to take up ½ cu in. if metal, and 1 cu in. if nonmetallic.

    (a) one
    (b) two
    (c) three
    (d) four

25. A(n) "_____" is a mechanically and electrically integrated grouping of modules with support structure including any attached system components such as inverter(s) or dc-to-dc converter(s) and attached associated wiring.

    (a) inverter
    (b) array
    (c) dc-to-dc converter
    (d) alternating-current photovoltaic module

26. The installation of PV equipment and all associated wiring and interconnections shall be performed only by _____.

    (a) licensed electricians
    (b) qualified personnel
    (c) master electricians
    (d) journeyman electricians

27. When mounting an enclosure in a finished surface, the enclosure shall be _____ secured to the surface by clamps, anchors, or fittings identified for the application.

    (a) temporarily
    (b) partially
    (c) never
    (d) rigidly

28. Article _____ covers the installation of large-scale PV electric supply stations with a generating capacity of not less than 5,000 kW and not under the electric utility control.

    (a) 690
    (b) 691
    (c) 705
    (d) 711

29. The area above the dedicated space required by 110.26(E)(1)(a) is permitted to contain foreign systems, provided protection is installed to avoid damage to the electrical equipment from condensation, leaks, or breaks in such foreign systems.

    (a) True
    (b) False

30. Article 400 covers general requirements, applications, and construction specifications for flexible cords and flexible cables.

    (a) True
    (b) False

Random Order | Final Exam B—Random Order

31. Service heads on raceways or service-entrance cables and gooseneck in service-entrance cables shall be located _____ the point of attachment, unless impracticable.

    (a) above
    (b) below
    (c) even with
    (d) any of these

32. Where portions of a cable raceway or sleeve are subjected to different temperatures and condensation is known to be a problem, the _____ shall be sealed to prevent the circulation of warm air to a colder section of the raceway or sleeve.

    (a) opening
    (b) cable
    (c) space
    (d) raceway or sleeve

33. For raceways terminating at a cable tray, a(an) _____ cable tray clamp or adapter shall be used to securely fasten the raceway to the cable tray system.

    (a) listed
    (b) approved
    (c) identified
    (d) marked

34. Where interconnected power production source output connections are made to circuit breakers _____ "line" and "load," the circuit breaker is considered suitable for backfeed.

    (a) not marked
    (b) labeled
    (c) identified as
    (d) listed for

35. EMT run between termination points shall be securely fastened within _____ of each outlet box, junction box, device box, cabinet, conduit body, or other tubing termination.

    (a) 12 in.
    (b) 18 in.
    (c) 2 ft
    (d) 3 ft

36. Direct-buried conductors, cables, or raceways, which are subject to movement by settlement or frost, shall be arranged to prevent damage to the _____ or to equipment connected to the raceways.

    (a) siding of the building
    (b) landscaping around the cable or raceway
    (c) enclosed conductors
    (d) expansion fitting

37. Neutral conductors for interconnected power production systems used solely for instrumentation, voltage detection, or phase detection can be sized in accordance with _____.

    (a) 250.66
    (b) 250.102
    (c) 250.122
    (d) 310.16

38. The supply-side bonding jumper on the supply side of services shall be sized according to the _____.

    (a) overcurrent device rating
    (b) ungrounded supply conductor size
    (c) service-drop size
    (d) load to be served

39. For interconnected power production systems, risks to personnel and equipment associated with the _____ could occur if an interactive electric power production source can operate as an intentional island.

    (a) primary source of power
    (b) power production system
    (c) primary source of power or power production system
    (d) possibility of a lightning strike

40. For supply-side connected interconnected power production source(s), the sum of the interconnected power source continuous current output ratings on a service, other than those controlled in accordance with 705.13, shall not exceed the ampacity of the _____.

    (a) service conductors
    (b) power production source output current
    (c) service disconnect rating
    (d) sum of all overcurrent protective devices

41. Where raceways are installed in wet locations above grade, the interior of these raceways shall be considered a _____ location.

    (a) wet
    (b) dry
    (c) damp
    (d) corrosive

42. According to Article 100, a "_____" is the machine that supplies the mechanical horsepower to a generator.

    (a) prime mover
    (b) motor
    (c) capacitor
    (d) starter

43. In judging equipment for approval, consideration(s) such as _____ shall be evaluated.

    (a) mechanical strength
    (b) wire-bending space
    (c) arcing effects
    (d) all of these

44. Where no overcurrent protection is provided for the PV circuit, an assumed overcurrent device rated in accordance with 690.9(B) shall be used to size the equipment grounding conductor in accordance with _____.

    (a) 250.66
    (b) 250.102(C)(1)
    (c) 250.122
    (d) Table 250.122

45. A device that provides a means to connect intersystem bonding conductors for _____ systems to the grounding electrode system is an "intersystem bonding termination."

    (a) limited-energy
    (b) low-voltage
    (c) communications
    (d) power and lighting

46. A "clothes closet" is defined as a _____ room or space intended primarily for storage of garments and apparel.

    (a) habitable
    (b) nonhabitable
    (c) conditioned
    (d) finished

47. A grounding electrode at a separate building or structure shall be required where one multiwire branch circuit serves the building or structure.

    (a) True
    (b) False

48. The ampacity of Type UF cable shall be that of _____ conductors in accordance with 310.14.

    (a) 60°C
    (b) 75°C
    (c) 90°C
    (d) 105°C

49. Where ungrounded supply conductors are paralleled in two or more raceways or cables, the bonding jumper for each raceway or cable shall be based on the size of the _____ conductors in each raceway or cable.

    (a) overcurrent protection for
    (b) grounded
    (c) ungrounded supply
    (d) sum of all

50. Bends in Type TC cable shall be made so as not to damage the cable. For TC Cable larger than 1 in. and up to 2 in. in diameter, without metal shielding, the minimum bending radius shall be at least _____ times the overall diameter of the cable.

    (a) two
    (b) three
    (c) five
    (d) seven

51. Interactive equipment intended to operate in parallel with electric power production sources shall be listed for interactive function or be _____ for interactive function and have a field label applied, or both.

    (a) tested
    (b) evaluated
    (c) approved
    (d) licensed

52. A "cable tray system" is a unit or assembly of units or sections and associated fittings forming a _____ system used to securely fasten or support cables and raceways.

    (a) structural
    (b) flexible
    (c) movable
    (d) secure

53. Where raceways contain insulated circuit conductors _____ AWG and larger, the conductors shall be protected from abrasion during and after installation by an identified fitting providing a smoothly rounded insulating surface.

    (a) 8
    (b) 6
    (c) 4
    (d) 2

54. A service consisting of 12 AWG service-entrance conductors requires a grounding electrode conductor sized no less than _____ AWG.

    (a) 10
    (b) 8
    (c) 6
    (d) 4

55. _____ is a raceway of circular cross section made of a helically wound, formed, interlocked metal strip.

    (a) Type MC cable
    (b) Type AC cable
    (c) LFMC
    (d) FMC

56. Type TC cable shall not be used where _____.

    (a) it will be exposed to physical damage
    (b) installed outside of a raceway or cable tray system, unless permitted in 336.10(4), 336.10(7), 336.10(9), and 336.10(10)
    (c) exposed to direct rays of the sun, unless identified as sunlight resistant
    (d) all of these

57. For transformers, other than Class 2 and Class 3, a means is required to disconnect all transformer ungrounded primary conductors. The disconnecting means shall be located within sight of the transformer unless the disconnect _____.

    (a) location is field marked on the transformer
    (b) is lockable open in accordance with 110.25
    (c) is nonfusible
    (d) location is field marked on the transformer and is lockable open in accordance with 110.25

58. The provisions of Article 690 apply to solar _____ systems, including inverter(s), array circuit(s), and controller(s) for such systems.

    (a) photoconductive
    (b) PV
    (c) photogenic
    (d) photosynthesis

59. A "ground-fault current path" is an electrically conductive path from the point of a ground fault through normally noncurrent-carrying conductors, equipment, or the earth to the _____.

    (a) ground
    (b) enclosure
    (c) electrical supply source
    (d) grounding electrode

60. Service conductors installed as unjacketed multiconductor cable shall have a minimum clearance of _____ ft from windows that are designed to be opened, doors, porches, balconies, ladders, stairs, fire escapes, or similar locations.

    (a) 3
    (b) 4
    (c) 6
    (d) 10

61. Feeder taps are permitted to be located at any point on the load side of the feeder overcurrent protective device.

    (a) True
    (b) False

62. Main bonding jumpers and system bonding jumpers shall not be smaller than specified in _____.

    (a) Table 250.102(C)(1)
    (b) Table 250.122
    (c) Table 310.16
    (d) Chapter 9, Table 8

63. Type NM cable shall be protected from physical damage by _____.

    (a) EMT
    (b) Schedule 80 PVC conduit
    (c) RMC
    (d) any of these

64. The "_____" is the point of connection between the facilities of the serving utility and the premises wiring.

    (a) service entrance
    (b) service point
    (c) overcurrent protection
    (d) beginning of the wiring system

65. Cable trays shall be supported at intervals in accordance with the installation instructions.

    (a) True
    (b) False

66. To prevent moisture from entering service equipment, service-entrance conductors shall _____.

    (a) be connected to service-drop conductors below the level of the service head
    (b) have drip loops formed on the individual service-entrance conductors
    (c) be connected to service-drop conductors below the level of the service head or have drip loops formed on the individual service-entrance conductors
    (d) be connected to service-drop conductors below the level of the service head and have drip loops formed on the individual service-entrance conductors

67. Metal wireways shall not be permitted for _____.

    (a) exposed work
    (b) hazardous locations
    (c) wet locations
    (d) severe corrosive environments

68. Article 348 covers the use, installation, and construction specifications for flexible metal conduit (FMC) and associated _____.

    (a) fittings
    (b) connections
    (c) terminations
    (d) ratings

69. Noncombustible surfaces that are broken or incomplete shall be repaired so there will be no gaps or open spaces greater than _____ in. at the edge of a cabinet or cutout box employing a flush-type cover.

    (a) $1/32$
    (b) $1/16$
    (c) $1/8$
    (d) $1/4$

70. The point of attachment of overhead premises wiring to a building shall in no case be less than _____ ft above finished grade.

    (a) 8
    (b) 10
    (c) 12
    (d) 15

71. The grounding of electrical systems, circuit conductors, surge arresters, surge-protective devices, and conductive normally noncurrent-carrying metal parts of equipment shall be installed and arranged in a manner that will prevent objectionable current.

    (a) True
    (b) False

72. Insulated conductors rated 600V with the letters "HH" in their designation have a _____ insulation rating.

    (a) 60°C
    (b) 75°C
    (c) 90°C
    (d) 105°C

Random Order | Final Exam B—Random Order

73. Connection of conductors to terminal parts shall ensure a thoroughly good connection without damaging the conductors and shall be made by means of _____.

    (a) solder lugs
    (b) pressure connectors
    (c) splices to flexible leads
    (d) any of these

74. In accordance with Article 690, a "functionally grounded system" has an electrical ground reference for operational purposes that is not _____ grounded.

    (a) effectively
    (b) sufficiently
    (c) solidly
    (d) any of these

75. Type MC cable containing four or fewer conductors, sized no larger than 10 AWG, shall be secured within _____ in. of every box, cabinet, fitting, or other cable termination.

    (a) 8
    (b) 12
    (c) 18
    (d) 24

76. Nominal battery voltage, as it relates to storage batteries, is the value of a(an) _____ of a given voltage class for convenient designation.

    (a) cell or battery
    (b) container
    (c) electrolyte
    (d) intertier connector

77. For one- and two-family dwelling units, all service conductors shall terminate in an emergency disconnecting means having a short-circuit current rating equal to or greater than the _____, installed in a readily accessible outdoor location.

    (a) demand load
    (b) peak demand load
    (c) available fault current
    (d) service conductor rating

78. The intersystem bonding termination shall _____.

    (a) be securely mounted and electrically connected to service equipment, the meter enclosure, or to an exposed nonflexible metallic service raceway, or be mounted at one of these enclosures and be connected to the enclosure or grounding electrode conductor with a minimum 6 AWG copper conductor
    (b) be securely mounted to the building or structure disconnecting means, or be mounted at the disconnecting means and be connected to the metallic enclosure or grounding electrode conductor with a minimum 6 AWG copper conductor
    (c) have terminals that are listed as grounding and bonding equipment
    (d) all of these

79. A permanent readily visible label indicating the highest maximum dc voltage in a PV system, calculated in accordance with 690.7, shall be provided by the installer at the _____ location(s).

    (a) dc PV system disconnecting means
    (b) PV system electronic power conversion equipment
    (c) distribution equipment associated with the PV system
    (d) any of these

80. For buildings with rapid shutdown, the rapid shutdown switch shall have a label that reads "RAPID SHUTDOWN SWITCH FOR SOLAR PV SYSTEM," installed within _____ ft of the switch.

    (a) 3
    (b) 6
    (c) 10
    (d) 25

81. Threadless couplings and connectors used with intermediate metal conduit shall be made _____.

    (a) rainproof
    (b) tight
    (c) moistureproof
    (d) wrenchtight

82. The minimum service-entrance conductor size shall have an ampacity not less than the maximum load to be served after the application of any _____ factors.

    (a) adjustment
    (b) correction
    (c) demand factors
    (d) adjustment or correction

83. Cable ties used to securely fasten flexible metal conduit shall be _____ for securement and support.

    (a) identified
    (b) labeled
    (c) marked
    (d) listed and identified

84. Joints between lengths of ENT, couplings, fittings, and boxes shall be made by _____.

    (a) a qualified person
    (b) set screw fittings
    (c) an approved method
    (d) exothermic welding

85. Horizontal runs of Type AC cable installed in wooden or metal framing members or similar supporting means shall be considered supported and secured where such support does not exceed _____ ft intervals.

    (a) 2
    (b) 3
    (c) 4½
    (d) 6

86. Type AC cable shall be supported and secured by _____.

    (a) staples
    (b) cable ties listed and identified for securement and support
    (c) straps
    (d) any of these

87. Type RMC conduit shall be permitted to be installed where subject to severe physical damage.

    (a) True
    (b) False

88. Type NM cable on a wall of an unfinished basement installed in a listed raceway shall have a _____ installed at the point where the cable enters the raceway.

    (a) suitable insulating bushing or adapter
    (b) sealing fitting
    (c) bonding bushing
    (d) junction box

89. Where a mast is used for overhead branch-circuit or feeder conductor support, it shall have adequate strength or be supported by braces or guys to safely withstand the strain imposed by the conductors.

    (a) True
    (b) False

90. PV system circuits installed on or in buildings shall include _____ to reduce shock hazard for firefighters.

    (a) ground-fault circuit protection
    (b) arc-fault circuit protection
    (c) a rapid shutdown function
    (d) automated power transfer

91. Where a premises wiring system contains feeders supplied from more than one nominal voltage system, each ungrounded conductor of a feeder shall be identified by phase or line and system by _____, or other approved means.

    (a) color coding
    (b) marking tape
    (c) tagging
    (d) any of these

92. Conductors in raceways shall be _____ between outlets, boxes, devices, and so forth.

    (a) continuous
    (b) installed
    (c) copper
    (d) in conduit

93. Article _____ covers the use, installation, and construction specifications for intermediate metal conduit (IMC) and associated fittings.

    (a) 342
    (b) 348
    (c) 352
    (d) 356

94. Metal boxes shall be _____ in accordance with Article 250.

    (a) grounded
    (b) bonded
    (c) secured
    (d) grounded and bonded

95. Where an interconnected power source connection is made to a feeder, the feeder shall have an ampacity _____ percent of the power source output circuit current.

    (a) equal to 125
    (b) greater than 125
    (c) not greater than 125
    (d) equal to 125 percent of the power source output circuit current, or greater than 125

96. The minimum working space on a circuit for equipment operating at 120 volts-to-ground, with exposed live parts on one side and no live or grounded parts on the other side of the working space, is _____ ft.

    (a) 1
    (b) 3
    (c) 4
    (d) 6

97. When a building is supplied with a(n) _____ fire sprinkler system, ENT shall be permitted to be used within walls, floors, and ceilings, exposed or concealed, in buildings exceeding three floors above grade.

    (a) listed
    (b) identified
    (c) NFPA 13
    (d) NFPA 72

98. Flexible metal conduit shall be securely fastened by a means approved by the authority having jurisdiction within _____ of termination.

    (a) 6 in.
    (b) 10 in.
    (c) 1 ft
    (d) 10 ft

99. Conductor terminal and splicing devices shall be _____ for the conductor material and they shall be properly installed and used.

    (a) listed
    (b) approved
    (c) identified
    (d) all of these

100. Where the main bonding jumper is a wire or busbar and is installed from the grounded conductor terminal bar or bus to the equipment grounding terminal bar or bus in the service equipment, the _____ shall be permitted to be connected to the equipment grounding terminal, bar, or bus to which the main bonding jumper is connected.

    (a) equipment grounding conductor
    (b) grounded service conductor
    (c) grounding electrode conductor
    (d) system bonding jumper

INDEX

Description	Rule	Page
A		
Armored Cable (Type AC)		
Bending Radius	320.24	319
Boxes and Fittings	320.40	321
Conductor Ampacity	320.80	321
Construction	320.100	322
Definition	320.2	317
Equipment Grounding Conductor	320.108	322
Exposed Work	320.15	318
In Accessible Attics or Roof Spaces	320.23	319
Listing Requirements	320.6	317
Securing and Supporting	320.30	319
Through or Parallel to Framing Members	320.17	318
Uses Not Permitted	320.12	318
Uses Permitted	320.10	318
B		
Branch Circuits		
Branch-Circuit Rating	210.18	86
Conductor Sizing	210.19	86
Identification for Branch Circuits	210.5	84
Multiple Branch Circuits	210.7	85
Multiwire Branch Circuits	210.4	82
Overcurrent Protection	210.20	88
Permissible Loads, Multiple-Outlet Branch Circuits	210.23	90
Receptacle Rating	210.21	89
Buildings Supplied by a Feeder		
Disconnecting Means	225.31	105
Disconnecting Means Location	225.32	105
Grouping of Disconnects	225.34	106
Identification of Multiple Supplies	225.37	106
Maximum Number of Disconnects	225.33	105
Number of Supplies	225.30	104
Rating of Disconnecting Means	225.39	106

Description	Rule	Page
C		
Cabinets		
Damp or Wet Locations	312.2	289
Deflection of Conductors	312.6	292
Enclosures	312.5	290
Overcurrent Device Enclosures	312.8	292
Position in Walls	312.3	290
Repairing Gaps in Noncombustible Surfaces	312.4	290
Cable Trays		
Bushed Conduit and Tubing	392.46	408
Cable and Conductor Installation	392.20	408
Cable Splices	392.56	408
Cable Tray Installations	392.18	407
Definition	392.2	405
Equipment Grounding Conductor	392.60	409
Expansion Splice Plates	392.44	408
Securing and Supporting	392.30	408
Uses Not Permitted	392.12	407
Uses Permitted	392.10	405
Conductors		
Ampacities for Conductors Rated 0V to 2,000V	310.14	279
Ampacities of Insulated Conductors in Raceways, Cables, or Buried	310.16	287
Ampacity Tables	310.15	280
Conductor Construction and Application	310.4	270
Conductor Identification	310.6	273
Conductors	310.3	269
Single-Phase Dwelling Services and Feeders	310.12	276
Uses Permitted	310.10	273
D		
Definitions		
Definitions	100	17

Index

Description	Rule	Page

E

Electrical Metallic Tubing (Type EMT)
Bends	358.24	383
Couplings and Connectors	358.42	385
Definition	358.2	381
Equipment Grounding Conductor	358.60	385
Listing Requirements	358.6	381
Number of Bends (360°)	358.26	383
Number of Conductors	358.22	383
Reaming	358.28	383
Securing and Supporting	358.30	384
Trade Size	358.20	382
Uses Not Permitted	358.12	382
Uses Permitted	358.10	382

Electrical Nonmetallic Tubing (Type ENT)
Bends	362.24	390
Bushings	362.46	391
Definition	362.2	387
Equipment Grounding Conductor	362.60	391
Joints	362.48	391
Listing	362.6	387
Number of Bends (360°)	362.26	390
Number of Conductors	362.22	389
Securing and Supporting	362.30	390
Trade Sizes	362.20	389
Trimming	362.28	390
Uses Not Permitted	362.12	389
Uses Permitted	362.10	387

Energy Storage Systems
Charge Control	706.33	510
Circuit Sizing and Current	706.30	509
Definitions	706.2	506
Directory (Identification of Power Sources)	706.21	509
Disconnect	706.15	507
General	706.20	508
Listing	706.5	507
Maximum Voltage	706.9	507
Multiple Systems	706.6	507
Overcurrent Protection	706.31	510
Qualified Personnel	706.3	506
Storage Batteries	706.8	507
System Requirements	706.4	506

F

Feeders
Conductor Identification	215.12	97
Conductor Sizing	215.2	92
Ground-Fault Protection of Equipment	215.10	97
Overcurrent Protection Sizing	215.3	96

Flexible Cords and Flexible Cables
Ampacity of Flexible Cords and Flexible Cables	400.5	414
Protection from Damage	400.17	417
Pull at Joints and Terminals	400.14	416
Suitability	400.3	413
Types of Flexible Cords and Flexible Cables	400.4	414
Uses Not Permitted	400.12	415
Uses Permitted	400.10	414

Flexible Metal Conduit
Bends	348.24	361
Definition	348.2	359
Equipment Grounding and Bonding Conductors	348.60	362
Listing Requirements	348.6	359
Number of Bends (360°)	348.26	361
Number of Conductors	348.22	360
Securing and Supporting	348.30	361
Trade Size	348.20	360
Trimming	348.28	361
Uses Not Permitted	348.12	359
Uses Permitted	348.10	359

G

General
Approval of Conductors and Equipment	110.2	45
Arc Flash Hazard Warning	110.16	59
Available Fault Current	110.24	63
Boxes or Fittings	300.15	257
Code Arrangement	90.3	10
Conductor Material	110.5	46
Conductor Sizes	110.6	46
Conductor Termination and Splicing	110.14	52
Conductors	300.3	240
Deteriorating Agents	110.11	49
Electrical Continuity	300.10	252
Enforcement	90.4	11
Equipment Short-Circuit Current Rating	110.10	48
Examination of Equipment for Product Safety	90.7	14
Exit Enclosures (Stair Towers)	300.25	267
High-Leg Conductor Identification	110.15	59
Identification of Disconnecting Means	110.22	62
Induced Alternating Currents in Ferrous Metal Parts	300.20	262

Index | G

Description	Rule	Page
Inserting Conductors in Raceways	300.18	261
Interrupting Rating (Overcurrent Protective Devices)	110.9	47
Length of Free Conductors	300.14	256
Lockable Disconnecting Means	110.25	63
Mandatory Requirements and Explanatory Material	90.5	13
Markings	110.21	61
Mechanical and Electrical Continuity of Conductors-Splices and Pigtails	300.13	255
Mechanical Continuity	300.12	254
Mechanical Execution of Work	110.12	50
Mounting and Cooling of Equipment	110.13	52
Number and Size of Conductors in a Raceway	300.17	259
Panels Designed to Allow Access	300.23	267
Protection Against Corrosion and Deterioration	300.6	250
Protection Against Physical Damage	300.4	243
Purpose of the *NEC*	90.1	7
Raceways Exposed to Different Temperatures	300.7	251
Raceways in Wet Locations Above Grade	300.9	251
Scope of the *NEC*	90.2	8
Securing and Supporting	300.11	252
Spaces About Electrical Equipment	110.26	63
Spread of Fire or Products of Combustion	300.21	264
Suitable Wiring Methods	110.8	47
Supporting Conductors in Vertical Raceways	300.19	261
Underground Installations	300.5	246
Use and Product Listing (Certification) of Equipment	110.3	46
Voltage Rating of Electrical Equipment	110.4	46
Wiring in Ducts and Plenum Spaces	300.22	265
Wiring Integrity	110.7	47

Generators

Description	Rule	Page
Ampacity of Conductors	445.13	436
Disconnecting Means and Emergency Shutdown	445.18	436
Listing	445.6	435
Marking	445.11	435

Grounding and Bonding

Bonding for Fault Current

Description	Rule	Page
Bonding Communications Systems	250.94	207
Bonding Equipment Containing Service Conductors	250.92	204
Bonding Loosely Jointed Metal Raceways	250.98	209
Bonding Metal Parts Containing 277V and 480V Circuits	250.97	209
Bonding of Piping Systems and Exposed Structural Metal	250.104	212
Bonding Other Enclosures	250.96	208
General	250.90	204
Lightning Protection Systems	250.106	216
Neutral Conductor, Bonding Conductors, and Bonding Jumpers	250.102	210

Enclosure, Raceway, and Service Cable Connections

Description	Rule	Page
Equipment Connected by Cord and Plug	250.114	216
Equipment Grounding Conductor Installation	250.120	222
Identification of Equipment Grounding Conductors	250.119	221
Metal Enclosures	250.109	216
Other Enclosures	250.86	204
Restricted Use of Equipment Grounding Conductors	250.121	223
Service Raceways and Enclosures	250.80	204
Sizing Equipment Grounding Conductors	250.122	223
Types of Equipment Grounding Conductors	250.118	218

General

Description	Rule	Page
Clean Surfaces	250.12	166
Connection of Grounding and Bonding Connectors	250.8	166
Objectionable Current	250.6	162
Performance Requirements for Grounding and Bonding	250.4	156
Protection of Ground Clamps and Fittings	250.10	166

Grounding Electrode System and Grounding Electrode Conductor

Description	Rule	Page
Auxiliary Grounding Electrodes	250.54	195
Common Grounding Electrode	250.58	196
Grounding Electrode Conductor	250.62	196
Grounding Electrode and Bonding Connection to Grounding Electrodes	250.68	201
Grounding Electrode Conductor Installation	250.64	196
Grounding Electrode Conductor Termination Fittings	250.70	203
Grounding Electrode Installation Requirements	250.53	190
Grounding Electrode System	250.50	186
Grounding Electrode Types	250.52	187
Sizing Grounding Electrode Conductor	250.66	200

Methods of Equipment Grounding Conductor Connections

Description	Rule	Page
Connecting Receptacle to an Equipment Grounding Conductor	250.146	229
Continuity and Attachment of EGC in Boxes	250.148	232
Cord-and-Plug-Connected	250.138	227
Equipment Connected by Permanent Wiring Methods	250.134	226
Equipment Secured to Grounded Metal Supports	250.136	227
Frames of Ranges, Ovens, and Clothes Dryers	250.140	227
Neutral Conductor for Effective Ground-Fault Current Path	250.142	228

Index

Description	Rule	Page

G (continued)

Grounding and Bonding (continued)

System Grounding and Bonding

Description	Rule	Page
Buildings Supplied by a Feeder	250.32	183
Generators—Portable and Vehicle- or Trailer-Mounted	250.34	185
Grounding	250.24	168
Grounding for Supply Side of the Service Disconnect	250.25	172
High-Impedance Grounded Systems	250.36	186
Main Bonding Jumper and System Bonding Jumper	250.28	173
Separately Derived Systems	250.30	174
Systems Required to be Grounded	250.20	167
Ungrounded Systems	250.21	168

I

Interconnected Electric Power Production Sources

General

Description	Rule	Page
Circuit Sizing and Current	705.28	500
Definitions	705.2	489
Disconnect	705.20	500
Equipment Approval	705.6	490
Ground-Fault Protection	705.32	502
Identification of Power Sources	705.10	490
Interrupting and Short-Circuit Current Rating	705.16	500
Load-Side Source Connections	705.12	493
Loss of Utility Power	705.40	502
Overcurrent Protection	705.30	501
Power Control Systems	705.13	499
Supply-Side Source Connections	705.11	491
System Installation	705.8	490
Unbalanced Interconnections	705.45	502
Wiring Methods	705.25	500

Microgrid Systems

Description	Rule	Page
Primary Power Source Connection	705.60	504
System Operation	705.50	504

Intermediate Metal Conduit (Type IMC)

Description	Rule	Page
Bends	342.24	348
Bushings	342.46	350
Couplings and Connectors	342.42	350
Definition	342.2	347
Dissimilar Metals	342.14	348
Equipment Grounding Conductor	342.60	351
Listing Requirements	342.6	347
Number of Bends (360°)	342.26	348
Number of Conductors	342.22	348
Reaming	342.28	348
Securing and Supporting	342.30	349
Trade Size	342.20	348
Uses Permitted	342.10	348

L

Liquidtight Flexible Metal Conduit (Type LFMC)

Description	Rule	Page
Bends	350.24	365
Definition	350.2	363
Equipment Grounding and Bonding Conductors	350.60	366
Listing Requirements	350.6	363
Number of Bends (360°)	350.26	365
Number of Conductors	350.22	364
Securing and Supporting	350.30	365
Trade Size	350.20	364
Trimming	350.28	365
Uses Not Permitted	350.12	364
Uses Permitted	350.10	363

Liquidtight Flexible Nonmetallic Conduit (Type LFNC)

Description	Rule	Page
Bends	356.24	379
Definition	356.2	377
Equipment Grounding Conductor	356.60	379
Fittings	356.42	379
Listing Requirements	356.6	377
Number of Bends (360°)	356.26	379
Number of Conductors	356.22	378
Securing and Supporting	356.30	379
Trade Size	356.20	378
Uses Not Permitted	356.12	378
Uses Permitted	356.10	377

M

Metal-Clad Cable (Type MC)

Description	Rule	Page
Bending Radius	330.24	326
Conductor Ampacities	330.80	328
Definition	330.2	323
Equipment Grounding Conductor	330.108	329
Exposed Work	330.15	325
In Accessible Attics or Roof Spaces	330.23	326
Listing Requirements	330.6	324
Securing and Supporting	330.30	326
Through or Parallel to Framing Members	330.17	325
Uses Not Permitted	330.12	325
Uses Permitted	330.10	324

Description	Rule	Page
Multioutlet Assemblies		
Through Partitions	380.76	399
Uses Not Permitted	380.12	399
Uses Permitted	380.10	399

N

Description	Rule	Page
Nonmetallic-Sheathed Cable (Type NM)		
Accessible Attics and Roof Spaces	334.23	335
Bending Radius	334.24	335
Boxes and Fittings	334.40	337
Conductor Ampacity	334.80	337
Definition	334.2	331
Equipment Grounding Conductor	334.108	338
Exposed Work	334.15	333
Listing Requirements	334.6	331
Securing and Supporting	334.30	336
Through or Parallel to Framing Members	334.17	334
Uses Not Permitted	334.12	333
Uses Permitted	334.10	332

O

Description	Rule	Page
Outlet, Pull, and Junction Boxes; Conduit Bodies; and Handhole Enclosures		
Conductors That Enter Boxes or Conduit Bodies	314.17	304
Covers and Canopies	314.25	308
Damp or Wet Locations	314.15	296
Flush-Mounted Box Installations	314.20	304
Handhole Enclosures	314.30	315
Metal Boxes	314.4	296
Nonmetallic Boxes	314.3	295
Outlet Box Requirements	314.27	309
Repairing Noncombustible Surfaces	314.21	305
Sizing Outlet Boxes	314.16	296
Sizing Pull and Junction Boxes	314.28	311
Support of Boxes	314.23	306
Surface Extensions	314.22	306
Wiring to be Accessible	314.29	314
Outside Circuits		
Attachment of Overhead Conductors	225.16	100
Clearance for Overhead Conductors	225.18	101
Clearances from Buildings	225.19	102
Masts as Supports	225.17	100
Minimum Conductor Size and Support	225.6	99
Raceway Seals	225.27	104
Raceways on Exterior Surfaces of Buildings or Other Structures	225.22	103
Trees for Conductor Support	225.26	103

Description	Rule	Page
Overcurrent Protection		
Circuit Breakers		
Applications	240.85	150
Arc Energy Reduction—Circuit Breakers	240.87	152
Indicating	240.81	149
Markings	240.83	149
Reconditioned Equipment	240.88	153
Series Ratings	240.86	151
Fuses		
Arc Energy Reduction—Fuses	240.67	149
Disconnecting Means for Fuses	240.40	147
Edison-Base Fuses	240.51	147
General		
Definitions	240.2	132
Ground-Fault Protection of Equipment	240.13	138
Location in Circuit	240.21	140
Location of Overcurrent Protective Devices at Premises	240.24	145
Other Articles (Overcurrent Protection of Equipment)	240.3	133
Overcurrent Protection of Conductors	240.4	133
Phase Conductor Overcurrent Device	240.15	139
Protection of Flexible Cords, Flexible Cables, and Fixture Wires	240.5	137
Standard Ampere Ratings	240.6	137
Supplementary Overcurrent Protection	240.10	138
Vertical Position	240.33	147

P

Description	Rule	Page
Panelboards		
Arrangement of Busbars and Conductors	408.3	429
Clearance for Conductors Entering Bus Enclosures	408.5	431
Clearances	408.18	432
Equipment Grounding Conductor	408.40	433
Field Identification	408.4	430
Neutral Conductor Terminations	408.41	434
Overcurrent Protection	408.36	432
Panelboard Orientation	408.43	434
Panelboards in Damp or Wet Locations	408.37	433
Reconditioning of Equipment	408.8	432
Short-Circuit Current Rating	408.6	432
Unused Openings	408.7	432
Power and Control Tray Cable (Type TC)		
Bending Radius	336.24	340
Definition	336.2	339
Listing Requirements	336.6	339
Uses Not Permitted	336.12	340
Uses Permitted	336.10	339

Index

Description	Rule	Page

R

Rigid Metal Conduit (Type RMC)
Bends	344.24	355
Bushings	344.46	358
Couplings and Connectors	344.42	357
Definition	344.2	353
Dissimilar Metals	344.14	354
Equipment Grounding Conductor	344.60	358
Listing Requirements	344.6	354
Number of Bends (360°)	344.26	355
Number of Conductors	344.22	354
Reaming	344.28	355
Securing and Supporting	344.30	355
Trade Size	344.20	354
Uses Permitted	344.10	354

Rigid Polyvinyl Chloride Conduit (Type PVC)
Bends	352.24	372
Bushings	352.46	373
Definition	352.2	369
Equipment Grounding Conductor	352.60	374
Expansion Fittings	352.44	373
Joints	352.48	374
Number of Bends (360°)	352.26	372
Number of Conductors	352.22	371
Securing and Supporting	352.30	372
Trade Size	352.20	371
Trimming	352.28	372
Uses Not Permitted	352.12	370
Uses Permitted	352.10	369

S

Service-Entrance Cable (Types SE and USE)
Bending Radius	338.24	343
Definitions	338.2	341
Listing Requirements	338.6	342
Uses Not Permitted	338.12	343
Uses Permitted	338.10	342

Services

General
Clearances on Buildings	230.9	110
Conductors Considered Outside a Building	230.6	109
Not to Pass Through a Building	230.3	109
Number of Services	230.2	107
Raceway Seals	230.8	110
Service Conductors Separate from Other Conductors	230.7	109
Vegetation as Support	230.10	110

Overhead Service Conductors
Means of Attachment	230.27	113
Overhead Service Conductor Size and Rating	230.23	111
Point of Attachment	230.26	112
Service Masts as Support	230.28	113
Vertical Clearance for Overhead Service Conductors	230.24	112

Service Disconnect Overcurrent Protection
Connected on Supply Side of the Service Disconnect	230.82	126
Emergency Disconnects	230.85	128
Ground-Fault Protection of Equipment	230.95	129
Grouping of Disconnects	230.72	125
Location	230.91	129
Manually or Power Operated	230.76	126
Number of Service Disconnects	230.71	125
Overload Protection—Where Required	230.90	128
Rating of Disconnect	230.79	126
Service Disconnect Requirements	230.70	124

Service Disconnect—General
Marking for Service Disconnect	230.66	123
Service Equipment—Enclosed or Guarded	230.62	122
Surge Protection	230.67	123

Service-Entrance Conductors
Cable Supports	230.51	120
Conductor Sizing	230.42	115
High-Leg Conductor Identification	230.56	122
Number of Service-Entrance Conductor Sets	230.40	115
Overhead Service Locations	230.54	121
Protection Against Physical Damage	230.50	120
Raceways to Drain	230.53	121
Spliced Conductors	230.46	119
Wiring Methods	230.43	119

Underground Service Conductors
Installation	230.30	114
Protection Against Damage	230.32	114
Underground Service Conductor Size and Rating	230.31	114

Solar Photovoltaic (PV) Systems

General
Alternating-Current Modules and Systems	690.6	455
Arc-Fault Circuit Protection	690.11	467
Circuit Current and Conductor Sizing	690.8	460
Connection to Other Power Sources	690.59	483
Definitions	690.2	451
Energy Storage Systems	690.71	483
Equipment Grounding and Bonding	690.43	478
General Requirements	690.4	454
Grounding Electrode System	690.47	480

Description	Rule	Page
Maximum PV System Direct-Current Circuit Voltage	690.7	456
Overcurrent Protection	690.9	465
PV Equipment Disconnecting Means to Isolate PV Equipment	690.15	470
PV System Disconnect	690.13	469
Rapid Shutdown	690.12	467
Self-Regulated PV Charge Control	690.72	484
Size of Equipment Grounding Conductors	690.45	479
Stand-Alone Systems	690.10	467

Markings and Labels

Description	Rule	Page
Direct-Current PV Circuit Label	690.53	481
Energy Storage	690.55	482
Identification of Power Sources	690.56	482
Interactive System Point of Interconnection	690.54	482

Wiring Methods

Description	Rule	Page
Access to Boxes	690.34	478
Component Interconnections	690.32	477
Connectors (Mating)	690.33	477
Wiring Methods	690.31	472

Solar Photovoltaic Systems Electric Supply Stations

Description	Rule	Page
Arc-Fault Mitigation	691.10	486
Conformance of Construction to Engineered Design	691.7	486
Definitions	691.2	485
Direct-Current Operating Voltage	691.8	486
Disconnect for Isolating Photovoltaic Equipment	691.9	486
Engineered Design	691.6	486
Equipment	691.5	486
Fence Bonding and Grounding	691.11	486
Scope	691.1	485
Special Requirements for Large-Scale PV Electric Supply Stations	691.4	485

Stand-Alone Systems

Description	Rule	Page
Equipment Approval	710.6	513
General	710.15	514
Identification of Power Sources	710.10	514
Stand-Alone Inverter Input Circuit Current	710.12	514

Storage Batteries

Description	Rule	Page
Battery and Cell Terminations	480.4	444
Battery Interconnections	480.12	446
Battery Locations	480.10	446
Battery Support Systems	480.9	445
Definitions	480.2	443
Direct-Current Disconnect Methods	480.7	445
Ground-Fault Detection	480.13	446
Insulation of Batteries	480.8	445
Wiring and Equipment Supplied from Batteries	480.5	445

Surface Metal Raceways

Description	Rule	Page
Definition	386.2	401
Equipment Grounding Conductor	386.60	403
Listing Requirements	386.6	402
Number of Conductors	386.22	402
Securing and Supporting	386.30	403
Separate Compartments	386.70	403
Size of Conductors	386.21	402
Splices and Taps	386.56	403
Uses Not Permitted	386.12	402
Uses Permitted	386.10	402

Switches

Description	Rule	Page
Accessibility and Grouping	404.8	423
Damp or Wet Locations	404.4	422
Electronic Control Switches	404.22	428
General-Use Snap Switches, Dimmers, and Control Switches	404.9	425
Grounding of Enclosures	404.12	427
Indicating	404.7	422
Mounting of Snap Switches, Dimmers, and Control Switches	404.10	426
Rating and Use of Snap Switches	404.14	427
Switch Connections	404.2	419
Switch Enclosures	404.3	421
Switch Marking	404.20	427

T

Transformers

Description	Rule	Page
Disconnecting Means	450.14	441
Grounding and Bonding	450.10	440
Overcurrent Protection	450.3	439
Transformer Accessibility	450.13	440
Ventilation	450.9	440

U

Underground Feeder and Branch-Circuit Cable (Type UF)

Description	Rule	Page
Ampacity	340.80	346
Bends	340.24	346
Definition	340.2	345
Equipment Grounding Conductor	340.108	346
Insulation	340.112	346
Listing Requirements	340.6	345
Uses Not Permitted	340.12	346
Uses Permitted	340.10	345

W | Index

Description	Rule	Page
Wireways		
Conductors Connected in Parallel	376.20	394
Construction	376.100	398
Definition	376.2	393
Number of Conductors and Ampacity	376.22	394
Splices, Taps, and Power Distribution Blocks	376.56	397
Supports	376.30	396
Uses Not Permitted	376.12	394
Uses Permitted	376.10	393
Wireway Sizing	376.23	395

Notes

ABOUT THE AUTHOR

Mike Holt—Author

Founder and President
Mike Holt Enterprises
Groveland, Florida

Mike Holt is an author, businessman, educator, speaker, publisher and *National Electrical Code* expert. He has written hundreds of electrical training books and articles, founded three successful businesses, and has taught thousands of electrical *Code* seminars across the US and internationally. His electrical training courses have set the standard for trade education, enabling electrical professionals across the country to take their careers to the next level.

Mike's approach to electrical training is based on his own experience as an electrician, contractor, inspector and teacher. Because of his struggles in his early education, he's never lost sight of how hard it can be for students who are intimidated by school, by their own feelings towards learning, or by the complexity of the *NEC*. As a result of that, he's mastered the art of explaining complicated concepts in a straightforward and direct style. He's always felt a responsibility to his students and to the electrical industry to provide education beyond the scope of just passing an exam. This commitment, coupled with the lessons he learned at the University of Miami's MBA program, have helped him build one of the largest electrical training and publishing companies in the United States.

Mike's one-of-a-kind presentation style and his ability to simplify and clarify technical concepts explain his unique position as one of the premier educators and *Code* experts in the country. In addition to the materials he's produced, and the extensive list of companies around the world for whom he's provided training, Mike has written articles that have been seen in numerous industry magazines including, *Electrical Construction & Maintenance (EC&M), CEE News, Electrical Design and Installation (EDI), Electrical Contractor (EC), International Association of Electrical Inspectors (IAEI News), The Electrical Distributor (TED), Power Quality (PQ)*, and *Solar Pro*.

Mike's ultimate goal has always been to increase electrical safety and improve lives and he is always looking for the best ways for his students to learn and teach the *Code* and pass electrical exams. His passion for the electrical field continues to grow and today he is more committed than ever to serve this industry.

His commitment to pushing boundaries and setting high standards extends into his personal life. Mike's an eight-time Overall National Barefoot Waterski Champion with more than 20 gold medals, and many national records, and he has competed in three World Barefoot Tournaments. In 2015, at the tender age of 64, he started a new adventure—competitive mountain bike racing. Every day he continues to find ways to motivate himself, both mentally and physically.

Mike and his wife, Linda, reside in New Mexico and Florida, and are the parents of seven children and six grandchildren. As his life has changed over the years, a few things have remained constant: his commitment to God, his love for his family, and doing what he can to change the lives of others through his products and seminars.

Special Acknowledgments

My Family. First, I want to thank God for my godly wife who's always by my side and also for my children.

My Staff. A personal thank you goes to my team at Mike Holt Enterprises for all the work they do to help me with my mission of changing peoples' lives through education. They work tirelessly to ensure that in addition to our products meeting and exceeding the educational needs of our customers, we stay committed to building life-long relationships with them throughout their electrical careers.

The National Fire Protection Association. A special thank you must be given to the staff at the National Fire Protection Association (NFPA), publishers of the *NEC*—in particular, Jeff Sargent for his assistance in answering my many *Code* questions over the years. Jeff, you're a "first class" guy, and I admire your dedication and commitment to helping others understand the *NEC*. Other former NFPA staff members I would like to thank include John Caloggero, Joe Ross, and Dick Murray for their help in the past.

ABOUT THE ILLUSTRATOR

Mike Culbreath—Illustrator

Mike Culbreath
Graphic Illustrator
Alden, Michigan

Mike Culbreath has devoted his career to the electrical industry and worked his way up from apprentice electrician to master electrician. He started working in the electrical field doing residential and light commercial construction, and later did service work and custom electrical installations. While working as a journeyman electrician, he suffered a serious on-the-job knee injury. As part of his rehabilitation, Mike completed courses at Mike Holt Enterprises, and then passed the exam to receive his Master Electrician's license. In 1986, with a keen interest in continuing education for electricians, he joined the staff to update material and began illustrating Mike Holt's textbooks and magazine articles.

Mike started with simple hand-drawn diagrams and cut-and-paste graphics. Frustrated by the limitations of that style of illustrating, he took a company computer home to learn how to operate some basic computer graphics software. Realizing that computer graphics offered a lot of flexibility for creating illustrations, Mike took every computer graphics class and seminar he could to help develop his skills. He's worked as an illustrator and editor with the company for over 30 years and, as Mike Holt has proudly acknowledged, has helped to transform his words and visions into lifelike graphics.

Originally from south Florida, Mike now lives in northern lower Michigan where he enjoys hiking, kayaking, photography, gardening, and cooking; but his real passion is his horses. He also loves spending time with his children Dawn and Mac and his grandchildren Jonah, Kieley, and Scarlet.

Mike Culbreath-Special Acknowledgments

I would like to thank Eric Stromberg, an electrical engineer and super geek (and I mean that in the most complimentary manner, this guy is brilliant), for helping me keep our graphics as technically correct as possible. I would also like to thank all our students for the wonderful feedback to help improve our graphics.

A special thank you goes to Cathleen Kwas for making me look good with her outstanding layout design and typesetting skills; to Toni Culbreath who proofreads all of my material; and to Dawn Babbitt who has assisted me in the production and editing of our graphics. I would also like to acknowledge Belynda Holt Pinto, our Executive Vice-President, Brian House for his input (another really brilliant guy), and the rest of the outstanding staff at Mike Holt Enterprises, for all the hard work they do to help produce and distribute these outstanding products.

And last but not least, I need to give a special thank you to Mike Holt for not firing me over 30 years ago when I "borrowed" one of his computers and took it home to begin the process of learning how to do computer illustrations. He gave me the opportunity and time needed to develop my computer graphics skills. He's been an amazing friend and mentor since I met him as a student many years ago. Thanks for believing in me and allowing me to be part of the Mike Holt Enterprises family.

ABOUT THE MIKE HOLT TEAM

There are many people who played a role in the production of this textbook. Their efforts are reflected in the quality and organization of the information contained in this textbook, and in its technical accuracy, completeness, and usability.

Technical Writing

Daniel Brian House

Brian House is Vice President of Digital and Technical Training at Mike Holt Enterprises and a permanent member of the video teams. He played a key role in editing this textbook, coordinating the content, and researching to assure the technical accuracy and flow of the information and illustrations presented.

Editorial and Production

A special thanks goes to **Toni Culbreath** for her outstanding contribution to this project. She worked tirelessly to proofread and edit this publication. Her attention to detail and her dedication is irreplaceable.

Dan Haruch is the newest member of our technical team. His skillset and general knowledge of the *NEC*, combined with his work ethic and ability to work with other members of the production team, were a major part of the successful publication of this textbook.

Many thanks to **Cathleen Kwas** who did the design, layout, and production of this textbook. Her desire to create the best possible product for our customers is greatly appreciated.

Also, thanks to **Paula Birchfield** who was the Production Coordinator for this product. She helped keep everything flowing and tied up all the loose ends. She, **Jeff Crandall** and **Kirsten Shea** did a great job proofing the final files prior to printing.

Video Team

The following special people provided technical advice in the development of this textbook as they served on the video team along with author **Mike Holt** and graphic illustrator **Mike Culbreath**.

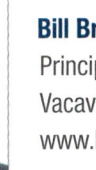

Bill Brooks
Principal Engineer
Vacaville, California
www.BrookSolar.com

Bill Brooks has over 30 years of experience designing, installing, and evaluating grid-connected PV systems. He holds B.S. and M.S. degrees in Mechanical Engineering from North Carolina State University and is a registered Professional Mechanical and Electrical Engineer. More than 15,000 installers and inspectors have attended his courses and he's written several important technical manuals for the industry throughout the U.S. and the world. His field troubleshooting skills have been valuable in determining where problems occur, and to focus training on those issues of greatest need. His recent publications include the *Expedited Permit Process for PV Systems*, the *Field Inspection Guidelines for PV Systems*, and *Understanding the CalFire Solar PV Installation Guidelines*, as well as articles in *IAEI* and *SolarPro* magazines.

Bill is actively involved in the development of PV codes and standards including IEEE-929 and IEEE1547 (PV Utility Interconnection), the *National Electrical Code* Article 690 (Solar Photovoltaic Systems), and IEC TC82 (International PV Standards). He's an active participant on many codes and standards panels including Code-Making Panel 4 of the *NEC*, and UL1703 and UL1741 Standards Technical Panels.

He was a member of the California Office of the State Fire Marshal's (Cal Fire) PV Task force that developed the Solar Photovoltaic Installation Guideline, which became the model for national fire regulation. In addition, he chaired the NFPA Large-Scale PV Electric Supply Station task group, the NFPA Firefighter Safety and PV systems task group, and two of the Article 690 task groups for Code-Making Panel 4 for the 2020 *NEC*.

Bill enjoys helping people make progress toward reaching their God-given potential. His interests include sailing, motorcycle riding, performance automobiles, home theater, and all types of music.

Video Team | About the Mike Holt Team

Daniel Brian House
Mike Holt Enterprises
Leesburg, Florida

Brian House is Vice President of Digital and Technical Training at Mike Holt Enterprises, and a Certified Mike Holt Instructor. Starting in the 1990s Brian owned and ran a contracting firm that did everything from service work to designing energy-efficient lighting retrofits, exploring "green" biomass generators, and partnering with residential PV companies.

He began teaching seminars in 2000 after joining the elite group of instructors who attended Mike Holt's Train the Trainer boot camp. Brian was personally selected for development by Mike Holt after being named as one of the top presenters in that class. He now travels around the country to teach Mike Holt seminars to groups that include electricians, instructors, the military, and engineers. His first-hand experience as an electrical contractor, along with Mike Holt's instructor training, gave him a teaching style that is practical, straightforward, and refreshing.

Brian is high-energy, with a passion for doing business the right way. He expresses his commitment to the industry and his love for its people whether he's teaching, working on books, or developing instructional programs. Brian also leads the Mike Holt Enterprises apprenticeship and digital products teams. They're creating cutting-edge training tools and partnering with apprenticeship programs nation-wide to help them take their curriculum to the next level.

Brian and his wife Carissa have shared the joy of their four children and many foster children during 22 years of marriage. When not mentoring youth at work or church, he can be found racing mountain bikes with his kids or fly fishing on Florida's Intracoastal Waterway. He's passionate about helping others and regularly engages with the youth of his community to motivate them into exploring their future.

Jim Rogers
Inspector of Wires for Town of Oak Bluffs
Vineyard Haven, Massachusetts

James J. Rogers is currently the inspector of wires for the town of Oak Bluffs, Massachusetts, the owner/operator of Bay State Inspectional Agency, and an active instructor of the *National Electrical Code* on a national basis. Jim currently represents IAEI as the principal member and Chairman of CMP-4 and is a principal member of the NFPA 303 committee on boatyards and marinas. He's the Cape and Islands Chapter delegate and secretary to the Eastern Section, and serves on the Massachusetts Electrical Code Committee and the Massachusetts Electrical Interpretations Committee. Jim also conducts forensic investigations of electrical injury accidents and fire scenes and serves on multiple Underwriter's Laboratories, Standard Technical Panels representing enforcement.

On a personal note, Jim has been married to his wife Kathy for 40 years. They have two sons; Adam, a fire protection engineer at Georgetown University; and Jeremie, a police officer for the town of West Tisbury. Jeremie is the proud father of Jim and Kathy's first grandson, Greyson Rogers. When time allows, Jim's favorite hobby is playing golf and Kathy has now taken up the game as well.

Eric Stromberg, P.E.
Electrical Engineer/Instructor
Los Alamos, New Mexico

Eric Stromberg has a bachelor's degree in electrical engineering and is a professional engineer. He started in the electrical industry when he was a teenager helping the neighborhood electrician. After high school, and a year of college, Eric worked for a couple of different audio companies, installing sound systems in a variety of locations from small buildings to baseball stadiums. After returning to college he worked as a journeyman wireman for an electrical contractor.

After graduating from the University of Houston, Eric took a job as an electronic technician and installed and serviced life safety systems in high-rise buildings. After seven years he went to work for Dow Chemical as a power distribution engineer. His work with audio systems had made him very sensitive to grounding issues and he took this experience with him into power distribution. Because of this expertise, Eric became one of Dow's grounding subject matter experts. This is also how Eric met Mike Holt, as Mike was looking for grounding experts for his 2002 Grounding vs. Bonding video.

Eric taught the *National Electrical Code* for professional engineering exam preparation for over 20 years, and has held continuing education teacher certificates for the states of Texas and New Mexico. He was on the electrical licensing and advisory board for the State of Texas, as well as on their electrician licensing exam board. Eric now works for a Department of Energy research laboratory in New Mexico, where he's responsible for the electrical standards as well as being a part of the laboratory's AHJ.

Eric's oldest daughter lives with her husband in Zurich, Switzerland, where she teaches for an international school. His son served in the Air Force, has a degree in Aviation logistics, and is a pilot and owner of an aerial photography business. His youngest daughter is a singer/songwriter in Los Angeles.

A Special Thanks

The week of the scheduled video recording, severe measures were put into place to combat the spread of the novel Coronavirus (COVID-19). Many companies prohibited their employees from travelling, and two of our team members were unable to make the trip. We want to acknowledge them for their commitment to this product and for participating remotely for most of the duration of the 3-day recording. Their participation and input was a valued part of this recording.

Jason Fisher has been in the PV industry for more than 20 years providing technical training, design review, performance modelling and validation, system optimization, commissioning and troubleshooting. He serves as the principal representative for the Solar Energy Industries Association (SEIA) on the *NEC* Code-Making Panel 4. Jason is a licensed master electrician, a NABCEP™ Certified PV Installation Professional, and a UL Certified PV System Installer.

Rebecca Hren is a licensed electrical contractor, NABCEP-certified PV Installation Professional, and a member of the NABCEP board and PV Installation Professional Exam Committee. She has over a decade of experience working in the PV industry as a system designer and installer. She teaches PV system design, authors technical articles for PV trade magazines, has co-authored two books on renewable energy, and has presented workshops at solar industry conferences around the world, including Solar Power International and Intersolar North America, India, and Middle East.

Notes

Save 25% On These Best-Selling Libraries

Understanding the NEC® Complete Training Library

This library makes it easy to learn the Code and includes the following best-selling textbooks and videos:

Understanding the National Electrical Code® Volume 1 Textbook
Understanding the National Electrical Code® Workbook, Art 90-480
Understanding the National Electrical Code® Volume 2 Textbook
Bonding and Grounding Textbook
General Requirements videos
Wiring and Protection videos
Bonding and Grounding videos
Wiring Methods and Materials videos
Equipment for General Use videos
Special Occupancies and Special Equipment videos
Limited Energy and Communications Systems videos

Product Code: 20UNDLIBMM   List Price: ~~$675.00~~   Now only $506.25*

Bonding and Grounding Training Package

Bonding and Grounding is one of the least understood and most important articles in the NEC.® This program focuses on Article 250 but also addresses grounding rules found throughout the Code Book. The textbook and videos are informative and practical, and include in one single place, all articles that relate to bonding and grounding. The full-color illustrations help break down the concepts and make them easier to understand. This topic is at the core of most power quality and safety issues, making this program a must-have for everyone in the industry. Order your copy today.

Library includes:

Bonding and Grounding Textbook
Bonding and Grounding videos

Product Code: 20BGMM   List Price: ~~$325.00~~   Now only $243.75*

Leadership and Life Skills Training Library

Mike shares his insight and knowledge on the skills and disciplines you need to be able to understand who you are, make goals, and work to achieve them. He gives you the tools to clear the path to understand what your personal success looks like, how to cultivate a winning attitude and employ great communications skills. Continuous improvement is necessary to learn how to embrace change, conflict and failure. Whatever your current position or goals, you'll learn tips and processes that will help you raise your game.

Package includes:

Leadership Skills Textbook
Life Skills Textbook
Life Skills videos
Life Skills MP3s

Product Code: LEADMM   List Price: ~~$225.00~~   Now only $168.75*

---

* Prices subject to change. Discount applies to price at time of order.

Call Now 888.NEC.CODE (632.2633)

& mention discount code: B20SOLB25

Mike Holt Enterprises

Save 25% On These Best-Selling Libraries

Understanding the NEC® Complete Training Library

This library makes it easy to learn the Code and includes the following best-selling textbooks and videos:

Understanding the National Electrical Code® Volume 1 Textbook
Understanding the National Electrical Code® Workbook, Art 90-480
Understanding the National Electrical Code® Volume 2 Textbook
Bonding and Grounding Textbook
General Requirements videos
Wiring and Protection videos
Bonding and Grounding videos
Wiring Methods and Materials videos
Equipment for General Use videos
Special Occupancies and Special Equipment videos
Limited Energy and Communications Systems videos

Product Code: 20UNDLIBMM   List Price: $675.00   Now only $506.25*

Bonding and Grounding Training Package

Bonding and Grounding is one of the least understood and most important articles in the NEC.® This program focuses on Article 250 but also addresses grounding rules found throughout the Code Book. The textbook and videos are informative and practical, and include in one single place, all articles that relate to bonding and grounding. The full-color illustrations help break down the concepts and make them easier to understand. This topic is at the core of most power quality and safety issues, making this program a must-have for everyone in the industry. Order your copy today.

Library includes:

Bonding and Grounding Textbook
Bonding and Grounding videos

Product Code: 20BGMM   List Price: $325.00   Now only $243.75*

Leadership and Life Skills Training Library

Mike shares his insight and knowledge on the skills and disciplines you need to be able to understand who you are, make goals, and work to achieve them. He gives you the tools to clear the path to understand what your personal success looks like, how to cultivate a winning attitude and employ great communications skills. Continuous improvement is necessary to learn how to embrace change, conflict and failure. Whatever your current position or goals, you'll learn tips and processes that will help you raise your game.

Package includes:

Leadership Skills Textbook
Life Skills Textbook
Life Skills videos
Life Skills MP3s

Product Code: LEADMM   List Price: $225.00   Now only $168.75*

---

* Prices subject to change. Discount applies to price at time of order.

Call Now 888.NEC.CODE (632.2633)
& mention discount code: B20SOLB25

 Mike Holt Enterprises